Exposition
of
I & II Samuel

Exposition
of
I & II Samuel

Matthew Henry,
John Gill
&
Arthur W. Pink

Sovereign Grace Publishers, Inc.
P.O. Box 4998
Lafayette, IN 47903
2001

Exposition of I & II Samuel
Copyright © 2001
By Jay P. Green, Sr.
All Rights Reserved

ISBN 1-58960-052-5

Printed In the United States of America
By Lightning Source, Inc.

CONTENTS

AN

EXPOSITION

OF THE FIRST BOOK OF

SAMUEL.

INTRODUCTION

This book, and that which follows it, bear the name of Samuel in the title, not because he was the penman of them (except of so much of them as fell within his own time, to the twenty-fifth chapter of the first book, in which we have an account of his death), but because the first book begins with a large account of him, his birth and childhood, his life and government; and the rest of these two volumes that are denominated from him contains the history of the reigns of Saul and David, who were both anointed by him. And, because the history of these two kings takes up the greatest part of these books, the Vulgar Latin calls them the *First* and *Second Books of the Kings,* and the two that follow the *Third* and *Fourth,* which the titles in our English Bible takes notice of with an *alias: otherwise called the First Book of the Kings,* &c. The LXX. call them the first and second *Book of the Kingdoms.* It is needless to contend about it, but there is no occasion to vary from the Hebrew verity. These two books contain the history of the last two of the judges, *Eli* and *Samuel,* who were not, as the rest, men of war, but priests (and so much of them is an appendix to the book of Judges), and of the first two of the kings, *Saul* and *David,* and so much of them is an entrance upon the history of the kings. They contain a considerable part of the sacred history, are sometimes referred to in the New Testament, and often in the titles of David's Psalms, which, if placed in their order, would fall in these books. It is uncertain who was the penman of them; it is probable that Samuel wrote the history of his own time, and that, after him, some of the prophets that were with David (Nathan as likely as any) continued it. This first book gives us a full account of Eli's fall and Samuel's rise and good government, chapter 1—8. Of Samuel's resignation of the government and Saul's advancement and mal-administration, chapters 9-15. The choice of David, his struggles with Saul, Saul's ruin at last, and the opening of the way for David to the throne, chapters 16-31. And these things are written for our learning.

CHAPTER 1.

"Now there was a certain man of Ramathaimzophim, of Mount Ephraim, and his name was Elkanah, the son of Jeroham, the son of Elihu, the son of Tohu, the son of Zuph, an Ephrathite. And he had two wives. The name of the one was Hannah, and the name of the other was Peninnah. And Peninnah had children, but Hannah had no children. And this man went out of his city from year to year, to worship and to sacrifice to the Lord of hosts in Shiloh. And the two sons of Eli, Hophni and Phinehas, the priests of the Lord were there. And when the time came that Elkanah offered, he gave portions to Peninnah his wife, and to all her sons and her daughters. But to Hannah he gave a worthy portion, for he loved Hannah. But the Lord had shut up her womb. And her foe also provoked her grievously, in order to make her fret, because the Lord has shut up her womb. And as he did so year by year, when she went up to the house of the Lord, so she provoked her. Therefore she wept and did not eat. Then her husband Elkanah said to her, Hannah, why do you weep? And why do you not eat? And why is your heart grieved? Am I not better to you than ten sons?" — 1 Samuel 1:1-8.

We have here an account of the state of the family into which Samuel the prophet was born. His father's name was Elkanah, a Levite, and of the family of the Kohathites (the most honourable house of that tribe) as appears, 1 Chron. 6:33,34. His ancestor Zuph was an Ephrathite, that is, of Bethlehem-Judah, which was called *Ephrathah*, Ruth 2. There this family of the Levites was first seated, but one branch of it, in process of time, removed to Mount Ephraim, from which Elkanah descended. Micah's Levite came from Bethlehem to Mount Ephraim, Judg. xvii. 8. Ministers' families are as movable as any. Perhaps notice is taken of their being originally Ephrathites to show their alliance to David. This Elkanah lived at Ramah, or Ramathaim, which signifies *the double Ramah*, the higher and lower town, the same with Arimathea of which Joseph was, here called *Ramathiam-zophim*. Zophim signifies *watchmen;* probably they had one of the schools of the prophets there for prophets are called *watchmen:* the Chaldee paraphrase calls Elkanah a *disciple of the prophets.* But it seems to me that it was in Samuel that prophecy revived, before this time there being, for a great while, no open vision, *ch.* iii. 1. Nor is there any mention of a prophet of the Lord from Moses to Samuel, except Judg. vi. 8. So that we have no reason to think that there was any nursery or college of prophets here till Samuel founded one, *ch.* xix. 19, 20. This is the account of Samuel's parentage, and the place of his nativity. Let us now take notice of the state of the family.

families in a particular manner. Ministers should be patterns of family religion. Elkanah went up at the solemn feasts to the tabernacle at Shiloh, to *worship and to sacrifice to the Lord of hosts.* I think this is the first time in scripture that God is called *the Lord of hosts — Jehovah Sabaoth*, a name by which he was afterwards very much called and known. Probably Samuel the prophet was the first that used this title of God, for the comfort of Israel, when in his time their hosts were few and feeble and those of their enemies many and mighty; then it would be a support to them to think that the God they served was Lord of hosts, of all the hosts both of heaven and earth; of them he has a sovereign command, and makes what use he pleases of them. Elkanah was a country Levite, and, for aught that appears, had not any place or office which required his attendance at the tabernacle, but he went up as a common Israelite, with his own sacrifices, to encourage his neighbors and set them a good example. When

8

he sacrificed he worshipped, joining prayers and thanksgivings with his sacrifices. In this course of religion he was constant, for he went up yearly. And that which made it the more commendable in him was, 1. That there was a general decay and neglect of religion in the nation. Some among them worshipped other gods, and the generality were remiss in the service of the God of Israel, and yet Elkanah kept his integrity; whatever others did, his resolution was that he and his house should serve the Lord. 2. That Hophni and Phinehas, the sons of Eli, were the men that were now chiefly employed in the service of the house of God; and they were men that conducted themselves very ill in their place, as we shall find afterwards; yet Elkanah went up to sacrifice. God had then tied his people to one place and one altar, and forbidden them, under any pretence whatsoever, to worship elsewhere, and therefore, in pure obedience to that command, he attended at Shiloh. If the priests did not do their duty, he would do his. Thanks be to God, we, under the gospel, are not tied to any one place or family; but the pastors and teachers whom the exalted Redeemer has given to his church are those only whose ministration tends to the *perfecting of the saints* and the *edifying of the body of Christ,* Eph. iv. 11, 12. None have dominion over our faith; but our obligation is to those that are the helpers of our holiness and joy, not to any that by their scandalous immoralities, like Hophni and Phinehas, make the sacrifices of the Lord to be abhorred, though still the validity and efficacy of the sacraments depend not on the purity of him that administers them.

II. Yet it was a divided family, and the divisions of it carried with them both guilt and grief. Where there is piety, it is a pity but there should be unity. The joint-devotions of a family should put an end to divisions in it.

1. The original cause of this division was Elkanah's marrying two wives, which was a transgression of the original institution of marriage, to which our Saviour reduces it. Matt. xix. 5, 8, *From the beginning it was not so.* It made mischief in Abraham's family, and Jacob's, and here in Elkanah's. How much better does the law of God provide for our comfort and ease in this world than we should, if we were left to ourselves! It is probable that Elkanah married Hannah first, and, because he had not children by her so soon as he hoped, he married Peninnah, who bore him children indeed, but was in other things a vexation to him. Thus are men often beaten with rods of their own making.

2. That which followed upon this error was that the two wives could not agree. They had different blessings; Peninnah, like Leah, was fruitful and had many children, which should have made her easy and thankful, though she was but a second wife, and was less beloved; Hannah, like Rachel, was childless indeed, but she was very dear to her husband, and he took all occasions to let both her and others know that she was so, and many a *worthy portion he gave her.* (v. 5), and this should have made her easy and thankful. But they were of different tempers: Peninnah could not bear the blessing of fruitfulness, but she grew haughty and insolent; Hannah could not bear the affliction of barrenness, but she grew melancholy and discontented: and Elkanah had a difficult part to act between them.

(1.) Elkanah kept up his attendance at God's altar notwithstanding this unhappy difference in his family, and took his wives and children with him, that, if they could not agree in other things, they might agree to worship God together. If the devotions of a family prevail not to put an end to its divisons, yet let not the divisions put a stop to the devotions.

(2.) He did all he could to encourage Hannah, and to keep up her spirits under her affliction, v. 4, 5. At the feast he offered peace-offerings, to supplicate for peace in his family; and when he and his family were to eat their share of the sacrifice, in token of their communion with God and his altar, though he carved to Peninnah and her children competent portions, yet to Hannah he gave a worthy portion, the choicest piece that came to the table, the piece (whatever it was) that used to be given on such occasions to those that were most valued; this he did in token of his love to her, and to give all possible assurances of it. Observe, [1.] Elkanah loved his wife never the less for her being barren. *Christ loves his church*, notwithstanding her infirmities, her barrenness; and *so ought men to love their wives*, Eph. v. 25. To abate our just love to any relation for the sake of any infirmity which they cannot help, and which is not their sin but their affliction, is to make God's providence quarrel with his precept, and very unkindly to add affliction to the afflicted. [2.] He studied to show his love so much the more because she was afflicted, insulted, and low-spirited. It is wisdom and duty to support the weakest, and to hold up those that are run down. [3.] He showed his great love to her by the share he gave her of his peace offerings. Thus we should testify our affection to our friends and relations, by abounding in prayer for them. The better we love them the more room let us give them in our prayers.

(3.) Peninnah was extremely peevish and provoking. [1.] She upbraided Hannah with her affliction, despised her because she was barren, and gave her taunting language, as one whom Heaven did not favour. [2.] She envied the interest she had in the love of Elkanah, and the more kind he was to her the more was she exasperated against her, which was all over base and barbarous. [3.] She did this most when they *went up to the house of the Lord*, perhaps because then they were more together than at other times, or because then Elkanah showed his affection most to Hannah. But it was very sinful at such a time to show her malice, when pure hands were to be lifted up at God's altar without wrath and quarrelling. It was likewise very unkind at that time to vex Hannah, not only because then they were in company, and others would take notice of it, but then Hannah was to mind her devotions, and desired to be most calm and composed, and free from disturbance. The great adversary to our purity and peace is then most industrious to ruffle us when we should be most composed. When the *sons of God* come to *present themselves before the Lord Satan* will be sure to *come among them*, Job. i. 6. [4.] She continued to do this from year to year, not once or twice, but it was her constant practice; neither deference to her husband nor compassion to Hannah could break her of it. [5.] That which she designed was to make her fret, perhaps in hopes to break her heart, that she might possess her husband's heart solely, or because she took a pleasure in her uneasiness, nor could Hannah gratify her more than by fretting. Note, It is an evidence of a base disposition to delight in grieving those that are melancholy and of a sorrowful spirit, and in putting those out of humour that are apt to fret and be uneasy. We ought to hear one another's burdens not add to them.

(4.) Hannah (poor woman) could not bear the provocation: *She wept, and did not eat*, v. 7. It made her uneasy to herself and to all her relations. She did not eat of the feast; her trouble took away her appetite, made her unfit for any company, and a jar in the harmony of family-joy. It was of the *feast upon the sacrifice* that she *did not eat*, for they were not to *eat of the holy things in their mourning*, Deut. xxvi. 14; Lev. x. 19. Yet it was her infirmity so far to give way to the sorrow of the world as to unfit herself for holy joy in God. Those that are of a fretful spirit, and are apt to lay provocations too much to heart, are enemies of themselves, and strip themselves very much of the comforts both of life and godliness. We find that God took notice of this ill effect of discontents and disagreements in the conjugal relation, that the parties aggrieved *covered the altar of the Lord with tears, insomuch that he regarded not the offering*, Mal. ii. 13.

Elkanah said what he could to her to comfort her. She did not upbraid him with his unkindness in marrying another wife as Sarah did, nor did she render to Peninnah railing for railing, but took the trouble wholly to herself, which made her an object of much compassion. Elkanah showed himself extremely grieved at her grief. (v. 8): *Hannah, why weepest thou?* [1.] He is much disquieted to see her thus overwhelmed with sorrow. Those that by marriage are made one flesh ought thus far to be of one spirit too, to share in each other's troubles, so that one cannot be easy while the other is uneasy. [2.] He gives her a loving reproof for it: *Why weepest thou? And why is thy heart grieved?* As many as God loves he rebukes, and so should we. He puts her upon enquiring into the cause of her grief. Though she had just reason to be troubled, yet let her consider whether she had reason to be troubled to such a degree, especially so much as to be taken off by it from eating of the holy things. Note, Our sorrow upon any account is sinful and inordinate when it diverts us from our duty to God and embitters our comfort in him, when it makes us unthankful for the mercies we enjoy and distrustful of the goodness of God to us in further mercies, when it casts a damp upon our joy in Christ, and hinders us from doing the duty and taking the comfort of our particular relations. [3.] He intimates that nothing should be wanting on his part to balance her grief: *"Am not I better to thee than ten sons?* Thou knowest thou hast my entire affection, and let that comfort thee."* Note, we ought to take notice of our comforts, to keep us from grieving excessively for our crosses; for our crosses we deserve, but our comforts we have forfeited. If we should keep the balance even, we must look at that which is for us, as well as that which is against us, else we are unjust to Providence and unkind to ourselves. *God hath set the one over-against the other* (Eccl. vii. 14) and so should we.

"So Hannah rose up after they had eaten in Shiloh and after they had drunk. Now Eli the priest sat on a seat by a post of the temple of the Lord. And she was in bitterness of soul and prayed to the Lord, and wept sorely. And she vowed a vow and said, O Lord of hosts, if You will indeed look upon the affliction of Your servant and remember me, and not forget Your servant, but will give to Your handmaid a son, then I will give him to the Lord all the days of his life, and no razor shall come on his head. And as she continued praying before the Lord, Eli noticed her mouth. Now Hannah spoke in her heart — only her lips moved, but her voice was not heard. Therefore Eli thought she had become drunk. And Eli said to her, How long will you be drunken? Put your wine away from you! And Hannah answered, No, my lord, I am a woman of sorrowful spirit. I have neither drunk wine nor strong drink, but have poured out my soul before the Lord. Do not count your servant to be a daughter of Belial, for out of the abundance of my meditation and grief I have spoken until now. Then Eli answered and said, Go in peace, and the God of Israel grant to you your petition that you have asked of Him. And she said, Let your servant find grace in your sight. So the woman went her way and ate, and her face was no longer sad" — 1 Samuel 1: 9-18.

Ver. 9. *Hannah rose up after they had eaten in Shiloh, and after they had drunk,* &c.] After dinner, after Elkanah and Peninnah, and their children, had eaten heartily, and drunk freely, and made a comfortable meal, and even a feast of it, at the place where the tabernacle and altar were, and their peace-offerings were offered up, part of which they had been regaling themselves with. The Targum is, "after she had eaten in Shiloh, and after she had drunk;" for upon the entreaty of her husband, and to make him easy, she might be prevailed upon to eat somewhat, though it might be but little; and to drink, though it was but water; for as for wine and strong drink, she declared afterwards she had not drunk, ver. 15: *now Eli the priest sat upon a seat by a post of the temple of the Lord;* for so the tabernacle was called, and sometimes the temple is called a tabernacle, Jer. x. 20. Now at the door-posts and side of the threshold of the temple of the Lord, as the Targum; at the entrance of the great court of the Israelites Eli had a seat placed, on which he sat; this must be at the gate of the court of the tabernacle, by the pillars of it; for in the court itself none afterwards might sit but kings of the family of David; here Eli sat as a high-priest and judge, to give advice in difficult cases, and to try and judge all causes that were brought before him; some say that he was on this day constituted a high-priest, and others say he was now made a judge; but no doubt he was both high-priest and judge before this time.

Ver. 10. *And she was in bitterness of soul,* &c.] Because of her barrenness, and the taunts and reflections she had met with on that account; her life was bitter to her, she could take no pleasure in any of the comforts of it: *and prayed unto the Lord, and wept sore;* her prayer was with strong crying and tears; it was very fervent and affectionate; she prayed most vehemently, and wept bitterly. This perhaps was about the time of the evening sacrifice, about three or four o'clock in the afternoon: seeing it was after dinner that she arose up and went to prayer in the house of God, at the door of the tabernacle, or near it, as it should seem by the notice Eli took of her, who sat there.

Ver. 11. *And she vowed a vow,* &c.] Which might be confirmed by her husband; otherwise the vow of a woman, if disapproved of by her husband, was not valid, Numb. xxx. 8; and Elkanah might make the same vow his wife did, and so it stood; for as this was a vow of Nazariteship, it is a tradition of the Jews, that a man may vow his son to be a Nazarite, but a woman may not; but as this instance contradicts the tradition, they endeavour to explain away this vow, as it may respect a Nazarite, as will be observed hereafter: *and said, O Lord of hosts;* this is properly the first time this title was used by any that we know of; for though it is expressed in ver. 3, there it is used as the words of the writer of this history, and so long after this prayer was put up; see the note there; and it is an observation in the Talmud, that from the day God created the world, no man called him the Lord of hosts till Hannah came and called him so: *if thou wilt indeed look upon the affliction of thine handmaid;* the sorrow of heart she had, the reproach she met with, on account of her having no children: *and remember me, and not forget thine handmaid;* which petitions are the same in other words, and are repeated to denote her vehemence and importunity in prayer, and may allude to usages among men, that will look upon a person in distress, and turn away and forget them, and never think of them more; which she deprecates may not be her case with God: *but wilt give unto thine hand-maid a man-child, or, a seed of men;* a son in the midst of men, as the Targum; such as is desirable by men, as a male child for the most part is; though some Jewish writers interpret it of the seed of righteous, wise, and understanding men, such as be fit to serve the Lord, which seems to be a sense foreign to the text; a man-child she asks, because no other could serve the Lord in the temple; and that she meant by this phrase such an one is clear, because she vowed that a razor should not come on his head, which is never said of females, as Kimchi observes: *then will I give him unto the Lord all the days of his life;* to serve him, and minister unto him in the sanctuary; being born a Levite, it was incumbent on him to serve the Lord, and he had a right to his service; but then a common Levite did not enter on it till 25 or 30 years of age, and was not always serving, but was dismissed from it at 50; but the child she vows, if the Lord would give her such an one, should be trained up in his service from its infancy, and continue in it all the days of its life; and was to be also a perpetual Nazarite, as Samson was, as follows: and there shall no razor come upon his head; as was not to come upon a Nazarite during his Nazariteship, Numb. vi. 5; and as such a vow made by a woman contradicts the tradition of the Jews before mentioned, they give another sense of this clause; as the Targum, which paraphrases it, "and the fear of man shall not be upon him;" but about this there is a division; but that Samuel was a Nazarite, and a perpetual one, is the sense of their best interpreters.

Ver. 12. *And it came to pass, as she continued praying before the Lord,* &c.] Being very earnest and importunate with him to grant her request, and therefore repeated her petition, and prolonged her prayer, being unwilling to let the Lord go, until she had a promise, or some satisfaction, that she should have the thing she asked; some think she continued an hour in prayer: *that Eli marked her mouth;* observed the motion of her lips, and no doubt her distorted countenance, and lift-up eyes and hands, but chiefly the former; not knowing what the woman was at, and what could be the meaning of such motions.

Ver. 18. *Now Hannah, she spake in her heart,* &c.] It was mental prayer she used, some ejaculations of her mind she sent up to God, which she was sensible were well known to him, and she needed not to express vocally: *only her lips moved;* as her heart indited, and sent up her petitions, as if she had used words and phrases in form; *but her voice was not heard;* that she might not be seen to be ostentatious in her prayer, and that she might not interrupt others in their devotions: and she knew that her voice was not necessary with respect to God: therefore Eli thought she had been drunken; by the motions she made, and gestures she used, as if she was muttering something to herself, and by her long continuance therein, and it being after a feast she had been at with her husband, and the rest of the family; from all which Eli concluded this must be the case.

Ver. 14. *And Eli said unto her, how long wilt thou be drunken?* &c.] What, every day drunk? what, continually in this wicked practice? when will it be left off? for Eli might have observed on other days, and at other times, odd looks, and a strange behaviour in her, which he took for the effects of drinking too much wine: or how long will this drunken fit last? she had been a considerable time as he thought in it, and it was not gone off yet: the Targum is, "how long wilt "thou behave like a fool, or a mad woman?" as drunken people generally do act, as if they were fools, or mad: *put away thy wine from thee;* not as if she had any with her there to drink of, but he advises her, since it had such an effect upon her, to abstain from it, and wholly disuse it, and so break off such a habit and custom she had got into; or he would have her go home and sleep it out, and wait till she had digested it, and the strength of it was gone off, before she came to such a place of devotion and worship; from hence the Jews say it may be learnt, that a drunken person ought not to pray.

Ver. 15. *And Hannah answered and said, no, my lord,* &c.] That is not my case, you have greatly mistaken it; she answered with great mildness and meekness, without falling into a passion at such a scandalous imputation upon her, and with great respect and reverence to Eli, suitable to his office; so in after-times the high-priest used to be addressed after this manner, particularly on the day of atonement, *lord high-priest*, do so and so; indeed these words of Hannah are interpreted as not so very respectful, as if the sense was, not a lord art thou in this matter; nor does the Holy Ghost dwell upon you; which you have sufficiently shown, or you would never have suspected me of drunkenness: *I am a woman of a sorrowful spirit;* depressed with trouble and grief on account of afflictions: if she was drunk, it was not with wine, but with sorrow: *or a woman of a hard spirit;* which is sometimes taken in an ill sense, and, according to Abarbinel, is here denied by her, who connects this clause with the preceding thus; not, my lord, am I a woman of a hard spirit, or such a hardened wretch, and such an impudent woman, as I must be, were it so, to come drunk into the house of God, and pretend to pray unto him: *I have drunk neither wine nor strong drink;* not any sort of intoxicating liquors that day, neither wine new or old, as the Targum: *but have poured out my soul before the Lord;* the affliction of it, as the same paraphrase; the grievances and distresses, the complaints of her soul, which were many, and which she had poured out before the Lord freely and plentifully, and which had taken up some time to do it; see Psal. lxii. 8, and the title of Psal. cii.; where phrases similar to this are used, and which seem to be taken from hence.

Ver. 16. *Count not thine handmaid for a daughter of Belial,* &c.] A yokeless, a lawless, impudent, and abandoned creature; one of the wickedest, vilest, and most profligate wretches; as she must be to come drunk into the sanctuary of God; see 1 Sam. xxv. 17, 25. Drunkenness in man is an abominable crime, but much more in a woman. The Romans forbade wine to women, and drunkenness in them was a capital crime, as adultery, or any other; and indeed a drunken woman is liable to all manner of sin: *for out of the abundance of my complaint and grief have I spoken hitherto;* out of the abundance of the heart the mouth will speak, whether it is a matter of trouble or of joy; the heart of Hannah was full of grief, and her mouth full of complaints, on which she had long dwelt, in order to give vent thereunto, and ease herself.

Ver. 17. *Then Eli answered and said, go in peace,* &c.] He found he was mistaken in her, and that her discourse was not only sober and rational, but religious and spiritual; and therefore dismisses her in peace, and bids her not distress herself with what he had said to her, nor with any thing she had met with from others, or from the Lord; but expect peace and prosperity, and particularly success in what she had been engaged, and had been solicitous for: *and the God of Israel grant thee thy petition that thou hast asked of him;* which may be considered either as a prayer for her, he joining with her in a request to the Lord, that what she had asked might be granted; or as a prophecy that so it would be, it being revealed to him by the Holy Ghost, as the high-priest of the Lord; or impressed by an impulse upon his spirit that the favour asked would be given; and therefore she might go home in peace, and with satisfaction of mind.

Ver. 18. *And she said let thine handmaid find grace in thy sight,* &c.] She had found favour in his sight she perceived, and she desires it might be continued and increased; and that as he had prayed for her, he would still use his interest at the throne of grace for her: *so the woman went her way;* took her leave of Eli, and went from the tabernacle to her husband; *and did eat;* what remained of the peace-offerings, which were to be eaten that night, and not left till the morning; and though she would not eat her dinner, her heart was so full of grief, yet she could now make a good supper, being eased and relieved in her mind: *and her countenance was no more sad;* sorrowful and dejected, but cheerful, brisk, and lively; believing that her prayers, and those of the high-priest, would be answered.

"And they rose up in the morning early and worshipped before the Lord, and returned, and came to their house to Ramah. And Elkanah knew Hannah his wife, and the Lord remembered her. Therefore when the time had come after Hannah had conceived, she bore a son and called his name Samuel, saying, Because I have asked him of the Lord. And the man Elkanah and all his house went up Shiloh to offer to the Lord the yearly sacrifice and his vow. But Hannah did not go up. For she said to her husband, I will not go up until the child is weaned, and then I will bring him so that he may appear before the Lord and stay there forever. And Elkanah her husband said to her, Do what seems good to you. Stay until you have weaned him. Only the Lord establish His word. So the woman stayed and gave her son suck until she weaned him. And when she had weaned him, she took him up with her, with three bulls and one ephah of flour, and a bottle of wine, and brought him to the house of the Lord in Shiloh. And the child was young. And they killed a bull and brought the child to Eli. And she said, O my Lord, as your soul lives, my Lord, I am the woman who stood by you here, praying to the Lord. For this child I was praying, and the Lord has given me my petition which I asked of him. Therefore I have returned him to the Lord. As long as he lives he shall be given to the Lord. And he worshipped the Lord there" — II Samuel 1:19-28.

Here is, I. The return of Elkanah and his family to their own habitation, when the days appointed for the feast were over, v. 19. Observe how they improved their time at the tabernacle. Every day they were there, even that which was fixed for their journey home, they worshipped God; and they rose up early to do it. It is good to begin the day with God. Let him that is the first have the first. They had a journey before them, and a family of children to take with them, and yet they would not stir till they had worshipped God together. Prayer and provender do not hinder a journey. They had spent several days now in religious worship, and yet they attended once more. We should not be weary of well-doing.

II. The birth and name of this desired son. At length the Lord remembered Hannah, the very thing she desired (v. 11), and more she needed not desire, that was enough, for then she conceived and bore a son. Though God seem long to forget his people's burdens, troubles, cares, and prayers, yet he will at length make it to appear that they are not out of his mind. This son the mother called *Samuel,* v. 20. Some make the etymology of this name to be much the same with that of *Ishmael — heard of God,* because the mother's prayers were remarkably heard, and he was an answer to them. Others, because of the reason she gives for the name, make it to signify *asked of God.* It comes nearly to the same; she designed by it to perpetuate the remembrance of God's favour to her in answering her prayers. Thus she designed, upon every mention of his name, to take the comfort to herself and to give God the glory of that gracious condescension. Note, Mercies in answer to prayer are to be remembered with peculiar expressions of thankfulness, as Ps. cxvi. 1, 2. How many seasonable deliverances and supplies may we call *Samuels, asked of God;* and whatever is so we are in a special manner engaged to devote to him. Hannah intended by this name to put her son in the mind of the obligation he was under to be the Lord's, in consideration of this, that he was asked of God and was at the same time dedicated to him. A child of prayer is in a special manner bound to be a good child. Lemuel's mother reminds him that he was the *son of her vows,* Prov. xxxi. 2.

III. The close attendance Hannah gave to the nursing of him, not only because he was dear to her, but because he was devoted to God, and for him she nursed him. She therefore nursed him herself, and did not hang him on another's breast. We ought to take care of our children, not only with an eye to the law of nature as they are ours, but with an eye to the covenant of grace as they are given up to God. See Ezek. xvi. 20,21. This sanctifies the nursing of them, when it is done as unto the Lord. Elkanah went up every year to worship at the tabernacle, and particularly to perform his vow, perhaps some vow he had made distinct from Hannah's if God would give him a son by her, v. 21. But Hannah, though she felt a warm regard for the courts of God's house, begged leave of her husband to stay at home; for the women were not under any obligation to go up to the three yearly feasts, as the men were. However Hannah had been accustomed to go, but now desired to be excused, 1. Because she would not be so long absent from her nursery. *Can a woman forget her sucking child?* We may suppose she kept constantly at home, for, if she had gone any where, she would have gone to Shiloh. Note, God will have mercy and not sacrifice. Those that are detained from public ordinances by the nursing and tending of little children may take comfort from this instance, and believe that, if they do that with an eye to God, he will graciously accept them therein, and though they tarry at home they shall divide the spoil. 2. Because she would not go up to Shiloh till her son was big enough, not only to be taken thither, but to be left there; for, if once she took him thither, she thought she could never find in her heart to bring him back again. Note, Those who are stedfastly resolved to pay their vows may yet see good cause to defer the payment of them. *Every thing is beautiful in its season.* No animal was accepted in sacrifice till it had been for some time under the dam, Lev. xxii. 27. Fruit is best when it is ripe. Elkanah agrees to what she proposes (v. 23): *Do what seemeth thee good.* So far was he from delighting to cross her that he referred it entirely to her. *Behold how good and pleasant a thing it is,* when yoke-fellows thus draw even in the yoke, and accommodate themselves to one another, each thinking well of what the other does, especially in words of piety and charity. He adds a prayer: *Only the Lord establish his word,* that is, "God preserve the child through the perils of his infancy, that the solemn vow which God signified his acceptance of, by giving us the child, may be performed in its season, and so the whole matter may be accomplished." Note, Those that have in sincerity devoted their children to God may with comfort pray for them, that God will establish the word sealed to them at the same time that they were sealed for him.

IV. The solemn entering of this child into the service of the sanctuary. We may take it for granted that he was presented to the Lord at forty days old, as all the firstborn were (Luke ii. 22,23): but this is not mentioned, because there was nothing in it singular; but now that he was weaned he was presented, not to be redeemed. Some think it was as soon as he was weaned from the breast, which, the Jews say, was not till he was three years old; it is said she gave him suck till she had weaned him, v. 23. Others think it was not till he was weaned from childish things, at eight or ten years old. But I see no inconvenience in admitting such an extraordinary child as this into the tabernacle at three years old, to be educated among the children of the priests. It is said (v. 24), *The child was young,* but, being intelligent above his years, he was no trouble. None can begin too soon to be religious. *The child was a child,* so the Hebrew reads it, in his learning-age. For *whom shall he teach knowledge* but *those that are* newly *weaned from the milk and drawn from the breasts?* Isa. xxviii. 9. Observe how she presented her child, 1. With a sacrifice; no less than three bullocks, with a meat-offering for each, v. 24. A bullock, perhaps, for each year of the child's life. Or one for a burnt-offering, another for a sin-offering, and the third for a peace-offering. So far was she from thinking that, by presenting her son to God, she made God her debtor, that she thought it requisite by these slain offerings to seek God's acceptance of her living sacrifice. All our covenants with God for ourselves and ours must be made by sacrifice, the great sacrifice. 2. With a grateful acknowledgment of God's goodness in answer to prayer. This she makes to Eli, because he had encouraged her to hope for an answer of peace (v. 26,27): *"For this child I prayed.* Here it was obtained by prayer, and here it is resigned to the prayer-hearing God. You have forgotten me, my lord, but I who now appear so cheerful am the woman, the very same, that three years ago stood by thee here weeping and praying, and this was the child I prayed for." Answers of prayer may thus be humbly triumphed in, to the glory of God. Here is a living testimony for God. "I am his witness that he is gracious (see Ps. lxvi. 16-19); for this mercy, this comfort, I prayed, *and the Lord has given me my petition."* See Ps. xxxiv. 2, 4, 6. Hannah does not remind Eli of it by adverting to the suspicion he had formerly expressed; she does not say, "I am the woman whom you passed that severe censure upon; what do you think of me now?" Good men ought not to be upbraided with their infirmities and oversights. They have themselves repented of them; let them hear no more of them. 3. With a full surrender of all her interest in this child unto the Lord. (v. 28): *I have lent him to the Lord as long as he liveth.* And she repeats it, because she will never revoke it: *He shall be* (a dodand) *lent* or given *to the Lord.* Not that she designed to call for him back, as we do what we lend, but she uses this word *Shaol, lent,* because it is the same word that she had used before (v. 20, *I asked* him of the Lord), only in another conjugation. And (v. 27) the Lord gave me the petition which I *asked (Shaalti,* in Kal), therefore *I have lent him (Hishilti,* the same word in Hiphil), and so it gives another etymology of his name *Samuel,* not only *asked of God,* but *lent to God.* And observe, (1.) Whatever we give to God, it is what we have first asked and received from him. All our gifts to him were first his gifts to us. *Of thy own, Lord, have we given thee,* 1 Chron. xxix. 14, 16. (2.) Whatever we give to God may upon this account be said to be *lent* to him, that though we may not recal it, as a thing lent, yet he will certainly repay it, with interest, to our unspeakable advantage, particularly what is given *to his poor,* Prov. xix. 17. When by baptism we dedicate our children to God, let us remember that they were his before by a sovereign right, and that they are ours still so much the more to our comfort. Hannah reigns him to the Lord, not for a certain term of years, as children are sent apprentices, but *durante vita — as long as he liveth, he shall be lent unto the Lord,* a Nazarite for life. Such must our covenant with God be, a marriage-covenant; as long as we live we must be his, and never forsake him.

Lastly, The child Samuel did his part beyond what could have been expected from one of his years; for of him that seems to be spoken, *He worshipped the Lord there,* that is, *he said his prayers.* He was no doubt extraordinarily forward (we have known children that have discovered some sense of religion very young), and his mother, designing him for the sanctuary, took particular care to train him up to that which was to be his work in the sanctuary. Note, Little children should learn betimes to worship God. Their parents should instruct them in his worship and bring them to it, put them upon engaging in it as well as they can, and God will graciously accept them and teach them to do better.

CHAPTER 2.

"And Hannah prayed and said, My heart rejoices in the Lord, my horn is exalted in the Lord. My mouth is enlarged over my enemies, because I rejoice in Your salvation. There is none holy as the Lord, for there is none beside You. And there is no rock like our God. Talk no more so very proudly. Remove arrogancy out of your mouth, for the Lord is a God of knowledge, and by Him actions are weighed. The bows of the mighty men are broken, and they that stumbled are girded with strength. They that were full have hired themselves out for bread, and they that were hungry ceased — so that the barren has borne seven, and she that has many children has become feeble. The Lord kills and makes alive. He brings down to the grave, and brings up. The Lord makes poor, and makes rich. He brings low, and lifts up. He raises up the poor out of the dust, and lifts up the beggar from the dunghill to set them among princes and to make them inherit the throne of glory — for the pillars of the earth are the Lord's, and He has set the world upon them. He will keep the feet of His saints, and the wicked shall be silent in darkness, for by strength shall no man prevail. The foes of the Lord shall be broken to pieces. Out of heaven He shall thunder on them. The Lord shall judge the ends of the earth. And He shall give strength to the horn of His king, and exalt the horn of His annointed" — 1 Samuel 2: 1-10.

And Hannah prayed and said, &c.] She had prayed before, but that was mental, this vocal; she had prayed and was answered, and had what she prayed for, and now she gives thanks for it; and thanksgiving is one kind of prayer, or a part of it; see 1 Tim. ii. 1, Phil. iv. 6; wherefore though what follows is a song, it was expressed in prayer; and therefore it is said she prayed, and that by a spirit of prophecy, as the Targum; hence she is by the Jews reckoned one of the seven prophetesses; and indeed in this song she not only relates the gracious experiences of divine goodness she had been favoured with, and celebrates the divine perfections, and treats of the dealings of God with men, both in a way of providence and grace; both prophesies of things that should be done hereafter in Israel, and particularly of the Messiah and of his kingdom. There is a great likeness in this song to the song of the Virgin Mary; compare ver. 1, with Luke i. 46, 47; and ver. 2, with ver. 49, and ver. 4, 8, with ver. 51, 53: *my heart rejoiceth in the Lord;* not in her son the Lord had given her, but in the goodness and kindness of the Lord in bestowing him on her, as an answer of prayer; which showed great condescension to her, the notice he took of her, the love he had to her, and his well-pleasedness in her, and his acceptance of her prayer through Christ; she rejoiced not in her husband, nor in the wealth and riches they were possessed of, nor in any creature-enjoyments, but in the Lord, the Giver of all; nor in her religious services and sacrifices, but in the Lord Christ, through whom her duties were acceptable to God, and who was the antitype of the sacrifices offered; and it is in the Person, offices, the grace of Christ, that we should alone rejoice; see Phil. iv. 4, and iii. 3; this joy of Hannah's was not worldly, but spiritual; not outward, but inward; not hypocritical, but the real and hearty: *mine horn is exalted in the Lord;* which supposes that she had been in a low estate, was crest-fallen, and her horn was defiled in the dust, as Job says was his case, ch. xvi. 15; when God had shut up her womb, and her adversary upbraided she could not eat her food, and prayed in the bitterness of her soul; but now she could lift up her horn and her head, as horned creatures, to whom the allusion is, do, when they are lively and strong; now she could look pleasant and cheerful, and even triumph, being raised to a high estate, and greatly favoured of the Lord, to whom she ascribes this change of her state and circumstances: it was owing to his power and grace that she was thus strengthened and exalted; as it is owing to the same, that the people of God, who are in a low estate by nature, are raised out of it in conversion, and brought into an open state of grace and favour with God, and put into the possession of rich blessings and mercies, and have hope of eternal glory, on account of which they can exult and triumph; *my mouth is enlarged over mine enemies;* meaning Peninnah, and those that provoked her, and upbraided her with her barrenness, to whom she was not able to make any reply; but now her mouth was opened, and she could speak largely, and did; not in a way of reproach and reviling, in retaliation for what she had met with from others; but in prayer to God, to whom she could come with open mouth, and use freedom and boldness, and plead with importunity, fervency, and in faith, and in praise and thanksgiving to him for the great and good things he had done for her, and would now freely and largely speak of them to others; to some, her friends, to their joy and pleasure; and to others, her enemies, to their grief and confusion: *because I rejoice in thy salvation;* not only in temporal salvation wrought by the Lord for her, whereby she was delivered from the reproach of barrenness, through a son being given unto her; but in spiritual and eternal salvation, through the Messiah, she had knowledge of, and faith in, as appears from ver. 10; as all believers in him do, as it is contrived by the wisdom of God, wrought out by Christ, and applied by his Spirit; it being so great, so suitable, so perfect and complete, entirely free, and of an everlasting duration; see Psal. xx. 5, Isa. xxv. 9.

There is *none holy as the Lord,* &c.] From the consideration of what the Lord had done for her, which had filled her heart and mouth with joy and praise, she is led to celebrate the perfections of God, and begins with his holiness, in which he is glorious, and which appears in all his ways and works; he is, essentially, originally, independently, perfectly, and immutably holy, as others are not. Angels are holy, but not of themselves; their holiness is from the Lord; nor is it perfect in comparison of his, and therefore they cover their faces while they celebrate that perfection of his; nor immutable, at least not naturally so, as the loss of it in those that fell demonstrates. Of men, some under the legal dispensation were holy, not truly, but in a typical and ceremonial sense; some are not outwardly and hypocritically holy, and only so in the sight of men, not in the sight of God; and those that are truly holy, being called to holiness, and have the principle of it implanted in them, and live holy lives and conversations; yet though there is a likeness of the holiness of God in them, being made partakers of the divine nature; it is far from an equality to it; for the holiness of the best of men is imperfect; they are not without sin in them nor without sin committed by them, and perfection is disclaimed by them all; but the Lord is without iniquity, just and true is he; none in his nature, nor in any of his works, not the least shadow thereof: *for there is none besides thee;* there is no God besides him; no being but what is of him, and none is holy but by him: the holiness of angels is from him: the holiness of Adam in innocence was of him; and all the holiness of his chosen ones comes from him, to which they are chosen by him, and which is secured in that choice unto them, and are sanctified by God the Father in Christ, and through the Spirit: *neither* is there *any rock like our God;* the word *rock* is used for Deity, and sometimes for a false one, Deut. xxxii. 31; and so it may here, and the sense be, there is no god like to our God; there is indeed none besides him; there are fictitious gods, and nominal ones, as the idols of the Gentiles, and who are so in an improper and figurative sense, as magistrates; but there is but one true and living God; nor is there any like him for the perfections of his nature, and the blessing of his goodness, whether in providence or grace. Under this metaphor of rock, our Lord Jesus Christ is often signified; he is the rock of Israel, the rock of refuge, and of salvation; and there is no rock can do what he does, hide and shelter from the justice of God; there is no rock like him for strength and duration; none like him for a foundation to build upon, or for safety and protection from the wrath of God, and the rage of men, see Psal. xviii. 31.

Talk no more so exceeding proudly, &c.] At such a high rate, in such an overbearing manner, as if above every one; this may have respect to Peninnah, and all that joined with her to provoke Hannah to anger, and make her fret, insulting and triumphing over her, because she had not children, as they had: but now their mouths would be stopped, and their talk over, and not give themselves the haughty airs they had done, at least there would be no occasion for them: *let not arrogancy come out of your mouth;* arrogating to themselves, and to their merits, what they enjoyed, as children, riches, &c., when all come from the Lord; or what is *hard,* intolerable, which bears so hard on those to whom it is said, that it cannot be borne with: or what is *old,* and trite, old sayings concerning barren women, as if of no use in the world, and disagreeable to God, and as having no share in his favour. The Targum renders the word by reproaches, or blasphemies: *for the Lord is a God of knowledge;* or *knowledges;* of perfect knowledge; he knows all persons and things; he knows himself, his perfections, purposes, thoughts, words and works; he knows all his creatures, animate and inanimate, rational and irrational, angels and men; the hearts of all men; all that they say, all their hard sayings, all their proud, haughty, overbearing expressions, calumnies, and reproaches, as well as all they think and all they do, good or bad; and God will sooner or later convince them of and punish them for their hard speeches against his people: and he is the Author of all knowledge, natural, civil, spiritual, and evangelical: *and by him actions are weighed;* his own actions; his works *ad intra;* his purposes and decrees, the counsels of his will, and the thoughts of his heart, the things of his mind are set upon, all his appointments and designs, his whole will and pleasure; all are pondered by him, and are formed with the utmost wisdom, and for the best ends and purposes; and all his actions and works without, whether of creation, providence, and grace, all are weighed and done according to infinite wisdom, unerring justice and truth; all respecting things temporal or spiritual, what relate to the outward estate of men, or to their everlasting happiness: all the actions of men, as they are known unto him, they are weighed and examined by him, whether they proceed from a right principle to a right end or no; upon which, many actions, thought to be good, are not found to be so, and others, though good, yet not found perfect before God; so that there is no justification nor salvation by the best: or the sense is, such actions as are done well, they are *directed to him;* as they are ordained by him that men should walk in them, they are for his use, and are done with a view to his glory. There is a double reading of these words; the marginal, which we follow, is *to* or *by him* actions are directed or weighed; but the textual reading is a negative, *actions are not weighed* or numbered; the works of God cannot be comprehended, or the actions of men are not disposed and ordered without his will and pleasure, or cannot be performed unless he wills or permits; and all are disposed of, overruled, and directed, to answer his own ends and purposes.

Ver. 4. *The bows of the mighty men are broken,* &c.] Hannah, from relating gracious experiences, and celebrating the divine perfections of holiness, omniscience, and sovereignty, passes on to take notice of the dealings of God with men in providence and grace; *bows* are here put all military arms, which men of might and war make use of, and which God can easily break in pieces, and so make war to cease in the earth, and hinder warlike men from doing what they design and attempt: they are enfeebled and weakened by him, and their hands cannot perform their enterprises: so the bows of Satan, and his principalities and powers, are broken, and his fiery darts are quenched, and the people of the Lord enabled to stand against him, and wrestle with him and them, being strong in the Lord, and in the power of his might, as it follows; *and they that stumbled are girt with strength;* who, though weakness, are ready to stumble at every thing they meet with in the way; yet, being girded with strength by the Lord, are able to do great exploits, as David did, that being his case, Psal. xviii. 29, 32; so such as are weak in grace, in faith, in knowledge, and ready to stumble at every trial and exercise, let it come from what quarter it will; yet being girded by the Lord with strength, are able to exercise grace, perform duty, go through every service they are called to, whether in a way of doing or suffering, to bear the yoke and cross of Christ, to oppose every enemy, to walk on in the ways of God, and to persevere in faith and holiness to the end.

They that are *full have hired out themselves for bread,* &c.] Such as have been full of the good things of this life have been stripped of all, and reduced to such circumstances as to be obliged to hire themselves out to persons to labour under them for their bread. Hannah has either respect to some instances she had known, or prophecies of what would be hereafter, and was fulfilled in the Israelites, when in the hands of the Egyptians and Assyrians, Lam. iv. 6; and may be exemplified in the case of the prodigal son, Luke xv. 13-16; and is true of such who have larger gifts, but not grace, and which they exercise for lucres sake, and are mere hirelings; and of self-righteous persons who are full of themselves, of their goodness and righteousness, purity and power; are quite mercenary do all they do for gain, work for life, and labour for perishing meat, and for that which is not bread, and is unsatisfying; *and they that were hungry ceased;* that is, from being hungry, being filled with good things, having a large and sufficient supply to satisfy their craving desire, Luke i. 53. Such are the changes sometimes in providence, that those who have lived in great plenty and fulness are obliged to work for their bread; and, on the other hand, such as have been starving, and in famishing circumstances, have been brought into very plentiful and affluent ones. The *hungry,* in a spiritual sense, are such who hunger and thirst after Christ, and his righteousness, for justification before God; after him and his blood for the remission of their sins, and the cleansing of their souls; after him, and salvation by him, in whom alone it is to be had; after a view of interest in him, and a greater degree of knowledge of him; and after more communion with him in his word and ordinances; and after the enjoyment of them for that purpose: now when they enjoy what they are craving after, they cease to hire out themselves for bread, as others do; they do not cease from working, but from dependence on their works, on which they cannot feed and live, having found and got other and better bread to feed upon; they cease to be hungry, for they are filled and satisfied with the love of God, with the righteousness of Christ, with the blessings of grace, and salvation by him, with the goodness of his house, and with all the fulness of God and Christ; and so having what satisfies them, they desire no other food, shall no more want, or be in a starving condition any more, especially this will be the case hereafter: *so that the barren hath borne seven;* meaning herself, who had born many, even five children besides Samuel, ver. 20, 21; which either was the case before this song was delivered; or rather what she believed would be the case after Eli had blessed her, and prayed for the children by her; seven being a number put for many, Prov. xxiv. 16, Isa. iv. 1; *and she that hath many children is waxed feeble;* and incapable of bearing more, and stripped of what she had; this may be understood of Peninnah, concerning whom the Jews have this tradition, which Jarchi relates, that when Hannah bore one child, Peninnah buried two; and whereas Hannah had five, Peninnah lost all her ten children. This may be applied to the case of the Gentiles and Jewish churches, under the Gospel dispensation, when more were the children of the desolate or barren, the Gentiles, than of the married wife, the Jews, Isa. liv. 1.

Ver. 6. *The Lord killeth, and maketh alive,* &c.] Which is true of different persons; some he takes away by death, and others he preserves and continues in life; and of the same persons, whom God removes by death, and restores them to life again, of which there are instances both in the Old and New Testament; and be they which they will, both are of God, he is the great Disposer of life and death. Death is of him; it is by his appointment; it is sent by his order; and when it has a commission from him, there is no resisting it; and let it be brought about by what means it will, still it is of God: and life is of him; it is first given by him, and it is preserved by him; and though taken away, it shall be restored at the resurrection of the dead; of which some interpret this clause, as Kimchi and Ben Gersom observe; and what is here said is true, in a spiritual sense; the Lord kills by the law, or shows men that they are dead in sin, and in a law-sense; and he makes alive by his Spirit, through the Gospel, quickening such who were dead in trespasses and sins; which is his own work, and the effect of divine power and grace; see the note on Deut. xxxii. 39; *he bringeth down to the grave, and bringeth up;* he brings some very near to the grave, to the very brink of it; so that in their own apprehensions, and in the opinion of their friends, they are just dropping into it, and no hope of recovery left; when he says to them Return, and brings them back from the pit, and delivers them from going into it, Job xxxiii. 22, 28, 30, Psal. xc. 3; and even when they are laid in it, he brings up out of it again, as in the case of Lazarus, and which will be the case in the resurrection, John v. 28, 29.

The Lord maketh poor, and maketh rich, &c.] Which is true in a natural sense of the same persons, as might be exemplified in the case of Job; and of different persons, as in the parable of the rich man and Lazarus; for both poverty and riches are of God, see Prov. xxii. 2, and xxx. 8. Poverty is of God; for though it is sometimes owing to a man's own conduct, yet that there is such a difference among men in general, that some should be poor, and others rich, is owing to the wise providence of God, that men may be dependent on one another. Riches are of God, and are the gifts of his bountiful providence; for though they are oftentimes the fruits of industry and diligence as means, yet not always; and whenever they are, they are to be ascribed to the blessing of God attending the diligent hand. This is also true in a spiritual sense; for though spiritual poverty is owing to the fall of Adam, and to the actual sins and transgressions of men, whereby they become poor and miserable, yet all this is not without the knowledge and will of God; and it is he that makes men sensible of their poverty, and then makes them rich in spiritual things, with his own grace, and the blessings of it, with the riches of grace here, and of glory hereafter; all which flow from the good will of God, who has laid up much for his people, bestowed much on them, and entitles them to more; and which come to them through the poverty of Christ, who, though he was rich, became poor, that they through his poverty might be made rich, 2 Cor. viii. 9; *he bringeth low, and lifteth up;* which has been verified in the same persons, as in Job, Nebuchadnezzar, *&c.*, and in different persons, for he puts down one, and raises up another; so he rejected Saul from being king, and took David from the sheepfold, debased Haman, and raised Mordecai to great dignity, and, in a spiritual sense, the Lord shows men the low estate and condition they are brought into by sin, humbles them under a sense of it, brings down their proud spirits to sit at the feet of Jesus, and to submit to him, and to his righteousness; and he lifts them up by his Son out of their fallen, captive, and miserable estate and by his Spirit and grace brings them out of the horrible pit of nature into the state of grace; sets them upon the rock, Christ, and makes their mountain to stand strong by the discoveries of his love, and will at last lift them up to glory, and place them on the same throne with Christ.

He raiseth up the poor out of the dust, and lifteth up the beggar from the dunghill, &c.] This is but a further illustration of what is before expressed. Literally; such poor as are beggars, are those that are extremely poor, that sit in the dust and beg, and have nothing but a dunghill to lie on; yet God is able to raise and lift up persons in such an extremely low condition to a very high one: spiritually; such are the poor, who are poor in spirit, and spiritually poor, and are sensible of it, and they, and they only, are beggars, For all that are poor, as they are not sensible of their poverty, so they beg not; but some are and beg; they knock at the door of grace and mercy; their language is petitionary, they entreat the grace and mercy of God; their posture is standing, and waiting till they have an answer; they are importunate, and will not easily take a denial; and they observe all opportunities to get relief, and are thankful for every thing that is given them. Their condition, in which they are, is represented by the *dust* and *dunghill;* which in general denotes that they are in a mean estate, in a sinful one, and in a very polluted and loathsome one; in this condition the Lord finds them, when he calls them by his grace; and from this he raises and lifts them up by his Spirit and grace, out of which they could never have raised themselves; and in which estate of sin and misery they must have lain, had he not exerted his powerful efficacious grace, in bringing them into a glorious one, next described; *to set* them *among princes;* the people of God called by grace, who are the sons of the King of kings by adoption, manifested in their regeneration and faith; have a princely spirit, the spirit of adoption, a free, generous, and bountiful one: live and look like princes, are well fed and clothed, and attended; have the riches of princes, and are heirs of a kingdom; and to be set among them is to be made one, and ranked as such; to have a place and a name in the church, and among the people of God; to sit down with them at the table of the Lord, and have communion with them; *and to make them inherit the throne of glory;* eternal glory and happiness, which as it is signified by a kingdom and crown, so by a throne, and is the same with Christ's, Rev. iii. 21; and therefore must be a glorious one; and this is had by way of inheritance; not obtained by industry, nor purchased with money; but comes by adoption, grace, and belongs only to children, is a bequest of our heavenly Father, and comes through the death of Christ the Testator; and this phrase denotes not barely the right unto, but the possession of his happiness and glory; *for the pillars of the earth are the Lord's, and he hath set the world upon them;* the earth has its foundations on which it is laid, and its pillars by which it is supported; but these are no other than the power and providence of God; otherwise the earth is hung upon nothing, in the open circumambient air; and that God can and does do this may well be thought, and to do all the above things in providence and grace, related in the preceeding verses; in the support, and for the proof of which, this is observed.

Figuratively, the pillars of the earth may design the princes of the world, the supreme rulers of it, and civil magistrates, who are sometimes called corner-stones, and the shields of the earth, Zech. x. 4, Psal. xlvii. 9; and so pillars because they are the means of cementing, supporting, and protecting the people of the earth, and of preserving their peace and property. Likewise good men may be meant in a figurative sense, who, as they are the salt of the earth, are the pillars of it, for whose sake it was made, and is supported, and continued in being; the church is the pillar and ground of truth; and every good man is a pillar in the house of God; and especially ministers of the Gospel; see Rev. iii. 12, 1 Tim. iii. 15, Gal. ii. 9, Prov. ix. 1.

He will keep the feet of his saints, &c.] Now follow promises and prophecies of future things respecting the Israel of God, either in a literal or spiritual sense. By *his saints* are meant not angels, though they are his holy ones, but men, and a body of them; who though unholy in themselves, nor can they make themselves holy, yet are made so by the grace of God, in consequence of electing grace, by which they are chosen to be holy, from Christ the source and spring of all holiness, by the Holy Spirit of God, as the efficient cause, and which is done in effectual vocation; hence they live holy lives and conversations, though not altogether without sin in the present state. The word also signifies such to whom God has been kind and gracious, and on whom he had bestowed blessings of goodness, and who are bountiful and beneficent to others. These are the Lord's whom he has set apart for himself and has sanctified in Christ, and by his Spirit; and of these he is Keeper, not angels, nor ministers of the word, nor themselves, but the Lord himself is the Keeper of them; and who is an able, faithful, tender and compassionate, constant and everlasting Keeper of them; and particularly he keeps their *feet,* he indeed keeps their whole persons, their bodies and souls; the members of their bodies, and the powers of their souls, their head, their heart, their affections, from turning aside from him; he guides, directs, and orders all their actions, and goings; he keeps their feet in his own ways, where he has guided them: he keeps them in Christ the way, and in all the paths of faith, truth, righteousness, and holiness, and in the way everlasting: he keeps them from falling; for though they are liable to fall into sin, and by temptation, and from a lively exercise of grace, yet not totally and finally; they are secured from it by his love to them; the promises he has made them; his power exerted on their behalf; their being in the hands of Christ, and the glory of all the Three Persons concerned herein: *and the wicked shall be silent in darkness:* sin has spread darkness over all human nature; every man is born and brought up in darkness, and walks in it: a state of unregeneracy is a state of darkness, in which wicked men continue; and they are in the dark about God, the perfections of his nature, his mind and will, word and worship; about Christ, and the way of life, peace, and salvation by him; about their own state and condition by nature, and the danger they are in: about the nature and necessity of regeneration; and about the scriptures, and the doctrines of the Gospel; and living and dying in such a state, darkness, blackness of darkness, is their portion for ever: so the Targum, "the wicked "in hell in darkness shall be judged:" and it is said they shall be *silent* in it; they are quiet, easy and content in the state of natural darkness in which they are; they neither do nor will understand; they do not care to come to the light; but shun the means of light and knowledge; they have nothing to say of God, of Christ, of the Spirit of God, or of divine things; they can talk enough of evil things, and pour them out in great plenty, but not of any good; and when their evils are charged upon them by the law, their mouths are stopped, and they pronounced guilty, and have nothing to say why justice and judgment should not take place; and so they will be silent and speechless at the great day of judgment. Some interpret it, they shall be *cut off in darkness;* so Kimchi and Ben Melech; that is, by death, by the hand of God, by the sword of justice: *for by strength shall no man prevail;* which is a reason both why God will keep his saints, and why the wicked shall be silent, or cut off and perish: with respect to good men, they are not saved, kept, and preserved by their own strength; they are not saved without a righteousness, without regeneration, without repentance towards God, and faith in Christ; neither of which they can perform in their own strength; nor can a saint keep himself from, or prevail over his spiritual enemies of himself, not over sin, nor Satan, nor the world; but it is by the power of God that he is kept through faith unto salvation: and with respect to wicked men, these shall not prevail by their strength over good men, or the church, who are built upon a rock, against which the gates of hell cannot prevail; nor can the wicked so prevail by their strength as to hinder their being cut off, and cast into other darkness; they have no power over the spirit to retain it in the day of death; and whether they will or no, they shall be cast into hell, and go into everlasting punishment.

The adversaries of the Lord shall be broken to pieces, &c.] Or Jehovah, Father, Son, and Spirit, *shall break in pieces those that contend with him;* with the Lord or with his people or with Samuel particularly; for this may be considered as a prophecy of Hannah concerning her son, what God would do for him against his enemies, that should rise up, contend, and fight with him, as the Philistines; of whom Ben Gersom interprets it, whom the Lord discomfited and broke to pieces; see the literal fulfilment of this prophecy in ch. vii. in a spiritual sense all wicked men are the enemies of God, and of his people, and sooner or later shall be broken to pieces. Some, in a good sense; when they are smitten with the words of his mouth, cut to the heart, and made contrite; are humbled and brought into subjection to him, and their enmity slain and abolished, and they filled with love to him; and are so broken to pieces, that they have nothing to depend upon, or trust in life or salvation, but apply to Christ alone for it. Others, in an ill sense; and the meaning is, that the wicked shall be utterly destroyed by the Lord, with an everlasting destruction, with an incurable and irreparable one; shall be broken in pieces like a potter's vessel, which can never be put together again, see Psal. ii. 9, Rev. ii. 27; *out of heaven shall he thunder upon them;* as the Lord did upon the Philistines in the times of Samuel, when Israel were engaged in war with them, ch. vii. 10. And the last vial of the wrath of God, poured out upon his adversaries the antichristian states, will be attended with thunders and lightnings, Rev. xvi. 17, 18; it denotes the terrible manner in which God will destroy his adversaries; the Septuagint version is, *the Lord ascended to heaven and thundered;* hence Procopius Gazeus, following this version, says, Hannah prophesied of the taking up of the Saviour, and of the mission of the Holy Ghost, and of the preaching of the apostles, and of the second coming of Christ, as follows; *the Lord shall judge the ends of the earth;* not the land of Israel by Samuel, as some interpret it, see ch. vii. 15-17; but of the whole world, and may refer to the government of it in general by the Lord, or to the judgment of it by his Son, for he judges none, but has committed all judgment to him; who at his first coming judged the world, by the ministry of the word in Judea and in the Gentile world, by setting up ordinances, and by qualifying and constituting persons to act in the government of his church under him; and at his spiritual coming he will take to himself his great power and reign, and judge the whore of Babylon; and at his last or second coming he will judge the whole world, quick and dead, righteous and wicked: *and he shall give strength unto his king;* either who was made king in the times of Samuel; Saul, who was the first of the kings of Israel, or David, whom Samuel anointed; and it is true of them both, that the Lord gave them strength to fight with, and conquer their enemies; or rather the Lord's anointed, or Messiah; *and exalt the horn of his anointed;* and so the Targum paraphrases the words, "he shall give strength "to his king, and enlarge the kingdom of his Messiah;" with which Kimchi agrees, and says, the thing is doubled or repeated, for the King is the Messiah; and to him the words are applied by other Jewish writers, ancient and modern. Christ is King over all, angels and men, particularly he is King of saints; he is Jehovah's King, set up and anointed by him from everlasting; was in time promised as such, and in the fulness of time came in that character, and at his ascension to heaven was made and declared Lord and Christ; and through the success of his Gospel in the world has appeared yet more so, and will be still more manifest in the latter day, when he shall be King over all the earth, and especially in his personal reign. Now when *strength* is said to be given him, this must be understood either of strength given to him in human nature, to perform the great work of our redemption and salvation, which required great strength; as a Divine Person he needed none, as man he did; or of that strength communicated to him as Mediator, to give unto his people, in whom they have both righteousness and strength; or rather of that power and dominion given him as King particularly; all power in heaven and in earth were given at his resurrection, and will appear more fully hereafter, when his kingdom will be from sea to sea, and his dominion from the river to the ends of the earth, see Dan. vii. 13, 14. And the same thing is meant by *horn,* which is an emblem of strength, power, dominion, and glory; hence he himself is called the horn of David, and the horn of salvation; it is a name and title given to kings, Dan. vii. 24, Rev. xvii. 12; in allusion to the horns of beasts, in which their strength lies to defend themselves, and annoy their enemies; and the exaltation of him prophesied of may respect and include his resurrection from the dead, ascension to heaven, session at the right hand of God, the judgment of all committed to him, and the glorious exercise of his kingly office in the spiritual and personal reigns. This is the first time we meet with the word Messiah, or anointed, as ascribed to a Divine Person, the Son of God; who has this name or title from his being anointed, not with material oil, but with the oil of gladness, with the Holy Ghost, and his gifts and graces without measure; and who is called the Lord's anointed, because he was anointed by his Father to be Prophet, Priest, and King, or invested by him with those offices even from eternity, see Psal. ii. 6, Prov. viii. 22, 23; and which was more manifestly declared at his birth, his baptism, and ascension to heaven; see Luke ii. 40, 52, Acts x. 37, 38; and ii. 36.

"And Elkanah went to Ramah to his house. And the child served the Lord before Eli the priest. Now the sons of Eli were sons of Belial. They did not know the Lord. And the priest's custom with the people was, that when any man offered sacrifice, the priest's servant came while the flesh was boiling, with a flesh-hook of three teeth in his hand. And he stuck it in the pan or kettle or cauldron or pot. All that the flesh-hook brought up the priest took for himself. So they did in Shiloh to all the Israelites that came there. Also before they burned the fat, the priest's servant came and said to the man who sacrificed, Give flesh to roast for the priest. For he will not have boiled flesh from you, but raw! And if any man said to him, Let them not fail to burn the fat at once, and then take as your soul desires — then he would answer him, No! But you shall give it to me now! And if not, I will take it by force. So the sin of the young men was very great before the Lord. For men hated the offering of the Lord. But Samuel served before the Lord, a child girded with a linen ephod. Moreover his mother

*made him a little coat, and brought it to him from year to year when she came
up with her husband to offer the yearly sacrifice. And Eli blessed Elkanah and
his wife, and said, May the Lord give you seed of this woman for the loan which
is loaned to the Lord. And they went to their own home. And the Lord visited
Hannah so that she conceived, and she bore three sons and two daughters. And
the child Samuel grew before the Lord. Now Eli was very old, and heard all that
his sons did to all Israel, and how they lay with the women who gathered at the
door of the tabernacle of the congregation. And he said to them, Why do you do
such things? For I hear of your evil dealings from all people. No, my sons, for it
is no good report that I hear. You make the Lord's people to cry out. If one man
sins against another, the judge shall judge him. But if a man sins against the
Lord, who shall plead for him? But they did not listen to the voice of their
father, because the Lord desired to kill them. And the child Samuel grew up and
was in favor both with the Lord and also with men"* — 1 Samuel 2: 11-26.

And Elkanah went to Ramah to his house, &c.] Of which see ch. i. 19. This
was after he had offered the sacrifices at the feast, worshipped the Lord, and
Hannah had delivered her prayer or song of praise, and both had committed
Samuel to the care of Eli, and left with him: *and the child did minister unto the
Lord before Eli the priest;* he had not only read in the book of the law, but
learned to sing the praises of God vocally, and to play upon an instrument of
music, used in the service of God in those times, and to light the lamps in the
tabernacle, and open and shut the doors of it, and the like; which were suitable
to his age, and which might not be quite so tender as some have thought; or this
may respect some small beginnings in the ministry of the sanctuary, in which he
gradually increased under the inspection, guidance, and instruction of Eli, which
is meant by ministering before him; the Targum is, "in the life of Eli the priest;"
he began the ministration before his death. *Now the sons of Eli were sons of
Belial, &c.*] Not that Eli their father was Belial, a wicked man; but though they
had so good a father, they were very wicked men, unprofitable abandoned
wretches, that cast off the yoke of the law of God, and gave themselves up to all
manner of wickedness: *they knew not the Lord;* not that they had no knowledge
of God in theory, or were real atheists, but they were so practically; they denied
him in works, they had no love to him, nor fear of him, and departed from his
ways and worship, as much as if they were entirely ignorant of him; so the
Targum, "they did not know to fear "before the Lord," or serve him; or, as
Kimchi, "they did not know the way of the Lord," that is practically.

And the priest's custom with the people was, &c.] Not what was according to
the will and law of God, but which the sons of Eli had introduced; and in which
they were followed by the rest of the priests, and so it became an established
custom, and had the force of a law, statute, or judgment, as the word signifies:
that *when any man offered sacrifice;* not any sort of sacrifice, for if it was a
burnt-offering, it was wholly consumed by fire, and in that the following custom
could not take place; and if it was a sin-offering, that was eaten by the priests,
and so there was no need of taking such a method as after related; but a
peace-offering, part of which belonged to the Lord, the fat that was burnt, and
the breast and shoulder to the priest, and the rest to the owner, who made a
feast of it for his family and friends: *the priest's servant came while the flesh was
in seething:* that is while those parts were boiling for the owner and his family;
which was done in some part of the tabernacle, as afterwards in the temple:
with a flesh-hook of three teeth in his hand; with a three-forked instrument,
with which he was sent by order of the priest that slew the sacrifice, and offered
it, to whom belonged the parts before mentioned, allowed him by the law; but

not content with these, he sent his servant, while the rest were boiling, with such an instrument as here described to draw up more of the boiling-pot.

And he struck it into the pan, or kettle, or cauldron, or pot, &c.] Whatever vessel was made use of, larger or lesser, according to the quantity of flesh the owner boiled for himself and friends, the trident the priest's servant brought with him, he struck into the boiler to the bottom of it: *all that the flesh-hook brought up the priest took for himself;* as his own property; whereas no part of it all belonged to him, he having had the breast and shoulder delivered to him in the first place: and yet, by this method, all that he could drag up with this three-forked instrument he claimed as his own; which might be much, that would hang upon three teeth of it, or in which they were fastened; and, according to Abarbinel, each of them would bring up a pound of flesh, and perhaps more: *so they did in Shiloh, unto all the Israelites that came thither;* to offer their sacrifices, which was the proper place for them, the tabernacle and altar being there; and men of all ranks and degrees were treated alike; princes and people, rich and poor; the custom universally obtained, and all sorts of men met with the same usage.

Also before they burnt the fat, &c.] Which belonged to the Lord, and was to be offered to him by fire, in the first place, as it ought to be; and the order of sacrificing required that he should have his part first before the priest or the owner: but so impious were the priests become, that *the priest's servants came, and said to the man that sacrificed;* not to the priest that offered, but to the man that brought his sacrifice to be offered by the priest; *give flesh to roast for the priest;* meaning, not what was his by law, as the breast and shoulder, though for these he ought to have stayed until the fat was offered to the Lord; but other parts of the peace-offering, which he had no right unto, for roasting or boiling, and yet in an imperious manner demanded it by his servant; *for he will not have sodden flesh of thee, but raw;* though this was not the only reason of this demand, because he liked roast meat better than boiled; but because the three-forked flesh-hook did not always bring up the best pieces out of the boiling-pot; and therefore he resolved to have flesh raw, that he might have the best, as well as dress it to his own liking.

And if any man said unto him, let him not fail to burn the fat presently, &c.] Or stay till they have offered the fat, as the Targum; let that be done in the first place, which may be quickly done, in a very little time, and let as much haste be made as can be to do it: *and then take* as much *as thy soul desireth:* by which it appears that the men that brought the sacrifice had more religion at heart, and were more concerned for the honour and glory of God than the priest; being willing to suffer in their property, but could not bear that the Lord should be dishonoured, and so rudely treated: they were willing the priests should take what they pleased of theirs, though they had no right to any; only they desired the Lord might be served first, which was but reasonable: *then he would answer him,* nay, *but thou shalt give it* me *now, and if not, I will take it by force;* signifying, he would not stay till the fat was burnt, and the Lord had his portion, but he would have it directly; and if he would not give it him freely, he would take it whether he would or no; to such a height of insolence and impiety were the priests arrived, as to put it in the power of their servants to make such wicked demands, and treat God, and those that brought their sacrifices to him, in such a contemptuous manner.

Wherefore the sin of the young men was great before the Lord, &c.] That is, the sons of Eli; for they were the ringleaders who set these bad examples, which other priests followed, and therefore the sin is ascribed to them; and which was sadly aggravated by taking what was not their own, and by taking it in a forcible manner, and before the Lord had his part in the offering, and all this done in the tabernacle, in the presence of God; which plainly showed that they had not the fear of God before their eyes, nor any sense of his omniscience and omnipresence, any more than of his holiness and justice: *for men abhorred the offering of the Lord;* it was irksome and disagreeable to them to bring their sacrifices, when they saw the law of God was not attended to, and the rules of sacrificing were not observed; such contempt of God, such abuse of sacrifices, such injury done to the sacrificers, and such covetousness and sensuality in priests, that it even set the people against sacrifices, and made them loath them, and neglect to bring them. And this aggravated the sin of the young men, though the sacrificers were not excused hereby, ver. 24.

But Samuel ministered before the Lord, &c.] The ministration of Samuel, though a child, is observed both before and after the account of the ill behaviour and wickedness of Eli's sons; partly to the shame and disgrace of them, and as serving to aggravate their sin, and make it appear the more black and heinous; and partly to his honour and reputation, that he was not corrupted and turned aside from God by their evil practices. The phrase here used is different from that in ver. 11; there he is said to minister before Eli, under his direction and guidance, but here before the Lord; being now engaged in higher services, and which he could perform without the assistance of Eli, as in the presence of God more immediately; it seems to have respect to him when more grown in age, stature, knowledge, and experience, though here related: yet still being *a child;* not got out of his childhood, or arrived to manhood: *girded with a linen ephod;* such as priests used to wear, but not Levites in common, nor extraordinary persons on extraordinary occasions, see 1 Sam. xxii. 18, 2 Sam. vi. 14. This seems to be a peculiar favour, and a special honour which Eli granted to Samuel when so very young, on account of the grace of God bestowed on him in a wonderful manner; and because brought up in the tabernacle as a holy person, and a Nazarite; and because his birth was foretold, and he asked of God, as his name signified as Procopius Gazeus observes.

Moreover, his mother made him a little coat, &c.] Suitable to his stature; this was an outer coat to wear over others, and this also was such an one as the priests wore; it is the same word that is used for the priest's *robe,* Exod. xxviii. 4; and this, it is very likely, was altogether of her own spinning, and weaving, and making up; which were works women did in those times: and this Hannah did partly out of her great love to her son Samuel, and partly to lessen the expense that Eli, or the congregation, were at in the maintenance of him; and the Talmudists observe, that a priest might wear a garment, and minister in it, if his mother made it; and they give instances of priests, Ishmael and Eleazar, for whom their mothers made garments: *and brought it to him from year to year;* for it seems this was only to be worn at festivals, and not on common days; and therefore she did not leave it with him, but took it home with her, and brought it again at the returning festival; *when she came up with her husband to offer the yearly sacrifice;* whether at the passover, or at Pentecost, or at the feast of tabernacles; and it is very probable she came with her husband at them all, yearly; for though she was not by the law obliged thereunto, yet her religious zeal and devotion, and her great desire to see her son as often as she could, induced her to come.

And Eli blessed Elkanah and his wife, &c.] Not only the first time they brought Samuel to him, and left him with him; but every year they came to worship, as the Jewish commentators mostly interpret it: *and said, the Lord give thee seed of this woman;* children by her, year after year: *for the loan which is lent to the Lord;* instead of Samuel, who was asked of the Lord and given to him again; and as they were thereby in some measure deprived of him, and could not always enjoy him, and be delighted with him, Eli prayed for them, and gave them his benediction as a priest, that they might be favoured with other children, who might be of delight and service to them when in old age: *and they went unto their own home;* at Ramah, as in ver. 11; or *to his place, Elkanah's;* hence Kimchi concludes that Hannah was of another city originally: but the Targum is, "to their place;" and indeed, what was now the place or home of the one, was of the other.

And the Lord visited Hannah, &c.] In a way of mercy, approving and confirming the blessing of Eli; or rather granting the blessing he prayed for, by giving her power to conceive, bear, and bring forth children, as the following words explain it: *so that she conceived and bare three sons and two daughters;* whereby the prophecy of Hannah was fulfilled, ver. 5, and was no doubt matter of great joy to her, though of these children we nowhere else read, nor even of their names. Josephus says, Elkanah had other sons by Hannah, and three daughters; which agrees not with the text: *and the child Samuel grew before the Lord;* in age and stature, in grace and goodness, and improved much in the worship and service of God, both in theory and practice of it; or became great with him, high in his esteem and favour, and was blessed with much of his presence, and with large gifts of his grace.

Now Eli was very old, &c.] It is very probable he was now about 90 years of age, since when he died he was 98, ch. iv. 15; which is observed to show his incapacity for the discharge of his office, and inspection into public affairs; which gave his sons an opportunity of acting the wicked part they did without reproof, and with impunity, Eli knowing nothing of it; and accounts in some measure for the gentle reproof he gave them, when he did know of it; for being old, he was not so full of spirit and vigour, and more propense to tenderness and mercy: besides, his sons were grown up and married, and he had less authority over them; though he ought to have considered himself not as a father only, but as a high-priest and judge of Israel, and performed his office as such; however, it must be a great affliction to him in his old age, and added to the weight of it, that his sons should behave so unworthily as they did: *and heard all that his sons had done unto Israel;* who, besides what was by the law allowed them, took flesh out of the pot as it was boiling, and demanded raw flesh to roast before the fat was offered up to the Lord; and in this manner they used all, without distinction, that came with their sacrifices: *and how they lay with the women that assembled at the door of the tabernacle of the congregation;* not that they lay with them at the door in a public beastly manner; but the women that came thither they decoyed into their own apartments, or into some of the courts of the tabernacle, and there debauched them: who these women were, and what their business at the tabernacle, is not easy to say; some think they came about business which belonged to women to do there, as to wash and clean the rooms, to sew and spin, and the like; but one would think that these latter works should be done, not at the door of the tabernacle, but in some apartment in it, or rather at their own houses, for the use of it: the Targum is, that they there assembled to pray, which is more likely, and that they were devout women; who came there in large numbers, for the word used has the signification of armies; to perform religious exercises in fasting, and praying, and bringing sacrifices to be offered for them: though they do not seem to be such, as was Anna the prophetess, Luke ii. 37; who made their abode in the tabernacle, and served God night and day with fastings and prayers, since these were only at the door of the tabernacle; nor were there in the tabernacle conveniences for such persons, as afterwards in the temple. The Jews, for the most part, by these understand lying-in-women, who came with their offerings for purification, attended with many other women, their relations, friends, and neighbours, and which especially, when several met together on such an occasion, made a crowd at the door of the tabernacle; and some are of opinion that these men did not lie with them, or debauch them, according to the literal sense of the word; but that they delayed the offering of their nests of doves they brought, so that they were forced to stay all night, and could not return home; and because by this means they were restrained from their husbands, it is reckoned as if these men had lain with them; and which they think is confirmed, in that the man of God sent to Eli, after mentioned, takes no notice of this lewdness of theirs, only of their ill behaviour as to sacrifices; but the text is so express for their debauchery, that it cannot be denied.

And he said unto them, why do ye such things? &c.] As to impose upon the people that bring their offerings, by taking more than is due, and in a very indecent and imperious manner; and especially to defile the women when they came to worship: these were very scandalous sins, and deserved a more severe reprimand, and indeed a greater chastisement than by mere words; Eli should have rebuked them more sharply, and laid open the evil of their doings, and as a judge punished them for them: *for I hear of your evil doings by all this people;* the inhabitants of Shiloh, or who came thither to worship, who were continually making their complaints to Eli; which still shows his backwardness to reprove them in the manner he did until he was obliged to it by the continual remonstrances of the people against the practices of his sons; he did not attend to the information he had from a few persons, until it became general.

Nay, my sons, &c.] This seems to be too soft and smooth an appellation, too kind and endearing, considering the offence they were guilty of, and were now reproving for; rather they deserved to be called sons of Belial, the children of the devil, than sons of Eli, or brutes and shameless wretches, and such like hard names: *for it is no good report that I hear;* a very bad one; far from being good, scarce any thing worse could have been said of them; to rob persons of the flesh of their offerings, when there was a sufficient allowance made for them by law, and to be so impious as to require what was not their due, and even before the Lord had his; and to debauch the women that came to religious worship, and that in the sacred place of worship, they also being priests of the Lord, and married men; sins very shocking and sadly aggravated, and yet Eli treats them in this gentle manner: *ye make the Lord's people to transgress;* by causing them to forbear to bring their sacrifices, being used in such an injurious and overbearing way; and by decoying the women into uncleanness, and by setting examples to others: or, *to cry out;* as in the margin of our Bibles, to exclaim against them for their exhorbitant and lewd practices; so the Targum, "the "people of the Lord murmur because so ill used by "them:" this clause may be read in connexion with the former, *it is no good report that I hear,* which *ye cause to pass through the Lord's people;* ye occasion the people to speak ill of you everywhere, in the camp of Israel, throughout the whole nation; the report as it is bad, it is general, is in every one's mouth; so Maimonides interprets it; with which Jarchi and others agree.

If one man sin against another, the judge shall judge him, &c.] When one man does an injury to another in his person and property, the case is brought before the judge, he hears it, examines into it, and determines upon it, and does justice, orders that the injured person have satisfaction made him, and so the matter is ended: *but if a man sin against the Lord, who shall entreat for him?* all sin is in some sense against God, as it is contrary to his nature, and a breach of his law, and especially bold, daring, presumptuous sins; but there are some sins that are more immediately and particularly against God, as sins against the first table of the law, which relates to the worship of God, and such were the sins of Eli's sons in the affair of sacrifices; all sin against God is aggravated by the perfections of his nature, and made tremendous, as being against a God of strict justice, of unspotted purity and holiness, and who is omniscient, omnipresent, and omnipotent; and by the relation and connexion there is between God and men, he is their Creator and Preserver, the God of their lives and mercies, and of all the blessings they enjoy, and yet sin against him! who will entreat the favour of God for such persons, ask pardon for them, and beseech the Lord to be propitious and merciful to them? who on earth will do it? such persons are scarce and rare, few care to stand up in the gap between God and sinners: in some cases they ought not, in others they cannot; Eli suggests by this question, that he could not, even for his own sons; and who in heaven can or will do it? not saints departed, who know nothing of what is done below nor angels, only the Lord Jesus Christ; he is the only Mediator between God and men, who has engaged his heart to approach unto God and men, and interpose between him and sinful men, and has made peace and reconciliation by his blood, and is become the propitiation for sin, and ever lives to make intercession for transgressors, and is always prevalent and successful in his mediation and intercession; excepting him, there is none to entreat for those that have sinned against the Lord, see 1 John ii. 1, 2. In answer to this question, *who shall entreat for him?* the Jews say, repentance and good works; but these are insufficient advocates for a sinner, without the atoning sacrifice of Christ, who is the only propitiation for sin, and upon which a plea for pardon can only be founded: *notwithstanding they hearkened not unto the voice of their father:* to his reproofs and counsels, his reasonings and expostulations; though his rebukes were so gentle, and this last reasoning of his so close and strong, so nervous and striking; *because the Lord would slay them;* it was his purpose and decree, his will and pleasure, to cut them off for their wickedness; wherefore he gave them up to a judicial blindness, and hardness of heart, as he did Pharaoh, so that they were proof against all advice, admonitions, and arguments used with them: some choose to read the words, *therefore the Lord would slay them,* because they were disobedient to the voice of their father; but the former sense is best; for his will to destroy them was not so much for their disregard to the reproofs of their father, in which he himself was culpable, as for their breach of his laws.

And the child Samuel grew up, &c.] Increased in stature and in grace, grew more and more in all respects, and better and better, whilst Eli's sons grew worse and worse; the contrast between these make the one to shine and appear illustrious, and the other to look the blacker; or *he went on, and grew, and was good;* as he preceded on in years, and grew in stature, he appears more and more to be a good man, a virtuous, holy, and gracious person: *and was in favour both with the Lord, and also with men;* the Lord was pleased to give him some tokens of his favour, that he delighted in him, that he was well-pleasing in his sight, and that his person and services were acceptable to him; and the more Eli's sons disgusted the people by their ill lives and conduct, the greater esteem among them did Samuel obtain by his becoming life and conversation: all admired him, spoke well of him, and thanked God that in such bad times he was raising up one among them, of whom they had the most hopeful prospect of usefulness to them.

'And there came a man of God to Eli and said to him, Thus says the Lord: Did I plainly appear to the house of your father, when they were in Egypt in Pharaoh's house? And did I choose him out of all the tribes of Israel to be My priest, to offer on My altar, to burn incense, to wear an ephod before me? And did I give to the house of your father all the offerings made by fire from the children of Israel? Why, then, do you kick at My sacrifice and My offering, which I have commanded in My house? Do you honour your sons above Me, to make yourselves fat with the best of all the offerings of Israel My people? Therefore the Lord God of Israel says, I said indeed that your house and the house of your father should walk before Me forever. But now the Lord says, Be it far from Me. For those who honour Me I will honor, and those that think little of Me shall be lightly regarded. Behold, the days come when I will cut off your arm and the arm of your father's house, so that there shall not be an old man in your house. And you shall see a rival in My house, in all the good which shall be done to Israel. And there shall not be an old man in your house forever. And that man of yours whom I shall not cut off from My altar shall be left in order to make your eyes fail and to grieve your heart. And all the increase of your house shall die in the flower of their age. And this shall be a sign to you, which shall come on your two sons, on Hophni and Phinehas — in one day both of them shall die. And I will raise up a faithful priest to Myself, one who shall do according to that which is in My heart and in My mind. And I will build him a sure house, and he shall walk before My anointed forever. And everyone who is left in your house shall come and bow down to him for a piece of silver and a piece of bread. And they shall say, I beg you, put me in one of the priests' offices so that I may eat a piece of bread" — 1 Samuel 2: 27-36.

Eli reproved his sons too gently, and did not threaten them as he should, and therefore God sent a prophet to him to reprove him sharply, and to threaten him, because, by his indulgence of them, he had strengthened their hands in their wickedness. If good men be wanting in their duty, and by their carelessness and remissness contribute any thing to the sin of sinners, they must both expect to hear of it and to smart for it. Eli's family was now nearer to God than all *the families of the earth, and therefore he will punish them,* Amos iii. 2. The message is sent to Eli himself, because God would bring him to repentance and save him; not to his sons, whom he had determined to destroy. And it might have been a means of awakening him to do his duty at last, and so to have prevented the judgment, but we do not find it had any great effect upon him. The message this prophet delivers from God is very close.

I. He reminds him of the great things God had done for the house of his fathers and for his family. He appeared to Aaron in Egypt (Exod. iv. 27,) in the house of bondage, as a token of further favour which he designed for him, v. 27. He advanced him to the priesthood, entailed it upon his family, and thereby dignified it above any of the families of Israel. He entrusted him with honourable work, to offer on God's altar, *to burn incense,* and to wear that ephod in which was the breast-plate of judgment. He settled upon him an honourable maintenance, a share out of *all the offerings made by fire,* v. 28. What could he have done more for them, to engage them to be faithful to him?' Note, The distinguishing favours we have received from God, especially those of the spiritual priesthood, are great aggravations of sin, and will be remembered against us in the day of account, if we profane our crown and betray our trusts, Deut. xxxii. 6; 2 Sam. xii. 7, 8.

II. He exhibits a high charge against him and his family. His children did wickedly, and he connived at it, and thereby involved himself in the guilt; the indictment therefore runs against them all, v. 29. 1. His sons had impiously profaned the holy things of God: *"You kick at my sacrifice which I have commanded;* not only trample upon the institution as a mean thing, but spurn at it as a thing you hate to be tied up to." They did the utmost despite imaginable to the offerings of the Lord when they committed all that outrage and rapine about them that we read of, and violently plundered the pots on which, in effect, *Holiness to the Lord* was written (Zech. xiv. 20), and took that fat to themselves which God had appointed to be burnt on his altar. 2. Eli had bolstered them up in it, by not punishing their insolence and impiety: "Thou for thy part *honourest thy sons above me,"* that is, "thou hadst rather see my offerings disgraced by their profanation of them than see thy sons disgraced by a legal censure upon them for so doing, which ought to have been inflicted, even to suspension and deprivation *ab officio et beneficio — of their office and its emoluments.* Those that allow and countenance their children in any evil way, and do not use their authority to restrain and punish them, do in effect *honour them more than God,* being more tender of their reputation than of his glory and more desirous to humour them than to honour him. 3. They had all shared in the gains of the sacrilege. It is to be feared that Eli himself, though he disliked and reproved the abuses they committed, yet did not forbear to eat of the roast meat they sacrilegiously got, v. 15. He was a *fat heavy man* (ch. iv. 18), and therefore it is charged upon the whole family (though Hophni and Phinehas were principally guilty), *You make yourselves fat with the chief of all the offerings.* God gave them sufficient to feed them, but that would not suffice; they made themselves fat, and served their lusts with that which God was to be served with. See Hos. iv. 8.

III. He declares the cutting off of the entail of the high priesthood from his family (v. 30): *"The Lord God of Israel,* who is jealous for his own honour and Israel's, says, and lets thee know it, that thy commission is revoked and superseded." *I said, indeed, that thy house, and the house of thy father* Ithamar (for from that younger son of Aaron Eli descended), *should walk before me for ever.* Upon what occasion the dignity of the high priesthood was transferred from the family of Eleazar to that of Ithamar does not appear; but it seems this had been done, and Eli stood fair to have that honour perpetuated to his posterity. But observe, the promise carried its own condition along with it: *They shall walk before me for ever,* that is, "they shall have the honour, provided they faithfully do the service." *Walking before God* is the great condition of the covenant, Gen. xvii. 1. Let them set me before their face, and I will set them before my face continually (Ps. xli. 12), otherwise not. But now the Lord says, *Be it far from me.* "Now that you cast me off you can expect no other than that I should cast you off; you will not walk before me as you should, and therefore you shall not." Such wicked and abusive servants God will discard, and turn out of his service. Some think there is a further reach in this recal of the grant, and that it was not only to be fulfilled shortly in the deposing of the posterity of Eli, when Zadok, who descended from Eleazar, was put in Abiathar's room, but it was to have its complete accomplishment at length in the total abolition of the Levitical priesthood by the priesthood of Christ.

IV. He gives a good reason for this revocation, taken from a settled and standing rule of God's government, according to which all must expect to be dealt with (like that by which Cain was tried, Gen. iv. 7): *Those that honour me I will honour, and those that despise me shall be lightly esteemed.*

1. Observe in general, (1.) That God is the fountain of honour and dishonour; he can exalt the meanest and put contempt upon the greatest. (2.) As we deal with God we must expect to be dealt with by him, and yet more favourably than we deserve. See Ps. xviii. 25, 26.

2. Particularly, (1.) Be it spoken, to the everlasting reputation of religion or of serious godliness, that it gives honour to God and puts honour upon men. By it we seek and serve the glory of God, and he will be behind-hand with none that do so, but here and hereafter will secure their glory. The way to be truly great is to be truly good. If we humble and deny ourselves in any thing to honour God, and have a single eye to him in it, we may depend upon this promise, he will put the best honour upon us. See John xii. 26. (2.) Be it spoken, to the everlasting reproach of impiety or profaneness, that this does dishonour to God (despises the greatest and best of beings, whom angels adore) and will bring dishonour upon men, for those that do so shall be lightly esteemed; not only God will lightly esteem them (that perhaps they will not regard, as those that honour him value his honour, of whom therefore it is said, *I will honour them*), but they shall be lightly esteemed by all the world; the very honour they are proud of shall be laid in the dust; they shall see themselves despised by all mankind, their names a reproach; when they are gone, their memory shall rot, and, when they rise again, it shall be to everlasting shame and contempt. The dishonour which their impotent malice puts upon God and his omnipotent justice will return upon their own heads, Ps. lxxix. 12.

V. He foretells the particular judgments which should come upon his family, to its perpetual ignominy. A curse should be entailed upon his posterity, and a terrible curse it is, and shows how jealous God is in the matters of his worship and how ill he takes it when those who are bound by their character and profession to preserve and advance the interests of his glory are false to their trust, and betray them. If God's ministers be vicious and profane, *of how much sorer punishment will they be thought worthy,* here and for ever, than other sinners! Let such read the doom here passed on Eli's house, and tremble. It is threatened,

1. That their power should be broken (v. 31): *I will cut off thy arm, and the arm of thy father's house.* They should be stripped of all their authority, should be deposed, and have no influence upon the people as they had had. God *would make them contemptible and base.* See Mal. ii. 8, 9. The sons had abused their power to oppress the people and encroach upon their rights, and the father had not used his power, as he ought to have done, to restrain and punish them, and therefore it was justly threatened that the arm should be cut off which was not stretched out as it should have been.

2. That their lives should be shortened. He was himself an old man; but instead of using the wisdom, gravity, experience, and authority of his age, for the service of God and the support of religion, he had suffered the infirmities of age to make him more cool and remiss in his duty, and therefore it is here threatened that none of his posterity should live to be old, v. 31, 32. It is twice spoken: "*There shall not be an old man in thy house for ever;*" and again (v. 33), "*All the increase of thy house,* from generation to generation, *shall die in the flower of their age,* when they are in the midst of the years of their service," so that though the family should not be extinct, yet it should never be considerable, nor should any member of it come to be eminent in his day. Bishop Patrick relates, out of some of the Jewish writers, that long after this, there being a family in Jerusalem none of which commonly lived above eighteen years, upon search it was found that they descended from the house of Eli, on which this sentence

was passed.

3. That all their comforts should be embittered. (1.) The comfort they had in the sanctuary, in its wealth and prosperity: *Thou shalt see an enemy in my habitation.* This was fulfilled in the Philistines' invasions and the mischiefs they did to Israel, by which the country was impoverished (ch. xiii. 19), and no doubt the priests' incomes were thereby very much impaired. The captivity of the ark was such an act of hostility committed upon God's habitation as broke Eli's heart. As it is a blessing to a family to see *peace upon Israel* (Ps. cxxviii. 5, 6), so the contrary is a sore judgment upon a family, especially a family of priests. (2.) The comfort of their children: *"The man of thine whom I shall not cut off by an untimely death* shall live to be a blot and burden to the family, a scandal and vexation to his relations; he shall be to *consume thy eyes* and *grieve thy heart,* for his foolishness or his sickliness, his wickedness or his poverty." Grief for a dead child is great, but for a bad child often greater.

4. That their substance should be wasted and they should be reduced to extreme poverty (v. 36): *"He that is left alive in thy house* shall have little joy of his life, for want of a livelihood; he shall come and crouch to the succeeding family for a subsistence." (1.) He shall beg for the smallest alms — *a piece of silver* (and the word signifies the *least piece) and a morsel of bread.* See how this answered the sin. Eli's sons must have the best pieces of flesh, but their sons will be glad of a *morsel of bread.* Note, Want is the just punishment of wantonness. Those who could not be content without dainties and varieties are brought, they or theirs, to want necessaries, and the Lord is righteous in thus visiting them. (2.) He shall beg for the meanest office: *Put me into somewhat belonging to the priesthood* (as it is in the original); *make me as one of the hired servants,* the fittest place for a prodigal. Plenty and power are forfeited when they are abused. They should not be able to pretend to any good preferment, nor to any place at the altar, but should petition for some poor employment, be the work ever so hard and the wages ever so small, so they might but get bread. This, it is probable, was fully accomplished when Abiathar, who was of Eli's race, was deposed by Solomon for treason, and he and his turned out of office in the temple (1 Kings ii. 26, 27), by which it is easy to think his posterity were reduced to the extremities here described.

5. That God would shortly begin to execute these judgments in the death of Hophni and Phinehas, the sad tidings of which Eli himself should live to hear: *This shall be a sign to thee,* v. 34. When thou hearest it, say, "Now the word of God begins to operate; here is one threatening fulfilled, from which I infer that all the rest will be fulfilled in their order." Hophni and Phinehas had many a time sinned together, and it is here foretold that they should die together both in one day. Bind these tares in a bundle for the fire. This was fulfilled, ch. iv. 11.

VI. In the midst of all these threatenings against the house of Eli, here is mercy promised to Israel (v. 35): *I will raise me up a faithful priest.* 1. This was fulfilled in Zadoc, of the family of Eleazar, who came into Abiathar's place in the beginning of Solomon's reign, and was faithful to his trust; and the high priests were of his posterity as long as the Levitical priesthood continued. Note, The wickedness of ministers, though it destroy themselves, yet it shall not destroy the ministry. How bad soever the officers are, the office shall continue always to the end of the world. If some betray their trust, yet others shall be raised up that will be true to it. God's work shall never fall to the ground for want of hands to carry it on. The high priest is here said to *walk before God's anointed* (that is, David and his seed) because he wore the breast-plate of judgment, which he was to consult, not in common cases, but for the king, in the affairs of state. Note,

Notwithstanding the degeneracy we see and lament in many families, God will secure to himself a succession. If some grow worse than their ancestors, others, to balance that, shall grow better. 2. It has its full accomplishment in the priesthood of Christ, that merciful and faithful high priest whom God raised up when the Levitical priesthood was thrown off, who in all things did his father's mind, and for whom God will build a sure house, build it on a rock, so that the gates of hell cannot prevail against it.

And the child Samuel served the Lord before Eli. And the word of the Lord was precious in those days. There was no open vision. And at that time, when Eli had lain down in his place, and his eyes began to become dim so that he could not see — and before the lamp of God went out in the temple of the Lord, where the ark of God was, and Samuel had lain down — the Lord called Samuel. And he answered, Here am I. And he ran to Eli, and said, Here am I. For you called me. And he said, I did not call — lie down again. And he went to lie down. And the Lord called still again, Samuel! And Samuel arose and went to Eli and said, Here am I, for you called me. And he answered, I did not call, my son. Lie down again. Now Samuel did not know the Lord, neither was the word of the Lord revealed to him. And the Lord called Samuel again the third time. And he arose and went to Eli and said, Here am I, for you called me. And Eli saw that the Lord had called the child. Therefore, Eli said to Samuel, Go lie down, and if He calls you, you shall say, Speak, Lord, for Your servant hears. So Samuel went to lie down in his place. And the Lord came and stood and called as at other times, Samuel, Samuel! Then Samuel answered, Speak, for Your servant hears" — 1 Samuel 3: 1-10.

And the child Samuel ministered unto the Lord before Eli. And the word of the Lord was precious in those days; *there was* no open vision. And it came to pass at that time, when Eli *was* laid down in his place, and his eyes began to wax dim, *that* he could not see; And ere the lamp of God went out in the temple of the Lord, where the ark of God *was*, and Samuel was laid down *to sleep;* That the Lord called Samuel: and he answered, Here *am* I. And he ran unto Eli, and said Here *am* I; for thou calledst me. And he said, I called not; lie down again. And he went and lay down. And the Lord called yet again, Samuel. And Samuel arose and went to Eli, and said, Here *am* I; for thou didst call me. And he answered, I called not, my son; lie down again. Now Samuel did not yet know the Lord, neither was the word of the Lord yet revealed unto him. And the Lord called Samuel again the third time. And he arose and went to Eli, and said, Here *am* I; for thou didst call me. And Eli perceived that the Lord had called the child. Therefore Eli said unto Samuel, Go, lie down: and it shall be, if he call thee, that thou shalt say, Speak, Lord; for thy servant heareth. So Samuel went and lay down in his place. And the Lord came, and stood, and called as at other times, Samuel, Samuel. Then Samuel answered, Speak; for thy servant heareth.

To make way for the account of God's revealing himself first to Samuel, we are here told, 1. How industrious Samuel was in serving God, according as his place and capacity were (v. 1): *The child Samuel,* though but a child, *ministered unto the Lord before Eli.* It was an aggravation of the wickedness of Eli's sons that the child Samuel shamed them. They rebelled against the Lord, but Samuel ministered to him; they slighted their father's admonitions, but Samuel was observant of them; he ministered before Eli, under his eye and direction It was the praise of Samuel that he was so far from being influenced by their bad example that he did not in the least fall off, but improved and went on. And it was a preparative for the honours God intended him; he that was thus faithful in a little was soon after entrusted with much more. Let those that are young be humble and diligent, which they will find the surest way to preferment. Those are fittest to rule who have learnt to obey. 2. How scarce a thing prophecy then was, which made the call of Samuel to be the greater surprise to himself and the greater favour of Israel: *The word of the Lord was precious in those days.* Now and then a man of God was employed as a messenger upon an extraordinary occasion (as ch. ii. 27), but there were no settled prophets, to whom the people might have recourse for counsel, nor from whom they might expect the discoveries of the divine will. And the rarity of prophecy made it the more precious, for what there was (it seems) was private: *There was no open vision,* that is, there were none that were publicly known to have visions. Perhaps the impiety and impurity that prevailed in the tabernacle, and no doubt corrupted the whole nation, had provoked God, as a token of his displeasure, to withdraw the Spirit of prophecy, till the decree had gone forth for the raising up of a more faithful priest, and then, as an earnest of that, this faithful prophet was raised up.

The manner of God's revealing himself to Samuel is here related very particularly, for it was uncommon.

"And the Lord said to Samuel, Behold, I will do a thing in Israel at which both the ears of everyone who hears it shall tingle. In that day I will do against Eli all that which I have spoken as to his house. When I begin, I will also make an end. For I have told him that I will judge his house forever for the iniquity which he knows, because his sons made themselves vile and he did not restrain them. And therefore I have sworn to the house of Eli that the iniquity of Eli's house shall not be purged with sacrifice or offering forever. And Samuel lay until morning and opened the doors of the house of the Lord. And Samuel feared to show Eli the vision. Then Eli called Samuel and said, Samuel, my son. And he answered, Here am I. And he said, What is the thing that the Lord has said to you? Please do not hide it from me. God do so to you and more also if you hide anything from me of all the things that He said to you. And Samuel told him all the things and hid nothing from him. And he said, It is the Lord; let Him do what seems good to Him " — 1 Samuel 3: 11-18

And the Lord said to Samuel, &c.] The voice of the Lord continued speaking to him: *behold, I will do a thing in Israel;* which may be particularly interpreted of the taking of the ark, and the slaying of the two sons of Eli: and which is elsewhere represented as the Lord's doing, for the sins of Eli's family, Psal. lxxviii. 61, 62; *at which both the ears of every one that heareth it shall tingle;* be struck with horror and amazement, and quite stunned, and know not what to think or say, like persons surprised with a violent clap of thunder, which strikes their ears so strongly, that the noise of it is not soon gone from them; this was verified in Eli, and in his daughter-in-law particularly, who, at the news of the above things, the one fell backwards and broke his neck, and the other fell into labour and died; and all Israel were struck with astonishment at these things.

In that day I will perform against Eli all things which I have spoken concerning his house, &c.] Or family, that is, by the man of God, ch. ii. 27; as that he would cut off the strength of it, that there should not be an old man in it; and such as remained should be reduced to the utmost poverty and meanness: this shows that that prophecy was antecedent to this, contrary to the sense of some: *when, I begin, I will also make an end;* not immediately, and at once, but by degrees, he began in the death of Hophni and Phinehas, and went on in the slaughter of Abimelech, and the 85 priests at Nob, in the times of Saul, and finished in the thrusting out of Abiathar from the priesthood, in the times of Solomon, whereby that family was brought to disgrace and poverty.

For I have told him that I will judge his house for ever, &c.] That is, bring his judgments upon them, which should continue on them to their utter destruction; this, as to the substance, he said before by the man of God: *for the iniquity which he knoweth;* for the iniquity of his sons, which he was thoroughly informed of, and fully acquainted with by others; and somewhat of which he must have been sensible of, and seen with his own eyes, and therefore was inexcusable: *because his sons made themselves vile;* mean and contemptible in the sight of men, abhorred and accursed in the sight of God, by taking the flesh of the sacrifices of the people, which did not belong to them, who came to sacrifice, and by debauching the women that came to the door of the tabernacle for religious service. It is said this clause was originally written, *because his sons made light of me;* or cursed the Lord, and is one of the eighteen places called the correction of the Scribes, who corrected it as we have it; and it may be observed, the Septuagint version is, *because his sons spake ill of God;* or cursed him; however, this they did, they preferred their lusts, and the indulging of them, to the honour and glory of God: this Eli knew, *and he restrained them not;* from their evil practices; he did not make use of his authority, neither as a father, and especially not as a high-priest, and the judge of Israel, who ought not only to have sharply reproved them, which he did not, but to have censured or punished them, and turned them out of their office: *did not frown upon them,* as in the margin of our Bibles; he did not knit his brows, or wrinkle up his face, and by his countenance show his displeasure at their proceedings, but in an easy, smooth, gentle manner, expostulated with them about them.

And therefore I have sworn unto the house of Eli, &c.] Either had done this before, which was signified to him by the man of God, or did swear now for the confirmation of threatenings, and to assure the certain performance of them: *that the iniquity of Eli's house shall not be purged with sacrifice nor offering for ever;* not even typically, which was all that legal sacrifice could do; and not so that the priesthood should ever return to the family again, as the office of high-priesthood never did; or, as Abarbinel interprets it because of sacrifice and offerings, that the iniquity of Eli's sons were guilty of in taking the flesh of the sacrifice and offerings, which did not belong to them, and before the Lord had his part, should never be expiated.

And Samuel lay until the morning, &c.] It is not said he slept; it can hardly be thought he should, when it is considered what a new, strange, and uncommon thing had befallen him; what honour had been conferred on him, a child, that the Lord should vouchsafe to speak and communicate his mind to him, and what dreadful things were said of Eli's family; all which must greatly affect his mind, and keep him waking: however, he lay musing thereon until morning, and then arose, *and opened the doors of the house of the Lord;* as he had used to do, and which was the business of the Levites; though he had been so highly honoured, he was not elated with it, nor thought himself above so low and mean an employment in the house of God; nor did he run to Eli or others, boasting of what he had met with that night, but modestly and carefully attended to what was his common and constant employment every morning: *and Samuel feared to shew Eli the vision;* the vision of prophecy, as the Targum; what God had foretold should befall him and his family, lest he should be grieved on more accounts than one; partly because he, an old man, a high-priest, and judge of Israel, was overlooked and neglected, and the prophecy was delivered to a child, and not to him; and partly because of the sad things that should come upon his family.

Then Eli called Samuel, &c.] Perceiving he was risen by the opening of the doors of the tabernacle, which he might hear; and observing he did not come to him as usual, to know whether he wanted any thing, and being impatient to hear what was said to him of the Lord: *and he said, Samuel, my son;* called him by his name, and in a very tender and affectionate manner, the more to engage him to hasten to him, and thereby also putting him in mind of his filial duty to obey him: *and he answered, here* am *I*; ready to attend and perform any service enjoined him.

And he said, what is the thing that the Lord *hath said unto thee?* &c.] The word *Lord* is not in the text, but it is *that it hath said;* the voice that had so often called him in the night, and which yet Eli knew was the voice of the Lord; and as it was, he was sensible there was something of importance said, and he had great reason to believe it respected him and his family; and the rather he might conclude this, by what the man of God had lately said to him, whose words perhaps he had too much slighted, questioning his authority; and therefore the Lord took this way and method to assure him that what was said came from him; for hereby Eli was fully convinced that this voice Samuel heard was of the Lord, and so what was said must be from him, and this he was impatient to know: *I pray thee, hide it not from me;* and he not only besought and entreated him, but adjured him, as in the next clause: *God do so to thee, and more also, if thou hide any thing from me of all the things that he said unto thee;* it is the form of an oath or curse, wishing that God would do some great evil to him, and more than he chose to express, if he concealed any thing from him that had been told him. So Kimchi and Abarbinel take it to be an oath; and Josephus and Procopius Gazeus on the place say, that Eli obliged Samuel by oaths and curses to declare what had been said to him.

And Samuel told him every whit, and hid nothing from him, &c.] And so approved himself to be a faithful prophet of God, and man of God, as he is afterwards called; the whole counsel of God is to be declared by his servants the prophets, and the ministers of his word; nothing is to be concealed, which it is the will of God should be made known, whether it be pleasing or displeasing to man: *and he said,* it is *the Lord;* that has said it, and there is nothing to be said against it, and that will do it; and there is no resisting him: or *the Lord* is *he;* who has a sovereign right to all his creatures, and may dispose of them as he pleases; he is all-wise, and does all things well; he is holy and righteous in all his ways and works, and there is no unrighteousness in him; he is faithful to his word, whether in a way of promise or threatening; and all he does to his people is in love, mercy, and kindness: *let him do what seemeth him good;* not what seems good to men, or is so in their esteem, but what seems good to the Lord, who knows what is best for his people, and can do nothing but what is good; all is good he does; there is nothing but goodness in him, and nothing but goodness comes from him; he does good, and nothing else, and even when he afflicts his people; all he does is well done in creation, providence, and grace: and Eli's desire is, that he would fulfil the good pleasure of his will; he appears to be in an excellent temper, not surly and morose, taking it ill that such a message should be sent him by a child; nor was he unaffected with the case of his family, but humbly submitted to the will of God, and acquiesces in it as good, and neither arraigns his justice, nor murmurs at his providences.

"And Samuel grew, and the Lord was with him and let none of his words fall to the ground. And all Israel, from Dan even to Beersheba, knew that Samuel was established to be a prophet of the Lord. And the Lord appeared again in Shiloh. For the Lord revealed Himself to Samuel in Shiloh by the word of the Lord" — 1 Samuel 3: 19-21.

And Samuel grew, &c.] Not only in years and stature, but in grace and goodness, in wisdom, knowledge, and understanding, both with respect to things natural and spiritual, and in esteem, credit, and reputation among men: *and the Lord was with him;* he was not only in favour with men, but with God; and had fresh and repeated tokens of the grace and good will of God towards him; he indulged him with his presence, and assisted him in his service, and prospered and succeeded him in all things in which he was engaged. The Targum is, "the Word of the Lord was "his help;" the essential Word of God, the Messiah: *and did let none of his words fall to the ground;* in allusion either to water that falls to the ground, and becomes useless, or to an arrow falling out of the bow, and to the ground, before it reaches the mark, and so unsuccessful; or to any weapon of war, sword or spear, falling out of the hand of the soldier, whereby he is disarmed and rendered unserviceable: and these words, according to Kimchi, and in which he is followed by Abarbinel, are to be understood, not only of the words which he spake by the Holy Ghost under a Spirit of prophecy, and had their exact accomplishment; but his common words, which were spoken by weight and measure, as the last expresses it, and which were delivered out according to the rules of justice, probity, and truth: and so he failed not of performing that which he had said or of doing what was right, whereby Israel knew he was fit, prepared, and designed to be a prophet of the Lord, as in the following verse; but it seems rather to have respect to the things predicted by him under a Spirit of prophecy concerning Eli and his house, which soon began to be fulfilled.

And all Israel, from Dan even unto Beersheba, &c.] That is, from the most northern border of the land of Israel, on which Dan lay, to the utmost border of it southward, where Beersheba was, the fame of Samuel for his piety, prudence, and prophecy, was spread abroad; so that all *knew that Samuel* was *established* to be a *prophet of the Lord;* or that he was *faithful* to God and man, to be credited in what he said; and so a fit man to be a prophet of the Lord, being eminently qualified with gifts by him for that office; the Targum is, "that Samuel was faithful in "the words of the prophecy of the Lord," in relating them.

And the Lord appeared again in Shiloh, &c.] In the tabernacle there; he had appeared before to Samuel, when he called him, and declared to him what he designed and resolved to do to Eli and his family, and now appeared again to him in the same place before the battle of the Israelites with the Philistines, of which there is an account in the following chapter. Such appearances had not been usual in Shiloh for a long time, but were now renewed and repeated: *for the Lord revealed himself to Samuel by the Word of the Lord;* by Christ, the Word of the Lord, who appeared to him, it is probable, in a human form, as he was wont to do to the patriarchs and prophets, and by whom the Lord revealed his mind and will unto them, being the Angel of his presence, and the Messenger of his covenant; or by giving him a word of command to be delivered by him to the children of Israel, and which is expressed and delivered in the next chapter.

"And the word of Samuel came to all Israel. Now Israel went out against the Philistines to battle and pitched beside Ebenezer. And the Philistines pitched in Aphek. And the Philistines put themselves in order against Israel. And when they joined battle, Israel was beaten before the Philistines. And they killed about four thousand men of the army in the field. And when the people had come to the camp, the elders of Israel said, Why has the Lord beaten us today before the Philistines? Let us bring the ark of the covenant of the Lord out of Shiloh to us, so that when it comes among us it may save us out of the hand of our enemies. So the people sent to Shiloh in order to bring the ark of the covenant of the Lord of hosts from there, the ark which dwells between the cherubim. And the two sons of Eli, Hophni and Phinehas, were there with the ark of the covenant of God. And when the ark of the covenant of the Lord came into camp, all Israel shouted with a great shout, so that the earth rang again. And when the Philistines heard the noise of the shout, they said, What does the noise of this great shout in the camp of the Hebrews mean? And they understood that the ark of the Lord had come into the camp. And the Philistines were afraid, for they said, God has come into the camp. And they said Woe to us! For there has not been such a thing until now. Woe to us! Who shall deliver us out of the hand of these mighty gods? These are the gods that struck the Egyptians with all the plagues in the wilderness. Be strong and fight like men, O Philistines, so that you may not be slaves to the Hebrews, as they have been to you. Be men and fight!"
— 1 Samuel 4:1-9.

The first words of this paragraph, which relate to Samuel, that *his word came to all Israel,* seem not to have any reference to the following story, as if it was by any direction of his that the Israelites went out against the Philistines. Had they consulted him, though but newly initiated as a prophet, his counsel might have stood them in more stead than the presence of the ark did; but perhaps the princes of Israel despised his youth, and would not have recourse to him as an oracle, and he did not as yet interpose in public affairs; nor do we find any mention of his name henceforward till some years after (ch. vii. 3), only *his word came to all Israel,* that is, people from all parts that were piously disposed had recourse to him as a prophet and consulted him. Perhaps it is meant of his prophecy against the house of Eli. This was generally known and talked of, and all that were serious and observing compared the events here related, when they came to pass, with the prophecy, and saw it accomplished in them. Here is,

I. A war entered into with the Philistines, v. 1. It was an attempt to throw off the yoke of their oppression, and would have succeeded better if they had first repented and reformed, and so begun their work at the right end. It is computed that this was about the middle of the forty years' dominion that the Philistines had over Israel (Judg. xiii. 1) and soon after the death of Samson; so Bishop Patrick, who thinks the slaughter he made at his death might encourage this attempt; but Dr. Lightfoot reckons it forty years after Samson's death, for so long Eli judged, v. 18.

II. The defeat of Israel in that war, v. 2. Israel, who was the aggressors, were smitten, and had 4000 men kipped upon the spot. God had promised that one of them should chase a thousand; but now, on the contrary, *Israel is smitten before the Philistines.* Sin, the accursed thing, was in the camp, and gave their enemies all the advantage against them they could wish for.

III. The measures they concerted for another engagement. A council of war was called, and, instead of resolving to fast and pray and amend their lives, so ill taught were they (and no wonder when they had such teachers) that, 1. They quarrelled with God for appearing against them. (v. 3): *Wherefore has the Lord smitten us?* If they meant this as an enquiry into the clause of God's displeasure, they needed not go far to find that out. It was plain enough; Israel had sinned, though they were not willing to see it and own it. But it rather seems that they expostulate boldly with God about it, are displeased at what God has done, and dispute the matter with him. They own the hand of God in their trouble (so far was right): "It is the Lord that has smitten us;" but, instead of submitting to it, they quarrel with it, and speak as those that are angry at him and his providence, and not aware of any just provocation they have given him: "Wherefore shall we, that are Israelites, be smitten before the Philistines? How absurd and unjust is it!" Note, The foolishness of man perverts his way, and then his heart *frets against the Lord.* (Prov. xix. 3) and finds fault with him. 2. They imagined that they could oblige him to appear for them the next time by bringing the ark into their camp. The elders of Israel were so ignorant and foolish as to make the proposal (v. 3), and the people soon put it in execution, v. 4. They sent to Shiloh for the ark, and Eli had not courage enough to detain it, but sent his ungodly sons, Hophni and Phinehas, along with it, at least permitted them to go, though he knew that wherever they went the curse of God went along with them. Now see here, (1.) The profound veneration the people had for the ark. "O send for that, and it will do wonders for us." The ark was, by institution, a visible token of God's presence. God had said that he would dwell *between the cherubim,* which were over the ark and were carried along with it; now they thought that, by paying a great respect to this sacred chest, they should prove themselves to be Israelites indeed, and effectually engage God Almighty to appear in their favour. Note, It is common for those that have estranged themselves from the vitals of religion to discover a great fondness for the rituals and external observances of it, for those that even deny the power of godliness not only to have, but to have in admiration, the form of it. The temple of the Lord is cried up, and the ark of the Lord stickled for with a great deal of seeming zeal by multitudes that have no regard at all for the Lord of the temple and the God of the ark, as if a fiery concern for the name of Christianity would atone for a profane contempt of the thing. And yet indeed they did but make an idol of the ark, and looked upon it to be as much an image of the God of Israel as those idols which the heathen worshipped were of their gods. To worship the true God, and not to worship him as God, is in effect not to worship him at all. (2.) Their egregious folly in thinking that the ark, if they had it in their camp, would certainly *save them out of the hand of their enemies,* and bring victory back to their side. For, [1.] When the ark set forward Moses prayed, *Rise up, Lord, and let thy enemies be scattered,* well knowing that it was not the ark moving them, but God appearing for them, that must give them success; and here were no proper means used to engage God to favour them with his presence; what good then would the ark do them, the shell without the kernel? [2.] They were so far from having God's leave to remove his ark that he had plainly enough imitated to them in his law that when they were settled in Canaan his ark should be settled in the place that he should choose (Deut. xii. 5, 11), and that they must come to it, not it to them. How then could they expect any advantage by it when they had not a just and legal possession of it, nor any warrant to remove it from its place? Instead of honouring God by what they did, they really affronted him. Nay, [3.] If there had been nothing else to invalidate their expectations from the ark, how could they expect it should bring a blessing when Hophni and Phinehas were the men that carried it? It would have given too much countenance to their villany if the ark had done any kindness to Israel while it was in the hands of those graceless priests.

IV. The great joy there was in the camp of Israel when the ark was brought into it (v. 5): *They shouted, so that the earth rang again.* Now they thought themselves sure of victory, and therefore gave a triumphant shout before the battle, as if the day was without fail their own, intending, by this mighty shout, to animate themselves and their own forces, and to intimidate their adversaries. Note, Carnal people triumph much in the external privileges and performances of religion, and build much upon them, as if these would infallibly save them, and as if the ark, God's throne, in the camp, would bring them to heaven, though the world and the flesh should be upon the throne in the heart.

V. The consternation into which the bringing of the ark into the camp of Israel put the Philistines. The two armies lay so near encamped that the Philistines heard the shout the Israelites gave on this great occasion. They soon understood what it was they triumphed in. (v. 6), and were afraid of the consequences. For, 1. It had never been done before in their days: *God has come into their camp*, and therefore *woe unto us* (v. 7), and again, *woe unto us*, v. 8. The name of the God of Israel was formidable even to those that worshipped other gods, and some apprehensions even the infidels had of the danger of contending with them. Natural conscience suggests this, that those are in a woeful condition who have God against them. Yet see what gross notions they had of the divine presence, as if the God of Israel were not as much in the camp before the ark came thither, which may very well be excused in them, since the notions the Israelites themselves had of that presence were no better. "O," say they, "this is a new design upon us, more frightful than all their statagems, for *there has not been such a thing heretofore;* this was the most effectual course they could take to dispirit our men and weaken their hands." 2. When it had been done in the days of old, it had wrought wonders: *These are the gods that smote the Egyptians with all the plagues in the wilderness*, v. 8. Here they were so much out in their history as in their divinity: the plagues of Egypt were inflicted before the ark was made and before Israel came into the wilderness; but some confused traditions they had of wonders wrought by or for Israel when this ark was carried before them, which they attributed, not to Jehovah, but to the ark. Now, say they, *Who shall deliver us out of the hand of these mighty gods?* taking the ark for God, as well they might when the Israelites themselves idolized it. Yet, it should seem, they scarcely believed themselves when they spoke thus formidably of *these mighty gods*, but only bantered; for instead of retreating, or proposing conditions of peace, which they would have done had they been really convinced of the power of Israel's God, they stirred up one another to fight so much the more stoutly; this surprising difficulty did but sharpen their resolution (v. 9): *Be strong and quit yourselves like men.* The commanders inspired bold and generous thoughts into the minds of their soldiers when they bade them remember how they had lorded it over Israel, and what an intolerable grief and shame it would be if they flinched now, and suffered Israel to lord it over them.

"And the Philistines fought, and Israel was beaten, and each one of them fled to his tent. And there was a very great slaughter, for there fell thirty thousand footmen of Israel. And the ark of God was taken. And Hophni and Phinehas, the

two sons of Eli, were slain" — 1 Samuel 4: 10-11.

And the Philistines fought, &c.] With great ardour and spirit, quitted themselves like men of valour and courage, their case being desperate as they imagined, since God was in the camp of Israel; *and Israel was smitten:* were routed and beaten: *and they fled every man into his tent;* such of them as escaped the sword of the Philistines fled to their own houses in the several cities from whence they came; so the Targum, "every man to his city;" so that their army was quite broken up: *and there was a very great slaughter;* far greater than in the first battle: *for there fell of Israel* 30,000 *footmen;* their army chiefly, if not altogether, consisting of footmen, there being few horses in Israel; and if any cavalry now, these may be supposed to flee; before they lost only 4,000, now 30,000; so that the ark was no security to them, which was suffered, to show their vain trust and confidence in it.

And the ark of God was taken &c.] By the Philistines; which was suffered partly as a punishment to the Israelites, for fetching it from the tabernacle without the will of God, and for their vain confidence in it; and partly that the Philistines might have an experiment of the power and might of God, as procopius Gazeus observes, by what they would suffer through having it among them; some have thought that this was an emblem of Christ being delivered into the hands of the Gentiles, and of the Gospel being translated from the Jews to them: *and the two sons of Eli, Hophni and Phinehas, were slain;* which fulfilled the prophecy of the man of God, that they should both die in one day, ch. ii. 34. It is very probable they stood fast by the ark, and chose rather to die than to give it up freely; having received a charge from their father, that if the ark was taken, not to desire life, nor dare to come into his presence more, as Josephus relates.

"And a man of Benjamin ran out of the army. And he came to Shiloh the same day with his clothes torn and with earth on his head. And when he came, lo, Eli sat on a seat by the wayside watching. For his heart trembled for the ark of God. And when the man came to the city and told it, all the city cried out. And when Eli heard the noise of the crying, he said, What does the noise of this tumult mean? And the man hurried in and told Eli. Now Eli was ninety-eight years old, and his eyes were dim so that he could not see. And the man said to Eli, I am he who came out of the army, and I fled today out of the army. And he said, What is done there, my son? And the messenger answered and said, Israel has fled before the Philistines and there has been a great slaughter among the people also. And also your two sons, Hophni and Phinehas, are dead, and the ark of God is taken. And when he spoke of the ark of God, he fell backward off his seat, by the side of the gate. And his neck broke, and he died, for he was an old man, and heavy. And he had judged Israel forty years" — 1 Samuel 4: 12-18.

Tidings are here brought to Shiloh of the fatal issue of their battle with the Philistines. Bad news flies fast. This soon spread through all Israel; every man that fled to his tent brought it, with too plain a proof of it, to his neighbours. But no place was so nearly concerned as Shiloh. Thither therefore an express posted away immediately; it was a man of Benjamin; the Jews fancy it was Saul. *He rent his clothes, and put earth upon his head,* by these signs to proclaim the sorrowful news how much he himself was affected with it, v. 12. He went straight to Shiloh with it; and here we are told,

I. How the city received it. *Eli sat in the gate* (v. 13, 18), but the messenger was loth to tell him first, and therefore passed him by, and told it in the city, with all the aggravating circumstances; and now *both the ears of every one that heard it tingled,* as was foretold, ch. iii. 11. Their hearts trembled, and every face gathered blackness. *All the city cried out* (v. 13), and well they might, for, besides that this was a calamity to all Israel, it was a particular loss to Shiloh, and the ruin of that place; for, though the ark was soon rescued out of the hands of the Philistines, yet it never returned to Shiloh again; their candlestick was removed out of its place, because they had *left their first love,* and their city dwindled, and sunk, and came to nothing. Now God *forsook the tabernacle of Shiloh,* they having driven him from them; and the tribe of Ephraim, which had for 340 years been blessed with the presence of the ark in it, lost the honour (Ps. lxxviii. 60, 67), and, some time after, it was transferred to the tribe of Judah, the *Mount Sion which he loved,* as it follows there (v. 68), because the men of Shiloh knew not *the day of their visitation.* This abandoning of Shiloh Jerusalem is long afterwards reminded of, and told to take warning by. Jer. vii. 12, "*Go see what I did to Shiloh.* From this day, this fatal day, let the desolations of Shiloh be dated." They had therefore reason enough to cry out when they heard that the ark was taken.

II. What a fatal blow it was to old Eli. Let us see, 1. With what fear he expected the tidings. Though old, and blind, and heavy, yet he could not keep his chamber when he was sensible the glory of Israel lay at stake, but placed himself by the way-side, to receive the first intelligence; for *his heart trembled for the ark of God,* v. 13. His careful thoughts represented to him what a dishonour it would be to God, and what an irreparable loss to Israel, if the ark should fall into the Philistines' hands, with what profane triumphs the tidings would be told in Gath and published in the streets of Ashkelon. He also apprehended what imminent danger there was of it. Israel had forfeited the ark (his own sons especially) and the Philistines would aim at it; and now the threatening comes to his mind, that he should *see an enemy in God's habitation* (ch. ii. 32); and perhaps in his own heart reproached him for not using his authority to prevent the carrying of the ark into the camp. All these things made him tremble. Note, All good men lay the interest of God's church nearer their hearts than any secular interest or concern of their own, and cannot but be in pain and fear for them if at any time they are in peril. How can we be easy if the ark be not safe? 2. With what grief he received the tidings. Though he could not see, he could hear the *tumult* and *crying of the city,* and perceived it to be the voice of lamentation, and mourning, and woe; like a careful magistrate, he asks, *What means the noise of this tumult?* v. 14. He is told there is an express come from the army, who relates the story to him very distinctly, and with great confidence, having himself been an eye-witness of it, v. 16, 17. The account of the defeat of the army, and the slaughter of a great number of the soldiers, was very grievous to him as a judge; the tidings of the death of his two sons, of whom he had been so indulgent, and who, he had reason to fear, died impenitent, touched him in a tender part as a father; yet it was not for these that his heart trembled: there is a greater concern upon his spirit, which swallows up the loss; he does not interrupt the narrative with any passionate lamentations for his sons, like David for Absalom, but waits for the end of the story not doubting but that the messenger, being an Israelite, would, without being asked, say something of the ark; and if he could but have said, "Yet the ark of God is safe, and we are bringing it home," his joy for that would have overcome his grief for all the other disasters, and have made him easy; but, when the messenger concludes his story with, *The ark of God is taken,* he is struck to the heart, his spirits fail, and, it should seem, he swooned away, fell off his seat, and partly with the fainting, and partly with the fall, he died immediately, and never spoke a word more. His heart was broken first, and then his neck. So fell the high priest and judge of Israel, so fell his heavy head when he had lived within two of 100 years, so fell the crown from his head when he had judged Israel about forty years: thus did his sun set under a cloud, thus were the folly and wickedness of those sons of his, whom he had indulged, his ruin at last. Thus does God sometimes set marks of his displeasure in this life upon good men who have misconducted themselves, that others may hear, and fear, and take warning. A man may die miserably and yet not die eternally, may come to an untimely end and yet the end be peace. Dr. Lightfoot observes that Eli died the death of an unredeemed ass, whose neck was to be broken, Exod. xiii. 13. Yet we must observe, to Eli's praise, that it was the loss of the ark that was his death, not the slaughter of his sons. He does, in effect, say, "Let me fall with the ark, for what pious Israelite can live with any comfort when God's ordinances are removed?" Farewell all in this world, even life itself, if the ark be gone.

"And his daughter-in-law, Phinehas's sife, was with child, ready to be delivered. And when she heard the tidings of the ark of God was taken, and that her father-in-law and her husband were dead, she bowed herself and travailed, for her pains came on her. And about the time of her death the women that stood by her said to her, Do not fear, for you have borne a son. But she did not answer, neither did she pay attention to it. And she named the child Ichabod, saying, The glory has departed from Israel — because the ark of God has been taken, and because of her father-in-law and her husband. And she said, The glory is departed from Israel -- for the ark of God is taken" — 1 Samuel 4: 19-22.

We have here another melancholy story, that carries on the desolations of Eli's house, and the sorrowful feeling which the tidings of the ark's captivity excited. It is concerning the wife of Phinehas, one of those ungracious sons of Eli that had brought all this mischief on Israel. It cost her her life, though young, as well as that of her father-in-law, that was old; for many a green head, as well as many a hoary head, has been brought by sorrow to the grave: it worketh death. By what is here related of her it appears,

I. That she was a woman of a very tender spirit. Providence so ordered it that, just at this time, she was near her time; and our Saviour hath said, *Woe to those that are with child*, or *give suck*, in such days as these, Matt. xxiv. 19. So little joy will there then be in the birth, even of a man-child, that it will be said, *Blessed are the wombs that bear not*, Luke xxiii. 29. The amazing news coming at this unhappy juncture, it put her into labour, as great frights or other strong passions sometimes do. When she heard of the death of her father-in-law whom she reverenced, and her husband whom, bad as he was, she loved, but especially of the loss of the ark, *she travailed, for her pains came* thickly *upon her* (v. 19), and the tidings so seized her spirits, at a time when they needed all possible supports, that, though she had strength to bear the child, she, soon after, fainted and died away, being very willing to let life go when she had lost the greatest comforts of her life. Those who are drawing near to that trying hour have need to treasure up for themselves comforts from the covenant of grace, to balance, not only the usual sorrows, but anything extraordinary that may add to the grief which they do not foresee. Faith, at such a time, will keep from fainting, Ps. xxvii. 13.

II. That she was a woman of a very gracious spirit, though matched to a wicked husband. Her concern for the death of her husband and father-in-law was an evidence of her natural affection; but her much greater concern for the loss of the ark was an evidence of her pious and devout affection to God and sacred things. The former helped to hasten her travail, but it appears by her dying words that the latter lay nearer her heart (v. 22): *She said, The glory has departed from Israel,* not lamenting so much the sinking of that particular family to which she was related as the general calamity of Israel in the captivity of the ark. This, this was it that was her grief, that was her death.

1. This made her regardless of her child. The women that attended her, who it is likely were some of the first rank in the city, encouraged her, and, thinking that her concern was mostly about the issue of her pains, when the child was born, *said unto her, Fear not,* now the worst is past, *for thou hast borne a son* (and perhaps it was her first-born), *but she answered not, neither did she regard it.* The sorrows of her travail, if she had no other, would have been *forgotten, for joy that a man-child was born into the world.* John xvi. 21. But what is that joy, (1.) To one that feels herself dying? No joy but that which is spiritual and divine will stand us in any stead then. Death is too serious a thing to admit the relish of any earthly joy; it is all flat and sapless then. (2.) What is it to one that is lamenting the loss of the ark? Small comfort could she have of a child born in Israel, in Shiloh, when the ark is lost, and is a prisoner of the land of the Philistines. What pleasure can we take in our creature-comforts and enjoyments if we want God's word and ordinances, especially if we want the comfort of his gracious presence and the light of his countenance? *As vinegar upon nitre, so is he that sings songs to such* *heavy hearts.*

2. This made her give her child a name which should perpetuate the remembrance of the calamity and her sense of it. She has nothing to say to the child, only it being her province, now that her husband was dead, to name the child, she orders them to call it *Ichabod,* that is, *Where is the glory?* Or, *Alas for the glory!* or, *There is no glory* (v. 21), which she thus explains with her dying lips (v. 22): "*The glory has departed from Israel; for the ark of God is taken,.* Call the child inglorious, for so he is; the beauty of Israel is lost, and there appears no hope of ever retrieving it; never let the name of an Israelite, much lest a priest, carry glory in it any more, now that the ark is takne." Note, (1.) The purity and plenty of God's ordinances, and the tokens of his presence in them, are the glory of any people, much more so than their wealth, and trade, and interest, among the nations. 2. Nothing is more cutting, more killing, to a faithful Israelite, than the want and loss of these. If God go, the glory goes and all good goes. Woe unto us if he depart!

"And the Philistines took the ark of God and brought it from Ebenezer to Ashdod. When the Philistines took the ark of God, they brought it into the house of Dagon and set it beside Dagon. And when those of Ashdod arose early on the next day, behold, Dagon had fallen on his face to the earth before the ark of the Lord. And they took Dagon and set him in his place again. And when they arose early on the next morning, behold, Dagon had fallen on his face to the earth before the ark of the Lord. And the head of Dagon, and both the palms of his hands, were cut off on the threshold. Only the stump of Dagon was left to him. Therefore neither the priests of Dagon, nor any that come into Dagon's house, tread on the threshold of Dagon in Ashdod to this day" — 1 Samuel 5: 1-5.

And the Philistines took the ark of God, &c.] Which fell into their hands, Israel being beaten, and caused to flee, and the priests that had the care of the ark slain; and when possessed of it, they did not destroy it, nor take out of it what was in it, only took it up; *and brought it from Ebenezer unto Ashdod;* Ebenezer was the place where the camp of Israel was pitched, ch. iv. 1, and near to which the battle was fought. Ashdod was one of the five principalities of the Philistines, the same with Azotus, Acts viii. 40. The distance between those two places, according to Bunting, was 160 miles; though one would think the distance from each other was not so great: why it was carried to Ashdod is not plain; perhaps it might be the nearest place of note in their country; and certain it is that it was one of their most famous cities, if not most famous; see the note on Isa. xx. 1, and had a famous idol temple in it.

When the Philistines took the ark of God, &c.] And had brought it to Ashdod; *they brought it into the house of Dagon;* a temple dedicated to that idol, and in which his image stood; of which see the note on Judg. xvi. 33; *and set it by Dagon;* by the side of him, either in honour to the ark, as Abarbinel, designing to give it homage or adoration, as to their own deity; for though the Gentiles did not choose to change their gods, yet they would add the gods of other nations to them, and such the Philistines might take the ark to be: or else, as Procopius Gazeus, they brought it into their idol's temple, as a trophy of victory, and as a spoil taken from their enemies, and which they dedicated to their idol. Laniado observes, that the word here used signifies servitude, as in Gen. xxxiii. 15; and that the ark was set here to minister to, or serve their god Dagon. The temple of Dagon at Ashdod or Azotus was in being in the times of the Maccabees, and was burnt by Jonathan, 1 Maccab. x. 83, 84.

And when they of Ashdod arose early on the morrow, &c.] Either the people, the inhabitants of the place, who came early to pay their devotions to their idol, before they went on their business; or the priests of the idol, who came to sacrifice in the morning: *and, behold, Dagon was fallen upon his face to the earth before the ark of the Lord;* as if he was subject to it, and giving adoration to it, and owing it was above him, and had superior power over him: *and they took Dagon, and set him in his place again:* having no notion that it was owing to the ark of God, or to the God of Israel, that he was fallen, but that it was a matter of change.

And when they arose early on the morrow morning, &c.] For the same purpose as before; unless they had any curiosity to indulge, to see whether the ark and Dagon agreed better together, if they had any suspicion that the former mischance was to be attributed to some variance and disagreement between them: *behold, Dagon was fallen upon his face to the ground before the ark of the Lord;* again, and in a worse condition than before: *and the head of Dagon, and both the palms of his hands, were cut off upon the threshold;* of the temple, upon which he fell with such force, that the threshold cut off his head, and both his hands; which signified he had neither wisdom to contrive for his own safety, nor strength and power to defend himself; and therefore of what advantage could he be to his votaries? This may be an emblem of the fall of idolatry in the Gentile world, before the preaching of Christ and his Gospel in it; or of the idol of man's righteousness, which is set up, though it cannot stand against the righteousness of Christ, and of man's renouncing that, when convinced of the weakness and insufficiency of it, and submitting to the righteousness of Christ: *only* the stump *of Dagon was left to him;* his body, as the Targum, his head and hands being cut off; or, as it is in the Hebrew text, only Dagon was left; that is, the fishy part of this idol; for *Dag* signifies a fish; and, as Kimchi relates, this idol, from the navel upwards, had the form of a man, and from thence downwards the form of a fish; and it was the lower part that was left; see the note on Judg. xvi. 23.

Therefore neither the priests of Dagon, nor any that came into Dagon's house, &c.] Neither the priests that continually attended the worship and service of Dagon, nor the people that came there to pay their devotions to him: *tread on the threshold of Dagon in Ashdod unto this day;* but used to leap over it, either reckoning it sacred because touched by their idol, which fell upon it; or rather, as it should seem, in a way of detestation, because it had been the means of cutting off the head and hands of their idol; and this custom not only continued to the latter days of Samuel, the writer of this book; but even among the Philistines in one place or another to the times of Zephaniah, who seems to allude to it, ch. i. 9. In aftertimes there was another deity worshipped at Ashdod; according to Masius, the Philistine Venus, or Astarte, was worshipped in this place; though perhaps she may be no other than Ategatis, or Adergatis, which with Selden, is only a corruption of Addirdag, the magnificent fish, in which form Dagon is supposed to be; so the Phoenician goddess Derceto, worshipped at Ascalon, had the face of a woman, and the other part was all fish; though Ben Gersom says Dagon was in the form of a man, and which is confirmed by the Complutensian edition of the Septuagint, which on ver. 4, reads *the soles of his feet were cut off;* which is a much better reading than the common one; *the soles of his hands,* which is not sense; by which it appears that he had head, hands, and feet; wherefore it seems most likely that he had his name from Dagon signifying corn; see the note on Judg. xvi. 23.

"But the hand of the Lord was heavy on the people of Ashdod, and He destroyed them and struck them with hemorrhoids, Ashdod and the borders of it. And when the men of Ashdod saw that it was so, they said, The ark of the God of Israel shall not stay with us. For His hand is sore on us and on Dagon our god. Therefore they sent and gathered all the lords of the Philistines to them.

And they said, What shall we do with the ark of the God of Israel? And they answered, Let the ark of the God of Israel be carried around to Gath. And they carried the ark of the God of Israel around. And after they had carried it around, the hand of the Lord was against the city with a very great destruction. And He struck the men of the city, both small and great, and they had hemorrhoids in their secret parts. So they sent the ark of God to Ekron. And as the ark of God came to Ekron, the Ekronites cried out, saying, They have brought around the ark of the God of Israel to us in order to kill us and our people. So they sent and gathered together all the lords of the Philistines and said, Send away the ark of the God of Israel, and let it go again to its own place, so that it does not kill us and our people. For there was a deadly destruction throughout the city. And the men that did not die were stricken with the hemorrhoids. And the cry of the city went up to the heavens" — 1 Samuel 5: 6-12.

The downfall of Dagon (if the people had made a good use of it, and had been brought by it to repent of their idolatries and to humble themselves before the God of Israel and seek his face) might have prevented the vengeance which God here proceeds to take upon them for the indignities done to his ark, and their obstinate adherence to their idol, in defiance of the plainest conviction. *Lord, when thy hand is lifted up they will not see, but they shall see,* Isa. xxvi. 11. And, if they will not see the glory, they shall feel the weight, of God's hand, for so the Philistines did. *The hand of the Lord was heavy upon them* (v. 6), and he not only convinced them of their folly, but severely chastised their insolence. 1. *He destroyed them,* that is, cut many of them off by a sudden death, those, we may suppose, that had most triumphed in the captivity of the ark. This is distinguished from the disease with which others were smitten. At Gath it is called *a great destruction* (ver. 9), *a deadly destruction,* v. 11. And it is expressly said (v. 12) that those who were *smitten with the emerods were the men that died not* by the other *destruction,* which probably was the pestilence. They boasted of the great slaughter which their sword had made among the Israelites, ch. iv. 10. But God lets them know that though he does not see fit to draw Israel's sword against them (they were unworthy to be employed), yet God had a sword of his own, with which he could make no less dreadful execution among them, which if he whet, and *his hand take hold on judgment, he will render vengeance to his enemies,* Deut. xxxii. 41, 42. Note, Those that contend with God, his ark, and his Israel, will infallibly be ruined at last. If conviction conquer not, destruction shall. 2. Those that were not destroyed *he smote with emerods* (ver. 6), *in their secret parts* (ver. 9), so grievous that (v. 12) the *cry went up to heaven,* that is, it might be heard a great way off, and perhaps, in the extremity of their pain and misery, they cried, not to Dagon, but to the God of heaven. The Psalmist, speaking of this sore judgment upon the Philistines, describes it thus: God *smote his enemies in the hinder parts,* and *put them to a perpetual reproach,* Ps. lxxviii. 66. The emerods (which we call the piles, and perhaps it was then a more grievous disease than it is now) is threatened among the judgments that would be the fruit of the curse, Deut. xxviii. 27. It was both a painful and shameful disease; a vile disease for vile deserts. By it God would humble their pride, and put contempt upon them, as they had done upon his ark. The disease was epidemical, and perhaps, among them, a new disease.

Ashdod was smitten, and the coasts thereof, the country round. For contempt of God's ordinances, *many are weak and sick, and many sleep,* 1 Cor. xi. 30. 3. The men of Ashdod were soon aware that it was *the hand of God, the God of Israel,* v. 7. Thus they were constrained to acknowledge his power and dominion, and confess themselves within his jurisdiction, and yet they would not renounce Dagon and submit to Jehovah; but rather, now that he touched their bone and their flesh, and in a tender part, they were ready to curse him to his face, and instead of making their peace with him, and courting the stay of his ark upon better terms, they desired to get clear of it, as the Gadarenes, who, when they had lost their swine, desired Christ to *depart out of their coasts.* Carnal hearts, when they smart under the judgments of God, would rather, if it were possible, put him far from them than enter into covenant and communion with him, and make him their friend. Thus the men of Ashdod resolve, *The ark of the God of Israel shall not abide with us.* 4. It is resolved to change the place of its imprisonment. A great council was called, and the question proposed to all the lords was, "What shall we do with the ark?" And at last it was agreed that it should be carried to Gath, v. 8. Some superstitious conceit they had that the fault was in the place, and that the ark would be better pleased with another lodging, further off from Dagon's temple; and therefore, instead of returning it as they should have done, to its own place, they contrive to send it to another place. *Gath* is pitched upon, a place famed for a race of giants, but their strength and stature are no fence against the pestilence and the emerods: the men of that city were smitten, *both great and small* (v. 9), both dwarfs and giants, all alike to God's judgments; none so great as to over-top them, none so small as to be over-looked by them. 5. They were all at last weary of the ark, and very willing to get rid of it. It was sent from Gath to Ekron, and, coming by order of council, the Ekronites could not refuse it, but were much exasperated against their great men for sending them such a fatal present (v. 10): *They have sent it to us to slay us and our people.* The ark had the tables of the law in it; and nothing more welcome to faithful Israelites than the word of God (to them it is a *savour of life unto life*) but to uncircumcised Philistines, that persist in enmity to God, nothing more dreadful nor unwelcome: to them it is a *savour of death unto death.* A general assembly is instantly called, to advise about *sending the ark again to its place,* v. 11. While they are consulting about it, the hand of God is doing execution; and their contrivances to evade the judgment do but spread it. Many drop down dead among them. Many more are raging ill of the emerods, v. 12. What shall they do? Their triumphs in the captivity of the ark are soon turned into lamentations, and they are as eager to quit it as ever they had been to seize it. Note, God can easily make Jerusalem a burdensome stone to all that heave at it, Zech. xii. 3. Those that fight against God will soon have enough of it, and, first or last, will be made to know that none ever hardened their hearts against him and prospered. The wealth that is got by fraud and injustice, especially that which is got by sacrilege and robbing God, though swallowed greedily, and rolled under the tongue as a sweet morsel, must be vomited up again; for, till it be, the sinner shall not *feel quietness in his belly,* Job xx. 15-20.

CHAPTER 6

"And the ark of the Lord was in the country of the Philistines seven months. And the Philistines called for the priests and the diviners, saying, What shall we do to the ark of the Lord? Tell us what we shall send with it to its place. And they said, If you send away the ark of the God of Israel, do not send it empty. But in any case return Him a trespass — offering. Then you shall be healed, and it shall be known to you why His hand is not removed from you. Then they said, What shall be the trespass — offering which we shall return to him? And they answered, Five golden hemorrhoids, and five golden mice, for the number of the lords of the Philistines. For one plague was on you all, and on your lords — therefore you shall make images of your hemorrhoids, and images of your mice which mar the land. And you shall give glory to the God of Israel. Perhaps He will lighten His hand from off you, and from off your gods, and from off your land. Why then do you harden your hearts, as the Egyptians and Pharaoh hardened their hearts? When He had worked wonderfully among them, did they not let the people go, and did they not depart? Now therefore make a new cart, and take two milk cows on which there has come no yoke, and tie the cows to the cart, and bring their calves home from them. And take the ark of the Lord and lay it on the cart. And put the jewels of gold which you return to Him for a trespass — offering in a box beside it. And send it away so that it may go. And watch — if it goes up by the way of its own border to Bethshemesh, then He has done us this great evil. But if not, then we shall know that it is not His hand that struck us. It was a chance that happened to us" 1 Samuel 6: 1-9.

The first words of the chapter tell us how long the captivity of the ark continued — it was *in the country of the Philistines seven months. In the field of the Philistines* (so it is in the original), from which some gather that, having tried it in all their cities, and found it a plague to the inhabitants of each, at length they sent it into the open fields, upon which mice sprang up out of the ground in great multitudes, and destroyed the corn which was now nearly ripe and marred the land. With that judgment they were plagued. (v. 5), and yet it is not mentioned in the foregoing chapter; so God let them know that wherever they carried the ark, so long as they carried it captive, they should find it a curse to them. *Cursed shalt thou be in the city, and cursed in the field*, Deut. xxviii. 16. But most take it to signify, as we render it, *The country of the Philistines*. Now, 1. Seven months Israel was punished with the absence of the ark, that special token of God's presence. How bare did the tabernacle look without it! How was the holy city now a desolation, and the holy land a wilderness! A melancholy time no doubt it was to the good people among them, particularly to Samuel; but they had this to comfort themselves with, as we have in the like distress when we are deprived of the comfort of public ordinances, that, wherever the ark is, *the Lord is in his holy temple, the Lord's throne is in heaven*, and by faith and prayer we may have access with boldness to him there. We may have God nigh unto us when the ark is at a distance. 2. Seven months the Philistines were punished with the presence of the ark; so long it was a plague to them, because they would not send it home sooner. Note, Sinners lengthen out their own miseries by obstinately refusing to part with their sins. Egypt's plagues would have been fewer than ten if Pharaoh's heart had not been hardened not to let the people go. But at length it is determined that the ark must be sent back; there is no remedy, they are undone if they detain it.,

I. The priests and the diviners are consulted about it, v. 2. They were supposed to be best acquainted both with the rules of wisdom and with the rites of worship and atonement. And the Israelites being their neighbours, and famed above all people for the institutions of their religion, they had no doubt the curiosity to acquaint themselves with their laws and usages; and therefore it was proper to ask them, *What shall we do to the ark of Jehovah?* All nations have had a regard to their priests, as the men whose lips keep knowledge. Had the Philistines diviners? We have divines, of whom we should enquire wherewith we shall *come before the Lord* and *bow ourselves before the most high God.*

II. They give their advice very fully, and seem to be very unanimous in it. It was a wonder they did not, as friends to their country give it, *ex officio — officially*, before they were asked. 1. They urge it upon them that it was absolutely necessary to send the ark back, from the example of Pharaoh and the Egyptians, v. 6. Some, it may be, were loth to yield, and were willing to try it out with the ark awhile longer, and to them they apply themselves: *Wherefore. do you harden your hearts, as the Egyptians and Pharaoh did?* It seems they were well acquainted with the Mosaic history, and could cite precedents out of it. This good use we should make of the remaining records of God's judgments upon obstinate sinners, we should by them be warned not to harden our hearts as they did. It is much cheaper to learn by other people's experience than by our own. The Egyptians were forced at last to let Israel go; therefore let the Philistines yield in time to let the ark go. 2. They advise that, when they sent it back, they should send a trespass-offering with it, v. 3. Whatever the gods of other nations were, they knew the God of Israel was a jealous God, and how strict he was in his demands of sin-offerings and trespass-offerings from his own people; and therefore, since they found how highly he resented the affront of holding his ark captive, those with whom he had such a quarrel must *in any wise return him a trespass-offering*, and they could not expect to be healed upon any other terms. Injured justice demands satisfaction. So far natural light instructed men. But when they began to contrive what that satisfaction should be, they became wretchedly vain in their imaginations. But those who by wilful sin have imprisoned the truth in unrighteousness, as the Philistines did the ark (Rom. i. 18), may conclude that there is no making their peace with him whom they have thus injured but by a sin-offering; and we know but one that can take away sin. 3. They direct that this trespass-offering should be an acknowledgment of the punishment of their iniquity, by which they might take shame to themselves as conquered and yielding, and guilty before God, and might *give glory to the God of Israel* as their mighty conquerer and most just avenger, v. 5. They must make images of the *emerods*, that is, of the swellings and sores with which they had been afflicted, so making the reproach of that shameful disease perpetual by their own act and deed (Ps. lxxviii. 66), also images of the *mice that had marred the land*, owning thereby the almighty power of the God of Israel, who could chastise and humble them, even in the day of their triumph, by such small and despicable animals. These images must be made of gold, the most precious metal, to intimate that they would gladly purchase their peace with the God of Israel at any rate, and would not think it bought too dearly with gold, *with much fine gold.* The *golden emerods* must be, in number, five, according to the *number of the lords,* who, it is likely, were all afflicted with them, and were content thus to own it; it was advised that the *golden mice* should be five too, but, because the whole country was infested with them, it should seem, upon second thoughts, they sent more of them, *according to the number both of the fenced cities and of the country villages,* v. 18. Their priests reminded them that *one plague was on them all;* they could not blame one another, for they were all guilty, which they were plainly told by being all plagued. Their proposal to offer a trespass-offering for their offence was conformable enough to divine revelation at that time; but to send such things as these for trespass-offerings was very foreign, and showed them grossly ignorant of the methods of reconciliation appointed by the law of Moses; for there it appears all along that it is blood, and not gold, that makes atonement for the soul. 4. They encourage them to hope that hereby they would take an effectual course to get rid of the plague: *You shall be healed,* v. 3. For, it seems, the disease obstinately resisted all the methods of cure their physicians had prescribed. "Let them therefore send back the ark, and then," say they, *"It shall be known to you why his hand is not removed from you,* that is, by this it will appear whether it is for your detaining the ark that you are thus plagued; for, if it be, upon your delivering it up the plague will cease." God has sometimes put his people upon making such a trial, whether their reformation would not be their relief. *Prove me now herewith, saith the Lord of hosts,* Mal. iii. 10; Hag. ii. 18, 19. Yet they speak doubtfully (v. 5): *Peradventure he will lighten his hand from off you;* as if now they began to think that the judgment might come from God's hand, and yet not be removed immediately upon the restitution of the ark; however that was the likeliest way to obtain mercy. Take away the cause and the effect will cease. 5. Yet they put them in a way to make a further trial whether it was the hand of the God of Israel that had smitten them with these plagues or no. They must, in honour of the ark, put it on a new cart or carriage, to be drawn by two milch-cows, that had calves daily sucking them (v. 7), unused to draw, and inclined to home, both for the sake of the crib where they were fed and of the calves they nourished, and, besides, altogether unacquainted with the road that led towards the land of Israel. They must have no one to lead or drive them, but must take their own way, which, in all reason, one might expect, would be home again; and yet, unless the God of Israel, after all the other miracles he has wrought, will work one more, and by an invisible power lead these cows, contrary to their natural instinct and inclination, to the land of Israel, and particularly to Bethshemesh, they will retract their former opinion, and will believe it was not the hand of God that smote them, but it was a chance that *happened to them,* v. 8, 9. Thus did God suffer himself to be tempted and prescribed to, after he had been otherwise affronted, by these uncircumcised Philistines. Would they have been content that the honour of Dagon, their god, should be put upon such an issue as this? See how willing bad men are to shift off their convictions of the hand of God upon them, and to believe, when they are in trouble, that it is *a chance that happens to them;* and, if so, the rod has no voice which they are concerned to hear or heed.

"And the men did so. And they took two milk cows and tied them to the cart and shut up their calves at home. And they laid the ark of the Lord on the cart, and the box with the mice of gold and the images of their hemorrhoids. And the cows took the straight way to the way of Bethshemesh, going along the highway, lowing as they went. And they did not turn aside to the right or to the left. And the lords of the Philistines went after them to the border of Bethshemesh. And the people of Bethshemesh were reaping their wheat-harvest in the valley. And they lifted up their eyes and saw the ark, and rejoiced to see it. And the cart came into the field of Joshua, a Bethshemite, and stood there beside a great stone. And they cut the wood of the cart and offered the cows as a burnt offering to the Lord. And the Levites took down the ark of the Lord and the box that was in it, in which the jewels of gold were, and put them on the great stone. And the men of Bethshemesh offered burnt offerings and sacrifices the same day to the Lord. And when the five lords of the Philistines had seen it they returned to Ekron the same day. And these are the golden hemorrhoids which the Philistines returned for a trespass offering to the Lord — one for Ashdod, one for Gaza, one for Askelon, one for Gath, and one for Ekron. And the golden mice were according to the number of all the cities of the Philistines belonging to the five lords, of fenced cities and of country villages, even to the great stone of Abel, on which they set down the ark of the Lord. This stone remains to this day in the field of Joshua the Bethshemite" — 1 Samuel 6: 10-18.

We are told,

I. How the Philistines dismissed the ark, v. 10, 11. They were made as glad to part with it as ever they had been to take it. As God had fetched Israel out of the house of bondage, so now he fetched the ark out of its captivity, in such a manner as that *Egypt was glad when they departed*, Ps. cv. 38. 1. They received no money or price for the ransom of it, as they hoped to do, even beyond a king's ransom. Thus it is prophesied of Cyrus (Isa. xlv. 13), *He shall let go my captives, not for price nor reward.* Nay, 2. They gave jewels of gold, as the Egyptians did to the Israelites, to be rid of it. Thus the ark that was carried into the land of the Philistines, a trophy of their victory, carried back with it trophies of its own and lasting monuments of the disgrace of the Philistines. Note, God will be no loser in his glory, at last, by the successes of the church's enemies against his ark, but will get himself honour from those that seek to do dishonour to him.

II. How the kine brought it to the land of Israel, v. 12. They *took the straight way to Bethshemesh*, the next city of the land of Israel, and a priest's city, *and turned not aside.* This was a wonderful instance of the power of God over the brute creatures, and, all things considered, no less than a miracle, that cattle unaccustomed to the yoke should draw so even, so orderly, and still go forward, — that, without any driver, they should go from home, to which all tame creatures have a natural inclination, and from their own calves, to which they had a natural affection, — that, without any director, they should go the straight road to Bethshemesh, a city eight or ten miles off, never miss the way, never turn aside into the fields to feed themselves, nor turn back home to feed their calves. They went on lowing for their young ones, by which it appeared that they had not forgotten them, but that nature was sensible of the grievance of going from them; the power of the God of nature therefore appeared so much the greater, in overruling one of the strongest instincts of nature. These two kine, says Dr. Lightfoot, knew their owner, their great owner (Isa. i. 3), whom Hophni and Phinehas knew not, to which I may add they brought home the ark to shame the stupidity of Israel, that made no attempt to fetch it home. God's providence is conversant about the motions even of brute-creatures, and serves its own purposes by them. The lords of the Philistines, with a suitable retinue no doubt, went after them, wondering at the power of the God of Israel; and thus those who thought to triumph over the ark were made to go like menial servants after it.

III. How it was welcomed to the land of Israel: *The men of Bethshemesh were reaping their wheat-harvest,* v. 13. They were going on with their worldly business, and were in no care about the ark, made no enquiries what had become of it; if they had, it is likely they might have had private intelligence beforehand of its coming, and might have gone to meet it, and conduct it into their own border. But they were as careless as the people that *ceiled their own houses* and *let God's house lie waste.* Note, God will in his own time effect the deliverance of his church, not only though it be fought against by its enemies, but though it be neglected by its friends. Some observe that the returning ark found the men of Bethshemesh, not idling or sporting in the streets of the city, but busy, reaping their corn in their fields, and well employed. Thus the tidings of the birth of Christ were brought to the shepherds when they were *keeping their flock by night.* The devil visits idle men with his temptations. God visits industrious men with his favours. The same invisible hand that directed the kine to the land of Israel brought them into the field of Joshua, and in that field they stood, some think for the owner's sake, on whom, being a very good man, they suppose God designed to put this honour. I rather think it was for the sake of the great stone in that field, which was convenient to put the ark upon, and which is spoken of, v. 14, 15, 18. Now, 1. When the reapers *saw the ark, they rejoiced* (v. 13); their joy for that was greater than the joy of harvest, and therefore they left their work to bid it welcome. When the Lord turned again the captivity of his ark they were *like men that dream; then was their mouth filled with laughter,* Ps. cxxvi. 1, 2. Though they had not zeal and courage enough to attempt the rescue or ransom of it, yet, when it did come, they bade it heartily welcome. Note, The return of the ark, and the revival of holy ordinances, after days of restraint and trouble, cannot but be matter of great joy to every faithful Israelite. 3. They offered up the kine for a burnt-offering, to the honour of God, and made use of the wood of the cart for fuel, v. 14. Probably the Philistines intended these, when they sent them, to be a part of their trespass-offering, to make atonement, v. 3, 7. However, the men of Bethshemesh looked upon it as proper to make this use of them, because it was by no means fit that they should be put to any other use; never shall that cart carry any common thing that has once carried that sacred symbol of the divine presence: and the kine had been under such an immediate guidance of heaven that God had, as it were, already laid claim to them; they were servants to him, and therefore must be sacrifices to him, and no doubt were accepted, though females, whereas, in strictness, every burnt-offering was to be a male. 3. They deposited the ark, with a chest of jewels that the Philistines presented, upon the great stone in the open field, a cold lodging for the ark of the Lord and a very mean one; yet better so than a Dagon's temple, or in the hands of the Philistines. It is desirable to see the ark in its habitation in all the circumstances of solemnity and splendour; but better have it upon a great stone, in the fields of the wood, than be without it. The intrinsic grandeur of instituted ordinances ought not to be diminished in our eyes by the meanness and poverty of the place where they are administered. As the burning of the cart and cows that brought home the ark might be construed to signify their hopes that it should never be carried away again out of the land of Israel, so the setting of it upon a great stone might signify their hopes that it should be established again upon a firm rock. 4. They offered the sacrifices of thanksgiving to God, some think upon the great stone, more probably upon an altar of earth made for the purpose, v. 15. And, the case being extraordinary, the law for offering at the altar in the court of the tabernacle was dispensed with, and the more easily because Shiloh was now dismantled; God himself had forsaken it, and the ark, which was its chief glory, they had with them here. Bethshemesh, though it lay within the lot of the tribe of Dan, yet belonged to Judah, so that this accidental bringing of the ark hither was an indication of its designed settlement there, in process of time; for, when God *refused the tabernacle of Joseph, he chose the tribe of Judah*, Ps. lxxviii. 67, 68. It was one of those cities which were assigned out of the lot of Judah to the *sons of Aaron*, Josh. xxi. 16. Whither should the ark go but to a priests' city? And it was well they had those of that sacred order ready (for though they are here called *Levites* v. 15, yet it should seem they were priests) both to take down the ark and to offer the sacrifices. 5. The lords of the Philistines returned to Ekron, much affected, we may suppose, with what they had seen of the glory of God and the zeal of the Israelites, and yet not reclaimed from the worship of Dagon; for how seldom *has a nation changed its gods, though they were no gods!* Jer. ii. 11. Though they cannot but think the God of Israel *glorious in holiness and fearful in praises*, yet they are resolved they ill cleave because he is theirs. 6. Notice is taken of the continuance of the great stone in the same place; there it is *unto this day* (v. 18), because it remained a lasting memorial of this great event, and served to support the traditional history by which it was transmitted to posterity. The fathers would say to the children, "This is the stone upon which the ark of God was set when it came upon the Philistines' hands, a thing never to be forgotten."

"And He struck the men of Bethshemesh because they had looked into the ark of the Lord. He even struck among the people seventy men — fifty chief men, And the people lamented because the Lord had struck many of the people with a great slaughter. And the men of Bethshemesh said, Who is able to stand before this holy Lord God? And to whom shall He go up from us? And they sent messengers to the people of Kirjathjearim, saying, The Philistines have brought again the ark of the Lord. Come down and bring it up to yourselves" — 1 Samuel 6: 19-21.

And he smote the men of Bethshemesh, &c.] That is, God smote them, though they had received the ark with such expressions of joy, and had offered sacrifices on account of it; yet sinning in one particular after mentioned, which was highly resented, they were smitten by him with a thunderbolt, as Josephus says: *because they had looked into the ark of the Lord;* which was forbidden the

Levites, Numb. iv. 20; out of curiosity these men opened the ark, to see whether the Philistines had taken any thing out of it, or put any thing into it; and this, when in the tabernacle, being only to be seen by the high-priest; and supposing they should never have the same opportunity again, to look upon the tables of the law which were in it, took it; and the rather they might be emboldened to this action, since it had been in the hands of the uncircumcised Philistines, who had profaned it; and as yet not restored to its pristine purity, holiness, and place; *even he smote of the people, 50,000 and 70 men;* but as Bethshemesh was but a small place, a village, as Josephus calls it, and it seems not likely that there should be such a number of persons in it, and especially that should look into the ark; or that God, who is good and merciful, should destroy so large a number for this offence, however he might think fit to make an example of some, it is thought that the case was not as our version represents it. Some who think there were so many slain, yet distinguish them, 70 of the elders of the people, and 50,000 of the congregation, or common people, as the Targum; which accounts not for the difficulty at all; others think that only 70 of the men of Bethshemesh died, and that 50,000 were such as flocked out of the country on this occasion; but as this was on the same day the ark came into those parts, it can hardly be thought that so great a number should be got together so soon; and still less that they should all of them open the ark, and look into it. Abarbinel is of opinion that only 70 men of Bethshemesh were slain, and that the other 50,000 were the Philistines, that died on account of the ark while it was among them; and reads the words, *with the men of Bethshemesh he smote — even he smote of the people 70;* that is, of the men of Bethshemesh; 50,000, that is of the Philistines, and so this gives the sum of all that died on account of the ark, both whilst it was in the hands of the Philistines, and when returned to Bethshemesh, which is not an improbable sense, but others, and perhaps more truly, think that only 70 persons were smitten with death; for the order in which this account is given is different from all others in the Hebrew text, the lesser number being put first with a considerable distinguishing accent upon it, whereas the greater number is always expressed first; it stands thus, *of the people 70 men; 50,000 men: 5,000,* according to the Syriac and Arabic versions, Josephus is express for it that only 70 men were slain, and so some of the ancient Jews, who say that these 70 were equal to 50,000 because of their superior excellency and dignity, as Ben Gersom observes, being the priests of the Lord, or the sanhedrim; but Bochart's sense seems to be preferable to all others, that there is a defect of the particle, *out of* and so to be read, either *seventy men out of fifty thousand;* that out of the 50,000 that flocked on this occasion from divers parts, 70 were smitten for the reason before given; or rather 70 *men 50 out of* 1,000 *men;* that is, a 20th part of the number of them, so that, out of 1,4000,70 men were struck with death for their curiosity. Something of this story seems to be retained by tradition among the Heathens; we are told, that when Troy was taken an ark was found, in which was the image of Bacchus; which being opened by Eurypylus, he was struck with madness as soon as he saw the image; *and the people lamented, because the Lord had smitten* many *of the people with a great slaughter;* I see no occasion for the supplement *many;* it was a great slaughter, if we consider the awful manner in which it was made, by thunder and lightning, as may be supposed; however, by an immediate stroke from heaven; and the persons on whom it was made, men of a sacred character, priests and Levites; and a great number, considering it was but a small city. Hence the place was called Abel, which signifies weeping, mourning, lamentation, ver. 18.

And the men of Bethshemesh said, who is able to stand before this holy Lord God, &c.] The Targum is, "before the ark of this holy Lord God;" which is said either by way of complaint of the severity of God, and the strictness of his justice; or in reverence of his holiness, acknowledging their imperfection, sin, and guilt, by reason of which they could not stand before him; nor can any, but on account of the mercy-seat over the ark, or through Christ, his blood, righteousness, and sacrifice: *and to whom shall he go up from us?* that is, the ark, the symbol of God's presence, which they seem to be desirous of parting with; being unworthy of it, and conscious of their impurity in comparison of God that dwelt in it; and of their weakness to give the honour and reverence that was due unto it; and yet they knew not who were fit for it, or would choose to receive it, because of the danger they were liable to through every inadvertency in them, and irreverence of that.

And they sent messengers to the inhabitants of Kirjath-jearim, &c.] Which was a city further on in the tribe of Judah, and lay among some woods, from whence it had its name, and was formerly called Kirjath-baal, from Baal's being worshipped there; of which see Josh. xv. 9; they might choose to send hither to fetch the ark from them, because it was at a greater distance from the Philistines, their city Bethshemesh being on the borders of them; and because it might be a place of greater eminence and strength, and besides lay in the way to Shiloh, whereby they might suppose it was intended to be had; unless Shiloh was before this time destroyed: *saying, the Philistines have brought again the ark of the Lord;* which they doubted not would be good news to them: *come ye down, and fetch it up to you;* but say not one word of the reason of this request, lest it should discourage them; but rather represent it as a favour to them, and an honour done them, as indeed it was. Kirjath-jearim seems to have stood on an eminence in comparison of Bethshemesh, and therefore it is said to come down from the one, and go up to the other. That Bethshemesh was in a valley see ver. 13; and this on a hill. ch. vii. 1.

"And the men of Kirjath-jearim came and brought up the ark of the Lord. And they brought it to the house of Abinadab in the hill. And they sanctified Eleazar his son to keep the ark of the Lord. And the ark remained in Kirjath-jearim a long time — for it was twenty years. And all the house of Israel yearned after the Lord" — 1 Samuel 7: 1-2.

And the men of Kirjath-jearim came, and fetched up the ark of the Lord, &c.] From Bethshemesh, which was near unto them as Josephus says; they made no difficulty of fetching it, but gladly received it; for if they knew of what happened to the men of Bethshemesh, they knew it was not owing to the presence of the ark among them, but to their irreverent behaviour to it; and though Kirjath-jearim was not a Levite city, and so the men of it could not bear the ark themselves, yet they might have proper persons from Bethshemesh to do this service: *and brought it into the house of Abinadab in the hill;* which hill was within the city of Kirjath-jearim, and is mentioned either to distinguish this Abinadab that dwelt on it from another of the same name in the city, as Kimchi observes; or else to remark the propriety of the place, and the reason of the choice of it for the ark to be placed in; hills and high places being in those times accounted fittest for sacred services to be performed in, as well as places of safety; who this man was is not certain. Josephus says he was a Levite, but if so he could only be a sojourner in this place; however he might be, as he suggests he was, a man of great esteem for religion and righteousness: *and sanctified Eleazar his son to keep the ark of the Lord;* not only to watch it that it might not be taken away, but to keep persons from it, from touching it, or using it irreverently; and such as were not allowed to come nigh it; as well as to keep the place clean where it was put; and for this he was appointed by the priests, or the elders of the city; and was set apart for this service, and prepared for it by washings and sacrifices; and the rather he and not his father was invested with this office, because he was a young man, and his father might be old and decrepit; and this his son also a holy good man, wise and prudent, and active and zealous for God, and true religion; and on all accounts a fit person for this post.

And it came to pass, while the ark abode in Kirjath-jearim, that the time was long, &c.] It could not be less than between 40 and 50 years, for it remained here until the times of David, who removed it from hence after he was made king over all Israel, and when he had reigned over Judah 7 years, and from the death of Eli to that time, which included the government of Samuel and Saul, it could not be less than what has been hinted: *for it was twenty years;* not that this was all the time the ark was at Kirjath-jearim, but it was so long there before it was much taken notice of, and sought unto, and the Lord by it; there was a great neglect of God, and his worship, which through the means of Samuel began to revive about this time, as it follows: *and all the house of Israel lamented after the Lord;* became sensible of their evil doings, and repented of them, and sought the Lord with fasting, and prayer, and tears: bewailed their backslidings and revoltings from him, and cried after a departing God.

"And Samuel spoke to all the house of Israel, saying, If you do return to the

Lord with all your hearts, then put away the strange gods and Ashtaroth from among you, and prepare your hearts to the Lord, and serve Him only. And He will deliver you out of the hand of the Philistines. Then the children of Israel did put away Baalim and Ashtaroth and served only the Lord. And Samuel said, Gather all Israel to Mizpeh, and I will pray for you to the Lord. And they came together to Mizpeh and drew water and poured it out before the Lord, and fasted on that day. And they said there, We have sinned against the Lord. And Samuel judged the children of Israel in Mizpeh" — 1 Samuel 7: 3-6.

We may well wonder where Samuel was and what he was doing all this while, for we have not had him so much as named till now, since ch. iv. 1, not as if we were unconcerned, but his labours among his people are not mentioned till there appears the fruit of them. When he perceived that they began to *lament after the Lord* he struck while the iron was hot, and two things he endeavoured to do for them, as a faithful servant of God and a faithful friend to the Israel of God: —

I. He endeavoured to separate between them and their idols, for *there* reformation must begin. He *spoke to all the house of Israel* (v. 3), going, as it should seem, from place to place, an itinerant preacher (for we find not that they were gathered together till v. 5), and wherever he came this was his exhortation, *"If you do indeed return to the Lord,* as you seem inclined to do, by your lamentations for your departure from him and his from you, then know, 1. That you must renounce and abandon your idols, *put away the strange gods,* for your God will admit no rival; put them away from you, each one from himself, nay, and put them *from among you,* do what you can, in your places, to rid them out of the country. Put away Baalim, the strange gods, and Ashtaroth, the strange goddesses," for such also they had. Or Ashtaroth, is particularly named because it was the best-loved idol, and that which they were most wedded to. Note, True repentance strikes at the darling sin, and will with a peculiar zeal and resolution put away that, the sin which most *easily besets us.* 2. "That you must make a solemn business of returning to God, and do it with a serious consideration and a stedfast resolution, for both are included in *preparing the heart,* directing, disposing, establishing, the heart unto the Lord. 3. That you must be wholly for God, for him and no other, *serve him only,* else you do not serve him at all so as to please him. 4. That this is the only way and a sure way to prosperity and deliverance. Take this course, and *he will deliver you out of the hand of the Philistines;* for it was because you forsook him and served other gods that he delivered you into their hands." This was the purport of Samuel's preaching, and it had a wonderfully good effect (v. 4): *They put away Baalim and Ashtaroth,* not only quitted the worship of them, but destroyed their images, demolished their altars, and quite abandoned them. *What have we to do any more with idols?* Hos. xiv. 8; Isa. xxx. 22.

II. He endeavoured to engage them for ever to God and his service. Now that he had them in a good mind he did all he could to keep them in it.

1. He summons all Israel, at least by their elders, as their representatives, to meet him at Mizpeh (v. 5), and there he promises to pray for them. And it was worth while for them to come from the remotest part of the country to join with Samuel in seeking God's favour. Note, Ministers should pray for those to whom they preach, that God by his grace would make the preaching effectual.

And, when we come together in religious assemblies, we must remember that it is as much our business there to join in public prayers as it is to hear a sermon. He would pray for them that, by the grace of God, they might be parted from their idols, and that then, by the providence of God, they might be delivered from the Philistines. Ministers would profit their people more if they did but pray more for them.

2. They obey his summons, and not only come to the meeting, but conform to the intentions of it, and appear there very well disposed, v. 6.

(1.) *They drew water and poured it out before the Lord*, signifying, [1.] Their humiliation and contrition for sin, owning themselves as water spilt upon the ground, which cannot be gathered up again (2 Sam. xiv. 14), so mean, so miserable, before God, Ps. xxii. 14. The Chaldee reads it, *They poured out their hearts in repentance before the Lord.* They wept rivers of tears, and sorrowed after a godly sort, for it was before the Lord and with an eye to him. [2.] Their earnest prayers and supplications to God for mercy. The soul is, in prayer, poured out before God, Ps. lxii. 8. [3.] Their universal reformation; they thus expressed their willingness to part with all their sins, and to retain no more of the relish or savour of them than the vessel does of the water that is poured out of it. They were free and full in their confession, and fixed in their resolution to cast away from them *all their transgressions.* Israel is now *baptized from their idols*, so Dr. Lightfoot. [4.] Some think it signifies their joy in the hope of God's mercy, which Samuel had assured them of. This ceremony was used with that signification at the feast of the tabernacles, John vii. 37, 38, and see Isa. xii. 3. Taking it in this sense, it must be read, *They drew water after they had fasted.* In the close of their humiliation they thus expressed their hope of pardon and reconciliation.

(2.) *They fasted*, abstained from food, afflicted their souls, so expressing repentance and exciting devotion.

(3.) They made a public confession: *We have sinned against the Lord*, so giving glory to God and taking shame to themselves. And, if we thus confess our sins, we shall find our God *faithful and just to forgive us our sins.*

3. Samuel judged them at that time in Mizpeh, that is, he assured them in God's name, of the pardon of their sins, upon their repentance, and that God was reconciled to them. It was a judgment of absolution. Or he received informations against those that did not leave their idols, and proceeded against them according to law. Those that would not judge themselves he judged. Or now he settled courts of justice among them, and appointed the terms and circuits which he observed afterwards, v. 16. Now he set those wheels a-going; and, whereas before he acted only as a prophet, now he began to act as a magistrate, to prevent their relapsing into those sins which now they seemed to have renounced.

"And when the Philistines heard that the children of Israel had come together to Mizpeh, the rulers of the Philistines went up against Israel. And when the children of Israel heard, they were afraid of the Philistines. And the children of Israel said to Samuel, Do not cease from crying to the Lord our God for us, so that He will save us out of the hand of the Philistines. And Samuel took a

Samuel cried to the Lord for Israel, and the Lord heard him. And as Samuel was offering up the burnt-offering, the Philistines drew near to battle against Israel. But the Lord thundered with a great thunder on that day on the Philistines and troubled them. And they were beaten before Israel. And the men of Israel went out of Mizpeh and pursued the Philistines. And they struck them until they came to Bethcar. Then Samuel took a stone and set it between Mizpeh and Shen and called the name of it Ebenezer, saying, The Lord has helped us until now" — 1 Samuel 7: 7-12.

And when the Philistines heard that the children of Israel were gathered together to Mizpeh, &c.] Not knowing it was upon a religious account; but supposing they met to concert schemes and measures to cast off their yoke, and deliver themselves out of their hands; and were preparing to take up arms, and fall upon them: *the lords of the Philistines went up against Israel;* with forces out of their several principalities united to fight with them; judging it advisable to lose no time, but attack them before they were well prepared and provided to defend themselves: *and when the children of Israel heard it, they were afraid of the Philistines;* because they were unarmed, and not at all prepared for war, and having no expectation of it.

And the children of Israel said to Samuel, &c.] To whom they applied, not as the general of their forces, but as the prophet of the Lord; believing his prayers for them would be of more avail to them than an army of men ever so numerous, or so well accoutred: *cease not to cry unto the Lord our God for us;* he had been praying for them that day, and they desired he would continue praying for them, well knowing that the effectual fervent prayer of a righteous man avails much; they knew their salvation was of the Lord, and that he only could save them, and that he must be sought unto for it; and as Samuel had an interest in him, they beg he would continue to make use of it on their behalf; in which they expressed their trust in God, their regard to means, the duty of prayer, and the high esteem they had of the prophet of the Lord, whom they entreat to pray for them; *that he will save us out of the hands of the Philistines;* who were now coming up against them, and who had for a long time tyrannised over them.

And Samuel took a sucking lamb, &c.] Which it might be, and not more than eight days old, for under that it might not be sacrificed. Exod. xxii. 30; *and offered it for a burnt-offering wholly unto the Lord;* the whole of it was burnt, skin and all whereas, the skin was the priest's in other burnt-offerings; and this is remarked as one of the three things in which it differed from other offerings; the word being feminine, the Jews gather from hence, as Jarchi notes, that females might be offered at a private altar; *and Samuel cried unto the Lord for Israel;* not only offered a sacrifice for them, but prayed for them; *and the Lord heard him;* and answered him, either by causing fire to come down on the sacrifice, by which it was consumed, or by the voice of thunder, which frighted and discomfited the Philistines; and the event of things manifestly showed it.

And as Samuel was offering up the burnt-offering, &c.] Which he might do by a priest, as Ben Gersom suggests, he being a prophet, and an extraordinary person, and this an extraordinary case, he might do it himself, as Gideon and others, as well as offer it in another place than where the tabernacle was; Shiloh *suckling lamb and offered it for a burnt-offering wholly to the Lord. And* being now destroyed, persons and places for sacrifice were now dispensed with: and before Samuel had made an end of offering the sacrifice, the *Philistines drew near to battle against Israel;* and were come as far almost as Mizpeh, where Israel were, and Samuel was sacrificing: *but the Lord thundered with a great thunder on that day upon the Philistines;* which fulfilled Hannah's prophecy ch. ii. 10; and this, as Josephus says, was attended with lightning, which flashed in their faces, and shook their weapons out of their hands, so that they fled disarmed; and also with an earthquake, which caused gaps in the earth, into which they fell: *and discomfited them:* disturbed, affrighted them, and threw them into confusion and disorder, as well as destroyed many of them: *and they were smitten before Israel;* the meaning of which is not that they fled before them, and were killed by them; but that before Israel could come out against them, and fight with them, they were smitten and destroyed, many of them by the thunder and lightning, and by the earth opening upon them, and devouring them; for this phrase, *before Israel,* denotes time, as Abarbinel observes, and not place.

And the men of Israel went out of Mizpeh, &c.] To which they were encouraged by the hearing or perceiving that the army of the Philistines was discomfited by the thunder, and lightning, and earthquake: *and pursued the Philistines;* who, when they came out, were fleeing from the opening earth, and affrighted with thunder and lightning, and many were killed and all put in disorder; so that they stayed not to engage in battle with Israel, and who had nothing to do but to pursue their enemy: *and smote them:* with what weapons of war they could get at Mizpeh, and with what some might have with them for private use, and in common wear; but more especially with the weapons of the Philistines, which they in their confusion and fright had thrown away: *until* they came *under Bethcar;* a place so called; *car* signifies a lamb; here might be formerly a temple dedicated to the lamb, unless it had its name in the memory of the lamb Samuel now offered, which was followed with success. Josephus calls this place Correa; and in the Targum it is Bethsaron, which signifies a fruitful field or champaign country.

And Samuel took a stone, and set it, &c.] Not for worship, but as a monument of the victory obtained by the help of God: and this he placed *between Mizpeh and Shen;* which latter signifies a *tooth,* and designs the precipice of a rock which jets out, and hangs over in the form of one: *and called the name of it Ebenezer;* which signifies *the stone of help;* and is the same place which by anticipation has this name, ch. iv. 1; so that in the self-same place where the Israelites were twice beaten by the Philistines, and the ark taken, was this salvation wrought for them: *saying, hitherto hath the Lord helped us;* this was but the beginning of their deliverance from the Philistines, and which was owing to the help of the Lord; and as he had began to help them, they might hope and encourage themselves that he would go on to help them until their deliverance was completed: however, they with Samuel thought it their duty, which was right, to acknowledge what the Lord had done for them, and perpetuate the memory of it, though they could not be sure of what he would do for them hereafter; yet as they were sensible of, and thankful for this instance of his goodness, they hope for more, and had their dependence on him for future success against their enemies.

*"So the Philistines were beaten, and they did not come any more to the border
of Israel. And the hand of the Lord was against the Philistines all the days of
Samuel. And the cities which the Philistines had taken from Israel were given
back to Israel, from Ekron even to Gath. And Israel delivered the borders of it
out of the hands of the Philistines. And there was peace between Israel and the
Amorites. And Samuel judged Israel all the days of his life. And he went from
year to year in a circuit to Bethel and Gilgal and Mizpeh and judged Israel in all
those places. And his return was to Ramah, for his house was there. And he
judged Israel there. And he built an altar there to the Lord"* — 1 Samuel 7:
13-17.

So the Philistines were subdued, &c.] Not that their country was conquered, or
they made subject and become tributaries to Israel; but they were so humbled,
as not to attempt to give the people of Israel any further trouble and distress,
who were now delivered from their oppression and tyranny: *and came
no more into the coast of Israel;* at this time they did not gather together their
forces dispersed, nor raise and bring a new army into the land of Israel; they
contented themselves with placing garrisons on the coast, but did not attempt to
enter and invade them any more; that is, for a long time, even until Samuel was
grown old, and the people would have a king, and had one, which offended the
Lord, and then he suffered them to be distressed by them again; but whilst
Samuel was alone governor they came no more, though they did quickly after
Saul was made king, as it follows; *the hand of the Lord was against the
Philistines all the days of Samuel;* not all the days of his life, but all the days of
his sole government, which restrained them from making incursions into the land
of Israel; and indeed in after-times, when they did come forth to make war with
them, the battle was against them during the times of Samuel.

*And the cities which the Philistines had taken from Israel were restored to
Israel, &c.*] We nowhere read that the Israelites went out to war with them, and
took these cities from them by besieging and assaulting them; but they made a
demand of them after the above victory obtained, by which the Philistines were
so intimidated, that they quietly surrendered them to them: *from Ekron even
unto Gath, and the coasts thereof, did Israel deliver out of the hands of the
Philistines:* not by dint of sword, but by demand, to which they submitted; and
though Ekron, if not Gath, fell to the tribe of Judah by lot, yet were never in
their possession; and so are to be understood exclusively here, that not they, but
the cities and towns that lay between them and the coasts thereof, which the
Philistines had seized upon, these they were obliged to deliver up again to Israel;
and if Ekron and Gath were delivered, they were not long held by them, for we
soon read of them as in the hands of others; *and there was peace between Israel
and the Amorites;* who were a principal nation of the Canaanites, and are put for
the whole of them that remained; and so Josephus calls them the remnant of the
Canaanites; these, finding the Philistines were subdued, were quiet and
peaceable, and gave Israel no more trouble.

And Samuel judged Israel all the days of his life.] Not only before Saul was
made king, but afterwards; for though he had not the exercise of the supreme
government of the nation, yet he might act as a judge under Saul, and hear and
try causes brought before him, and execute justice and judgment; and as a
prophet he taught and instructed the people, and reformed abuses among them;

and besides, he held and exercised his extraordinary office, to which he was raised up of God, and even took upon him to reprove Saul himself, and to kill Agag. The Jews say he judged Israel 13 years only, 11 by himself, and two with Saul; but his government must be much larger, his with Saul is reckoned 40 years, Acts xiii. 21.

And he went from year to year in circuit, &c.] As judges do; or *from the year in the year,* from the time of the year in the year, as the Targum, from the middle of it, that is, every half-year; and so Josephus says, that he went twice a year in circuit; and the places he went to, and where he held his courts of judicature, were *Bethel, and Gilgal, and Mizpeh;* by Bethel is not meant Shiloh, as Abarbinel, for that was now destroyed; nor Kirjath-jearim, where the ark was, for it would have been called by its name; but the same Bethel that was near to Ai, and not far from Shiloh, and was in the tribe of Benjamin, as all those places were. Gilgal was where the tabernacle, ark, and camp of Israel were first pitched, when they came over Jordan, and Mizpeh where the people used to be assembled on occasion, see ver. 5, 6: *and judged Israel in all those places;* who came from all parts hither with their causes, and for advice and counsel in all cases, at the returning periods.

And his return was to Ramah, &c.] When he had gone his circuit, he came back to this city, which was his native place, and where his father and mother had dwelt, see chi. i.; *for there* was *his house;* and his father's house before him, and perhaps the same, ch. i. 19; *and there he judged Israel;* here was his fixed residence, and here he was always to be met with, except when on his circuit; and hither the people of Israel might repair from all parts, to have justice done them between man and man, or receive information in matters of difficulty and importance: *and there he built an altar unto the Lord;* to offer his own sacrifices, and the sacrifices of people, either by himself, or by a priest, when the people came to have justice administered to them; or to desire him to pray for them, teach and instruct them, or to give them advice. Shiloh being destroyed, and no place appointed for the tabernacle and altar, the Jews say, high places for a private altar were unlawful, and even for one that was not a priest to offer: these things, though settled by law, yet were for a time dispensed with, until things could be fixed in their proper place and order.

CHAPTER 8

"And when Samuel was old, he made his sons judges over Israel. Now the name of his first-born was Joel, and the name of his second was Abiah, judges in Beersheba. And his sons did not walk in his ways, but turned aside after ill gain and took tribes and perverted judgment" — 1 Samuel 8: 1-3.

Two sad things we find here, but not strange things: — 1. A good and useful man growing old and unfit for service (v. 1): *Samuel was old,* and could not judge Isreal, as he had done. He is not reckoned to be past sixty years of age now, perhaps not so much; but he was a man betimes, was full of thoughts and cares when he was a child, which perhaps hastened the infirmities of age upon him. The fruits that are the first ripe keep the worst. He had spent his strength and spirits in the fatigue of public business, and now, if he think to shake himself as at other times, he finds he is mistaken: old age has cut his hair. Those that are in the prime of their time ought to be busy in doing the work of life: for, as they go into years, they will find themselves less disposed to it and less able for it. 2. The children of a good man turning aside, and not treading in his steps. Samuel had given his sons so good an education, and they had given him such good hopes of their doing well, and gained such a reputation in Israel, that he made them judges, assistants to him awhile, and afterwards deputies under him at Beersheba, which lay remote from Ramah, v. 2. Probably the southern countries petitioned for their residence there, that they might not be necessitated to travel far with their causes. We have reason to think that Samuel gave them their commissions, not because they were his sons (he had no ambition to entail the government upon his family, any more than Gideon had), but because, for aught that yet appeared, they were men very fit for the trust; and none so proper to ease the aged judge, and take some of the burden off him, as (*ceteris paribus — other things being equal*) his own sons, who no doubt were respected for their good father's sake, and, having such an advantage at setting out, might soon have been great if they had but been good. But, alas! *his sons walked not in his ways* (v. 3), and, when their character was the reverse of his, their relation to so good a man, which otherwise would have been their honour, was really their disgrace. *Degeneranti genus opprobrium — A good extraction is a reproach to him that degenerates from it.* Note, Those that have the most grace themselves cannot give grace to their children. It has often been the grief of good men to see their posterity, instead of treading in their steps, trampling upon them, and, as Job speaks, *marring their path.* Nay, many that have begun well, promised fair, and set out in the right path, so that their parents and friends have had great hopes of them, yet afterwards have turned aside to bypaths, and been the grief of those of whom they should have been the joy. When Samuel's sons were made judges, and settled at a distance from him, then they discovered themselves. Thus, (1.) Many that have been well educated, and have conducted themselves well while they were under their parents. eye, when they have gone abroad into the world and set up for themselves have proved bad. Let none therefore be secure either of themselves or theirs, but depend on divine grace. (2.) Many that have done well in a state of meanness and subjection have been spoiled by preferment and power. Honours change men's minds, and too often

69

for the worse. It does not appear that Samuel's sons were so profane and vicious as Eli's sons; but, whatever they were in other respects, they were corrupt judges, they *turned aside after lucre*, after *the mammon of unrighteousness*, so the Chaldee reads it. Note, *The love of money is the root of all evil*. It is pernicious in any, but especially in judges. Samuel had taken no bribes (ch. xii. 3), but his sons had, though, no doubt, he warned them against it when he made them judges; and then they perverted judgment. In determining controversies, they had an eye to the bribe, not to the law, and enquired who bid highest, not who had right on his side. It is sad with a people when the public justice that should do them right, being perverted, does them the greatest wrong.

"Then all the elders of Israel gathered themselves together and came to Samuel to Ramah. And they said to him, Behold, you are old, and your sons do not walk in your ways. Now make us a king to judge us like all the nations. But the thing was evil in the eyes of Samuel when they said, Give us a king to judge us. And Samuel prayed to the Lord. And the Lord said to Samuel, Listen to the voice of the people in all that they say to you. For they have not rejected you, but they have rejected Me, that I should not reign over them. According to all the works which they have done since the day that I brought them up out of Egypt even until this day — works with which they have forsaken Me and served other gods — so they do also to you. Now therefore listen to their voice. However, still protest solemnly to them and show them the kind of king who shall reign over them. And Samuel told all the words of the Lord to the people who asked a king of him. And he said, This will be the kind of king who shall reign over you. He shall take your sons and appoint them for himself, for his chariots, and to be his horsemen. And some shall run before his chariots. And he will appoint for himself captains over thousands, and captains over fifties. And some will have to plow his ground, and reap his harvest, and make his weapons of war and things for his chariots. And he will take your daughters to be perfumers and cooks and bakers. And he will take your fields and your vineyards and your oliveyards, the best, and give them to his servants. And he will take the tenth of your seed and of your vineyards and give it to his officers and to his servants. And he will take your slaves and your slave-girls, and your finest young men, and your asses, and put them to his work. He will take the tenth of your sheep, and you shall be his servants. And you shall cry out in that day because of your king whom you have chosen, and the Lord will not hear you in that day. But the people refused to obey the voice of Samuel. And they said, No, but we will have a king over us, so that we also may be like all the nations, so that our king may judge us and go out before us and fight our battles. And Samuel heard all the words of the people, and he repeated them in the ears of the Lord. And the Lord said to Samuel, Listen to their voice and make them a king. And Samuel said to the men of Israel, Every man go to his city" — 1 Samuel 8: 4-22.

We have here the starting of a matter perfectly new and surprising, which was the setting up of kingly government in Israel. Perhaps the thing had been often talked of among them by those that were given to change and affected that which looked great. But we do not find that it was ever till now publicly proposed and debated. Abimelech was little better than a titular king, though he is said to reign over Israel (Judges ix. 22), and perhaps his fall had for a great while rendered the title of king odious in Israel, as that of Tarquinius did among the Romans; but, if it had, by this time the odium was worn off, and some bold steps are here taken towards so great a revolution as that amounted to. Here is,

I. The address of the elders to Samuel in this matter (v. 4, 5): They *gathered themselves together*, by common consent; and not in a riotous tumultuous manner, but with the respect due to his character, they came to him to his house at Ramah with their address, which contained,

1. A remonstrance of their grievances: in short, *Thou art old, and thy sons walk not in thy ways.* Many a fairer occasion that people had had to ask a king, when they were oppressed by their neighbours or embroiled at home for want of *a king in Israel*, but a small thing will serve factious spirits for a colour to desire a change. (1.) It was true that Samuel was old; but if that made him less able to ride the circuit, and sit long on the bench, yet it made him the more wise and experienced, and, upon that account, the fitter to rule. If he was old, had he not grown old in their service? And it was very unkind, ungrateful, nay, and unjust, to cast him off when he was old, who had spent his days in doing them good. God had saved his youth from being despicable (ch. iii. 20), yet they make his old age so, which should have been counted worthy of double honour. If old people be upbraided with their infirmities, and laid aside for them, let them not think it strange; Samuel himself was so. (2.) It was true that his sons did not walk in his ways; the more was his grief, but they could not say it was his fault: he had not, like Eli, indulged them in their badness, but was ready to receive complaints against them. And, if that had been the thing desired, we may well suppose, upon the making out of the charge of bribery against them he would have superseded their commissions and punished them. But this would not content the elders of Israel; they had another project in their head.

2. A petition for the redress of these grievances, by setting a king over them: *Make us a king to judge us like all the nations.* Thus far it was well, that they did not rise up in rebellion against Samuel and set up a king for themselves, *vi et armis — by force;* but they applied to Samuel, God's prophet, and humbly begged of him to do it. But it appears by what follows that it was an evil proposal and ill made, and was displeasing to God. God designed them a king, a man after his own heart, when Samuel was dead; but they would anticipate God's counsel, and would have one now that Samuel was old. They had a prophet to judge them, that had immediate correspondence with heaven, and therein they were great and happy above any nation, none having God *so nigh unto them* as they had, Deut. iv. 7. But this would not serve; they must have a king to judge them with external pomp and power, like *all the nations.* A poor prophet in a mantle, though conversant in the visions of the Almighty, looked mean in the eyes of those who judged by outward appearance; but a king in a purple robe, with his guards and officers of state, would look great: and such a one they must have. They knew it was in vain to court Samuel to take upon him the title and dignity of a king, but he must appoint them one. They do not say, "Give us a king that is wise and good, and will judge better than thy sons do," but, "Give us a king," any body that will make but a figure. Thus foolishly did they forsake their own mercies, and, under pretence of advancing the dignity of their nation to that of their neighbours, did really thrust themselves down from

their own excellency, and profane their crown by *casting it to the ground.*

II. Samuel's resentment of this address, v. 6. Let us see how he took it. 1. It cut him to the heart. Probably it was a surprise to him, and he had not any intimation before of their design, which made it the more grievous. The thing displeased Samuel; not when they upbraided him with his own infirmities and his children's irregularities (he could patiently bear what reflected on himself and his own family), but it *displeased him when they said, Give us a king to judge us,* because that reflected upon God and his honour. 2. It drove him to his knees; he gave them no answer for the present, but took time to consider what they proposed, and prayed unto the Lord for direction what to do, spreading the case before him and leaving it with him, and so making himself easy. Samuel was a man much in prayer, and we are encouraged *in everything to make our requests known to God,* Phil. iv. 6. When any thing disturbs us, it is our interest, as well as our duty, to show before God our trouble, and he gives us leave to be humbly free with him.

III. The instruction God gave him concerning this matter. Those that in straits seek to God shall find him nigh unto them, and ready to direct them. He tells him,

1. That which would be an allay to his displeasure. Samuel was much disturbed at the proposal: it troubled him greatly to see his prophetic office thus slighted, and all the good turns he had done to Israel thus ungratefully returned; but God tells him he must not think it either hard or strange. (1.) He must not think it hard that they had put this slight upon him, for they had herein put a slight upon God himself: *"They have not rejected thee* only, but *they have rejected me.* I share with thee in the affront," v. 7. Note, If God interest himself in the indignities that are done us, and the contempts that are put upon us, we may well afford to bear them patiently; nor need we think the worse of ourselves if *for his sake we bear reproach* (Ps. lxix. 7), but rather rejoice and count it an honour, Col. i. 24. Samuel must not complain that they were weary of his government, though just and gentle, for really they were weary of God's government; this was what they disliked: *They have rejected me, that I should not reign over them.* God *reigns over the heathen* (Ps. xlvii. 8), over all the world, but the government of Israel had hitherto been, in a more peculiar manner than ever any government was, a Theocracy, a divine government; their judges had their call and commission immediately from God; the affairs of their nation were under his peculiar direction. As the constitution, so the administration of their government, was by *Thus saith the Lord;* this method they were weary of, though it was their honour and safety, above any thing so long as they kept in with God. They were indeed so much the more exposed to calamities if they provoked God to anger by sin, and found they could not transgress at so cheap a rate as other nations could, which perhaps was the true reason why they desired to stand upon the same terms with God that other nations did. (2.) He must not think it strange, nor marvel at the matter, for they do as they always have done: *According to all the works which they have done, since the day that I brought them out of Egypt, so do they unto thee,* v. 8; They had at first been so very respectful and obsequious to Samuel that he began to hope they were cured of their old stubborn disposition; but now he found himself deceived in them, and must not be surprised at it. They had always been

rude to their governors, witness Moses and Aaron; nay, *They have forsaken me and served other gods;* the greatness of their crime, in affecting new gods, may make this crime of affecting new governors seem little. Samuel might expect they would deal treacherously, for they were called *transgressors from the womb,* Isa. xlviii. 8. This had been *their manner from their youth up,* Jer. xxii. 21.

2. He tells him that which would be an answer to their demand. Samuel would not have known what to say if God had not instructed him. Should he oppose the motion, it would bespeak a greater fondness of power and dominion than did become a prophet, and an indulgence of his sons. Should he yield to the motion, it would look like the betraying of his trust, and he would become accessory to all the bad consequences of a change. Aaron sinned in gratifying the people when they said, *Make us gods;* Samuel dares not therefore comply with them when they say, *Make us a king,* but he gives them, with assurance, the answer God sent them.

(1.) He must tell them that *they shall have a king. Hearken to the voice of the people,* v. 7, and again, v. 9. Not that God was pleased with their request, but, as sometimes he crosses us in love, so at other times he gratifies us in wrath; he did so here. When they said, *Give us a king and princes he gave them a king in his anger* (see Hos. xiii. 10, 11), as he gave them quails, Ps. cvi. 15; lxxviii. 29. God bade Samuel humour them in this matter, [1.] That they might be beaten with their own rod, and might feel, to their cost, the difference between his government and the government of a king; see 2 Chron. xii. 8. It soon appeared how much worse their condition was, in all respects, under Saul, than it had been under Samuel. [2.] To prevent something worse. If they were not gratified, they would either rise in rebellion against Samuel or universally revolt from their religion and admit the gods of the nations, that they might have kings like them. Rather than so, let them have a king. [3.] God knows how to bring glory to himself out of it, and to serve his own wise purposes even by their foolish counsels.

(2.) But he must tell them, withal, that when they have a king they will soon have enough of him, and will, when it is too late, repent of their choice. This he must *protest solemnly to them* (v. 9), that, if they would have a king to rule them, as the eastern kings ruled their subjects, they would find the yoke exceedingly heavy. They looked only at the pomp or magnificence of a king, and thought that would make their nation great and considerable among its neighbours, and would strike a terror upon their enemies; but he must bid them consider how they would like to bear the charges of that pomp, and how they would endure that arbitrary power which the neighbouring kings assumed. Note, Those that set their hearts inordinately upon any thing in this world ought, for the moderating of their desires, to consider the inconveniences as well as the conveniences that will attend it, and to set the one over against the other in their thoughts. Those that set their hearts inordinately upon any thing in this world ought, for the moderating of their desires, to consider the inconveniences as well as the conveniences that will attend it, and to set the one over against the other in their thoughts. Those that subnit to the government of the world and the flesh are told plainly what hard masters they are, and what a tyranny the dominion of sin is; and yet they will exchange God's government for it.

IV. Samuel's faithful delivery of God's mind to them, v. 10. He *told them all the words of the Lord*, how ill he resented it, that he construed it a rejoicing of him, and compared it with their serving other gods, — that he would grant their request if they insisted on it, but withal had ordered him to represent to them the certain consequences of their choice, that they would be such that if they had any reason left them, and would allow themselves to consult their own interest, they would withdraw their petition, and beg to continue as they were. Accordingly he lays before them, very particularly, what would be, not the right of a king in general, but *the manner of the king that should reign over them*, according to the pattern of the nations, v. 11. Samuel does not speak (as bishop Patrick expounds it) of a just and honest right of a king to do these things, for his right is quite otherwise described in that part of Moses's law which concerns the king's duty, but such a right as the kings of the nations had then acquired. *This shall be the manner of the king*, that is, "thus he must support his dignity at the expense of that which is dearest to you, and thus he will abuse his power, as those that have power are apt to do; and having the militia in his hand, you will by under a necessity of submitting to him."

1. If they will have such a king as the nations have, let them consider, (1.) That king must have a great retinue, abundance of servants to wait on him, grooms to look after his chariots and horses, gentlemen to ride about with him, and footmen to run before his chariots. This is the chief grandeur of princes, and the imaginary glory of great men, to have a multitude of attendants. And whence must we have these? "Why, he will take your sons, who are free-born, have a liberal education, and whom you now have at your own disposal, and will *appoint them for himself*," v. 11. They must wait upon him, and be at his beck; those that used to work for their parents and themselves must work for him, *ear his ground, and reap his harvest* (v. 12), and count it their preferment, too, v. 16. This would be a great change. (2.) He must keep a great table; he will not be content to dine with his neighbours upon a sacrifice, as Samuel used to do (ch. ix. 13); but he must have a variety of dainty dishes, forced meats, and sweet-meats, and delicate sauces; and who must prepare him these? "Why, he will take your daughters, the most ingenious and handy of them, whom you hoped to prefer to houses and tables of their own; and, whether you be willing or no, they must be his confectioners, and cooks, and bakers, and the like." (3.) "He must needs have a standing army, for guards and garrisons; and your sons, instead of being elders of your cities, and living in quiet and honour at home, must be captains over thousands and captains over fifties, and must be disposed of at the pleasure of the sovereign." (4.) "You may expect that he will have great favourites, whom, having dignified and ennobled, he must enrich, and give them estates suitable to their honour; and which way can he do that, but out of your inheritances? v. 14. *He will take your fields and vineyards*, which descended to you from your ancestors, and which you hoped to leave to your posterity after you, *even the best of them*; and will not only take them to himself (you could bear that better), but he will *give them to his servants*, who will be your masters, and bear rule over that for which you have laboured, How will you like that?" 5. "He must have great revenues to maintain his grandeur and power with; and whence must he have them but from you? He will take the tenth of the fruits of your ground (v. 15), and your cattle, v. 17. You think the

tenths, the double tenths, which the law of God has appointed for the support of the church, grievous enough, and grudge the payment of them; but, if you have a king, there must issue another tenth out of your estates, which will be levied with more rigor, for the support of the royal dignity. Consider the expense with the magnificence, and whether it will quit cost."

2. These would be their grievances, and (1.) They would have none but God to complain to. Once they complained to the prince himself, and were answered, according to the manner of the king, Your *yoke is heavy, and I will add to it,* 1 Kings xii. 11. (2.) When they complained to God he *would not hear them,* v. 18. Nor could they expect that he should, both because they had been deaf to his calls and admonitions, and this trouble, in particular, they had brought upon themselves by rejecting him, and would not believe when he told them what would come of it. Note, When we bring ourselves into distress by our own irregular desires and projects we justly forfeit the comfort of prayer and the benefit of divine aids, and, if God be not better to us than we deserve, must have our relief in our own hands, and then it is bad with us.

V. The people's obstinancy in their demand, v. 19,20. One would think such a representation of the consequences as this was, coming from God Himself, who can neither deceive by his word nor be deceived in his knowledge, should have prevailed with them to waive their request: but their hearts were upon it, right or wrong, good or evil: *"We will have a king over us,* whatever God or Samuel say to the contrary; we will have a king, whatever it cost us, and whatever inconvenience we bring upon ourselves or our posterity by it." See their folly. 1. They were quite deaf to reason and blind to their own interest. They could not answer Samuel's arguments against it, nor deny the force of them, and yet they grow more violent in their request, and more insolent. Before it was, *"Pray, make us a king;"* now it is, *"Nay, but we will have a king;* yea, that we will, because we will; nor will we bear to have any thing said against it." See the absurdity of inordinate desires, and how they rob men of their reason. 2. They could not stay God's time. God had intimated to them in the law that, in due time, Israel should have a king (Deut. xvii. 14,15), and perhaps they had some intimation that the time was at hand; but they are all in haste: "We, in our day, will have this king over us." Could they but have waited ten or twelve years longer they would have had David, a king of God's giving in mercy, and all the calamities that attended the setting up of Saul would have been prevented. Sudden resolves and hasty desires make work for a long and leisurely repentance. 3. That which they aimed at in desiring a king was not only, as before, that they might be like the nations, and levelled with the one above whom God had so far advanced them, but that they might have one to judge them, and to go out before them when they took the field, and to fight their battles. Foolish people and unwise! Could they ever desire a battle better fought for them than the last was, by Samuel's prayer and God's thunder? ch. vii. 10. Was victory hereby too sure to them? And were they fond of trying the chance of war at the same uncertainty that others did? So sick, it seems, were they of their privileges: and what was the issue? Their first king was slain in a battle, which none of their judges ever were; so was Josiah, one of the last and best.

VI. The dismissing of them with an intimation that very shortly they should have what they asked. 1. *Samuel rehearsed all their words in the ears of the*

Lord, v. 21. Not but that God perfectly knew it, without Samuel's report; but thus he dealt faithfully between God and Israel, as a prophet, returning the answer to him that sent him, and thus he waited on God for further direction. God is fully acquainted with the state of the case we are in care and doubt about, but he will know it from us. His rehearsing it *in the ears of the Lord* intimates that it was done in private; for the people were not disposed to join with him in prayer to God for direction in this matter; also it bespeaks a holy familiarity, to which God graciously admits his people: they speak in the ears of the Lord, as one friend whispers with another; their communion with God is *meat they have to eat which the world knows not of,* John iv. 32. 2. God gave direction that they should have a king, since they were so inordinately set upon it (v. 22): *"Make them a king,* and let them make their best of him, and thank themselves if that very pomp and power which they are so eager to see their sovereign in be their plague and burden." *So he gave them up to their own hearts' lusts.* Samuel told them this, but sent them home for the present, *every man to his city;* for the designation of the person must be left to God; they had now no more to do. When God saw fit to notify the choice to Samuel they should hear further from him; in the mean time let them keep the peace and expect the issue.

CHAPTER 9.

"Now there was a man of Benjamin, whose name was Kish, the son of Abiel, the son of Zeror, the son of Bechorath, the son of Aphiah, a Benjamite, a mighty man of power. And he had a son whose name was Saul, a choice young man and a handsome one. And there was not a more handsome one than he among all the children of Israel. From his shoulders and upward he was taller than any of the people" — 1 Samuel 9:1-2.

Now there was a man of Benjamin, &c.|Of the tribe of Benjamin, which had its name from the youngest son of Jacob, and one of this tribe was the first king of Israel: *whose name was Kish*; whom the apostle calls Cis, Acts xiii. 21; and Josephus Cises; his name, according to Hillerus signifies *ensnared;* for what reason it was given him is not certain: *the son of Abiel;* in 1 Chron. viii. 33, and ix. 39; he is called Ner that begat Kish; and in this book, ch. xiv. 50, 51; Ner and Kish are represented as brethren, the sons of Abiel: to reconcile this, it may be observed, that Ner being the elder brother, on the death of his father Abiel, had the care and bringing up of his younger brother Kish; and therefore when he is said to beget him, the meaning is, not that he was the parent of him, but the bringer up of him; or rather, as Kimchi thinks, Abiel, had two sons, one of which was Ner; and that he had two sons, one that was called after his own name, Ner, who was the father of Abner; and the other Kish, the father of Saul: *the sons of Zeror, the son of Bechorath, the son of Aphiah, a Benjamite;* of these persons we nowhere else read: *a mighty man of power;* not a man of riches, or of authority, neither a wealthy man, nor a magistrate, for his family was mean and contemptible, ver. 21, and ch. x. 27: but a man of great strength, an able-bodied man, and of great natural fortitude, and courage of mind.

And he had a son whose name was Saul, &c.|Of this name was the great apostle of the Gentiles before his conversion, and was of the same tribe also, but very different in stature; he was a little man, this a large tall man, like his father perhaps; *a choice young man, and a goodly;* ch. ii. of a goodly aspect, a comely man, tall and well-shaped, in the prime of his age, a very agreeable person, one among a thousand: and there was *not among the children of Israel a goodlier person than he;* meaning not for the endowments of his mind, or his moral character and behaviour. There might be as good, or better men than he, on such accounts, but for his outward appearance, his bodily shape, and the dignity of his person: *from his shoulders and upwards he was higher than any of the people;* this description of him is enlarged upon and explained, to show that he was just such a person the people were desirous of having king over them, such a one as the nations about them had; and it was usual with the eastern people, and so with the Greeks and Romans, to choose persons to the highest offices of magistracy that made a personable appearance superior to others, and is what they often take notice of, as a recommendation of them as princes. Herodotus reports of the Ethiopians, that they judged the largest of the people, and him who had strength according to his bigness, most worthy to be king. And the same writer observes, that among the many thousands of men of the army of Xerxes, there was not one who for comeliness and largeness was so worthy of the empire as Xerxes himself; so Ulysses, because of his tallness, was the more acceptable to the people of Corfu; so Alexander's captains, it is said, might be thought to be kings for their beautiful form, tallness of body, and greatness of strength and wisdom. Julius Caesar is said to be of high stature; and so Domitian; Virgil represents Turnus as in body more excellent than others, and by the entire head above them; and Anchises as walking statelier and higher than the rest; among the many encomiums Pliny gives of Trajan, as to his outward form and appearance, this is one, *proceritas corporis*, tallness of body, being higher than others; the Gentiles had a notion that such men came nearer to the dieties, and looked more like them; so Diana is described as taller than any of the nymphs and goddesses. Solomon, according to Josephus, chose such young men to ride horses, and attend his person, when he himself rode, who were conspicuous for their height, and greatly above others.

"And the asses of Kish, Saul's father, were lost. And Kish said to his son Saul, Now take one of the servants with you and rise and go look for the asses. And they passed through Mount Ephraim, and passed through the land of Shalisha, but they did not find them. Then they passed through the land of Shalim, and did not. And he passed through the land of the Benjamites, but they did not find them. And when they had come to the land of Zuph, Saul said to his servant who was with him, Come and let us return — lest my father quit caring for the asses and be anxious about us. And he said to him, Look, now, in this city is a man of God, and an honorable man. All that he says surely comes to pass. Now let us go there. Perhaps he can show us our way that we should go. Then Saul said to his servant, But behold, if we go, what shall we bring the man? For the bread in our vessels is gone, and there is no present to bring to the man of God. What do we have? And the servant answered Saul again and said, See, I have here at hand the fourth part of a shekel of silver. I will give it to the man of God to tell us our way. (In the old days in Israel, when a man went to inquire of God, he spoke in this way — Come, let us go to the seer — for a prophet was in the old days called a seer.) Then Saul said to his servant, Your word is good. Come, let us go. So they went into the city where the man of God was" — 1 Samuel 9:3-10.

Here is, I. A great man rising from small beginnings. It does not appear that Saul had any preferment at all, or was in any post of honor or trust, till he was chosen king of Israel. Most that are advanced rise gradually, but Saul, from the level with his neighbors, stepped at once into the throne, according to that of Hannah, He *raiseth up the poor out of the dust, to set them among princes*, 1 Sam. ii. 8. Saul, it should seem, though he was himself married and had children grown up, yet lived in his father's house, and was subject to him. Promotion comes not by chance nor human probabilities, but God is the judge.

II. A great event arising from small occurrences. How low does the history begin! Having to trace Saul to the crown, we find him first employed as meanly as any we meet with called out to preferment.

1. Saul's father sends him with one of his servants to seek some asses that he had lost. It may be they had no way then to give public notice of such a number of asses strayed or stolen out of the grounds of Kish the Benjamite. A very good law they had to oblige men to bring back an ox or an ass that went astray, but it is to be feared that was, as other good laws, neglected and forgotten. It is easy to observe here that those who have must expect to lose, that it is wisdom to look after what is lost, that no man should think it below him to know the state of his flocks, that children should be forward to serve their parents' interests. Saul readily went to *seek his father's asses* v. 3,4. His taking care of the asses is to be ascribed, not so much to the humility of his spirit as to the plainness and

simplicity of those times. But his obedience to his father in it was very commendable. *Seest thou a man diligent in his business,* and dutiful to his superiors, willing to stoop and willing to take pains? he does as Saul stand fair for preferment. The servant of Kish would be faithful only as a servant, but Saul as a son, in his own business, and therefore he was sent with him. Saul and his servants travelled far (probably on foot) in quest of the asses, but in vain: they found them not. He missed of what he sought, but had no reason to complain of the disappointment, for he met with the kingdom, which he never dreamed of.

2. When he could not find them, he determined to return to his father (v. 5), in consideration of his father's tender concern for him, being apprehensive that if they staid out any longer his aged father would begin to fear, as Jacob concerning Joseph, that an evil beast had devoured them or some mischief had befallen them; he will *leave caring for the asses,* as much as he was in care about them, and *will take thought for us.* Children should take care that they do nothing to grieve or frighten their parents, but be tender of their tenderness.

3. His servant proposed (for, it should seem, he had more religion in him than his master) that, since they were now at Ramah, they should call on Samuel, and take his advice in this important affair. Observe here, (1.) They were close by the city where Samuel lived, and that put it into their heads to consult him (v. 6): *There is in this city a man of God.* Note, Wherever we are we should improve our opportunities of acquainting ourselves with those that are wise and good. But there are many that will consult a man of God, if he comes in their way, that would not go a step out of their way to get wisdom. (2.) The servant spoke very respectfully concerning Samuel, though he had no personal knowledge of him, but by common fame only: *He is a man of God, and an honourable man.* Note, Men of God are honourable men, and should be so in our eyes. Acquaintance with the things of God, and serviceableness to the kingdom of God, put true honour upon men, and make them great. This was the honour of Samuel, as a man of God, that *all he saith comes surely to pass.* This was observed concerning him when he was a young prophet (ch. iii. 19), *God did let none of his words fall to the ground;* and still it held true. (3.) They agreed to consult him concerning *the way that they should go; peradventure he can show us.* All the use they would make of the man of God was to be advised by him whether they should return home, or, if there were yet any hopes of finding the asses, which way they must go next — a poor business to employ a prophet about! Had they said, "Let us give up the asses for lost, and, now that we are so near the man of God, let us go and learn from him the good knowledge of God, let us consult him how we may order our conversations aright, and enquire the law at his mouth, since we may not have such another opportunity, and then we shall not lose our journey" — the proposal would have been such as became the Israelites; but to make prophecy, that glory of Israel, serve so mean a turn as this, discovered too much what manner of spirit they were of. Note, Most people would rather be told their fortune than told their duty, how to be rich than how to be saved. If it were the business of the men of God to direct for the recovery of lost asses, they would be consulted much more than they are now that it is their business to direct for the recovery of lost souls; so preposterous is the care of most men! (4.) Saul was thoughtful what present they should bring to the man of God, what fee they should give him for his advice (v. 7): *What shall we bring the man?* They could not present him, as Jeroboam's wife did Ahijah, with loaves and cakes (1 Kings xiv. 3), for their bread was spent; but the servant bethought himself that he had in his pocket the fourth part of a shekel, about seven-pence halfpenny in value, and *that* he would give to the man of God to direct them, v.

8. "That will do," says Saul; *"let us go,"* v. 10. Some think that when Saul talked of giving Samuel a fee he measured him by himself, or by his sons, as if he must be hired to do an honest Israelite a kindness, and was like the false prophets, that *divined for money*, Mic. iii. 11. He came to him as a fortune-teller, rather than as a prophet, and therefore thought the fourth part of a shekel was enough to give him. But it rather seems to be agreeable to the general usage of those times, as it is to natural equity, that those who sowed spiritual things should reap not only eternal things from him that employs them, but temporal things from those for whom they are employed. Samuel needed not their money, nor would he have denied them his advice if they had not brought it (it is probable, when he had it, he gave it to the poor); but they brought it to him as a token of their respect and the value they put upon his office; nor did he refuse it, for they were able to give it, and, though it was but little, it was the widow's mite. But Saul, as he never thought of going to the man of God till the servant proposed it, so, it should seem, he mentioned the want of a present as an objection against their going; he would not own that he had money in his pocket, but, when the servant generously offered to be at the charge, then, "Well said," says Saul; "come, let us go." Most people love a cheap religion, and like it best when they can devolve the expense of it on others. (5.) The historian here takes notice of the name then given to the prophets: they called them *Seers*, or *seeing men* (v. 9), not but that the name *prophet* was then used, and applied to such persons, but that of seers was more in use. Note, Those that are prophets must first be seers; those who undertake to speak to others of the things of God must have an insight into those things themselves.

"And as they went up the hill to the city, they found young girls going out to draw water. And they said to them, Is the seer here? And they answered them and said, He is. Behold, he is before you. Hurry now, for he came today to the city, for there is a feast of the people today in the high place. As soon as you have come to the city, you shall immediately find him before he goes up to the high place to eat. For the people will not eat until he comes, because he blesses the feast. Afterwards those who have been invited eat. Now therefore go up, for about this time you shall find him. And they went up into the city. When they had come into the city, behold, Samuel came out across from them to go up to the high place. Now the Lord had told Samuel in his ear a day before Saul came, saying, Tomorrow about this time I will send you a man out of the land of Benjamin. And you shall anoint him to be the leader over My people Israel, so that he may save My people out of the hand of the Philistines. For I have looked on My people because their cry has come to Me. And when Samuel saw Saul, the Lord said to him, Behold the man of whom I spoke to you! This one shall reign over My people" — 1 Samuel 9: 11-17.

Here, I. Saul, by an ordinary enquiry, is directed to Samuel, v. 11-14. Gibeah of Saul was not twenty miles from Ramah where Samuel dwelt, and was near to Mizpeh where he often judged Israel, and yet, it seems, Saul had lived so very privately, and had taken so little notice of public affairs, that he had never seen Samuel, for when he met him (v. 18) he did not know him, so that there was no cause to suspect any secret compact or collusion between them in this matter. *I knew him not*, says John the Baptist concerning Christ, John i. 31. Yet I do not think it any commendation to Saul that he was a stranger to Samuel. However,

1. The maid-servants of Ramah, whom they met with at the places of drawing water, could give him and his servant intelligence concerning Samuel; and very

particular they were in their directions, v. 12, 13. We should always be ready to give what assistance we can to those that are enquiring after God's prophets, and to further them in their enquiries. Even the maid-servants could tell them, (1.) That there was a sacrifice that day in the high place, it being either an ordinary festival or an extraordinary day of prayer and thanksgiving, with which sacrifices were joined. The tabernacle being deprived of the ark, the altar there had not now the reputation it formerly had, nor were they confined to it, as they would be when God had again chosen a place to put his name in; and therefore now other places were allowed. Samuel had built an altar at Ramah (ch. vii. 17), and here we have him making use of that altar. (2.) That Samuel came that day to the city, either from his circuit or from his country seat. He was such a public person that his movements were generally known. (3.) That the people would not eat till Samuel came, not only because he was the worthiest person, and they ought in good manners to stay for him, and he was, as some think, the maker of this feast, the sacrifice being offered at his charge and upon his account; but because, as a man of God, whoever made the feast, *he* must bless the sacrifice, that is, those parts of the sacrifice which they feasted upon, which may be considered, [1.] As a common meal, and so this is an instance of the great duty of craving a blessing upon our meat before we partake of it. We cannot expect benefit from our food without that blessing, and we have no reason to expect that blessing if we do not pray for it. Thus we must give glory to God as our benefactor, and own our dependence upon him and our obligations to him. Or, [2.] As a religious assembly. When the sacrifice was offered, which was the ceremony, Samuel blessed it, that is, he prayed over it, and offered up spiritual sacrifices with it, which were the substance; and afterwards, when the holy duties were performed, they did eat. Let the soul first be served. The feast upon the sacrifice being a sacred rite, it was requisite that it should in a particular manner be blessed, as is the Christian eucharist. They feasted in token of their reconciliation to God by virtue of the sacrifice, and their participation of the benefits of it; and Samuel blessed the feast, that is, he prayed to God to grace the solemnity with his special presence, that it might answer those great ends. Bishop Hall observes what a particular account those maid-servants could give of the usages of those sacred feasts, and infers from it that, "where there is the practice and example of piety in the better sort, there will be a reflection of it upon the meanest. It is no small advantage to live in religious places; for we shall be much to blame if all goodness fall beside us."

2. Saul and his servant followed the directions given them, and very opportunely met Samuel going to the high place, the synagogue of the city, v. 14. This seemed purely accidental, but the divine providence ordered it for the forwarding of this great event. The wise God serves very great and certain purposes by very small and casual occurrences. A sparrow falls not to the ground without our Father.

II. Samuel, by an extraordinary revelation, is informed concerning Saul. He was a seer, and therefore must see this in a way peculiar to himself.

1. God had told him, the day before, that he would, at this time, send him the man that should serve the people of Israel for such a king as they wished to have, *like all the nations,* v. 15, 16. He *told him in his ear,* that is, privately, by a secret whisper to his mind, or perhaps by a still small voice, some soft and gentle sounds conveyed to his ear, probably when he was praying in secret for direction in that and other affairs of the nation. He had spoken *in the ears of the Lord* (ch. viii. 21), and now God *spoke in his ear,* in token of friendship and familiarity, for *he revealeth his secret to his servants the prophets,* as secrets in

their ear, Amos iii. 7. God told him before, that it might not be a surprise to him; and perhaps it was in expectation of it that he appointed the feast and the sacrifice, for the imploring of God's blessing upon this great and important affair, though he might keep the particular occasion in his own breast, God having only told it to him in his ear. The Hebrew phrase is, *He uncovered the ear of Samuel,* to which some allude for the explication of the way of God's revealing himself to us; he not only speaks, but *uncovers our ear.* We have naturally a covering on our ears, so that we perceive not what God says (Job xxxiii. 14), but, when God will manifest himself to a soul, he uncovers the ear, says, *Ephphatha, Be opened;* he takes *the veil from off the heart,* 2 Cor. iii. 16. Though God had, in displeasure, granted their request for a king, yet here he speaks tenderly of Israel; for even in *wrath he remembers mercy.* (1.) He calls them again and again his people; though a peevish and provoking people, yet mine still. (2.) He sends them a man to be captain over them, that they might not be a body without a head, and to *save them out of the hand of the Philistines,* which perhaps was more than many of them aimed at in desiring a king. (3.) He does it with a gracious respect to them and to their cry: *I have looked upon my people,* and *their cry has come unto me.* as the tender mother humours the forward child, lest it should break his heart. And, (as bishop Patrick observes), though he would not hear their cry to relieve them against the oppression of their kings (ch. viii. 18), yet he was so gracious as to make those kings instruments of their deliverance from the oppression of their neighbours, which was more than they had reason to expect.

2. When Saul came up towards him in the street God again whispered Samuel in the ear (v. 17): *Behold the man whom I spoke to thee of!* Saul being a man of unusual stature, it is natural to think that Samuel fixed his eye upon him at a distance, and perhaps looked the more wistfully towards him because the hour had now come when God would send him the man that should be king of Israel, and he fancied this might be he; but, that he might be fully satisfied, God told him expressly, *That is the man* that shall *restrain* (for magistrates are heirs of restraint) *my people Israel.*

"Then Saul drew near to Samuel in the gate and said, I beg you, tell me where the seer's house is. And Samuel answered Saul and said, I am the seer. Go up before me to the high place. For you shall eat with me today, and tomorrow I will let you go and will tell you all that is in your heart. And as for your asses that were lost three days ago, do not set your mind on them. For they are found. And on whom is all the desire of Israel? Is it not on you and on all your father's house? And Saul answered and said, Am I not a Benjamite, of the smallest of all the tribes of Israel? And is not my family the least of all the families of the tribe of Benjamin? Why then do you speak so to me? And Samuel took Saul and his servant and brought them into the parlor. And he made them sit in the chief place among those who had been invited, about thirty persons. And Samuel said to the cook, Bring that part which I gave you, of which I said to you, Set it beside you. And the cook took up the shoulder and that which was on it and set it before Saul. And Samuel said, Behold that which is reserved! Set it before you and eat. For until this time it has been kept for you, since I said, I have invited the people. So Saul ate with Samuel that day. And when they had come down from the high place into the city, Samuel talked with Saul on the top of the house. And they arose early. And about the spring of the day Samuel called Saul to the top of the house, saying, Up! so that I may send you away. And Saul arose, and both of them went out, he and Samuel, outside. And

as they were going down to the end of the city, Samuel said to Saul, Tell the servant to go on before us (and he went on), but you stand still awhile, so that I may show you the word of God" — 1 Samuel 9: 18-27.

Then Saul drew near to Samuel in the gate, &c.] Either at the door of his own house, just as he was coming out of it, or within the gate of the city; as Saul entered that, Samuel come to it, in order to go through it to the high place, which it is probable was without the city; wherefore it is very properly said that Samuel came out to meet them, ver. 14; *and said, tell me, I pray thee, where the seer's house is;* one knows not which to wonder at most, the simplicity and humility of Samuel to be in so plain a habit, unattended by servants, and yet going to a public festival, so that he seemed to be no other than a common man, to be inquired of whereabouts his house was; or the ignorance of Saul, who had lived so long in the world, and so near Samuel, and yet had never seen and knew not the chief magistrate in the nation, so famous both for his civil and religious character.

And Samuel answered Saul, and said, I am the seer, &c.] For he supposed, by inquiring for his house, that his business was with him; wherefore this he said, not as boasting of his character and office, or in the pride and vanity of his mind, but merely for information-sake: *go up before me unto the high place;* instead of returning home with him, he invited him to go to the place of feasting, as the Targum, whither he was going to partake of the entertainment there; and he bids him go before him, either because he was an old man, and could not go his pace, or he had business to do by the way, or this was in honour to Saul, whom he knew was to be the king of Israel: *for ye shall eat with me today;* he and his servant, at the public feast: he insisted upon his dining, or it may be rather supping with him: *and tomorrow I will let thee go;* for it being in the evening when this feast was, he could not depart that night, but must stay till morning, and then he is promised to dismiss him: *and will tell thee all that is in thine heart;* answer all questions he had in his mind to ask him, for which he came into the city, and inquired for his house. The Jews have a tradition that it was in the heart of Saul that he should be a king, having in a vision seen himself placed on the top of a palm-tree, which was a sign of royalty, and this Samuel told him.

And as for thine asses that were lost three days ago, &c.] Which, according to Kimchi, is to be understood not of the time from whence they were lost, but to be reckoned from the time that Saul had been seeking of them; so the Targum, "as to the business of the asses, which are lost to thee, and thou art come to seek them today, these three days:" though it is probable enough that the same day they were lost Saul set out to seek them. Now Samuel telling him of the asses that were lost, and of the time of their being lost, or of his seeking them, so exactly, before ever he said a word to him about them, must at once convince him that he was a true prophet, and which must prepare him to give credit to all that he should hereafter say to him: *set not thy mind on them, for they are found;* of the truth of which he could not doubt, after he had said the above words; and which he said to make his mind easy, that he might the more cheerfully attend the feast, and be the more willing to stay all night: *and on whom is all the desire of Israel?* which was to have a king; in this they were unanimous, and who so fit and proper as Saul, it is intimated, whom Samuel knew God had chosen and appointed to be king over them? is it *not on thee, and on all thy father's house?* not that the Israelites had their eye on Saul, and their desire after him to be their king, though he was such an one as they wished for;

but that as this desire of theirs was granted, it would issue and terminate in him and his family; he should be advanced to the throne, which would be attended with the promotion of his father's house, as Abner particularly, who was his uncle's son, and was made the general of the army.

And Saul answered and said, am not I a Benjamite, &c.] Or the son of Jemini, the name of one of his ancestors, see ver. 1; or rather, as the Targum, a son of the tribe of Benjamin: *of the smallest of the tribes of Israel?* having been greatly reduced, even to the number of 600 men, by the fatal war between that tribe and the rest, on account of the Levite's concubine, and is called little Benjamin, Psal. lxviii. 27: *and my family the least of all the families of the tribe of Benjamin;* the smallest in number, had the least share of authority in the tribe, and of land and cattle, wealth and substance: *wherefore then speakest thou so to me?* Saul presently understood Samuel's meaning, that he should be chosen king of Israel, the affair of a king being at this time in every one's mind and mouth; but could not believe that one of so small a tribe, and which sprung from the youngest son of Jacob, and of so mean a family, would be raised to such dignity, but that a person of great figure and character would be pitched upon; and therefore he took Samuel to be in joke, as Josephus says, and not in earnest.

And Samuel took Saul and his servant, and brought them into the parlour, &c.] The dining-room of the house, which belonged to the high place: *and made them sit in the chiefest place among them that were bidden;* and who very probably were the principal persons in the city; and yet Saul was placed at the head of them by Samuel, to convince him that what he had said to him was in earnest, and to do him honour before all the people; and for the sake of him, and to show his respect to him, he placed his servant, his minister, also in the chief place with him; what was reckoned the highest and most honourable places at table, see the note on Matt. xxiii. 6. The guests were placed by the master of the feast according to their rank: and the dignity of the person, as Jarchi observes, was known by his manners and place of sitting: *which* were *about* 30 *persons;* more or less; Josephus says 70, disagreeing with the text, the Targum, Syriac, and Arabic versions, but agreeing with the Septuagint.

And Samuel said unto the cook, &c.] That dressed and prepared the food for the entertainment of the guests: *bring the portion which I gave thee;* to dress; for part of the provisions of the feast was Samuel's, and the other part of the people's that brought the peace-offerings: *of which I said unto thee, set it by thee;* do not bring it in with the rest, but keep it in the cook-room till called for.

And the cook took up the shoulder, and that which was upon it, &c.] Meaning either, as some think, some sauce that was poured on it, or garnish about it; or the thigh, as the Targum, and so Jarchi, Kimchi, and others; or rather the breast, as a more ancient Jew; since this joined to the shoulder before separated, and in sacrifices went along with it; though most think this was the left shoulder and breast, because the right shoulder and breast of the peace-offerings were given to the priest, to be eaten by him and his sons, Lev. vii. 34; but in those unsettled times, with respect to sacrifices, many things were dispensed with; and Samuel, though a Levite, might officiate as a priest, and so the right shoulder and breast often belonged to him as such; and this best accounts for his having the disposal of it; and upon this extraordinary occasion, Saul, though not the son of a priest, might be admitted to eat of it, it being the choicest part, and fit to be set before one designed to be a king; and to show that he was to live in friendship with the priests of the Lord, and to take care of and protect the ministerial function: *and set it before Saul;* by the direction of Samuel no doubt, as a token of honour and respect unto him; it being usual in other countries to commend the best dishes, or best pieces of flesh, to the more excellent and worthy persons at table; and this was, as Josephus calls it, a royal portion; the arm or shoulder, especially the right arm being a symbol of strength, may denote that strength which was necessary for him to bear the burden of government, to protect his people, and fight in defence of them; and the breast being the seat of wisdom and prudence, of affection and love, may signify how necessary such qualities were for kingly government, to know how to go in and out before the people, and be heartily concerned for their good: *and* Samuel *said, behold that which is left;* not by the guests, and what they could not eat; for till Samuel came they did not begin to eat; and as for this part, it was but just brought in, and was never set before the guests, but it was left by Samuel in the hands of the cook, and reserved for the use of Saul: *set* it *before thee,* and *eat;* it was already set before him, but he would have him keep it by him, and eat of it, and make his meal of it, it being the best dish at the table: *for unto this time* hath it *been kept for thee;* by which he gave him to understand that he knew of his coming before-hand, and therefore had made this provision for him; and which might serve to persuade him of the truth and certainty of what he had hinted to him: since *I said I have invited the people;* not the thirty persons before mentioned, for it does not appear that they were invited by Samuel, but rather by those who brought the peace-offerings, who had a right to invite any of their friends they thought fit: but by *the people* are meant Saul and his servant; for in the eastern languages two or three persons, and even one, are called a people; and this Samuel had said to his cook, when he bid him set by the shoulder, and what was on it, because he had invited some, for whom he had designed it: *so Saul did eat with Samuel that day;* they dined together.

And when they came down from the high place into the city, &c.] After the feast was ended; and though Ramah itself was situated on an eminence, yet it seems this high place was higher than that, being without the city upon a hill, and therefore they are said to come down from the one to the other; or they came down from the high place, and then ascended the hill to the city: Samuel *communed with Saul upon the top of the house;* of Samuel's house; when they were come thither, Samuel took Saul up to the roof of his house, which was flat, as the roofs of houses in this country were; see Deut. xxii. 8; on which they could walk to and fro, and converse together; hence you read of preaching and praying on house-tops, Matt. x. 27, Acts x. 9; what they communed about is not said, but may be guessed at, that it was about Saul's being made king; of the certainty of it, by divine designation: of the manner of executing that office wisely and justly; about the objections Saul had made of the smallness of his tribe and family; and of Samuel's willingness to resign the government to him, with other things of the like kind.

And they arose early, &c.] Neither of them being able to sleep, as Abarbinel supposes; not Samuel for thinking what he was to do the next morning, anoint Saul king over Israel; nor Saul for what Samuel had hinted to him about the desire of all Israel being upon him, and for the honour they had together afterwards: *and it came to pass about the spring of the day;* or the *ascents of the morning,* when day was about to break, before the sun was up: *that Samuel called Saul to the top of the house;* where they had conversed together the evening before: *saying, up, that I may send thee away;* meaning, not rise from his bed, for he was risen; but that he would prepare to set out on his journey, that Samuel might take his leave of him for the present, when he had accompanied him some part of the way, as he intended; and he was the more urgent upon him, because there was something to be done before people were stirring: *and Saul arose, and they went out both of them, he and Samuel, abroad;* out of Samuel's house, without-doors, into the street.

And *as they were going down to the end of the city,* &c.] That end of it that led the way to the place where Saul was going. As this city was built on a hill, going to the end of it was a declivity, a descent: *Samuel said to Saul, bid the servant pass on before us;* being another man's servant, he did not choose of himself to bid him go on, but desired his master to order him go before them, that he might not hear what Samuel had to say to Saul, or see what he did unto him; for as the choice of Saul to be king was to be declared by lot, as coming from the Lord, all those precautions were taken of rising early, and going abroad, and sending the servant before them, that it might not be thought that Samuel did this of himself: *and he passed on;* his master bidding him: *but stand thou still a while;* that he might hear the better, and more attentively than in walking; such a posture was most fitting also for what to be done, anointing him with oil: *that I may shew thee the word of God;* tell him more of the mind of God concerning his being king, and declare more fully the word, will, and decree of God about that matter, by an action which would put it out of all doubt that he was the man God designed to be king, as in the following chapter.

"Then Samuel took a phial of oil and poured it on his head, and kissed him, said, Is it not because the Lord has anointed you to be captain over his inheritance? When you have departed from me today, then you shall find two men by Rachel's tomb in the border of Benjamin at Zelzah. And they will say to you, The asses which you went to seek are found. And lo, your father has quit caring for the asses and sorrows for you, saying, What shall I do for my son? Then you shall go forward from there, and you shall come to the plain of Tabor. And there you shall meet three men going up to God to Bethel, one carrying three kids, and another carrying three loaves of bread, and another carrying a bottle of wine. And they will greet you and give you two loaves of bread, which you shall take from their hands. After that you shall come to the hill of God, where the garrison of the Philistines is. And when you have come there to the city, you shall meet a company of prophets coming down from the high place with a psaltery and tabret and a pipe and a harp before them. And they shall prophesy. And the Spirit of the Lord will come upon you, and you shall prophesy with them and shall be turned into another man. And when these signs have come to you, you will do as you shall find occasion, for God is with you. And you shall go down before me to Gilgal. And, behold, I will come to you, you will do as you shall find occasion, for God is with you" — 1 Samuel 10: 1-8.

Samuel is here executing the office of a prophet, giving Saul full assurance from God that he should be king, as he was afterwards, according to these prophecies which went before of him.

I. He *anointed him* and *kissed him*, v. 1. This was not done in a solemn assembly, but it was done by divine appointment, which made up the want of all external solemnities, nor was it ever the less valid for its being done in private, under a hedge, or, as the Jews say, by *a fountain*. God's institutions are great and honourable, though the circumstances of their administration be ever so mean and despicable. 1. Samuel, by anointing Saul, assured him that it was God's act to make him king: *Is it not because the Lord hath anointed thee?* And, in token of that, the high priest was anointed to his office, to signify the conferring of those gifts upon him that were requisite for the discharge of its duties, and the same was intimated in the anointing of kings; for whom God calls he qualifies, and suitable qualifications furnish good proof of a commission. These sacred unctions, then used, pointed at the great Messiah, or anointed one, the king of the church, and high priest of our profession, who was anointed with the oil of the Spirit, not by measure, but without measure, and above all the priests and princes of the Jewish church. It was common oil, no doubt, which Samuel used, and we read not of his blessing it or praying over it. But it was only a vial of oil that he anointed him with, the vessel brittle, because his kingdom would soon be cracked and broken, and the quantity small, because he had but little of the Spirit conferred upon him to what David had, who was therefore anointed with a horn of oil, as were Solomon and Jehu with a box of oil. 2. By kissing him, he assured him of his own approbation of the choice, not only for his consent to it, but his complacency in it, though it abridged his power and eclipsed his glory and the glory of his family. *"God has anointed thee,"* says Samuel, *"to be king, and I am satisfied and very well pleased, in pledge of which take this kiss."* It was likewise a kiss of homage and allegiance; hereby he not only owns him to be king, but his king, and in this sense we are commanded to *kiss the Son*, Ps. ii. 12. God has anointed him, and therefore we must thus acknowledge him to do homage to him. In Samuel's explication of the ceremony, he reminds him, (1.) Of the nature of the government to which he is called. He was anointed to be a captain, a commander indeed, which bespeaks honour and power, but a commander in war, which bespeaks care, and toil, and danger. (2.) Of the origin of it: *The Lord hath anointed thee.* By him he ruled, and therefore must rule for him, in dependence on him, and with an eye to his glory. (3.) Of the end of it. It is over his inheritance, to take care of that, protect it, and order all the affairs of it for the best, as a steward whom a great man sets over his estate, to manage it for his service and give an account of it to him.

II. For his further satisfaction he gives him some signs, which should come to pass immediately, this very day; and they were such as would not only confirm the word of Samuel in general, and prove him a true prophet, but would confirm this word to Saul in particular, that he should be king. 1. He should presently meet with some that would bring him intelligence from home of the care his father's house was in concerning him, v. 2. These he would meet hard by Rachel's sepulchre. The first place Samuel directed him to was a sepulchre, the sepulchre of one of his ancestors, for Rachel died in travail with Benjamin; there he must read a lecture of his own mortality, and now that he had a crown in his eye must think of his grave, in which all his honour would be laid in the dust. Here two men would meet him, perhaps sent on purpose to look after him, and would tell him the asses were found, and his father was in pain concerning him, saying, *What shall I do for my son?* He would reckon it happened well that he met with these messengers; and it is good to eye Providence in favourable conjunctures (though the matter be minute) and to be encouraged to trust it in greater matters. 2. He should next meet with others going to Bethel, where, it should seem, there was a high place for religious worship, and these men were bringing their sacrifices thither, v. 3, 4. It was a token for good to one that was designed for the government of Israel, wherever he came, to meet with people going to worship God. It is supposed that those kids and loaves, and the bottle of wine which the three men had with them, were designed for sacrifice, with the meat-offerings and drink-offerings that were to attend the sacrifice; yet Samuel tells Saul that they will give him two of their loaves, and he must take them. Such a present would look to us now like the relieving of a beggar. Saul must hereafter remember the time when he received alms, and must therefore be humble and charitable to the poor. But perhaps it would then be construed as a fit present for a prince; and, as such, Saul must receive it, the first present that was brought to him, by such as knew not what they did, nor why they did it, but God put it into their hearts, which made it the more fit to be a sign to him. These two loaves, which were the first tribute paid to this newly anointed king, might serve for an admonition to him not to spend the wealth of his crown in luxury, but still to be content with plain food. Bread is the staff of life. 3. The most remarkable sign of all would be his joining with a company of prophets that he should meet with, under the influence of a spirit of prophecy, which should at that time come upon him. What God works in us by his Spirit serves much more for the confirming of faith than any thing wrought for us by his providence. He here (v. 5, 6) tells him, (1.) Where this would happen: *At the hill of God* where there was a *garrison of the Philistines,* which is supposed to be near Gibeah, his own city, for there was the Philistines' garrison, ch. xiii. 3. Perhaps it was one of the articles of Samuel's agreement with them that they should have a garrison into that place, and thence God raised up the man that should chastise them. There was a place that was called the *hill of God,* because of one of the schools of the prophets built upon it; and such respect did even Philistines themselves pay to religion that a garrison of their soldiers suffered a school of God's prophets to live peaceably by them, and did not only not dislodge them, but not restrain nor disturb the public exercises of their devotion. (2.) Upon what occasion; he should meet *a company of prophets with music before them, prophesying,* and with them he should join himself. These prophets were not (as it should seem) divinely inspired to foretel things to come, nor did God reveal himself to them by dreams and visions, but they employed themselves in the study of the law, in instructing their neighbours, and in the acts of piety, especially in praising God, wherein they were wonderfully assisted and enlarged by the Spirit of God. It was happy for Israel that they had not only prophets, but companies of prophets, who gave them good instructions and set them good examples, and helped very much to keep up religion among them. Now the word of the Lord was not precious, as it had been when Samuel was first raised up, who had been instrumental in founding these colleges, or religious houses, whence, it is probable, the synagogues took their rise. What a pity was it that Israel should be weary of the government of such a man, who though he had not, as a man of war, expelled the Philistines, yet (which was a greater kindness to Israel) had, as a man of God, settled the schools of the prophets! Music was then used as a proper means to dispose the mind to receive the impressions of the good Spirit, as it did Elisha's, 2 Kings iii. 15. But we have no reason to look for the same benefit by it now, unless we saw it as effectual as it was then in Saul's case, to drive away the evil spirit. These prophets had been at the high place, probably offering sacrifice, and now they came back singing psalms. We should come from holy ordinances with our hearts greatly enlarged in holy joy and praise. See Ps. cxxxviii. 5. Saul should find himself strongly moved to join with them, and should be turned thereby *into another man* from what he had been while he lived in a private capacity. The Spirit of God, by his ordinances, changes men, wonderfully transforms them; Saul, by praising God in the communion of saints, became another man, but whether a new man or no may be questioned.

"And it was so, that when he had turned his back to go from Samuel, God gave him another heart. And all those signs came to pass that day. And when they came there to the hill, behold, a company of prophets met him. And the Spirit of God came on him, and he prophesied among them. And when all who knew him before saw that, behold, he prophesied among the prophets, then the people said to one another, What is this that has happened to the son of Kish? Is Saul also among the prophets? And one from the same place answered and said, But who is their father? Therefore it became a proverb, Is Saul also among the prophets? And when he had made an end of prophesying, he came to the high place. And Saul's uncle said to him and to his servant, Where did you go? And he said, To look for the asses. And when we saw that they were nowhere to be found, we came to Samuel. And Saul's uncle said, Tell me, please, what Samuel

said to you. And Saul said to his uncle, He told us plainly that the asses were found. But he did not tell him of the matter of the kingdom of which Samuel spoke" — 1 Samuel 10: 9-16.

Saul has now taken his leave of Samuel, much amazed, we may well suppose, at what has been done to him, almost ready to question whether he be awake or no, and whether it be not all a dream. Now here we are told,

I. What occurred by the way, v. 9. Those signs which Samuel had given him came to pass very punctually; but that which gave him the greatest satisfaction of all was this, he found immediately that God had given him *another heart*. A new fire was kindled in his breast, such as he had never before been acquainted with: seeking the asses is quite out of his mind, and he thinks of nothing but fighting the Philistines, redressing the grievances of Israel, making laws, administering justice, and providing for the public safety; these are the things that now fill his head. He finds himself raised to such a pitch of boldness and bravery as he never thought he should be conscious of. He has no longer the heart of a husbandman, which is low, and mean, and narrow, and concerned only about his corn and cattle; but the heart of a statesman, a general, a prince. Whom God calls to any service he will make fit for it. If he advance to another station, he will give another heart, to those who sincerely desire to serve him with their power.

II. What occured when he came near home. They came to *the hill* (v. 10), that is, to *Gibeah*, or *Geba*, which signifies *a hill*, and so the Chaldee here takes it as a proper name; he met with the prophets as Samuel had told him, and the Spirit of God came upon him, strongly and suddenly (so the word signifies), but not so as to rest and abide upon him. It came on so as to go off quickly. However, for the present, it had a strange effect upon him; for he immediately joined with the prophets in their devotion, and that with as much decorum and as great a transport of affection as any of them: *He prophesied among them.* Now,

1. His prophesying was publicly taken notice of, v. 11, 12. He was now among his acquaintance, who, when they saw him among the prophets, called one another to come and see a strange sight. This would prepare them to accept him as a king, though one of themselves, when they had seen how God had advanced him to the honour of a prophet. The seventy elders prophesied before they were made judges, Num. xi. 25. Now, (1.) They all wondered to see Saul among the prophets: *What is this that has come to the son of Kish?* Though this school of the prophets was near his father's house, yet he had never associated with them, nor shown them any respect, perhaps had sometimes spoken slightly of them; and now to see him prophesying among them was a surprise to them, as it was long after when his namesake, in the New Testament, preached that gospel which he had before persecuted, Acts ix. 21. Where God gives another heart it will soon show itself. (2.) One of them, that was wiser than the rest, asked, "*Who is their father,* or instructor? Is it not God? Are they not all taught of him? Do they not all owe their gifts to him? And is he limited? Cannot he make Saul a prophet, as well as any of them, if he please?" Or, "Is not Samuel their father?" Under God, he was so; and Saul had now lately been with him, which, by his servant, he might know. No marvel for him to prophesy who lay last night under Samuel's roof. (3.) It became a proverb, commonly used in Israel, when

they would express their wonder at a bad man's either becoming good, or at least being found in good company, *Is Saul among the prophets?* Note, Saul among the prophets is a wonder to a proverb. Let not the worst be despaired of, yet let not an external show of devotion, and a sudden change for the present, be too much relied on; for Saul among the prophets was Saul still.

2. His being anointed was kept private. When he had done prophesying, (1.) It should seem he uttered all his words before the Lord, and recommended the affair to his favour, for he went straight *to the high place* (v. 13), to give God thanks for his mercies to him and to pray for the continuance of those mercies. But, (2.) He industriously concealed from his relations what had passed. His uncle, who met with him either at the high place or as soon as he came home, examined him, v. 14. Saul owned, for his servant knew it, that they had been with Samuel, and that he told them the asses were found, but said not a word of *the kingdom*, v. 14, 15. This was an instance, [1.] Of his humility. Many a one would have been so elated with this surprising elevation as to proclaim it upon the house-top. But Saul, though he might please himself in it among his neighbours. The heirs of the kingdom of glory are well enough pleased that *the world knows them not*, 1 John iii. 1. [2.] Of his prudence. Had he been forward to proclaim it, he would have been envied, and he knew not what difficulty that might have created him. Samuel had communicated it to him as a secret, and he knows how to keep counsel. Thus it appears that he had another heart, a heart fit for government. [3.] Of his dependence upon God. He does not go about to make an interest for himself, but leaves it to God to carry on his own work by Samuel, and, for his own part, sits still, to see how the matter will fall.

"And Samuel called the people together to the Lord at Mizpeh. As he said to the children of Israel, Thus says the Lord God of Israel, I brought up Israel out of Egypt, and delivered you out of the hand of the Egyptians, and out of the hand of all kingdoms, and of those who oppressed you. And you have this day rejected your God, who Himself saved you out of all your adversities and your tribulations. And you have said to Him, you shall set a king over us. Now therefore present yourselves before the Lord by your tribes and by your thousands. And when Samuel had caused all the tribes of Israel to come near, the tribe of Benjamin was taken. When he had caused the tribe of Benjamin to come near by their families, the family of Matri was taken, and Saul the son of Kish was taken. And when they looked for him, he could not be found. Therefore they inquired of the Lord further, if the man would still come to that place. And the Lord answered, Behold, he has hidden himself among the stuff. And they ran and brought him from there. And when he stood among the people, he was higher than any of the people from his shoulders and upward. And Samuel said to all the people, Do you see him whom the Lord has chosen, that there is none like him among all the people? And the people shouted, and said, Let the king live! Then Samuel told the people what kind of kingdom it was to be. And he wrote it in a book and laid it up before the Lord. And Samuel sent all the people away, every man to his house. And Saul also went home to Gibeah. And a band of men went with him, whose hearts God had touched. But the children of Belial said, How shall this man save us? And they despised him and brought him no presents. But he said nothing" — 1 Samuel 10:17-27.

And Samuel called the people together unto the Lord at Mizpeh.] Not that in Gilead, but in the tribe of Benjamin, where the people had been before convened on a certain occasion, ch. vii. 3; and the people called together could not be every individual of the nation, but the heads and elders of the people, their representatives, and who were summoned by the orders of Samuel; perhaps by a herald making proclamation and cry of the same, as the word signifies; and these were gathered together to the Lord, to have the following affair transacted before him, and under his guidance and direction; the priest perhaps being here with the Urim and Thummim, as Kimchi thinks, and who also conjectures that the ark might be brought hither at this time, the symbol of the Divine Presence: though wherever the church and people of God were gathered together in his name, in a solemn manner, there the Lord was.

And said unto the children of Israel, &c.] In the name of the Lord, using the phrase which the prophets used when they spoke in the name of the Lord: *thus saith the Lord God of Israel;* the great Jehovah, the Being of beings, the covenant-God of his people Israel: *I brought up Israel out of Egypt;* when in bondage there, with a mighty hand and stretched-out arm, by means of signs and wonders done by the hands of Moses and Aaron; the Lord working mightily with them, and thereby inclining Pharaoh and his people to let them go: *and delivered you out of the hand of the Egyptians;* at the Red sea, drowning them in it, when they threatened Israel with an utter destruction: *and out of the hand of all kingdoms,* and *of them that oppressed you;* as the Arabic writers, the kingdoms of Og and Bashan in their way to Canaan, and the Mesopotamians, Moabites, Canaanites, Midianites, Ammonites, and Philistines, in the times of the judges; all which is observed to show their ingratitude, and aggravate their guilt.

And ye have this day rejected your God, &c.] As their king, by desiring another to be set over them: *who himself saved you out of all your adversities and your tribulations;* that they had been in at any time in Egypt, in their passage through the wilderness to Canaan, and after they were settled there: *ye have said unto him,* nay, *but set a king over us;* they did as good as say God should not be their King, but they would have one set over them like the kings of the nations about them; Samuel reminds them of this their request and resolution to have a king, which they had expressed some time ago, that it might appear to them that this was wholly of their own seeking; the motion came from themselves, and not from the Lord, nor from Samuel, and therefore, whatever ill consequences might follow upon it, they had none to blame but themselves: *now therefore present yourselves before the Lord by your tribes, and by your thousands;* by the heads of their tribes, and by the rulers of the thousands into which their tribes were divided, that it might be known either by Urim and Thummim, or rather by casting lots, out of which tribe, and out of which thousand, house, and family in it, their king was to be chosen; which method, as it would clearly appear to be a choice directed by the Lord, so it would prevent all contention and discord among themselves.

And when Samuel had caused all the tribes to come near, &c.] The heads and representatives of them to the place where the lots were cast: *the tribe of Benjamin was taken;* the lot fell upon that tribe for the choice of a king out of it; not the tribe of Reuben, who was the first-born, nor the tribe of Judah, to whom the kingdom was promised, but the tribe of Benjamin, the least of all the tribes, and which sprung from the youngest son of Jacob, as it were probable, to the expectation of all.

And when he had caused the tribe of Benjamin to come near by their families, &c.] By the heads of them, to have lots cast for them, out of which of the families the king should be chosen: *the family of Matri was taken;* that is, by lot: the lot fell upon that family for the choice of a king out of them; in the account of the families of the tribe of Benjamin, 1 Chron. viii. no mention is made of this family, nor any where else, and yet no doubt there was such a family, and Saul was of it; it seems to have its name from the butt or mark arrows were shot at; some of the Benjaminites being famous for their skill in darting and slinging, and perhaps this family might be so; *and Saul the son of Kish was taken;* the lot being cast upon the men in the family of Matri, though it is not expressed, fell upon Saul; for though he was not there, as Jarchi observes, the lot fell upon him; for their names were written on a piece of paper, and put into a box, and the prophet put in his hand and took out one, and on that was the name of Saul, and this was the manner of the lot: *and when they sought him, he could not be found;* because he had hid himself, as in the next verse; it is very probable, and indeed plain that he was in this assembly at the first opening of it; and knowing what Samuel had said and done to him, and perceiving in what way the lot was going concerning the same, the tribe of Benjamin being taken, he concluded how it would issue, and therefore left the assembly, and hid himself, as follows.

Therefore they inquired of the Lord further, &c.] Or again, by lot, by which they knew who the person was that was chosen king, but they did not know where he was, and therefore inquire further how they must come at him; and this inquiry was made either before the high priest by Urim and Thummim, or by Samuel the prophet of the Lord: and the inquiry was, *if the man should yet come thither;* whether he was already come, or would come there, and if not, what methods they must take to find him: *and the Lord answered, behold, he hath hid himself among the stuff;* the word signifies household stuff, vessels, utensils, arms, &c., which the people had brought along with them for their use, and were laid up in some one place; and among these baggages Saul hid himself, hoping that if he was not found they would proceed to another choice, so free from ambition was he, and such was his modesty: nor does this seem to be affected and dissembled, but real; though afterwards, when he was settled in the kingdom, he did not care to part with it, and sought to kill David, whom he looked upon as his rival: there were many things which now concurred, that made him uneasy and unwilling to assume the government of the people; partly the envy and ill will of some of them, which he must expect: chiefly the sense he had of his own unfitness for such an office, being of a mean family, and having had so mean an education, and so little knowledge of the maxims of government; and besides, must at once, as soon as on the throne, enter into a war with the Ammonites; but what might most of all distress him, he perceived by Samuel's speech to the people, that the affair of a king was displeasing to the Lord, though he condescended to grant the people's request; and therefore what comfort and happiness could he expect in such a situation?

And they ran and fetched him thence, &c.] Being in haste to see their king elect, and proclaim him: *and when he stood among the people;* being brought among them, and presented to them: *he was higher than any of the people, from the shoulders, and upwards;* which made him look very graceful and majestic; height of stature, and a comely form, as Kimchi observes, recommend to royal dignity; and make the people stand more in awe of a prince, and have always been reckoned among all other nations to make a prince venerable, see the note on ch. ix. 2.

CHAPTER 11

"Then Nahash the Ammonite came up and camped against Jabesh – gilead. And all the men of Jabesh said to Nahash, Make a covenant with us, and we will serve you. And Nahash the Ammonite answered them, By this I will make a covenant with you, that I may put out all your right eyes and lay it for a reproach on all Israel. And the elders of Jabesh said to him, Bear with us seven days, so that we may send messengers to all the borders of Israel. And then if there is no man to save us, we will come out to you. Then the messengers came to Gibeah of Saul and told the news in the ears of the people. And all the people lifted up their voices and wept" — 1 Samuel 11: 1-4.

Then Nahash the Ammonite came up, and encamped against Jabesh-gilead, &c.] A month after, as in the Septuagint and Vulgate Latin versions, that is a month after Saul was chosen king; so Josephus: this prince was preparing for war against Israel before, which they hearing of, requested they might have a king to go before them in battle, ch. xii. 12; but now he actually marched from his own country, and besieged Jabesh-gilead, a city in the land of Gilead, from whence it had its name, and lay in the half-tribe of Manasseh, on the other side Jordan, see Judg. xxi. 8. It lay near to the Ammonites, and was part of the country they laid claim to in the times of Jephthah, which they now renewed, and attempted to gain it by force. This Nahash was king of the Ammonites, as he is called in the Targum, and by Josephus, and so in the Arabic version, see ch. xii. 12; *and all the men of Jabesh-gilead said unto Nahash, make a covenant with us;* they desired to be his allies and confederates, live in peace and friendship with him, and enjoy their religion and liberties on certain conditions they were willing to come into; and this was the sense of them all, or at least the greatest part, which showed a mean and abject spirit in them, to make no defiance of themselves, but as soon as besieged to move for a capitulation. This doubtless arose from a sense of their weakness, not being able to hold it out long, and from an apprehension that their brethren the Israelites on the other side Jordan, could give them no assistance, being in an unsettled condition, having chosen a king, and he scarce on the throne, and the Philistines having great power over them: *and he will serve thee;* not as slaves, but as tributaries; they were willing to pay a yearly tax to him.

And Nahash the Ammonite answered them, &c.] In a very haughty and scornful manner: *on this* condition *will I make* a covenant *with you, that I may thrust out all your right eyes;* some Jewish writers go into a mystical and allegorical sense of these words, as that Nahash ordered the book of the law to be brought, which was their right eye, that he might erase out of it these words, *an Ammonite or Moabite shall not enter into the congregation of the Lord;* others understand it of the sanhedrim, which were the eyes of Israel; and others, which come a little nearer to the sense, of the slingers and archers, the desire of the eyes of Israel; and who, by having their right eyes thrust out, would be in a great measure spoiled for taking aim; for the words are to be understood literally; the intention of Nahash was to disable them for war, and that they might become quite unfit for it, as Josephus observes; the left eye being under the shield, as it usually was in war, and the right eye plucked out, they would be as blind men: he did not choose to have both their eyes thrust out, for then they could have been of no use and service to him as slaves or tributaries; *and lay it*

95

for a reproach upon all Israel; that they did not come up to the relief of their brethren, and defend them, and signifying that they must all expect the same treatment from him.

And the elders of Jabesh said, &c.] The magistrates and principal men of the city: *give us seven days' respite, that we may send messengers to all the coast of Israel;* that is, cease from besieging them, from throwing in darts into the city, or any other missive weapons, and from attempting to break open the gates, or break down the walls of it, and storm it; such a space of time they desire, which was as litle as could be granted, to go and return in, and without this it would not be a reproach to all Israel, if they were ill used by them, since they had no knowledge of their case, nor time to come up to their assistance: *and then if there be no man to save us, we will come out to thee;* and submit to be used at thy pleasure. And it seems that this was granted by Nahash out of a bravado, and to reproach and insult all Israel, and bid them defiance; with whom he sought to quarrel, having a design upon their land, and knowing very well their condition, being awed by the Philistines; and having just chosen a king, and he an inexperienced man in the affairs of war, and had no army; nor was it likely that one could be assembled in so short a time, and come to the relief of this people, and therefore he thought himself safe enough in granting their request.

Then came the messengers to Gibeah of Saul, &c.] Where he was born, and brought up, and now dwelt; and he being elected king, it brought an honour to the place; and from hence had this name, to distinguish it from the others, and this is the first time it was so called. Now the messengers from Jabesh came hither directly, because they knew that Saul, the chosen king, dwelt here, and the Benjaminites of all the tribes, had great reason to show regard to them, since it was from hence they had 400 wives, when they were reduced to 600 men only, in order to raise up their tribe: *and told the tidings in the ears of the people;* Saul being not at home in the city, but in the fields, they report to them the hardships their city was under, being besieged by the Ammonites, and threatened that if not relieved in such a time, all their right eyes would be plucked out; *and all the people lifted up their voices, and wept;* moved with sympathy to their brethren, and who by their intermarriage with them were nearly related to them: and who might fear they would not stop there, but having taken that place would march forward, and come to them, and use them in like manner; the thought of which was very distressing to them.

"*And, behold, Saul came after the herd out of the field. And Saul said, What is wrong with the people that they weep? And they told him the news of the men of Jabesh. And the Spirit of God came on Saul when he heard those tidings and his anger was kindled greatly. And he took a yoke of oxen and cut them in pieces, and sent them throughout all the borders of Israel by the hands of messengers, saying, Whoever does not come forth after Saul and after Samuel, so shall it be done to his oxen. And the fear of the Lord fell on the people, and they came out with one consent. And when he numbered them at Bezek, the children of Israel were three hundred thousand, and the men of Judah thirty thousand. And they said to the messengers that came, So shall you say to the men of Jabesh-gilead, Tomorrow by the time the sun is hot, you shall have help. And the messengers came and told the men of Jabesh, and they were glad.*

Therefore the men of Jabesh said, Tomorrow we will come out to you, and you shall do with us all that seems good to you. And on the next day, Saul put the people in three companies, and they came into the middle of the army at the morning watch. And they killed the Ammonites until the heat of the day. And the ones who remained were scattered, so that two of them were not left together" — 1 Samuel 11: 5-11.

What is here related turns very much to the honour of Saul, and shows the happy fruits of that other spirit with which he was endued. Observe here,

I. His humility. Though he was anointed king, and accepted by his people, yet he did not think it below him to know the state of his own flocks, but went himself to see them, and came in the evening, with his servants, *after the herd out of the field,* v. 5. This was an evidence that he was not puffed up with his advancement, as those are most apt to be that are raised from a mean estate. Providence had not yet found him business as a king; he left all to Samuel; and therefore, rather than be idle, he would, for the present, apply himself to his country business again. Though the sons of Belial would, perhaps, despise him the more for it, such as were virtuous and wise, and loved business themselves, would think never the worse of him. He had no revenues settled upon him for the support of his dignity, and he was desirous not to be burdensome to the people, for which reason, like Paul, he worked with his hands; for, if he neglect his domestic affairs, how must he maintain himself and his family? Solomon gives it as a reason why men should look well to their herds because *the crown doth not endure to every generation,* Prov. xxvii. 23, 24. Saul's did not; he must therefore provide something surer.

II. His concern for his neighbours. When he perceived them in tears, he asked, *"What ails the people that they weep?* Let me know, that, if it be a grievance which can be redressed, I may help them, and that, if not, I may weep with them."* Good magistrates are in pain if their subjects are in tears.

III. His zeal for the safety and honour of Israel. When he heard of the insolence of the Ammonites, and the distress of a city, a mother in Israel, *the Spirit of God came upon him,* and put great thoughts into his mind, *and his anger was kindled greatly,* v. 6. He was angry at the insolence of the Ammonites, angry at the mean and sneaking spirit of the men of Jabesh-Gilead, angry that they had not sent him notice sooner of the Ammonites' descent and the extremity they were likely to be reduced to. He was angry to see his neighbours weeping, when it was fitter for them to be preparing for war. It was a brave and generous fire that was now kindled in the breast of Saul, and such as became his high station.

IV. The authority and power he exerted upon this important occasion. He soon let Israel know that, though he had retired to his privacy, he had a care for the public, and knew how to command men into the field, as well as how to drive cattle out of the field, v. 5, 7. He sent a summons to all the coasts of Israel, to show the extent of his power beyond his own tribe, even to all the tribes, and ordered all the military men forthwith to appear in arms at a general rendezvous in Bezek. Observe, 1. His modesty, in joining Samuel in commission with himself. He would not execute the office of a king without a due regard to that of a prophet. 2. His mildness in the penalty threatened against those that should disobey his orders. He hews a yoke of oxen in pieces, and sends the pieces to the several cities of Israel, threatening, with respect to him who should decline the public service not, "Thus shall it be done to *him*," but, "Thus shall it be done to his *oxen*." God had threatened it as a great judgment (Deut. xxviii. 31), *Thy ox shall be slain before thy eyes, and thou shalt not eat thereof.* It was necessary that the command should be enforced with some penalty, but this was not nearly so severe as that which was affixed to a similar order by the whole congregation, Judg. xxi. 5. Saul wished to show that his government was more gentle than that which they had been under. The effect of this summons was that the militia, or trained bands, of the nation, *came out as one man,* and the reason given is, because *the fear of the Lord fell upon them.* Saul did not affect to make them fear him, but they were influenced to observe his orders by the fear of God and a regard to him who had made Saul their king and them members one of another. Note, Religion and the fear of God will make men good subjects, good soldiers, and good friends to the public interests of their country. Those that fear God will make conscience of their duty to all men, particularly to their rulers.

V. His prudent proceedings in this great affair, v. 8. He numbered those that came in to him, that he might know his own strength, and how to distribute his forces in the best manner their numbers would allow. It is the honour of princes to know the number of their men, but it is the honour of the King of kings, that *there is not any number of his armies,* Job xxv. 3. In this muster, it seems, Judah, though numbered by itself, made no great figure; for, as it was one tribe of twelve, so it was but an eleventh part of the whole number, 30,330, though the rendezvous was at Bezek, in that tribe. They wanted the numbers, or the courage, or the zeal for which that tribe used to be famous; so low was it, just before the sceptre was brought into it in David.

VI. His faith and confidence, and (grounded thereon) his courage and resolution, in this enterprise. It should seem that those very messengers who brought the tidings from Jabesh-Gilead Saul sent into the country to raise the militia, who would be sure to be faithful and careful in their own business, and them he now sends back to their distressed countrymen, with this assurance (in which, it is probable, Samuel encouraged him): *"Tomorrow,* by such an hour, before the enemy can pretend that the seven days have expired, *you shall have deliverance,* v. 9. Be you ready to do your part, and we will not fail to do ours. Do you sally out upon the besiegers, while we surround them." Saul knew he had a just cause, a clear call, and God on his side, and therefore doubted not of success. This was good news to the besieged Gileadites, whose right eyes had wept themselves dry for their calamities, and now began to fail with looking for relief and to ache in expectation of the doom of the ensuing day, when they must look their last; the greater the exigence the more welcome the deliverance. When they heard it they were glad, relying on the assurances that were sent to them. And they sent into the enemies' camp (v. 10) to tell them that next day they would be ready to meet them, which the enemies understood as an intimation that they despaired of relief, and so were made the more secure by it. If they took not care, by sending out scouts, to rectify their own mistake, they must thank themselves if they were surprised: the besieged were under no obligation to give them notice of the help they were assured of.

VII. His industry and close application to this business. If he had been bred up to war from his youth, and had led regiments as often as he had followed droves, he could not have gone about an affair of this nature more dexterously nor more diligently. When the Spirit of the Lord comes upon men it will make them expert even without experience. A vast army (especially in comparison with the present usage) Saul had now at his foot, and a long march before him, nearly six miles, and over Jordan too. No cavalry in his army, but all infantry, which he divides into three battalions, v. 11. And observe, 1. With what incredible swiftness he flew to the enemy. In a day and a night he came to the place of action, where his own fate, and that of Israel, must be determined. He had passed his word, and would not break it; nay, he was better than his word, for he promised help next day, *by that time the sun was hot* (v. 9), but brought it before day, *in the morning-watch*, v 11. Whom God helps he *helps right early*, Ps. xlvi. 5. 2. With what incredible bravery he flew upon the enemy. Betimes in the morning, when they lay dreaming of the triumphs they expected that day over the miserable inhabitants of Jabesh-Gilead, before they were aware he was in the midst of their host; and his men, being marched against them in three columns, surrounded them on every side, so that they could have neither heart nor time to make head against them.

Lastly, to complete his honour, God crowned all these virtues with success. Jabesh-Gilead was rescued, and the Ammonites were totally routed; he had now the day before him to complete his victory in, and so complete a victory it was that those who remained, after a great slaughter, were scattered so that *two of them were not left together* to encourage or help one another, v. 11. We may suppose that Saul was the more vigorous in this matter, 1. Because there was some alliance between the tribe of Benjamin and the city of Jabesh-Gilead. That city had declined joining with the rest of the Israelites to destroy Gibeah, which was then punished as their crime, but perhaps was now remembered as their kindness, when Saul of Gibeah came with so much readiness and resolution to relieve Jabesh-Gilead. Yet that was not all; two-thirds of the Benjamites that then remained were provided with wives from that city (Judg. xxi. 14), so that most of the mothers of Benjamin were daughters of Jabesh-Gilead, for which city Saul, being a Benjamite, had therefore a particular kindness; and we find they returned his kindness, ch. xxxi. 11, 12. 2. Because it was the Ammonites' invasion that induced the people to desire a king (so Samuel says, ch. xii. 12), so that if he had not done his part, in this expedition, he would have disappointed their expectations, and for ever fortified their respect.

"And the people said to Samuel, Who is he that said, Shall Saul reign over us? Bring the men so that we may put them to death. And Saul said, There shall not a man be put to death today — for today the Lord has worked salvation in Israel. Then Samuel said to the people, Come and let us go to Gilgal and renew the kingdom there. And all the people went to Gilgal. And there they made Saul king before the Lord in Gilgal, and there they sacrificed sacrifices of peace offerings before the Lord. And there Saul and all the men of Israel rejoiced greatly" — 1 Samuel 11: 12-15.

And the people said unto Samuel, &c.] By which it seems that Samuel accompanied Saul in this expedition; though it is some what difficult to account for it, that a man of his years should be able to attend so quick a march that Saul made: it may be, therefore, that he might follow after him gently, and meet him quickly after the battle was fought, when the people made the following speech to him; *who is he that said, shall Saul reign over us?* is such a mean inexperienced man fit to rule over us? who can bear his government, and submit to it? what can be expected from him, that he should deliver and save us out of the hands of our enemies? in this they had respect to the sons of Belial, and what they said, ch. x. 27; but now it appeared he was sufficiently qualified, and God had made him an instrument of salvation, and was a proper person to be king over them: *bring the men, that we may put them to death;* so transported were they with affection to Saul, and indignation against those men.

And Saul said, &c.] Preventing Samuel from giving an answer, being ready to forgive injuries; as it was in his power as a king, and him only, to pardon those persons that treated him in so ill a manner, and it was policy so to do, especially in the beginning of his reign; and it plainly appears that this temper did not always continue with him; though there is no reason to believe otherwise, that this was now owing to his lenity as well as his prudence: *there shall not be a man put to death this day;* who by their appearance to his summons had testified their obedience, and by their courage and valour had showed their attachment to him, and to the interest of their country. Ben Gersom takes the sense to be, that it might be right after, but not on this day to put them to death; or that this was an artifice of Saul to deliver those men out of the hands of the Israelites, suggesting as if it was his intention hereafter to put them to death, though not now, for the following reason: *for to-day the Lord hath wrought salvation in Israel;* he does not ascribe the victory to the quick dispatch he made, to his wisdom and prudence in forming the scheme he did, and to his valour and courage, and that of his troops, but to the power and goodness of God.

Then said Samuel to the people, &c.] Agreeing to what Saul had said, and in order to put them off from demanding the lives of the offenders, and willing to take them whilst they were in a good disposition: *come, and let us go to Gilgal;* which was the nearest place to them, on the other side Jordan, from which they now were, and where the children of Israel first encamped when they passed over Jordan, where the tabernacle and ark first were, and an altar was built, and where meetings used to be held on certain occasions; all which might be reasons why Samuel proposed to go to this place. According to Bunting, this place was 36 miles from Jabesh-gilead: *and renew the kingdom there;* that is, recognize Saul, own and declare him king of Israel.

And all the people went to Gilgal, &c.] Agreed to the motion, and marched along with Saul and Samuel thither: *and there they made Saul king before the Lord in Gilgal;* that is they declared him to be king there; he was inaugurated into, and invested with his office, otherwise it was God only that made him king, who only had the power of making one, see Acts ii. 36. Josephus says, that Samuel anointed him with the holy oil; and so the Septuagint version here renders it, and Samuel anointed Saul there to be "king," and it is not improbable that as he privately anointed him, he did it publicly also; if not at the election of him, when at this time; and it is observable that in the next chapter, and not before, he is called the Lord's anointed. Now this was *before the Lord;* in this place; this being, as Abarbinel observes, a sanctified place, where the tabernacle and ark of God had been; and he supposes it probable that the ark was brought hither; but it was enough that the people and congregation of the Lord were here, and who, when assembled in his name, his presence was with them: *and there they sacrificed sacrifices of peace-offerings before the Lord;* where an altar was built, and on which they offered these peace-offerings by way of thanksgiving, partly for the victory obtained over the Ammonites, and partly for the renewal of the kingdom to Saul, and their unanimity in it, as well as to implore and obtain future peace and prosperity: *and there Saul, and all the people of Israel, rejoiced greatly;* they in their king, and he in the good will of his people, and both in the great salvation God had wrought for them.

CHAPTER 12.

"And Samuel said to all Israel, Behold, I have listened to your voice in all that you said to me and have made a king over you. And now, behold, the king walks before you. And I am old and gray headed, and, behold, my sons are with you. And I have walked before you from my childhood to this day. Behold, here I am. Witness against me before the Lord and before His anointed. Whose ox have I taken? Or whose ass have I taken? Or whom have I defrauded? Whom have I oppressed? Or from whose hand have I received a bribe, to blind my eyes with it? And I will restore it to you. And they said, You have not defrauded us or oppressed us. And you have not taken anything from any man's hand. And he said to them, The Lord is witness against you, and His anointed is witness this day, that you have not found anything in my hand. And they answered, He is witness" — 1 Samuel 12: 1-5.

Here, I. Samuel gives them a short account of the late revolution, and of the present posture of their government, by way of preface to what he had further to say to them, v. 1, 2. 1. For his own part, he had spent his days in their service; he began betimes to be useful among them, and had continued long so: *"I have walked before you,* as a guide to direct you, as a shepherd that leads his flock (Ps. lxxx. 1), *from my childhood unto this day."* As soon as he was illuminated with the light of prophecy, in his early days, he began to be a burning and shining light to Israel; "and now my best days are done: *I am old and gray-headed;"* therefore they were the more unkind to cast him off, yet therefore he was the more willing to resign, finding the weight of government heavy upon his stooping shoulders. He was old, and therefore the more able to advise them, and the more observant they should have been of what he said, for *days shall speak* and *the multitude of years shall teach wisdom;* and there is a particular reverence due to the aged, especially aged magistrates and aged ministers. "I am old, and therefore not likely to live long, perhaps may never have an opportunity of speaking to you again, and therefore take notice of what I say." 2. As for his sons, *"Behold"* (says he), *"they are with you,* you may, if you please, call them to an account for any thing they have done amiss. They are present with you, and have not, upon this revolution, fled from their country. They are upon the level with you; if you can prove them guilty of any wrong, you may prosecute them now by a due course of law, punish them, and oblige them to make restitution." 3. As for their new king, Samuel had gratified them in setting him over them (v. 1): *"I have hearkened to your voice in all that you said to me,* being desirous to please you, if possible, and make you easy, though to the discarding of myself and family; and now will you hearken to me, and take my advice?" The change was now perfected: *"Behold, the king walketh before you"* (v. 2); he appears in public, ready to serve you in public business. Now that you have made yourselves like the nations in your civil government, and have cast off the divine administration in that, take heed lest you make yourselves like the nations in religion and cast off the worship of God.

II. He solemnly appeals to them concerning his own integrity in the administration of the government (v. 3): *Witness against me, whose ox have I taken?* Observe,

1. His design in this appeal. By this he intended, (1.) To convince them of the injury they had done him in setting him aside, when they had nothing amiss to charge him with (his government had no fault but that it was too cheap, too easy, too gentle), and also of the injury they had done themselves in turning off

101

one that did not so much as take an ox or an ass from them, to put themselves under the power of one that would take from them their fields and vineyards, nay, and their very sons and daughters (ch. viii. 11), so unlike would the manner of the king be from Samuel's manner. (2.) To preserve his own reputation. Those that heard of Samuel's being rejected as he was would be ready to suspect that certainly he had done some evil thing, or he would never have been so ill treated; so that it was necessary for him to make this challenge, that it might appear upon record that it was not for an iniquity in his hands that he was laid aside, but to gratify the humour of a giddy people, who owned they could not have a better man to rule them, only they desired a bigger man. There is a just debt which every man owes to his own good name, especially men in public stations, which is to guard it against unjust aspersions and suspicions, that we may finish our course with honour as well as joy. (3.) As he designed hereby to leave a good name behind him, so he designed to leave his successor a good example before him; let him write after his copy, and he will write fair. (4.) He designed, in the close of his discourse, to reprove the people, and therefore he begins with a vindication of himself; for he that will, with confidence, tell another of his sin, must see to it that he himself be clear.

2. In the appeal itself observe,

(1.) What it is that Samuel here acquits himself from. [1.] He had never, under any pretence whatsoever, taken that which was not his own, ox or ass, had never distrained their cattle for tribute, fines, or forfeitures, nor used their service without paying for it. [2.] He had never defrauded those with whom he dealt, nor oppressed those that were under his power. [3.] He had never taken bribes to pervert justice, nor was ever biassed by favour or affection to give judgment in a cause against his conscience.

(2.) How he calls upon those that had slighted him to bear witness concerning his conduct: *"Here I am; witness against me.* If you have any thing to lay to my charge, do it *before the Lord and the king,* the proper judges." He puts honour upon Saul, by owning himself accountable to him if guilty of any wrong.

III. Upon this appeal he is honourably acquitted. He did not expect that they would do him honour at parting, though he well deserved it, and therefore mentioned not any of the good services he had done them, for which they ought to have applauded him, and returned him the thanks of the house; all he desired was that they should do him justice, and that they did (v. 4), readily owning, 1. That he had not made his government oppressive to them, nor used his power to their wrong. 2. That he had not made it expensive to them: *Neither hast thou taken aught of any man's hand* for the support of thy dignity. Like Nehemiah, he did *not require the bread of the governor* (Neh. v. 18), had not only been righteous, but generous, had *coveted no man's silver, or gold, or apparel,* Acts xx. 33.

IV. This honourable testimony borne to Samuel's integrity is left upon record to his honour (v. 5): *"The Lord is witness,* who searcheth the heart, *and his anointed is witness,* who trieth overt acts;" and the people agree to it: *"He is witness."* Note, The testimony of our neighbours, and especially the testimony of our own consciences for us, that we have in our places lived honestly, will be our comfort under the slights and contempts that are put upon us. Demetrius is a happy man, that has a *good report of all men and of the truth itself,* 3 John 12.

"And Samuel said to the people, It is the Lord who made Moses and Aaron, and who brought your fathers up out of the land of Egypt. Now therefore stand still,

so that I may reason with you before the Lord of all the righteous acts of the Lord which He did to you and to your fathers. When Jacob had come into Egypt, and your fathers cried to the Lord, then the Lord sent Moses and Aaron, who brought forth your fathers out of Egypt and made them live in this place. And when they forgot the Lord their God, He sold them into the hand of Sisera, captain of the army of Hazor, and into the hand of the Philistines, and into the hand of the king of Moab, and they fought against them. And they cried to the Lord, and said, We have sinned because we have forsaken the Lord and have served Baalim and Ashtaroth. But now deliver us out of the hand of our enemies and we will serve You. And the Lord sent Jerubbaal, and Bedan, and Jephthah, and Samuel and delivered you out of the hand of your enemies on every side, and you lived safely. And when you saw that Nahash the king of the children of Ammon came against you, you said to me, No, but a king shall reign over us — when the Lord your God was your King. Now, therefore, behold the king whom you have chosen, whom you have desired! And, behold, the Lord has set a king over you! If you will fear the Lord, and serve Him, and obey His voice, and not rebel against the commandment of the Lord, then both you and also the king who reigns over you shall continue following the Lord your God. But if you will not obey the voice of the Lord, but rebel against the commandment of the Lord, then the hand of the Lord shall be against you as it was against your fathers" — 1 Samuel 12: 6-15.

And Samuel said unto the people, &c.] Having cleared and established his own character, he proceeds to lay before the people some of the great things God had done for them formerly, and quite down to the present time, the more to aggravate their ingratitude in rejecting God as their King: it is *the Lord that advanced Moses and Aaron;* raised them from a low estate, the one in a foreign country in Midian, the other in bondage in Egypt, to be deliverers, guides, and governors of his people Israel. Kimchi thinks this refers to what goes before, and that the sense is, that God, that raised Moses and Aaron to great honour and dignity, was a witness between him and the people; in which he is followed by some Christian interpreters. Ben Gersom makes mention of the same, but rather approves of the connexion of the words with what follows, as does Abarbinel, and is doubtless most correct; the Targum is, "who hath done mighty things by the hands of Moses and Aaron;" *and that brought your fathers up out of the land of Egypt;* when they were in bondage there, and that by the means of Moses and Aaron, by whose hands he wrought signs and wonders, and inflicted plagues on the Egyptians, which made them willing at last to let Israel go.

Now therefore stand still, &c.] Keep your place, and do not as yet break up the assembly, but wait a little longer patiently, and with reverence and attention hearken to what I have further to say: *that I may reason with you before the Lord;* as in his presence, and which he observes to command the greater awe upon their mind, and the greater regard to the subject of his discourse and resolutions; which would be, *of all the righteous acts of the Lord, which he did to you and to your fathers:* not only in a way of judgment delivering them into the hands of their enemies, when they sinned against him, but rather in a way of mercy and kindness in delivering them out of their hands.

When Jacob was come into Egypt, &c.] With his family to see his son Joseph, and dwelt there; or rather the posterity of Jacob are meant, who settled in Egypt, and continued there many years, and at length were oppressed by the Egyptians, and brought into hard bondage: *and your fathers cried unto the Lord;* by reason of their bondage, for help and deliverance: *then the Lord sent*

Moses and Aaron, which brought forth your fathers out of Egypt; after various messages carried by them from the Lord to Pharaoh king of Egypt, and after many signs and wonders wrought by them, by which the heart of that king was at last brought to consent to their dismission: *and made them dwell in this place;* the land of Canaan; they conducted them through the Red sea, guided them through the wilderness, and accompanied them, especially Moses, to the borders of the land of Canaan; for neither of them went into it, but died before the people's entrance there. Joshua, the successor of Moses, of whom Samuel makes no mention, introduced Israel into it; though Moses and Aaron, as they were the instruments of bringing them out of Egypt, were the cause, by conducting them through the wilderness, and by their prayers, counsels, and instructions, of their entrance into and settlement in it: besides, Moses appointed Joshua in his stead, and ordered him to lead the people there, and directed to the division of the land among them, yea, two tribes and a half were settled by him on the other side Jordan; the Septuagint, Vulgate Latin, Syriac, and Arabic versions, read in the singular number, *he made them dwell, that is, the Lord.*

And when they forgot the Lord their God, &c.] The worship of the Lord their God, as the Targum; that is, they fell into idolatry, which is a plain instance and proof of forgetfulness of God; for such that neglect his worship, and serve idols, may be truly said to forget him: *he sold them into the hand of Sisera, captain of the host of Hazor;* who was general of the army of Jabin king of Canaan, who reigned in Hazor, Judg. iv. 2; where they are said to be sold into the hands of Jabin, here into the hands of Sisera; because it is highly probable he was sent against them by Jabin, and subdued them, as he afterwards was sent by him, when they rebelled against him, and were delivered out of his hand: *and into the hand of the Philistines;* as they were in and before the times of Samson, Judg. xiii. 1; *and into the hand of the king of Moab;* as in the times of Ehud, Judg. iii. 14, 15; the exact order of these things is not observed; *and they fought against them;* the king of Moab, Sisera, and the Philistines, and overcame them, and so they fell into their hands.

And they cried unto the Lord, &c.] When in the hands of their enemies, and in bondage to them, and cruelly oppressed by them: *and said, we have sinned;* the word for *said* is in the Cetib, or written text, singular, and in the Keri, or marginal reading, plural; and may signify, that every one of them had a sense of their sin, and made acknowledgment of it; their confession was universal, as their sin was: *because we have forsaken the Lord;* the Word of the Lord, as the Targum; *and have served Baalim and Ashtaroth;* see the notes on Judg. ii. 11, 13: *but now deliver us out of the hand of our enemies, and we will serve thee;* they did not ask for a king to go before them, and fight their battles, as they did now, but applied to the Lord for deliverance, promising to serve him as their King and their God.

And the Lord sent Jerubbaal, &c.] Or Gideon, as the Targum, for Jerubbaal was the name given to Gideon, when he first became a judge, Judg. vi. 23; *and Bedan;* if this was one of the judges, he must have two names, or is one that is not mentioned in the book of Judges; the Targum interprets it of Samson; so Jerom, for the word may be rendered *in Dan;* one in Dan, who was of the tribe of Dan, as Samson was; and it was in the camp of Dan the Spirit of God first came upon him; and Kimchi observes that it is the same as Bendan the son of Dan, that is, a Danite; and though he was after Jephthah, yet is set before him, because he was a greater man than he; and this way go the generality of Jewish writers; but a man of this name being among the posterity of Manasseh, 1 Chron. vii. 17; Junius, and who is followed by others, thinks that Jair is meant, and is so called to distinguish him from a more ancient Jair, the son of Manasseh, and with whom the order of the judges better agrees, see Numb. xxxii. 41, Judg.

x. 3, 4; but the Septuagint, Syriac, and Arabic versions read Barac; and he may rather be thought to be meant, because he was the instrument of delivering Israel out of the hand of Sisera, the captain of the host of Hazor before mentioned, ver. 9; and agrees with the words of the apostle, Heb. xi. 32; who mentions those judges much in the same order:*and Jephthah, and Samuel;* meaning himself, who was the last of the judges, and who speaks of himself as of a third person, as Lamech does, Gen. iv. 23; and this he did not out of ostentation, but to observe that God had made him an instrument of delivering them out of the hand of the Philistines, which must be fresh in their memory, as he had made use of others before him, when he sent judges, and not kings, and therefore they had no need to ask a king. The Syriac and Arabic versions read Samson instead of Samuel, and which also agrees best with Heb. xi. 32; *and delivered you out of the hands of your enemies on every side;* not the judges but the Lord; for the word for *delivered* is of the singular number: *and ye dwelled safe:* in the greatest security and confidence, without any fear of enemies having God their king in the midst of them, and stood in no need of any other king to protect and defend them.

And when ye saw that Nahash the king of the children of Ammon came against you, &c.] Or *but yet;* however, notwithstanding though the Lord had been so kind and gracious to them, as to raise up judges one after another to deliver them, when they cried unto him, yet when they perceived that Nahash the Ammonite was preparing to make war with them, instead of applying to the Lord for his protection, they desired to have a king to go before them, and fight their battles, as follows: *nay, but a king shall reign over us;* though Samuel told them they had no need of one: *when the Lord your God* was *your King;* and would put their trust in him; and he himself Samuel was their judge, and would be their general and commander, and they had experience of success under him to the utter destruction of their enemies, ch. vii. 10; and yet, notwithstanding all this, they insisted upon it to have a king. According to Abarbinel, this preparation of Nahash to war with them is after they had asked for a king, and was a punishment of them for their request; and yet they repented not of it, but in effect said, though Nahash, and all the enemies in the world, come against us, he will not go back from our request, but insist on it, that we have a king to reign over us; such was their obstinacy and perverseness.

Now therefore behold the king whom ye have chosen, and *whom ye have desired,* &c.] For though God chose their king for them, it was at their request: they chose to have a king, and desired one, and they approved of and consented to, and confirmed the choice he had made, and it was in effect their own: *and behold, the Lord hath set a king over you;* he gratified them in their desires; though he did not suffer them to make themselves a king, he suffered them to have one, and he gave them one; this power he reserved to himself of setting up and pulling down kings at his pleasure.

If ye will fear the Lord, and serve him, and obey his voice, &c.] All worship and service of God, and obedience to his word and ordinances, should spring from fear and reverence of him; and therefore the whole of worship, both external and internal, is sometimes expressed by the fear of the Lord: *and not rebel against the commandment of the Lord:* break it, and thereby exasperate him, and provoke him to wrath and bitterness: *then shall both ye, and also the king that reigneth over you, continue following the Lord your God;* the Targum is, "after the worship of the Lord your God;" which was their duty to do, and is expressed in the preceding clauses: and this therefore is rather a promise of some benefit and privilege to their duty, and to encourage them to it, since it stands opposed to the threatening of punishment in the next verse; and the words in the original are, *then shall ye,* &c., *be after the Lord your God:* that is, though they had in effect rejected the Lord from being their King, by asking and having one; yet notwithstanding, if they and their king were obedient to the commands of the Lord, he would not cast them off, but they should follow him as their Guide, Leader, and Director, and he would protect and defend them as a shepherd does his sheep that follow after him; so Jarchi takes it to be a promise of long life and happiness to them and their king, "ye shall be established to length of days, both ye and the king."

But if ye will not obey the voice of the Lord, but rebel against the commandment of the Lord, &c.] They and their king, by sinning, disregarding his precepts, both affirmative and negative: *then shall the hand of the Lord be against you;* by sending some judgments upon them, as famine, sword, or pestilence, particularly captivity and subjection to their enemies; *as it was against your fathers;* who had no king; and it is suggested that their case, who had one, would be no better than theirs; their king would not be able to save them from the hand of God: the words in the original are, *and against your fathers;* which is interpreted in the Talmud of their fathers dead, and in their graves, and of their enemies digging them up, and taking them out in contempt; but much better, by Kimchi, of their kings, who are, or should be, fathers of their subjects, as Augustus Caesar was called the father of his; and so the Septuagint version renders it, *and upon their king;* signifying that both they and their king should feel the weight of the hand of the Lord, if they rebelled against him.

"Now therefore stand and see this great thing which the Lord shall do before your eyes. Is it not wheat harvest today? I will call to the Lord and He shall send thunder and rain, so that you may perceive and see that your wickedness is great — your wickedness which you have done in the sight of the Lord, in asking a king for you. So Samuel called to the Lord. And the Lord sent thunder and rain that day. And all the people greatly feared the Lord and Samuel. And all the people said to Samuel, Pray for your servants to the Lord your God, so that we will not die. For we have added this evil to all our sins, to ask a king for us. And Samuel said to the people, Do not fear. You have done all this wickedness. Yet do not turn aside from following the Lord, but serve the Lord with all your heart. And do not turn aside after vanities, which cannot profit nor deliver. For they are vain. For the Lord will not forsake His people for His great name's sake — because it has pleased the Lord to make you His people. Moreover, as for me, God forbid that I should sin against the Lord in ceasing to pray for you. But I will teach you the good and the right way. Only fear the Lord and serve Him in truth with all your heart. For consider what great things He has done for you. But if you shall still do wickedly, you shall be consumed, both you and your king" — 1 Samuel 12: 16-25.

Two things Samuel here aims at: —

I. To convince the people of their sin in desiring a king. They were now rejoicing before God in and with their king (ch. xi. 15), and offering to God the sacrifices of praise, which they hoped God would accept; and this perhaps made them think that there was no harm in their asking a king, but really they had done well in it. Therefore Samuel here charges it upon them as their sin, as wickedness, *great wickedness in the sight of the Lord.* Note, Though we meet with prosperity and success in a way of sin, yet we must not therefore think the more favourably of it. They have a king, and if they conduct themselves well their king may be a very great blessing to them, and yet Samuel will have them perceive and see that their *wickedness was great in asking a king.* We must never think well of that which God in his law frowns upon, though in his providence he may seem to smile upon it. Observe,

1. The expressions of God's displeasure against them for asking a king. At Samuel's word, God sent prodigious thunder and rain upon them, at the season of the year when, in that country, the like was never seen or known before, v. 16-18. Thunder and rain have natural causes and sometimes terrible effect. But Samuel made it to appear that this was designed by the almighty power of God on purpose to convince them that they had done very *wickedly in asking a king;* not only by its coming in an unusual time, in wheat-harvest, and this on a fair clear day, when there appeared not to the eye any signs of a storm, but by his giving notice of it before. Had there happened to be thunder and rain at the time when he was speaking to them, he might have improved it for their awakening and conviction, as we may in a like case: but, to make it no less than a miracle, before it came, (1.) He spoke to them of it (v. 16, 17): *Stand and see this great thing.* He had before told them to *stand and hear* (v. 7); but, because he did not see that his reasoning with them affected them (so stupid were they and unthinking), now he bids them *stand and see.* If what he said in a *still small voice* did not reach their hearts, nor his doctrine which dropped as the dew, they shall hear God speaking to them in dreadful claps of thunder and the great rain of his strength. He appealed to this as a sign: "*I will call upon the Lord, and he will send thunder, will* send it just now, to confirm the word of his servant, and to make you see that I spoke truly when I told you that God was angry with you for *asking a king.*" And the event proved him a true prophet; the sign and wonder came to pass. (2.) He spoke to God for it. Samuel called unto the Lord, and, in answer to his prayer, even while he was yet speaking, *the Lord sent thunder and rain.* By this Samuel made it to appear, not only what a powerful influence God has upon this earth, that he could, of a sudden, when natural causes did not work towards it, produce this dreadful rain and thunder, and bring them out of his treasures (Ps. cxxxv. 7), but also what a powerful interest *he* had in heaven, that God would thus *hearken to the voice of a man* (Josh. x. 14) and answer him *in the secret place of thunder,* Ps. lxxxi. 7. Samuel, that son of prayer, was still famous for success in prayer. Now by this extraordinary thunder and rain sent on this occasion, [1.] God testified his displeasure against them in the same way in which he had formerly testified it, and at the prayer of Samuel too, against the Philistines. *The Lord discomfited them with a great thunder,* ch. vii. 10. Now that Israel rebelled, and vexed his Holy Spirit, he turned to be their enemy, and fought against them with the same weapons which, not long before, had been employed against their adversaries, Isa. lxiii. 10. [2.] He showed them their folly in desiring a king to save them, rather than God or Samuel, promising themselves more from an arm of flesh than from the arm of their king *thunder with a voice like God?* Job xl. 9. Could their prince command such forces as the prophet could by his prayers? [3.] He intimated to them that how serene and prosperous soever their condition seemed to be now that they had a king, like the weather in wheat-harvest, yet, if God pleased, he could soon change the face of their heavens, and persecute them with his tempest, as the Psalmist speaks.

2. The impressions which this made upon the people. It startled them very much, as well it might. (1.) *They greatly feared the Lord and Samuel.* Though when they had a king they were ready to think they must fear him only, God made them know that *he is greatly to be feared* and his prophets for his sake. Now they were rejoicing in their king, God taught them to rejoice with trembling. (2.) They owned their sin and folly in desiring a king: *We have added*

to all our sins this evil, v. 19. Some people will not be brought to a sight of their sins by any gentler methods than storms and thunders. Samuel did not extort this confession from them till the matter was settled and the king confirmed, lest it should look as if he designed by it rather to establish himself in the government than to bring them to repentance. Now that they were *flattering themselves in their own eyes, their iniquity was found to be hateful,* Ps. xxxvi. 2. (3.) They earnestly begged Samuel's prayers (v. 19); *Pray for thy servants, that we die not.* They were apprehensive of their danger from the wrath of God, and could not expect that he should hear their prayers for themselves, and therefore they entreat Samuel to pray for them. Now they see their need of him whom awhile ago they slighted. Thus many that will not have *Christ to reign over them* would yet be glad to have him intercede for them, to turn away the wrath of God. And the time may come when those that have despised and ridiculed praying people will value their prayers, and desire a share in them. *"Pray,"* (say they) *"to the Lord thy God;* we know not how to call him ours, but, if thou hast any interest in him, improve it for us."

II. He aims to confirm the people in their religion, and engage them for ever to cleave unto the Lord. The design of his discourse is much the same with Joshua's, ch. xxiii. and xxiv.

1. He would not that the terrors of the Lord should frighten them from him, for they were intended to frighten them to him (v. 20): *"Fear not; though you have done all this wickedness* and though God is angry with you for it, yet do not therefore abandon his service, nor *turn from following him." Fear not,* that is, "despair not, fear not with amazement, the weather will clear up after the storm. Fear not; for, though God will frown upon his people, yet he will not forsake them (v. 22) *for his great name's sake;* do not you forsake him then." Every transgression in the covenant, though it displease the Lord, yet does not throw us out of covenant, and therefore God's just rebukes must not drive us from our hope in his mercy. The fixedness of God's choice is owing to the freeness of it; we may therefore hope he will not forsake his people, because it has *pleased him to make them his people.* Had he chosen them for their good merits, we might fear he would cast them off for their bad merits; but, choosing them *for his name's sake,* for his name's sake he will not leave them.

2. He cautions them against idolatry: *"Turn not aside* from God and the worship of him" (v. 20, and again v. 21); "for if you turn aside from God, whatever you turn aside to, you will find it is a vain thing, that can never answer your expectations, but will certainly deceive you if you trust to it; it is a broken reed, a broken cistern." Idols are so; they are vanity and a lie: whatever we make a god of, we shall find it so. Creatures in their own place are good things, but when put in God's place they are vain things. Idols could not profit those that sought to them in their wants, nor deliver those that sought them in their straits, for they were vain, and not what they pretended to be. *An idol is nothing in the world,* 1 Cor. viii. 4.

3. He comforts them with an assurance that he would continue his care and concern for them, v. 23. They desired him to pray for them, v. 19. He might have said, "Go to Saul, the king that you have put in my room," and get him to pray for you; but so far is he from upbraiding them with their disrespect to him that he promised them much more than they asked. (1.) They asked it of him as a favour; he promised it as a duty, and startles at the thought of neglecting it. *Pray for you!* says he, *God forbid that I should sin against the Lord in not doing it.* Note, It is a sin against God not to pray for the Israel of God, especially for those of them that are under our charge: and good men are afraid of the guilt of

omissions. (2.) They asked him to pray for them at this time, and upon this occasion, but he promised to continue his prayers for them and not to cease as long as he lived. Our rule is to *pray without ceasing:* we sin if we restrain prayer in general, and in particular if we cease praying for the church. (3.) They asked him only to pray for them, but he promised to do more for them, not only to pray for them, but to teach them. though they were not willing to be under his government as a judge, he would not therefore deny them his instructions as a prophet. And they might be sure he would teach them no other than the *good and the right way:* and the right way is certainly the good way: the way of duty is the way of pleasure and profit.

4. He concludes with an earnest exhortation to practical religion and serious godliness, v. 24, 25. The great duty here pressed upon us is to *fear the Lord.* He had said (v. 20), *"Fear not* with a slavish fear," but here, "Fear the Lord, with a filial fear. As the fruit and evidence of this, serve him in the duties of religious worship and of a godly conversation, in truth and sincerity, and not in show and profession only, with your heart, and *with all your heart* not dissembling, not dividing. And two things he urges by way of motive: — (1.) That they were bound in gratitude to serve God, considering *what great things he had done for them,* to engage them for ever to his service. (2.) That they were bound in interest to serve him, considering what great things he would do against them if they should still do wickedly: *"You shall be destroyed* by the judgments of God, *both you and your king* whom you are so proud of and expect so much from, and who will be a blessing to you if you keep in with God." Thus, as a faithful watchman, he gave them warning, and so delivered his own soul.

"Saul reigned one year. And when he had reigned two years over Israel, Saul chose three thousand men of Israel for himself — two thousand of these were with Saul in Michmash and in Mount Bethel, and a thousand were with Jonathan in Gibeah of Benjamin. And of the rest of the people, he sent each man to his tent. And Jonathan struck the company of the Philistines that was in Geba, and the Philistines heard of it. And Saul blew the trumpet throughout all the land, saying Let the Hebrews hear. And all Israel heard say that Saul had struck a garrison of the Philistines, and also that Israel stank in the nostrils of the Philistines. And the people were called together to Gilgal after Saul. And the Philistines gathered themselves together to fight with Israel — thirty thousand chariots, and six thousand horsemen, and people like the sand which is on the seashore in multitude. And they came up and pitched in Michmash, eastward from Bethaven. When the men of Israel saw that they were in a tight place (for the people were distressed,) then the people hid themselves in caves, and in thickets, and in rocks, and in high places, and in pits. And some of the Hebrews went over Jordan to the land of Gad and Gilead. As for Saul, he was still in Gilgal, and all the people followed him trembling" — 1 Samuel 13: 1-7.

Saul reigned one year, &c.] Or *the son of a year in his reigning;* various are the senses given of these words: some interpret them, Saul had a son of a year old when he began to reign, Ishbosheth, and who was forty years of age when his father died, 2 Sam. ii. 10; others, who understand the words of Saul himself, think there is an *ellipsis*, or defect of the number, and that it may be supplied, that Saul was the son of thirty or forty years, or whatsoever age he may be supposed to be at when he began his reign: others take the words in a figurative sense, that he was like a child of a year old, for purity and innocence; so the Targum "as the son of a year, in whom there are no faults, so was Saul when he reigned;" or he was but a year old, reckoning from the time he was turned into another man, and had another heart, which was immediately after he was anointed king at Ramah by Samuel; or he was but a year old with respect to his kingdom: the inauguration of a king is *natalisimperii*, the birth-day of his kingdom, and therefore the words are well enough rendered by us, *Saul, reigned one year;* which is to be reckoned either from his unction at Ramah, or rather from his election at Mizpeh, to the renewal of the kingdom at Gilgal: and when he *had reigned two years over Israel;* which the Jewish chronologers make to be the whole of his reign, which is not probable, considering the many things done in his reign, the many battles he fought with all his enemies on every side of him, and his long persecution of David; and there were no less than three high-priests in his reign; Josephus says he reigned 18 years in the life-time of Samuel, and 22 years after his death, in all 40; which agrees with Acts xiii. 21. Some interpret he reigned two years well, and the rest in a tyrannical way; or that at the end of two years, when David was anointed, the kingdom was not reckoned to him, but to David; and to this purpose Dr. Lightfoot writes, that he had been king one year from his first anointing by Samuel at Ramah, to his second anointing by him at Gibeah (Gilgal I suppose he means); and he reigned after this two years more, before the Lord cast him off, and anointed David; and the time he ruled after that was not a rule, but a tyranny and persecution; but the sense Ben Gersom gives is best of all, that one year had passed from the time of his being anointed, to the time of the renewal of the kingdom at Gilgal; and when he had reigned two years over Israel, then he did what follows, chose 3000 men, &c. In the first year of his reign was done all that is recorded in the preceding chapter; and when he had reigned two years, not two years more, but two years in all, then he did what is related in this chapter.

Saul chose him 3,000 *men of Israel,* &c.] Out of the 300,000 that went with him to fight the Ammonites, and returned with him to Gilgal where he now was, and had stayed as may be supposed about a year, since now he had reigned two years. These 3,000 men some of them doubtless were appointed as a guard about his person, and the rest were a standing army to preserve the peace of the nation, to protect them from their enemies, to watch the motions of the Philistines, and to be ready on any sudden invasion: whereof 2,000 *were with Saul in Michmash, and in Mount Bethel; Michmash,* according to Bunting, was 4 miles from Gilgal. Jerom says, in his time it was shown a large village on the borders of Elia, or Jerusalem, retaining its ancient name, 9 miles distant from it, near the village of Rama. Adrichomius says it is now called Byra, and Mr. Maundrell observes, that it is supposed by some to be the same with Beer, whither Jotham fled after he had delivered his parable. Judg. ix. 21; Michmash is in the Misnah celebrated for the best wheat being brought from it; and near to it, as appears from hence, was Bethel, and the mount of that name; and so Jerom speaks of Bethel as over against Michmash; and this mount very probably is the same said to be on the east of Bethel, where Abraham built an altar, Gen. xii. 8; for Michmash lay to the east of Bethel: *and* 1,000 *were with Jonathan in Gibeah of Benjamin:* the native place of Saul, and this Jonathan was the son of Saul, ver. 16. According to Bunting, Gibeah, where Jonathan was stationed, was eight miles from Mishmash: *and the rest of the people he sent every man to his tent;* to their own houses; or, as the Targum, to their cities; these were they that came at his summons, and were numbered at Bezek, and went with him to the relief of Jabesh-gilead, and had been with him ever since, and now dismissed.

And Jonathan smote the garrison of the Philistines that was *in Geba,* &c.] No the same with Gibeah of Benjamin, as Jarchi; for it can hardly be thought that Jonathan should place himself with his thousand men where the Philistines had a garrison; or that if this was the same with that in the preceding verse, that it should be called by another name in this; but Gebeah and Geba were two places, as Kimchi observes, both indeed in the tribe of Benjamin, and it is very probably not far from one another; see Josh. xviii. 24, 28. This seems to be the same with the hill of God, where was a garrison of the Philistines, ch. x. 5; who after their defeat by Samuel contented themselves with some strong holds and garrisons in some parts of the land to keep Israel in awe: the Targum understands this of a single person, a governor of the Philistines in this place, whom Jonathan slew, and so Jarchi; and according to R. Isaiah he was one that was appointed to gather the tax for them: *and the Philistines heard of it;* which alarmed them, and made them prepare for war: *and Saul blew the trumpet throughout all the land;* not he in person, for he was at Gilgal, as the next verse shows; but he ordered it to be blown, being aware of the preparations the Philistines were making to attack him: *saying, let the Hebrews hear;* both what sin had done, and what the Philistines were doing.

And all Israel heard say that Saul had smitten a garrison of the Philistines, &c.] For though it was smitten by Jonathan, yet it was by the order of Saul, and so ascribed to him: it seems to be a concerted thing to fall upon the garrison of the Philistines, and get them out of their hands, and so deliver Israel entirely from them; but it was impolitic in Saul, if he had such a scheme in his head, to disband his large army, as he had lately done; *and that Israel also was had in abomination with the Philistines;* who were highly incensed against them by this action, and vowed revenge; the name of an Israelite was abhorred by them; and perhaps this action might be attended with much craft and cruelty; and if these garrisons were held by agreement, they might charge them with perfidy, with breach of articles; and so their name was made to stink among them, as the word signifies: *and the people were called together after Saul to Gilgal;* by sound of trumpet.

And the Philistines gathered themselves together to fight with Israel, &c.] To prevent their further encroachments on them, and designs against them; for they perceived they intended to cast off their yoke, and free themselves entirely from them: 30,000 *chariots, and* 6,000 *horsemen;* it may seem incredible that so small a people as the Philistines were, who only were possessed of five cities, or lordships, with the villages belonging to them, except what they had taken from Israel; and even if assisted by the Tyrians, as the author of Ecclesiasticus says, ch. xlvi. 20; though he seems to have respect not to this time, but when Samuel discomfited them, ch. vii. 10. I say it may seem incredible that they should bring such a number of chariots into the field; wherefore this must either be understood of 30,000 men that fought in chariots, as Lyra interprets it, and in which sense it is plain and certain the word *chariots* is sometimes used, as in 2 Sam. x. 18, 1 Kings xx 21, 1 Chron. xix 18; or else of some sort of carriages, not chariots of war, at least not all of them; but what were brought to carry the baggage of their infantry, which was very large, and to, carry away the goods and substance of the Israelites; some have thought that there is a mistake of the copier, who instead of three, read thirty, so Capellus; and the rather because in the Arabic and Syriac versions it is only three thousand; but even this is too great a number, understood of chariots of war; for never any people in the world was known to have so many chariots of war; Pharaoh in his large host had but 600, Exod. xiv. 7; Jabin king of Canaan had indeed 900, Judg. iv. 3; and David took from the king of Zobah 1,000 chariots; but whether they were all chariots of war is not certain, 2 Sam. viii. 4. Solomon indeed had 1,400 chariots, but they did not appear to be chariots of war, but some for use, and some for state and grandeur. Wherefore, if a mistake in the copy is admitted of, and this can be confirmed by some MSS. yet we must recur to one or other of the above sense; some of them must be understood of other sort of carriages, or of men that fought in these chariots; and allowing ten men to a chariot, which seems to be the usual number by comparing 2 Sam. x. 18, with 1 Chron. xix. 18; then 3,000 men will fill 300 chariots, which are as many as it can well be thought the Philistines had. Zerah the Ethiopian, who brought into the field an army of 1,000,000 men, had no more than 800 chariots, 2 Chron. xiv. 9; and no more had Antiochus Eupator in his army, 2 Maccab. xiii. 2. Darius in his vast army had but 200, and in the very large one which Mithridates brought against the Romans there was but 100; and now 3,000 men in 300 chariots were but a proportion to 6,000 horsemen, which in those times and countries was a large cavalry: *and the people as the sand which is on the sea-shore in multitude;* the infantry was so large as not to be numbered; however, the phrase denotes a great multitude of them; Josephus says there were 300,000 foot: *and they came up, and pitched in Michmash, eastward from Bethaven;* where Saul, before he went to Gilgal, had his quarters, ver. 2; Bethaven Jeroboam had set up the worship of the calves there, Hos. iv. 15; it signifying the house of vanity or iniquity.

When the men of Israel saw they were in a strait, for the people were distressed, &c.] By reason of the vast army that the Philistines brought into the field, greatly superior to theirs, and were likely to be encompassed by them on every side; so that nothing but destruction was expected, which gave them the utmost anxiety and uneasiness; though Abarbinel refers this last clause, not to the people of Israel, but to the people of the Philistines, and takes it in this sense, *for the people drew nigh;* the army of the Philistines was approaching, and got near to them; and so they were in great danger of being quickly attacked by them, and destroyed, their numbers being so great: *then the people did hide themselves in caves;* of which there were many in the land of Judea, capable of receiving a large number, as the cave of Adullam, the cave of Engedi, &c., and such as the Israelites made to hide themselves when oppressed by the Midianites, Judg. vi. 2; *and in thickets;* woods and forests, or among thorns as Jarchi; where there was a very great number of brambles and thorn-bushes; some, as Kimchi, interpret the word of munitions, garrisons, and fortified places, to which they betook themselves: *in rocks, and in high places, and in pits;* in the holes of rocks and mountains, particularly in Mount Ephraim; see ch. xiv. 22; and where there were any pits or ditches, high or deep places, where they might be out of sight, and be sheltered from their enemies.

And some of the Hebrews went over Jordan to the land of Gad and Gilead, &c.] As far off as they could from the Philistines, who lay on the west of the land of Israel, and these countries were to the east. Kimchi observes, that the land of Reuben is not mentioned, which was on the other side Jordan also; because that was nearer to it than what was inhabited by Gad, and the half-tribe of Manasseh; and therefore they chose to go further, thinking themselves there safer: *as for Saul, he was yet in Gilgal;* where he stayed till Samuel should come to him, as directed, ch. x. 8; to have his advice and counsel: *and all the people followed him trembling;* all that were with him, the army as distinct from the common people; they abode by him, and were at his command, and were ready to go where he should direct them; but with trembling hearts when they saw the panic of the people, fleeing into holes and corners, and considered what a huge host the Philistines were coming upon them with, and Samuel their prophet not with them to encourage and counsel them.

"And he stayed seven days, according to the time that Samuel had set. But Samuel did not come to Gilgal. And the people were scattered from him. And Saul said, Bring a burnt-offering and peace-offerings here to me. And he offered the burnt-offering. And as soon as he had made an end of offering the burnt-offering, behold, Samuel came. And Saul went out to meet him so that he might greet him. And Samuel said, What have you done? And Saul said, Because I saw that the·people were scattered from me, and that you did not come within the days appointed, and that the Philistines gathered themselves together at Michmash, therefore I said, The Philistines will come down now on me to Gilgal, and I have not made supplication to the Lord. Therefore I forced myself and offered a burnt-offering. And Samuel said to Saul, You have done foolishly. You have not kept the commandment of the Lord your God, which He commanded you. For now the Lord would have established your kingdom upon Israel forever. But now your kingdom shall not go on. The Lord has sought a man after His own heart for Himself; and the Lord has commanded him to be captain over His people, because you have not kept that which the Lord commanded you" — 1 Samuel 13: 8-14.

Here is, I. Saul's offence in offering sacrifice before Samuel came. Samuel, when he anointed him, had ordered him to tarry for him seven days in Gilgal, promising that, at the end of those days, he would be sure to come to him, and both offer sacrifices for him and direct him what he should do. This we had ch.

x. 8. Perhaps that order, though inserted here, was given him afterwards, or was given in him as a general rule to be observed in every public congress at Gilgal, or, as is most probable, though not mentioned again, was lately repeated with reference to this particular occasion; for it is plain that Saul himself understood it as obliging him from God now to stay till Samuel came, else he would not have made so many excuses as he did for not staying, v. 11. This order Saul broke. He staid till the seventh day, yet had not patience to wait till the end of the seventh day. Perhaps he began to reproach Samuel as false to his word, careless of his country, and disrespectful of his prince, and thought it more fit that Samuel should wait for him than he for Samuel. However, 1. He presumed to offer sacrifice without Samuel, and nothing appears to the contrary but that he did it himself, though he was neither priest nor prophet, as if, because he was a king, he might do any thing, a piece of presumption which king Uzziah paid dearly for, 2 Chron. xxvi. 16, &c. 2. He determined to engage the Philistines without Samuel's directions, though he had promised to *show him what he should do.* So self-sufficient Saul was that he thought it not worth while to stay for a prophet of the Lord either to pray for him or to advise him. This was Saul's offence, and that which aggravated it was, (1.) That, for aught that appears, he did not send any messenger to Samuel, to know his mind, to represent the case to him, though he had enough about him that were swift enough of foot at this time. (2.) That when Samuel came he rather seemed to boast of what he had done than to repent of it; for he *went forth to salute him,* as his brother-sacrificer, and seemed pleased with the opportunity he had of letting Samuel know that he needed him not, but could do well enough without him. He went out to *bless him,* so the word is, as if he now thought himself a complete priest, empowered to bless as well as sacrifice, whereas he should have gone out to be blessed by him. (3.) That he charged Samuel with breath of promise: *Thou camest not within the days appointed* (v. 11), and therefore if any thing was amiss Samuel must bear the blame, who was God's minister; whereas he did come according to his word, before the seven days had expired. Thus the *scoffers of the latter days* think the promise of Christ's coming is broken, because he does not come in their time, though it is certain he will come at the set time. (4.) That when he was charged with disobedience he justified himself in what he had done, and gave no sign at all of repentance for it. It is not sinning that ruins men, but sinning and not repenting, falling and not getting up again. See what excuses he made, v. 11, 12. He would have this act of disobedience pass, [1.] For an instance of his prudence. The people were most of them scattered from him, and he had no other way than this to keep those with him that remained and to prevent their deserting too. If Samuel neglected the public concerns, he would not. [2.] For an instance of his piety. He would be thought very devout, and in great care not to engage the Philistines till he had by prayer and sacrifice engaged God on his side: *"The Philistines,"* said he, *"will come down upon me, before I have made my supplication to the Lord,* and then I am undone. What! go to war before I have said my prayers! Thus he covered his disobedience to God's command with a pretence of concern for God's favour. Hypocrites lay a great stress upon the external performances of religion, thinking thereby to excuse their neglect of the *weightier matters of the law.* And yet, lastly, He owns it went against his conscience to do it: *I forced myself and offered a burnt-offering,* perhaps boasting that he had broken through his convictions and got the better of them, or at least thinking this extenuated his fault, that he knew he should not have done as he did, but did it with reluctancy. Foolish man! to think that God would be well pleased with sacrifices offered in direct opposition both to his general and particular command.

II. The sentence passed upon Saul for this offence. Samuel found him standing by his burnt-offering, but, instead of an answer of peace, was sent to him with heavy tidings, and let him know that *the sacrifice of the wicked is an abomination to the Lord,* much more when he brings it, as Saul did, *with a wicked mind.* 1. He shows him the aggravations of his crime, and says to this king, *Thou art wicked,* which it is not for any but a prophet of the Lord to say, Job xxxiv. 18. He charges him with being an enemy to himself and his interest — *Thou hast done foolishly,* and a rebel to God and his government — *"Thou hast not kept the commandment of the Lord thy God,* that commandment wherewith he intended to try thy obedience." Note, Those that disobey the commandments of God do foolishly for themselves. Sin is folly, and sinners are the greatest fools. 2. He reads his doom (v. 14): *"Thy kingdom shall not continue* long to thee or thy family; God has his eye upon another, *a man after his own heart,* and not like thee, that will have thy own will and way." The sentence is in effect the same with *Mene tekel,* only now there seems room left for Saul's repentance, upon which this sentence would have been reversed; but, upon the next act of disobedience, it was made irreversible, ch. xv. 29. And no,w, better a thousand times he had continued in obscurity tending his asses than to be enthroned and so soon dethroned. But was not this hard, to pass so severe a sentence upon him and his house for a single error, an error that seemed so small, and in excuse for which he had so much to say? No, *The Lord is righteous in all his ways* and does no man any wrong, *will be justified when he speaks and clear when he judges.* By this, (1.) He shows that there is no sin little, because no little god to sin against; but that every sin is a forfeiture of the heavenly kingdom, for which we stood fair. (2.) He shows that disobedience to an express command, though in a small matter, is a great provocation, as in the case of our first parents. (3.) He warns us to *take heed of our spirits,* for that which to men may seem but a small offence, yet to him that knows from what principle and with what disposition of mind it is done, may appear a heinous crime. (4.) God, in rejecting Saul for an error seemingly little, sets off, as by a foil, the lustre of his mercy in forgiving such great sins as those of David, Manasseh, and others. (5.) We are taught hereby how necessary it is that we *wait on our God continually.* Saul lost his kingdom for want of two or three hours' patience.

"And Samuel arose and went up from Gilgal to Gibeah of Benjamin. And Saul numbered the people present with him, about six hundred men. And Saul, and Jonathan his son, and the people present with them, stayed in Gibeah of Benjamin. But the Philistines camped in Michmash. And the spoilers came out of the camp of the Philistines in three companies. One company turned to the way to Ophrah, to the land of Shual. And another company turned to the way to Bethhoron. And another company turned to the way of the border that looks toward the valley of Zeboim toward the wilderness. Now there was no smith found throughout all the land of Israel. For the Philistines said, Lest the Hebrews make swords or spears. But all the Israelites went down to the Philistines, each one to sharpen his plow and its blade, and his axe, and his pick-axe. And they had the file for the pick-axe, and for the blades, and for the forks, and for the axes, and to sharpen the goads. So in the day of battle there was neither sword nor spear found in the hand of any of the people that were with Saul and Jonathan. But with Saul and with Jonathan his son there was found sword and spear. And the garrison of the Philistines went out to the passage of Michmash" — 1 Samuel 13: 15-23.

And Samuel arose, &c.] Seemingly in wrath and displeasure, not staying to offer up the peace-offerings which remained; and though no mention is made of Saul's going with him, yet it seems as if he did, or at least quickly followed him, as appears from the next verse: *and got him up from Gilgal unto Gibeah of Benjamin;* the native place of Saul, thereby directing Saul where he should go, and which might be a stronger place than Gilgal; or however where he might expect to be joined by more persons of his own tribe, as well as in the first place protect and defend that; and it looks by Samuel's going thither, though he was displeased with Saul, yet that he did not intend to forsake him directly and entirely: *and Saul numbered the people that were present with him, about* 600 *men;* which was done either before he left Gilgal, or as soon as he came to Gibeah; so great a desertion was there from him, that of the 3,000 first chosen by him, and of the people after called and gathered to him at Gilgal, only 600 remained with him; a small number indeed to encounter so large an army the Philistines had brought into the field, and which therefore Saul could not face.

And Saul, and Jonathan his sons, &c.] Who were now joined to their men, on Saul's coming to Gibeah: *and the people that were present with them;* the 600 men before numbered: *abode in Gibeah of Benjamin;* being perhaps a strong fortified place, not choosing to go forth to meet the army of the Philistines, so vastly superior to them: *but the Philistines encamped at Michmash;* the old quarters of Saul before he went to Gilgal, ver. 2.

And the spoilers came out of the camp of the Philistines in three companies, &c.] Saul not daring to come out to fight them, and there being none throughout the land to oppose them, they sent out three companies of soldiers to ravage and spoil the country; of so little use and service was a king to Israel, they were so extremely desirous of; and this was suffered, to convince them of their vain confidence in him, and that their trust ought to be in the Lord their God; never was their country more exposed to rapine and violence than now; *one company turned unto the way that leadeth to Ophrah;* a city in the land of Benjamin, of which see Josh. xviii. 23; and lay south-west from Michmash, where the army of the Philistines were: *unto the land of Shual;* which the Targum paraphrases, "the land of the south:" it seems to have had its name from the multitude of foxes in it, Shual signifying a fox.

And another company turned the way to Bethhoron, &c.] Of which name there were two cities, the upper and nether, and both in the tribe of Ephraim, of which see Josh. xvi. 3, 5; this lay north-west from the camp of the Philistines at Michmash; eight miles from it, according to Bunting: *and another company turned to the way of the border, that looketh towards the valley of Zeboim, toward the wilderness;* and take this to be the Zeboim which was destroyed with Sodom and Gomorrah; and the wilderness, the wilderness of Jordan; but as that, so the valley in which it stood, was turned into a bituminous lake; this seems to be a city in the land of Benjamin, Neh. xi. 34; near to which was a valley, and this towards the wilderness of Jericho, and so lay eastward; the Targum calls it the valley of vipers, perhaps from its being infested with many; and so David de Pomis says it is the name of a place where plenty of serpents were found, and which he says were called so because of the variety of colours in them; with which agrees Kimchi's note on the place; they seem to mean serpents spotted, as if they were painted and died of various colours, as the Hebrew word which is thus paraphrased signifies: according to Bunting, it was eight miles from Michmash.

Now there was no smith found throughout all the land of Israel, &c.] The Philistines, when they ruled over them, having removed them into their own country, and forbid any to learn or exercise that trade in Israel; *for the Philistines said, lest the Hebrews make swords or spears;* this they did to prevent their having arms, and the use of them, that they might not rebel against them, and fight with them, and overcome them; it was a piece of policy to keep them subject to them; so Nebuchadnezzar, when he conquered the Jews and carried them captive, took care particularly to carry away their smiths, and left none but the poorest sort of people in the land, 2 Kings xxiv. 14, Jer. xxiv. 1; and Porsena, king of the Etrusci, when he made a covenant with the Romans, upon the expulsion of their kings, made this a condition of peace with them, that they should use no iron but in husbandry. When this course was taken by the Philistines with the Israelites, and how long it had continued, is not certain; it is probable it might be in the space of forty years they ruled over Israel, in which Samson was born, for we never read of any sword or spear that he made use of; and though there were two battles in the time of Eli, in both which Israel were beaten, they might make use only of bows and arrows, slings, and stones, clubs, &c., as also in the battle of Saul with the Ammonites; and as for the defeat of the Philistines in the time of Samuel, it was by thunder; and though the Philistines were then subdued, yet, as Samuel grew old, they regained their power in a good measure, and the Israelites had not spirit enough to oppose them, nor diligence and industry to learn and revive the trade of smiths among them; not even for what was necessary to husbandry, as the following verse shows.

But all the Israelites went down to the Philistines, &c.] Were obliged to go into Palestine, into some one or other of the cities of the Philistines, or to their garrisons, where the trade of a smith was exercised; *to sharpen every man his share and his coulter;* which are the parts of the plough made of iron, with which the earth is cut and thrown up: *and his ax and his mattock;* or pick-axe: with the one wood is felled and cut, and with the other stones are dug; and each of these for their several uses needed sharpening; and when they did, they were obliged to go to the Philistines to have them done, they having no smiths among them.

Yet they had a file for the mattocks, and for the coulters, and for the forks, and for the axes, &c.] Those that would not go to the Philistines, or were not able, or thought it too much trouble, these kept files by them to sharpen those several instruments with upon occasion; though the words are by some rendered in connexion with the preceding, to this sense, that they went to the Philistines to sharpen them, *when the mouths,* or edges, *of the mattocks, coulters,* &c., *were dull; or blunt;* and so needed sharpening: *and* even *to sharpen the goads;* with which they pricked and pushed on the oxen in ploughing, when sluggish and remiss.

So it came to pass in the day of battle, &c.] When that drew near, and they were called to it, and obliged to flight or flee, or surrender: *that there were neither sword nor spear found in the land of any of the people that were with Saul and Jonathan;* which was not owing to their leaving them behind in the camp, or casting them away from them through fear, as they followed Saul with trembling, but to the cause now mentioned. In what manner some preceding battles were fought with the Philistines and Ammonites, notwithstanding, have been accounted for on ver. 19; but it is strange that the Israelites did not furnish themselves with the arms of the Philistines at the defeat of them in Ebenezer, ch. vii. 10, 11; and with the arms of the Ammonites at Jabesh-gilead, ch. xi. 11; and that such a warlike prince as Saul appeared at his first setting out to be, should not in the first place take care to provide armour for his men by some means or another; for that those that left him should have arms, and not those that abode with him, does not seem reasonable. It may be the Benjamites, being expert in slinging, were indifferent to and neglected the use of any other weapon, or method of fighting, *but with Saul and with Jonathan his son was there found;* swords and spears, and with them only.

And the garrison of the Philistines went out to the passage of Michmash.] According to Jarchi, these two places, Michmash where the Philistines were, and Gibeah where Saul and Jonathan were, lay on two hills over against each other, and there was a valley between them; and the garrison of the Philistines drew nigh to the passage of Michmash, which led to the side of Gibeah, to the valley between them, either with an intention to besiege Gibeah, or to dare Israel to come out and fight them: but rather it seems to be some strong pass between the rocks near Michmash, where the garrison placed themselves to guard and keep against any sudden surprise; see ch. xiv. 4. The Targum is, "the governor of the Philistines went out to the ford or passage of Michmash;" and Kimchi interprets it of the princes or generals of the army; these might go to mark out a camp, and pitch upon a proper place to draw in a line of battle.

CHAPTER 14.

"Now there was a day that Jonathan the son of Saul said to the young man who bore his armour, Come and let us go over to the Philistines' garrison which is on the other side. But he did not tell his father. And Saul stayed in the furthest part of Gibeah under a pomegranate tree which is in Migron. And the people who were with him were about six hundred men. And Ahiah, the son of Ahitub, Ichabod's brother, the son of Phinehas, the son of Eli, the Lord's priest in Shiloh, was wearing an ephod. And the people did not know that Jonathan was gone. And between the passages by which Jonathan sought to go over to the Philistines' garrison there was a sharp rock on the one side and a sharp rock on the other side. And the name of the one was Bozez, and the name of the other Seneh. The front of the one was north over against Michmash, and the other southward over against Gibeah. And Jonathan said to the young man who bore his armor, Come, and let us go over to the garrison of these uncircumcised. It may be that the Lord will work for us. For there is no restraint to the Lord, to save by many or by few. And his armor-bearer said to him, Do all that is in your heart. Turn, for behold, I am with you according to your heart. Then Jonathan said, Behold, we will go over to these men, and we will show ourselves to them. If they say to us, stay until we come to you, then we will stand still in our place and will not go up to them. But if they say this, Come up to us — then we will go up, for the Lord has delivered them up into our hand. And this shall be a sign to us. And both of them showed themselves to the garrison of the Philistines. And the Philistines said, Behold, the Hebrews come forth out of the holes where they have hidden themselves. And the men of the garrison answered Jonathan and his armour-bearer and said, Come up to us, and we will show you a thing. And Jonathan said to his armor-bearer, Come up after me, for the Lord has delivered them into the hand of Israel. And Jonathan climbed up on his hands and feet, and his armor-bearer after him. And they fell before Jonathan, and his armor-bearer killed after him. And that first slaughter which Jonathan and his armor-bearer made, was about twenty men, within as it were a half acre of land which a yoke of oxen might plow. And there was trembling in the army, in the field, and among all the people. The garrison and the spoilers also trembled, and the earth quaked — so it was a very great trembling" — 1 Samuel 14: 1-15.

We must here take notice,

I. Of the goodness of God in restraining the Philistines, who had a vast army of valiant men in the field, from falling upon that little handful of timorous trembling people that Saul had with him, whom they would easily have swallowed up at once. It is an invisible power that sets bounds to the malice of the church's enemies, and suffers them not to do that which we should think there is nothing to hinder them from.

II. Of the weakness of Saul, who seems here to have been quite at a loss, and unable to help himself. 1. He pitched his tent under a tree, and had but 600 men with him, v. 2. Where were now the 3000 men he had chosen, and put such a confidence in? ch. xiii. 2. Those whom he trusted too much to failed him when he most needed them. He durst not stay in Gibeah, but got into some obscure place, in the uttermost part of the city, under a pomegranate-tree, under *Rimmon* (so the word is), *Ha-Rimmon*, that Rimmon near Gibeah, in the caves of which those 600 Benjamites that escaped his themselves, Judg. xx. 47. Some think that there Saul took shelter, so mean and abject was his spirit, now that he had fallen under God's displeasure, every hour expecting the Philistines upon him, and thereby the accomplishment of Samuel's threatening, ch. xiii. 14.

Those can never think themselves safe that see themselves cast out of God's protection. 2. Now he sent for a priest, and the ark, a priest from Shiloh, and the ark from Kirjath-jearim, v. 3, 18. Saul had once offended by offering sacrifice himself, ch. xiii. 9. Now he resolves never to fall into that error again, and therefore sends for a priest, and hopes to compromise the matter with God Almighty by a particular reformation, as many do whose hearts are unhumbled and unchanged. Samuel, the Lord's prophet, had forsaken him, but he thinks he can make up that loss by commanding Ahiah, the Lord's priest, to attend him, and *he* will not make him stay for him nor reprove him, as Samuel had done, but will do just as be hids him, v. 18, 19. Many love to have such ministers as will be what they would have them to be, and prophesy smooth things to them; and their caressing them because they are priests, they hope, will atone for their enmity to those ministers that deal faithfully and plainly with them. He will also have the ark brought, perhaps to upbraid Samuel, who in the days of his government, for aught that appears, had not made any public use of it; or in hopes that this would make up the deficiency of his forces; one would have supposed that they would never bring the ark into the camp again, since, the last time, it not only did not save them, but did itself fall into the Philistines' hands. But it is common for those that have lost the substance of religion to be most fond of the shadows of it, as here is a deserted prince courting a deserted priest.

III. Of the bravery and piety of Jonathan, the son of Saul, who was much fitter than the father to wear the crown. "A sweet imp (says bishop Hall) out of a crab-stock."

1. He resolved to go *incognito — unknown to any one*, into the camp of the Philistines; he did not acquaint his father with his design, for he knew he would forbid him; nor the people, for he knew they would all discourage him, and, because he resolved not to heed their objections, he resolved not to hear them, nor ask their advice, v. 1, 3. Nor had he so great an opinion of the priest as to consult him, but, being conscious of a divine impulse putting him upon it, he threw himself into the mouth of danger, in hope of doing service to his country. The way of access to the enemies' camp is described (v. 4, 5) as being peculiarly difficult, and their natural entrenchments impregnable, yet this does not discourage him; the strength and sharpness of the rocks do not harden and whet his resolutions. Great and generous souls are animated by opposition and take a pleasure in breaking through it.

2. He encouraged his armour-bearer, a young man that attended him, to go along with him in this daring enterprise, (v. 6): "*Come, and let us* put our lives in our hands, *and go over to the* enemies' *garrison*, and try what we can do to put them into confusion." See whence he draws his encouragements. (1.) "They are uncircumcised, and have not the seal of the covenant in their flesh, as we have. Fear not, we shall do well enough with them, for they are not under the protection of God's covenant as we are, cannot call him theirs as we can, by the sign of circumcision." If such as are enemies to us are also strangers to God, we need not fear them. (2.) "God is able to make us too victorious over their unnumbered regiments. *There is no restraint in the Lord*, no limitation to the holy One of Israel, but it is all one to him *to save by many or by few.*" This is a truth easily granted in general, that it is all alike to Omnipotence what the instruments are by which it works; and yet it is not so easy to apply it to a particular case; when we are but few and feeble then to believe that God can not only save us, but save by us, this is an instance of faith, which, wherever it is, shall obtain a good report. Let this strengthen the weak and encourage the timid: let it be pleaded with God for the enforcing of our petitions and with

ourselves the silencing of our fears: *It is nothing with God to help, whether with many or with those that have no power,* 2 Chron. xiv. 11. (3.) "Who knows but he that can use us for his glory will do it? *It may be the Lord will work for us,* work with us, work a sign or miracle for us." So the Chaldee. We may encourage ourselves with hope that God will appear for us, though we have not ground on which to build an assurance. An active faith will venture far in God's cause upon an *it may be.* Jonathan's armour-bearer, or esquire, as if he had learned to carry, not his arms only, but his heart, promised to stand by him and to follow him whithersoever he went, v. 7. We have reason to think that Jonathan felt a divine impulse and impression putting him upon this bold adventure, in which he was encouraged by his servant's concurrence, otherwise the danger was so great which he ran upon that he would have tempted God rather than trusted him. And perhaps he had an actual regard to that word of Joshua (Josh. xiii. 10), *One man of you shall chase a thousand,* borrowed from Moses, Deut. xxxii. 30.

3. How bold soever his resolution was, he resolved to follow Providence in the execution of it, which, he believed, would guide him *with its eye* (Ps. xxxii. 8), and which therefore he would carefully attend and take hints of direction from. See how he put himself upon Providence, and resolved to be determined by it. "Come" (says he to his confidant), we will discover ourselves to the enemy, as those that are not afraid to look them in the face (v. 8), and then, if they be so cautious as to bid us stand, we will advance no further, taking it for an intimation of Providence that God would have us act defensively, and we will prepare as well as we can to give them a warm reception (v. 9); but if they be so presumptuous as to challenge us, and the first sentinel we meet with bid us march on, we will push forward, and make as brisk an onset, assuredly gathering thence that it is the will of God we should act offensively, and then not doubting but he will *stand by us,"* v; 10. And upon this issue he puts it, firmly believing, as we all should, (1.) That God has the governing of the hearts and tongues of all men, even of those that know him not, nor have any regard to him, and serves his own purposes by them, though they mean not so, neither do their hearts think so. Jonathan knew God could discover his mind to him if he pleased, and would do it, since he depended upon him, as surely by the mouth of a Philistine as by the mouth of a priest. (2.) That God will, some way or other, direct the steps of those that *acknowledge him in all their ways,* and seek unto him for direction, with full purpose of heart to follow it. Sometimes we find most comfort in that which is least our own doing, and into which we have been led by the unexpected, but well observed, turns of Providence.

4. Providence gave him the sign he expected, and he answered the signal. He and his armour-bearer did not surprise the Philistines when they were asleep, but discovered themselves to them by day-light, v. 11. The guards of the Philistines, (1.) Disdained them, upbraided them with the cowardice of many of their people, and looked upon them to be of the regiment of sneakers: *Behold, the Hebrews come forth out of their holes.* If some of Christ's soldiers play the coward, others that play the man may perhaps be upbraided with it. (2.) They defied them (v. 12): *Come, and we will show you a thing,* as if they came like children to gaze about them; but meaning, as Goliath (ch. xvii. 44), that they would *give them as meat to the fowls of the air.* They bantered them, not doubting but to make a prey of them. This greatly emboldened Jonathan. With it he encouraged his servant; he had spoken with uncertainty (v. 6): *It may be the Lord will work for us;* but now he speaks with assurance (v. 12): *The Lord has delivered them,* not into our hands (he sought not his own glory), but *into the hand of Israel,* for he aimed at nothing but the advantage of the public. His

faith being thus strengthened, no difficulty can stand before him; he climbs up the rock upon all four (v. 13), though he has nothing to cover him, nor any but his own servant to second him, nor any human probability of any thing but death before him.

5. The wonderful success of this daring enterprise. The Philistines, instead of falling upon Jonathan, to slay him, or take him prisoner, fell before him (v. 13) unaccountably, upon the first blow he gave. They fell, that is, (1.) They were many of them slain by him and his armour-bearer, v. 14. Twenty Philistines fell presently. It was not so much the name of Jonathan that made them yield so tamely (though some think that this become terrible to them, since he smote one of their garrisons, ch. xiii. 3), but it was God's right hand and his arm that got him this victory. (2.) The rest were put to flight, and fell foul upon one another (v. 15): *There was trembling in the host.* There was no visible cause for fear; they were so numerous, bold, and advantageously posted; the Israelites had fled before them; not an enemy nade head against them, but one gentleman and his man; and yet they shook like an aspen-leaf. The consternation was general: they all trembled; even *the spoilers,* those that had been most bold and forward, shared in the common fright, the joints of their loins were loosed, and their knees smote one against another, and yet none of them could tell why or wherefore. It is called *a trembling of God* (so the original phrase is), signifying not only, as we render it, a very great trembling, which they could not resist nor reason themselves clear of, but that it was supernatural, and came immediately from the hand of God. He that made the heart knows how to make it tremble. To complete the confusion, even the earth quaked, and made them ready to fear that it would sink under them. Those that will not fear the eternal God, he can make afraid of a shadow. See Prov. xxi. 1; Isa. xxxiii. 14.

"And the watchmen of Saul in Gibeah of Benjamin looked, and behold, the multitude melted away, and they went on beating down one another. Then said Saul to the people who were with him, Number now and see who is gone from us. And when they had counted, behold, Jonathan and his armour-bearer were not there. And Saul said to Ahiah, Bring the ark of God here. For the ark of God was at that time with the children of Israel. And while Saul talked to the priest, the noise that was in the army of the Philistines went on and grew greater. And Saul said to the priest, Withdraw your hand. And Saul and all the people that were with him gathered themselves together. And they came to the battle. And, behold, every man's sword was against his fellow. There was a very great destruction. Moreover the Hebrews that were with the Philistines before that time, who went up with them into the camp all around, even they also turned to be with the Israelites who were with Saul and Jonathan. Likewise all the men of Israel who had hidden themselves in Mount Ephraim, when they heard that the Philistines fled, even they also followed hard after them in the battle. So the Lord saved Israel that day, and the battle passed over to Bethaven" — 1 Samuel 14: 16-23.

We have here the prosecution and improvement of the wonderful advantages which Jonathan and his armour-bearer gained against the Philistines.

I. The Philistines were, by the power of God, set against one another. They melted away like snow before the sun, and *went on beating down one another* (v. 16), for (v. 20) *every man's sword was against his fellow.* When they fled for fear, instead of turning back upon those that chased them, they reckoned those only their enemies that stood in their way, and treated them accordingly. The

Philistines were very secure, because all the swords and spears were in their hands. Israel had none except what Saul and Jonathan had. But now God showed them the folly of that confidence, by making their own swords and spears the instruments of their destruction, and more fatal in their own hands than if they had been in the hands of Israel. See the like done, Judg. vii. 22; 2 Chron. xx. 23.

II. The Israelites were hereby animated against them.

1. Notice was soon taken of it by the watchmen of Saul, those that stood sentinel at Gibeah, v. 16. They were aware that the host of the enemy was in great confusion, and that a great slaughter was made among them, and yet, upon search, they found none of their own forces absent, but only Jonathan and his servant (v. 17), which no doubt greatly animated them, and assured them that it could be no other than the Lord's doing, when there was no more of man's doing than what those two could do against a great host.

2. Saul began to enquire of God, but soon desisted. His spirit had not come down so far as to allow him to consult Samuel, though, it is probable, he was near him; for we read (ch. xiii. 15) that he had come to Gibeah of Benjamin; but he called for the ark (v. 18), desiring to know whether it would be safe for him to attack the Philistines, upon the disorder they perceived them to be in. Many will consult God about their safety that would never consult him about their duty. But, perceiving by his scouts that the noise in the enemy's camp increased, he commanded the priest that officiated to break off abruptly: *"Withdraw thy hand* (v. 19), consult no more, wait no longer for an answer. He was very unwise indeed if (as some think) he forbade him to lift up his hands in prayer; for when Joshua was actually engaged with Amalek Moses continued still to lift up his hands. It is rather a prohibition to his enquiring of the Lord, either, (1.) Because he now thought he did not need an answer, the case was plain enough. And yet the more evident it was that God did all the more reason he had to enquire whether he would give him leave to do any thing. Or, (2.) Because now he would not stay for it; he was in such haste to fight a falling enemy that he would not stay to make an end of his devotions, nor hear what answer God would give him. A little thing will divert a vain and carnal mind from religious exercises. He that believeth will not make haste, such haste as this, nor reckon any business so urgent as not to allow time to take God along with him.

3. He, and all the little force he had, made a vigorous attack upon the enemy; and all the people *were cried together* (so the word is, v. 20), for want of the silver trumpets wherewith God appointed them to sound an alarm in the day of battle, Num. x. 9. They summoned them together by shouting, and their number was not so great but that they might soon be got together. And now they seem bold and brave when the work is done to their hands. Our Lord Jesus has conquered our spiritual enemies, routed and dispersed them, so that we are cowards indeed if we will not stand to our arms when it is only to pursue the victory and to divide the spoil.

4. Every Hebrew, even those from whom one would least have expected it, now turned his hand against the Philistines. (1.) Those that had deserted and gone over to the enemy, and were among them, now fought against them, v. 21. Some think, they were such as had been taken prisoners by them, and now they were as goads in their sides. It rather seems that they went in to them voluntarily, but, now that they saw them falling, recovered the hearts of Israelites, and did valiantly for their country. (2.) Those that had fled their colours, and hid themselves in the mountains, returned to their posts, and joined in with the pursuers (v. 22), hoping by their great zeal and officiousness, now that the

danger was over and the victory sure, to atone for their former cowardice. It was not much to their praise to appear now, but it would have been more their reproach if they had not appeared. Those are remiss and faint-hearted indeed that will not act in the cause of God when they see it victorious, as well as righteous. Thus all hands were at work against the Philistines, and every Israelite slew as many as he could, without sword or spear; yet it is said (v. 23) it was *the Lord that saved Israel that day*. He did it by them, for without him they could do nothing. *Salvation is of the Lord.*

"And the men of Israel were distressed that day. For Saul had commanded the people, saying, Cursed is the man that eats any food until evening, so that I may be avenged on my enemies. So none of the people tasted any food. And all the men of the land came to a woods, and there was honey on the ground. And when the people had come into the woods, behold, the honey dropped. But no man put his hand to his mouth, for the people feared the oath. But Jonathan did not hear when his father commanded the people with the oath. Therefore he put forth the end of the rod that was in his hand and dipped it in a honeycomb, and put his hand to his mouth. And his eyes were enlightened. Then one from the people answered and said, Your father strictly charged the people with an oath, saying, Cursed is the man who eats any food this day. And the people were weary. Then Jonathan said, My father has troubled the land. I beg you, see how my eyes have been enlightened because I tasted a little of this honey. How much more if the people had happened to eat freely today of the spoil of their enemies which they found? For would not there have been a much greater slaughter among the Philistines? And they struck the Philistines that day from Michmash to Aijalon, and the people were very faint. And the people flew on the spoil and took sheep and oxen and calves and killed them on the ground. And the people ate them with the blood. Then they told Saul, saying, Behold, the people sin against the Lord in that they eat meat with the blood. And he said, You have transgressed. Roll a great stone to me this day. And Saul said, Disperse yourselves among the people and say to them, Let each man bring his ox here, and each man his sheep, and kill them here and eat. And do not sin against the Lord in eating with the blood. And each man of all the people brought his ox in his hand that night and killed them there. And Saul built an altar to the Lord. The same was the first altar that he built to the Lord" — 1 Samuel 14: 24-35.

And the men of Israel were distressed that day, &c.] By reason of the following order Saul gave with an oath, forbidding any to taste meat till evening, when the people were faint and weary, which is the common sense of interpreters; but Jarchi interprets it, the men of Israel were ready, forward, and hasty, and drew nigh to fight with the Philistines, and so refer it to the persons before mentioned, who came out of their lurking-places; and this sense is approved of by Abarbinel; *for*, or *and Saul had adjured the people;* or *willed* them, signified to them his will and pleasure, which would not have been so much amiss, had he had not annexed a curse to it, as follows; *saying, cursed be the man that eateth* any *food until the evening;* or *bread*, which comprehends all food, and among the rest honey; the design of which was, that no time might be lost, and that he might make the victory over the Philistines, and their destruction, as complete as possible; though it may seem a little too hard and severe upon the people, and too imperious in him, as well as imprudent; since a little refreshment would have animated and enabled them to have pursued their enemies with more ardour and vigour: yet by the lot afterwards made, it seems to have been countenanced by the Lord: *that I may be avenged on mine enemies;* who long tyrannised over the people of Israel, more or less for many years, and lately had sadly spoiled and plundered them: *so none of the people tasted any food;* so observant were they of, and so obedient to the order of their king, and so much awed by the oath or imprecation annexed to it; though they were faint and hungry, and had an opportunity of refreshing themselves as follows, which was no small temptation to disobedience.

And all they of *the land came to a wood,* &c.] Which lay between Bethaven and Aijalon; by whom are meant not all the inhabitants of the land of Israel, but all that came with Saul and Jonathan, and that joined them in the pursuit: *and there was honey upon the ground;* which dropped upon it, as in the following verse, or where it was produced by bees; for Aristotle reports, that bees in some places make their combs upon the ground; this was wild honey, which Diodorus Siculus speaks of as common in Arabia, and which perhaps John the Baptist ate of, Matt. iii. 4. Jarchi says, this was the honey of canes, or sugar-canes, which grew in the land of Israel: and affirms from Nathan an Ishmaelite, that in the Ishmaelitish or Arabic language they call honey sugar; but neither of these can be proved.

And when the people came into the wood, behold the honey dropped, &c.] Either from trees, which produced it; so Diodorus Siculus speaks of trees in some countries which produce honey; or from the sugar-canes, as Jarchi; or rather from the honeycombs which were framed in trees by bees; so Hesiod speaks of bees making their nests or combs in trees. Ben Gersom thinks that bee-hives were placed here in rows by the way-side from whence the honey flowed; or *went,* or there was a going of it; perhaps the combs being pressed by the Philistines as they fled: the land of Canaan was a land flowing with milk and honey; *but no man put his hand to his mouth;* that is, took not any of the honey and ate it, though it was so near at hand, and there was plenty of it: *for the people feared the oath;* Saul adjured them by, or the imprecation he made on the person that should eat any food that day.

But Jonathan heard not when his father charged the people with the oath, &c.] Which charge was given, either before he came from Gibeah, before he came to Jonathan, or whilst pursuing, when Jonathan was with another party either fighting or pursuing: *wherefore he put forth the end of the rod that* was *in his hand;* the staff with which he walked, or rather the spear which he carried in his hand, and fought his enemies with: *and dipped it in an honeycomb;* or sugar-cane, as Jarchi: or in wood honey, as the margin of our Bibles; but best, in the honeycomb, as the word is rendered, Cant. v. 1; and so the Targum, into the nest of honey *and he put his hand to his mouth;* first he took the honey off the top of his rod, and then put it to his mouth and ate it; *and his eyes were enlightened;* which before were dim and dull through want of food, which is a common case: but became brisk and lively on eating the honey, nourishment being presently communicated, and he refreshed with it, and his spirits revived; and which quickly appeared in the briskness and sparkling of his eyes; honey being of a subtle nature, gives immediate refreshment and vigour: hence this phrase is frequently used by Jewish writers for refreshment, after hunger, fatigue, and weariness; and which virtue is ascribed by them to fine bread, wine, oil, and particularly to honey.

Then answered one of the people, and said, &c.] To Jonathan, who might direct and encourage the people to do as he had done, at least so he did by his example, if not by words; the latter is not improbable; and therefore one of the men that came along with Saul, and had now joined Jonathan, and who heard what Saul had said, replied, *thy father straitly charged the people with an oath;* gave them a strict charge, with an oath or imprecation annexed to it: *saying, cursed be the man that eateth* any *food this day:* that is, until the evening, as in ver. 24; *and the people were faint:* which is either the observation of the writer of the book; or it may be the words of the man, imputing the faintness of the people to this adjuration of Saul's restraining them from good; or as taking notice how strictly the people observed it, though they were hungry, faint, and weary.

Then said Jonathan, my father hath troubled the land, &c.] The people of the land, as the Targum, the soldiers in his army; afflicted and distressed them, and made them uneasy in their minds, like troubled waters; the Arabic version is, "my father hath sinned against the people;" hath done them injury by forbidding them to eat. This was not wisely said by Jonathan; how much soever his father was to be blamed, it did not become him as a son thus to reflect upon him, and it might have tended to mutiny and sedition: *see I pray you, how mine eyes have been enlightened, because I tasted a little of this honey;* the benefit he received by it was very visible; it might easily be discerned that he was greatly refreshed with it, and his spirits invigorated by it; it was to be seen in the cheerfulness of his countenance and the briskness of his eyes: and he suggests it would have had the same effect upon the people, had they eaten of it, as he had done.

How much more, if haply the people had eaten freely to day of the spoil of their enemies which they found? &c.] That is, had they been allowed to eat freely of the provisions of bread, wine, &c., they found in the enemy's camp, they would have been much more refreshed and strengthened than it could be supposed he was with eating a little honey; if that had had such an effect upon him, of what service would a full meal have been to the people? *for had there not been now a much greater slaughter among the Philistines?* the people would have had more strength to smite them, and would have pursued them with greater ardour and swiftness, and so have made a greater slaughter among them than they had; he intimates that Saul's end would have been better answered by suffering the people to eat, than by forbidding them.

And they smote the Philistines that day from Michmash to Aijalon, &c.] Michmash was the place where the camp of the Philistines was when Jonathan first attacked them, and from whence they fled, and they were pursued by the Israelites that day as far as Aijalon. There was a city of this name in the tribe of Dan, famous for the moon standing still in a valley adjoining it, in the time of Joshua, ch. x. 12, and xix. 42; and another in the tribe of Zebulon, Judg. xii. 12; but they both seem to be at too great a distance to be the place here meant, which rather seems to be Aijalon in the tribe of Judah, 2 Chron. xi. 10; according to Bunting, it was 12 miles from Michmash: *and the people were very faint;* as they might well be, with pursuing the enemy so many miles, and doing so much execution among them, without eating any food.

And the people flew upon the spoil, &c.] Like a swift and ravenous bird, as the eagle, and which seems to have its name in Greek from this word, see Isa. xlvi. 11. When the evening was come, and they were free from the oath of Saul, and being extremely hungry, faint, and weary, they were even ravenous for food, and with the greatest haste and eagerness laid hold on what came first to hand: *and took sheep, and oxen, and calves, and slew* them *on the ground;* and there they lay in their blood, which in such a position could not run out freely as when slain and hung up; *and the people did eat them with the blood;* they were so hungry they could not stay the dressing of them, but ate them raw with the blood in them, not being squeezed or drained out, at least not half boiled or roasted. Some of the Jewish Rabbins are of opinion that these were their peace offerings; and that their fault was, that they ate of them before the blood was sprinkled, whilst it was in the basin; but this was common food, which, being hungry, they were eager of, and could not wait the proper dressing of it, according to the law of God. The phrase is by some rendered *by, upon,* or *about* the blood, and think it refers to an idolatrous custom of the Heathens, who, sacrificing to demons, sat down round about the blood, and ate their food; see the notes on Lev. xix. 26; and Ezek. xxxiii. 25; to which may be added, that Homer represents the infernal spirits as gathered together at a ditch where the blood of an animal was shed, to drink of it, that they might know and foretell things to come, as particularly Tiresias the Theban.

Then they told Saul, &c.] Some that were more conscientious and religious, were more circumspect, and strictly attended to the laws forbidding the eating of blood, and were concerned at the indecent behaviour of others, and therefore thought fit to acquaint Saul with it, to restrain it: *behold, the people sin against the Lord, in that they eat with the blood;* by breaking the laws of God respecting the eating of blood in Gen. ix. 4, Lev. iii. 17, and vii. 26, 27, and xvii. 10, 11; especially in Lev. xix. 26; *and he said, ye have transgressed;* the above laws of God; that is, Saul said to some persons who were accused of the breach of them, and were ordered to come before him, and did come: *roll a great stone unto me this day;* pointing, perhaps, at one which lay at some distance from him, and which he ordered to be rolled to him; this was done, that the creatures might be slain on it, and their blood drawn out from them, or to offer sacrifice upon, and indeed for both.

And Saul said, disperse yourselves among the people, &c.] In the camp, some one way, and some another, and make proclamation throughout it: this he said to some of his officers, whom he sent out as heralds, to publish his will and pleasure: *and say unto them, bring me hither every man his ox, and every man his sheep, and slay* them *here;* on the great stone he had ordered to roll to the place where he was: *and eat* them; in the same place, being rightly slain, and the blood let out; all this was to be done, the slaying of the beasts, and eating them, in the presence of Saul, and under his inspection, that every thing might be done decently, and in order, and according to the law of God; *and sin not against the Lord, in eating with the blood;* as some of them had done, ver. 32: *and all the people brought every man his ox with him;* and his sheep also, though not expressed, yet to be supplied, from the preceding clause; and these every man brought *with him that night;* the Jewish Rabbins are divided about these creatures slain, whether for sacrifices or common food; and those that think sacrifices are meant dispute whether it was lawful to slay them in the night, which some allow to be lawful, if on a small and private altar, but not upon a large and public one; but these were slain no doubt for common food, which all agree might be slain in the night: *and slew* them *there;* before Saul, and on the great stone rolled unto him.

And Saul built an altar unto the Lord, &c.] To offer peace-offerings upon, in thankfulness for the victory obtained over his enemies, or sin-offerings to make atonement for the sin of the people, perhaps both however the former: *the same was the first altar, that he built unto the Lord;* for though he had offered sacrifice at Gilgal, there was an altar ready built for him: or *he began to build;* he laid the first stone of it, and the builders built upon it; so some others say, that he was the first of the kings that built an altar to the Lord; others, the first of the judges that built one: though Gideon built one, it was for his own private use, not for all Israel, as this, as R. Isaiah; but Ben Gersom, and so Abarbinel, refer this to the great stone Saul ordered to be rolled to him, and take the sense to be, that that began to be built an altar to the Lord; that was the beginning of one; for he did not now stay to finish it, being eager on his pursuit of the Philistines, as follows.

"And Saul said, Let us go down after the Philistines by night and spoil them until the morning light, and let us not leave a man of them. And they said, Do whatever seems good to you. Then the priest said, Let us draw near here to God. And Saul asked counsel of God: Shall I go down after the Philistines? Will you deliver them into the hand of Israel? But He did not answer him that day. And Saul said, Draw near here, all the chief of the people, and know and see what this sin has been this day. For, as the Lord lives, He who is saving Israel, though it is in Jonathan my son, he shall surely die. But there was not a man among all the people who answered him. Then he said to all Israel, You be on one side, and Jonathan my son and I will be on the other side. And the people said to Saul, Do what seems good to you. Therefore Saul said to the Lord God of Israel, Give a perfect lot. And Saul and Jonathan were taken, but the people escaped. And Saul said, Cast lots between me and Jonathan my son. And Jonathan was taken. Then Saul said to Jonathan, Tell me what you have done. And Jonathan told him and said, I did but taste of a little honey with the end of the rod that was in my hand, and, lo, I must die. And Saul answered, God do so and more also, for you shall surely die, Jonathan. And the people said to Saul, Shall Jonathan die, who has worked out this great salvation in Israel? God forbid! As the Lord lives, there shall not one hair of his head fall to the ground, for he was worked with God this day. So the people rescued Jonathan, so that he did not die. Then Saul went up from following the Philistines. And the Philistines went to their own place" -- 1 Samuel 14: 36-46.

Here is, I. Saul's boasting against the Philistines. He proposed, as soon as his soldiers had got their suppers, to pursue them all night, and *not leave a man of them,* v. 36. Here he showed much zeal, but little discretion; for his army, thus fatigued, could as ill spare a night's sleep as a meal's meat. But it is common for rash and foolish men to consider nobody but themselves, and, so that they may but have their humour, not to care what hardships they put upon those that are under them. However, the people were so obsequious to their king that they would by no means oppose the motion, but resolved to make the best of it, and, if he will go on, they will follow him: *Do whatsoever seemeth good to thee.* Only the priest thought it convenient to go on with the devotions that were broken off abruptly (v. 19), and to consult the oracle: *Let us draw near hither unto God.* Princes and great men have need of such about them as will thus be their remembrancers, wherever they go, to take God along with them. And, when the priest proposed it, Saul could not for shame reject the proposal, but *asked counsel of God* (v. 37): *"Shall I go down after the Philistines?* And shall I speed?"

II. His falling foul on his son Jonathan: and the rest of this paragraph is wholly concerning him; for, while he is prosecuted, the Philistines make their escape. We know not what mischief may ensue upon one rash resolve.

1. God, by giving an intimation of his displeasure, put Saul upon searching for an accursed thing. When, by the priest, he consulted the oracle, God *answered him not,* v. 37. Note, When God denies our prayers it concerns us to enquire what the sin is that has provoked him to do so. *Let us see where the sin is,* v. 38. For God's ear is not heavy that it cannot hear, but it is sin that separates between us and him.

If God turns away our prayer, we have reason to suspect it is for some iniquity regarded in our hearts, which we are concerned to find out, that we may put it away, may mortify it, and put it to death. Saul swears by his Maker that whoever was the Achan that troubled the camp, by eating the forbidden fruit, should certainly die, though it were Jonathan himself, that is, though ever so dear to himself and the people, little thinking that Jonathan was the man (v. 39): *He shall surely die*, the curse shall be executed upon him. But none of the people answered him, that is, none of those who knew Jonathan had broken the order would inform against him.

2. Jonathan was discovered by lot to be the offender. Saul would have lots cast between himself and Jonathan on the one side, and the people on the other, perhaps because he was as confident of Jonathan's innocency in this matter as of his own, v. 40. The people, seeing him in a heat, durst not gainsay anything he proposed, but acquiesced: *Do as seemeth good unto thee*. Before he cast lots, he prayed that *God would give a perfect lot* (v. 41), that is, make a full discovery of this matter, or, as it is in the margin, that he would show the innocent. This was with an air of impartial justice. Judges should desire that truth may come out, whoever may suffer by it. Lots should be cast with prayer, because they are a solemn appeal to Providence, and by them we beg of God to direct and determine us (Acts i. 24), for which reason some have condemned games that depend purely upon lot or chance as making too bold with a sacred thing. Jonathan at length was taken (v. 42), Providence designing hereby to countenance and support a lawful authority, and to put an honour upon the administration of public justice in general, reserving another way to bring off one that had done nothing worthy of death.

3. Jonathan ingenuously confesses the fact, and Saul, with an angry curse, passes sentence upon him. Jonathan denies not the truth, nor goes about to conceal it, only he thinks it hard that he must *die for it*, v. 43. He might very fairly have pleaded his invincible ignorance of the law, or have insisted upon his merit, but he submitted to the necessity with a great and generous mind: "God's and my father's will be done:" thus he showed as much valour in receiving the messengers of death himself as in sending them among the Philistines. It is as brave to yield in some cases as it is in other cases to fight. Saul is not mollified by his filial submission nor the hardness of his case; but as one that affected to be thought firm to his word, and much more to his oath; even when it bound him hardest, with another imprecation he gives judgment upon Jonathan (v. 44): "*God do so and more also* to me if I do not execute the law upon thee, *for thou shalt surely die, Jonathan.*" (1.) He passed this sentence too hastily, without consulting the oracle. Jonathan had a very good plea in arrest of the judgment. What he had done was not *malum in se — bad in itself*; and, as for the prohibition of it, he was ignorant of that, so that he could not be charged with rebellion or disobedience. (2.) He did it in fury. Had Jonathan been worthy to die, yet it would have become a judge, much more a father, to pass sentence with tenderness and compassion, and not with such an air of triumph, like a man perfectly divested of all humanity and natural affection. Justice is debased when it is administered with wrath and bitterness. (3.) He backed it with a curse upon himself if he did not see the sentence executed; and this curse did return upon his own head. Jonathan escaped, but God did so to Saul, and more also; for he was rejected of God and made anathema. Let none upon any occasion dare to use such imprecations as these, lest God say Amen to them, and *make their own tongues to fall upon them*, Ps. lxiv. 8. This stone will return upon him that rolleth it. Yet we have reason to think that Saul's bowels yearned towards

Jonathan, so that he really punished himself, and very justly, when he seemed so severe upon Jonathan. God made him feel the smart of his own rash edict, which might make him fear being again guilty of the like. By all these vexatious accidents God did likewise correct him for his presumption in offering sacrifice without Samuel. An expedition so ill begun could not end without some rebukes.

4. The people rescued Jonathan out of his father's hand, v. 45. Hitherto they had expressed themselves very observant of Saul. What seemed good to him they acquiesced in, v. 36, 40. But, when Jonathan is in danger, Saul's word is no longer a law to them, but with the utmost zeal they oppose the execution of his sentence: "*Shall Jonathan die* — that blessing, that darling, of his country? Shall that life be sacrificed to a punctilio of law and honour which was so bravely exposed for the public service, and to which we owe our lives and triumphs? No, we will never stand by and see him thus treated whom God delights to honour." It is good to see Israelites zealous for the protection of those whom God has made instruments of public good. Saul had sworn that Jonathan should die, but they oppose their oath to his, and swear he shall not die: *As the Lord liveth there shall not* only not his head, but not *a hair of his head fall to the ground.*" They did not rescue him by violence, but by reason and resolution; and Josephus says they made their prayer to God that he might be loosed from the curse. They plead for him that *he has wrought with God this day;* that is, "he has owned God's cause, and God has owned his endeavours, and therefore his life is too precious to be thrown away upon a nicety." We may suppose Saul had not so perfectly forgotten the relation of a father but that he was willing enough to have Jonathan rescued, and well pleased to have that done which yet he would not do himself: and he that knows the heart of a father knows not how to blame him.

5. The design against the Philistines is quashed by this incident (v. 46): *Saul went up from following them,* and so an opportunity was lost of completing the victory. When Israel's shields are clashing with one another the public safety and service suffer by it.

"*So Saul took the kingdom over Israel and fought against all his enemies on every side — against Moab, and against the children of Ammon, and against Edom, and against the king of Zobah, and against the Philistines. And wherever he turned himself, he troubled them. And he gathered an army and struck the Amalekites and delivered Israel out of the hands of those who spoiled them. Now the sons of Saul were Jonathan, and Ishui and Melchishua. And the names of his two daughters: the name of the first born was Merab, and the name of the younger was Michal. And the name of Saul's wife was Ahinoam, the daughter of Ahimaaz. And the name of the captain of his army was Abner, the son of Ner, Saul's uncle. And Kish was the father of Saul. And Ner the father of Abner was the son of Abiel. And there was heavy war against the Philistines all the days of Saul. And when Saul saw any strong man, or any brave man, he took him to himself*" — 1 Samuel 14: 47-52.

So Saul took the kingdom over Israel, &c.] Which seemed to be almost taken from him when he was shut up in Gibeah, and the Philistines ravaged his country at pleasure; but now, having obtained a victory over them, he recovered his kingdom, and reassumed his power and authority; or he was now strengthened in it, as Kimchi interprets it; the people seeing that he succeeded in his wars with their enemies, they readily submitted to his government without any hesitation, and obeyed his commands; so the Targum, "Saul prospered in the kingdom over Israel; and, according to Abarbinel, these words will admit of another sense, that whereas, after he was anointed and made king, he followed the herd, and attended rustic affairs, but now, after this victory over the Philistines, he took upon him the state and majesty of a king, and no more concerned himself with his farm and cattle, but betook himself wholly to regal and military affairs, as follows: *and fought against all his enemies on every side;* who invaded his kingdom from different quarters; he defended himself against them, and preserved his kingdom: *against Moab, and against the children of Ammon;* who lay on the east of him: *and against Edom; which was on the southern border of his land: and against* the *king of Zobah;* a part of Syria, which was to the north of the land of Israel, and was near Damascuts, see 2 Sam. viii. 3, 5, and, according to Benjamin of Tudela, the same with Haleb, or Aleppo. There never were but two kings of it, Rehob and Hadadezer, who lived in the reigns of Saul and David, 2 Sam. viii. 3, *and against the Philistines;* who were on the western border of the land of Canaan: *and whithersoever he turned himself, he vexed* them; disturbed and disquieted them, and made them very uneasy; he terrified and distressed them: the Targum is he *condemned* them, he treated him as wicked and ungodly persons, and punished them as such.

And he gathered an host, &c.] A large army; for after the battle with the Ammonites he disbanded his army, and sent them home, retaining only 3,000 men, and these deserted him to 600, which were all the men he had with him, when he gought last with the Philistines; but now, finding he had enemies on every side of him, he gathered a numerous host to defend his country against them, and particularly to attack the people next mentioned: *and he smote the Amalekites;* a people that Israel, by the law of God, were bound to destroy, and blot out their name; a particular account of his expedition against them is given in the following chapter: *and delivered Israel out of the hands of them that spoiled them;* the nations before mentioned, Moabites, Ammonites, Edomites, Syrians, and Philistines.

And the sons of Saul were Jonathan, &c.] Who seems to be his first-born, of whom, his valour and success, we read in this and the preceding chapter: *and Ishui;* the same with Abinadab, 1 Chron., viii. 33, and ix. 39; for he had two names: *and Melchishua;* and besides these three there was another, whose name was Ishbosheth, sometimes called Eshbaal, 2 Sam. ii. 8, 1 Chron. viii. 33; who succeeded him in the kingdom; for which reason Abarbinel thinks he is not mentioned here, because he was a king; though it is generally supposed the reason why these only are named is, because they went out to war with him, and died with him, but this did not; he had other children by a concubine, or secondary wife, whose name was Rizpah, not mentioned here, 2 Sam. xxi. 8; *and the names of his two daughters* were these, *the name of the first-born Merab;* who was afterwards married to Adriel the Meholathite, ch. xviii. 19; *and the name of the younger, Michal;* who became the wife of David, ch. xviii. 27.

And the name of Saul's wife was *Ahinoam, the daughter of Ahimaaz,* &c.] Who very probably was the mother of all the above children, and therefore taken notice of; and Abarbinel conjectures that Ishbosheth was not a son of her's but the son of Saul by another wife, and which he takes to be another reason why he is not mentioned here; but though Saul had a concubine, we nowhere read of his having another wife: *and the name of the captain of his host* was *Abner the son of Ner, Saul's uncle;* not Abner, but Ner, was Saul's uncle; for Kish the father of

Saul, and Ner, were brothers, as Josephus says, and as appears from the next verse; and Abner was cousin-german to Saul, whom he raised and advanced to be captain of his army, and a very valiant man he was: we hear of him again in this history, and in the beginning of David's reign.

And Kish was *the father of Saul,* &c.] See ch. ix. 1: *and Ner the father of Abner* was *the son of Abiel;* this Abiel was the father both of Kish and Ner, and the grandfather of Saul, see ch. ix. 1.

And there was sore war against the Philistines all the days of Saul, &c.] For notwithstanding the late victory over them, and slaughter made among them, they recovered themselves, and came out again to battle, and gave Saul a great deal of trouble, and he at last died in battle with them: *and when Saul saw any strong man, or any valiant man, he took him unto him;* to be his body-guard, as Josephus says; or for soldiers and officers and his army, even such, as the same writer observes, that exceeded others in comeliness of person, and in largeness and tallness; such as were in some measure like himself, that were strong, able-bodied men, and of courage, and valour, and fortitude of mind.

"Samuel said to Saul, The Lord sent me to anoint you to be king over His people, over Israel. Now therefore listen to the voice of the words of the Lord. Thus says the Lord of hosts, I remember that which Amalek did to Israel, how he laid wait for him in the way when he came up from Egypt. Now go and strike Amalek, and completely destroy all that they have, and do not spare them. But kill both man and woman, infant and suckling, ox and sheep, camel and ass. And Saul gathered the people together and numbered them in Telaim, two hundred thousand footmen and ten thousand men of Judah. And Saul came to a city of Amalek and laid wait in the valley. And Saul said to the Kenites, Go! Depart! Get away from among the Amalekites, lest I destroy you with them. For you showed kindness to all the children of Israel when they came up out of Egypt. So the Kenites departed from among the Amalekites. And Saul struck the Amalekites from Havilah, until you come to Shur, which is over across from Egypt. And he took Agag the king of the Amalekites alive. And he completely destroyed all the people with the edge of the sword. But Saul and the people spared Agag and the best of the sheep and of the oxen and of the fatlings and the lambs, and all that was good, and would not completely destroy them. But everything that was vile and refuse they completely destroyed" – 1 Samuel 15: 1-9.

Here, I. Samuel, in God's name, solemnly requires Saul to be obedient to the command of God, and plainly intimates that he was now about to put him on trial, in one particular instance, whether he would be obedient or no, v. 1. And the making of this so expressly the trial of his obedience did very much aggravate his disobedience. 1. He reminds him of what God had done for him: *"The Lord sent me to anoint thee to be a king.* God gave thee thy power, and therefore he expects thou shouldst use thy power for him. He put honour upon thee, and now thou must study how to do him honour. He made thee king over Israel, and now thou must plead Israel's cause and avenge their quarrels. Thou art advanced to command Israel, but know that thou art a subject to the God of Israel and must be commanded by him." Men's perferment, instead of releasing them from their obedience to God, obliges them so much the more to it. Samuel had himself been employed to anoint Saul, and therefore was the fitter to be sent with these orders to him. 2. He tells him, in general, that, in consideration of this, whatever God commanded him to do he was bound to do it: *Now therefore hearken to the voice of the Lord.* Note, God's favours to us lay strong obligations upon us to be obedient to him. This we must render, Ps. cxvi. 12.

II. He appoints him a particular piece of service, in which he must now show his obedience to God more than in any thing he had done yet. Samuel premises God's authority to the command: *Thus says the Lord of hosts,* the Lord of all hosts, of Israel's hosts. He also gives him a reason for the command, that the severity he must use might not seem hard: *I remember that which Amalek did to Israel,* v. 2. God had an ancient quarrel with the Amalekites, for the injuries they did to his people Israel when he brought them out of Egypt. We have the story, Exod. xvii. v. 8, &c., and the crime is aggravated, Deut. xxv. 18. He basely smote the hindmost of them, and feared not God. God then swore that he would have *war with Amalek from generation to generation,* and that in process of time he *would utterly put out the remembrance of Amalek;* this is the work that Saul is now appointed to do (v. 3): *"Go and smite Amalek.* Israel is now strong, and the measure of the iniquity of Amalek is now full; now go and make a full riddance of that devoted nation." He is expressly commanded to kill and slay all before him, *man and woman, infant and suckling,* and not spare them out of pity; also *ox and sheep, camel and ass,* and not spare them out of covetousness. Note, 1. Injuries done to God's Israel will certainly be reckoned for sooner or later, especially the opposition given them when they are coming out of Egypt. 2. God often bears long with those that are marked for ruin. The sentence passed is not executed speedily. 3. Though he bear long, he will not bear always. The year of recompence for the controversy of Israel will come at last. Though divine justice strikes slowly it strikes surely. 4. The longer judgment is delayed many times the more severe it is when it comes. 5. God chooses out instruments to do his work that are fittest for it. This was bloody work, and therefore Saul who was a rough and severe man must do it.

III. Saul hereupon musters his forces, and makes a descent upon the country of Amalek. It was an immense army that he brought into the field (v. 4): 200,000 *footmen.* When he was to engage the Philistines, and the success was hazardous, he had but 600 attending him, ch. xiii. 15. But now that he was to attack the Amalekites by express order from heaven, in which he was sure of victory, he had thousands at his call. But, whatever it was at other times, it was not now for the honour of Judah that their forces were numbered by themselves, for their quota was scandalously short (whatever was the reason), but a twentieth part of the whole, for they were but 10,000, when the other ten tribes (for I except Levi) brought into the field 200,000. The day of Judah's honour drew near, but had not yet come. Saul numbered them in *Telaim,* which signifies *lambs.* He numbered them *like lambs* (so the vulgar Latin), numbered them *by the paschal lambs* (so the Chaldee), allowing ten to a lamb, a way of numbering used by the Jews in the later times of their nation. Saul drew all his forces to the *city of Amalek,* that city that was their metropolis (v. 5), that he might provoke them to give them battle.

IV. He gave friendly advice to the Kenites to separate themselves from the Amalekites among whom they dwelt, while this execution was in doing, v. 6. Herein he did prudently and piously, and, it is probable, according to the direction Samuel gave him. The Kenites were of the family and kindred of Jethro, Moses's father-in-law, a people that dwelt in tents, which made it easy for them, upon every occasion, to remove to other lands not appropriated. Many of them, at this time, dwelt among the Amalekites, where, though they dwelt in tents, they were fortified by nature, for *they put their nest in a rock,* being hardy people that could live any where, and affected fastnesses, Num. xxiv. 21. Balaam had foretold that they should be wasted, Num. xxiv. 22. However Saul must not waste them. But, 1. He acknowledges the kindness of their ancestors to Israel, when they came out of Egypt. Jethro and his family had been very helpful and serviceable to them in their passage through the wilderness, had been to them instead of eyes, and this is remembered to their posterity many ages after. Thus a good man leaves the divine blessing for an inheritance to his children's children; those that come after us may be reaping the benefit of our good works when we are in our graves. God is not unrighteous to forget the kindnesses shown to his people; but they shall be remembered another day, at furthest in the great day, *and recompensed in the resurrection of the just. I was hungry, and you gave me meat.* God's remembering the kindness of the Kenites' ancestors in favour to them, at the same time when he was punishing the injuries done by the ancestors of the Amalekites, helped to clear the righteousness of God in that dispensation. If he entail favours, why may he not entail frowns? He espouses his people's cause, so as to *bless those that bless them;* and therefore so as to *curse those that curse them,* Num. xxiv. 9; Gen. xii. 3. They cannot themselves requite the kindnesses nor avenge the injuries done them, but God will do both. 2. He desires them to remove their tents from among the Amalekites: *Go, depart, get you down from among them.* When destroying judgments are abroad God will take care to separate between the precious and the vile, and to hide the meek of the earth in the day of his anger. It is dangerous being found in the company of God's enemies, and it is our duty and interest to *come out from among them,* lest we share in their sins and plagues, Rev. xviii. 4. The Jews have a saying, *Woe to the wicked man and woe to his neighbour.*

V. Saul prevailed against the Amalekites, for it was rather an execution of condemned malefactors than a war with contending enemies. The issue could not be dubious when the cause was just and the call so clear: *He smote them* (v. 7), *utterly destroyed them,* v. 8. Now they paid dearly for the sin of their ancestors. God sometimes *lays up iniquity for the children.* They were idolaters, and were guilty of many other sins, for which they deserved to fall under the wrath of God; yet, when God would reckon with them, he fastened upon the sin of their ancestors in abusing his Israel as the ground of his quarrel. Lord, How unsearchable are thy judgments, yet how incontestable is thy righteousness!

VI. Yet he did his work by halves, v. 9. 1. He *spared Agag,* because he was a king like himself, and perhaps in hope to get a great ransom for him. 2. He spared the best of the cattle, and destroyed only the refuse, that was good for little. Many of the people, we may suppose, made their escape, and took their effects with them into other countries, and therefore we read of Amalekites after this; but that could not be helped. It was Saul's fault that he did not destroy such as came to his hands and were in his power. That which was now destroyed was in effect sacrificed to the justice of God, as the God to whom vengeance belongeth; and for Saul to think the torn and the sick, the lame and the lean, good enough for that, while he reserved for his own fields and his own table the firstlings and the fat, was really to honour himself more than God.

"Then the word of the Lord came to Samuel saying, It grieves Me that I have set up Saul to be king. For he has turned back from following Me and has not done My commandments. And it grieved Samuel, and he cried out to the Lord all night. And when Samuel rose up early in the morning to meet Saul, they said to Samuel, Saul came to Carmel, and behold, he set up a place for himself and has gone around and passed on and gone down to Gilgal. And Samuel came to Saul. And Saul said to him, You are blessed of the Lord. I have done the commandment of the Lord. And Samuel said, What then does this bleating of the sheep in my ears mean? And what is the lowing of the oxen which I hear? And Saul said, They have brought them from the Amalekites. For the people spared the best of the sheep and of the oxen to sacrifice to the Lord your God. And the rest we have completely destroyed. Then Samuel said to Saul, Wait, and I will tell you what the Lord has said to me tonight. And he said to him, speak. And Samuel said, When you were little in your own sight, were you not made the head of the tribes of Israel? And the Lord anointed you king over Israel. And the Lord sent you on a journey and said, Go and completely destroy the sinners, the Amalekites, and fight against them until they have been destroyed. Why then did you not obey the voice of the Lord? Why did you fly upon the spoil and do evil in the sight of the Lord? And Saul said to Samuel Yes, I have obeyed the voice of the Lord, and have gone the way which the Lord sent me, and have

brought Agag the king of Amalek, and have completely destroyed the Amalekites. But the people took sheep and oxen from the spoil, the best of the things which should have been completely destroyed, to sacrifice to the Lord your God in Gilgal. And Samuel said, Does the Lord have as much delight in burnt-offerings and sacrifices, ad in obeying the voice of the Lord? Behold, to obey is better than sacrifice! To listen is better than the fat of rams! For rebellion is like the sin of witchcraft, and stubbornness is like iniquity and idol-worship. Behold! You have rejected the Lord! He has also rejected you from being king!" — 1 Samuel 15: 10-23.

Saul is here called to account by Samuel concerning the execution of his commission against the Amalekites; and remarkable instances we are here furnished with of the strictness of the justice of God and the treachery and deceitfulness of the heart of man. We are told,

I. What passed between God and Samuel, in secret, upon this occasion, v. 10, 11. 1. God determines Saul's rejection, and acquaints Samuel with it: *It repenteth me that I have set up Saul to be king.* Repentance in God is not, as it is in us, a change of his mind, but a change of his method or dispensation. He does not alter his will, but wills an alteration. The change was in Saul: *He has turned back from following me;* this construction God put upon the partiality of his obedience, and the prevalency of his covetousness. And hereby he did himself make God his enemy. God repented that he had given Saul the kingdom and the honour and power that belonged to it: but he never repented that he had given any man wisdom and grace, and his fear and love; these gifts and callings of God are without repentance. 2. Samuel laments and deprecates it. *It grieved Samuel* that Saul had forfeited God's favour, and that God had resolved to cast him off; and he *cried unto the Lord all night,* spent a whole night in interceding for him, that this decree might not go forth against him. When others were in their beds sleeping, he was upon his knees praying and wrestling with God. He did not thus deprecate his own exclusion from the government nor was he secretly pleased, as many a one would have been, that Saul, who succeeded him, was so soon laid aside, but on the contrary prayed earnestly for his establishment, so far was he from desiring that woeful day. The rejection of sinners is the grief of good people; God delights not in their death, nor should we.

II. What passed between Samuel and Saul in public. Samuel, being sent of God to him with these heavy tidings, went, as Ezekiel, in *bitterness of soul,* to meet him, perhaps according to an appointment when Saul went forth on this expedition, for Saul had come to Gilgal (v. 12), the place where he was made king (ch. xi. 15), and where now he would have been confirmed if he had approved himself well in this trial of his obedience. But Samuel was informed that Saul had set up a triumphal arch, or some monument of his victory, at Carmel, a city in the mountains of Judah, seeking his own honour more than the honour of God, for he set up this place (or *hand,* as the word is) for himself (he had more need to have been repenting of his sin and making his peace with God than boasting of his victory), and also that he had marched in great state to Gilgal, for this seems to be intimated in the manner of expression: *He has gone about, and passed on, and gone down,* with a great deal of pomp parade. There Samuel gave him the meeting, and,

1. Saul makes his boast to Samuel of his obedience, because that was the thing by which he was now to signalize himself (v. 13): *"Blessed be thou of the Lord,* for thou sentest me upon a good errand, in which I have had great success, and *I*

have performed the commandment of the Lord." It is very likely, if his conscience had not flown in his face at this time and charged him with disobedience, he would not have been so forward to proclaim his obedience; for by this he hoped to prevent Samuel's reproving him. Thus sinners think, by justifying themselves, to escape being *judged of the Lord;* whereas the only way to do that is by *judging ourselves.* Those that boast most of their religion may justly be suspected of partiality and hypocrisy in it.

2. Samuel convicts him by a plain demonstration of his disobedience. "Hast thou performed the commandment of the Lord? *What means then the bleating of the sheep?* v. 14. Saul would needs have it thought that God Almighty was wonderfully beholden to him for the good service he had done; but Samuel shows him that God was so far from being a debtor to him that he had just cause of action against him, and produces for evidence the *bleating of the sheep, and the lowing of the oxen,* which perhaps Saul appointed to bring up the rear of his triumph, but Samuel appeals to them as witnesses against him. He needed not go far to disprove his professions. The noise the cattle made (like the *rust of the silver,* Jam. v. 3) would be a *witness against him.* Note, It is no new thing for the plausible professions and protestations of hypocrites to be contradicted and disproved by the most plain and undeniable evidence. Many boast of their obedience to the command of God; but what mean then their indulgence of the flesh, their love of the world, their passion and uncharitableness, and their neglect of holy duties, which witness against them?

3. Saul insists upon his own justification against this charge, v. 15. The fact he cannot deny; the sheep and oxen were brought from the Amalekites. But, (1.) It was not his fault, for *the people spared them;* as if they durst have done it without the express orders of Saul, when they knew it was against the express orders of Samuel. Note, Those that are willing to justify themselves are commonly very forward to condemn others, and to lay the blame upon any rather than take it to themselves. Sin is a brat that nobody cares to have laid at his doors. It is the sorry subterfuge of an impenitent heart, that will not confess its guilt, to lay the blame on those that are tempters, or partners, or only followers in it. (2.) It was with a good intention: "It was *to sacrifice to the Lord thy God.* He is thy God, and thou wilt not be against any thing that is done, as this is, for this honour." This was a false plea, for both Saul and the people designed their own profit in sparing the cattle. But, if it had been true, it would still have been frivolous, for God hates robbery for burnt-offering. God appointed these cattle to be sacrificed at his altar; for he will be served in his own way, and according to the rule he himself has prescribed. Nor will a good intention justify a bad action.

4. Samuel overrules, or rather overlooks, his plea, and proceeds, in God's name, to give judgment against him. He premises his authority. What he was about to say was what the Lord had said to him (v. 16), otherwise he would have been far from passing so severe a censure upon him. Those who complain that their ministers are too harsh with them should remember that, while they keep to the word of God, they are but messengers, and must say as they are bidden, and therefore be willing, as Saul himself here was, that they should *say on.* Samuel delivers his message faithfully. (1.) He reminds Saul of the honour God had done him in making him king (v. 17), *when he was little in his own sight.* God regarded the lowness of his state and rewarded the lowliness of his spirit. Note, Those that are advanced to honour and wealth ought often to remember their mean beginnings, that they may never think highly of themselves, but always study to do great things for the God that has advanced them. (2.) He lays before

him the plainness of the orders he was to execute (v. 18): *The Lord sent thee on a journey;* as easy was the service, and so certain the success, that it was rather to be called a *journey* then a *war.* The work was honourable, to destroy the sworn enemies of God and Israel; and had he denied himself, and set aside the consideration of his own profit so far as to have destroyed all that belonged to Amalek, he would have been no loser by it at last, nor have gone this *warfare on his own charges.* God would no doubt have made it up to him, so that he should have no need of spoil. And therefore, (3.) He shows him how inexcusable he was in aiming to make a profit of his expedition, and to enrich himself by it (v. 19): *"Wherefore then didst thou fly upon the spoil,* and convert that to thy own use which was to have been destroyed for God's honour?"* See what evil the love of money is the root of; but see what is the sinfulness of sin, and that in it which above any thing else makes it evil in the sight of the Lord. It is disobedience: *Thou didst not obey the voice of the Lord.*

5. Saul repeats his vindication of himself, as that which, in defiance of conviction, he resolved to abide by, v. 20, 21. He denies the charge (v. 20): *"Yea, I have obeyed,* I have done all I should do;" for he had done all which he thought he needed to do, so much wiser was he in his own eyes than God himself. God bade him kill all, and yet he puts in among the instances of his obedience that he had brought Agag alive, which he thought was as good as if he had killed him. Thus carnal deceitful hearts think to excuse themselves from God's commandments with their own equivalents. He insists upon it that he has *utterly destroyed the Amalekites* themselves, which was the main thing intended; but, as to the spoil, he owns it should have been *utterly destroyed;* so that he knew his *Lord's will,* and was under no mistake about the command. But he thought that would be wilful waste; the cattle of the Midianites was taken for a prey in Moses's time (Num. xxxi. 32, &c.), and why not the cattle of the Amalekites now? Better it should be a prey to the Israelites than to the fowls of the air and the' wild beasts; and therefore he connived at the people's carrying it away. But it was their doing and not his; and, besides, it was for *sacrifice to the Lord* here at Gilgal, whither they were now bringing them. See what a hard thing it is to convince the children of disobedience of their sin and to strip them of their fig leaves.

6. Samuel gives a full answer to his apology, since he did insist upon it, v. 22, 23. He appeals to his own conscience: *Has the Lord as great delight in sacrifices as in obedience?* Though Saul was not a man of any great acquaintance with religion, yet he could not know this, (1.) That nothing is so pleasing to God as obedience, no, not sacrifice and offering, and the fat of rams. See here what we should seek and aim at in all the exercises of religion, even acceptance with God, that he may delight in what we do. If God be well pleased with us and our services, we are happy, we have gained our point; but otherwise *to what purpose is it?* Isa. i. 11. Now here we are plainly told that humble, sincere, and conscientious obedience to the will of God, is more pleasing and acceptable to him than *all burnt-offerings and sacrifices.* A careful conformity to moral precepts recommends us to God more than all ceremonial observances, Mic. vi. 6-8; Hos. vi. 6. Obedience is enjoined by the eternal law of nature, but sacrifice only by a positive law. Obedience was the law of innocency, but sacrifice supposes sin come into the world, and is but a feeble attempt to take that away which obedience would have prevented. God is more glorified and self more denied by obedience than by sacrifice. It is much easier to bring a bullock or lamb to be burnt upon the altar than to bring *every high thought into obedience* to God and the will subject to his will. Obedience is the glory of angels (Ps. cii.

20), and it will be ours. (2.) That nothing is so provoking to God as disobedience, setting up our wills in competition with his. This is here called *rebellion* and *stubbornness*, and is said to be as bad as *witchcraft* and *idolatry*, v. 23. It is as bad to set up other gods as to live in disobedience to the true God. Those that are governed by their own corrupt inclinations, in opposition to the command of God, do, in effect, consult the *teraphim* (as the word here is for idolatry) or the diviners. It was obedience that made us all sinners (Rom. v. 19), and this is the malignity of sin, that is the *transgression of the law*, and consequently it is *enmity to God*, Rom. viii. 7. Saul was a king, but, if he disobey the command of God, his royal dignity and power will not excuse him from the guilt of rebellion and stubbornness. It is not the rebellion of the people against their prince, but of a prince against God, that this text speaks of.

7. He reads his doom: in short, *"Because thou hast rejected the word of the Lord,* hast *despised it* (so the Chaldee), hast *made nothing of it* (so the LXX.), hast cast off the government of it, therefore he has *rejected thee,* despised and made nothing of thee, but cast thee off *from being king.* He that made thee king has determined to unmake thee again."* Those are unfit and unworthy to rule over men who are not willing that God should rule over them.

"And Saul said to Samuel, I have sinned. For I have disobeyed the commandment of the Lord and your words, because I feared the people and obeyed their voice. Now therefore I beg you, pardon my sin and turn again with me so that I may worship the Lord. And Samuel said to Saul, I will not return with you, for you have rejected the word of the Lord, and the Lord has rejected you from being king over Israel. And as Samuel turned around to go away, he laid hold on the skirt of his mantle, and it tore. And Samuel said to him, The Lord has torn the kingdom of Israel from you today and has given it to a neighbour of yours who is better than you. And also the strength of Israel will not lie or repent, for He is not a man that He should repent. Then he said, I have sinned. Yet honor me now, I beg you, before the elders of my people and before Israel. And turn again with me so that I may worship the Lord your God. So Samuel turned again after Saul, and Saul worshipped the Lord" — 1 Samuel 15: 24-31.

And Saul said unto Samuel, I have sinned, &c.] This confession of his sin does not appear to be ingenuous, cordial, and sincere, and was made chiefly for the sake of getting the sentence of rejecting him from being king reversed: *for I have transgressed the commandment of the Lord, and thy words;* which last seems to be added to collogue with Samuel, and to ingratiate himself with him; and Abarbinel thinks that Saul suspected that Samuel had aggravated the matter of himself, and that he did not really transgress the words of the Lord, but as the words of Samuel, and therefore according to the words of Samuel he had sinned, but not according to the words of the Lord only; *because I feared the people;* Doeg the Edomite, who was reckoned as all of them, Jarchi says: this was a mere excuse of Saul's he stood in no fear of the people, he kept them in awe, and did as he would with them, as a sovereign prince: *and obeyed their voice;* in sparing the best of the cattle; so he pretended, when it was his own will, and the effect of his covetousness.

Now therefore, I pray thee, pardon my sin, &c.] It can hardly be thought that Saul was so ignorant as to imagine that Samuel could pardon his sin, as committed against God, which none but God can do, but that he would forgive it, so far as he had offended him; or rather his meaning is, that as he was a prophet of the Lord, and had great interest in him, that he would make use of it on his behalf, and pray to God that his sin might be forgiven him, and the sentence reversed concerning his rejection from the kingdom; which perhaps is the chief thing he means by the pardon of his sin, which sometimes means no more than adverting a threatened judgment, or freedom from punishment: *and turn again with me;* to Gilgal, for he was come out from thence to meet Samuel, having heard that he was coming: *that I may worship the Lord;* by offering sacrifice, either in thankfulness for the victory obtained, or to atone for his sin, and seek pardon for it, or both; this he thought would be a motive and inducement to Samuel to go along with him.

And Samuel said unto Saul, I will not return with thee, &c.] Not being satisfied with his repentance and confession, he still extenuating his sin, and laying the blame of it on the people. This he said by way of resentment, and as expressing his indignation at him, though he afterwards did return with him on a change of his mind; which a good man may be allowed to make, without any imputation of falsehood or a lie unto him: *for thou hast rejected the word of the Lord, and the Lord hath rejected thee from being king over Israel;* which is repeated from ver. 23; for the confirmation of it, and to let Saul know that his pretended confession and repentance had made no alteration in the decree and sentence of God respecting the kingdom.

And as Samuel turned about to go away, &c.] From Saul, a different way from Gilgal, perhaps towards his own city Ramah, with an intention to have nothing more to say to Saul, or to do with him, or to see his face no more; so displeased was he with him; *he laid hold upon the skirt of his mantle;* in order to detain him, and prevent his departure from him, and his going a different way; *and it rent;* Samuel twitching away from him with great vehemence and warmth. The Jewish Rabbins are divided about this, whose skirt was rent; some say it was Samuel that rent the skirt of Saul, and by this signified to him, that he that cut off the skirt of his garment should reign in his stead; whereby Saul knew that David would be king when he cut off the skirt of his robe, ch. xxiv. 4, 20; others, that Samuel rent the skirt of his own mantle himself, which is the way of good men when things are not right; but the plain sense is, that Saul rent the skirt of Samuel's mantle, which, when Samuel saw, he understood what that rent was a sign of, as expressed in the following verse.

And Samuel said unto him, the Lord hatn rent the kingdom of Israel from thee this day, &c.] Seeing his mantle rent by Saul, he took occasion from thence to predict, and no doubt it was impressed on his mind by the Spirit of God, that his kingdom should be in a like manner rent from him, on account of his own evil conduct and behaviour; and from this day forward he might expect it: the sentence was gone forth from God, and it would not be reversed; and by a like sign was signified the rending of the ten tribes from the kingdom of Solomon in his son Rehoboam, 1 Kings xi. 30, 31; *and hath given it to a neighbour of thine,* that is *better than thou;* who was David, a man after God's own heart, that would fulfil his will, who was more holy, just, and wise than Saul; whose works were better and juster than his, as the Targum; who was an Israelite, of the same nation and religion as his, and so his neighbour; and though he was not of the same tribe, yet of a neighbouring tribe; Benjamin, and Judah, of which tribe David was, joining closely to one another. It is highly probable that at this time Samuel knew not personally who he was that was designed to be made king in his room, though under the direction of the Spirit of God he thus describes him; for after this he is bid to go to Jesse's family, from thence to anoint a king, and several passed before him ere the Lord pointed out the proper person to him.

And also the strength of Israel will not lie nor repent, &c.] Neither of the evil which he had threatened to Saul in taking away the kingdom from him; nor of the good which he had promised to David in giving it to him; nor of his purpose and promise to Israel to protect and defend them, save and deliver them from the Philistines, and continue them a nation and kingdom: and for the confirmation of all this, this title or character of the Lord is given, *the strength of Israel;* hence he cannot lie, which is the effect of weakness; nor repent or change his mind, as men do, when something unforeseen arises, which hinders the execution of their first design, and which through weakness they cannot surmount: and hence God would support Israel as a nation, and strengthen them against their enemies, and work deliverance and salvation for them: or *the victory of Israel;* the author of Israel's victories, and to whom they are to be ascribed, and who is able to give them more, and would; and as he did especially by David, to whom the kingdom is promised: or *the eternity of Israel;* that gives firmness, permanency, and duration to them; all which is true of Israel in a spiritual sense; he gives them spiritual strength, victory over their enemies, sin, Satan, and the world, permanent duration, everlasting salvation, immortality, and eternal life: *for he is not a man, that he should repent;* men are weak and feeble, and cannot perform what they propose or promise, and therefore repent; but God, the Strength of Israel, is able to perform whatever he has purposed or promised, and therefore repents not; men are changeable in their minds, and repent of their first thoughts and designs; but God is unchangeable, and never alters his counsels, breaks his covenant, reverses his blessings, repents of his gifts, nor changes his affections to his Israel. Abarbinel says this may be understood of Saul, and so be given as a reason why God would not repent of the evil he had threatened him with, because he was a man that repented not of his sin: but the first sense is best, and agrees with and is confirmed by Numb. xxiii. 19.

Then he said, I have sinned, &c.] So he had said before, ver. 24; but his confession there was attended with an extenuation of his sin, pleading in excuse of it that it was through fear of the people, but here it is without any; and yet by what follows it appears to be not ingenuous and sincere, but hypocritical; *yet honour me now, I pray thee, before the elders of my people and before Israel;* with his company; since should he be slighted openly by the Lord, and by his prophet, he would fall into contempt both with the principal men, and with the common people: wherefore he seemed more concerned for the loss of honour and reputation with the people than for his sin against God, which is always the case of hypocrites; *and turn again with me, and worship the Lord thy God;* see the note on ver. 25.

So Samuel turned again after Saul, &c.] Though he before said he would not, ver. 26; yet he did, changing his mind, as he might without being chargeable with a lie; and he also might have an impulse from the Lord so to do, and which he did not in order to worship with Saul, which it does not appear he did, but rather the contrary; but that Saul might not be despised by the people, and his authority lessened, whilst he continued the king; and that he might do what Saul had neglected to do, destroy Agag; *and Saul worshipped the Lord;* alone, by offering sacrifice to him.

"*Then Samuel said, Bring here to me Agag the king of the Amalekites. And Agag came to him daintily. And Agag said, Surely the bitterness of death is past. And Samuel said, As your sword has made women childless, so shall your mother be childless among women. And Samuel cut Agag in pieces before the Lord in*

Gilgal. Then Samuel went to Ramah. And Saul went up to his house to Gibeah of Saul. And Samuel came no more to see Saul until the day of his death. But Samuel mourned for Saul. And the Lord repented that He had made Saul king over Israel" — 1 Samuel 15: 32-35.

Samuel, as a prophet, is here set over kings, Jer. i. 10.

I. He destroys king Agag, doubtless by such special direction from heaven as none now can pretend to. He *hewed Aga in pieces.* Some think he only ordered it to be done; or perhaps he did it with his own hands, as a sacrifice to God's injured justice (v. 33), and sacrifices used to be cut in pieces. Now observe in this,

1. How Agag's present vain hopes were frustrated: He *came delicately,* in a stately manner, to show that he was a king, and therefore to be treated witn respect, or in a soft effeminate manner, as one never used to hardship, that *could not set the sole of his foot to the ground for tenderness and delicacy* (Deut. xxviii. 56), to move compassion: and he said, "Surely, now that the heat of the battle is over, *the bitterness of death is past,* v. 32. Having escaped the sword of Saul," that man of war, he thought he was in no danger from Samuel, an old prophet, a man of peace. Note, (1.) There is bitterness in death, it is terrible to nature. *Surely death is bitter,* so divers versions read those words of Agag; as the LXX. read the former clause, *He came trembling.* Death will dismay the stoutest heart. (2.) Many think the bitterness of death is past when it is not so; they put that evil day far from them which is very near. True believers may, through grace, say this, upon good grounds, though death be not past, the bitterness of it is. *O death! where is thy sting?*

2. How his former wicked practices were now punished. Samuel calls him to account, not only for the sins of his ancestors, but his own sins: *Thy sword has made women childless,* v. 33. He trod in the steps of his ancestors' cruelty, and those under him, it is likely, did the same; justly therefore is all the righteous blood shed by Amalek required of this generation, Matt. xxiii. 36. Agag, that was delicate and luxurious himself, was cruel and barbarous to others. It is commonly so: those who are indulgent of their appetites are not less indulgent of their passions. But blood will be reckoned for; even kings must account to the King of kings for the guiltless blood they shed or cause to be shed. It was that crime of king Manasseh which the Lord would not pardon, 2 Kings xxiv. 4. See Rev. xiii. 10.

II. He deserts king Saul, takes leave of him (v. 34), and *never came any more to see him* (v. 35), to advise or assist him in any of his affairs, because Saul did not desire his company nor would he be advised by him. He looked upon him as rejected of God, and therefore he forsook him. Though he might sometimes see him accidentally (as ch. xix. 24), yet he never came to see him out of kindness or respect. Yet he *mourned for Saul,* thinking it a very lamentable thing that a man who stood so fair for great things should ruin himself so foolishly. He mourned for the bad state of the country, to which Saul was likely to have been so great a blessing, but now would prove a curse and a plague. He mourned for his everlasting state, having no hopes of bringing him to repentance. When he wept for him, it is likely, he made supplication, but the Lord had *repented that he had made Saul king,* and resolved to undo that work of his, so that Samuel's prayers prevailed not for him. Observe, We must mourn for the rejection of sinners, 1. Though we withdraw from them, and dare not converse familiarly with them. Thus the prophet determines to leave his people and go from them, and yet to *weep day and night for them,* Jer. ix. 1, 2. 2. Though they do not mourn for themselves. Saul seems unconcerned at the tokens of God's displeasure which he lay under, and yet Samuel mourns day and night for him. Jerusalem was secure when Christ wept over it.

CHAPTER 16.

"And the Lord said to Samuel, How long will you mourn for Saul, since I have rejected him from reigning over Israel? Fill your horn with oil and go. I will send you to Jesse of Bethlehem. For I have provided a king for me among his sons. And Samuel said, How can I go? If Saul hears, he will kill me. And the Lord said, take a heifer with you and say, I have come to sacrifice to the Lord. And call Jesse to the sacrifice, and I will show you what you shall do. And you shall anoint to Me the one I name to you. And Samuel did that which the Lord spoke and came to Bethlehem. And the elders of the town trembled at his coming and said, Do you come peaceably? And he said, Peaceably. I have come to sacrifice to the Lord. Sanctify yourselves and come with me to the sacrifice. And he sanctified Jesse and his sons and called them to the sacrifice" — 1 Samuel 16: 1-5.*

Samuel had retired to his own house in Ramah, with a resolution not to appear any more in public business, but to addict himself wholly to the instructing and training up of the sons of the prophets, over whom he presided, as we find, ch. xix. 20. He promised himself more satisfaction in young prophets than in young princes; and we do not find that, to his dying day, God called him out to any public action relating to the state, but only here to anoint David.

I. God reproves him for continuing so long to mourn for the rejection of Saul. He does not blame him for mourning on that occasion, but for exceeding in his sorrow: *How long wilt thou mourn for Saul?* v. 1. We do not find that he mourned at all for the setting aside of his own family and the deposing of his own sons; but for the rejecting of Saul and his seed he mourns without measure, for the former was done by the people's foolish discontent, this by the righteous wrath of God. Yet he must find time to recover himself, and not go mourning to his grave, 1. Because God has rejected him, and he ought to acquiesce in the divine justice, and forget his affection to Saul; if God will be glorified in his ruin, Samuel ought to be satisfied. Besides, to what purpose should we weep? The decree has gone forth, and all his prayers and tears cannot prevail for the reversing of it, 2 Sam. xii. 22, 23. 2. Because Israel shall be no loser by it, and Samuel must prefer the public welfare before his own private affection to his friend. "Mourn not for Saul, for I *have provided me a king.* The people provided themselves a king and he proved bad, now I will provide myself one, *a man after my own heart."* See Ps. lxxxix. 20; Acts xiii. 22. "If Saul be rejected, yet Israel shall not be *as sheep having no shepherd.* I have another in store for them; let thy joy of him swallow up thy grief for the rejected prince."

II. He sends him to Bethlehem, to anoint one of the sons of Jesse, a person probably not unknown to Samuel. *Fill thy horn with oil.* Saul was anointed with a glass vial of oil, scanty and brittle, David with a horn of oil, which was more plentiful and durable; hence we read of a *horn of salvation in the house of his servant David,* Luke i. 69.

III. Samuel objects the peril of going on this errand (v. 2): *If Saul hear it, he will kill me.* By this it appears, 1. That Saul had grown very wicked and outrageous since his rejection, else Samuel would not have mentioned this. What impiety would he not be guilty of who durst kill Samuel? 2. That Samuel's faith was not so strong as one would have expected, else he would not have thus feared the rage of Saul. Would not he that sent him protect him and bear him out? But the best men are not perfect in their faith, nor will fear be wholly cast out any where on this side heaven. But this may be understood as Samuel's desire of direction from heaven how to manage this matter prudently, so as not to expose himself, or any other, more than needed.

IV. God orders him to cover his design with a sacrifice: *Say, I have come to sacrifice;* and it was true he did, and it was proper that he should, when he came to anoint a king, ch. xi. 15. As a prophet, he might sacrifice when and where God appointed him; and it was not at all inconsistent with the laws of truth to say he came to sacrifice when really he did so, though he had also a further end, which he thought fit to conceal. Let him give notice of a sacrifice, and invite Jesse (who, it is probable, was the principal man of the city) and his family to come to the feast upon the sacrifice; and, says God, *I will show thee what thou shalt do.* Those that go about God's work in God's way shall be directed step by step, wherever they are at a loss, to do it in the best manner.

V. Samuel went accordingly to Bethlehem, not in pomp, or with any retinue, only a servant to lead the heifer which he was to sacrifice; yet *the elders of Bethlehem trembled at his coming,* fearing it was an indication of God's displeasure against them and that he came to denounce some judgment for the iniquities of the place. Guilt causes fear. Yet indeed it becomes us to stand in awe of God's messengers, and to tremble at his word. Or they feared it might be an occasion of Saul's displeasure against them, for probably they knew how much he was exasperated at Samuel, and feared he would pick a quarrel with them for entertaining him. They asked him, *"Comest thou peaceably?* Art thou in peace thyself, and not flying from Saul? Art thou at peace with us, and not come with any message of wrath?" We should all covet earnestly to stand upon good terms with God's prophets, and dread having the word of God, or their prayers, against us. When the son of David was born king of the Jews all Jerusalem was troubled, Matt. ii. 3. Samuel kept at home, and it was a strange thing to see him so far from his house; they therefore concluded it must needs be some extraordinary occasion that brought him, and feared the worst till he satisfied them (v. 5): *"I come peaceably, for I come to sacrifice,* not with a message of wrath against you, but with the methods of peace and reconciliation; and therefore you may bid me welcome and need not fear my coming; therefore *sanctify yourselves,* and prepare to join with me in the sacrifice, that you may have the benefit of it." Note, Before solemn ordinances there must be a solemn preparation. When we are to offer spiritual sacrifices it concerns us, by sequestering ourselves from the world and renewing the dedication of ourselves to God, to sanctify ourselves. When our Lord Jesus came into the world, though men had reason enough to tremble, fearing that his errand was to condemn the world, yet he gave full assurance that he came peaceably, for he came to sacrifice, and he brought his offering along with him: *A body hast thou prepared me.* Let us sanctify ourselves, that we may have an interest in his service. Note, Those that come to sacrifice should come peaceably; religious exercises must not be performed tumultuously.

VI. He had a particular regard to Jesse and his sons, for with them his private business lay, with which, it is likely, he acquainted Jesse at his first coming, and took up his lodging at his house. He spoke to all the elders to *sanctify themselves,* but he *sanctified Jesse and his sons* by praying with them and instructing them. Perhaps he had acquaintance with them before, and it appears (ch. xx. 29, where we read of the sacrifices that family had) that it was a devout religious family. Samuel assisted them in their family preparations for the public sacrifice, and, it is probable, chose out David, and anointed him, at the family-solemnities, before the sacrifice was offered or the holy feast solemnized. Perhaps he offered private sacrifices, like Job, *according to the number of them all* (Job i. 5), and, under colour of that, called for them all to appear before him. When signal blessings are coming into a family they ought to sanctify themselves.

"And when they had come, he looked at Eliab and said, Surely the Lord's anointed is before Him. But the Lord said to Samuel, Do not look at his face or on his height, because I have refused him. For the Lord does not see as man sees. For man looks on the outward appearance, but the Lord looks on the heart. Then Jesse called Abinadab and made him pass before Samuel. And he said, The Lord has not chosen this one. Then Jesse made Shammah to pass by. And he said, The Lord has not chosen this one. Again, Jesse made seven of his sons to pass before Samuel. And Samuel said to Jesse, The Lord has not chosen these. And Samuel said to Jesse, Are all your children here? And he said, There remains yet the youngest, and behold, he keeps the sheep. And Samuel said to Jesse, Send and bring him. For we will not sit down until he comes here. And he sent and brought him in. Now he was ruddy, and altogether of a beautiful face and handsome to look at. And the Lord said, Arise! Anoint him! For this is the one. Then Samuel took the horn of oil and anointed him in the midst of his brothers. And the Spirit of the Lord came on David from that day forward. So Samuel rose up and went to Ramah" — 1 Samuel 16: 6-13.

If the sons of Jesse were told that God would provide himself a king among them (as he had said, v. 1), we may well suppose they all made the best appearance they could, and each hoped he should be the man; but here we are told,

I. How all the elder sons, who stood fairest for the preferment, were passed by.

1. Eliab, the eldest, was privately presented first to Samuel, probably none being present but Jesse only, and Samuel thought he must needs be the man: *Surely this is the Lord's anointed,* v. 6. The prophets themselves, when they spoke from under the divine direction, were as liable to mistake as other men; as Nathan, 2 Sam. vii. 3. But God rectified the prophet's mistake by a secret whisper to his mind: *Look not on his countenance,* v. 7. It was strange that Samuel, who had been so wretchedly disappointed in Saul, whose countenance and stature recommended him as much as any man's could, should be so forward to judge of a man by that rule. When God would please the people with a king he chose a comely man; but, when he would have one after his own heart, he should not be chosen by the outside. Men judge by the sight of the eyes, but God does not, Isa. xi. 3. *The Lord looks on the heart,* that is, (1.) He knows it. We can tell how men look, but he can tell what they are. Man looks on the eyes (so the original word is), and is pleased with the liveliness and sprightliness that appear in them; but God looks on the heart, and sees the thoughts and intents of that. (2.) He judges of men by it. The good disposition of the heart, the holiness or goodness of that, recommends us to God, and is *in his sight of great price* (1 Pet. iii. 4), not the majesty of the look, or the strength and stature of the body. Let us reckon that to be true beauty which is within, and judge of men, as far as we are capable, by their minds, not their mien.

2. When Eliab was set aside, Abinadad and Shammah, and, after them, four more of the sons of Jesse, seven in all, were presented to Samuel, as likely for his purpose; but Samuel, who now attended more carefully than he did at first to the divine direction, rejected them all: *The Lord has not chosen these,* v. 8, 10. Men dispose of their honours and estates to their sons according to their seniority of age and priority of birth, but God does not. *The elder shall serve the younger.* Had it been left to Samuel, or Jesse, to make the choice, one of these

would certainly have been chosen; but God will magnify his sovereignty in passing by some that were most promising as well as in fastening on others that were less so.

II. How David at length was pitched upon. He was the youngest of all the sons of Jesse; his name signifies *beloved,* for he was a type of the beloved Son. Observe, 1. How he was in the fields, *keeping the sheep* (v. 11), and was left there, though there was a sacrifice and a feast at his father's house. The youngest are commonly the fondlings of the family, but, it should seem, David was least set by of all the sons of Jesse; either they did not discern or did not duly value the excellent spirit he was of. Many a great genius lies buried in obscurity and contempt; and God often exalts those whom men despise and gives *abundant honour to that part which lacked.* The Son of David was he whom men despised, *the stone which the builders refused,* and yet he was *a name above every name.* David was taken *from following the ewes to feed Jacob* (Ps. lxxviii. 71), as Moses from keeping the flock of Jethro, an instance of his humility and industry, both which God delights to put honour upon. We should think a military life, but God saw a pastoral life (which gives advantage for contemplation and communion with heaven), the best preparative for kingly power, at least for those graces of the Spirit which are necessary to the due discharge of that trust which attends it. David was keeping sheep, though it was a time of sacrifice; for there is mercy that takes precedence of sacrifice. 2. How earnest Samuel was to have him sent for: "*We will not sit down* to meat" (perhaps it was not the feast upon the sacrifice, but a common meal) "*till he come hither;* for, if all the rest be rejected, this must be he." He that was designed not to sit at table at all is now waited for as the principal guest. If God will exalt those of low degree, who can hinder? 3. What appearance he made when he did come. No notice is taken of his clothing. No doubt that was according to his employment, mean and coarse, as shepherds' coats commonly are, and he did not change his clothes as Joseph did (Gen. xli. 14); but he had a very honest look, not stately, as Saul's, but sweet and lovely: *He was ruddy, of a beautiful countenance, and goodly to look to* (v. 12), that is, he had a clear complexion, a good eye, and a lovely face; the features were extraordinary, and there was something in his looks that was very charming. Though he was so far from using any art to help his beauty that his employment exposed it to the sun and wind, yet nature kept its own, and, by the sweetness of his aspect, gave manifest indications of an amiable temper and disposition of mind. Perhaps his modest blush, when he was brought before Samuel, and received by him with surprising respect, made him look much the handsomer. 4. The anointing of him. The Lord told Samuel in his ear (as he had done, ch. ix. 15) that this was he whom he must anoint, v. 12. Samuel objects not to the meanness of his education, his youth, or the little respect he had in his own family, but, in obedience to the divine command, took his horn of oil and *anointed him* (v. 13), signifying thereby, (1.) A divine designation to the government, after the death of Saul, of which hereby he gave him a full assurance. Not that he was at present invested with the royal power, but it was entailed upon him, to come to him in due time. (2.) A divine communication of gifts and graces, to fit him for the government, and make him a type of him who was to be the Messiah, the anointed One, who received the Spirit, not by measure, but without measure. He is said to be anointed *in the midst of his brethren,* who yet, possibly, did not understand it as a designation to the government, and therefore did not envy David (as Joseph's brethren did him), because they saw no further marks of dignity put upon him, no, not so much as a coat of divers colours. But bishop Patrick reads it, *He anointed him from the midst of his brethren,* that is, he singled him out from the rest, and privately anointed him, but with a charge to keep his own counsel, and not to let his own brethren know it, as by what we find (ch. xvii. 28), it should seem, Eliab did not. It is computed that David was now about twenty years old; if so, his trouble by Saul lasted ten years, for he was thirty years old when Saul died. Dr. Lightfoot reckons that he was about twenty-five, and that his troubles lasted but five years. 5. The happy effects of this anointing: *The Spirit of the Lord came upon David from that day forward,* v. 13. The anointing of him was not an empty ceremony, but a divine power went along with that instituted sign, and he found himself inwardly advanced in wisdom, and courage, and concern for the public, with all the qualifications of a prince, though not at all advanced in his outward circumstances. This would abundantly satisfy him that his election was of God. The best evidence of our being predestinated to the kingdom of glory is our being sealed with the Spirit of promise, and our experience of a work of grace in our own hearts. Some think that his courage, by which he slew the lion and the bear, and his extraordinary skill in music, were the effects and evidences of the Spirit's coming upon him. However, this made him the sweet psalmist of Israel, 2 Sam. xxiii. 1. Samuel, having done this, went to Ramah in safety, and we never read of him again but once (ch. xix. 18), till we read of his death; now he retired to die in peace, since his eyes had seen the salvation, even the sceptre brought into the tribe of Judah.

"But the Spirit of the Lord departed from Saul, and an evil spirit from the Lord terrified him. And Saul's servants said to him, Behold now, an evil spirit from God terrifies you. Let our lord now command his servants who are before you to seek out a man who is a skillful player on a harp. And when the evil spirit from God is on you, he shall play with his hand, and you shall be well. And Saul said to his servants, Give me now a man who can play well, and bring him to me. Then one of the servants answered and said, Behold, I have seen a son of Jesse the Bethlehemite who is skillful in playing, and a mighty, brave man, and a man of war, and prudent in speech. And he is a person of good form, and the Lord is with him. Therefore Saul sent messengers to Jesse and said, Send me your son David, who is with the sheep. And Jesse took an ass loaded with bread and a bottle of wine and a kid and sent them by his son David to Saul. And David came to Saul and stood before him. And he loved him greatly, and he became his armor-bearer. And Saul sent to Jesse saying, I ask you, let David stand before me, for he has found favor in my sight. And it came to pass, when the evil spirit from God was on Saul, that David took a harp and played with his hand. So Saul was refreshed and was well, and the evil spirit departed from him" — 1 Samuel 16: 14-23.

But the Spirit of the Lord departed from Saul, &c.] As a spirit of prophecy as at first, as a spirit of wisdom and prudence in civil government, and as a spirit of fortitude and courage, as the Targum: *and an evil spirit from the Lord troubled him;* the reverse of the former, which by the permission of God, and as a punishment to him for his sins, came upon him; he seemed to be a demoniac, as Josephus represents him, as if possessed with the devil: by whom he was almost suffocated and strangled, as well as was distracted in his counsels, and became weak and foolish; lost all courage and greatness of mind, was timorous and fearful, and started at every thing, and was full of envy, suspicion, rage and despair.

And Saul's servants said unto him, &c.] His courtiers, who observing him to act in a frantic manner, to be dull and melancholy, timorous, and irresolute, unsteady, divided, and distressed; or his physicians, who were called in to assist him, and remove his disorder from him: *behold, now an evil spirit from God troubleth thee;* the disorder was not from any natural cause, or any bodily disease, and therefore out of the reach of physicians to do any service, but was from an evil spirit suffered of God to harrass and disturb him.

Let our lord now command thy servants which are before thee, &c.] Meaning either themselves or some of a more inferior rank, who were in some post and office at court, waiters there, such as yeomen of the guards: *to seek out a man who is a cunning player on the harp;* a musical instrument much in use in those days: *and it shall come to pass, when the evil spirit from God is upon thee;* when in a melancholy mood, and Satan takes the advantage of it to distress and terrify, to spread the gloom, and stir up evil passions, and promote distraction and confusion: *that he shall play with his hand;* upon the harp, that being not an instrument of wind, but of hand-music: *and thou shalt be well:* music being a means of cheering the spirits, and removing melancholy and gloomy apprehensions of things, and so of restoring to better health of body and disposition of mind; and that music has such an effect on the bodies and minds of men is certain from observation and experience in all ages. Music has been found to be medicine to various diseases, not only for the curing of the bite of vipers, and of the tarantula, but for easing the pains of the sciatica, and for helping persons labouring under the disorders of the phrensy; and Pythagoras used to compose the mind, and remove the perturbations of it, by the use of the harp, the thing here advised to. *And Saul said unto his servants,* &c.] Approving of, and pleased with the advice they gave: *provide me now a man that can play well, and bring him to me;* for, being a sovereign prince, he could command whom he would to attend to his person and service.

Then answered one of the servants, &c.] Which the Jews say was Doeg the Edomite, who out of envy and ill-will to David, spake of him, that Saul might have an opportunity of slaying him; but this is not at all likely; rather it was one of David's friends and acquaintance, that was desirous of promoting him at court, and no doubt was directed to that motion by the overruling providence of God: *and said, behold, I have seen a son of Jesse the Bethlehemite;* he does not mention the name of his son, but so describes him, that he might be easily known by those who knew any thing of the family of Jesse; besides it was sufficient that he was one of Jesse's sons, to find him out: that is *cunning in playing:* that is, on the harp; has good skill in music, and is expert in it; *and a mighty valiant man;* as appeared by his encountering with and slaying the lion and the bear; an event now past, as very probable: *and a man of war;* some think this character of him was given after the affair of his fighting with Goliath and killing him, but here put by a prolepsis or anticipation; and indeed if David had been taken into Saul's court before that affair, it is difficult to account for Saul's ignorance of him, since he must be so near him, and so often with him, as his musician and armour-bearer; though that difficulty may be removed, as may be observed in its proper place: *and prudent in matters;* in his talk and conversation, and conduct and behaviour; knew how to carry himself, even in a prince's court: *and a comely person;* which always recommended to the courts of the eastern nations; see the note on Dan. i. 4; *and the Lord is with him;* prospering and succeeding him in whatsoever he was engaged; and seeing the Lord is with him, it might be expected the evil spirit would depart from Saul, when this person, with whom the Lord was, was in his presence. The Targum is, "the Word of the Lord is for his help;" all that is said of him showed that he was fit to be in the palace of a king, and a proper person to be with Saul in his present circumstances. *Wherefore Saul sent messengers to Jesse,* &c.] For David; not choosing to take him without his leave, though Samuel suggests that kings would do so, ch. viii. 11; *and said, send me David, thy son, which is with the sheep;* he had learnt his name, and what was his employment; and which last he mentions not by way of contempt, it not being reckoned mean and despicable even in the sons of great parsonages, in those times and countries, to attend flocks and herds: so with the Arabs, as Philo testifies, young men and maids of the most illustrious families fed cattle; and with the ancient Romans, the senator fed his own sheep. Paris, son of Priamus, king of Troy, is said to feed his father's oxen and sheep; and Saul himself had done the same; but to describe him particularly. *And Jesse took an ass* laden *with bread,* &c.] Laden with a load of bread, as the Targum; with as much as it could carry, or was used to carry: the Septuagint version is, an omer of bread, which was as much as a man could eat in one day; and, according to Kimchi and Ben Melech, it may be interpreted a heap of bread, agreeably to the use of the word in Judg. xv. 16; *and a bottle of wine;* or a skin of wine, a leather bag or sack, which held more than our bottles: the Targum is, a flagon of wine: *and a kid;* of the goats, as the same Targum: *and sent* them *by David his son unto Saul;* some think that Jesse suspected that Saul had got the secret of David's being anointed, and was fearful that he had a design upon his life, and therefore sent this present by his son to pacify him, and ingratiate him unto him: but rather he sent it as a token of respect and subjection to his sovereign, and according to the custom of those times, when men used to carry presents when they waited upon princes, and indeed in their common visits; and do in the eastern countries to this day; see the note on ch. ix. 7.

And David came to Saul, and stood before him, &c.] As a servant, and ministered to him in the way, and for the purpose for which he was sent: *and he loved him greatly;* being a comely person, and a well-behaved youth, and especially as he was serviceable to him with his music, in driving away melancholy from him: *and he became his armour bearer;* that is, he appointed him to this office, though we never read that he exercised it; nor did he go with Saul in this capacity to the battle related in the following chapter: it may be literally rendered: *and he was to him a bearer of vessels, or instruments;* and Abarbinel thinks this is to be understood not of instruments of war, but of instruments of music to play with; which he brought in and bare before him when he went in to the king.

And Saul sent to Jesse, saying, let David, I pray thee, stand before me, &c.] Continue in his service; which was great condescension in him, and great respect shown to Jesse, not to detain his son without his leave, and to ask it as a favour of him: *for he hath found favour in my sight;* was very acceptable to him, which must be very pleasing to Jesse to hear; especially if he was in any fear that Saul had an ill design upon him, when he first sent for him.

And it came to pass, when the evil *spirit from God was upon Saul,* &c.] See ver. 14, 15, though the word *evil* is not in the text here: wherefore Abarbinel thinks that this here was the Spirit of God, which stirred up in him thoughts of divine things, put him in mind of what God had said, that he had rejected him from being king, and had rent the kingdom from him; and this filled him with grief and trouble, and he became melancholy: *that David took an harp, and played with his hands;* upon it; and, as Josephus says, at the same time sung hymns and psalms; made use both of vocal and instrumental music: *so Saul was refreshed, and was well;* became cheerful, his grief was removed, his black and gloomy apprehensions of things were dispersed, and he was cured of his melancholy disorder for the present: *and the evil spirit departed from him;* at least for a while; he had his fits and intervals: of the effects of music in a natural way, see the note on ver. 16; though no doubt the music of David was more than natural, being attended with the power and blessing of God, in order to raise his fame and credit at court.

ARTHUR W. PINK'S

INTRODUCTION TO LIFE OF DAVID.

The life of David marked an important epoch in the unfolding of God's purpose and plan of redemption. Here a little and there a little God made known the grand goal toward which all His dealings tended. At sundry times and in divers manners God spake in times past. In various ways and by different means was the way prepared for the coming of Christ. The work of redemption, with respect to its chief design, is carried on from the fall of man to the end of the world by successive acts and dispensations in different ages, but all forming part of one great whole, and all leading to the one appointed and glorious climax.

"God wrought many lesser salvations and deliverances for His church and people before Christ came. Those salvations were all but so many images and forerunners of the great salvation Christ was to work out when He should come. The church during that space of time enjoyed the light of Divine revelation, or God's Word. They had in a degree the light of the Gospel. But all those revelations were only so many forerunners and earnests of the great light which He should bring who came to be 'the Light of the world.' That whole space of time was, as it were, the time of night, wherein the church of God was not indeed wholly without light: but it was like the light of the moon and stars, that we have in the night; a dim light in comparison with the light of the sun. The church all that time was a minor: see Gal. 4: 1-3" (Jon. Edwards).

We shall not here attempt to summarize the Divine promises and pledges which were given during the earlier ages of human history, nor the shadows and symbols which God then employed as the prefigurations of that which was to come: to do so, would require us to review the whole of the Pentateuch. Most of our readers are more or less familiar with the early history of the Israelitish nation, and of what that history typically anticipated. Yet comparatively few are aware of the marked advance that was made in the unfolding of God's counsels of grace in the days of David. A wonderful flood of light was then shed from heaven on things which were yet to come, and many new privileges were then vouchsafed into the O. T. Church.

In the preceding ages it had been made known that the Son of God was to become incarnate, for none but a Divine person could bruise the Serpent's head (cf. Jude 9), and He was to do so by becoming the woman's "Seed" (Gen. 3: 15). To Abraham God had made known that the Redeemer should (according to the flesh) descend from him. In the days of Moses and Aaron much had been typically intimated concerning the Redeemer's priestly office and ministry. But now it pleased God to announce that particular person in all the tribes of Israel from which Christ was to proceed, namely, David. Out of all the thousands of Abraham's descendants, a most honourable mark of distinction was placed upon the son of Jesse by anointing him to be king over his people. This was a notable step toward advancing the work of redemption. David was not only the ancestor of Christ, but in some respects the most eminent personal type of Him in all the O. T.

"God's beginning of the kingdom of His church in the house of David, was, as it were, a new establishing of the kingdom of Christ; the beginning of it in a state of such visibility as it thenceforward continued in. It was as it were God's planting the root, whence that branch of righteousness was afterwards to spring

152

up, that was to be the everlasting King of His church; and therefore this everlasting King is called the *branch from the stem of Jesse:* "And there shall come forth a rod out of the stem of Jesse, and a branch shall grow out of his roots' (Isa. 11: 1). 'Behold the days come, saith the Lord, that I will raise up unto David a righteous Branch, and a King shall reign and prosper' (Jer. 23: 5). So Christ, in the New Testament, is called *'the root and offspring of David',* Rev. 22: 16" (Work of Redemption by Jon. Edwards, 1757).

It is deserving of our closest attention and calls for our deepest admiration that each advance which was made in the unfolding of the counsels of Divine grace occurred at those times when human reason would have least expected them. The first announcement of the Divine incarnation was given not while Adam and Eve remained in a state of innocency, but after they had rebelled against their Maker. The first open manifestation and adumbration of the everlasting covenant was made after all flesh had corrupted its way on earth, and the flood had almost decimated the human race. The first announcement of the particular people from which the Messiah would spring, was published after the general revolt of men at the tower of Babel. While the wondrous revelation found in the last four books of the Pentateuch was made not in the days of Joseph, but after the whole nation of Israel had apostatised (see Ezek. 20: 5-9).

The principle of which attention has been directed in the above paragraph received further exemplification in God's call of David. One has but to read through the book of Judges to discover the terrible deterioration which succeeded the death of Joshua. For upwards of five centuries a general state of lawlessness prevailed: "In those days there was no king in Israel: *every* man did that which was right in his *own* eyes" (Judges 21: 25). Following this was Israel's demand for a king, and that, that they might "be *like* all the nations" (1 Sam. 8:20); therefore did Jehovah declare, "I gave thee a king in Mine anger, and took him away in My wrath" (Hos. 13:11). He too was an apostate, and his history ends by his consulting a witch (1 Sam. 28), and perishing on the battlefield (1 Sam. 31).

Such is the dark background upon which the ineffable glory of God's sovereign grace now shone forth; such is the historical setting of the life of him we are about to consider. The more carefully this be pondered, the more shall we appreciate the marvelous interposition of Divine mercy at a time when the prospects of Israel seemed wellnigh hopeless. But man's extremity is always God's opportunity. Even at that dark hour, God had ready the instrument of deliverance, "a man after His own heart." But who he was, and where he was located, none but Jehovah knew. Even Samuel the prophet had to be given a special Divine revelation in order to identify him. And this brings us to that portion of Scripture which introduces to us, David as a youth.

"And the Lord said unto Samuel, How long wilt thou mourn for Saul, seeing I have rejected him from reigning over Israel? fill thine horn with oil, and go, I will send thee to Jesse the Bethlehemite: for I have provided Me a king among his sons" (1 Sam. 16:1). This is the sequel to what is recorded in 1 Sam. 16: 10-12. Saul had despised Jehovah, and now he was rejected by Him (1 Sam. 15:23). True, he continued to occupy the throne for some little time, nevertheless, Saul was no longer owned of God. An important principle is here illustrated, which only the true Spirit-taught can appreciate: — a person, an institution, a corporate company, is often rejected by God secretly, a while before this solemn fact is evidenced outwardly; Judaism was abandoned by the Lord immediately before the cross (Matt. 23:38), yet the temple stood until A. D. 70!

God had provided Him a king among the sons of Jesse the Bethlehemite, and, as Micah 5:2 informs us, Bethlehem Ephratah was "little among the thousands of Judah." Ah, "God hath chosen the foolish things of the world to confound the wise; and God hath chosen the weak things of the world to confound the things which are mighty; and base things of the world, and things which are despised, hath God chosen, and things which are not, to bring to naught things that are" (1 Cor. 1:27,28). And why? "That no flesh should glory in His presence" (v. 29). God is jealous of His own honour, and therefore is He pleased to select the most unlikely and unpromising instruments to execute His pleasure (as the unlettered fishermen of Galilee to be the first heralds of the Cross), that it may the more plainly appear the power is His alone.

The principle which we have just named received further illustration in the particular son of Jesse which was the one chosen of God. When Jesse and his sons stood before Samuel, it is said of the prophet that "He looked on Eliab and said, Surely the Lord's anointed is before Him" (1 Sam. 16:6). But the prophet was mistaken. And what was wrong with Eliab? The next verse tells us, "But the Lord said unto Samuel, Look not on his countenance, or on the height of his stature; because I have refused him: for the Lord seeth not as man seeth; for man looketh on the outward appearance, but the Lord looketh on the heart" (v. 7). Ah, my reader, this is solemn and searching: it is at your *heart* the Holy One looks! What does He see in you? — a heart that has been purified by faith (Acts 15:9), a heart that loves Him supremely (Deut. 6:5), or a heart that is still "desperately wicked" (Jer. 17:9)?

One by one the seven sons of Jesse passed in review before the prophet's eye, but the "man after God's own heart" was not among their number. The sons of Jesse had been called to the sacrifice (v. 5), and, apparently, the youngest was deemed too insignificant by his father to be noticed on this occasion. But "the counsel of the Lord that *shall* stand" (Prov. 19:21), so inquiry and then request is made that the despised one should be sent for. "And he sent, and brought him in. Now he was ruddy, withal of a beautiful countenance, and goodly to look to. And the Lord said, Arise, anoint him: for this is he" (v. 12). Most blessed is it to compare these words with what is said of our Lord in Song of Sol. 5: 10, 16, "my Beloved is white and ruddy, the chiefest among ten thousands. . . His mouth is most sweet: yea, He is altogether lovely."

The principle of Divine election is designed for the humbling of man's proud heart. Very striking and solemn is it to see that, all through, God ignored that in which the flesh glories. Isaac, and not Ishmael (Abraham's firstborn), was the one selected by God. Jacob, and not Esau, was the object of His eternal love. The Israelites, and not the Egyptians, the Babylonians, or the Greeks, was the nation chosen to shadow forth this blessed truth of God's sovereign foreordination. So here the eldest sons of Jesse were all "rejected" by Jehovah, and David, the youngest, was the one of God's appointing. It should be observed too that David was the *eighth* son, and all through Scripture that numeral is connected with a *new beginning:* suitably then (and ordained by Divine providence) was it that *he* should be the one to mark a fresh and outstanding epoch in the history of the favoured nation.

The elect of God are *made manifest* in time by the miracle of regeneration being wrought within them. This it is which has always *distinguished* the children of God from the children of the devil; Divine calling, or the new birth, is what *identifies* the high favourites of Heaven. Thus it is written, "whom He did predestinate, them He also called" (Rom. 8:30) — called out of darkness into His marvelous light (1 Pet. 2:9). This miracle of regeneration, which is the birth-mark of God's elect, consists of a complete *change of heart*, a renewing of it, so that God becomes the supreme object of its delight, the pleasing of Him its predominant desire and purpose, and love for His people its characteristic note. God's *chosen* are transformed into the *choice* ones of the earth, for the members of Christ's mystical body are predestinated to be "conformed to the image" of their glorious Head; and thus do they, in their measure, in this life, "show forth" His praises.

Beautiful is it to trace the fruits or effects of regeneration which were visible in David at an early age. At the time Samuel was sent to anoint him king, he was but a youth, but even then he evidenced, most unmistakably, the transforming power of Divine grace. "And Samuel said unto Jesse, Are here all thy children? And he said, There remaineth yet the youngest, and, *behold*, he *keepeth the sheep*" (1 Sam. 16:11). Thus the first sight we are given of David in God's Word presents him as one who had a heart (a shepherd's care) for those who symbolized the people of God. "Just as before, when the strength of God's people were being wasted under Pharaoh, Moses, their deliverer, was hidden as a shepherd in a wilderness; so, when Israel was again found in circumstances of deeper, though less ostensible, peril, we again find the hope of Israel concealed in the unknown shepherd of an humble flock" (David by B. W. Newton).

An incident is recorded of the shepherd-life of David that plainly denoted his character and forecast his future. Speaking to Saul, ere he went forth to meet Goliath, he said, "thy servant kept his father's sheep, and there came a lion, and a bear, and took a lamb out of the flock: and I went out after him, and smote him, and delivered it out of his mouth: and when he arose against me I caught him by his beard, and smote him, and slew him" (1 Sam. 17:34, 35). Observe two things. First, the loss of one poor lamb was the occasion of David's daring. How many a shepherd would have considered *that* a thing far too trifling to warrant the endangering of his own life! Ah, it was love to that lamb and faithfulness to his charge which moved him to act. Second, but how could a youth triumph over a lion and a bear? Through faith in the living God: he trusted in Jehovah, and prevailed. Genuine faith in God is ever an infallible mark of His elect (Titus 1:1).

There is at least one other passage which sheds light on the spiritual condition of David at this early stage of his life, though only they who are accustomed to weigh each word separately are likely to perceive it. "Lord, remember David, and all his afflictions: How he sware unto the Lord, and vowed unto the mighty God of Jacob; Surely I will not come into the tabernacle of my house, nor go up into my bed; I will not give sleep to mine eyes, or slumber to mine eyelids, until I find out a place for the Lord, an habitation for the mighty God of Jacob. Lo, we heard of it *at Ephratah:* we found it in the fields of the wood" (Psa. 132:1-6). A careful reading of the whole Psalm reveals to us the interests of the youthful David's heart. There, amid the pastures of Bethlehem Ephratah, he was deeply concerned for *Jehovah's* glory. In closing, let us note how conspicuous was the *shepherd* character of David in his early days. Anticipating for a moment that which belongs to a later consideration, let us thoughtfully observe how that after David had rendered a useful service to king Saul, it is recorded that, "David went and returned from Saul to feed his father's sheep at Bethlehem" (1 Sam. 17:15). From the attractions (or distractions) of the court, he returned *to the fold* — the influences of an exalted position had not spoiled him for humble service! Is there not a word here for a pastor's heart: the evangelistic field, or the Bible-conference platform, may furnish tempting allurements, but your duty is to the "sheep" over which the good Shepherd has placed you. Take heed to the ministry you have aeceived of the Lord, that you fulfill it.

Fellow-servant of God, your sphere may be an humble and inconspicuous one; the flock to which God has called you to minister may be a small one; but *faithfulness* to your trust is what is required of you. There may be an Eliab ready to taunt you, and speak contemptuously of "those *few* sheep in the wilderness" (1 Sam. 17:28), as there was for David to encounter; but regard not their sneers. It is written, "His Lord said unto him, Well done, thou good and faithful servant: thou hast been faithful over a few things, I will make thee ruler over many things: enter thou into the joy of thy Lord" (Matt. 25:21).

As David was faithful to his trust in the humble sphere in which God first placed him, so he was rewarded by being called to fill a more important position, in which there too he honourably acquitted himself: "He chose David also for His servant, and took him from the sheepfolds: from following the ewes great with young He brought him to feed Jacob, His people, and Israel His inheritance. So he fed them according to *the integrity of his heart;* and guided them by the skilfulness of his hands" (Psa. 78:70-72).

In our last article we called attention to the *time* in which David's lot was cast. The spirituality of Israel had indeed fallen to a low ebb. The law of God was no longer heeded, for "every man did that which was right in his own eyes" (Judges 21:25). The terrible failure of the priesthood stands out clearly in the character of Eli's sons (1 Sam. 2:22). The nation as a whole had rejected Jehovah that He should not reign over them (1 Sam. 8:7). The one then on the throne was such a worthless reprobate that it is written, "The Lord repented that He had made Saul king over Israel (1 Sam. 15:35). The utter contempt which the people paid to the sacred tabernacle appears in the dreadful fact that it was suffered to languish in "the fields of the wood" (Psa. 132:6). Well, then, might our patriarch cry out, "Help Lord, for the godly man ceaseth" (Psa. 12:1).

But though the righteous government of God caused Israel to be sorely chastised for their sins, He did not completely abandon them. Where sin abounded, grace did much more abound. Amid the prevailing darkness, almighty power sustained, here and there, a light unto Himself. The heart of one feeble woman laid hold of Jehovah's strength: "He raiseth up the poor out of the dust, and lifteth up the beggar from the dunghill, to set them among princes, and to make them inherit the throne of glory; for the pillars of the earth are the Lord's and He hath set the world upon them. He will keep the feet of His saints, and the wicked shall be silent in darkness: for by strength shall no man prevail. The adversaries of the Lord shall be broken to pieces; out of heaven shall He thunder upon them: the Lord shall judge the ends of the earth, and He *shall* give strength unto His King, and exalt the horn of His *Anointed*" (1 Sam. 2:8-10). That was the language of true faith, and faith is something which God never disappoints. Most probably Hannah lived not to *see* the realization of her Spirit-inspired expectations, but in "due season" they were realized.

How encouraging and comforting ought the above to be to the little remnant of God's heritage in this "cloudy and dark day!" To outward sight, there is now much, very much, to distract and dishearten. Truly "men's hearts are failing them for fear, and for looking after those things which are coming on the earth" (Luke 21:26). But, blessed be His name, "the Lord, hath *His* way in the whirlwind" (Nah. 1:3). Faith looks beyond this scene of sin and strife, and beholds the Most High upon His throne, working "all things after the counsel of His own will" (Eph. 1:11). Faith lays hold of the Divine promises which declare, "at eveningtide it shall be light" (Zech. 14:7); and "When the enemy shall come in like a flood, the Spirit of the Lord shall lift up a standard against him" (Isa. 59:19). In the meantime God's grace is sufficient for the feeblest who really trusts Him.

Samuel was given by God in response to the prayers of Hannah, and who can doubt that David also was the answer to the earnest supplications of those who sought Jehovah's glory. And the Lord's ear has not grown heavy that it can no longer hear; yet the *actions* of present-day professing Christians say they believe that it has! If the diligence which is now paid to the ransacking of daily newspapers in search for sensational items which are regarded as "signs of the times," and if the time that is now given to Bible conferences was devoted to confession of sin and crying unto God to raise up a man after His own heart, whom He would use to bring back His wayward people into the paths of righteousness, it would be spent to much greater profit. Conditions are not nearly so desperate today as they were at the close of the "dark ages," nor even as bad as they were when God raised up Whitefield. To your knees, my brethren: God's arm is not shortened that it cannot save.

Now not only was the raising up of David a signal demonstration of Divine grace working in the midst of a people who deserved nought but untempered judgment, but, as pointed out in the preceding paper, it marked an important stage in the unfolding of God's counsels, and a further and blessed adumbration of what had been settled upon in the everlasting covenant. This has not been sufficiently emphasized by recent writers, who, in their zeal to stress the *law* element of the Mosaic economy, have only too often overlooked the *grace* element which was exercised throughout. No "new dispensation" was inaugurated in the days of David, but a most significant advance was made in the Divine foreshadowings of that kingdom over which the Messiah now rules. The Mediator is not only the arch Prophet and high Priest, but He is also the King of kings, and *this* it is which was now to be specifically typified. The *throne*, as well as the altar, belongs to Christ!

From the days of Abraham, and onwards for a thousand years, the providential dealings of God had mainly respected that people from whom the Christ was to proceed. But now attention is focussed on that particular person whence He was to spring. It pleased God at this time to single out the specific man of whom Christ was to come, namely, David. "David being the ancestor and great type of Christ, his being solemnly anointed to be king over his people, that the kingdom of His church might be continued in his family forever, may in some respects be looked on as an anointing of Christ Himself. Christ was as it were anointed in him; and therefore Christ's anointing and David's anointing are spoken of under *one* in scripture: 'I have found David My servant; with My holy oil have I anointed him' (Psa. 89:20). And David's throne and Christ's are spoken of as one: 'And the Lord shall give Him the throne of His father David' (Luke 1:32). 'David — knowing that God had sworn with an oath to him, that of the fruit of his loins, according to the flesh, He would raise up Christ to sit on his throne,' Acts 2:30" (Jon. Edwards).

The *typical* character of David's person presents a most precious line of study. His very name signifies "the Beloved." His being an inhabitant of Bethlehem was ordained to point to that place where the Darling of God's heart was to be born. His "beautiful countenance" (1 Sam. 16:13), spoke of Him who is "fairer than the children of men." His occupation as a shepherd set forth the peculiar relation of Christ to God's elect, and intimated the nature of His redemptive work. His faithful discharge of the pastoral office forecast the love and fidelity of the great Shepherd. His lowly occupation before he ascended the throne prefigured the humiliation of the Saviour's prior to His glorious exaltation. His victory over Goliath symbolized the triumph of Christ over the great enemy of God and His people. His perfecting of Israel's worship and instituting of a new ecclesiastical establishment, anticipated Christ as the Head and Law-giver of His church.

But it is in the *anointing* of David that we reach the most notable feature of our type. The very name or title "Christ" means "the Anointed" One, and David was the first of Israel's kings who thus foreshadowed Him. True, Saul also was anointed, but he furnished a solemn contrast, being a dark foreboding of the antichrist. At an earlier period, Aaron had been anointed unto the sacerdotal office (Lev. 8:12); and, at a later date, we read of Elisha the prophet being anointed (1 Kings 19:16). Thus the threefold character of the Mediator's office as Prophet, Priest, and Potentate was fully typed out centuries before He was openly manifested here on earth.

It is a remarkable fact that David was anointed *three* times. First, privately at Bethlehem (1 Sam. 16:13). Second, by the men of Judah (2 Sam. 2:4). Third, by the elders of Israel (2 Sam. 5:3). So also was that august One whom he foreshadowed. This will appear the more evident if we quote the following: "Then Samuel took the horn of oil, and anointed him in (or "from") the midst of his brethren: and *the Spirit of the Lord came upon David* from that day forward" (1 Sam. 16:13). Concerning our Lord, His humanity was miraculously conceived and sanctified by the Spirit and endowed with all graces in the Virgin's womb (Luke 1: 35). Second, He was publicly "anointed with the Spirit" (Acts 10:38) at His baptism, and thus equipped for His ministry — see Isa. 61:1. Third, at His ascension He was "anointed with the oil of gladness above His fellows" (Psa. 45:6, 7). It was to *this* that the anointing of David more especially pointed.

It is striking to observe that God anointed David *after* Saul, to reign in his room. He took away the crown from him who was higher in stature than any of his people, and gave it to one who resided in Bethlehem, which was "little among the thousands of Judah" (Micah 5:2). In this way was God pleased to prefigure the fact that He who, when on earth, was "despised and rejected of men," should take the kingdom from the great ones of the earth. At a later date, this was more expressly revealed, for in the Divine interpretation of Nebuchadnezzar's dream Daniel declared, "In the days of these kings shall the God of heaven set up a kingdom, which shall never be destroyed: and the kingdom shall not be left to other people, but it shall break in pieces and consume all these kingdoms, and it shall stand forever. Forasmuch as thou sawest that the Stone was cut out of the mountain without hands, and that it break in pieces the iron, the brass, the clay, the silver, and the gold; the great God hath made known to the king what shall come to pass hereafter" (Dan. 2:44,45).

It was the mediatorial reign of Christ which David foreshadowed, and of which he prophesied: "Thy throne, O God, is forever and ever: the sceptor of Thy kingdom is a right sceptor" (Psa. 45:6). That "throne" is His *mediatorial* throne, and that "sceptor" is the symbol of authority over His mediatorial kingdom. Those metaphors are here applied to Christ as setting forth His kingly office, together with His dignity and dominion, for the throne whereon He sits is "the throne of the Majesty in the heavens" (Heb. 8:1). "Thou lovest righteousness, and hatest wickedness: therefore, God, Thy God, hath anointed Thee with the oil of gladness above Thy fellows" (Psa. 45:7). This is in contrast from the days when He was "a Man of sorrows and acquainted with grief." It denotes His triumph and exaltation. It was at His ascension that He was "crowned with glory and honor" (Heb. 2:7).

Just as the priestly office and work of Christ were foreshadowed by Melchizedek and Aaron, so the kingship and kingdom of the Mediator were typed out by both David and Solomon. It would lead us too far afield to enlarge upon this very much, but the interested reader will do well to ponder such Scriptures as 2 Sam. 7: 12-16; Isa. 16:5; Jer. 23:5, 6; 33: 14-17; Acts 13:34; Rev. 3:7; 5:5. And let us not be robbed of the preciousness of these passages by the attempts of "dispensationalists" who would have us believe they belong only to the future. In many instances their insistance of *literalizing* many portions of Holy Writ has resulted in the *carnalizing* of them, and the missing of their true and *spiritual* import. Let the reader beware of any system of interpretation which takes away from the Christian any portion of God's word: *all* Scripture is "profitable for *doctrine*" (2 Tim. 3:16).

Between the first and the third anointings of David, or between Samuel's consecrating of him to the kingly office and his actually ascending the throne, there was a period of severe trials and testings, during which our patriarch passed through much suffering and humiliation. Here too we may discern the accuracy of our type. David's Son and Lord trode a path of unspeakable woe between the time when the Holy Spirit first came upon Him and His being exalted to the right hand of the Majesty on high. It is indeed blessed to read through the first book of Samuel and take note of the series of wonderful providences by which God preserved David's life until the death of Saul; but it is yet more precious to see in these so many adumbrations of what is recorded in such passages as Matt. 2:16; John 4:29; John 8:59; John 10:31, 39, etc.

Ere passing on, let us seek to make practical application unto ourselves of what has just been referred to above. God promised Abraham a son, in whom all the nations of the earth should be blessed (Gen. 12:3), yet he performed it not for thirty years (Gen. 21:2). God anointed David king over Israel, yet before the kingdom was actually given to him, his faith was severely tested, and he was called on to endure many sore buffetings. He was hated, persecuted, outlawed, and hunted like a partridge on the mountains (1 Sam. 26:20, etc.). Yet was he enabled to say, "I waited patiently for the Lord, and He inclined unto me, and heard my cry" (Psa. 40:1). So the Christian has been begotten to a glorious inheritance, but "we *must* through *much* tribulation enter into the kingdom of God" (Acts 14:22). It is only "through faith and patience (we) inherit the promises" (Heb. 6:12).

Another thing which God did at that time toward furthering the great work of redemption was His inspiring David to show forth Christ and His salvation in Divine songs. David was endowed with the spirit of prophecy, and is called "a prophet" (Acts 2:29,30) so that here too he was a type of Christ. "This was a great advancement that God made in this building; and the light of the Gospel, which had been gradually growing from the fall, was exceedingly increased by it; for whereas before there was but here and there a prophecy given of Christ in a great many ages, now here Christ is spoken of by David abundantly, in multitudes of songs, speaking of His incarnation, life, death, resurrection, ascension into heaven, His satisfaction, intercession; His prophetical, kingly, and priestly office; His glorious benefits, in this life and that which is to come; His union with the church, and the blessedness of the church in Him; the calling of the Gentiles. All these things concerning Christ and His redemption are abundantly spoken of in the book of Psalms (Jon. Edwards).

To quote again from this Spirit-taught man, "Now first it was that God proceeded to choose a particular city out of all the tribes of Israel to place His name there. There is several times mention made in the law of Moses of the children of Israel's bringing their oblations to the place which God should choose, as Deut. 12:5-7; but God had never proceeded to it till now. The tabernacle and ark were never pitched, but sometimes in one place, and sometimes in another; but now God proceeded to choose Jerusalem. The city of Jerusalem was never thoroughly conquered or taken out of the hands of the Jebusites, till David's time. It is said in Joshua 15:63, 'As for the Jebusites, the inhabitants of Jerusalem, the children of Judah could not drive them out.' But now David wholly subdued it, as we have an account in 2 Sam. 5. And now God proceeded to choose that city to place His name there, as appears by David's bringing up the ark thither soon after; and therefore this is mentioned afterwards as the first time God proceeded to choose a city to place His name there: 2 Chron. 6:5, 6; 12:13.

"The city of Jerusalem is therefore called the *holy city;* and it was the greatest type of the church of Christ in all the O. T. It was redeemed by David, the captain of the hosts of Israel, out of the hands of the Jebusites to be God's city, the holy place of His rest forever, where He would dwell; as Christ, the Captain of His people's salvation redeemed His church out of the hands of devils, to be His holy and beloved city. And therefore how often does the Scripture, when speaking of Christ's redemption of His church, call it by the names of *Zion, and Jerusalem!* This was the city that God had appointed to be the place of the first gathering and erecting of the Christian Church after Christ's resurrection, of that remarkable pouring out of the Spirit of God on the apostles and primitive Christians, and the place whence the Gospel was to sound forth into all the world; the place of the first Christian Church, that was to be, as it were, the mother of all other churches in the world; agreeably to that prophecy, Isa. 2:3, 4: 'out of Zion shall go forth the law, and the word of the Lord from Jerusalem' " (Work of Redemption).

"Now the Philistines gathered their armies together, and had gathered together at Shochoh, which belongs to Judah, and pitched between Shochoh and Azekah, in Ephesdammin. And Saul and the men of Israel had gathered together and pitched by the valley of Elah. And they set the battle in order against the Philistines. And the Philistines stood on a mountain on the one side, and Israel stood on a mountain on the other side. And there was a valley between them. And a champion came out of the camp of the Philistines, named Goliath, from Gath, whose height was six cubits and a span. And he had a helmet of bronze on his head, and he was armor-coated with bronze. And the weight of the coat was five thousand shekels of bronze. And he had greaves of bronze on his legs and buckler of bronze between his shoulders. And the staff of his spear was like a weaver's beam. And his spear's head weighed six hundred shekels of iron. And one went in front of him, carrying a shield. And he stood and cried to the armies of Israel, and said to them, Why have you come out to set your battle in order? Am I not a Philistine, and are you not servants to Saul? Choose your man and let him come down to me. If he is able to fight with me, then we will be your servants. But if I prevail against him and kill him, then you shall be our servants and serve us. And the Philistine said, I defy the armies of Israel today. Give me a man, so that we may fight together. When Saul and all Israel heard those words of the Philistine, they were dismayed and greatly afraid. Now David was the son of that Ephrathite of Bethlehem in Judah whose name was Jesse. And Jesse had eight sons. And the man was an old man in the days of Saul. And

the three oldest sons of Jesse went and followed Saul to the battle. And the names of his three sons that went to the battle were Eliab the first-born, and next to him Abinadab, and the third Shammah. And David was the youngest. And the three oldest followed Saul. And David was going and returning from Saul to feed his father's sheep at Bethlehem. And the Philistine drew near morning and evening, and presented himself forty days. And Jesse said to David his son, Now take your brothers an ephah of this parched grain, and these ten loaves, and run to the camp to your brothers. And carry these ten cheeses of milk to the captain of their thousand, and see how your brothers are faring, and take their pledge. Now Saul, and they, and all the men of Israel, were in the valley of Elah fighting with the Philistines. And David rose up early in the morning and left the sheep with a keeper. And he got up and went, as Jesse had commanded him. And he came to the path as the army was going forth to fight and shouting the war-cry. For Israel and the Philistines had put the battle in order, army against army. And David left his baggage in the hand of the keeper of the baggage and ran into the army. And he came and greeted his brothers. And as he talked with them, behold, the champion came up, the Philistine of Gath, Goliath by name, out of the armies of the Philistines, and spoke according to the same words. And David heard" — I Samuel 17:1-23. (KJ II)

In our last article we contemplated David's anointing; in our present study an entirely different experience in his varied career is before us. The two halves of 1 Sam. 16 present a series of striking contrasts. In the former we behold David called to occupy the throne, in the latter he is seen entering the place of service. There we see the Spirit of the Lord coming upon David (v. 13), here we behold the Spirit of the Lord departing from Saul (v. 14). In the one David is anointed with the holy oil (v. 13), in the other Saul is troubled with an evil spirit (v. 14). Samuel was "mourning" (v. 1), Saul is "refreshed" (v. 23). Samuel approached Jesse with an heifer for sacrifice (v. 2), Jesse sends David to Saul with bread, wine, and a kid for feasting (v. 20). David was acceptable in God's sight (v. 12), here he found favour in Saul's eyes (v. 22). Before he was tending the sheep (v. 11), now he is playing the harp in the palace (v. 23).

God did not set David upon the throne immediately: after his "anointing" came a season of testing. The coming of the Spirit upon him was followed by his having to face the great Enemy. Thus it was with David's Son and Lord, the One whom, in so many respects, he foreshadowed. After the descent of the Holy Spirit upon Him at His baptism, Christ was tempted of the Devil for forty days. So here: the next thing we read of is David's being sent to calm Saul who was terrified by an evil spirit, and shortly after that he goes forth to meet Goliath — figure of Satan. The principle which is here illustrated is one that we do well to take to heart: patience has to be tested, humility manifested, faith strengthened, before we are ready to enter into God's best for us; we must use rightly what God has given us, if we desire Him to give us more.

"But the Spirit of the Lord departed from Saul, and an evil spirit from the Lord troubled him" (1 Sam. 16:14). Exceedingly solemn is this, the more so when we consider that which precedes it. In 15:1-3 the Lord, had, through Samuel, given a definite commission unto Saul to "utterly destroy Amelek, and all that they had." Instead of so doing, he compromised: "But Saul and the people spared Agag, and the best of the sheep, and of the oxen, and of the fatlings, and the lambs, and all that was good, and would not utterly destroy them" (15:9). When faced by God's faithful prophet, the king's excuse was "the people spared the best of the sheep and the oxen to sacrifice unto the Lord" (v.

15). Then it was that Samuel said, "Hath the Lord as great delight in burnt offerings and in sacrifices, as in *obeying* the voice of the Lord? Behold, to obey is *better* than sacrifice, to hearken than the fat of rams" (v. 22).

Saul had openly defied the Lord by deliberately disobeying His plain commandment. Wherefore the prophet said unto him, "For rebellion is as the sin of witchcraft, and stubbornness is as iniquity and idolatry. Because thou hast rejected the word of the Lord, he hath also rejected thee from being king" (v. 23). And now we come to the dreadful sequel. "The Spirit of the Lord departed from Saul, and an evil spirit from the Lord troubled him." Having forsaken God, God forsook him. Rightly did Matthew Henry say upon this verse: "They that drive the good Spirit away from them, do of course become a prey to the evil spirit. If God and His grace do not rule us, sin and Satan will have possession of us."

"But the Spirit of the Lord departed from Saul, and an evil spirit from the Lord troubled him" (16:14). Great care needs to be taken against our reading into these words what is really not in them, otherwise we shall make one part of Scripture contradict another. The Holy Spirit had never been given to Saul as the Spirit of regeneration and sanctification: but He had been given to him as a Spirit of prophecy (see 10:10 and contrast 28:6), and as a Spirit of wisdom for temporal rule, thus fitting him for the discharge of his royal duties. In like manner, when we read that "God gave him *another* heart" (10:9), this must not be confounded with "a new heart" (Ezek. 36:26) — the "another heart" was not in a moral and spiritual sense, but only in a way of wisdom for civil government, prudence to rule, courage to fight against his enemies, fortitude against difficulties and discouragements.

It is a serious mistake to suppose that because the Holy Spirit has not come as the Spirit of regeneration and sanctification unto many professors, that therefore He has not come to them at all. Many *are* "made partakers of the Holy Spirit" as the Spirit of "enlightenment" (Heb. 6:4), of spiritual aspirations (Num. 24:2, etc.), of deliverance from the "pollutions of the world" (2 Pet. 2:20), who are never brought from death unto life. There are common operations of the Spirit as well as special, and it behooves all of us to very seriously and very diligently examine our hearts and lives for the purpose of discovering whether or not the Holy Spirit indwells *us* as a *Sanctifier,* subduing the flesh, delivering from worldliness, and conforming to the image of Christ. "When men grieve and quench the Spirit by wilful sin, He departs, and will not strive" (Matt. Henry).

The servants of Saul were uneasy over the king's condition, realizing that an evil spirit from God was tormenting him. They therefore suggested that a man who had skill in playing the harp should be sought out, saying, "And it shall come to pass, when the evil spirit from God is upon thee, that he shall play with his hand, and thou shalt be well" (v. 16). Such is the best counsel which poor worldlings have to offer unto those in trouble. As Matt. Henry says, "How much better friends had they been to him, if they had advised him, since the evil spirit was from the Lord, to make his peace with God by true repentance, to send for Samuel to pray with him, and intercede with God for him; then might he not only have had some present relief, but the good Spirit would have returned."

How many whose consciences have convicted them of their careless, sinful, Godless ways, and who have been startled by the presence of an eternity in Hell, have been ruined forever by following a course of drowning the concerns of the soul by regaling and delighting the senses of the body. "Eat, drink, and be merry" is the motto of the world, and every effort is made to stifle all anxiety about the near prospect of a time arriving when instead of being able to go on so doing, not even a drop of water will be available to ease their unbearable sufferings. Let the younger readers seriously ponder this. "Rejoice, O young man, in thy youth; and let thy heart cheer thee in the days of thy youth, and walk in the ways of thine heart, and in the sight of thine eyes: but know thou, that for all these things God will surely bring thee unto judgment" (Ecc. 11:9).

The suggestion made by his servants appealed to Saul, and he gave his consent. Accordingly one of them told him, "Behold, I have seen a son of Jesse the Bethlehemite, that is cunning in playing, and a mighty valiant man, and a man of war, and prudent in matters, and a comely person, and the Lord is with him" (v. 18). A high character is here accorded David, as one well fitted for the strange part he was to play. Not only was his person suited for the court, not only was he skilled upon the harp, but he was known for his courage and wisdom. The terming of him "a mighty valiant man" intimates that his single-handed victory over the lion and the bear (17:37) had already been noised abroad. Finally, it was known that "the Lord is with him." How this illustrates and demonstrates the fact that one who has received the Spirit as the Spirit of regeneration and sanctification gives clear evidence of it to others! Where a miracle of grace has been wrought in the heart, the fruits of it will soon be unmistakably manifested to all around. Very searching is this. Can those with whom we come into daily contact *see* that "the Lord is with" the writer and the reader? O to let our light "*so* shine before men, that they may see our good works, and glorify our Father which is in heaven" (Matt. 5:16).

"Wherefore Saul sent messengers unto Jesse, and said, Send me David thy son, which is with the sheep" (v. 19). Little did Saul think that in giving this order he was inviting to his palace the very one of whom Samuel had said "The Lord hath rent the kingdom of Israel from thee this day, and hath given it to a neighbour of thine, better than thou" (15:28)! How marvelously does God, working behind the scenes, bring His own purpose to pass! Verily "man's goings are of the Lord," and well may we say "how can a man then understand his own way?" (Prov. 20:24). Yet while we are quite incapable of analyzing either the philosophy or psychology of it, let us admire and stand in awe before Him of whom it is written "For of Him, and through Him, and to Him, are *all things:* to whom be glory forever," Amen (Rom. 11:36).

"Wherefore Saul sent messengers unto Jesse, and said, send me David thy son, which is with the sheep" (v. 19). What a *testing* for David was this! He who had been anointed unto an office wherein he would command and rule over others, was now called on to serve. Lovely is it to mark his response: there was no unwillingness, no delay. He promptly complied with his father's wishes. It was also a testing of his courage: might not Saul have learned his secret, and now have designs upon his life? might not this invitation to the palace cover a subtle plot to destroy him! Ah, "the angel of the Lord encampeth round about them that fear Him, and delivereth them," and where God is truly feared, the fear of man disappears.

"And Jesse took an ass laden with bread, and a bottle of wine, and a kid, and sent them by David his son unto Saul" (v. 20). What a beautiful typical picture is here presented to us. It was the dire need of poor Saul which moved Jesse to send forth his anointed son: so it was a world lying in sin unto which the Father sent His Beloved. Behold David richly laden with presents for the king: Jesse sent him forth not with weapons of warfare in his hands, but with the tokens of his good will. So the Father sent forth His Son "not to condemn the world" (John 3:17), but on an errand of grace and mercy unto it.

"And David came to Saul." Yes, at his father's bidding he freely left his home: though the anointing oil was upon him, he went forth not to be ministered unto, but to minister. How blessedly this foreshadowed Him of whom it is written, "Who, being in the form of God, thought it not robbery to be equal with God: But made Himself of no reputation, and took upon Him the form of a servant, and was made in the likeness of men: And being found in fashion as a man, He humbled Himself, and became obedient unto death" (Phil. 2:6-8). O that writer and reader may be so filled with His Spirit, that not only shall we unmurmuringly, but joyfully, perform our Father's bidding.

"And David came to Saul." Admire again the wondrous working of God. David had been called to reign over Israel, but the time had not yet arrived for him to occupy the throne. An unsophisticated shepherd-boy needed training. Observe then how the providence of God ordered it that for a season he should dwell in the royal court, thus having full opportunity to note its ways, observe its corruptions, and discover its needs. And mark it well, this was brought about *without* any scheming or effort either on his own part or of that of his friends. An evil spirit from the Lord troubled the king: the courtiers were exercised, and proposed a plan to him: their plan met with Saul's approval: David was mentioned as the one who should be sent for: the king assented, Jesse raised no demurs, David was made willing; and thus, working secretly but surely, God's purpose was accomplished. It is only the eye of faith that looks above the ordinary happenings of daily life and sees the Divine hand ordering and shaping them for the accomplishment of God's counsels and the good of His people.

An important principle is here illustrated: when God has designed that any Christian should enter *His* service, His providence concurs with His grace to prepare and qualify him for it, and often it is by means of God's providences that the discerning heart perceives the Divine will. God opened the door into the palace without David having to force or even so much as knock upon it. When *we* assume the initiative, take things into our own hands, and attempt to hew a path for ourselves, we are acting in the energy of the flesh. "Commit thy way unto the Lord: trust also in Him, and He shall bring it to pass . . . Rest in the Lord, and wait patiently for Him" (Psa. 37:5-7). Obedience to these exhortations is not easy to flesh and blood, yet they must be complied with if we are not to miss God's best. The more we appropriate and act upon such Divine precepts, the more clearly will the hand of God be seen when it intervenes on our behalf: the feverish activities of natural zeal only raise a cloud of dust which conceal from us the beauties of Divine providence.

"And David came to Saul, and stood before him: and he loved him greatly; and he became his armourbearer. And Saul sent to Jesse, saying, Let David, I pray thee, stand before me; for he hath found favour in my sight" (vv. 21,22). Here too we may perceive and admire the secret workings of God's providence. "The king's heart is in the hand of the Lord, as the rivers of water: *He* turneth it whithersoever He will" (Prov. 21:1). It was the Divine purpose, and for David's good, that he should spend a season at the court; therefore did the Lord incline Saul's heart toward him. How often we lose sight of this fact. How apt we are to attribute the favour and kindness of people toward us to any thing rather than to the Lord! O my reader if God has given you favour in the eyes of your congregation, or your employer, or your customers, give Him the glory and the thanks for it.

"And it came to pass, when the evil spirit from God was upon Saul, that David took an harp, and played with his hand: so Saul was refreshed, and was well, and the evil spirit departed from him" (v. 23). Here we see the readiness of David to perform every task which God allotted him. In this he evidenced his moral fitness for the important role he was yet to fill. "Thou hast been faithful over a few things, I will make thee ruler over many things" (Matt. 25:21), expresses an important principle in the government of God, and one which we do well to take to heart. If I am careless in fulfilling my duties as a Sunday school teacher, I must not be surprised if God never calls me to the ministry. And if I am unfaithful in teaching and disciplining my own children, I must not be surprised if God withholds His power and blessing when I seek to teach the children of others.

The power of David's harp to quiet the spirit of Saul and to temporarily drive away the demon, ought not to be attributed either to the skill of the player or to the charm of music. Instead, it must be ascribed alone to the Lord, who was pleased to *bless* this means to these ends. The instrument, be it weak or strong, likely or unlikely, is utterly powerless in and of itself. Paul may plant and Apollos may water, but there will be no increase unless *God gives it.* In view of 17:55, 56 some have concluded that what has been before us in the closing verses of chap. 16 is placed out of its chronological order. But there is no need to resort to such a supposition. Moreover, 17:15 plainly refutes it. How long David remained in the palace we know not, but probably for quite some time; after which he returned again unto his humbler duties in the sheepfold.

"And all the men of Israel, when they saw the man, ran from him and were very much afraid. And the men of Israel said, Have you seen this man that has come up? Surely he has come up to defy Israel. And the king will enrich the man who kills him with great riches; and he will give him his daughter and make his father's house tax-free in Israel. And David spoke to the men who stood by him, saying, What shall be done to the man who kills this Philistine and takes away this shame from Israel? For who is this uncircumcised Philistine that he should defy the armies of the living God? And the people answered him in this way, saying, So shall it be done to the man who kills him. And Eliab his oldest brother heard when he spoke to the man. And Eliab's anger was kindled against David, and he said, Why did you come down here? And with whom have you left those few sheep in the wilderness? I know your pride and the naughtiness of your heart. For you have come down so that you might see the battle. And David said, What have I done now? Is there not a cause? And he turned from him toward another and spoke in the same way. And the people answered him again in the same way. And when the words which David spoke were heard, they told them before Saul. And he sent for him. And David said to Saul, Let no man's heart fail because of him. Your servant will go and fight with this Philistine. And Saul said to David, You are not able to go against this Philistine to fight with him. For you are but a youth, and he is a man of war from his youth. And David said to Saul, Your servant kept his father's sheep, and a lion and a bear came and took a lamb out of the flock. And I went out after it and struck it and delivered the lamb out of its mouth. And when it rose against me, I caught it by the beard and struck it and killed it. Your servant killed both the lion and the bear And this uncircumcised Philistine shall be like one of them, since he has defied the armies of the living God. And David added, The Lord who delivered me out of the paw of the bear, He will deliver me out of the hand of this Philistine. And Saul said to David, Go, and may the Lord be with you. And Saul armed David with his armor, and he put a helmet of bronze on his head. He also put an armor-coat on him. And David girded his sword on his armor, and he tried to go. But he had not tested it. And David said to Saul, I

cannot go with these, for I have not tested them. And David took them off. And he took his staff in his hand, and he chose five smooth stones out of the brook for himself and put them in a shepherd's vessel which he had, even in a bag. And his sling was in his hand. And he drew near the Philistine. And the Philistine came on and drew near David. And the man who bore the shield went in front of him. And when the Philistine looked around and saw David, he disdained him. For he was only a youth, and ruddy, and of a beautiful face. And the Philistine said to David, Am I a dog that you come to me with sticks? And the Philistine cursed David by his gods. And the Philistine said to David, Come to me and I will give your flesh to the birds of the air and to the beasts of the field. And David said to the Philistine, You come to me with a sword and with a spear and with a shield. But I come to you in the name of the Lord of hosts, the God of the armies of Israel, whom you have defiled. The Lord will deliver you into my hand today, and I will strike you and take your head from you. And I will give the bodies of the army of the Philistines to the birds of the air today, and to the wild beasts of the earth, so that all the earth may know that there is a God in Israel. And all this multitude shall know that the Lord does not save with sword and spear; for the battle is the Lord's, and He will give you into our hands. And when the Philistines rose and came and drew near to meet David, David hurried and ran toward the army to meet the Philistine. And David put his hand into his bag and took a stone from there. And he threw it with his sling and struck the Philistine in his forehead, so that the stone sank into his forehead. And he fell on his face to the earth. So David prevailed over the Philistine with a sling and with a stone. And he struck the Philistine and killed him. But there was no sword in the hand of David. Then David ran and stood on the Philistine. And he took out his sword and drew it out of its sheath and killed him, and cut off his head with it. And when the Philistines saw that their champion was dead, they fled. And the men of Israel and Judah pursued the Philistines until you come to the valley, and to the gates of Ekron. And the wounded of the Philistines fell down by the way to Shaaraim, even to Gath and to Ekron. And the children of Israel returned from chasing after the Philistines, and they spoiled their tents. And David took the head of the Philistine and brought it to Jerusalem. But he put his armor in his tent. And when Saul saw David go forth against the Philistine, he said to Abner, the captain of the army, Abner, whose son is this young man? And Abner said, As your soul lives, O king, I cannot tell. And the king said, You go ask whose son the young man is. And as David returned from the slaughter of the Philistine, Abner took him and brought him before Saul, with the head of the Philistine in his hand. And Saul said to him, Whose son are you, young man? And David answered, I am the son of your servant Jesse of Bethlehem" — 1 Samuel 17:24-58. (KJ II)

When Samuel denounced Saul's first great sin and announced that his kingdom should not continue, he declared, "The Lord hath sought Him a man after His own heart" (1 Sam. 13:14). To this, allusion was made by the apostle Paul in his address in the synagogue at Antioch, "He raised up unto them David to be their king; to whom also He gave testimony, and said, I have found David the son of Jesse, a man after Mine own heart, which shall fulfill all My will" (Acts 13:22). A truly wondrous tribute was this unto the character of David, yet one which the general course of his life bore out. The dominant characteristic of our patriarch was his unfeigned and unsurpassed devotion to God, His cause, and His Word. Blessedly is this illustrated in what is now to be before us. The man after God's own heart is the one who is out and out for Him, putting His honour and glory before all other considerations.

1 Sam. 17:15 supplies a precious link between what was considered in our last lesson and what we are now about to ponder. There we are told, "But David went and returned from Saul to feed his father's sheep at Bethlehem." Knowing that he was to be the next king over Israel, natural prudence would suggest that his best policy was to remain at court, making the most of his opportunities, and seeking to gain the goodwill of the ministers of state; but instead of so doing, the son of Jesse returned to the sheepfold, leaving it with God to work out His will concerning him. No seeker after self-aggrandisement was David. The palace, as such, possessed no attractions for him. Having fulfilled his service unto the king, he now returns to his father's farm.

"Now the Philistines gathered together their armies to battle, and were gathered together at Shochoh" (1 Sam. 17:1). Josephus (Antiq. 50:6, c. 9, sect. 1) says that this occurred not long after the things related in the preceding chapter had transpired. It seems likely that the Philistines had heard of Samuel's forsaking of Saul, and of the king's melancholy and distraction occasioned by the evil spirit, and deemed it a suitable time to avenge themselves upon Israel for their last slaughter of them (chap. 14). The enemies of God's people are ever alert to take advantage of their opportunities, and never have they a better one than when their leaders provoke God's Spirit and His prophets leave them. Nevertheless, it is blessed to see here how that God makes the "wrath of man" to praise Him (Psa. 76:10).

"And Saul and the men of Israel were gathered together and pitched by the valley of Elah, and set the battle in array against the Philistines" (17:2) The king had been relieved, for a season at least, of the evil spirit; but the Spirit of the Lord had not returned to him, as the sequel plainly evidences. A sorry figure did Saul and his forces now cut. "And there went out a champion out of the camp of the Philistines, named Goliath of Gath . . . . And he stood and cried unto the armies of Israel, and said unto them, Why are ye come out to set your battle in array? Am not I a Philistine, and ye servants to Saul? choose you a man for you, and let him come down to me. If he be able to fight with me, and to kill me, then will we be your servants; but if I prevail against him, and kill him, then shall ye be our servants, and serve us. And the Philistine said, I defy the armies of Israel this day; give me a man, that we may fight together. When Saul and all Israel heard those words of the Philistine, they were dismayed, and greatly afraid" (vv. 4, 8-11). Ere pondering the haughty challenge which was here thrown down, let us point out (for the strengthening of faith in the inerrancy of Holy Writ) a small detail which exhibits the minute accuracy and harmony of the Word.

In Numb. 13, we read that the spies sent out by Moses to inspect the promised land, declared, "The land through which we have gone to search it, is a land that eateth up the inhabitants thereof; and all the people that we saw in it are men of a great stature. And there we saw the *giants* the sons of *Anak* which come of the giants" (vv. 32, 33). Now link up with this Josh. 11:21, 22, "And at that time came Joshua, and cut off *the Anakims* from the mountains . . . . there was none of the Anakims left in the land of the children of Israel: only in Gaza, in *Gath*, and in Ashdod, there *remained.*" Here in our present passage it is stated, quite incidentally, that Goliath belonged to "Gath!" Thus, in the mouth of three witnesses — Moses, Joshua, and Samuel — is the word established, concurring as they do in a manner quite artless, to verify a single particular. How jealous was God about His Word! What a sure foundation faith has to rest upon!

Goliath pictures to us the great Enemy of God and man, the Devil, seeking to battle-field of faith! It is the genuine denying of self, the daily taking up of the prodigious size (probably over eleven feet) symbolized the great power of Satan. His accoutrements (compare the word "armour" in Luke 11:22!) figured the fact that the resources of flesh and blood can not overcome Satan. His blatant challenge adumbrated the roaring of the lion, our great adversary, as he goes about "seeking whom he may devour" (1 Pet. 5:8) His declaration that the Israelites were but "servants to Saul" (v. 8) was only too true, for they were no longer in subjection to the Lord (1 Sam. 8:7). The dismay of Saul (v. 11) is in solemn contrast from his boldness in 11:5-11 and 14:47, when the Spirit of the Lord was upon him. The terror of the people (v. 11) was a sad evidence of the fact that the "fear of the Lord" (11:7) was no longer upon them. But all of this only served to provide a background from which the courage of the man after God's own heart might the more evidently appear.

The terrible giant of Gath continued to menace the army of Israel twice a day for no less than forty days — a period which, in Scripture, is ever associated with probation and testing. Such a protracted season served to make the more manifest the impotency of a people out of communion with God. There was Saul himself, who "from his shoulders and upward was higher than any of the people" (9:2). There was Jonathan who, assisted only by his armour-bearer, had, on a former occasion, slain twenty of the Philistines (14:14). There was Abner, the captain of the host (14:50), a "valiant man" (26:15), but he too declined Goliath's challenge. Ah, my reader, the best, the bravest of men, are no more than what God makes them. When He renews not his courage, the stoutest heart is a coward. Yet God does not act arbitrarily, rather is cowardice one of the consequences of lost communion with Him: "The righteous are bold as a lion" (Prov. 28:1).

Man's extremity is God's opportunity. But He does not always, nor generally, act immediately, when we are brought low. Now, he*"waits to be gracious"* (Isa. 30:18), that our helplessness may be the more fully realized, that His delivering hand may be seen the more clearly, and that His merciful interposition may be the more appreciated. But even at this time, when all seemed lost to Israel, when there was none in her army that dared to pick up the gauntlet which Goliath had thrown down, God had His man in reserve, and in due time he appeared on the scene and vindicated the glorious name of Jehovah. The instrument chosen seemed, to natural wisdom and military prudence, a weak and foolish one, utterly unfitted for the work before him. Ah, it is just such that God uses, and why? That the honour may be His, that "no flesh should glory in His presence" (1 Cor. 1:29). Before considering the grand victory which the Lord wrought through David, let us carefully ponder the training which he had received in the school of God. This is deeply important for our hearts.

It was away from the crowds, in the quietude of pastoral life, that David was taught the wondrous resources which there are in God available to faith. There, in the fields of Bethlehem, he had, by Divine enablement, slain the lion and the bear (v. 34, 35). This is ever God's way: He teaches in secret that soul which He has elected shall serve Him in public. Ah, my reader, is it not just at this point that we may discover the explanation of our failures? — it is because we have not sufficiently cultivated the "secret place of the most High" (Psa. 91:1). *That* is our primary need. But do we really esteem communion with God our highest privilege? Do we realize that walking with God is the source of our strength?

There had been direct dealings between David's soul and God out there in the solitude of the fields, and it is only thus that any of us are taught how to get the victory. Have you yet learned, my brother or sister, that the closet is the great terrify, and bring into captivity those who bear the name of the Lord. His cross, the knowing how to cast down imaginations and every high thing that exalteth itself against the knowledge of God, and the bringing into captivity every thought to the obedience of Christ (2 Cor. 10:5). Let the foe be met and conquered in private and we shall not have to mourn defeat when we meet him in public. O may the Holy Spirit impress deeply upon each of our hearts the vital importance of coming forth from the presence of God as we enter upon any service unto Him: *this* it is which regulates the difference between success and failure. Note how the blessed Redeemer acted on this principle: Luke 6:12, 13, etc.!

"And Jesse said unto David his son, Take now for thy brethren an ephah of this parched corn, and these ten loaves, and run to the camp to thy brethren; And carry these ten cheeses unto the Captain of their thousand, and look how thy brethren fare, and take their pledge" (vv. 17, 18). Another beautiful type is this of our Saviour going about His Father's business, seeking the good of His *brethren:* a similar one is found in Gen. 37:13, 14. But without staying to develop this thought, let us observe how God was directing all things to the accomplishment of His purpose. Jesse had eight sons (16:10, 11), and only three of them had joined Saul's army (17:13), so that five of them were at home; yet David, the youngest, was the one sent — though Jesse knew it not, God had work for *him* to do. Nothing happens by chance in this world: *all* is controlled and directed from on High (John 19:11).

"And David rose up early in the morning, and left the sheep with a keeper, and took, and went, as Jesse had commanded him; and he came to the trench, as the host was going forth to fight, and shouted for the battle" (v. 20). How this evidenced the readiness and eagerness of David to obey his father's orders! Again we may look from the type to the Antitype, and hear Him say, "Lo, I come, to do Thy will, O God" (Heb. 10:7). Blessed it is to mark that David was as mindful of his father's sheep as he was of his commands: his leaving them "with a keeper," evidenced his care and fidelity in the discharge of his office. His faithfulness in a few things fitted him to be ruler over many things. He who is best qualified to command, is the one who had, previously, learned to obey.

"God's providence brought him to the camp very seasonably, when both sides had set the battle in array, and as it should seem were more likely to come to an engagement than they had yet been all the forty days (v. 21). Both sides were now preparing to fight. Jesse little thought of sending his son to the army just in that critical juncture; but the wise God orders the time, and all the circumstances, of actions and affairs, so as to serve His design of securing the interests of Israel, and advancing the man after His own heart" (Matt. Henry).

Though he had only just completed a long journey, we are told that David "ran into the army, and came and saluted his brethren" (v. 22). This reminds of Prov. 22:29 "Seest thou a man diligent in his business? he shall stand before kings." As David talked with his brethren, Goliath came forth again and repeated his challenge. The whole army was "sore afraid" (v. 24), and though reminding one another of the promised reward awaiting the one who slew the giant, none dared to venture his life — such inducements as Saul offered, sink into utter insignificance when *death* confronts a man. David mildly expostulated with those who stood near him, pointing out that Goliath was defying "the armies of the living God" (v. 26).

"And Eliab his eldest brother heard when he spake unto the men; and Eliab's anger was kindled against David, and he said, Why camest thou down hither? and with whom hast thou left those few sheep in the wilderness? I know thy pride, and the naughtiness of thine heart; for thou art come down that thou mightest see the battle" (v. 28). How this reminds us of what is said of David's Son and Lord in John 1:11, etc. There is a lesson here which every true minister of Christ does well to take to heart, for by so doing he will be forearmed against many a disappointment and discouragement. Sufficient for the disciple to be as his Master: if the incarnate Son was not appreciated, His agents should not expect to be — "For if I yet pleased men, I should not be the servant of Christ (Gal. 1:10). Not only will men in general be displeased, but even the people of God, when in a low state, will neither understand nor value the actings of *faith*. The man of God must be prepared to be misinterpreted and to stand alone.

Blessed it is to mark David's reply to the cruel taunt of his brother: it was a real testing of his meekness, but when he was reviled, he reviled not again. Nor did he attempt any self-vindication, or explanation of his conduct — such had been quite wasted upon one with such a spirit. First, he simply asked "What have I done": what fault have I committed to be thus chided; reminding us of our Lord's meek reply under a much stronger provocation — "Why smitest thou Me?" (John 18:23). Second, he said, "Is there not a cause?" This he left with him: there *was* a cause for his coming to the camp: his father had sent him: the honour of Israel — sullied by Goliath — required it; the glory of God necessitated it. Third, he "turned from him toward another" (v. 30).

David's speaking to one and another soon reached the ears of Saul, who accordingly sent for him (v. 31). To the king, he at once said, "Let no man's heart fail because of him; thy servant will go and fight with this Philistine" (v. 32); only to be met with this reply, "Thou art not able to go against this Philistine to fight with him." Ah, "Those that undertake great and public services must not think it strange if they be discountenanced and opposed by those from whom they have reason to expect support and assistance. But must humbly go on with their work, in the face not only of their enemies' threats, but of their friends sleights and suspicions" (M. Henry). The langauge used by him in the presence of the king was not the bravado of a boaster, but the God-honouring testimony of a man of faith. Saul and his people were in despair as the consequence of their being occupied with the things of sight: the man of faith had a contemptuous disdain for Goliath because he viewed him from God's viewpoint — as His enemy, as "uncircumcised." Note how he attributed his previous successes to the Lord, and how he improved them to count upon Him for further victory: see v. 37.

The response made by Saul unto David's pleading was solemnly ludicrous. First, he said "Go, and the Lord be with thee," which were idle words on such lips. Next we read that "Saul armed David with his own armour" (i. e., with some that he kept in his armory), in which he had far more confidence than in God. But David quickly perceived that such was unsuited to him: the one who has much to do with God in secret, cannot employ worldly means and methods in public; the man of faith has no use for carnal weapons. Such things as ecclesiastical titles, dress, ritualistic ceremonies, which are imposing to the eye of the natural man, are but bubbles and baubles to the spiritual. "And David put them off him" (v. 39), and advanced to meet the haughty Philistine with only a sling and five smooth stones. Should it be asked, But are we not justified in using *means?* The answer is, Yes, the means which *God* supplies (the "smooth stones"), but not that which man offers — his "armour."

"When the Philistine looked about and saw David, he disdained him" (v. 42). First, Eliab had taunted, then Saul had sought to discourage, and now Goliath scorns him. Ah, the one who (by grace) is walking by faith is neither chilled by a cold reception nor cooled by outward difficulties: it looks away from both, unto

Him with whom it has to do. If God be "for us" (Rom. 8:31), it matters not who be against us. Nevertheless, faith has to strengthen its fiber, to give occasion for its exercise. Well may writer and reader pray, "Lord, increase our faith."

The Philistine blustered, "cursed David by his gods" (v. 43), and vowed he would give his flesh unto the fowls and beasts. But it is written, "the race is not to the swift, nor the battle to the strong" (Eccl. 9:11); and again, "God resisteth the proud" (James 4:6). The response made by David at once revealed the secret of his confidence, the source of his strength, and the certainty of his victory: "I come to thee in the name of the Lord of hosts, the God of the armies of Israel, whom thou hast defied" (v. 45). Ah, "the name of the Lord is a strong tower, the righteous runneth into it, and is safe" (Prov. 18:10).

The reader is so familiar with the blessed sequel that little comment on it is required. Faith having brought God into the scene could announce the victory in advance (v. 46). One stone in its hand was worth more than all the Philistines armour on the giant of unbelief. And why? Because that stone, though flung by David's sling, was directed and made efficacious by the hand of God. It is pitiable to find how some of the best commentators missed the real point here. Verse 5 begins the description of Goliath's armour by saying "he had a helmet of brass upon his head": some have suggested this fell off when he lifted up his hand to curse David by his gods (v. 43); others supposed he left the visor open that he might see the better. But David's stone did not enter his eye, but his "forehead" — Divine power sent it through the helmet of brass! In David's cutting off his head (v. 51) we have a foreshadowment of what is recorded in Hebrews 2:14.

CHAPTER 18.

"And when he had finished speaking to Saul, the soul of Jonathan was joined with the soul of David, and Jonathan loved him as he did his own Soul. And Saul took him that day and would not let him go home to his father's house any more. Then Jonathan and David made a covenant, because he loved him as his own soul. And Jonathan stripped himself of the robe that he wore and gave it to David, it and all his clothing, even to his sword and to his bow and to his girdle. And David went out wherever Saul sent him, behaving himself wisely. And Saul set him over the men of war, and it was good in the sight of all the people, and also in the sight of Saul's servants. And when David had returned from the slaughter of the Philistines, as they came the women came out of all cities of Israel, singing and dancing, to meet King Saul with tabrets, with joy, and with instruments of music. And the women answered as they played, and said, Saul has slain his thousands, and David his ten thousands. And Saul was very angry, and the saying made him angry. And he said, They have given David ten thousands, and to me they have given only thousands. And what more can he have but the kingdom? And Saul eyed David from that day and forward. And on the next day the evil spirit from God came on Saul, and he prophesied in the midst of the house. And David played with his hand, as at other times. And there was a javelin in Saul's hand. And Saul threw the javelin. For he said, I will strike David even to the wall. And David drew back out of his presence twice. And Saul was afraid of David, because the Lord was with him and had departed from Saul" — 1 Samuel 18:1-12.

Had we sought a topical title for this article, "The Price of Popularity" might well have been selected. The 17th chapter of 1 Samuel closes by recounting the memorable victory of David over Goliath the Philistine giant; the 18th chapter informs us of a number of things which formed the sequel to that noteable achievement. There is much which those who are ambitious and covetous of earthly honour do well to take to heart. An accurate portrayal is given of different phases and features of human nature that is full of instruction for those who will duly ponder the same. Much is condensed into a small compass, but little imagination is required in order to obtain a vivid conception of what is there presented. One scene after another is passed in rapid review, but amid them all, the man after God's own heart acquitted himself admirably. May the Lord enable each of us to profit from what is here recorded for our learning.

"And it came to pass, when he had made an end of speaking unto Saul, that the soul of Jonathan was knit with the soul of David, and Jonathan loved him as his own soul" (1 Sam. 18:1 and cf. vv. 3, 4). Let us admire here the tender grace of God, and behold an illustration of a blessed principle in His dealings with us. Jonathan was the son of Saul, and, therefore (ordinarily), 'heir apparent to the throne.' But, as we have seen, David had been anointed unto that position. There was, therefore, occasion for Jonathan to look upon David as his rival, and to be filled with jealousy and hatred against him. Instead, his heart is united unto him with a tender affection. This should not be attributed to the amiability of his character, but is to be ascribed unto Him in whose hand are all our hearts and ways.

What we have just called attention to above, is not sufficiently recognized and pondered in these evil days, no, not even by the people of God. There is nothing recorded of Jonathan which really shows that he was a saved man, but not a little to the contrary — particularly in the closing scenes of his life. When, then,

the heart of a man of the world is drawn out to a saint, when he shows kindness
unto him, we should always discern the secret workings of God's power,
graciously exercised for us. He who employed ravens to feed His servant Elijah
(1 Kings 17), often moves the hearts and minds of unregenerate people to be
kind toward His children. It was the Lord who gave Joseph "favour in the sight
of the keeper of the prison" (Gen. 39:21), the Israelites "favour in the sight of
the Egyptians" (Ex. 3:21) at the time of their exodus, Esther in the sight of king
Ahasuerus (Est. 5:2). It is so still; and we only honour God when we perceive
and own this, and praise Him for it.

David's finding favour in the eyes of Jonathan was the more noteworthy, in
that the envy and enmity of Saul was soon stirred against him. What a mercy
from God was it, then, for David to have a true friend in his enemy's household!
— the value of it will come before us later. It was by this means that our hero
received warning and his safety was promoted. In like manner, there are few of
God's children unto whom He does not, in critical seasons, raise up those who
are kindly disposed toward them, and who in various ways help and succour
them. Thus it has been in the life of the writer, and we doubt not, with many of
our readers also. Let us admire the Lord's goodness and adore his faithfulness in
thus giving us the sympathy and assistance of unsaved friends in a hostile world.

"And Saul took him that day, and would let him go no more home to his
father's house" (v. 2). The purpose of God concerning David was beginning to
ripen. First, He had so over-ruled things, that Saul had sent for him to attend the
king occasionally in his fits of melancholia. But now David was made a
permanent member of the court. This was but fitting in view of the promise
which had been made to him by the king before he encountered Goliath: that if
victorious, Saul's daughter should be given to him to wife (17:25). Thus was
David being fitted for his royal duties. It is blessed when we are able to realize
that each providential change in our lives is another step toward the
accomplishing of the Divine counsels concerning us.

"And David went out whithersoever Saul sent him, and behaved himself wisely:
and Saul set him over the men of war, and he was accepted in the sight of all the
people, and also in the sight of Saul's servants" (v. 5). Beautiful it is to behold
here the humility and fidelity of the one upon whom the anointing oil already
rested: diligently had he fulfilled his trust in the sheepfold at Bethlehem,
dutifully did he now carry out the orders of the king. Let this be duly laid to
heart by any who are tempted to chafe under the situation which they now
occupy. "Whatsoever thy hand findeth to do, do it with thy might" (Ecc. 9:10),
defines the duty of each one of us. The teaching of the New Testament is, of
course, the same: "Not slothful in business; fervent in spirit" (Rom. 12: 11).
Whatever position you occupy, dear reader, no matter how humble or
distasteful, "whatsoever ye do, do it heartily, as to the Lord, and not unto men"
(Col. 3:23).

"And behaved himself wisely." How very few do so! How many have, through
injudicious conduct, not only hindered their spiritual progress, but ruined their
earthly prospects. Such a word as the one now before us needs to be turned into
prayer — believing, fervent, persevering. Especially is that counsel timely unto
the young. We need to ask God to enable us to carry ourselves wisely in every
situation in which He has placed us: that we may redeem the time, be on our
guard against temptations, and perform each duty to the very best of our ability.
"Be ye wise as serpents, and harmless as doves" (Matt. 10:16), does not mean,
be compromisers and temporisers, tricky and deceitful; but, take into
consideration the fickleness of human nature and trust none but God. In David's

behaving himself "wisely" he points again unto Him of whom God said, "Behold, My Servant shall deal prudently" (Isa. 52:13).

Saul now set David "over the men of war": though not made commander-in-chief, some high military office was given him, possibly over the king's bodyguard. This was a further step toward the equipping of David for his life's work: there was much fighting ahead of him, powerful enemies of Israel which had to be conquered; thus was God making all things "work together" for his good. What a change from the obscurity and peace of pastoral life, to becoming a courtier and soldier. "And he was accepted in the sight of all the people, and also in the sight of Saul's servants." God gave their future ruler favour in the eyes both of the common people and of the court. How this reminds us of what is recorded of the Antitype: "And Jesus increased in wisdom and stature, and in favour with God and man" (Luke 2:52).

"And it came to pass as they came, when David was returned from the slaughter of the Philistine, that the women came out of all cities of Israel, singing and dancing, to meet king Saul, with tabrets, with joy, and with instruments of music. And the women answered as they played, and said, Saul hath slain his thousands, and David his ten thousands" (vv. 6, 7). How this incident served to make manifest the low spiritual state into which the nation of Israel had now sunk. "Out of the abundance of the heart the mouth speaketh" (Matt. 12:34): the language we employ, is a sure index to the condition of our souls, "They are *of* the world, therefore *speak* they of the world" (1 John 4:5). It is indeed distressing, yet ought not to be surprising, that so very, very few professing Christians in their general conversation with each other, "minister grace unto the hearers" (Eph. 4:29) — not surprising, because the great majority of them are strangers to the power of godliness.

The language used by the women of Israel when celebrating the death of Goliath and the defeating of the Philistines, gave plain indication that their hearts and minds were occupied only with the human victors. "God was not in all their thoughts" (Psa. 10:4). Alas that this is so often the case today: we are living in an age of hero worship, and Christendom itself is infected by this evil spirit. Man is eulogized and magnified on every hand, not only out in the world, but even in the so-called churches, Bible conferences, and religious periodicals — seen in the advertising of the speakers, the printing of their photos, and the toadying to them. O how little hiding behind the cross, how little self-effacement there is today. "Cease ye from *man*" (Isa. 2:22), needs to be placed in large letters over the platforms of all the big religious gatherings in this man-deifying age. No wonder the Holy Spirit is "grieved" and "quenched," yet where are the voices being raised in faithful protest?

"And the women answered as they played, and said, Saul hath slain his thousands, and David his ten thousands." What a sad contrast was this from what we find recorded in Ex. 15! A far greater overthrow of the enemy was witnessed by Israel at the Red Sea, than what had just taken place in the valley of Elah (1 Sam. 17:19). Yet we do not find the mothers of these women of Israel magnifying Moses and singing *his* praises. Instead, we hear Miriam saying to her sisters, "Sing ye to the Lord, for *He* hath triumphed gloriously: the horse and his rider hath He thrown into the sea" (v. 21). Jehovah was there given His true place, the victory being ascribed to Him and not to the human instruments. See to it dear reader, that — no matter what the common and evil custom be to the contrary — you give *all* the glory to Him unto whom alone it rightfully belongs.

"And Saul was very wrath, and the saying displeased him; and he said, They have ascribed unto David ten thousands, and to me they have ascribed but thousands: and what can he have more but the kingdom?" (v. 8). The song of the women was not only dishonouring to God, but was impolitic as well. As we saw in v. 15, David "behaved himself *wisely*"; but the conduct of Israel's daughters was in sharp contrast therefrom. The honouring of David above Saul, was more than the king's proud heart could endure: the activity of the "flesh" in the women acted upon the "flesh" in him. Unable to rejoice in what God had wrought through the superior praises of David being sung; he could not tolerate the thought of being second.

Perhaps someone may be inclined to raise the question, Why did not God restrain those women from exalting David in song above Saul (as He could easily have done), and thus prevented the rising of the king's jealousy? Several answers may be returned to this query: it subserved God's purpose, and promoted the spiritual good of David. God often withholds His curbing hand in order that it may the better appear what is in fallen and unregenerate man. Were He not to do so, the distinction between the children of God and the children of the Devil would not be so evident. Moreover, David was being flattered, and flattery is ever a dangerous thing; therefore does God often wisely and mercifully check our proud hearts from being unduly elated thereby, by causing some to think and speak evil of us.

"For every great and good work a man must expect to be envied by his neighbor: no distinction or pre-eminence can be so unexceptionably obtained, but it will expose the possessor to slander and malice, and perhaps to the most fatal consequences. But such trials are very *useful* to those who love God, they serve as a counterpoise to the honour put upon them, and check the growth of pride and attachment to the world; they exercise them to faith, patience, meekness, and communion with God; they give them a fair opportunity of exemplifying the amiable nature and tendency of true godliness, by acting with wisdom and propriety in the most difficult circumstances; they make way for increasing experience of the Lord's faithfulness, in restraining their enemies, raising them up friends, and affording them His gracious protection; and they both prepare them for those stations in which they are to be employed, and open their way to them: for in due time modest merit will shine forth with double lustre" (T. Scott).

Ere passing on, let it be remembered that each detail of this chapter, and every thing in the Old Testament Scriptures, is "written for our learning" (Rom. 15:4). Especially does it need to be emphasized for the benefit of the young, that lavish commendations from those who admire and love us, in such a world as this, often prove a real injury; and in all cases every thing should be avoided which can excite and envy opposition — except the performance of our duty to God and man. "Woe unto you when all men shall speak well of you" (Luke 6:26). During the twelve years he was in the pastorate, the writer deemed it expedient to retire into the vestry as soon as the service was over: the "flesh" loves to hear the eulogies of the people, but they are not conducive to humility. "Seekest thou great things for thyself? *seek them not*" (Jer. 45:5).

"And Saul eyed David from that day and forward" (v. 9). Perceiving that David was looked upon favourably by the people (v. 5), jealous of the praise which was accorded him (v. 7), fearful that he might soon lose the kingdom (v. 8), Saul now regarded the slayer of Goliath with a malignant eye. Instead of looking upon David with esteem and gratitude, as he should have done because of his gallant behaviour, he jealously observed his ways and actions, biding his time to do him injury. What a solemn example does this provide of the inconstancy of poor human nature! Only a little before Saul had "loved him greatly" (16:21), and now he hated him. Beware, my reader, of the fickleness of the human heart. There is only One who can truthfully say "I change not" (Mal. 3:6).

If David was counting upon the stability of Saul's affection for him, if he concluded that his military prowess had established him in the king's favour, he was now to meet with a rude awakening. Instead of gratitude, there was cruel envy; instead of kindly treatment, his very life was sought. And this too is recorded for our instruction. The Holy Scriptures not only unveil to us the attributes of God, but they also reveal to us the character of man. Fallen human nature is faithfully depicted as it actually is. The more attentively God's Word be pondered and its teachings and principles absorbed, the better will we be fortified against many a bitter disappointment. There is no excuse for any of us being deceived by people: if we took to heart the solemn warnings which the Bible furnishes, we should be far more upon our guard, and would heed such exhortations as are found in Psa. 146:3, Prov. 17:18, Jer. 9:4; 17:5; Micah. 7:5.

"And it came to pass on the morrow, that the evil spirit from God came upon Saul, and he prophesied in the midst of the house. And David played with his hand, as at other times; and there was a javelin in Saul's hand. And Saul cast the javelin; for he said, I will smite David even to the wall. And David avoided out of his presence twice" (vv. 10, 11). How swiftly troubles follow on the heels of triumphs! What a contrast between hearing the acclaiming songs of the women, and dodging a murderous weapon! And yet how true to life! Well, then, does each of us need to seek grace that we may learn to hold everything down here with a light hand. Rightly did one of the Puritans counsel, "Build not thy nest in any earthly tree, for the whole forest is doomed to destruction." It is only as the heart is set upon things above that we find an object which will never disappoint nor pall.

"The evil spirit came from God upon Saul." Yes, the wicked as well as the righteous, evil spirits as well as holy angels, are under the absolute and immediate control of God, cf Judges 9:23. But let us not miss the solemn *connection* between what is recorded in v. 9 and in v. 10: when we indulge jealousy and hatred, we give place to the Devil (Eph. 4:26, 27). "And he prophesied:" all prophesyings are not inspired by the Holy Spirit, that is why we need to heed 1 John 4:1. Observe the enemy's subtilty: no doubt Saul's prophesying was designed to take David off his guard — he would least expect an attempt on his life at such a time. Blessed is it to note that after avoiding the deadly weapon cast at him, David did not pick it up and hurl it at Saul; instead, he quietly withdrew from his presence. May like grace be granted unto both writer and reader when tempted to retaliate upon those who wrong us.

"Therefore Saul moved him away from himself and made him his captain over a thousand. And he went out and came in before the people. And David behaved himself wisely in all his ways. And the Lord was with him. Therefore when Saul saw that he behaved himself very wisely, he was afraid of him. But all Israel and Judah loved David, because he went out and came in before them. And Saul said to David, Behold, I will give you my older daughter Merab for a wife. Only you must be brave for me and fight the Lord's battles. For Saul said, Let not my hand be on him, but let the hand of the Philistines be on him. And David said to Saul, Who am I, and what is my life, or my father's family in Israel, that I should be son-in-law to the king? But at the time when Merab, Saul's daughter, should have been given to David, she was given to Adriel the Meholathite to be his wife. And Saul's daughter Michal loved David. And they told Saul, and the thing

pleased him. And Saul said, I will give her to him, so that she may be a trap to him, and so that the hand of the Philistines may be against him. Therefore Saul said to David, Today you shall be my son-in-law the second time. And Saul commanded his servant, saying, Talk with David secretly and say, Behold, the king delights in you, and all his servants love you. Now therefore be the king's son-in-law. And Saul's servants spoke these words in the ears of David. And David said, Does it seem to you a light thing to be a king's son-in-law, since I am a poor man and of little worth? And the servants of Saul told him saying, This is the way David spoke. And Saul said, You shall say this to David, The king does not desire any dowry except a hundred foreskins of the Philistines, to be avenged of the king's enemies. But Saul thought to make David fall by the hand of the Philistines. And when his servants told David these words, it was right in the eyes of David to be the king's son-in-law. And the days were not fulfilled. Therefore David arose and went forth, he and his men. And they killed two hundred men of the Philistines. And David brought their foreskins, and they gave them in full number to the king so that he might be the king's son-in-law. And Saul gave him his daughter Michal for a wife. And Saul saw and knew that the Lord was with David, and that Michal, Saul's daughter, loved him. And Saul was still more afraid of David. And Saul became David's enemy continually. Then the leaders of the Philistines came forth. And after they came forth, David behaved himself more wisely than all the servants of Saul, so that his name was very precious" — 1 Samuel 18:12-30. (KJ II)

Human nature is very apt to turn eyes of envy upon those who occupy exalted positions. It is commonly supposed that they who are stationed in seats of eminence and honour enjoy many advantages and benefits which are denied those beneath them; but this is far more imaginary than real, and where true is offset by the added responsibilities incurred and the more numerous temptations which are there encountered. What was before us in our last article ought to correct the popular delusion. David on the plains of Bethlehem was far better off than David in the king's household: tending the sheep was less exciting than waiting upon Saul. Amid the green pastures he was free from jealous courtiers, the artificial etiquette of the palace, and the javelin of a mad monarch. The practical lesson to be learned by us is, to be contented with the lowly position which the providence of God has assigned us. And why should those who are joint-heirs with Christ be concerned about the trifles and toys of this world?

Resuming now at the point where we broke off, we next read, "And Saul was afraid of David, because the Lord was with him, and was departed from Saul" (1 Sam. 18:12). The word for "afraid" here is a milder one than that employed in v. 15, and might be rendered "apprehensive." The king was becoming increasingly uneasy about the future. Consequent upon his disobedience, the prophet of God had plainly told Saul, "Because thou hast rejected the word of the Lord, He hath also rejected thee from being king," and then he added, "The Lord hath rent the kingdom of Israel from thee this day, and hath given it to a neighbour of thine, that is better than thou" (15:23, 28). While he was probably ignorant of David's anointing (16:13), it is plain that Saul was now growing more fearful that the man who had vanquished Goliath was he whom Jehovah had selected to succeed him.

First, it was evident to all that the Lord had given the young shepherd the victory over Goliath, for none had dared, in his own courage, to engage the mighty giant. Second, David's behaving himself so wisely in every position assigned him, and his being "accepted in the sight of all the people, and also in the sight of Saul's servants" (18:5), indicated that he would be popular with the masses were he to ascend the throne. Third, the song of the women caused the jealous king to draw his own conclusion: "they have ascribed unto David ten thousands, and to me they have ascribed thousands, and what can he have more but *the kingdom?*" (v. 8). And now that his personal attack upon David's life had been frustrated (v. 11), Saul was apprehensive, for he saw that the Lord was with David, while he knew that He had forsaken himself.

"And Saul was afraid of David, because the Lord was with him" (v. 12). The proofs that the special favour of God rested upon David were too plain and numerous for Saul to deny. Jehovah was protecting and preserving, prospering and succeeding David, giving him victory over his enemies and acceptance in the sight of the people. Ah, my reader, when the smile of the Lord is resting upon any of His saints, even the wicked are obliged to take note of and acknowledge the same. The chief captain of Abimelech's host admitted to Abraham "God is *with thee* in all that thou doest" (Gen. 21:22) — what a testimony was that from a heathen! When Joseph was in the house of Potiphar, we are told, "And his master *saw* the Lord was with him" (Gen. 39:3). Can those among whom our lot is cast perceive that the special blessing of Heaven is resting upon us? If not, our hearts ought to be deeply exercised before God.

"And Saul was afraid of David, because the Lord was with him, and was departed from Saul." An additional cause of Saul's alarm was the knowledge that the Lord had departed from him, and therefore was he destitute of strength of mind and courage, wisdom and prudence, and had become mean and abject, and exposed to the contempt of his subjects. The reference is to 16:14. A solemn warning is this for us. It was because of his rebellion against the Lord, that Saul was now deserted of God. How often God withdraws His sensible and comforting presence from His people, through their following of a course of self-will. "He that hath My commandments and keepeth them, he it is that loveth Me: and he that loveth Me shall be loved of My Father, and I will love him, and will *manifest* myself to him" (John 14:21).

"Therefore Saul removed him from him, and made him his captain over a thousand; and he went out and came in before the people" (v. 13). Solemn indeed is it to behold how Saul acted here. Instead of humbling himself before God, he sought to rid himself of the man whose presence condemned him. Instead of judging himself unsparingly for the sin which had caused the Spirit of God to leave him, the wretched king was loath to look any more at the one upon whom Jehovah's favour manifestly rested. How differently did sinning David act at a later date! Behold him as he cries, "For I acknowledge my transgressions, and my sin is ever before me. Against Thee, Thee only, have I sinned, and done this evil in Thy sight . . . Cast me not away from Thy presence; and take not Thy Holy Spirit from me" (Psa. 51:3, 4, 11). Ah, here is the great difference between the unregenerate and regenerate: the one harden themselves in their sin, the other are broken before God on account of it.

"Therefore Saul removed him from him, and made him his captain over a thousand; and he went out and came in before the people." But let us admire again the hand of God over-ruling, yea, directing, the reprobate monarch's actions to the carrying out of His own designs. Though it was hatred of his person that caused the king to remove David from the court, and perhaps partly to please his subjects and partly because he hoped he might be slain in battle, that our hero was now made captain over a regiment; yet this only served the more to ingratiate him with the people, by affording him the opportunity of leading them to victory over their enemies. Abundant opportunity was thus afforded to all Israel to become acquainted with David and all his ways.

Let us also take note of another line in the typical picture here. Though anointed king of Israel (16:13), David was, nevertheless, called upon to endure the hatred of the ruling power. Thus it was with David's Son the Lord. The One who lay in Bethlehem's manger was none other than "*Christ* ("the Anointed") the Lord" (Luke 2:11), and "born King of the Jews" (Matt. 2:2); yet the king of Judea sought His life (Matt. 2:16) — though fruitlessly, as in our type. So too at a later date, when His public ministry had begun, we read that, "the Pharisees went out and held a council against Him, how they might destroy Him" (Matt. 12:14). Blessed is it to see how that, instead of attempting to take things into his own hands, David was content to quietly wait the time which God had appointed for his coronation. In like manner, our blessed Lord willingly endured the "sufferings" before He entered into His "glory." May Divine grace grant unto us all needed patience.

"And David behaved himself wisely in all ways; and the Lord was with him" (v. 14). Observe that little word "all," and turn it into prayer and practice. Whether on the farm, in the court, or on the battlefield, the man after God's own heart conducted himself prudently. Here too he foreshadowed Him of whom it was declared "He hath done *all* things *well*" (Mark 7:37). Let this ever be our desire and aim. "And the Lord was with him," protecting and prospering. That word in 2 Chron. 15:2 still holds good, "The Lord is with you, while ye be with Him: and if ye seek Him, He will be found of you; but if ye forsake Him, He will forsake you." If we diligently seek to cultivate a daily walk with God, all will be well with us.

"Wherefore when Saul saw that he behaved himself very wisely, he was afraid of him. But all Israel and Judah loved David, because he went out and came in before them" (vv. 15, 16). When the God-forsaken king perceived that he had gained no advantage against David, but that instead he succeeded in all his undertakings, and was more and more in favour with the people, Saul was greatly alarmed, lest the hour was drawing near when the kingdom should be rent from him and given to his rival. When the wicked discern that the awe and blessing of God is upon the righteous, they are "afraid" of them: thus we read that "Herod feared John, knowing that he was a just man and an holy" (Mark 6:20). When it is known that God is in the assemblies of His saints, even the great ones of the earth are convinced and rendered uneasy: see Psa. 48:2-6.

"And Saul said to David, Behold my elder daughter Merab, her will I give thee to wife: only be thou valiant for me, and fight the Lord's battles. For Saul said, Let not mine hand be upon him, but let the hand of the Philistines be upon him" (v. 17). This was said not in friendship and good-will to David, but as designed to lay a snare for him. Thoroughly obsessed with envy, the king was unable to rest. If it could be accomplished without incurring direct guilt, he was determined to encompass David's destruction. Formerly he had made a personal attack upon his life (18:11), but now he feared the people, with whom David was so popular (v. 16); so Saul deemed it wiser to devise this vile plot. He would have David work out his own doom. Remarkable is it to note that this was the very way in which Saul's own career was ended — he was slain by the Philistines: see 1 Sam. 31:1-5.

"Only be thou valiant for me and fight the Lord's battles. For Saul said, Let not mine hand be upon him, but let the hand of the Philistines be upon him." Was this incident before David when he wrote, "The words of his mouth were smoother than butter, but war was in his heart; his words were softer than oil, yet were they drawn swords" (Psa. 55:21)! How unspeakably dreadful was this:

here was a man with murder in his heart, deliberately plotting the death of a fellow-creature; yet, at that very moment, talking about "fighting *the Lord's* battles"! O how often is the vilest hypocrisy cloaked with spiritual language! How easy it is to be deceived by fair *words!* How apt would be the bystanders, who heard this pious language of Saul, to conclude that the king was a very godly man. Ah, my reader, learn well this truth: it is *actions* which speak louder than words.

"And David said unto Saul, Who am I? and what is my life, or my father's family in Israel, that I should be son-in-law to the king"? (v. 18). Some of the commentators have supposed that Saul promised David his daughter to wife at the time when he went forth to engage Goliath; but there is nothing in Scripture which directly supports this. What is recorded in 17:25 was the words of Israel, and not of the king — they *supposed* he would do this and more. When Saul's proposal was made known to him, the modesty and humility of David was at once manifested. Some think that the reference made by David to his "family," had in view his descent from Ruth the Moabitess.

It is blessed to behold the lowly spirit which was displayed by David on this occasion. No self-seeking time-server was he. His heart was occupied in faithfully performing each duty assigned him, and he aspired not after earthly honours and fleshly advantages. "Who am I?" at once evidenced the mean estimate which he entertained of himself. Ah, *that* is the man whom the Lord uses and promotes: "God resisteth the proud, but giveth grace unto the humble" (James 4:6). "And what is my life?", breathes the same sentiment: the pitting of *my* life against the Philistine is no equivalent to receiving the *king's* daughter in marriage. Here again we see the subject of these articles adumbrating the perfections of his Lord: "learn of Me, for I am meek and *lowly in heart"* (Matt. 11:29) gives us what the modesty of David but imperfectly represented. Let writer and reader earnestly seek grace to heed that word "not to think of himself more highly than he ought to think; but to think soberly" (Rom. 12:3).

"But it came to pass at the time when Merab Saul's daughter should have been given to David, that she was given unto Adriel the Meholathite to wife" (v. 19). What was the word of such a man worth? Be very slow, dear reader, in resting upon the promises of a fallen creature. No doubt the perfidy of the king in so grossly affronting David was designed to anger him: such shameful treatment was calculated to stir up to mutiny one who had the right to claim the fulfillment of Saul's agreement; and thus the king thought he could gain an advantage against him. It is striking and solemn to discover that the curse of God rested upon that marriage; for the five sons born by Merab to the Meholathite (brought up by Michal) were delivered into the hands of the Gibeonites, and "hanged" (2 Sam. 21:8,9).

"And Michal Saul's daughter loved David: and they told Saul, and the thing pleased him. And Saul said, I will give him her, that she may be a snare to him, and that the hand of the Philistines may be against him" (vv. 20, 21). A new opportunity now presented itself unto the wicked king's purpose. Michal, another of his daughters, fell in love with David: he therefore proposed to give her to him for a wife instead of Merab, hoping that he would now have opportunity of bringing about his death. But let us look beyond the Devil-possessed monarch, and behold and admire the wondrous ways of Him who maketh "all things work together for good" to them that love Him. Just as of old the Lord turned the heart of the daughter of Pharaoh unto Moses and thus foiled the evil designs of her father to destroy all the male children of the Hebrews, so He now drew out the affections of Michal unto David, and used her to thwart the murderous intentions of Saul: see 19:11-17. What a proof that *all* hearts are in God's hands!

Conscious that his own word would have no weight with him, the king slyly employed his servants to gain David's confidence. They were commanded to commune with him "secretly," and to assure him "the king hath *delight* in thee, and all of his servants love thee: now therefore be the king's son-in-law" (v. 22). When the secret restraints of God are withdrawn from them "the heart of the sons of men is fully set in them to do evil" (Eccl. 8:11). They will scruple at nothing, but employ any and every means to hand for accomplishing their evil designs: they will flatter and praise or criticize and condemn, advance or abase, the object of their spleen, as best serves their purpose.

When his servants made known unto Saul David's reply, the real design of the king became apparent. "The condition of the marriage must be that he kill a hundred Philistines, and, as proof that those he had slain were uncircumcised, he must bring in their foreskins cut off. This would be a great reproach upon the Philistines, who hated circumcision, as it was an ordinance of God; and perhaps David's doing this would the more exasperate them against him; and make them seek to be revenged on him, which was the thing Saul desired and designed" (M. Henry). Even to such a stipulation David did not demur: knowing that God was with him, jealous of His glory to slay His enemies, he went forth and killed double the number required. Verily, God maketh the wrath of man to praise Himself (Psa. 76:10).

When David was informed of the king's intention, his reply again evidenced the lowliness of his heart: "Seemeth it to you a light thing to be a king's son-in-law, seeing that I am a poor man, and lightly esteemed?" — by the king (v. 23). From what follows, it seems evident that David was here pointing out his inability to bring the king's daughter the dowry that might be expected: compare Genesis 29:18; 34:12; Exodus 22:16, 17. Beautifully has Matthew Henry, in his comments on this verse, pointed out: "If David thus magnified the honour of being son-in-law to the king, how highly then should we think of it to be the sons (not in law, but in Gospel) to the King of kings! 'Behold what manner of love the Father hath bewtowed upon us!' (1 John 3:1). Who are we that we should be thus dignified?" Utterly unable as we were to bring any "dowry" to recommend us unto God.

At the close of 1 Sam. 18 there is a very striking word recorded which supplies a most blessed line in the typical picture that was furnished by the man after God's own heart. There we read, "David behaved himself more wisely than all the servants of Saul; so that his name was much set by" — the marginal reading is still more suggestive: "so that his name was *precious.*" What a lovely foreshadowing was this of Him whose "Name" is "as ointment poured forth" (Song of Sol. 1:3)! Yes, both to His Father and to His people the name of Christ is "much set by." He has "obtained a more excellent name" than angels bear (Heb. 1:4); yea, He has been given "a name which is above every name" (Phil. 2:9). "Precious" beyond description is that Name unto His own: they plead it in prayer (John 14:13); they make it their "strong tower" (Prov. 18:10).

CHAPTER 19.

"And Saul said to Jonathan his son, and to all his servants, that they should kill David. But Jonathan, Saul's son, loved David very much. And Jonathan told David, saying, My father Saul seeks to kill you. Now therefore, I beg you, be careful until morning, and stay in a secret place, and hide yourself. And I will go out and stand beside my father in the field where you are, and I will talk about you with my father. And I will tell you what I see. And Jonathan spoke good of David to Saul his father. And he said to him, Do not let the king sin against his servant, against David, because he has not sinned against you, and because his works have been very good toward you. For he took his life in his hand and killed the Philistines, and the Lord worked out a great salvation for all Israel. You saw it and rejoiced! Why then will you sin against innocent blood, to kill David without a cause? And Saul listened to the voice of Jonathan. And Saul swore, As the Lord lives, he shall not be killed! And Jonathan called David, and Jonathan showed him all these things. And Jonathan brought David to Saul, and he was in his presence as in times past. And there was war again. And David went out and fought with the Philistines and killed them with a great slaughter. And they fled from him. And the evil spirit from the Lord was on Saul as he sat in his house with his javelin in his hand. And David played with his hand. And Saul thought to strike David even to the wall with the javelin. But he slipped away out of Saul's presence, and he struck the javelin into the wall. And David ran and escaped that night. Saul also sent messengers to David's house to watch him and to kill him in the morning. And David's wife Michal told him saying, If you do not save your life tonight, tomorrow you shall be killed. So Michal let David down through a window. And he left. And he hurried away and escaped. And Michal took an image and laid it in the bed, and put a pillow of goats' hair at his head, and covered it with a cloth. And when Saul sent messengers to take David, she said, He is sick. And Saul sent the messengers again to see David, saying, Bring him up to me in the bed so that I may kill him. And when the messengers had come in, behold, there was an image in the bed with a pillow of goats' hair at its head. And Saul said to Michal, Why have you deceived me so and sent away my enemy so that he has escaped? And Michal answered Saul, He said to me, Let me go — why should I kill you? So David fled, and escaped, and came to Samuel to Ramah, and told him all that Saul had done to him. And he and Samuel went and lived in Naioth. And it was told Saul, saying, Behold, David is at Naioth in Ramah. And Saul sent messengers to take David. And when they saw the company of the prophets prophesying, and Samuel standing as appointed over them, the Spirit of God was on the messengers again the third time, and they prophesied also. Then he also went to Ramah and came to a great wall that is in Sechu. And he asked and said, Where are Samuel and David? And one said, Behold they are at Naioth in Ramah. And he went there to Naioth in Ramah. And the Spirit of God was on him also, and he went on and prophesied, until he came to Naioth in Ramah. And he stripped off his clothes also, and prophesied before Samuel in the same way, and lay down maked all that day and all that night. Therefore they say, Is Saul also among the prophets?" — I Samuel 19:1-24.

"And Saul spoke to Jonathan his son, and to all his servants, that they should kill David" (1 Sam. 19:1). How vivid and how solemn is the contrast presented between the last sentence of the preceding chapter and the opening one of this! And yet perhaps the spiritually-minded would hardly expect anything else. When

181

the "name" of the "Beloved" (for that is what "David" signifies) is "much set by," we are prepared to see the immediate raging of the Enemy — personified here by Saul. Yes, the picture here presented to our view is true to life. Nothing is more calculated to call into action the enmity of the Serpent against the woman's Seed than the extolling of His "name," with all that that scripturally includes. It was thus in the days of the apostles. When they announced that "There is none other Name under heaven given among men whereby we must be saved" (Acts 4:12), the Jewish leaders "commanded them not to speak at all nor teach in the name of Jesus" (v. 18); and because they heeded not, the apostle's were "beaten" and again commanded "not to speak in the name of Jesus" (Acts 5:40).

The previous plot of Saul upon David's life had failed. Instead of his being slain by the Philistines, they fell under the hand of David, and the consequence was that the son of Jesse became more esteemed than ever by the people. His name was held in high honour among them. Thus it was too with his Antitype: the more the chief priests and Pharisees persecuted the Lord Jesus, the more the people sought after Him: "From that day forth they took counsel together for to put Him to death. . .and the Jews' passover was nigh at hand: and many went out of the country up to Jerusalem before the passover, to purify themselves. Then they sought for Jesus" (John 11:53, 55, 56). So it was after His ascension: the more His witnesses were persecuted, the more the Gospel prospered. There seems little room for doubt that the death of Stephen was one of the things used by God to convict him who afterwards became the mighty apostle to the Gentiles. When the early church was assailed, we are told, "Therefore they that were scattered abroad went everywhere preaching the Word" (Acts 8:4). Thus does God make the wrath of man to praise Him.

Saul was growing desperate, and now hesitated not to make known unto his own son his fierce hatred of David. Yet here again we may behold and admire the directing hand of Providence, in the king's not concealing his murderous desire from Jonathan. The son shared not his father's enmity, accordingly we read, "But Jonathan Saul's son delighted much in David: and Jonathan told David, saying, Saul my father seeketh to kill thee: now therefore, I pray thee, take heed to thyself until the morning, and abide in a secret place, and hide thyself: and I will go out and stand beside my father in the field where thou art, and I will commune with my father of thee; and what I see, that I will tell thee" (19:1, 2). It is blessed to see such true and disinterested friendship for it should not be forgotten that Jonathan was the natural heir to the throne. Here we see him faithfully acquainting David of his danger, and counselling him to take precautionary measures against it.

Not only did Jonathan warn his beloved friend of the evil intentions of his father, but he also intreated the king on his behalf. Beautiful it is to see him interceding before Saul (vv. 4, 5), at the imminent risk of bringing down his anger upon his own head. Jonathan reminded Saul that David had never wronged him; so far from it, he had delivered Israel from the Philistines, and had thus saved the king's throne; why then should he be so set upon shedding "innocent blood." Jonathan must not here be regarded as a type of Christ, rather is he a vivid contrast. Jonathan's plea was based upon David's personal merits. It is very opposite in the case of the Christian's Intercessor. Our great High Priest appears before the King of the universe on behalf of His people not on the ground of any good *they* have done, but solely on the ground of that perfect satisfaction or obedience which *He* offered to Divine justice on their behalf; no merits of theirs can He plead, but His own perfect sacrifice prevails for them.

Jonathan's intercession was successful: "And Saul hearkened unto the voice of Jonathan" (v. 6). He not only gave his son a fair hearing, but was duly impressed by the arguments used, and was convicted for the present that he was wrong in seeking the life of David. Yet here again the intercession of Jonathan and that of the Lord Jesus for His people are in striking contrast: the former had naught but a temporary and transient effect upon his father, whereas that of our Advocate is eternally efficacious — forever be His name praised. "And Saul sware, As the Lord liveth, he shall not be slain" (v. 6). Once more we see how easy it is for wicked men to make use of pious expressions, and appear to superficial observers very godly men. The sequel shows of what little value is the solemn oath of a king, and warns us to place no confidence in the engagements of earthly rulers. They who are acquainted with the Scriptures are not surprised when even national and international treaties become only worthless "scraps of paper."

Reassured by Jonathan, David returned to Saul's household (v. 7). But not for long: a fresh war (probably local, and on a small scale) broke out with the Philistines. This called for David to resume his military activities, which he did with great success (v. 8), killing many of the enemy and putting the remainders to flight. A blessed example does the man after God's own heart here set us. Though serving a master that little appreciated his faithful efforts, nay, who had vilely mistreated him, our hero did not refuse to perform his present duty. "David continues his good services to his king and country. Though Saul had requited him evil for good, and even his usefulness was the very thing for which Saul envied him, yet he did not therefore retire in sullenness, and decline public service. Those that are ill paid for doing good, yet must not be weary of well-doing, remembering what a bountiful benefactor our heavenly Father is" (Matt. Henry).

"And the evil spirit from the Lord was upon Saul, as he sat in his house with his javelin in his hand" (v. 9). The opening word of this verse seems to intimate that the fresh victory of David over the Philistines stirred up the spiteful jealousy of the king, and thus by "giving place to the devil" (Eph. 4:26, 27) became susceptible again to the evil spirit. "And David played with his hand," no doubt upon the harp. One who had been so successful upon the battlefield, and was held in such honour by the people, might have deemed such a service as beneath his dignity; but a gracious man considers no ministry too humble by which he may do good to another. Or, he might have objected on the basis of the danger he incurred the last time he performed this office for Saul (18:10), but he counted upon God to preserve him in the path of duty.

"And Saul sought to smite David even to the wall with the javelin" (v. 10). In view of his so recently acceding to his son's intercession and swearing that David should not be slain, our present verse furnishes an illustration of a solemn and searching principle. How often unsaved people, after sudden conviction have *resolved* to break from their evil doings and serve the Lord, but only after a short season to return to their course of sin, like a washed sow to her wallowing in the mire (2 Pet. 2:22). Where there has been no miracle of mercy wrought within the heart, no change of disposition, and where there is no dependence upon Divine grace for needed strength, resolutions, however sincere and earnest, seldom produce any lasting effect. Unmortified lusts quickly break through the most solemn vows; where the fear of God does not possess the heart, fresh temptations soon arouse the dormant corruptions, and this gives Satan good opportunity to regain complete mastery over his victim.

"But he slipped away out of Saul's presence, and he smote the javelin into the wall; and David fled, and escaped that night" (v. 10). How wonderful is the care of God for His own! Though invisible, how real are His protecting arms! ' Not a shaft of hate can hit, till the God of love sees fit." What peace and stability it brings to the heart when faith realizes that "The angel of the Lord encampeth round about them that fear Him, and delivereth them" (Psa. 34:7). Men may be filled with malice against us, Satan may rage and seek our destruction, but none can touch a hair of our heads without God's permission. The Lord Almighty is the "Shield and Buckler," the "Rock and Fortress" of all those who put their trust in Him. Yet note that David was not foolhardy and wreckless. Faith is not presumptuous: though we are to trust Him, we are forbidden to *tempt* the Lord; therefore it is our duty to retire when men seek our hurt — cf. Matt. 10:23.

"Saul also sent messengers unto David's house, to watch him, and to slay him in the morning: and Michal David's wife told him, saying, If thou save not thy life tonight, tomorrow shalt thou be slain" (v. 11). Saul was thoroughly aroused: chagrined by his personal failure to kill David, he now sent his guards to assassinate him. These were to surround his house and wait till daylight, rather than enter and run the risk of killing some one else, or allowing him to make his escape during the confusion and darkness. But man proposes, and God disposes. The Lord had other services for David to perform, and the servant of God is immortal until the work allotted him has been done. This time the king's own daughter, who had married David, was the one to befriend him. In some way she had learned of her father's plan, so at once took measures to thwart it. First, she acquainted her husband of his imminent danger.

Next we are told, "so Michal let David down through a window; and he went, and fled, and escaped" (v. 12). In like manner, Rahab had let down the spies from her house in Jericho, when the king's messengers were in quest of him; and as the disciples let down the apostle Paul at Damascus, to preserve him from the evil designs of the Jews. Though the doors were securely guarded, David thus escaped through a window, and fled swiftly and safely away. It is of deep interest at this point to turn to the 59th Psalm, the heading of which (inspired, we believe) tells us it was written "when Saul sent, and they watched the house to kill him." In his critical situation, David betook himself to prayer: "Deliver me from mine enemies, O my God: defend me from them that rise up against me. Deliver me from the workers of iniquity, and save me from bloody men. For, lo, they lie in wait for my soul: the mighty are gathered against me; not for my transgression, nor for my sin, O Lord" (Psalm 59:1-3). Blessed is it to see that ere he completed the Psalm, full assurance of deliverance was his: "But I will sing of Thy power, yea, I will sing aloud of Thy mercy *in the morning*" (v. 16).

"And Michal took an image, and laid it in the bed, and put a pillow of goats' hair for his bolster, and covered it with a cloth, and when Saul sent messengers to take David, she said, He is sick" (vv. 13, 14). Water will not rise above its own level. We cannot expect the children of this world to act according to heavenly principles. Alienated as they are from the life of God (Eph. 4:18), utter strangers to Him in experience (Eph. 2:12), they have no trust in Him. In an emergency they have no better recourse than to turn unto fleshly schemings and devisings. From a natural viewpoint Michal's fidelity to her husband was commendable, but from a spiritual standpoint her deceit and falsehood was reprehensible. The one who commits his cause and case unto thy Lord, *trusting* also in Him to bring to pass His own wise purpose and that which shall be for his own highest good (Psa. 37:5), has no need to resort unto tricks and deceits. Does not David's having yoked himself to an unbeliever supply the key to his painful experiences in Saul's household!

"And Saul sent the messengers again to see David, saying, Bring him up to me in the bed, that I may slay him" (v. 15). Bent on David's destruction, the king gave orders that, sick or not he should be carried into his presence, and this for the specific purpose of slaying him by his own hand. Base and barbarous was it to thus triumph over one whom he thought was sick, and to vow the death of one that, for all he knew, was dying by the hand of nature. Spurred on by him who is "a murderer from the beginning" (John 8:44), the savage cruelty of Saul makes evident the extreme danger to which David was exposed: which, in turn, intensifies the blessedness of God's protection of him. How precious it is for the saint to know that the Lord places Himself as the Shield between him and his malicious Foe! "As the mountains are round about Jerusalem, so the Lord is round about His people from henceforth even forever" (Psa. 125:2).

When the servants returned to and entered Michal's house, her plot was exposed and the flight of David discovered (v. 16). Whereupon the king asked his daughter, "Why hast thou deceived me so, and sent away mine enemy, that he is escaped?" (v. 17). How thoroughly blurred is the vision of one who is filled with envy, anger and hatred! He who had befriended Saul again and again, was now regarded as an "enemy." There is a solemn lesson for us in this: if pride, prejudice, or self-seeking rule our hearts, we shall regard those who are our wisest counsellors and well-wishers as foes. Only when our eye be single is our whole body full of light. Solemn is it to note Michal's answer to Saul: "He said unto me, Let me go; why should I kill thee?" (v. 17), thereby representing David as a desperate man who would have slain her had she sought to block his escape. Still more solemn is it to find the man after God's own heart married to such a woman!

"So David fled, and escaped, and came to Samuel to Ramah, and told him all that Saul had done to him. And he and Samuel went and dwelt in Naioth" (v.18). It was by Samuel he had been anointed, and through him he had first received the promise of the kingdom. Probably David now sought God's prophet for the strengthening of his faith, for counsel as to what he should do, for comfort under his present troubles, for fellowship and prayer: it was through Samuel he was now most likely to learn the mind of the Lord. And too, he probably regarded asylum with Samuel as the most secure place in which he could lodge. Naioth was close to Ramah, and there was a school of the prophets: if the Philistines gave no disturbance to the "hill of God" and the prophets in it (10:5), it might be reasonably concluded that Saul would not.

"And it was told Saul, saying, Behold, David is at Naioth in Ramah." And Saul sent messengers to take David: and when they saw the company of the prophets prophesying and Samuel standing as appointed over them, the Spirit of God was upon the messengers, who were so much taken up with the religious exercises, they neglected the errand on which they had been sent. How this reminds us of the Pharisees and chief priests sending officers to apprehend Christ, but who instead of executing their commission, returned to their masters, saying, "Never man spake like this Man" (John 7:32, 45, 46)! Saul sent others of his servants, a second and a third time, to seize David, but with the same result as before (v. 21). Saul now therefore went forth in person to seek and slay David, but before he reached the place where David was, the Spirit of God came upon him and threw him into a kind of trance, in which he continued all day and night; giving David plenty of time to escape. Such strange methods does Jehovah sometimes employ in bringing to naught the efforts of His enemies against His servants.

CHAPTER 20

"And David fled from Naioth in Ramah and came and said before Jonathan, What have I done? What is my iniquity? And what is my sin before your father, that he seeks my life? And he said to him, Far be it! You shall not die! Behold, my father will do nothing either great or small that he will not show to me. And why should my father hide this thing from me? It is not so. And David again said passionately, Your father certainly knows that I have found grace in your eyes. And he said, Do not let Jonathan know this, lest he be full of sorrow. But truly as the Lord lives, and as your soul lives, there is only a step between me and death. Then Jonathan said to David, Whatever your soul desires, I will even do it for you. And David said to Jonathan, Behold, tomorrow is the new moon, and I should not fail to sit at table with the king. But let me go so that I may hide myself in the field until the third day at evening. If your father misses me at all, then say, David earnestly asked permission from me that he might run to his city Bethlehem. For there is a yearly sacrifice there for all the family. If he says, It is well, your servant shall have peace — but if he is very angry, be sure that evil is determined by him. Therefore you shall deal kindly with your servant, for you have brought your servant into a covenant of the Lord with you. But if there is any iniquity in me, kill me yourself. For why should you bring me to your father? And Jonathan said, Far be it from you. For if I knew certainly that evil was determined by my father to come on you, then would I not tell you? Then David said to Jonathan, Who shall tell me? Or what if your father answers you roughly? And Jonathan said to David, Come, and let us go into the field. And both of them went out into the field. And Jonathan said to David, By the Lord, the God of Israel, when I have sounded out my father about this time tomorrow or the third day, behold, if there is good toward David, then shall I not send to you and show it to you? If it pleases my father to do you evil, then may the Lord do so and much more to Jonathan if I do not show it to you and send you away so that you may go in peace. And may the Lord be with you, as He has been with my father. And you shall not only show me the kindness of the Lord while I still live, so that I do not die, but you shall not cut off your kindness from my house forever, no, not when the Lord has cut off the enemies of David, every one, from the face of the earth. So Jonathan made a covenant with the house of David, saying, Let the Lord even require it at the hand of David's enemies. And Jonathan caused David to swear again, because he loved him. For he loved him as he loved his own soul. Then Jonathan said to David, Tomorrow is the new moon. And you shall be missed, because your seat is empty.
And when you have stayed three days, then you shall go down quickly and come to the place where you hid yourself when the business was in hand. And you shall remain by the stone Ezel. And I will shoot three arrows on the side, as though I shot at a mark. And, behold, I will send a lad saying, Go find the arrows. If I carefully say to the lad, Look! The arrows are on this side of you, take them — then you may come, for peace is there to you, and no hurt, as the Lord lives. But if I say this to the young man, Look! The arrows are behind you — go your way, for the Lord has sent you away. And as to the matter which you and I have spoken of, behold, may the Lord be between you and me forever. So David hid himself in the field. And when the new moon had come, the king sat down to eat meat. And the king sat on his seat as at other times, on a seat by the wall. And Jonathan arose, and Abner sat at Saul's side, and David's place was empty. But Saul did not speak anything that day. For he thought, Something has happened to him, he is not clean. Surely, he is not clean. And on

187

the next day, the second day of the month, David's place was empty. And Saul said to his son Jonathan, Why does the son of Jesse not come to eat, either yesterday or today? And Jonathan answered Saul, David earnestly asked of me to go to Bethlehem — and he said, Let me go, I beg you, for our family has a sacrifice in the city. And my brother has summoned me. And now, if I have found favour in your eyes, please let me get away and see my brothers. Therefore he does not come to the king's table. Then Saul's anger was kindled against Jonathan, and he said to him, You son of a perverse, rebellious woman, do I not know that you have chosen the son of Jesse to your own confusion, and to the shame of your mother's nakedness? For as long as the son of Jesse lives on the earth, you shall not be established, nor your kingdom. So send now and bring him to me, for he shall surely die. And Jonathan answered Saul his father and said to him, Why should he be killed? What has he done? And Saul threw a javelin at him to strike him, and by this Jonathan knew that his father was determined to kill David. So Jonathan rose from the table in fierce anger, and ate no food the second day of the month. For he was grieved for David, because his father had shamed him. And in the morning Jonathan went out into the field at the time appointed with David. And a little lad was with him. And he said to this lad, Run now, find the arrows which I shoot. As the lad ran, he shot an arrow behind him. And when the lad had come to the place of the arrow which Jonathan had shot, Jonathan cried after the lad and said, Is not the arrow beyond you? And Jonathan cried after the lad, Make haste and hurry, do not wait. And Jonathan's lad gathered up the arrows and came to his master. But the lad did not know anything. Only Jonathan and David knew the matter. And Jonathan gave his weapons to his lad and said to him, Go, carry them to the city. And as soon as the lad had gone, David rose out of a place toward the south and fell on his face to the ground. And he bowed himself three times. And they kissed one another, and wept with one another, until David restrained himself. And Jonathan said to David, Go in peace because we have both sworn in the name of the Lord, saying, The Lord be between me and you, and between my seed and your seed, forever. And he rose and went away. And Jonathan went into the city" — 1 Samuel 20:1-42.

The picture which the Holy Spirit has given in Scripture of David's character and life is a composite one. It is somewhat like a painting in which the dominant colours are white, black and gold. In many details David has left an example which we do well to follow. In other respects he presents a solemn warning which we do well to heed. In other features he was a blessed type of Christ. Thus, the meeting together of these three distinct things in David may well be likened unto a composite picture. Nor do we exercise a wrong spirit (providing our motive be right), or sully the grace of God by dwelling upon the sad defects in the character of the Psalmist or the failures in his life; rather will the Spirit's design be realized and our souls be the gainers if we duly take to heart and turn them into earnest prayer, that we may be delivered from the snares into which he fell.

At the close of our last article we saw how that, to escape the murderous hatred of Saul, David took refuge with Samuel at Naioth. Thither did his relentless enemy follow him. But wondrously did God interpose. Three times the messengers which the king had sent to arrest David were restrained and awed by the power of the Holy Spirit. Not only so, but when Saul himself came in person, the Spirit of God subdued and threw him into a kind of ecstatic trance. One would have thought that this signal intervention of God for David had quieted all his fears, and filled his soul with praise and thanksgiving unto Him who had shown Himself strong on his behalf. Was it not plain that God did not intend Saul to harm the one whom His prophet had anointed? Ah, but David too was a man of like passions with us, and unless Divine grace wrought effectually *within* him, no outward providences would avail to spiritualise him. The moment the Lord leaves us to ourselves (to try us, to show what we are), a fall is certain.

Instead of continuing at Naioth, quietly waiting the next token of God's goodness, David became alarmed, and took matters into his own hands. Instead of being occupied with the Divine perfections, David now saw only a powerful, inveterate, blood-thirsty enemy. Accordingly, the next thing we read is, "And David fled from Naioth in Ramah" (20:1): true he "fled" from Saul, but he also turned his back upon Samuel. "And came and said before Jonathan, What have I done? What is mine iniquity? and what is my sin before thy father, that he seeketh my life?" It is solemn to see David preferring a conference with Jonathan rather than the prophet of God. As usual, the key is hung upon the door; the opening verse of this chapter explains to us what is found in the later ones. It was "natural" that David should turn for help to a "friend," but was it *spiritual?*

Do not the questions David put to Jonathan reveal to us the state of his heart? The "I," "mine," "my," "my," show plainly enough the condition of his mind. God was not now in all his thoughts, yea, *He* was not mentioned at all. The repeated attempts of Saul upon his life had thoroughly unnerved him, and his "there is but a step between me and death" (20:3), intimates plainly that unbelieving fears now possessed him. Ah, David needed to turn unto an abler physician than Jonathan if his feverish anxiety was to be allayed: only One was sufficient for laying a calming and cooling hand upon him. O how much the saint loses when he fails to acknowledge the Lord in all his ways (Prov. 3:6). But worse: when communion is broken, when the soul is out of touch with God, temptation is yielded unto and grievous sin is committed. It was so here. Afraid that Saul's anger would return when his absence from the table was noted, but fearful to take his place there, David bids Jonathan utter a deliberate lie on his behalf (20:5, 6). May this speak loudly to each of our hearts, warning of the fearful fruits which issue from severed fellowship with the Lord.

The first false step David had taken was in marrying the daughter of Saul, for it is evident from the sacred narrative that she was no suited partner for the man after God's own heart. His second mistake was his fleeing from Naioth, and thus turning his back upon the prophet of God. His third failure was to seek aid of Jonathan. The true character of his "friend" was exhibited on this occasion: seeing David so perturbed, he had not the moral courage to acknowledge the truth, but sought to pacify him with a prevarication (20:2). Surely Jonathan could not be ignorant of Saul's having thrown the javelin at David, of the instructions given to the servants to slay him (19:11), of the messengers sent to arrest him (19:20), and of his going after David in person (19:22). But all doubt is removed by "Saul spake *to Jonathan* his son, and to all his servants, that they should *kill* David" (19:1). Jonathan deliberately equivocated in 20:2, and "evil communications corrupt good manners" (1 Cor. 15:33): thus it was here — David lied too (20:5, 6).

We do not propose to go over this 20th chapter verse by verse, for we are not now writing a commentary upon 1 Samuel. A plan was agreed upon by Jonathan whereby he should ascertain the latest attitude of his father and acquaint David with the same. A solemn covenant was entered into between them: Jonathan here, and David much later (2 Sam. 9), faithfully carried out its terms. The words "David hid himself in the field" (v. 24 and cf. 35, 41), at once expose his lie in v. 6, though the commentators have glossed it over. When David was missed from the king's table and inquiry was made, Jonathan repeated the lie which David had suggested to him. Thereupon the king reviled his son, and declared that David "shall surely die" (v. 31). When Jonathan sought to expostulate, and ask why David should be slain, Saul threw his javelin at him. The meeting between Jonathan and David in the field, and their affectionate leave-taking is touchingly described (vv. 41, 42).

"Then came David to Nob to Ahimelech the priest" (21:1). When a real saint is out of touch with God, when he is in a backslidden state, his conduct presents a strange enigma and his inconsistent ways are such as no psychologist can explain. But much that is inexplicable to many (even to ill-informed believers) is solved for us by Gal. 5:17: "for the flesh lusteth against the spirit, and the spirit against the flesh: and these are contrary the one to the other; so that ye cannot do the things that ye would." Here we have set forth the conflict of the two "natures" in the Christian, the irreconcilable opposition between the two mainsprings of conduct, the "flesh" and the "spirit." According as one or the other of these two principles is actuating and dominating the saint, such will be his course of action. The final clause of this verse has a double force: the presence of the "flesh" hinders the "spirit" from completely realizing its desires in this life (Rom. 7:15-25); the presence of the "spirit," prevents the "flesh" from fully having its way.

Gal. 5:17 supplies the key to many a mysterious experience in the life of a Christian, and sheds much light on the checkered histories of O. T. saints. We might add many paragraphs at this point by illustrating the last sentence from the lives of Noah, Abraham, Isaac, Jacob, Joseph, Moses, Joshua, Elijah, etc., but instead, we will confine our attention to the leading subject of these articles. In his meeting the attacks of the wild animals (17:34-36), in his devotion for the tabernacle (Psa. 132:1-7), in his engagement with Goliath, the "spirit" was uppermost in David, and therefore was the Lord before his heart. There had been severe testings of courage and faith, but his trust in the Lord wavered not. Then followed a season in the king's household, where it was much harder to preserve this spirituality. Then Saul turned against him, and again and again sought his life. Deprived of the outward means of grace, David's faith flagged, and as it flagged fears replaced it, and instead of being occupied with the Lord, his powerful foe filled his vision.

In his flight from Saul, David first sought unto Samuel, which shows that the "flesh" in him was not completely regnant, as it never is in a truly regenerate soul: "Sin shall not have *dominion* over you" (Rom. 6:14) — it shall not render you its absolute slave. But in his flight from Samuel and his turning to Jonathan for help, we see the "flesh" more and more regulating his actions — still plainer manifested in the falsehood which he put into his friend's mouth. And now his flight unto Ahimelech and the manner in which he conducted himself, the anointed eye may discern the conflict which was at work within him. It now seemed clear unto David that no change for the better was to be expected in Saul: as long as the king was alive, he was in danger. An outcast from the court, he now became a lonely wanderer, but before he journeyed farther afield, his heart was drawn first to Nob, whither the tabernacle had been removed.

Various motives and considerations seem to have moved David in his repairing to Nob. Foreseeing that he must now be an exile, he wished to take leave of the tabernacle, not knowing when he should see it again. It is plain from many of his Psalms that the sorest grief of David during the time of his banishment was his isolation from the house of God and his restraint from public ordinances: "How amiable are Thy Tabernacles, O Lord of hosts! My soul longeth, yea, even fainteth for the courts of the Lord. . . For a day in Thy courts is better than a thousand. I had rather be a doorkeeper in the house of my God, than to dwell in the tents of wickedness" (Psa. 84:1, 2, 10 and cf. 42:3, 4 etc.) Second, it seems clear from 1 Sam. 22:10 that David's purpose was to enquire of the Lord through the high priest, to obtain directions from Him as to his path. Third, from what follows here, it appears that food was also his quest.

"And Ahimelech was afraid at the meeting of David" (21:1). Evidently the high priest had heard of David's having fallen under the displeasure of Saul, and so concluded that he was a fugitive. Knowing the type of man the king was, Ahimelech was fearful of endangering his own life by entertaining David. "And said unto him, Why art thou alone, and no man with thee?" That there were some "young men" with him is clear from v. 4 and also Matt. 12:3, yet having won such renown both in camp and court, it might well be expected that David should be accompanied by a suitable equipage. The disdain which the high priest showed for David the outcast, illustrates the merciless attitudes of the world toward a fallen and impoverished hero.

"And David said unto Ahimelech the priest, The king hath commanded me a business, and hath said unto me, Let no man know any thing of the business whereabout I send thee, and what I have commanded thee: and I have appointed my servants to such and such a place" (v. 2). Here again we see David guilty of a gross untruth. How solemn to find the Psalmist of Israel telling a deliberate lie at the threshold of the house of God, whither he had come to enquire the mind of the Lord. Verily, each one of us has real need to pray "Remove from me the way of lying" (Psa. 119:29). David's heart quailed under the embarrassing question of the priest, and he who had dared to meet single-handed the Philistine giant was now afraid to speak the truth. Ah, there cannot be the calm and courage of faith, where faith itself is inoperative. Elijah shrank not from meeting the four hundred prophets of Baal, yet later he fled in terror from Jezebel. Peter dared to step out of the ship onto the sea, yet trembled before a maid. "Wherefore let him that thinketh he standeth, take heed lest he fall."

It is easier to trust God in days of sunshine than in times of gloom and darkness. "David had often, indeed, before known difficulty and danger: from the day of his conflict with Goliath he had known little else: but then, there was this difference — in former difficulties he had been enabled to triumph. Some ray of brightness had gilded every cloud; some honour awaited him out of each affliction. But now, God seemed no longer to interfere on his behalf. The fell enmity of Saul was allowed to take its course; and God interfered not, either to subdue or to chasten. He appeared no longer to intend raising David above circumstances, but to allow him to be overcome by them. David's heart seemed unable to bear this. To trust God whilst overcoming is one thing; to trust Him when being overcome is another" (B. W. Newton).

David now asked Ahimelech for five loaves of bread (v. 3): bear in mind that he stood at the door of the tabernacle, and not before the priest's personal residence. All that was to hand were the twelve loaves which had rested for a week on the golden table in the sanctuary, and which, being replaced at once by twelve more, became the property of the priests and their families. Assuring Ahimelech that he and his men met the requirements of Ex. 19:15, David pressed for the bread being given to him. To what a low estate had the son of Jesse fallen: now that Saul's rooted malice was generally known the people would be afraid and unwilling to befriend him. In Matt. 12 we find the Lord

Jesus vindicating this action, which shows us that the ordinances of religion may be dispensed with where the preservation of life calls for it: ritual observances must give way to moral duties, and in the case of urgent providential necessity that is permissible which ordinarily may not be done.

"Now a certain man of the servants of Saul was there that day, detained before the Lord; and his name was Doeg, an Edomite, the chiefest of the herdmen that belonged to Saul" (v. 7). And yet in *his* hearing David had preferred his urgent request. Surely natural common sense would have prompted him to act with more prudence. Ah, my reader, when the saint is in a backslidden state of soul, he often acts more foolishly than does the man of the world. This is a righteous judgment of God upon him. He has given us His Word to walk by, and that Word is one of *wisdom*, containing salutary counsel. We turn from it at our peril and irreparable loss. To lean unto our own understanding is to court certain disaster. Yet, when communion with God is broken, this is exactly what we do. Then it is that we are suffered to reap the bitter fruits of our evil ways and made to feel the consequences of our folly.

Next, David asked Ahimelech for a weapon, and was told that the only one available was "the sword of Goliath," which had been preserved in the tabernacle as a monument of the Lord's goodness to Israel. When told of this, David exclaimed, "There is none like that, give it to me." Alas, alas, how had the mighty fallen. "Surely it augured ill for David, that *his* hand — that hand which had placed the sword of Goliath in the sanctuary of the God of Israel — that hand which had once taken the pebble and the sling as the symbol of its strength, because it trusted in the Lord of hosts, — it augured ill that his hand should be the first to withdraw the giant weapon from its resting place in order that he might transfer to *it* a measure, at least, of that confidence which he was withdrawing from God. How different the condition of David now, and on the day of Goliath's fall! Then, trusting in the God of Israel, and associated with Israel, he had gone out in owned weakness; but now, forsaking Israel and the land of Israel, he went forth armed with the sword of Goliath, to seek friendship and alliance with the Philistines, the enemies of Israel, and the enemies of God" (B. W. Newton). Thus David now set forth, provisioned (temporarily, at least) and armed. But at what a cost? The unsuspecting priest had believed David's lies, and assured by him that Saul had commissioned him, feared not the presence of Doeg the king's servant (v. 7). But he paid dearly for listening, against his better judgment, to David's falsehoods. That treacherous Edomite informed Saul (22:9, 10), and later he was ordered by the enraged king to reek a fearful vengeance: "And Doeg the Edomite turned, and he fell upon the priests, and slew on that day fourscore and five persons that did wear a linen ephod. And Nob, the city of the priests smote he with the edge of the sword, both men and women, children and sucklings, and oxen, and asses, and sheep" (1 Sam. 22:18, 19). Such were some of the fearful results of David's lies, as he afterwards acknowledged to the one remaining child of Ahimelech: "I have occasioned the death of all the persons of thy father's house" (1 Sam. 22:22). May it please the Holy Spirit to powerfully move both writer and reader to lay to heart the whole of this solemn incident, that we may daily pray with increasing earnestness, "Lead us not into temptation, but deliver us from evil."

CHAPTER 21.

"Then David came to Nob to Ahimelech the priest. And Ahimelech was afraid at the meeting of David. And he said to him, Why are you alone and no man with you? And David said to Ahimelech the priest, The king has commanded me a business and has said to me, Let no man know of the business about which I send you, and what I have commanded you. And I have sent servants to such and such a place. Now, therefore, what is under your hand? Give me five loaves of bread in my hand, or what there is to be found. And the priest answered David and said, There is no common bread under my hand, but there is holy bread if the young men have kept themselves at least from women. And David answered the priest and said to him, Truly women have been kept from us for about three days, since I came out. And the vessels of the young men are holy, and in a way the bread is common — the more so since today there are other loaves to be made holy in the vessel. So the priest gave him holy bread. For there was no bread there but the showbread that was taken from before the Lord in order to put hot bread in on the day when it was taken away. Now a certain man from the servants of Saul was there that day, held there before the Lord. And his name was Doeg, an Edomite, the chief of Saul's herdmen" 1 Samuel 21:1-7.

There are times when God's tender love for His people *seems* to be contradicted by the sore testings which He sends upon them, times when His providences appear to clash with His promises; then it is that faith is tested, and so often fails; then it is also that the superabounding grace of God is evidenced by delivering the one who has given way to unbelief. These principles are illustrated again and again on the pages of Holy Writ, especially in the O. T., and one of their chief values is for us to lay them to heart, turn them into earnest prayer, and seek to profit from them. God forbid that we should "wrest" them to our destruction (2 Pet. 3:16). God forbid that we should deliberately sin in order that grace may abound (Rom. 6:1,2). And God forbid that we should take the failures of those who preceded us as excuses for our own grievous falls, thus endeavouring to shelter behind the faults of others. Rather let us seek grace to regard them as danger-signals, set up to deter us from slipping into the snares which tripped them.

To Abraham God promised a numerous seed (Gen. 12:2), but His providences seemed to run counter to the fulfillment. Sarah was barren! But the sterility of her womb, presented no difficulty to Omnipotence. Nor was there any need for Abraham to attempt a fleshly compromise, by seeking a son through Hagar (Gen. 16). True, for a while, his plan appeared to succeed, but the sequel not only demonstrated the needlessness for such a device, but in Ishmael a bitter harvest was reaped. And this is recorded as a warning for us. To Jacob God said, "Return unto the land of thy fathers, and to thy kindred, and I will be with thee" (Gen. 31:3). During the course of his journey, messengers informed him that Esau was approaching with four hundred men, and we read that "Jacob was greatly afraid and distressed" (32:7). How human! True, and how sad, how dishonouring to God! What cause for fear was there when Jehovah was with him? O for grace to "trust in Him at all times" (Psa. 62:8).

Learn, dear brethren and sisters, that faith must be tested — to prove its genuineness. Yet only He who gives faith, can maintain it; and for this we must constantly seek unto Him. What has just been before us receives further illustration in the subject of these articles. David was the king elect, yet another wore the crown. The son of Jesse had been anointed unto the throne, yet Saul was now bitterly persecuting him. Had God forgotten to be gracious? No, indeed. Had He changed His purpose? That could not be (Mal. 3:6). Why, then, should the slayer of Goliath now be a fugitive? He had been appointed to be master of vast treasures, yet he was now reduced to begging bread (21:3). Faith, *must* be tested, and we *must* learn by painful experience the bitter consequences of *not trusting* in the Lord with all our hearts, and the evil fruits which are borne whenever we lean unto our own understandings, take matters into our own hands, and seek to extricate ourselves from trouble.

Concerning Hezekiah we read that "God left him, to try him, that he might know all that was in his heart" (2 Chron. 32:31). None of us knows how weak he is till God withdraws His upholding grace (as He did with Peter) and we are left to ourselves. True, the Lord has plainly told us that "without Me ye can do nothing." We think we believe that word, and in a way we do; yet there is a vast difference between the noncalling into question of a verse of Scripture, an assenting to its verity, and an inward acquaintance with the same in our own personal history. It is one thing to believe that I am without strength or wisdom, it is another to *know* it through actual experience. Nor is this, as a rule, obtained through a single episode, any more than a nail is generally driven in securely by one blow of the hammer. No, we have to learn, and re-learn, so stupid are we. The Truth of God has to be burned into us in the fiery furnace of affliction. Yet this ought not to be so, and would not be so if we paid more heed to these O. T. warnings, furnished in the biographies of the saints of yore.

In our last article we saw that, following the murderous attack of Saul upon him, David fled to Naioth. But thither did his relentless enemy follow him. Wondrously did God interpose on His servant's behalf. Yet, being a man of like passions with ourselves, and the supernatural grace of God not supporting him at the time, instead of David's fears being thoroughly removed, and his waiting quietly with Samuel to receive a word of Divine guidance, he was occupied with his immediate danger from Saul, and after vainly conferring with Jonathan, took things into his own hands and fled to Nob. There he lied to the priest, by means of which he obtained bread, but at the fearful cost of Saul reeking vengeance through Doeg in slaying eighty-five of those who wore the linen ephod. Disastrous indeed are the consequences when we have to seek our own way and hew out a path for ourselves. How differently had things turned out if David had trusted the Lord, and let Him to undertake for him!

God is all-sufficient in Himself to supply all our need (Phil. 4:19) and to do for us far more exceeding abundantly above all that we ask or think (Eph. 3:20). This He can do either in an immediate way, or mediately if He sees fit to make use of creatures as instruments to fulfil His pleasure and communicate what He desires to impart to us. God is never at a loss: all things, all events, all creatures, are at His sovereign disposal. This foundational truth of God's all-sufficiency should be duly improved by us, taking heed that we do not by our thoughts or actions reflect upon or deny this Divine perfection. And this we certainly do when we use *unlawful* means to escape imminent dangers. Such was the case with Abram (Gen. 20) and Isaac (Gen. 26) when they denied their wives, concluding that that was a necessary expedient to save their lives — as though God were not able to save them in a better and more honourable way. Such we shall see was the case with David at Ziklag.

We also made brief reference in our last article to the fact that when the saint is out of touch with God, when he is in a backslidden state, his behaviour is so different from his former conduct, so inconsistent with his profession, that his actions now present a strange enigma. And yet that enigma is capable of simple solution. It is only in God's light that any of us "see light" (Psa. 36:9). As the Lord Jesus declares, "he that followeth Me shall not walk in darkness" (John

8:12). Yes, but it is only as we are really "following" Him, our hearts engaged with the example which He has left us, that we shall see, know, and take that path which is pleasing and honouring to Him. There is only one other alternative, and that is seeking to please either our fellows or ourselves, and where this is the case, only confusion and trouble can ensue.

When communion with God (who is "light") is severed, nothing but spiritual darkness is left. The world is a "dark place" (2 Pet. 1:19), and if we are not ordering our steps by the Word (Psa. 119:105), then we shall flounder and stumble. "The backslider in heart shall be filled with *his own* ways" (Prov. 14:14), not with the "ways" of God (Psa. 103:7). Where fellowship with the Lord is broken, the mind is no longer illuminated from Heaven, the judgment is clouded, and a lack of wisdom, yea, folly itself, will then characterise all our actions. Here is the key to much in our lives, the explanation of those "unwise doings," those "foolish mistakes" for which we have had to pay so dearly — we were not controlled by the Holy Spirit, we acted in the energy of the flesh, we sought the counsel of the ungodly, or followed the dictates of common sense.

Nor is there any determining to what lengths the backslider may go, or how foolishly and madly he may not act. Solemnly is this illustrated in the case now before us. As we saw in the preceding paper, David was worried at being unarmed, and asked the high priest if there were no weapon to hand. On being informed that the only one available was "the sword of Goliath," which had been preserved in the tabernacle as a memorial of the Lord's goodness to His people, David exclaimed, "There is none like it, give it me" (1 Sam. 21:9). Alas, "how had the fine gold become dim"! He who when walking in the fear of the Lord had not hesitated to advance against Goliath with nothing in his hand save a sling, now that the fear of man possessed him, places his confidence in a giant's sword. Perhaps both writer and reader are inclined to marvel at this, but have we not more reason to *mourn* as we see in this incident an accurate portrayal of many of our past failures?

"And David arose, and fled that day for fear of Saul, and went to Achish the king of Gath" (1 Sam. 21:10). Fearing that Saul would pursue him were he to make for any other part of the land of Israel, and not being disposed to organize a company against him, David took refuge in Gath of the Philistines. But what business had he in the territory of God's enemies? None whatever, for he had not gone there in *His* interests. Verily, "oppression maketh a wise man mad" (Eccl. 7:7). Few indeed conduct themselves in extreme difficulties without taking some manifestly false step: we should therefore "watch and pray that we enter not into temptation" (Matt. 26:41), earnestly seeking from God the strength which will alone enable us to successfully resist the Devil.

"And David arose, and fled that day for fear of Saul, and went to Achish the king of Gath." It is evident from what follows that David hoped he would not be recognized. Thus it is with the backslidden Christian as he fraternizes with the world: he attempts to conceal his colours, hoping that he will not be recognized as a follower of the Lord Jesus. Yet behold the consummate folly of David: he journeyed to Gath with "the sword of Goliath" in his hands! Wisdom had indeed deserted him. As another has said, "Common prudence might have taught him, that, if he sought the friendship of the Philistines, the sword of Goliath was not the most likely instrument to conciliate their favour." But where a saint has grieved the Holy Spirit, even common sense no longer regulates him.

"And the servants of Achish said unto him, Is not this David the king of the land? did they not sing one to another of him in dances, saying Saul hath slain his thousands and David his ten thousands?" (v. 11). God will not allow His people to remain incognito in this world. He has appointed that they should "be blameless and harmless, the sons of God, without blame in the midst of a crooked and perverse nation among whom" they are to "shine as lights in the world" (Phil. 2:15), and any efforts of theirs to annual this, He will thwart. Abraham's deception was discovered: Peter's attempt to conceal his discipleship failed — his very speech betrayed him. So here: David was quickly recognized. And thus it will be with us. And mercifully is this the case, for God will not have His own to settle down among and enjoy the friendship of His enemies.

"And David laid up these words in his heart, and was sore afraid of Achish the king of Gath" (v. 12). What right had David to be at Gath? None whatever, and God soon caused circumstances to arise which showed him that he was out of his place, though in wondrous mercy He withheld any chastisement. How sad to hear of him who had so courageously advanced against Goliath now being "sore afraid"! "The righteous are bold as a lion" (Prov. 28:1); yes, the "righteous," that is, they who are right with God, walking with Him, and so sustained by His grace. Sadder still is it to see how David now acted: instead of casting himself on God's mercy, confessing his sin, and seeking His intervention, he had recourse to deceit and played the fool.

"And he changed his behaviour before them, and feigned himself mad in their hands, and scrabbled on the doors of the gate, and let his spittle fall down upon his beard" (v. 13). Afraid to rely upon the man whose protection he had sought, the anointed of God now feigned himself to be crazy. It was then that he learned experimentally "It is better to trust in the Lord than to put confidence in princes" (Psa. 118:9). The king elect "feigned himself mad": "such was the condition into which David had sunk himself. Saul himself could scarcely have wished for a deeper degradation" (B. W. Newton). Learn from this, dear reader, what still indwells the true saint, and which is capable of any and every wickedness but for the restraining hand of God. Surely we have need to pray daily "Hold Thou me up, and I shall be safe" (Psa. 119:117).

"Then said Achish unto his servants, Lo, ye see the man is mad: wherefore then have ye brought him to me? Have I need of mad men, that ye have brought this fellow to play the mad man in my presence? Shall this fellow come into my house?" (vv. 14, 15). How evident is it to the anointed eye, from the whole of this incident, that the Holy Spirit's object here was not to glorify David, but to magnify the longsuffering grace of God, and to furnish salutary instruction and solemn warning for us? Throughout the Scriptures the character of man is accurately painted in the colours of reality and truth.

Many are the lessons to be learned from this sad incident. Though ingenious falsehoods may seem to promote present security, yet they insure future disgrace. They did for Abraham, for Isaac, for Jacob, for Peter, for Ananias. Leaning unto his own understanding conducted David to Gath, but he soon learned from the shame of his folly that he had not walked in wisdom. Not only was David deeply humiliated, by this pitiful episode, but Jehovah was grievously dishonoured thereby. Marvelous indeed was it that he escaped with his life: this can only be attributed to the secret but invincible workings of His power, moving upon the king of the Philistines, for as the title of Psa. 34 informs us, "Achish drove him away, and he departed." Such was the means which an infinitely merciful God used to screen His child from imminent danger.

From Gath David fled to the cave of Adullam. Blessed is it to learn of the repentant and chastened spirit in which the servant of God entered it. The 34th Psalm was written by him then (as its superscription informs us), and in it the Holy Spirit has given us to see the exercises of David's heart at that time. There we find him blessing the Lord, his soul making his boast in Him (vv. 1-3). There we hear him saying, "I sought the Lord, and He heard me, and delivered me from all my fears" (v. 4). There he declares, "This poor man cried, and the Lord heard him, and saved him out of all his troubles. The angel of the Lord encampeth round about them that fear Him, and delivereth them" (vv. 6, 7).

But it was more than praise and gratitude which filled the restored backslider. David had learned some valuable lessons experimentally. Therefore we hear him saying, "Come ye children, hearken unto me: I will teach you the fear of the Lord. What man is he that desireth life, and loveth many days, that he may see good? Keep thy tongue from evil, and thy lips from speaking guile. Depart from evil, and do good; seek peace and pursue it" (vv. 11:14). "He had proved the evil of lying lips and a deceitful tongue, and now was able to warn others of the pitfall into which he had fallen" (B. W. Newton). But it is blessed to mark that he warned, not as one who was left to reap the harvest of his doings, but as one who could say, "The Lord redeemeth the soul of His servants, and none of them that trust in Him shall be desolate" (v. 22).

CHAPTER 22.

"And David left there and escaped to the cave Adullam. And when his brothers and all his father's house heard it, they went down there to him. And everyone who was in distress, and everyone who was in debt, and everyone who was bitter of soul gathered themselves to him. And he became a captain over them. And there were about four hundred men with him" — 1 Samuel 22:1-2.

At the close of the preceding article, we saw the backslider restored to communion with God. As David then wrote, "Many are the afflictions of the righteous" — most of them brought upon ourselves through sinful folly — "but the Lord delivereth him out of them all" (Psa. 34:19). Yet, in His own good time. The hour had not yet arrived for our patriarch to ascend the throne. It would have been a simple matter for God to have put forth His power, destroyed Saul, and given His servant rest from all his foes. And this, no doubt, is what the energetic nature of David had much preferred. But there were other counsels of God to be unfolded before He was ready for the son of Jesse to wield the scepter. Though *we* are impulsive and impetuous, God is never in a hurry; the sooner we learn this lesson, the better for our own peace of mind, and the sooner shall we "Rest in the Lord, and wait patiently for Him" (Psa. 37:7).

"God had designs other than the mere exaltation of David. He intended to allow the evil of Saul and of Israel to exhibit itself. He intended to give to David some apprehension of the character of his own heart, and to cause him to learn subjection to a greater wisdom than his own. He intended also to prove the hearts of His own people Israel; and to try how many among them would discern that the Cave of Adullam was the only true place of excellency and honour in Israel" (B. W. Newton). Further discipline was needed by David, if he was to learn deeper lessons of dependency upon God. Learn from this, dear reader, that though God's *delays* are trying to flesh and blood, nevertheless they are ordered by perfect wisdom and infinite love. "For the vision is yet for an appointed time, but at the end it shall speak, and not lie: though it tarry, wait for it; because it will surely come" (Habak. 2:3).

"David therefore departed thence, and escaped to the cave Adullam" (1 Sam. 22:1). Still a fugitive, David left the land of the Philistines, and now took refuge in a large underground cavern, situated, most probably, not far from Bethlehem. To conceal himself from Saul and his blood-thirsty underlings, our hero betook himself to a cave — it is probable that the Holy Spirit made reference to this in Heb. 11:38. The high favourites of Heaven are sometimes to be located in queer and unexpected places. Joseph in prison, the descendants of Abraham labouring in the brick-kilns of Egypt, Daniel in the lion's den, Jonah in the whale's belly, Paul clinging to a spar in the sea, forcibly illustrate this principle. Then let us not murmur because we do not now live in as fine a house as do some of the ungodly; *our* "mansions" are in Heaven!

"David therefore departed thence, and escaped to the cave Adullam." It is blessed to learn how David employed himself at this time; yet close searching has to be done before this can be ascertained. The Bible is no lazy man's book: much of its treasure, like the valuable minerals stored in the bowels of the earth, only yield up themselves to the diligent seeker. Compare Prov. 2:1-5. By noting the superscriptions to the Psalms (which, with many others, we are satisfied are Divinely inspired), we discover that two of them were composed by "the sweet singer of Israel" at this time. Just as the 34th casts its welcome light upon the close of 1 Sam. 21, so Psalm 57 and 142 illuminate the opening verses of 1 Sam.

22.

The underground asylum of David made an admirable closet for prayer, its very solitude being helpful for the exercise of devotion. Well did C. H. Spurgeon say, "Had David prayed as much in his palace as he did in his cave, he might never have fallen into the act which brought such misery upon his latter days." We trust the spiritual reader will, at this point, turn to and ponder the 57th and 142nd Psalms. In them he will perceive something of the exercises of David's heart. From them he may derive valuable instruction as to how to pray acceptably unto God in seasons of peculiar trial. A careful reading of the 57th Psalm will enable us to follow one who began it amid the gloomy shadows of the cavern, but from which he gradually emerged into the open daylight. So it often is in the experiences of the believer's soul.

Perhaps the 142nd Psalm was composed by David before the 57th: certainly it brings before us one who was in deeper anguish of soul. Blessed indeed is it to mark the striking contrast from what is here presented to us and what was before us as we passed through 1 Sam. 20 and 21. There we saw the worried fugitive turning to Jonathan, lying to Ahimelech, playing the madman at Gath. But vain was the hope of man. Yet how often we have to pass through these painful experiences and bitter disappointments before we thoroughly learn this lesson! Here we behold the son of Jesse turning to the only One who could do him any real good. "I cried unto the Lord with my voice . . . I poured out my complaint before Him. I showed before Him my trouble" (vv. 1, 2). This is what we should do: thoroughly unburden our hearts unto Him with whom we have to do. Note how, at the close of this Psalm, *after* he had so freely poured out his woes, David exclaimed, "Thou *shalt* deal bountifully with me"!

"And Jonathan loved him as his own soul . . . all Israel and Judah loved David" (1 Sam. 18:1, 16). Now their love was tested, now an opportunity was furnished them to manifest their affections for him. This was the hour of David's unpopularity: he was outlawed from the court; a fugitive from Saul, he was dwelling in a cave. Now was the time for devotion to David to be clearly exhibited. But only those who truly loved him could be expected to throw in their lot with an hated outcast. Strikingly is this illustrated in the very next words.

"And when his brethren and all his father's house heard it, they went down thither to him" (1 Sam. 22:1). Ah, true love is unaffected by the outward circumstances of its object. Where the heart is genuinely knit to another, a change in his fortunes will not produce a change in its affections. David might be, in the eyes of the world, in disgrace; but that made no difference to those who *loved* him. He might be languishing in a cavern, but that was all the more reason why they should show their kindness and demonstrate their unswerving loyalty. Among other things, this painful trial enabled David to discover who were, and who were not, his real friends.

If we look beneath the surface here, the anointed eye should have no difficulty in discerning another striking and blessed type of David's Son and Lord. First, a type of Him when He tabernacled among men, in "the days of His flesh." How fared it then with the Anointed of God? By title the throne of Israel was His, for He was born "the King of the Jews" (Matt. 2:2). That God was with him was unmistakably evident. He too "behaved Himself wisely in all His ways." He too performed exploits: healing the sick, freeing the demon-possessed, feeding the hungry multitude, raising the dead. But just as Saul hated and persecuted David, so the heads of the Jews — the chief priests and Pharisees — were envious of and hounded Christ. Just as Saul thirsted for the blood of Jesse's son, the leaders of

Israel (at a later date) thirsted for the blood of God's Son.

The analogy mentioned above might be drawn out at considerable length, but at only one other point will we here glance, namely, the fact of the solemn foreshadowment furnished by David as first the friend and benefactor of his nation, now the poor outcast. Accurately did he prefigure that blessed One, who when here was "the Man of sorrows and acquainted with grief." Trace His path as the Holy Spirit has described it in the New Testament. Behold Him as the unwanted One in this world of wickedness. Hear His plaintive declaration, "The foxes have holes, and the birds of the air have nests; but the Son of Man hath not where to lay His head" (Matt. 8:20). Read too "And every man went unto his own house; Jesus went unto the mount of Olives" (John 7:53; 8:1); and it is evident that David's Lord was the Homeless Outcast in this scene.

But were there none who appreciated Him, none who loved Him, none who were willing to be identified with and cast in their lot with Him who was "despised and rejected of men"? Yes, there were some, and these, we believe, are typically brought before us in the next verse of the scripture we are now pondering: "And every one that was in distress, and everyone that was in debt, and every one that was discontented, gathered themselves unto him" (1 Sam. 22:2). What a strange company to seek unto God's anointed! No mention is made of the captains of the army, the men of state, the princes of the realm, coming unto David. No, they, with all like them, preferred the court and the palace to the cave of Adullam.

Is not the picture an accurate one, dear reader? Is it not plain again that these O. T. records furnish something more than historical accounts, that there is a typical and spiritual significance to them as well. If David be a type of Christ, then those who sought him out during the season of his humiliation, must represent those who sought unto David's Son when He sojourned on this earth. And clearly they did so. Read the four Gospels, and it will be found that, for the most part, those who sought unto the Lord Jesus, were the poor and needy; it was the lepers, the blind, the maimed and the halt, who came unto Him for help and healing. The rich and influential, the learned and the mighty, the leaders of the Nation, had no heart for Him.

But what is before us in the opening of 1 Sam. 22 not only typed out that which occurred during the earthly ministry of Christ, but it also shadowed forth that which has come to pass all through this Christian era, and that which is taking place today. As the Holy Spirit declared through Paul, "For ye see your calling brethren, how that not many wise men after the flesh, not many mighty, not many noble, are called: but God hath chosen the foolish things of the world to confound the wise; and God hath chosen the weak things of the world, to confound the things which are mighty; and base things of the world, and things which are despised, hath God chosen, yea, and things which are not, to bring to nought the things which are: That no flesh should glory in his presence" (1 Cor. 1:26-29).

The second verse of 1 Sam. 22 sets before us a striking Gospel picture. Note, first, that those who came to David were *few in number:* "about four hundred." What a paltry retinue! What a handful compared with the hosts of Israel! But did Christ fare any better in the days of His flesh? How many friends stood around the cross, wept at His sepulchre, or greeted Him as he burst the bars of death? How many followed Him to Bethany, gazed at His ascending form, or gathered in the upper room to await the promised Spirit? And how is it today? Of the countless millions of earth's inhabitants what percentage of them have even heard the Gospel? Out of those who bear His name, how many evidence that they are denying self, taking up their cross daily, and following the example which He has left, and thus proving themselves by the only badge of discipleship which He will recognize? A discouraging situation, you say. Not at all, rather is it just what faith expects. The Lord Jesus declared that His flock is a "little one" (Luke 12:32). that only "few" tread that narrow way which leadeth unto life (Matt. 7:14).

Second, observe again the particular *type of people* who sought out David: they were "in distress, in debt, and discontented." What terms could more suitably describe the condition they are in when the redeemed first seek help from Christ! "In debt": in all things we had come short of the glory of God. In thought, word, and deed, we had failed to please Him, and there was marked up against us a multitude of transgressions. "In distress"; who can tell out that anguish of soul which is experienced by the truly convicted of the Holy Spirit? Only the one who has actually experienced the same, knows of that unspeakable horror and sorrow when the heart first perceives the frightful enormity of having defied the infinite Majesty of heaven, trifled with His longsuffering, slighted His mercy again and again.

"Discontented." Yes, this line in the picture is just as accurate as the others. The one who has been brought to realize he is a spiritual pauper, and who is now full of grief for his sins, is discontented with the very things which till recently pleased him. Those pleasures which fascinated, now pall. That gay society which once attracted, now repells. O the emptiness of the world to a soul which God hath smitten with a sense of sin! The striken one turns away with disgust from that which he had formerly sought after so eagerly. There is now an aching void within, which nothing without can fill. So wretched is the convicted sinner, he wishes he were dead, yet is terrified at the very thought of death. Reader, do you know anything of such an experience, or is all this the language of an unknown tongue to you?

Third, these people who were in debt, in distress, and discontented, *sought out* David. They were the only ones who did so; it was *a deep sense of need* which drove them to him, and a hope that he could relieve them. So it is spiritually. None but those who truly feel that they are paupers before God, with no good thing to their credit, absolutely destitute of any merits of their own, will appreciate the glad tidings that Christ Jesus came into this world to pay the debt of such. Only those who are smitten in their conscience, broken in heart, and sick of sin, will really respond to that blessed word of His, "Come unto Me all ye that labour and are heavy-laden, and I will give you rest." Only those who have lost all heart for this poor world, will truly turn unto the Lord of glory.

Fourth, the spiritual picture we are now contemplating is not only a type of the first coming to Christ of His people, but also of their subsequent *going forth* "unto Him without the camp" (Heb. 13:13). Those who sought David in the Cave of Adullam turned their backs upon both the court of Saul and the religion of Judaism. There was none to pity them there. Who cared for penniless paupers? Who had a heart for those in distress? So it is in most of the churches today. Those who are "poor in spirit" have nothing in common with the self-satisfied Laodiceans. And how "distressed" in soul are they over the worldliness that has come in like a flood, over the crowds of unregenerate members, over the utter absence of any scriptural discipline. And what is to be the attitude and actions of God's grieved children toward those having nothing more than a form of godliness? This, "from such turn away" (2 Tim. 3:5). Identify yourself with Christ on the outside; walk alone with Him.

Fifth, "And he became a *captain over them*" (1 Sam. 22:2). Important and striking line in the picture is this. Christ is to be received as "Lord" (Col. 2:6) if

He is to be known as Saviour. Love to Christ is to be evidenced by "keeping His commandments" (John 14:15). It mattered not what that strange company had been who sought unto David, they were now his servants and soldiers. They had turned away from the evil influence of Saul, to be subject unto the authority of David. This is what Christ requires from all who identify themselves with Him. "Take My *yoke* upon you" is His demand (Matt. 11:29). Nor need we shrink from it, for He declares "My yoke is easy, and My burden is light."

And David went from there to Miz-peh of Moab. And he said to the king of Moab, Please, let my father and my mother come forth and be with you until I know what God will do for me. And he brought them before the king of Moab. And they lived with him all the time that David was in the stronghold. Leave and go into the land of Judah. And David left and came to the forest of Har-eth. When Saul heard that David was discovered, and the men that were with him (now Saul abode in Gib-e-ah under a tree in Ra-mah, having his spear in his hand. And all his servants were standing about him), then Saul said to his servants that stood around him, Hear now, you Benjamites. Will the son of Jesse give every one of you fields and vineyards and make you all captains of thousands and captains of hundreds? How is it that all of you have conspired against me, and none have shown me that my son has made a covenant with the son of Jesse, and none of you is sorry for me or shows me that my son has stirred up my servant against me, to lie in wait as at this day? Then Do-eg the E-dom-ite, who was set over the servants of Saul, answered and said, I saw the son of Jesse coming to Nob, to A-him-e-lech the son of A-hi-tub. And he asked of the LORD for him and gave him food and gave him the sword of Go-li-ath the Philistine. Then the king sent to call A-him-e-lech the priest, the son of A-hi-tub, and all his father's house, the priests that were in Nob. And they came, all of them, to the king. And Saul said, Hear now, you son of A-hi-tub. And he answered, here I am, my lord. And Saul said to him, Why have you conspired against me, you and the son of Jesse, in that you have given him bread and a sword, and have asked of God for him, that he should rise against me to lie in wait as at this day? Then A-him-e-lech answered the king and said, And who is so faithful among all your servants as David, who is the king's son-in-law, and who goes at your bidding, and who is honourable in your house? Did I then begin to ask of God for him? Be it far from me. Do not let the king charge anything to his servant, or to all the house of my father. For your servant knew nothing of all this, more or less. And the king said, A-him-e-lech, you shall surely die, you and all your father's house. And the king said to the guard that stood around him, Turn and kill the priests of the LORD, because their hand also is with David, and because they knew when he fled and did not tell me. But the servants of the king would not put forth their hand to fall on the priests of the LORD. And the king said to Do-eg, You turn and fall on the priests. And Do-eg the E-dom-ite turned, and he fell on the priests. And on that day he killed eighty-five persons who wore a linen ephod. And he struck Nob, the city of the priests, with the edge of the sword, both men and women, children and babes, and oxen, and asses, and sheep with the edge of the sword. And one of the sons of A-him-e-lech the son of A-hi-tub, named A-bi-a-thar, escaped and fled after David. And A-bi-a-thar told David that Saul had slain the LORD's priests. And David said to A-bi-a-thar, I knew that day, when Do-eg the E-dom-ite was there, that he would surely tell Saul. I have caused the death of all the persons of your father's house. You stay with me. Do not fear. For he who seeks my life seeks your life. But you shall be safe with me. — 1 Samuel 22:3-23.

In our last article we left David in the Cave of Adullam. An incident is recorded in 2 Sam. 23 which throws an interesting light on the spiritual life of our hero at this time. "And three of the thirty chief went down and came to David in the harvest-time unto the cave of Adullam: and the troop of the Philistines pitched in the valley of Rephaim. And David was then in an hold, and the garrison of the Philistines was then in Bethlehem. And David longed, and said, Oh, that one would give me drink of the water of the well of Bethlehem, which is by the gate! And the three mighty men brake through the hosts of the Philistines, and drew water out of the well of Bethlehem, that was by the gate, and took and brought it to David: nevertheless he would not drink thereof, but poured it out unto the Lord. And he said, Be it far from me, O Lord, that I should do this: is not this the blood of the men that went in jeopardy of their lives? Therefore he would not drink of it" (vv. 13-17).

No doubt the trials of his present lot had called to David's mind his happy life at home. The weather being hot, he expressed a longing for a drink from the family well of Bethlehem, though with no thought that any of his men would risk their lives to procure it for him. Yet this is precisely what happened: out of deep devotion to their outlawed captain, three of them fought their way through a company of the Philistines who were encamped there, and returned to David with the desired draught. Touched by their loyalty, stirred by their self-sacrifice, David felt that water obtained at such risk was too valuable for him to drink, and was fit only to be "poured out unto the Lord" as a "drink-offering." Beautifully has Matthew Henry made application of this, thus: "Did David look upon that water as very precious, which was got but with the hazard of these men's blood, and shall not we much more value those benefits for the purchasing of which our blessed Saviour shed His blood"?

We quote from another who has commented upon this incident. "There is something peculiarly touching and beautiful in the above scene, whether we contemplate the act of the three mighty men in procuring the water for David, or David's act in pouring it out to the Lord. It is evident that David discerned, in an act of such uncommon devotedness, a sacrifice which none but the Lord Himself could duly appreciate. The odor of such a sacrifice was far too fragrant for him to interrupt it in its ascent to the throne of the God of Israel. Wherefore he, very properly and very graciously, allows it to pass him by, in order that it might go up to the One who alone was worthy to receive it, or able to appreciate it. All this reminds us, forcibly, of that beautiful compendium of Christian devotedness set forth in Phil. 2:17,18: 'Yea, and if I be poured out upon the sacrifice, and service of your faith, I joy and rejoice with you all; for this cause ye also joy and rejoice with me.' In this passage, the apostle represents the Philippian saints in their character as priests, presenting a sacrifice and performing a priestly ministration to God; and such was the intensity of his self-forgetting devotedness, that he could rejoice in his being poured out as a drink-offering upon their sacrifice, so that all might ascend, in fragrant odor to God" (C. H. M.).

Some commentators have denied that the above touching episode occurred during that section of David's history which we are now considering, placing it at a much later date. These men failed to see that 1 Chron. 11:15 and 2 Sam. 23 recounts things out of their chronological order. If the reader turn back to 1 Sam. 17:1; 19:8, etc., he will see that the Philistines were quite active in making raids upon Israel at this time, and that David, not Saul, was the principal one to withstand them. But now he was no longer in the position to engage them. Saul, as we shall see in a moment, had dropped all other concerns and was confining his whole attention to the capture of David: thus the door was then wide open for the Philistines to continue their depredations. Finally, be it said, all that is recorded after David came to the throne, makes it altogether unlikely that the Philistines were then encamped around Bethlehem, still less that the king should seek refuge in the cave of Adullam.

"And David went thence to Mizpeh of Moab: and he said unto the king of Moab: Let my father and my mother, I pray thee, come forth, and be with you, till I know what God will do for me. And he brought them before the king of Moab: and they dwelt with him all the while that David was in the hold" (1 Sam. 22: 3, 4). We are convinced that what has been before us in the above paragraphs supplies the key to that which is here recorded. In 22:1 we learn that "all his family" had come to David in the Cave. From 16:1 we learn that their home was in Bethlehem: but the Philistines were now encamped there (2 Sam. 23:14), so they could not return thither. David did not wish his parents to share the hardships involved by his wanderings, and so now he thoughtfully seeks an asylum for them. Blessed is it to see him, in the midst of his sore trials, "honouring his father and his mother." Beautifully did this foreshadow what is recorded in John 19:26, 27.

While Saul was so bitterly opposed to David, there was no safety for his parents anywhere in the land of Israel. The deep exercises and anguish of David's heart at this time are vividly expressed in Psa. 142, the Title of which reads, "A Prayer when he was in the Cave." "I cried unto the Lord with my voice, with my voice unto the Lord did I make my supplication. I poured out my complaint before Him: I showed before Him my trouble. When my spirit was overwhelmed within me, then Thou knowest my path. In the way wherein I walked have they privily laid a snare for me. I looked on my right hand, and beheld, but there was no man that would know me: refuge failed me; no man cared for my soul. I cried unto Thee, O Lord: I said, Thou art my refuge and my portion in the land of the living. Attend unto my cry; for I am brought very low; deliver me from my persecutors, for they are stronger than I. Bring my soul out of prison, that I may praise Thy name: the righteous shall compass me about; for Thou shalt deal bountifully with me." Blessed is it to mark the note of confidence in God in the closing verse.

"And David went thence to Mizpeh of Moab: and he said unto the king of Moab, let my father and mother, I pray thee, come forth, and be with you." What was it induced David to trust his parents unto the protection of the Moabites? We quote, in part, from the answer given by J. J. Blunt in his very striking book "Undesigned Coincidences in the O. and N. T." "Saul, it is true, had been at war with them, whatever he might then be, — but so had he been with every people round about; with the Ammonites, with the Edomites, with the kings of Zobah. Neither did it follow that the enemies of Saul, as a matter of course, would be the friends of David. On the contrary, he was only regarded by the ancient inhabitants of the land, to which ever of the local nations they belonged, as the champion of Israel; and with such suspicion was he received amongst them, notwithstanding Saul's known enmity towards him, that before Achish king of Gath, he was constrained to feign himself mad, and so effect his escape. . .

"Now what principle of preference may be imagined to have governed David when he committed his family to the dangerous keeping of the Moabites? Was it a mere matter of chance? It might seem so, as far as appears to the contrary in David's history, given in the books of Samuel; and if the book of Ruth had never come down to us, to accident it probably would have been ascribed. But this short and beautiful historical document shows us a *propriety* in the selection of Moab above any other for a place of refuge to the father and mother of David; since it is there seen that the grandmother of Jesse, David's father, was actually a *Moabitess;* Ruth being the mother of Obed, and Obed the father of Jesse. And, moreover, that Orpah, the other Moabitess, who married Mahlon at the time when Ruth married Chilion his brother, remained behind in Moab after the departure of Naomi and Ruth, and remained behind with a strong feeling of affection, nevertheless, for the family and kindred of her deceased husband taking leave of them with tears (Ruth 1:14). She herself then, or at all events, her descendants and friends might still be alive. Some regard for the posterity of Ruth, David would persuade himself, might still survive amongst them. . .

"Thus do we detect, not without some pains, a certain fitness, in the conduct of David in this transaction which makes it to be a real one. A forger of a story could not have fallen upon the happy device of sheltering Jesse in Moab simply on the recollecting of his Moabitish extraction two generations earlier; or, having fallen upon it, it is probable he would have taken care to draw the attention of his readers towards his device by some means or other, lest the evidence it was intended to afford of the truth of the history might be thrown away upon them. As it is, the circumstance itself is asserted without the smallest attempt to explain or account for it. Nay, recourse must be had to another book of Scripture, in order that the coincidence may be seen."

Unto the king of Moab David said, "Let my father and my mother, I pray thee, come forth and be with you, till I know what God will do for me." Slowly but surely our patriach was learning to acquiesce in the appointments of God. Practical subjection unto the Lord is only learned in the school of experience: the theory of it may be gathered from books, but the actuality has to be hammered out on the anvil of our hearts. Of our glorious Head it is declared, "Though He were a Son, yet learned He obedience by the things which He suffered" (Heb. 5:8). This word of David's also indicates that he was beginning to feel the need of waiting upon God for directions: how much sorrow and suffering would be avoided did *we* always do so. His "what God will do *for* me," rather than "with me," indicated a hope in the Lord.

"And the prophet Gad said unto David, Abide not in the hold; depart, and get thee into the land of Judea. Then David departed, and came into the forest of Hareth" (v. 5). In the light of this verse, and together with 22:23, we may see that "the excellent" of the earth (Psa. 16:3) were more and more gathering to him who was a type of Christ in His rejection. Here we see the prophet of God, with him, and shortly afterwards he was joined by the high priest — solemn it is to contrast the apostate Saul, who was now deserted by both. David had been humbled before God, and He now speaks again to him, not directly, but mediately. Two reasons may be suggested for this: David was not yet fully restored to Divine communion, and God was honouring His own institutions — the prophetic office: cf. 23:9-11.

"And the prophet Gad said unto David, Abide not in the hold; depart, and get thee into the land of Judah." It is quite clear from the language of this verse that at the time God now spoke to His servant through the prophet, he had not returned to the Cave of Adullam, but had sought temporary refuge in some stronghold of Moab. Now he received a call which presented a real test to his faith. To appear more openly in his own country would evidence the innocency of his cause, as well as display his confidence in the Lord. "The steps of a good man are ordered by the Lord" (Psa. 37:23), yet the path He appoints is not the one which is smoothest to the flesh. But when God calls, we must respond, and leave the issue entirely in His hands.

"When Saul heard that David was discovered, and the men that were with him, (now Saul abode in Gibeah under a tree in Ramah, having his spear in his hand, and all his servants standing about him); then Saul said unto his servants" etc. Here the Spirit takes up again another leading thread around which the history of 1 Samuel is woven. Having traced the movements of David since the leaving of his home (19:11, 12) up to the Cave of Adullam and his now receiving orders to return to the land of Judea, He follows again the evil history of Saul. The king had apparently set aside everything else, and was devoting himself entirely to the capture of David. He had taken up his headquarters at Gibeah: the "spear in his hand" showed plainly his blood-thirsty intentions.

The news of David's return to Judea, soon reached the ears of Saul, and the fact that he was accompanied by a considerable number of men, probably alarmed him not a little, fearful that the people would turn to his rival and that he would lose his throne. His character was revealed again by the words which he now addressed to his servants (v. 7), who were, for the most part, selected from his own tribe. He appealed not to the honour and glory of Jehovah, but to their cupidity. David belonged to Judah, and if he became king then those who belonged to the tribe of Benjamin must not expect to receive favours at his hands — neither rewards of land, nor positions of prominence in the army.

"All of you have conspired against me, and there is none that showeth me that my son hath made a league with the son of Jesse, and there is none of you that is sorry for me, or showeth unto me that my son hath stirred up my servant against me, to lie in wait, as at this day" (v. 8). Here Saul charges his followers with having failed to reveal to him that which he supposed they knew, and of showing no concern for the circumstance in which he was then placed; this he construed as a conspiracy against him. His was the language of ungovernable rage and jealousy. His son is charged as being ringleader of the conspirators, merely because he would not assist in the murder of an excellent man whom he loved! True, there was a covenant of friendship between Jonathan and David, but no plot to destroy Saul, as he wildly imagined. But it is the nature of an evil person to regard as enemies those who are not prepared to toady to him or her in everything.

It was in response to Saul's bitter words to his men, that Doeg the Edomite made known David's secret visit to Ahimelech, and his obtaining victuals and the sword of Goliath (vv. 9, 10). Nothing was mentioned of the high priest being imposed upon, but the impression was left that he joined with David in a conspiracy against Saul. Let us learn from this that we may "bear false witness against our neighbour" as really and disastrously by maliciously *withholding* part of the truth, as by deliberately inventing a lie. When called upon to express our opinion of another (which should, generally, be declined, unless some good purpose is to be served thereby), honesty requires that we impartially recount what is in his favour, as well as what makes against him. Note how in His addresses to the seven churches in Asia, the Lord commended the good, as well as rebuked that which was evil.

The terrible sequel is recorded in vv. 11-19 Ahimelech and all his subordinate priests were promptly summoned into the king's presence. Though he was by rank the second person in Israel, Saul contemptuously called the high priest "the son of Ahitub" (v. 12). Quietly ignoring the insult, Ahimelech addressed the king as "my lord," thus giving honour to whom honour was due — the occupant of any office which God has appointed is to be honoured, no matter how unworthy of respect the man may be personally. Next, the king charged the high priest with rebellion and treason (v. 13). Ahimelech gave a faithful and ungarnished account of his transaction with David (vv. 14, 15). But nothing could satisfy the incensed king but death, and orders were given for the whole priestly family to be butchered.

One of the sons of Ahimelech, named Abiathar, escaped. Probably he had been left by his father to take care of the tabernacle and its holy things, while he and the rest of the priests went to appear before Saul. Having heard of their bloody execution, and before the murderers arrived at Nob to complete their vile work of destroying the wives, children and flocks of the priests, he fled; taking with him the ephod and the urim and thummim, and joined David (v. 21). It was then that David wrote the 52nd Psalm. Three things may be observed in connection with the above tragedy. First, the solemn sentence which God had pronounced against the house of Eli was now executed (2:31-36; 3:12-14) — thus the iniquities of the fathers were visited upon the children. Second, Saul was manifestly forsaken of God, given up to Satan and his own malignant passions, and was fast ripening for judgment. Third, by this cruel carnage David obtained the presence of the high priest, who afterwards proved a great comfort and blessing to him (23:6, 9-13; 30:7-10) — thus did God make the wrath of man to praise Him and work together for good unto His own.

Then they told David, saying, Behold, the Philistines are fighting against Ke-i-lah and they are robbing the threshing-floors. Therefore David asked of the LORD, saying, Shall I go and strike these Philistines? And the LORD said to David, Go and strike the Philistines and save Ke-i-lah. And David's men said to him, Behold, we are afraid here in Judah. How much more then if we come to Ke-i-lah against the armies of the Philistines? Then David inquired of the LORD still again. And the LORD answered him and said, Arise, go down to Ke-i-lah. For I will deliver the Philistines into your hand. So David and his men went to Ke-i-lah and fought with the Philistines. And they brought away their cattle and struck them with a great slaughter. So David saved the people of Ke-i-lah. And when A-bi-a-thar the son of A-him-e-lech fled to David to Ke-i-lah, he came down with an ephod in his hand. And it was told Saul that David had come to Ke-i-lah. And Saul said, God has delivered him into my hands, for he is shut in by entering into a town that has gates and bars. And Saul called all the people together to war, to go down to Ke-i-lah to besiege David and his men. And David knew that Saul secretly planned evil against him. And he said to A-bi-a-thar the priest, Bring the ephod here. Then David said, O LORD God of Israel, Your servant has surely heard that Saul seeks to come to Ke-i-lah, to destroy the city for my sake. Will the men of Ke-i-lah deliver me up into his hand? Will Saul come down as Your servant has heard? O LORD God of Israel, I beg of You, tell Your servant. And the LORD said, He will come down. Then David said, Will the men of Ke-i-lah deliver me and my men into the hand of Saul? And the LORD said, They will deliver you up. Then David and his men, about six hundred, arose and left Ke-i-lah and went wherever they could go. And it was told to Saul that David had escaped from Ke-i-lah. And he did not go forth. And David stayed in the wilderness in strongholds and remained in a mountain in the wilderness of Ziph. And Saul looked for him every day, but God did not deliver him into his hands. – 1 Samuel 23:1-14.

The first section of 1 Sam. 23 (which we are now to look at) presents some striking contrasts. In it are recorded incidents exceedingly blessed, others fearfully sad. David is seen at his best, Saul at his worst. David humbly waits on the Lord, Saul presumes upon and seeks to pervert His providences. Saul is indifferent to the wellbeing of his own subjects, David delivers them from their enemies. David at imminent risk rescues the town of Keilah from the marauding Philistines; yet so lacking are they in gratitude, that they were ready to hand him over unto the man who sought his life. Though the priests of the Lord, with their entire families, had been brutally slain by Saul's orders, yet the awful malice of the king was not thereby appeased: he is now seen again seeking the life of David, and that at the very time when he had so unselfishly wrought good for the nation.

It is instructive and helpful to keep in mind the *order* of what has been before us in previous articles, so that we may perceive one of the important spiritual lessons in what is now to be before us. David had failed, failed sadly. We all do; but David had done what many are painfully slow in doing: he had humbled himself before the Lord, he had repented of and confessed his sins. In our last paper, we saw how that David had been restored, in considerable measure at least, to communion with the Lord. God had spoken to him through His prophet. Light was now granted again on his path. The word was given him to return to the land of Judah (22:5). That word he had heeded, and now we are to see how the Lord *used* him again. Strikingly does this illustrate 1 Pet. 5:6: "Humble yourselves therefore under the mighty hand of God, that He may exalt you in due time."

"Then they told David, Behold, the Philistines fight against Keilah, and they rob the threshingfloors" (1 Sam. 23:1). Here we may see another reason (more than those suggested at the close of our last article) why God had called David to return to the land of Judah: He had further work for him to do there. Keilah was within the borders of that tribe (Josh. 15:21, 44). It was a fortified town (v. 7), and the Philistines had laid seige to it. The "threshingfloors" (which were usually situated outside the cities: Judges 6:11, Ruth 3:2, 15) were already being pilfered by them. Who it was that acquainted David with these tidings we know not.

"Therefore David inquired of the Lord, saying, Shall I go and smite these Philistines?" (v. 2). Very blessed is this, and further evidence does it supply of David's spiritual recovery. Saul was neglecting the public safety, but the one whom he was hounding was concerned for it. Though he had been ill treated, David was not sulking over his wrongs, but instead was ready to return good for evil, by coming to the assistance of one of the king's besieged towns. What a noble spirit did he here manifest! Though his hands were full in seeking to hide from Saul, and provide for the needs of his six hundred men (no small task!), yet David unselfishly thought of the welfare of others.

"Therefore David inquired of the Lord, saying, Shall I go and smite these Philistines?" This is very beautiful. Having been anointed unto the throne, David considered himself the protector of Israel, and was ready to employ his men for the public weal. He had an intense love for his country, and was desirous of freeing it from its enemies, yet he would not act without first seeking counsel of the Lord: he desired that *God* should appoint his service. The more particularly we seek direction from God in fervent prayer, and the more carefully we consult the sacred Scriptures for the knowledge of His will, the more He is honoured, and the more we are benefited.

"And the Lord said unto David, Go, and smite the Philistines, and save Keilah" (v. 2). Where God is truly sought — that is, sought sincerely, humbly, trustfully, with the desire to learn and do that which is pleasing to Him — the soul will not be left in ignorance. God does not mock His needy children. His word declares, "In all thy ways acknowledge Him, and He *shall* direct thy paths" (Prov. 3:6). So it was here. The Lord responded to David's inquiry — possibly through the prophet Gad — and not only revealed His will, but gave promise that he should be successful.

"And David's men said unto him, Behold, we be afraid here in Judah: how much more then if we come to Keilah against the armies of the Philistines?" (v. 3). This presented a real test to David's confidence in the Lord, for if his men were unwilling to accompany him, how could he expect to relieve the besieged town? His men were obviously "afraid" of being caught between two fires. Were they to advance upon the Philistines and Saul's army should follow them up in the rear, then where would they be? Ah, their eyes were not upon the living God, but upon their difficult "circumstances," and to be occupied with these is always discouraging to the heart. But how often has a man of God, when facing a trying situation, found the unbelief of his professed friends and followers a real hindrance. Yet he should regard this as a test, and not as an obstacle. Instead of paralyzing action, it ought to drive him to seek succour from Him who never fails those who truly count upon His aid.

"Then David inquired of the Lord yet again" (v. 4). This is very precious. David did not allow the unbelieving fears of his men to drive him to despair. He could hardly expect them to walk by *his* faith. But he knew that when God works, He works at both ends of the line. He who had given him orders to go to the relief of Keilah, could easily quiet the hearts of his followers, remove their fears, and make them willing to follow his lead. Yes, with God "all things are possible." But He requires to be "inquired of" (Ezek. 36:37). He delights to be "proved" (Mal. 3:10). Oft He permits just such a trial as now faced David in order to teach us more fully His sufficiency for every emergency.

"Then David inquired of the Lord yet again." Yes, this is blessed indeed. David did not storm at his men, and denounce them as cowards. That would do no good. Nor did he argue and attempt to reason with them. Disdaining his own wisdom, feeling his utter dependency upon God, and more especially for their benefit — to set before them a godly example — he turned once more unto Jehovah. Let us learn from this incident that, the most effectual way of answering the unbelieving objections of faint-hearted followers and of securing their co-operation, is to refer them unto the promises and precepts of God, and set before them an example of complete dependency upon Him and of implicit confidence in Him.

"And the Lord answered him and said, Arise, go down to Keilah: for I will deliver the Philistines into thine hand" (v. 4). How sure is the fulfillment of that promise, "Them that honour Me, I will honour" (1 Sam. 2:30)! We always lose by acting independently of God, but we never lose by seeking counsel, guidance and grace from Him. God did not ignore David's inquiry. He was not displeased by his asking a second time. How gracious and patient He is! He not only responded to David's petition, but He gave an answer more explicit than at the first, for He now assured His servant of entire victory. May this encourage many a reader to come unto God with every difficulty, cast every care upon Him, and count upon His succour every hour.

"So David and his men went to Keilah, and fought with the Philistines, and brought away their cattle, and smote them with a great slaughter. So David saved the inhabitants of Keilah" (v. 5). Animated by a commission and promise from God, David and his men moved forward and attacked the Philistines. Not only did they completely rout the enemy, but they captured their cattle, which supplied food for David's men, that they were probably in much need of. How this furnishes an illustration of "Him that is able to do exceeding abundantly *above* all that we ask or think, according to the power that worketh in us" (Eph. 3:20)! God not only overthrew the Philistines and delivered Keilah, but as well, bountifully provided David's army with a supply of victuals.

"And it came to pass, when Abiathar the son of Ahimelech fled to David to Keilah, that he came down with an ephod in his hand" (v. 6). This was a further reward from the Lord unto David for obeying His word. As we shall see later, the presence of the high priest and his ephod with him, stood David in good stead in the future. We may also see here a striking example of the absolute control of God over all His creatures: it was David's visit to Ahimelech that had resulted in the slaying of all his family: well then might the only son left, feel that the son of Jesse was the last man whose fortunes he desired to share.

"And it was told Saul that David was come to Keilah. And Saul said, God hath delivered him into mine hand; for he is shut in, by entering into a town that hath gates and bars" (v. 7). Surely David's signal victory over the common enemy should have reconciled Saul to him. Was it not abundantly clear that God was with him, and if *He* were with him, who could be against him? But one who is abandoned by the Lord can neither discern spiritual things nor judge righteously, and therefore his conduct will be all wrong too. Accordingly we find that instead of thinking how he might most suitably reward David for his courageous and unselfish generosity, Saul desired only to do him mischief. Well might our patriarch write, "They regarded me evil for good to the spoiling of my soul" (Psa. 35:12).

"And Saul said, God hath delivered him into mine hand; for he is shut in, by entering into a town that hath gates and bars." How easy it is for a jaundiced mind to view things in a false light. When the heart is wrong, the providences of God are certain to be mis-interpreted. Terrible is it to behold the apostate king here concluding that God Himself had now sold David into his hands: that man has sunk to a fearful depth who blatantly assumes that the Almighty is working to further his wicked plans. While David was at large, hiding in caves and sheltering in the woods, he was hard to find; but here in a walled town, Saul supposed he would be completely trapped when his army surrounded it.

"And Saul called all the people together to war, to go down to Keilah, to besiege David and his men" (v.8). If we omit the last clause and read on through the next verse, it will be seen that the unscrupulous Saul resorted to a dishonest ruse. To make war against the Philistines was the ostensible object which the king set before his men; to capture David was his real design. The last clause of v. 8 states Saul's secret motive. While pretending to oppose the common enemy, he was intending to destroy his best friend. Verily, the Devil was his father, and the lusts of his father he would do.

"And David knew that Saul secretly practised mischief against him; and he said to Abiathar, the priest, Bring hither the ephod" (v. 9). Yes, "the secret of the Lord is with them that fear Him" (Psa. 25:14). Ah, but *only* with them that truly "fear" Him. "If any man walk in the day, he stumbleth not" (John 11:9). "He that followeth Me," said Christ, "shall not walk in darkness" (John 8:12). O what a blessed thing it is, dear reader, to have light upon our path, to *see* the enemy's snares and pitfalls. But in order to this, there must be a walking with Him who is "the Light." If we are out of communion with the Lord, if we have for the moment turned aside from the path of His commandments, then we can no longer perceive the dangers which menace us.

"And David knew that Saul secretly practised mischief against him." This is very blessed, and recorded for our instruction. We ought not to be ignorant of Satan's devices (2 Cor. 2:11), nor shall we be if our hearts are right with God. Observe carefully that this 9th verse opens with the word "And," which announces the fact that it is connected with and gives the sequel to what has gone before. And what *had* preceded in this case? First, David had sought counsel of the Lord (v. 2). Second, he had refused to be turned aside from the path of duty by the unbelieving fears of his followers (v. 3). Third, he had maintained an attitude of complete dependency upon the Lord (v. 4). Fourth, he had definitely obeyed the Lord (v. 5). And now God rewarded him by acquainting him with the enemy's designs upon him. Meet the conditions, my brother or sister, and you too shall know when the Devil is about to attack you.

David was not deceived by Saul's guile. He knew that though he had given out to his men one thing, yet in his heart he purposed quite another. "Then said, David, O Lord God of Israel, Thy servant hath certainly heard that Saul seeketh to come to Keilah, to destroy the city for my sake" (v. 10). This too is very blessed: once more David turns to the living God, and casts all his care upon Him (1 Pet. 5:7). Observe well his words: he does not say "Saul purposeth to slay *me*," but he seeketh to destroy *the city* for my sake," on my account. Is it not lovely to see him more solicitous about the welfare of others, than the preserving of his own life!

"Will the man of Keilah deliver me up into his hands? will Saul come down, as

Thy servant hath heard? O Lord God of Israel, I beseech Thee tell Thy servant. And the Lord said, He will come down" (v. 11). It is to be noted that the two questions here asked by David were not orderly put, showing the perturbed state of mind he was then in. We should also observe the manner in which David addressed God, as "Lord God of Israel" (so too in v. 10), which was His *covenant* title. It is blessed when we are able to realize the covenant-relationship of God to us (Heb. 13:20, 21), for it is ever an effectual plea to present before the Throne of Grace. The Lord graciously responded to David's supplication and granted the desired information, reversing the order of his questions. God's saying "he (Saul) will come down" (that is his purpose), here manifested His omniscience, for He knows all contingencies (possibilities and likelihoods), as well as actualties.

"Then said David, Will the man of Keilah deliver me and my men into the hand of Saul?" (v. 12). Wise David, He had good cause to conclude that after so nobly befriending Keilah and delivering it from the Philistines, that its citizens would now further his interests, and in such case, he and his own men could defend the town against Saul's attack. But he prudently refrained from placing any confidence in their loyalty. He probably reasoned that the recent cruel massacre of Nob would fill them with dread of Saul, so that he must not count upon their assistance. Thus did he seek counsel from the Lord. And so ought we: we should never confide in help from others, no, not even from those we have befriended, and from whom we might reasonably expect a return of kindness. No ties of honour, gratitude, or affection, can secure the heart under powerful temptation. Nay, we know not how *we* would act if assailed by the terrors of a cruel death, and left without the immediate support of Divine grace. We are to depend *only* upon the Lord for guidance and protection.

"And the Lord said, They will deliver thee up" (v. 12). This must have been very saddening to David's heart, for base ingratitude wounds deeply. Yet let us not forget that the kindness of other friends whom the Lord often unexpectedly raises up, counterbalances the ingratitude and fickleness of those we have served. God answered David here according to His knowledge of the human heart. *Had* David remained in Keilah, its inhabitants would have delivered him up upon Saul's demand. But he remained not, and escaped. Be it carefully noted that this incident furnishes a clear illustration of human responsibility, and is a strong case in point against bald Fatalism — taking the passive attitude that what is to be, must be.

"Then David and his men, which were about six hundred, arose and departed out of Keilah, and went whithersoever they could go. And it was told Saul that David was escaped from Keilah, and he forebare to go forth. And David abode in the wilderness in strong-holds, and remained in a mountain in the wilderness of Ziph. And Saul sought him every day, but God delivered him not into his hand" (vv. 13, 14). This too is blessed: David was willing to expose himself and his men to further hardships, rather than endanger the lives of Keilah! Having no particular place in view, they went forth wherever they thought best. The last half of v. 14 shows God's protecting hand was still upon them, and is Jehovah's reply to Saul's vain and presumptuous confidence in v. 7.

And David saw that Saul had come out to seek his life. And David was in the wilderness of Ziph in a woods. And Jonathan, Saul's son, arose and went to David in the woods and strengthened his hand in God. And he said to him, Do not fear, for the hand of Saul my father shall not find you. And you shall be king over Israel, and I shall be next to you. And my father Saul knows that also.

And the two of them made a covenant before the LORD. And David stayed in the woods, and Jonathan went to his house. Then the men of Ziph came up to Saul to Gib-e-ah, saying, Does not David hide himself with us in strongholds in the woods, in the hill of Ha-chi-lah, which is on the south of Je-shi-mon? Now therefore, O king, come down according to all the desire of your soul to come down. And our part is to deliver him into the king's hand. And Saul said, Blessed are you from the LORD, for you have pity on me. I beg you, go prepare still more, and know and see the place where his foot is, and who has seen him there, For I am told that he deals very wisely. Watch therefore and take knowledge of all the lurking-places where he hides himself, and come to me again with the certainty. And I will go with you. And if he is in the land, I will search him out throughout all the thousands of Judah. And they arose and went to Ziph before Saul. But David and his men were in the wilderness of Ma-on, in the plain on the south of Je-shi-mon. Saul and his men also went to look for him. And they told David. And he came down from the rock and stayed in the wilderness of Ma-on. And when Saul heard, he followed David in the wilderness of Ma-on. And Saul went on this side of the mountain, and David and his men on that side of the mountain. And David hurried to get away for fear of Saul. For Saul and his men were surrounding David and his men, to catch them. But a messenger came to Saul, saying, Hurry and come! For the Philistines have invaded the land. And Saul turned back from pursuing after David and went against the Philistines. Therefore they called that place, The Dividing Rock. And David went up from there and lived in strongholds at En-ge-di. 1 Samuel 23:15-29.

Many are the afflictions of the righteous" (Psa. 34:19): some internal, others external; some from friends, others from foes; some more directly at the hand of God, others more remotely by the instrumentality of the Devil. Nor should this be thought strange. Such has been the lot of all God's children in greater or less degree. Nor ought we to expect much comfort in a world which so basely crucified the Lord of glory. The sooner the Christian makes it his daily study to pass through this world as a stranger and pilgrim, anxious to depart and be with Christ, the better for his peace of mind. But it is natural to cling tenaciously to this life and to love the things of time and sense, and therefore most of the Lord's people have to encounter many buffetings and have many disappointments before they are brought to hold temporal things with a light hand and before their silly hearts are weaned from that which satisfies not.

There is scarcely any affliction which besets the suffering people of God that the subject of these articles did not experience. David, in the different periods of his varied life, was placed in almost every situation in which a believer, be he rich or poor in this world's goods, can be placed. This is one feature which makes the study of his life of such practical interest unto us today. And this also it was which experimentally fitted him to write so many Psalms, which the saints of all ages have found so perfectly suited to express unto God the varied feelings of their souls. No matter whether the heart be cast down by the bitterest grief, or whether it be exultant with over-flowing joy, nowhere can we find language more appropriate to use in our approaches unto the Majesty on High, than in the recorded sobs and songs of him who tasted the bitters of cruel treatment and base betrayals, and the sweetness of human success and spiritual communion with the Lord, as few have done.

Oftentimes the providences of God seem profoundly mysterious to our dull perceptions, and strange unto us do appear the schoolings through which He passes His servants; nevertheless faith is assured that Omniscience makes no mistakes, and He who is Love causes none of His children a needless tear. Beautifully did C. H. Spurgeon introduce his exposition of Psa. 59 by saying, "Strange that the painful events in David's life should end in enriching the repertoire of the national minstrelsy. Out of a sour, ungenerous soil spring up the honey-bearing flowers of psalmody. Had he never been cruelly hunted by Saul, Israel and the church of God in after ages would have missed this song. The music of the sanctuary is in no small degree indebted to the trials of the saints. Affliction is the tuner of the harps of sanctified songsters." Let every troubled reader seek to lay this truth to heart and take courage.

"And David abode in the wilderness in strong holds, and remained in a mountain in the wilderness of Ziph. And Saul sought him every day but God delivered him not into his hand" (1 Sam. 23:14). It is blessed to behold David's self-restraint under sore provocation. Though perfectly innocent, so far as his conduct toward Saul was concerned, that wicked king continued to hound him without any rest. David had conducted himself honourably in every public station he filled, and now he has to suffer disgrace in the eyes of the people as a hunted out-law. Great must have been the temptation to put an end to Saul's persecution by the use of force. He was a skilled leader, had six hundred men under him (v. 13), and he might easily have employed strategy, lured his enemy into a trap, fallen upon and slain him. Instead, he possessed his soul in patience, walked in God's ways, and waited God's time. And the Lord honoured this as the sequel shows.

Ah, dear reader, it is written, "He that is slow to anger is better than the mighty; and he that ruleth his spirit than he that taketh a city" (Prov. 16:32). O for more godly self-control; for this we should pray earnestly and oft. Are you, like David was, sorely oppressed? Are you receiving evil at the hands of those from whom you might well expect good? Is there some Saul mercilessly persecuting you? Then no doubt you too are tempted to take things into your own hands, perhaps have recourse to the law of the land. But O tried one, suffer us to gently remind you that it is written, "Avenge not yourselves, but rather give place unto wrath . . . vengeance is Mine; I will repay, saith the Lord. Therefore if thine enemy hunger, feed him; if he thirst, give him drink" (Rom. 12:19, 20). Remember too the example left us by the Lord Jesus, "Who, when He was reviled, reviled not again; when He suffered, He threatened not; but committed Himself to Him that judgeth righteously" (1 Pet. 2:23).

"And David saw that Saul was come out to seek his life: and David was in the wilderness of Ziph in a wood" (v. 15). How this illustrates what we are told in Gal. 4:29, "But as then he that was born after the flesh persecuted him that was born after the Spirit, even so it is now"! And let us not miss the deeper spiritual meaning of this: the opposition which Isaac encountered from Ishmael adumbrated the lustings of the "flesh" against "the spirit." There is a continual warfare within every real Christian between the principle of sin and the principle of grace, commonly termed "the two natures." There is a spiritual Saul who is constantly seeking the life of a spiritual David: it is the "old man" with his affections and appetites, seeking to slay the new man. Against his relentless attacks we need ever to be on our guard.

"And David saw that Saul was come out to seek his life: and David was in the wilderness of Ziph in a wood." "Ziph" derived its name from a city in the tribe of Judah: Josh. 15:25. It is surely significant that "Ziph" signifies "a refining-place": possibly the "mountain" there (v. 14) was rich in minerals, and at Ziph there was a smelter and refiner. Be this as it may, the spiritual lesson is here written too plain for us to miss. The hard knocks which the saint receives from a hostile world, the persecutions he endures at the hands of those who hate God, the trials through which he passes in this scene of sin, may, and should be, improved to the good of his soul. O may many of the Lord's people prove that these "hard times" through which they are passing are a "refining place" for their faith and other spiritual graces.

"And Jonathan Saul's son arose, and went to David into the wood, and strengthened his hand in God. And he said unto him, Fear not: for the hand of Saul my father shall not find thee; and thou shalt be king over Israel, and I shall be next unto thee; and that also Saul my father knoweth. And they two made a covenant before the Lord: and David abode in the wood, and Jonathan went to his house" (vv. 16-18). These verses record the final meeting on earth between David and the weak, vacillating Jonathan. Attached to David as he was by a strong natural affection, yet he lacked grace to throw in his lot with the hunted fugitive. Refusing to join with his father in persecuting David, yet the pull of the palace and the court was too strong to be resisted. He stands as a solemn example of the spiritual compromiser, of the man who is naturally attracted to Christ, but lacking a supernatural knowledge of Him which leads to full surrender to Him. That he "strengthened David's hand in God" no more evidenced him to be a regenerate man, than do the words of Saul in v. 21. Instead of his words in v. 17 coming true, he fell by the sword of the Philistines on Gilboa.

"Then came up the Ziphites to Saul to Gibeah, saying, Doth not David hide himself with us in strong holds in the wood, in the hill of Hachilah, which is on the south of Jeshimon? Now therefore, O King, come down according to all the desire of thy soul to come down; and our part shall be to deliver him into the king's hand" (vv. 19, 20). Alas, what is man, and how little to be depended upon! Here was David seeking shelter from his murderous foe, and that among the people of his own tribe, and there were they, in order to curry favour with Saul, anxious to betray him into his hands. It was a gross breach of hospitality, and there was no excuse for it, for Saul had not sought unto nor threatened them. It mattered not to them though innocent blood were shed, so long as they procured the smile of the apostate monarch. That Day alone will show how many have fallen victims before those who cared for nothing better than the favour of those in authority.

"And Saul said, Blessed be ye of the Lord; for ye have compassion on me" (v.21). Thankfully did Saul receive the offer to these treacherous miscreants. Observe well how he used the language of piety while bent on committing the foulest crime! Oh my reader, for your own good we beg you to take heed unto this. Require something more than fair words, or even religious phrases, before you form a judgment of another, and still more so before you place yourself in his power. Promises are easily made, and easily broken by most people. The name of God is glibly taken upon the lips of multitudes who have no fear of God in their hearts. Note too how the wretched Saul represented himself to be the aggrieved one, and construes the perfidy of the Ziphites as their loyalty to the king.

"Go, I pray you, prepare yet, and know and see his place where his haunt is, and who hath seen him there: for it is told me that he dealeth very subtilly. See therefore, and take knowledge of all the lurking places where he hideth himself, and come ye again to me with the certainty and I will go with you: and it shall come to pass, if he be in the land, that I will search him out throughout all the thousands of Judah" (vv. 22, 23). Before he journeyed to Ziph, Saul desired more specific information as to exactly where David was now located. He knew that the man he was after had a much better acquaintance than his own of that section of the country. He knew that David was a clever strategist: perhaps he had fortified some place, and the king wished for details, so that he might know how large a force would be needed to surround and capture David and his men. Apparently Saul felt so sure of his prey, he considered there was no need for hurried action.

The news that the Ziphites had proven unfaithful reached the ears of David, and though the king's delay gave him time to retreat to the wilderness of Maon (v. 24), yet he was now in a sore plight. His situation was desperate, and none but an Almighty hand could deliver him. Blessed is it to see him turning at this time unto the living God and spreading his urgent case before Him. It was then that he prayed the prayer which is recorded in Psa. 54, the superscription of which reads "A Psalm of David, when the Ziphites came and said to Saul, Doth not David hide himself with us?" In it we are given to hear him pouring out his heart unto the Lord; and unto it we now turn to consider a few of its details.

"Save me, O God, by Thy name, and judge me by Thy strength" (Psa. 54:1). David was in a position where he was beyond the reach of human assistance: only a miracle could now save him, therefore did he supplicate the miracle-working God. Without any preamble, David went straight to the point and cried, "Save me, O God." Keilah would not shelter him, the Ziphites had basely betrayed him, Saul and his men thirsted for his blood. Other refuge there was none; God alone could help him. His appeal was to His glorious "Name," which stands for the sum of all His blessed attributes; and to His righteousness — "judge me by Thy strength" signifies, Secure justice for me, for none else will give it me. This manifested the innocency of his cause. Only when our case is pure can we call upon the power of Divine justice to vindicate us.

"Hear my prayer, O God; give ear to the words of my mouth" (Psa. 54:2). How *we* need to remember and turn unto the Lord when enduring the contradiction of sinners against ourselves: to look above and draw strength from God, so that we be not weary and faint in our minds. Well did C. H. Spurgeon write, "As long as God hath an open ear we cannot be shut up in trouble. All other weapons may be useless, but all-prayer is evermore available. No enemy can spike this gun." "For strangers are risen up against me, and oppressors seek after my soul: they have not set God before them. Selah" (Psa. 54:3). Those who had no acquaintance with David, and so could have no cause for ill-will against him, were his persecutors; strangers were they to God. In such a circumstance it is well for us to plead before God that we are being hated for *His* sake.

We must not here expound the remainder of this Psalm. But let us note three other things in it. First, the marked change in the last four verses, following the "Selah" at the end of v. 3. On that word there Spurgeon wrote, "As if he said, 'Enough of this, let us pause.' He is out of breath with indignation. A sense of wrong bids him suspend the music awhile. It may also be observed, that more pauses would, as a rule, improve our devotions: we are usually too much in a hurry." Second, his firm confidence in God and the assurance that his request would be granted: this appears in vv. 4-6, particularly in the "He *shall* reward evil unto mine enemies" — the "cut them off" was not spoken in hot revenge, but as an Amen to the sure sentence of the last Judge. Third, his absolute confidence that his prayer was answered: the "hath delivered me" of v. 7 is very, very striking, and with it should be carefully compared and pondered Mark 11:24.

It now remains for us to observe *how* God answered David's prayer. "And they arose, and went to Ziph before Saul: but David and his men were in the wilderness of Maon, in the plain of the south of Jeshimon" (v. 24). The term "wilderness' is rather misleading to English ears: it is not synonymous with desert, but is in contrast from cultivated farmlands and orchards, often signifying a wild forest. "And when Saul heard that, he pursued after David in the wilderess of Maon. And Saul went on this side of the mountain, and David and his men on that side of the mountain: and David made haste to get away for fear of Saul; for Saul and his men compassed David and his men round about to take them" (vv. 25, 26). How often is such the case with us: some sore trial presses, and we cry unto God for relief, but before His answer comes, matters appear to get worse. Ah, that is in order that His hand may be the more evident.

David's plight was now a serious one, for Saul and his men had practically enveloped them, and only a "mountain," or more accurately, a steep cliff, separated them. Escape seemed quite cut off: out-numbered, surrounded, further flight was out of the question. At last Saul's evil object appeared to be on the very point of attainment. But man's extremity is God's opportunity. Beautifully did Matthew Henry comment, "This mountain (or cliff) was an emblem of the Divine Providence coming between David and the destroyer, like the pillar of cloud between the Israelites and the Egyptians." Yet, a few hours at most, and Saul and his army would either climb or go around that crag. Now for the striking and blessed sequel.

"But there came a messenger unto Saul, saying, Haste thee, and come; for the Philistines have invaded the land. Wherefore Saul returned from pursuing after David, and went against the Philistines: therefore they called that place The rock of divisions. And David went up from thence and dwelt in strong holds at Engedi" (vv. 27-29). How marvelously and how graciously God times things! He who orders all events and controls all creatures, moved the Philistines to invade a portion of Saul's territory, and tidings of this reached the king's ear just at the moment David seemed on the brink of destruction. Saul at once turned his attention to the invaders, and thus he was robbed of his prey and God glorified as his Protector. Thus, without striking a blow, David was delivered. O how blessed to know that the same God is *for* His people today, and without them doing a thing He can turn away those who are harassing. God *does* hear and answer the prayer of faith! David and his little force now had their opportunity to escape, and fled to the strong holds of Engedi, on the shore of the Dead Sea.

And when Saul had returned from following the Philistines, he was told, Behold, David is in the wilderness of En-ge-di. Then Saul took three thousand chosen men out of all Israel and went to seek David and his men on the rocks of the wild goats. And he came to the sheepcotes by the way, where there was a cave. And Saul went in to cover his feet. And David and his men remained in the sides of the cave. And the men of David said to him, Behold, this is the day of which the LORD said to you, Behold, I will deliver your enemy into your hand so that you may do to him as it shall seem good to you. Then David arose and cut off the skirt of Saul's robe secretly. 1 Samuel 24: 1-4.

We began our last article by quoting "many are the afflictions of the righteous," the remainder of the verse reading "but the Lord delivereth him out of them all" (Psa. 34:19). This does not mean that God always rescues the afflicted one from the physical danger which menaces him. No indeed, and we must be constantly on our guard against carnally interpreting the Holy Scriptures. It is quite true that there are numerous cases recorded in the Word where the Lord was pleased to graciously put forth His power and extricate His people from situations where death immediately threatened them: the deliverance of Israel at the Red Sea, Elijah from the murderous intentions of Ahab and Jezebel, Daniel from the lions' den, being striking illustrations in point. Yet the slaying of Abel by Cain, the martyrdom of Zechariah (Matt. 23:35), the stoning of Stephen, are examples to the contrary. Then did the promise of Psa. 34:19 fail in these latter instances? No indeed they received a yet more glorious fulfillment, for they were finally delivered out of this world of sin and suffering.

David was the one whose hand was moved by the Holy Spirit to first pen Psalm 34:19, and signally was it fulfilled in his history in a physical sense. Few men's lives have been more frequently placed in jeopardy than was his, and few men have experienced the Lord's delivering hand as he did. But there was a special reason for that, and it is this to which we would now call attention. David was one of the progenitors of Israel's Messiah, and it is indeed striking and blessed to note the wonderful works of God of old in His miraculously preserving the chosen seed from which Christ, after the flesh, was to spring. Indeed it is this more particularly, which supplies the key to many a Divine interposition on behalf of the patriachs and others, who were in the immediate line from which Jesus of Nazareth issued.

Strikingly does this appear in the history of Abraham, Isaac, and Jacob, who for so many years dwelt in the midst of the Canaanites. The inhabitants of that land were heathen, and most wicked, as Gen. 15:16 intimates. Abraham and his descendants were exposed to them as sojourners in the land, and men are most apt to be irritated by the peculiar customs of strangers. It was, then, a most remarkable dispensation of Providence which preserved the patriarchs in the midst of such a people: see Psa. 105:42, "Thus was this handful, this little root that had the blessing of the Redeemer in it, preserved in the midst of enemies and dangers; which was not unlike to the preserving of the ark in the midst of the tempestuous deluge" (Jon. Edwards). Wondrously too did God preserve the infant nation of Israel in Egypt, in the wilderness, and on their first entering the promised land.

Still more arresting is the illustration which this principle receives in the Divine preserving of the life of him who was more immediately and illustriously the sire of Christ. How often was there but a step betwixt David and death! His encountering of the lion and bear in the days of his shepherd life, which, without Divine intervention, could have rent him in pieces as easily as they caught a lamb from his flock; his facing Goliath, who was powerful enough to break him across his knee, and give his flesh to the beasts of the field as he threatened; the exposing of his life to the Philistines, when Saul required one hundred of their foreskins as a dowry for his daughter; the repeated assaults of the king by throwing his javelin at him; the later attempts made to capture and slay him; — yet from all these was David delivered. "Thus was the precious seed that virtually contained the Redeemer and all the blessings of redemption, wondrously preserved, when all earth and hell were conspired against it to destroy it" (Jonathan Edwards).

But we must now turn to our present lesson, a lesson which records one of the most striking events in the eventful life of David. Well did Matthew Henry point out, "We have hitherto had Saul seeking an opportunity to destroy David, and, to his shame, he could never find it; in this chapter David had a fair opportunity to destroy Saul, and, to his honour, he did not make use of it; and his sparing Saul's life was as great an instance of God's *grace in* him, as the presrving of his own life was of God's *providence over* him." Most maliciously had Saul sought David's life, most generously did David spare Saul's life. It was a glorious triumph of the spirit over the flesh, of grace over sin.

"And it came to pass, when Saul was returned from following the Philistines, that it was told him, saying, Behold, David is in the wilderness of Engedi" (1 Sam. 24:1). From these words we gather that Saul had been successful in turning back the invading Philistines. This illustrates a solemn principle which is often lost sight of: human success is no proof of Divine approbation. The mere fact that a man is prospering outwardly, does not, of itself, demonstrate that his life is pleasing unto the Lord. No one but an infidel would deny that it was *God* who enabled Saul to clear his land of the Philistines, yet we err seriously if we conclude from this that He delighted in him. As oxen are fattened for the slaughter, so God often ripens the wicked for judgment and damnation by an abundance of His temporal mercies. The immediate sequel shows clearly what Saul still was.

"And it came to pass, when Saul was returned from following the Philistines, that it was told him, saying, Behold, David is in the wilderness of Engedi." This may be regarded as a testing of Saul, for every thing that happens in each of our lives tests us at some point or other. Miserably did Saul fail under it. Nothing in the outward dispensations of God change the heart of man: His chastisements do not break the stubborn will, nor His mercies melt the hard heart. Nothing short of the regenerating work of the Spirit can make any man a new creature in Christ Jesus. The success with which God had just favoured his military enterprise against the Philistines, made no impression upon the reprobate soul of the apostate king. Pause for a moment, dear reader, and face this question, Has the goodness of God brought *you* to repentance?

"Then Saul took three thousand chosen men out of all Israel, and went to seek David and his men upon the rocks of the wild goats" (v. 2). What a terribly solemn illustration does this verse supply of what is said in Eccl. 8:11, "Because sentence against an evil work is not executed speedily, therefore the heart of the sons of men is *fully* set in them to do evil." Wicked men are often interrupted in their evil courses, yet they return unto them when the restraint is removed, as if deliverance from trouble were only given that they should add iniquity unto iniquity. It was thus with Pharaoh: time after time God sent a plague which stayed that vile monarch's hand, yet as soon as respite was granted, he hardened his heart again. So Saul had been providentially blocked while pursuing David, by the invading Philistines; but now, as soon as this hindrance was removed, he redoubled his evil efforts. O unsaved reader, has it not been thus with you? Your course of self-pleasing was suddenly checked by an illness, your round of pleasure-seeking was stopped by a sick-bed. Opportunity was given for you to consider the interests of your immortal soul, to humble yourself beneath the mighty hand of God. Perhaps you did so in a superficial way, but what has been the sequel? Health and strength have been mercifully restored by God, but are they being used for His glory, or are you now vainly pursuing the phantoms of this world harder than ever?

Ought not the very invasion of the Philistines to have changed Saul's attitude toward the one whom he was so causelessly and relentlessly pursuing? Ought he not to have realized now more forcibly than ever, that he needed David at the head of his army to repulse the common enemy? And O unsaved reader, is not the case very much the same with thee? The faithful servant of God, who has your interests at heart, you despise; that Christian friend who begs you to consider the claims of Christ, the solemnities of an unending eternity, the certain and terrible doom of those who live only for this life, you regard as a "kill-joy." Saul is now in the torments of Hell, and in a short time at most *you* will be there too, unless you change your course and beg God to change your heart.

Let us turn our thoughts once more unto David. As we saw at the close of our last article, in answer to believing prayer, God granted him a striking deliverance from the hand of his enemy. Yet that deliverance was but a brief one. Saul now advanced against him with a stronger force than before. Does not every real Christian know something of this in his own spiritual experience? It is written that "we must through *much* tribulation enter into the kingdom of God" (Act 14:22). Troubles come, and then a respite is granted, and then new troubles follow on the heels of the old ones. Our spiritual enemies will not leave us in peace very long; nevertheless, they are a blessing in disguise if they drive us to our knees. Very few souls thrive as well in times of prosperity as they do in seasons of adversity. Winters' frosts may necessitate warmer clothes, but they also kill the flies and garden pests.

David had now betaken himself unto "The rocks of the wild goats." Thither Saul and his large army follow him. Once more God undertook for him, and that in a striking way. "And he came to the sheepcotes by the way, where was a cove; and Saul went in to cover his feet: and David and his men remained in the sides of the cave" (v. 3). In that section of Palestine there are large caves, partly so by nature, partly so by human labour, for the sheltering of sheep from the heat of the sun; hence we read in the Song of Sol. 1:7 of "where thou makest thy flock to rest at noon." In one of these spacious caverns, David, and some of his men at least, had taken refuge. Thither did Saul, separated apparently from his men, now turn, in order to seek repose. Thus, by a strange carelessness (viewed from the human standpoint), Saul places himself completely at David's mercy.

"And the men of David said unto him, Behold the day of which the Lord said unto thee, Behold, I will deliver thine enemy into thine hand, that thou mayest do to him as it shall seem good unto thee" (v. 4). David's men at once saw the hand of the Lord in this unexpected turn of events. So far, so good. None but an infidel believes in things happening by chance, though there are many infidels now wearing the name of "Christian." There are no accidents in a world which is governed by the living God, for "of Him, and through Him, and to Him, are all things: to whom be glory forever. Amen" (Rom. 11:36). Therefore does faith perceive the hand of God in every thing which enters our lives, be it great or small. And it is only as we recognize His hand moulding all our circumstances, that God is honoured, and our hearts are kept in peace. O for grace to say at all times, "It is the Lord: let Him do what seemeth Him good" (1 Sam. 3:18).

"And the men of David said unto him, Behold the day of which the Lord said unto thee, Behold, I will deliver thine enemy into thine hand, that thou mayest do to him as it shall seem good unto thee." It is not difficult to trace the line of thought which was in their minds. They felt that here was an opportunity too good to be missed, an opportunity which Providence itself had obviously placed in David's way. One stroke of the sword would rid him of the only man that stood between him and the throne. Not only so, but the slaying of this apostate Saul would probably mean the bringing back of the whole nation unto the Lord. How many there are in Christendom today who believe that the end justifies the means: to get "results" is the all-important thing with them — *how* this is done matters little or nothing. Had such men been present to counsel David they had argued, Be not scrupulous about slaying Saul, see how much good it will issue in!

"What a critical moment it was in David's history! Had he listened to the specious counsellors who urged upon him to do what Providence, seemingly, had put in his way, his life of faith would have come to an abrupt end. One stroke of his sword, and he steps into a throne! Farewell poverty! Farewell the life of a hunted goat. Reproaches, sneers, defeat, would cease; adulations, triumphs, riches would be his. But his at the sacrifice of faith; at the sacrifice of a humbled will, ever waiting on God's time; at the sacrifice of a thousand precious experiences of God's care, God's provision, God's guidance, God's tenderness. No, even a throne at that price is too dear. Faith will wait" (C. H. Bright).

But there is a deeper lesson taught here, which every Christian does well to take thoroughly to heart. It is this: we need to be exceedingly cautious *how we interpret* the events of Providence and what conclusions we draw from them, lest we mistake the opportunity of following out our own inclinations for God's approbation of our conduct. God had promised David the throne, had His time now come for removing the one obstacle which stood in his way? It looked very much like it. Saul had shown no mercy, and there was not the least likelihood that he would do so; then was it God's will that David should be His instrument for taking vengeance upon him? It seemed so, or why should He have delivered him into his hand! David had cried to God for deliverance and had appealed unto Divine Justice for vindication (Psa. 54:1), had the hour now arrived for his supplication to be answered? The unexpected sight of Saul asleep at his feet, made this more than likely. How easy, how very easy then, for David to have made an erroneous deduction from the event of Providence on this occasion!

God was, in reality, *testing* David's faith, testing his patience, testing his piety. The testing of his faith lay in submission to the Word, which plainly says, "thou shalt not kill," and God had given him no exceptional command to the contrary. The testing of his patience lay in his quietly waiting God's time to ascend the throne of Israel: the temptation before him was to take things into his own hands and rush matters. The testing of his piety lay in the mortifying of his natural desires to avenge himself, to act in grace, and show kindness to one who had sorely mistreated him. It was indeed a very real testing, and blessed is it to see how the spirit triumphed over the flesh.

The application of this incident to the daily life of the Christian is of great practical importance. Frequently God tests *us* in similar ways. He so orders his providences as to try our hearts and make manifest what is in them. How often we are exercised about some important matter, some critical step in life, some change in our affairs involving momentous issues. We distrust our own wisdom, we want to be sure of God's will in the matter, we spread our case before the Throne of Grace, and ask for light and guidance. So far, so good. Then, usually, comes the testing: events transpire which seem to show that it *is* God's will for us to take a certain step, things appear to point plainly in that direction. Ah, my friend, that may only be God trying your heart. If, notwithstanding your praying over it, your *desires* are really set upon that object or course, then it will be a very simple thing for you to misinterpret the events of Providence and jump to a wrong conclusion.

An accurate knowledge of God's Word, a holy state of heart (wherein self is judged, and its natural longings mortified), a broken will, are absolutely essential in order to clearly discern the path of duty in important cases and crises. The safest plan is to *deny* all suggestions of revenge, covetousness, ambition, and impatience. A heart that is established in true godliness will rather interpret the dispensations of Providence as trials of faith and patience, as occasions to practice self-denial, than as opportunities for self-indulgence. In any case, "he that believeth shall not make haste" (Isa. 28:16). "Commit thy way unto the Lord; trust also in Him; and He shall bring it to pass. . .Rest in the Lord, and wait patiently for Him" (Psa. 37:5, 7). O for grace to do so; but such grace has to be definitely, diligently, and daily sought for. A.W.P.

And afterward David's heart struck him because he had cut off Saul's skirt. And he said to his men, The LORD forbid that I should do this thing to my master, the LORD's anointed, to stretch forth my hand against him, since he is the anointed of the LORD. So David cut off his servants with these words and did not allow them to rise against Saul. But Saul rose up out of the cave and went on his way. David also arose afterward and went out of the cave and cried after Saul, saying, My lord the king! And when Saul looked behind him, David stooped with his face to the earth and bowed himself. And David said to Saul, Why do you hear man's words, saying, Behold, David seeks your hurt? Behold, your eyes have seen today how the LORD had delivered you today into my hand in the cave. And some urged me to kill you. But my eye spared you. And I said, I will not put forth my hand against my lord, for he is the LORD's anointed. And my father, see! Yes, see the skirt of your robe in my hand! For in that I cut off the skirt of your robe and did not kill you, you know and see that there is neither evil nor transgression in my hand, and I have not sinned against you. Yet you hunt my soul, to take it. May the LORD judge between me and you, and may the LORD avenge me of you. But my hand shall not be on you. As the proverb of the ancients says, Wickedness comes forth from the wicked. But my hand shall not be on you. After whom has the king of Israel come out? After whom do you pursue? After a dead dog? After a flea? May the LORD therefore be judge, and judge between you and me, and see, and plead my cause, and deliver me out of your hand. 1 Samuel 24:5-15.

In our last we left the apostate king of Israel asleep in the cave of Engedi, the very place which had been made a refuge by David and his followers. There Saul lay completely at the mercy of the man whose life he sought. David's men were quick to perceive their advantage, and said to their master "Behold the day of which the Lord said unto thee, Behold I will deliver thine enemy into thine hand, that thou mayest do to him as it shall seem good unto thee" (1 Sam. 24:4). A real temptation presented itself to the sweet Psalmist of Israel, and though he was not completely overcome by it, yet he did not emerge from the conflict without a wound and a stain. "Then David arose, and cut off the skirt of Saul's robe privily." How true it is that "evil communications corrupt good manners" (1 Cor. 15:33)! Did this incident come back to his mind when, (probably) at a later date, the Spirit of God moved him to write "Blessed is the man that walketh not in the counsel of the ungodly" (Psa. 1:1)? Possibly so; at any rate, we find here a solemn warning which each of us does well to take to heart.

"And it came to pass afterward that David's heart smote him, because he had cut off Saul's skirt" (1 Sam. 24:5): which means, his conscience accused him, and he repented of what he had done. Good is it when our hearts condemn us for what the world regards as trifles. Though David had done no harm to the king's person, and though he had given proof it was in his power to slay him, nevertheless his action was a serious affront against the royal dignity. No matter what be the personal character of the ruler, because of his office, God commands us to "honour the king" (1 Pet. 2:17). This is a word concerning which all of us need reminding, for we are living in times when an increasing number "despise dominion, and *speak evil* of dignities" (Jude 8). God takes note of this!

"David's heart smote him, because he had cut off Saul's skirt." With this should be compared 1 Sam. 24:10, "And David's heart smote him after that he numbered the people. And David said unto the Lord, I have sinned greatly in that I have done: and now, I beseech Thee, O Lord, take away the iniquity of Thy servant; for I have done very foolishly." From these passages it is evident that David was blest with a tender conscience, which is ever a mark of true spirituality. In solemn contrast therefrom, we read of those "having their conscience seared with a hot iron" (1 Tim. 4:2), and of some "being past feeling" (Eph. 4:19), which is a sure index of those who have been abandoned by God. David soon regretted his rash action and realized he had sinned. May God graciously grant unto reader and writer a sensitive conscience.

"And he said unto his men, The Lord forbid that I should do this thing unto my master, the Lord's anointed, to stretch forth mine hand against him, seeing he is the anointed of the Lord" (v. 6). How honest of David! He not only repented before God of his rash conduct, but he also confessed his wrong- doing unto those who had witnessed the same. It requires much grace and courage to do this, yet nothing short of it is required of us. Moreover, we know not to whom God may be pleased to bless a faithful and humble acknowledgement of our sins. David now let his men know plainly that he was filled with abhorrence for having so insulted his sovereign Lord. Observe how that it was his looking at things from the *Divine* viewpoint which convicted him: he now regarded Saul not as a personal enemy, but as one whom *God* had appointed to reign as long as he lived.

"So David stayed his servants with these words, and suffered them not to rise against Saul" (v. 7). "Stayed" here signifies, pacified or quieted them, hindering them from laying rough hands upon the king. The first word of this verse is deeply significant: "So," in this manner, by what he had just said — how evident that God clothed his words with power! Few things have greater weight with men than their beholding of *reality* in those who bear the name of the Lord. David had honoured God by calling the attention of his men to the fact that Saul was His "anointed," and now He honoured David by causing his honest confession to strike home to the hearts of his men. Thus, by restraining his followers David returned good for evil to him from whom he had received evil for good.

"But Saul rose up out of the cave, and went on his way" (v. 7). Utterly unconscious of the danger which had threatened him, the king awoke, arose, and went forth out of the cave. How often there was but a step betwixt us and death, and we knew it not. Awake or asleep, our times are in God's hands, and with the Psalmist faith realized "*Thou* holdest my soul in life" (66:9). None can die a moment before the time his Maker has appointed. Blessed is it when the heart is enabled to rest in God. Each night it is our privilege to say, "I will both lay me down in peace, and sleep: for Thou, Lord, only makest me dwell in safety" (Psa. 4:8). But how unspeakably solemn is the contrast between the cases of the godly and the wicked: the one is preserved for eternal glory, the other is reserved unto everlasting fire. Such was the difference between David and Saul.

"David also arose afterward and went out of the cave, and cried after Saul, saying, My lord the king" (v. 8). "Though he would not take the opportunity to slay him, yet he wisely took the opportunity, if possible, to slay his enmity by convincing him that he was not such a man as he took him for" (Matt. Henry). In thus revealing himself to Saul, David intimated that he still entertained an honourable opinion of his sovereign: this was further evidenced by the respectful language which he employed. "And when Saul looked behind him, David stooped with his face to the earth, and bowed himself." How surprised the blood-thirsty monarch must have been in hearing himself addressed by the one whose life he sought! The posture of David was not that of a cringing criminal, but of a loyal subject. In what follows we have one of the most respectful, pathetic, and forcible addresses ever made to one of earth's rulers.

"And David said to Saul, Wherefore hearest thou men's words, saying, Behold, David seeketh thy hurt?" (v. 9). It is beautiful to see how David commences his speech to the king, wherein he endeavours to show how much he was wronged in being so relentlessly persecuted, and how much he desired Saul to be reconciled to him. Most graciously did David throw the blame upon Saul's courtiers, rather than upon the king himself. In the question here asked Saul, it was suggested that his prejudice against David had been provoked by slanderous reports from others. Herein important instruction is furnished us as to what method to follow when seeking to subdue the malice of those who hate us: proceeding on the assumption that it is not the individual's own enmity against us, but that it has been unjustly stirred up by others. Particularly does this apply to those in authority: respect is due unto them, and where they err, due allowance should be made for their having been ill-informed by others.

It is the practical application of the teaching of Scripture to the details of our own lives which is so much needed today. Of what real value is a knowledge of its history or an understanding of its prophecies, if they exert no vital influence upon our conduct? God has given us His Word not only for our information, but as a law to walk by, and every chapter in it contains important rules for us to appropriate and put into practice. What is before us above supplies a timely case in point. How often differences arise between men, breaches between friends, and misunderstandings between fellow-Christians; and how rarely do we see the spirit displayed by David unto Saul, exercised now in efforts to effect a reconciliation! Let us earnestly seek grace to profit from the lovely and lowly example here set before us.

"Behold, this day, thine eyes have seen how that the Lord had delivered thee today into mine hand in the cave: and some bade me kill thee: but mine eyes spared thee; and I said, I will not put forth mine hand against my lord, for he is the Lord's anointed" (v. 10). First, David had refrained from reproaching or sharply expostulating Saul, now he shows that there was no ill-will in his own heart against him. He appealed to the most decisive proof that he had no intention of injuring him. The king had been completely at his mercy, and his men had urged him to dispatch his enemy, but pity for the helpless monarch had restrained him. Moreover, the fear of God governed him, and he dared not to lay violent hands upon His "anointed." By such mild measures did David seek to conciliate his foe. Let us take a leaf out of his copybook, and seek by acts of kindness to prove unto those that harbour false thoughts against us that Satan has misled them.

"Moreover, my father, see, yea, see the skirt of thy robe in my hand: for in that I cut off the skirt of thy robe, and killed thee not, know thou and see that there is neither evil nor transgression in mine hand, and I have not sinned against thee; yet thou huntest my soul to take it" (v. 11). "He produceth undeniable evidence to prove the falseness of the suggestion upon which Saul's malice against him was grounded. David was charged with seeking Saul's hurt: 'see,' saith he, 'yea, see the skirt of thy robe: let this be a witness for me, and an unexceptional witness it is; had that been true which I am accused of, I had now had thy head in my hand, and not the skirt of thy robe; for I could as easily have cut off that as this" (M. Henry). Well for us is it when we can go to one filled with unjust suspicions against us, and confirm our words with convincing proofs of our good-will.

It is very touching to see David here reminding Saul that there was a more intimate relation between them than that of king and subject; he had been united in marriage to his daughter, and therefore does he now address him as "my father" (v. 11). Here was an appeal not only to his honour, but to his affection: from a monarch one may expect justice, but from a parent we may surely look for affection. David might have addressed Saul by a hard name, but he sought to "overcome evil with good." Blessedly did he here prefigure his Lord, who, at the time of his arrest in the garden, addressed the treacherous Judas not as "Betrayer" or "Traitor," but "Friend." Nothing is gained by employing harsh terms, and sometimes "A soft answer turneth away wrath" (Prov. 15:1).

"The Lord judge between me and thee, and the Lord avenge me of thee: but mine hand shall not be upon thee" (v. 12). David now appealed unto a higher court. First, he desires that Jehovah Himself shall make it appear who was in the right and who in the wrong. Second, he counts upon the retribution of Heaven if Saul should continue to persecute him. Third, he affirms his steadfast resolution that no matter what he might suffer, nor what opportunities might be his to avenge himself, he would not do him hurt, but leave it with God to requite the evil. This was indeed a mild method of reasoning with Saul, and the least offensive way of pointing out to him the injustice of his conduct. If men would deal thus one with another how much strife could be avoided, and how many quarrels be satisfactorily ended!

"As saith the proverb of the ancients, Wickedness proceedeth from the wicked: but mine hand shall not be upon thee" (v. 13). This intimates that it is permissible for us to make a right use of the wise sayings of others, particularly of the ancients, even though they are not directly inspired of God. Such aphorisms as "Look before you leap," "Too many cooks spoil the broth," "All is not gold that glitters," are likely to stand us in good stead if they are stored in the memory and duly pondered. In days gone by, such proverbs were frequently spoken in the hearing of children (we are thankful that they were in ours), and the general absence of them today is only another evidence of the decadence of our times.

"As saith the proverb of the ancients, Wickedness proceedeth from the wicked: but mine hand shall not be upon thee." The use which David here made of this proverb is obvious: he reminds Saul that a man is revealed by his actions. As a tree is known by its fruits, so our conduct makes manifest the dispositions of our hearts. It was as though David said, "Had I been the evil wretch which you have been made to believe, I would have had no conscience of taking away your life when it was in my power. But I could not: my heart would not let me." Though the dog barks at the sheep, the sheep do not snap back at the dog.

"After whom is the king of Israel come out? after whom dost thou pursue? after a dead dog, after a flea" (v. 14). Here David descends and reasons with Saul on the lowest grounds: in your own judgment I am a worthless fellow, then why go to so much trouble over me! Is it not altogether beneath the dignity of a monarch to take so much pains in hunting after one who is not worthy of his notice? In likening himself to a "flea," David, by this simile, depicts not only his own weakness, but the circumstances he was in: obliged to move swiftly from place to place, and therefore not easily taken; and if captured, of no value to the king. Why then be so anxious to give chase to one so inconspicuous? "To conquer him would not be his honour, to attempt it only his disparagement. If Saul would consult his own reputation he would slight such an enemy (supposing he were really his enemy), and would think himself in no danger from him." If Saul had a spark of generosity in him, the humble carriage of David here would surely abate his enmity.

"The Lord therefore be Judge, and judge between me and thee, and see, and plead my cause, and deliver me out of thine hand" (v. 15). Having pleaded his case so forcibly, David now solemnly warned his enemy that Jehovah would judge righteously between them, deliver him out of his hand, and avenge his cause upon him. When we are innocent of the suspicions entertained against and preferred upon us, we need not fear to leave the issue with God. This is what our Lord Himself did: "When he suffered, He threatened not; but committed Himself to Him that judgeth righteously" (1 Pet. 2:23). Assured that God would, in due time, vindicate him, David acted faith upon Him and rested in His faithfulness. The justice of God should ever be the refuge and comfort of those who are wrongfully oppressed: the day is coming when the Judge of all the earth shall recompense every evil-doer, and reward all the righteous.

A brief analysis of what we may term David's "defence," teaches us what methods we should follow when seeking to show a person that we have given no cause for his malice against us. First, David asked Saul if he had not been unjust in listening to slanders against him (v. 9)? Second, he pointed out that because the fear of God was upon him, he dared not sin presumptuously (v. 10). Third, he appealed to his own actions in proof thereof (v. 11). Fourth, he affirmed he had no intention to retaliate and return evil for evil (v. 12). Fifth, he argued that the known character of a person should prevent others from believing evil reports about him (v. 13). Sixth, he took a lowly place, shaming pride by humility (v. 14). Seventh, he committed his case unto the justice of God (v. 15).

And when David had made an end of speaking these words to Saul, Saul said, Is this your voice, my son David? And Saul lifted up his voice and wept. And he said to David, You are more righteous than I, for you have rewarded me with good, but I have rewarded you evil. And you have shown today how you have dealt well with me, because when the LORD had delivered me into your hand, you did not kill me. For if a man finds his enemy, will he let him go completely away? Therefore may the LORD reward good for what you have done to me today. And now, behold, I know well that you shall surely be king, and that the kingdom of Israel shall be established in your hand. Now swear therefore to me before the LORD that you will not cut off my seed after me, and that you will not destroy my name out of my father's house. And David swore to Saul. And Saul went home, but David and his men went up into the stronghold. — 1 Samuel 24:16-22.

"He that is slow to anger is better than the mighty; and he that ruleth his spirit than he that taketh a city" (Prov. 16:32). A man who is "slow to anger" is esteemed by the Lord, respected by men, is happy in himself, and is to be preferred above the strongest giant that is not master of self. Alexander the great conquered the world, yet in his uncontrollable wrath, slew his best friends. Being "slow to anger" is to take time and consider before we suffer our passions to break forth, that they may not transgress due bounds; and he who can thus control himself is to be esteemed above the mightiest warrior. A rational conquest is more honourable to a rational creature than triumph by brute force.

The most desirable authority is self-government. The conquest of ourselves and our own unruly passions, requires more regular and persevering management than does the obtaining of a victory over the physical forces of an enemy. The conquering of our own spirit is a more important achievement than the taking of a foe's fortress. He that can command his temper is superior to him that can successfully storm a fortified town. Natural courage, skill and patience, may do the one; but it requires the grace of God and the assistance of the Holy Spirit to do the other. Blessedly was all this exemplified by David in that incident which has occupied our attention in the last two articles. He had been sorely provoked by Saul, yet when the life of his enemy was in his hand, he graciously spared him, and returned good for evil.

"A soft answer turneth away wrath" (Prov. 15:1). Strikingly was this illustrated in what is now to be before us. A child of God is not to rest satisfied because *he* has not originated strife, but if others begin it, he must not only not continue it, but endeavour to end it be molifying the matter. Better far to pour oil on the troubled waters, than to add fuel to the fire. "The wisdom that is from above is first pure, then peaceable, gentle, easy to be intreated, full of mercy and good fruits, without partiality, and without hypocrisy" (James 3:17). We are to disarm resentment by every reasonable concession. Mild words and gentle expressions, delivered with kindness and humility, will weaken bitterness and scatter the storm of wrath. Note how the Ephraimites were pacified by Gideon's mild answer (Judge 8:1-13). The noblest courage is shown when we withstand our own corruptions, and overcome enemies by kindness.

"Forgive us our sins, for we also forgive every one that is indebted to us" (Luke 11:4). Wherein does this forgiving of others consist? First, in withholding ourselves from revenge. "Forbearing one another and forgiving one another, if any man have a quarrel against any" (Col. 3:13): "forbearing and forgiving" are inseparably connected. Some men will say, We will do to him as he has done to us; but God bids us, "Say *not* I will do so to him as he hath done unto me, I will render to the man according to his work" (Prov. 24:29). Corrupt nature thirsts for retaliation, and has a strong inclination that way; but grace should check it. Men think it a base thing to put up with wrongs and injuries; but this it is which gives a man a victory over himself, and the truest victory over his enemy, when he forbears to revenge.

By nature there is a spirit in us which is turbulent, revengeful, and desirous of returning evil for evil; but when we are able to deny it, we are ruling our own spirit. Failure so to do, being overcome by passion, is moral weakness, for our enemy has thoroughly overcome us when his injuring to us prevails to our breaking of God's laws in order to retaliate. Therefore we are bidden "Be not overcome of evil, but overcome evil with good" (Rom. 12:21): then is grace victorious, and then do we manifest a noble, brave, and strong spirit. And wondrously will God bless our exemplifications of His grace, for it is often His way to shame the party that did the wrong, by overcoming him with the meekness and generosity of the one he has injured. It was thus in the case of David and Saul, as we shall now see.

"And it came to pass, when David had made an end of speaking these words unto Saul, that Saul said, Is this thy voice, my son David? And Saul lifted up his voice, and wept" (1 Sam. 24:16). Though his mind was so hostile to David, and he had cruelly chased him up and down, yet he now saw that the one he was pursuing had foreborne revenge when it was in his power, he was moved to tears. In like manner, when the captains of the Syrians, whom the prophet had temporarily blinded, were led to Samaria, fully expecting to be slain there, we are told that the king "prepared great provisions for them: and when they had eaten and drunk, he sent them away." And what was the sequel to such kindness unto their enemies? This: it so wrought upon their hearts, their bands "came no more into the land of Israel" (2 Kings 6:20-23). May these incidents speak loudly unto each of our hearts.

"And it came to pass, when David had made an end of speaking these words unto Saul, that Saul said, Is this thy voice, my son David? And Saul lifted up his voice and wept." Let us pause and adore the restraining power of God. Filled with wrath and fury, so eager to take David's life, Saul, instead of attempting to kill him, had stood still and heard David's speech without an interruption. He who commands the winds and the waves, can, when He pleases, still the most violent storm within a human breast. But more; Saul was not only awed and subdued, but melted by David's kindness. Observe the noticeable change in his language: before, it was only "the son of Jesse," now he says, "my son, David." So deeply was the king affected, that he was moved to tears; yet, like those of Esau, they were not tears of real repentance.

"And he said to David, Thou art more righteous than I: for thou hast rewarded me good, whereas I have rewarded thee evil" (v. 17). Saul was constrained to acknowledge David's integrity and his own iniquity, just as Pharaoh said, "I have sinned against the Lord your God, and against you" (Ex. 10:16); and as many today will own their wrong-doing when shamed by Christians returning to them good for evil, or when impressed by some startling providence of God. But such admissions are of little value if there is no change for the better in the lives of those who make them. Nevertheless, this acknowledgement of Saul's made good that word of God's upon which He had caused His servant to hope: "He shall bring forth thy righteousness as the light, and thy judgment as the noonday" (Psa. 37:6). They who are careful to maintain "a conscience void of offence toward God and man" (Acts 24:16). may safely leave it unto Him to secure the credit of it.

"This fair confession was sufficient to prove David innocent, even his enemy himself being judge; but not enough to prove Saul himself a true penitent. He should have said, 'Thou art righteous, and I am wicked,' but the utmost he will own is this, 'Thou art more righteous than I.' Bad men will commonly go no farther than this in their confessions: they will own they are not so good as some others are; there are that are better than they, more righteous" (M. Henry). Ah, it takes the supernatural workings of Divine grace in the heart to strip us of all our fancied goodness, and bring us into the dust as self-condemned sinners. It requires too the continual renewings of the Holy Spirit to *keep us in the dust,* so that we truthfully exclaim, "Not unto us, O Lord, not unto us, but unto Thy name give glory, for Thy mercy and for Thy truth's sake" (Psa. 115:1).

"And thou hast showed this day how that thou hast dealt well with me: forasmuch as when the Lord had delivered me into thine hand, thou killest me not" (v. 18). This is striking: even the most desperate sinners are sometimes amenable to acts of kindness. Saul could not but own that David had dealt far more mercifully with him, than he would have done with David if their position had been reversed. He acknowledged that he had been labouring under a misapprehension concerning his son, for clear proof had been given that David was of a far different stamp than what he had supposed. "We are too apt to suspect others to be worse affected towards us than they really are, and than perhaps they are proved to be; and when afterwards our mistake is discovered, we should be forward to recall our suspicions as Saul doth here" (M. Henry).

"And thou hast showed this day how that thou hast dealt well with me: forasmuch as when the Lord had delivered into thine hand, thou killest me not." In view of the later sequel, this is also exceedingly solemn. Saul not only recognizes the magnanimity of David, but he perceives too the providence of God: he owns that it was none other than the hand of Jehovah which had placed him at the mercy of the man whose life he had been seeking. Thus it was plain that God was *for* David, and who could hope to succeed *against* him! How this ought to have deterred him from seeking his hurt afterwards; yet it did not: his "goodness was as a morning cloud, and as the early dew it goeth away" (Hos. 6:4). Alas, there are many who mourn for their sins, but do not truly repent of them; weep bitterly for their transgressions, and yet continue in love and league with them; discern and own the providences of God, yet do not yield themselves to Him.

"For if a man find his enemy, will he let him go well away?" (v. 19). No, this is not the customary way among men. "Revenge is sweet" to poor fallen human nature, and few indeed refuse to drink from this tempting cup when it is presented to them. And if there be more lenity shown unto fallen enemies today than there was in past ages, it is not to be ascribed unto any improvement in man, but to the beneficent effects of the spread of Christianity. That this is the case may be clearly seen in the vivid contrasts presented among nations where the Gospel is preached, and where it is unknown: the "dark places" of the earth are still "full of the habitations of cruelty" (Psa. 74:20).

"For if a man find his enemy, will he let him go well away? wherefore the Lord reward thee good for that thou hast done unto me this day" (v. 19). Strange language this for a would-be murderer! Yes, even the reprobate have spurts and flashes of seeming piety at times, and many superficial people who "believeth every word": (Prov. 14:15) are deceived thereby. "Seemingly pious" we say, for after all, those fair words of Saul were empty ones. Had he really meant what he said, would he not personally and promptly have rewarded David himself? Of course he would. He was king; he had power to; it was his bounden duty to re-instate David in the bosom of his family, and bestow upon him marks of the highest honour and esteem. But he did nothing of the sort. Ah, dear reader: do not measure people by what they say; it is *actions* which speak louder than words.

"And now, behold, I know well that thou shalt surely be king, and that the kingdom of Israel shall be established in thine hand" (v. 20). The realization that

God had appointed David to succeed him on the throne, was now forced upon Saul. The providence of God in so remarkably preserving and prospering him, his princely spirit and behaviour, his calling to mind of what Samuel had declared, namely, that the kingdom should be given to a neighbour of his, better than he (15:18) — and such David was by his own confession (v. 17); and the portion cut off his own robe — which must have been a vivid reminder of Samuel rending his mantle, when he made the solemn prediction; all combined to convince the unhappy king of this. Thus did God encourage the heart of His oppressed servant, and support his faith and hope. Sometimes He deigns to employ strange instruments in giving us a message of cheer.

"Sware now therefore unto me by the Lord, that thou wilt not cut off my seed after me, and that thou wilt not destroy my name out of my father's house" (v. 21). Under the conviction that God was going to place David upon the throne of Israel, Saul desired from him the guaranty of an oath, that he would not, when king, extirpate his posterity. What a tribute this was unto *the reality* of David's profession! Ah, the integrity, honesty, veracity of a genuine child of God, is recognized by those with whom he comes into contact. They who have dealings with him know that *his* word is his bond. Treacherous and unscrupulous as Saul was, if David promised in the name of the Lord to spare his children, he was assured that it would be fulfilled to the letter. Reader, is *your* character thus known and respected by those among whom you move?

"Sware now therefore unto me by the Lord, that thou wilt not cut off my seed after me, and that thou wilt not destroy my name out of my father's house." How tragically this reveals the state of his heart. Poor Saul was more concerned about the credit and interests of his family in this world, than he was of securing the forgiveness of his sins before he entered the world to come. Alas, there are many who have their seasons of remorse, are affected by their dangerous situations, and almost persuaded to renounce their sins; they are convinced of the excellency of true saints, as acting from superior principles to those which regulate their own conduct, and cannot withhold from them a good word; yet are they not thereby humbled or changed, and sin and the world continue to reign in their hearts until death overtakes them.

"And David sware unto Saul. And Saul went home; but David and his men gat them unto the hold" (v. 22). David was willing to bind himself to the promise which Saul asked of him, and accordingly swore to it on oath. Thus he has left us an example to "be subject unto the higher powers" (Rom. 13:1). His later history evidences how he respected his oath to Saul, by sparing Mephibosheth, and in punishing the murderers of Ishbosheth. It is to be noted that David did not ask Saul to sware unto him, that he would no more seek his life; knowing him too well to trust in a transient appearance of friendliness, and having no confidence in his word. Nor should we deliberately place a temptation in the way of those lacking in honour, by seeking to extract from them a definite promise.

"And Saul went home; but David and his men gat them up unto the hold." David did not trust Saul, whose inconstancy, perfidy, and cruel hatred, he full well knew. He did not think it safe to return unto his own house, nor to dwell in the open country, but remained in the wilderness, among the rocks and the caves. The grace of God will teach us to forgive and be kind unto our enemies, but not to trust those who have repeatedly deceived us; for malice often seems dead, when it is only dormant, and will ere long revive with double force. "They that, like David, are innocent as doves, must thus, like David, be wise as serpents" (M. Henry). Note how v. 22 pathetically fore-shadowed John 7:53 and 8:1.

Here then is the blessed victory that David gained over Saul, not by treacherous stealth, or by brute force; but a moral triumph. How complete his victory was that day, is seen in the extent to which that haughty monarch humbled himself before David, entreating him to be kind unto his offspring, when he should be king. But the great truth for us to lay hold of, the central lesson here recorded for our learning is that, David first gained the victory over himself, before he triumphed over Saul. May writer and reader be more diligent and earnest in seeking grace from God that, we may not be overcome by evil, but that we may "overcome evil with good."

The incident which is now to engage our attention may seem, at first sight, to contain in it little of practical importance for our hearts. If so, we may be sure that our vision is dim. There is nothing trivial in Holy Writ. Everything which the Spirit has recorded therein has a voice for us, if only we will seek the hearing ear. Whenever we read a portion of God's Word, and find therein little suited to our own case and need, we ought to be humbled: the fault is in us. This should at once be acknowledged unto God, and a spiritual quickening of soul sought from Him. There should be a definite asking Him to graciously anoint our eyes (Rev. 3:18), not only that we may be enabled to behold wondrous things in His Law, but also that He will make us of quick discernment to perceive *how* the passage before us *applies to ourselves* — what are the particular lessons we need to learn from it. The more we cultivate this habit, the more likely that God will be pleased to open His Word unto us.

It is the *practical* lessons to be learned from each section that all of us are in so much need of, and this is uppermost in our mind in the composing of this present series of articles. What, then, is there here for us to take to heart? David, in his continued wanderings, applies to a well-to-do farmer for some rations for his men. The appeal was suitably timed, courteously worded, and based upon a weighty consideration. The request was presented not to a heathen, but to an Israelite, to a member of his own tribe, to a descendant of Caleb; in short, to one from whom he might reasonably expect a favourable response. Instead, he met with a rude rebuff, and a provoking insult. Obviously, there is a *warning* here for us in the despicable meanness of Nabal, which turned into prayer for Divine grace to preserve us from being inhospitable and unkind to God's servants.

But it is with David that we are chiefly concerned. In our last three lessons we have seen him conducting himself with becoming mildness and magnanimity, showing mercy unto the chief of his enemies. There we saw him resisting a sore temptation to take matters into his own hands, and make an end of his troubles by slaying the chief of his persecutors, when he was thoroughly in his power. But here our hero is seen in a very different light. He meets with another trial, a trial of a much milder nature, yet instead of overcoming evil with good, he was in imminent danger of being overcome with evil. Instead of exercising grace, he is moved with a spirit of revenge; instead of conducting himself so that the praises of God are "*shown* forth" (1 Pet. 2:9), only the works of the flesh are seen. Alas, how quickly had the fine gold become dim! And how are we to account for this? and what are the lessons to be learned from it?

Is the reader surprised as he turns from the blessed picture presented in the second half of 1 Sam. 24 and ponders the almost sordid actions of David in the very next chapter? Is he puzzled to account for the marked lapse in the conduct of him who had acted so splendidly toward Saul? Is he at a loss to explain David's spiteful attitude toward Nabal? If so, he must be woefully ignorant of *his own* heart, and has yet to learn a most important lesson: that no man stands a moment longer than Divine grace upholds him. The strongest are weak as water immediately the power of the Spirit is withdrawn; the most mature and experienced Christian acts foolishly the moment he be left to himself; none of us has any reserve strength or wisdom in himself to draw from: our source of sufficiency is *all* treasured up for us in Christ, and as soon as communion with Him be broken, as soon as we cease looking alone to Him for help, we are helpless.

What has just been stated above is acknowledged as true by God's people in general, yet many of their thoughts and conclusions are glaringly inconsistent therewith — or why be so surprised when they hear of some eminent saint experiencing a sad fall! The "eminent saint" is not the one who has learned to walk alone, but he who most feels his need of leaning harder upon the "ever-lasting arms." The "eminent saint" is not the one who is no longer tempted by the lusts of the flesh and harassed by the assaults of Satan, but he who knows that in the flesh there dwelleth no good thing, and that only *from Christ* can his "fruit" be found (Hos. 14:8). Looked at in themselves, the "fathers" in Christ are just as frail and feeble as the "babes" in Christ. Left to themselves, the wisest Christians have no better judgment than has the new convert. Whether God is pleased to leave us upon earth another year or another hundred years, all will constantly need to observe that word "Watch and pray, that ye enter not into temptation: the spirit indeed is willing, but the flesh is weak" (Matt. 26:41).

And God has many ways of teaching us the "weakness" of the flesh. One of these receives striking illustration in the incident to be before us, and which has no doubt been painfully realized in the experience of each Christian reader: that in some great crisis we have been enabled to stand our ground, strong in faith, whereas before some petty trial we have broken down and acted as a man of the world would act. It is thus that God stains our pride, subdues our self-sufficiency, and brings us to the place of more real and constant dependence upon Himself. It is the "little foxes" (Song of Sol. 2:15) that spoil the vines, and it is our reaction unto the lesser irritations of every-day life which most reveal us to ourselves — humbling us through our failures, and fitting us to bear with more patience the infirmities of our brethren and sisters in Christ.

Who would have thought that he who had taken so meekly the attacks of the king upon his life, should have waxed so furious when a farmer refused a little food for his men! Rightly did Thos. Scott point out, "David had been on his guard against anger and revenge when most badly used by Saul, but he did not expect such reproachful language and insolent treatment from Nabal: he was therefore wholly put off his guard; and in great indignation he determined to avenge himself." Lay this well to heart dear reader: a small temptation is likely to prevail after a greater has been resisted. Why so? Because we are less conscious of our need of God's delivering grace. Peter was bold before the soldiers in the Garden, but became fearful in the presence of a maid. But it is time for us to consider some of the details of our passage.

CHAPTER 25

And Samuel died. And all the Israelites were gathered together. And they lamented him and buried him in his house at Ra-mah. And David arose and went down to the wilderness of Par-an. And there was a man of Ma-on whose possessions were in Carmel. And the man was very important. And he had three thousand sheep and a thousand goats. And he was shearing his sheep in Carmel. Now the name of the man was Na-bal, and the name of his wife was Ab-i-gail. And she was a woman of good understanding and of a beautiful form. But the man was surly and evil in his doings. And he was of the house of Caleb. And David heard in the wilderness that Na-bal was shearing his sheep. And David sent out ten young men. And David said to the young men, Go up to Carmel and go to Na-bal, and greet him in my name. And you shall say this to him who lives prosperously, Peace be to you, and peace be to your house, and peace be to all that you have. And now I have heard that you have shearers. Now we did not hurt your shepherds who were with us; neither was there anything missing to them all the while they were in Carmel. Ask your young men, and they will tell you. Therefore let the young men find favor in your eyes, for we come in a good day. Please give whatever comes to your hand to your servants and to your son David. And when David's young men came, they spoke to Na-bal according to all those words in the name of David, and stopped. And Na-bal answered David's servants and said, Who is David? And who is the son of Jesse? There are many servants nowadays who break away, each one from his master. Shall I then take my bread and my water and my meat that I have killed for my shearers, and give it to men about whom I know not where they come from? So David's young men turned their way and went again. And they came and told him all those things. And David said to his men, Let each man put on his sword. And they each put on his sword, and David also put on his sword. And about four hundred men went up after David, and two hundred stayed by the stuff. — 1 Samuel 25:1-13.

"And Samuel died; and all the Israelites were gathered together and lamented him, and buried him in his house at Ramah" (1 Sam. 25:1). How often will people sorrow outwardly for one when dead to whom they did not care to listen when living. There had been a time when Samuel was appreciated by Israel, particularly when they were feeling the pressure of the Philistine yoke; but more recently he has been despised (1 Sam. 8). They had preferred a king to the prophet, but now Saul was proving such a disappointment, and the breach between the king and David showed no signs of being healed, they lamented the removal of Samuel.

"And David arose, and went down to the wilderness of Paran" (25:1). David too was despised by the greater part of the nation. Once he had been the hero of their songs, but now he was homeless, outlawed, and few cared to own him. Learning of Samuel's death, he probably thought that his danger was greater than ever, for the prophet was more than friendly disposed toward him. He no doubt concluded that Saul's malice would be now more unrestrained than ever. Taking advantage of "all the Israelites" being gathered together, to mourn the death of Samuel, he left Engedi to sojourn for a while in other parts. But let us note well the ominous hint given in the words "and *went down* to the wilderness of Paran."

We have next presented to our notice the one to whom David made his appeal (1 Sam. 25:2, 3). From the character given to him by the Holy Spirit, not much good might be expected from him. His name was "Nabal" which signifies "a fool," and none is a greater fool than he who thinks only of number one. He was a descendant of Caleb, which is mentioned here as an aggravation of his wickedness: that he should be the degenerate plant of so noble a vine. We are told that this man was "very great": not in piety, but in material possessions, for he had very large flocks of sheep and goats. His wife was of a beautiful countenance "and of good understanding," but her father could not have been so, or he would not have sacrificed her to a man who had nothing better to recommend him than earthly wealth. Poor woman! she was tied to one who was "churlish and evil in his doings": greedy and grasping, sour and cross-tempered.

"And David heard in the wilderness that Nabal did shear his sheep. And David sent out ten young men, and David said unto the young men, Get you up to Carmel, and go to Nabal, and greet him in my name" (vv. 4, 5). The season for shearing the sheep was a notable one, for wool was a leading commodity in Canaan. With such a very large flock, a considerable number of extra hands would have to be hired by Nabal, and a plentiful supply of provisions prepared. From 2 Sam. 13:23 it appears that it was the custom in those days to combine feasting and merriment with the shearing: compare also Gen. 38:13. It was a time when men were generally disposed to be hospitable and kind. As to how far David was justified in appealing to man, rather than spreading his need before God alone, we undertake not to decide — it is certainly not safe to draw any inference from the sequel.

"And thus shall ye say to him that liveth, Peace be both to thee, and peace be to thine house, and peace be unto all that thou hast. And now I have heard that thou hast shearers: now thy shepherds which were with us, we hurt them not, neither was there ought missing unto them, all the while they were in Carmel. Ask thy young men, and they will show thee. Wherefore let the young men find favour in thine eyes: for we come in a good day: give, I pray thee, whatsoever cometh to thine hand unto thy servants, and to thy son David" (vv. 6-8). The request to be presented before Nabal was one which the world would call respectful and tactful. The salutation of peace bespoke David's friendly spirit. Reminder was given that, in the past, David had not only restrained his men from molesting Nabal's flocks, but had also protected them from the depredations of invaders — compare vv. 14-17. He might then have asked for a reward for his services, but instead he only supplicates a favour. Surely Nabal would not refuse his men a few victuals, for it was "a good day," a time when there was plenty to hand. Finally David takes the place of a "son," hoping to receive some fatherly kindness from him.

But as we examine this address more closely, we note the low ground which was taken: there was nothing spiritual in it! Moreover, we fully agree with Matt. Henry's comments on the opening words of v. 6. "Thus shall ye say to him that liveth as Nabal did, with abundance of the wealth of this world about them; whereas, in truth, those that live in pleasure are dead while they live (1 Tim. 5:6). This was, methinks, too high a compliment to pass upon Nabal, to call him the man that liveth: David knew better things — that 'in God's favour is life', not in the world's smiles; and, by the rough answer, he was well enough served for this too smooth address to such a muckworm."

"And when David's young men came, they spake to Nabal according to all those words in the name of David, and ceased" (v. 9). This verse serves to illustrate another important principle: not only are God's children more or less *revealed* by their reaction to and conduct under the varied experiences they encounter, but the presence of God's servants *tests* the character of those with whom they come into contact. It was so here. A golden opportunity was afforded Nabal of showing kindness to the Lord's "anointed," but he seized it not. Alas, how many there are who know not the day of their visitation. Nabal had no heart for David, and clearly was this now made manifest. So too the selfishness and carnality of professors frequently becomes apparent by their failure to befriend the servants of God, when chances to do so are brought right to their door. It is a grand and holy privilege when the Lord sends one of His prophets into your neighborhood, yet it may issue in a fearfully solemn sequel.

"And Nabal answered David's servants, and said, Who is David? And who is the son of Jesse? there be many servants now a days that break away every man from his master. Shall I then take my bread, and my water, and my flesh, that I have killed for my shearers, and give it unto men, whom I know not whence they be?" (vv. 10, 11). What an insulting answer to return unto so mild a request! To justify a refusal he stooped to heaping insults on the head of David. It was not a total stranger who had applied to him, for Nabal's calling him "the son of Jesse" showed he knew well who he was; but, absorbed with schemes of selfish acquisition he cared not for him. Let it be duly noted that in acting in such a heartless manner Nabal clearly disobeyed Deut. 15:7-11. Nabal's repeated use of the word "my" in v. 11 reminds us of the other rich "fool" in Luke 12:18-20.

"So David's young men turned their way, and went again, and came and told him all those sayings" (v. 12). Highly commendable was their conduct. "Young men" are often hot-blooded and hot-headed, and act impetuously and rashly; but they admirably restrained themselves. The language of Nabal had been offensive, but instead of returning railing for railing, they treated him with silent contempt and turned their backs upon him: such churls are not entitled to any reply. It is blessed to see they did not use force, and attempt to take what ought to have been freely given to them. Never are the children of God justified in so doing: we must ever seek grace to maintain a good conscience, "in all things willing to live honestly" (Heb. 13:18). Oft times the best way for overcoming a temptation to make a wrathful reply, is to quietly turn away from those who have angered us.

"And came and told him all those sayings." Here we are shown how the servants of Christ are to act when abused. Instead of indulging the spirit of revenge, they are to go and spread their case before their Master (Luke 14:21). It was thus the perfect Servant acted: of Him it is written, "Who, when He was reviled, reviled not again; when He suffered, He threatened not; but committed His cause to Him that judgeth righteously" (1 Pet. 2:23). Ofttimes God brings us into trying situations to reveal unto us whether we are "acknowledging Him in *all* our ways" (Prov. 3:6), or whether there is still a measure of self-sufficiency at work in our hearts — our response to the trial makes manifest which be the case.

And what was David's response? How did *he* now react unto the disappointing tidings brought back by his men? Did he, as the *servant* of God, meekly bear Nabal's taunts and cutting reproach? Did he cast his burden on the Lord, looking to Him for sustaining grace (Psa. 55:22)? Alas, he acted in the energy of the flesh. "And David said unto his men, Gird ye on every man his sword. And they girded on every man his sword; And David also girded on his sword" (v. 13). David neither betook himself to prayer nor reflected upon the matter, but hurriedly prepared to avenge the insult he had received.

True, the ingratitude which Nabal had shown, and the provoking language he had used, were hard to endure — too hard for mere flesh and blood, for human nature ever wants to vindicate itself. His only recourse lay in God: to see *His* hand in the trial, and to seek grace to bear it. But momentarily David forgot that he had committed his cause unto the Lord, and took matters into his own hands. And why did God permit this breakdown? That no flesh should glory in His presence (1 Cor. 1:29). "This must be the reason why such-like episodes are found in the lives of all the Lord's servants. They serve to demonstrate that these servants were not any better flesh than other men, and that it was not more richly endowed brains that gave them faith of devotedness, but simply the *supernatural* power of the Holy Spirit" (C. H. Bright).

But one of the young men told Ab-i-gail, Na-bal's wife, saying, Behold! David sent messengers out of the wilderness to greet our master, and he flew on them. But the men were very good to us, and we were not hurt. And we did not miss anything as long as we were going to and fro among them, when we were in the fields. They were a wall to us both by night and day all the while we were with them keeping the sheep. Now then, know and consider what you will do, for evil is determined against our master and against all his household. For he is a son of Be-li-al, so that a man cannot speak to him. Then Ab-i-gail hurried and took two hundred loaves, and two bottles of wine, and five sheep ready dressed, and five measures of parched grain, and a hundred clusters of raisins and laid them on asses. And she said to her servants, Go on before me. Behold, I am coming after you. But she did not tell her husband Na-bal. And it was so, as she rode on the ass, that she came down under cover of the mountain. And behold, David and his men came down across from her. And she met them. Now David had said, Surely in vain I have kept all that this fellow has in the wilderness, so that nothing was missed of all that belonged to him. And he has requited me evil for good. So and more also may God do to the enemies of David, If I leave by the morning light of all that belongs to him any that waters against the wall. When Ab-i-gail saw David, she hurried and dismounted from the ass and fell before David on her face. And she bowed herself to the ground. And she fell at his feet and said, On me, my lord, on me let this iniquity be. And, I beg you, let your handmaid speak in your ears, and hear the words of your handmaid. I beg you, do not let my lord regard this man of Be-li-al, Na-bal. For as his name is, so is he. Na-bal is his name, and foolishness is with him. But your handmaid did not see the young men of my lord, whom you sent. Now therefore, my lord — as the LORD lives and as your soul lives, since the LORD has withheld you from coming to shed blood, and from avenging yourself with your own hand — now let your enemies, and those that seek to do evil to my lord, be as Na-bal. Now this present which your handmaid has brought to my lord, let it even be given to the young men who follow my lord. I beg you to forgive the trespass of your handmaid. For the LORD will certainly make a sure house for my lord, because my lord fights the battles of the LORD, and evil has not been found in you all your days. Yet a man has risen to pursue you and to seek your soul. But the soul of my lord shall be bound in the bundle of life with the LORD your God. And as to the souls of your enemies, He shall sling them out, as out of the middle of a sling. And when the LORD has done to my lord according to all the good that He has spoken about you and has made you ruler over Israel, this shall be no stumbling to you or offence of heart to my lord, either that you have shed blood without cause or that my lord has avenged himself. But when the LORD has dealt well with my lord, then remember your handmaid. And David said to Ab-i-gail, Blessed be the LORD God of Israel, who sent you to meet me today.

And blessed is your advice, and blessed are you who have kept me from coming today to shed blood, and from avenging myself by my own hand. For truly, as the LORD God of Israel lives, who has kept me back from hurting you — unless you had hurried and come to meet me, surely there would not have been left to Na-bal by the morning light any that waters against the wall. So David received from her hand that which she had brought him, and said to her, Go up in peace to your house. See, I have listened to your voice and have accepted your person. 1 Samuel 25:14-35.

In our last article we saw how that God submitted David unto a testing of quite another character and from a different quarter than those he had previously been tried by. Hitherto, the thorn in his side had been none other than the king of Israel, to which we may add the callous indifference toward him of the nation at large. But now he was unexpectedly rebuffed by an individual farmer, from whon he had sought some victuals for his men. "His churlish soul, adding insult to injury, dismissed the messenger of David with contumely and scorn. It is a hard thing to endure. David had endured, and was enduring much. He was suffering from the active enmity of Saul, and from the dull apathy of Israel. But both were great, and so to speak, dignified enemies. Saul was Israel's king; and Israel were God's people. It seemed comparatively honourable to be persecuted by *them:* but it was a far different thing to endure the reproach of one so despicable as Nabal. 'Surely in vain,' said David, 'have I kept all that this fellow hath in the wilderness.' " (B. W. Newton).

What made the trial more poignant to David's soul, was the fact that he himself had acted honourably and kindly toward Nabal. When on a previous occasion, he had sojourned in those parts, he had not only restrained his own men from preying upon Nabal's flocks, but had been a defence to them from the wandering bands of the Philistines. It was, then, the least that this wealthy sheep-owner could do, to now show his appreciaton and make present of a little food to David's men. Instead, he mocked them. Ingratitude is always trying to flesh and blood, but more so when it is coupled with gross injustice. Yet often God is pleased to try His people in this way, calling upon them to receive treatment which they feel is quite "uncalled for," yea, positively "unjust." And why does God permit this? For various reasons: among others, to furnish us opportunities to *act out what we profess!*

The reaction of David unto this trial is recorded for our learning: for us to lay to heart, and turn into earnest prayer. "And David said unto his men, Gird ye on every man his sword. And they girded on every man his sword; and David also girded on his sword" (1 Sam. 25:13). Well may we ask, Had he been so long in the school of affliction and not yet learned patience! "He forgot that all suffering, all reproach, that is *for God's sake*, is equally honourable, whether it come from a monarch, or from a churl. His proud spirit was roused, and he who had refused to lift up his hand against Saul, and had never unsheathed his sword against Israel: he who was called to fight, not for his *own sake*, against his *own* enemies, but for the *Lord's sake* against the *Lord's* enemies, he -- David, forgot his calling, and swore that Nabal should expiate his offence in blood" (B. W. N.).

And how are we to account for his lapse? Wherein, particularly, was it that David failed? In being unduly occupied with the second cause, the human instrument; his eyes were upon man, rather than upon God. When his men returned with their disappointing tidings he ought to have said with Job, "Shall we receive good at the hand of God, and shall we not receive evil?" (2:10). Ah, it is easy for us to say what David *ought* to have said, but do we act any better when we are similarly tested? Alas, has not both writer and reader full reason to bow his head in shame! Far be it from us, who thoroughly deserve them ourselves, to throw stones at the beloved Psalmist. Nevertheless, the Holy Spirit has faithfully recorded his failures, and the best way for us to profit from them is to trace them back to their source, and seek grace to avoid repeating them.

Above we asked the question, Had David been so long in the school of affliction and not yet learned patience? This leads us to enquire, *What is patience?* Negatively, it is meekly receiving as *from God* whatever enters our lives, a saying from the heart, "The cup which my Father hath given me, shall I not drink it?" (John 18:11). Positively, it is a persevering continuance in the path of duty, not being overcome by the difficulties of the way. Now to accept as from God whatever enters our lives requires us to cultivate the habit of seeing *His* hand in every thing: just so long as we are unduly occupied with secondary causes and subordinate agents, do we destroy our peace. There is only one real haven for the heart, and that is to "rest in the Lord," to recognize and realize that "of Him, and through Him, and to Him, are *all* things" (Rom. 11:36): ever seeking to learn His lesson in each separate incident.

It is blessed to know that "The steps of a good man are ordered by the Lord," and that "though he fall, he shall not be utterly cast down: for the Lord upholdeth his hand" (Psa. 37:23, 24). Yes, and ofttimes though we trip, He keeps us from falling. Where it is the genuine desire of the heart to please the Lord in all things, He will not let us go far wrong; where the will is sincerely bent God-wards, He will not suffer Satan to prevail. Thus it was here with David. To answer the Fool (Nabal) according to his folly (Prov. 26:4) was just what the devil desired, and momentarily he had gained an advantage over him. But the eyes of the Lord were upon His tempted servant, and graciously did He now move one to deter him from accomplishing his vindictive purpose. Let us admire His providential workings.

First, we are told that, "But one of the young men told Abigail, Nabal's wife, saying, Behold, David sent messengers out of the wilderness to salute our master; and he railed on them. But the men were very good unto us, neither missed we any thing, as long as we were conversant with them, when we were in the fields: They were a wall unto us both by night and by day, all the while we were with them keeping the sheep. Now therefore know and consider what thou wilt do; for evil is determined against our master, and against all his household: for he is such a son of Belial, that a man cannot speak to him" (vv. 14-17). One of Nabal's servants acquainted his mistress with what had transpired, confirming, be it noted, what was said, by David's men in v. 7. He probably drew the logical inference that David would avenge his insult, and anxious for his own safety, as well as the other members of the household, and yet not daring to voice his fears unto Nabal, he informed Abigail.

How wondrously God makes all things "work together" for the good of His own. How perfect are His ways: fulfilling His own secret and invincible designs, yet leaving quite free the instruments who, unconsciously, fulfill them. The providential machinery to restrain the impetuous David was now set in motion. A servant of Nabal's, moved by nothing higher than the instinct of self-preservation (so far as *his* consciousness went), warns his mistress of their impending danger. Now mark, secondly, her response: she did not laugh at the servant, and tell him his fears were groundless; nor was she suddenly paralyzed by feminine fright at the alarming tidings. No, a hidden Hand calmed her heart and directed her mind. Accepting the warning, she acted promptly, setting out at once with an elaborate present to placate the angry David; a present that would meet the immediate needs of his hungry men: see vv. 18, 19.

There are some who have criticised this action of Abigail's, dwelling upon the last clause of v. 19: "But she told not her husband Nabal." Such a criticism is a very superficial conclusion. What Abigail did was necessary for the protection of the family. Perceiving that Nabal's stubbornness would ruin them all, the exegencies of the situation fully justified her conduct. It is true she owed allegiance to her husband, but her first and great duty was to take measures to protect their lives: inferior interests must always be sacrificed to secure the greater — our property to preserve our lives, our very lives to preserve our souls. As we shall see, vv. 24, 28 make it clear that she acted from no disloyalty to Nabal. Nevertheless, it is an extraordinary case which is here before us, and so *not* to be used as an example.

And what of David at this time? Was he recovered from his outburst of anger? No, indeed, or there had been no need for Abigail's mission of conciliation. The words of Nabal were still rankling within his heart. Hear him as he petulantly declares, "Surely in vain have I kept all that this fellow hath in the wilderness, so that nothing was missed of all that pertained unto him: and he hath requited me evil for good" (v. 21). He repented of the kindness shown Nabal, feeling now that it had been wasted upon him, that he was devoid of gratitude and incapable of appreciating the good turn shown him. But God is "kind to the unthankful and to the evil," and bids us "Be ye therefore merciful" (Luke 6:35, 36).

Ah, to cultivate that attitude we must seek grace to *mortify* the spirit of pride which desires recognition, and that bitterness which rises when we are slighted.

Not only was David chafing under the ingratitude and taunts of Nabal, but he was still bent on revenge: as v. 23 show, he had determined to slay every male in Nabal's household. This was unjust and cruel in the extreme, and if God suffered him to carry out such a design, had greatly sullied his character and given his enemies an immense advantage against him. So determined was he, that he confirmed his intention with an oath, which was rash and savoured of profanity. See here, dear reader, what even the child of God is capable of when grace is not active within him. The realization of this ought to make us walk very softly, and work out our salvation with "fear and trembling." It is for this reason that God so often withdraws from us the power of His Spirit: that we may know what is yet in our hearts (2 Chron. 32:31), and be humbled before Him.

How blessedly God *times* His mercies. Here was David pre-meditating evil, yea, on the point of carrying out his wicked purpose. But there was one, sent by the Lord, already on the way to deliver him from himself. Ah, dear reader, have not you and I often been the recipient of similar favours from Heaven? Were there not times, be they recalled to our deep shame, where *we* had determined upon a course dishonouring to our Lord; when, all praise unto Him, some one crossed our path, and we were delayed, hindered, deterred. That some one may not have spoken to us as definitely as Abigail did unto David: rather perhaps *their* errand was of quite another nature, which at the time we may have resented as a nuisance for interrupting us; but now, as we look back, do we not see the kind hand of God withholding us from carrying out an evil purpose!

Apparently David was already on his way to execute his evil intention when Abigail met him (v. 20). Blessed it is to see the place which she now took: "When Abigail saw David, she hasted, and lighted off the ass, and fell before David on her face and bowed herself to the ground; and fell at his feet" (v.v. 23, 24). This was not mere adulation, and it was something more than an oriental salutation: it was *faith's acknowledgment* of the "anointed of the Lord." Nabal had insulted him as a run-away slave, but his wife owns him as a superior, as her king in the purpose of God. Her address to him on this occasion (vv. 24-31) is deserving of close study, but we can only offer a few brief remarks upon it.

It is to be carefully noted that Abigail did not upbraid David for cherishing the spirit of revenge and tell him that it ill-became his character and calling: it had not been seemly for *her* to do; rather did she leave it for his conscience to accuse him. She did not excuse her husband's conduct, nor did the present case allow her to hide his infirmity, but she sought to turn his well-known character for rashness and insolence (v. 25) into an argument with David, why he should lay aside his resentment. "She intimated that Nabal (whose name means 'folly'), intended no peculiar affront to him, but only spoke to his usual way of treating those who applied to him; and it was beneath a person of David's reputation and eminence to notice the rudeness of such a man" (T. Scott).

Abigail's piety comes out clearly in v. 26. Possibly she percceived a change in David's countenance, or more probably she felt in her spirit that the object before her was now gained; but instead of attributing this unto her pleading, or the present she had brought, she ascribed it solely unto the restraining grace of God: "the Lord hath withholden thee from coming to shed blood, and from avenging thyself with thine own hand." Thus alone is God honoured and given His proper place, when we freely impute unto *His* working all that is good in and from our fellow-creatures. Beautiful too is it to behold how she shields her churlish husband: "upon me, my lord, upon me, let this iniquity be" (v. 24), "I pray thee, forgive the trespass of thine handmaid" (v. 28). She took upon herself the blame for the ill-treatment of his men, and says, "If thou wilt be angry, be angry against *me*, rather than with my poor husband."

Next, we behold her strong faith: "the Lord will certainly make my lord a sure house" (v. 28). She makes reference unto the future to draw his heart from the present. As another has said, "To the heir of a kingdom, a few sheep could have but little attraction; and one who knew that he had the anointing oil of the Lord upon his head, might easily bear to be called a run-away servant." Ah, it is ever the office of faith to look beyond present circumstances and difficulties, on to the time of deliverance; only thus do we begin to judge things from *God's* viewpoint. Then she pointed out that David was fighting "the battles of the Lord" (v. 28), and therefore it was not for him to think of avenging an insult to himself.

Her closing words in vv. 29-31 are very beautiful. First, she makes reference to the relentless persecution of Saul, but in becoming loyalty to the throne speaks of him as "a man" rather than "the king," and assures David in most striking language that his life should be preserved (v. 29). Second, looking away from his abject condition, she confidently contemplated the time when the Lord would make him "ruler over Israel": how heartening was this unto the tried servant of God! Thus too does God often send us a word of comfort when we are most sorely tried. Third, she pleaded with David that he would let his coming glory regulate his present actions, so that in that day, his conscience would not reproach him for previous follies. If we kept more before us the judgment-seat of Christ, surely our conduct would be more regulated thereby. Finally, she besought David to remember her, his "handmaid," when he should ascend the throne.

" 'As an earring of gold, and an ornament of fine gold, so is a wise reprover upon an obedient ear" (Prov. 25:12). Abigail was a wise reprover of David's passion, and he gave an obedient ear to the reproof according to his own principle: 'Let the righteous smite me, it shall be a kindness' (Psa. 141:5): never was such an admonition either better given or better taken" (M. Henry). Herein are the children of God made manifest; they are tractable, open to conviction, willing to be shown their faults; but the children of the devil ("sons of Belial") are like Nabal — churlish, stubborn, proud, unbending. Ah, my reader, lay this to heart: if we will listen to faithful counsellors now, we shall be delivered from much folly and spared bitter regrets in the future.

God blessed this word of Abigail's to David, so that he was now able to view the whole transaction and his own bitter spirit and purpose, in a true light. First, he praises God for sending him this check in a sinful course (v. 32): it is a true mark of spirituality when we discern and own the Lord's hand in such deliverances. Second, he thanked Abigail for so kindly interposing between him and the sin he was about to commit (v. 33): ah, we must not only receive a reproof patiently, but *thank* the faithful giver of it. Note that instead of speaking lightly of the evil he premeditated, David emphasized its enormity. Third, he dismissed her with a message of peace, and accepted her offering. The whole shows us wise men are open to sound advice, even though it comes from their inferiors; and that oaths must not bind us to do that which is evil.

Finally, let us point out for the benefit of preachers, that we have in the above incident a blessed picture of an elect soul being drawn to Christ. 1. Abigail was yoked to Nabal: so by nature we are wedded to the law as a covenant of works, and it is "against us" (Col. 2:14). 2. She was barren to Nabal: see Rom. 7:1-4. 3. It was tidings of impending doom which caused her to seek David (v. 17). 4. She took her place in the dust before him (v. 23). 5. She came to him confessing "iniquity" (v. 24). 6. She sought "forgiveness" (v. 28). 7. She was persuaded of David's goodness (v. 28). 8. She owned his exaltation (v. 30). 9. She, like the dying thief, begs to be "remembered" (v. 31). 10. David granted her request, accepted her person, and said, "Go in peace" (v. 35)!

Some of our readers may wonder why we have given to the present article such a title, and what bearing it has upon the contents of 1 Sam. 26: if so, we would ask them to thoughtfully ponder the closing verses of the preceding chapter. Much is lost by many readers of the Bible through failing to observe the connection between the ending of one chapter and the beginning of another: even when incidents which are totally distinct and different follow each other, a spiritual eye may often discern an intimate moral relation between them, and therein many valuable lessons may be learned. Such is the case here. At first glance there appears to be no logical link uniting the further uncalled-for attack of Saul upon David, and his having taken unto himself a wife a little before; but the two things *are* related as is effect to cause, and here is to be found the key which opens to us the Divine significance of what is now to be before us.

"The way of transgressors is hard" (Prov. 13:15). No doubt the primary reference in these words is to the wicked, yet the principle of them unquestionably holds good in the case of the redeemed. In the keeping of God's commandments there is "great reward" (Psa. 19:11), in this life (1 Tim. 4:8) as well as in that which is to come; but in the breaking of God's commandments bitter chastening is sure to follow. Wisdom's ways are ways of pleasantness, and all her paths are peace (Prov. 3:17), but he who departs from Wisdom's ways and follows a course of self-will, must expect to smart for it. So it was now in the experience of David. It is true that in case of marital infidelity the Mosaic law permitted the innocent one to obtain a divorce and marry again; but it made no provision for a plurality of wives, and *that* was what David was now guilty of; and for his sin he was sorely chastised.

Ah, my reader, let this truth sink deep into thine heart: God is exercising a moral government over the saved as well as the unsaved, and He will no more wink at the sins of the one than He will of the other. David was saved by grace through faith apart from any good works as the meritorious cause, as truly as we are; but he was also called to be holy in all manner of conversation or behaviour, as we are. Grace does not set aside the requirements of Divine holiness, instead, it reigns "through righteousness' (Rom. 5:21). And when one who has been saved by grace fails to deny "ungodliness and worldly lusts" (Titus 2:12), then the chastening rod of God falls upon him, that he may be a "partaker of His holiness" (Heb. 12:10). And this, be it noted, is not only a part of the Father's dealings with His *children*, but it is also a part of His ways with His *subjects* as the Moral Ruler of this world.

As we suggested in the 7th article of this series, it was David's being united in marriage to the unbelieving Michal, which accounts for the painful experiences he passed through while a member of Saul's household. Trials do not come upon us haphazardly; no, they come from the hand of God. Nor does He act capriciously, but according to the righteous principles of His government. In an earlier chapter we saw how that God graciously protected David when the Devil-driven king sought his life, and how that He moved him to return home. Why, then, should His restraining hand be removed, and Saul allowed to go forth again on a blood-thirsty mission? Why should the brief respite David had enjoyed now be so rudely borken? The answer is that God was again using his enemy to chasten David for his recent sin, that he might, by painful experience, learn anew that the way of transgressors *is* hard.

"O that thou hadst hearkened to My commandments! then had thy peace been as a river, and thy righteousness as the waves of the sea" (Isa. 48:18). What a difference it makes whether the ways of a Christian please or displease the Ruler of this world: it is the difference of having God *for*, or having Him *against* us — not in the absolute sense, not in the eternal sense, but in His *governmental* dealings with us. When the heart be right with God, then He shows Himself strong on our behalf (2 Chron. 16:9). When our ways please Him, then He makes even our enemies to be at peace with us (Prov. 16:7). Then how diligently should we guard our hearts and ponder the path of our feet (Prov. 4:23, 26). Carelessness invites disaster; disobedience ensures chastening; sinning will withhold good things from us (Jer. 5:25).

It is very important to see that while the penal and eternal consequences of the Christian's sins have been remitted by God, because atoned for by Christ, yet the disciplinary and temporal effects thereof are not cancelled — otherwise the saints would never be sick or die. It is not God in His absolute character, acting according to His ineffably holy nature, but God in His official character, acting according to the principles of His righteous government, which deals with the present conduct of His people, rewarding them for their obedience and chastening for disobedience. Hence, when God makes use of the Devil and his agents, to scourge His people, it is not unto their ultimate destruction, but unto their present plaguing and disciplining. And this is exactly what we see in our present lesson: Saul was allowed to disturb David's rest, but not to take his life. In like manner, the Devil is often permitted to whip us, but never to devour us.

"And the Ziphites came unto Saul to Gibeah, saying, Doth not David hide himself in the hills of Hachilah, which is before Jeshimon?" (1 Sam. 26:1). The reader may remember that the Ziphites had shown themselves unfriendly towards David on a former occasion. Was it not then a hazardous thing for him to return unto those parts! How are we to account for his acting so injudiciously, and thus courting danger? Ah, let us recall what was pointed out under 21:1 in article 8. When the soul is out of touch with God, when fellowship with Him has been broken by giving way to the lusts of the flesh, the judgment is dulled, and imprudent conduct is sure to be the effect. It is not without reason that godliness is so often designated "wisdom" (e.g. Psa. 90:12), and that a course of evil doing is termed "folly."

David had acted imprudently in marrying Abigail; he had committed a grave sin in taking unto wife Ahinoam. We say he had acted "imprudently" in marrying Abigail. The *time* was not propitious for that. He was then a homeless wanderer, and in no condition to give unto a wife the care and devotion to which she is entitled. Holy Scripture declares, "to everything there is a season" (Eccl. 3:1). While on this point, let it be said that, in the judgment of the writer, young men who are out of work and have no good prospects of soon obtaining any, are acting imprudently, yea, rashly, in getting married. Let them possess their souls in patience (Luke 21:19) and wait a more favourable season, and not tempt God. So too those in straitened circumstances who continue having an increase in their families are imprudent, nay, disobeying 1 Cor. 7:29. These are days for practicing *self-denial.*

"And the Ziphites came unto Saul to Gibeah, saying, Doth not David hide himself in the hills of Hachilah, which is before Jeshimon?" If we venture upon the enemy's territory we must expect to be harassed by him. It is probable these Ziphites were fearful that should David succeed Saul on the throne, then he would avenge himself upon them for their previous perfidy: if so, they were now the more anxious that he should be captured and slain. Afraid to tackle him themselves, they sent word to the king of David's present whereabouts. Their message presented a temptation for Saul to return again unto that evil course which he had abandoned, temporarily at least: thus does one evil-doer encourage another in wickedness.

"Then Saul arose, and went down to the wilderness of Ziph, having three thousand chosen men of Israel with him, to seek David in the wilderness of Ziph" (v. 2). Poor Saul, his goodness was a a morning cloud, and as the early dew it vanished away. "How soon do unsanctified hearts lose the good impressions which their convictions have made upon them, and return with the dog to their vomit" (M. Henry). O what need has even the Christian to pray earnestly unto God, that since he still has so much of the tinder of corruption left within, the sparks of temptation may be kept far from him, lest when they come together they are "set on fire of hell" (James 3:6). The providential restraint of God in causing Saul to leave off pursuing David because the Philistines were invading his territory, had wrought no change *within* him: his evil disposition towards God's anointed was the same as ever; and now that the favourable opportunity to seize David presented itself, he gladly made the most of it.

The action of Saul here provides a solemn illustration of a well known principle: if sin be not dethroned and mortified, it will soon recover its strength, and when a suitable temptation is presented, break out again with renewed force. How often do the servants of God witness souls under deep conviction, followed by a marked reformation, which leads them to believe that a genuine work of grace has taken place within them; only to see them, a little later, return to their sins and become worse than ever. So here: upon receiving word from the Ziphites, Saul's enmity and malice revived, and, like Pharaoh of old, he again hardened his heart, and determined to make another effort to remove his rival. And thus it is with many a one who has been sobered and awed by the Word: after a brief season, Satan and his agents suggest such thoughts as tend to rekindle the smothered flame, and then the lusts of the flesh are again allowed free play. O my reader, beg God to *deepen* your convictions and write His law on your heart.

"And Saul pitched in the hill Hachilah, which is before Jeshimon, by the way. But David abode in the wilderness, and he saw that Saul came after him into the wilderness. David therefore sent out spies, and understood that Saul was come in very deed" (vv. 3, 4). "David neither fled, nor went out to meet Saul, when he was fully certified that he was actually come forth to destroy him! Had a much greater army of uncircumcised Philistines marched against him, he would doubtless have faced them with his small company, and trusted in God for the event; but he would not fight against the 'Lord's anointed,' " (T. Scott).

"David therefore sent out spies, and understood that Saul was come in very deed." From the previous verse it would seem David had perceived that some large force was advancing into that part of the country where he and his men were now quartered. Though not certain as to who was at the head of the approaching army, he probably suspected that it was none other than Saul, and therefore did he now sent out spies to make sure. He would not fully believe that the king had again dealt so basely with him, till he had the clearest proof of it: thereby does he set us an example not to believe the worst of our enemies till we are really forced to do so by incontestable evidence.

"And David arose, and came to the place where Saul had pitched; and David beheld the place where Saul lay, and Abner the son of Ner, the captain of his hosts; and Saul lay in the trench, and the people pitched round about him" (v. 5). Most likely it was in the dusk of the evening that David now went forward to reconnoitre, surveying from close range the order of Saul's camp and the strength of its entrenchments. Though he knew the Lord was his Protector, yet he deemed it necessary to be upon his guard and make use of means for his safety. Well for us when we act as wisely as serpents, but as harmless as doves. It is to be noted that David did not entrust this critical task unto any of his underlings, but performed it in person. The leader ought always to take the lead in the most difficult and dangerous tasks.

"Then answered David and said to Ahimelech the Hittite, and to Abishai the son of Zeruiah, brother to Joab, saying, Who will go down with me to Saul to the camp? And Abishai said, I will go down with thee" (v. 6). David now addressed himself unto two of those who were, most likely, his closest attendants, asking who was bold enough to volunteer in accompanying him on an exceedingly dangerous enterprise — that of two men entering a camp of three thousand soldiers. There is little room to doubt that David was prompted by the Spirit to act thus, from whom he probably received assurance of Divine protection: thereby he would be afforded another opportunity of demonstrating to Saul and Israel his innocency. Ahimelech was probably a proselyted Hittite, and not having that faith in the God of Israel which such a severe testing called for, held back. But Abishai, who was David's own nephew (1 Chron. 2:15, 16), readily agreed to accompany David.

"So David and Abishai came to the people by night: and, behold, Saul lay sleeping within the trench, and his spear stuck in the ground at his bolster: but Abner and the people lay around about him" (v. 7). What an extraordinary situation now presented itself before the eyes of David and his lone companion? Where was the guard? Had the watchmen failed at their point of duty? There was none to sound an alarm: the entire camp was wrapped in slumber so profound that, though the two uninvited visitors walked and talked in their midst, none was aroused. Ah, how easily can *God* render impotent an entire host of enemies! All the forces of nature are under His immediate control: He can awaken from the sleep of death, and He can put the living into such a heavy sleep that none can awaken them. There was Saul and all his forces as helpless as though they were in fetters of iron.

"Then said Abishai to David, God hath delivered thine enemy into thine hand this day: now therefore let me smite him, I pray thee, with the spear even to the earth at once, and I will not smite him the second time" (v. 8). In view of what had transpired in the cave (24:4-6), no doubt Abishai thought that though David scrupled to kill Saul with his own hand, yet he would allow one of his officers to slay him: thus would an end be put to the difficulties and dangers unto himself and his adherents, by cutting off at one blow their inveterate prosecutor; the more so, since Providence had again placed Saul in their power apparently for this very purpose. This illustrates the fact that often it requires as much godly resolution to restrain the excesses of zealous but unspiritual friends, as it does to stand firm against the rage of incensed enemies.

A powerful temptation was here set before David. Had their positions been reversed, would Saul hesitate to slay him? Why, then, should David allow sentiment to prevail? Moreover, did it not look as though *God* had arranged things to this very end? The previous opportunity was not nearly so strongly marked as this one: Saul had, as it were, accidentally wandered into the cave; but here was something extraordinary — the entire camp was wrapped in a supernatural slumber. Furthermore, his attendant urges upon him that it *was* the will of God to now takes things into his own hand. But David was not to be moved from his loyalty to the throne. First, he told Abishai that it would be *sinful* to lay violent hands upon one whose person was sacred (v. 10), for Saul had been appointed by God and anointed for his office. Second, he declared it was *unnecessary:* God would, sooner or later, cut him off (vv. 10, 11). Remembering how the Lord had just before smitten Nabal, he left it to Him to avenge his cause.

"So David took the spear and the cruse of water from Saul's bolster; and they gat them away, and no man saw it, nor knew it, neither awaked; for they were all asleep; because a deep sleep from the Lord was fallen upon them" (v. 12). Here we see David as a type of Christ in His wonderful forbearance toward His enemies, and in His faith in God: 1 Pet. 2:23. David's procedure was an effective method of convincing Saul that he *could* have slain him. And what a proof to the king that the Lord had departed from him, and was protecting David! "Thus do we lose our strength and comfort when we are careless and secure, and off our watch" (M. Henry), gives the practical lesson for us in Saul's losing his spear and cruse of water.

And Ab-i-gail came to Na-bal. And behold, he held a feast in his house like the feast of a king. And Na-bal's heart was merry within him, for he was very drunk. Therefore she did not tell him anything, more or less, until the morning light. But in the morning, when the wine had gone out of Na-bal and his wife had told him these things, his heart died within him and he became like a stone. And about ten days afterward the LORD struck Na-bal so that he died. And when David heard that Na-bal was dead, he said, Blessed is the LORD who has pleaded the cause of my reproach from the hand of Na-bal and has kept His servant from evil. For the LORD has returned the wickedness of Na-bal on his own head. And David sent and spoke with Ab-i-gail, to take her to himself for a wife. And when the servants of David had come to Abigail, at Carmel, they spoke to her, saying, David sent us to you to take you to himself for a wife. And she arose and bowed herself on her face to the earth and said, Behold, let your handmaid be a servant to wash the feet of the servants of my lord. And Abigail hurried and arose. And she rode on an ass, with five of her maidens who went after her. And she followed the messengers of David and became his wife. David also took Ahinoam of Jezreel. And they were also, both of them, his wives. But Saul had given his daughter Michal, David's wife, to Phalti the son of Laish, who was of Gallim. — 1 Samuel 25:36-44.

"Behold, the righteous shall be recompensed in the earth: much more the wicked and the sinner" (Prov. 11:31). This is a most appropriate verse with which to introduce the passage that is to engage our attention, for each of its clauses receives striking illustration in what is now to be before us. The closing verses of 1 Sam. 25 supply both a blessed and a solemn sequel to what is found earlier in the chapter. There we saw the wicked triumphing, and the righteous being oppressed. There we saw the godly wife of the churl, Nabal, graciously and faithfully befriending the outcast David. Here we behold the hand of God's judgment falling heavily upon the wicked, and the hand of His grace rewarding the righteous.

"Behold, the righteous shall be recompensed in the earth: much more the wicked and the sinner." Of all the hundreds of Solomon's inspired proverbs this is the only one which is prefaced by the word "Behold." This at once intimates that a subject of great importance is here in view, bidding us fix the eyes of our mind upon the same with close and admiring attention. That subject is the *providential dealings* of God in human affairs, a subject which has fallen sadly into disfavor during the last two or three generations, and one concerning which much ignorance and error now widely prevails. Three things are clearly signified by Prov. 11:31: first, that God disposes the affairs of all His creatures; second, that He pleads the cause of the innocent and vindicates His oppressed people; third, that He plagues and over-throws evil-doers.

Practically all professing Christians believe that there is a *future* day of retribution, when God shall reward the righteous and punish the wicked; but comparatively few believe God *now* does so. Yet the verse with which we have opened expressly declares that "The righteous shall be recompensed *in the earth*," It is impossible to read the Scriptures with an unprejudiced mind and not see this truth exhibited in the history of individuals, families, and nations. Cain murdered Abel: a mark was set upon him by God, and he cried, "my punishment is greater than I can bear." Noah was a just man and walked with God: he and his family were preserved from the flood. Pharaoh persecuted the Hebrews, and is drowned at the Red Sea. Saul thirsts for David's life, and is slain in battle. Of the Lord we must say, "Verily, He is a God that judgeth in the earth" (Psa. 58:11).

And now comes the "Dispensationalist" with his objection: All that you have said above obtained during the O. T. dispensation, but in this Christian era it is not so; we are shut up to faith. How ridiculous. Has God vacated His throne? Is He no longer shaping human affairs? Is His governmental justice no longer operative? Why, the most signal example in all history of God's "recompensing" the wicked and the sinner in the earth, has transpired in this *Christian* dispensation! It was in A. D. 70 that God publicly executed judgment upon Jerusalem for the Jews' rejection and crucifixion of their Messiah, and the condition of that people throughout the earth ever since, has been a perpetual exemplification of this solemn truth. The same principle has been repeatedly manifested in the establishment of Christianity upon the ruins of its oppressors. As to Christians being "shut up to faith," so were the O. T. saints just as much as we are: Habak. 2:1-4.

But let us notice a more formidable objection. Have there not been many righteous souls who were falsely accused, fiercely persecuted, and who were not vindicated on earth by God? Have there not been many of the wicked who have prospered temporally, and received no retribution in this life? First, let it be pointed out that God does not always respond immediately. The writer (who is not yet fifty) has lived long enough to see more than one or two who traded on the Sabbath, oppressed widows, and despised all religion, brought to want. Second, there is a happy medium between denying (on the one hand) that God is not now acting at all in the capacity of Judge, and insisting (on the other hand) that *every* man fully reaps in this life what he has sown.

Here, as everywhere, the *truth* lies between two extremes. If God were to visibly reward every righteous act and punish every evil-doer in this life, much of the work pertaining to the great Day of Judgment would be forestalled. But if God never honours in this world those who honour Him, or punishes those who openly defy Him, then we should be without any pre-intimations of that Great Assize, other than what is revealed in those Scriptures of Truth which very few so much as read. Therefore, in His providential government of this world, God wisely gives sufficiently clear manifestations of His love and righteousness and hatred of unrighteousness, as to leave all without excuse concerning what may be expected when we stand before Him to be fully and finally judged. While there are sufficient cases of godliness apparently passing unrewarded and examples of evil-doers prospering, as to leave full room for the exercise of faith that the righteousness of God shall yet be completely vindicated; nevertheless, there are also a sufficient number of clear demonstrations before our eyes of God's vengeance upon the wicked to awe us that *we* sin not.

"And Abigail came to Nabal; and behold, he held a feast in his house, like the feast of a king; and Nabal's heart was merry within him, for he was very drunken: wherefore she told him nothing, less or more until the morning light" (v. 36). Recall the circumstances. Only a little while previously Nabal had offered a gross insult to one who was in dire need, and who had several hundred men under his command. Measured by the standards of the world that insult called for retaliation, and so felt the one who had received it. David had sworn to revenge himself by slaying Nabal and every male member of his household, and v. 23 makes it plain that he was on his way to execute that purpose. But for the timely intervention of his wife, Nabal had been engaged in a hopeless fight to preserve his life; and here we see him feasting and drunken!

As Abigail furnishes a typical illustration of a needy sinner coming to Christ and being saved by Him (see close of last arricle), so Nabal affords us a solemn portrayal of one who despises Christ and perished in his sins. Let preachers develop the leading points which we here note down in passing. See the false security of sinners when in dire danger: Eccl. 8:11. Observe how one who grudges to give to God for the relief of His poor, will lavishly spend money to satisfy his lusts or make a fair show in the flesh: Luke 16:19-21. O how many there are more concerned about having what they call "a good time," than they are in making their peace with God: Isa. 55:2. So sottish are some in the indulging of their appetites that they sink lower than the beasts of the field: Isa. 1:3. It is adding insult to injury when the sinner not only breaks God's laws but abuses His mercies: Luke 14:18-20. Remember people are intoxicated with other things besides "wine" — wordly fame, wordly riches, wordly pleasures.

Yes, the fool Nabal vividly portrays the case of multitudes all around us. The curse of God's broken law hanging over them, yet "feasting" as though all is well with their souls for eternity. The sword of Divine justice already drawn to smite them down, yet their hearts "merry" with "the pleasures of sin for a season."

The Water of Life neglected, but "drunken" with the intoxicating things of this perishing world. A grave awaiting them in a few days' time, but flirting with death during the brief and precious interval. In such a benumbed and giddy state, that it would be the casting of pearls before swine for the godly to speak seriously unto them. O how securely the Devil holds his victims! O the beguiling and paralyzing effects of sin! O the utterly hopeless condition of the unsaved, unless a sovereign God intervenes, works a miracle of grace, and snatches them as brands from the burning!

"But it came to pass in the morning, when the wine was gone out of Nabal, and his wife had told him these things, that his heart died within him, and he became as a stone" (v. 37). The day of danger had been spent in revelling, the night in intoxicated stupefaction, and now he is called, as it were, to account. The sacred narrative records no reproaches that Abigail made: they were not necessary — the guilty conscience of Nabal would perform its own office. Instead, she merely told her husband of what had transpired. Her words at once dispelled his dreams, shattered his peace, and sank his spirits. Most probably, he was over-come with fright, that, notwithstanding his wife's kindly overtures, David would swifty take vengeance upon him. Filled with bitter remorse, now it was too late to repent, giving way to abject despair, Nabal's heart "became as a stone." See here a picture of the poor worldling when facing death, and the terrors of the Almighty overwhelming him. See here the deceitfulness of carnal pleasures: over-night his heart merry with wine, now paralyzed with horror and terror. Yes, the "*end of that mirth is heaviness*" (Prov. 14:13); how different the joys which God gives!

"And it came to pass about ten days after, that the Lord smote Nabal, that he died" (v. 38). What a fearfully solemn termination to a wasted life! Nabal's course was one of folly, his end was that of "the fool." Here was a man "very great" (v. 2), who had boastfully spoken of "*my* bread, *my* flesh, *my* shearers" (v. 11); who had scorned David, and spent his time in excessive self-gratification; now arrived at the close of his earthly journey, with nothing before him but "the blackness of darkness forever." He seems to have lain in a senseless stupor for ten days, induced either by the effects of his intoxication, or from the horror and anguish of his mind, and this was completed by the immediate stroke of the power and wrath of God, cutting him off out of the land of the living. Such is, my reader, the doom of every one who despises and rejects Christ as Lord and Saviour.

"And it came to pass about ten days after, that the Lord smote Nabal, that he died." Not only is the case of Nabal a solemn example of a careless, giddy, reckless sinner, suddenly cut off by God whilst giving himself up to the indulgence of the flesh, when the sword of Divine judgment was suspended over his head; but we also see in his death an exhibition of the faithfulness of God, an illustration of Rom. 12:19: "Dearly beloved, avenge not yourselves, but rather give place unto wrath: for it is written, Vengeance is Mine; I will repay, saith the Lord." Not only is it sinful for the saint to avenge himself when unjustly insulted and ill treated, but it is quite unnecessary. In due time Another will do it far more effectually for him.

"And when David heard that Nabal was dead, he said, Blessed be the Lord, that has pleaded the cause of my reproach from the hand of Nabal, and hath kept His servant from evil: for the Lord hath returned the wickedness of Nabal upon his own head" (v. 39). It is not that David was guilty of unholy glee over the wretched end of one who had wronged him, but that he rejoiced in the display of *God's* glory, of the exercise of Divine justice, and the triumphing of piety over iniquity. Therein lies the real key to a number of passages which many of our moderns suppose breathe only a vengeful spirit: as though God erected a lower standard of holiness in O. T. times than is now given to us. Such was not the case: the law, equally with the Gospel, required *love* for the neighbour.

As this subject has been so sadly wrested by "Dispensationalists," let us add a few words here. Take for example Psalm 58:10, "The righteous shall rejoice when he seeth the vengeance: he shall wash his feet in the blood of the wicked." Superficial people say, "But *that* is altogether contrary to the spirit of *this* dispensation!" But read on: "So that a man shall say, Verily there is a reward for the righteous: verily He is a God that judgeth in the earth" (v. 11). It was not the exercise of a spirit of malice, which took delight in seeing the destruction of *their* foes: no indeed: for in the O. T. the Divine command was, *"Rejoice not when thine enemy falleth"* (Prov. 24:17). Instead, it was the heart bowing in worship before the governmental dealings of God, adoring that Justice which gave unto the wicked their due. And where the heart is not completely under the dominion of maudlin sentimentality, there will be rejoicing *today* when some notoriously wicked character is manifestly cut down by the holy hand of God: so it will be at the end of this dispensation: see Rev. 18:20; 19:1,2.

Ere passing on to the next verses, let us take notice of David's thankful acknowledgement of God's restraining grace: "Blessed be the Lord, that hath pleaded the cause of my reproach from the hand of Nabal, and hath *kept* His servant from evil" (v. 39). If we carefully reviewed the details of each day, we should frequently find occasion to admire the sin-preventing providences of God. We may well adopt the language of the Psalmist at the close of a beautiful illustration of the Divine mercies: "Whoso is wise, shall understand the loving-kindness of the Lord" (Psa. 107:43). Let us never miss an opportunity of praising God when He graciously keeps us from committing any evil we had premeditated.

"And David sent and communed with Abigail, to take her to him to wife. And when the servants of David were come to Abigail to Carmel, they spake unto her, saying, David sent us unto thee, to take thee to him to wife" (vv. 39, 40). The stroke of God's judgment had freed Abigail from a painful situation, and now the workings of His providence rewarded her righteousness. God gave her favour in the eyes of His anointed. David was charmed not only with the beauty of her person and the prudence of her character, but also with her evident piety — the most valuable quality of all in a wife. Abigail being now a widow, and David's own wife living in adultery, he sent messengers with a proposal of marriage to her. This line in the type is strikingly accurate: the Lord Jesus does not court His wife immediately, but employs the ministers of the Gospel, endued with the Holy Spirit, to woo and win sinners unto Himself.

"And she arose, and bowed herself on her face to the earth, and said, Behold, let thine handmaid be a servant to wash the feet of the servants of my lord" (v. 41). Very beautiful is it to see the great modesty and humility with which such a wealthy woman received the advances of David, deeming herself unworthy of such an honour, yea, having such respect for him that she would gladly be one of the meanest servants of his household. She accepted his proposal, and thereby added still another line to this typical picture of conversion: note how in the margin of 2 Chron. 30:8 faith is represented as to "give the *hand* unto the Lord"!

"And Abigail hasted, and arose, and rode upon an ass, with five damsels of hers that went after her; and she went after the messengers of David, and became his wife" (v. 42). Most blessed is this. At the time, David was an homeless wanderer, outlawed; yet Abigail was willing not only to forsake her own house and comfortable position, but to share his trials and endure hardships for his sake. Nevertheless, she knew it would be only for a brief season: she married *in faith*, assured of the fulfillment of God's promises (v. 30) and confident that in due course she would "reign with him"! And this is what true conversion is: a turning of our back upon the old life, willing to suffer the loss of all things for Christ, with faith looking forward to the future.

"David also took Ahinoam of Jezreel, and they were also both of them his wives. But (or "for") Saul had given Michal his daugher, David's wife, to Phalti the son of Laish, which was of Gallim" (vv. 43, 44). Polygamy, though not in accord with either the law of nature or the law of God, was a custom which prevailed in those degenerate days, which some good men gave in to, though they are not to be commended for it. In taking Ahinoam of Jezreel to wife (and later several others: 2 Sam. 3), David followed the corruption of the times, but from the beginning it was not so, nor is it permissible now since Christ has ushered in "the times of reformation": Matt. 19:4-6.

CHAPTER 26.

And the Ziphites came to Saul at Gibeah, saying, Does not David hide himself in the hill of Hachilah, which is before Jeshimon? Then Saul arose and went down to the wilderness of Ziph to seek David in the wilderness of Ziph, having three thousand chosen men of Israel with him. And Saul pitched in the hill of Hachilah, which is before Jeshimon, by the way. But David stayed in the wilderness, and he saw that Saul came after him into the wilderness. Then David sent out spies and knew that Saul had come indeed. And David arose and came to the place where Saul had pitched. And David looked at the place where Saul lay, and on Abner the son of Ner, the captain of his army, And Saul lay in the trench with the people pitched around him. Then David answered and said to Ahimelech the Hittite, and to Abishai the son of Zeruiah, the brother of Joab, saying, Who will go down with me to the camp to Saul? And Abishai said, I will go down with you. So David and Abishai came to the people by night. And, behold, Saul lay sleeping in the tent, and his spear was stuck in the ground at his head. But Abner and the people lay around him. Then Abishai said to David, God has shut up your enemy into your hand this day. Now therefore, I beg you, let me strike him with the spear even to the earth at once, and I will not strike the second time. And David said to Abishai, Do not destroy him. For who can stretch forth his hand against the LORD's anointed and be guiltless? And David said, As the LORD lives, the LORD shall strike him — or his day shall come to die — or he shall go down to battle and perish. But the LORD forbid that I should stretch forth my hand against the LORD's anointed. But now, I ask you to take the spear that is at his head and the cruse of water, and let us go. So David took the spear and the cruse of water from Saul's head. And they got away, and no man saw or knew, neither did they awake. For they were all asleep, because a deep sleep from the LORD had fallen on them. Then David went over to the other side and stood on the top of a hill afar off, a great space between them. And David cried to the people and to Abner the son of Ner, saying, Do you not answer, Abner? Then Abner answered and said, Who are you that cries to the king? And David said to Abner, Are you not a man? And who is like you in Israel? Why then have you not kept your lord the king? For there came one of the people in to destroy your lord the king. This thing that you have done is not good. As the LORD lives, because you have not kept your master, the LORD's anointed, you are worthy to die. And now see where the king's spear is, and the cruse of water that was at his head. And Saul knew David's voice and said, Is this your voice, my son David? And David said, It is my voice, my lord, O king. And he said, Why does my lord pursue after his servant this way? For what have I done? Or what evil is in my hand? Now therefore, I beg you, let my lord the king hear the words of his servant. If the LORD has stirred you up against me, let Him accept an offering. But if it is the children of men, they are cursed before the LORD. For they have driven me out today from living within the inheritance of the LORD, saying, Go serve other gods. Now therefore, let not my blood fall to the earth before the face of the LORD. For the king of Israel has come out to seek a flea, as when one hunts a partridge in the mountains. Then Saul said, I have sinned, Return, my son David, for I will never do you harm any more, because my life was precious in your eyes this day. Behold, I have played the fool and have greatly erred. And David answered and said, Behold, the king's spear! And let one of the young men come over and get it. May the LORD give to every man his righteousness and his faithfulness. For the LORD delivered you into my hand today, but I would not *stretch forth my hand against the LORD's anointed. And behold, as your life was precious in my eyes this day, so let my life be precious in the eyes of the LORD, and let Him deliver me out of all tribulation. Then Saul said to David, Blessed are you, my son David. You shall both do great things and also shall still prevail. So David went on his way, and Saul returned to his place.* 1 Samuel 26:1-25.

"There are few periods in the life of David in which his patient endurance was displayed more conspicuously than in his last interview with Saul. Saul had once more fallen into his power; but David again refused to avail himself of the advantage. He would not deliver himself by means that God did not sanction, nor stretch out his hand against the Lord's anointed. Recognition of the excellency of David, and confession of his own sin, was extorted, even from the lips of Saul" (B. W. Newton).

In the preceding article we followed David and his lone attendant as they entered the camp of Saul, and secured the king's spear and the cruse of water which lay at his head. Having accomplished his purpose, David now retired from his sleeping enemies. Carrying with him clear evidence that he had been in their very midst, he determined to let them know what had transpired, for he was far from being ashamed of his conduct — when our actions are innocent, we care not who knows them. David now stations himself within hailing distance, yet sufficiently removed that they could not come at him quickly or easily. "Then David went over to the other side and stood on the top of an hill afar off; a great space between them" (1 Sam. 26:13). This was evidently on some high point facing the "hill of Hachilah" (v. 3), a wide valley lying between.

"And David cried to the people, and to Abner the son of Ner, saying, Answerest thou not, Abner?" (v. 14). David now hailed the sleeping camp with a loud voice, addressing himself particularly unto Abner, who was the general of the army. Apparently had to call more than once before Abner was fully aroused. "Then Abner answered and said, Who art thou that criest to the king?" Probably those were words both of anger and contempt: annoyance at being so rudely disturbed from his rest, and scorn as he recognized the voice of the speaker. Abner had so lightly esteemed David and his men, that he had not considered it necessary to keep awake personally, nor even to appoint sentinels to watch the camp. The force of his question was, Whom do you think *you* are, that you should address the monarch of Israel! Let not the servants of God deem it a strange thing that those occupying high offices in the world consider them quite beneath their notice.

"And David said to Abner, art not thou a valiant man? and who is like to thee in Israel? wherefore then hast thou not kept thy lord the king? for there came one of the people in to destroy the king thy lord" (v. 15). David was not to be brow-beaten. "The wicked flee when no man pursueth: but the righteous are bold as a lion" (Prov. 28:1). Where the fear of God rules the heart, man cannot intimidate. Paul before Agrippa, Luther before the Diet of Worms, John Knox before bloody queen Mary, are cases in point. My reader, if you tremble before worms of the dust, it is because you do not tremble before God. David boldly charged Abner with his criminal neglect. First, he reminded him that he was a valiant "man," i.e. a man in office, and therefore duty bound to guard the person of the king. Second, he bantered him in view of the high position he held. Third, he informed him of how the king's life had been in danger that night as the result of his culpable carelessness. It was tantamount to telling him he was disgraced forever.

"This thing is not good that thou hast done. As the Lord liveth, ye are worthy to die, because ye have not kept your master, the Lord's anointed" (v. 16). By martial law Abner and his officers had forfeited their lives. It should be duly noted that David was not here speaking as a private person to Saul's general, but as the servant and mouthpiece of God, as is evident from "as the Lord liveth." "And now, see where the king's spear is, and the cruse of water that was at his bolster." David continued to banter him: the force of this word was, Who is *really* the king's friend — you who neglected him and left him exposed, or I that spared him when he was at my mercy! You are stirring up Saul against me, and pursuing me as one who is unfit to live; but *who*, now, is worthy to die? It was plainly a case of the biter being bit.

"And Saul knew David's voice, and said, Is this thy voice, my son David?" (v. 17). The king at once recognized the voice of him that was denouncing Abner, and addressed him in terms of cordial friendship. See here another illustration of the instability and fickleness of poor fallen man: one day thirsting after David's blood, and the next day speaking to him in terms of affection! What reliance can be placed in such a creature? How it should make us the more revere and adore the One who declares, "I am the Lord, I change not" (Mal. 3:6). "And David said, it is my voice, my lord, O king" (v. 17). Very beautiful is this. Though David could not admire the variableness and treachery of Saul's character, yet he respected his office, and is here shown paying due deference to the throne: he not only owned Saul's crown, but acknowledged that he was *his* sovereign. Tacitly, it was a plain denial that David was the rebellious insurrectionist Saul had supposed.

"And he said, Wherefore doth my lord thus pursue after his servant? for what have I done? or what evil is in mine hand?" (v. 18). Once more (cf. 1 Sam. 24:11, etc.) David calmly remonstrated with the king: what ground was there for his being engaged in such a blood-thirsty mission? First, David was not an enemy, but ready to act as his "servant" and further the court's interests; thus he suggested it was against Saul's own good to persecute one who was ready to do his bidding and advance his kingdom. Equally unreasonable and foolish have been other rulers who hounded the servants of God: none are more loyal to the powers that be, none do as much to really strengthen their hands, as the true ministers of Christ; and therefore, they who oppose them are but forsaking their own mercies.

Second, by pursuing David, Saul was driving him from his master and lawful business, and compelling to flee the one who wished to follow him with respect. O the exceeding sinfulness of sin: it is not only unreasonable and unjust (and therefore denominated "iniquity"), but cruel, both in its nature and in its effects. Third, he asked, "What have I done? or what evil is in mine hand?" Questions which a clear conscience (and that only) is never afraid of asking. It was the height of wickedness for Saul to persecute him as a criminal, when he was unable to charge him with any crime. But let us observe how that by these honest questions David was a type of Him who challenged His enemies with "which of you convicteth Me of sin?" (John 8:46), and again, "If I have spoken evil, bear witness of the evil; but if well, why smitest thou Me?" (John 18:23).

"Now therefore, I pray thee, let my lord the king hear the words of his servant. If the Lord have stirred thee up against me, let Him accept an offering" (v. 19). It is likely that David had paused and waited for Saul to make reply to his searching queries. Receiving no answer, he continued his address. David himself now suggested two possible explanations for the king's heartless course. First, it might be that the Lord Himself was using him thus to righteously chastise His servant for some fault. It was *the Divine side* of things which first engaged David's mind: "If the Lord hath stirred thee up against me." This is a likelihood which should always exercise the conscience of a saint, for the Lord "does not afflict willingly" (Lam. 3:33), but usually because *we* give Him occasion to use the rod upon us. Much of this would be spared, if we kept shorter accounts with God and more unsparingly judged ourselves (1 Cor. 11:31). It is always a timely thing to say with Job, "Show me wherefor Thou contendest with me" (10:2).

Should the Lord convict him of any offense, then "let him accept an offering": David would then make his peace with God and present the required sin offering. For the Christian, this means that, having humbled himself before God, penitently confessed his sins, he now pleads afresh the merits of Christ's blood, for the remission of their governmental consequences. But secondly, if God was not using Saul to chastise David (as indeed He was), then if evil men had incited Saul to use such violent measures, the Divine vengeance would assuredly over-take them — they were accursed before God. It is blessed to note the mildness of David on this occasion: so far from reviling the king, and attributing his wickedness unto the evil of his own heart, every possible excuse was made for his conduct.

"But if they be the children of men, cursed be they before the Lord; for they have driven me out this day from abiding in the inheritance of the Lord, saying, Go, serve other gods" (v. 19). This was what pained David the most: not the being deprived of an honourable position as servant to Saul, not the being driven from home, but being exiled from Canaan and cut off from the public means of grace. No longer could he worship in the tabernacle, but forced out into the deserts and mountains, he would soon be obliged to leave the Holy Land. By their actions, his enemies were saying in effect, "Go, serve other gods": driving him into a foreign country, where he would be surrounded by temptations. It is blessed to see that it was the having to live among *idolators*, and not merely among *strangers*, which worried him the more.

Ah, nought but the sufficiency of Divine grace working in David's heart could, under such circumstances, have kept him from becoming utterly disgusted with the religion which Saul, Abner, and his fellows professed. But for *that*, David had said, "If these be Israelites,' then let me become and die a Philistine!" Yes, and probably more than one or two readers of this article have, like the writer, passed through a similar situation. We expect unkind, unjust, treacherous, merciless, treatment at the hands of the world; but when they came from those whom we have regarded as true brethren and sisters in Christ, we were shaken to the very foundation, and but for the mighty power of the Spirit working within, would have said, "If *that* is Christianity, I will have no more to do with it!" But, blessed be His name, God's grace *is* sufficient.

"Now therefore, let not my blood fall to the earth before the face of the Lord: for the king of Israel is come out to seek a flea, as when one doth hunt a partridge in the mountains" (v. 20). In these words David completed his address to Saul. First, he gave solemn warning that if he shed his blood, it would fall before the face of the Lord, and *He* would not hold him guiltless. Second, he argued that it was far beneath the dignity of the monarch of Israel to be chasing the son of Jesse, whom he here likens unto "a flea" — an insignificant and worthless thing. Third, he appeals again to the king's conscience by resembling his case to men hunting a "partridge" — an innocent and harmless bird, which when attacked by men offers no resistance, but flies away; such had been David's attitude. Now we are to see what effect all this had upon the king.

"Then said Saul, I have sinned: return, my son David; for I will no more do thee harm, because my soul was precious in thine eyes this day; behold, I have played the fool, and have erred exceedingly" (v. 21). This is more than the wretched king had acknowledged on a former occasion, and yet it is greatly to be feared that he had no true sense of his wickedness or genuine repentance for it. Rather was it very similar to the remorseful cry of Judas, when he said, "I have sinned in that I have betrayed the innocent blood" (Matt. 27:4). These words of Saul's were the bitter lament of one who, too late, realized he had made shipwreck of his life. He owned that he had sinned — broken God's law — by so relentlessly persecuting David. He besought his son to return, assuring him that he would do him no more injury; but he must have realized that *his* promises could not be relied upon. He intimated that David's magnanimity had thoroughly melted his heart, which shows that even the worst characters are capable of recognizing the good deeds of God's people.

"Behold, I have played the fool, and have erred exceedingly." O what a fool he had been: in opposing the man after God's own heart, in alienating his own son, in so sorely troubling Israel, and in bringing madness and sorrow upon himself! And how exceedingly had he "erred": by driving away from his court the one who would have been his best friend, by refusing to learn his lesson on the former occasion (1 Sam. 24), by vainly attempting to fight against the Most High! Unsaved reader, suffer us to point out that these words, "I have played the fool, and have erred exceedingly" are the wail of the lost in Hell. Now it is too late they realize what fools they were in despising the day of their opportunity, in neglecting their souls' eternal interests, in living and dying in sin. They realize they "erred exceedingly" in ignoring the claims of God, desecrating His holy Sabbaths, shunning His Word, and despising His Son. Will this yet be *your* cry?

"And David answered and said, Behold the king's spear! and let one of the young men come over and fetch it" (v. 22). This at once shows the estimate which David placed on the words of the king: he did not dare to trust him and return the spear in person, still less accompany him home. Good impressions quickly pass from such characters. No good words or fair professions entitle those to our confidence who have long sinned against the light. Such people resemble those spoken of in James 1:23, 24, who hear the Word and do it not, and are like unto a man "beholding his natural face in a glass: for he beholdeth himself, goeth his way, *and straighway forgetteth* what manner of man he was." Thus it was with Saul; he now said that he had sinned, played the fool and erred exceedingly, yet this deterred him not from seeking unto the witch of Endor!

"The Lord render to every man his righteousness and his faithfulness: for the Lord delivered thee into my hand today, but I would not stretch forth mine hand against the Lord's anointed" (v. 23). This was very solemn, David now appealed to God to be the Judge of the controversy between himself and Saul, as One who was inflexibly just to render unto every man according to his works. David's conscience is quite clear in the matter, so he need not hesitate to ask the righteous One to decide the issue: good for us is it when we too are able to do likewise. In its final analysis, this verse was really a prayer: David asked for Divine protection on the ground of the mercy which he had shown to Saul.

"And, behold, as thy life was much set by this day in mine eyes, so let my life be much set by in the eyes of the Lord, and let Him deliver me out of all tribulation" (v. 24). It is to be noted that David made no direct reply to what Saul had said, but his language shows plainly that he placed no reliance in the king's promises. He does not say, "As thy life was much set by this day in mine eyes, so let my life be much set by in *thine* eyes," but rather, "in the eyes of the

Lord." His confidence was in God alone, and though further trials awaited him, he counted upon His power and goodness to bring him safely through them.

"Then Saul said to David, Blessed be thou, my son David: thou shalt both do great things, and also shalt still prevail" (v. 25). Such were the final words of Saul unto David: patient faith had so far prevailed as to extort a blessing even from its adversary. Saul owned there was a glorious future before David, for he who humbleth himself shall be exalted. There was a clear conviction in the king's mind that David was favoured by God, yet that conviction in nowise checked him in his own downward course: convictions which lead to no amendment only increase condemnation. "So David went on his way, and Saul returned to his place" (v. 25). Thus they parted, to meet no more in this world. Saul went forward to his awful doom; David waited God's time to ascend the throne. –

After Saul's departure (1 Sam. 26:25), David took stock of his situation, but unfortunately he left God out of his calculations. During tedious and trying delays, and especially when outward things seem to be all going against us, there is grave danger of giving way to unbelief. Then it is we are very apt to forget former mercies, and fear the worst. And when faith staggers, obedience wavers, and self-expedients are frequently employed, which later, involve us in great difficulties. So it was now with the one whose varied life we are seeking to trace. As David considered the situation he was still in, remembered the inconstancy and treachery of Saul, things appeared very gloomy to him. Knowing full well the kings' jealousy, and perhaps reasoning that he would now regard him with a still more evil eye, since God so favoured him, David feared the worst.

"The moment in which faith attains any triumph, is often one of peculiar danger. Self-confidence may be engendered by success, and pride may spring out of honour that humility has won; or else, if faithfulness, after having achieved its victory, still finds itself left in the midst of danger and sorrow, the hour of triumph may be succeeded by one of undue depression and sorrowful disappointment. And thus it was with David. He had obtained this great moral victory; but his circumstances were still unchanged. Saul yet continued to be king of Israel: himself remained a persecuted outcast. As the period, when he had before spared the life of Saul, had been followed by days of lengthened sorrow, so he probably anticipated an indefinite prolongation of similar sufferings, and his heart quailed at the prospect" (B. W. Newton).

Solemn is it to mark the contrast between what is found at the close of 1 Sam. 26 and that which is recorded in the opening verses of the next chapter. To question the faithfulness and goodness of God is fearful wickedness, though there are some who regard it as a very trivial offense; in fact, there are those who wellnigh exalt the doubts and fears of Christians into fruits and graces, and evidences of great advancement in spiritual experience. It is sad indeed to find a certain class of men petting and pampering people in unbelief and distrust of God, and being in this matter unfaithful both to their Master and to the souls of His saints. Not that we are an advocate for smiting the feeble of the flock, but their *sins* we must denounce. Any teaching which causes Christians to pity themselves for their failings and falls, is evil, and to deny that doubting the loving kindness of God is a very heinous offense, is highly reprehensible.

And David said in his heart, I shall now perish one day by the hand of Saul.
There is nothing better for me than that I should speedily escape into the land of
the Philistines. And Saul shall despair of seeking me any more in any border of
Israel, and so I shall escape out of his hand. And David arose. And he passed over
with the six hundred men that were with him to Achish the son of Maoch, king
of Gath. And David lived with Achish of Gath, he and his men, every man with
his household — David with his two wives, Ahinoam of Jezreel, and Abigail of
Carmel, Nabal's wife. 1 Samuel 27:1-3.

"And David said in his heart, I shall now perish one day by the hand of Saul:
there is nothing better for me than that I should speedily escape into the land of
the Philistines" (1 Sam. 27:1). "And yet the hour of Saul's fall and of his own
deliverance was close at hand. The Lord was about to interfere, and to extricate
His faithful servant from his long and sore afflictions. Almost the very last hour
of his trial under Saul had come, yet at that last moment he failed: so hard is it
for 'patience to have her *perfect* work.' David had just said, '*Let the Lord* deliver
me out of all tribulation.' It was a strong, and no doubt a sincere expression of
confidence in God; but the feeling of the heart, as well as the expression of the
lips, may often exceed the reality of our spiritual strength, and therefore, not
unfrequently, when strong expressons have been used, they who have used them
are tested by some peculiar trial; that so, if there be weakness, it may be
detected, and no flesh glory in the presence of God" (B. W. Newton).

"And David said in his heart, I shall now perish one day by the hand of Saul."
Such a conclusion was positively erroneous. There was *no evidence in proof*
thereof: he had been placed in perilous positions, before, but God had never
deserted him. His trials had been many and varied, but God had always made for
him "a way to escape" (1 Cor. 10: 13). It was therefore *contrary* to the
evidence. Once he had said, "thy servant slew both the lion and the bear, and this
uncircumcised Philistine shall be as one of them' (1 Sam. 17:36). Why not
reason like that now? and say "Thy servant slew Goliath, was delivered from the
javelin of a madman, escaped the evil devices of Doeg, and so he shall continue
to escape out of the hand of Saul!" Moreover, David's rash conclusion was
contrary to promise: Samuel had poured upon his head the anointing oil as
God's earnest that he should be king — how then could he be slain by Saul?

How is David's unbelief to be accounted for? "First, because he was a man. The
best of men are men at the best, and man at his best is such a creature that well
might David himself say, 'Lord, what is man?' . . . If faith never gave place to
unbelief, we might be tempted to lift up the believer into a demi-God, and think
him something more than mortal. That we might see that a man full of faith is
still a man, that we might glory in infirmities, since by them the power of God is
the more clearly proved, therefore God was pleased to let the feebleness of man
grievously show itself. Ah, it was not David who achieved those former victories,
but *God's grace* in David; and now, when that is removed for a moment, see
what Israel's champion becomes."

"Second, David had been exposed to a very long trial; not for one week, but
for month after month, he had been hunted like a partridge, upon the
mountains. Now a man could bear one trial, but a perpetuity of tribulations is
very hard to bear . . . Such was David's trial: always safe, but always harassed;
always secure through God, but always hunted about by his foe. No place could
give him any ease. If he went unto Keilah, then the citizens would deliver him

up; if he went into the woods of Ziph, then the Ziphites betrayed him; if he went even to the priest of God, there was that dog of a Doeg to go to Saul, and accuse the priest; even in Engedi or in Adullam he was not secure; secure, I grant you, in God, but always persecuted by his foe. Now, this was enough to make the wise man mad, and to make the faithful man doubt. Do not judge too harshly of David; at least judge just as hardly of yourselves.

"Third, David had passed through some strong excitements of mind. Just a day or so before he had gone forth with Abishai in the moonlight to the field where Saul and his hosts lay sleeping. They passed the outer circle where the common soldiers lay, and quietly and stealthily the two heroes passed without awakening any. They came at last to the spot where the captains of the hundreds slept, and they trod over their slumbering bodies without arousing them. They reached the spot where Saul lay, and David had to hold back Abishai's hand from slaying him; so he escaped from this temptation, as he had aforetime. Now, brethren, a man may do these great things helped by God, but do you know it is a sort of natural law with us, that after a strong excitement *there is a re-action!* It was thus with Elijah after his victory over the prophets of Baal: later, he ran from Jezebel, and cried 'Let me die.'

"But there was another reason, for we are not to exculpate David. He sinned, and that not merely through infirmity, but through evil of heart. It seems to us that David had *restrained prayer.* In every other action of David you find some hint that he asked counsel of the Lord . . . But this time what did he talk with? Why, with the most deceitful thing that he could have found — with his own heart. . .Having restrained prayer, he did the fool's act: he forgot his God, he looked only at his enemy, and it was no wonder that when he saw the strength of the cruel monarch, and the pertinacity of his persecution, he said 'I shall one day fall before him.' Brothers and sisters, would you wish to hatch the egg of unbelief till it turns into a scorpion? Restrain prayer! Would you see evils magnified and mercies diminish? Would you find your tribulations increased sevenfold and your faith diminished in proportion? Restrain prayer!" (Condensed from C. H. Spurgeon).

"I shall now perish one day." Ah, has not this been the cry of man a Satan-harassed saint! He looks within and sees what God has done for him: that he has desires and aspirations which he never had before conversion, so that the things he once hated he now loves. He realizes there has been a radical change, such as mere nature could not possibly effect, and his spirit rejoices in the hope set before him. *But* he also sees so very much corruption within him, and finds so much weakness that aids and abets that corruption; he sees temptations and sore trials awaiting him, and cold despondency falls upon his heart, and doubts and questions vex his mind. He is tripped up and has a bad fall, and then Satan roars in his ear, "Now God has forsaken thee," and he is almost ready to sink into despair.

"And David arose, and he passed over with the six hundred men that were with him unto Achish, the son of Maoch king of Gath" (v. 2). Under the pressure of trial, *relief* is what the flesh most desires, and unless the mind be stayed upon God, there is grave danger of seeking to take things into our own hands. Such was the case with David: having leaned unto his own understanding, being occupied entirely with the things of sight and sense, he now sought relief in his own way, and followed a course which was the very opposite to that which the Lord had enjoined him (1 Sam. 22:5). There God had told him to depart from the land of Moab and go into the land of Judah, and there He had marvelously preserved him. How this shows us what poor weak creatures the best of us are, and how low our graces sink when the Spirit does not renew them!

In what is here before us (v. 2), we are shown the ill effects of David's unbelief. "First, it made him do a foolish thing; the same foolish thing which he had rued once before. Now we say a burnt child always dreads the flame; but David had been burnt, and yet, in his unbelief, he puts his hand into the same fire again. He went once to Achish, king of Gath, and the Philistines identified him, and being greatly afraid, David feigned himself mad in their hands, and they drove him away. Now he goes to the same Achish again! Yes, and mark it, my brethren, although you and I know the bitterness of sin, yet if we are left to our own unbelief, we shall fall into the same sin again. I know we have said, 'No; never, never; I know so much by experience what an awful thing this is.' Your experience is not worth a rush to you apart from the continual restraints of grace. If your faith fail, everything else goes down with it; and you hoary-headed professor, will be as big a fool as a very boy, if God lets you alone.

"Second, he went over to the Lord's enemies. Would you have believed it: he that killed Goliath, sought a refuge in Goliath's land; he who smote the Philistines trusts in the Philistines; nay, more, he who was Israel's champion, becomes the chamberlain to Achish, for Achish said, 'Therefore will I make thee keeper of my head forever,' and David became thus the captain of the body-guard of the king of Philistia, and helped preserve the life of one who was the enemy of God's Israel. Ah, if we doubt God, we shall soon be numbered among God's foes. Inconsistency will win us over into the ranks of His enemies, and they will be saying, 'What do these Hebrews here?' 'The just shall live by faith, but if any man draw back, My soul shall have no pleasure in him' — the two sentences are put together as if the failure of our faith would surely lead to a turning back to sin.

"Third, he was on the verge of still worse sin — of overt acts of warfare against the Lord's people. David's having become the friend of Achish, when Achish went to battle against Israel, he said to him, 'Know thou assuredly, that thou shalt go with me to battle, thou and thy men'; and David professed his willingness to go. We believe it was only a feigned willingness; but then, you see, we convict him again of falsehood.. . .It is true that God interposed and prevented him fighting against Israel, but this was no credit to David, for you know, brethren, we are guilty of a sin, even if we do not commit it, if we are willing to commit it. The last effect of David's sin was this: it brought him into great trial" (C. H. Spurgeon).

O my readers, what a solemn, solemn, warning is all of this for our hearts! How it shows us the wickedness of unbelief and the fearful fruits which that evil root produces. It is true that David had no reason to trust Saul, but he had every reason to continue trusting God. But alas, unbelief is the sin of all others which doth so easily beset us. It is inherent in our very nature, and it is more impossible to root it out by any exertions of ours, than it is to change the features of our countenances. What need is there for us to cry daily, "Lord, I believe, help *Thou* mine unbelief" (Mark 9:24). Let me see in David myself, my very nothingness. O to fully realize that in our best moments we can never trust ourselves to little, nor God to much.

"And David arose, and he passed over with the six hundred men that were with him unto Achish, the son of Maoch, king of Gath" (v. 2). Here we see David not only forsaking the path of duty, but joining interests with the enemies of God: this we must never do; no, not even for self-preservation, or out of care for our family. As another has said, "It is in one sense, a very easy matter to get out of the place of trial; but then we get out of the place of blessing also." Such is generally, if not always the case, with the children of God. No matter how sore the trial, how pressing our circumstances, or how acute our need, to "rest in the Lord, wait patiently for Him" (Psa. 37:7), is not only the course which most honours Him, but which, in the long run, spares us much great confusion and trouble which results when *we* seek to extricate ourselves.

"And David dwelt with Achish at Gath, he and his men, every man with his household" (v. 3). David's circumstances upon entering into Gath this time were very different from what they had been on a previous occasion (1 Sam. 21:10-15): then he entered secretly, now openly; then as a person unknown, now as the recognized enemy of Israel's king; then alone, now with six hundred men; then he was driven hence, now he probably had been invited thither. Apparently he met with a kindly reception — probably because the king of Gath now hoped to use him in his own service: either that he could employ David against Israel, or secure an advantageous alliance with him, if ever he came to the throne. Thus the plan of David appeared to meet with success: at last he found a quiet dwelling-place. Providence seemed to be smiling upon him, and none but an anointed eye could have discerned otherwise.

"And David dwelt with Achish at Gath, he and his men, every man with his household, even David with his two wives: Ahinoam the Jezreelitess and Abigail the Carmelitess, Nabal's wife" (v. 3). Ah, has not the Holy Spirit supplied the key (in the second half of this verse) which explains to us David's sad lapse? It was his "*two* wives" which had displeased the Lord! We entitled the last article but one David's "chastening" and sought to point out the connection between what is found at the end of 1 Sam. 25 and that which is recorded in 1 Sam. 26, namely, the renewed attack of Saul upon him. That Divine "chastening" was now continued, and may be discerned by the spiritual eye in a variety of details.

In this article we have sought to show the awfulness of unbelief, and the evil character of the fruits that issue from it; and how that the graces of the strongest Christian soon became feeble unless they are renewed by the Spirit. But let it be now pointed out that God does not act capriciously in this: if our graces be not renewed, the fault lies in ourselves. It is by working backward from effect to cause, that we may here learn the most important lesson of all. (1) David sinned grievously in seeking refuge among the enemies of the Lord. (2) He went to them without having sought Divine guidance. (3) He leaned unto his own under-standing, and reasoned that it was best for him to go to Gath. (4) He acted thus because he had given way to unbelief. (5) He gave way to unbelief because his faith was not Divinely renewed and prayer in him had been choked. (6) His faith was not renewed because *the Holy Spirit was grieved over his sin!* Re-read these six points in their inverse order!

And Saul was told that David had fled to Gath. And he never again looked for him. And David said to Achish, If I have now found grace in your eyes, let them give me a place in some town in the country so that I may live there. For why should your servant live in the royal city with you? Then Achish gave him Ziklag that day. Therefore Ziklag belongs to the kings of Judah to this day. And the time that David lived in the country of the Philistines was a full year and four months. And David and his men went up and invaded the Geshurites, and the Gezrites, and the Amalekites. For those nations were of old the people of the land, as you go to Shur, even to the land of Egypt. And David struck the land and did not leave either a man or woman alive. And he took away the sheep and the oxen and the asses and the camels and the clothing, then returned and came to Achish. And Achish said, Where have you made a raid today? And David said,

Against the south of Judah, and against the south of the Jerahmeelites, and against the south of the Kenites. And David saved neither man or woman alive to bring news to Gath, saying, Lest they should tell on us, saying, This is what David did, and so will be his manner all the while he lives in the country of the Philistines. And Achish believed David, saying, He has made his people Israel utterly hate him — therefore he shall be my servant forever. 1 Samuel 27:4-12.

One of the chief differences between the Holy Spirit's description of Biblical characters and the delineations in human biographies is, that the former has faithfully presented their failures and falls, showing us that they were indeed men of "like passions with us"; whereas the latter (with very rare exceptions) record little else than the fair and favourable side of their subjects, leaving the impression they were more angelic than human. Biographies need to be read sparingly, especially modern ones, and then with due caution (remembering that there is much "between the lines" not related), lest a false estimate of the life of a Christian be formed, and the *honest* reader be driven to despair. But God has painted the features of Biblical characters in the colours of reality and truth, and thus we find that "as in water face answereth to face, so the heart of man to man" (Prov. 27:19).

The *practical* importance (and it is *that* which should ever be our first and chief quest as we read and ponder the Scriptures) of what has just been pointed out should preserve both preacher and hearer from a one-sided idea of Christian experience. A saint on earth is not a sinless being; nor, on the other hand, does sin have complete dominion over him. In consequence of both the "flesh" and the "spirit" still indwelling him, in "*many* things" he offends (James 3:2), and in many things he pleases God. The "old man" is not only still alive (though the Christian is to "reckon" it as being *judicially* dead before God: (Rom. 6:11), but is constantly active; and though Divine grace restrain it from breaking forth into much outward evil, yet it defiles all our inner being, and pollutes our best endeavours both Godward and manward: Rom. 7:14-25. Nevertheless, the "new man" is also active, producing that which is glorifying to God.

It is because of this *dual* experience of the Christian that we are ever in danger of concentrating too much on the one aspect, to the ignoring of the other. Those with a pessimistic turn of mind, or whose body suffers from a torpid liver, need to watch against dwelling too much on the gloomy side of the Christian life, and spending too much time in Job and the Lamentations, to the neglect of the later Psalms and the epistle to the Philippians. In the past, a certain class of writers occupied themselves almost exclusively with the contemplation of human depravity and its fearful workings in the saint, conveying the idea that a constant mourning over indwelling sin and groaning over its activities was the only mark of high spiritual experience. Such people are only happy when they are miserable. We counsel those who have been strongly influenced by such teaching, to turn frequently to John's Gospel, chapters 14 to 17, and turn each verse into prayer *and praise.*

On the other side, those with a buoyant temperament and optimistic turn of mind need to watch against the tendency to appropriate and meditate upon the promises to the almost total ignoring of the precepts of Scripture; to strive against lightness and superficiality, and to be careful they do not mistake exuberance of natural spirits for the steadier and deeper flow of spiritual joy. To be all the time dwelling upon the Christian's standing, his privileges and blessings, to the neglect of his state, obligations and failures, will beget pride and self-righteousness. Such people need to prayerfully ponder Rom. 7, the first half of Heb. 12, and much in 1 Peter. Sinful self and all its wretched failures should be sufficiently noticed so as to keep us in the dust before God. Christ and His great salvation should be contemplated so as to lift us above self and fill the soul with thanksgiving.

The above meditations have been suggested by that portion of David's life which is now to engage our attention. The more it be carefully pondered, the more should we be delivered from entertaining an erroneous conception of the experience and history of a saint. Not that we are to seize upon these sad blemishes in David to *excuse* our own faults — no indeed, that would be wickedness of the worst kind; but we are to be *humbled* by the realization that the same evil nature indwells *us,* and produces works in you and me equally vile. Those who are *surprised* that the Psalmist should act as he here did, must be woefully ignorant of the "plague" of their own hearts, and blind unto sins in their own lives which are just abominable in the sight of the Holy One as were those of David's.

In our last article we saw that, unbelief and fear so gained the upperhand over David, that he exclaimed, "I shall now perish one day by the hand of Saul: there is nothing better for me than that I should speedily escape into the land of the Philistines" (1 Sam. 27:1). And yet, probably only a short while before, this same David had declared, "Though an host should encamp against me, my heart shall not fear: though war should rise against me, in this will I be confident" (Psa. 27:3). Yes, and has not the reader, when in close communion with the Lord, and when the sails of faith were fully spread and filled with the breeze of the Spirit, said or felt the same? And, alas that it should be so, has not this confidence waned, and then disappeared before some fresh trial! How these sad lapses should show us *ourselves,* and produce real humility and self abasement. How often expressions from our own lips in the past condemn us in the present!

Then we pointed out that, "under the pressure of trial, *relief* is what the flesh most desires." Perhaps the reader may ask, "but is not that natural? Yes indeed, but is it *spiritual?* Our first desire in trial, as in everything else, should be that *God* may be honoured, and for this, we should earnestly seek grace to so conduct ourselves that we may "glorify the Lord in the fires" (Isa. 24:15). Our next concern should be that our *soul* may profit from the painful experience and for this we should beg the Lord to graciously *sanctify it* unto our lasting good. But alas, when unbelief dominates us, *God* is forgotten, and deliverance, our own ease, obsess the mind; and hence it is that — unless Divine grace interpose — we seek relief in the wrong quarter and by unspiritual means. Thus it was here with David: he and his men passed over unto Achish, the king of Gath.

"And David dwelt with Achish, he and his men, every man with his household" (v. 3). From these words it seems that Achish, the Philistine, made no demur against David and his men entering his territory; rather does it look as though he met with a friendly and kindly reception. Thus, from present appearances — the obtaining, at last, a quiet dwelling-place — it seemed that the fleshly plan of David was meeting with real success, that Providence was smiling upon him. Yes, it is often this way *at first* when a Christian takes things into his own hands: to carnal reason the sequel shows he did the right thing. Ah, but later on, he discovers otherwise. One false step is followed by another, just as the telling of a lie is usually succeeded by other lies to cover it. So it was now with David: he went from bad to worse.

"And it was told Saul that David was fled to Gath: and he sought no more again for him" (v. 4). This too would seem to confirm the thought that David had acted wisely, and that God was blessing his worldly scheme, for his family and people now rested safely from the approaches of their dreaded foe. But when everything is going smoothly with the Christian, and the enemy ceases to harass him, then is the time, generally speaking, when he needs to suspect that something is wrong with his testimony, and beg God to show him what it is. Nor was Saul's cessation of hostility due to any improvement of character, but because he dared not to come where David now was. "Thus many seem to leave their sins, but really their sins leave them; they would persist in them if they could (M. Henry).

"And David said unto Achish, If I have now found grace in thine eyes, let them give me a place in some town in the country, that I may dwell there: for why should thy servant dwell in the royal city with thee?" (v. 5). David knew from experience how jealous were kings and their favourites, so to prevent the envy of Achish's courtiers he deemed it well not to remain too near and receive too many favours at his hands. Probably the idolatry and corruption which abounded in the royal city made David desirous of getting his family and people removed therefrom. But in the light of the sequel, it seems that the principal motive which prompted him to make this request was, that he might have a better opportunity to fall upon some of the enemies of Israel without the king of Gath being aware of it. The practical lesson for us is, that when we forsake the path of God's appointment a spirit of restlessness and discontent is sure to possess us.

David presented his request to Achish very modestly: "give me a place in *some* town in the country that I may dwell there," where they could enjoy greater privacy and more freedom from the idolatry of the land. Six hundred men and their families would crowd the royal city, and might prove quite a burden; while there was always the danger of the subjects of Achish regarding David as a *rival* in state and dignity. But to what a low level had God's anointed descended when he speaks of himself as the "servant" of Achish! How far from communion with the Lord was he, when one of the uncircumcised is to choose his dwelling-place for him! A child of God is "the Lord's *free* man" (1 Cor. 7:22): Yes, but to maintain this in a practical way, he must walk in faith and obedience to Him; otherwise he will be brought in bondage to the creature, as David was.

"Then Achish gave him Ziklag that day:" (v. 6). Originally this city had been given to the tribe of Judah, (Josh. 15:31), then to Simeon (Josh. 19:1,5), though it seems that neither of them possessed it, but that it came into the hands of the Philistines. "Wherefore Ziklag pertained unto the kings of Judah unto this day." Being given unto David, who shortly after became king, this section was annexed to the crown-lands, and ever after it was part of the portion of the kings of Judah: so that it was given to David not as a temporary possession, but, under God, as a permanent one for his descendants. Truly, the ways of the Lord are past finding out.

"And the time that David dwelt in the country of the Philistines was a full year and four months" (v. 7). "But rest reached by self-will or disobedience is anything rather than peace to the heart that fears God, and loves His service. David could not forget that Israel, whom he had forsaken, were God's people; nor that the Philistines, whom he had joined were God's enemies. He could not but remember his own peculiar relation to God, and to His people — for Samuel had anointed him, and even Saul had blessed him as the destined king of Israel. His conscience therefore, must have been ill at ease; and the stillness and rest of Ziklag would only cause him to be more sensible of its disquietude" (B. W. Newton).

"And David and his men went up, and invaded the Geshurites, and the Gezrites, and the Amalekites: for those nations were of old the inhabitants of the land" (v. 8). "When the consciences of God's servants tells them that their position is wrong, one of their devices not unfrequently is, to give themselves, with fresh energy, to the attainment of some right end; as if rightly directed, or successful energy, could atone for committed evil, and satisfy the misgivings of a disquieted heart. Accordingly, David, still retaining the self-gained rest of Ziklag, resolved that it should not be the rest of inactivity, but that he would thence put forth fresh energies against the enemies of God and of His people. The Amalekites were nigh. The Amalekites were they of whom the Lord had sworn that He would have war with Amalek from generation to generation. David therefore went up against them, and triumphed" (B. W. Newton).

Those which David and his men invaded were some of the original tribes which inhabited Canaan, and were such as had escaped the sword of Saul, and had fled to more distant parts. His attack upon them was not an act of cruelty, for those people had long before been divinely sentenced to destruction. Yet though they were the enemies of the Lord and His people, David's attack upon them was ill timed, and more likely than not the chief motive which prompted him was the obtaining of food and plunder for his forces. "Nothing could be more complete than his success: 'He smote the land, and left neither man nor woman alive; and took away the sheep, and the oxen, and the asses, and the camels, and the apparel.' Ziklag was enriched with spoil, and that the spoil of the enemies of the Lord. What prosperity then could be greater — what apparently more immediately from God?" (B.W. Newton).

A solemn warning, which we do well to take to heart, is pointed for us in vv. 8, 9, namely, not to measure the right or wrong of a course of conduct by the *success* which appears to attend it. This principle is now being flagrantly disregarded, the scripturalness or unscripturalness of an action concerns few professing Christians today: so long as it seems to produce good results, this is all that matters. Women are tolerated in the pulpit, worldly devices are brought into the "church," fleshly and high-pressure methods are adopted by "evangelists," and so long as crowds are drawn, the young people "held," and "converts" made, it is argued that the end justifies the means. If "souls are being saved," the great majority are prepared to wink at almost anything today, supposing that the "blessing of God" (?) is a sure proof that nothing serious is wrong. So the children of Israel might have reasoned when the waters flowed from the rock which Moses disobediently smote in his anger. So David might have concluded when such success attended his attack upon the Amalekites! To judge by visible results is walking by sight; to measure everything by Holy Writ and reject all that is out of harmony therewith, is walking by faith.

"And David smote the land, and left neither man nor woman alive, and took away the sheep, and the oxen, and the asses, and the camels, and the apparel, and returned and came to Achish" (v. 9). Mark well the closing words of this verse: one had thought that Achish was the last man whom David would wish to see at this time. It had been far more prudent had he returned quietly to Ziklag, but as we pointed out in a previous article, when a saint is out of communion with God, and controlled by unbelief, he no longer acts according to the dictates of common sense. A striking and solemn illustration of that fact is here before us. O that writer and reader may lay this well to heart: *faith and wisdom* are inseparably linked together. Nothing but folly can issue from an unbelieving heart, that is, from a heart which has not been won by divine grace.

"And Achish said, Whither have ye made a road today?" (v. 10). No doubt the king of Gath was surprised, as he had reason to be, when he saw David and his men so heavily laden with their booty, and therefore does he inquire where they had been. Sad indeed is it to hear the reply given: "And David said, Against the south of Judah, and against the south of the Jerahmeelites, and against the south of the Kenites." Though not a downright lie, yet it was an equivocation, made with the design of deceiving, and therefore cannot be defended, nor is it to be imitated by us. David was not willing that Achish should know the truth. He did not now play the part of a madman, as he had on a former occasion, but fearful of losing his self-chosen place of protection, he dissembles unto the king. The Amalekites were fellow-Canaanites with the Philistines, and if not in league with them, Achish and his people would probably be apprehensive of danger by harbouring such a powerful foe in their midst, and would want to expel them. To avoid this, David resorted to deception. O what need has writer and reader to pray daily, "Lead us not into temptation, but deliver us from evil."

Following his local incursion upon and victory over the Amalekites, David, instead of quietly making for Ziklag, more imprudently "came to Achish" (1 Sam. 27:9). Seeing him so heavily laden with the spoils which had been taken, the king inquired where he had been. David feared to tell Achish that he had been destroying Israel's enemies and the Philistines' friends, and therefore returned a misleading answer. David had taken precaution to cover his tracks, for we are told that he "saved neither man nor woman alive, to bring tidings to Gath, saying, Lest they should tell on us, saying, So did David, and so will be his manner all the while he dwelleth in the country of the Philistines" (27:11).

Forgetful of God and the many tokens he had already received of His protecting care, David dissembled. Achish was thoroughly deceived, for we read, "Achish believed David, saying, He hath made his people Israel utterly to abhor him; therefore he shall be my servant forever" (27:12).

Probably it was his persuading Jonathan to tell his father that he had gone about his business, telling Abimelech an untruth, his prevarications before Achish, and some other instances, which caused David, when later he penitently reflected upon them, to pray "Remove from me the way of lying" (Psa. 119:29). This seems to have been David's "besetting sin," or the particular inclination of his corrupt nature. Now when we are foiled by any sin, we should take careful pains lest we settle into a "way" or course of sinning; for as a branch which has once been in the flame is now more susceptible to fire, so the committing of any sin renders us more liable to form a habit of that evil.

Humiliating as may be the acknowledgment of it, the fact remains that every one of us needs to cry fervently unto God "Remove from me the way of lying." Because we are descended from parents who, at the beginning, preferred the Devil's lie to God's truth, we are strongly inclined unto lying; yea, it is so much a part of our fallen nature that none but God can remove it from us. How many indulge in exaggeration, which is a form of lying. How many deceive by gestures and actions, which is another form of it. How many make promises (in their letters, for example, vowing they will soon write again) which they never fulfill. Worse still, how many lie unto God by false appearances: going through the form of prayer, feigning to be very pious outwardly, when their hearts and minds are upon the things of the world. Of old God said, "Ephraim compasseth Me about with lies: and the house of Israel with deceit" (Hos. 11:12): God sees through all vain shows, and will not be mocked.

And in those days the Philistines gathered their armies together for war, to fight with Israel. And Achish said to David, You surely know that you shall go with me to battle, you and your men. And David said to Achish, Surely you know what your servants can do. And Achish said to David, Therefore I will make you keeper of my head forever. Now Samuel was dead, and all Israel had mourned him and buried him in Ramah, even in his own city. And Saul had put away those that had familiar spirits, and the wizards, out of the land. And the Philistines gathered themselves together and came and pitched in Shunem. And Saul gathered all Israel together, and they pitched in Gilboa. And when Saul saw the army of the Philistines, he was afraid, and his heart greatly trembled. And when Saul inquired of the LORD, the LORD did not answer him, neither by dreams, nor by Urim, nor by prophets. Then Saul said to his servants, Seek me a woman who has a familiar spirit, so that I may go to her and inquire of her. And his servant said to him, Behold, there is a woman who has a familiar spirit at Endor. And Saul disguised himself and put on other clothing. And he went. And two men went with him. And they came to the woman by night. And he said, I beg you, divine to me by the familiar spirit, and bring me up the man whom I shall name to you. And the woman said, You know what Saul has done — how he has cut off those that have familiar spirits, and the wizards, out of the land. Why then do you lay a snare for my life, to cause me to die? And Saul swore to her by the LORD, saying, As the LORD lives there shall no punishment happen to you for this thing. — 1 Samuel 28:1-10.

The consequences of David's lie soon became apparent. "And it came to pass in those days, that the Philistines gathered their armies together for warfare, to fight with Israel. And Achish said unto David, Know thou assuredly, that thou shalt go out with me to battle, thou and thy men" (1 Sam. 28:1). Probably this was about the last thing he expected. Poor David! he was indeed in a tight place now, so tight that it seemed impossible for him to turn either way. On the one hand, to refuse the king's request would not only be to run the danger of angering him, with what that would most likely entail, but would appear the height of ingratitude in return for the kindness and protection which had been given to him and his people. On the other hand, to accept Achish's proposal meant being a traitor to Israel.

This sore dilemma in which David found himself, is recorded for *our* learning. It is a solemn warning of what we may expect if we forsake the path of God's precepts. If we enter upon a wrong position, then, trying and unpleasant situations are sure to arise — situations which our consciences will sharply condemn, but from which we can see no way out of. When we deviate from the path of duty, in the slightest degree, each circumstance that follows will tend to draw us farther aside. Once a rock starts downhill, it gains momentum with every bound that it takes. Then how watchful we need to be against the *first* false step. yea, how earnestly should we pray, "Hold Thou me up, and I shall be safe" (Psa. 119:117)! Satan rests not satisfied for the Christian to yield one "little" point, and knows full well our doing so greatly lessens our resistance to his next temptations.

For the sake of younger readers, let us enlarge a little more upon this point. To go any where we ought not, will bring us into temptations that it will be almost impossible to resist. To seek the society of non-Christians is to play with fire, and to accept favours from them will almost certainly result in our getting burned. To compromise one point, will be followed by letting down the bars at others. For a young lady to accept the attentions of an undesirable young man, makes it far harder to reject his later advances. Once you accept a favour — even if it be but a "joy-ride" in an auto — you place yourself under an obligation, and though you be asked to pay a high price in return, yet if you demur, "ingratitude" is what you are likely to be charged with. Then go slow, we beg you, in accepting favours from any, especially from those who are likely to take an unfair advantage of you.

David had done wrong in seeking protection from Saul in the land of the Philistines, and now the king of Gath required service from him in return. War being determined against Israel, Achish asks the assistance of David and his men. Yes, when the Christian turns unto the world for help, he must expect to be asked to pay the world's price for the same. Needless intimacies with the avowed enemies of godliness, and the receiving of favours from them, quickly reduces us to be unfaithful to God or ungrateful to our benefactors. To what a strait had the false position of David reduced him: if he promised to fight against Israel, and then broke his word, he would be guilty of treachery; if he fought against Israel, he would alienate the affections of his own people, and expose himself to the reproach of having slain Saul. It seemed impossible that he should extricate himself from this dilemma with a good conscience and clear reputation.

"And David said to Achish, Surely thou shalt know what thy servant can do" (28:2). Probably David was quite undecided how to act, and cherished a secret hope that the Lord would help him out of his great difficulty; yet this by no means excused him for returning an insincere and evasive answer. "And Achish said to David, Therefore will I make thee keeper of mine head forever." The king of Gath understood his reply as a promise of effectual assistance, and so determined to make him the captain of his bodyguard. At the time David was too much swayed by the fear of man to refuse attendance upon Achish.

"Now Samuel was dead, and all Israel had lamented him, and buried him in Ramah, even in his own city" (v. 3). This seems to be brought in for the purpose of intimating why the Philistines should make an attack upon Israel at this time: the knowledge of the prophet's death had probably emboldened them. When death has removed ministers of God, or persecution has banished them (as it had David), a land is deprived of its best defence. "And Saul had put away those that had familiar spirits, and the wizards, out of the land" (v. 3). This is mentioned as an introduction to what follows unto the end of the chapter: it serves to emphasize the inconstancy of Saul: it illustrates the worthlessness of the temporary reformation of professors, who ultimately return to their wallowing in the mire.

"And the Philistines gathered themselves together, and came and pitched in Shunem: and Saul gathered all Israel together, and they pitched in Gilboa. And when Saul saw the host of the Philistines, he was afraid, and his heart greatly trembled" (vv. 4, 5). Had he been in communion with God, there would be no need for such a fear, but he had provoked the Holy One to forsake him. Saul's excessive terror arose chiefly from a guilty, conscience: his contempt of Samuel, his murdering the priests and their families, his malicious persecution of David. Probably he had a premonition that this attack of the Philistines foreboded his approaching doom.

"And when Saul inquired of the Lord, the Lord answered him not" (v. 6). Unspeakably solemn is this: the case of one abandoned by God. It was under urgent terror, and not as a preparation for repentance, that Saul now sought unto the Lord. He did not "inquire" of Him till his doom was sealed, till it was too late, for God will not be mocked. O unsaved reader, heed that call, "seek ye the Lord *while He may be found*, call ye upon Him *while he is near*" (Isa. 55:6); otherwise God may yet say of thee, as of those of old, "These men have set up their idols in their hearts, and put the stumblingblock of their iniquity before their face: should I inquired of at all *by them?*" (Ezek. 14:3).

"And when Saul enquired of the Lord, the Lord answered him not" (v. 6). Some see a contradiction between this statement and what is said in 1 Chron. 10:13, 14, "So Saul died for his transgression which he committed against the Lord, against the word of the Lord, which he kept not, and also for asking of a familiar spirit, to enquire; and enquired not of the Lord." The "literalists" of the day, those who are incapable of seeing beneath the bare letter of the Word, may well be stumbled by a comparison of the two passages; but he who is taught the *spiritual* meaning of the Scriptures perceives no difficulty. There is much that passes for "prayer" among men (when they are in great physical distress) which unto God is no more than the "howling" of beasts: see Hos. 7:14. Saul "enquired" in a hypocritical manner, which the Lord would not regard at all. The ear of the Lord is open unto none save those of a broken heart and a contrite spirit.

"Then said Saul unto his servants, Seek me a woman that hath a familiar spirit, that I may go to her, and enquire of her. And his servants said to him, Behold, there is a woman that hath a familiar spirit at Endor" (v. 7). Here we behold the fearful wickedness of one who was righteously abandoned by God. Fearful presumption was it for Saul to deliberately and definitely resort unto one who practiced diabolical arts. Only a little before, he had banished from the land those who had "familiar spirits" (v. 3), known today as "mediums." It illustrates the fact that apostates frequently commit those very sins which they once were most earnest in opposing. We shall not follow Saul through the remainder of this chapter, but pass on to the 29th, where the Holy Spirit continues the narrative about the Philistines and David.

"Now the Philistines gathered together all their armies to Aphek; and the Israelites pitched by a fountain which is in Jezreel. And the lords of the Philistines passed on by hundreds, and by thousands; but David and his men passed on in the rear with Achish" (29:1, 2). "If David had told the truth, Achish would never have dreamed of enrolling him amongst the hosts of the Philistines. It was his own contrivance that had brought him there. He, who so well knew how to discriminate between the Philistines and the armies of the living God; and who, on the ground of that distinction, had so often sought and obtained the assistance of the God of Israel, now found himself leagued with the enemies of God for the destruction of God's people. He who had so distinctly refused to stretch out his hand against the Lord's anointed, was now enrolled with those very hosts who were about to shed the blood of Saul, and of Jonathan too, upon the mountains of Gilboa. Such was the terrible circumstances in which David suddenly found himself. He seems to have looked upon them as hopeless, nor do we read of his attempting any remedy.

"But David had not ceased to be the subject of care to the great Shepherd of Israel. He had wandered, and was to be brought back. The secret providence of God again interfered, and separated him from the camp of the Philistines" (B. W. Newton). Yes, man's extremities are (so to speak) God's opportunities, and from the dilemma which David could see no way out of, he graciously extricated him; without his having to move a finger, a door was opened for his deliverance. The means which the Lord employed upon this occasion should cause us to bow in adoration before the High Sovereign over all, and deepen our trust in Him.

"Then said the princes of the Philistines, What do these Hebrews here? And Achish said unto the princes of the Philistines, Is not this David, the servant of Saul the king of Israel, which hath been with me these days, or these years, and I have found no fault in him since he fell unto me this day" (v. 3). God has various ways of delivering His people from their difficulties. While the ungodly pursue their own purposes and follow out their own plans, God secretly influences them to such determinations as subserve the good of His saints. These "princes" of the Philistines were not those of the immediate court of Achish, but lords of other principalities, who were confederates with him. These now opposed the design of Achish to use David and his men in the forthcoming battle.

"And the princes of the Philistines were wroth with him; and the princes of the Philistines said unto him, Make this fellow return, that he may go again to his place which thou hast appointed him, and let him not go down with us to battle, lest in the battle he be an adversary to us; for wherewith should he reconcile himself unto his master? should it not be with the heads of these men? Is not this David, of whom they sang one to another in dances, saying Saul slew his thousands, and David his ten thousands?" (29:4,5). "Though God might justly have left David in his difficulty, to chasten him for his folly, yet because his heart was upright with Him, He would not suffer him to be tempted above what he was able, but with the temptation made a way for his escape (1 Cor. 10: 13). A door was opened for his deliverance out of this strait. God inclined the hearts of the Philistine princes to oppose his being employed in this battle, and to insist upon him being dishonoured; and thus their enmity befriended him, when no friend he had was capable of doing him such a kindness" (Matt. Henry).

The esteem and affection of the wicked often become snares to us; but reproaches, contempt, injurious suspicions, prove beneficial, and the ill-usage of the ungodly by which we are driven from them is much better for us than their friendship which knits us to them. "When worldly people have no evil to say to us, but will bear testimony to our uprightness, we need no more from them; and this we should aim to acquire by prudence, meekness, and a blameless life. But their *flattering* commendations are almost always purchased by improper compliances, or some measure of deception, and commonly cover us with confusion. It is seldom prudent to place great confidence in one who has changed sides, except as the fear of God influences a real convert to conscientious fidelity" (T. Scott). It is striking to note the particular thing which God made use of to influence those Philistine lords against David: it was the song which the women of Israel had sung in David's honour, and which now for the third time brought him into dishonour — so little are the flatteries of people worth! they stir up jealousy and hatred in others; yet in the hand of God it became the instrument of David's deliverance.

Achish now summoned David into his presence and said, "Wherefore now return, and go in peace, that thou displease not the lords of the Philistines" (v. 7). No doubt David secretly rejoiced at this deliverance from his sore dilemma, yet he was unwilling that the king of Gath should know it; he prevaricated again, making an appearance of concern for being so summarily dismissed. "And David said unto Achish, But what have I done? and what hast thou found in thy servant so long as I have been with thee unto this day, that I may not go fight against the enemies of my lord the king" (v. 8). Sad it is to see the anointed of God dissembling and speaking in such a manner of His people. But Achish was not to be moved, and said, "Wherefore now rise up early in the morning with thy master's servants that are come with thee; and as soon as ye be up early in the morning and have light, depart" (v. 10). Marvelous deliverance was this from his ensnaring service, yet without the slightest credit to David: it was nought but the sovereign grace of God which freed him from the snare of the fowler.

Then the woman said, Whom shall I bring up to you? And he said, Bring me up Samuel. And when the woman saw Samuel, she cried with a loud voice. And the woman spoke to Saul, saying, Why have you deceived me? For you are Saul! And the king said to her, Do not be afraid, For what did you see? And the woman said to Saul, I saw gods coming up out of the earth. And he said to her, What is his form? And she said, An old man comes up, and he is covered with a cloak. And Saul saw that it was Samuel, and he stooped with his face to the ground and bowed himself. And Samuel said to Saul, Why have you disturbed me, to bring me up? And Saul answered, I am grievously distressed, for the Philistines are warring against me. And God has left me and does not answer me any more, either by prophets or by dreams. Therefore I have called you so that you may make known to me what I should do. Then Samuel said, Why then do you ask me, since the LORD has left you and has become your enemy? And the LORD has done for Himself as He spoke by me. For the LORD has torn the kingdom out of your hand and has given it to your neighbor, to David. Because you did not obey the voice of the LORD, nor execute His fierce wrath on Amalek, therefore the LORD has done this thing to you now. Moreover, the LORD will also deliver Israel with you into the hand of the Philistines. And tomorrow you and your sons shall be with me. The LORD also shall deliver the army of Israel into the hand of the Philistines. Then Saul immediately fell headlong on the earth. And he was sorely afraid because of the words of Samuel. And there was no strength in him, for he had eaten no bread all day or all night. And the woman came to Saul and saw that he was sorely troubled, and said to him, Behold, your handmaid has obeyed your voice, and I have put my life in my hand and have listened to your words which you spoke to me. Now therefore, I beg you, listen also to the voice of your handmaid, and let me set a bit of bread before you, and eat, so that you may have strength when you go on your way. But he refused and said, I will not eat. But his servants, together with the woman, urged him. And he listened to their voice. So he arose from the earth and sat on the bed. And the women had a fat calf in the house. And she hurried and killed it, and took flour and kneaded it, and baked unleavened bread with it. And she brought it before Saul, and before the servants. And they ate. Then they rose and went away that night. — 1 Samuel 28:11-25.

"Preserve me, O God: for in Thee do I put my trust" (Psa. 16:1). This is a prayer which, in substance at least, every child of God frequently puts up to his heavenly Father. He feels his own insufficiency, and calls upon One who is all-sufficient. He realizes how incompetent he is to defend and protect himself, and seeks the aid of Him whose arms are all-mighty. If he is in his right mind, before starting out on a journey, when any particular danger threatens him, and ere settling down for the night's repose, he commits himself into the custody and care of Him who never slumbers or sleeps. Blessed privilege! Wise precaution! Happy duty! The Lord graciously keep us in a spirit of complete dependence upon Himself.

"The Lord *preserveth* all them that love Him" (Psa. 145:20). Most Christians are readier to perceive the fulfillment of this precious promise when they have been delivered from some physical danger, than when they were preserved from some moral evil; which shows how much more we are governed by the natural than the spiritual. We are quick to own the preserving hand of God when a disease epidemic avoids our home, when a heavy falling object just clears our path, or when a swiftly-moving auto just misses the car we are in; but we ought to be just as alert in discerning the miraculous hand of God when a powerful temptation is suddenly removed from us, or we are delivered from it.

"But the Lord is faithful, who shall stablish you, and keep you from evil" (2 Thess. 3:3). The Lord's people are surrounded with a variety of evils within and without. They have sin in them, and it is the cause and fountain of all the evil and misery which they at any time feel and experience. There is the Evil one without, who endeavours at times to bring great evil upon them. But the Lord "keepeth His people from evil," not that they are exempted wholly and altogether from evil. Yet they are kept from being overcome by and engulfed in it. Though they fall, they shall not be utterly cast down, for the Lord upholdeth them with His right hand.

Wondrous are the ways in which God *preserves* His saints. Many a one has been withheld from that success in business on which he had fondly set his heart: it was God delivering him from those material riches which would have ruined his soul! Many a one was disappointed in a love affair: it was God delivering from an ungodly partner for life, who would have been a constant hindrance to your spiritual progress! Many a one was cruelly treated by trusted and cherished friends: it was God breaking what would have proved an unequal yoke! Many a parent was plunged into grief by the death of a dearly loved child: it was God, in His mercy, taking away what would have proved an idol. Now we see these things through a glass darkly, but the Day will come, dear reader, when we shall perceive clearly that it was the *perserving* hand of our gracious God thus dealing with us at those very times when all seemed to be working against us.

The above meditations have been suggested by what is recorded in 1 Sam. 29. At the close of our last article we saw how mercifully God interposed to deliver His servant from the snare of the fowler. Through his unbelief and self-will, David had got into a sore dilemma. Seeking help from the ungodly, he had placed himself under obligations to the king of Gath. Pretending to be the friend of the Philistines and the enemy of his own people, Achish was now determined to employ David and his men upon the attack which was planned against Israel. Then it was that the Lord interposed and *preserved* the object of His love from falling into much graver evil. He now graciously made "a way to escape" (1 Cor. 10:13), lest His poor erring child should be tempted above that which he was able.

And *how* was that "way to escape" opened for him? Ah, *this* is the point which we wish to particularly direct our attention unto. It was not by means of any visible or outward work, but through the inward and secret operations of His power. The Lord turned against David the hearts of the other "lords of the Philistines" (1 Sam. 29:3-5); and in consequence, Achish was obliged to part with his services. Ah, my reader, how often was the Lord secretly working *for* you, when He turned the heart of some worldling *against* you! If we were more spiritual, this would be perceived more clearly and frequently by us, and we should then render unto our gracious Deliverer the praise which is His due. David's discharge from the service of Achish was just as much a miracle as was his deliverance from the enmity of Saul; it was as truly the working of God's *preserving* power to rouse the jealousy and enmity of the Philistine lords against David, as it was to shield him from the javelin which the demon-possessed king hurled at him (1 Sam. 18:11).

"So David and his men rose up early to depart in the morning to return into the land of the Philistines. And the Philistines went up to Jezreel" (1 Sam. 29:11). Commanded by the king of Gath so to do (v. 10), there was no other prudent alternative. Thus the snare was broken, and David was now free to return unto his own city, not knowing (as yet) how urgently his presence was needed there. Stealing away amid the shadows of the dawn, the flight of David and his men was scarcely any less ignominious than was the banishment of back-slidden Abraham from Egypt (Gen. 12: 20). Though God often extricates His people from the dangerous situations which their unbelief brings them into, nevertheless, He makes them at least taste the bitterness of their folly. But, as we shall see, the shame which the Philistine lords put upon David, turned to his advantage in various ways. Thus does God, sometimes, graciously over-rule unto good even our failures and falls.

"So David and his men rose up early to depart in the morning to return into the land of the Philistines. And the Philistines went up to Jezreel." Delivered from a sore dilemma, a heavy burden removed from his shoulders, we may well suppose it was with a light heart that David now led his men out of the camp of Achish. Blithely unconscious of the grievous disappointment awaiting them, David and his men retraced their steps to Ziklag, for it was there he had deposited all that was chiefly dear to him on earth: his wives and his children were there, it was there he had formed a rest for himself — but, apart from God! Ah, how little do any of us know what a day may bring forth: how often is a happy morning followed by a night of sadness: much cause have we while in this world to "rejoice with trembling" (Psa. 2:11).

Though David had now been delivered from his false position as an ally of Achish against Israel, not yet had he been brought back to God. Deep exercises of heart were required for this, and He who preserveth His people from fatal back-sliding saw to it that His erring servant should not escape. Though He is the God of all grace, yet His grace ever reigns "through righteousness," and never at the expense of it. Though His mercy delivers His saints from the sad pitfalls into which their folly leads them, usually, He so orders His providences, that they are made to smart for their wrong-doing; and the Holy Spirit uses this to convict them of their sins, and they, in turn, *condemn themselves* for the same. The means employed by God on this occasion were drastic, yet surely not more so than the case called for.

"And it came to pass, when David and his men were come to Ziklag on the third day, that the Amalekites had invaded the south, and Ziklag, and smitten Ziklag, and burned it with fire" (30:1). After a three days' march from the camp of Achish, hoping to find rest in their homes and joy in the bosom of their families, here was the scene upon which the eyes of David and his men now fell! What a bitter moment must this have been for our hero! His little all had vanished: he returns to the place where his family and possessions were, only to find the city a mass of smoking ruins, and those whom he loved no longer there to welcome him. When we leave our families (though it be for only a few hours) we cannot foresee what may befall them, or ourselves, ere we return; we ought therefore to commit each other to the protection of God, and to render unto Him unfeigned thanks when we meet again in peace and safety.

"And had taken the women captives, that were therein: they slew not any, either great or small, but carried them away, and went on their way" (30:2). Let us learn from this that it is the part of wisdom, on *all* occasions, to moderate our expectation of earthly comforts, lest we should by being over-sanguine, meet with the more distressing disappointment. Behold here the restraining power of the Lord, in preventing the Amalekites from slaying the women and children. "Whether they spared them to lead them in triumph, or to well them, or to use them for slaves, God's hand must be acknowledged, who designed to make use of the Amalekites for the correction, but not for the destruction, of the house of David" (Matt. Henry). Blessed is it to know that even in wrath God remembers "mercy" (Hab. 3:2).

"And had taken the women captives, that were therein: they slew not any, either great or small, but carried them away, and went on their way." From this we may also see how sorely David was now being chastened for being so forward to go with the Philistines against the people of God. Hereby the Lord showed him he had far better have stayed at home and minded his own business. "When we go abroad, in the way of our duty, we may comfortably hope that God will take care of our families, in our absence, *but not otherwise*" (Matt. Henry). No, to count upon the Lord's protection, either for our selves or for our loved ones, when we enter forbidden territory, is wicked presumption and not faith. It was thus the Devil sought to tempt Christ: Cast Thyself down from the pinnacle of the temple, and the angels shall safeguard Thee.

"So David and his men came to the city, and behold it was burned with fire; and their wives, and their sons, and their daughters, were taken captives. Then David and the people that were with him lifted up their voice and wept, until they had no more power to weep" (vv. 3, 4). Ah, now he was tasting the bitterness of being without the full protection of God. As a homeless wanderer, hunted like a partridge upon the mountains, despised by the Nabal's who dwelt at ease in the land, yet never before had he known the like of this. But now, under the protection of the king of Gath, and with a city of his own, he learns that without *God's shelter* he is exposed indeed. Learn from this, dear reader, how much we lose when we enter the path of self-will. In the first shock of disappointment, David could only weep and wail; all appeared to be irrevocably lost.

"It was indeed no wonder that David's heart was stricken. He had never before known what it was to be smitten like this by the chastening hand of God. Of late he had seemed even more than ordinarily to be the subject of His care: but now the relation of God seemed suddenly changed into one of severity and wrath. During the year that David had watched his father's flock, during his residence in the courts of Saul, during the time of his sorrowful sojourn in the wilderness, during his late eventful history in Ziklag, he had never experienced anything but kindness and preservation from the hand of God. He had become so long accustomed to receive sure protection from God's faithful care, that he seems to have calculated on its uninterrupted continuance. He had lately said, 'The Lord render unto every man his righteousness . . . and let Him deliver me out of all tribulation.' But now the Lord Himself seemed turned into an enemy, and to fight against him. Nor could the conscience of David have failed to discern the reason. It must have owned the justice of the blow. Thus, however, the bitterness of his agony would be aggravated, not lessened" (B. W. Newton).

"And David's two wives were taken captives, Abinoam the Jezreelitess and Abigail the wife of Nabal the Carmelite" (v. 5). Why did the historian, after specifically stating in v. 2 that the Amalekites had "taken the women captives," enter into this detail? Ah, is the answer far to seek? Is it not the Holy Spirit making known to us the prime cause of the Lord's displeasure against David? His "*two* wives" was the occasion of the severing of his communion with the Lord, which, as we have seen, was at once followed by Saul's renewed attack (see 25:43, 44 and 26:1, 2), his unbelieving fear (27:1), and his seeking help from the ungodly (27:2, 3). We mention this because it supplies *the key* to all that follows from 25:44, and because so far as we know no other writer has pointed it out.

"And David was greatly distressed: for the people spake of stoning him, because the soul of all the people was grieved (bitter), every man for his sons and for his daughters" (v. 6). Poor David! one trouble was added to another. Heartbroken over the loss of his family, and the burning of his city, additional distress was occasioned by the murmuring and mutiny of his men. They considered the entire blame rested upon their leader, for having journeyed to Achish and left the city of Ziklag defenseless, and because he had provoked the Amalekites and their allies (27:8, 9) by his inroad upon them, who had now availed themselves of the opportunity to avenge the wrong. "Thus apt are we, when in trouble, to fly into a rage against those who are in any way the occasion of our troubles, when we overlook the Divine providence and have no due regard to *God's hand* in it" (M. Henry).

"On all past occasions he had ever found some to sympathize with, and to console him in his afflictions. In the house of Saul, he had had the affection of Jonathan, and the favour of many beside: even in the wilderenss, six hundred out of Israel had joined him, and had faithfully struggled with him through many a day of difficulty and danger: but now, they too abandon him. Enraged at the sudden calamity, (for they also were bereaved of everything) — stung to the quick by a sense of its bitter consequences — imputing all to David (for it was he who had guided them to Ziklag) — even they who shrunk not from the sorrows of the cave of Adullam, and who had braved all the dangers of the wilderness, forsook him now. They all turned fiercely upon him as the author of their woe, and spake of stoning him. Thus stricken of God, execrated by his friends, bereaved of all that he loved, David drank of a cup which he never tasted before. He had earned it for himself. It was the fruit of his self-chosen Ziklag" (B. W. Newton).

And what was the Lord's purpose in these sore trials which now came upon David? It was not to crush him and sink him into despair. No, rather was it with the design of moving him to "humble himself beneath His mighty hand" (1 Pet. 5:6), confess his wrong-doing, and be restored to happy fellowship. God's heaviest chastenings of "His own" are sent in love and for the benefit of their subjects. But to enter into the good of them, to afterward enjoy "the peaceable fruit of righteousness" therefrom, the recipient of those chastenings *must be* "exercised thereby" (Heb. 12:11): he must bow beneath the rod, yea, "hear" and "kiss" it, before he will be the spiritual gainer. Thus it was with the subject of these articles, as will appear in the immediate sequel.

CHAPTER 29.

Now the Philistines gathered together all their armies to Aphek. And the Israelites pitched by a fountain which is in Jezreel. And the princes of the Philistines passed on by hundreds and by thousands. But David and his men passed on in the rear with Achish. Then the leaders of the Philistines said, What are these Hebrews doing here? And Achish said to the leaders of the Philistines, Is this not David the servant of Saul the king of Israel, who has been with me these days, or these years — and I have found no fault in him since he fell to me, until this day? And the princes of the Philistines were angry with him. And the princes of the Philistines said to him, Make this fellow return so that he may go again to his place which you have marked out for him. And do not let him go down with us to battle, lest in the battle he become an enemy to us. For with what should he reconcile himself to his master? Should it not be with the heads of these men? Is not this David, of whom they sang to one another in dances, saying, Saul killed his thousands, and David his ten thousands? Then Achish called David and said to him, Surely, as the LORD lives, you have been upright, and your going out and your coming in with me in the army is good in my sight. For I have not found evil in you since the day of your coming to me until today. But the princes do not favor you. Therefore return now, and go in peace so that you do not displease the princes of the Philistines. And David said to Achish, But what have I done? And what have you found in your servant so long as I have been with you to this day, that I may not go fight against the enemies of my lord the king? And Achish answered and said to David, I know that you are good in my sight, like an angel of God. But the princes of the Philistines have said, He shall not go up with us to the battle. Therefore now, rise up early in the morning with your master's servants who have come with you. And as soon as you are up early in the morning, and have light, depart. So David and his men rose up early to leave in the morning, to return to the land of the Philistines. And the Philistines went up to Jezreel. — 1 Samuel 29:1-11.

In our last we directed attention to the gracious manner in which the Lord put forth His interposing hand to deliver David from that snare of the fowler into which his unbelief and folly had brought him. Ere passing on to the immediate sequel, let us pause and admire the blessed way in which God *timed* His intervention. "To everything there is a season. . .He hath made everything beautiful in *His time*" (Eccl. 3:1, 11): equally so in the spiritual realm as in the natural. Probably every Christian can look back to certain experiences in life when his circumstances were suddenly and unexpectedly changed. At the time, he understood not the meaning of it, but later was able to perceive the wisdom and goodness of Him who shaped his affairs. There have been occasions when our situation was swiftly altered, by factors over which we had no control, which called for us to move on: but the sequel showed it was God opening our way to go to the help of others who sorely needed us. So it was now with David.

"My times are in Thy hand" (Psa. 31:15). Yes, my "times" of tarrying, and my "times" of journeying; my "times" of prosperity, and my "times" of adversity; my "times" of fellowship with the saints, and my "times" of isolation and loneliness; each and all are ordered by God. It is blessed to know this, and more blessed still when the heart is permitted to rest thereon. Nothing is more quieting and stabalizing to the soul than the realization that everything was ordained by omniscience, and is now ordered by infinite love: that He who eternally decreed the hour of my birth, has fixed the day of my departure from

274

this world; that my "times" of youth and health, and my "times" of infirmity and sickness, are equally in *God's* hands. He knows *when* it is best to bring me out of a distressing situation, and His mercy opens the way when it is His time for me to make a move.

While David and his men were in the camp of Achish, the Amalekites took advantage of their absence, fell upon the unprotected Ziklag, burned it, and carried away captive all the women and children. Their husbands and fathers knew nothing of this: no, *but God did,* and He had designs of mercy toward them. Their sad case seemed a hopeless one indeed, but appearances are deceptive. Though they were unaware of the fact, God had already set moving the means for their deliverance. Unlike us, God is never too early, and He is never too late. Had David and his men been discharged by Achish a week sooner, they had been on hand to defend Ziklag, and a needed chastisement and a great blessing from it had been missed! Had they returned home a week later, they had probably been too late to recover their loved ones. Admire, then the *timeliness of* God's freeing David from the yoke of the Philistines.

"So David and his men came to the city, and, behold, it was burned with fire; and their wives, and their sons, and their daughters, were taken captives. Then David and the people that were with him lifted up their voice and wept, until they had no more power to weep" (1 Sam. 30:3, 4). Observe, there was no turning unto God, or seeking to cast their care upon Him! They were completely overwhelmed by shock and grief. Perhaps the reader knows something of such a state from painful experience. A heavy financial reverse which plunged the soul into dark gloom; or a sudden bereavement came, and in the bitterness of grief all seemed to be against you, and even the voice of prayer was silenced. Ah, David and his men are not the only ones who have been overwhelmed by trouble and anguish.

"And David was greatly distressed; for the people spake of stoning him, because the soul of all the people was grieved, every man for his sons, and every man for his daughters" (v. 6). The turning against him of his faithful followers was the final ingredient in the bitter cup which David was now called on to drink. But even this was of God: if one stroke of His chastening rod avails not, it must be followed by another; and if necessary, yet others, for our holy Father will not suffer His wayward children to remain impenitent indefinitely. So it was here: the sight of Ziklag in ruins, and the loss of his family did not bring David to his knees; so yet other measures are employed. The anger of his men aroused him from his lethargy, the menacing of his own life by intimate friends was the way God took to bring him back unto Himself.

"But David encouraged himself in the Lord his God" (v. 6). Here is where light broke into this dark scene, yet care needs to be taken lest we make a wrong use of the same. No one sentence in God's Word is to be interpreted as an isolated unit, but scripture must be compared with scripture. Much is included in the words now before us, far more than any human writer is capable of fully opening up. Attention needs to be directed unto three things: first, what is pre-supposed in David's "encouraging himself in the Lord;" second, what is signified thereby; third, what followed the same. If we take into consideration the *real* character of David as "the man after God's own heart," if we bear in mind the whole context recounting his sad lapses, and, above all, if we view our present verse in the light of the Analogy of Faith, little difficulty should be experienced in 'reading between the lines.'

"But David encouraged himself in the Lord his God." Ah, much is implied here. David could not *truly* "encourage himself in the Lord" until there had been *previous* exercises of heart: conviction, contrition, confession, necessarily preceded comfort and consolation. "He that covereth his sins shall not prosper: but whoso confesseth and forsaketh them shall have mercy" (Prov. 28:13): that enunciates an unchanging principle in God's governmental dealings, with unconverted and converted alike. Had there been no repentance on David's part, no unsparing condemnation of himself, no broken-hearted acknowledgement unto God of his failures, he would have been "encouraging himself" in *sin!* and that would be "turning the grace of our God into lasciviousness." Not only has Christ died to save His people from the penalty of their sins, but He has also procured the Holy Spirit to work in them a hatred for the vileness of their sins! And as there is no forgiveness and cleansing for the saint without confession (1 John 1:9), so there is no acceptable "confession" save that which issues from a contrite heart.

There is great need today for the above principles to be explained unto and pressed upon professing Christians. Neither God's glory will be maintained nor the good of His people promoted, if we conceal and are silent about the requirements of His righteousness. God's mercy is exercised in a way of holiness: where there is no repentance, there is no forgiveness; where there is no turning away from sin, there is no blotting out of sins. Something more is required than simply asking God to be gracious unto us for Christ's sake. There are many who quote "the blood of Jesus Christ His Son cleanseth us from all sin" (1 John 1:7), but there are few indeed who faithfully point out that that precious promise is specifically qualified with, "IF *we walk in the light* as He is in the light." If we avoid the searching light of God's holiness, if we hide, excuse, repent not of and refuse to make daily confession of our sins, then the blood of Christ certainly *does not* "cleanse" us from all sin. To insist on the contrary is grossly dishonouring to the Blood, and is to make Christ the Condoner of evil!

Weigh well the following: "If they pray toward this place, and confess Thy name, *and turn from their sin*, when Thou afflictest them: *then* hear Thou in Heaven, and forgive the sin of Thy servants. . .If Thy people go out to battle against their enemy, whithersoever Thou shalt send them, and shall pray unto the Lord toward the city which Thou hast chosen, and toward the house that I have built for Thy name: then hear Thou in Heaven their prayer and their supplication, and maintain their cause. If they sin against Thee (for there is no man that sinneth not), and Thou be angry with them, and deliver them to the enemy, so that they carry them away captives unto the land of the enemy, far or near; Yet if they shall bethink themselves in the land whither they were carried captives, *and repent*, and make supplication unto Thee in the land of them that carried them captives, saying, We have sinned, and have done perversely, we have committed wickedness; and so *return* unto Thee *with all their heart*, and with all their soul, in the land of their enemies, which led them away captive, and pray unto Thee. . . *Then hear Thou their prayer* and their supplication in heaven Thy dwelling-place, and maintain their cause, *and forgive* Thy people that have sinned against Thee" (1 Kings 8:35, 36, 44-50). And God is still the same. No change of "dispensation" effects any alteration in His character, or in anywise modifies His holy requirements: with Him there is "no variableness neither shadow of turning" (James 1:27).

"But David encouraged himself in the Lord his God." Having sought to indicate what is *pre-supposed* by those words, let us now briefly consider what is *signified* by them. The same *Holy* Spirit who convicts the backslidden saint of his sins, works in him a sincere repentance, and moves him to frankly and freely confess them to God, *also* gives him a renewed sense of the abounding mercy of

God, strengthens faith in His blessed promises, and reminds him of His unchanging faithfulness (1 John 1:9): and thus the contrite heart is enabled to rest in the infinite grace of God; and being now restored to communion with Him, the soul "encourages" itself in His perfections. Thus, just as the Holy Spirit delivers the saint from heeding Satan's counsel to hide his sins, so also does He rescue him from Satan's attempts to sink him in despair after he is convicted of his sins.

"But David encouraged himself in the Lord his God." This means that he reviewed afresh the everlasting covenant which God had made with him in Christ, that covenant "ordered in all things and sure." It means that he recalled God's past goodness and mercy towards him, which reassured his heart for the present and the future. It means that he contemplated the omnipotency of the Lord and realized that nothing is too hard for Him, no situation is hopeless unto His mighty power, for *He* is able to over-rule evil unto good, and bring a clean thing out of an unclean. It means that he remembered God's promises to bring him safely to the throne, and though he knew not how his immediate trouble would disappear, without doubting, *he hoped in God*, and confidently counted upon His undertaking for him. O Christian reader, when we are at our wit's end, we should not be at faith's end. See to it that all is right between your soul and God, and then trust in His sufficiency.

When all things were against him, David's faith was stirred into exercise: he turned unto the One who had never failed him, and from whom he had so sadly departed. Ah, blessed is the trial, no matter how heavy; precious is the disappointment, no matter how bitter, that issues thus. To penitently return unto God means to be back again in the place of blessing. Better, far better, to be in the midst of the black ruins of Ziklag, surrounded by a threatening mob, than to be in the ranks of the Philistines fighting against His people. Have we, in any way, known what bitter disappointment means? and have we in the midst of it turned unto Him who has smitten us, and "encouraged" ourselves in Him? If so, then like David, we may say, "Before I was afflicted, I went astray; but now have I kept Thy Word" (Psa. 119:67).

O that it may please the Lord to bless this article unto some sorely-distressed soul, who is no longer enjoying the light of His countenance, but who is beneath His chastening frowns. You may be borne down by sorrow and despondency, but no trouble is too great for you to find relief in God: in the One who has, in righteousness, sent this sorrow upon you. Humble yourself beneath His mighty hand, acknowledge to Him your sins, count upon the multitude of His mercies, and seek grace to rest upon His comforting promises. When faith springs up amidst the ruins of blighted hopes, it is a blessed thing. What has just been before us marked a turning-point in David's life; may it be so in yours. "Cast thy burden upon the Lord, and He shall sustain thee" (Psa. 55:22).

O my reader, be you saved or unsaved, none but God can do you good, relieve your distress, remove the load from your heart, and bring blessing into your life. If you refuse to humble yourself before Him, lament the course of self-will which you followed, and turn from the same, you are your own worst enemy and are forsaking your own mercies. But if you will take your place before Him in the dust, repent of your wickedness, and seek grace to live henceforth in subjection to His will, then pardon, peace, joy, awaits you. No matter how sadly you have failed in the past, nor what light and favours you sinned against, if you will own it all in brokenness of heart unto the Lord, He is ready to forgive.

"And David said to Abiathar the priest, Ahimelech's son, I pray thee, bring me hither the ephod. And Abiathar brought thither the ephod to David. And David enquired at the Lord, saying, Shall I pursue after this troop? shall I overtake them?" (vv. 7, 8). Here we see the first *result* which followed David's turning back unto God. It is blessed to observe that the Holy Spirit has thrown a veil of silence over what took place in secret between David and the Lord, as He has over Christ's private interview with Peter (1 Cor. 15:5). But after telling us of David's encouraging himself in the Lord, He now reveals the reformation which took place in his conduct. Nothing was said of David's seeking counsel from God when he journeyed to Achish (27:2), but now that he is restored to happy fellow-ship, he will not think of taking a step without asking for Divine guidance.

Very blessed indeed is what is recorded in vv. 7, 8. Moses had laid it down as a law that the leader of Israel should "stand before" (Eleazar) the priest, who shall ask counsel for him after the judgment of Urim before the Lord: at his word shall they go out, and at his word they shall come in" (Num. 27:21), and in compliance therewith, David turned to the priest, and bade him seek the mind of the Lord as to how he should now act in this dire emergency. Learn from this that *obedience* to the revealed will of God is the best evidence of having been restored to communion with Him. Of course it is, for it is the very nature of love to seek *to please* its object. Let us test, then, *our* practical relation to God, not by our feelings nor by our words, but by the extent to which we are in actual subjection to Him, and walking in a spirit of dependency upon Him.

Notice here how indwelling grace triumphed over the promptings of the flesh. Mere nature would urge that David's only possible course was to rush after the Amalekites and seek to rescue any of the women and children who might yet be alive. But David was now delivered from his impetuous self-confidence; his soul was again "like a weaned child." God was now to order all the details of his life. Alas most of us have to receive many hard knocks in the by-paths of folly, before we are brought to this place. It is indeed much to be thankful for when the feverish restlessness of the flesh is subdued, and the soul truly desires God to *lead us* step by step: progress may not *seem* so swift, but it certainly will be more sure. The Lord graciously lay His quieting hand upon each of us, and cause us to look unto a rest in Himself alone.

CHAPTER 30.

And when David and his men had come to Ziklag on the third day, the Amalikites had invaded the south and Ziklag and had struck Ziklag and burned it with fire. And they had taken captive the women who were in it. They did not kill any, either small or great, but carried them away and went on their way. So David and his men came to the city. And, behold, it was burned with fire, and their wives and their sons and their daughters had been taken captives. Then David and the people who were with him lifted up their voice and wept, until they had no more power to weep. And David's two wives had been taken captive, Ahinoam of Jezreel, and Abigail, the wife of Nabal of Carmel. And David was greatly distressed, for the people spoke of stoning him — because the soul of all the people was grieved, each one for his sons and for his daughters. But David encouraged himself in the LORD his God. And David said to Abiathar the priest, Ahimelech's son, Please bring the ephod here to me. And Abiathar brought the ephod there to David. And David inquired of the LORD, saying, Shall I go after this troop? Shall I overtake them? And He answered him, Go! For you shall surely overtake them and will without fail recover all. So David went, he and the six hundred men that were with him, and came to the brook Besor, where those who were left behind stayed. But David pursued, he and four hundred men. For two hundred stayed behind, who were so faint that they could not go over the brook Besor. And they found an Egyptian in the field and brought him to David and gave him bread, and he ate. And they made him drink water. And they gave him a piece of a cake of figs, and two clusters of raisins. And when he had eaten, his spirit came again to him. For he had eaten no bread or drunk water for three days and three nights. And David said to him, To whom do you belong? And where do you come from? And he said, I am a young man of Egypt, servant to an Amalekite. And my master left me because three days ago I fell sick. We made an invasion on the south of the Cherethites, and on that which belongs to Judah, and on the south of Caleb. And we burned Ziklag with fire. And David said to him, Can you bring me down to this company? And he said, Swear to me by God that you will neither kill me nor deliver me into the hands of my master, and I will bring you down to this company. — 1 Samuel 30:1-15.

We are now to be engaged with *the blessed sequel to* David's putting matters right between his soul and God, and his encouraging himself in the Lord. At the close of the preceding article we saw that the first result of his returning to God was that he summoned the high priest with his ephod, and "inquired of the Lord" whether or not he should pursue after those who had burned Ziklag and carried away his wives captive. This exemplifies a principle which is ever operative when there has been a true reformation of heart: our own wisdom and strength are disowned, and Divine help and guidance are earnestly sought. Herein are we able to check up the state of our souls and discover whether or not we are really walking with the Lord. Backsliding and a spirit of independency ever go together; contrariwise, communion with God and dependence upon Him are never separated.

As we pointed out in our last, the Mosaic law required that Israel's ruler should stand before the priest, who would ask counsel for him as to whether he should go out or no (Num. 27:21). In like manner, the saint today is bidden to "Commit thy way unto the Lord, trust also in Him, and He shall bring it to pass" (Psa. 37:5). No step in life should be taken, be it great or small, without first

279

waiting upon God for direction: "If any of you lack wisdom, let him ask of God, that giveth to all liberally, and upbraideth not; and it shall be given him" (James 1:5). To seek not wisdom from above, is to act in self-sufficiency and self-will; to honestly and earnestly apply for that wisdom, betokens a heart in subjection to God, desirous of doing that which is pleasing to Him.

"In all thy ways acknowledge Him": if this be faithfully done, then we may be fully assured that "and He shall direct thy paths" (Prov. 3:6). The serious trouble into which David fell when he sought refuge in the land of Gath, had arisen immediately from failure *to enquire of the Lord;* but now he consulted Him through the high priest: "Shall I pursue after this troop? shall I overtake them?" (1 Sam. 30:8). Blessed indeed is this. Would that we might learn to imitate him, for our fleshly efforts to undo the consequences of our unbelief and folly, only cause us to continue going on in the same path which brought God's chastening upon us; and this is certain to end in further disappointment. "Be still, and know that I am God" is the word we need to heed at such a time: to unsparingly judge ourselves, and suffer the hand that has smitten to now lead in *His* path, is the only way to recovery. Only then do we give evidence that disappointment and sorrow have been *blest* to our souls.

Unspeakably precious is it to note the Lord's response to David's inquiry: "And He answered him, Pursue: for thou shalt surely overtake them, and without fail recover all" (v. 8). "See the goodness and perfectness of the grace of God. There was no delay in this answer — no reserve — no ambiguity; more even was told than David had asked. He was told not only that he might pursue, but that he should surely recover all. In a moment the black cloud of sorrow, that had hung so darkly over David's soul, was gone: agony gave place to joy: and he whom his companions had been dooming to death, stood suddenly before them as the honoured servant of the Lord his God, commissioned to pursue and to conquer. He did pursue, and all was as God had said" (B. W. Newton).

"So David went, he and the six hundred men that were with him" (1 Sam. 30:9). The force of this can only be perceived and appreciated by recalling what was before us in v. 6: "David was greatly distressed, for the people spake of stoning him"! What a change we behold now! The enmity of his men has been stilled, and they are again ready to follow their leader. Herein we see the third consequence of David's spiritual return and encouraging himself in the Lord. First, he had submitted to the Divine order, and sought guidance from God. Second, he had promptly received a gracious response, the Lord granting the assurance he so much desired. And now the power of God fell upon the hearts of his men, entirely subduing their mutiny, and making them willing, weary and worn as they were, to follow David in a hurried march after the Amalekites. O how much do we lose, dear reader, when we fail to right matters with God!

"So David went, he and the six hundred men that were with him." Here is David's response to the word he had received from God through the high priest. Without taking rest or refreshment, he at once set out in pursuit of the ravagers. Tired and weak as he well might be, David was now nerved to fresh endeavours. Ah, is it not written, "They that wait upon the Lord shall *renew their strength;* they shall mount up with wings as eagles; they shall run, and not be weary; they shall walk, and not faint" (Isa. 40:31). So it ever is. If we truly desire spiritual guidance of the Lord, and humbly and trustfully seek it from Him, our inner man will be renewed, and we shall be empowered to follow the path of His ordering.

"And came to the brook Besor, where those that were left behind stayed" (v.

9). This teaches us that when we *are* in the current of the revealed will of God, all will not, necessarily, be plain sailing. We must be prepared to meet with difficulties and obstacles even in the path of obedience. It was *by faith* in the word that he had received from Jehovah that David turned from the ruins of Ziklag, and faith must be *tested*. A severe trial now confronted David: fatigued from their former journey and their spirits further depressed by the sad scene they had gazed upon, many of his men, though willing, were unable to proceed farther; and he left no less than two hundred behind at the brook Besor.

"But David pursued, he and four hundred men: for two hundred abode behind, which were so faint that they could not go over the brook Besor" (v. 10). Considerate of the state of his men, David would not drive or force those who were faint to accompany him. Further proof was this that our hero was now again in communion with God, for "*He* knoweth our frame, He remembereth that we are dust" (Psa. 103:14) — alas, how often do those who profess His name seem to forget this. But though his company was now reduced by one third, and, as v. 17 plainly intimates, was far inferior to the forces of the Amalekites, yet David relied implicitly on the Word of the Lord, and continued to push forward.

"And they found an Egyptian in the field, and brought him to David, and gave him bread, and he did eat; and they made him drink water. And they gave him a piece of a cake of figs, and two clusters of raisins; and when he had eaten, his spirit came again to him: for he had eaten no bread, nor drunk any water, three days and three nights. And David said unto him. To whom belongest thou? and whence art thou? And he said, I am a young man of Egypt, servant to an Amalekite; and my master left me, because three days agone I fell sick. We made an invasion upon the south of the Cherethites, and upon the coast which belongeth to Judah, and upon the south of Caleb; and we burned Ziklag with fire. And David said to him, Canst thou bring me down to this company? And he said, Sware unto me by God, that thou wilt neither kill me, nor deliver me into the hands of my master, and I will bring thee down to this company" (vv. 11-15). We shall consider these verses from two angles: as they add to what has been before us above; as they contain a lovely Gospel picture.

In the verses just quoted we may perceive the seventh consequence which followed David's righting things with God. First, he encouraged himself in the Lord: v. 6. Second, he submitted to the Divine order and sought guidance from God: vv. 7, 8. Third, he obtained light for his path and assurance of God's help: v. 8. Fourth, the power of God fell upon the hearts of his men, subduing their mutiny (v. 6) and making them willing to follow him on a difficult and daring enterprise: v. 9. Sixth, grace granted him to overcome a sore trial of faith: v. 10. And now we are to observe how the Lord showed Himself strong on their behalf by ordering His providences to work in his favour. Such are some of the Divine mercies which we may confidently expect when the channel of blessing between our souls and God is no longer choked by unjudged and unconfessed sins.

A most remarkable intervention of Divine providence is here before us. David was pursuing the Amalekites, and from this incident we gather that he knew not in which direction they had gone, nor how far ahead they were. God did not work a miracle for them, but by natural means provided him with a needed guide. The men of David came across one in a field, who was sick and famished. He turned out to be an Egyptian slave, whom his master had barbarously abandoned. Upon being brought to David, he furnished full particulars, and after receiving assurance that his life should be spared, agreed to conduct David and his men to the place where the Amalekites were encamped. Let us admire the various details in this wondrous secret provision which God now made for David, and the combined factors which entered into it.

First, stand in awe of the high sovereignty of God which suffered this Egyptian slave to fall sick: v. 13. Second, in permitting his master to act so unhumanly, by leaving him to perish by the wayside: v. 13. Third, in moving David's men to spare his life (v. 11), when they had every reason to believe he had taken part in the burning of Ziklag. Fourth, in the fact that he was himself an Egyptian and not an Amalekite (v. 11) — had he been the latter, they were bound to kill him: Deut. 25:19. Fifth, in moving David to show him kindness: v. 11. Sixth, in causing the food given to so quickly revive him: v. 12. Seventh, in inclining him to freely answer David's inquiries and be willing to lead him to the camp of the Amalekites. Each of these seven factors had to combine, or the result had never been reached: God made "all things *work together*" for David's good. So He does for us: His providences, day by day, work just as wondrously on our behalf.

Approaching these verses (11-15) now from another angle, let us see portrayed in them a beautiful type of a lost sinner being saved by Christ. There are so distinct lines in this lovely Gospel picture that we can here do little more than point out each one separately. 1. *His citizenship:* "And they found an Egyptian in the field" (v. 11). In Scripture Egypt is a symbol of the world: the moral world to which the unregenerate belong and in which they seek their satisfaction. As another has said, "It had its beginning in Cain's day, when he 'went out from the presence of the Lord,' and he and his descendants builded cities, sought out witty inventions of brass and iron, manufactured musical instruments, and went in for a good time generally, in forgetfulness of God. And that continues to this day. The land of Egypt figures this. There Pharaoh, type of Satan, ruled and tyrannized."

2. *His woeful condition:* "I fell sick" (v. 13). Such is the state of every descendant of fallen Adam. An awful disease is at work in the unregenerate: that disease is *sin,* and "sin, when it is finished, bringeth forth death" (James 1:15). It is sin which has robbed the soul of its original beauty: darkening the understanding, corrupting the heart, perverting the will, and paralyzing all our faculties so far as their exercise Godward is concerned. But not only was this Egyptian desperately sick, he was *starving:* he had had nothing to eat or drink for three days. Well might he cry, "I perish with hunger" (Luke 15:17).

3. *His sad plight:* "my master left me, because three days agone I fell sick" (v. 13). He was a slave, and now that his master thought he would be of no further use to him, he heartlessly abandoned him and left him to perish. "And that is the way the devil treats his servants. He uses them as his tools as long as he can. Then, when he cannot use them any more, he leaves them to their folly. Thus he treated Judas, and hosts of others before and since" (C. Knapp).

4. *His deliverance:* "And brought him to David" (v. 11). No doubt he was too weak and ill to come of himself; and even had he the ability, he had never used it thus, for David was an utter stranger to him! Thus it is with the unregenerate sinner and that blessed One whom David foreshadowed. Therefore did Christ say, "No man can come to Me, except the Father which hath sent Me draw him" (John 6:44). Each of God's elect is "brought" to Christ by the Holy Spirit.

5. *His deliverer.* No doubt this half-dead Egyptian presented a woe-begone spectacle, as he was led or carried into the presence of the man after God's own heart. But his very ruin and wretchedness drew out the compassion of David toward him. Thus it is with the Saviour: no matter what ravages sin has wrought, nor how morally repulsive it has made its victim, Christ never refuses to receive and befriend one whom the Father draws to Him.

6. *His entertainment:* "And gave him bread, and he did eat; and they made him drink water. And they gave him a piece of a cake of figs, and two clusters of raisins" (vv. 11, 12). Precious line in our picture is this of the Divine grace which is stored up in Christ. None brought to Him by the Spirit are ever sent empty away. How this reminds us of the royal welcome which the prodigal received and the rich fare that was set before him.

7. *His confession:* When David asked him to whom he belonged and whence he came, he gave an honest and straight-forward reply: "He said, I am a young man of Egypt, servant to an Amalekite" (v. 13). Strikingly did this adumbrate the fact that when an elect sinner has been brought to Christ, and been given the bread and water of life, he takes his proper place, and candidly acknowledges what he was and is by nature. "If we confess our sins, He is faithful and just to forgive us" (1 John 1:9).

8. *His obligation:* "And David said, Canst thou bring me down to this company?" (v. 15). In this we may see how David pressed his claims upon the one whom he had befriended, though it is blessed to mark that it was more in the form of an appeal than a direct command. In like manner, the word to the converted is, "I beseech you therefore, brethren, by the mercies of God, that ye present your bodies a living sacrifice, holy, acceptable unto God, which is your reasonable service" (Rom. 12:1).

9. *His desire for assurance:* "And he said, "Sware unto me by God, that thou wilt neither kill me, nor deliver me into the hands of my master, and I will bring thee down to this company" (v. 15). There could be no joy in the service of his new master until assured that he should not be returned unto the power of his old one. Blessed is it to know that Christ delivers His people not only from the wrath to come, but also from the dominion of sin.

10. *His gratitude:* "And when he had brought him down" (v. 16). He was now devoted to the interests of David, and did as he requested. So Christians are told, "For we are His workmanship, created in Christ Jesus *unto good works*" (Eph. 2:10). O for grace to serve Christ as ardently as we did sin and Satan in our unregenerate days.

And when he had brought him down, behold, they were spread abroad on all the earth, eating and drinking and dancing, because of all the great spoil that they had taken out of the land of the Philistines and out of the land of Judah. And David struck them from the twilight even to the evening of the next day. And not a man of them escaped, except four hundred young men who rode on camels and fled. And David recovered all that the Amalekites had carried away. And David rescued his two wives. And there was nothing lacking to them, great or small, sons or daughters, either spoil or anything that they had taken to themselves. David recovered all. And David took all the flocks and the herds which they drove before those other cattle. And he said, This is David's spoil. And David came to the two hundred who were so faint that they could not follow David, whom they had made also to stay at the brook Besor. And they went forth to meet David, and to meet the people who were with him. And when David came near the people, he greeted them. Then all the wicked men and men of Belial among the men who went with David answered and said, Because they did not go with us, we will not give them anything of the spoil that we have recovered, except to every man his wife and his children, so that they may lead them away and depart. Then David said, My brothers, you shall not do so with that which the LORD has given us. For he has kept us alive and has delivered into our hand the company that came against us. For who will listen to you in this matter? But as his part is that goes down to the battle, so shall be his part that stays by the stuff. They shall divide alike. And from that day forward he made it a statute and an ordinance for Israel to this day. And when David came to Ziklag, he sent some of the spoil to the elders of Judah, to his friends, saying, Behold, a present for you from the spoil of the enemies of the LORD — to the ones who were in Bethel, and to the ones who were in south Ramoth, and to the ones who were in Jattir, and to the ones who were in Aroer, and to the ones who were in Siphmoth, and to the ones who were in Eshtemoa, and to the ones who were in Rachal, and to the ones who were in the cities of the Jerahmeelites, and to the ones who were in the cities of the Kenites, and to the ones who were in Hormah, and to the ones who were in Chorashan, and to the ones who were in Athach, and to the ones who were in Hebron, and to all the places where David himself and his men had been among them. — 1 Samuel 30:16-31.

"And when he had brought him down, behold, they were spread abroad upon all the earth, eating and drinking, and dancing, because of all the great spoil that they had taken out of the land of the Philistines and out of the land of Judah. And David smote them from the twilight even unto the evening of the next day: and there escaped not a man of them, save four hundred young men, which rode upon camels, and fled" (1 Sam. 30:16, 17). We resume at the point where we left off in our last. These verses form a solemn sequel to those previously pondered, and set before us the other side of the picture which was then considered.

The Amalekites, in all probability, knew that the Israelites and Philistines were engaged in fighting each other, a considerable distance away, and supposed that David and his men were assisting the king of Gath. Deeming themselves secure, they imprudently began to riot and make merry over the abundance of spoils they had captured, without so much as placing guards to give notice of an enemy's approach. They lay not in any regular order, much less in any military formation, but were scattered in groups, here and there. Consequently, David and his little force came upon them quite unawares, and made a dreadful slaughter of them. How often when men say, "Peace and safety, sudden destruction cometh upon them, as travail upon a woman with child, and they shall not escape" (1 Thess. 5:3).

Just as the sick and abandoned Egyptian who was befriended by David typified one of God's elect being saved by Christ, so these flesh-indulging Amalekites portray careless sinners who will yet be destroyed by Him. Solemnly is this announced in 2 Thess. 1:7-9, "The Lord Jesus shall be revealed from heaven with His mighty angels, in flaming fire taking vengeance on them that know not God, and that obey not the Gospel of our Lord Jesus Christ; who shall be punished with everlasting destruction from the presence of the Lord, and from the glory of His power." And again, "Behold, the Lord cometh, with ten thousands of His saints, to execute judgment upon all, and to convince all that are ungodly among them of all their ungodly deeds, which they had ungodly committed, and of all their hard speeches which ungodly sinners have spoken against Him" (Jude 14, 15).

Yet, such unspeakably solemn warnings as those which God has given in His Word have no restraining effect upon the unconcerned and Satan-drugged world. The vast majority of our fellows live as though there were no eternity to come, no judgment-day when they must appear before God, give an account of the deeds they have done in the body, and be sentenced according to their works.

They know full well how brief and uncertain this life is: at short intervals their companions are cut down by the hand of death, but no lasting serious impressions are made upon them. Instead, they continue in their pleasure-loving whirl, impervious to the Divine threatenings, deaf to the voice of conscience, disregarding any entreaties or admonitions which they may receive from Christian friends or the servants of God.

O how tragically true to the present-day life of the world is the gay scene presented to us in the verses we are now pondering. Those care-free Amalekites were "eating and drinking and dancing." In their fancied security they were having what the young people of this degenerate age call "a good time." There was an abundance of food to hand, why then should they deny those lusts of the flesh which war against the soul? They had been successful in spoiling their neighbours, why then should they not "celebrate" and make merry? All were in high spirits, why then should they not fill the air with music and laughter? Yes, similar is the fatal reasoning of multitudes today. But mark well the fearful sequel: "And David smote them from the twilight even unto the evening of the next day." Alas, what was their carnal security worth!

David was just as truly a type of Christ in his slaying of the Amalekites as he was in befriending the poor Egyptian. Ah, dear reader, he who saves those who submit to Him as their Lord and trust in Him as their Redeemer, shall as surely judge and destroy them who despise and reject Him. He will yet say, "But those Mine enemies, which would not that I should reign over them, bring hither, and slay before Me" (Luke 19:27). How will it fare with *you* in that Day? The answer to this question will be determined by whether or not you have truly received Him as a Prophet to instruct you, as Priest to atone for your sins, as King to regulate and reign over your heart and life. If you have not already done so, seek grace from above to throw down the weapons of your warfare against Him and surrender yourself wholly to Him.

"The young man of Egypt was with David when he came upon the Amalekites. He once belonged to their company and was one of them. Had he not been separated from them he would have surely shared their fate. If unconverted, you are of that world of sinners 'whose judgment now for a long time lingereth not.' Turn from it now ere the vengeance of God destroys you with it. God has borne with it long. The sins of Christendom reach up to Heaven, and cry for vengeance. Christ is your only refuge. Come to Him now, and, like Noah in the ark and Lot in the mountain, you will be safe from the sweeping storm. Like the young man of Egypt, you will be taken out of the world and away from this scene before the stroke descends. You will appear with Christ, along with those ten thousand holy ones who accompany Him when He comes to earth to war and judge" (C. Knapp).

Let us now return to our narrative and seek its practical teaching for the Christian today. "And when he had brought him down, behold, they were spread abroad upon all the earth, eating and drinking, and dancing, because of all the great spoil that they had taken out of the land of Judah" (v. 16). How many miles it was that the befriended Egyptian led David and his men we do not know, but probably some considerable distance: that they were supernaturally strengthened for their strenuous exertions after their previous fatigue, we cannot doubt. Justly did God make use of this poor Egyptian, basely abandoned, as an instrument of death to the Amalekites.

"And David smote them from the twilight even unto the evening of the next day: and there escaped not a man of them, save four hundred young men, which rode upon camels and fled. And David recovered all that the Amalekites had carried away: and David rescued his two wives. And there was nothing lacking to them, neither small nor great, neither sons nor daughters, neither spoil nor anything that they had taken to them: David recovered all" (vv. 17-19). Here is the blessed sequel to all that has occupied us in the preceding verses of this chapter. What a proof that David's heart was now perfect toward the Lord, for most manifestly did He here show Himself strong on his behalf, by granting such signal success to his endeavours. Ah, when our sins are forsaken and forgiven, and we act by the Lord's directions, we are very likely to recover what we lost by our previous folly.

"And David took all the flocks and the herds, which they drove before those other cattle, and said, This is David's spoil" (v. 20). The seeming ambiguity of this language is removed if we refer back to what is said in v. 16: the Amalekites had successfully raided other places before they fell upon Ziklag. The spoil they had captured was kept separate, and the cattle which they had taken in the territory of Philistia and Judah David claimed for his own portion: the noble use which he made of the same we shall see in a moment.

"And David came to the two hundred men which were so faint that they could not follow David, whom they had made also to abide at the brook Besor: and they went forth to meet David, and to meet the people that were with him: and when David came near to the people, he saluted them" (v. 21). The expression "whom they had *made* to abide by the brook Besor" shows plainly that those fatigued men earnestly desired to follow David further, and had to be constrained not to do so. Typically, it tells us that all Christians are not equally strong in the Lord: compare 1 John 2:13. The Hebrew word for "saluted" signifies "he asked them of peace," which means, he enquired how they did, being solicitous of their welfare. Though all Christians are not alike spiritually robust, all are equally dear unto Christ.

"Then answered all the wicked men and men of Belial, of those that went with David, and said, Because they went not with us, we will not give them ought of the spoil that we have recovered, save to every man his wife and his children, that they may lead them away, and depart" (v. 22). In the most favoured company there will be found selfish men, who being ungrateful to God for His kindness and favours will desire to enrich and pamper themselves, leaving their fellows to starve, for all they care. Even amid David's band were certain sons of Belial, wicked men, of a covetous and grasping disposition. No doubt they were the ones who took the lead in suggesting that David be "stoned" (v. 6). Their real character was here made quite evident: in their evil suggestion we may see how the heart of David was tested.

"Then said David, Ye shall not do so, my brethren, with that which the Lord hath given us, who hath preserved us, and delivered the company that came against us into our hand" (v. 23). David's reply to the selfish suggestion of some of his grasping followers was meek, pious, and righteous, and it prevailed unto their silencing. Note how gently he replied even to the sons of Belial, addressing them as "my brethren"; but observe that he, at the same time, maintained his dignity as the general-in-chief, by directly denying their request. Yet it was not a mere arbitrary assertion of his authority: he followed his "Ye shall not do so" with powerful reasonings.

First, he reminded these selfish followers that, the spoil which had been taken from the Amalekites was *not theirs* absolutely, but that "which the Lord hath given us." Therein David inculcated an important principle which is to regulate us in the discharge of our Christian stewardship: freely we have received from

God, and therefore freely we should give unto others. Miserliness in a child of God is a practical denial of how deeply he is indebted unto Divine grace. Second, he reminded them of how mercifully the Lord had "preserved" them when they attacked a people who greatly out-numbered them, and how He had also "delivered" the Amalekites into their hands. They must not ascribe the victory unto their own prowess, and therefore they could not claim the booty as wholly belonging unto themselves. It is not a time to give way to a spirit of greed when the Lord has particularly manifested His kindness to us.

Third, he pointed out that their evil suggestion most certainly would not commend itself unto any wise, just, and right-thinking people: "For who will hearken unto you in this matter?" (v. 24). When the people of God are in the majority, they will vote down the propositions of the covetous; but when the unregenerate are allowed to outnumber them in their assemblies, woe unto them. Fourth, David reminded them that those who tarried at Besor did so out of no disloyalty or unwillingness: they had fought valiantly in the past, and now they had faithfully done their part in guarding the "stuff" or baggage, and so were entitled to a share of the spoils: "But as his part is that goeth down to the battle, so shall his part be that tarrieth by the stuff: they shall part alike" (v. 24).

The whole of the above illustrates the fact that when a backsliding believer has been restored to communion with God, he is now in a state of soul to enjoy his recovered possessions: they will no longer be a snare unto him. When God takes something from us to teach us a needed lesson, He can, after we have learned that lesson, restore it to us again. Often, though not always, He does so. Faith is now dominant again, and receives the recovered blessings from the hand of God. One who has been truly restored, like David, who knew what his own failure has been, will permit of no such selfishness as the sons of Belial advocate. Those who had stayed at home, as it were, should share in the victory. That was true *largeness of heart,* which ever marks one who has learned in God's school.

But there are always some who would wish to stint those possessing less faith and energy, yet he who realizes something of his own deep indebtedness to Divine grace rejoices to give out to others what he has gained. When the Lord is pleased to open up some part of His precious Word unto one of His servants he, with enlarged heart welcomes every opportunity to pass on the same to others. But how often there are those who seek to pour cold water on his zeal, urging that it is not "wise" or "timely," yea, that such teaching may prove "dangerous." While it is not fitting that we should take the childrens' bread and cast it to the dogs, on the other hand it is sinful to withhold any portion of the Bread of Life from hungry souls. If God has restored to us any portion of His truth, we owe it to the whole Household of Faith to impart it unto as many as will receive it.

"And when David came to Ziklag, he sent of the spoil unto the elders of Judah, even to his friends, saying, Behold a present for you of the spoil of the enemies of the Lord" (v. 26). "David not only distributed of the spoil to all who had followed him in the wilderness, and shared his dangers there — he also remembered that there were some, who, though they had refused to quit their position in Israel, and had shrunk (as well they might) from the cave of Adullam, did nevertheless love and favour him. Yet though they had drawn back from following him, and had declined to partake of his cup of sorrow, David, in the hour of his triumph, refused not to them participation in his joy. Such is the liberality of a heart that has sought and found its portion in *grace"* (B. W. Newton)

Very blessed is what we find recorded in these closing verses of 1 Sam. 30. Those who view God as the Giver of their abundance will dispense of it with equity and liberality: they will seek to restrain injustice in others (v. 23), establish useful precedents (v. 25), and share with friends (vv. 26-31). The Amalekites had spoiled some of those parts of Judah mentioned in vv. 26-31 (see vv. 14, 16), and therefore did David now send relief to those sufferers: it was the part of justice to restore what had been taken from them. Moreover, he had a grateful remembrance of those friends who secretly favoured him during the time of Saul's persecution, and who had sheltered and relieved his men in the time of this distress (v. 31). Instead of selfishly enriching himself, he generously befriended others, and gave them proof that the Lord was with him.

Fearfully divergent may be the effects produced on different persons who pass under the same trials and blessings. The "sons of Belial" companied with David during the night of his sorrow (as Judas did with Christ), and were also made the recipients of his mercies; yet they now evidenced a state of soul which marked them in God's sight as "wicked men" (v. 22). What more abhorrent to God than that which would narrow the expansiveness of grace: what more hateful in His sight than a selfishness which sought to extract out of His free favours an excuse for enriching itself by despising others — cf. John 12:4-6. But how different with David: from the ruins of Ziklag he rose, step by step, to a higher faith: manifesting dependency upon God, seeking His guidance, obtaining energy to pursue the enemy, and exercising largeness of heart in sharing the spoils with all. Thereby did he furnish an eminent foreshadowing of Him who "took the prey from the mighty" (Isa. 49:24), "led captivity captive, and *gave gifts unto men*" (Eph. 4:8).

Now the Philistines fought against Israel. And the men of Israel fled from before the Philistines and fell down wounded in Mount Gilboa. And the Philistines followed hard on Saul and on his sons. And the Philistines killed Jonathan and Abinadab and Malchishua, Saul's sons. And the battle went hard against Saul. And the archers hit him, and he was sorely wounded by the archers. Then Saul said to his armor-bearer, Draw your sword and thrust me through with it, lest these uncircumcised ones come and thrust me through and abuse me. But his armor-bearer would not, for he was very much afraid. Therefore Saul took a sword and fell on it. And when his armor-bearer saw that Saul was dead, he fell likewise on his sword and died with him. So Saul died, and his three sons, and his armor-bearer, and all his men that same day together. And when the men of Israel who were on the other side of the valley, and those who were on the other side Jordan, saw that the men of Israel fled and that Saul and his sons were dead, they abandoned the cities and fled. And the Philistines came and lived in them. And on the next day, when the Philistines came to strip the slain, they found Saul and his three sons fallen in Mount Gilboa. And they cut off his head and stripped off his armor and sent into the land of the Philistines all around, to publish it in the house of their idols and among the people. And they put his armor in the house of Ashtaroth, and they fastened his body to the wall of Bethshan. And when the people of Jabesh in Gilead heard of what the Philistines had done to Saul, all the brave men arose and traveled all night. And they took the body of Saul and the bodies of his sons from the wall of Bethshan and came to Jabesh and burned them there. And they took their bones and buried them under a tree at Jabesh, then fasted seven days. — 1 Samuel 31:1-13.

The final chapter of 1 Sam. presents to us an unspeakably solemn and terrible scene, being concerned not with David, but with the termination of Saul's earthly life. In these articles we have said very little about him, but here one or two paragraphs concerning his tragic career and its terrible close seem in place. A solemn summary of this, from the *Divine* side, is found in Hos. 13:11, when at a later date, God reminded rebellious Israel, "I gave them a king in Mine anger, *and took him away in My wrath*": the reference being to Saul.

The history of Saul properly begins at the 8th chapter. There we behold the revolted heart of Israel, which had departed further and further from Jehovah, desiring a human king in His stead. Though Samuel the prophet faithfully remonstrated, and space was given them to repent of their rash decision, it was in vain: they were determined to have their own way. "Nevertheless the people. . said, Nay, but we will have a king over us, that we also may be like all the nations; and that our king may judge us, and go out before us, and fight our battles" (8:19, 20). Accordingly, God, "in His anger," delivered them up to their own hearts' lusts and suffered them to be plagued by one who proved a disappointment and curse to them, until, by his godless incompetency, he brought the kingdom of Israel to the very verge of destruction.

From the *human* side of things, Saul was a man splendidly endowed, given a wonderful opportunity, and had a most promising prospect. Concerning his physique we are told, "Saul was a choice young man, and a goodly: and there was not among the children of Israel a goodlier person than he: from his shoulders and upward he was higher than any of the people" (9:2). Regarding his acceptability unto his subjects, we read that when Samuel set him before them, that "all the people shouted, and said, God save the king" (10:24): more, "there went with him a band of men, whose hearts God had touched" (10:26), giving the young king favor in their eyes. Not only so, but "the Spirit of the Lord came upon Saul" (11:6), equipping him for his office, and giving proof that God was ready to act if he would submit to His yoke.

Yet notwithstanding these high privileges, Saul, in his spiritual madness, played fast and loose with them, ruined his life, and by disobeying and defying God, lost his soul. In the 13th chapter of 1 Sam. we find Saul tried and found wanting. The prophet left him for a little while, bidding him go to Gilgal and wait for him there, till he should come and offer the sacrifices. Accordingly we are told "he tarried seven days, according to the set time that Samuel had appointed." And then we read, "but Samuel came not to Gilgal, and the people were scattered from him" — having lost their confidence in the king to lead them against the Philistines to victory. Petulent at the delay, Saul presumptuously invaded the prophet's prerogative and said, "Bring hither a burnt offering to *me*, and peace offerings, and *he* offered the burnt offering" (13:9). Thus did he forsake the word of the Lord and break the first command he received from Him.

In the 15th chapter we see him tested again by a command from the Lord: "Thus saith the Lord of hosts, I remember that which Amalek did to Israel, how he laid wait for him in the way, when he came up from Egypt. Now go and smite Amalek and utterly destroy *all* that they have, and spare them not: but slay both man and woman, infant and suckling, ox and sheep, camel and ass" (vv. 2, 3). But again he disobeyed: "But Saul and the people *spared* Agag, and the best of the sheep, and of the oxen, and of the fatlings, and the lambs, and all that was good, and *would not* utterly destroy them" (v. 9). Then it was that the prophet announced, "Behold, to obey is better than sacrifice, and to hearken than the fat of rams. For rebellion is as the sin of witchcraft, and stubbornness is as iniquity and idolatry. Because thou hast rejected the word of the Lord, He hath also rejected thee from being king" (vv. 22, 23). From that point Saul rapidly went from bad to worse: turning against David and relentlessly seeking his life, shedding the blood of God's priests (22: 18, 19), till at last he scrupled not to seek the aid of the Devil himself (28:7, 8).

And now the day of recompense had come, when he who had advanced steadily from one degree of impiety to another, should miserably perish by his own hand. The Divine account of this is given in 1 Sam. 31. The Philistines had joined themselves against Israel in battle. First, Saul's own army was defeated (v. 1); next, his sons, the hopes of his family, were slain before his eyes (v. 2); and then the king himself was sorely wounded by the archers (v. 3). Fearful indeed is what follows: no longer able to resist his enemies, nor yet flee from them, the God-abandoned Saul expressed no concern for his soul, but desired only that his life might be dispatched speedily, so that the Philistines might not gloat over him and torture his body.

First, he called upon his armour-bearer to put an end to his wretched life, but though his servant niether feared God nor death, he had too much respect for the person of his sovereign to lift up his hand against him (v. 4). Whereupon Saul became his own murderer: "Saul took a sword and fell upon it"; and his armour-bearer, in a mad expression of fealty to his royal master, imitated his fearful example. Saul was therefore the occasion of his servant being guilty of fearful wickedness, and "perished not alone in his iniquity." As he had lived, so he died: proud and jealous, a terror to himself and all about him, having neither the fear of God nor hope in God. What a solemn warning for each of us! What need is there for both writer and reader to heed that exhortation, "Take heed, brethren, lest there be in any of you an evil heart of unbelief in departing from the living God" (Heb. 3:12).

The cases of Ahithopel (2 Sam. 17:23), Zimri (1 Kings 16:18) and Judas the traitor (Matt. 27:5) are the only other instances recorded in Scripture of those who murdered themselves. The awful sin of suicide seems to have occurred very rarely in Israel, and not one of the above cases is extenuated by ascribing the deed unto insanity! When the character of those men be examined, we may perceive not only the enormity of the crime by which they put an end to their wretched lives, but the unspeakably fearful consequences which must follow the fatal deed. How can it be otherwise, when men either madly presume on the mercy of God or despair of it, in order to escape temporal suffering or disgrace, despise His gift of life, and rush headlong, uncalled, unto His tribunal? By an act

of direct rebellion against God's authority (Ex. 20:13), and in daring defiance of His justice, suicides fling themselves on the bosses of Jehovah's buckler, with the guilt of unrepented sin on their hands.

"And it came to pass on the morrow, when the Philistines came to strip the slain, that they found Saul and his three sons fallen in mount Gilboa. And they cut off his head, and stripped off his armour, and sent into the land of the Philistines round about, to publish it in the house of their idols, and among the people. And they put his armour in the house of Ashtaroth: and they fastened his body to the wall of Bethshan" (31:8-10). Though Saul had escaped torture at their hands, his body was signally abused — adumbrating, we doubt not, the awful suffering which his soul was now enduring, and would continue to endure forever. Saul's self-inflicted death points a most solemn warning for us to earnestly watch and pray that we may be preserved from both presumption and despair, and Divinely enabled to bear up under the trials of life, and quietly to hope for the salvation of the Lord (Lam. 3:26), that Satan may not tempt us to the horrible sin of self-murder, for which the Scriptures hold out *no* hope of forgiveness.

II SAMUEL

CHAPTER 1.

Now after the death of Saul, when David had returned from the slaughter of the Amalekites, and after David had stayed two days in Ziklag, on the third day, behold, a man came out of the camp from Saul with his clothes torn and earth on his head. And when he came to David, he fell to the earth and bowed to him. And David said to him, Where do you come from? And he said to him, I have escaped out of the camp of Israel. And David said to him, How did the matter go? I beg you, tell me. And he answered, The people have fled from the battle, and many of the people also have fallen and are dead. And Saul and his son Jonathan are dead also. And David said to the young man who told him, How do you know that Saul and his son Jonathan are dead? And the young man who told him said, As I happened by chance on Mount Gilboa, behold, Saul leaned on his spear. And, lo, the chariots and horsemen followed hard after him. And when he looked behind him, he saw me, and called to me. And I answered, Here am I. And he said to me, Who are you? And I answered him, I am an Amalekite. He said to me again, I beg you, stand over me and kill me, for anguish has come on me, because my life is still whole in me. So I stood over him and killed him, because I was sure that he could not live after he had fallen. And I took the crown that was on his head, and the bracelet that was on his arm, and have brought them here to my lord. Then David took hold on his clothes and tore them. And likewise all the men who were with him. And they mourned and wept and fasted until evening, for Saul and for his son Jonathan, and for the people of the LORD, and for the house of Israel, because they had fallen by the sword. And David said to the young man who told him, Where are you from? And he answered, I am the son of a stranger, an Amalekite. And David said, Why were you not afraid to stretch forth your hand to destroy the LORD's anointed? And David called one of the young men and said, Go near and fall on him. And he struck him so that he died. And David said to him, Your blood shall be on your head, for your mouth has testified against you, saying, I have slain the LORD's anointed. And David mourned with this mourning over Saul and over his son Jonathan. (Also he told them to teach the children of Judah the use of the bow. Behold, it is written in the book of Jasher.) The beauty of Israel is slain on your high places! How are the mighty fallen! Tell it not in Gath, do not let it be known in the streets of Askelon, lest the daughters of the Philistines rejoice, lest the daughters of the uncircumcised triumph. You mountains of Gilboa, let there be no dew, and let there be no rain on you, or fields of offerings. For there the shield of the mighty has been tarnished, the shield of Saul, without being anointed with oil. From the blood of the slain, from the fat of the mighty, the bow of Jonathan did not turn back, and the sword of Saul did not return empty. Saul and Jonathan were lovely and pleasant in their lives, and in their death they were not divided. They were swifter than eagles; they were stronger than lions. Daughters of Israel, weep over Saul, who clothed you in scarlet and with other delights, who put ornaments of gold on your clothes. How are the mighty fallen in the midst of the battle! O Jonathan, you were slain in your high places. I am distressed for you, my brother Jonathan. Very pleasant you have been to me. Your love to me was wonderful, more than the love of women. How are the mighty fallen and the weapons of war lost! — II Samuel 1.

"Now it came to pass after the death of Saul, when David was returned from the slaughter of the Amalekites, and David had abode two days in Ziklag" (2

292

Sam. 1:1). David had returned to Ziklag, where he was engaged with dividing the spoil he had captured and in sending presents to his friends (1 Sam. 30:26-31). "It was strange he did not leave some spies about the camps to bring him early notice of the issue of the engagement (between the Philistines and the army of Saul): a sign he desired not Saul's woeful day, nor was impatient to come to the throne, but willing to wait till those tidings were brought to him, which many a one would have sent more than half way to meet. He that believeth does not make haste, takes good news when it comes, and is not weary while it is in the coming" (Matthew Henry).

"It come even to pass on the third day, that, behold, a man came out of the camp from Saul with his clothes rent, and earth upon his head: and so it was, when he came to David, that he fell to the earth, and did obeisance. And David said unto him, From whence comest thou? And he said unto him, Out of the camp of Israel am I escaped. And David said unto him, How went the matter? I pray thee, tell me. And he answered, That the people are fled from the battle, and many of the people also are fallen and dead; and Saul and Jonathan his son are dead also" (2 Sam. 1:2-4). This Amalekite presented himself as a mourner for the dead king, and as a loyal subject to the one who should succeed Saul. No doubt he prided himself that he was the first to pay homage to the sovereign-elect, expecting to be rewarded for bringing such good news (4:10); whereas he was the first to receive sentence of death from David's hands.

"And David said unto the young man that told him, How knowest thou that Saul and Jonathan be dead? And the young man that told him said, As I happened by chance upon mount Gilboa, behold, Saul leaned upon his spear; and, lo, the chariots and horsemen followed hard after him. And when he looked behind him, he saw me, and called unto me. And I answered, here am I. And he said unto me, Who art thou? And I answered him, I am an Amalekite. And he said unto me again, stand, I pray thee, upon me, and slay me, for anguish is come upon me, because my life is yet whole in me. So I stood upon him, and slew him, because I was sure that he could not live after that he was fallen: and I took the crown that was upon his head, and the bracelet that was on his arm, and have brought them hither unto my lord" (vv. 5-10). This is one of the passages seized by atheists and infidels to show that "the Bible is full of contradictions," for the account here given of Saul's death by no means tallies with what is recorded in the previous chapter. But the seeming difficulty is easily solved: 1 Sam. 31 contains God's description of Saul's death; 2 Sam. 1 gives man's fabrication. Holy Writ records the lies of God's enemies (Gen. 3:4) as well as the true statements of His servants.

From 1 Sam. 31:4 it is definitely established that Saul murdered himself, and *was dead* before his armour-bearer committed suicide. That is the unerring record of the Holy Spirit Himself, and must not be questioned for a moment. In view of this, it is quite evident that the Amalekite who now communicated to David the tidings of Saul's death, lied in a number of details. Finding Saul's body with the insignia of royalty upon it — which evidenced both the conceit and rashness of the infatuated king: going into battle with the crown upon his head, and thus making himself a mark for the Philistine archers — he seized them (v. 10), and then formed his story in such a way as he hoped to ingratiate himself with David. Thus did this miserable creature seek to turn the death of Saul to his own personal advantage, and scrupled not to depart from the truth in so doing; concluding, from the wickedness of his own heart, that David would be delighted with the news he communicated.

By the death of Saul and Jonathan the way was now opened for David to the throne. "If a large proportion of Israel stood up for the rights of Ishbosheth, who was a very insignificant person (2 Sam. 2-4), doubtless far more would have been strenuous for Jonathan. And though *he* would readily have given place, yet his brethren and the people in general would no doubt have made much more opposition to David's accession to the kingdom" (T. Scott). Yet so far was David from falling into a transport of joy, as the poor Amalekite expected, that he mourned and wept; and so strong was his passion that all about him were similarly affected: "Then David took hold on his clothes, and rent them; and likewise all the men that were with him: And they mourned and wept, and fasted until even, for Saul, and for Jonathan his son, and for the people of the Lord, and for the house of Israel; because they were fallen by the sword" (vv. 11, 12).

"Rejoice not when thine enemy falleth; and let not thine heart be glad when he stumbleth" (Prov. 24:17). There are many who secretly wish for the death of those who have injured them, or who keep them from honors and estates, and who inwardly rejoice even when they pretend to mourn outwardly. But the grace of God subdues this base disposition, and forms the mind to a more liberal temper. Now will the spiritual soul exult in the prospect of worldly advancement, for he realizes that such will increase his responsibilities, that he will be surrounded by greater temptations, and called to additional duties and cares. David mourned for Saul out of good will, without constraint: out of compassion, without malice; because of the melancholy circumstances attending his death and the terrible consequences which must follow, as well as for Israel's being triumphed over by the enemies of God.

"And David said unto the young man that told him, Whence art thou? And he answered, I am the son of a stranger, an Amalekite. And David said unto him, How wast thou not afraid to stretch forth thine hand to destroy the Lord's anointed? And David called one of the young men, and said, Go near, and fall upon him. And he smote him that he died. And David said unto him, Thy blood be upon thy head; for thy mouth hath testified against thee, saying, I have slain the Lord's anointed" (vv. 13-16). As an Amalekite, he was devoted to destruction (Deut. 25:17-19), and as the elect-king, David was now required to put the sentence into execution.

The last nine verses of our chapter record the "lamentation" or elegy which David made over Saul and Jonathan. Not only did David rend his clothes, weep, and fast over the decease of his arch-enemy, but he also composed a poem in his honour: 2 Sam. 1:17-27. Nor was it mere sentiment which prompted him: it was also because he looked upon Saul as Israel's "king," the "anointed" of God (v. 16). This elegy was a noble tribute of respect unto Saul and of tender affection for Jonathan. First, he expressed sorrow over the fall of the mighty (v. 19). Second, he deprecated the exultations of the enemies of God in the cities of the Philistines (v. 20). Third, he celebrated Saul's valour and military renown (vv. 21, 22). Fourth, he touchingly mentioned the fatal devotion of Jonathan to his father (v. 23). Fifth, he called upon the daughters of Israel, who had once sung Saul's praises, to now weep over their fallen leader (v. 24). Sixth, his faults are charitably veiled! Seventh, nothing could truthfully be said of Saul's piety, so David would not utter lies — how this puts to shame the untruthful adulations found in many a funeral oration! Eighth, he ended by memorializing the fervent love of Jonathan for himself.

And after this David inquired of the LORD, saying, Shall I go up into any of the cities of Judah? And the LORD said to him, Go up! And David said, Where shall I go? And He said, To Hebron. So David went up there, and his two wives also, Ahinoam of Jezreel and Abigail of Carmel, Nabal's wife. And David brought up his men that were with him, each man with his household. And they lived in the cities of Hebron. And the men of Judah came. And they anointed David king over the house of Judah there. And they told David, saying, The men of Jabeshgilead were the ones who buried Saul. And David sent messengers to the men of Jabeshgilead. And he said to them, Blessed are you of the LORD, that you have shown this kindness to your lord, to Saul, and have buried him. And now may the LORD show kindness and truth to you. And I also will repay you this kindness, because you have done these things. Therefore now let your hands be strengthened, and be brave. For your master Saul is dead, and also the house of Judah have anointed me king over them. But Abner the son of Ner, captain of Saul's army, took Ishbosheth the son of Saul and brought him over to Mahanaim. And he made him king over Gilead, and over the Ashurites, and over Jezreel, and over Ephraim, and over Benjamin and over all Israel. — II Samuel 2:1-9.

The news of Saul's death had been received by the exiled David in characteristic fashion. He first flamed out in fierce anger against the lying Amalekite, who had hurried with the tidings, hoping to curry favor with him by pretending that he had killed Saul on the field of battle. A short shrift and a bloody end were his, And then the wrath gave place to mourning. Forgetting the mad hatred and relentless persecution of his late enemy, thinking only of the friendship of his earlier days and his official status as the anointed of the Lord, our hero cast over the mangled corpses of Saul and Jonathan the mantel of his noble elegy, in which he sings the praise of the one and celebrates the love of the other. Not until those offices of justice and affection had been performed, did he think of himself and the change which had been affected in his own fortunes.

It seems clear that David had never regarded Saul as standing between himself and the kingdom. The first reaction from his death was not, as it would have been with a less devout and less generous heart, a flush of gladness at the thought of the empty throne; but instead, a sharp pang of grief from the sense of an empty heart. And even when he began to comtemplate his immediate future and changed fortunes he carried himself with commendable self-restraint. At the time David was still a fugitive in the midst of the ruins of Ziklag, but instead of rushing ahead, "making the most of his opportunity," and seizing the empty throne, he sought directions from the Lord. Ah, we not only need to turn unto God in times of deep distress, but equally so when His outward providences appear to be working decidedly in our favour.

David would do nothing in this important crisis of his life — when all which had for so long appeared a distant hope, now seemed to be rapidly becoming a present fact — until his Shepherd should lead him. Impatient and impetuous as he was by nature, schooled to swift decisions, followed by still swifter actions, knowing that a blow struck speedily while all was chaos and despair in the kingdom, might at once set him on the throne; nevertheless, he held the flesh, carnal policy, and the impatience of his followers in check, to hear what God would say. To a man of David's experience it must have appeared that now was the opportune moment to subdue the remaining adherents of the fallen Saul, rally around himself his loyal friends, grasp the crown and the scepter, vanquish the gloating Philistines, and secure unto himself the kingdom of Israel. Instead, he refused to take a single step until Jehovah had signified *His will* in the matter.

The manner in which David conducted himself on this occasion presents an example which we do well to take to heart and punctually emulate. The important principle of action which was here exemplified has been well expressed by another: "If we would possess temporal things with a blessing, we must not eagerly seize upon them, nor be determined by favorable events or carnal counsel: but we must observe the rules of God's Word, and pray for His direction; using those means, and those only, which He has appointed or allowed, and avoid all evil, or 'appearance of evil,' in our pursuit of them: and then whatever else we fail in, we shall be directed in the way to the kingdom of heaven" (T. Scott). "Trust in the Lord with all thine heart; and lean not unto thine own understanding. In all thy ways acknowledge Him, and *He shall direct thy paths*" (Prov. 3:5, 6).

To "acknowledge" the Lord in all our ways means, that instead of acting in self-sufficiency and self-will, we seek wisdom from above in every undertaking of our earthly affairs, beg God to grant us light from His Word on our path, and seek His honor and glory in all that we attempt. Thus it was now with David: "And it came to pass after this, that David inquired of the Lord, saying, Shall I go up into any of the cities of Judah?" (2 Sam. 2:1). This is very blessed, and should be linked with all that was before us in 1 Sam. 30:6-31. What is here recorded of David supplies further proof of his having been restored from backsliding. Previously he had *left* the cities of Judah "inquiring" of his own heart (1 Sam. 27:1), but now he would only think of *returning* thither as God might conduct him. Alas, that most of us have to pass through many painful and humiliating experiences ere we learn this lesson.

"David inquired of the Lord, saying, Shall I go up into any of the cities of Judah?" Though the Lord had promised him the kingdom, though he had already been anointed by Samuel unto the same, and though Saul was now dead, David was not hasty to take matters into his own hands, but desired to submit himself unto God's directions and act only according to His revealed will. This evidenced the fact that he really trusted in Him who had promised him the kingdom, to give it to him in His own due time and manner; and thus he would possess it with a clear conscience, and at the same time avoid all those appearances of evil with which he might know the remaining adherents of Saul would be ready to charge him. So fully did he fulfill the word of his early Psalm: "my Strength! upon Thee will I wait" (59:9). We never lose anything, my reader, by believing and patiently waiting upon God; but we are always made to suffer when we take things into our own hands and rush blindly ahead.

"Shall I go up into any of the cities of Judah?" David was prepared to go where the Lord bade him. His particular inquiry about "the cities *of Judah*" was because that was his own tribe and the one to which most of his friends belonged. "And the Lord said, Go up": that is, from Ziklag into the territory of Judah, though He did not specify any particular city. This is usually the Lord's method: to first give us a *general* intimation of His will for us, and later more specific details little by little. He does not make known to us the whole path at once, but keeps us dependent upon Himself for light and strength, step by step. This is for our good, for our training, though it be a trying of our patience. Patience is a grace of great price in the sight of God, and it is only developed by discipline. May grace be diligently sought and divinely bestowed so that we shall heed that exhortation, "let patience have her perfect work" (James 1:4).

"And the Lord said unto him, Go up": the absence of anything more definite was a *testing* of David. Had the flesh been dominant in him at this time, he would have eagerly jumped to the conclusion that he was fully justified in leaving Ziklag immediately and taking prompt measures to obtain the kingdom. Blessed is it to see how he responded to the test: instead of rushing ahead, he continued to wait on the Lord for more explicit instructions, and asked, "*Whither* shall I go up?" (v. 1) — to which part of Judah, Jerusalem or where? He had paid dearly in the past for taking journeys which the Lord had not ordered, and for residing in places which He had not named for him; and now he desired to move only as God should appoint. Reader, have you yet reached this point in your spiritual experience: have you truly surrendered unto the lordship of Christ, so that you have turned over to Him the entire government and disposing of your life? If not, you know not how much peace, joy, and blessing you are missing.

"And He said, Unto Hebron" (v. 1). This is recorded for our encouragement. The Lord is never wearied by our asking! Nay, the more childlike we are, the better for us; the more we cast *all* our care upon Him (1 Pet. 5:7), the more we seek counsel of Him, the more He is honored and pleased. Has He not told us, "In *everything* by prayer and supplication, with thanksgiving let your requests be made known unto God" (Phil. 4:6)? That means just what it says, and we are greatly the losers, and God is dishonored, just in proportion to our disregard of that privilege and duty. The old hymn is true when it says, "O what peace we often forfeit, O what needless pains we bear, All because we do not carry, Everything to God in prayer." The readiness of Jehovah to respond unto David's inquiry, is a sure intimation of His willingness to hear us; for He is "The *same*, yesterday, and today, and forever."

"And He said, Unto *Hebron*." There is a spiritual beauty in this word which can only be perceived as we compare scripture with scripture. In the O. T. "Hebron" stands typically, for *communion*. This may be seen from the first mention of the word: "Then Abram removed his tent, and came and dwelt in the plain of Mamre, which is in Hebron, and built there *an altar* unto the Lord" (Gen. 13: 15). Again, "So he (Jacob) sent him (Joseph, on an errand of mercy to his brethren) out of the vale of Hebron" (Gen. 37:14) — figure of the Father sending the Son on a mission of grace unto His elect. "And they gave Hebron unto Caleb" (Judges 1:20): the place of fellowship became the portion of the man who followed the Lord "fully" (Num. 14:24). How fitting, then that the restored David should be sent back to "Hebron" — it is ever back unto *communion* the Lord calls His wandering child. O how thankful we should be when the Holy Spirit restores us to communion with God, even though it be at the cost of disappointment and sorrow (Ziklag) to the flesh.

"So David went up to Hebron" (2 Sam. 2:2). God had graciously granted him the needed word of guidance, and he followed out the same. O that all his actions had been controlled by the same rule: how much trouble and grief he had then escaped. But they were not; and this makes the more solemn the contrast presented in the next statement: "And his two wives also, Abinoam the Jezreelitess, and Abigail Nabal's wife the Carmelite" (v. 2). Here was the one blot on the otherwise fair picture: the lusts of the flesh obtruded themselves; yes, immediately after his having sought guidance from God! — what a warning for us: we are never safe a single moment unless upheld by the arm of Omnipotence. As we have seen in earlier articles, Divine chastisement was the sequel to what we read of in 1 Sam. 25:44, so now we may be assured that his retention of "two wives" omened ill for the future. The closing verses of our lesson show plainly that he missed God's best.

"And his men that were with him did David bring up, every man with his household: and they dwelt in the cities of Hebron" (v. 3). Those who had been David's companions in tribulation were not forgotten now that he was moving forward toward the kingdom. Blessed foreshadowment was this of, "If we suffer, we shall also reign with Him" (2 Tim. 2:12).

"And the men of Judah came, and there they anointed David king over the house of Judah" (v. 4). David had been *privately* anointed as Saul's successor (1 Sam. 16:12,13), now the principal princes in the tribe of Judah *publicly* owned him as their king. They did not take it upon themselves to make him king over all Israel, but left the other tribes to act for themselves. No doubt in this they acted according to the mind of David, who had no desire to force himself on the whole nation at once, preferring to obtain government over them by degrees, as Providence should open his way. "See how David rose gradually: he was first appointed king in reversion, then in possession of one tribe only, and at last over all the tribes. Thus the kingdom of the Messiah, the Son of David, is set up by degrees: He is Lord of all by Divine designation, but 'we see not *yet* all things put under Him': Heb. 2:8" (M. Henry).

"And David sent messengers unto the men of Jabesh-Gilead, and said unto them, Blessed by ye of the Lord, that ye have showed this kindness unto your lord, even unto Saul, and have buried him" (v. 5). David expressed his appreciation of what the men of Jabesh had done in rescuing the bodies of Saul and his sons from the Philistines, and for the kindly care they had taken of them. He pronounced the blessing of the Lord upon them, which probably means that he asked Him to reward them. By thus honouring the memory of his predecessor he gave evidence that he was not aiming at the crown from any principles of carnal ambition, or from any enmity to Saul, but only because he was called of God to it.

"And now the Lord show kindness and truth unto you: and I also will requite you this kindness, because ye have done this thing" (v. 6). David not only prayed God's blessing upon those who honoured the remains of Saul, but he promised to remember them himself when opportunity afforded. Finally, he bade them fear not the Philistines, who might resent their action and seek revenge — especially as they no longer had a head over them; but *he*, as king of Judah, would take their part and assist them: "Therefore now let your hands be strengthened and be ye valiant: for you master Saul is dead, and also the house of Judah have anointed me king over them" (v. 7). Thus did he continue to show his regard for the late king. By sending a deputation to Jabesh, David instituted a conciliatory measure toward the remaining adherents of Saul.

"But Abner the son of Ner, captain of Saul's host, took Ishbosheth the son of Saul, and brought him over to Mahanaim" (v. 8). This is a solemn "But," traceable, we believe, to the "two wives" of v. 2! David was not to come to the throne of all Israel without further opposition. Abner was general of the army, and no doubt desired to keep his position. He took Ishbosheth, apparently the only son of Saul now left, to Mahanaim, a city on the other side of the Jordan, in the territory of Gath (Josh. 13:24-26): partly to keep the men of Jabesh-Gilead in awe and prevent their joining with David, and partly that he might be at some distance both from the Philistines and from David, where he might mature his plans. "Ishbosheth" signifies "a man of shame": he was not considered fit to accompany his father to battle, yet was now deemed qualified to occupy the throne to the exclusion of David.

"And made him king over Gilead, and over the Ashurites, and over Jezreel, and over Ephraim, and over Benjamin, and over all Israel" (v. 9). The nation in general had rejected the "Judges" whom God had raised up for them, and had demanded a king; and now in the same rebellious spirit, they refused the prince which the Lord had selected for them. In type it was Israel preferring Barabbas to Jesus Christ. Abner prevailed till he got all the tribes of Israel, save Judah, to own Ishbosheth as their king. All this time David was quiet, offering no resistance: thus keeping his oath in 1 Sam. 24:21, 22!

"The believer's progress must be gradual: his faith and his graces must be proved, and his pride subdued, before he can properly endure any kind of prosperity: and for these purposes the Lord often employs the perverseness of his brethren, without their knowledge or contrary to their intention. In the professing church few honour those whom the Lord will honour: before Jesus came, and in each succeeding generation, the very builders have rejected such as Heaven intended for eminent situations; and His servants must be conformed to Him. Ambition, jealousy, envy, and other evil passions, cause men to rebel against the Word of God, but they generally attempt to conceal their real motives under plausible pretenses. The believer's wisdom, however, consists in waiting quietly and silently under injuries, and in leaving God to plead his cause, except it be evidently his duty to be active" (T.Scott).

Ishbosheth, Saul's son, was forty years old when he began to reign over Israel, and he reigned two years. But the house of Judah followed David. And the time that David was king in Hebron over the house of Judah was seven years and six months. And Abner the son of Ner, and the servants of Ishbosheth the son of Saul, went out from Mahanaim to Gibeon. And Joab the son of Zeruiah, and the servants of David, went out and met together by the pool of Gibeon. And they sat down, the one on the one side of the pool and the other on the other side of the pool. And Abner said to Joab, Let the young men now arise and play before us. And Joab said, Let them arise. Then there arose and went over twelve from Benjamin, who belonged to Ishbosheth the son of Saul, and twelve of the servants of David. And each one caught his fellow by the head, and thrust his sword in his fellow's side, so that they fell down together. Therefore that place was called the Field of Blades, which is in Gibeon. And there was a very grievous battle that day. And Abner and the men of Israel were beaten before the servants of David. And there were three sons of Zeruiah there, Joab and Abishai and Asahel. And Asahel was as light of foot as a wild roe. And Asahel ran after Abner, and in going he did not turn to the right hand or to the left from following Abner. Then Abner looked behind him and said, Are you Asahel? And he answered, I am. And Abner said to him, Turn aside to your right hand or to your left, and lay hold on one of the young men, and take his armor. But Asahel would not turn aside from following him. And Abner said again to Asahel, Turn aside from following me — why should I strike you to the ground? How then should I hold up my face to Joab your brother? However he refused to turn aside. So Abner struck him with the blunt end of the spear under the fifth rib, so that the spear came out behind him. And he fell down there and died in the same place. And everyone who came to the place, where Asahel fell down and died, stood still. Joab and Abishai also ran after Abner. And the sun went down when they had come to the hill of Ammah, which lies before Giah by the way of the wilderness of Gibeon. And the children of Benjamin gathered themselves together after Abner and became one troop and stood on the top of a hill. Then Abner called to Joab and said, Shall the sword devour forever? Do you not know that it will be bitterness in the latter end? How long shall it be then before you command the people to return from chasing their brothers? And Joab said, As God lives, unless you had spoken, surely then in the morning the people would have gone up each one from following his brother. So Joab blew a trumpet, and all the people stood still and did not pursue after Israel any more. And they did not fight any more. And Abner and his men walked all that night through the plain and passed over Jordan and went through all Bithron, and they came to Mahanaim. And Joab returned from following Abner. And when he had gathered all the people together, nineteen men and Asahel were missing from David's servants. But the servants of David had stricken three hundred and sixty men of Benjamin and of Abner's men, who died. And they took Asahel and buried him in the tomb of his father, which was in Bethlehem. And Joab and his men traveled all night, and they came to Hebron at the break of day. — II Samuel 2:9-32.

It is a wonderful thing when a wayward believer is brought back to the place of fellowship with God, as David had been, though it necessarily involves added obligations. It is *sin* which causes us to leave that place, and though at first sin be a sweet morsel unto the flesh, yet it soon turns bitter, and ultimately becomes as wormwood and gall unto him who has yielded to it. "The way of transgressors is hard" (Prov. 13:14): the wicked prove the full truth of that fact in the next world, where they discover that "the wages of sin is death" — a death agonizing in its nature and eternal in its duration. But even in this life the transgressor is usually made to feel the hardness of that way which his own mad self-will has chosen, and especially in this the case with the believer, for the harvest of *his* ill sowings is reaped — mainly, at least — in this world. The Christian, equally with the non-Christian, is a subject under the government of God, and *doubly* is *he* made to realize that God cannot be mocked with impunity.

Strikingly and solemnly was this fact exemplified in the history of Israel during O. T. times; *this* principle supplies the key to all God's governmental dealings with them. The history of no nation has been nearly so checkered as *theirs:* no people was ever so sorely and so frequently afflicted as the favoured descendants of Jacob. From the death of Joshua unto the days of Malachi we find one judgment after another sent from God upon them. Famines, pestilence, earthquakes, internal dissensions and external assaults from the surrounding nations, followed each other in rapid succession, and were *repeated* again and again. There were brief respites, short seasons of peace and prosperity, but for the most part it was one sore trouble after another. God did not deal *thus* with any other nation during the Mosaic economy. It is true that heathen empires suffered, and ultimately collapsed under the weight of their lasciviousness, but in the main God "suffered all nations to walk in their own ways" (Acts 14:16), and "the times of this ignorance God winked at" (Acts 17:30).

Far otherwise was it with His own covenant people. This has surprised many; yet it should not. Unto Israel God said, "You only have I known of all the families of the earth." Yes, and that has been commonly recognized by readers of the O. T., but what immediately follows has very largely been lost sight of — "*therefore* I will punish you for all your iniquities" (Amos 3:2). Ah, it was *not* "You only have I known of all the families of the earth, *therefore* will I *wink* at your sins, excuse *your* faults, and pass over your transgressions. No, no; far from it. It was unto Israel that God had revealed Himself, it was "in Judah He was known," and therefore would He manifest before their hearts and eyes His ineffable holiness and inflexible justice. Where they were loose and lax, despising God's authority, and recklessly and brazenly breaking His laws, He would *vindicate His honour* by making it appear how much He hated sin, and hates it most of all in those who are *nearest* to Him! See Ezek. 9:6!

That is why another of Israel's prophets announced unto those who had, under a temporal covenant, been taken into a bridal relation to Jehovah, "she hath received of the Lord's hand *double* for all *her* sins" (Isa. 40:2). Does that strike the reader as strange? But why should it? Are not the sins of the professing poeple of God *doubly heinous* to those committed by them who make no profession at all? What comparison was there between the sins of the nation of Israel and the sins of the heathen who were without the knowledge of the true God? The sins of the former were sins *against light,* against an open and written revelation from Heaven, against the abounding goodness and amazing grace of God toward them; and therefore must He, in His holiness and righteousness, make the severest example *of them.* Make no mistake upon that point: God will either be sanctified *by* or *upon* those who have been taken unto a place of (even outward) nearness to Himself: see Lev. 10:3.

Thus, Amos 3:2 becomes *a prophecy* of God's dealings with Christendom. The great difference which existed between the nation of Israel and the Gentiles, finds its parallel in this era between Christendom (the sphere where Christianity is professedly acknowledged) and the heathen world. But with this additional solemn consideration: increased privileges necessarily entail increased responsibilities. Under this Christian era a far higher and grander revelation of God has been made in and through and by the Lord Jesus Christ, than ever the *nation* of Israel had in O. T. times. If then Israel's *despising* of God in His inferior revelation was followed by such awful consequences to the temporal welfare of their people under the old covenant, what *must* be the consequences of the *despising* of God in His highest revelation under the new covenant? "See that ye refuse not Him that speaketh. For if they escaped not who refused Him that spake on earth, *much more* shall not we escape if we turn away from Him that speaketh from heaven" (Heb. 12:25).

But what has all the above to do with the life of David? Much every way. God dealt with individual saints, who had been taken into spiritual nearness to Himself on the same principles, governmentally, (that is, in the ordering of their temporal affairs), as He treated with the Nation as a whole, which enjoyed only outward nearness to Himself, Hence, *as* David sowed in his conduct so he reaped in his circumstances. As *we* have seen in the last few articles, God had acted in marvelous grace with the son of Jesse, and following his repentance and putting things right with the Lord, had unmistakably shown Himself strong on his behalf, ending by bringing him to "Hebron" which speaks of *fellowship.* Thus, David had now reached the point, where God said to him, as it were, "sin no more, *lest a worse thing come upon thee"* (John 5:14).

Should it be asked, "But what has all of this to do with us? *We* are living in the 'Dispensation of Grace,' and God deals with people now — both nations collectively, and saints individually — very differently from what He did in O. T. times." That is a great mistake: a glaring, and a horrible one. Glaring it certainly is, for Rom. 15:4 expressly states, "Whatsoever things were written *aforetime* were written for our learning": but what *could* we "learn" from the ways of God with His people of old if He is now acting from entirely different principles? Nothing whatever; in fact, in that case, the less we read the O. T., the less we are likely to be confused. Ah, my reader, in the N.T. also we read that "judgment must begin at *the house of God*" (1 Pet. 4:17). *Christians* are also warned, "Be not deceived, God is not mocked: for whatsoever a man soweth, that shall he also reap" (Gal. 6:7). Horrible too is such a mistake, for it represents the immutable God *changing* the principles of His government.

What has been pointed out in the above paragraphs is something more than an interesting and instructive item of historical information, explaining much that is to be met with in the O. T. Scriptures, throwing light upon God's dealings with the nation of Israel collectively and with its prominent men individually; it is also of vital moment *for Christians to day.* "Righteousness and judgment are the habitation" of God's "throne" (Psa. 97:2), and *our* temporal affairs are regulated and determined according to the same principles of God's moral government as were those of His people in by gone ages. If the distinguishing favours of God do not restrain from sin, they most certainly will not exempt us from Divine chastisement. Nay, the greater the Divine privileges enjoyed by us, the nearer we are brought unto God in a way of profession and favour, the more quickly will He notice our inconsistencies and the more severely will He deal with our sins.

"He that despised Moses' law died without mercy under two or three witnesses: of how much *sorer punishment,* suppose ye, shall he be thought worthy, who hath trodden under foot the Son of God, and hath counted the blood of the covenant, wherewith he was sanctified, an unholy thing, and hath done despite unto the Spirit of Grace?" (Heb. 10:28,29). Here is a statement of the broad principle which we have been seeking to explicate and illustrate. True, in this particular passage the application of it is made unto apostates, but the fact is plainly enough revealed that the greater the privileges enjoyed the greater the obligations entailed, and the greater the guilt incurred when those obligations are ignored. The same prinicple applies (though the consequences are different) in the contrast between the sins of the Christian and the non-Christian. The sins of the former are more heinous than those of the latter. How so? Because God is far more dishonoured by the sins of those who bear His name than by those who make no profession at all.

The same principle, as it applies to gradation by contrast, holds good of the individual Christian in different stages of his own life. The more light God gives him, the more practical godliness He requires from him; the more favours he receives and privileges he enjoys, the more responsible is he to bear increased fruit. So too a sin committed by him may receive comparatively light chastisement; but let it be repeated and he may expect the rod to fall more heavily upon him. In like manner, God may bear long with one of His backslidden children, and though the path of recovery be a thorny one, yet will he exclaim "I richly deserved far severer treatment." But when the backslider has been restored and brought back into communion with God, another departure from Him is likely to be attended with far worse consequences than the former one was.

"But there is forgiveness with Thee, that Thou mayest be *feared"* (Psa. 130:4). Yes, "feared," not trifled with, not that we may the more confidently give free rein to our lusts. A true apprehension of the Divine mercy will not embolden unto sin, but will deepen our hatred of it, and make us more earnest in striving to abstain from it. A spiritual apprehension of God's abounding grace toward us, so far from begetting carelessness, produces increased carefulness, lest we displease One so kind and good. It is just because the Christian has been sealed by the Spirit unto the day of redemption, that he is exhorted to watchfulness lest he "grieve" Him. The more the heart truly appreciates the infinitude of God's wondrous love unto us, the more will its language be, "How can I do this great wickedness against Him!"

"But there is forgiveness with Thee, that Thou mayest be feared." Not a slavish and servile fear, but the fear of the Lord which is "the beginning of wisdom": that fear which reverences, loves, worships, serves and obeys Him. Genuine gratitude for God's pardoning grace will move the soul unto suitable filial conduct: it works a fear of being carried away from the heavens of His conscious presence by the insidious current of worldliness. It is jealous lest anything be allowed that would mar our communion with the Lover of our souls. Where the pardoning mercy of God is thankfully esteemed by the soul, it calls to mind the fearful price which was paid by Christ so that God could righteously forgive His erring people, and *that* consideration melts the heart and moves to loving obedience.

"But there is forgiveness with Thee, that Thou mayest be feared." Yes, once more we say "feared," and not "trifled with." The word unto backsliders, who have been pardoned and graciously restored to fellowship with God, is, "Let them not *turn again* to folly" (Psa. 85:8): that is, let them beware of any cooling of their affections, and slipping back into their old ways; let them pray earnestly and strive resolutely against a sinful trading with God's mercy and a turning of His grace into lasciviousness. We serve a jealous God, and must needs therefore be incessantly vigilant against sin. If we are not, if we do "return again to folly," then most surely will His rod fall more heavily upon us; and not only will our inward peace be disturbed, but our outward circumstances will be made to sorely trouble us.

That principle was plainly enunciated in the threatening which the Lord made unto Israel of old: "And if ye will not be reformed by Me by *these* things, but will walk contrary unto Me; then will I also walk contrary unto you, and will punish you *yet seven times* for your sins" (Lev. 26:23,24). If the first sensible tokens of God's displeasure do not attain their end in the humbling of ourselves beneath His mighty hand and the reforming of our ways, if His lesser judgments do not lead to this, then He will surely send sorer judgments upon us. Ezra recognized this principle when, after the remnant had come out of Babylon, he said, "After all that is come upon us for our evil deeds, and for our great trespass, seeing that Thou our God hast punished us less than our iniquites deserved, and hast given us such deliverance as this; should we *again* break Thy commandments, and join these abominations? wouldest not Thou be angry with us till Thou hast consumed us, so that there should be no remnant nor escaping?" (9:13, 14). Then let *us* beware of trifling with God, particularly so after He has recovered us from a season of backsliding.

Instead of taking up the details of 2 Sam. 2:9-32 (the passage which immediately follows the verses considered in the preceding article), we felt this topical one would prove much more helpful in paving the way for those which are (D. V.) to follow. Those verses record an encounter between the rival factions. The gauntlet was thrown down by Abner, the general of the followers of Ishbosheth (Saul's son), and the challenge was accepted by Joab, who headed the military forces of David. Neither side brought their full army into the field, and the slaughter was but small (v. 30). The men of Abner, the aggressor, were routed, and at the close of the day their captain begged for peace (v. 26). Knowing the pacific intentions of David, and his lothness to make war upon the house of Saul, Joab generously called a halt (v. 28); and each side made their way homeward (vv. 29-32).

And now a word upon the title we have given to this article, and we must close. David was now located at Hebron, which signifies communion or fellowship. The men of Judah had made him their king (2 Sam. 2:4), which though a step toward it, was by no means the complete fulfilment of the promise that he should be king "over *Israel*" (1 Sam. 16:1, 13). David made kindly overtures unto "the men of Jabesh-Gilead," the followers of the late Saul (v. 5), expressing the hope they would now show fealty to him (v. 7). Would the Lord continue showing Himself strong on his behalf, by turning the hearts of the rival faction toward him? The need for this was evident (vv. 7-10), yet it was easy for God to heal that breach and give David favour in the eyes of all. Would He do so? How far will the present conduct of David warrant this? for God will not place a premium on sin. David was now *put to the test:* how he acquitted himself we must leave for the next section.

CHAPTER 3.

Now there was long war between the house of Saul and the house of David. But David became stronger and stronger, and the house of Saul became weaker and weaker. And sons were born to David in Hebron. And his first-born was Amnon, the son of Ahinoam of Jezreel. And his second was Chileab, of Abigail of Carmel, the wife of Nabal, And the third was Absalom, the son of Maacah the daughter of Talmai king of Geshur. And the fourth was Adonijah, the son of Haggith. And the fifth was Shephatiah, the son of Abital. And the sixth was Ithream, by Eglah, David's wife. These were born to David in Hebron. And while there was war between the house of Saul and the house of David, Abner made himself strong for the house of Saul. And Saul had a concubine whose name was Rizpah, the daughter of Aiah. And Ishbosheth said to Abner, Why have you gone in to my father's concubine? Then Abner was very angry for the words of Ishbosheth, and said, Am I a dog's head, who shows kindness against Judah this day to the house of Saul your father, to his brothers and to his friends, and have not delivered you into the hand of David? Am I a dog's head that you charge me today with a fault concerning this woman? So may God do to Abner, and more also, unless, as the LORD has sworn to David, even so I do to him — to transfer the kingdom from the house of Saul, and to set up the throne of David over Israel and over Judah, from Dan even to Beersheba. And he could not answer Abner a word again, because he feared him. And Abner sent messengers to David on his behalf, saying, Whose is the land? — saying also, Make your covenant with me, and, behold, my hand shall be with you, to bring about all Israel to you. And he said, Good! I will make a league with you, but one thing I ask of you. That is, that you shall not see my face unless you first bring Michal, Saul's daughter, when you come to see my face. And David sent messengers to Ishbosheth, Saul's son, saying, Deliver my wife Michal, whom I betrothed to me for a hundred foreskins of the Philistines. And Ishbosheth sent and took her from her husband, from Phaltiel the son of Laish. And her husband went along with her, weeping behind her, to Bahurim, Then Abner said to him, Go, return! and he returned. And Abner had a talk with the elders of Israel, saying, You sought for David in times past to be king over you. Now then do it, for the LORD has spoken of David, saying, By the hand of My servant David I will save My people Israel out of the hand of the Philistines, and out of the hand of all their enemies. And Abner also spoke in the ears of Benjamin. And Abner went also to speak in the ears of David in Hebron all that seemed good to Israel, and all that seemed good to the whole house of Benjamin. So Abner came to David at Hebron, and twenty men came with him. And David made a feast for Abner and the men who were with him. And Abner said to David, I will arise and go, and will gather all Israel to my lord the king, so that they may make a covenant with you, and so that you may reign over all that your heart desires. And David sent Abner away, and he went in peace. And, behold, the servants of David and Joab came from pursuing a troop. And they brought in a great spoil with them. But Abner was not with David in Hebron, for he had sent him away, and he had gone in peace. When Joab and all the army that was with him had come, they told Joab, saying, Abner the son of Ner came to the king, and he has sent him away, and he has gone in peace. Then Joab came to the king and said, What have you done? Behold, Abner came to you. Why is it that you have sent him away, and he has completely gone? You know Abner the son of Ner, that he came to deceive you, and to know your going out and your coming in, and to know all that you do. And when Joab had come out from David, he sent messengers after Abner, who brought him again from the well of Sirah. But David did not know it. And when Abner had returned to Hebron, Joab took him aside in the gate to speak with him quietly. And he struck him there under the fifth rib, so that he died, for the blood of Asahel his brother. And afterward when David heard, he said, My kingdom and I are guiltless before the LORD forever from the blood of Abner the son of Ner. Let it rest on the head of Joab, and on all his father's house. And let there not fail from the house of Joab one who has an issue, or who is a leper, or who leans on a staff, or who falls on the sword, or who lacks bread. So Joab and Abishai his brother killed Abner, because he had slain their brother Asahel at Gibeon in the battle. And David said to Joab and to all the people who were with him. Tear you clothes and gird yourselves with sackcloth and mourn before Abner. And king David followed the bier. And they buried Abner in Hebron. And the king lifted up his voice and wept at the grave of Abner. And all the people wept. And the king mourned over Abner and said, Did Abner die like a fool dies? Your hands were not bound, or your feet put into fetters – as a man falls before wicked men, so you fell. And all the people wept again over him. And when all the people came to David to eat food while it was still day, David swore, saying, So let God do to me, and more also, if I taste bread or anything else until the sun is down. And all the people took notice, and it pleased them, as whatever the king did pleased all the people. For all the people and all Israel understood that day that it was not of the king to kill Abner the son of Ner. And the king said to his servants, Do you not know that there is a prince and a great man fallen this day in Israel? And I am weak this day, though anointed king. And these men, the sons of Zeruiah, are too hard for me. The LORD shall reward the doer of evil according to his wickedness. – II Samuel 3.

And when Saul's son heard that Abner was dead in Hebron, his hands were feeble, and all the Israelites were troubled. And Saul's son had two men that were captains of bands. The name of the one was Baanah, and the name of the other was Rechab, the sons of Rimmon of Beeroth, of the children of Benjamin. For Beeroth also was counted to Benjamin, and the men of Beeroth fled to Gittaim and were strangers there until this day. (And Jonathan, Saul's son, had a son who was lame in his feet. He was five years old when the news of Saul and Jonathan came out of Jezreel. and his nurse took him up and fled. And as she made haste to flee, he fell and became lame. And his name was Mephibosheth.) And Rechab and Baanah, the sons of Rimmon of Beeroth, went and came about noon to the house of Ishbosheth, who lay in a bed at noon. And they came there into the midst of the house, as though they would have brought wheat. And they struck him under the fifth rib. And Rechab and his brother Baanah escaped. For when they came to the house, he lay in his bed in his bedroom. And they struck him and killed him and beheaded him and took his head and got away through the plain all night. And they brought the head of Ishbosheth to David at Hebron. And they said to the king, Behold, the head of Ishbosheth the son of Saul, your enemy who sought your life! And the LORD has avenged my lord the king to day of Saul and of his seed. And David answered Rechab and his brother Baanah, the sons of Rimmon of Beeroth. And he said to them, As the LORD lives, who has redeemed my soul out of all adversity, when one told me, saying, Behold, Saul is dead, thinking to have brought good news, I took hold of him and killed him in Ziklag — which was the reward I gave him for his news. How much more, when wicked men have slain a righteous person in his own house on his bed? Shall I not therefore now require his blood of your hand and take you away from the earth? And David commanded his young men, and they killed them and cut off their hands and their feet. And they hanged them up over the pool in Hebron. But they took the head of Ishbosheth and buried it in the tomb of Abner in Hebron. — II Samuel 4.

In our last article (so far as the application of the principles enunciated therein related to him who is the principal subject of this series) we endeavoured to show that very much hinged on the manner in which David now conducted himself. A most important crisis had been reached in his life. The time which he spent at Hebron constituted the dividing-line in his career. On the one side of it was what we may designate as the period of his rejection, when the great majority of the people clave unto Saul, who hounded him from pillar to post; on the other side of it, was the period of his exaltation when he reigned over the nation. When pondering the different events which happened in the first stage of his career, we sought to point out the moral connection between them, seeking to trace the relation between the personal conduct of David and the various circumstances which the governmental dealings of God brought about as the sequel. We propose, by Divine aid, to follow a similar procedure in taking up the details under the second stage of his career.

In article 20 we saw how David displeased the Lord by his taking unto himself two wives (1 Sam. 25:43,44), and in article 22 we noticed how one sin led to another; while in article 24 we observed the Divine chastisement which followed. In article 26 we dwelt upon David's putting things right with God and encouraging himself in the Lord, following which we traced out the blessed results which ensued (articles 27, 28), terminating in his being restored to full fellowship with the Lord, as was typified by God's directing him to "Hebron." There he received a "token for good" (Psa. 86:17) in the reception which he met with from the men of his own tribe, who came and "anointed David over the house of Judah" (2 Sam. 2:4): that was indeed a promising intimation that if his ways continued to please the Lord, He would make "even his enemies to be at peace with him" (Prov. 16:7). On the other hand, that "token for good" only becomes the more solemn in the light of all that follows.

How much there is in the later chapters of 2 Sam. which makes such pathetic and tragic reading. Few men have experienced such sore social and domestic trials as David did. Not only was he caused much trouble by political traitors in his kingdom, but, what was far more painful, the members of his own family brought down heavy grief upon him. His favourite wife turned against him (6:20-22), his daughter Tamar was raped by her half brother (13:14), his son Ammon was murdered (13:28,29). His favourite son Absalom sought to wrest the kingdom from him, and then he was murdered (18:14). Before his death, another of his sons, Adonijah, sought to obtain the throne (1 Kings 1:5), and he too was murdered (1 Kings 2:24,25). Inasmuch as the Lord never afflicts willingly (Lam. 3:33), but only as our sins occasion it, how are these most painful family afflictions to be accounted for?

If the Holy Spirit has been pleased to furnish us with any explanation of the sore trials which David encountered in his later life, or if He has supplied us with materials that serve to throw light upon what is recorded in the second half of 2 Sam., then that explanation must be sought for or that illuminating material must be enquired after, in the *early* chapters of that book. That is a principle of great importance in order to a right understanding of the Scriptures. As a general rule, God hangs the key for us right on the door itself: in other words, the opening chapters (often the first verses) contain a clear intimation or forecast of what follows. True, in some cases, this is more apparent than in others, yet concerning each one of the sixty-six books of the Bible, it will be found that the closer be the attention given unto its introduction, the easier will it be to follow the development of its theme. Such is obviously the case here in 2 Sam.

"Now there was long war between the house of Saul and the house of David: but David waxed stronger and stronger, and the house of Saul waxed weaker and weaker" (2 Sam. 3:1). The battle referred to at the end of the previous chapter, though it went so greatly in favour of David, did not put an end to the warfare between him and Ishbosheth. Though Saul himself was no more, yet his son and subjects refused to quietly submit to David's sceptre. For another five years they continued to manifest their defiance, and many were the skirmishes which took place between his men and the loyal subjects of David. The latter was loth to employ harsh measures against them, and probably his magnanimity and mildness were mistaken for weakness or fear, and encouraged his opponents to renew their efforts for his overthrow. But little by little they were weakened, until Ishbosheth was willing to make a league with David.

"Now there was long war between the house of Saul and the house of David: but David waxed stronger and stronger, and the house of Saul waxed weaker and weaker." The contents of this verse may well be taken as a type of the conflict which is experienced in the heart of the Christian. David, exalted to be king over Judah, may be regarded as a figure of one of God's elect when he has been lifted out of the miry clay (into which the fall of Adam plunged him) and his feet set upon the Rock of ages. As 1 Sam. 2:8 declares, "He raiseth up the poor out of the dust, and lifteth up the beggar from the dunghill, to set them among princes, and to make them inherit the throne of glory." But is all now henceforth peace and joy? Far from it. Inward corruption is there, and is ever assailing the principle of grace which was imparted at regeneration: "the flesh lusteth against the spirit, and the spirit against the flesh" (Gal. 5:17). What is the outcome? Is the flesh victorious? No, it may annoy, it may win minor skirmishes, but little by little the flesh is weakened and the spirit strengthened, until at the last sin is completely destroyed.

"Now there was long war between the house of Saul and the house of David." Thus the kingdom of Israel was rent asunder by civil war. That it should last so long, when David was clearly in the right, has presented quite a problem to the commentators. Personally, we regard the contnets of this verse as a plain intimation *that David was missing God's best.* This is an expression we use rather frequently in these pages, so perhaps a definition of it here will not be amiss. For the benefit of our Calvinistic friends (and the editor is not ashamed to confess that he is a "high Calvinist"), let it be pointed out that it is by no means equivalent to affirming that God's counsels may be thwarted by us. No indeed, puny man can no more defeat the eternal purpose of the Almighty than he can cause the sun to cease from shining or the ocean from rolling. "But our God is in the heavens: He hath done *whatsoever* He hath pleased" (Psa. 115:3).

There is a vast difference between the *promises* of God and His eternal *decrees:* many of the former are conditional, whereas the latter are immutable, dependent upon nothing for their fulfilment save the omnipotence of God. In saying that many of the Divine promises recorded in Holy Writ are "conditional" we do not mean they are uncertain and unreliable, no; we mean that they are infallible declarations of what God will do or give *providing* we follow a certain course of conduct: just as the Divine threatenings recorded in Scripture are declarations of what God will do or inflict *if* a certain course be pursued. For example, God has declared "Them that honour Me, I will honour" (1 Sam. 2:30). But suppose we *fail* to "honour" God, suppose we do not obtain that enabling grace which He is ever ready to give unto those who earnestly seek it in a right way — what then? The same verse tells us: "And they that despise Me shall be lightly esteemed."

Take for instance the declaration made in Josh. 1:8, "This book of the law shall not depart out of thy mouth; but thou shalt meditate therein day and night, that thou mayest observe to do according to all that is written therein: for *then* thou shalt make thy way prosperous, and *then* thou shalt have good success." First, let it be pointed out that that verse has nothing whatever to do with the eternal destiny of the soul; instead, it relates only to the present life of the saint. In it God tells us that *if* we give His holy Word the first place in our thoughts and affections, and regulate both our inner and outer life by its teaching, *then* He will make our way "prosperous" and we shall have "good success." This does not mean that we shall become millionaires, but that by heeding the rules of His Word, we shall escape those rocks upon which the vast majority of our fellows make shipwreck, and that the *blessing of God* will rest upon our lives in all their varied aspects and relations; an all-wise and sovereign God determining both the kind and measure of the "success" which will be most for His glory and our highest good.

Nor are the principles enunciated in Josh. 1:8 to be restricted in their application to those who lived under the old covenant: inasmuch as the governmental ways of God remain the same in all ages, those principles hold good in all dispensations. From the beginning of human history it has always been true, and to the end of history it will continue so to be, that "no good thing will He withhold from *them that walk uprightly*" (Psa. 84:11). On the other hand, it is equally a fact that those who are not subject to God's Word, who follow instead the devices of their own hearts and give way to the lusts of the flesh, suffer adversity and come under the rod of Divine chastisement; of them it has to be said, "Your sins have withholden good things from you" (Jer. 5:25). In other words, they have missed God's best: not that they have failed to obtain any blessing which He had eternally decreed should be theirs, but they have not entered into the good of what God's Word promises should be the *present* portion of those who walk in obedience thereto.

"O that My people had hearkened unto Me, and Israel had walked in My ways! I should soon have subdued their enemies, and turned My hand against their adversaries. The haters of the Lord should have submitted themselves unto Him: but their time should have endured forever. He should have fed them also with the finest of the wheat; and with honey out of the rock should I have satisfied thee" (Psa. 81:13-16). What could be plainer than that! Those verses need present no difficulty to the high Calvinist, nor is there anything in them which will support the Arminian delusion that having created men free moral agents, God is unable to do with and for them what he desires, without reducing them to mere machines. This passage is not treating of the eternal counsels of God, but of His governmental dealings with men in this life.

The key to the above verses is found in their immediate context: "But My people would not hearken to My voice; and Israel would none of Me. So I gave them unto their own hearts' lust; and they walked in their own counsels" (Psa. 81:11, 12). The children of Israel walked contrary — not to the eternal purpose of Jehovah, but — to His revealed will. They would not submit to the rules laid down in God's Word, but in their self-will and self-pleading determined to have their own way; in consequence, *they missed God's best for them in this life.* Instead of His subduing their enemies, He allowed those enemies to subdue them; instead of providing abundant harvests, He sent them famines; instead of giving them pastors after His own heart, He suffered false prophets to deceive.

Many more are the passages which might be quoted from the Old and N.T. alike, which set forth the same great fact, warning us that if we walk contrary to the Scriptures we shall certainly suffer for it, both in soul and body, both in our estate and circumstances, in this life; failing to enter into those blessings — spiritual and temporal — which the Word promises to those who are in subjection to it. That is as true today as it was under the old economy, and it supplies the key to many a problem, and explains much in God's governmental dealings with us. It certainly supplies the key to David's life, and explains why the chastening rod of God fell so heavily upon himself and his family. Bear in mind carefully what has been said above, read the passage which now follows, and then there is no reason why we should be surprised at all that is found unto the end of 2 Sam.

"And unto David were sons born in Hebron: and his first born was Ammon, of Ahinoam the Jezreelitess. And his second, Chileab, of Abigail the wife of Nabal the Carmelite; and the third, Absalom, the son of Maacah the daughter of Talmai, king of Geshur. And the fourth, Adonijah the son of Haggith; and the fifth, Shephatiah the son of Abital. And the sixth, Ithream, by Eglah David's wife. These were born to David in Hebron" (2 Sam. 3:2-5). In the light of all that has been said in the preceding article and in this one up to here, there is little need for us to attempt any lengthy comments upon these unpleasant verses. Here we see David giving way to the lust of the flesh, and practicing polygamy; and as he sowed to the flesh in his family life, so in the flesh he reaped corruption in his family. Three of the above-mentioned sons were murdered!

The subject of polygamy as a whole is too large a one for us to deal with here, nor can we discuss it at length as it bore upon the lives of the different patriarchs. God's original creation of only one man and one woman indicated from the beginning that monogamy was the Divine order for man to heed (Matt. 19:4,5). The first of whom we read in Scripture that had more wives than one, was Lamech (Gen. 4:19), who was of the evil line of Cain. And while Moses, because of the hardness of Israel's heart (Matt. 19:8) introduced the statute of divorce, yet nowhere did the Mosaic law sanction a plurality of wives. The limitation of one wife only is plainly suggested by such scriptures as Prov. 5:18 and 18:22.

"Thou shalt in any wise set him king over thee, whom the Lord thy God shall choose; one from among thy brethren shalt thou set king over thee: thou mayest not set a stranger over thee, which is not thy brother. But he shall not multiply horses to himself. . .*neither shall he multiply wives to himself,* that his heart turn not away" (Deut. 17:15-17). Here was a definite and express law which the *kings* of Israel were required to obey, and thereby set before their subjects an example of sobriety and marital fidelity. And this was the commandment which David so flagrantly disobeyed, for no sooner was he anointed "king over the house of Judah" (2 Sam. 2:4), than he began to *multiply* "wives" unto himself (3:2-5). Not only so, but when Abner sought to make a league with him, David laid it down as a condition that his first wife, Michal, who had been given to another man (1 Sam. 25:44) must be restored to him (2 Sam. 3:13), which was an open violation of Deut. 24:1-4.

A little later on we read, "And David took him more concubines and wives out of Jerusalem, after he was come from Hebron" (2 Sam. 5:13). Here, then was David's besetting sin, to which he yielded so freely — little wonder that his son Solomon followed in his footsteps! And a Holy God will not tolerate evil, least of all in those whom He has made leaders over His people. Though in the main David's life was pleasing to God, and though he was endowed with so many spiritual excellencies, yet there was this one sad weakness. His giving way to it brought down long and severe chastenings, and the record of it as a whole — the sowing and the consequent reaping — is for our learning and warning. Learn, then, dear reader, that even when restored from backsliding and brought back to fellowship with God, your only safety lies in earnestly crying to Him daily "Hold Thou me up, and I shall be safe" (Psa. 119:117).

Then all the tribes of Israel came to David to Hebron. And they spoke, saying, Behold, we are your bone and your flesh. Also in time past, when Saul was king over us, you were he who led Israel out and brought them in. And the LORD said to you, You shall feed My people Israel, and you shall be a captain over Israel. So all the elders of Israel came to the king at Hebron. And king David made a covenant with them in Hebron before the LORD. And they anointed David king over Israel. David was thirty years old when he began to reign, and he reigned forty years. In Hebron he reigned over Judah seven years and six months, and in Jerusalem he reigned thirty-three years over all Israel and Judah. — II Samuel 5:1-5.

Inasmuch as it is not our design to write a verse by verse commentary on the books of Samuel, but rather to study the life of David, we pass over what is found in the remainder of 2 Sam. 3 and 4 and come to the opening verses of chapter five. In the interval between what was before us in our last article and the incident we are now to contemplate, the providence of God has been working on David's behalf. His principal opponents had met with a summary and tragic end, and the way was now cleared for the purpose of God concerning our hero, to receive its accomplishment. Viewing him typically, it is indeed striking to observe how that David's path to the throne was marked by *bloodshedding*. From the human side, Saul, Jonathan, and later, Ishbosheth, stood in the way, and none of them died a natural death; by the hand of violence was each one removed!

We cannot regard as accidental, or as a trivial detail, what has just been pointed out above. There is nothing trivial in the imperishable Word of God: everything recorded therein has a profound significance, if only we have eyes to see it. Here, the deeper meaning of these details is not hard to discern: David, in all the essential features of his history (his failures excepted), foreshadowed the Lord Jesus, and, as we know, *His* path to the throne was a long one of bloodshedding. True, the Lord Jesus was "born King of the Jews," as David also had been born into the royal tribe of Judah. True, Christ had been "anointed" (Matt. 3; Acts 10:38), prophet, priest, and king, years before His coronation; as David also had been "anointed" to the royal office (1 Sam. 16:13). Yet, it was not until after His precious blood was shed at Calvary, that God exalted Christ to be a "Prince" unto the *spiritual* "Israel" (Acts 2:36; 5:31); as it was not until after the bloodshedding of Saul, Jonathan, and Ishbosheth, that David became king.

Upon the death of Abner and Ishbosheth the tribes of Israel were left without a leader. Having had more than sufficient of the rule of Saul and Ishbosheth over them, they had no inclination to make a further experiment by setting another of Saul's family on the throne, and having observed the prosperous state of Judah under the wise and benign government of David, they began to entertain higher and more honourable thoughts of the "man after God's own heart." That illustrates an important principle in God's dealings with those whom He has marked out for salvation. There has to be a turning from Satan unto God, from the service of sin unto subjection to Christ. *That* is what true conversion is: it is a change of masters: it is a saying from the heart, "O Lord our God, other lords besides Thee have had dominion over us; but by *Thee only* will we make mention of Thy name" (Isa. 26:13).

But conversion is preceded by conviction. There is wrought in the soul a dissatisfaction with the old master, before there is begotten desires towards the new Master. Sin is made to be realized as a bitter thing, before there is an hungering and thirsting after righteousness. The cruel bonds of Satan must be felt, before there is any longing to be made free by Christ. The prodigal son was made to feel the wretchedness of the far country, before he had any thought of journeying toward the Father's house. Clearly is this principle exemplified and illustrated in the case of these men who now sought unto David, desiring that he should be king over them. They had had more than enough of what the prophet Samuel had faithfully warned them (1 Sam. 8:11-18)! They had no desire for any other of the house of Saul to reign over them, but were now desirous of submitting themselves to *David's* scepter.

Unspeakably blessed, then, is the typical picture here presented to our view. In the voluntary coming unto David of those men of the different tribes, following their unhappy lot under the reigns of Saul and Ishbosheth, we have adumbrated the outcome of the Holy Spirit's operations in the hearts of God's elect when He draws them to Christ. He first makes them discontented with their present lot. He gives them to realize there is no real and lasting satisfaction to be found in the service of sin and in continuing to follow a course of opposition to God and His Christ. He creates within the soul an aching void, before He reveals the One who alone can fill it. In short, He makes us thoroughly discontented with our present portion before He moves us to seek the true riches. The Hebrews must be made to groan under their merciless taskmasters in Egypt, before they were ready to start out for the promised land.

"Then came all the tribes of Israel to David unto Hebron, and spake, saying, Behold, we are thy bone and thy flesh. Also in time past, when Saul was king over us, thou wast he that leddest out and broughtest in Israel: and the Lord said to thee, Thou shalt feed My people Israel, and thou shalt be a captain over Israel. So all the elders of Israel came to the king to Hebron; and king David made a league with them in Hebron before the Lord: and they anointed David king over Israel" (2 Sam. 5:1-3). Ah, note well the opening word, "Then": after a period of no less than seven and a half years since the death of Saul: v. 5.

After the death of the apostate king, and following David's recognition by the royal tribe, "It might have been expected that all Israel would have been ready to welcome him. Had it not long ago been declared by the lips of Samuel, that God had forsaken the house of Saul? Had not this been acknowledged by Saul himself? Had not God by the destruction on Gilboa, finally set His seal to the truth of His denunciations? And was it not evident, that the strength and blessing that had departed from Saul, had accompanied the dishonoured sojourn of David in the wilderness? The might of Israel was there. There were they who were able to break through the host of the Philistines, and to draw from the well of Bethlehem, when Bethlehem and its waters were in the grasp of the enemy. There too, was the Psalmody of Israel. And yet, despite every indication that God had given — careless alike of the tokens of His favour towards David, and of His displeasure towards themselves — the tribes of Israel continued to reject the chosen servant of God; and Judah only welcomed him.

"The son of Saul, though feeble and unknown, was preferred to David; and David left the wilderness, only to be engaged in a long and destructive struggle with those who should have welcomed him as the gift of God for their blessing. So slowly does the hand of God effectuate its purposes — so resolute are men in refusing to recognize any thing save that which gratifies the tendencies of their nature, or approves itself to the calculation of their self-interest. For seven years and six months, Abner and all the tribes of Israel fiercely assailed David: and yet afterwards, they were not ashamed to confess, that they knew that David was he whom God had destined to be the deliverer of Israel. They knew this, and yet for seven years they sought to destroy him; and no doubt, all the while, spoke of themselves, and were spoken of by others, as conscientious men fulfilling an apprehended duty in adhering to the house of Saul. So easy is it to speak well of evil, and to encourage iniquity by smooth words of falsehood.

"At last, however, God accomplished the long cherished desire of His servant's heart — the desire that He had Himself implanted — and David became the head and governor of Israel" (B. W. Newton). Yes, at last the hearts of these rebels were subdued; at last they were willing to submit themselves unto David's scepter. Ah, note well dear reader, *the particular character* in which David was owned by them: "thou shalt be a *captain over Israel.*" As we have pointed out in the introductory paragraphs, the surrender of the men of the eleven tribes unto David, was a type of the sinner's *conversion.* This presents to us a vital and fundamental aspect of salvation which has wellnigh disappeared from modern "evangelism." What is conversion? true and saving conversion, we mean. It is far, far more than a believing that Jesus Christ is the incarnate Son of God, and that He made an atonement for our sins. Thousands believe that who are yet dead in trespasses and sins!

Conversion consists not in believing certain facts or truths made known in Holy Writ, but lies in the complete surrender of the heart and life to a Divine person. It consists in a throwing down of the weapons of our rebellion against Him. It is the total disowning of allegiance to the old master — Satan, sin, self, and a declaring "we *will* have this Man to reign over us" (Luke 19:14). It is owning the claims of Christ and bowing to His rights of absolute dominion over us. It is taking His yoke upon us, submitting unto His scepter, yielding to His blessed will. In a word, it is "receiving Christ Jesus *the Lord*" (Col. 2:6), giving Him the throne of our hearts, turning over to Him the control and regulation of our lives. And, my reader, nothing short of this is a Scriptural *conversion:* anything else is a make-believe, a lying substitute, a fatal deception.

In the passage now before us, these Israelites, who had for so long resisted the claims of David, serving under the banner of his adversary instead, now desired the king of Judah to be *their* king. It is evident that a great change had been *wrought in them* — wrought in them by God, though He was pleased to use circumstances to incline toward or prepare for that change: we purposely qualify our terms, for it should be quite obvious that no mere "circumstances" could have wrought *such* a change in their attitude toward the ruler of God's appointment, unless He had so "used" or influenced them by the same. So it is in connection with conversion: the distressing "circumstances" of a sinner may be used of the Spirit to convict him of the vanity of everything beneath the sun, and to teach him that no real heart satisfaction is to be found in mere *things* — even though those "things" may be an earthly mansion, with every thing in it that the flesh craves; but He must perform a miracle of grace within the soul before any descendant of Adam is willing to pay full allegiance to Christ as *King!*

"Behold, we are thy bone, and thy flesh" (v. 1). What a precious line in our typical picture is this! After conviction and conversion follows spiritual illumination. The Holy Spirit is given to glorify Christ: to take of the things concerning Him and reveal them to those whom He draws to the Saviour (John 14:16). After a soul has been brought death unto life by His mighty and sovereign operations, the Spirit of God *instructs* him; shows him the marvelous relation which Divine grace has given him to the Redeemer. He discovers to him the glorious fact of his *spiritual union* with Christ, for "he that is *joined to the Lord* in one spirit" (1 Cor. 6:17). He reveals to the quickened children of God's family the amazing truth that they are members of that mystical Body of which Christ is the Head, and thus we are "members of His body, of His flesh, and of *His bones*" (Eph. 5:30).

It is precious to see that these words of all the tribes of Israel, "we are thy bone and thy flesh," were used by them *as a plea.* They had long ignored his rights and resisted his claims. They had been in open revolt against him, and deserved nought but judgment at his hands. But now they humbled themselve before him, and pleaded their near relation to him as a reason why he should forgive their ill-usage of him. They were his brethren, and on that ground they sought his clemency. And *this* is the very ground on which the Spirit-instructed believer sues for mercy from God in Christ. "Forasmuch then as the children are partakers of flesh and blood, He also Himself likewise took part of the same. . . Wherefore in all things it behooved Him to be made like unto His brethren that He might be a merciful and faithful high priest" (Heb. 2:14, 17). What confidence does the apprehension of this impart to the penitent heart of the Satan-harassed and sin-distressed saint!

O dear Christian reader, beg God to make this transcendant and precious fact more real and moving to thy heart. The Saviour is not one who, like the cherubin and seraphim, is far removed from thee in the scale of being. True, He *is* very God of very God, the Creator of the ends of the earth, the King of kings and Lord of lords, but he is *also* one who was "born of woman," who became Man, who is bone of thy bone, and flesh of thy flesh, and therefore "He is not ashamed to call us *brethren*" (Heb. 2:11). And for the same reason He can be touched with the feeling of our infirmities" (Heb. 4:15), and "in that He Himself hath suffered being tempted, He is able to succour them that are tempted" (Heb. 2:18). Then hesitate not to approach Him with the utmost freedom and pour out thy heart unreservedly before Him. He will not reprove thee any more than David did his erring brethren. Take full encouragement from this endearing relation: we are the *brethren* of Christ; He is our *kinsman* Redeemer!

"Also in time past, when Saul was king over us, thou wast he that leddest out and broughtest in Israel; and the Lord said to thee, Thou shalt feed My people Israel, and thou shalt be a captain over Israel" (v. 2). This too is very blessed when we look through the type to the antitype. These humbled revolters now praised David for his *former* services, which before they had overlooked; and now acknowledged the Lord's appointment of him, which before they had resisted. So it is in the experience of the converted. While in the service of Saul (Satan) we have no appreciation of the work Christ has done and no apprehension of the position of honour to which God has elevated Him: the depths of humiliation into which the Beloved of the Father entered and the unspeakable suffering which He endured on behalf of His people, melted not our hearts; nor did the scepter which He now wields bring us into loving subjection to Him. But conversion alters all this!

But more: "the Lord said to thee, thou shalt feed My people Israel, and thou shalt be a captain over Israel." They not only praised David for his former services, but recognizing him as the Divinely appointed *shepherd* of Israel they determined to put themselves under his protection, desiring that he would rule over them in tenderness and righteousness, for their safety and comfort, and that he would lead them forth to victory over his enemies. This too finds its counterpart in the history of those who are truly converted: they realize they have many foes, both within and without, which are far too powerful for them to conquer, and therefore do they "commit the keeping of their souls *to Him*" (1 Pet. 4:19), assured that "He is able to keep. . .against that Day" (2 Tim. 1:12). Yes, He who is bone of our bone and flesh of our flesh is *"mighty* to save," "able to save unto the uttermost them that come unto God by Him" (Heb. 7:25).

1 Chron. 12:23-40 supplies fuller light upon the opening verses of 2 Sam. 5. There we are shown not only the numbers which came unto David from each tribe, and with what zeal and sincerity they came, but also *the gracious reception they met with*. The one whom they had so grievously wronged did not

refuse to accept them, but instead gave them a hearty and royal welcome: "And there they were with David three days (typically, now on *resurrection* ground), eating and drinking" (v. 39) — at perfect ease in his presence; "for there was *joy* in Israel" (v. 40). Blessed be God, the Saviour of sinners has declared, "All that the Father giveth Me shall come to Me; and him that cometh to Me I will in no wise cast out" (John 6:37). Hallelujah!

The long-hunted exile has now been elevated to the throne: his principal enemies are in their graves, and David is exalted over the kingdom of Israel. There is not a little in the opening chapters of 2 Sam. which we have passed over, as being outside the scope of this series of papers; yet they record several details that present some lovely traits in the character of our hero. As we have previously pointed out, the news of the death of Saul and Jonathan was received by David with no carnal joy, but instead with magnanimous grief (2 Sam. 1:17). He had never regarded the apostate king and her favourite son as standing between him and the kingdom, and his first feeling on their fall was not — as it had been in a less generous heart — a flush of gladness at the thought of the empty throne, but instead a sharp pang of pain that the anointed of God had been grievously dishonoured and degraded by the enemies of Israel (2 Sam. 1:20).

Even when he began to contemplate his new prospects, there was no hurried taking of matters into his own hands, but instead, a calm and reverent inquiring of the Lord (2 Sam. 2:1). He would do nothing in this crisis of his fortunes, when all which had been so long a hope seemed to be nearing its realization, until his Shepherd should lead him. Curbing his naturally impetuous disposition, refusing to take swift action and subdue his remaining opponents, holding in check the impatient ambitions of his own loyal followers, he waited to hear what *God* had to say. Few men have exercised such admirable self-restraint as David did under the circumstances which confronted him when his long-persecuting oppressor was no longer there to contest the field with him. Blessedly did he fulfill the vow of earlier years: "my Strength! upon Thee will I wait" (Psa. 59:9).

Even before the death of Saul, the strength of David's forces had been rapidly increased by a constant stream of fugitives from the confusion and misery into which the kingdom had fallen. Even Benjamin, Saul's own tribe, sent him some of its famous archers — a sure token of the king's waning fortunes. The hardy men of Manasseh and Gad, "whose faces were like the faces of lions, and were as swift as roes upon the mountains" (1 Chron. 12:8) sought his standard; while from his own tribe recruits "day by day came to David to help him, until it was a great host like the host of God" (1 Chron. 12:22). With such forces, it is evident that he could easily and quickly have subdued any scattered troops of the former dynasty. But he made no such attempt, and took no measures whatever to advance any claims to the crown. He preferred God to work out things *for* him, instead of *by* him!

When he was settled at Hebron he followed the same trustful and patient policy, not merely for a few days or weeks, but for a period of upwards of seven years. The language of the history seems to denote a disbanding of his army, or at least to their settling down to domestic life in the villages around Hebron, without any thought of winning the kingdom by force of arms. His elevation to the partial monarchy which he at first possessed was not from his own initiative, but was from the spontaneous act of "the men of Judah" who came to him and anointed him "king over the house of Judah" (1 Sam. 2:4). Then followed a feeble but lingering opposition to David, headed by Saul's cousin Abner, rallying around the late king's incompetent son Ishbosheth, whose name significantly means "man of shame."

The brief narrative which we have of the seven years spent by the still youthful David at Hebron, presents him in a very loveable light. The same gracious temper which had marked his first acts after Saul's death is strikingly brought out in 2 Sam. 2:2-4. "He seems to have left the conducting of the (defensive) war altogether to Joab, as though he shrank from striking any personal blow for his own advancement. When he did interfere, it was on the side of peace, to curb and chastise ferocious vengeance and dastardly assassination. The incidents recorded all go to make up a picture of rare generosity, of patiently waiting for God to fulfill His purposes, of longing that the miserable strife between the tribes of God's inheritance should end. He sends grateful messages to Jabesh-Gilead; he will not begin the conflict with the insurgents. The only actual fight recorded is provoked by Abner, and managed with unwonted mildness by Joab.

"The generosity of his nature shines out again in his indignation at Joab's murder of Abner, though he was too meek to avenge it. There is no more beautiful picture in this life than that of his following the bier where lay the bloody corpse of the man who had been his enemy ever since he had known him, and sealing the reconciliation which Death even makes in noble souls, by the pathetic dirge he chanted over Abner's grave (3:31). We have a glimpse of his people's unbounded confidence in him, given incidentally when we are told that his sorrow pleased them, 'as whatsoever the king did pleased all the people' (3:36). We have a glimpse of the feebleness of his new monarchy as against the fierce soldier who had done so much to make it, in his acknowledgment that he was yet weak (3:39)" (Alex. Maclaren).

The final incident of David's reign over Judah in Hebron was his execution of summary justice upon the murderers of the poor puppet-king Ishbosheth (4:12), upon whose death the whole resistance to David's power collapsed. Immediately after, the elders of all the tribes came up to Hebron, with the tender of the (5:1-3). They offered it upon the triple grounds of kingship, of his military service in Saul's reign, and of the Divine promise of the throne. A solemn pact was made, and David was "anointed" in Hebron "king over Israel": a king not only by Divine right, but also a constitutional monarch, chosen by popular election, and limited in his powers. The *evangelical* significance of this event we considered in the preceding article; other points of interest connected therewith are now to engage our attention.

This crowning of David king over all Israel was, first, the fulfilment of one of the great prophecies of Scripture. "Judah, thou art he whom thy brethren shall praise: thy hand shall be in the neck of thine enemies; thy father's children shall bow down before thee" (Gen. 49:8). Let it be carefully noted that the clause "thy hand shall be in the neck of thine enemies" is placed *between* "thy brethren shall praise thee" and "thy father's children shall bow down before thee"; and that immediately following this, Judah's victories over the enemies of God's people is again pointed out: "Judah is a lion's whelp: from the prey, my son, thou art gone up" (v. 9).

The above prophecy intimated the exalted position which Judah, when compared with the other tribes, was to occupy: Judah was to be the fore-champion in Israel's warfare against their enemies, God having empowered him with conquering power over the foes of his kingdom. The commencement of this in the life of David is plainly intimated in 2 Sam. 5:1-3. David's hand had been "in the neck of Israel's enemies": seen in his memorable victory over Goliath, the Philistine giant; following which we observe the begun-fulfillment of "thy brethren shall praise thee" in the song of the women, "Saul hath slain his thousands and David his ten thousands" (1 Sam. 18:6). So also here in 2 Sam. 5 the elders of the eleven tribes "bowed down before him" when they nominated him their king, and that, specifically, in view of the fact that he had triumphantly led out and brought in Israel's army in times past (v. 2)!

This leads us, in the second place, to contemplate the coronation of David as a blessed foreshadowment of the exaltation of his greater Son and Lord. This is so obvious that there is little need for us to amplify it at much length — though the interested reader would find it profitable to prayerfully trace out for himself other details in it. The life and activities of David are plainly divided into two main parts, though the second part was of very much longer duration than the first: thus it is also in the mediatorial work of Him whom he pointed to. In the first section of his career, he who was born at Bethlehem (1 Sam. 16:1) and "anointed" of God (16:13), wrought some mighty works (1 Sam. 17:34-36, 49) which clearly demonstrated that the Lord was with him: for the antitype see Luke 2:11, Acts 10:38). The fame of David was sung by many, which stirred up the jealousy and enmity of the ruling power (1 Sam. 18:7, 8): for the antitype see Matt. 21:15!

The enmity of Saul against David was exceeding bitter, so that he thirsted for his blood (1 Sam. 18:29): compare Matt. 12:14. From that time forth David became a homeless wanderer (1 Sam. 22:1): compare Matt. 8:20. A little company of devoted souls gathered around him (1 Sam. 22:2), but the nation as a whole despised and rejected him: compare John 1:11, 12. This was the period of his *humiliation,* when the anointed of God suffered privation and persecution at the hands of his enemies. True, he could (as we have seen above) have taken matters into his own hands, and grasped the kingdom by force of arms; but he steadily refused to do so, preferring to meekly and patiently wait *God's* time for him to ascend the throne: compare Matt. 26:52. In these and many other respects, our hero blessedly foreshadowed the character and career of his suffering but greater Son and Lord.

But the time had now arrived when the season of David's humiliation was over, and when he entered into that position of *honour and glory* which God had long before ordained for him: "they anointed David king over Israel" (2 Sam. 5:3). In his coronation we have a precious adumbration of the ascension of Christ, and His exaltation unto "the right hand of the Majesty on high" (Heb. 1:3), when He "took upon Him the form of a servant" and "made Himself of no reputation" was "highly exalted" and given "a Name which is above every name" (Phil. 2:7-10). As we are told in Acts 5:31 "Him hath God exalted with His right hand to be *a Prince* and a Saviour, for to give repentance to (the spiritual) Israel." The recorded deeds of David after he came to the throne, which will come before us (D. V.) in the articles to follow, also strikingly prefigured the work and triumphs of our exalted and glorified Redeemer.

And now, in the third place, let us inquire, How did the fugitive bear this sudden change of fortune? What were the thoughts of David, what the exercises of his heart, now that this great dignity, which he never sought, became his? The answer to our question is supplied by Psa. 18 which (see the superscription) he "spoke in the day that the Lord delivered him from *all* his enemies, and from the hand of Saul," that is, when the Lord brought to an end the opposition of Saul's house and followers. In this Psalm the Holy Spirit has recorded the breathings of David's spirit and graciously permits us to learn of the first freshness of thankfulness and praise which filled the soul of the young king upon his accession to the throne. Here we are shown the bright spiritual beginnings of the new monarchy, and are given to see how faithfully the king remembered the vows which as an exile had been mingled with his tears.

"It is one long outpouring of rapturous thankfulness and triumphant adoration, which streams from a full heart in buoyant waves of song. Nowhere else, even in the Psalms — and if not there, certainly nowhere else — is there such a continuous tide of unmingled praise, such magnificence of imagery, such passion of love to the delivering God, such joyous energy of conquering trust. It throbs throughout with the life-blood of devotion. All the terror, and pains, and dangers of the weary years — the black fuel for the ruddy glow — melt into warmth too great for smoke, too equable to blaze. The plaintive notes that had so often wailed from his heart, sad as if the night wind had been wandering among its chords, have all led up to this rushing burst of full-toned gladness. The very blessedness of heaven is anticipated, when sorrows gone by are understood and seen in their connection with the joy to which they have led, and are felt to be the theme for deepest thankfulness" (A. Maclaren).

It is blessed to note that this 18th Psalm is entitled, "A Psalm of David, the *servant* of the Lord," upon which C. H. Spurgeon remarked, "David, although at this time a king, calls himself "the servant of the Lord,' but makes no mention of his royalty: hence we gather that he counted it a higher honour to be the Lord's servant than to be Judah's king. Right wisely did he judge. Being possessed of poetical genius, he *served* the Lord by composing this Psalm for the use of the Lord's house." We cannot here attempt a full analysis of its contents, but must glance at one or two of its more prominent features.

The first clause strikes the keynote: "I will love Thee, O Lord, my strength." "That personal attachment to God, which is so characteristic of David's religion, can no longer be pent up in silence, but gushes forth like some imprisoned stream, broad and full even from its wellhead" (A. Maclaren). Scholars have pointed out that the intensity of David's adoration on this occasion moved him to employ a word which is never used elsewhere to express man's emotions towards God, a word so strong that its force is but feebly expressed if we render it "*from my heart* do I love Thee." The same exalted spiritual fervour is seen again in the loving accumulation of Divine names which follow — no less than eight are used in v. 2! — as if he would heap together in a great pile all the rich experiences of that *God* (which all names utterly fail to express) which he had garnered up in his distresses and deliverances.

In vv. 3 and 4 David recalls pathetically the past experiences when, like an animal caught in the nets, those who hunted him so relentlessly were ready to close in upon and seize their prey. "In his distress," he says, "I called upon the Lord and cried unto my God" (v. 4). Though it was but the call of one weak solitary voice, unheard on earth, it reached Heaven, and the answer shook all creation: "He heard my voice out of His temple:. . .Then the earth shook and trembled" (vv. 6, 7 etc.). One saint in his extremity put in motion the mighty powers of Omnipotence: overwhelming is the contrast between cause and effect. Wonderful as the greatness, equally marvelous is the swiftness of the answer: "*Then* the earth shook."

It is blessed to note how David ascribes *all* to the power and grace of the Lord. "For *by Thee* I have run through a troop; and by my God have I leaped over a wall. . .It is *God* that girdeth me with strength, and maketh my way perfect. . . Thou hast also given me the shield of Thy salvation: and Thy right hand hath holden me up, and Thy gentleness hath made me great. . .It is *God* that avengeth me, and subdueth the people under me . . . .Therefore will I give thanks unto Thee, O Lord, among the heathen, and sing praises unto Thy name. Great deliverance giveth He to His king; and showeth mercy to His anointed, to David, and to his seed for evermore" (vv. 29, 32, 35, 47, 50).

And the king and his men went to Jerusalem, to the Jebusites, the people of the land, who spoke to David, saying, Unless you take away the blind and the lame, you shall not come in here — thinking, David cannot come in here. But David took the stronghold of Zion — the same is the city of David. And David said on that day, Whoever gets up to the watercourse and smites the Jebusites, and the lame and the blind who are hated of David's soul, shall be chief and captain — because they said, The blind and the lame shall not come into the house. So David lived in the fort and called it the city of David. And David built all around, from Millo and inward. And David went on and became great, and the LORD God of hosts was with him. And Hiram king of Tyre sent messengers, and cedar trees, and carpenters, and masons to David. And they built David a house. And David saw that the LORD had established him king over Israel, and that He had made his kingdom sure for His people Israel's sake. And David took more concubines and wives out of Jerusalem, after he had come from Hebron. And there were still more sons and daughters born to David. These are the names of those who were born to him in Jerusalem — Shammua, and Shobab, and Nathan, and Solomon, also Ibhar, and Elishua, and Nepheg, and Japhia, and Elishama, and Eliada and Eliphalet. — II Samuel 5:6-16.

In 2 Sam. 5:6-9 a brief record is given of David wresting the stronghold of Zion out of the hands of the Canaanites, and of his making it the capital of his kingdom. This, it is to be noted, is the first thing recorded of our hero after all the tribes of Israel had made him their king. By noting that order we obtain the key to the typical significance of the incident which is now to be considered by us. In the previous article we pointed out that the coronation of David, after the season of his humiliation, was a beautiful foreshadowing of the exaltation of his Son and Lord, the enthronement on High of that blessed One who had been, in the main, despised and rejected by men on the earth. It therefore follows that the noble exploits of David after he came to the throne, strikingly prefigured the work and triumphs of our ascended and glorified Redeemer. It is thus, by looking beneath the mere historical upon the pages of the O. T., that we discover "in the volume of the Book" it is written of *Christ*.

The long-cherished desire of David's heart — implanted there by God Himself — had been accomplished, and he was now the head and governor of Israel. His real work had only just commenced, his most glorious achievements were still to be accomplished. His being crowned king over all Israel was but preparatory unto the royal conquests he was to make. His previous exploits only served to manifest his qualifications for the honoured position and the important work which God had appointed him. So it was with the Antitype. The enthronement of the Mediator at the right hand of the Majesty on high was but the introduction to the stupendous undertaking which God had assigned Him, for "He must reign till He hath put all enemies under His feet" (1 Cor. 15:25) — a very plain intimation that His "reign" has already commenced. The life-work, death, and resurrection of the Lord Jesus, simply laid the foundation upon which His royal conquests are now being achieved.

It is a great and serious mistake made by many to suppose that the Lord Jesus is now *inactive,* and to regard His being "seated" as denoting a state of inertia — such Scriptures as Acts 7:55 and Rev. 2:1 ought at once to correct such an idea. The word "sat" in scripture marks an end *and a beginning:* the process of preparation is ended, and the established order is begun (cf. Gen. 2:2; Acts 2:3) We say again that the real work of Christ (His atonement but laying the foundation thereof) began only after He was invested with "all power (i. e. 'authority') in heaven and in earth" (Matt. 28:18). This was plainly announced in the Messianic Psalms: after God has set His king upon His holy hill of Zion, He was to ask of Him and the heathen would be given Him for His inheritance, and He would reign over them with a "rod of iron" (Psa. 2). "*Rule* Thou in the midst of Thine enemies," was the Father's word to Him (Psa. 110).

To His chosen servants the Lord Jesus declared "Lo, I am with you alway, unto the end of the world" (Matt. 28:20). On the day of Pentecost Peter declared, "Therefore being by the right hand of God exalted, and having received of the Father the promise of the Holy Spirit, *He* (Jesus) hath shed forth this, which ye now see and hear" (Acts 2:33). Later, we are told, "they went forth, and preached everywhere, *the Lord working with them*, and confirming the Word with signs following" (Mark 16:20). There is much in the book of Revelation which makes known to us the various activities in which the ascended Saviour is engaged, into which we cannot enter. But sufficient has here been produced to show that the King of saints is now wielding His mighty scepter to good effect.

Most blessedly was that which has been before us above typed out by the crowned David. Upon his ascension to the throne he was far from indulging in ease of self-luxuriation. It was now that his best achievements were accomplished. In that section of 2 Sam. which we are entering we behold David capturing the stronghold of Zion, vanquishing the Philistines, providing a resting-place for the holy ark, and being concerned in building a temple for the worship of Jehovah. So blessed is each of these incidents, so rich is their typical and spiritual import, that we purpose, the Lord enabling, to devote an article unto the separate consideration of each of them. May the Spirit of Truth graciously undertake for both writer and reader, giving us eyes to see and hearts to appreciate the "wondrous things" hidden away in this portion of God's Holy Word.

"And the king and his men went to Jerusalem, unto the Jebusites" (v. 6). "If Salem, the place which Melchizedek was king of, was Jerusalem (as seems probable from Psa. 76:2), it was famous in Abraham's time; Joshua in his times found it the chief city of the south part of Canaan: Josh. 10:1,3. It fell to Benjamin's lot (Josh. 18:28), but joined close to Judah's (Josh. 15:8). The children of Judah had taken it (Judges 1:8), but the children of Benjamin suffered the Jebusites to dwell among them (Judges 1:21). Now the very first exploit David did after he was anointed king over all Israel, was to gain Jerusalem out of the hands of the Jebusites; which, because it belonged to Benjamin, he could not well attempt till that tribe, which long adhered to Saul's house, submitted to him" (Matt. Henry).

"And the king and his men went to Jerusalem unto the Jebusites, the inhabitants of the land: which spake unto David, saying, Except thou take away the blind and the lame, thou shalt not come in hither: thinking, David cannot come in hither (v. 6). The wording of the second half of this verse appears rather ambiguous, and we believe the translation given in the "Companion Bible" is to be preferred, "thou shalt not come hither, for the blind and the lame shall drive thee away." It was the language of utter contempt. The Jebusites were so assured of the impregnability of their stronghold that they considered the feeblest of their men would be quite sufficient to defend it against any attack of David and his army.

The "Jebusites" were Canaanites who inhabited the country surrounding Jerusalem, and who occupied the fortress of Zion. The tribe of Judah had once failed to drive them out (Josh. 15:63), and later the children of Benjamin met with no more success (Judges 1:21). So secure did they now deem themselves that when David purposed its capture, they met him with insulting ridicule. In this we have an illustration of the fact that the enemies of God are often most confident of their strength when the day of their fall is most imminent. Thus also it frequently appears in the history of the salvation of God's elect: their case seems to be the most hopeless immediately before the hand of Divine mercy snatches them as brands from the burning. Thus it was with the dying thief, delivered at the eleventh hour; with Saul of Tarsus, as he was persecuting the church; with the Philippian jailor, as he was on the point of committing suicide. Man's extremity is God's opportunity.

"Nevertheless, David took the stronghold of Zion: the same is the city of David" (v. 7). The literal or material "Zion" was a steep hill which lay just outside Jerusalem, to the south west, on which had been built a fortress to protect the city. It had two heads or peaks: Moriah, on which the temple was afterwards erected, and the other on which was built the future residence of the kings of Israel. So steep and inaccesible was Zion that, like a smaller Gibraltar, it had remained in the hands of Israel's foes. But undeterred by the natural difficulties and unmoved by the contemptuous confidence of the Jebusites, David succeeded in wresting it from the enemy, and became the founder of that Jerusalem which existed from that time onwards.

"Nevertheless David took the stronghold of Zion: the same is the city of David." Previously, he had reigned for seven years over Judah "in Hebron" (v. 5), but now that he had been anointed king over all Israel he cast his eyes toward Jerusalem, as a preferable metropolis, and a more suitable seat of his extending empire. But as long as the hill of Zion was occupied by the military Jebusites, they would retain their command of the lower city. His first step, therefore, was, by the help of God, to dispossess the enemy of their stronghold. There David henceforth dwelt, as a conqueror, as in a castle (1 Chron. 11:7); there he fixed his royal abode, and there he swayed his scepter over the whole land of Israel, from Dan to Beersheba.

"So David dwelt in the fort, and called it the city of David. And David built round about from Millo and inward" (v. 9). Millo seems to have been the townhall, or statehouse, a place of public convention (compare 2 Kings 12:20, 2 Chron. 32:5). Around Millo David erected such buildings as became his capital or seat of government, for the reception of the court which he kept. "And David went on and grew great, and the Lord God of hosts was with him" (v. 10). The tide of fortune had turned, and the once despised fugitive now waxed great in power and reputation, in wealth and honour, subduing his enemies, and enlarging his dominion. But all his success and prosperity was entirely owing to Jehovah showing himself strong on his behalf: without His enablement, none of us can accomplish anything good: John 15:5.

Now there would be little or no difficulty in our perceiving the typical significance of the above were it not that so many of our minds have been blinded by the errors of modern "dispensationalism." A careful study of the connections in which "Zion" is found in the Psalms, and Prophets, makes it clear that "Zion" was the name by which the O. T. Church was usually called. "For the Lord hath chosen Zion; He hath desired it for His habitation. This is My rest forever: here will I dwell; for I have desired it. I will abundantly bless her provision: I will satisfy her poor with bread. I will also clothe her priests with salvation: and her saints shall shout aloud for joy. There will I make the horn of David to bud: I have ordained a lamp for Mine Anointed" (Psa. 132:13-17). Let the dubious (and also the interested) reader ponder such verses in Psa. 74:2; 87:5; 102:13; 128:5; 133:3; Isa. 51:16.

The O. T. Church was designated "Zion" after the mount on which the Temple was built, whither the tribes of Israel went up to worship Jehovah, who dwelt between the cherubim. This name was duly transferred to the N. T. Church, which is grafted into the Old, as the teaching upon the "olive" tree in Rom. 11 shows, and as the Holy Spirit in Eph. 2:19-22 and 3:6 expressly states. Such passages as Rom. 11:26 (note carefully it is *out* of Sion" and *not* "unto Sion");

Heb. 12:22; 1 Pet. 2:6; Rev. 14:1, make it plain that the N.T. Church is denominated "Sion," for the Church is now God's abode upon earth, His "temple" (2 Cor. 6:16), His "city" (Eph. 2:19), His "Jerusalem" (Gal. 4:26 — "which is above" is not to be understood astronomically, but means "which *excells*"). Thus, all that is spoken of "Zion," of "the city of God," of "Jerusalem" in the O. T. in a *spiritual* way belongs unto Christians now, and is for their faith to appropriate and enjoy.

The history of Jerusalem and Zion (for they are inseparably connected) accurately foreshadowed what is found spiritually in the antitype. The first reference to the same in Scripture presents that city as being under the benign sceptre of Melchizedek (Gen. 14:18): so, originally, the Church was blest with all spiritual blessings in Christ (Eph. 1:3). But, next, we see this city no longer in subjection to the servant of God, but fallen into the hands of the heathen: so the Church apostatised in Adam, God's elect sinking to the natural level of the non-elect. Zion now became inhabited by a race who were under the curse of God (Gen. 9:25): so, in consequence of the Fall, God's elect were by nature "the children of wrath even as others" (Eph. 2:3). For centuries Zion refused to be subject unto the people of God (Josh. 15:63; Judges 1:21); so the Gentiles were "aliens from the commonwealth of Israel" etc. (Eph. 2:11, 12).

But, eventually, Zion was subdued and captured by David, and made his royal residence, the Temple also being erected upon one of its mounts. Thus the stronghold of the enmey was converted into a habitation of God, and became the throne of His government upon earth. Wondrous figure was this of Christ's conquest of the *Gentile Church* (Acts 15:14) unto Himself, wresting it out of the hand of the Enemy, bringing it into subjection unto Himself, and setting up His throne in the hearts of its individual members. Announcement to this effect was made by the Saviour when He delcared, in view of His immediate death (v. 32), "Now shall the Prince of this world be cast out" (John 12:31). Satan was to be dethroned and driven from his dominion, so that Christ would "draw" unto Himself many of those over whom the Devil had reigned (Eph. 2:2). It is to be noted that the tense of the verb there denotes that the "casting out" of Satan would be as *gradual* as the "drawing" (Alford).

At the Cross the Lord Jesus "spoiled principalities and powers," and at His ascension He "made a show of them openly, triumphing over them in it" (Col. 2:15 and cf. Eph. 4:8). At Calvary Satan's hold over the world was broken: "the Prince of this world is judged" (John 16:11). Then it was that the "strong man" (the devil) was "overcome" by One stronger than himself, his armour being taken from him, and his "spoils" (captives) divided (Luke 11:21, 22). And a *manifestation* of this fact is made every time an elect soul is "delivered from the power of darkness and translated into the kingdom of God's dear Son" (Col. 1:13). Christ's frequent casting out of demons from the bodies of men during the days of His flesh presaged His delivering the souls of His redeemed from the dominion of Satan during this Gospel era.

That which our present type sets forth is not the Lord Jesus paying the ransom-price for the purchase of His people (particularly, those among the *Gentiles*), but His actual redeeming or delivering them from the power of the enemy. As David's capture of Zion *followed* his coronation, so that work his conquest prefigured pointed to the victorious activities of Christ *after* His ascension. It is that which was foretold in Psa. 110:1-3. First, "Sit Thou at My right hand." Second, "The Lord shall send the rod of Thy strength (the Gospel in the power of the Spirit) out of Zion." Third, "Thy people shall be willing in the day of Thy power." One by one those whom the Father gave to Christ are subdued by His grace, made willing to throw down the weapons of their warfare against His Son, and His throne is set up in their hearts (2 Cor. 10:5).

It is beautiful to note that the meaning of the word Zion is "sunny" or "shone upon," as facing the south, basking the rays of the warm sun. So the spiritual Zion, delivered by Christ (through His post-ascension activities) from the dominion of Satan, has been brought into the unclouded favour of God. The type is completed by what we read of in 2 Sam. 5:11, "And Hiram king of Tyre sent messengers to David, and cedar trees, and carpenters, and masons: and they built David a house." In the sending of those messengers to David by *Hiram*, proffering to build him a house, we have the foreshadowment of Christ's being acknowledged by the *Gentiles* (cf. Isa. 60:3), and their being built into His spiritual house (Eph. 2:22; 1 Pet. 2:5).

But when the Philistines heard that they had anointed David king over Israel, all the Philistines came up to seek David. And David heard and went down to the hold. The Philistines also came and spread themselves in the valley of Rephaim. And David inquired of the LORD, saying, Shall I go up to the Philistines? Will You deliver them into my hand? And the LORD said to David, Go up! For I will surely deliver the Philistines into your hand. And David came to Baal-perazim, and David struck them there, and said, The LORD has broken forth on my enemies before me, like the breaking forth of waters. Therefore he called the name of that place Baal-perazim. And there they left their images, and David and his men burned them. And the Philistines came up still again and spread themselves in the valley of Rephaim. And when David inquired of the LORD, He said, You shall not go up, but go around behind them and come upon them over across from the mulberry trees. And when you hear the sound of marching in the tops of the mulberry trees, then you shall stir yourself — for then the LORD shall go out before you to strike the army of the Philistines. And David did so, as the LORD had commanded him. And he struck the Philistines from Geba until you come to Gazer. — II Samuel 5:17-25.

"But when the Philistines heard that they had anointed David king over Israel, all the Philistines came up to seek David" (2 Sam. 5:17). The civil war in Israel, which had continued for several years, having been brought to an end, and the whole nation being now united under the government of David, he had thereby become much more powerful. Probably hearing, too, of David's capture of Jerusalem (v. 7) and of the friendship shown him by Hiram king of Tyre (v. 11), the Philistines now thought it was high time to bestir themselves and put an end to his prowess. Accordingly they assembled a great army against him, but were overthrown, though not annihilated.

The typical significance of the above (by which we mean its prophetic and dispensational foreshadowings) points to much that is recorded in the book of Acts, which, in turn, presages that which was to obtain more or less throughout the whole of this Christian era. As soon as the kingdom of Christ had been set up in the world, it was vigorously attacked by the powers of darkness, which, by the combined forces of Jews and Gentiles, sought to overthrow it. Definite proof of this is found in Acts 4, where we read of the arrest of Peter and John, their being summoned before the Sanhedrin, being threatened by them, and subsequently released. On returning to their own company and reporting their experiences, they all "with one accord" quoted from the second Psalm, which some — probably with good reason — conclude was written by David just after his victory over the Philistines.

That part quoted from the second Psalm was, "Why did the heathen rage, and the people imagine vain things? The kings of the earth stood up, and the rulers were gathered together against the Lord, and against His Christ" (Acts 4:25, 26). This is a clear intimation from the Spirit Himself that the substance of these verses is by no means to be restricted unto the opposition made by the powers of evil (through their human emissaries) against Christ personally during the days of his flesh, but include also Christ mystical, His Church, and is a prophetic intimation of the continuous enmity of the Serpent against the woman's Seed, i. e., Christ and His people. But as the remainder of the second Psalm shows, all such opposition will prove futile, for "He must reign till He hath put all enemies under His feet" (1 Cor. 15:25).

In this article, however, we do not propose to develop at length the prophetic application of David's victories over the Philistines, but rather shall we endeavor to concentrate upon the spiritual and practical bearings of the same. Surely *this* is what our poor hearts stand most in need of in this "cloudy and dark day" — that which, under God's blessing, will better equip us to fight the good fight of faith; that which will instruct and encourage for running the race that is set before *us*. There is a "time" and "season" for everything. While it is our happy privilege to admire and study the handiwork of God in creation, yet neither the pleasure of beholding the beautiful flowers nor investigating the mystery of the planets would be in order if an enemy were at our doors, and we were called upon to defend our lives. The same principle applies to concentrating upon one or more of the many different departments of Scripture study.

It was to carry forward the conquest of Canaan — begun by Joshua, but long interrupted (see Judges 1:21-36) that God had raised up David. "And Abner had communicated with the elders of Israel, saying, Ye sought for David in times past to be king over you: now then do it; for the Lord hath spoken of David, saying, By the hand of My servant David I will save My people Israel out of the hand of the Philistines, and out of the hand of all their enemies" (2 Sam. 3: 17, 18). Chief among Israel's enemies were the Philistines. They had long been a serious menace to God's people, and eventually succeeded in slaying Saul and his sons (1 Sam. 31:1-6). But now the time had come for God to stain their pride, fight against them, and overthrow their forces. "The triumphing of the wicked is short" (Job. 20:5): so discovered Pharaoh, Haman, Rabshakeh, Nero; and so shall it be with those who now oppose the Lord and His people.

"But when the Philistines heard that they had anointed David king over Israel, all the Philistines came up to seek David" (2 Sam. 5:17). First of all let us behold and admire here the providential dealings of God: "For of Him, and through Him, and to Him are all things" (Rom. 11:36). Nothing happens by chance in this world, and the actions of the wicked are just as truly controlled, yea, and directed, by the Governor of this world, as are those of the righteous. It was of the Lord that these Philistines threatened Israel at this time, and therein we may perceive His grace toward His servant. They were the enemies of Jehovah, and belonged to the people He had commanded Israel to destroy. But to take the initiative against them, David might feel was the height of ingratitude, for on two occasions the Philistines had given him protection when sorely persecuted by Saul (1 Sam. 27:1-3; 28:1,2). By God's moving the Philistines to take the initiative, David's scruples were subdued.

Though David had ascended the throne of Israel, this did not deter his former enemies; rather did it excite their jealousy and stirred them up to come against him. Therein we may find an illustration of Satan's ways against the saints. Whenever an advance step is taken for God, or whenever honour is put upon the true King and Christ is given His proper place in our arrangements, the enemy is on hand to oppose. Let Abraham return unto "the place of the altar" and at once there is strife between his herdsmen and those of Lot (Gen. 13:4-7). Let Joseph receive a Divine revelation in a dream, and immediately the cruel envy of his brethren is stirred against him (Gen. 37). Let Elijah triumph over the false prophets upon Carmel, and Jezebel threatens his life. Many such cases are also found in the book of Acts. These are recorded for *our* instruction. To be forewarned is to be forearmed.

Let, then, the attack of the Philistines upon David right after his coronation *warn us* against finding security in any spiritual prosperity we may have been blest with. High altitudes are apt to make the head dizzy. No sooner had David made Zion his own city, and that to the glory of the Lord, than the Philistines came up against him. The very next words after the boastful "Lord, by Thy favour Thou hast made *my* mountain to stand *strong,*" are, "Thou didst hide Thy face, and I was troubled" (Psa. 30:7). Our "strength" is to maintain a conscious *weakness* (2 Cor. 12:10). Every spiritual advance needs to be accompanied by watchfulness and prayer. "Let not him that girdeth on his armour boast himself as he that putteth it off" (1 Kings 20:11)!

"The Philistines also came and spread themselves in the valley of Rephaim" (v. 18). The valley of Rephaim was but a very short distance from Jerusalem: no doubt the Philistines expected to make themselves masters of that strategic city before David had time to complete the fortification of it. In the words "spread themselves" indication is given that their force was a large one: *"all* the Philistines" (v. 17) probably denotes that their five principalities (1 Sam. 6:16, 18) were here combined together. Little did they realize that they were rushing onward to their destruction, for they knew not the might of David's scepter nor the power of Jehovah who had exalted him. The Philistines were unaware of the fact that the living God was *for* David, as He had not been for Saul.

Let us now consider David's response unto the threatening presence of the Philistine hosts. "And David enquired of the Lord, saying, Shall I go up to the Philistines? Wilt Thou deliver them into mine hand?" (v. 19). This is very blessed, accentuated by the final clause in v. 17, which is in marked contrast from what is recorded in v. 18: in the one we read "and David heard of it, and *went down* to the hold"; in the other we are told that the Philistines "came and *spread themselves* in the valley of Rephaim." In sharp antithesis from the self-confident Pharisees, David took a lowly place and evidenced his dependence upon God. Instead of accepting their challenge and immediately engaging them in battle, David turned to the Lord and inquired *His* will for him. O that writer and reader may cultivate this spirit more and more: it is written "In all thy ways *acknowledge Him*", and the promise is, "And he shall direct thy paths" (Prov. 3:6).

"And David inquired of the Lord, saying, Shall I go up to the Philistines? wilt Thou deliver them into mine hand"? Not as the mighty man of valour did he impetuously rush ahead, but as the man submissive to his God did the king here act: most probably it was through Abiathar, by means of the urim and thummim in his ephod, that the Lord's mind was sought. His inquiry was twofold: concerning his duty and concerning his success: "his conscience asked the former, his prudence the latter. (Matt. Henry). His first concern was to make sure he had a Divine commission against the Philistines. In view of 2 Sam. 3:18 his duty seemed clear, but the question was, Is it *God's* time for me to act *now!* His second concern was whether the Lord would prosper his efforts, for he realized that victory was entirely dependent upon God — unless *He* delivered the

Philistines into his hand, all would be in vain.

"And the Lord said unto David, Go up: for I will doubtless deliver the Philistines into thine hand" (v. 19). He who has said, "Seek ye My face" will not mock that soul who sincerely and trustfully responds with, "my *heart* said unto Thee, Thy face, Lord, will I seek" (Psa. 27:8). Gods of wood and stone, the idols of earthly fame and material wealth, will fail their devotees in the hour of need, but the living God will not disappoint those who are subject unto Him and seek His aid in the time of emergency. The Lord is ever "a very *present* help in trouble" (Psa. 46:1), and the sure promise is "Draw nigh to God, and He will draw nigh to you" (James 4:8). The Divine ordering of our ways, the directing of our steps, is urgently needed by all of us, nor will it be withheld if sought after the appointed order.

"And the Lord said unto David, Go up: for I will doubtless deliver the Philistines into thine hand." This also is recorded for *our* instruction and comfort; then let us earnestly seek faith to appropriate the same and make it *our own*. Those words were graciously spoken by the Lord to encourage and nerve David for the battle. We too are called upon to *fight the good fight of Faith.*" Yes, and it is only as *faith* is in exercise, only as the Divine promises are actually *laid hold of* (expectantly *pleaded* before God), that we shall fight with good success. Has not God said *to us* He will "bruise Satan under your feet shortly" (Rom. 16:20); how *that* ought to animate us for the conflict! If we lay hold of that promise we shall be able to exclaim, "I therefore so run, *not as uncertainly; so* fight I, not as one that beateth the air" (1 Cor. 9:26).

"And David came to Baalperazim, and David smote them there, and said, The Lord hath broken forth upon mine enemies before me, as the breach of waters" (v. 20). Here, too, David has left a noble example for us to follow, and the more closely we do so, the more will God be honored, and the more will further successes be assured for us. Having obtained mercy to be dependent, David found grace to be humble, and ascribed the victory unto its true Author: *"The Lord* hath broken forth upon mine enemies before me" — as when a swollen river bursts its banks and carries all before it. In every forward step, in every resistance of temptation, in every success in service, learn to acknowledge "yet not I, but the grace of God which was with me" (1 Cor. 15:10). May writer and reader be delivered from the self-praising, boastful, Laodicean spirit of this evil age, saying, "Not unto us, O Lord, not unto us, but unto Thy name give glory" (Psa. 115:1).

"And there they left their images, and David and his men burned them" (v. 21). No doubt the Philistines had expected both protection and help from their idols, but they failed them in the hour of need: equally vain and impotent will prove any visible or material thing in which we put our trust. Now they were unwilling to preserve such gods as were unable to preserve them: "God can make men sick of those things that they have been most fond of, and compel them to desert what they doted upon, and cast even the idols of silver and gold to the moles and bats (Isa. 2:20)" (M. Henry). In *burning* the idols of the Philistines, David not only made clean work of his victory, but *obeyed* God's order in Deut. 7:5: "thou shalt. . .burn their graven images with fire."

"And the Philistines came up yet again, and spread themselves in the valley of Rephaim" (v. 22). Yes, even though we have the promise "Resist the Devil, and he will flee from you" (James 4:7), there is no assurance given that he will not return. He departed from the Saviour only "for a season" (Luke 4:13), and thus it is with His followers. Yet let not his return to the attack discourage us: it is but a summons to renewed waiting upon God, seeking *fresh* strength from Him daily, hourly. "And when David inquired of the Lord, He said" (v. 23). On this second occasion also David sought Divine guidance: even though he had been successful in the first battle, he realized that further victory depended entirely upon the Lord, and for that he must be completely subject to Him.

"Thou shalt not go up: fetch a compass behind them, and come upon them over against the mulberry trees. And let it be, when thou hearest the sound of a going in the tops of the mulberry trees, that then thou shalt bestir thyself: for then shall the Lord go out before thee, to smite the hosts of the Philistines" (vv. 23, 24). This is very striking: here was the same enemies to be met, in the same place, and under the same Lord of hosts, and yet God's answer now is the very opposite of the previous one: then it was, "Go up;" now it is "Go not up," but make for their rear — circumstances may seem identical to human sight, yet on each occasion God is to be sought unto, trusted and obeyed, or victory cannot be insured. A real test of obedience was this for David, but he did not argue or decline to respond; instead, he meekly bowed to the Lord's will. *Here* is the man "after God's own heart" — who waited upon the Lord, and acted by His answer when it was given. Nor did he lose by it: 'The Lord shall go before thee to smite the hosts of the Philistines': God is ready to do still greater things when we own what He has already done for us!

"And David did so, as the Lord had commanded him: and smote the Philistines from Geba until thou come to Gazer" (v. 25). "David observed his orders, waited God's motions, and stirred then, and not till then" (M. Henry). Complete success was granted him: God performed His promise and routed all the enemy's forces. How that should encourage *us!* "When the kingdom of the Messiah was to be set up, the apostles, who were to beat down the devil's kingdom, must not attempt anything till they receive the promise of the Spirit, who 'came with a sound from Heaven, as of a rushing mighty wind' (Acts 2:2), which was typified by this 'sound of a going in the tops of the mulberry trees'; and when they heard that, they must bestir themselves, and did so: they went forth conquering and to conquer" (M. Henry).

For lack of space we were obliged to omit from the preceding article a number of important points upon the closing verses of 2 Sam. 5; so we will use them here as the introduction for this one. We saw how that when the Philistines came up against David (2 Sam. 5:18), he "inquired of the Lord" what he should do (v. 19), and God responded with the gracious assurance that the enemy should be delivered into his hands; which was accordingly accomplished. Then we saw that other Philistines came up against him again (v. 22). Taking nothing for granted, David once more sought unto the Lord for Divine instructions. Therein we are taught the duty of acknowledging God in *all* our ways (Prov. 3:6), and His gracious readiness to grant needed light for our path, for "whatsoever things were written aforetime, were written for *our* learning" (Rom. 15:4). The whole of that blessed incident reveals some valuable and precious lessons on the intensely practical subject of *Divine guidance.*

David did not act mechanically when the Philistines came against him the second time, and do according as God had instructed him on the first occasion; instead, he definitely inquired of Him *again!* Circumstances may *seem identical* to our dim vision, nevertheless, it is our duty and wisdom to wait upon the Lord on *all* occasions, trustfully seeking His instructions, implicitly obeying when His will is made clear to us through His Word. In no other way can victory over the lusts of the flesh and the subtle wiles of the devil, be insured. As we saw in our last, the Lord *did not* give David the same answer on the second occasion as He had given him in the first. His response was quite different: the first time He said, "Go up" (v. 21); the second time He said, "thou shalt not go up, but fetch a compass behind them" etc. It is at *that* point, particularly, there is important instruction for us.

On the first occasion the Lord said unto David, "Go up, for I will doubtless deliver the Philistines into thine hand" (v. 19). But on the second, He said, Thou shalt not go up, but fetch a compass behind them, and come upon them over against the mulberry trees. And let it be, when thou hearest the sound of a going in the tops of the mulberry trees, that then thou shalt bestir thyself: for then shall the Lord go out before thee, to smite the host of the Philistines" (vv. 23, 24). That made a *greater demand* upon David's faith, patience, and submission, than the former order did. It was humbling to the pride of the flesh not to make an open and frontal attack. It called for quite a march to circle around and get to their rear. And when he got there, he must *wait* until he heard a movement in the boughs of the mulberry trees; and waiting is much harder than rushing ahead. The lesson here is, that as we grow in grace and progress in practical godliness, the Lord requires fuller and fuller submission to Himself.

"And let it be, when thou hearest the sound of a going in the tops of the mulberry trees." This was the equivalent of the word that was given to Israel at the Red Sea, as they saw the Egyptians bearing down upon them: "Stand still, and see the salvation of the Lord." The mulberry trees could not move of themselves: David was to tarry till a breath from the Lord stirred them: he was to wait till he heard the wind (emblem of the Spirit!) stirring their leaves. He was not to go to sleep, but to remain alert for the Lord's signal. The lesson here is, that while we are waiting for our Lord, we must diligently observe the providential motions of God: "Continue in prayer, *and watch* in the same" (Col. 4:2).

"When thou hearest the sound of a going in the tops of the mulberry trees, that *then* thou shalt bestir thyself:" that is, David was to *respond* to the intimation which God had graciously given him. The practical lesson for us is obvious: when the Lord has made known His will, prompt action is required. There is a time to stand still, and a time to move. "Go forward" was the second word to Israel at the Red Sea. Strange as it may seem, there are many who fail at this very point. They arrive at some crisis in life: they seek unto the Lord for directions: His providential "pillar of cloud" goes before them, but they do not "bestir" themselves and follow it. It is only mocking God to ask Him for light when we respond not to what He *has* given. Listen attentively for *His* "sound of a going" and when you have heard it, act.

Observe the blessed and assuring promise which accompanied the directions to David at that time, "For then shall the Lord go out before thee, to smite the host of the Philistines" (v. 24). If we carefully compare that with what is said in v. 20, it will be seen that the Lord wrought *more manifestly* on this second occasion than He did on the first. There we are simply told "and *David* smote them," though he promptly ascribed his victory unto God. But here the Lord promised that *He* would smite the Philistines. The comforting lesson for us is, that if we duly wait upon God, implicitly obey His instructions – no matter how "unreasonable" they seem, nor how distasteful; if we diligently watch every movement of His providence, and "bestir" ourselves when His will is clear, then we may assuredly count upon Him showing Himself strong on our behalf.

There is a blessed sequel to the above incident recorded in 1 Chron. 14:16, 17, which is not mentioned in 2 Sam., "David therefore did as God commanded him; and they smote the host of the Philistines from Gibeon even to Gazer. And the fame of David went out into all lands; and the Lord brought the fear of him upon all nations." God will be no man's debtor: He always rewards those who keep His commandments. He not only enabled David to vanquish the Philistines, but He also honoured the one who had honoured Him, by causing his fame to go abroad, so that all nations were afraid to attack him. And is it not equally the case now, that where there is a soul who is fully subject to Himself, He causes even Satan to feel he is but wasting his time to assail such an one! Compare Prov. 16:7.

The next thing we are told of David after his triumph over the Philistines, is the godly concern he now evidenced for the ark. This is exceedingly beautiful, manifesting as it does the deep spirituality of our hero, and showing again the propriety of his being designated "the man after God's own heart." David's first thought after he was firmly seated as king over all Israel, was the enthronement in Jerusalem of the long-forgotten ark, that sacred coffer which held supreme place among the holy vessels of the tabernacle; that ark concerning which the Lord had said to Moses, "Thou shalt put the mercy seat above upon the ark; and in the ark thou shalt put the testimony that I shall give thee. And *there* I will meet with thee, and I will commune with thee from above the mercy seat, from between the two cherubim which are on the ark of the testimony" (Ex. 25:21, 22).

That ancient symbol of the presence of the true King, had passed through many vicissitudes since the days when it had been carried around the walls of Jericho. In the degenerate times of the Judges, it had been superstitiously carried into battle, as though it were merely a magical mascot, and righteously did God mock their impious expectations: "the ark of God" fell into the hands of the uncircumcised. The Philistines carried it in triumph through their cities, and then housed it in the temple of Dagon. But again Jehovah vindicated His honour, and the ark was sent back to Israel in dismay. It had been joyfully welcomed by the inhabitants of Bethshemesh: then, alas, unholy curiosity moved them to look within the sacred chest, and the Lord smote them "with a great slaughter" (1 Sam. 6:19).

The ark was then removed to the forest seculsion of Kerjath-jearim (the city or village of the woods) and placed in the house of Abinadab, where it lay neglected and forgotten for over fifty years. During the days of Saul, they "inquired not at it" (1 Chron, 13:3). But from his days as a youth, David was deeply exercised over the dishonour done to the Lord's throne: "Lord, remember David, and all his afflictions: How he sware unto the Lord, and vowed unto the mighty God of Jacob; surely I will not come into the tabernacle of my house, nor go up into my bed; I will not give sleep to mine eyes, nor slumber to mine eyelids, until I find out a place for the Lord, *a habitation for* the mighty God of Jacob. Lo, we heard of it at Ephratah: we found it in the fields of the wood" (Psa. 132:1-6). He had resolved to establish a place where Jehovah's worship could be celebrated, a house where the symbol of His presence should be fixed and communion with His people established.

CHAPTER 6.

Again David gathered together all the chosen men of Israel, thirty thousand. And David arose and went with all the people that were with him from beyond Baale of Judah, to bring up the ark of God from there, whose name is called by the name of the LORD of hosts who dwells between the cherubims. And they set the ark of God on a new cart and brought it out of the house of Abinadab that was in Gibeah. And Uzzah and Ahio, the sons of Abinadab, drove the new cart.
— II Samuel 6:1-3.

Now that he was established over the kingdom of Israel, David did not forget his early vows, but forthwith proceeded to put them into execution. "Again, David gathered together all the chosen men of Israel, thirty thousand. And David arose, and went with all the people that were with him from Baale of Judah, to bring up from thence the ark of God, whose name is called by the name of the Lord of hosts that dwelleth between the cherubim" (2 Sam. 6:1, 2). No doubt it was with a full heart that David now acted, with deep longings after God, with fervent rejoicings in Him (see v. 5). No doubt he painted a bright picture, as he anticipated the blessings which would follow the ark being rightfully honoured. Alas, how his hopes were dashed to the ground! Sad indeed was the immediate sequel.

"And they set the ark of God upon a new cart, and brought it out of the house of Abinadab that was in Gibeah: and Uzzah and Ahio, the sons of Abinadab, drave the cart. And they brought it out of the house of Abinadab which was in Gibeah, accompanying the ark of God: and Ahio went before the ark. And David and all the house of Israel played before the Lord on all manner of instruments made of fir wood, even on harps, and on psalteries, and on timbrels, and on cornets, and on cymbals. And when they came to Nachon's threshingfloor, Uzzah put forth his hand to the ark of God, and took hold of it; for the oxen shook it. And the anger of the Lord was kindled against Uzzah, and God smote him there for his error; and there he died by the ark of God. And David was displeased, because the Lord had made a breach upon Uzzah: and he called the name of the place the breach of Uzzah to this day" (vv. 3-8). Some exceedingly solemn lessons are pointed in this passage, and they are recorded for *our* warning; alas that they are so widely disregarded in Christendom today.

"To bring back therefore the Ark from the place of its dishonour; to bring it again into the bosom of Israel; to make it once more that which Israel should seek unto and enquire at: and above the establish it in the citadel of Zion, the place of sovereign supremacy and strength, these were the immediate objects of David's desires. Herein he was fulfilling his office of king, in giving supremacy to God and to His truth. But the servants of God have not unfrequently to learn, that the pursuit of a right end, does not necessarily imply the employment of right means" (B. W. Newton). This is the first thing here to take to heart.

"And they set the ark of God upon a new cart." By so doing they were guilty of a serious error. In the fervency of his zeal, David ignored the precepts of God. The Lord had given very definite instructions as to the order which must be followed when the ark was to be moved. Through Moses Jehovah had said, "When the camp setteth forward, Aaron shall come, and his sons, and they shall take down the covering veil, and *cover the ark of* testimony with it: and shall put thereon the covering of badgers' skins, and shall spread over it a cloth wholly of blue, and shall *put in the staves thereof*" (Num. 4:5, 6). The sacred ark was to be duly hidden from the gaze of curious, but it does not appear that this detail was attended to by David! Nor was that all: "And when Aaron and his sons have made an end of covering the sanctuary, as the camp is to set forward: after that, the sons of Kohath shall come to bear it" (Num. 4:15); "they should bear *upon their shoulders*" (Num. 7:9).

The will of God was plainly revealed: the ark was to be covered, staves were to be inserted in the rings in its ends, and it was to be carried on the shoulders of the Kohathites. Nothing had been said about placing it on "a new cart:" *that* was a human invention, and *contrary* to the instructions of the Lord. David's desire was holy, his motive was pure, but *he went about things in a wrong way*, and dire were the consequences. Now there are two ways of doing the work of the Lord, two ways of acquitting ourselves when engaged in His service: strictly following what is prescribed for us in the written Word of God, or following *our own* ideas and inclinations — or following the example of other men, which amounts to the same thing. Alas, how much the later is now in evidence; how often are right things being done in a wrong way!

The due order for the removing of the ark had been plainly made known by God in His written Word. Jehovah had given express command that the ark should be covered with the sacred curtains, committed to the charge of a Divinely-selected set of men, and it *must* be carried on their "shoulders," and in no other way. That was *God's* way: to move it on a cart drawn by cattle was *man's* way. Some might think the latter was to be preferred. Some might consider it was such a "little" matter as to be of no consequence. Some might conclude that as their object was right and their motive pure, that even though they ignored *the prescribed mode* of performing the duty, they might surely count upon the Divine blessing. *What the Lord thought* of their procedure is evidenced in the tragic sequel.

But how are we to account for David's serious failure to heed the commands of God? What is the explanation of the "confusion" which here attended his well-meant and praise-worthy effort? Let us go back again to the beginning of 2 Sam. 6, and read carefully its first three verses. Notice, dear reader, a very significant *omission;* observe closely the solemn contrast between his conduct in 2 Sam. 5:19 and 5:23, and what is said of him here. Each time the Philistines came up against him, David "inquired of the Lord," but nothing is said of *that* now he purposed to conduct the ark unto a suitable habitation for it! Need we wonder, then, at what follows? If, *God's* blessing be not definitely sought, how can it be rightfully expected? If *prayer* does not precede and accompany our very best actions, what are they likely to amount to! If in *any* of our ways God be not "acknowledged," be not surprised if they lead to disaster.

"And David *consulted with the captains* of thousands and hundreds, with every leader. And David said unto all the congregation of Israel, If it seem good *unto you*, and that it be of the Lord our God, let us send abroad unto our brethren everywhere, that are left in all the land of Israel, and with them also to the priests and Levites which are in their cities and suburbs, that they may gather themselves unto us. And let us bring again the ark of our God to us" (1 Chron. 13:1-3). Instead of "inquiring of the Lord," David had conferred with his officers. There was *no need whatever* for him to "consult" with any human being, for the *will of the Lord* was already upon record! And what was the policy suggested by the "leaders?" Why, to imitate the ways of the religious world around them! The Philistine "priests' had counselled that the ark be returned to Israel upon "a new cart" (1 Sam. 5:2-11), and now David — under the advice of his officers — "set the ark of God upon *a new cart*" (2 Sam. 6:3)!

And they brought it out of the house of Abinadab which was at Gibeah, going with the ark of God. And Ahio went before the ark. And David and all the house of Israel played before the LORD on all kinds of instruments made of fir wood, even on harps, and on psalteries, and on timbrels, and on cornets and on cymbals. And when they came to Nachon's threshingfloor, Uzzah reached toward the ark of God, and took hold of it, for the oxen stumbled. And the anger of the LORD was kindled against Uzzah. And God struck him there for his error. And he died there by the ark of God. — II Samuel 6:4-7.

Our principal design in this David-series of articles is to emphasise the fact that the O.T. is far, far more than a historical record of events which happened thousands of years ago, and to make it manifest that every part of God's Word is full of important truth which is urgently needed by us today. The business of the Bible teacher is twofold: to give an accurate *interpretation* of the meaning of Holy Writ, and to make *application* of its contents to the hearts and lives of his hearers or readers. By "making application," we mean, the pointing out and the pressing upon ourselves of the practical lessons which each passage contains, seeking to heed its warnings, appropriate its encouragements, obey its precepts, and put in a claim to its promises. Only thus does it become a living and profitable Word *to us.*

The first verses of 2 Sam. 6 record an incident which needs to be prayerfully laid to heart by every one whom God has separated unto His service. It chronicles a most blessed action on the part of David, who had in view naught but the honour and glory of the Lord. But alas, that action was sadly marred by permitting the fervency of his zeal to ignore the precepts of God. He was anxious that the long-neglected and dishonoured Ark should be suitably housed in Zion. His desire was good and his motive was pure, but his execution of the same met with the open displeasure of the Lord. It is not sufficient to have a worthy purpose and a proper spirit: God's work must be performed *in the right way:* that is, according to the rules of His prescribing; anything other than that is but a species of self-will.

There seem to be a great many in Christendom today who are desirous of doing good, but they are exceedingly lax and careless in the mode and manner their desires are carried out. They act as though the means used and the methods employed mattered little or nothing, so long as their aim and end is right. They are creatures of impulse, following the dictates of mere whim and sentiment, or imitating the examples of others. They seem to have no concern for *God's standard,* study not His Word diligently to discover what laws and rules the Lord has given for the regulation of our conduct in His "service." Consequently, they are governed by the flesh, rather than the Spirit, so that it frequently happens that they do good things *in a wrong way;* yea, in a manner directly opposed to *God's* way as revealed in His Word.

There are many "church officers" who are anxious to see the pews occupied and their treasury well filled, and so, "socials," "ice-cream suppers," and other worldly attractions are employed to draw the crowd. There are many preachers who are anxious to hold the young people, and so "athletic clubs," social entertainments, are introduced to secure that end. There are many evangelists who are anxious to "make a good show," secure "results," and be able to herald so many hundreds of "converts" at the close of their "campaigns," and so fleshly means are used, high pressure methods are employed to bring this about: "decision cards," the "sawdust trial," the "penitent form" are called in to their aid. There are many Sunday School teachers who are anxious to hold the interest of their class, and so "prizes" are given, "picnics" are arranged, and other devices are resorted to.

Apparently it does not occur to these "leaders" to *challenge* their own actions, to weigh them in "the balances of the sanctuary," to inquire how near or how far they measure up to the Divine standard: so long as such means and methods seem right *to them*, or are in general vogue in other "churches," and so long as they appear to "succeed," nothing else matters. But in a coming day, GOD is going to ask of them "who hath required *this* at your hand?" (Isa. 1:12)! None of the devices mentioned by us above have one particle of scriptural authority to warrant their use; and it is *by the Scriptures* that each of us will yet be *judged!* *All* things must be done "according to the pattern" (Heb. 8:5; Ex. 25:40) which God has furnished us; and woe will it yet be unto us if we have disregarded *His* "pattern" and substituted another of our own.

The terrible confusion which now prevails so extensively in Christendom is no excuse whatever for us falling into line with it: *"thou shalt not* follow a multitude to do evil" (Ex. 23:1). No matter how "peculiar" he may be thought, no matter how "unpopular" he may be because of it, *faithfulness* is what God requires from each of His servants (1 Cor. 4:2). And "faithfulness" means doing the work which God has appointed *in the way which He has prescribed.* Expedience may have grasped the helm; compromise may be the order of the day; principles may be valued because of their "practicability" rather than because of their *scripturalness;* but that alters not one whit the strict discharge of duty which the Lord requires from each of His servants. Unless that fact be clearly realized, we read in vain the solemn incident recorded in 2 Sam. 6.

The laxity which now obtains in so many professedly "Christian" circles is indeed appalling. Unconverted men are allowed to occupy positions which none but Christ's true servants have any title to stand in. Women are allowed to speak in public before a mixed audience, in open violation of 1 Cor. 14:34 The "sprinkling" of a few drops of water on an infant's head is substituted for the scriptural immersion of believers only. Human convenience is consulted when the Lord's death is to be remembered, and His "supper" is changed into the *morning* "breaking of bread." Leavened bread, rather than *"this* bread" (1 Cor. 11:26), is used to set forth the immaculate person of the Redeemer. And if one dares to raise a voice in protest against these innovations — no matter how gently and lovingly — he is called "legalistic" and a "troubler in Israel." But even that must not move the one who covets his *Master's* "Well done."

"And they set the ark of God upon a new cart" (2 Sam. 6:3). In so doing, David and his counsellors (1 Chron. 13:1) committed a serious fault: they ignored the Divinely appointed order and substituted their own arrangements. The Lord had given express commands in Num. 4:5, 6; 15:7,9 as to *how* the sacred ark was to be carried when it should be moved from one place to another; and He requires unquestioning obedience to all His regulations. It is true that David was moved on this occasion with a deep concern for Jehovah's honour and glory. It is true that is was the urgings of *love for Him* which prompted his noble action; but He has said, "If ye love Me, keep My commandments" (John 14:15) — love must flow in the *appointed* channels; it must be *directed by* the Divine precepts, if it is to please its Object.

"God is a Spirit: and they that worship Him must worship Him in spirit and in truth" (John 4:24): among other things that means, God must be worshipped according to *the pattern* He has given us in His Word. There are many Protestants who can see clearly the human inventions, superstitious innovations, and unscriptural practices of the Romanists, in their "elevation of the mass," the vestments of their "priests," the burning of incense, the worship of images, and the adoration of the mother of our Saviour. The unwarrantable introduction of such devices are patent to multitudes of Protestants, yet they are blind *to their own* unscriptural and antiscriptural ways! Listen, my reader: anything we introduce into "the service of the sanctuary," into the worship of God, for which we have no "thus saith the Lord," is nothing but a species of *"will* worship" (Col. 2:23), and must be abandoned by us.

As we pointed out in our last article, the counsel given to David by the "leaders" in Israel, was patterned after the invention of the heathen. The "priests" of the Philistines had sent back the ark on "a new cart" drawn by oxen (1 Sam. 6). And history has repeated itself. If many of the means and methods which are now used in much so-called "Divine worship" and "Christian work" were challenged, if a *reason* were demanded for their employment, the best that could be given would be, *Others* are using them. But no scriptural authority could be cited. The "leaders" in Israel might have argued that the device used by the Philistines "succeeded" and that God "blessed" their arrangements. Ah, but the Philistines had not God's Word in their hands; but Israel had! In like manner, many now argue "God blesses" these women preachers and many other things for which we have no "thus saith the Lord," But, as we shall see, God *cursed* Israel's flagrant violation of His commands!

The outstanding fact which concerns us as we seek to ponder and *profit from* this solemn incident in David's life is, that *he acted without Divine orders:* he introduced something into the Divine worship for which he had *no* "thus saith the Lord." And the lesson to be learned therefrom is to rigidly scrutinize our own actions – the things we do, *the way in which* we do them, the means we employ – and ask, Are these *appointed by God?* There is much apparent reverence and devotion among the Papists, but is it acceptable to the Lord? Ah, my readers, if very much of the "Christian service" of earnest, zealous, enthusiastic Protestants were weighed in the balances of Holy Writ, it would be "found wanting:" nor am I guiltless if found in association and fellowship with the same – no, no matter how much I protest against it all. Individual loyalty to Christ, personal obedience to His commands, is what is demanded of each one of us.

It may be thought that David was ignorant of what was recorded in Num. 4 and 7, and so was not so seriously to blame; but the validity of such a conclusion is more than doubtful, as we shall show (D.V.) in the next article. Again; it may be supposed that David considered the regulations given in the days of Moses pertained only to Israel while they were on the march in the wilderness, and did not apply to his own case; but this defence of David also breaks down before a passage we hope to consider in our next chapter. Even were the case as just supposed, his bounden duty would have been to first "ask counsel of the Lord," and inquire *"Whereon* shall the ark be placed?" Instead he conferred with flesh and blood (1 Chron. 13:1) and followed their advice.

David's efforts proved a failure. And sooner or later all effort on the part of the "Church," or of the individual Christian, which is not strictly according to the Word of the Lord will prove a failure: it will be but "wood, hay, stubble" (1 Cor. 3:12) in the day of Divine testing and reward. God has magnified His Word above all His name (Psa. 138:2), and He demands that His servants shall do all things according to the plan and manner which He has prescribed. When he commanded Moses to build the tabernacle, He bade him do so according to the "pattern" which He showed him in the mount (Ex. 25:40): there was no room for human opinion or preference. And if we would serve Him *acceptably*, then we must go according to *His* way, and not ours. The right attitude for us was expressed by Peter when he said, "Nevertheless, at Thy word, I will let down the net" (Luke 5:5): he acted according to Christ's instruction, and was blest!

"And when they came to Nachon's threshingfloor, Uzzah put forth his hand to the ark of God, and took hold of it; for the oxen shook it" (2 Sam. 6:6). Yes, as the marginal rendering tells us, "the oxen *stumbled.*" And do you suppose that was an accident? No, indeed there are *no* "accidents" in a world which is presided over by the living God. Not even a hair can fall from our head till the moment He *decreed* for it to happen. But not only is everything directed by God, but there is also a significance, a meaning, a message, in the smallest occurrences, had we but eyes to see and hearts to understand. "The oxen stumbled:" of course they did; what else could be expected! There can be naught but "confusion" when the Divine order is departed from. In the stumbling of those oxen the Lord was *making manifest* David's disorder.

"Uzzah put forth his hand to the ark of God, and took hold of it." He feared it would be overthrown, and so he wished to avert such a disaster. Like David's design in seeking a honourable habitation for the ark, Uzzah's purpose was good, and his motive pure; but like David, he also *disregarded God's written law.* See here one sin leading to another! See how David's conferring with flesh and blood, following the counsel of the "leaders," and emulating the way of the heathen, was now succeeded by the priest's son committing an act of sacrilege. Alas, alas, how much will the present-day "leaders" in Christendom yet have to answer for, because of their setting such an evil example before others, and thus encouraging the "young people" to lightly esteem the holy and authoritative precepts of God.

"And the anger of the Lord was kindled against Uzzah, and God smote him there for his error; and there he died by the ark of God" (v. 7). The Lord God will not be mocked. Plainly had He declared that, even the Kohathites, who were appointed to carry the ark by staves on their shoulders, "shall *not touch* any holy things, *lest they die*" (Num. 4:15). God not only keeps His promises, but He also *fulfills His threats!* So Uzzah, found, and so will every other disregarder of His commandments yet discover.

"He, whose name is *Jealous*, was greatly offended. The sincere, the well-meaning man, having no command, nor any example for what he did, fell under Jehovah's anger, and lost his life, as the reward of his officiousness. And as the Holy Spirit has recorded the fact so circumstantially, we have reason to consider it *as a warning to all*, of the danger there is in tampering with positive ordinances; and as a standing evidence that God will have His cause supported, and His appointments administered, *in His own way*. The case of Saul, and the language of Samuel, to that disobedient monarch, inculcate the same thing: 'the people,' said Saul to the venerable prophet, 'took of the spoil, sheep and oxen, to sacrifice unto the Lord thy God in Gilgal. And Samuel said, Hath the Lord as great delight in burnt offerings and sacrifices, as *in obeying the voice* of the Lord? Behold, to obey is better than sacrifice, and to hearken than the fat of rams': 1 Sam. 15:21-23" (A. Booth, 1813).

It is solemn to recall that no Divine judgment fell upon the Philistines when *they* placed the holy ark upon a cart and sent it back to Israel: but "the anger of the Lord *was* kindled against Uzzah!" How plainly this shows us that God will suffer from the world what *He will not tolerate* in His professing people, who bear His holy name. That is why it will be "more tolerable" for Sodom and Gomorrah in the Day of Judgment, than it will be for Divinely-enlightened, highly favoured, and loud-boasting Capernaum. The same principle will obtain when Christendom comes to be judged. Better to have lived and died in the ignorance of darkest Africa, than to have had God's Word in our hands and set at naught its laws!

And David was displeased because the LORD had broken forth on Uzzah. And he called the name of the place Perez-uzzah to this day. And David was afraid of the LORD that day, and said, How shall the ark of the LORD come to me? So David would not remove the ark of the LORD to him to the city of David. But David carried it aside into the house of Obed-edom the Gittite. And the ark of the LORD stayed in the house of Obed-edom the Gittite three months. And the LORD blessed Obed-edom and all his household. — II Samuel 6:8-11.

As we have seen in the preceding articles, after his coming to the throne of Israel and his victories over the Philistines, David evidenced a godly concern for the holy ark, which had been so grievously and so long neglected. Zealous of the Divine glory, he had resolved to establish a place where Jehovah's worship should be celebrated and where the symbol of His presence should be securely housed. Accordingly, he gathered all the leaders of Israel together to bring the sacred coffer to Jerusalem (2 Sam. 6:1). But, alas, instead of heeding the Divinely-given instructions for such an occasion and placing the ark upon the shoulders of the Levites, he followed the evil example of the heathen and placed it upon a new cart. In so doing he ignored the plainly revealed will of God, and substituted a human device. The work which David undertook was indeed a good one, his motive was pure, and his design was praiseworthy, but it was executed in a wrong way. He introduced into the Divine worship that for which he had no "Thus saith the Lord."

David did not inquire whether *God* had any will in the matter and ask, Whereon shall the holy ark be placed? Rather did he confer with flesh and blood. It was at *that* point he made his fatal mistake, and it is this which we need to take carefully to heart. Instead of consulting the Holy Scriptures, he sought counsel of men. It is true that he "consulted with the captains of thousands and hundreds and with every leader" (1 Chron. 13:1), but as Job 32:9 tells us "great men are not always wise," and so it proved on this occasion. Instead of reminding David of the instructions which the Lord had given through Moses (Num. 4:5, 6; 15:7, 9), they, apparently, advised him to follow the way of the uncircumcised (1 Sam 6:7,8). By so doing, David spoiled his fair enterprise, and incurred the displeasure of God. A good beginning had a bad ending because of departure from the Divinely-prescribed rules of procedure.

The above incident has been recorded for our learning, especially for those of us who are engaged in the Lord's service. It points a solemn warning. It shows the imperative need for zeal to be rightly directed, for there is "a zeal of God, but not according to knowledge" (Rom. 10:2); this is, a zeal to further the cause of God and bring glory unto His name, which is not regulated by that knowledge which His Word supplies. In our fervency to extend the kingdom of Christ, to spread His Gospel, to point souls unto Him, we are apt to forget His precepts, and do *His* work in *our* way. The danger is very real, and in this restless age of great activity now a few are being ensnared by this very evil. Many are so eager about the quantity of their service, they pay too little attention to the quality of it: they are anxious to be active in the Master's vineyard, but they do not sufficiently consult His guide-book as to *how* their activities must be conducted.

David's well meant effort turned out a failure. The Lord manifested His displeasure. David, accompanied by a large number of musicians, went before the ark, playing "on all manner of instruments" (2 Sam. 6:5). But when

Nachon's threshingfloor was reached, the oxen drawing the cart on which the sacred chest reposed, stumbled, and Uzzah put forth his hand to steady it. "And the anger of the Lord was kindled against Uzzah, and God smote him there for his error; and there he died by the ark of God" (v. 7). A tragic check was this unto the joyous procession — one which should have produced deep heart-searchings and penitential confession of failure. Has not God said, "Provoke Me not, and I will do you no harm" (Jer. 25:6)? Therefore, when He *does* afflict, ought we not to inquire as to wherein we have "provoked" Him!

Though the displeasure of God was plainly manifested, yet it did not at first produce the proper effect. "And David was displeased, because the Lord had made a breach upon Uzzah" (v. 8). Apparently a measure of self-complacency was at work in David's heart over the important service he was engaged in — for honouring the ark which had been neglected for so long. Now that things had gone contrary to *his* expectations, he was disconcerted, peeved, "displeased," or as the Hebrew word really signifies, "angry." His anger was not a righteous indignation against Uzzah for his affronting God, but because his own plans had gone awry. His own pride was wounded: the drastic cutting off of Uzzah by Divine judgment would not advance *him* in the eyes of his subjects; rather was he now humiliated before them. But the fault was his own, and he ought to have manfully shouldered the blame, and not acted like a peeved child.

"And David was displeased (angry) because the Lord had made a breach upon Uzzah" (v. 8). When the rod of God descends upon us, we are but adding sin to sin if we become enraged thereby: this is "despising" the chastening of the Lord, which is expressly forbidden (Heb. 12:5). "And he called the name of the place Perez-uzzah to this day"(v. 8), which, as the margin tells us, signifies "the *breach* of Uzzah." Thus did David memorialize the stroke of God as a warning for posterity to beware of rashness and irreverence. A solemn contrast may be seen here from what is recorded in 2 Sam. 5:20, where David changed the name of "the valley of Rephaim" unto "Baal-perazim" — "the place of *breaches*" — because "the Lord hath broken forth upon mine enemies." In the one he was celebrating God's goodness, in the other he was solemnizing God's judgment.

The conduct of David on this occasion was very deplorable, for it is highly reprehensible to be angered by any of the Lord's dealings. But in the light of such warnings, *our* petulency is far worse. David ought to have humbled himself beneath the mighty hand of God (1 Pet. 5:6), confessed his failure and corrected his fault (Prov. 28:13), and owned God's righteousness in thus taking vengeance on his inventions (Psa. 99:8). By so doing he would have put the blame where it belonged, have set a good example before others, and vindicated the Lord. Instead, his pride was hurt, his temper was inflamed, and blessing was missed. Alas, how often has writer and reader failed in a similar manner. How rarely have we heeded that injunction, "Wherefore glorify ye the Lord in the fires" (Isa. 24:15): one way of doing which is to judge ourselves unsparingly and own the need of the flames to purge away our dross.

"And David was afraid of the Lord that day, and said, How shall the ark of the Lord come to me?" (v. 9). The transition is very easy from sudden zeal and joy to fretfulness and dejection. We are, naturally, creatures of extremes, and the pendulum quickly swings from earnestness to indolence, from jubilation to commiseration. He who dares one day to face singlehanded the four hundred prophets of Baal, next day flees from the threat of Jezebel. He who feared not to draw his sword in the presence of armed soldiers, trembled before a maid. They who sang so heartily at the Red Sea, murmured a little later when their food-supplies gave out. Few maintain an even keel amid the varying tides of life.

A. measure of servile fear now possessed David, and he would not venture to bring the ark any nearer his own immediate residence, lest he too should be destroyed. That holy vessel of the tabernacle which had been the object of his veneration, now became an occasion of dread.

With the death of Uzzah a fear came upon David. This exemplifies an important principle: fear always follows where faith is not in exercise. Said the prophet, "I will trust and not be afraid" (Isa. 12:2). When the timorous disciples awoke the Saviour because of their storm-tossed ship, He said, "Why are ye fearful? O ye *of little faith*" (Matt. 8:26). When a spirit of trembling seizes the heart it is a sure sign that faith is at a low ebb. The promise is, "Thou wilt keep him in perfect peace whose mind is stayed on Thee, *because he trusteth* in Thee" (Isa. 26:3). Thus, the fear of David on this occasion is easily accounted for: his faith was eclipsed. Learn this valuable lesson, dear reader: as soon as you are conscious of sinking of heart, uneasiness, or alarm, cry unto the Lord for a strengthening of your faith. Say with the Psalmist, "What time I am afraid, I will trust in Thee" (Psa. 56:3).

There is another important principle exemplified by David's attitude on this occasion: his faith was inoperative because his *walk* was not according to the revealed will of the Lord. It is true that faith is the gift of God, and that, unaided, we cannot call it into operation after it is received. Every exercise of faith, every increase thereof, is to be ascribed unto the gracious influence of the Holy Spirit. But let it not be forgotten that *He* is the *Holy* Spirit, and will not put a premium upon wrong-doing. When our ways are contrary to the Rule which we are to walk by, the Spirit is grieved. When we act in self-will, and then refuse to judge ourselves under the mark of God's displeasure, His blessed operations are withheld. Fearfulness is a sign that faith is inactive, and inactive faith is an evidence that the Spirit is grieved; and that, in turn denotes that our walk is displeasing to God. Learn, then, dear reader, to "Consider your ways" (Hag. 1:5) when conscious that faith is at a low ebb: clean out the choked channel and the waters shall flow freely again.

"And David was afraid of the Lord that day, and said, How shall the ark of the Lord come to me?" Does it not seem strange that David should ask such a question when the Lord had given clear and definite instructions as to *how* the ark should be conducted from place to place? Stranger still, sadder far, that he would not make right the wrong which he had committed. But alas, it is not easy to condemn ourselves when we have departed from God's ways: even though the providential smile of the Lord be changed into a frown, we are loath to humble ourselves before Him. How this reveals the "desperate wickedness" which still remains in our hearts, and how the realization of this ought to remove pride far from us, cause us to marvel increasingly at God's longsuffering with us, and make us more patient toward our erring brethren.

"So David would not remove the ark of the Lord unto him, into the city of David: but David carried it aside into the house of Obed-edom, the Gittite" (v. 10). Instead of correcting his fault, we now see David forsaking his own mercy (Jonah 2:8). The ark was the symbol of the Lord's manifest presence, and *that* should be the one thing above all others desired and cherished by the saint. Moses was deeply conscious of this when he said, "If Thy presence go not with me, carry us not up hence" (Ex. 33:15). Ah, but to enjoy the manifest presence of God we must be in the path of obedience: "he that hath My commandments, and *keepeth* them, he it is that loveth Me, and he that loveth Me shall be loved of My Father, and I will love him, and will *manifest* Myself to him" (John 14:21). Was it not because he felt he was out of the way of subjection to God's revealed will that caused David to now abandon his purpose of bringing up the ark to Jerusalem? It was a guilty conscience which made him "afraid of the Lord."

There is a fear of God which is becoming, spiritual, excellent; but there is also a fear of God which is hurtful, carnal, worthless: the one is servile, the other filial. There is a slavish fear which springs from hard thoughts of God, and there is a holy and laudable fear which issues from lofty thoughts of His majesty. The one is a terror produced in the mind by apprehensions of evil, the other is a reverential awe of God which proceeds from right views of His infinite perfections. The one is the fear of wrath, such as Adam had in Eden, when he was afraid and hid himself; and such as the demons have, who "believe and tremble" (James 2:19). The other is a fear of displeasing One who is gracious, like children have to dear parents. The one is our treasure, the other our torment; the one drives from God, the other draws to God; the one leads to despair, the other to godly activities (Heb. 11:7). The one is the product of a guilty conscience, the other is the fruit of an enlightened understanding.

There is a natural fear and there is a spiritual fear of God. The one hates Him, like a slave his cruel master; the other loves God, as a child respects and reveres his father. The one dreads God because of His power and wrath; the other venerates God because of His holiness and sovereignty. The one engenders to bondage, the other conduces to worship. Perfect love casts out the former (1 John 4:18), appropriating God's promises leads to the furtherance of the latter (2 Cor. 7:1). When we are walking with God in the light of His Word, a filial fear directs our ways; but when we depart from His statutes and a guilty conscience torments us, then a servile fear possesses our hearts. Hard thoughts are entertained of God, and we dread His anger. The soul is no longer at ease in His presence, and instead of viewing Him as our loving Father, we shrink from Him and regard Him as a hard Master. Such was the condition of David at this time. Alarmed by the Divine judgment upon Uzzah, he was afraid to have anything more to do with the ark.

"But David carried it aside into the house of Obed-edom the Gittite," That was David's loss; but, as we shall see, it was Obed-edom's gain. The ark was both the symbol of God's manifested presence in the midst of Israel, and a notable type of the person of the Lord Jesus. In the placing of the ark in the house of Obed-edom, following the unbelief of David, there was a prophetic hint given of the Gentiles receiving what Israel failed to appreciate — so marvelously does God overrule even the failures of His people. Obed-edom was a Gittite, and the "Gittites" were *Philistines* (Josh. 13:3), the inhabitants of Gath (1 Chron. 20:5); yet many of them were devoted to the person and interests of David (2 Sam. 5:18-21). Thus it was dispensationally: "It was necessary that the Word of God should first have been spoken to you (Jews): but seeing ye put it from you, and judge yourselves unworthy of everlasting life, lo, we turn to the Gentiles" (Acts 13:46).

"And the ark of the Lord continued in the house of Obed-edom the Gittite three months" (v. 11). After the awful death of Uzzah, and the fear of David to have anything further to do with the ark, it had scarcely been surprising had this Gittite refused to shelter the sacred coffer. As a Philistine, it is likely that he was acquainted with the trouble it had caused in the temple of Dagon (1 Sam. 5:2-4), and of the plague it brought upon the Ashdodites" (1 Sam. 5:6). Anxious enough were they to get rid of the ark (1 Sam. 6), yet now we find one of their countrymen providing a home for it in his own house. Doubtless he had been truly converted unto the Lord, and therefore esteemed whatever pertained to His worship. It is beautifully significant that his name "Obed" means *servant*, and here we find him rendering a true service unto God.

"And the Lord blessed Obed-edom, and all his household" (v. 11). Need we be surprised at this? God will be no man's debtor: as He declared, "Them that honour Me, I will honour" (1 Sam. 2:30). It is ever so. After Laban had received the fugitive Jacob into his family, he acknowledged. "I have learned by experience that the Lord hath blessed me for thy sake" (Gen. 30:27). When His servant was befriended by Potiphar, we read, "The Lord blessed the Egyptian's house for Joseph's sake" (Gen. 39:5). Through giving shelter unto God's prophet the widow of Zarephath was rewarded by having her son restored to life (1 Kings 17:23). How much more may we be sure of receiving God's rich blessing when His dear Son — to whom the ark pointed — is given the throne of our hearts.

"And the Lord blessed Obed-edom, and all his household." By the indwelling Spirit the Lord has promised to manifest Himself to the believer. The presence of the Lord in our lives and in our homes is the limitless source, if we will, of Divine blessing. The blessing will depend upon our *servant* attitude to that Presence or Spirit. If we take the place of a true "Obed," surrendering ourselves to His sway, the Lord will make our way prosperous. If in all things we give Christ the pre-eminence, so far from being the losers thereby, we shall be immeasurably the gainers, both now and hereafter. O may He who moved Obed to take in the ark, open our hearts to receive Christ in all His fulness.

And they told king David, saying, The LORD has blessed the house of Obed-edom, and all that belongs to him, because of the ark of God. So David went and brought up the ark of God from the house of Obed-edom into the city of David with gladness. And it happened that when those who bore the ark of the LORD had gone six steps, he sacrificed oxen and fatlings. And David danced before the LORD with all his might. And David was girded with a linen ephod. So David and all the house of Israel brought up the ark of the LORD with shouting, and with the sound of the trumpet. And as the ark of the LORD came to the city of David, Michal, Saul's daughter, looked through a window and saw king David leaping and dancing before the LORD. And she despised him in her heart. And they brought in the ark of the LORD and set it in its place in the midst of the tabernacle that David had pitched for it. And David offered burnt offerings and peace offerings before the LORD. And as soon as David had made an end of offering burnt offerings and peace offerings, he blessed the people in the name of the LORD of hosts. And he gave out among all the people, among the whole multitude of Israel, to the women as well as men, to everyone a cake of bread and a good piece of meat, and a flagon of wine. So all the people departed, each one to his house. Then David returned to bless his household. And Michal the daughter of Saul came out to meet David and said, How glorious was the king of Israel today, who uncovered himself today before the slave-girls of his servants, as a worthless one shamelessly uncovers himself! And David said to Michal, It was before the LORD, who chose me before your father, and before all his house, to appoint me ruler over the people of the LORD, over Israel. Therefore I will play before the LORD. And I will be still lower than this and will be base in my own sight. And of the slave-girls of whom you have spoken of, them I shall be had in honor. Therefore Michal the daughter of Saul had no child to the day of her death. — II Samuel 6:12-23.

"And it was told king David, saying, The Lord hath blessed the house of Obed-edom, and all that pertaineth unto him, because of the ark of God. So

David went and brought up the ark of God from the house of Obed-edom into the city of David with gladness" (2 Sam. 6:12). There are five things to be observed here. First, the Lord's blessing of a man is a very real and evident thing. Second, it is so patent that others take notice thereof. Third, they perceive why it is that the blessing of God is bestowed. Fourth, so impressed are they therewith, they mention it to others. Fifth, the effect which the evident blessing of the Lord of Obed-edom had upon David. Let us briefly ponder each of these points, and pray that their distinct messages may find lodgment in our hearts.

First, the Lord's blessing of a man is a very real and evident thing. "All these blessings shall come on thee, and overtake thee, if thou shalt hearken unto the voice of the Lord thy God. . .Blessed shall be thy basket, and thy store; blessed shalt thou be when thou comest in, and blessed shalt thou be when thou goest out", etc. (Deut. 28:2, 5, 6). In view of our recent sections on "Dispensationalism" we shall not take space now in replying to those who say "such promises are not for us:" suffice it to point out that *God's governmental ways* are the same in all dispensations. "The blessing of the Lord, it maketh rich, and He added no sorrow with it" (Prov. 10:22): for the meaning of the word "rich" see v. 4 — in the former the means is in view, in the latter the Source; in neither verse does spiritual "riches" exclude material ones. "No good thing will He withhold from them that walk uprightly" (Psa. 84:11).

Second, God's blessing of a person is so obvious that others are obliged to take notice thereof. So much so was this the case with Isaac, that Abimelech and two of his chief men went to him and said, "We certainly saw that the Lord was with thee" (Gen. 26:28) — what a testimony was that! Of the one who purchased Joseph it is recorded, "And his master *saw* that the Lord was with him and that the Lord made all that he did to prosper in his hand" (Gen. 39:3) — do people now see this is the case *with us*? "And Saul saw and knew that the Lord was with David" (1 Sam. 18:28). The wicked may not read God's Word, but they do the lives of His people, and are quick to perceive when His blessing is upon them; and the recognition of *that* has far more weight than anything they say!

Third, nor are men ignorant of *the reason why* the Lord prospers those with whom He is pleased. This is evident from the case now before us: "And it was told king David, saying, The Lord hath blessed the house of Obed-edom and all that pertaineth unto him, *because of* the ark of God." This is very striking: they traced the effect back to the cause: they recognised that God had honoured the one who had honoured Him. The same prinicple is illustrated again in Acts 4:13, "Now when they saw the boldness of Peter and John, and perceived that they were unlearned and ignorant men, they marvelled; and *they took knowledge* of them that they had been with Jesus." The men who drew this deduction were not regenerate, but the most notorious enemies of Christ; nevertheless they were right in attributing the spiritual graces of the apostles unto their fellowship with the Saviour.

Fourth, the recognition of God's evident blessing upon those whose ways are pleasing in His sight is voiced by men unto their fellows. It was so in the incident now before us. When it was so apparent that Obed-edom was being blessed in all his affairs, some went and informed the king thereof. Ah, my readers, we little know what impression is being made upon our neighbours by God's governmental dealings with us, nor how they speak one to another when it is manifest that His smile is upon us. How we should plead this before God in prayer, that He would enable us so to walk that we may not miss His best, and this that *His* name may be glorified through those around us taking note of the fact that "godliness with contentment (Greek "a sufficiency") *is great gain*" (1

Tim. 6:6).

Fifth, the effect which this news had upon David. As he had perceived God's frown in His stroke upon Uzzah, so now he discerned God's smile in Obed-edom's prosperity. It was clear to him that the ark was not a burdensome object, for so far from being the loser, he who had provided a home for it had been noticeably blest of the Lord. This encouraged David to resume his original design of bringing the sacred coffer to Jerusalem: his fears were now stilled, his zeal was rekindled. "The experience which others have of the gains of godliness, should encourage us to be religious. Is the ark a blessing to others's homes? let us bid it welcome to ours" (Matt. Henry). Do we perceive that those who are most yielded to the Lord make the best progress spiritually? then let that be an incentive to fuller consecration on our part.

"He restoreth my soul: He leadeth me in the paths of righteousness for His name's sake" (Psa. 23:4). In restoring the souls of His erring people, God does not act uniformly: according to His lovingkindness, unerring wisdom, and sovereign pleasure, He is pleased to use and bless a variety of means. Sometimes it is by a process of disappointment, withering the gourd under which we luxuriated, blowing upon that in which we had promised ourselves satisfaction. Sometimes it is by the application of a verse of Scripture, searching our conscience or melting our heart. Sometimes it is by a sore calamity, like the death of a loved one, which casts us back more closely upon the Lord for strength and comfort. In the case now before us it was the words of friends, who reported to David the blessing which the presence of the ark had brought to the family of Obed-edom.

The effect of David's restoration of soul is seen very blessedly in 1 Chron. 15:2, 3, 12, 13. "Then David said, None ought to carry the ark of God but the Levites; for them hath the Lord chosen to carry the ark of God, and to minister unto Him forever. And David gathered all Israel together to Jerusalem, to bring up the ark of the Lord unto his place, which he had prepared for it. And said unto them, Ye are the chief of the fathers of the Levites: sanctify yourselves, both ye and your brethren, that ye may bring up the ark of the Lord God of Israel unto the place that I have prepared for it. For because ye did it not at the first the Lord our God made a breach upon us, for that we sought Him not after the due order." There are several things in these verses which we do well to note.

First, David now gave the Lord His proper place in his plans and submitted to the regulations which He had given. He learned from painful experience that God's work must be done in God's prescribed way, if His approval and blessing was to rest upon the same. None but those whom God had specifically appointed must carry the sacred ark: this was one of the duties assigned the Levites, who had been definitely set apart unto the Lord's service. The application of this to our own day is obvious. The ark was a type of Christ: the carrying of the ark from place to place prefigured the making known of Christ through the preaching of the Gospel. Only those are to preach the Gospel whom God has specially called, separated, and qualified for His holy service. For others to invade this sacred office is but to introduce confusion and incur God's displeasure.

Second, David now realized that suitable preparation must precede holy activities: "Sanctify yourselves, both ye and your brethren, that ye may bring up the ark of the Lord God of Israel unto the place that I have prepared for it:" let the reader compare Exodus 19:10:15; 2 Chron. 29:5. Those who carried the ark must cleanse themselves from all ceremonial pollution and compose themselves for the solemn service of the Lord: only thus would they strike reverence upon the people. The same principle holds good in this Christian dispensation: "The

Lord hath made bare His holy arm in the eyes of all the nations. . .*be ye clean,* that bear the vessels of the Lord" (Isa. 52:10, 11). Those whom God has separated unto the sacred ministry of the Gospel must be "an example of the believers, in word, in conversation, in love, in spirit, in faith, in purity" (1 Tim. 4:12 and cf. 2 Tim. 2:21,22) — God's servants today are to "sanctify" themselves for the discharge of their honourable duties by repentance, confession, faith, prayer, and meditation, availing themselves constantly of that precious Fountain which has been opened for sin and uncleanness.

Third, David owned his previous failures: "The Lord our God made a breach upon us, for that we sought Him not after the due order." In like manner, Daniel acknowledged, "O Lord, righteousness belongeth unto Thee, but unto us confusion of faces as at this day; to the men of Judah, and to the inhabitants of Jerusalem, and unto all Israel, that are near, and that are far off, through all the countries whither Thou hast driven them, because of their trespass that they have trespassed against Thee" (9:7). "The life of faith is little more than a series of falls and restorations, errors and corrections displaying, on the one hand, the sad weakness of man, and on the other, the grace and power of God" (C.H.M.).

"So the priests and the Levites sanctified themselves to bring up the ark of the Lord God of Israel. And the children of the Levites bare the ark of God upon their shoulders with the staves thereon, as Moses commanded according to the word of the Lord" (1 Chron. 15:14, 15). All was now carried out "after the due order." God requires obedience in small things as well as great. And due notice is taken and record made by Him of all our actions. Blessed is it to behold these Levites now being governed, in every detail, by the revealed will of the Lord. "*Then* we make a good use of the judgments of God on ourselves and others, when we are awakened by them to reform and amend whatever has been amiss" (M. Henry). O that each of us may have more and more occasion for saying "Before I was afflicted, I went astray, but now have I *kept* Thy law" (Psa. 119:67).

"So David, and the elders of Israel, and the captains over thousands, went to bring up the ark of the covenant of the Lord out of the house of Obed-edom *with joy*" (1 Chron. 15:25). That is no small part of the present reward which God bestows upon His obedient people. Satan would feign seek to persuade us that a strict compliance with all the statutes of Holy Writ would be irksome. One of his favourite dogmas is, Law-keeping brings one into bondage. That is one of his lies. The Psalmist was better instructed: said he, "And I will walk *at liberty,* for I seek Thy precepts" (119:45): the more we practice the precepts of Scripture, the more are we delivered from the dominion of sin. God fills the heart of the obedient with gladness; hence, the reason why there is so much gloom and unhappiness among Christians to-day is because their obedience is so half-hearted and spasmodic.

"And it came to pass when God *helped* the Levites that bare the ark of the covenant of the Lord, that they offered seven bullocks and seven rams" (1 Chron. 15:26). God is honoured when we acknowledge His assistance — for without Him we can do nothing — even in those things which fall within the compass of our natural powers. But more especially should we own His aid in all our spiritual exercises: "Having therefore obtained help of God, I continue unto this day, witnessing" (Acts 26:22). These Levites were in need of special help, for remembering the fate of Uzzah, they were likely to tremble when they took up the ark; but God calmed their fears and strengthened their faith. God enabled them to discharge their duty decently and orderly, without any mishap.

"And it came to pass when God *helped* the Levites that bare the ark of the covenant of the Lord, that they offered seven bullocks and seven rams." This is wonderful. Everything was changed now: there was no stumbling, no thrusting forth of presumptuous hands to steady a shaking ark, no judgment from God; instead, His evident smile was upon them. It is ever thus: when God's work is done in God's way, we may confidently count upon His help. Go against the Word of God, and He is against us, as we shall discover sooner or later; but go according to the Word and God will bless us. "And they went forth, and preached everywhere, the Lord *working with them,* and confirming the Word with signs following" (Mark 16:20).

"And it was so, that when they that bare the ark of the Lord had gone six paces, he sacrificed oxen and fatlings" (2 Sam. 6:13). Probably David offered this sacrifice unto God with a twofold design: to make an atonement for his former errors, and as a thank-offering for present mercies. Great must have been his gratitude and joy when he perceived that all was now well. *"Then* we are likely to speed (prosper) in our enterprises when we begin with God, and give diligence to make our peace with Him. When we attend upon God in holy ordinances, our eye must be to the great Sacrifice, to which we owe it that we are taken into covenant and communion with God" (M. Henry).

"And David danced before the Lord with all his might; and David was girded with a linen ephod" (2 Sam. 6:14). The ordinances of God are to be performed with joy as well as reverence. In seeking to preserve a becoming decorum and sobriety, we need to be on our guard against lapsing into a cold and stilted perfunctoriness. No doubt there are certain occasions when higher expressions of joy are more suited than at others. It was so here. After his previous disappointment David was now transported with delight. His exultation of mind was manifested in his leaping for gladness, which he did "with all his might." "We ought to serve the Lord with our whole body and soul, and with every endowment or capacity we possess; our religious affections cannot be too intense, if properly directed; nor our expressions of them too strong, provided 'all be done decently and in order,' according to the spirit of the dispensation under which we live (Thos. Scott).

"And David was girded with linen ephod." On this auspicious occasion, David laid aside his royal robes, and, as taking the lead in the worhsip of God he wore a linen ephod. This was the ordinary garb of the priests when officiating, yet it was also used in religious exercises by those who were not priests, as the case of Samuel shows: 1 Sam. 2:18. The Spirit of God has here duly noted the fact that, though king over all Israel, David deemed it no disparagement to appear in the clothing of a minister of the ark; yet let it not be supposed that he was making any attempt to encroach upon the priestly office. The practical lesson for us in this detail is, that instead of decking ourselves out in worldly finery, we should be garbed plainly when we attend the public worship of God.

In conclusion it should be pointed out that the best expositors, ancient and modern, have regarded Psalm 24 as a sacred song composed by David on the glad occasion of the ark being brought to Jerusalem. The joy and triumph, the awe and the memories of victory which clustered around the dread symbol of the presence of the Lord, are wonderfully expressed in that choral piece. It is divided into two parts. The first replies to the question, "Who shall ascend into the hill of the Lord? or who shall stand in His holy place?" — an evident echo of the terror-stricken exclamation of the Bethshemites (1 Sam. 6:20). The answer is given in a description of the men who dwell with God. The second half deals with the correlative inquiry "Who is the King of glory?" And the answer is, The God who comes to dwell with men.

Inexpressibly blessed is v. 7. As the procession reached the walls of Jerusalem, and ere the ark — type of Christ — entered, the cry was made "Lift up your heads, O ye gates; and be ye lift up, ye everlasting doors; and the King of glory shall come in." It was as though their towering portals were too low. How clearly David recognized his own derived power, and the real Monarch of whom he was but the shadowy representative! The newly conquered city was summoned to admit its true Conqueror, whose throne was the ark, which was expressly named "the glory" (1 Sam. 4:21), and in whose train the earthly king followed as a subject and a worshipper.

In the closing verses of 2 Sam. 6 there is to be seen a mingling of the lights and shadows: the blessed fruits of the Spirit appear, but the evil works of Satan are also evident. As it often is in the natural world, so we find it in the moral realm — conflicting forces clash with each other: sunshine and rain, calm and storm, summer and winter, constantly alternate. That which is spread before our senses in nature, is but an external adumbration of what exists in the invisible: two mighty beings, diametrically opposed to each other, the Lord God and the devil, are ever at work. Such too is the life of the individual Christian, for he is a miniature replica of the world: in him "the flesh lusteth against the spirit, and the spirit against the flesh: and these are contrary the one to the other, so that ye cannot do the things that ye would" (Gal. 5:17), and consequently in his experience there is ever a mingling of the lights and shadows.

Before it ended, the joyful day of David's bringing up of the ark to Jerusalem was overcast by a domestic cloud. There was one in his own household who was incapable of entering into the fervour of his heart toward God, who was irritated by his devotion, and who bitterly condemned his zeal: one who was near and dear to him railed upon the king for his earnestness in Jehovah's cause and service. The enmity of the Serpent was stirred by the honour accorded the holy ark, the procession of the Levites, the jubilation of Israel's ruler, and the offerings which had been presented before the Lord. The anointed eye has no difficulty in discerning behind Michal him who is the inveterate Enemy of God and His people, and in her biting denunciation of David, the Christian of today may learn what to expect from those who are not one with him in the Lord.

Our last article closed at the verse "So David and all the house of Israel brought up the ark of the Lord with shouting, and with the sound of the trumpet" (2 Sam. 6:16). Our present lesson opens with "and as the ark of the Lord came into the city of David, Michal, Saul's daughter, looked through a window, and saw king David leaping and dancing before the Lord, and she despised him in her heart" (v. 16), and, as we shall see from the sequel, that secret hatred of David was shortly after vented in open opposition. Let not those who are engaged in the happy service of the Lord be surprised when they encounter antagonism; when, so far from their efforts being appreciated by all, there will be some who decry and denounce them. It was so with the prophets; it was so with Christ's fore-runner; it was so with the Lord of glory Himself; it was so with His apostles; and it will continue to be so with all His faithful servants unto the end of time. It cannot be otherwise while Satan is out of the Pit.

"And as the ark of the Lord came into the city of David, Michal, Saul's daugher, looked through a window, and saw king David leaping and dancing before the Lord; and she despised him in her heart" (2 Sam. 6:16). Saul himself had grievously neglected the public worship of Jehovah, and his daughter appears to have had no sense of the importance and value of heavenly things. It could hardly be expected that a woman who had idols, "teraphim," in her house (1 Sam. 19:13), cared anything for the holy ark, and hence she regarded her husband with scorn as she beheld his show of gratitude and joy. Poor creature, though a king's daugher, and married to the present monarch of Israel, Michal was quite incapable of entering into the gladness and zeal of the man after God's own heart. "The natural man receiveth not the things of the Spirit of God, for they are foolishness unto him; neither can he know them, because they are spirtually discerned" (1 Cor. 2:14).

Yes, not only is the natural man (the unregenerate) unable to apprehend the things of the Spirit, but that of which He is the Author appears as "foolishness" unto him. When the Lord Jesus was so occupied in ministering unto the needy multitude that He and His disciples "could not so much as eat bread," we are told that His kinsmen "went out to lay hold on Him: for they said, He is *beside Himself*" (Mark 3:21). When the apostles began to "speak with other tongues," the wondrous works of God, some mocked and said, "These men are full of new wine" (Acts 2). When Paul reasoned so earnestly with Agrippa, he answered "thou art beside thyself; much learning doth make thee mad" (Acts 26:24). And, my reader, there is something seriously lacking in you and me if similar charges are not made against us today!

The world will tolerate religion so long as its carnal repose is not disturbed; yea, while it provides a garb to hide its shame, the world approves. But let the high claims of God be pressed, let it be insisted on that HE demands the *first* place in our affections, thoughts, and lives, and such a message is at once distasteful. The professing Christian who attends the church on Sunday and the theatre during the week, who contributes occasionally to missionary societies but underpays his servants and overcharges his customers, is commended for his broad-mindedness and shrewdness. But the real Christian who lives in the fear of the Lord all the day long, and who conducts himself as a stranger and pilgrim in this scene, is condemned as a bigot and puritan. Let the saint weep over the dishonouring of his Lord by many that bear His name, or leap for joy in His service as David did, and like David he will be dubbed a fanatic and his whole-heartedness will be similarly censured.

"And they brought in the ark of the Lord, and set it in his place in the midst of the tabernacle that David had pitched for it: and David offered burnt offerings and peace offerings before the Lord" (v. 17). The word "tabernacle" does not signify a building made of wood or stone, but rather a tent. Joshua had erected such an one centuries before, but doubtless that had decayed and perished long ago. It is to be noted that David did not bring the ark into his own residence, but into a separate curtained canopy, which he had provided for it. In the days of Solomon a more stately temple was built to house the sacred coffer. As the ark was so manifestly a figure of Christ, its abiding first in a lowly tent and then in a magnificent edifice, no doubt foreshadowed the twofold state of the Saviour: first in humiliation, and then in glory.

"And David offered burnt offerings and peace offerings before the Lord." Now that his noble design had been completely effected, David presented suitable sacrifices unto the Lord. His object in so doing was probably twofold: to express his deep gratitude unto God for the success of his undertaking, and to supplicate a continuance of His favours. An important lesson for us is therein inculcated: praises are to mingle with our prayers: God is to be recognized and owned amid our joys, as well as sought unto under our sorrows. "Is any among you afflicted? let him pray. Is any merry? let him sing psalms" (James 5:13): the first is easily remembered, but the latter is often forgotten. God has appointed "feasts as well as "fasts," for He is to be given the first place by us at all times.

"And as soon as David had made an end of offering burnt offerings and peace offerings, he blessed the people in the name of the Lord of Hosts" (v. 18). This seems to have been an official act, consonant with the position to which God had instated him. The expression occurs first in Gen. 14:19, where we find that Melchizedek, priest of the Most High, "blessed" Abraham. At a later date, Moses (Ex. 39:43), Joshua (Josh. 22:6), and Solomon (1 Kings 8:14) "blessed the people:" in each case it was their leaders who did so. The added words that David "blessed the people in the name of the Lord of hosts" signifies that he, formally and authoritatively, pronounced His blessing upon those who had been committed to his care.

As a prophet of God, and as king over the people, it was both David's privilege and duty to do so, "without all contradiction, the less is blessed of the better" (Heb. 7:7). In this act we may see David prefiguring his greater Son and Lord. Of Him it is recorded, "And He led them out as far as to Bethany, and He lifted up His hands, and *blessed* them. And it came to pass, while He blessed them, He was parted from them, and carried up into heaven" (Luke 24:50, 52). There we behold Christ as the Prophet unto and the King over the Church, officially blessing its ministers: that was His final act ere He left this earth and took His place on high, to administer all the blessings which He had purchased for His people; and unto the end of the age the efficacy of His benediction abides. If by grace the writer and reader be among those whom *He* has blest, then are we blessed indeed.

"And he dealt among all the people, even among the whole multitude of Israel, as well as to women as men, to every one a cake of bread, and a good piece of flesh, and a flagon of wine. So all the people departed every one to his house" (v. 19). Those who accompanied David on his joyous undertaking were now bounteously feasted: having presented his thank offerings unto the Lord, presents were now made to the people. "When the heart is engaged in cheerfulness, that should open the hand in liberality: as they to whom God is merciful, ought to show mercy in forgiving; so they to whom God is bountiful, ought to exercise bounty in giving" (Matt. Henry). Compare Esther 9:22: the feast of Purim, celebrating the Jews' deliverance from the plot of Haman, was observed with "sending portions one to another, and gifts to the people." By this act David confirmed his interest in the people, and would endear himself to them, so that they would be encouraged to attend him again should he have occasion to call them. The typical significance is obvious.

"Then David returned to bless his household" (v. 20). In attending to his official duties, David did not overlook his domestic responsibilites. "Ministers must not think that their public performances will excuse them from their family worship: but when they have, with their instructions and prayers, blessed the solemn assemblies, they must return in the same manner to bless their households, for with them they are in a particular manner charged" (Matt. Henry). Nor must they be deterred from the discharge of this obligation and privilege should there be those under their roof whose hearts do not accompany them in such holy exercises: God must be honoured by the head of the house and the family altar maintained, no matter how much Satan may oppose the same.

"And Michal the daughter of Saul came out to meet David, and said, How glorious was the king of Israel today, who uncovered himself today in the eyes of the handmaids of his servants, as one of the vain fellows shamelessly uncovereth himself!" (v. 20). Being a total stranger to the zeal for God which filled David, incapable of appreciating his elevation of heart over the bringing home of the ark, she regarded his joyous dancing as unbecoming a king, and imagined he was demeaning himself in the eyes of his subjects. Having no heart herself for God, she despised the exuberance of one who had. Being obsessed with thoughts of temporal dignity and glory, she looked upon David's transports of religious fervour in the midst of his people, as degrading to his high office. "David *the brave captain,* leading forth the people to battle and returning with them in triumph, she admired; but David *the saint,* leading the people in the ordinances of God, and setting before them the example of fervency of spirit in His service, she despised" (Thos. Scott).

Base ingratitude was this for Michal to thus revile the very one who had been so devoted to her that he had declined to accept a crown unless she was restored to him (2 Sam. 3:13). Fearful sin was this to insult and denounce her lord, whom God required her to reverence. Having secretly scorned him in her heart, she now openly chides with her lips, for "out of the abundance of the heart the mouth speaketh." She was highly displeased with his deep veneration for the holy ark, and basely misrepresented his conduct by charging him with indecent dancing before it. There can be no doubt that her charge was a false one, for it is a common thing for those who have no piety themselves to paint others in false colours and hold them up as the most odious characters.

But the wicked conduct of Michal is not difficult to account for: at heart she was a partisan of the fallen house of Saul, and a despiser of Jehovah and His worship. As she grew older, her character had hardened in its lines and became more and more like her father's in its insatiable pride, and in its half dread and half hatred of David. Now she poured forth her venom in these mocking jibes. Because David had laid aside his royal robes, and had girded himself in a plain "linen ephod" (v. 14), she vilely charged him with immodesty. O how empty professors hate the true pilgrim spirit! Nothing riles them more than to see the children of God refusing to conform to the extravagant and flesh-pleasing fashions of the world, and instead, dress and act as becometh the followers of Him, who, when here, "had not where to lay His head."

"And David said unto Michal, It was before the Lord, which chose me before thy father, and before all his house, to appoint me ruler over the people of the Lord, over Israel; therefore will I play before the Lord" (v. 21). David now vindicated himself. He had no reason to be ashamed of his conduct, for what he had done was only for the glory of God. No matter through what distorted lens the evil eyes of Michal might view it, his conscience was clear. If our own hearts condemn us not, we need not be troubled over the censures of the ungodly. Moreover, had not God recently elevated him to the throne? Then it was but fitting that he should show his jubilant gratitude. There was an implied reproof in his reference to Saul and "all his house:" God had not been honoured in *their* courts — all the more reason, then, why He should be publicly magnified now.

"And I will yet be more vile than thus, and will be base in mine own sight; and of the maidservants which thou hast spoken of, of them shall I be had in honour" (v. 22). David replies to Michal's evil charge in the language of irony, which was suitably "answering a fool according to her folly" (Prov. 26:5). The force of his words is, If because of my setting aside the showy robes of imperial majesty and clothing myself in plain linen, and dancing before the ark of God's glory, I am regarded by *you* as mean, then I, who am but "dust and ashes" in the sight of the Almighty, will humble myself yet more before Him; and so far from the common people despising me for the same, they will esteem one who takes a lowly place before the Lord. The more we be condemned for well doing, the more resolute should we be in it.

"Therefore Michal the daughter of Saul had no child unto the day of her death" (v. 23). Thus did God punish David's wife for her sin. "She unjustly reproached David for his devotion, and therefore God justly put her under the perpetual reproach of barrenness. They that honour God, He will honour; but those that despise Him, and His servants and service, shall be lightly esteemed" (Matt. Henry). There is a searching application of this verse which holds good today. We often hear quoted the first half of 1 Sam. 2:30, but the second half is not so frequently cited. It is just as true that they who "despise" the Lord shall be "lightly esteemed" by Him, as those who "honour" Him shall be "honoured" by Him. A solemn example of this is found here: in mocking David, Michal insulted his Master! Beware how you slight or speak evil against God's servants, lest spiritual "barrenness" be your portion!

And when the king sat in his house, and when the LORD had given him rest all around from all his enemies, the king said to Nathan the prophet, See now, I live in a house of cedar, but the ark of God dwells within curtains. And Nathan said to the king, Go, do all that is in your heart, for the LORD is with you. And that night the word of the LORD came to Nathan, saying, Go and tell My servant David, Thus says the LORD, shall you build Me a house for Me to dwell in? For I have not lived in any house since the day that I brought up the children out of Egypt until this day, but have walked in a tent and in a tabernacle. In all the places in which I have walked with all the children of Israel, did I speak a word with any of the tribes of Israel, whom I commanded to feed My people Israel, saying, Why do you not build Me a house of cedar? Now therefore, so shall you say to My servant David, Thus says the LORD of hosts: I took you from the sheepcote, from following the sheep, to be ruler over My people, over Israel. And I was with you wherever you went and have cut off all your enemies out of your sight, and have made you a great name like the name of the great men who are in the earth. Moreover I will appoint a place for My people Israel and will plant them so that they may dwell in a place of their own and move no more. Neither shall the children of wickedness afflict them any more, as before. And even from the time that I commanded judges to be over My people of Israel, so I will cause you to rest from all your enemies. Also the LORD tells you that He will make you a house. And when your days are fulfilled, and you shall sleep with your fathers, I will set up your seed after you, who shall come out of your bowels, And I will make his kingdom sure. He shall build a house for My name, and I will establish the throne of his kingdom forever. I will be his Father, and he shall be My son. If he commits iniquity, I will chasten him with the rod of men, and with the stripes of the children of men. But My mercy shall not leave him, as I took it from Saul, whom I put away before you. And your house and your kingdom shall be made sure forever before you. Your throne shall be established forever. According to all these words, and according to all this vision, so Nathan spoke to David. — II Samuel 7:1-17.

How often has "success" been the ruination of those who have experienced it! How often has worldly advancement been followed by the deterioration of spirituality! It is good to see that such was far from being the case with David. In the 35th article of this series we called attention to the blessed manner in which David conducted himself after coming to the throne. So far from indulging in ease and self-luxuriation, it was now that his best achievements were accomplished. First, he captured the stronghold of Zion; next he vanquished the Philistines; then he provided a restingplace for the holy ark; and now he evidenced his deep concern to build a temple for the worship of Jehovah. So blessed is each of these incidents, so rich are they in their spiritual and typical import, we proposed to devote a section unto the separate consideration of each of them. By the Lord's gracious enabling we have accomplished our purpose concerning the first three, and now we turn to the fourth.

"And it came to pass, when the king sat in his house, and the Lord had given him rest round about from all his enemies" (2 Sam. 7:1). This brings before us a restful interlude in the strenuous and eventful life of our hero. As we have seen in earlier chapters, David had been called upon to gird on the sword again and again; and as we shall see in what follows, considerable fighting yet lay before him. Moreover, little opportunity had been given him in previous years for quietness and repose: during Saul's life and also under the reign of Ishbosheth, David was much harried, and forced to move from place to place; so too in the future, disquieting and distressing experiences lay before him. But here in 2 Sam. 7 a very different picture is set before us: for a brief season the Lord granted His servant rest.

What has been pointed out above finds its counterpart, more or less, in the lives of all Christians. For the most part, their experience both outward and inward closely resembles that of David's. Christians are called upon to wage a warfare against the flesh, the world, and the devil, to "Fight the good fight of faith." Those inveterate enemies of the new man give him little rest, and often when he has been enabled by Divine grace to achieve a notable victory, he quickly discovers that fresh conflicts await him. Yet, amid his outward troubles and inward strifes, he is occasionally granted a little breathing-spell, and as he sits in his house it can be said of him, "The Lord hath given him rest round about from all his enemies."

As it is in nature, so it is in grace: after the storm comes a peaceful calm. The Lord is very merciful and tender in His dealings with His own. Amid many disheartenings, He grants encouragements along the way. "There hath no temptation taken you, but such as is common to man: but God is faithful, who will not suffer you to be tempted above what ye are able; but will with the temptation also make a way to escape, that ye may be able to bear it" (1 Cor. 10:13). After the toil of trying service, He says, "Come ye yourselves apart into a desert place, and *rest awhile*" (Mark 6:31). After a long stretch of the dreary sands of the wilderness, He brings us to come Elim "where are twelve wells of water, and three score and ten palm trees" (Ex. 15:27). After some unusually fierce conflict with Satan, the Lord grants a season of peace, and then, as in David's case, we have rest "from all our enemies."

And with what was David's mind employed during the hour of repose? Not upon worldly trifles or fleshly indulgences, but with the honour of God: "That the king said unto Nathan the prophet, See, now, I dwell in an house of cedar, but the ark of God dwelleth within curtains" (7:2). This is very blessed and furnishes a true insight to the character of him whom the Lord Himself declared to be "a man after His own heart." There are few things which afford a surer index to our spirituality — or the lack of it — than how we are engaged in our hours of *leisure*. When the conflict is over, and the sword is laid down, we are very apt to relax and become careless about spiritual concerns. And then it is, while off our guard, that Satan so often succeeds in gaining an advantage over us. Far different was it with him whose history we are here pondering.

"The king said unto Nathan the prophet, See, now, I dwell in a house of cedar, but the ark of God dwelleth within curtains." Observe, first, that in this season of rest David's companion was "the prophet." Let that speak loudly to us! A godly companion is an invaluable aid to the preserving of spirituality when we are enjoying a little rest. Hours of recreation would prove hours of *re-creation* indeed, if they were spent in godly converse with someone who lives near to the Lord. David here supplied proof of his own assertion, "I am a companion of all that fear Thee, and of them that keep Thy precepts" (Psa. 119:63). A person is not only *known* by the company he or she keeps, but is *moulded* thereby: "He that walketh with wise men, shall be wise; but a companion of fools shall be destroyed" (Prov. 13:20). Seek as your friends, dear reader, those who are most Christlike in their character and conversation.

Next, observe what it was which occupied David's heart while he sat in his palace in the company of Nathan the prophet' "See, now, I dwell in an house of cedar, but the ark of God dwelleth within curtains." How this, too, reveals the beatings of David's heart! One cannot but contrast what we have here with the haughty words of Nebuchadnezzar: "Is not this great Babylon, that I have built for the house of the kingdom, by the might of my power, for the honour of *my* majesty?" (Dan. 4:30). Instead of being occupied with his achievements and self-satisfied with the position which he now occupied, David was concerned about the lowly abode of God's ark. Very beautiful indeed is it to see the recently crowned monarch solicitous, not for the honour of his own majesty, but for the glory of Him whom he served.

It is not often that those in high places manifest such interest in spiritual things: would that more of the Lord's people who are entrusted with a considerable amount of this world's goods were more exercised in heart over the prospering of His cause. There are not many who make conscience over-spending far more upon themselves than they do for furthering the service of God. In this generation, when the pilgrim character of the saints is well-nigh obliterated, when separation from the world is so largely a thing of the past, when self-indulgence and the gratification of every whim is the order of the day, few find their rest disturbed in the conviction that the worship is languishing. Thousands of professing Christians think more about the welfare of their pet dogs than they do in seeing that the needs of God's servants and impoverished believers are met, and spend more on the upkeep of their motorcars than they do in the support of missionaries. Little wonder that the Holy Spirit is quenched in so many places.

"And Nathan said to the king, Go, do all that is in thine heart; for the Lord is with thee" (v. 3). A certain class of writers who delight in criticising almost everyone and everything, and who pretend unto a deeper insight of spiritual things than all who went before them, condemn both David and Nathan on this occasion, which seems to us close akin to the complaint of Judas when Mary lavished her costly ointment upon the Saviour. Nothing is said in the record here that David actually purposed to build Jehovah a temple, but only that he was troubled because one was not yet erected. Whatever conclusion Nathan may have drawn therefrom, he was careful to say nothing to modify David's godly concern, but rather sought to encourage his spiritual aspirations. Alas, how many today are ready to snub earnestness, quench zeal, and hinder those who have more love for perishing souls than they have.

Nathan was better taught in Divine things than some of those who have traduced him. He was quick to perceive that such unselfishness and godly concern as the king manifested was good evidence that the Lord was with him, for such spiritual exercises of heart proceed not from mere nature. Had David been actuated by a "legalistic" spirit as one of his foolish detractors supposed — deploring it with an "alas, alas!" — God's faithful servant had promptly rebuked, or at least corrected him. But instead of so doing, he says, "Go, do all that is in thine heart; for the Lord is with thee." O that more of this so-called "legality" were in evidence today — a heart melted by the Lord's abounding mercies, anxious to express its gratitude by furthering His cause and service. But it is hardly to be expected that those who so strenuously oppose the Law's being a rule of life for the Christian, should have any clear ideas on either grace or what constitutes "legality."

"And it came to pass that night, that the word of the Lord came unto Nathan" (v. 4). In the brief notes on this verse found in "The Companion Bible" it is there stated that, "After these words ('that night') all the MSS. (manuscripts) have a hiatus, marking a solemn pause." The design of the ancient Hebrews may have been to connect this passage with Gen. 15:12-17, which is another *night* scene. It both a wondrous revelation was made by the Lord: in both His great purpose concerning the Messiah and Mediator received an unfolding: in both a remarkable adumbration was made respecting the contents of the Everlasting Covenant.

"Go and tell My servant David, Thus saith the Lord, Shalt thou build Me an house for Me to dwell in?" (v. 5), or, as it is said in 1 Chron. 17:4, "Thou shalt not build Me an house to dwell in." Some may suppose that these words make it quite clear that David *had* definitely determined to erect a temple unto Jehovah. But we rather regard these statements as the gracious construction which God placed upon the holy concern of His servant, just as the Saviour sweetly interpreted the loving devotion of Mary's anointing as "against the day of My burying hath she kept this" (John 12:7); and, as in a coming day He will yet say unto those on His right hand, "I was an hungered, and ye gave *Me* meat: I was thirsty, and ye gave *Me* drink; I was a stranger, and ye took *Me* in" (Matt. 25:35 etc.).

"For if there be first a willing mind, it is accepted according to that a man hath, not according to that he hath not" (2 Cor. 8:12). It is the disposition and desire of the heart which God regards, and sincere intentions to do good are approved by Him, even though His providences do not permit the execution of them. Thus it was in David's case. He was concerned that the sacred ark should be under curtains, while he dwelt in a ceiled house. That holy concern was tantamount unto a willingness on his part to honour the Lord's worship by a stately temple, and *this* is the construction which God graciously placed upon it, accepting the will for the deed. Though David had not formally planned to build the temple, God so *interpreted* the exercises of his mind; just as when a man looks lustfully upon a woman, Christ *interprets* this as "adultery" itself (Matt. 5:28).

We have dwelt the longer upon this point because the commentators have quite missed the force of it. Not only so, but some teachers, who are looked upon in certain circles as wellnigh infallible in their expositions, have falsely charged David with "legality." Now that the Lord had elevated him from the sheepcote to the throne, and had given him rest from all his enemies, David's concern for the dwellingplace of the ark is twisted into his desire to so something *for* the Lord as payment of all He had done for him. Such men err "not knowing the scriptures." One verse of the Word is sufficient to refute their childish misconceptions, and establish what we have said above: "And the Lord said unto David my father, Whereas it was in thine heart to build an house unto My name, thou *didst well* (not "thou was moved by a legalistic spirit") that it was in thine heart" (1 Kings 8:18).

We do not propose to comment in detail upon the remainder of the Lord's message through Nathan, but rather will we generalize our remarks upon the same. First, the Lord made touching mention of His own infinite condescension in graciously accommodating Himself unto the stranger and pilgrim character of His people (v. 6). The great Jehovah had deigned to "*walk with* the children of Israel." What an amazing and heart-melting word is that in Lev. 25:23 "The land shall not be sold forever: for the land is Mine; for ye are strangers and sojourners *with* Me." David himself had laid hold of that word, as his statement in Psa. 39:12 clearly shows, "Hold not Thy peace at my tears: for I am a stranger *with Thee*, and a sojourner as all my fathers were." Until Israel were settled in their inheritance an humble tent had served the Lord's requirements. In this He has left *us* an example to follow: pomp and parade, extravagance and luxury, ill become those who have here "no continuing city."

Second, as yet the Lord had given no definite instruction for the erection of an imposing edifice for His worship (v. 7), and until He did, a *tent* of His appointing, was better than a *temple* of man's devising. Our desires, even of usefulness, must be governed by His precepts. Whatever be our spiritual aspirations, they must be regulated by the revealed will of God. He assigns unto every one his own work, and each of us should thankfully and faithfully attend to our own proper business. For example, no matter how strong the sisters may yearn to engage in public preaching, since they have received no commission from the Lord so to do, they are required to "keep silence in the churches." O to be satisfied with the place which God has allotted *us*, to discharge earnestly the duty which He has appointed us, and leave to others whom He has chosen, the more honourable work. The temple was to bear the name of Solomon, and not that of David.

Third, David was reminded of the wondrous things which God had already wrought for him, so that while he was not called unto the building of the temple, nevertheless, he *was* one of the favourites of Heaven (v. 8). Moreover, God had made him signally victorious over all his foes, and had advanced him unto high honour among the nations (v. 9). Let us be thankful for the mercies which God *has* bestowed, and not repine for any which He sees fit to withhold. Fourth, the happy future of his people was assured him (v. 10), from which he might well conclude that, when *they* were more securely established, then would be the time for the erection of a permanent house of worship. Finally, God announces rich blessings as being entailed upon David's family, for from *his* seed should issue, according to the flesh, the promised Messiah and Mediator (vv. 11-16). Thus, instead of David's building for the Lord a material and temporal house, the Lord would build for *him* a spiritual house which would abide "for ever." Thus we see that a "willing mind" (2 Cor. 8:12) is not only accepted, but richly *rewarded*. "Now unto him that is able to do exceeding abundantly above all that we ask or think, according to the power that worketh in us, unto Him be glory in the Church, by Christ Jesus throughout all ages, world without end. Amen." (Eph. 3:20,21).

In the preceding article we looked upon David while he was permitted to enjoy a brief season of repose, following the trying experiences through which he had passed ere he came to the throne. He might well have found in the many trials and vicissitudes of his past life leisure as well as their toil to God, and will serve with thankofferings in peace Him whom they invoked with earnest supplication in battle. As another has said, "Prosperity is harmless only when it is accepted as an opportunity for fresh forms of devotion, and not as an occasion for idle self-indulgence." Thus it was with our hero. He was not spoiled by success; his head was not made giddy by the height he now occupied; the Lord was not forgotten when prosperity smiled upon him. Instead, he was deeply concerned about the honour of God, especially at there being no suitable place for His public worship.

As David sat alone in his palace, meditating, there can be little doubt that one so conversant with the Scriptures as he was, would turn in thought to the ancient promise, "When He giveth you rest from all your enemies round about, so that ye dwell in safety, then there shall be a place which the Lord your God shall choose to cause His name to dwell there" (Deut. 12:10, 11). It was *that* word, we believe, which caused our hero to say unto Nathan, "See, now, I dwell in a house of cedar, but the ark of God dwelleth within curtains" (2 Sam. 7:2). Israel's king felt more or less rebuked by his own ease and comfort, and regarded his tranquility not as a season for selfish indolence, but rather as a call to serious reflection upon the interests of God's cause or kingdom. He could not bear the thought of lavishing more upon self than upon the service of Him to whom he owed everything.

The response made by the Lord unto the spiritual exercises of His servant was indeed blessed. Through the prophet He gave David a much fuller revelation of what was in *His* heart toward him: "I will set up thy seed after thee. . .I will establish the throne of his kingdom forever. . .thine house and thy kingdom shall be established forever" (vv. 10-12). God made known His purpose to confer upon the posterity of David a special favour, which He had not granted even to Abraham, Moses, or Joshua, namely, establish them upon the throne of Israel. Moreover, it was declared of his seed who should be set up after him, "He shall build an house for My name" (v. 13). If we are spared, this will be considered in more detail under "The Divine Covenants" (when we reach the "Davidic"): suffice it now to say, the ultimate reference was a *spiritual* one in the person and kingdom of the Lord Jesus Christ.

While there was much in the revelation now granted to David which was well calculated to evoke gratitude and praise, yet there was one omission from it that presented a real test of his submission, humility, and patience. While there was abundant cause for thanksgiving, that *his* posterity should continue to occupy the throne, and his own son build an house for Jehovah's name (and fame), yet that *he* was denied this honour, had been resented by one who was proud and filled with a sense of his own importance. David's longings were not to be realized during his own lifetime, and though he should be permitted to gather together much of the material for the future temple, yet *he* would not be permitted to see the finished product itself. Here, then, was a real trying of his character, and it is blessed to see how he endured and met the same.

How often it falls out that one sows and another reaps: one set of men labour, and another generation is permitted to enter into the benefits of their toil. Nor should we complain at this, seeing that our sovereign and all-wise God has so ordered it. David did not complain, nor did he manifest any petulant disappointment at the crowning of his hopes being deferred to a future time. Instead, as we shall see, he sweetly bowed to God's pleasure and adored Him for the same. Ah, my readers, our prayers may yet move God to send a gracious revival, yet that happy event may not come during *our* lifetime. The faithful labours of God's servants today may not immediately transform the present "wilderness" state of Zion into a fruitful garden, yet if they be the means of plowing and harrowing the ground as a necessary preliminary thereto, ought we not to gladly acquiesce?

Then king David went in and sat before the LORD. And he said, Who am I, O Lord GOD? And what is my house, that You have brought me this far? And this was yet a small thing in Your sight, O Lord GOD. But You have spoken also of Your servant's house for a great while to come. And is this the manner of men, O Lord GOD? And what can David say more to You? For You, Lord GOD, know Your servant. For Your word's sake, and according to Your own heart, You have done all these great things to make Your servant know. — II Samuel 7:18-21.

In the passage which is now to be before us, we behold the effects which God's wondrous revelation through Nathan had upon the soul of David. "Then went king David in, and sat before the Lord; and he said, Who am I, O Lord God? and what is my house, that Thou hast brought me hitherto?" (2 Sam. 7:18). Inexpressibly blessed is this. Such tidings as had just fallen on his ears, would have puffed up many a man, filled him with a sense of his own importance, and caused him to act arrogantly toward his fellows. Far otherwise was it with "the man after God's own heart." Filled with joyful amazement at Jehovah's infinite condescension, David at once left the royal palace and betook himself to the humble tent which housed that sacred ark, there to pour out his heart in adoration and praise. There is nothing like a feeling sense of God's sovereign, free, and rich *grace*, to melt the soul, humble the heart, and stir unto true and acceptable worship.

"Then went king David in, and sat before the Lord" (2 Sam. 7:18). This is in designed contrast from v. 1: there the king "sat in his house;" here he is seen in the tabernacle, before Jehovah. The word *"sat* before the Lord," probably refers to his *continuance* in the tabernacle, rather than to the posture in which he prayed. "And he said, Who am I, O Lord God? and what is my house, that Thou hast brought me hitherto?" (v. 18). How few kings there are who have such a realization of their lowliness as this! All sense of personal greatness vanished when David came into the presence of the great Jehovah. Ah, my reader, when *the Lord* is truly before us, "I" sinks into utter insignificance! But it is only as we are absorbed with His perfections — His infinitude, His majesty, His omnipotency — that self will be lost sight of.

"Who am I? O Lord God? and what is my house?" How these words bring before us the deep humility of David! Truthfully could he say, "Lord my heart is not haughty, nor my eyes lofty" (Psa. 131:1). A number of illustrations of this lovely grace may be cited from the record of David's life. His being content to follow his mean vocation as a shepherd, till God called him to a higher office. He never affected the royal diadem, neither would it have been any grief of heart to him had God passed him by, and made another king. His words to Abishai concerning Saul, "Destroy him not: for who can stretch forth his hand against the Lord's anointed, and be guiltless?" (1 Sam. 26:9) show plainly that he was not coveting the crown, and was quite content for the son of Kish to continue occupying the throne of Israel.

It is beautiful to see how often this spirit of lowliness and self-abnegation appears in "the man after God's own heart." When he went forth to engage Goliath, it was not in the confidence of his own skill, but with the holy assurance "This day will *the Lord* deliver thee into mine hand" (1 Sam. 17:46). When Saul lay helpless before him, he took no credit unto himself, but said to the king, *"the Lord* had delivered thee today into mine hand" (1 Sam. 24:10). When Abigail was used to quiet his passionate spirit, he exclaimed, "Blessed be the Lord God of Israel, which sent thee this day to meet me" (1 Sam. 25:32); and when Nabal was dead, "Blessed be the Lord, that hath pleaded the cause of my reproach. . .and hath kept His servant from evil" (v. 39). After his notable victory over the Amalekites he said, "Ye shall not do so, my brethren, with that which *the Lord* hath given us, who hath preserved us, and delivered the company that came against us into our hand" (1 Sam. 30:23). Humility is that grace which gives the Lord His proper place.

Distrusting his own wisdom, we find David "enquiring of the Lord" again and again (1 Sam. 23:2,4; 30:8; 2 Sam. 2:1; 5:19; etc.). This is another sure mark of genuine humility: that spirit which is afraid to trust in our own knowledge, experience, and powers, and seeks counsel and direction from above. When for his prowess Saul called him to court and promised to give him Michal to wife, he answered "Seemeth it to you a light thing to be a king's son-in-law, seeing that I am a poor man, and lightly esteemed?" (1 Sam. 18:23). Note the love he bore to those who admonished him for his sins: "Let the righteous smite me: it shall be a kindness: and let him reprove me; it shall be an excellent oil, which shall not break my head" (Psa. 141:5): far meaner people do not take it so kindly! In all his heroical acts he sought not his own honour, but God's: "Not unto us, O Lord, not unto us, but unto Thy name give glory" (Psa. 115:1).

Mark his submission to God under chastisement: "And the king said unto Zadok, Carry back the ark of God into the city: if I shall find favour in the eyes of the Lord, He will bring me again, and show me both it, and His habitation: But if He thus say, I have no delight in thee: behold, here am I, let Him *do to me as seemeth good unto Him*" (2 Sam. 15:25,26). In all his dealings with God, he dared not trust in his own righteousness, but wholly took refuge in the covenant of grace: "If Thou, Lord, shouldest mark iniquities, O Lord, who shall stand?" (Psa. 130:3). "Enter not into judgment with Thy servant: for in Thy sight shall no man living be justified" (Psa. 143:2). When a man can find all this in himself, he may honestly say, "Lord, *my* heart is not haughty" (Psa. 131:1). Yet, David was not perfect, and the remains of pride still indwelt him, as they do each of us — till we get rid of the flesh, we shall never be completely rid of pride. Psa. 30:6 and 2 Sam. 24:2 show his vain glory creeping out.

We have dwelt the more largely upon David's *humility*, because in this day of Laodicean conceit and boasting, it needs to be emphasised that, as a general rule, those whom God has used most mightily have not been men who were distinguished for abnormal natural powers or gifts, but instead *by deep humility*. See this admirable trait in Abraham: "I am but dust and ashes" (Gen. 18:27); in Moses, "Who am I, that I should go unto Pharaoh, and that I should bring forth the children of Israel out of Egypt?" (Ex. 3:11); in Christ's forerunner, "He must increase, but I must decrease" (John 3:30); in Paul, "I am the least of the apostles, that am not meet to be called an apostle, because I persecuted the church of God" (1 Cor. 15:9). O that Divine grace may make us "little in our own eyes."

But again we would notice it was while David was "before the Lord" that he said, "Who am I?" So too it was while he was in the immediate presence of the Lord that Abraham confessed himself to be "but dust and ashes." In like manner, it was when the great I Am revealed Himslef at the burning bush that Moses asked, "Who am I that I should go unto Pharaoh?" It was when Job could say, "now mine eye seeth Thee" — in all Thine awful sovereignty (see context) — that he cried, "wherefore I abhor myself" (45:5). It was when Isaiah saw Jehovah "sitting upon a throne high and lifted up," that he bemoaned "woe is me, for I am undone" (Isa. 6:5). It was when he stood face to face with the Lord Jesus in theophanic manifestation that Daniel owned "my comeliness was turned in me into corruption" (10:8). And my brethren if *we* were more in the Lord's presence and had closer dealing with Him, pride would be more largely subdued in us.

"And what is my house, that Thou hast brought me hitherto?" David continued in the same lowly strain. His "house" pertained to the royal tribe; he was the immediate descendant of the prince of Judah, so that he was connected with the most honourable family in Israel; yet such fleshly distinctions were held very lightly by him. The "Thou hast brought me hitherto" — to the throne, to rest from all his enemies — gave to God the rightful glory. "It intimates that he could not have reached this himself by his own management, if God had not brought him to it. All our attainments must be looked upon as God's vouchsafements" (Matt. Henry).

"And this was yet a small thing in Thy sight, O Lord God; but Thou hast spoken also of Thy servant's house for a great while to come. And is this the manner of man, O Lord God?" (v. 19). Having owned the goodness of the Lord upon him "hitherto," David now turns to comment upon the glorious things which God had promised for the future. The latter so immeasurably outweighed the former, that he sums up his own establishment over the kingdom as "this was yet a small thing in Thy sight, O Lord God." We believe this throws light upon the word "sat" in the previous verse, which has presented a difficulty unto the commentators — who point out that this is the only place in Scripture where a saint is represented as being seated while engaged in prayer. But are we not rather to regard the term as denoting that David was in an attitude of most carefully surveying the wonderful riches of Divine grace toward him, instead of defining his posture while engaged in his devotions?

The whole of 2 Sam. 7 is to be viewed as the blessed and instructive sequel to what is presented to us in the opening verse. God had tenderly given His servent a season of rest that he might receive a fuller revelation of what was in *His* heart toward him. And now he is in the sacred tabernacle, pondering over what he had heard through Nathan. As he meditated, Divine light and understanding broke in upon him, so that he was enabled, in measure at least, to penetrate the mysterious depths of that wondeful prophecy. The golden future was now opened to him, shining with more than earthly glory and bliss. "He beheld in spirit another Son than Solomon, another Temple than that built of stones and cedar, another Kingdom than the earthly one on whose throne he sat. He beholds a sceptre and a crown, of which his own on Mount Zion were only feeble types — dim and shadowy images" (Krummacher's "David and the God man").

Beautifully does this come out in his next words: "And is this the manner of man, O Lord God? And what can David say more unto Thee? for Thou, Lord God, knowest Thy servant. For Thy word's sake, and according to Thine own heart, hast Thou done all these great things, to make Thy servant know them" (vv. 19-21) — in the light of which knowledge, he no doubt penned the 40th, 45th and 110th Psalms. The last clause of v. 19 should be translated, more literally, "This is the law of *the* Man, the Lord God," namely, "The Man" of Psalm 8:5, 6 and of Psalm 80:17! David was now given to realise that the blessed promises which had been given to him through the prophet would be made good in the person of the Messiah, who should yet issue from his own loins, who would be "The Man," yet none other than "the Lord God" incarnate. Yes, God reveals His secrets to the lowly, but hides them from those who are wise and prudent in their own esteem.

Therefore, You are great, O LORD God. For there is none like You, and there is no God besides You, according to all that we have heard with our ears. And what one nation in the earth is like Your people, like Israel, whom God went to redeem for a people to Himself, and to make Himself a name, and to do for you great things, even fearful things for Your land, before Your people, whom You redeemed to Yourself from Egypt, from the nations and their gods? For You have confirmed to Yourself Your people Israel to be a people to You forever. And You, LORD, have become their God. And now, O LORD God, the word that You have spoken concerning Your servant, and concerning his house: establish it forever, and do as You have said. And let Your name be magnified forever, saying, The LORD of hosts is the God over Israel. And let the house of Your servant David be established before You. For You, O LORD of hosts, God of Israel, have revealed to Your servant, saying, I will build you a house. Therefore Your servant has found in his heart to pray this prayer to You. And now, O LORD God, You are that God, and Your words are true, and You have promised this goodness to Your servant. And now, let it please You to bless the house of Your servant so that it may continue forever before You. For You, O Lord GOD, have spoken it. And with Your blessing let the house of Your servant be blessed forever. — II Samuel 7:22-29.

The latter part of 2 Sam. 7 contains the prayer made by David in the tabernacle, following the gracious revelation which he had received from the Lord through Nathan (vv. 5-16). This prayer is among the "whatsoever things were written aforetime, were written for our learning" (Rom. 15:4). It contains valuable instruction which we do well to take to heart. It makes known that which is a valuable preliminary-aid unto stimulating the spirit of prayer. It shows us the attitude of soul which most becomes the creature when desirous of drawing nigh unto the great Creator. It reveals some of the elements which are found in those supplications that gain the ear of God and which "availeth much." If the Christian of today paid more attention unto the prayers *of Scripture*, both of the Old and New Testaments alike, and sought to pattern his invocations after theirs, there is little doubt they would be more acceptable and effectual.

We pointed out in our last that David's *sitting* before the Lord denoted his earnest attention unto the message he had received from Him, his careful pondering of it, his devout surveying of the riches of Divine grace which were then spread before his mind's eye. This preceded his prayer, and supplies a valuable hint for us to heed. Meditation upon the discoveries which God has made to us of His goodness, of His bounty, of the glorious things contained in His covenant, is a wondrous stimulant to the spirit of devotion and a suitable preparative for an approach into the Mercy-seat. To review God's past dealings with us, and to mix faith with His promises for the future, kindle the fires of gratitude and love. As we attend upon what God has spoken to us, when our consciences are pricked or our affections stirred, then is the best time to retire to our closets and pour out our hearts before Him.

Generally it is but an idle excuse — if not something worse — when the Christian complains that his heart is cold and the spirit of prayer is quite inactive within him. Where this be the case, it must be shamefacedly confessed to God, accompanied by the request that He may be pleased to heal our malady and bring us back again into communion with Himself. But better still, the *cause* of the complaint should be corrected: nine times out of ten it is because the Word has been neglected — if read at all, mechanically, without holy reflection and personal appropriation. The soul is likely to be in a sickly state if it be not regularly fed and nourished by the Bread of life. There is nothing like *meditating* upon God's promises for warming the heart: "While I *was musing* the fire burned: then spake I with my tongue" (Psa. 39:3).

We commented in our last upon the deep humility manifested by David on this occasion. This too is recorded for our learning. If we are becomingly to approach the Most High, there must be the taking of a lowly place before Him. This is the chief design of prayer, the prime reason why God has appointed this holy ordinance: for the *humbling* of the soul — to take our proper place in the dust, to kneel before the Lord as beggars, dependent upon His bounty; to stretch forth empty hands, that He may fill them. Alas that so often man, in his pride and perverseness, turns the footstool of mercy into the bench of presumption, and instead of supplicating becomes guilty of dictating unto the Almighty. Ah, my readers, take careful note that, He who prayed "Not as I will, but as Thou wilt," was *on His face* before the Father (Matt. 26:39).

We cannot forbear from inserting a word of warning at this point concerning many of the so-called "prayer meetings" of this degenerate day. In our "Sound the Alarm" articles (some time ago), we urged our readers to separate themselves from those "churches" where Christ is dishonoured by false doctrine, by fleshly attractions, by worldly devices for raising money, by refusing to maintain a Scriptural discipline. Some of God's people who are more or less "outside the (apostate) camp," yet felt free to attend undenominational "prayer meetings." Alas, they little realise the spiritual dangers (diseases) to which they expose themselves, and the likelihood of their becoming infected by the evil example set before them. The "prayers" (?) they will hear, are, for the most part, highly insulting to the Lord — how can it be otherwise, when they issue from those who sit under erroneous teaching and are mixed up with the Laodicean abominations of the day.

Now in seeking to ponder David's pattern prayer — having duly noted above what preceded it, let us seek to profit from the various features found in it. First, observe that *all is ascribed to free grace.* "And what can David say more unto Thee? for Thou, Lord God, knowest Thy servant. For Thy word's sake, and according to Thine own heart, hast Thou done all these great things, to make Thy servant know them" (vv. 20, 21). David's heart was deeply moved by a sense of God's sovereign benignity: that such blessings should be bestowed upon him and his posterity was more than he could understand. He was lost in wonderment: words utterly failed him, as his "what can David say more unto Thee?" evidences, And is it not thus, at times, with every true believer? As he contemplates the abounding of God's mercies, the richness of His gifts, the supernal future promised him, is he not moved to exclaim, "What shall I render unto the Lord for all His benefits toward me?" (Psa. 116:12).

Realizing his own nothingness and unworthiness (v. 18), viewing the future glories assured him (v. 19), knowing there was nothing in himself which merited any such blessings, David traces them to their true cause: "For Thy Word's sake, and according to Thine own heart, hast Thou done all these great things" (v. 21). It is the *personal* "Word" which he had in mind, Him of whom it is declared, "In the beginning was the Word, and the Word was with God, and the Word was God" (John 1:1). It was an acknowledgement "for *Christ's* sake" Thou hast so honoured me! "And according to Thine own heart" signifies, according to His gracious counsels, out of His own mere good pleasure. Yes, those, and those alone, are the springs of all God's dealings with us: He blessed His people for the sake of His beloved Son, "according to the riches of His grace" and "according to His good pleasure which He hath purposed in Himself" (Eph. 1:7, 9).

Second, *the greatness of God is apprehended and extolled.* "Wherefore Thou art great, O Lord God: for there is none like Thee, neither is there any God beside Thee, according to all that we have heard with our ears" (v. 22). It is blessed to observe that David's sense of God's goodness in nowise abated his awesome veneration of the Divine majesty. There is ever a danger at this point: we may be so occupied with God's love as to forget His holiness, so appreciative of His tenderness as to ignore His omnipotency. It is most needful that we should hold the balance here, as everywhere else; hence did the Saviour instruct us to say "Our Father, who art in Heaven" — the latter words reminding us of the exalted dignity of the One who has deigned to adopt us into His family. Apprehensions of God's amazing grace toward us must not crowd out the realization of His infinite exaltation above us.

God's greatness should be duly acknowledged by us when we seek an audience with the Majesty on high: it is but ascribing to Him the glory which is His due. Prayer is reduced to a very low level if it is to be confined unto the presenting of requests. The soul needs to be so absorbed with the Divine perfections that the worshipper will exclaim, "Who is like unto Thee, O Lord, among the gods? who is like Thee, glorious in holiness, fearful in praises, doing wonders?" (Ex. 15:11). God's supreme excellency is to be reverently and freely owned by us. It was owned by Solomon, "Lord God of Israel, there is no God like Thee, in heaven above, or on earth beneath" (1 Kings 8:23). It was by Jehoshaphat, "O Lord God of our fathers, art not Thou God in heaven? and rulest not Thou over all the kingdoms of the heathen? and in Thine hand is there not power and might, so that none is able to withstand Thee?" (2 Chron. 20:6). It was by Jeremiah, "Forasmuch as there is none like unto Thee, O Lord; Thou art great, and Thy name is great in might. Who would not fear Thee, O king of nations?" (10:6,7). What examples are these for us to take to heart. The more we heartily acknowledge God's greatness, the more likely is He to answer our requests.

Third, *The special goodness of God to His people is owned.* "And what one nation in the earth is like Thy people, like Israel, whom God went to redeem for a people to Himself, and to make Him a name, and to do for you great things and terrible?" (v. 23). As none of the "gods" of the heathen could be compared to Jehovah, so none among the people's of the earth have been so highly favoured and so richly blest as His privileged "Nation" (Matt. 21:43; 1 Pet. 2:9). O what praise is due unto God for His distinguishing mercy and discriminating grace unto His elect. "We are bound to give thanks *always* to God for you, brethren beloved of the Lord, because God hath from the beginning chosen you to salvation" (2 Thess. 2:13). The special blessings of God call for special acknowledgement: the "redemption" which we have in and by Christ Jesus demands our loudest hosannas. There is far too little praise in our prayers today: its absence denotes a low state of spirituality — occupation with self, instead of with the Lord. It is written "whoso offereth praise, glorifieth Me" (Psa. 50:23).

Fourth, *the Covenant of Grace is celebrated.* "For Thou hast confirmed to Thyself Thy people Israel to be a people unto Thee forever; and Thou, O, Lord, art become their God" (v. 24). In the light of the whole context, it is evident that the *spiritual* "Israel" is here in view, contemplated as being taken into covenant relationship with the triune Jehovah. For, whenever a people is said to be *God's* people, and He avows Himself as their God, it is the covenant relationship which is in view. Thus it was in the promise to Abraham: "And I will establish My covenant between Me and thee and thy seed after thee in their generations for an everlasting covenant, *to be a God* unto thee, and to thy seed after thee" (Gen. 17:7). Thus it is under the new covenant, "I will be to them *a God*, and they shall be to Me *a people*" (Heb. 8:10). It greatly encourages and emboldens the praying soul to bear this in mind.

Fifth, *a believing pleading of the promises.* "And now, O Lord God, the word that Thou hast spoken concerning Thy servant, and concerning his house, establish it forever, and *do as Thou hast said*" (v. 25). This is very blessed, and most important for us to emulate. In these words the faith of David was expressed in two ways: in *believing* God's word, in pleading its accomplishment. That should be the very heart of our petitionary prayers: laying hold of the Divine promise, and pleading for its fulfilment. God is not only a Speaker, but a Doer as well: "God is not a man, that He should lie; neither the son of man, that

He should repent: hath He said, *and shall He not do it?* or hath He spoken, and shall He not make it good?" (Num. 23:19). Ah, but it is one thing to mentally assent to such a declaration, but it is quite another for the heart to be really influenced thereby, and for the praying soul to appropriate that fact.

True faith looks to a *promising* God, and expects Him to be a *performing* God too: "Faithful is He that calleth you, who *also will do it*" (1 Thess. 5:4). The business of faith in prayer is to appropriate God's Word to our own case and beg for it to be made good unto us. Jacob did this: "*And Thou saidest,* I will surely do thee good, and make thy seed as the sand of the sea" (Gen. 32:10). David is another noteable example: "Remember the word unto Thy servant, upon which Thou hast caused me to hope" (Psa. 119:49) — "hope" in Scripture signifies far more than a vague and uncertain longing: it denotes a confident expectation. That confident expectation was his because his faith rested upon the sure promise of Jehovah, and that promise he here reverently reminds God. Glance through this 119th Psalm, dear reader, and observe how frequently David requested God to act "according to Thy word" — vv. 25, 28, 41, 58, etc.

"Do as Thou hast said." Faith has no other foundation to rest upon but the Word of God. One of God's chief ends in giving us His Word was that His people might appropriate the same unto themselves (John 20:31; 1 John 5:13). Nothing honours Him more than for us to count upon His making it good to us (Rom. 4:20). Now whatever may be our case, there is something in the Word exactly suited thereto, and it is our privilege to lay hold of the same *and plead it* before God. Are we groaning under sin's defilement? then plead Isa. 1:18. Are we bowed down with a sense of our backslidings? then plead Jer. 3:22. Do we feel so weak as to have no strength for the performance of duty? then plead Isa. 40:29-31. Are we perplexed as to our path and in urgent need of Divine guidance? then plead Prov. 3:6 or James 1:5. Are you sorely harassed with temptation? then plead 1 Cor. 10:13. Are you destitute and fearful of starving to death? then plead Phil. 4:19. Reverently urge the promise and plead "Do as Thou hast said."

Sixth, *the supreme desire: that God might be glorified.* "And let Thy name be magnified forever, saying, The Lord of hosts is the God over Israel: and let the house of Thy servant David be established before Thee. For Thou, O Lord of hosts, God of Israel, hast revealed to Thy servant, saying I will build thee an house: therefore hast Thy servant found in his heart to pray this prayer unto Thee" (vv. 26, 27). This must be the supreme desire and the chief in all our praying: "Whatsoever ye do, do all to the glory of God" (1 Cor. 10:31). The prayer which Christ has given for our pattern begins with "Hallowed by Thy name," and ends with "Thine is the glory." The Lord Jesus ever practiced what He preached: "Now is My soul troubled, and what shall I say?. . .Father, *glorify* Thy name" (John 12:27); so too at the beginning of His High Priestly prayer, "Father, the hour is come; glorify Thy Son, that Thy Son also may glorify Thee" (John 17:1). O that more of His spirit may possess us: that the honour of God may be our great concern, His glory our constant aim.

Seventh, *a final pleading for God to make good His Word.* "And now, O Lord God, Thou art that God, and Thy words be true, and Thou hast promised this goodness unto Thy servant: therefore now let it please Thee to bless the house of Thy servant, that it may continue forever before Thee: for Thou, O Lord God, hast spoken it; and with Thy blessing let the house of Thy servant be blessed forever" (vv. 28, 29). David built his hopes upon the fidelity of God: "I intreated Thy favour with my whole heart: be merciful unto me *according to* Thy Word" (Psa. 119:58) — I desire no more, I expect no less. We may be bold to ask for all God has engaged to give. As Matthew Henry said, "It is by turning God's promises into petitions that they are turned into performances." How necessary it is then that we should diligently acquaint ourselves with the Scriptures, so that we ask not "amiss" (James 4:3). How necessary that the Word dwell in us richly, that we may act in faith, nothing doubting.

Our space is exhausted. Ponder carefully, dear reader, these seven features or elements in David's God-honouring prayer, and seek the help of the Holy Spirit to pattern your supplications after his.

CHAPTER 8.

And after this David struck the Philistines and humbled them, And David took Metheg-ammah out of the hand of the Philistines. And he struck Moab and measured them with a line, casting them down to the ground. Even with two lines he measured to put to death, and with one full line to keep alive. And so the Moabites became David's servants, bringing gifts. David also struck Hadadezer, the son of Rehob, king of Zobah, as he went to recover his border at the river Euphrates. And David took from him a thousand chariots, and seven hundred horsemen and twenty thousand footmen. And David hamstrung all the chariot horses but kept enough of them for a hundred chariots. And when the Syrians of Damascus came to rescue Hadadezer king of Zobah, David killed twenty-two thousand men of the Syrians. Then David put troops in Syria of Damascus. And the Syrians became servants to David, bringing gifts. And the LORD preserved David wherever he went. And David took the shields of gold that were on the servants of Hadadezer and brought them to Jerusalem. And from Betah, and from Berothai, cities of Hadadezer, king David took very much copper. When Toi king of Hamath heard that David had struck all the army of Hadadezer, then Toi sent Joram his son to king David, to greet him and bless him, because he had fought against Hadadezer and had struck him. For Hadadezer had wars with Toi. And Joram brought with him vessels of silver and vessels of gold, and vessels of copper, which also king David dedicated to the LORD, with the silver and gold that he had dedicated from all nations which he subdued: of Syria, and of Moab, and of the children of Ammon, and of the Philistines, and of Amalek, and of the spoil of Hadadezer son of Rehob, king of Zobah. And David became famous when he returned from striking the Syrians in the valley of salt, eighteen thousand men. And he stationed troops in Edom. He put garrisons throughout all Edom, and all the men of Edom became David's servants. And the LORD preserved David wherever he went. And David reigned over all Israel. And David did judgment and justice to all his people. And Joab the son of Zeruiah was over the army. And Jehoshaphat the son of Ahilud was recorder. And Zadok the son of Ahitub, and Ahimelech the son of Abiathar, were the priests. And Seraiah was the scribe. And Benaiah the son of Jehoiada was over both the Cherethites and the Pelethites. And David's sons were chief rulers.
— II Samuel 8:1-18;

2 Samuel 8 opens with, "And after this it came to pass, that David smote the Philistines, and subdued them: and David took Metheg-ammah out of the hand of the Philistines. And he smote Moab. . .David smote also Hadadezer" (vv. 1-3). The thoughtful reader may well ask, What is there here for me? Why are such matters as these recorded in God's Word, to be read by His people in all generations? Are they merely a bare account of incidents which happened thousands of years ago? If so, they can hardly hold for me anything more than what is of historical interest. But such a conclusion will be far from satisfactory to a devout inquirer, who is assured there is something of profit for his soul in *every* portion of his Father's Word. But how to ascertain the spiritual value and practical lessons of such verses is that which sorely puzzles not a few: may it please the Lord to now enable us to render them some help at this point.

Whilst it be true that none but the One who inspired the Holy Scriptures can open to any of us their hidden depths and rich treasures, yet it is also true that He places no premium upon sloth. It is the prayerful and meditative reader who is rewarded by the Holy Spirit's illumination of the mind, giving him to behold

365

wondrous things out of God's Law. "The soul of the sluggard desireth, and hath nothing: but the soul of the *diligent* shall be made fat" (Prov. 13:4). If, then, any verse of Scripture is to really speak to our hearts, there has to be not only a crying unto God for the hearing ear, but there must be a girding up the loins of our minds and a careful pondering of each word in the verse.

"And after this it came to pass, that David smote the Philistines and subdued them: and David took Metheg-ammah out of the hand of the Philistines. And he smote Moab. . .David smote also Hadadezer." As he carefully weighs these statements, the spiritually-minded can hardly fail to discern One more eminent than David, even his greater Son and Lord. Here we may clearly behold in type the Lion of the tribe of Judah (to which tribe the son of Jesse belonged!), springing upon and overcoming His enemies. In figure, it is the Lord as "a man of war" (Ex. 15:3), going forth "conquering and to conquer" (Rev. 6:2), of whom it is written "For He must reign till He hath put all enemies under His feet" (1 Cor. 15:25). Yet, precious as this is, it fails to direct us to the practical application of the passage unto our own particular case.

The question, then, returns upon us, What direct message is there in these verses for the Christian today? Not simply what curious signification may be found to amuse him during a few minutes' recreation, but what practical lessons are here inculcated which can be turned to useful account in his struggle to live the Christian life. Nothing short of *that* should be before the Satan-harassed, sin-afflicted, temptation-tried soul, when he turns to the Word of God for help, instruction, strength and comfort. Nor will God fail him if he seeks in the right spirit — confessing his deep need, pleading the all-prevailing Name of Christ, asking God to grant him for the Redeemer's sake that wisdom, understanding and faith he sorely craves. Yet, let us add, prayer is not designed to encourage laziness, for it is not a substitute for diligent effort: the Scriptures must be "searched" (John 5:39) and "studied" if they are to yield food to the soul.

But *how* is the devout and anxious reader to get at the spiritual meaning and practical value of the verses quoted above? Well, the first thing to observe is that the central thing in them is, *David overcoming his enemies*. Put in *that* form, the application to ourselves is obvious. David is here to be viewed as a type of the Christian who is menaced by powerful foes both within and without. These are not to be suffered to lord it over the believer, but are to be engaged in mortal combat. Second, we note that David is not said to have exterminated or annihilated those enemies, but to have "subdued" them (v. 11), which is true to the type, and supplies a key to its practical interpretation. Third, we must pay due attention unto the time-mark which is given in the opening verse — "And *after this* it came to pass that David smote the Philistines" — for this is another key which unlocks for us its meaning. It is by attending carefully unto such details that we are enabled to burrow beneath the surface of a verse.

"And *after this* it came to pass that David smote the Philistines." These words look back to what was before us in 7:1, "And it came to pass, when the king sat in his house, and the Lord had given him rest round about from all his enemies." May we not apply these words to the first coming of a sinner to Christ, heavily laden with a conscious load of guilt, sorely pressed by the malicious foes of his soul, now finding *spiritual rest* in the only One in whom and from whom it is to be obtained. Hitherto David had been assailed again and again by the surrounding heathen, but now the Lord granted him a season of repose. That season had been spent in sweet communion with God, in the Word (2 Sam. 7:4-17) and prayer (2 Sam. 7:18-29). Blessed indeed is that, but let it be duly noted that communion with God is intended to animate us for the discharge of duty. It is not upon flowery beds of ease that the believer is conducted to Heaven. Being led beside the still waters and being made to lie down in green pastures is a blissful experience, yet let it not be forgotten that it is a means to an end — to supply strength for the carrying out of our obligations.

"And after this it came to pass, that David smote the Philistines and subdued them." We may observe a very noticeable change here: previously the Philistines had been the aggressors. In 2 Sam. 5 we read, "But when the Philistines heard that they had anointed David king over Israel, all the Philistines came up to seek David. . .the Philistines also came and spread themselves in the valley of Rephaim. . .And the Philistines came up yet again" (vv. 17, 18, 22). From their assaults God had graciously given His servant "rest" (2 Sam. 7:1). But now he evidently received a commission from the Lord to make war upon them. Thus it is in the initial experience of the Christian. It is a sense of sin — its vileness, its filthiness, its guilt, its condemnation — which drives him to Christ, and coming to Christ, he finds "rest." But having obtained forgiveness of sins and peace of conscience, he now learns that he must "strive against sin" (Heb. 12:4) and fight the good fight of faith. Now that the young believer has been delivered from the wrath to come, he discovers that he must "endure hardness as a good soldier of Jesus Christ" (2 Tim. 2:3), and spare not anything within him which opposes God.

"And after this it came to pass, that David smote the Philistines, and subdued them." While these words may be legitimately applied to the *initial* experience of the believer, they are by no means to be restricted there unto. They contain a principle which pertains to the Christian life as a whole, and to every stage thereof. That principle is that, before we are fitted to engage our spiritual enemies we must first spend a season in communion with God: only thus and only then can strength be obtained for the conflict which lies before us. Renewed efforts to subdue our persistent foes can only be made (with any degree of success) as we are renewed by the Spirit in the inner man, and that is only to be obtained by feeding on the Word (2 Sam. 7:4-17) and by prayer (2 Sam. 7:18-29) — and two chief means for communion with God.

"And David took Metheg-ammah out of the hand of the Philistines." Here our passage passes from the general to the particular, and a most important practical truth is here inculcated. This is another case when Scripture has to be compared with Scripture in order to understand its terms. 1 Chron. 18 is parallel with 2 Sam. 8, and by comparing the language of the opening verse of the former we are enabled to arrive at the meaning of our text: "Now after this it came to pass, that David smote the Philistines, and subdued them, and took *Gath and her towns* out of the hand of the Philistines." Thus "Metheg-ammah" has reference to "Gath and her towns" Now Gath (with its suburbs) was the metropolis of Philistia, being a fortified city on a high hill (2 Sam. 2:24). In our text it is called "Metheg-ammah" which means "the bridle of the mother city." It had long acted as a "bridle" or curb upon Israel, serving as a barrier to their further occupation of Canaan. So much, then, for the etymological and historical meaning: now for the typical.

What was denoted spiritually by "Gath and her towns?" In seeking the answer to this question let us carefully bear in mind the three details mentioned above: Gath occupied a powerful eminence, it was the metropolis or mother-city, it had served as a "bridle" upon Israel. Surely the practical application of this to ourselves is not difficult: is it not some *master* lust in our souls or *dominant* sin in our lives which is here represented? And is it not *this* which is to occupy first attention in the welfare against our spiritual foes. Of what avail is it to dress a vision which faith brought to him? This, "And he saw it and *was glad.*" In like wound while the blood-stream itself remains poisoned? What use would it be to guard chickens against cats and dogs when the wolf is allowed to assail them? Saul might slay all the other Amalekites, but for sparing "Agag *the king,*" the kingdom was rent from him (1 Sam. 15). Loudly ought that to speak unto our hearts today.

It is not the eyelashes which require trimming, but the "eye" itself which must be plucked out; it is not the fingernails which need paring, but the "right hand" which must be cut off (Matt. 5:29, 30), if the Christian would make any headway in overcoming his inward corruptions. It is to his special "besetting sin" he must direct his attention. No truce is to be made with *it,* no excuses offered for it. No matter how firmly entrenched it may be, nor how long it has held sway, grace must be diligently and persistently sought to conquer it. That darling sin which has so long been cherished by an evil heart must be slain: if it be "spared," as Saul spared Agag, it will slay us. The word of mortification is to begin at the place where sin has its strongest hold upon us.

The subduing of the Philistines, and particularly the capture of Gath, was vitally essential if Israel was to gain their rights, for as yet they were not in full possession of the land to which, by the Divine promise, they were entitled. Canaan had been given to them by God as their heritage, but valiant effort, hard fighting, was called for, in order to bring about their occupation of the same. This is a point which has sorely puzzled many. It is clear from Scripture that the land of Canaan was a figure of Heaven, but there is no *fighting* in Heaven! True, but the believer is not yet in Heaven; nevertheless, Heaven ought to be in him, by which we mean that even now the believer should be walking in the daily enjoyment of that wondrous portion which is now his by having been made a joint-heir with Christ. Alas, how little is this fact appreciated by the majority of God's dear people today, and how little are they experimentally *possessing* "Their possessions" (Obad. 17).

It is greatly to be regretted that so many of the saints relegate to *the future* the time of their victory, joy, and bliss; and seem content to live in the present as though they were spiritual paupers. For example, how very generally are the words "For so an entrance shall be ministered unto you abundantly into the everlasting kingdom of our Lord and Saviour Jesus Christ" (2 Pet. 1:11) regarded as referring to the time of the believer's glorification. But there is nothing whatever in the context to warrant such a view, nothing required in it to understand that "abundant entrance" as belonging to a day to come, nothing to justify us postponing it at all in our thoughts. Instead, there is much against it. In the preceding verses the apostle is exhorting the believer to make his calling and election "sure," and this by adding to his faith "virtue" etc. (vv. 5-7), assuring him that by so doing he shall "never fall," and adding "for *so* an entrance shall be ministered unto you abundantly."

Legally, the believer has already been "delivered from the power of darkness and translated into the kingdom of God's dear Son" (Col. 1:13), but experimentally an "abundant entrance" thereinto is dependent upon his spiritual growth and the cultivation of his graces. The believer has already been begotten unto "an inheritance incorruptible, and undefiled, and that fadeth not away, reserved in Heaven" for him (1 Pet. 1:4), but his practical *enjoyment* thereof turns upon the exercise of faith. "Abraham," said Christ, "rejoiced to see My day" (John 8:56): and *how* did the patriarch "see" it? Why, *by faith,* for there was no other way in which he could see it: by the exercise of faith in the sure promises of God. And what was the effect upon Abraham of this entrancing manner, the believer now is to use the long distance lens of faith and view his promised inheritance, and *rejoice* therein; then will "the joy of the Lord" be his strength" (Neh. 8:10).

Israel had a valid title to the land of Canaan: it was theirs by the gift of God. But enemies sought to prevent their occupation of it: and enemies seek to hinder the Christian from faith's appropriation and enjoyment of *his* "inheritance." And what are those enemies? Chiefly, the lusts of the flesh, sinful habits, evil ways. *Faith cannot be in healthy exercise while we yield to the lusts of the flesh.* How many a saint is sighing because his faith is so feeble, so spasmodic, so fruitless. Here is the cause: allowed sin! Faith and sin are opposites, opponents, and the one cannot flourish until the other be subdued. It is vain to pray for more faith until we start in earnest to mortify our lusts, crucify our Christ-dishonouring corruptions, and wrestle with and overcome our besetting sins; and that can only be accomplished by fervently and untiringly seeking enabling grace from on High.

"David *smote* the Philistines, and *subdued* them." In figure that represents the believer waging unsparing warfare upon all within him that is opposed to God, "denying ungodliness and worldly lusts" in order that he may "live soberly, righteously and godly in this present world" (Titus 2:12). It represents the believer doing what the apostle speaks of in 1 Cor. 9:27, "But I *keep under* my body, and bring it into subjection:" his "body" there referring not so much to the physical, as to the "old man" within, the "body of sin" (Rom. 6:6), "this body of death" (Rom. 7:24 margin); or as it is spoken of elsewhere as "the body of the sins of the flesh" (Col. 2:11). Indwelling sin is spoken of in these passages as a "body" because it has, as it were, a complete set of members or faculties of its own; and these must be *subdued* by the Christian: "Casting down imaginations, and every high thing that exalteth itself against the knowledge of God, and bringing into captivity every thought to the obedience of Christ" (2 Cor. 10. 5).

"And David took Metheg-ammah out of the land of the Philistines." Typically this turns, as we have previously said, from the general unto the particular — from the work of mortification as a whole to the crucifying of a special sin which prevails against the saint. In figure it represents the believer concentrating his attention upon and conquering his master lust or chief besetting sin, that "mother" evil which is the prolific source of so many iniquities, that "bridle" which has for so long hindered his entering into God's best for him.

In the preceding section we pointed out that the central thing in 2 Sam. 8 is David overcoming his enemies, and this, in order that Israel might enter their rightful portion — occupy and enjoy the inheritance which God had given them. In order to this, hard fighting was entailed. We also called attention to the fact that 2 Sam. 8 opens with the word "And," which requires us to observe what immediately goes before. In 2 Sam. 7 we find God giving David "rest round from all his enemies" (v. 1), and that he spent this season of repose in communion with the Lord — over His Word, (vv. 4:17) and in prayer (vv. 18-29). Following which he evidently received a commission from on High to attack and conquer his most formidable foes, for we are next told "and after this it came to pass, that David smote the Philistines, and subdued them" (v. 1).

The spiritual application unto the believer of the above is very striking and blessed. The "rest" given to David from those who had assailed him typifies, first, the initial coming to Christ of a convicted and sin-weary soul, and finding rest in Him; and second, it typifies the restraining hand of God laid upon the sinful lusts of the Christian, granting him a little respite from their assaults. This is necessary if there is to be sweet and profitable communion with the thrice holy God, for the soul is in no condition to rejoice in His perfections while sin is raging within him; therefore does the Lord, in His mercy, frequently lay His powerful hand upon us, subduing our iniquities (Micah 7:19). Then it is we should improve the opportunity be feeding upon the Word of promise and by pouring out our hearts before God in thanksgiving, praise, and adoring worship. Thus David used his "rest," and so should we; for by so doing new strength will be obtained for further conflicts.

David's smiting of the Philistines and subduing them is a figure of the work of mortification to which God calls the Christian: "Mortify therefore your members which are upon the earth: fornication, uncleanness, inordinate affection, evil concupiscence and covetousness" (Col. 3:5). The clear call of God to His people is "Let not sin therefore reign in your mortal body, that ye should obey it in the lusts thereof" (Rom. 6:12). The Christian must not suffer his fleshly lusts to lord it over him, but is to engage them in mortal combat, refusing to spare anything in him which is opposed to God. David's taking of "Metheg-ammah" (which means "the bridle of the mother") out of the hands of the Philistines, speaks of the believer devoting his special attention unto his master lust or besetting sin, for until *that* be (by grace) conquered there can be no real experimental progress in spiritual things: "Wherefore putting away lying, speak every man truth to his neighbour. . .Let him that stole, steal no more. . Let no corrupt communication proceed out of your mouth" (Eph. 4:25, 28, 29).

Now David's subduing of the Philistines and his capture of Metheg-ammah their chief stronghold, was imperatively necessary if Israel was to gain possession and occupy their inheritance, and it is *this* fact which we desire to press most upon the reader. The Christian has been begotten unto a blessed and eternal inheritance in Heaven: from his eventual entrance into it Satan cannot keep him, but from his present possession and enjoyment thereof he seeks by might and main to rob him; and unless the believer be duly instructed and steadfastly resists him, then the Enemy will prove only too successful. Alas that so few of the Lord's people realise *what* their present privileges are; alas that so many of them relegate unto the future what is theirs *now* in title; alas that they are so ignorant of Satan's devices and so dilatory in seeking to resist the great robber of their souls.

The believer has, *even now*, a rich and wondrous portion in Christ: a portion which is available and accessible unto *faith*: "For all things *are* yours; whether Paul, or Apollos, or Cephas, or the world, or life, or death, or things present, or things to come; *all* are yours; and ye are Christ's, and Christ is God's" (1 Cor. 3:21-23). But O how little are we impressed by such glorious declarations as these; how little do we enter into them in a practical way; how little do we *appropriate* them. We are much like the man who died in poverty, knowing not that a valuable estate had been left to him. Instead of setting our affections upon things above, we act as though there was nothing there for us until we pass through the portals of the grave. "In Thy presence is fulness of joy; at Thy right hand there are pleasures for evermore" (Psa. 16:11) — *now* as well as in the future!

O what a tremendous difference it makes whether or not the Christian be living in the present enjoyment of his eternal inheritance. What power could the attractions of this world have for one whose heart is on high? None at all. Instead, they would appear to him in their true light, as worthless baubles. How little would he be affected by the loss of a few temporal things: not making them his "treasure" or chief good, the loss of them could neither destroy his peace nor kill his joy — "And took joyfully the spoiling of your goods, knowing *in yourselves* that ye have in heaven a better and an enduring substance" (Heb. 10:34). How little would tribulation and suffering move us from a steady pressing forward along the path of duty: "who for the joy *that was set before Him* (by faith) endured the cross, despising the shame" (Heb. 12:2).

But for the present enjoyment of our eternal inheritance *faith* must be in exercise, for "Faith is the substance of things hoped for, the evidence of things not seen" (Heb. 11:1). Faith is that which gives visibility and tangibility to that which is invisible to sight. Faith is that which gives *reality* to the things which hope is set upon. Faith brings near what is far off. Faith lifts the heart above the things of time and sense: "By faith Moses, when he was come to years, refused to be called the son of Pharaoh's daughter; choosing rather to suffer affliction with the people of God, than to enjoy the pleasures of sin for a season; esteeming the reproach of Christ greater riches than the treasures in Egypt: *for he had respect unto* the recompence of the reward" (Heb. 11:24-26). Ah, the "recompence of the reward" was a living reality unto Moses, and under the elevating power thereof the flesh-inviting offer of Egypt's princess was powerless to drag him down. And, my reader, if "our citizenship is in Heaven" (Phil. 3:20) *in a practical way*, so far from the baits of Satan tempting us, they will repel.

But, as we pointed out in the preceding section, faith cannot be in healthy operation while the work of mortification be neglected. If we yield to the solicitations of our fleshly and worldly lusts, if we fail to crucify our besetting sins, if any evil be "allowed" by us, then faith will be suffocated and rendered inactive. Just as both the Canaanites and the Israelites could not possess the promised land at one and the same time — one being compelled to yield occupancy to the other — so neither can faith and sin rule the heart at one and the same time. The idolatrous Canaanites already had possession of the promised land when God gave it to them, and *only by hard fighting* could the Israelites secure it for themselves. In like manner sinful lusts originally possess the heart of the Christian, and it is only by hard fighting that they can be dispossessed and the heart be filled with Heaven.

As the Canaanites were vanquished, the Israelites occupied their places. Thus it must be spiritually. The mortification of sin is in order to the vivification of spirituality. The garden-plot must first be clear of weeds and rubbish before it is ready for the vegetables and flowers to be planted therein. Hence the oft-repeated word is "Cease to do evil, Learn to do well" (Isa. 1:16,17), "depart from evil and do good" (Psa. 34:14), "hate the evil and love the good" (Amos 5:15) — the second cannot be attended to until the first be accomplished. "Put off concerning the former conversation the old man, which is corrupt according to the deceitful lusts. . .Put on the new man, which after God is created in righteousness and true holiness" (Eph. 4:22, 24). That is God's unchanging order throughout: we must "cleanse ourselves from all filthiness of the flesh and of the spirit," if we would "perfect holiness in His fear."

How instructive and how very striking is the order in Obad. 17, "But upon mount Zion shall be deliverance, and there shall be holiness; and the house of Jacob shall possess their possessions." First, there is deliverance upon "mount Zion," which is where *Christ* is, for in Psa. 2:6 God declares, "Yet have I set My King upon My holy hill of Zion." Only by Christ can the sin-harassed believer obtain "deliverance" from those enemies which are ever threatening to destroy his peace, joy, and usefulness. Second, following the "deliverance" is the promise of "holiness," which is a positive thing, a moral quality of purity, with the added signification of devotedness unto God. But note this cannot be before the "deliverance!" Third, there is then the assurance that God's people shall *possess their possessions*," that is, actually enjoy them, live in the power thereof.

"And he smote Moab" (v. 2). In order to get at the practical application of this unto ourselves it will be necessary to go back to earlier scriptures. From Gen. 19:36, 37 we learn that Moab was the incestuous son of backslidden Lot. Their territory was adjacent to the land of Canaan, the Jordan dividing them (Num. 22:1; 31:12). It was Balak the king of the Moabites who hired Balaam to curse Israel (Num. 22:4, 5). Her daughters were a snare to the sons of Israel (Num. 25:1). Her land also proved to be a snare unto Naomi and her family (Ruth 1:1). God used the Moabites as one of His scourges upon His wayward people in the days of the Judges (3:12-14). No Moabite was suffered to enter into the congregation of the Lord unto the tenth generation (Deut. 23:3). It was foretold that Christ would "smite" them (Num. 24:17). In the last reference to them in Scripture we read, "Surely Moab shall be as Sodom" (Zeph. 2:9).

From the above facts it is clear that the Moabites were a menace unto Israel, and that there should be no fellowship between them. But the particular point which we need to define is, exactly what do the Moabites symbolize? The answer to this question is not difficult to discover: they figured the world away from God, but more particularly, the world bordering on the domain of faith. It is not the world-bordering Church, but the Church-bordering *world*, ever inviting the people of God to leave their own heritage and come down to their level. The Moabites were *near* to Israel both by birth and locality. There was a long and a strong border-line between them, namely, the Jordan, the river of death, and *that* had to be crossed before the people of God could enter their domain. Moab, then, typifies the world *near* the Church; in other words, Moab stands for a mere *worldly profession* of the things of God.

"But God forbid that I should glory, save in the cross of our Lord Jesus Christ, by which the world hath been crucified unto me and I unto the world" (Gal. 6:14). The cross of Christ is the antitype of the Jordan. It is by the cross the Christian is separated from the world. While the principle of the cross — the principle of self-sacrifice, death to sin — rules the Christian, he is preserved from the blandishments of the world. But as soon as the principle of the cross — mortification, the denying of self — ceases to dominate, we fall victims to the fair "daughters of Moab," and commit spiritual adultery with them (Num. 25:1); in other words, our testimony degenerates into a mere profession; we cease to be heavenly pilgrims, and vital godliness becomes a thing of the past. "Every fair attractive worldly delight that makes us forget our true Home is a 'daughter of Moab' " (F. C. Jennings).

"And he smote Moab." The spiritual application of this to us today, is, we must be uncompromising in our separation from an apostate Christendom, and unsparingly mortify every desire within us to flirt with worldly churches and an empty profession. For a child of God to come under the power of "Moab" is to have his usefulness, power, and joy, replaced with wretchedness, impotency, and dishonour. Hence our urgent need of *obeying* that emphatic command, "Having a form of godliness, but denying the power thereof: *from such turn away*" (2 Tim. 3:5). It is not that we are called upon to *fight against* the modern "Moabites" (as Israel did under the O.T. dispensation) but to *mortify* that within us which lusts after their attractions. In sparing one third of the Moabites and in receiving "gifts" from them, David temporized — the sad sequel is found in 2 Kings 3:4, 5 and what follows.

We do not have sufficient light and discernment to follow out all the details of 2 Sam. 8 and give the spiritual application of them unto ourselves, but several other obvious points in the chapter claim our attention. "David smote also Hadadezer" (v. 3); "David slew of the Syrians two and twenty thousand men" (v. 5). How *numerous* are the (spiritual) enemies which the people of God are called upon to engage! It is to be carefully noted that David did not quit when he had subdued the Philistines and the Moabites, but continued to assail other foes! So the Christian must not become weary in well doing: no furloughs are granted to the soldiers of Jesus Christ: they are called on to be "stedfast, unmoveable, *always* abounding in the work of the Lord" (1 Cor. 15:58), i.e. the work or task which the Lord has assigned them, which, as the immediate context shows, is to gain the victory over *sin*.

Let us now anticipate a criticism which some of the Lord's people may feel ready to make against what we have said in this and the previous article: Have you not been arguing in favour of self-sufficiency and creature-ability? No, indeed; yet, on the other hand, we are no advocate for Christian impotency, for there is a vital difference between the regenerate and unregenerate as to spiritual helplessness. The way to get more faith and more strength is to *use* what we already have. But we are far from affirming that the Christian is able to overcome his spiritual foes in his own might. So with David. Considering the vast numbers which composed the ranks of his numerous enemies, David and his small force could never have won such great victories had not *the Lord* undertaken for him.

"And the Lord preserved David whithersoever he went" (v. 6): note the exact repetition of these words in v. 14. Here is the explanation of David's success: he fought not in his own strength. So the Christian, fighting the good fight of faith, though weak in himself, is energized by Divine grace. David's onslaught upon the Philistines and the Moabites was in line with the promises of God in Gen. 15:18 and Num. 24:17, and most probably they nerved him for the battle. Thus it should be with the Christian. It is his privilege and duty to remind God of His promises and *plead* them before Him: such promises as "I will subdue all thine enemies" (1 Chron. 17:10), and "sin shall not have dominion over you" (Rom. 6:14). O to be able to say "Thou hast girded me with strength unto the battle: Thou hast subdued under me those that rose up against me" (Psa. 18:39).

We have space to consider only one point: "Which also king David did dedicate unto the Lord, with the silver and gold that he had dedicated of all nations which he subdued" (v. 11). While David destroyed the idols, he dedicated to God all the vessels of silver and gold which he took from his enemies. So while the Christian strives to mortify every lust, he must consecrate unto the Lord all his natural and spiritual endowments. Whatever stands in opposition to God must be crucified, but that which may glorify Him must be dedicated to His service. This point is a very blessed one: David entirely *changed the destination* of this silver and gold: what had previously adorned the idolaters, was afterwards used in the building of the temple. The spiritual application of this is found in "as yet have yielded your members servants to uncleanness and unto iniquity, even so now yield your members servants to righteousness unto holiness" (Rom. 6:19). May the Lord graciously add His blessing unto all that has been before us.

And David said, Is there still any that is left from the house of Saul, that I may show him kindness for Jonathan's sake? And the house of Saul had a servant whose name was Ziba. And when they had called him to David, the king said to him, Are you Ziba? And he said, Your servant is he. And the king said, Is there not yet a man of the house of Saul, so that I may show the kindness of God to him? And Ziba said to the king, Jonathan still has a son, who is lame in his feet. And the king said to him, Where is he? And Ziba said to the king, Behold, he is in the house of Machir, the son of Ammiel, in Lodebar. Then king David sent and brought him out of the house of Machir the son of Ammiel, from Lodebar. Now when Mephibosheth, the son of Jonathan, the son of Saul, had come to David, he fell on his face and bowed to him. And David said, Mephibosheth! And he answered, Behold your servant! And David said to him, Do not fear, for I will surely show you kindness for Jonathan your father's sake. And I will restore you all the land of Saul your father. And you shall eat bread at my table forever. And he bowed himself and said, What is your servant, that you should look on such a dead dog as I am? Then the king said to Ziba, Saul's servant, and said to him, I have given to your master's son all that belonged to Saul and to all his house. And you and your sons and your servants shall till the land for him, and you shall harvest, so that your master's son may have food to eat. But Mephibosheth your master's son shall eat bread always at my table. Now Ziba had fifteen sons and twenty servants. Then Ziba said to the king, According to all that my lord the king has commanded his servant, so shall your servant do. As for Mephibosheth, he shall eat at my table like one of the king's sons. And Mephibosheth had a young son, whose name was Micha. And all that lived in the house of Ziba were servants to Mephibosheth. So Mephibosheth lived in Jerusalem. For he always sat at the king's table. And he was lame in both his feet. — II Samuel 9:1-13.

2 Samuel 9 presents to us one of the loveliest scenes in the life of David. To properly appreciate it we need to recall his earlier experiences, particularly the unkind treatment he received from the hands of Saul. We will only refer briefly now to the jealousy which was awakened in that king's heart when he heard the women celebrating in song the victory of Jesse's youthful son over Goliath. How that later he sought to kill David again and again by throwing a javelin at him. Finally, how that David had to flee for his life and how relentlessly the king pursued him, determining to kill him. But things had been completely altered. Saul and his sons were slain in battle, and David has ascended the throne of Israel. A most admirable spirit did our hero now display: instead of using his royal power tyrannically or maliciously, he put it to a most noble use: to return good for evil, to extend pity to the descendant of his foe, to befriend one who might well have feared death at the hands, was David's next act.

"And David said, Is there yet any that is left of the house of Saul, that I may show him kindness for Jonathan's sake?" (2 Sam. 9:1). First of all let us observe the pathos of such a question. 1 Chron. 8:33 furnishes a list of Saul's sons, but now his family had been so reduced by the judgments of God that inquiry has to be made "is there yet *any* that is left of the house of Saul?" How true it is that "the sins of the fathers are visited upon the children" — O that more parents would take this to heart. But, second, let us note the benevolent design of David: he sought any possible survivor of Saul's family, not that he might imprison or slay, but that he might show him "kindness." Let our dispensational friends note that this was under the era of Law! — even then, wherever the Holy Spirit possessed a soul, the spirit triumphed over the flesh; blessedly did it do so in the case now before us.

It seems evident from what follows in the sacred narrative that none of the courtiers could answer their royal master's question. It is not at all likely that *they* were interested in such matters. No doubt they remembered the trouble which the opposition of Ishbosheth — the last of Saul's sons — had caused, and hoped that his family had now become entirely extinct. But David was not to be deterred, and continued asking. It was no passing whim which had actuated him. "Jonathan" was before his heart, and for *his* "sake" he was determined to show clemency and display his magnanimity. At length they brought to David an old retainer of Saul's family, who knew well the sad state into which it was fallen; and to him also David said, "Is there not yet any of the house of Saul, that I may show the kindness of God unto him?" (v. 3).

But beautiful as was David's conduct on this occasion, something yet more blessed was shadowed forth by it, and upon that we would particularly concentrate our attention. As other writers on this sweet incident have pointed out, David as monarch over Israel suggests to us God upon His throne in Heaven: David showing kindness to the family of his arch-enemy, foreshadowed God's dealing in grace with sinners. The name of the one whom David befriended, the place he had hitherto occupied, the condition he was then in, the wondrous portion he received, all typified the case of those upon whom God bestows saving mercy. The picture here presented is perfect in its accuracy in every detail, and the more closely it be examined, the more clearly will its evangelical character appear. O that our hearts may be melted by its exquisite light and shade.

"And David said, Is there yet any that is left of the house of Saul, that I may show him kindness for Jonathan's sake?" Let us first observe that *David* was the one who here *took the initiative*. No overtures were made unto him by the one remaining descendant of Saul; the king himself was the one to make the advance. So it is in the antitype: it is not the sinner, but God, who makes the first move. Through the Gospel He makes overtures of mercy, and in each instance of salvation He is found of them that seek Him not. "All we *like sheep* have gone astray" (Isa. 53:6), and it is the nature of a lost sheep to wander farther and farther afield. The shepherd must do the seeking, for sheep astray never go after the shepherd — true alike both naturally and spiritually. It was God who sought out Abraham in Ur, Jacob at Bethel, Moses in Midian, Saul of Tarsus on the road to Damascus, and not they who sought unto Him.

Next, we may notice *the object* of David's quest. It was not one who had befriended him during the days of his own dire need. Nor was it one whom men of the world would call "a deserving case." Nor was it one from whom David could expect anything again in return. Instead, it was one immediately descended from his most merciless and implacable foe; it was one who was hiding away from him; it was one who had nothing of his own, having lost his heritage. How accurate the picture! The Gospel of God's grace is not seeking those who have something of their own to commend them unto the Lord, nor does it offer salvation in return for service to be rendered afterwards. Its inestimable riches are for worthless wretches, spiritual paupers, lost and undone sinners; and those riches are freely proffered "without money and without price."

But let us pay attention to *the motive which actuated David*. Very beautiful is this line in our typical picture. "And David said, Is there yet any that is left of the house of Saul, that I may show kindness *for Jonathan's sake."* Here was what moved the king to make overtures of mercy toward the house of his sworn enemy. Though there was nothing whatever in Saul's survivor to commend him unto the royal favour, David found a reason *outside* of him, in that bond of love and friendship which existed between his own heart and Jonathan. And thus it is too in the antitype: "For we ourselves also *were* sometime foolish, disobedient, deceived, serving divers lusts and pleasures, living in malice and envy, hateful, hating one another. But after that *the kindness* and pity of God our Saviour toward man appeared, *not by works of righteousness which we have done,* but according to His mercy He saved us, by the washing of regeneration and renewing of the Holy Spirit; which He shed on us abundantly *through Jesus Christ our Saviour"* (Titus 3:3-6). It is because of Another that God is gracious to His people: "God *for Christ's sake* hath forgiven you" (Eph. 4:32).

One more item completes this point, and a very striking one it is. When Ziba, Saul's servant, had been found and brought to David, the king asked, "Is there not yet any of the house of Saul, that I may show the *kindness of God* unto him?" (v. 3). This language goes further than his words in the first verse. It takes us back to 1 Sam. 20. There we find Jonathan acted the part of a *mediator* between Saul and David (vv. 27—34). There too we read of a solemn "covenant" (vv. 16, 17, 42) between Jonathan and David, in which the latter swore to show "kindness unto the house of the former forever: "Jonathan caused David to sware again, because he loved him: for he loved him as he loved his own soul" (v. 17). It was to *that* incident the words of David "that I may show the kindness *of God* unto him" looked back: it was that "kindness of which God Himself had been the witness; it was *covenant* "kindness" which he had promised to exercise.

Thus, the one who here obtained kindness at the hands of the king, received favour not because of anything *he* had done, nor because of any personal worthiness he possessed, but wholly on account of a covenant promise which had been made *before he was born.* So it is with those toward whom God now acts in free and sovereign grace. It is not because of any personal claims they have upon Him, but because of the love He bears toward the Mediator, that He shows "kindness." Nor is that all: long, long before they first saw the light, God entered into a covenant with Christ, promising to extend mercy unto all who belonged to His "house:" "Wherein God, willing more abundantly to show unto the heirs of promise, the immutability of His counsel, confirmed it *by an oath:* that by two immutable things, in which it was impossible for God to lie, we might have a strong consolation, who have fled for refuge to lay hold upon the hope set before us" (Heb. 6:17, 18). It is "through the blood of *the everlasting covenant"* that God makes His people "perfect in every good work to do His will" (Heb. 13:20, 21).

Next, let us look more closely at this one to whom David showed "the kindness of God" — covenant-kindness. First, his name, for no detail here is meaningless. The son of Jesse was called "Mephibosheth" (v. 6), which signifies *"a shameful thing."* How accurately does that appellation describe the natural man! "We are all as an unclean thing" (Isa. 64:6) says God's Word — polluted by sin. We are by birth and practice thoroughly depraved and corrupt. Our understanding is darkened so that we cannot apprehend spiritual things, our wills are opposed to God's, our hearts are desperately wicked, our consciences are seared, our strength spent in the service of Satan; and in the sight of the Holy One our very righteousnesses are "as filthy rags." "A shameful thing," then, we truly are: "from the sole of the foot even unto the crown of the head there is no soundness" in us by nature, but instead "wounds and bruises and putrefying sores" (Isa. 1:6). O what cause have we to cry with the leper "Unclean! unclean!" and say with Job "I am vile.

Second, Mephibosheth was a *fugitive from David.* When news reached the survivors of his family that Saul and his sons had been slain in battle, and David had ascended the throne, Mephibosheth and his nurse fled in terror: "he was five years old when the tidings came of Saul and Jonathan out of Jezreel, and his nurse took him up, *and fled"* (2 Sam. 4:4). They were anxious to keep out of David's way. So it is with the sinner. He is afraid of God, and seeks to banish Him from his thoughts. The knowledge of God's holiness, power and omniscience fills him with dismay, and he seeks to have nothing to do with Him. "The wicked flee when no man pursueth." It was thus with Adam at the beginning. After his transgression, no sooner did he hear the voice of the Lord, than he hid himself among the trees of the Garden: A guilty conscience renders God an object of terror to the wicked.

Third, Mephibosheth was *a cripple.* He was "lame of his feet" (2 Sam. 4:4): as the closing words of our chapter state, he "was lame on *both* his feet" (v. 13). How accurately that portrays the condition of those who are out of Christ! The natural man is *unable* to run in the path of God's commandments, or tread the narrow way which leadeth unto Life. He is a spiritual cripple: "without strength" (Rom. 5:6). The utter inability of the unregenerate to meet God's requirements and walk acceptably before Him, is a truth written plain across the Scriptures, though it is given little place indeed in modern preaching. The greatness of man, the freedom of his will, his ability to accept Christ any time, is now the sweet opiate which is chloroforming millions. "No man *can come to Me except* the Father which hath sent Me draw him" (John 6:44): how those words of Christ's attest the solemn fact that the sinner is "lame of *both* his feet!"

Fourth, Mephibosheth became a cripple *through a fall:* "and his nurse took him up and fled: and it came to pass, as she made haste to flee that he fell, and *became* lame" (2 Sam. 4:4). What a truly marvellous book the Bible is! Yet how it needs eyes anointed by the Divine Inspirer in order to perceive its wonders and beauties! How obvious it is to those favoured with spiritual discernment that we have here far more then a historical account pertaining to a single individual: that it is rather a *typical* picture having a *universal* application. Man was not originally created in the condition he is now in. Man was very far from being "lame on both his feet" when his Maker proclaimed him "very good." The faculties of man's soul have become spiritually crippled as the result of *the fall* — our fall in Adam. In consequence of that fall, "they that are in the flesh *cannot* please God" (Rom. 8:8).

Fifth, *the place where Mephibosheth resided.* It was not at Jerusalem, No, indeed; none out of Christ live there. Jerusalem signifies "the foundation of peace" and as Holy Writ truly declares, "There is no peace, saith the Lord, unto the wicked" (Isa. 48:22): how can there be while they despise Him in whom alone peace is to be found. "But the wicked are like the troubled sea, when it cannot rest" (Isa. 57:20) — discontented, dissatisfied. No, it was not at Jerusalem that poor Mephibosheth resided. Instead, he dwelt at "Lo-debar" (2 Sam. 9:4), which means, "the place *of no pasture."* What a significant line in our picture is this, so obviously drawn by more than a human artist. How aptly does it portray the world in which we live, the world which is away from God, which lieth in the wicked one. It is a world which provides no food for the soul: it is a great "howling wilderness" so far as spiritual provisions are concerned. Yet how little is that fact realised by those who are in it and of it.

"Lo-debar" is written across all the varied fields of this world, though the great masses of people realise it not. Multitudes are seeking to find something to fill that void in the heart which God should occupy. They seek satisfaction in sport, in novel reading, in an endless round of pleasure, in making money, in fame; but soul satisfaction is not to be found in such *things* — things which perish with the using of them. Despising Him who is "the true Bread," the "Bread of life," no food is to be found here but "the *husks* that the swine" feed upon. The prodigal son discovered that when he left his patrimony and went into the far country: "I perish with hunger" was his plaintive cry. Life, peace, joy, satisfaction, are to be found only in the Lord.

One other point and we must conclude this section: *the provision* David made for Mephibosheth. There was this poor creature, belonging to a family that was in rebellion against David, lame in both feet, and dwelling in the place of no pasture. And here was the king upon his throne, with purpose of heart to show him kindness for the sake of another. What, then, was the next move? Did David send a message of welcome, inviting him to come to Jerusalem? Did he notify Mephibosheth that if he "did his part" mercy should be accorded him? Did he forward the cripple a pair of crutches, bid him make use of them, and hobble to Jerusalem as best he could? No, indeed; had anything like *that* been David's policy, our typical picture had failed completely to exhibit "the kindness *of God*" unto those on whom He bestows His so great salvation. God does much more than provide "means of grace."

"Then king David sent and *fetched* him" (v. 5). This blessed item shadows forth the efficacious work of the Holy Spirit in those whom God brings unto Himself. Had He done nothing more than give His Son to die for sinners, and then sent forth His servants with the Gospel invitation, *none* had ever been saved. This is clear from the parable of the Great Supper: men were bade to come and assured that "all things were now ready." And what was their response? This, "they all with one consent began to make excuse" (Luke 14:18). But God was not to be foiled, and said to the servant (the Spirit), "Go out quickly into the streets and lanes of the city, *and bring in* hither the poor, and the maimed, and the halt, and the blind." Thank God for *bringing* grace; that He does *all*, both for and in His people.

> "'Twas the same grace that spread the feast,
> That gently forced me in;
> Else I had still refused to taste,
> And perished in my sin."

Behind the noble magnanimity exercised by David toward the last descendant of his arch-enemy Saul, we may perceive the shining forth of the glory of God's grace unto His fallen and sinful people. Alas, how feeble are our apprehensions of this wonderful attribute of God, how altogether inadequate our best efforts to set forth its excellency! Those who are the most indebted to the Divine favour, are most conscious of the poverty of their language to express the gratitude and praise, the admiration and adoration which is due from them. When the poor outcast and crippled son of Jonathan was brought from Lo-debar to Jerusalem, and was received not only with kindness, but accorded a place in the king's family and given a seat at David's own table, he must have found words to utterly fail him. And when a slave of sin and captive of Satan is not only set free by Christ but made a joint heir with Him, he is lost in wonderment. Eternity will be required to render unto God that worship to which He is entitled.

Grace is the oppostie of justice. Justice gives to each his exact due: it shows no favour and knows no mercy. It gives impartially to all the precise wages which they have earned. But grace is free favour, unwarranted and unmerited by the recipients of it. Grace is the very last thing to which rebellious sinners are entitled; to talk of *deserving* "grace" is a contradiction in terms. Grace is purely a matter of charity, exercised sovereignly and spontaneously, attracted by nothing praiseworthy in its object. Divine grace is the free favour of God in the bestowment of mercies and blessings upon those who have no good *in* them, and concerning whom no compensation is demanded *from* them. Nay more: Divine grace is not only shown to those who have no merit, but who are full of positive demerit; it is not only bestowed upon the ill-deserving, but the hell-deserving.

How completely grace sets aside *every* thought of personal desert, may be seen from a single quotation of Scripture: "Being justified freely by His grace" (Rom. 3:24). The word "freely" gives intensity to the term "grace," though the Greek does not convey the thought of abundance, but rather emphasizes its gratuitousness. The same word is rendered "without a cause" in John 15:25. There was nothing whatever in the Lord Jesus to deserve such vile treatment from the hands of His enemies, nothing whatever that He had done warranting such awful enmity on their part. In like manner, there is nothing whatever in any sinner to call forth the favourable regard of a holy God, nothing done by him to win His love; instead, everything to the contrary. Grace, then, is gratis; a free gift.

The very expression "the grace of God" implies and denotes that the sinner's condition is desperate to the last degree, and that God may justly leave him to perish; yea, it is a wonder of wonders that he is not already in hell. Grace is a Divine provision for those who are so depraved they cannot change their own nature, so averse from God they will not turn to Him, so blind they can neither see their malady nor the remedy, so dead spiritually that God must bring them out of their graves on to resurrection ground if ever they are to walk in newness of life. Grace is the sinner's last and only hope; if he is not saved by grace, he will never be saved at all. Grace levels all distinctions, and regards the most zealous religionist on the same plane as the most profligate, the chaste virgin as the foul prostitute. Therefore God is perfectly free to save the chiefest of sinners and bestow His mercy on the vilest of the vile. .

In our last, we got as far as Mephibosheth being actually brought into the presence of David. What a meeting was that! For the first time in his life this man now sees the one whom his grandfather had so mercilesssly and unrighteously persecuted. "Now when Mephibosheth the son of Saul, the son of Jonathan, was come unto David, he fell on his face, and did reverence" (v. 6). Fitting position was this to take for one whose very life hung upon the mere mercy of the king. What could he expect but to hear from his lips the sentence of death! There he lies, aptly portraying a trembling sinner, who, in his understanding and conscience, is brought, for the first time, face to face with the thrice holy God, with the One whom he has so long slighted, so wickedly ignored, so grievously offended. It was thus with Saul of Tarsus when the Lord first appeared to him: "he fell to the earth" (Acts 9:4). Reader, have you ever taken your place before Him in the dust?

Most probably David had never before seen Mephibosheth, yet he now addressed him in the most intimate terms: "And David said, Mephibosheth" (v. 6). It is blessed to see that the king was the first one to break the silence, showing us in type how God *takes. the initiative* at every point in connection with the saving of His people. This recalls to us that word of the apostle to the Galatians, "But now, after that ye have known God, *or rather* are known of God" (4:9). A single word was all that David yet uttered — "Mephibosheth" —

yet how much was expressed by it! How it reminds us of that precious declaration from the lips of the good Shepherd, "He calleth His own sheep *by name*" (John 10:3). When, at the burning bush, the Lord first revealed Himself to Israel's deliverer from Egypt, He said, "Moses, Moses" (Ex. 3:4). The first word of the Saviour to the one in the sycamore tree was "Zaccheus" (Luke 19:5). When he made known Himself unto the tear-blinded seeker at His sepulchre, it was by the single word, "Mary" (John 20:16). His first word to the persecutor of His church was "Saul" (Acts 9:4). Thus it was in our present incident. "And Mephilbosheth answered, Behold thy servant."

But the next word of David's was yet more blessed: "Fear not" (v. 7) he said to the cripple prostrate before him. There was no rebuke for his having so long kept away from him, no reproaching him because he was of the house of Saul; but instead, a word to assure him, to put him at his ease. O how this should comfort every contrite soul: we have nothing whatever to fear, once we take our place in the dust before the Lord. "God resisteth the proud, but giveth grace unto the humble" (James 4:6). Was it not thus with the Father, when the penitent prodigal cast himself on His mercy! No word of censure left His lips: instead He quickly assured him of His love. How this "fear not" of David to Mephibosheth reminds us of the same language found so often on the lips of the Redeemer when addressing His own! Wondrous is it to observe that, when the glorified Saviour appeared unto John in Patmos, when that apostle fell at His feet as dead, it was the same old familiar "Fear not" (Rev. 1:17) which reassured him.

Not only did David address Mephibosheth by name, and quiet his heart with a "Fear not," but he also added, "For I will surely show thee kindness for Jonathan thy father's sake, and will restore thee all the land of Saul thy father; and thou shalt eat bread at My table continually" (2 Sam. 9:7). This was grace pure and simple, wondrous grace, the "exceeding riches of grace." There was no contingency here, no bargain made, no conditions stipulated; but instead "I will *surely* show thee kindness." David did not say "If you do this or that" or "if you will keep your part of the contract, I will adhere to mine." No, no; it was free favour, gratuitous mercy, unmerited bounty; everything for nothing. David acted royally, like a king, for it becomes not a monarch to barter. How much more is this the case with the King of kings: He is "the God of all grace" (1 Pet. 5:10), and eternal life is a *gift* (Rom. 6:23) wherever He is pleased to bestow it. To preach salvation by works is not only to mock impotent sinners, but is to grossly insult the ineffable Jehovah.

And what effect did this astonishing kindness have upon Mephibosheth? Did it puff him up with self-importance, and cause him to act as though he was other than a poor cripple? No, indeed; such is never the effect of Divine grace applied to the heart, though often it is the case where airy notions of it sink no deeper than the head. "And he bowed himself, and said, What is thy servant, that thou shouldest look upon such a dead dog as I am?" (v. 8). Is not that truly beautiful? The exceeding kindness of David did not work in him self-elation and self-exaltation, but self-abasement: it wrought in him a deeper consciousness of his utter unworthiness before such unthought of favours. He was amazed that the king should even notice, much less favourably regard, such a worthless creature as he felt himself to be. Did he not now conduct himself in suitable accord with *his name*, when he called himself "a dead dog;" for "Mephibosheth" signifies "a shameful thing." And what is the name which Scripture gives to me? — sinner!: do I, by my attitude, own the truthfulness of it?

This line in our picture calls for particular notice in such a day as we are living in, wherein there is so much self-esteem, creature boasting, laodicean complacency and Pharisaic self-righteousness. O what a stench in the nostrils of the Almighty must be the reeking pride of modern Christendom. How little practical exemplification of that principle, "Let nothing be done through strife or vainglory; but in lowliness of mind let each esteem other better than themselves" (Phil. 2:3). How few feel, like Paul did, that they are "the chief of sinners." And why is this? Because the hearts of so very few are *really* touched and affected by the grace of God. Grace ever humbles. The goodness of God leadeth to repentance (Rom. 2:4). Where the kindness of God is truly felt in the soul we are "little in our own eyes." Just as the royal magnanimity of David bowed Mephibosheth before him, causing him to own that he was but "a dead dog," so when the love of God melts our hard hearts, we realize and own what unworthy wretches, vile creatures, and corrupt worms we are.

We must now consider the wondrous *portion* which was bestowed upon Mephibosheth as the result of the great kindness which David showed him, for this was a striking figure of the "riches" which Divine grace imparts to those who are blessed with all spiritual blessings in Christ. First, there was *life* for him, for the king refused to slay him when he was in his power. That his life was spared him was a notable act of clemency on the part of the monarch. Blessedly did this illustrate the abounding mercy of God unto those who have flouted His authority, broken His laws, and deserved naught but unsparing judgment at His hands: though the wages of sin is death, yet the gift of God is "eternal life" through Jesus Christ our Lord. Second, there was *peace* for him: David's "Fear not" was designed to allay his terror, quiet his heart, and set him at perfect ease in the presence of the king. So it is with the believer: "Therefore being justified by faith, we have peace with God" (Rom. 5:1).

Third, there was *an inheritance* for him. "Then the king called Ziba, Saul's servant, and said unto him, I have given unto thy master's son all that pertained to Saul and to all his house" (v. 9). What a truly wonderful line in our typical picture is that! — one, we are again constrained to say, which no merely human artist could have drawn. How it portrays to us the bounty of our God in bestowing upon poor bankrupt paupers the riches of His grace. Though we come to Him empty-handed, He does not suffer us to remain so. But there is something there yet more definite: Mephibosheth had restored to him the *forfeited* inheritance. The heritage which had originally belonged to Saul had been lost to his family. In like manner, through our first father's apostasy, we lost our primitive heritage, even the life, image, and blessing of God. Nor could *we* possibly do anything to regain it. But as David "for Jonathan's sake" restored unto Mephibosheth the estate of his fathers, so God for Christ's sake gives back to His people all that they lost in Adam.

Fourth, there was a *wondrous portion* granted him. Said David to Mephibosheth, "thou shalt eat bread at my table continually" (v. 7). What a tremendous contrast was that from being an outcast at Lo-debar — "the place of no pasture:" now to feast at the king's own table, and that, not merely for once, but "continually!" Truly it *was* the "kindness of God" which David showed unto him. How forcible this reminds us of what we find at the close of the parable of the prodigal son, when he who, having been "in want" in the far country, after his return in penitence, is feasted by his Father with the "fatted calf." Nothing short of giving us His best will satisfy the great heart of "the God of all grace:" and what is His "best" but *fellowship with Himself*, of which eating at His table is the symbol.

Fifth, there was *an honoured position* for him: "As for Mephibosheth said the king, he shall eat at my table, *as one of the king's sons*" (v. 11). He eats not as an alien or stranger, but as a member of the royal family. Not only was he sumptuously fed, but highly honoured: a place in the king's own palace was now his, and that, not as a servant, but as a son. How this makes us think of "Behold what manner of love the Father hath bestowed upon us, that *we* should be called *the sons of God"* (1 John 3:1)! O what a marvellous place does Divine grace give unto those that are the objects of it: all believers stand accepted as the children of God, the subjects of His everlasting favour. That is something which Saul never enjoyed, but for Jonathan's sake Mephibosheth now gained more than he had previously lost. So through Christ the believer obtains far, far more than he lost in Adam. Where sin abounds, grace does *much more* abound. "That as sin hath reigned unto death, even so might grace reign through righteousness unto eternal life by Jesus Christ our Lord" (Rom. 5:21). Under the king's table the crippled feet of Mephibosheth were *lost to sight:* in Christ all our deformities are hid!

There is a sequel, both pathetic and blessed, recorded in the later chapters of 2 Sam. which we will here briefly notice, for it provides a lovely completeness to all which has been before us. First, in 2 Sam. 16:1-4 we learn that when David fled from Absalom, Ziba the servant of Mephibosheth met the king with a liberal provision of food for his men. When David inquired where Mephibosheth was, Ziba answered him, "Behold, he abideth at Jerusalem: for he said, Today shall the house of Israel restore me the kingdom of my father." This is one of many warnings given to the saints in Scripture that they must be prepared for calumny and unkind treatment: often — as was the case here — by those from whom it should be the least expected.

Second, after Absalom's death, there went forth a company to do honour to the returned king. Among them was Mephibosheth, of whom it is said, that he "had neither dressed his feet, nor trimmed his beard, nor washed his clothes, from the day the king departed until the day he came again in peace" (2 Sam. 19:24). What a lovely picture does that present to us of a loyal soul, whose heart had remained true to the (temporarily) rejected king! How clearly Mephibosheth's condition evidenced *where his affections* had been during David's absence! David now repeated the tale which Ziba had told him, and is informed it was utterly false. Mephibosheth then cast himself on the spiritual discernment and sovereign pleasure of his royal master (vv. 27, 28). The king then put his heart to the test, suggesting that the land be divided between Mephibosheth and his servant — the same in principle as Solomon's proposal that the living child be divided between the two women who claimed it as hers.

Had Mephibosheth been the false-hearted wretch which Ziba has painted him, he had acquiesced promptly to David's suggestion, glad to escape so easily: "a wise settlement" he would have exclaimed. Instead, he nobly replied, "Yea, let him take all, forasmuch as my lord the king is come again in peace unto his own house" (2 Sam. 19:30). How that gave the lie to Ziba's accusation: how it demonstrated he was clear of any carnal covetousness. It was not *land* which he wanted: now that his beloved master had returned, he was quite satisfied. O how this should speak to and search us: are *our* affections set upon the Person of the absent King? Is it *His* presence that *we* long for above everything else?

And after this the king of the children of Ammon died, and his son Hanun reigned in his stead. Then said David I will show kindness to Hanun the son of Nahash, as his father showed kindness to me. And David sent to comfort him for his father, by the hand of his servants. And David's servants came to the land of the children of Ammon. And the princes of the children of Ammon said to Hanun their lord, Do you think that David honors your father, that he has sent comforters to you? Has not David sent his servants to you to search the city, and to spy it out, and to overthrow it? So Hanun took David's servants and shaved off half their beards, and cut off their garments in the middle, to their buttocks, and sent them away. When they told it to David, he sent to meet them, because the men were greatly ashamed. And the king said, Stay at Jericho until your beards are grown, and then return. And when the children of Ammon saw that they had begun to stink before David, the children of Ammon sent and hired the Syrians of Beth-rehob, and the Syrians of Zoba, twenty thousand footmen, and from king Maacah a thousand men, and from Ishtob twelve thousand men. And when David heard, he sent Joab and all the army of the mighty men. And the children of Ammon came out and put the battle in order at the entering in of the gate. And the Syrians of Zoba, and of Rehob, and Ishtob, and Maacah, were by themselves in the field. When Joab saw that the front of the battle was against him before and behind he chose from all the choice men of Israel and put them in order against the Syrians. And the rest of the people he delivered into the hand of Abishai his brother, so that he might put them in order against the children of Ammon. And he said, If the Syrians are too strong for me, then you shall help me. But if the children of Ammon are too strong for you, then I will come and help you. Be courageous and strengthen yourselves for our people and for the cities of our God. And may the LORD do that which seems good to Him. And Joab and the people who were with him drew near to the battle against the Syrians. And they fled before him. And when the children of Ammon saw that the Syrians had fled, then they fled also before Abishai and entered into the city. So Joab returned from the children of Ammon and came to Jerusalem. And when the Syrians saw that they were beaten before Israel, they gathered themselves together. And Hadarezer sent and brought out the Syrians who were beyond the river. And they came to Helam. And Shobach the captain of the host of Hadarezer went before them. And when David was told, he gathered all Israel together and crossed over Jordan and came to Helam. And the Syrians set themselves in order against David and fought with him. And the Syrians fled before Israel. And David killed the men of seven hundred chariots of the Syrians, and forty thousand horsemen, and struck Shobach the captain of their host, who died there. And when all the kings who were servants of Hadarezer saw that they were beaten before Israel, they made peace with Israel and served them. So the Syrians feared to help the children of Ammon any more. — II Samuel 10:1-19.

The next incident recorded in the life of David needs to be pondered from more than one viewpoint. This is intimated to us by the fact that in 2 Sam. 10 it is given immediately after the account of the grace which he showed unto Mephibosheth, whereas in 1 Chron. 19 it is placed right after a parallel account of what is mentioned to 2 Sam. 8. Yet though the context of 2 Sam. 10 and 1 Chron. 19 is so different, each of them opens with *the same* words: "And ('Now') it came to pass after this." Thereby it is suggested that inasmuch as this incident is described at length in almost identical language in 2 Sam. and 1

383

Chron., it possesses a *twofold* significance; and because it is given different settings, that it requires to be considered *separately* in its relation to each one. We shall endeavour, then, to follow up this clue, viewing the subject first as it comes immediately after what was before us in the preceding article.

The king of the Ammonites having died, David purposed to express a neighbourly and friendly sympathy for his son. Accordingly, he sent some of his servants "to comfort him." But instead of this kindly overture meeting with appreciation, it was regarded with distrustful suspicion. The princes of the Ammonites imagined that David had evil designs against their city, and that the men who had ostensibly come to console their bereaved master, were but spies, seeking information with a view to their overthrow. Whereupon Hanun the king grievously insulted his visitors and put them to an open shame. His action was a declaration of war against David, and so the king of Israel regarded it. The remainder of the chapter records the fighting to which their insult gave rise. But it is the typical and spiritual meaning of it with which we are desirous of being occupied. Nor should this be difficult to ascertain.

The link of connection between 2 Sam. 9 and 10 is obvious on the surface: the former opens with "and David said, Is there yet any that is left of the house of Saul, that I may *show him kindness* for Jonathan's sake?" the latter opens with, "And it came to pass after this, that the king of the children of Ammon died, and Hanun his son reigned in his stead. Then said David *I will show kindness* unto Hanun the son of Nahash, as his father showed kindness unto me." But with the exception of the words we have just italicised everything else is in sharp and solemn contrast. In 2 Sam. 9 David shows kindness to an Israelite; in 2 Sam. 10 he shows kindness to an Ammonite. In the former, it was to the descendant of his arch-enemy; in the latter, it was to the son of one who had befriended him. In the one, his gracious overtures were deeply appreciated; in the other, they were maliciously resented.

Now as we showed at length in our two articles upon 2 Sam. 9, that chapter gives us a most lovely typical picture of the free and sovereign grace of God unto His elect. What, then, is it which is distinctively prefigured here in 2 Sam. 10? In seeking the answer to this question, as we attend closely to each word used in the first five verses of it, we notice a further contrast: throughout 2 Sam. 9 it is David himself who is prominent; whereas in 2 Sam. 10 it is his ambassadors who occupy the center of the stage. In vv. 2-4 the *servants* of David are referred to no less than four times; whereas his servants are not mentioned once in the preceding chapter. Here, then, is the key to our incident; typically, it is the ambassadors of the Son of David who are in view.

"But after that the kindness and pity (margin) of God our Saviour toward *man* appeared" (Titus 3:4). And wherein is that "kindness and pity of God our Saviour" revealed? In the Gospel. And to whom is His Gospel to be preached? To "every creature" (Mark 16:15). There are some of our readers — preachers — who need reminding of this. Christ has commissioned His servants to preach the Gospel, to make known His "kindness and pity," not only to those who give evidence of having been awakened by the Holy Spirit, but also to the unregenerate. There is something seriously wrong with any creed or theological system which cramps and fetters the preacher in his free proclamation of the Gospel. They who imagine that the Gospel is only for the elect, err grievously. In order to "do the work of an evangelist" (2 Tim. 4:5) one does not have to embrace the errors of Arminians, and believe either in a general redemption or in the free will of fallen man.

In the parable of the Sower, Christ makes it very clear that *He* sowed the seed upon *all* parts of the field, and not on the "good ground" only. In the closing parable of Matt. 13, He represents the Gospel "net" as gathering in fish of all kinds, "bad" as well as "good." In the parable of the Great Supper, the servant is sent forth to say, "Come, for all things are now ready," and this, even unto those who "all with one consent began to make excuse" (Luke 14:17, 18) In the closing section of the parable of the two sons, Christ declared concerning the *elder* brother (the self-righteous, hard-hearted Pharisee) "therefore came his Father *out* and *entreated* him" (Luke 15:28). O my dear brethren in the ministry, seek grace and wisdom to make *your* ministry square with that of Christ's! HE did not allow the eternal decrees of God to tie His hands or muzzle His mouth.

It was the same with those that immediately succeeded Christ. It was to a *promiscuous* audience (Acts 3:9), to those who were unbelievers (v. 17), that Peter said, "Repent ye, therefore, and be converted, that your sins may be blotted out" (Acts 3:19)! "Then Philip went down to the city of Samaria, and preached Christ unto them" (Acts 8:5): we are not told that it was to a small and picked company, who had been quickened by the Spirit, but to "the *city* of Samaria" in general. And what was the theme of his preaching? *Christ!* — as an all-sufficient Saviour for the very chief of sinners. The apostle Paul was not cramped in his message: "Testifying both to the Jews, and also to the Greeks, repentance toward God, and faith toward our Lord Jesus Christ" (Acts 20:21): the impenitent He called upon *to* repent; and the unbelieving, he bade believe on the Saviour. Are not these very things recorded for *our* learning, as a precedent for us to follow!

That which we have sought to emphasise in the last three paragraphs receives striking illustration and confirmation in the incident we are here considering. If 2 Sam. 9 supplies a blessed representation of the kindness of God shown toward one of His elect, our present chapter gives an equally clear type of the overtures of the Lord's kindness extended unto the non-elect. Here is the reason why the two incidents are placed side by side: the one *supplements* the other. If in the last chapter we beheld the "kindness" of David manifested unto one with whom he was in covenant relationship, in the chapter now before us we see his "kindness" being shown to one who was outside the commonwealth of Israel, to one who was a heathen. And it is in *that* particular fact lies the typical beauty of our passage, and the great evangelical lesson which we need to learn from it.

"And it came to pass after this, that the king of the children of Ammon died, and Hanun his son reigned in his stead. *Then* said David, I will show kindness unto Hanun the son of Nahash" (2 Sam. 10:1, 2). It is only as we attend closely unto each detail here that we can appreciate the accuracy of our typical picture. *Death* provided the dark background for it. It was the decease of Nahash which supplied the opportunity for David to manifest the kindness of his heart! Once our minds are definitely focused on this item, what anointed eye can fail to perceive its spiritual signification? No "comfort" was needed by man in his unfallen state; the Gospel had been entirely unsuited to Adam during the brief season that he remained in unclouded communion with his Maker. But the entrance of sin entirely altered the case.

Adam's transgression cast a pall of blackness over the fair scene of Eden; nor was its darkness in anywise relieved till the light of the Gospel (Gen. 3:15) broke in on it. It is *sin* which exhibited the need for a Saviour; it was that spiritual *death* into which the fall plunged the whole family, which makes evident the glad tidings of life in Christ. The whole have no need of a physician, but they that are sick. And it was where sin abounded, that grace did much more abound.

The sin of men brought out the marvellous grace that was in the heart of God. The Lord had by no means acted unjustly, had He eternally doomed the whole human race when their father and federal head apostatized from Him. But He did not do so: in wrath He "remembered mercy."

Here, then, is the first line in our typical picture: *death* provides for it a suitable background. The more the awfulness be felt of that spiritual death which it adumbrated, the more will we appreciate the blessedness of that wondrous "comfort" which divine mercy hath provided. The terrible fall which brought in spiritual death was of such an aggravated nature that it left all whom Adam represented without excuse. The nature of our spiritual death is described in Eph. 4:18, "Having the understanding darkened, being *alienated from the life of God* through the ignorance that is in them, because of the blindness of their heart." It has wrought in us a carnal mind which "is enmity" against God (Rom. 8:7). Why, then, should the Lord have any regard for us? Why should He concern Himself about those who prefer darkness to light, evil to good, death to life? Had He totally abandoned us to our ruin and wretchedness, that had been all we deserved.

"Then said David, I will show kindness unto Hanun" (v. 2). Here is the second line in our typical picture, pointing us unto the One who is the Author of all that is good, gentle, sympathetic and unselfish in His creatures: and is Himself "of great kindness" (Jonah 4:2). O what kindness did the Lord show when He left Heaven's glory and came down to this sin-curst earth! What kindness for the Lord to take upon Himself the form of a servnat, and minister unto others rather than be ministered unto. What compassion He exhibited when in the presence of want, suffering and misery; what kindness when He "healed all manner of sickness and all manner of disease" (Matt. 4:23). Thus did the kindness of David shadow forth the infinitely greater kindness of his Son and Lord.

"And David sent to comfort him by the hand of his servants" (v. 2). This gives the third line in our typical picture. During the days of His flesh, Christ announced, "The Spirit of the Lord is upon Me, because He hath anointed Me to preach the Gospel to the poor; He hath sent Me to heal the brokenhearted, to preach deliverance to the captives, and recovering of sight to the blind, to set at liberty them that are bruised" (Luke 4:18). Since His ascension, He has continued this gracious ministry through His ambassadors and servants: 2 Cor. 5:20; Mark 16:20. O what a message of "comfort" have Christ's ministers for every poor sinner that will give ear to them: a message which makes known a way of escape from the wrath to come, that tells of how the forgiveness of sins may be obtained; how peace, joy, everlasting life and bliss may become our portion. The fourth line in our picture is given in the next words, "And the servants of David came into the land of the children of Ammon" (v. 2). Let those words be carefully weighed by those of us who may be inclined toward hyper-Calvinism — the term is justly warranted, for his own writings make it very clear that Calvin himself pressed the requirements of the Gospel (repentance and faith) upon all and sundry. These servants of David were not like Jonah, who demurred when called upon to preach unto the Ninevites. No, they made no objection against going *outside* the bounds of God's covenant people, and journeying to a place of idolators. As such, they prefigured the obedient servants of the Son of David, whose commission is "That repentance and remission of sins should be preached in His name among *all* nations" (Luke 24:47).

"And the princes of the children of Ammon said unto Hanun their lord, Thinkest thou that David doth honour thy father, that he hath sent comforters unto thee? hath not David rather sent his servants unto thee to search the city, and to spy it out, and to overthrow it?" (v. 3). Is any interpreter required here? Is not this next line in our picture so clear that it speaks for itself! The common experience of the Christian evangelist is identical in substance with that which befell the servants of David. Though his intentions are of the best, they are interpreted as being evil. Though he comes with a message of true "comfort," the poor blinded dupes of Satan regard him as a "kill-joy." Though his only object be to make known the "kindness" of his royal Master, the vast majority of those to whom he comes, resent his mission. Alas, that now, in many circles of professing Christians, the true servant of Christ is not wanted, but rather looked upon him with suspicion, as a "self-seeker" or "disturber of the peace."

"Wherefore Hanun took David's servants, and shaved off the one half of their beards, and cut off their garments in the middle, even to their buttocks, and sent them away" (v. 4). This line in our picture is also so obvious that it needs little comment from us. It foreshadowed the treatment which the Son of David's servants would receive from those whose welfare they sought. Those servants were mocked and insulted: not wanted, they were "sent away" in shame. Men today have other ways of insulting and disgracing the ministers of the Gospel beside the methods used by those Ammonites; but they are just as effective. Wrongful charges are made against them, false reports are spread, so that they are excluded from many places.

"When they told it unto David, he sent to meet them, because the men were greatly ashamed: and the king said, Tarry at Jericho until your beards be grown, and then return" (v. 5). Here is the sequel to the unkind treatment they had met with: the servants of David are called upon *to retire from the public eye.* They have to spend a season — one of some months at least — in seclusion, cut off from fellowship. One wonders how many today are, like the writer, "tarrying at Jericho!" Not a few "teachers" are now "removed into a corner" (Isa. 30:20), for the time hath come "when they will not endure sound doctrine" (2 Tim. 4:3). Concerning Israel of old we read, "But they mocked the messengers of God, and despised His words, and misused His prophets, until the wrath of the Lord arose against His people, till there was *no remedy"* (2 Chron. 36:16) — is this soon to be repeated in the history of Christendom?

The final line in our typical picture — occupying the remainder of 2 Sam. 10 — is a very solemn one: *David avenged his insulted servants.* He regarded the ignominy heaped on them, as a direct affront upon himself. Thus it is in the antitype. Concerning His ministers, Christ has said, "He that heareth you, heareth Me; and he that despiseth *you,* despiseth *Me"* (Luke 10:16). He regards the ill-usage of *them* as a declaration of war against *Himself.* He has said, "Touch not Mine anointed, and do My prophets *no* harm" (Psa. 105:15), and He will not be disobeyed with impugnity. Solemn is it to look forward to the time when those who have despised, slandered, insulted, and cast out His servants, will yet have to answer to the Son of David Himself.

Many and important are the lessons for the servants of Christ in this incident. Chief among them are: 1. They are to obediently carry out the orders of their royal Master, no matter how unreasonable they may appear or how distasteful they be unto themselves. 2. They must be prepared for their best intentions and kindest actions to expose them unto the basest suspicions. They must expect ingratitude, contempt and abuse; but sufficient for the servant to be as his Lord. 3. These things must not discourage them, for eventually, Christ Himself will plead their cause! 4. They must not attempt to avenge themselves, but rather follow the example left by their Master: 1 Pet. 2:23. 5. If now, for a season, they are required to "tarry at Jericho," they may take comfort from the fact that it is their Lord who has ordered that isolated seclusion.

And after the year had passed, at the time when kings go forth to battle, David sent Joab, and his servants with him, and all Israel. And they destroyed the children of Ammon and circled Rabbah. But David remained at Jerusalem. And one evening David arose from his bed and walked on the roof of the king's house. And from the roof he saw a woman washing herself. And the woman was very beautiful to look upon. And David sent and asked about the woman. And one said, Is not this Bathsheba, the daughter of Eliam, the wife of Uriah the Hittite? And David sent messengers and took her. And she came to him, and he lay with her. And when she had purified herself from her uncleanness, she returned to her house. — II Samuel 11:1-4.

"I have seen an end of all perfection; but Thy commandment is exceeding broad" (Psa. 119:96). The Chaldee Paraphrase renders this verse, "I have seen an end of all things about which I have employed my care; but Thy commandment is very large." The Syriac version reads, "I have seen an end of all regions and countries (that is, I have found the compass of the habitable world to be finite and limited), but Thy commandment is of vast extent." The contrast drawn by the Psalmist is between the works of the creature and the Word of the Creator. The most perfect of worldly things are but imperfect; even man, at his best estate, is "altogether vanity" (Psa. 39:5). We may quickly see "the end" or "the bound" of man's works, for the profoundest product of human wisdom is but shallow, superficial, and having its limits; but it is far otherwise with the Scriptures of Truth.

"But Thy commandment is exceeding broad." The Word partakes of the perfections of its Divine Author: holiness, inerrency, infinitude, and eternity, are numbered among its wondrous qualities. God's Word is so deep that none can fathom it (Psa. 36:6), so high that it is established in Heaven (Psa. 119:89), so long that it will endure forever (1 Pet. 1:23), so exceeding broad that one can measure it, so full that its contents will never be exhausted. It is such a rich storehouse of spiritual treasure, that no matter how many draw upon it, the wealth thereof remains undiminished. It has in it such an inconceivable vastness of wisdom, that no single verse in it has been fully fathomed by any man. No matter how many may have previously written upon a certain chapter, the Spirit can still reveal wonders and beauties in it never before perceived.

We are now to go over again the same passage which was before us in our last section, but this time it is to be considered from an entirely different viewpoint. Perhaps some explanatory remarks are called for at this point, that none of our readers may be confused. There are many portions of the Word that are not only capable of several legitimate applications, but which *require* to be pondered from distinct and separate angles. Oftentimes the same incident which manifests the goodness and grace of God, also exhibits the depravity and sin of man. Many parts of the life of Samson furnish most striking prefigurations of Christ, yet at the same time we see in them the grievous failures of Samson himself. The same dual principle is exemplified in the lives of other characters prominent in the O.T. Instead of being confused thereby, let us rather admire the wisdom of Him who has brought together things so diverse.

Moses erred sadly when, instead of trustfully responding promptly unto the Lord's call for him to make known His request unto Pharaoh, he gave way to unbelief and voiced one objection after another (Ex. 3 and 4); nevertheless in the same we may perceive a lovely exemplification of the self-diffidence of those called upon to minister in Divine things, and their personal sense of unfitness and utter unworthiness. The two things are quite distinct, though they are found in one and the same incident: the personal failure of Moses, yet his very failure supplying a blessed type of humility in the true servant of God. That which is found in 2 Sam. 10 affords a parallel: the action of David in expressing his condolence to the king of Ammonites supplies a beautiful type of Christ sending forth His servants with a message of comfort for sinners; yet, as we shall see, from a *personal* viewpoint, David's conduct was to be blamed.

The same thing is seen again in connection with Jonah. We have the Lord's own authority for regarding him as a type or "sign" of Himself (Matt. 12:39, 40), and marvellously did that prophet foreshadow the Saviour in many different details. But that in nowise alters or militates against the fact that, as we read the personal history of Jonah, we find some grievous sins recorded against him. Let it not seem strange, then, if our present exposition of 2 Sam. 10 differs so radically from our treatment of it in our last article: there is no "contradiction" between the two sections; instead, they approach the same incident from two widely separated angles. Our justification for so doing, lies in the fact that the incident is described in identical terms in 1 Chron. 19, yet its context there is *quite different* from 2 Sam. 9.

On this occasion, instead of admiring the lovely typical picture which 2 Sam. 10 set forth, we shall examine the personal conduct of David, seeking to take to heart the lessons and warnings which the same inculcates. "And it came to pass after this, that the king of the children of Ammon died, and Hanun his son reigned in his stead. Then said David, I will show kindness unto Hanun the son of Nahash, as his father showed kindness unto me. And David sent to comfort him by the hand of his servants for his father" (vv. 1, 2).

In seeking to get at the practical teaching of these verses, the first question which needs to be pondered is, *Why* did David send his servants with a message of comfort to the king of Ammon? What was the motive which prompted him? It is no sufficient answer to reply, The kindness of his heart; for that only changes the form of our inquiry to, *Why* should he determine to show kindness unto the head of this heathen tribe? And how are we to discover the answer to our question? By noting carefully the context: this time, the context of 1 Chron. 19; which is the same as the *remoter* context in 2 Sam. for 1 Chron 19 is parallel with 2 Sam. 9. And what do we find there? David engaging in warfare, subduing the Philistines (2 Sam. 8:1), the Moabites (v. 2), Hadadezer (v. 3), the Syrians (v. 5), placing garrisons in Edom, and setting in order the affairs of his kingdom (vv. 15-18.).

After engaging in so much fighting, it appears that David now desired a season of rest. This is borne out by what we are told in the very first verse of the next chapter: "And it came to pass, after the year was expired, at the time when kings go forth to battle, that David sent Joab, and his servants with him, and all Israel; and they destroyed the children of Ammon, and besieged Rabbah. *But David tarried still* at Jerusalem" (2 Sam. 11:1). Thus, in the light of the immediate context, both before and after what is recorded in 2 Sam. 10 and 1 Chron. 19, it seems clear that David's sending a message of comfort to Hanun after the death of his father, was a diplomatic move on his part to secure peace between the Ammonites and Israel. In other words, reduced to first principles, it was an attempt to promote amity between the ungodly and the godly. The Lord *blew upon this move*, and caused it to come to nought.

"Ye adulterers and adulteresses, know ye not that *the friendship* of the world is enmity with God?" (James 4:4). Yes, we may know it in theory, but alas, how often we disobey it in practice. God requires His people to be separated from the world, to be strangers and pilgrims therein, to have no close familiarity with its subjects, to refuse all "yokes" with them. And is not that both right and necessary? What fellowship can there be between those who love His Son and those who hate Him? between those who are subject to His sceptre and those who are in league with Satan? Yet, self evident as is this principle, how slow many of us are to conform our *ways* to its requirements! How prone we are to flirt with those who are the enemies of God.

But if *we* are careless and disobedient, *God* is faithful. In his love for us, He often causes worldlings to *repulse* our friendly advances, to wrongly interpret our kindly overtures, to despise, mock and insult us. If we will not keep on *our* side of the line which God has drawn between the kingdom of His Son and the kingdom of Satan, then we must not be surprised if He employs the wicked to drive us out of *their* territory. Herein lies the key, my reader, to many a painful experience which often perplexes the Christian. Why does a righteous God suffer me to receive such unjust and cruel treatment from those I wish to be "nice to?" God permits that "enmity" which *He* has placed between the seed of the serpent and the seed of the woman to burst out against the latter, because they were becoming too intimate with the former.

It is not only that God rebukes us for disregarding the line which He has drawn between the world and the Church, but that it is our spiritual profit which He designs to promote. "We know that all things work together for good to them that love God, to them who are the called according to His purpose" (Rom. 8:28). Yes, Christian reader, and that *"all* things" includes the present aloofness of some unsaved people who were once very friendly towards you; that "all things" includes the coldness of Christless relatives, the unkind attitude of neighbours, the unfriendliness of those who work side by side with you in the office, store, or workshop. God sees the *danger,* if you do not! Because of His love for you, He prevents your becoming drawn into alliances with those whose influence would greatly hinder your growth in grace. Then instead of chafing against the attitude of your fellows, thank the Lord for *His* faithfulness.

Against what has been said above it may be objected, But you surely do not mean that, in his separation from the world, the Christian must be unsociable and live like a hermit; or that God requires us to be uncivil and morose toward our fellow-creatures. No, dear reader, *that* is not our meaning. We are required to be "pitiful" and "courteous" (1 Pet. 3:8), and to "do good unto all, especially unto them who are of the household of faith" (Gal. 6:10). Moreover, the Christian must be very watchful against assuming an "I am holier than thou" attitude toward his fellow men. Nevertheless, there is a real difference between a respectful and kindly conduct toward the unsaved, and an undue intimacy with them — making close friends of them.

It may be further objected, But in David's case, it was proper and needful for him to act as **he** did, for v. 2 expressly states that Hanun's father had shown kindness to him. Then would it not have been rebukable ingratitude if David had failed to make some suitable return? Exactly what was the nature of that "kindness" which Nahash, the king of the Ammonites, had shown David, Scripture does not inform us; and therefore speculation is useless. But if David had *sought* some favour from him, as he did from Achish, the son of the king of Gath (1 Sam. 27:1-7), then he was guilty of turning aside from the high calling and privileged place of one whose dependency should be on the living God alone. When such is the case, when we place our confidence in man aɪ d lean upon the creature, we must not be surprised if God rebukes and foils our carnal hopes.

There is a principle involved here which it is important for us to be clear upon, but the application of which is likely to exercise those who are of a tender conscience. How far is it permissible for the Christian to receive favours from unbelievers? Something depends upon the relation borne to him by the one who proffers them; something upon the motive likely to be actuating the profferer; something upon the nature of what is proffered. Obviously, the Christian must never accept anything from one who has no right to tender it — a dishonest employee, for example. Nor must he accept anything which the Word of God condemns — such as an immodest dress, a ticket to the theatre, etc. Firmly must he refuse any favour which would bring him *under obligation* to a worldling: it is at *this* point that Satan often seeks to ensnare the believer — by bringing him under the power of the ungodly through becoming indebted to them.

But though we are not informed of how and when Nahash had befriended David, the Holy Spirit *has* placed on record an incident which reveals the character of this king: "Then Nahash the Ammonite came up and encamped against Jabesh-gilead: and all the men of Jabesh said unto Nahash, Make a covenant with us, and we will serve thee. And Nahash the Ammonite answered them, On this condition will I make a covenant with you, that I may thrust out all your right eyes, and lay it for a reproach upon all Israel" (1 Sam. 11:1, 2). Why, then, should David now show respect unto the memory of one who had evidenced himself such a cruel enemy of the people of God! It could not be any *spiritual* principle which actuated Israel's king on this occasion. A clear word for our guidance concerning those who are the open enemies of God is given us in, "Shouldest thou help the ungodly, and love them that hate the Lord!" (2 Chron. 19:2).

But not only should the evil character of Nahash have restrained David from showing respect to his memory, but *the race* to which he belonged ought to have been a separating barrier. He was an Ammonite, and as such under the interdict of the Lord, because that nation had refused to meet the children of Israel "with bread and with water in the way, when they came forth out of the land of Egypt," and they together with the Moabites (because they had hired Balaam against them) were debarred from entering into the congregation of the Lord, even to their tenth generation (Deut. 23:3, 4). But more: concerning both the Ammonites and the Moabites God expressly prohibited, "Thou shalt *not* seek their peace nor their good all thy days forever" (Deut. 23:6). David, then, disobeyed a plain command of God on this occasion.

As to whether or not David was personally acquainted with that particular Divine statute, we cannot say. Probably the only thought in his mind was to diplomatically time his effort to secure peace between the two nations. But God blew upon his political scheme, and in so doing gave warning unto His people throughout all generations that, only disappointment and vexation can be expected from their attempts to court the friendship of the ungodly. "And the princes of the children of Ammon said unto Hanun their lord, Thinkest thou that David doth honour thy father, that he hath sent comforters unto thee? hath not David rather sent his servants unto thee, to search the city, and to spy it out, and to overthrow it?" (2 Sam. 10:3). Treacherous minds always suspect other people of perfidy. Beware of those, my reader, who are ever ready to think the worst of others and place an evil construction on the most innocent actions.

"Wherefore Hanun took David's servants, and shaved off the one half of their beards, and cut off their garments, even to their buttocks, and sent them away" (v. 4). And why did God allow those princes to wrongly interpret David's kindness, and their king to heed them and now insult David by thus disgracing his ambassadors? Because He had far different designs than His servant. These men had filled up "the measure" of their iniquity (Gen. 15:16; Matt. 23:32): their hearts were ripe for ruin, and therefore were they hardened to their destruction (11:1). God had not forgotten what is recorded in 1 Sam. 11:1, 2, though it had taken place many years before. His mills "grind slowly," yet in the end, "they grind exceeding small."

And the woman conceived. And she sent and told David, and said, I am with child. And David sent to Joab, saying Send me Uriah the Hittite. And Joab sent Uriah to David. And when Uriah had come to him, David asked how Joab did, and how the people did, and how the war went. And David said to Uriah, Go down to your house and wash your feet. And Uriah left the king's house. And a gift from the king went out after him. But Uriah slept at the door of the king's house with all the servants of his lord. And he did not go down to his house. And when they told David, saying, Uriah did not go down to his house — David said to Uriah, Did you not come from your journey? Why then do you not go down to your house? And Uriah said to David, The ark and Israel and Judah abide in tents. And my lord Joab, and the servants of my lord, are camped in the open fields. Shall I then go to my house to eat and to drink and to lie with my wife? As you live, and as your soul lives, I will not do this thing. And David said to Uriah, Stay here today also, and tomorrow I will let you go. So Uriah stayed in Jerusalem that day and the next day. And when David had called him, he ate and drank before him. And he made him drunk. And at evening he went out to lie on his bed with the servants of his lord, but he did not go down to his house. — II Samuel 11:5-13.

A difficult and most unwelcome task now confronts us: to contemplate and comment upon the darkest blot of all in the fair character of David. But who are we, so full of sin in ourselves, unworthy to unloose his shoes, to take it upon us to sit in judgment upon the sweet Psalmist of Israel. Certainly we would not select this subject from personal choice, for it affords us no pleasure to gaze upon an eminent saint of God befouling himself in the mire of evil. O that we may be enabled to approach it with true humility, in fear and trembling, remembering that "as in water face answereth to face, so the heart of man to man." Only then may we hope to derive any profit from our perusal; the same applies to the reader. Before proceeding further, let each of us ask God to awe our hearts by the solemn scene which is to be before us.

It must be for God's glory and our profit that the Holy Spirit has placed on record this account of David's fearful fall, otherwise it would not have been given a permanent place on the imperishable pages of Holy Writ. But in order to derive any good from it for our souls, it is surely necessary that we approach this sad incident with a sober mind and in a spirit of meekness, "considering ourselves, lest we also be tempted" (Gal. 6:1). This inspired record is to be regarded as a Divine beacon, warning us of the rocks upon which David's life was wrecked; and a danger-signal, bidding us to be on our guard, lest we, through unwatchfulness, experience a similar calamity. Viewed thus, there are valuable lessons to be learned; instruction which will stand us in good stead if it be humbly appropriated.

The fearful fall of David supplies a concrete exemplification of many solemn statements of Scripture concerning the nature and character of fallen man. Its teaching in regard to human depravity is very pointed and unpalatable, and often has it been made a subject of unholy jest by godless scoffers. Such declarations as heart as, the imagination of man's heart is love from his youth" (Gen. 8:21), "the heart is deceitful above all things, and desperately wicked" (Jer. 17:9), "in my flesh dwelleth no good thing" (Rom. 7:18), and highly objectionable to human pride, yet *the truth* of them cannot be gainsaid. Fearful and forbidding as are such descriptions of fallen man, nevertheless their accuracy is illustrated and demonstrated again and again in the lives of Bible characters, as well as in the world to day.

Rightly has it been said that, "One of the most astounding demonstrations of the truth of the Bible is its unhesitating revelation and denunciation of sin, in the professed follower of God. It conceals nothing; on the contrary, it pulls aside the veil and discloses all. It condones nothing; instead, it either utters the terrible wrath of God against the guilty one, or records His judgments as they fall upon the unhappy sinner, even to the third and fourth generation (Ex. 34:7).

"It exalts Noah as a preacher of righteousness in an evil and violent generation; with equal faithfulness it records his drunkenness and shame (Gen. 9:20, 21). Abraham is set before us as a man of faith. In the hour of famine, instead of waiting in quietness upon God, he goes down into Egypt. Once there, he persuades his wife to misrepresent her relationship to him, and through the acted falsehood imperils his peace and her own (Gen. 12:12, 13). Lot falls away after his deliverance from Sodom, and through love of wine is subjected to the lust of his wanton daughters. Aaron and Miriam are filled with jealousy and speak evilly against Moses, their brother. Moses speaks unadvisedly with his lips, and is shut out from the land of promise. The white light of truth flashes on every page, and the faults, the follies, the sins and inexcusable iniquities of those who call themselves the people and servants of God, are seen in all their repulsive forms." (I.M. Haldeman).

Thus it was in the tragic case now before us. The fearful conduct of David reveals to us with terrible vividness that not only is the natural man a fallen and depraved creature, but also that the redeemed and regenerated man is liable to fall into the most heinous evil; yea, that unless God is pleased to sovereignly interpose, unwatchfulness on the part of the believer is certain to issue in consequences highly dishonouring to the Lord and fearfully injurious to himself. This it is which above all else makes our present portion so unspeakably solemn: here we behold the lusts of the flesh allowed full sway not by a man of the world, but by a member of the household of faith; here we behold a saint, eminent in holiness, in an unguarded moment, surprised, seduced, and led captive by the devil. The "flesh" in the believer is no different and no better than the flesh in an unbeliever!

Yes, the sweet Psalmist of Israel, who had enjoyed such long and close communion with God, still had the "flesh" within him, and because he *failed to mortify* its lusts, he now flung away the joys of Divine fellowship, defiled his conscience, ruined his soul's prosperity, brought down upon himself (for all his remaining years) a storm of calamities, and made his name and religion a target for the arrows of sarcasm and blasphemy of each succeeding generation. Every claim that God had upon him, every obligation of his high office, all the fences which Divine mercy had provided, were ruthlessly trampled under foot by the fiery lust now burning in him. He who in the day of his distress cried, "my soul thirsteth for God, for the living God" (Psa. 42:2) now lusted after a forbidden object. Alas, what is man? Truly "man at his best estate is altogether vanity" (Psa. 39:5).

But how are we to account for David's fearful fall? Why was it that he succumbed so readily in the presence of temptation? What was it that led up to and occasioned his heinous sin? These questions are capable of a twofold answer, according as we view them in the light of the high sovereignty of God or the responsibility of man; for the present we shall consider them from the latter viewpoint. And it is here we should derive the most practical help for our own souls; it is in tracing the *relation* between God's chastisements and what occasions them, between men's sins and what leads up to them, that we discover what is most essential for us to lay to heart. The reasons why Abraham "went *down* to Egypt" are revealed in the context. Peter's denial of Christ may be traced back to his self-confidence in following his Master "afar off." And, we shall see, the Divine record enables us to trace David's fall back to the springs which occasioned it.

"And it came to pass, after the year was expired, at the time when kings go forth to battle, that David sent Joab, and his servants with him, and all Israel; and they destroyed the children of Ammon, and besieged Rabbah. But David tarried still at Jerusalem. And it came to pass in an evening tide, that David arose from off his bed, and walked upon the roof of the king's house: and from the roof he saw a woman washing herself; and the woman was very beautiful to look upon. And David sent and inquired after the woman. And one said, Is not this Bathsheba, the daughter of Eliam, the wife of Uriah the Hittite? And David sent messengers, and took her; and she came in unto him, and he lay with her; for she was purified from her uncleanness: and she returned unto her house" (2 Sam. 11:1-4). We cannot do better than seek to fill in the outline of Matt. Henry on these verses: first, the occasions of the sin; second, the steps of the sin; third, the aggravations of the sin.

The occasions of or what led up to David's fearful fall are plainly intimated in the above verses. We begin by noticing the time-mark here mentioned: "And it came to pass after the year was expired, at the time when kings go forth to battle" (v. 1), which signifies, at the season of spring, after the winter is over. Following the period of enforced inactivity, upon the return of favourable weather, the military activities against the Ammonites were resumed: Joab and the army went forth, "BUT David tarried still at Jerusalem." Ominous "But," noting the Spirit's disapproval at the king's conduct. Here is the first key which explains what follows, and we do well to weigh it attentively, for it is recorded "for *our* learning" and warning. Reduced to its simplest terms, that which is here signified is, *David's failure to follow the path of duty.*

It is obvious that at this time the king's place — his accustomed one hitherto (see 10:17) — was at the head of his fighting men, leading them to the overthrow of Israel's enemies. Had he been out fighting the battles of the Lord, he had not been subject to the temptation which soon confronted him. It may appear a very trifling matter in our eyes that the king should tarry at Jerusalem: if so, it shows we sadly fail to view things in their proper perspective — it is never a trifling matter to forsake *the post of obligation*, be that post the most menial one. The fact is that we cannot count upon Divine protection when we forsake the path of duty. *That* was the force of our Saviour's reply when the devil bade him cast Himself down from the pinnacle of the temple; that pinnacle lay not in the path of His duty, hence His "thou shalt not tempt the Lord thy God."

David relaxed when he should have girded on the sword: he preferred the luxuries of the palace to the hardships of the battlefield. Ah, it is so easy to follow the line of least resistance. It requires grace (diligently sought) to "endure hardness as a good soldier of Jesus Christ" (2 Tim. 2:3). Alas that David had failed to profit from a previous failure along this same line: when he had *sought rest* among the Philistines at an earlier date, he fell readily into sin (1 Sam. 21:13); so it was now, when he sought ease in Jerusalem. The important principle here for the Christian to lay to heart is, David had *taken off his armour*, and therefore he was without protection when the enemy assailed him. Ah, my reader, this world is no place to rest in; rather is it the arena where faith has to wage its fight, and that fight is certain to be a losing one if we disregard that exhortation "Put on the whole armour of God, that ye may be able to stand against the wiles of the devil" (Eph. 6:11).

"And it came to pass in an eveningtide, that David arose from off his bed and walked upon the roof of the king's house." Here is the second thing for us to observe: not only had David shunned the post of duty, but he was guilty of *slothfulness*. It was not the slumbers of nighttime which the Spirit here takes notice of, for it was eveningtide when he "arose" — it was the afternoon which he had wasted in self-luxuriation. David had failed to redeem the time: he was not engaged either in seeking to be of use to others, or in improving himself. Laziness gives great advantage to the tempter: it was "while men slept" that the enemy "came and sowed tares among the wheat" (Matt. 13:29). It is written "The hand of the diligent shall bear rule (in measure, over his lusts), but the slothful shall be *under tribute*" (Prov. 12:24).

What a word is this "I went by the field of *the slothful*, and by the vineyard of the man void of understanding; and *lo*, it was all grown over with thorns, nettles had covered the face thereof, and the stone wall thereof was broken down" (Prov. 24:30, 31). Does not the reader perceive the *spiritual* meaning of this: the "field" is his life, open before all; the vineyard" (private property) is his heart. And what a state they are in: through idle neglect, filled with that which is obnoxious to God and worthless to men. "Then I saw, and considered it well: I looked upon it, and received instruction" (v. 32). Do *we?* do we lay it to heart and profit therefrom when we behold so many wrecked and fruitless lives around us — ruined by spiritual *indolence*. "Yet a little sleep, a little slumber, a little folding of the hands to sleep: So shall thy poverty come as one that travelleth; and thy want as an armed man" (vv. 33,34) — are not those verses a solemn commentary on 2 Sam. 11:2!

"And from the roof he saw a woman washing herself, and the woman was very beautiful to look upon." Here is the third thing: *a wandering eye*. In Isa. 33:15, 16 we are told concerning the one that "shutteth his eyes from seeing evil, he shall dwell on the heights, his place of defence shall be the munitions of rocks." Alas, this is what David did not do: instead, he suffered his eyes to dwell upon an alluring but prohibited object. Among his prayers was this petition. "Turn away mine eyes from beholding vanity" (Psa. 119:37), but we cannot expect God to answer us if we deliberately spy upon the privacy of others. We turn now to consider the actual steps in this fall.

"And David sent and enquired after the woman." He purposed now to satisfy his lust. He who had once boasted "*I will* behave myself wisely in a perfect way. O when wilt Thou come unto me? *I will* walk within my house with a perfect heart. *I will* set no wicked thing before mine eyes: I hate the work of them that turn aside; it shall not cleave to me. A froward heart shall depart from me: *I will not* know a wicked person" (Psa. 101:2-4), now determined to commit adultery. Note the repeated "I will" in the above passage, and learn therefrom how much the "free will" of man is worth!

"And David sent and enquired after the woman. And one said, is not this Bathsheba, the daughter of Eliam, the wife of Uriah the Hittite?" Here was calm deliberation and pre-meditation on the part of David. Here too was a merciful interposition on the part of God, for one of the king's servants dared to remind his royal master that the woman he was inquiring about was the *wife* of another.

How often does the Lord in His grace and faithfulness place some obstacle across our path, when we are planning something which is evil in His sight! It is this which renders our sin far worse, when we defiantly break through any hedge which the providence of God places about us. O that we may draw back with a shudder when such obstacles confront us, and not rush blindly like an ox to the slaughter.

"And David sent messengers, and took her; and she came in unto him, and he lay with her." The order is very solemn: first "he saw" (v. 2), then he "sent and inquired" (v. 3), and now "he lay with her." Yet that does not give us the complete picture: we need to go back to v. 1 in order to take in the entire scene, and as we do so, we obtain a vivid and solemn illustration of what is declared in James 1:14, 15. First, David was "drawn away of his lust" — of fleshly ease and indolence; second, he was then "enticed" — by the sight of a beautiful woman; third, "then when lust had conceived it brought forth sin" — that of premeditated adultery; and, as the terrible sequel shows, "sin when it was finished brought forth *death*" — the murder of Uriah her husband.

The *aggravations* of his sin were marked and many. First, David was no longer a hot-blooded youth, but a man of some fifty years of age. Second, he was not a single man, but one who already had several wives of his own — this is emphasised in 12:8, when God sent the prophet to charge him with his wickedness. Third, he had sons who had almost reached the age of manhood: what a fearful example for a father to set before them! Fourth, he was the king of Israel, and therefore under binding obligation to set before his subjects a pattern of righteousness. Fifth, Uriah, the man who he so grievously wronged, was even then hazarding his life in the king's service. And above all, he was a child of God, and as such, under bonds to honour and glorify His name.

And when David had called him, he ate and drank before him. And he made him drunk. And at evening he went out to lie on his bed with the servants of his lord, but he did not go down to his house. And in the morning David wrote a letter to Joab and sent it by the hand of Uriah. And he wrote in the letter, saying, Set Uriah in the forefront of the hottest battle, and draw back from him so that he may be stricken and die. And when Joab observed the city, he sent Uriah to a place where he knew brave men were. And the men of the city went out and fought with Joab. And some of the people of the servants of David fell. And Uriah the Hittite also died. Then Joab sent and told David all the things concerning the war. And he commanded the messenger saying, When you have made an end of telling the matters of the war to the king, and if it be so that the king's wrath arise, and he say to you, Why did you approach so near to the city when you fought? Did you not know that they would shoot from the wall? Who struck Abimelech the son of Jerubbesheth? Did not a woman cast a millstone on him from the wall, so that he died in Thebez? Why did you go near the wall? — then you shall say, Your servant Uriah the Hittite is dead also. So the messenger departed and came and showed David all that Joab had sent him for. And the messenger said to David, Surely the men prevailed against us and came out to us to the field, and we were on them even to the entering of the gate. And the shooters shot from off the wall on your servants, and some of the king's servants are dead, and your servant Uriah the Hittite is dead also. Then David said to the messenger, So you shall say to Joab, Do not let this thing displease you, for the sword devours one as well as another. Make your battle stronger against the city and overthrow it. And you encourage him. And when the wife of Uriah heard that Uriah her husband was dead, she mourned for her husband. And when her mourning was past, David sent and brought her to his house, and she became his wife and bore him a son. But the thing that David had done was evil in the eyes of the LORD. — II Samuel 11:13-27.

In the Psalms of David two very different characters come before us again and again. In some of those Psalms there is expressed the sorrows of one who is consciously *righteous,* suffering the reproaches of the wicked, yet assured of strength in God, and looking forward to that fulness of joy which is at His right hand. In other Psalms we hear the sobbings of a *convicted* conscience, a heart deeply exercised over personal transgression, seeking after Divine mercy, and being granted a blessed sense of the infinite sufficiency of Divine grace to meet his deep need. Now, those two characters in the Psalms correspond to the two principal stages in David's life as portrayed, respectively, in the 1st and 2nd books of Samuel. In 1st Samuel we see him brought from obscurity unto honour and peace, upheld by God in righteousness amid the persecution of the wicked. In the latter we behold his descending from honour, through sin, into degradation and turmoil, yet there learning the amazing riches of Divine grace to bear with and pardon one who fell into such deep mire.

Solemn indeed is the contrast presented of David in the two books of Samuel: in the former he is conqueror of the mighty Goliath: in the latter he is mastered by his own lusts: Now the sins of God's servants are recorded for our instruction: not for us to shelter behind and use for palliating our own offences, but for us to lay to heart and seek with all our might to avoid. The most effectual means against our repeating their sins is to keep from those things which lead up to or occasion them. In the preceding article we pointed out that David's fearful fall was preceded by three things: the laying aside of his armour at the very time it was his duty to gird on the sword; the indulging in slothful ease in the palace, when he should have been enduring hardness as a soldier on the battlefield; the allowing of a wandering eye to dwell upon an unlawful object, when he should have turned it away from beholding vanity.

"Watch and pray, that ye enter not into temptation: the spirit indeed is willing, but the flesh is weak" (Matt. 26:41). Prayer of itself is not sufficient: we have not fully discharged our duty when we have asked God to lead us not into temptation, but deliver us from evil. We must "watch" be on the alert, noting the direction of our desires, the character of our motives, the tendency of things which may be lawful in themselves, the influence of our associations. It is our *inner man* which we most need to watch: "Keep thy heart with all diligence, for out of it are the issues of life" (Prov. 4:23). Then, if we are faithful and diligent in "watching," out of a sense of our personal weakness and insufficiency, it is in order to "pray" counting on the help of our gracious God to undertake for us. To pray *without* "watching" is only to mock God, by seeking to shelve our responsibility.

Prayer was never designed by God as a substitute for personal effort and diligence, but rather as an adjunct thereto — to seek Divine grace for enabling us to be dutiful and faithful. "Continue in prayer, *and watch* in the same with thanksgiving" (Col. 4:2). Not only does God require us to "watch" *before* we pray, but we are also to "watch" immediately after. And again we say, that which we most need to watch is *ourselves.* There is a traitor within our own breast, ever ready and desirous of betraying us if allowed the opportunity of so doing. Who had thought that such an one as David would ever experience such a fearful fall as he had! Ah, my reader, not even a close walk with God, or a long life of eminent piety, will eradicate or even change the sinful nature which still abides in the saint. So long as we are in this world we are never beyond the reach of temptation, and nought but watchfulness and prayer will safeguard us from it.

Nor is it easy to say how low a real child of God may fall, nor how deeply he may sink into the mire, once he allows the lusts of the flesh their free play. Sin is insatiable: it is never satisfied. Its nature is to drag us lower and lower, getting more and more daring in its opposition to God; and but for His recovering grace it would carry us down to hell itself. Look at Israel: unbelieving at the Red Sea, murmuring in the wilderness, setting up the idolatrous calf at Sinai. Look at the course of Christendom as outlined in Rev. 2 and 3: beginning by leaving her first love, ending by becoming so mixed up with the world that Christ threatened to spue her out of His mouth. Thus it was with David: from lazing on his bed to allowing his eyes to wander, from gazing on Bathsheba to committing adultery with her, from adultery to murder, and then sinking into such spiritual deadness that for a whole year he remained impenitent, till an express messenger from God was needed to arouse him from his torpor.

"And the woman conceived, and sent and told David, and said, I am with child" (2 Sam. 11:5). Sooner or later the man or the woman who deliberately defies God and tramples His laws underfoot finds from painful experience that "the way of transgressors is hard." (Prov. 13:15). It is true that the final punishment of the wicked is in the next world, and it is true that for years some daring rebels appear to mock God with impugnity; nevertheless, His government is such that, even in this life, they are usually made to reap as they have sown. The pleasures of sin are but "for a season" (Heb. 11:25), and a very brief one at that; nevertheless "at the last it biteth like a serpent and stingeth like an adder" (Prov. 23:32). Make no mistake on that point, dear reader; "Be sure your sins will find you out" (Num. 32:23). It did so with David and Bathsheba, for now the day of reckoning had to be faced.

The penalty for adultery was death: "And the man that committeth adultery with another man's wife, even he that committeth adultery with his neighbour's wife, the adulterer and adulteress shall surely be put to death" (Lev. 20:10). Bathsheba now had good cause to fear the righteous wrath of her husband, and the enforcing of the dread sentence of the law. David, too, was faced with serious trouble: the one with whom he had had illicit intercourse was pregnant, and her own husband had been away from home for some time. The hidden works of darkness must soon be forced into the light for when Uriah returned the unfaithfulness of his wife would be discovered. This would give him the right to have her stoned, and though David, by virtue of his high position as king, might escape a similar fate, yet it was likely that his guilt would be proclaimed abroad and a general revolt be stirred up against him. But sad as was the predicament in which David now found himself, still sadder was the measure he resorted to in seeking to extricate himself.

Before taking up the doleful details in the inspired narrative, let us first seek to obtain a general idea of what follows — asking the reader to go over 2 Sam. 11:6-21 ere continuing with our comments. There was no thirsting for Uriah's blood on the part of David: it was only after all his carnal efforts had failed to use Uriah in covering his own sin, that the king resorted to extreme measures. Another before us has pointed out the awful parallel which here obtains between David and Pilate. The Roman governor thirsted not for the blood of the Saviour, rather did he resort to one expedient after another so as to preserve His life; and only after those had failed, did he give his official sanction to the crucifying of the Lord Jesus. Alas that the sweet Psalmist of Israel should here find himself in the same class with Pilate, but the flesh in the believer is no different from the flesh in the unbeliever, and when allowed its way it issues in the same works in both.

But the analogy between David and Pilate is even closer. What was it that caused David to sacrifice Uriah in order to shield himself? It was his love of the world, his determination to presreve his place and reputation among men at all costs. Love of his fair name in the world, resolved that under no circumstances would he be branded as an adulterer, so whatever stood in the way must be removed. He contrived various expedients to preserve his character, but these were baffled; so just as the lust of the eye led him to adultery with Bathsheba, now the pride of life goaded him to the murder of her husband. And was it not the same with Pilate? He had no murderous designs against Christ, but he put his own credit in the eyes of men before eveything else: he was Caeser's friend — the world's friend — and rather than risk any breach in that friendship Jesus must die.

"And David sent to Joab, saying, Send me Uriah the Hittite. And Joab sent Uriah to David" (v. 6). It was not unto the Lord that David now turned: *He* seems not to have been in his thoughts at all. Nor is He when sin has gained the ascendency over the saint. Alas that we are so slow, so reluctant, to put things right with God — by sincere repentance and humble confession — when we have displeased and dishonoured Him. No, David was far more anxious to conceal his crime and escape the temporal consequences of it, than he was to seek the forgiveness of the Lord his God. This too is recorded for our instruction. It is written, "He that covereth his sins shall not prosper" (Prov. 28:13), and there is no exception to that rule — O that Divine grace would cause each of us to lay it to heart and *act upon it.* Only God knows how many of His own people are now under His chastening rod, are lean in their souls and joyless in their hearts, because of failure at this very point.

Refusal to put things right with God and our fellows, by confessing our sins to the One and (so far as lies in our power) making restitution to the other, gives Satan a great advantage over us. A guilty conscience estranges the heart from God, so that it is no longer able to count upon His protection; the Spirit is grieved and withholds His grace, so that the understanding is unable to see things in His light. The soul is then in such a state that Satan's lies are acceptable to it, and then the whole course of conduct is more or less regulated by him. Carnal scheming takes the place of seeking wisdom from on high, stealth and trickery supplant openness and honesty, and self-interests absorb all the energies instead of seeking the glory of God and the good of others. This comes out very plainly in the deplorable sequel here: all of David's actions now show that he was actuated by Satan rather than dominated by the Holy Spirit.

"And when Uriah was come unto him, David demanded of him how Joab did, and how the people did, and how the war prospered" (v. 7). Having been summoned back from the scene of fighting, Uriah was given an audience with David under the pretence of supplying his royal master with an accurate account of how the hostilities were proceeding. In reality, those inquiries of the king were merely a blind to cover his real desire in having sent for Bathsheba's husband. Seemingly, David wished to convey to Uriah the impression that he had more confidence in *his* word concerning the progress of the war than that of any one else in Israel. But it is quite clear from what follows that David had called Uriah home for a very different purpose. How little *we* know the motives of those who ask us questions, and how it behooves us to heed exhortation "*put not* your confidence in princes" (Psa. 146:3).

"And David said to Uriah, Go down to thy house, and wash thy feet" (v. 8). This makes clearer the secret design of the king in summoning Uriah to Jerusalem. David was determined to spare himself the shame of its becoming known that he was guilty of adultery with Bathsheba, and the only way in which that could be avoided was by getting her husband back to spend a night or two at home, so that the child might be fathered on him. "And Uriah departed out of the king's house, and there followed him a mess of meat from the king" (v. 8). David was anxious that the one whom he designed to act as a cloak for his own sin should feel free to enjoy to the full the brief fulough now granted him. Again we say, how ignorant we often are of the subtle designs of some who may express good-will toward us by their presents.

"But Uriah slept at the door of the king's house with all the servants of his lord, and went not down to his house" (v. 9). How often the best-laid schemes of men meet with disappointment. It was so with Abraham's attempt in getting Sarah to pose as his sister; it was so with Jonah's efforts to avoid preaching to the Ninevites; it was so here. David was balked: he had failed to estimate aright the sterling qualties of the man he was dealing with. Uriah was not the one to give way to self-indulgence while his brethren were enduring the hardships of a military campaign. And should not this speak loudly to our hearts? Are the days in which *we* are living such that Christians are justified in seeking ease and fleshly gratification?

"And when they had told David, saying, Uriah went not down unto his house, David said unto Uriah, Camest thou not from thy journey? Why then didst thou not go down into thine house?" (v. 10). Instead of commending Uriah for his noble unselfishness, the king half reproved him. But David could not approve his conduct without condemning his own. Ah, my reader, they who criticise those who *live as* "strangers and pilgrims" in this scene (and they are few in number in this degenerate generation), calling them "strict," "straight-laced," "extremists," "puritanic," do but give themselves away. They who practice self-denial are thorns in the sides of those who wish to "make the most of both worlds" by pandering to their carnal desires.

"And Uriah said unto David, The ark, and Israel, and Judah, abide in tents: and my lord Joab, and the servants of my lord, are encamped in the open fields; shall I then go into mine house, to eat and to drink, and to lie with my wife? — as thou livest, and thy soul liveth, I will not do this thing" (v. 11). What a rebuke was this! The Lord and His people in the open fields, engaging the foes of Israel; David at home in his palace, enjoying his ease and indulging the desires of nature. How those noble words of Uriah should have melted David's heart! How they should have smitten his conscience for having yielded so vilely to his sinful passions and for so grievously wronging, in his absence, such a loyal subject! But alas, where the heart is no longer concerned for *God's* glory, it is incapable of receiving correction or rebuke from a fellow creature. David was filled with pride of reputation and the fear of man, and was determined to make Uriah serve for him as a screen from the public eye.

"And David said to Uriah, Tarry here to day also, and to morrow I will let thee depart. So Uriah abode in Jerusalem that day, and the morrow" (v. 12). When the heart is fully set upon doing evil, it refuses to be daunted by difficulties: if one method of obtaining the coveted end fails, it will try another. Alas that the same persistent determination does not characterise us when we are seeking that which is good: how easily we are discouraged then! Patience is a virtue, but it is prostituted to a base end when used in an evil course. Thus it was now: David refused to admit defeat, and hoped that by keeping Uriah in Jerusalem a little longer, his base desire might be realised.

"And when David had called him, he did eat and drink before him: and he made him drunk" (v. 13). To what awful lengths can sin carry a saint once he enters upon the downward path. The plan which David now resorted to was horrible indeed, deliberately endeavouring to make the faithful Uriah break his vow in v. 11. How sad to now see David the tempter of Uriah unto drunkenness — hoping that while his blood was heated, he would go home to his wife. But again he failed: "And at even he went out to lie on his bed with the servants of his lord, *but went not down to his house"* (v. 13). How this baffling of his plans should have aroused David's sleeping conscience, for, manifestly, God's providences were working *against* him. Worse was yet to follow: this we must leave for our next.

David's fearful fall into committing adultery with Bathsheba was now followed by a crime yet more odious. His unlawful child, soon to be born, he had sought to father upon Uriah; but his efforts had failed. A desperate situation now confronted him. He knew that if Uriah lived, he must discover his wife's unfaithfulness, and this the king was determined to prevent at all costs. Even though it meant adding sin to sin and sinking more deeply into the mire of evil, David must preserve his reputation before men. Here, again, we see the likeness between him and Pilate: each sought to preserve innocent blood *and* the world (a position of honour in it) for himself at the same time, and surrendered the former for the latter when they could not both be retained — the "pride of life" was so strong that to maintain it, the death of another was not scrupled at.

Once a man, even though he be a believer, disregards the claims of God, he is very liable to ignore the claims of human friendship. It was so in the sad case here before us. David now shrank not from going to any length. First, he had tempted Uriah to break his vow (2 Sam. 11:11). Second, he had endeavoured to make him drunk (11:13). And now he deliberately plotted the death of his devoted subject. He had rather that innocent blood be shed, and his whole army be threatened with defeat, than that his *own* good name should be made a scandal. See to what incredible lengths sin will urge even a child of God once he yields to its clamourings: adultery now occasioned murder! Oh my reader, what very real need there is for begging God to enable you to "pass the time of your sojourning here *in fear"* (1 Pet. 1:17)!

"When a man has so far given place to the devil as not only to commit scandalous sins, but to use disingenuous and base means of concealing them, and with sure prospect of having the whole exposed to public view; what would prevent his being pushed forward, by the same influence and from the same motives, to treachery, malice, and murder, till crimes are multiplied and magnified beyond computation, and till every nobler consideration is extinguished?" (T. Scott). Thus it was here: no matter what happened, David was resolved to maintain *his own* reputation. Sure proof was this that, at the time, he was completely dominated by Satan, as is shown by those words "lest being lifted up with *pride,* he fall into the condemnation of the devil" (1 Tim. 3:6). How we need to pray that God would mercifully *"hide* pride from" us (Job 33:17)!

Further proof that David was then thoroughly in the toils of Satan, may be seen in the subtle and vile tactics which he now resorted to. Thoroughly determined to cover his awful sin of adultery by committing still greater wickedness, he resolved to have poor Uriah put out of the way. "That innocent, valiant, and gallant man, who was ready to die for his prince's honour must die by his prince's hand" (Matt. Henry). Yes, but not directly; David was too cunning for that, and too anxious to preserve his own good name before men. He would not kill Uriah by his own hand, nor even bid his servants assassinate him, for his reputation had been destroyed by such a step. He therefore resorted to a more serpentine measure, which, though it concealed his own hand, was none the less heinous. The bravery of Uriah and his zeal for this country, suggested to the king the method of dispatching him.

"And it came to pass in the morning, that David wrote a letter to Joab, and sent it by the hand of Uriah. And he wrote in the letter, saying, Set ye Uriah in the forefront of the hottest battle, and retire ye from him, that he may be smitten, and die" (2 Sam. 11:14, 15). With cold-blooded deliberation David penned a note to the commander of his army, commanding him to station his faithful soldier in the place where he would be the most exposed to the assaults of the foe, and then leave him to his cruel fate. The king's letter, decreeing his death, was carried by Uriah himself, and delivered to Joab. The general did as his master had bidden, and Uriah was slain. David's abominable plan succeeded, and he whose accusations he so much feared, now lay silent in death — committed to an honourable grave, while his murderer's honour was sullied as long as this world lasts.

This terrible sin of David's was more laid to his charge by God than any other he committed: not only because of its gravity, and because it has given occasion to so many of His enemies to blaspheme, but also because it was more a deliberate and premeditated crime than an involuntary infirmity acting suddenly. How many of his failures are left on record: his lie to Ahimelech (1 Sam. 21:2), his dissimulation before the king of Gath (1 Sam. 21:12), his rash vow to destroy Nabal (1 Sam. 25:33), his unbelieving "I shall one day perish at the hand of Saul" (1 Sam. 27:1) his injustice in the matter of Mephibosheth and Ziba (2 Sam. 16:4), his indulgence of Absalom, his numbering of the people (2 Sam. 24); yet after his death God said, "David did that which was right in the eyes of the Lord, and turned not aside from any thing that He commanded him all the days of his life, *save only in the matter of Uriah the Hittite*" (1 Kings 15:5).

The immediate sequel is as sad and awful as is what has just been before us. When he received the tidings that his vile plot had succeeded, David callously said to the messenger, "Thus shalt thou say unto Joab, Let not this thing displease thee, for the sword devoureth one as well as another" (v. 25). There was no compunction that a loyal supporter had been cruelly murdered, no horror of heart at his own guilt in connection therewith, no grief that others besides Uriah had been sacrificed for his crime; instead, he pretended that it was but "the fortunes of war," and to be taken stoically. Disregarding the massacre his soldiers, David complimented Joab on the execution of his abominable order, and bade the messenger return "and encourage thou him."

"And when the wife of Uriah heard that Uriah her husband was dead, she mourned for her husband" (v. 26). What a vile mockery! Only God knows how often the outward "mourning" over the departed is but a hypocritical veil to cover satisfaction of heart for being rid of their presence. Even where that be not the case, the speedy re-marriage of weeping widows and widowers indicates how shallow was their grief. "And when the mourning was past, David sent and fetched her to his house, and she became his wife, and bare him a son. But the thing that David had done displeased the Lord" (v. 27). David had pleased himself, but he had grievously displeased the Lord! "Let none therefore encourage themselves in sin by the example of David, for if they sin as he did, they will fall under the displeasure of God as he did" (Matt. Henry).

The question has been asked, "Can a person who has committed such atrocious crimes, and so long remains impenitent, be indeed a child of God, a member of Christ, a temple of the Holy Spirit, and an heir of everlasting glory? Can one spark of Divine life exist unextinguished in such an ocean of evil?" Were we left to our own unaided judgment to make reply, most probably every last one of us would promptly answer, *No*, such a thing is unthinkable. Yet in the clear light of Holy Writ it is plain that such things *are* possible. Later, David made it manifest that he was a truly regenerated person by the sincerity and depth of his contrition and confession. Yet, let it be said that, no man while guilty of such sins, and before he *genuinely* repents of the same, can have any warrantable evidence to conclude that *he* is a believer; yea, everything points to the contrary. Though grace be not lost in such an awful case, Divine consolation and assurance is suspended.

But now the question arises, *Why did God permit* David to fall so low and sin so terribly? The first answer must be, To display His high and awe-inspiring *sovereignty*. Here we approach ground which is indeed difficult for us to tread, even with unshodden feet. Nevertheless it cannot be gainsaid that there is a marvellous and sovereign display of the Lord's grace toward His people in this particular respect, both before their calling and after. Some of the elect are permitted to sin most grievously in their unconverted state, whilst others of them, even in their unregenerate days, are wondrously preserved. Again; some of the elect after their conversion have been Divinely allowed to awfully fall into the most horrible impieties, whilst others of them are so preserved as never to sin wilfully against their consciences from the first conviction to the very close of their lives (Condensed from S.E. Pierce on Hosea 14:1).

This is a high mystery, which it would be most impious for us to attempt to pry into: rather must we bow our heads before it and say, "Even so, Father, for *so* it seemeth good in Thy sight." It is a solemn fact, from which there is no getting away, that some sin more before their conversion, and some (especially those saved in early life) sin worse after their conversion. It is also a plain fact that with some saints God most manifests His *restraining grace*, and with others His *pardoning* grace. Three things are to be steadily borne in mind in connection with the sins of the saints. God never regards sin as a trifle: it is *ever* that abominable thing which He "hates" (Jer. 44:4). Second, it is never to be excused or extenuated by us. Third, God's *sovereignty* therein must be acknowledged: whatever difficulties it may raise before our minds, let us hold fast the fact that God does as He pleases, and "giveth no account" of His actions (Job 33:13).

A second answer to the question, Why did God permit David to fall so fearfully and sin so grievously? may be: that we might have set before our eyes the more clearly the awful fact that "the heart is deceitful above all things, and desperately wicked" (Jer. 17:9). Unmistakably plain as is the meaning of those words, uttered by Him who cannot lie, yet how very slow we all are to *really* receive them at their face value, and acknowledge that they accurately describe the natural state of every human heart — that of the Man Christ Jesus alone excepted. But God has done more than make this bare statement: He has placed on record in His Word illustrations, exemplifications, demonstrations of its verity — notably so in allowing us to see the unspeakable wickedness that still remained in the heart of *David!*

Third, by suffering David to fall and sin as he did, God has graciously given a most solemn warning to believers in middle life — and elder Christians also. "Many conquerors have been ruined by their carelessness after a victory, and many have been spiritually wounded after great successes against sin. David was so; his great surprisal into sin was after a long profession, manifold experiences of God, and watchful keeping himself from his iniquity. And hence, in particular, hath it come to pass that the profession of many hath declined in their old age or riper time: they have given over the work of mortifying sin *before* their work was at an end. There is no way for us to pursue sin in its unsearchable habitation but by being endless in our pursuit. The command God gives in Col. 3:5 is *as necessary* for them to observe who are toward the end of their race, as those who are but at the beginning of it" (John Owen).

Fourth, the fearful fall of David made way for a display of the amazing grace of God in recovering His fallen people. If we are slow to receive what Scripture teaches concerning the depravity of the human heart and the exceeding sinfulness of sin, we are equally slow to *really* believe what it reveals about the covenant-faithfulness of God, the efficacy of Christ's blood to cleanse the foulest stain from those for whom it was shed, and the super-abounding grace of Him who is "the Father of mercies." Had David never sinned so grievously and sunken so low, he had never known those infinite depths of mercy which there are in the heart of God. Likewise, had his terrible sin, his subsequent broken-hearted confession, and his *pardon* by God, never been placed upon Divine record, not a few of God's people throughout the centuries had sunk in abject despair.

Fifth, to furnish a fatal stumbling-block to blatant rebels. "It is certain that thousands through succeeding generations have, by this fall of 'the man after God's own heart,' been prejudiced against true religion, hardened in infidelity, or emboldened in blasphemy; while others have thence taken occasion to commit *habitual wickedness* under a religious profession, and with presumptuous confidence, to the still greater discredit of the Gospel. It should, however, be considered, that all these have been, previously, either open enemies to true religion, or hypocritical pretenders to it: and it is the righteous purpose of God, that stumbling-blocks should be thrown in the way of such men, that they may 'stumble, and fall, and be snared, and taken, and perish:' It is His holy will thus to detect the secret malignity of their hearts, and to make way for the display of His justice in their condemnation. On the other hand, thousands, from age to age, have by this awful example been rendered more suspicious of themselves, more watchful, more afraid of temptation, more dependent on the Lord, and more fervent in prayer; and by means of David's fall, have, themselves, been preserved from falling" (T. Scott).

God, then, had wise and sufficient reasons, both for permitting David to sin so heinously and for placing the same upon imperishable record. Nor has any opposer or despiser of the Truth any just ground to sneeringly ask, Are *those* the fruits of grace and faith? We answer, No, they are not; instead, they are the horrible works of the flesh, the filth which issues from corrupt human nature. How strong must those inclinations be to evil, when they, at times, succeed in overcoming the oppositions of truth and grace dwelling in the heart of an eminent saint of God! And in the light of the context (2 Sam. 11:1, 2) how it behooves us to watch against the *beginnings* of negligence and self-indulgence, and keep at the utmost distance from that precipice over which David fell; begging God that it may please Him to deliver us from all forbidden objects.

But this incident presents another difficulty to some, namely, how to harmonize it with the declaration made in 1 John 3:15: "Ye know that no murderer hath eternal life abiding in him." It is really surprising that so many have experienced trouble in reconciling this with the case of David: as usual, the difficulty is self-created through ignoring the context. In 1 John 3:11 the apostle takes up the subject of the Christians' love one for another, whereby they make it manifest that they are *brethren* in Christ. The world (1) loves them not (2) hates them (3) will murder them whenever they dare — as Cain did Abel. But no real Christian has *such* a hatred in his heart against any "brother" in Christ. Nor had David. Uriah was not an Israelite, but an *"Hittite"* (2 Sam. 11:3, 1 Kings 15:5)!

In conclusion, let us point out some of the solemn lessons which we may learn from this sad incident. 1. Beware of the *beginnings* of sin: who had imagined that taking his ease when he should have been at the post of duty on the battlefield, had led to adultery and ended in murder. 2. See how refusal to put one serious wrong right, preferring concealment to confession, gives Satan a great advantage over us, to lead into yet worse evil! 3. Learn therefrom that there is no security in years, and that no *past* communion with God will safeguard us against temptations when we are careless in *the present*. 4. How fickle is poor human nature: David's heart smote him when he cut off Saul's skirt, yet later he deliberately planned the murder of Uriah. 5. Mark what fearful lengths pride will go to in order to maintain a reputation before men. 6. Behold how callous the heart will become once the strivings of consciences are disregarded. 7. Though we may succeed in escaping the wrath of our fellows, sin always meets with the displeasure of the Lord.

CHAPTER 12.

*And the LORD sent Nathan to David. And he came to him and said to him,
There were two men in one city, the one rich and the other poor. The rich man
had exceeding many flocks and herds, but the poor man had nothing except one
little ewe lamb which he had bought and nourished. And it grew up together
with him and with his children. It ate of his own food and drank from his own
cup, and lay in his bosom, and was to him like a daughter. And there came a
traveler to the rich man, and he spared to take of his own flock and of his own
herd to dress for the traveler that had come to him. But he took the poor man's
lamb and dressed it for the man who had come to him. And David's anger was
greatly kindled against the man. And he said to Nathan, As the LORD lives, the
man who has done this thing shall surely die. And he shall restore the lamb
fourfold, because he did this thing, and because he had no pity. And Nathan said
to David, You are the man! Thus says the LORD God of Israel, I anointed you
king over Israel, and I delivered you out of the hand of Saul. And I gave you
your master's house and your master's wives into your bosom. And I gave you
the house of Israel and of Judah. And if that was too little, I would have given to
you such and such things besides. Why have you despised the commandment of
the LORD, to do evil in His sight? You have killed Uriah the Hittite with the
sword, and have taken his wife to be your wife, and have killed him with the
sword of the children of Ammon. Now therefore, the sword shall never depart
from your house, because you have despised Me and have taken the wife of
Uriah the Hittite to be your wife. Thus says the LORD, Behold, I will raise up
evil against you out of your own house, and I will take your wives before your
eyes and give them to your neighbor. And he shall lie with your wives in the
sight of this sun. For you did it secretly, but I will do this thing before all Israel
and before the sun. And David said to Nathan, I have sinned against the LORD.
And Nathan said to David, The LORD also has put away your sin — you shall
not die. —* II Samuel 12:1-13.

An interval of some months elapsed between what is recorded in 2 Sam. 11 and
that which is found at the beginning of chapter 12. During this interval David
was free to enjoy to the full that which he had acquired through his wrongdoing.
The one obstacle which lay in the way of the free indulgence of his passion was
removed; Bathsheba was now his. Apparently, the king, in his palace, was secure
and immune. So far there had been no intervention of God in judgment, and
through out those months David had remained impenitent for the fearful crimes
he had committed. Alas, how dull the conscience of a saint may become. But if
David was pleased with the consummation of his vile plans, there was One who
was displeased. The eyes of God had marked his evil conduct, and the Divine
righteousness would not pass it by. "These things hast thou done, and I kept
silence," yet He adds "but I will reprove thee, and set them in order before thine
eyes" (Psa. 50:21).

God may suffer His people to indulge the lusts of the flesh and fall into
grievous sin, but He will not allow them to remain content and happy in such a
case: rather are they made to prove that "the way of transgressors is hard." In
Job 20 the Holy Spirit has painted a graphic picture of the
wretchedness experienced by the evil-doer. "Though wickedness be sweet in his
mouth, though he hide it under his tongue; though he spare it, and forsake it
not, but keep it still within his mouth; yet his meat in his bowels is turned, *it is
the gall of asps within him.* He hath swallowed down riches, and he shall vomit

them up again: God shall cast them out of his belly. He shall suck the poison of asps: the viper's tongue shall slay him. . .It shall go ill with him that is left in his tabernacle. The heavens shall reveal his iniquity" (vv. 12-16, 26, 27). Notably is this the case with backsliders, for God will not be mocked with impugnity.

The coarse pleasures of sin cannot long content a child of God. It has been truly said that "Nobody buys a little passing pleasure in evil at so dear a rate, or keeps it so short a time, as a good man." The conscience of the righteous soon reasserts itself, and makes its disconcerting voice heard. He may yet be far from true repentance, but he will soon experience keen remorse. Months may pass before he again enjoys communion with God, but self-disgust will quickly fill his soul. The saint has to pay a fearfully high price for enjoying "the pleasures of sin for a season." Stolen waters may be sweet for a moment, but how quickly his "mouth is filled with gravel" (Prov. 20:17) Soon will the guilty one have to cry out, "He hath made my chain heavy. . .He hath made me desolate: He hath filled me with bitterness. . .Thou hast removed my soul far off from peace" (Lam. 3:7, 11, 15, 17).

Though the inspired historian has not described the wretchedness of David's soul following his murder of Uriah, yet we may obtain a clear view of the same from the Psalms penned by him after his conviction and deep contrition. Those Psalms tell of a sullen closing of his mouth: "when I kept silence" (32:3). Though his heart must frequently have smitten him, yet he would not speak to God about his sin; and there was nothing else he could speak of. They tell of the inward perturbation and tumult that filled him: "My bones waxed old through *my roaring* all the day long" (32:3): groans of remorse were wrung from his yet unbroken heart. "For day and night Thy hand was heavy upon me" (v. 4) — a sense of the Divine holiness and power oppressed him, though it did not melt him.

Even a palace can afford no relief unto one who is filled with bitter remorse. A king may command his subjects, but he cannot quiet the voice of outraged conscience. No matter whether the sun of the morning was shining or the shades of evening were falling, there was no escape for David. "Day and night" God's heavy hand weighted him down: "my moisture is turned into the drought of summer" (he declared in v. 4) — it was as though some heated iron was scorching him: all the dew and freshness of his life was dried up. Most probably he suffered acutely in both body and soul. "Thus he dragged through a weary year — ashamed of his guilty dalliance, wretched in his self-accusation, afraid of God, and skulking in the recesses of his palace from the sight of the people."

"David learned, what we all learn (and the holier a man is, the more speedily and sharply the lesson follows on the heels of his sin), that every transgression is a blunder, that we never get the satisfaction which we expect from any sin, or if we do, we get something with it which spoils it all. A nauseous drug is added to the exciting, intoxicating drink which temptation offers, and though its flavour is at first disguised by the pleasanter taste of sin, its bitterness is persistent though slow, and clings to the palate long after that has faded away utterly" (Alex. Maclaren). With equal clearness does this appear in the 51st Psalm. "Restore unto me the joy of Thy salvation" (v. 12) he cries, for spiritual comforts had entirely deserted him. "O Lord, open Thou my lips; and my mouth shall show forth Thy praise" (v. 15): the dust had settled upon the strings of his harp because the Spirit within was grieved.

How could it be otherwise? So long as David refused to humble himself beneath the mighty hand of God, seeking from Him a spirit of true repentance, and freely confessing his great wickedness, there could be no more peace for him, no more happy communion with God, no further growth in grace. O my reader, we would earnestly press upon you the great importance of *keeping short accounts with God.* Let not guilt accumulate upon thy conscience: make it a point *each* night of spreading before Him the sins of the day, and seeking to be cleansed therefrom. Any great sin lying long upon the conscience, unrepented of, or not repented of as the matter requires, only furthers our indwelling corruptions: neglect causes the heart to be hardened. "My wounds stink and are corrupt *because of my foolishness"* (Psa. 38:5): it was his foolish neglect to make a timely application for the cure of the wounds that sin had made, which he there laments.

At the end of 2 Sam. 11 we read, "But the thing that David had done displeased the Lord," upon which Matthew Henry says, "One would think it should be followed that the Lord sent enemies to invade him, terrors to take hold on, and the messengers of death to arrest him. No, He sent *a prophet* to him" — "And the Lord sent Nathan unto David" (12:1). We are here to behold the exceeding riches of Divine grace and mercy: *such* "riches" that legal and self-righteous hearts have murmured at, as a making light of sin — so incapable is the natural man of discerning spiritual things: they are 'foolishness" unto him. David had wandered far, but he was not lost. "Though the righteous fall," yet it is written "he *shall not be* utterly cast down" (Psa. 37:24). O how tenderly God watches over His sheep! How faithfully He goes after and recovers them, when they have strayed! With what amazing goodness does He heal their backslidings, and continue to love them freely!

"And the Lord sent Nathan unto David" (12:1). It is to be duly noted that it was not David who sent for the prophet, though never did he more sorely need his counsel than now. No, it was *God* who took the initiative: it is ever thus, for we never seek Him, until He seeks us. It was thus with Moses when a fugitive in Midian, with Elijah when fleeing from Jezebel, with Jonah under the juniper tree, with Peter after his denial (1 Cor. 15:5). O the marvel of it! How it should melt our hearts. "If we believe not, yet *He* abideth faithful: He cannot deny Himself" (2 Tim. 2:13). Though He says, "I will visit their transgression with the rod, and their iniquity with stripes," it is at once added "Nevertheless My lovingkindness will I not utterly take from him, nor suffer My faithfulness to fail" (Psa. 89: 32, 33). So it was here: David still had an interest in that everlasting covenant "ordered in all things and sure" (2 Sam. 23:5).

"And the Lord sent Nathan unto David." Probably about a year had elapsed from what is recorded in the beginning of the preceding chapter, for the adulterous child was already born (12:14). Rightly did Matthew Henry point out "Though God may suffer His people to fall into sin, He will not suffer His people to lie still in it." No, God will exhibit His holiness, His righteousness, and His mercy in connection therewith. His holiness, by displaying His hatred of the same, and by bringing the guilty one to penitently confess it. His righteousness, in the chastening visited upon it; His mercy, in leading the backslider to forsake it, and then bestow His pardon upon him. What a marvellous and blessed exercise of His varied attributes! "For the iniquity of his covetousness was I wroth, and smote him: I hid Me, and was wroth, and he went on frowardly in the way of his heart. I have seen his ways, and will *heal him* (!!): I will lead him also and restore comforts unto him" (Isa. 57:17,18).

"And the Lord sent Nathan unto David." The prophet's task was far from being an enviable one: to meet the guilty king alone, face to face. As yet David had evinced no sign of repentance. God had not cast off His erring child, but He would not condone his grievous offences: all must come out into the light. The Divine displeasure must be made evident: the culprit must be charged and rebuked: David must judge himself, and then discover that where sin had abounded grace did much more abound. Wondrous uniting of Divine righteousness and mercy — made possible by the cross of Christ! The righteousness of God required that David should be faithfully dealt with; the mercy of God moved Him to send Nathan for the recovery of His strayed sheep. "Mercy and truth are *met together;* righteousness and peace have kissed each other" (Psa. 85:10).

Yes, Nathan might well have quailed before the commission which God now gave him. It was no easy matter to have to rebuke his royal master. Varied indeed are the tasks which the Lord assigns His servants. Often are they sent forth with a message which they well know will be most unpalatable to their hearers; and the temptation to tone it down, to take off its sharp edge, if not to substitute another which will be more acceptable, is both real and strong. Little do the rank and file even of God's people realise what it costs a minister of the Gospel to be *faithful* to his calling. If the apostle Paul felt his need of requesting prayer "that utterance may be given unto me, that I may open my mouth *boldly*" (Eph. 6:18,19), how much more do God's servants today need the support of the supplications of their brethren and sisters in Christ! for on every side the cry now is "speak unto us *smooth* things!"

On a previous occasion God had sent Nathan to David with a message of promise and comfort (7:4, 5, etc.); now he is ordered to charge the king with his crimes. He did not decline the unwelcome task, but executed it faithfully. Not only was his mission an unenviable one, but it was far from easy. Few things are more difficult and trying to one with a sensitive disposition than to be called upon to reprove an erring brother. In pondering the method here followed by the prophet — his line of approach to David's slumbering conscience — there is valuable instruction for those of us who may be called upon to deal with similar cases. *Wisdom* from on High (we do not say "tact," the *world's* term, for more often that word is employed to denote the serpentine subtleties of the serpent than the honest dealings of the Holy Spirit) is sorely needed if we are to be a real help to those who have fallen by the wayside — lest we either condone their offences, or make them despair of obtaining pardon.

"And the Lord sent Nathan unto David. And he came unto him, and said unto him, There were two men in one city; the one rich, and the other poor. The rich man had exceeding many flocks and herds: but the poor man had nothing, save one little ewe lamb, which he had bought and nourished up: and it grew up together with him, and with his children; it did eat of his own meat, and drink of his own cup, and lay in his bosom, and was unto him as a daughter. And there came a traveller unto the rich man, and he spared to take of his own flock and of his own herd, to dress for the wayfaring man that was come unto him; but took the poor man's lamb, and dressed it for the man that was come to him" (2 Sam. 12:1-4).

Nathan did not immediately charge David with his crimes: instead, he approached his conscience indirectly by means of a *parable* — clear intimation that he was out of communion with God, for He never employed *that* method of revelation with those who were walking in fellowship with Him. The method employed by the prophet had the great advantage of presenting the facts of the case before David *without* stirring up his opposition of self-love and kindling resentment against being directly rebuked; yet causing him to pass sentence against himself without being aware of it — sure proof that Nathan had been given wisdom from above! "There scarcely ever was any thing more calculated, on the one hand, to awaken emotions of sympathy, and, on the other, those of indignation, than the case here supposed; and the several circumstances by which the heart must be interested in the poor man's case, and by which the unfeeling oppression of his rich neighbour was aggravated" (T. Scott).

The prophet began, then, by giving an oblique representation of the vileness of David's offence, which was conveyed in such a way that the king's judgment was *obliged* to assent the gross injustice of which he was guilty. The excuselessness, the heartlessness, and the abominable selfishness of his conduct was depicted, though Uriah's loyal service and the king's ingratitude and treachery, and the murder of him and his fellow-soldiers, was not alluded to — is there not a hint here that, when reproving an erring brother we should *gradually* lead up to the worst elements in his offense? Yet obvious as was the allusion in Nathan's parable, David perceived not its application unto himself — how this shows that when one is out of touch with God, he is devoid of spiritual discernment: it is only in God's light that we can see light!

"And David's anger was greatly kindled against the man, and he said to Nathan, As the Lord liveth, the man that hath done this thing shall surely die" (v. 5). David supposed that a complaint was being preferred against one of his subjects. Forgetful of his own crimes, he was fired with indignation at the supposed offender, and with a solemn oath condemned him to death. In condemning the rich man, David unwittingly condemned himself. What a strange thing the heart of a believer is! what a medley dwells within it! — often filled with righteous indignation against the sins of others, while blind to its own! Real need has each of us to solemnly and prayerfully ponder the questions of Rom. 2:21-23. Self-flattery makes us quick to mark the faults of others, but blind to our own grievous sins. Just in proportion as a man is in love with his own sins, and resentful of being rebuked, will he be unduly severe in condemning those of his neighbors.

Having brought David to pronounce sentence upon a supposed offender for crimes of far less malignity than his own, the prophet now, with great courage and plainness, declared "*Thou* art the man" (v. 7), and speaks directly in the name of God: "Thus saith the Lord God of Israel." First, David is reminded of the signal favours which had been bestowed upon him (vv. 7,8), among them the "wives" or women of Saul's court, from which he might have selected a wife. Second, God was willing to bestow yet more (v. 8): had he considered anything was lacking, he might have asked for it, and had it been for his good the Lord had freely granted it — cf. Psa. 84:11. Third, in view of God's tender mercies, faithful love, and all-sufficient gifts, he is asked "Wherefore hast thou *despised* the commandment of the Lord, to do evil in His sight?" (v. 9). Ah, it is contempt of the Divine authority which is the occasion of all sin — making light of the Law and its Giver, acting as though its precepts were mere trifles, and its threats meaningless.

The desired result was now accomplished. "And David said unto Nathan, I have sinned against the Lord" (v. 13). Those words were not uttered lightly or mechanically, as the sequel shows; but this we must leave (D.V.) till our next article.

"The emperor Arcadius and his wife had a very bitter feeling towards Chrysostom, bishop of Constantinople. One day, in a fit of anger, the emperor said to one of his courtiers, 'I would I were avenged of this bishop!' Several then proposed how this should be done. 'Banish him and exile him to the desert,' said one, 'Put him in prison', said another. 'Confiscate his property,' said a third. 'Let him die,' said a fourth. Another courtier, whose vices Chrysostom had reproved, said maliciously, 'You all make a great mistake. You will never punish him by such proposals. If banished the kingdom, he will feel God as near to him in the desert as here. If you put him in prison and load him with chains, he will still pray for the poor and praise God in the prison. If you confiscate his property, you merely take away his goods from the poor, not from him. If you condemn him to death, you open Heaven to him. Prince, do you wish to be revenged on him? Force him to commit sin. I know him; *this man fears nothing in the world but sin.*' O that this were the only remark which our fellows could pass on you and me, fellow-believer" (From the *Fellowship* magazine).

We recently came across the above in our reading, and thought is would form a most suitable introduction to this section. What cause have we *to fear* SIN! — that "abominable thing" which God hates (Jer. 44:4), that horrible disease which brought death into the world (Rom. 5:12), that fearful thing which fouls the believer's garments and so often brings reproach upon the sacred Name which he bears. Yes, good reason, has each of us to *fear* sin, and to beg God that it may please Him to work in our hearts a greater horror and hatred of it. Is not this one reason why God permits some of the most eminent saints to lapse into outrageous evils, and place such upon record in His Word: that we should be more distrustful of ourselves, realising that *we* are liable to the same disgracing of our profession; yea, that we certainly shall fall into such unless upheld by the mighty hand of God.

As we have seen, David sinned, and sinned grievously. What was yet worse, for a long season he refused to acknowledge unto God his wickedness. A period of months went by ere he felt the heinousness of his conduct. Ah, my reader, it is the inevitable tendency of sin to deaden the conscience and harden the heart. Therein lies its most hideous feature and fatal aspect. Sin suggests innumerable excuses to its perpetrator and ever prompts to extenuation. It was thus at the beginning. When brought face to face with their Maker, neither Adam nor Eve evidenced any contrition; rather did they seek to vindicate themselves by placing the blame elsewhere. Thus it was with each of us whilst in a state of nature. Sin blinds and hardens, and nought but Divine grace can illumine and soften. Nothing short of the power of the Almighty can pierce the calloused conscience or break the sin-petrified heart.

Now God will not suffer any of His people to remain indefinitely in a state of spiritual insensibility: sooner or later He brings to light the hidden things of darkness, convicts them of their offenses, causes them to mourn over the same, and leads them to repentance. God employs a variety of means in accomplishing this, for in nothing does He act uniformly. He is limited to no one measure or method, and being sovereign He acts as seemeth good unto Himself. This may be seen by comparing some of the cases recorded in the Scriptures. It was a sense of God's awe-inspiring majesty which brought Job to repent of his self-righteousness and abhor himself (Job. 42:1-6). It was a vision of the Lord's exalted glory which made Isaiah cry out, "Woe is me! for I am undone; because I am a man of unclean lips" (Isa. 6:1-5). A sight of Christ's miraculous power moved Peter to cry "Depart from me, for I am a sinful man, O Lord" (Luke 5:8). Those on the day of Pentecost were "pricked in their heart" (Acts 2:37) by hearing the apostle's sermon.

In the case of David God employed *a parable* in the mouth of His prophet to produce conviction. Nathan depicted a case where one was so vilely treated that any who heard the account of it must perforce censure him who was guilty of such an outrage. For though it is the very nature of sin to blind its perpetrator, yet it does not take away his sense of right and wrong. Even when a man is insensible to the enormity of his own transgressions, he is still capable of discerning evil in others; yea, in most instances it seems that the one who has a beam in his own eye is readier to perceive the mote in his fellow's. It was according to this principle that Nathan's parable was addressed to David: if the king was slow to confess his own wickedness, he would be quick enough to condemn like evil in another. Accordingly the case was spread before him.

In the parable (2 Sam. 12:1-4) an appeal is made to both David's affections and his conscience. The position of Uriah and his wife is touchingly portrayed under the figure of a poor man with his "one little ewe lamb," which was dear to him and "lay in his bosom." The one who wronged him is represented as a rich man with "exceeding many flocks and herds," which greatly heightened his guilt in seizing and slaying the one lone lamb of his neighbour. The occasion of the offence, the temptation to commit it, is stated as "there came *a traveller* unto the rich man:" it was to minister unto *him* that the rich man seized upon the poor man's lamb. That "traveller" which came to him pictures the restless flesh, the active lusts, the wandering thoughts, the roving eyes of David in connection with Bathsheba. Ah, my reader, it is at *this* point we most need to be upon our guard. "Casting down imaginations, and every high thing that exalteth itself against the knowledge of God, and bringing into captivity every thought to the obedience of Christ" (2 Cor. 10:5).

"Keep thy heart with all diligence, for out of it are the issues of life" (Prov. 4:23). Part of that task lies in regulating our thoughts and repelling unlawful imaginations. True it is that we cannot prevent wandering thoughts from entering our minds nor evil imaginations from surging up within us, but we *are* responsible to resist and reject them. But this is what David failed to do: he *welcomed* this "traveller," he *entertained* him, he *feasted* him, and feasted him upon that which was *not lawful* — with that which belonged to another: pictured in the parable by the lamb belonging to his neighbour. And, my reader, it is when we give place to our sinful lusts, indulge our evil imaginations, feed our wandering thoughts upon that which is unlawful, that we pave the way for a sad fall. "Travellers" *will* come to us — the mind will be active — and our responsibility is to see that they are fed with that which is lawful: ponder Phil. 4:8 in this connection.

Nathan, then, traced the trouble back to its source, and showed what it was which occasioned and led up to David's fearful fall. The details of the parable emphasised the excuselessness, the injustice, the lawlessness, the wickedness of his crime. He already had wives of his own, why, then, must he rob poor Uriah of his! The case was so clearly put, the guilt of the offender so evidently established, the king at once condemned the offender, and said, "The man that hath done this thing shall surely die" (12:5). Then it was that the prophet turned and said to him, "*Thou* art the man." David did not flame forth in hot resentment and anger against the prophet's accusation; he made no attempt to deny his grievous transgression or proffer any excuses for it. Instead, he frankly owned "I have sinned against the Lord" (v. 13). Nor were those words uttered mechanically or lightly as the sequel so clearly shows, and as we shall now see.

David's slumbering conscience was now awakened, and he was made to realise the greatness of his guilt. The piercing arrow from God's quiver, which Nathan had driven into his diseased heart, opened to David's view the awfulness of his present case. Then it was that he gave evidence that, though woeful had been his conduct, nevertheless, he was not a reprobate soul, totally abandoned by God.

"The dormant spark of Divine grace in David's heart now began to rekindle, and before this plain and faithful statement of facts, in the name of God, his evasions vanished, and his guilt appeared in all its magnitude. He therefore was far from resenting the pointed rebuke of the prophet, or attempting any palliation of his conduct; but, in deep humiliation of heart, he confessed, 'I have sinned against the Lord.' The words are few; but the event proved them to have been the language of genuine repentance, which regards sin as committed against the authority and glory of the Lord, whether or not it have occasioned evil to any fellow-creature" (Thos. Scott).

In order to fully obtain the mind of God on any subject treated of in His Word, Scripture has to be diligently searched and one passage carefully compared with another — failure to observe this principle ever results in an inadequate or one-sided view. It is so here. Nothing is recorded in the historical account of Samuel about the deep exercises of heart through which David now passed; nothing is said to indicate the reality and depth of his repentance. For *that* we must turn elsewhere, notably to the penitential Psalms. There the Holy Spirit has graciously given us a record of what David was inspired to write thereon, for it is in the Psalms we find most fully delineated the varied experiences of soul through which the believer passes. There we may find an unerring description of every exercise of heart experienced by the saint in his journey through this wilderness scene; which explains why *this* book of Scripture has ever been a great favourite with God's people: therein they find *their own* inward history accurately described.

The two principal Psalms which give us a view of the heart exercises through which David now passed are the 51st and the 32nd. The 51st is evidently the earlier one. In it we see the fallen saint struggling up out of "the horrible pit and miry clay." In the latter we behold him standing again on firm ground with a new song in his mouth, even the blessedness of him "whose sin is covered". But both of them are evidently to be dated from the time when the sharp thrust of God's lancet in the hand of Nathan pierced David's conscience, and when the healing balsam of God's assurance of forgiveness was laid by the prophet upon his heart. The passionate cries of the sorely stricken soul (Psa. 51) are really the echo of the Divine promise — the efforts of David's faith to grasp and appropriate the merciful gift of pardon. It was the Divine promise *of* forgiveness which was the basis and encouragement of the prayer *for* forgiveness.

It is to be noted that the title affixed to the 51st Psalm is "A Psalm of David, when Nathan the prophet came unto him, after he had gone in to Bathsheba." Beautifully did Spurgeon point out in his introductory remarks, "When the Divine message had aroused his dormant conscience and made him see the greatness of his guilt, he wrote this Psalm. He had forgotten his psalmody while he was indulging his flesh, but he returned to his harp when his spiritual nature was awakened, and he poured out his song to the accompaniment of sighs and tears." Great as was David's sin, yet he repented, and was restored. The depths of his anguish and the reality of his repentance are evident in every verse. In it we may behold the grief and the desires of a contrite soul pouring out his heart before God, humbly and earnestly suing for His mercy. Only the Day to come will reveal how many sin-tormented souls have from this Psalm — "all blotted with the tears in which David sobbed out his repentance" found a path for backsliders in a great and howling desert.

"Although the Psalm is one long cry for pardon and restoration, one can discern an order and progress in its petitions — the order, not of an artificial reproduction of a past mood of mind, but the instinctive order in which the emotion of contrite desire will ever pour itself forth. In the Psalm all begins (v. 1), as all begins in fact, with the grounding of the cry for favour on 'Thy loving-kindness, The multitude of Thy tender mercies'; the one plea that avails with God, whose love is its own motive and its own measure, whose past acts are the standard for all His future, whose own compassions, in their innumerable numbers, are more than the sum of our transgressions, though these be 'more than the hairs of our head.' Beginning with God's mercy, the penitent soul can learn to look next upon its own sin in all its aspects of evil" (A. Maclaren).

The depth and intensity of the Psalmist's loathing of self is clearly revealed by the various terms he uses to designate his crime. He speaks of his "transgressions" (vv. 1, 3) and of his "iniquity" and "sin (vv. 2, 3). As another has forcibly pointed out, "Looked at in one way, he sees the separate acts of which he had been guilty — his lust, fraud, treachery, murder; looked at in another, he sees them all knotted together in one inextricable tangle of forked, hissing tongues, like the serpent-locks that coil and twist round a Gorgon head. No sin dwells alone; the separate acts have a common root, and the whole is matted together like the green growth on a stagnant pond, so that, by whatever filament it is grasped the whole mass is drawn towards you."

A profound insight into the essence and character of sin is here exhibited by the accumulated synonyms. It is "transgression," or as the Hebrew word might be rendered, "rebellion" — not merely the breach of an impersonal law, but the revolt of a subject's will against its true King; disobedience to God, as well as contravention of a standard. It is "iniquity" — perversion or distortion — acting unjustly or dealing crookedly. It is "sin" or "missing the mark," for all sin is a blunder, shooting wide of the true goal, whether regard be had for God's glory or our own well being and happiness. It is pollution and filth, from which nothing but atoning blood can cleanse. It is "evil" (v. 4), a vile thing which deserves only unsparing condemnation. It is a fretting leprosy, causing him to cry "Purge me with hyssop, and I shall be clean; wash me, and I shall be whiter than snow" (v. 7).

"Against Thee, Thee only, have I sinned, and done this evil in Thy sight" (v. 4). In these words David gives evidence of the sincerity of his contrition and proof that he was a regenerate man. It is only those possessing a spiritual nature that will view sin in the presence of God. The evil of all sin lies in its opposition to God, and a contrite heart is filled with a sense of the wrong done unto Him. Evangelical repentance mourns for sin because it has displeased a gracious God and dishonoured a loving Father. David, then, was not content with looking upon his evil in itself, or in relation only to the people who had suffered by it. He had been guilty of crimes against Bathsheba and Uriah, and even Joab whom he made his tool, as well as against all his subjects; but dark as those crimes were, they assumed their true character only when seen as committed *against God*.

"Behold, I was shapen in iniquity, and in sin did my mother conceive me" (v. 5). Many have been puzzled by this verse in the light of its setting, yet it should occasion no difficulty. Certainly it was not said by David in self-extenuation; rather was it to emphasise his own excuseless guilt. From the second half of v. 4 it is plain that he was vindicating God: *Thou* hadst nothing to do with my sin: it was all *mine* own — out of the proneness unto evil of my depraved nature. It was not Thou, but my own evil lusts, which tempted me. David was engaged in making *full* confession, and therefore did he acknowledge the defilement of his very nature. It was to humble himself, clear God, and magnify the Divine grace, that David said verse 5.

In the clear light of Psalm 51 we cannot doubt the reality, the sincerity, nor the depth of David's repentance and broken-hearted contrition. We close, then, with a brief quotation from Thos. Scott: "Let not any vile hypocrite, who resembles David in nothing but his transgressions, and who adds the habit of allowed sin to all other aggravations, buoy up his confidence with *his* example; let him first imitate David's humiliation, repentance, and other eminent graces, before he thinks himself, or requires others to consider him, as a backslider."

The inward experience of a believer consists very largely of growing discoveries of his own vileness and of God's goodness, of his own excuseless failures and of God's infinite forbearance, with a frequent alternation between gloom and joy, confession and thanksgiving. Consequently, the more he reads and meditates upon the Word, the more he sees how exactly suited it is to his case, and how accurately his own checkered history is described therein. The two leading themes of the Scriptures are *sin and grace:* throughout the Sacred Volume each of these is traced to its original source, each is delineated in its true character, each is followed out in its consequences and ends, each is illustrated and exemplified by numerous personal examples. Strange as it first sounds, yet it is true that, upon these two, *sin and grace*, do turn all the transactions between God and the souls of men.

The force of what has just been said receives clear and striking demonstration in the case of David. Sin in all its hideousness is seen at work within him, plunging him into the mire; but grace is also discovered in all its loveliness, delivering and cleansing him. The one serves as a dark background from which the other may shine forth the more gloriously. Nowhere do we behold so unmistakably the fearful nature and horrible works of sin than in the man after God's own heart, so signally favoured and so highly honoured, yet failing so ignominiously and sinking so low. Yet nowhere do we behold so vividly the amazing grace of God as in working true repentance in this notorious transgressor, pardoning his iniquity, and restoring him to communion. King Saul was rejected for a far milder offense: ah, *he* was not in the covenant! O the awe-inspiring sovereignty of Divine grace.

Not only has the Holy Spirit faithfully recorded the awful details of David's sin, He has also fully described the heart-affecting repentance of the contrite king. In addition thereto, He has shown us how he sought and obtained the Divine forgiveness. Each of these is recorded for our learning, and, we may add, for our comfort. The first shows us the fearful tendency of the flesh which still indwells the believer, with its proneness to produce the vilest fruit. The second makes known to us the lamentable work which we make for ourselves when we indulge our lusts, and the bitter cup we shall then be obliged to drink. The third informs us that grievous though our case be, yet it is not hopeless, and reveals the course which God requires us to follow. Having already considered the first two at some length, we will now turn to the third.

As it is in the Psalms that the Spirit has recorded the exercises of David's broken heart, so it is therein we learn of how he obtained the Divine pardon for his aggravated offences. We will begin by turning to one of the last of the "penitential" Psalms, which we believe was probably penned by David himself. "Out of the depths have I cried unto Thee, O Lord" (130:1). There are various "depths" into which God suffers His people, at times, to fall: "depths" of trial and trouble over financial losses, family bereavements, personal illness. There are also "depths" of sin and guilt, into which they may plunge themselves, with the consequent "depths" of conviction and anguish, of darkness and despair — through the hidings of God's face — and of Satanic opposition and despondency. It is these which are here more particularly in view.

The design of the Holy Spirit in this 130th Psalm was to express and represent in the person and conduct of the Psalmist the case of a soul entangled in the meshes of Satan, overwhelmed by the conscious guilt of sin, but relieved by a discovery of the grace of God, with its deportment upon and participation of that grace. We quote the helpful paraphrase of J. Owen in its opening verses. "O Lord, through my manifold sins and provocation I have brought myself into great distresses. Mine iniquities are always before me, and I am ready to be overwhelmed with them, as with a flood of waters; for they have brought me into depths, wherein I am ready to be swallowed up. But yet, although my distress be great and perplexing, I do not, I dare not, utterly despond and cast away all hopes of relief and recovery. Nor do I seek unto any other remedy, way, or means of relief, but I apply myself to Thee, Jehovah, to Thee alone. And in this my application unto Thee, the greatness and urgency of my troubles makes my soul urgent, earnest, and pressing in my supplication. Whilst I have no rest, I can give Thee no rest; oh, therefore, attend and hearken unto the voice of my crying!"

When the soul is in such a case — in "the depths" of distress and despondency — there is no relief for it *but in God,* fully unburdening the heart to Him. The soul cannot rest in such a state, and no deliverance is to be obtained from any creature helps. "Asshur shall not save us; we will not ride upon horses; neither will we say any more to the work of our hands, Ye are our gods: for *in Thee* the fatherless (the grief-stricken and helpless) findeth mercy" (Hos. 14:3). In God alone is help to be found. The vain things which deluded Romanists have invented — prayers "to the Virgin," penances, confession to "preists," fastings, masses, pilgrimages, works of compensation — are all "cisterns which hold no water." Equally useless are the counsels of the world to sin-distressed souls — to try a change of scenery, diversion from work, music, cheerful society, pleasure, etc. There is no peace but in the God of peace.

Now in his very lowest state the Psalmist *sought help* from the Lord, nor was his appeal in vain. And this is what *we* need to lay hold of when in similar circumstances: it is recorded to this very end. Dear Christian reader, however deplorable may be your condition, however dire your need, however desperate your situation, however intolerable the load on your conscience, your case *is not hopeless.* David cried, and was heard; he sought mercy, and obtained it; and the Divine promise to you and me is "let us therefore come boldly unto the Throne of Grace, that we may *obtain mercy,* and find grace to help in time of need" (Heb. 4:16). David was not the only one who cried unto God out of "the depths." Think of the prophet Jonah: following a course of self-will, deliberately fleeing from God's commandment, then cast into the sea and swallowed by the whale: yet of him too we read, "I cried by reason of mind affliction unto the Lord, and He heard me; out of the belly of hell cried I, and Thou *heardest* my voice" (2:2).

It was his hope in the plentitude of Divine grace that moved David to seek unto the Lord. "If Thou, Lord, shouldest mark iniquities, O Lord, who shall stand? But there is forgiveness with Thee, that Thou mayest be feared. I wait for the Lord, my soul doth *wait,* and in His word do I *hope*" (Psa. 130:3-5). In the third verse he owns that he could not stand before the thrice Holy One on the ground of his own righteousness, and that if God were to "mark iniquities," that is, impute them unto condemnation, then his case was indeed hopeless. In the 4th verse he humbly reminds God that there *was* forgiveness with Him, that He might be revered and adored — not trifled with and mocked, for Divine pardon is not a license for future self-indulgence. In the 5th verse he hopefully waits for some "token for good" (Psa. 86:17), some "answer of peace" (Gen. 41:16) from the Lord.

But it is in the 51st Psalm that we find David most definitely and most earnestly suing for God's pardon. The same intensity of feeling expressed in the use of so many words for sin, is revealed also in his reiterated synonyms for pardon. This petition comes from his lips again and again, not because he thought to be heard for his much speaking, but because of the earnestness of his longing. *Such* repetitions are signs of the persistence of faith, while those which last, like the prayers of Baal's priests "from morning till the time of evening sacrifice," indicate only the supplicant's doubts. The "vain repetition" against which the Lord warned, is not a matter of repeating the same form of request, but of mechanically multiplying the same — like the Romanist with his "pater noster's" — and supposing there is virtue and merit in so doing.

David prayed that his sins might be "blotted out" (v. 1), which petition conceives of them as being recorded against him. He prayed that he might be "washed" (v. 2). from them, in which they are felt to be foul stains, which require for their removal hard scrubbing and beating — for such is, according to some of the commentators, the force of the Hebrew verb. He prayed that he might be "cleansed" (v. 7), which was the technical word for the priestly cleansing of the leper, declaring him clear of the taint. There is a touching appropriateness in this last reference, for not only lepers, but those who had become defiled by contact with a dead body, were thus purified (Num. 19); and on whom did the taint of this corruption cleave as on the murderer of Uriah? The prayer in the original is even more remarkable, for the verb is formed from the word for "sin," and if our language permitted it, would be rendered "Thou shalt *un-sin* me."

"Create in me a clean heart, O God, and renew a right spirit within me" (Psa. 51:10). His sin had made manifest his weakness and sensuality, but his remorse and anguish evidenced that above and beyond all other desires was his abiding longing after God. The petitions of this Psalm clearly demonstrate that, despite his weakness and Satan's victory over him, yet the root of the Divine matter was in David. In asking God to *create* in him a clean heart, David was humbly placing himself on a level with the unregenerate: he realised too his own utter inability to quicken or renew himself — God alone can create either a new heart or a new earth. In asking for a right spirit, he was owning that God takes account of the state of our souls as well as the quality of our actions: a *"right* spirit" is a loving, trustful obedient, steadfast one, that none but God can either impart or maintain.

In the midst of his abased confessions and earnest cries for pardon, there comes with wondrous force and beauty the bold request for restoration to full communion: "Restore unto me the joy of Thy salvation" (v. 12). How that request evidenced a more than ordinary confidence in the rich mercy of God, which would efface all the consequences of his sin! But note well *the position* occupied by this petition: it *followed* his request for pardon and purity — apart from *those*, "joy" would be nought but vain presumption or insane enthusiasm. "And uphold me by Thy free Spirit" (v. 12). First, he had prayed "Take not Thy Holy Spirit from me" (v. 11) — an obvious reference to the awful judgment which fell upon his predecessor, Saul; here, assured that the previous petition is granted, and conscious of his own weakness and inability to stand, he asks to be supported by that One who alone can impart and maintain holiness.

Ere passing on to consider the gracious answer which David received, perhaps this is the best place to consider the question, Was he justified in asking God *for* forgiveness? or to put it in a form which may better satisfy the critical, Are we warranted in supplicating God for the pardon of our sins? for there are those today who insist that *we* occupy a different and superior relation to God than David did. It will no doubt surprise some of our readers that we raise such a question. One would naturally think it was so evident that we *ought* to pray for forgiveness, that none would question it; that such a prayer is so well founded upon Scripture itself, is so agreeable to our condition as erring believers, and is so honouring to God that we *should* take the place of penitent suppliants, acknowledging our offences and seeking His pardoning mercy, that no further proof is required. But alas, so great is the confusion in Christendom today, and so much error abounds, that we feel obliged to devote one or two paragraphs unto the elucidation of this point.

There is a group, more or less influential, who argue that it is dishonouring to the blood of Christ for any Christian to ask God to pardon his sins, quoting *"Having* forgiven you *all* trespasses" (Col. 2:13). These people confuse the impetration of the Atonement with its application, or in less technical terms, what Christ purchased for His people, with the Holy Spirit's making good the same to them in the court of their conscience. Let it be clearly pointed out that, in asking God for forgiveness, we do *not* pray as though the blood of Christ had never been shed, or as though *our* tears and prayers could make any compensation to Divine justice. Nevertheless, renewed sins call for renewed repentance: true, we do not then need another Redeemer, but we *do* need a fresh exercise of Divine mercy toward us (Heb. 4:16), and a fresh application to our conscience of the cleansing blood (1 John 1:7, 9).

The saints of old prayed for pardon: "For Thy name's sake, O Lord, pardon mine iniquity; for it is great" (Psa. 25:11). The Lord Jesus taught His disciples *to pray* "Forgive us our debts" (Matt. 6:12), and that prayer is assuredly for Christians today, for it is addressed to *"our Father!"* In praying for forgiveness we ask God to be gracious to us for *Christ's* sake; we ask Him *not* to lay such sins to our charge — "enter not into judgment with Thy servant" (Psa. 143:2); we ask Him for a gracious *manifestation* to us of His mercy to our conscience — "Make me *to hear* joy and gladness; that the bones which Thou hast broken may rejoice" (Psa. 51:8); we ask Him for the comforting proofs of His forgiveness, that we may again have "the joy of His salvation."

Now it is in the 32nd Psalm that we learn of the answer which "The God of all grace" (1 Pet. 5:10) granted unto His erring but penitent child. In his introductory remarks thereon Spurgeon said, "Probably his deep repentance over his great sin was followed by such blissful peace that he was led to pour out his spirit in the soft music of this choice song." The word "Maschil" at its head, signifies "Teaching:" "The experience of one believer affords rich instruction to others, it reveals the footsteps of the flock, and so comforts and directs the weak." At the close of the 51st Psalm David had prayed, "O Lord, open Thou my lips, and my mouth shall show forth Thy praise" (v. 15): here the prayer has been heard, and this is the beginning of the fulfillment of his vow.

" *Blessed* is he whose transgression is forgiven, whose sin is covered. Blessed is the man unto whom the Lord imputeth not iniquity, and in whose spirit there is no guile" (Psa. 32:1, 2). In the former Psalm David had begun with the plaintive cry for mercy; here he opens with a burst of praise, celebrating the happiness of the pardoned penitent. There we heard the sobs of a man in the agonies of contrition and abasement; here we have an account of their blessed issue. There we had the multiplied synonyms for sin and for the forgiveness which was desired; here is the many-sided preciousness of forgiveness *possessed,* which runs over in various yet equivalent phrases. The one is a psalm of wailing; the other, to use its own words, a "song of deliverance."

The joy of conscious pardon sounds out in the opening "*blessed* is the man," and the exuberance of his spirit rings forth in the melodious variations of the one thought of forgiveness in the opening words. How gratefully he draws on the treasures of his recent experience, which he sets forth as the "taking away" of sin — the removal of an intolerable load from his heart; as the "covering" of sin — the hiding of its hideousness from the all-seeing Eye by the blood of Christ; as the "imputing not" of sin — a debt discharged. How blessed the realisation that his own forgiveness would encourage other penitent souls — "*For this* shall every one that is godly pray unto Thee" (v. 6). Finally, how precious the deep assurance which enables the restored one to say, "Thou art my hiding place; Thou shalt preserve me from trouble; Thou shalt compass me about with songs of deliverance" (v. 7)!

Here, then, is hope for the greatest backslider, if he will but humble himself before the God of all grace. True sorrow *for* sin is followed by the pardon *of* sin: "If we confess our sins, He is faithful and just to forgive us our sins, and to cleanse us from all unrighteousness" (1 John 1:9). "Is it possible that such a backslider from God can be recovered, and admitted afterwards to comfortable communion with Him? Doubtless it is: 'for with the Lord there is mercy, and with Him there is plenteous redemption,' and He will never cast out one humble penitent believer, whatever his former crimes have been, nor suffer Satan to pluck any of His sheep out of His hand. Let then those who are fallen return to the Lord without delay, and seek forgiveness through the Redeemer's atoning blood" (T. Scott).

However, because by this deed you have given great occasion to the enemies of the Lord to blaspheme, this child that is born to you shall surely die. And Nathan left to go to his house. And the Lord struck the child that Uriah's wife bore to David, and it was very sick. David therefore prayed to God for the child. And David fasted and went in and lay all night on the earth. And the elders of his house arose and went to him, to raise him up from the earth. But he would not, neither did he eat bread with them. And on the seventh day the child died. And the servants of David feared to tell him that the child was dead. For they said, Behold, while the child was still alive we spoke to him, and he would not listen to our voice. How then will he trouble himself if we tell him that the child is dead? But when David saw that his servants whispered, David perceived that the child was dead. Therefore David said to his servants, Is the child dead? And they said, He is dead. Then David arose from the earth and washed, and anointed himself, and changed his clothing, and came to the house of the Lord and worshiped. Then he came to his house. And when he asked, they set bread before him and he ate. Then his servants said to him, What is this that you have done? You fasted and wept for the child while it was alive, but when the child was dead you arose and ate bread! And he said, While the child was still alive, I fasted and wept; for I said, Who can tell if God will be gracious to me so that the child may live? But now he is dead — why should I fast? Can I bring him back again? I shall go to him, but he shall not return to me. And David comforted his wife Bathsheba. And he went in to her and lay with her. And she bore a son. And he called his name Solomon. And the Lord loved him. And he sent by the hand of Nathan the prophet, and he called his name Jedidiah, because of the Lord. And Joab fought against Rabbah of the children of Ammon, and they took the royal city. And Joab sent messengers to David and said, I have fought

420

*against Rabbah and have taken the city of waters. Now therefore gather the rest
of the people together, and camp against the city and take it — lest I take the
city and it be called after my name. And David gathered all the people together
and went to Rabbah and fought against it and took it. And he took the king's
crown from off his head, the weight of which was a talent of gold with the
precious stones. And it was set on David's head. And he brought forth the spoil
of the city in great abundance. And he brought forth the people that were in it
and put them to laboring with saws and harrows of iron, and under axes of iron.
And he made them labor around the brick-kiln. And so he did to all the cities of
the children of Ammon. So David and all the people returned to Jerusalem. —
II Samuel 12:14-31.*

It may strike some readers as strange that our last section upon David's
forgiveness should be immediately followed by one upon his *chastening:* surely
if God had pardoned his transgressions we would not expect to hear of His rod
now being laid upon him. But there will be no difficulty if we carefully
distinguish between two of the principal offices which God sustains, namely, the
character of moral *Ruler* of the world, and that of the *Judge* of His creatures:
the one relating to His dealings with us in time, the other pertaining to His
passing formal sentence upon our eternal destiny; the one concerning His
governmental actions, the other His penal verdict. Unless this distinction be
plainly recognised and given a constant place in our thoughts, not only will our
minds be clouded with confusion, but our peace will be seriously undermined
and our hearts brought into bondage; worst of all, we shall entertain erroneous
ideas of God and sadly misinterpret His dealings with us in providence. How we
need to pray that "our love may abound yet more and more *in knowledge* and in
all judgment, that we may try things *that differ* (Phil. 1:9,10 margin).

"And David said unto Nathan, I have sinned against the Lord. And Nathan said
unto David, The Lord also hath put away thy sin; thou shalt not die. Howbeit,
because by this deed thou hast given great occasion to the enemies of the Lord
to blaspheme, the child also that is born unto thee shall surely die" (2 Sam.
12:13, 14). Here are the two things to which we have just called attention, and
placed moreover in immediate juxtaposition. The first exhibits to us the Lord in
His character as *Judge*, declaring that David had been pardoned for his great
transgression — such a word (spoken now by the Spirit in power to the
conscience of a penitent believer) is *anticipatory* of God's verdict at the Great
Assize. The second manifests the Lord in His character of *Ruler*, declaring that
His holiness required Him to take governmental notice of David's wickedness, so
that demonstration might be made that His laws cannot be broken with
impunity. Let us proceed to follow out this double thought a little further.

"He hath not dealt with us after our sins, nor rewarded us according to our
iniquities" (Psa. 103:10). Here is a verse which no believer will hesitate to set to
his seal that it is true, for he has abundant evidence thereof in his own personal
experience, and therefore will he positively affirm, If I received my just deserts, I
had been cast into hell long ago. Rightly did Spurgeon say on this passage, "We
ought to praise the Lord for what He has *not done,* as well as for what He has
wrought for us." O what cause has each Christian to marvel that his perverseness
and sottishness have not utterly exhausted God's patience. Alas that our hearts
are so little affected by the infinite forbearance of God: O that His goodness
may lead us to repentance.

Have we not abundant reason to conclude, because of our base ingratitude and
vile behaviour, that God would withhold from us the communications of His

Spirit and the blessings of His providence, cause us to find the means of grace profitless, and allow us to sink into a state of settled backsliding? Is it not a wonder that He does not so deal with us? Truly "He hath not dealt with us after our sins, nor rewarded us according to our iniquities." Any why? Because He dealt with Another "after our sins" and exacted from Him full satisfaction to His justice. And payment God cannot *twice* demand: first at my bleeding Surety's hand, and then again at mine. God rewarded Christ according to our iniquites, and now He rewards us according to Christ's merits. Hallelujah. Heaven be praised for such a Gospel. May this old, old truth, come with new power and sweetness unto our souls.

"He hath not dealt with us after our sins, nor rewarded us according to our iniquities." This is true *penally* (i.e. God's dealings with us as Judge) and with respect to the *eternal* consequences of our sins. Yet this does *not* mean that the sins believers commit are ignored by God as the moral Ruler of this world, that He refrains from dealings with us governmentally. The whole of His dealings with His people Israel (who were in covenant relationship with Him) shows otherwise. The New Testament also forbids such a conclusion: see Gal. 6:7; 1 Cor. 11:29, 30! Yet is must be remembered that God exercises His sovereignty in this, as in all things: the extent to which and the manner in which God makes His people smart for their "inventions" is determined by His own mere good pleasure.

Though God forgives His people their sins, yet He frequently gives them plain proof of His holy abhorrence of the same, and causes them to taste something of the bitter fruits which they bring forth. Another scripture which brings out this dual truth is, "Thou wast a God that forgavest them, though Thou tookest vengeance of their inventions" (Psa. 99:8). What could possibly be plainer than this: God pardoning His people, yet also manifesting His sore displeasure against their transgressions. A striking case in point — obviously included in Psa. 99:6-8 — is recorded in Ex. 32. There we see Israel worshipping the golden calf in the lascivious manner of the heathen. In response to the intercession of Moses, they were forgiven: "The Lord repented of the evil which He thought to do unto His people" (v. 14). Nevertheless, God took vengeance of their inventions, "And the Lord plagued the people, because they made the calf, which Aaron made" (v. 35).

Another exanple is seen in the case of the unbelief of Moses and Aaron at Meribah: though God pardoned the guilt of their anger as to eternal death, yet He took vengeance by not suffering them to conduct Israel into the promised land: see Num. 20:12, 24. And so it is still, as many a Christian discovers from sorrowful experience when God takes him to task for his sinful "inventions" and visits upon him His governmental displeasure. Yet this in nowise clashes with the fact that "He hath not dealt with us after our sins, nor rewarded us according to our iniquities." There is *mercy* in our chastenings, and no matter how heavily the rod may smite, we have good cause to say "And after all that is come upon us for our evil deeds, and for our great trespass, seeing that Thou our God hast punished us *less* than our iniquities deserve" (Ezra 9:13).

Ere passing on, let us anticipate the objection of some tried saints, whose case may be quite extreme. There are some who are smarting so severely beneath the chastening rod of God that to them it certainly seems that He *is* dealing with them "after their sins" and rewarding them "according to their iniquities." The light of His countenance is withheld from them, His providential dealings wear only a dark frown, and it appears very much as though He has "forgotten to be gracious." Ah, dear friend, if your heart is in any measure truly exercised before

God, then your case is far from being hopeless, and to you apply those words "Know therefore that God exacteth of thee less than thine iniquity deserveth" (Job 11:6). My brother, even your present *sufferings* are far, very far from being as great as your *sins*.

Now what we have sought to bring out above receives striking exemplification in the case of David. In a very real sense God did not deal with him after his sins, nor reward him according to his inquities; yet in another sense, He did. God sent a prophet to faithfully rebuke him, He wrought conviction and repentance in David, He heard his cry, blotted out his transgressions, as the 32nd Psalm so blessedly shows. Yet though God pardoned David as to the guilt of eternal death, saved his soul, and spared his life, yet He "took vengeance of his inventions." There was a needs-be why sore afflictions came upon him: the Divine holiness must be vindicated, His governmental righteousness must be manifested, a solemn warning must be given to wrong-doers, and David himself must learn that "the way of the transgressor is hard." O that writer and reader may lay this to heart and profit therefrom.

Through Nathan God said to David, "Wherefore hast thou despised the commandment of the Lord, to do evil in His sight? thou hast killed Uriah the Hittite with the sword, and hast taken his wife to be thy wife, and hast slain him with the sword of the children of Ammon. Now therefore the sword shall never depart from thine house; because thou hast desposed Me, and hast taken the wife of Uriah the Hittite to be thy wife. Thus saith the Lord, Behold, I will raise up evil against thee out of thine own house, and I will take thy wives before thine eyes, and give them unto thy neighbour, and he shall lie with thy wives in the sight of this sun" (2 Sam. 12:9-11). What a solumn exhibition of God's governmental righteousness! David must reap as he had sown. He had caused Uriah to be slain by the sword, and now God tells him "the sword shall never depart from thine house;" he had committed adultery with Bathsheba, and now he hears that his own wives shall be defiled. How true are those words "For with what judgment ye judge, ye shall be judged: and with what measure ye mete, it shall be measured to you again" (Matt. 7:2)!

God hath declared that "to the froward He will show Himself froward" (Psa. 18:26), and frequently does He punish sin *in its own kind*. Upon the burning lusts of the Sodomites He rained down fire and brimstone from heaven (Gen. 19:24). Jacob deceived his father by means of the skin of a kid (Gen. 29:16), and he in turn was thus deceived by his sons, who brought him Joseph's coat dipped in the blood of a kid (Gen. 37:31), saying he had been devoured by a wild beast. Because Pharaoh had cruelly ordered that the male infants of the Hebrews should be drowned (Ex. 1:22), the Egyptian king and all his hosts were swallowed up by the Red Sea (Ex. 14:28). Nadab and Abihu sinned grievously by offering "strange fire" unto the Lord, and accordingly they were consumed by fire from heaven (Lev. 10:1, 2). Adonibezek cut off the thumbs and toes of the kings he took in battle, and in like manner the Lord rewarded him (Judges 1:6,7). Agag's sword made women childless, and so his own mother was made childless by his being torn in pieces before the Lord (1 Sam. 15:33).

What proofs are these that "the eyes of the Lord are in every place, beholding the evil and the good" (Prov. 15:3). What evidences are these of the inflexible justice of God: none need fear but what the Judge of all the earth will "do right." What solemn intimations are they that in the Day to come each one shall be judged "according to his works." What warnings are these that God is not to be mocked. But let it not be forgotten that if it is written "He that soweth to the flesh shall of the flesh reap corruption: it is also added (though not nearly so frequently quoted) that "he that soweth to the Spirit shall of the Spirit reap life everlasting" (Gal. 6:8). The same principle of God's granting an exact quid pro quo applies to the service of His ministers: "He which soweth sparingly shall reap also sparingly; and he which soweth bountifully shall reap also bountifully" (2 Cor. 9:6) — the harvest shall not only be answerable to the seed and the reward to the work, but it will be greater or less according to the quantity and quality of the work.

Nor does the last-quoted passage mean that God is going to reward His ministers according to the fruit and success of their work, but rather according to the labour itself, be it little or much, better or worse: "Every man shall receive his own reward according to his own labour" (1 Cor. 3:8). God in His sovereignty may set His servant over a blind and perverse people (as He did Ezekiel), who so far from profiting from his ministry, add iniquity to their iniquity; nevertheless his work is with God (Isa. 49:4). So too with the rank and file of Christians the more bountifully they sow the seeds of good works, the more shall they reap; and the more sparingly they sow, the less will be the harvest: "Knowing that whatsoever good thing any man doeth, the same shall he receive of the Lord" (Eph. 6:8). What an incentive and stimulus should that be unto all of us: "Let us not be weary in well doing: for in due season we *shall* reap, if we faint not" (Gal. 6:9).

But to return to David. "And Nathan departed unto his house" (v. 15). The prophet had faithfully delivered his message, and now he withdrew from the court. It is very striking and blessed to see how God *honoured* His servant: He moved David to name one of his sons "Nathan" (1 Chron. 3:5), and it was from *him* Christ, according to the flesh, descended (Luke 3:31). "And the Lord struck the child that Uriah's wife bare unto David, and it was very sick" (v. 15). The prophet's words now began to receive their tragic fulfillment. Behold here the sovereignty of God: the parents lived, the child must die. See here too God's respect for His law: David had broken it, but He executes it, by visiting the sins of the father upon the son.

"David therefore besought God for the child; and David fasted, and went in, and lay all night upon the earth" (v. 16). It is touching to see this seasoned warrior so affected by the sufferings of his little one — proof of a broken heart and a contrite spirit, for the penitent are pitiful. It is true that the prophet had said, "The child also that is born unto thee shall surely die" (v. 14), yet David seems to have cherished the hope that this threat was but a *conditional* one, as in the case of Hezekiah: his words "while the child was yet alive I fasted and wept: for I said, Who can tell whether God will be gracious to me, that the child may live?" (v. 22) strongly appear to bear this out. In his fasting and lying all night upon the ground David humbled himself before the Lord, and evidenced both the sincerity of his repentance and the earnestness of his supplication. What is recorded in v. 17 illustrates the fact that the natural man is quite incapable of understanding the motives which regulate the conduct of believers.

"And it came to pass on the seventh day that the child died" (v. 18). No detail of Scripture is meaningless. It was on the eighth day that the male children of the Israelites were to be circumcised (Gen. 17:12, etc.), thus in the death of his son before it could receive the sign of the covenant a further proof was given David of God's governmental displeasure! Though it was a mercy to all concerned that the infant was removed from this world, yet inasmuch as its death had been publicly announced as a rebuke for their sin (v. 14), its decease was a manifest chastening from God upon David and Bathsheba.

"Then David arose from the earth, and washed, and anointed himself, and changed his apparel, and came into the house of the Lord, and worshipped: then he came to his own house; and when he required, they set bread before him, and he did eat" (v. 20). This is very beautiful, reminding us of Job's bowing beneath God's chastening rod and worshipping Him when he received tidings of the death of his children. How different was this from the disconsolate grief and rebellion against God which is so often displayed by worldings when *their* loved ones are snatched away from them. Weeping should never hinder worshipping: "Is any among you afflicted? let him pray" (James 5:13) How the terms of this verse rebuke the personal untidiness of some who attend public worship!

"And David comforted Bathsheba his wife, and went in unto her, and lay with her: and she bare a son, and he called his name Solomon: and the Lord loved him" (v. 24). Having meekly bowed before God's rod, humbled himself beneath His mighty hand, and publicly owned Him in worship, David now received a token of God's favour: "Behold, a son shall be born to thee, who shall be a man of rest; and I will give him rest from all his enemies round about: for his name shall be Solomon, and I will give peace and quietness unto Israel in his days" (1 Chron 22:9). The birth and name given to Solomon was an evidence that God *was reconciled* to David, as it was also an earnest of the tranquility which would obtain in Israel during his reign. Solomon was also named "Jedidiah" which signifies "beloved of the Lord" — signal demonstration of the *sovereignty* of Divine grace!

The chapter closes (vv. 26-31) with a brief account of Israel's capture of Rabbah, the royal city of the Ammonites. Further proof was this of God's grace unto David: he prospered his arms notwithstanding his aggravated sins. The additional chastisements which came upon him under the governmental dealings of God will be considered by us in the sections which follow.

CHAPTER 13.

And after this Absalom the son of David had a beautiful sister whose name was Tamar. And Amnon the son of David loved her. And Amnon was so troubled that he fell sick for his sister Tamar — for she was a virgin. And Amnon thought it hard for him to do anything to her. But Amnon had a friend, whose name was Jonadab, the son of David's brother Shimeah. And Jonadab was a very crafty man. And he said to him, Why are you, the king's son, lean from day to day? Will you not tell me? And Amnon said to him, I love Tamar, my brother Absalom's sister. And Jonadab said to him, Lay down on your bed and make yourself sick. And when your father comes to see you, say to him, I beg you, let my sister Tamar come and give me food and prepare the food in my sight so that I may see and eat it at her hand. So Amnon lay down and made himself sick. And when the king had come to see him, Amnon said to the king, I beg you, let my sister Tamar come and make me a couple of cakes in my sight, so that I may eat at her hand. Then David sent home to Tamar, saying, Go now to your brother Amnon's house and prepare food for him. So Tamar went to her brother Amnon's house. And he had lain down. And she took flour and kneaded it and made cakes in his sight, and baked the cakes. And she took a pan and poured them out before him. But he refused to eat. And Amnon said, Have all the men go out from me. And every man went out, away from him. And Amnon said to Tamar, Bring the food into the room so that I may eat out of your hand. And Tamar took the cakes which she had made and brought them into the room to Amnon her brother. And when she had brought them to him to eat, he seized her and said to her, Come lie with me, my sister. And she answered him, No, my brother, do not humble me. For no such thing ought to be done in Israel. Do not do this folly. And I — where shall I cause my shame to go? And as for you — you shall be as one of the fools in Israel. Now therefore, I beg you, speak to the king. For he will not withhold me from you. However, he would not listen to her voice; but being stronger than she, he forced her and lay with her. Then Amnon hated her with a great hatred. So that the hatred with which he hated her was greater than the love iwth which he had loved her. And Amnon said to her, Get up and go. And she said to him, There is no cause — this evil in sending me away is greater than the other that you did to me. But he would not listen to her. Then he called his servant who waited on him and said, Now put this woman out from me and bolt the door after her. And she had a robe of many colors on her, for the king's virgin daughters were clothed with such robes. Then his servant brought her out and bolted the door after her. And Tamar put ashes on her head and tore the robe of many colors that was on her. And she laid her hand on her head and went on, crying. And Absalom her brother said to her, Has Amnon your brother been with you? But say nothing now, my sister. He is your brother. Do not set your heart on this thing. So Tamar remained desolate in her brother Absalom's house. And when king David heard of all these things, he was very angry. And Absalom did not speak to his brother Amnon, either good or bad, for Absalom hated Amnon because he had forced his sister Tamar. And after two full years Absalom had sheepshearers in Baalhazor, which is beside Ephraim. And Absalom invited all the king's sons. And Absalom came to the king and said, Behold now, your servant has sheepshearers — I beg you, let the king and his servants go with your servant. And the king said to Absalom, No, my son, let us not all go now, lest we be too heavy on you. And he pressed him. He would not go, however, but blessed him. Then Absalom said, If not, please let my brother Amnon go with us? And the king said to him, Why should he go with you? But Absalom pressed him, so that he let Amnon and all the king's sons go with him. Now Absalom had commanded his servants, saying, Now watch when Amnon's heart is merry with wine, and when I say to you, Strike Amnon! — then kill him, do not fear. Have I not commanded you? Be courageous and be brave. And the servants of Absalom did to Amnon as Absalom had commanded. Then all the king's sons arose. And every man got on his mule and fled. And while they were in the way, news came to David, saying, Absalom has killed all the king's sons, and there is not one of them left. Then the king arose and tore his garments and lay on the earth. And all his servants stood by with their clothes torn. And Jonadab, the son of David's brother Shimeah answered and said, Let not my lord think that they have killed all the young men, the king's sons. For only Amnon is dead. For by the mouth of Absalom this has been determined from the day that he forced his sister Tamar. Now therefore do not let my lord the king take this thing to his heart, to think that all the king's sons are dead, for only Amnon is dead. But Absalom fled. And the young man that kept the watch lifted up his eyes and looked. And, behold, many people came by the way of the hillside behind him. And Jonadab said to the king. See, the king's sons come — as your servant said, so it is. And as soon as he had stopped speaking, behold, the king's sons came. And they lifted up their voice and wept with a great weeping. But Absalom fled and went to Talmai, the son of Ammihud, king of Geshur. And David mourned for his son every day. So Absalom fled and went to Geshur and was there three years. And king David longed to go forth to Absalom, for he was comforted about Amnon, since he was dead. — II Samuel 13:1-39.

The chastenings, which were the natural fruits of David's sins, quickly began to fall upon him. Though God had made with him a covenant "ordered in all things and sure" (2 Sam. 23:5), and though he was the man after His own heart, yet He was very far from regarding his sins lightly. The honour of Jehovah's name required that such transgressions as David's should be marked by no ordinary tokens of His displeasure. He had "given great occasion to the enemies of the Lord to blaspheme" (2 Sam. 12:14), and therefore did He proclaim His disapproval more loudly by suffering David to live and pass through one tremendous sorrow after another, than had He slain him instantly after his crime against Uriah. Yet we may also behold therein the faithfulness, wisdom, and grace of God towards His servant by using those very sorrows for the renewing of him in holiness; that this *was* accomplished appears blessedly in the sequel.

David was now to prove to the full the solemn truth of "Thine own wickedness shall correct thee, and thy backslidings shall reprove thee: know therefore and see that it is an evil thing and bitter that thou hast forsaken the Lord thy God, and that My fear is not in thee, saith the Lord God of hosts" (Jer. 2:19). It was through those nearest and dearest to himself that David was to experience what "an evil thing and bitter" it is to depart from the Lord. "Behold, I will raise up evil against thee out of *thine own house*" (2 Sam. 12:11) the Lord had declared. What must have been the feelings of his poor heart with this dread threat hanging over his family! How often do *we* moralize upon the wisdom and mercy of God in withholding from us a knowledge of the future: how it would spoil our present peace and comfort if we were acquainted with the trials and sorrows lying ahead of us; the more so if it were now revealed to us the evils which would yet overtake the members of our household. But the case was otherwise with David: *he knew* that the sore judgments of God were about to fall within his family circle!

One can readily imagine with what trepidation David would now look upon his several children, wondering upon which of them the Divine blow would first fall. The death of Bathsheba's infant was but the prelude of the fearful storm which was about to descend upon his loved ones. It seems quite clear from all that follows, one of the family-failings of David was that he had been too easy-going with and indulgent toward his children, allowing his natural affections to override his better judgment, instead of (as it should be) the judgment guiding the affections — it is not without reason and meaning that the head is set *above* the heart in our physical bodies! No doubt the fact that David had several wives made it much more difficult to rule his offspring as duty required — how one wrong leads to another!

As we have seen in earlier chapters, David was a man of strong natural passions, and the deep feelings he cherished for his children was in full accord therewith. The fear of his servants to tell him that his infant was dead (2 Sam. 12:18); the advice of Jonadab to Ammon, who had read David's disposition aright, to feign himself sick, that "when his father came to see him" (2 Sam. 13:5) he might proffer his requests; his "weeping so sore" for the death of this son, and then again, his anguish having subsided, "his soul longing to go forth" to the other son who had slain him (2 Sam. 13:39); and the final instructions to his officers touching the safety of Absalom, even when he was in arms against his father — "deal gently, for my sake, with Absalom" (2 Sam. 18:5) — being far more concerned with the care of his child than the outcome of the battle; are so many illustrations of this trait.

But that which throws light upon the doting fondness of David for his children, a fondness which caused him to set aside the clamant calls of duty, comes out in his failure to punish Amnon for his crime against Tamar, and his failure to punish Absalom for his murder of Amnon. What light is thrown upon this infirmity of David's when, in connection with Adonijah's rebellion, "his father had not displeased him at any time in saying, Why hast thou done so?" (1 Kings 1:6). Little wonder, then, that his own offspring were made a scourge to him. Alas, he followed far too closely the evil example of Eli, the high priest of Israel, of whom it is written, "his sons made themselves vile, and he restrained them not" (1 Sam. 3:13). Wisely did Thos. Scott say, "children are always uncertain comforts, but *indulged* children surely prove trials to pious parents, whose foolish fondness induces them to neglect their duty to God" — who *requires* them to duly discipline their offspring.

Yet David's children had been preserved from open wickedness in their early years: it was not until *their father* became guilty of aggravated crimes that the restraining hand of God was removed from *them*! How this should speak to the hearts of parents today: if *they* forsake the paths of righteousness, there is good reason to believe that God will chasten them by suffering *their offspring* to do likewise. Children in their youth naturally consider the evil example of their parents an excuse why they may follow in their steps; and grown up ones too are emboldened and confirmed in sin by the sinful conduct of fathers and mothers. "Let this be a warning to us to watch and pray against temptations, lest by the misconduct of one unguarded hour we should occasion such future consequences to our offspring, and such misery to ourselves throughout our future lives" (Thos. Scott).

It is both deeply instructive and unspeakably solemn to observe *the method* followed by the Lord in the execution of His awful threatenings through Nathan. It was not that David's palace was now burned by fire from heaven or razed to the ground by a cyclone. Nor was it that one of his sons was killed by a flash of lightning, and another swallowed up by an earthquake. No, *that* is not God's customary way: not by physical miracles, but by the operation of moral laws, is the retribution meted out by His government conducted. "God denounced the most grievous afflictions against the house of David on account of his conduct toward Uriah. Those afflictions were all executed in a way of Providence. . .Every part of the Divine sentence against David was executed by His providence without a miracle. Who can work like God?" (Alex. Carson). This is exceedingly striking and worthy of our closest attention, for it casts much light upon God's government over the world today.

Yes, the manner in which God's awful threatenings were fulfilled is most noteworthy: it was done in a way of *natural consequence* from David's own transgressions. The curse which God pronounced upon him corresponded exactly to the character of his iniquities. He had despised the commandment of the Lord (2 Sam. 12:9, namely, "Thou shalt not commit adultery") by taking to himself the wife of another man, and now the women of his own household should be defiled. He had become a man of blood in the butchery of Uriah, and now of blood his own family should be made to drink. He had yielded to his lusts, and by that same baneful passion in others was he to be scourged for the rest of his days. The *complexion* of his remaining years was set by his own conduct in the palace at Jerusalem! And though David himself was spared from the violent hand of the avenger, yet he was long made the spectacle of righteous suffering before the world.

In marked contrast from the opening of 2 Sam. 11, chapter 12 closes by showing us David occupying again his proper position. There he slighted the post of duty, but here he is seen at the head of his people fighting the battles of the Lord. In the previous case David was made to pay dearly for his fleshly ease, but here God prospered his efforts by delivering Rabbah into his hands. After the victory David and his army returned *to Jerusalem*, yet only for him to suffer one calamitous grief after another. The chapter which is now to be considered by us chronicles two of the most horrible crimes which ever disrupted the harmony of a family circle. One of David's sons now dishonours David's daughter, while another of his sons, after biding his time, revenged the outraged honour of his sister by murdering her seducer. Thus, lust and fraticide now desolated the king's own household.

David's children had learned the lesson which the fall of their father had taught them. Tragic indeed was the harvest the king now reaped, for a parent can have no sharper pang than the sight of his own sins reappearing in his children. "David saw the ghastly reflection of his unbridled passion in his eldest son's foul crime (and even a gleam of it in his unhappy daughter), and of his murderous craft in his second son's bloody revenge" (Alex. Maclaren). There is little need for us to dwell upon the revolting details. First, Amnon had determined to commit the fearful sin of incest against his half-sister, who was "fair" or beautiful (2 Sam. 13:1). Ah, how many a young woman has grieved because she was not pretty: alas, good looks often prove to be a fatal snare, and those endowed with them need to be doubly cautious.

The most solemn features of this first calamity may be seen in tracing the workings of God's righteous retribution in it. First, we have the Spirit's time mark in the opening words of our chapter, "and it came to pass after this," which, as we have intimated above, was when the king had returned *to Jerusalem* — where his own fearful fall had taken place! Second, Amnon was the king's oldest son (2 Sam. 3:2) andtherefore the one in immediate line for the throne, and probably the one he loved the most. Third, Amnon was at a loss to think of means for the gratification of his base desires, but there was at hand a cunning counsellor who promptly devised a plot whereby he succeeded, and that man was a nephew of David's (v. 3)! Fourth, the workings of Providence were such that David himself was made an unwilling accessory to his daughter's ravishment. When the king saw Amnon, who pretended to be sick, God not only withheld from him a discernment of his evil designs, but David was the one who sent for Tamar: as poor Uriah had been deceived by him, now he was deceived by his son!

After gross insult (v. 17) had been added to her grievous injury Tamar found a home with Absalom, who was her full brother. His question to her (v. 20) indicates that the character of Amnon was well known, which renders the more excuseless the king's consenting for his daughter to visit him. Yet "the counsel of the Lord, that *must* stand" (Prov. 19:21), and though it evidenced His "severity" (Rom. 11:22), nevertheless it was what even this world would designate a case of "poetic justice," so far as David was concerned. The more closely the case be examined the more will appear the righteous retribution which characterises it. As Joab had been so far from refusing to execute David's wicked plan, but had been a willing party to the same (2 Sam. 11:15, 16), so Jonadab instead of recoiling with horror from the vile design of Amnon, helped him to secure it!

"But when king David heard of all these things, he was very wroth" (v. 21). A severe testing of his character was now presented, for it must be remembered that as king he was the chief magistrate in Israel, and therefore under the highest obligations to see that the law of God was impartially enforced. Merely to be "very wroth" by no means met the requirements of the case: as the head of the nation it was his bounden, though exceedingly painful, duty, to see that his debauched son was punished. The law was very express concerning such a case (see Lev. 20:17), yet there is no intimation that David inflicted this penalty. Was it the workings of his own guilty conscience (calling to remembrance his sin), or parental softness toward his offspring which deterred him? Whichever it was, a dangerous precedent was set, for mildness unto transgressors by magistrates only serves to encourage greater evils. But though the king failed in his public duty, later on, the Lord dealt with Amnon, and in such a way as to greatly add to David's domestic trials.

"And Absalom spake unto his brother Amnon neither good nor bad, for Absalom hated Amnon because he had forced his sister Tamar" (v. 22). The Holy Spirit now introduces to our notice one of the most despicable, vile, and God-abandoned characters whose record is chronicled in the Scriptures. The first thing that we learn about him is his antecedents: he issued from a heathenish stock! His mother was a Gentile, the daughter of Talmai, king of Geshur (2 Sam. 3:3). The Geshurites were a fierce and intractable people, and the strain of their lawlessness passed into his blood. In taking Maacah unto himself David disobeyed a plain command of the Lord: "Neither shalt thou make marriages with them: thy daughter thou shalt not give unto his son, nor his daughter shalt thou take unto thy son" (Deut. 7:3). Need we wonder then that, having sown the wind David was made to reap the whirlwind? God will not be defied with impugnity.

"To Maacah were born Tamar and Absalom. Both were fair; both attractive. 'In all Israel there was none to be so much praised as Absalom for his beauty: from the sole of his foot even to the crown of his head there was no blemish in him.' David probably was proud of the attractiveness which adorned his house, and was willing to forget the source from which it sprang. The attractiveness wrought its effects; and as might be expected from the attractiveness of nature, the resulting consequences were sin and sorrow. The beauty of Tamar was the cause of sin and destruction to Amnon, who fell beneath the revengeful hand of Absalom his brother; and the attractiveness of Absalom wrought on the hearts of the men of Israel till they were drawn away from David and his throne. Such were the results of an attractiveness derived from sources foreign and forbidden to God's people" (B. W. Newton).

Little wonder that Mr. Newton went on to ask, "Has Christianity profited by the lesson, or has it also formed alliances with the stranger?" Alas, that these questions are so easily answered. One of the chief reasons why poor Christendom is in such a sad condition today is because she has been so largely attracted by that which makes an appeal to the flesh. Nor is this evil by any means restricted to Rome, with its ornate architecture, imposing ritual, appeal to the senses. The same thing, in varied forms, now blights the greater part of Protestantism. The plain exposition of the Scriptures is replaced by the popular topics of the day, congregational singing has been pushed into the background by professional vocalists in the choir, and all sorts of worldly devices are employed to "draw" the young people. All of this is but the present form of Israel being allured by the plysical attractions of a godless Absalom.

Singularly enough the meaning of "Absalom" is "the father of peace" but his was the peace of *a deceiver*. He was the child of him that was a liar and a murderer from the beginning, and he knew no other master — there is not a single intimation that *God* ever had any place in his thoughts. The deceitfulness and treachery of his character appears from the beginning. His words to Tamar were "hold now thy peace, my sister; he (Amnon) is thy brother: regard not this thing. So Tamar *remained* desolate in her brother Absalom's house" (v. 20), apparently with no suspicion of his murderous intentions. Meanwhile, "Absalom spake unto his brother neither good nor bad; for Absalom hated Ammon, because he had forced his sister Tamar." The spirit of revenge consumed him, and he only waited his time for a suitable opportunity to exercise it. Absalom was the rod appointed by the Lord for the further chastening of David; a rod, as we have seen, taken out of his own stem, his own child. "The mills of God grind slowly, but they grind exceeding small!"

Tamar, David's daughter, as we saw in our last, found an asylum in the home of Absalom, following the vile treatment which she had received from Amnon — another of David's sons, but by a different wife. Her brother, we are told, "hated Amnon, because he had forced his sister Tamar." Nor did Absalom's enmity abate at all with the passing of time, but merely waited an occasion which he deemed would be most suitable for taking his revenge. This only served to make more apparent his real character. There is an anger which is sinless, as is clear from "When He (Christ) had looked round about on them *with anger*, being grieved for the hardness of their hearts" (Mark 3:5). Yet there is so much of a combustible nature in the flesh of a Christian that he needs to turn into earnest prayer that exhortation, "Be ye angry, and sin not: let not the sun go down upon your wrath" (Eph. 4:26).

But the sun *had* gone down upon Absalom's wrath: a deadly fire burned in his heart which two full years had no power to quench, his crafty soul biding its time until a way opened to let out his rage on its victim. Implacable hatred burned in Absalom toward his half-brother as though it had been kindled but yesterday; and now his subtilty devised a sure passage for it. He was most manifestly a child of the devil, and the lusts of his father he was ready to willingly execute. The guide of the "serpent" now ministered unto the fury of the "lion," for those are the two predominant characteristics in the arch enemy of God and men. This is clear from the tactics he followed with our blessed Lord. First, we see his venomous guile in the Temptation, and then his fiendish cruelty at the Cross. Similarly does he work now, and thus it ever is with those whom he dominates.

"And it came to pass after two full years, that Absalom had sheepshearers in Baalhazor, which is beside Ephraim: and Absalom invited all the king's sons" (2 Sam. 13:23). Corresponding to the old English custom of "harvest-home," when a time of feasting and merriment followed the garnering of it, in Palestine the annual occasion of "sheepshearing" was made an event of festive celebration and of the coming together of relatives and friends. This is clear from Gen. 38:12, 13 and 1 Sam. 25:4, 36: for in the one we read, "and Judah was comforted (after the death of his daughter), and went up unto his sheepshearers in Timnath, with his friend," while in the other we are told that "Nabal did shear his sheep. . .and behold, he held *a feast* in his house, like the feast of a king; and Nabal's heart was merry within him, for he was very drunken."

During quite a lengthy interval Absalom had concealed his bitter hatred against his half-brother under an appearance of indifference, for we read that he "spake unto him neither good nor bad" (v. 22). But now Absalom deemed the time ripe for his murder. To cover his base design he invites "all the king's sons" to his feast, which he had purposed should be the place of execution for his unsuspecting victim. Only the last great Day will reveal how often treacherous designs have been cloaked by apparent kindness — Judas betrayed his Master not with a blow, but a kiss! In his long and varied experience the writer has found in every instance that his worst enemies fawned upon and flattered him to his face, and then stabbed him behind his back; yet sufficient for the servant to be as his Lord.

But Absalom went to yet greater pains to hide his base intention. "And Absalom came to the king and said, Behold now, thy servant hath sheepshearers; let the king, I beseech thee, and his servants go with thy servant" (v. 24). That was downright hypocrisy, for Absalom could have had no desire that David himself should be on the ground to witness the treachery against his son. Nor was the success of his cunning plot endangered by this specious move, for he had good reason to believe that his father would decline the invitation. Such indeed was the case: "And the king said to Absalom, nay my son, let us not all now go, lest we be chargeable unto thee." How that evidenced one of the many noble traits of David's character: his unselfish thoughtfulness of others — his kindly consideration by refusing to put his son to unnecessary expense. "And he pressed him," yet a little later sought to turn the hearts of all Israel against him and wrest the kingdom from his hand! "Howbeit he would not go, but blessed him" (v. 25), that is, pronounced a patriarchal benediction upon him.

"Then said Absalom, If not, I pray thee, let my brother Amnon go with us" (v. 26). Here was the real design of Absalom in pressing the king to be present himself at the forthcoming family-union and feast: having considerately declined his son's invitation, it would be doubly difficult to refuse his second request. Yet how this pretended deference unto David's parental authority exhibited the perfidy of Absalom! He was determined to get Amnon into his toils, yet veiled his bloodthirstiness under a pretence of affection and filial respect. "And the king said unto him, Why should he go with thee?" (v. 26). David was evidently somewhat uneasy or at least wondered what lay behind the outward show of Absalom's friendliness toward Anmon. But "The king's heart is in the hand of the Lord, as the rivers of water: He turneth it whithersoever He will" (Prov. 21:1); and so the sequel clearly demonstrated.

"But Absalom pressed him, that he let Amnon and all the king's sons go with him" (v. 27). Absalom prevailed against the king's better judgment. It may be that David yielded to his son's urgency from the fond hope that a full reconciliation would be effected between the two brothers, but whether or not that be the case, we must look higher and behold the over-ruling hand of God accomplishing His own counsel. The Lord had declared that "the sword shall never depart from thine house" and "I will raise up evil against thee out of thine own house" (2 Sam. 12:10, 11), and from the execution of that judgment there was no escape. Divine providence so directed things that David, by giving his consent for Amnon to attend the feast, became an unwitting accessory to Amnon's murder. How much heavier did this make the blow to the poor king's heart! Yet how absolutely just were the Divine dealings with him!

"Now Absalom had commanded his servants, saying, Mark ye now when Amnon's heart is merry with wine, and when I say unto you, Smite Amnon; then kill him, fear not: have not I commanded you; be courageous, and be valiant" (v. 28). Birds of a feather flock together: Absalom had succeeded in gathering around him unscrupulous menials who were ready to aid him in any villany. They knew that the Lord God had commanded "thou shalt *not* kill," yet were they ready to damn their souls in order to please their wicked master. The vilest characters are rarely at a loss to find those who will aid them in the blackest of crimes. The fearful impiety of the reprobate Absalom, appears in "when *I* say unto you, Smite Amnon, then kill him: fear not" — either God or man, be regardless of consequences. Such reckless abandon marks those who are given up by God.

But let us now observe how *the righteous retribution of God* appears in every detail of this incident. First, as David's murder of Uriah was not a sudden surprisal unto evil, but a thing deliberately premeditated in cold blood, so Absalom's removal of Amnon was callously planned beforehand, as v. 28 shows. Second, as the slaying of Uriah was a means to an end — that David might obtain Bathsheba; so the killing of Amnon was but a preliminary to Absalom's design of obtaining the kingdom — by removing his older brother who was heir to the throne. Third, as David did not slay Uriah by his own hand, but made Joab an accomplice, so Absalom involved his servants in the guilt of his crime — instead of striking the fatal blow himself. Fourth, as David made Uriah "drunk" before his death (11:13), so Amnon was struck down while "his heart was merry with wine!" Who can fail to see the superintending government of God here.

"And the servants of Absalom did unto Amnon as Absalom had commanded (v. 29). How little can we foresee when tragic calamity may smite a family reunion — "thou knowest not what a day may bring forth" (Prov. 27:1). How lightly we should hold the things of earth, for the most treasured of them are likely to be rudely snatched from us at any moment. The predicted "sword" is now drawn in David's house, and the rest of his sons knew not how soon *they* might fall victims to Absalom's bloodthirstiness. Therefore do we read, "Then all the king's sons arose, and every man gat him upon his mule, and fled" (v. 29). What an ending to a time of festivity! How vain are the pleasures of this poor world! How slender is the thread upon which hangs the lives even of king's sons!

"And it came to pass, while they were in the way, that tidings came to David, saying, Absalom hath slain all the king's sons, and there is not one of them left" (v. 30). How often the bearers of evil tidings make bad matters worse by excuselessly exaggerating them! Things were now represented unto David as being much blacker than they really were. There is a warning for *us* here: not to credit reports of evil until they are definitely corroborated. "Then the king arose, and tore his garments, and lay on the earth; and all his servants stood by with their clothes rent" (v. 31). How ready we are to believe the worst! Poor David was now as sorely afflicted by the false news brought to him as though it had been authentic. But alas, how slow we are to believe the Good News; such is fallen man — ready to receive the most egregious lie, but rejecting the authority of Divine Truth.

"And Jonadab, the son of Shimeah David's brother, answered and said, Let not my lord suppose that they have slain all the young men the king's sons; for Amnon only is dead: for by the appointment of Absalom this hath been determined from the day that he forced his sister Tamar" (v. 32). Jonadab appears to have had knowledge from the beginning that Absalom had definitely purposed to slay his brother, yet had he refrained from informing the king — so that he might use his influence to reconcile the two men, or at least take steps to prevent murder being done. Great indeed was the guilt of Jonadab. But again we perceive Providence overruling things. God sometimes permits the evil plots of men to come to light, so that their intended victims receive timely warnings (Acts 9:23-25), while in other instances He seals the mouths of those possessing such knowledge; and this as best subserves His own inexorable designs.

"But Absalom fled, and went to Talmai, the son of Ammihud, king of Geshur, and was there three years" (vv. 37, 38). By his foul crime the land of Israel had been defiled and his own life forfeited (Num. 35:33). He was now a debtor to that Law of which David was the guardian, for the king held his throne on the terms of reading the Law continually and obeying the same (Deut. 17:18-20). It is true that David had not executed punishment for Amnon's incest, but he could scarcely expect him to wink at barbarous fratricide. Nor could this abandoned wretch obtain protection in any of the "cities of refuge," for they afforded no shelter unto those who were guilty of willful murder. Only one alternative, then, was left him, and that was to flee unto his mother's people; and there it was that he found an asylum.

From the human side of things it seems a great pity that this fugitive from justice did not continue at Geshur, the place of his heathen origin: but the sentimental heart of his father yearned after him: "And the soul of king David longed to go forth unto Absalom, for he was comforted concerning Amnon" (v. 39). Time is a great healer, and after three years most of David's horror at Absalom's sin and grief over Amnon's death had worn off. "At first he could not find in his heart to do justice on him: now he can almost find in his heart to take him into his favour again. This was David's infirmity" (M. Henry). One can understand David's attitude, and his subsequent conduct, from a natural viewpoint; but from the spiritual side it betokened another sad lapse, for Divine holiness requires us to "*Crucify* the flesh with the affections and lusts" (Gal. 5:24): yes, dear reader, its "*affections*" as well as its "lusts." The claims of God must prevail over all natural inclinations to the contrary, and when they do not, we have to pay dearly, as David did.

We read nothing of Absalom's pining for a return unto his father, for he was devoid of even natural affection. Fierce, proud, utterly unscrupulous, he lacked any of the finer qualities of human nature. But "David longed to go forth unto Absalom," yet it seemed that this son on whom he wasted his affections was irredeemably lost to him. Absalom was guilty of murder, and the unchanging law of God commands, "Whoso sheddeth man's blood by man shall his blood be shed" (Gen. 9:6). How, then, was it possible for David to restore his erring son without defying the Divine requirements of *his* maintaining righteous government in Israel? It is to be duly noted that there is no word recorded of David seeking unto the Lord at this time. Ominous silence! The energies of nature now dominated him, and therefore there was no seeking of wisdom from above. This it is which casts light upon the dark scenes that follow.

The 14th chapter of 2 Sam. makes known to us how it came to pass that Absalom was brought back again to Jerusalem. The prime mover was Joab, who was what would be termed in present-day language an astute politician — an unprincipled man of subtle expediency. He was the leader of Israel's armies, and anxious to curry favour both with the king and his heir apparent. He knew that David doted upon Absalom and reasoned that any plausible device to bring him back would be acceptable to the king, and, at the same time, strengthen his own position in the royal favour. But the problem confronting him was, How might mercy rejoice against judgment? He knew too that while there might be a godly remnant who would oppose any open flouting of the Law, yet he counted on the fact that with the generality of Israel Absalom was their idol: see v. 25.

Joab therefore resorted to an artful subterfuge whereby David might be saved from disgracing the throne and yet at the same time regain his beloved son. He employed a woman to pose as a desolate widow and relate to the king a ficticious story, getting him to commit himself by passing judgment thereon. She is termed a "wise woman" (14:2), but *her* wisdom was the guile of the Serpent. Satan has no initiative, but always imitates, and in the tale told by this tool of Joab we have but a poor parody of the parable given through Nathan. The case she pictured was well calculated to appeal to the king's susceptibilities, and bring to mind his own sorrow. With artful design she sought to show that under exceptional circumstances *it would be permissible* to dispense with the executing of a murderer, especially when the issue involved the destruction of the last heir to an inheritance.

The story she related was far from being an accurate portrayal of the real facts of the case relating to Absalom. First, Absalom had not slain Amnon during a fit of sudden anger, nor had he murdered him when they were alone together (14:6); instead, he was slain by deliberate malice, and that, in the presence of his brethren. Second, there was no cruel persecution being waged against Absalom by those who coveted his inheritance (v. 7): but the righteous Law of God demanded his death! Third, Absalom was not the only remaining son of David (12:24,25), so that there was no immediate danger of the royal line becoming extinct, as the woman represented (14:7). These half-lies clearly indicated *the source* of this woman's "wisdom," and had David been in communion with God at the time, he had not been imposed upon or induced to deliver such an unholy judgment.

But apart from these glaring inaccuracies, the tale told by this woman made a touching appeal to the king's sentiments, and prevailed upon him. First, he hastily promised to protect her (v. 10), and then rashly confirmed the same by an oath (v. 11). Then she applied his concession to the case of Absalom and intimated that David was going against the interests of *Israel* (not displeasing *God*, be it noted!) in allowing his son to remain in exile (v. 13). Next she argued that since God in His sovereignty had spared David's life (notwithstanding his murder of Uriah), it could not be wrong for him to show leniency into Absalom (v. 13). Finally, she heaped flattery upon the king (v. 17). The sequel was that David willingly concluded his oath to this woman *obliged* him to recall Absalom

(v. 21), and accordingly he gave orders to Joab for him to be brought back.

Now Joab the son of Zeruiah saw that the king's heart was toward Absalom. And Joab sent to Tekoah and brought a wise woman from there. And he said to her, I beg you, pretend yourself to be a mourner, and put on mourning clothes now, and do not anoint yourself with oil. But be like a woman who has mourned for the dead for a long time. And come to the king and speak in this way to him. So Joab put the words in her mouth. And when the woman of Tekoah came to the king, she fell on her face to the ground and bowed to him. She said, Help, O king! And the king said to her, What ails you? And she answered, I am indeed a widow woman, and my husband is dead. And your handmaid had two sons, and the two of them fought together in the field. And there was no deliverer to part them, but the one struck the other and killed him. And behold, the whole family has risen against your handmaid. And they said, Deliver him who struck his brother so that we may kill him for the life of his brother whom he killed. And we will destroy the heir also. And so they shall put out my coal which is left and shall leave to my husband neither name nor remainder on the face of the earth. And the king said to the woman, Go to your house, and I will give command concerning you. And the woman of Tekoah said to the king, My lord, O king, may the guilt be on me and on my father's house. And may the king and his throne be without guilt. And the king said, Whoever says anything to you, bring him to me, and he shall not touch you any more. Then she said, I beg you, let the king remember the LORD your God, that you would not allow the revengers of blood to destroy any more, lest they should destroy my son. And he said, As the LORD lives, there shall not one hair of your son fall to the earth. Then the woman said, I beg you, let your handmaid speak one more word to my lord the king. And he said, Say on! And the woman said, Why then have you thought such a thing against the people of God? For the king speaks this thing as one who is at fault, in that the king does not bring his banished one home again. For we must all die, and we are as water spilled on the ground, which cannot be gathered up again. And God does not respect any person. Yet He does devise means so that His banished one may not be cast out from Him. Now therefore I have come to speak of this thing to my lord the king, because the people have made me afraid. And your handmaid said, I will now speak to the king. It may be that the king will do what his handmaid has asked. For the king will hear, to deliver his handmaid out of the hand of the man who would destroy me and my son together out of the inheritance of God. Then your handmaid said, The word of my lord the king shall now be comforting. For as an angel of God, so is my lord the king, to see what is good and bad. Therefore the LORD your God will be with you. Then the king answered and said to the woman, please, do not hide from me the thing that I shall ask you. And the woman said, Let my lord the king now speak. And the king said, Is the hand of Joab with you in all this? And the woman answered and said, As your soul lives, my lord the king, none can turn to the right hand or to the left from anything which my lord the king has spoken. For your servant Joab commanded me. And he put all these words in the mouth of your handmaid. Your servant Joab has done this thing to change the face of the matter. And my lord is wise according to the wisdom of an angel of God, to know all things that are in the earth. And the king said to Joab, See now, I have done this thing. Then go and bring the young man Absalom again. And Joab fell to the ground on his face and bowed and thanked the king. And Joab said, Today your servant knows that I have found grace in your sight, my lord, O king, in that the king has done what your servant has asked. So Joab arose and went to Geshur and brought Absalom to Jerusalem. And the king said, Let him turn to his own house, and let him not see my face. So Absalom returned to his own house and did not see the king's face. But in all Israel there was none to be so much praised as Absalom for his beauty. From the sole of his foot even to the crown of his head there was no blemish in him. And when he trimmed his head (for it was at every year's end that he trimmed it, because it was heavy on him, therefore he trimmed it), he weighed the hair of his head at two hundred shekels, according to the king's weight. And there were born three sons to Absalom, and one daughter, whose name was Tamar. She was a woman with a beautiful face. So Absalom lived two full years in Jerusalem and did not see the king's face. Therefore Absalom lived two full years in Jerusalem and did not see the king's face. Therefore Absalom sent to Joab, to send him to the king. But he would not come to him. And when he sent again a second time, he would not come. Therefore he said to his servants, See, Joab's field is near mine, and he has barley there. Go and set it on fire! And Absalom's servants set the field on fire. Then Joab arose and came to Absalom's house and said to him, Why have your servants set my field on fire? And Absalom answered Joab, Behold, I sent to you, saying, Come here so that I may send you to the king, to say, Why have I come from Geshur? It had been good for me to be there still. Now therefore let me see the king's face, and if there is any iniquity in me, let him kill me. So Joab came to the king and told him. And when he had called for Absalom, he came to the king and bowed himself on his face to the ground before the king. And the king kissed Absalom. — II Samuel 14:1-33.

It was fleshly sentiment, and not a concern for God's glory, which moved David to authorise Joab to bring back Absalom. Some of our readers may regard this as a harsh verdict and say, "Possibly the writer is not a parent, if he were, perhaps he would better understand the case before him. Was not David actuated by *love* for his erring son? Surely God does not expect His people to be without natural affection." Ah, dear reader, the claims of the Lord are both high and comprehensive, and His requirement much more exacting than many like to recognize. Right eyes are to be plucked out and right hands cut off (Matt. 5:29, 30) — things which are very dear to us — if they prove a hindrance to our treading the Narrow Way; and *that* is indeed a painful sacrifice, is it not? — so painful, that nothing short of the supernatural but sufficient grace of God can enable any of us thereunto.

"If any man come to Me," said the Lord Christ, "and hate not his father, and mother, and wife, and children, and brethren, and sisters, yea, and his own life also, he cannot be My disciple" (Luke 14:26). No wonder that he bade intending disciples to "set down first and count the cost" (Luke 14:28). Christ will be Lord of all, or He will not be Lord at all. He requires the throne of our hearts, and all other interests and inclinations must bow before His sovereign will. Alas, how little are *His* claims emphasised today! How His holy standard has been lowered! How His Gospel has been cheapened! How maudlin sentimentality now ousts the principles of holiness in the great majority of those who bear His name! How those who endeavour, in their feeble way, to press the Divine requirements are now condemned as being heartless and censorious.

"But surely a Christian is not required to become an unemotional stoic, devoid of all natural affection." No, indeed; grace in the heart does not harden, but softens. Nevertheless, holiness, and not carnal sentiment, is to dominate the

Christian. Natural affections are not to be granted a lawless license, but are to be *regulated* by the precepts of Scripture. A Christian is permitted to lament the death of a fellow-believer, yet is he bidden to "sorrow not even as others which have no hope" (1 Thess. 4:13). We are exhorted to *mortify* "inordinate affection" (Col. 3:5), that is, lawless and excessive fondness. And sometimes we have to choose — as David did — between honouring God by an obedience which requires us to set aside the yearnings of nature, or dishonour Him by yielding to fleshly emotions: in such a case self (the natural man) is to be *denied*.

Take it on its lowest ground. Do not those parents defeat their own ends who, from a *miscalled* "love," fail to deal sternly with the disobedience and defiance of their little ones; and who when their children are grown up, wink at their sins? How many a shiftless youth, whose every whim is gratified by his doting mother, develops into a worthless wastrel! How many a flighty daughter is allowed her own way, under the pretext of "letting her have a good time," only to end in her becoming a woman of the streets! Even the natural man is responsible to bring his affections under the control of his judgment, and not let his heart run away with his head. But the child of God is to be regulated by far higher and holier principles, and is to subordinate the yearnings of nature to the glory of God by obeying His commandments.

Now in his ordering Joab to fetch back Absalom from Geshur, David acted according to the dictates of "natural affection," and not out of any regard to the honour of the Lord. Joab knew how to work upon his weakness, as is evident from the success of his scheme through the woman of Tekoah. She so wrought upon his sentiments that he rashly gave a verdict in favour of the criminal depicted in her story; and then she persuaded him to restore his treacherous son. Yet nothing could possible justify him in disregarding the Divine Law, which cried aloud for the avenging of Amnon. God had given no commandment for his son to be restored, and therefore *His* blessing did not attend it. David paid dearly for his foolish pity, as we shall see from the sequel; and *that* is recorded for *our* learning. God grant that some parents at least who read these lines will take this solemn lesson to heart.

"So Joab arose and went to Geshur, and brought Absalom to Jerusalem. And the king said, Let him turn to his own house, and let him not see my face. So Absalom returned to his own house, and saw not the king's face" (vv. 23, 24). Previously we read that "David mourned for his son every day" and "the soul of the king David was consumed (margin) to go forth unto Absalom" (13:37, 39), whereas now that he is brought back to Jerusalem orders are given that he must *not* see the king's face. What a strange thing human nature is! What expedients it will resort to and compromises it will make in order to save its face. Possibly some of the more godly of David's counsellors had demurred at his flouting of the Law, and may be his own heart was uneasy over the step he had taken; and so as a sop to his conscience, and in order to quiet the censures of others, Absalom was confined to his own private dwelling.

Some writers are of the opinion that this measure of the king was designed for the humbling of his son, hoping that he would now be brought to see the heinousness of his sin and repent for it. But surely there had been sufficient time for that in his three years' sojourn in Geshur. No, we believe that what we have pointed out above is the more likely explanation. By permitting Absalom to return to his own house David exercised mercy, and by denying his entrance to the court he made a show of justice, persuading himself by this interdict he evidenced his abhorrence of Amnon's murder. Nevertheless the fact remained that, as chief magistrate in Israel, David had set aside the Divine law. Therefore he must not be surprised if his wayward son now resorts to further lawlessness, for there is no escape from the outworking of the principle of sowing and reaping.

"But in all Israel there was none to be so much praised as Absalom for his beauty: from the sole of his foot even to the crown of his head there was no blemish in him" (v. 25). How this reveals the low state of the Nation at that time! Absalom was not esteemed for his moral worth, for he was utterly lacking in piety, wisdom, or justice. His handsome physique was what appealed to the people. His abominable wickedness was ignored, but his person was admired — which only served to increase his arrogance, ending in his utter ruin. Alas, how often a corrupt mind indwells a sound body. How sad it is to observe our decadent generation valuing physical beauty and prowess more highly than moral virtues and spiritual graces. The allowing of his luxuriant hair to grow to such a length, and then afterwards weighing it (v. 26), shows the pride and effeminacy of the man. The three sons born to him (v. 27) evidently died at an early age: see 18:18.

"So Absalom dwelt two full years in Jerusalem, and saw not the king's face. Therefore Absalom sent for Joab, to have sent him to the king; but he would not come to him, and when he sent again the second time, he would not come" (vv. 28, 29). In the light of the immediate sequel it is clear that Absalom was chafing at his confinement (that he "sent for Joab" indicates he was virtually a prisoner in his own house) because it interfered with the development of his evil plans, and that the reason why he was anxious to be reconciled to the king was that he might obtain his liberty and thus be able to win the Nation over to himself. Probably this was the reason why Joab declined to visit him: suspecting his disloyal designs, knowing what a dangerous character he was to be at large.

"Therefore he said unto his servants, See, Joab's field is near mine and he hath barley there; go and set in on fire. And Absalom's servants set the field on fire" (v. 30). He was still the same self-willed character: "who is lord over us?" being the language of all his actions. The three years he had spent at Geshur and his two years of isolation in Jerusalem had wrought no change in him: his heart was not humbled and his pride was not mortified. Instead of being thankful that his life has been spared, he deems himself sorely wronged for being secluded from the court. Instead of being grateful to Joab for bringing him back from Geshur, he now takes a mean revenge upon him because he refused his present request. Such conduct displayed a self-will that would brook no denial; a man of violence ready to go to any lengths in order to have his own way. The fear of God was not on him, nor had he any respect for his neighbor.

"Then Joab arose, and came to Absalom unto his house, and said unto him, Wherefore have thy servants set my field on fire?" (v. 31). At first sight it seems strange after twice refusing to see Absalom, that now, after being insulted and injured, Joab should grant his request, and mediate for him with the king; yet a little reflection will make it clear. Joab was a shrewd politician, with his finger on the public's pulse, and he knew full well that Absalom stood high in the favour of the people (v. 25); and now that he had further proof of the fury and power of the man — his servants being ready at his bidding to do violence unto the property of the general of the army! — he was afraid to further cross his will; and probably, with an eye to the future, he also wished to keep in his good books.

"And Absalom answered Joab, Behold, I sent unto thee, saying, Come hither, that I may send thee to the king, to say, Wherefore am I come from Geshur? it had been good for me to have been there still: now therefore let me see the king's face; and if there be any iniquity in me, let him kill me" (v. 32). What an arrogant and insolent attitude to assume toward his royal parent: one which manifested the grossest ingratitude, a contempt for the king's authority, and a deliberate challenge for him to enfore the law. Rightly did M. Henry point out, "His message was haughty and imperious, and very unbecoming either a son or a subject. He undervalued the favour that had been showed him in recalling him from banishment, and restoring him to his own house. He denies his own crimes, though most notorious, and will not own that there was any iniquity in him, insinuating that, therefore, he had been wronged in the rebukes he had been under. He defies the king's justice, 'Let him kill me, if he can find it in his heart,' knowing he loved him too well to do it."

"So Joab came to the king, and told him: and when he had called for Absalom, he came to the king, and bowed himself on his face to the ground before the king; and the king kissed Absalom" (v. 33). Alas, notwithstanding his insulting rudeness Absalom prevailed upon the king to yield. His better judgment blinded by intemperate affection for his son, David invited Absalom to the palace. By prostrating himself before the king Absalom feigned submission to his authority, yet his heart was full of base designs to secure the throne for himself. David sealed his pardon with a kiss, instead of allowing the Law to take its course. As another has well said, "David's inordinate tenderness only paved the way for Absalom's open rebellion. Terrible warning! Deal tenderly with evil, and it will, assuredly, rise to a head and crush you in the end. On the other hand, meet evil with a face of flint, and victory is sure. Sport not with the serpent, but at once crush it beneath your feet."

Whilst all this trouble was brewing around David a strange passiveness seems to have crept over him, and to have continued till his flight before Absalom. The narrative is singularly silent about him. He appears to be paralyzed by the consciousness of his past sins: he orginated nothing. He dared not punish Amnon, and could only weep when he heard of Absalom's crime. He weakly craved for the return of the latter, but could not bring himself to send for him till Joab urged it. A flash of his old kingliness appeared for a moment in his refusal to see his son, but even that vanished when Joab chose to insist that Absalom should return to the court. He had no will of his own, but had become a mere tool in the hands of his fierce general — Joab having gained this hold over him by his complicity in Uriah's murder. At every step he was dogged by the consequences of his own wrong-doings, even though God had pardoned his sins.

Beautifully did Alex. Maclaren, in his little work "The Life of David as reflected in his Psalms," throw light upon this particular stage of his career, and we feel we cannot do our readers a better service than close this article with a rather lengthy quotation therefrom. "It is not probable that many Psalms were made in those dreary days. But the *forty-first* and *fifty-fifth* are, with reasonable probability, referred to this period by many commentators. They give a very touching picture of the old king during the four years in which Absalom's conspiracy was being hatched. It seems from the 41st that the pain and sorrow of his heart had brought on some serious illness, which his enemies had used for their own purposes and embittered by hypocritical condolences and ill-concealed glee. The sensitive nature of the Psalmist winces under their heartless desertion of him, and pours out its plaint in this pathetic lament. He begins with a blessing on those who 'consider the afflicted' — having reference, perhaps, to the few who were faithful to him in his languishing sickness. He passes thence to his own case, and, after humble confession of his sin — almost in the words of the 51st Psalm — he tells how his sick bed had been surrounded by different visitors.

"His disease drew no pity, but only fierce impatience that he lingered in life so long. 'Mine enemies speak evil of me — when will he die, and his name have perished?' One of them, in especial, who must have been a man in high position to gain access to the sick chamber, has been conspicuous by his lying words of condolence. 'If he come to see me, he speaketh vanity.' The sight of the sick king touched no chord of affection, but only increased the traitor's animosity — 'his heart gathered evil to itself' — and then, having watched his pale face for wished-for unfavourable symptoms, the false friend hurries from the bedside to talk of his hopeless illness — 'he goeth abroad, he telleth it.' The tidings spread, and are stealthily passed from one conspirator to another: 'all that hate me whisper together against me.' They exaggerate the gravity of his condition, and are glad because, making the wish the father to the thought, they believe him dying — 'a thing of Belial (i.e. a destructive disease) say they, is poured out upon him, and now that he lieth, he shall rise up no more.

"We should be disposed to refer the thirty-ninth Psalm also to this period. It, too, is the meditation of one in sickness, which he knows to be a Divine judgment for his sin. There is little trace of enemies in it; but his attitude is that of *silent submission,* while wicked men are disquieted around him — which is precisely the characteristic peculiarity of his conduct at this period. It consists of two parts (vv. 1-6 and 7-13), in both of which the subjects of his meditations are the same, but the tone of them different. His own sickness and mortality, and man's fleeting, shadowy life, are his themes. The former has led him to think of the latter.

"It may be observed that this supposition of a protracted illness, which is based upon these Psalms, throws light upon the singular passiveness of David during the maturing of Absalom's conspiracy, and may naturally be supposed to have favoured his schemes, an essential part of which was to ingratiate himself with suitors who came to the king for judgment, by affecting great regret that no man was deputed of the king to hear them. The accumulation of untried causes, and the apparent disorganisation of the judicial machinery, are well accounted for by David's sickness."

And after this Absalom prepared himself chariots and horses and fifty men to run before him. And Absalom rose up early and stood beside the way of the gate. And when any man who had a suit to come before the king for judgment, then Absalom called to him and said, What city are you from? And he said, Your servant is of one of the tribes of Israel. And Absalom said to him, See! Your matters are good and right. But no man from the king will hear you. Absalom also said, Oh that I might be made judge in the land, so that every man who has any suit or cause might come to me, and I would do him justice! And when any man came near to bow down to him, he put forth his hand and took him and kissed him. And in this way Absalom did to all Israel that came to the king for judgment. So Absalom stole the hearts of the men of Israel. And at the end of forty years, Absalom said to the king, I beg you, let me go and pay my vow which I have vowed to the LORD in Hebron. For your servant vowed a vow while I lived at Geshur in Syria, saying, If the LORD will indeed bring me again to Jerusalem, that I will serve the LORD. And the king said to him, Go in peace. So he arose and went to Hebron. But Absalom sent spies throughout all the tribes of Israel, saying, As soon as you hear the sound of the trumpet, then you shall say, Absalom reigns in Hebron! And with Absalom went two hundred called men out of Jerusalem. And they went in their honesty and did not know anything about Absalom's plans. And Absalom sent for Ahithophel of Giloh, David's counsellor, from his city Giloh, while he offered sacrifices. And the conspiracy was strong, for the people with Absalom grew more and more. — II Samuel 15:1-12.

"And it came to pass after this, that Absalom prepared him chariots and horses, and fifty men to run before him" (2 Sam. 15:1). The "after this" refers to what now followed upon David's receiving back into his favour the son who had murdered a brother (14:33). If a spark of gratitude had burned in his breast, Absalom would now have sought to do all in his power toward forwarding the interests of his indulgent father. But alas, so far from strengthening the hands of his royal parent, he sets to work to dethrone him. Absalom was now in the position to develop his vile plan of deposing David. The methods he followed thoroughly revealed what a godless and unscrupulous scoundrel he was. The first thing here recorded of him at once intimated his utter contempt of God and manifested his affinity with the heathen.

Jehovah requires His people to conduct themselves differently from the idolatrous nations surrounding them, and therefore He gave, among others, this law for the regulation of Israel's king: "But he shall not multiply *horses* to himself" (Deut. 17:16). It was in accord with this, that, when the King of kings formally presented Himself to Israel, He appeared "meek and sitting upon *an ass*" (Matt. 21:5), so perfectly did He honour the Law in every detail. But Absalom was of a totally different type: arrogant, proud, self-willed. All the other sons of David rode upon mules (2 Sam. 13:19), but nothing less than "chariots and horses" would satisfy this wicked aspirant to the kingdom.

The "fifty men to run before him" was a symbol of *royalty*: see 1 Sam. 8:11; 1 Kings 1:5. In acting thus, Absalom took advantage of his father's fond attachment and basely traded upon his weakness. Unauthorised by the king, yet not forbidden by him, he prepared an imposing retinue, which gave him a commanding status before the nation. Finding himself unchecked by the king, he made the most of his position to seduce the hearts of the people. By means of underhand methods, Absalom now sought to turn toward himself the affection of his father's subjects. From the employment of force (2 Sam. 14:30), he resorted to craftiness. As we have said before, these two are the leading characteristics of the devil: the *violence* of the "lion" and the *guile* of the "serpent," and thus it ever is with those whom he fully possesses.

"And Absalom rose up early, and stood beside the way of the gate: and it was so, that when any man that had a controversy came to the king for judgment, then Absalom called unto him, and said, Of what city art thou? And he said, Thy servant is of one of the tribes of Israel. And Absalom said unto him, See, thy matters are good and right; but there is no man deputed of the king to hear thee. Absalom said moreover, Oh that I were made judge in the land, that every man which hath any suit or cause might come unto me, and I would do him justice! And it was so, that when any man came nigh to him to do him obeisance, he put forth his hand, and took him, and kissed him. And in this manner did Absalom to all Israel that came to the king for judgment: so Absalom stole the hearts of the men of Israel" (2 Sam. 15:2-6).

A few explanatory comments are required upon some of the terms in the above verses. First, the "way of the gate" was the place of judgment, that is, of judicial assize (see Gen. 19:1; 23:10,18; 34:20; Ruth 4:1). "Thy matters" in v. 3 signifies "thy suit or cause" as in v. 4. The obvious intention of Absalom in stationing himself at this important centre was to ingratiate himself with the people. His "thy matters are good and right" to all and sundry alike, showed his determination to win them regardless of the requirements of justice or the claims of mercy. His "there is no one deputed of the king to hear thee" was a dastardly attempt to create prejudice and lower the sovereign in their eyes. His "Oh that I were made judge in the land" revealed the lusting of his heart; neither pleasure nor pomp contented him — he must have *power* too. His embracing of the common people (v. 5) was a display of (pretended) humility and geniality.

"So Absalom stole the hearts of the men of Israel," upon which Thos. Scott well said, "He did not gain their hearts by eminent services, or by a wise and virtuous conduct. But he affected to look great, as heir to the crown, and yet to be very condescending and affable to his inferiors: he pretended a great regard to their interests, and threw out artful insinuations *against David's administration*; he flattered every one who had a cause to be tried, with the assurance that he had right on his side; that, if it went against him, he might be led to accuse David and the magistrates of injustice. Though Absalom knew not how to obey, and deserves to die for his atrocious crime, yet he expressed a vehement desire to be judge over all the land, and suggested that suits should not then be so tedious, expensive, and partially decided as they were. This he confirmed by rising early and by apparent application; though it was other people's business, and not his own duty: and by such sinister arts, united with his personal attractions and address, he imposed upon multitudes all over the land to prefer so worthless a character to the wise, righteous, and pious David."

Ere proceeding further let us pause and ask the question, What is there here for *our own souls?* This should ever be the principal concern of our minds as we read the Word of God. Its historical sections are full of important practical teaching: many valuable lessons may be learned therefrom if only we have hearts to receive them. Ah, *that* is the point on which so much turns. There must be a readiness and willingness on my part if I am to profit spiritually from what I peruse; and for that, there must be *humility*. Only a lowly heart will perceive that *I* am likely to be attracted by the same baits which led to the downfall of others; that *I* am liable to the same temptations they met with, and that unless I guard the particular gate at which the Enemy succeeded in gaining an entrance into *their* souls, he will just as surely prevail over *me*. O for grace to heed the solemn warnings which are found in every incident we ponder.

Now look again at what is recorded here. "Absalom stole the hearts of the men of Israel." Surely *that* is the sentence which should speak most loudly to us. It was not the open enemies of David that he wrought upon, but his subjects. It was not the Philistines whom he enlisted but the people of God whom he seduced. Absalom sought to sow the seeds of discontent in their minds, to alienate their affections from David, to render them disloyal to their king. Ah, is not the lesson plain? Is there not one who is ever seeking to seduce the subjects of Christ? tempting them to revolt from allegiance to His sceptre, endeavouring to allure them into *his* service. Learn, then, dear friend, to look beneath the surface as you read the Holy Scriptures, to see through the historical details to the underlying principles that are therein illustrated, to observe the motives which prompted to action; and then *apply the whole to yourself.*

What had *you* done had you been one of those "men of Israel" whose hearts Absalom was seeking to divorce from David? The answer to that question would have turned entirely on one thing: was your heart satisfied with David? Of this tempter we read, "But in all Israel there was none to be so much praised as Absalom for his beauty: from the sole of his foot even to the crown of his head there was no blemish in him" (2 Sam. 14:25), thus there was everything about his person to appeal to "the lust of the *flesh.*" And as we have seen, "Absalom prepared him chariots and horses, and fifty men to run before him," thus there was an appeal to "the lust of the *eyes.*" Moreover, he promised to further the temporal interests of all who had "a controversy," that is, of all who considered they had a grievance and were being hardly dealt with: thus there was an appeal to "*the pride of life*" (1 John 2:16). Were those things more than sufficient to counterbalance the excellencies which David possessed?

Again we say, *Look beneath* the historical characters and discern those whom they typified! When Satan comes to tempt the subjects of the antitypical David he assumes his most alluring character and dangles before us that which appeals either to the lust of the flesh, the lust of the eye, or the pride of life. But mark it well, dear reader, that Satan's baits *have no attraction* for those who are in communion with and finding their joy in the Lord. And he knows that full well, and therefore does he seek to stir up enmity against Him. He knows he cannot cause a regenerate soul to dislike the *person of* the Lord, so he endeavours to create dissatisfaction with *His government over us.* It was so in the type: "there is no man deputed of the king to hear thee." Ah, it is here we most need to be on our guard: to resist every effort of Satan's to bring us to murmur at the Lord's providences. But we must turn from the spiritual application back again to the historical.

And what of David during this time? He could hardly have been totally ignorant of the perfidy of his son: some tidings must have reached him of the treacherous plot now on foot to depose him. Yet there is no hint that he took any steps to thwart Absalom. How, then, shall we account for *his apathy?* At the close of our last article we dwelt upon the strange passiveness which characterised David during this stage of his checkered career, suggesting that the explanation proferred by Alex. Maclaren was a most likely one and apparently confirmed by the Scriptures, namely, that during this period the king suffered from a severe and protracted sickness. That helpful writer called attention to the fact that many of the best commentators regard the 41st and 55th Psalms as being composed by David at this time. Having already given his brief remarks upon the former, we will now reproduce those upon the latter; suggesting that Psa. 55 be read through at this point.

"The fifty-fifth psalm gives some very pathetic additional particulars. It is in three parts: a plaintive prayer and portraiture of the psalmist's mental distress (vv. 1-8); a vehement supplication against his foes, and indignant recounting of their treachery (vv. 9-16); and, finally a prophecy of the retribution that is to fall upon them (vv. 17-23). In the first and second portions we have some points which help to complete our picture of the man. For instance, his heart 'wriths' within him, the 'terrors of death' are on him, 'fear and trembling' are come to him and 'horror' has covered him. All this points, like subsequent verses, to his knowledge of the conspiracy before it came to a head.

"The state of the city, which is practically in the hands of Absalom and his tools, is described with bold imagery. Violence and strife in possession of it, spies prowling about the walls day and night, evil and trouble in its midst, and destruction, oppression, and deceit — a goodly company — flaunting in its open spaces. And the spirit, the brain of the whole, is the trusted friend whom he had made his own equal, who had shared his secretest thoughts in private, who had walked next him in solemn processions to the temple. Seeing all this, what does the king do, who was once so fertile in resource, so decisive in counsel, so prompt in action? Nothing. His only weapon is prayer: 'As for me, I will call upon God; and the Lord will save me. Evening and morning, and at noon, will I pray, and cry aloud; and He shall hear my voice.'

"He lets it all grow as it list, and only longs to be out of all the weary coil of troubles. 'O that I had wings like a dove, then would I fly away and be at rest. Lo, I would flee far off, I would lodge in the wilderness. I would swiftly fly to my refuge from the raging wind, from the tempest.' The langour of his disease, love for his worthless son, consciousness of sin, and submission to the chastisement through 'one of his own house,' which Nathan had foretold, kept him quiet, though he saw the plot winding its meshes round him. And in this submission patient confidence is not wanting, though subdued and saddened, which finds expression in the last words of this psalm of the heavy laden, 'Cast thy burden upon the Lord, and He shall sustain thee. . .I will trust in Thee.' "

Much of what Absalom said to those whose hearts he stole had, no doubt, a measure of truth in it. The disorders and sorrows of David's house had borne heavily on the king: his energy flagged, his health was broken, and the influence of his throne proportionately weakened. Absalom saw the defects of his father's government, and perceived that others saw them too, and quicly and meanly he took advantage of the situation, deprecating David and extolling himself. Yet David idolized Absalom, indeed, this was one of his chief failures, and bitterly was he now made to smart for cherishing such a viper in his bosom. He knew that Absalom was exalting himself. He knew that the calling of God was not with him, but with Solomon (2 Sam. 7:12; 12:25). He knew that Absalom was godless, that the flesh ruled him in all his ways; and yet knowing all this, he interfered not to restrain him.

"And it came to pass after forty years, that Absalom said unto the king, I pray thee, let me go and pay my vow, which I have vowed unto the Lord, in Hebron" (15:7). We are not sure from what point these forty years date, but certainly not from the time of David's coronation, for in such a case we would now have arrived at the closing year of his reign, which is obviously not the case — see 2 Sam. 21:1. Possibly it is to be dated from the time of his first annointing (1 Sam. 16:13). At any rate, that which is most germane to our present line of meditation is, Absalom considered that his wicked plot was ripe for execution, hence he now proceeded to put the finishing touches to it. Nothing less than the kingdom itself was what he determined to seize.

"For thy servant vowed a vow while I abode at Geshur in Syria, saying, If the Lord shall bring me again indeed to Jerusalem, then I will serve the Lord. And the king said unto him, Go in peace. So he arose, and went to Hebron" (vv. 8, 9). Absalom's duplicity and hypocrisy appear in all their hideousness. He cloaked his insurrection under the guise of offering sacrifice unto Jehovah (Deut. 23:21-23) in performance of a vow which he pretended to have made. He had no love for his parent and no fear for his God, for he dared now to mock His worship with a deliberate lie. He cunningly imposed upon his poor father's hopes that at last his wayward son was becoming pious. No doubt David had often prayed for him, and now he supposed that his supplications were beginning to be answered. How delighted he would be to hear that Absalom desired to "serve the Lord," and therefore he readily gave his consent for him to go to Hebron.

"But Absalom sent spies throughout all the tribes of Israel, saying, As soon as ye hear the sound of the trumpet, then ye shall say, Absalom reigneth in Hebron" (v. 10). Let this be a warning to parents not to assume too readily that their children have experienced the new birth, but wait to see *the fruits* of the same. Instead of journeying to Hebron in order to worship Jehovah, Absalom's purpose was to be acclaimed monarch over Israel. "Hebron" was not only the place where he was born (2 Sam. 3:2, 3) but it was also where David had commenced his reign (2 Sam. 5:1-3). These "spies" that he sent forth were either his own trusted "servants" (14:30) or those whose hearts he had stolen from David and on whom he could now rely to further his evil scheme. Those who would hear this proclamation "Absalom reigneth" might draw whatever conclusion they pleased — that David was dead, or that he had relinquished the reins of government, or that the Nation at large preferred his attractive son.

"And with Absalom went two hundred men out of Jerusalem, that were called, and they went in their simplicity, and they knew not any thing" (v. 11). No doubt these "two hundred men" were persons of rank and prominence, being summoned to accompany the king's son to a sacred feast. Absalom's object was to awe the common people and give them the impression that David's cause was now being deserted at headquarters. Thus these men unwittingly contenanced Absalom's evil devices, for their presence signified that they supported his treason. This is a fair sample of the methods employed by unprincipled politicians to further their selfish ends, getting many to join their ranks or party under a complete misconception of the leader's real policy.

"And Absalom sent for Ahithophel, the Gilonite, David's counsellor, from his city, even from Giloh, while he offered sacrifices. And the conspiracy was strong, for the people increased continually with Absalom" (v. 12). The man whose aid Absalom now sought was a renowned statesman, apparently no longer on friendly terms with David. He was a fit tool for the insurrectionist, though in the end God turned his counsel into foolishness. The sovereignty which God displays in His providences is as patent as it is awe-inspiring. As He graciously raises up those to befriend His people in the hour of their need, so He has appointed those who are ready to help the wicked in the furthering of their evil plans. As there was an Ittai loyal to David, so there was an Ahithophel to counsel Absalom.

And there came a messenger to David saying, The hearts of the men of Israel are after Absalom. And David said to all his servants who were with him at Jerusalem, Arise, and let us flee! For otherwise we shall not escape from

Absalom. Hurry and leave so that he may not overtake us suddenly and bring evil on us and strike the city with the edge of the sword. And the king's servants said to the king, Behold, your servants will do whatever my lord the king shall choose. And the king went forth and all his household after him. And the king left ten women who were concubines to keep the house. — II Samuel 15:13-16.

There are few incidents in the checkered life of David more pathetic than the one which is now to engage our attention, illustrating as it also does the providential ups and downs and the alternating spiritual prosperity and adversity which is the lot of God's people on this earth. All is not unclouded sunshine with them, nor is it unrelieved gloom and storm. There is a mingling of both; joys and sorrows, victories and defeats, assistance from friends and injuries from foes, smiles from the Lord's countenance and the hidings of His face. By such changes opportunities are afforded for the development and exercise of *different* graces, so that we may, in our measure, "know how to be abased and how to abound. . . .both to be full and to be empty" (Phil. 4:12); and above all, that we may, amid varying circumstances, prove the unchanging faithfulness of God and His sufficiency to supply our every need.

David was called to leave the lowly plains of Bethlehem to participate in the honours of Saul's palace. From tending the flock he became the conqueror of Goliath and the popular hero of Israel. But soon Saul's friendship was changed to enmity, and David had to flee for his life, and for many weary months he was hunted as a partridge on the mountains. Subsequently his fortunes were again greatly altered, and from being an outcast he was crowned king of Israel. Then he was enabled to capture Jerusalem, the stronghold of Zion, which became "the city of David" (2 Sam. 5:7). There he established his court and thither he "brought up the ark of the Lord with shouting and with the voice of the trumpet" (2 Sam. 6:15). But now we are to behold him fleeing from Jerusalem and being separated from the holy ark: a fugitive once more, in humiliation and deep anguish.

Ah, my reader, if you be one of God's elect, expect not a smooth and easy path down here, but be prepared for varying circumstances and drastic changes. The Christian's restingplace is not in this world, for "here have we no continuing city" (Heb. 13:14). The Christian is a "pilgrim," on a journey; he is a "soldier," called on to fight the good fight of faith. The more this be realized, the less keen will be the disappointment when our ease is disturbed and our outward peace rudely broken in upon. "Many are the afflictions of the righteous," and if they come not to us in one form, they most certainly will in another. If we really "appropriate" *this* promise (!) then we shall not be so staggered when those afflictions come upon us. It is written that "we must through *much* tribulation enter into the kingdom of God" (Acts 14:22), and therefore we should make up our minds *to expect* the same, and to "think it not strange" (1 Pet. 4:12) when we are called upon to pass through "the fiery trial."

Affliction, tribulation, and fiery trial were now David's portion. "And there came a messenger to David, saying, The hearts of the men of Israel are after Absalom" (2 Sam. 15:13). Visualize the sad scene: the dark clouds of a threatened revolt had been steadily gathering, and now the storm bursts on the king's head. By this time David was some sixty years of age, with health and strength greatly impaired. Ahithophel, his trusted counseller, had deserted him, and Absalom his favourite son was now risen in rebellion against him. Not only his throne, but his very life was in danger, together with the lives of his wives and their little ones — Solomon was scarcely ten years old at this time. What, then, does the king do? Nothing! There was no calling of a counsel, no effort made to provision Jerusalem for the withstanding of a siege, no determination to stand his rightful ground and resist his lawless son.

"And David said, unto all his servants that were with him at Jerusalem, Arise, and let us flee; for we shall not else escape from Absalom: make speed to depart, lest he overtake us suddenly; and bring evil upon us, and smite the city with the edge of the sword" (v. 14). Now that at last the blow falls, David passively acquiesces in what he evidently felt to be God's righteous chastisement upon him. When the awful news arrives that Absalom had set up the standard of revolt at Hebron, David's only thought was immediate flight. The intrepid warrior was now almost cowardly in his eagerness to escape, and was prepared to give up everything without a blow. It seemed as though only a touch was needed to overthrow his throne. He hurries on the preparations for flight with nervous haste. He forms no plans beyond those of his earlier wish to fly away and be at rest.

That David had good reason to conclude the situation which now confronted him was a *just retribution* upon his own crimes is quite evident. First, the Lord had declared "I will raise up evil against thee out of thine own house" (2 Sam. 12:11), fulfilled here in the insurrection of his favourite son. Other evidences thereof will come before us later, but at this point we will consider, second, Ahithophel's joining hands with the rebel. No sooner had Absalom determined to execute his daring plan than he looked to Ahithophel. He appears, for some reason not specifically mentioned, to have confidently counted upon his cooperation; nor was he disappointed. "And Absalom sent for Ahithophel the Gilonite, David's counsellor, from his city, even from Giloh" (15:12). It is to be carefully noted that immediately after Ahithophel's coming to Absalom, we are informed, "And the conspiracy was strong, for the people *increased* continually with Absalom" (v. 12) -- intimating that Ahithophel was a host in himself.

"And the counsel of Ahithophel, which he counselled in those days, was as if a man had inquired at the oracle of God: so was all the counsel of Ahithophel both with David and with Absalom" (16:23): in view of this statement we need not be surprised that his joining heart and hand with Absalom so greatly strengthened his cause. There is no doubt that *he* was the chief instrument in this conspiracy, and the prime reason why so many in Israel turned from the king to his traitorous son. His official status and the great influence which he possessed over the people made Absalom glad to avail himself of his help, both to sink the spirits of David's party and to inspire his own with confidence, for Ahithophel was commonly regarded as a prophet. But *what was it* that made Ahithophel to respond so readily to Absalom's invitation, and cause him to find still greater favour in the eyes of the people, as one who had been grievously wronged and deserved to be avenged of his adversity?

To answer this question the Scriptures must be searched and passage carefully compared with passage. In the second half of 2 Sam. 23 the names are given of the thirty-seven men who formed the special body "guard" (v. 23) of David. Among them we find "Eliam the son of Ahithophel *the Gilonite*" (v. 34) and "Uriah the Hittite" (v. 39). Thus Eliam and Uriah were fellow-officers and would be much thrown together. Hence, we need not be surprised to learn that Uriah married the daughter of Eliam (see 2 Sam. 11:3). Thus Bathsheba, whom David so grievously wronged, was *the grand-daughter of Ahithophel*; and Uriah, whom he so cruelly murdered, was his grandson by marriage! Does not *this* fact explain why David's "familiar friend" (Psa. 41:9) became his deadly foe, and account for his readiness to aid Absalom -- thus seeking to avenge the dishonour brought upon his house.

Some years had passed since this dishonour had come upon the family of Ahithophel, and during that interval it appears that he had turned his back upon David and the court, and had quietly retired to his birthplace (15:12). Brooding over the grievous wrongs which David had done to his family, the spirit of revenge would rankle in his heart. It seems that Absalom was well aware of this, and perceived that Ahithophel was only waiting for a suitable opportunity to give vent to his feelings and execute his meditated wrath upon the head of David. Does not this explain why Absalom approached him *with confidence,* made known to him his treason, and counted on him welcoming the news and becoming his fellow-worker? Does not this also account for so many of the people transferring their allegiance from a throne which they knew to be defiled with adultery and murder to the rebellious son?

Not only does Ahithophel's blood-relationship to Bathsheba explain his readiness to take sides with Absalom against the king, and account for the common people's transference of loyalty, but it also supplies the key to David's own attitude and conduct at this time. It was additional evidence to him that *God* was now dealing with him for his sins — other proofs of this will come before us later, but we must not anticipate. And most blessed is it to observe him bowing so meekly to the Divine rod. David felt that to withstand Absalom would be to resist the Lord Himslef; therefore, instead of strengthening his forces in Jerusalem and maintaining his ground he flees. We cannot but admire the lovely fruit brought forth by the Spirit at this time in David's heart, for *to Him,* and not to mere nature, must be attributed that which is here presented to our view.

Long before this we had occasion to admire the beautiful spirit evidenced by David when suffering *for righteousness,* now we behold it again when he was suffering *for transgressions.* Then we saw him as *the martyr* in the days of Saul, bringing forth the fruits of meekness, patience, and confidence in God, willing to be hounded by Saul day after day, and refusing to take vengeance into his own hands and smite the Lord's anointed. But here we see David as *the penitent:* His sin has found him out, brought into remembrance before God, and he submissively bows his head and accepts the consequences of his wrongdoing. This is very beautiful, manifesting again the workmanship of the Spirit of God in David. He alone can quiet the turbulent heart, subdue the rebellious will, and mortify that innate desire to take matters into our own hands; as He alone can bring us to humble ourselves beneath the mighty hand of God, and hold our peace when He visits our iniquity "with stripes" (Psa. 89:32).

Yes, it is, as we said in our opening paragraph, *changing circumstances* that afford opportunity for the development and exercise of *different* graces. Some graces are of the active and aggressive kind, while others are of a passive order, requiring quite another setting for their display: some of the traits which mark the soldier on a battlefield, would be altogether out of place were he languishing on a bed of sickness. Spiritual joy and godly sorrow is equally beautiful in its season. It would be most incongruous to mourn while the Bridegroom was present, but it is fitting for the children of the Bridechamber to fast when He is absent. As there are certain vegetables, fruits, and flowers which cannot be grown in lands which are unvisited by nipping winds and biting frosts, so there are some fruits of the Spirit which are only produced in the soil of severe trials, troubles, and tribulations.

"And the king's servants said unto the king, Behold, thy servants are ready to do whatsoever my lord the king shall appoint" (v. 15). What we have just said above is equally pertinent to this verse: the sad situation confronting David revealed plainly the state of heart of those in his immediate employ. The revolt of Absalom and his stealing the hearts of so many of the people, afforded an opportunity for these servants of David to manifest *their* unswerving loyalty and deep devotion to their master. Very blessed is this, supplying as it does the sequel to what was before us in v. 6. There we saw that Absalom was a man well calculated to captivate the multitude. But let it be duly noted that he possessed no attractions for those who were nearest to David. That illustrates an important principle: while we maintain communion with Christ, the antitypical David, the baits of Satan will have no influence over us!

Let us observe too that changing circumstances are necessary in order to test the loyalty of those who are on intimate terms with us. Not only did this revolt of Absalom's provide an occasion for the manifestation of David's subjection to the will of God, but it also served to make unmistakably evident who were for and who were against him. Prosperity is often a mixed blessing, and adversity is far from being an unmixed calamity. When the sunshine of providence smiles upon a person, he is soon surrounded by those who profess great attachment to him; but when the dark clouds of providence cover his horizon, most of those fawning flatterers will quickly take their departure. Ah, my reader, it is worth something to discover who really *are* our friends, and therefore we should not murmur if it takes the shaking of our nest and the disrupting of our peace to make this plainly evident to us. Adversities are a gain when they expose to us the hypocrisy of an Ahithophel, and still more so when they prove the loyalty and love of the few who stand by us in the storm.

"And the king went forth, and all his household after him. And the king left ten women, which were concubines, to keep the house" (v. 16). The writer feels his heart awed as he reads the second half of this verse — a very prosaic statement, yet one possessing depths which no human mind can fathom. Apparently David acted quite freely when he made this simple domestic arrangement, yet really he could do no otherwise, for he was being *directed* by the unerring and invincible hand of God, unto the outworking of His own counsels. *David's* object in leaving behind the ten concubines was "to keep the house," that is, to maintain the palace in some order and cleanliness; but *God's* design was to make good His own word.

A part of the punishment which the Lord had announced should fall upon David for his evildoing was, "*I* will take thy wives before thine eyes, and give them unto thy neighbour, and he shall be with thy wives in the sight of this sun. For thou didst it secretly: but I will do this thing before all Israel" (2 Sam. 12:11, 12). The execution of that threat is recorded in, "So they spread Absalom a tent upon the top of the house and Absalom went in unto his father's concubines in the sight of all Israel" (16:22). The connecting link between the two is seen here in our present passage: "And the king left ten women which were concubines, to keep the house" (v. 16). Again, we say, David's object in leaving them behind was that they should "keep the house," but *God's* purpose was that they should be publicly insulted, raped by Absalom. Unspeakably solemn is this fact: *God directs* those actions which eventuate in evil as truly as He does those which terminate in good, Not only all events, but all persons, and their every action, are under the immediate control of the Most High.

"For of Him, and through Him, and to Him, are *all* things; to whom be glory forever." (Rom 11:36). Yet this neither makes God the "Author of sin" nor man an irresponsible creature: God is holy in all His ways, and man is accountable for all his actions. Whether or not we perceive the "consistency" of them, each of these basic truths must be held fast by us; nor must one be so maintained that the other is virtually negatived. Some will argue, If God has foreordained our every action, then we are no better than machines; others insist, If man is a free agent, his actions cannot be directed by God. But Holy Writ exposes the vanity of such reasonings: so far as David knew it was a voluntary act on his part when he decided to leave ten of his concubines in the house, nevertheless he was Divinely "constrained" in it for the accomplishment of God's purpose.

"And the king went forth, and all the people after him, and tarried in a place that was far off. And all his servants passed on beside him; and all the Cherethites, and all the Pelethites, and all the Gittites, six hundred men which came after him from Gath, passed on before the king" (vv. 17, 18). No, "fair weather friends" were these. They had enjoyed with him the calm, they would not desert him in the storm; they had shared the privileges of Jerusalem, they would not abandon him now that he had become a fugitive and outcast. It is striking to note that while Absalom "stole the hearts of the men of Israel," *all* the Cherethites, Pelethites, and Gittites remained steadfast to David — a foreshadowment of Christ, for whereas the Jewish nation despised and rejected Him, yet God's elect among the Gentiles have not been ashamed to be His followers.

And the king went forth, and all the people after him, and stayed in a place that was far off. And all his servants passed on beside him. And all the Cherethites, and all the Pelethites, and all the Gittites, six hundred men who came after him from Gath, passed on before the king. Then the king said to Ittai the Gittite, Why do you also go with us? Return to your place, and stay with the king. For you are a stranger and also an exile. Since you came only yesterday, should I make you go up and down with us today? Since I go where I may, you may return and take back your brothers. May mercy and truth be with you. And Ittai answered the king and said, As the LORD lives, and as my lord the king lives, surely in whatever place my lord the king shall be, whether in death or life, even there also will your servant be. And David said to Ittai, Go and pass over. And Ittai the Gittite passed over, and all his men, and all the little ones that were with him. And all the country wept with a loud voice, and all the people passed over. The king himself also passed over the brook Kidron, and all the people passed over, toward the way of the wilderness. And lo, Zadok came also, and all the Levites were with him, carrying the ark of the covenant of God. And they set down the ark of God. And Abiathar went up until all the people had finished passing out of the city. And the king said to Zadok, Carry the ark of God back into the city, If I shall find favor in the eyes of the LORD, He will bring me again and show it to me, and its dwelling place also. But if He says this, I have no delight in you — behold me, and let Him do to me as seems good to Him. — II Samuel 15:17-26.

The second half of 2 Sam. 15 displays a striking blending of lights and shadows: in David's darkest hour we not only see the shining forth of some of his own loveliest virtues, but we also behold his friends and followers at their best. It is the way of our gracious God to temper our severest crosses by mingling comforts with them. David's favourite son and his chief counsellor had both turned traitors against him, but the loyalty of part of his army, the faithfulness of the Levites, the sympathy expressed by those of the common people who witnessed his distress, afforded some real consolation to his stricken heart. In times of deep distress and seasons of sore despondency we are very apt to imagine that our enemies are more numerous than is actually the case, and that we have fewer friends than is really so; but David was now to discover that a goodly number were prepared to cleave to him at all costs.

It is not so much from the natural (though even here there is much that is praiseworthy) as the spiritual viewpoint that our passage needs to be pondered. The key to it lies in the state of David's heart at this time. He is to be viewed as *the penitent soul*, as one who realised that in justice he was being afflicted. He knew that his sin had found him out, that he was being lovingly yet righteously chastised for the same. He was filled with godly sorrow and mourned before Him whose Name had been so dishonoured by him. He humbly bows to God's rod and submissively receives its stroke. In this spirit he would be *alone* in his trouble, for he alone had sinned and provoked Jehovah: therefore does he counsel the Gittites to leave him. In the same lowly spirit he sends the ark — they symbol of Jehovah's manifested presence — back to Jerusalem: it was his chief joy, and *that* he felt he was not now entitled to taste.

But we will not generalize any further upon our passage, but consider its details. "Then said the king to Ittai the Gittite. Wherefore goest thou also with us? return to thy place, and abide with the king (Absalom, who now usurped the throne): for thou art a stranger, and also an exile. Whereas thou camest but yesterday, should I this day make thee go up and down with us? seeing I go hither I may, return thou, and take back thy brethren: mercy and truth be with thee" (2 Sam. 15:19, 20). What a lovely spirit did the king here evidence: in the midst of his own deep trouble, his thought and concern was for those about him, desiring them to escape the hardships and peril which now lay before him. What a gracious example for us to heed in this selfish age — that even in our sorest trials we must not impose upon those who are kind to us and load them with our troubles. "For every man shall bear his own burden" (Gal. 6:5).

It would appear that Ittai was the leader of the six hundred Gittites (v. 18). They had thrown in their lot with David while he sojourned in Gath of the Philistines, and followed him when he returned to the land of Israel: either because they believed that Philistia was doomed or, more likely, because they were attracted by David himself. They were now among the king's most faithful attendants, having accompanied him as he fled from the royal city. They would be a most useful body guard for him at this time, but in his noble generosity and tender compassion David desired to spare them the inconveniences and dangers which were now his portion. How this makes us think of David's Son and Lord, who, probably, at this identical place, said to those who had come to arrest Him, "If therefore ye seek Me, let these go their way" (John 18:8). The *Antitype* should ever be in mind as we read the O.T. Scriptures.

"And Ittai answered the king, and said, As the Lord liveth, and my lord the king liveth, surely in what place my lord the king shall be, whether in life or death, even there also will thy servant be" (v. 21). David desired to dismiss them, but their attachment to him and his cause was much stronger than that of many of the Israelites. Most blessed and striking is this, for David had nothing to offer them now save fellowship with him in his rejection and sufferings; yet they valued his companionship so highly that they refused to leave their stricken leader. Spiritually, that love of the brethren which is the fruit of the Spirit of Christ, when it is healthy and vigorous, will not be deterred through fears of hardship or danger, but will stand by and render assistance to those in affliction. Antitypically, this verse teaches us that we should cleave faithfully to Christ no matter how low His cause in the world may be.

"And David said to Ittai, Go and pass over. And Ittai the Gittite passed over, and all his men, and all the little ones that were with him" (v. 22). Such devotion as had been displayed by these loyal followers must have touched the king's heart, the more so as it proceeded from those who were of a heathen stock. From Ittai's words "as the Lord liveth" (v. 21), it would seem that they were influenced by David's religion as well as his person; and assuredly he would *not* have kept them so near him, or have said "mercy and truth be with thee" (v. 20), unless they had definitely renounced all idolatry. There is a seeming ambiguity in his words here "go and pass over," yet this disappears in the light of the next verse: it was the Kidron they crossed — thus they were given the place of chief honour, taking the lead and heading David's present company!

"And all the country wept with a loud voice, and all the people passed over" (v. 23). Though the multitude favoured Absalom, yet there were many who sympathised with David. It must indeed have been a hard heart which remained unmoved by such an affecting sight: the aged king forsaking his palace — with but a small retinue — fleeing from his own son — now seeking shelter in the wilderness! They had been less than human if they grieved not for poor David. And let it be duly noted that the Spirit has *recorded* their weeping, for God is not unmindful of genuine tears, either of personal repentance or pity for others. This mention of their weeping plainly teaches that *we* should feel deeply for those parents who are abused or ruined by their children.

"The king also himself passed over the brook Kidron, and all the people passed over, toward the way of the wilderness" (v. 23). This manifestly foreshadowed one of the most bitter episodes in our Lord's passion. Not only is this same brook mentioned in John 18:1 — the slight different in spelling being due to the change from the Hebrew to Greek — but there are too many points of analogy between David's and Christ's crossing of it to miss the merging of the type into the antitype. But before tracing these striking resemblances, let us — as its solemn historical interest requires — make a few remarks upon the brook itself.

Significantly enough "Kidron," or to use the more familiar spelling of John 18:1 "Cedron," signifies "black." It was aptly named, for it was a dark rivulet which ran through the gloomy valley of Moriah, which Josephus tells us was on the east side of Jerusalem. It lay between the bases of the temple hill and the mount of Olivet. Into this brook was continually emptied the sewage of the city, as well as the filth from the temple sacrifices for sin. This was the "unclean place without the city" (Lev. 14:40, 45), where the excrements of the offerings were deposited and carried away by the waters of this brook. In a figure it was the sins and iniquities of the people which were being washed away from before God's face — from the temple, where He dwelt in Israel's midst.

It is interesting to note there are other references to "Kidron" in the O.T., and what is recorded in connection therewith is in striking and solemn harmony with what we have just pointed out above. This brook not only (later) received the filth of the city and the refuse from the temple, but into its foul waters the godly kings of Judah cast the ashes of the idols they had destroyed: see 2 Chron. 15:16; 30:14; 2 Kings 23:4, 6. Over this unclean brook our blessed Saviour passed on His dolorous way to Gethsemane, where His holy soul loathed our iniquities put into His "cup," represented by this filthy and nasty Cedron. That foul brook served as a suitable reminder of the deep mire (Psa. 69:2) into which Christ was about to sink. Nothing could be more repulsive and nauseating than the soil and waters of this brook, and nothing could be more loathsome to the Holy One than to be encompassed with all the guilt and filth of sin belonging to His people.

But let us now consider the points of resemblance between the type and antitype. First, it was at this brook the humiliating flight of David began, and the crossing of the same marked the commencement of the Saviour's "Passion" (Acts 1:3). Second, it was as the despised and rejected king that David now went forth, and so it was with the Redeemer as He journeyed to Gethsemane. Third, yet David was not entirely alone: a little company of devoted followers, still clung to him; thus it was with the Antitype. Fourth, Ahithophel, his familiar friend, had now joined forces with his enemies: in like manner, Judas had gone forth to betray Christ to His foes. Fifth, though the multitude favoured Absalom, some of the common people sympathized with and "wept" for David; so, while the general cry against the Lord Jesus was "crucify Him," nevertheless, there were those who wept and bewailed Him (Luke 23:27).

"And lo Zadok also, and all the Levites were with him, bearing the ark of the covenant of God: and they set down the ark of God; and Abiathar went up, until all the people had done passing out of the city" (v. 24). This spoke well for David, that even the Levites, and the high priest himself, were prepared to throw in their lot with him in the day of his rejection. Notwithstanding his sad failures, the ministers of the tabernacle knew full well the affection which the sweet Psalmist of Israel had for them and their office. The policy which Absalom had followed in order to curry favour with the people had not appealed at all to these servants of the Lord, and therefore they steadfastly adhered to the king, in spite of the drastic change in his fortunes. Alas, how often has it been otherwise, when the religious leaders turned traitors at the time the ruling monarch most needed their support and ministrations.

Ministers of God should always set an example of submission and loyalty to "the powers that be" (Rom. 13:1), and more especially should they openly manifest their fealty unto those rulers who have countenanced and protected them in their pious labours, when those rulers are opposed by rebellious subjects. "Fear God: honour the king" (1 Pet. 2:17) are joined together in Holy Writ, and if the ecclesiastical leaders fail to render obedience to this Divine precept, how can we expect that those who are under their charge will do better? "They that are friends to the ark in their prosperity, shall find it a friend to them in their adversity. Formerly, David would not rest till he had found a restingplace for the ark (Psa. 132); and now, if the priests may have their mind, the ark shall not rest till David returns to his restingplace" (Matt. Henry).

"And the king said unto Zadok, Carry back the ark of God into the city: if I shall find favour in the eyes of the Lord, he will bring me again, and show me both it and His habitations" (v. 25). This too is very impressive, bringing out as it does the better side of David's character. The presence of the Levites, and particularly of the ark, would have considerably strengthened the king's cause. That ark had figured prominently in Israel's history, and the very sight of it would hardly have failed to stir the hearts of the people. Moreover, it was the recognised symbol of God's presence, esteemed by David more highly than anything else. But the king, like Eli of old, was very solicitous for the welfare of the sacred coffer, and therefore he refused to expose it to the possible insults of Absalom and his faction. He "preferred Jerusalem — the honour of the Lord — above his chief joy" (Psa. 137:6). Furthermore, David knew that he was under the Divine rebuke, and so felt himself to be unworthy for the ark to accompany him, and therefore while he was being chastised for his sins, he refused to pretend that God was on his side.

"If I shall find favour in the eyes of the Lord, He will bring me again, and show me both it and His habitation." Clearly, David recognised that everything hinged upon *the unmerited "favour"* of the Lord. This is a point of considerable importance, for our modern dispensationalists suppose that Israel was under such a stern regime of Law that the grace of God was virtually unknown, yea, that, He did *not* exercise it till Christ appeared — a view based on an entirely erroneous interpretation of John 1:17. This is a great mistake, for the O.T. Scriptures make it unmistakeably clear that God's free grace is the foundation of all blessing: see Num. 14:8; Deut. 10:15; 1 Kings 10:9; 2 Chron. 9:8; Acts 7:46. It is very blessed to observe David's "If I shall find favour in the eyes of the Lord, He will bring me back again and show me not 'my place,' but — both it and *His* habitation:" he valued the humble tabernacle far more highly than his own throne and honour!

"But if He thus say, I have no delight in thee: behold, here am I, let Him do to me as seemeth good unto Him" (v. 26). Precious submission was this. The Lord was rebuking him for his sins, and he knew not what would be the outcome. He humbled himself beneath the mighty hand of God, and left the issue to His sovereign pleasure. He hoped for the best, but was prepared for the worst. He realised that he deserved to suffer the continued displeasure of the Holy One, and therefore did he commit the outcome of his cause unto God's sovereign grace. Mark it carefully, dear reader, that David saw *God's* disciplinary hand in this dark hour of Absalom's revolt, and *that* preserved him, in measure at least, both from rebellion against Heaven and the fear of man. The more *we* discern the controlling hand of the Most High in all events, the better for our peace of mind.

There is much important and precious instruction for our hearts in this incident. It is a true act *of faith* when we yield ourselves to that sovereign pleasure of God wherein He is "gracious to whom He will be gracious, and will show mercy on whom He will show mercy" (Ex. 33:19); yes, just as truly so as when we appropriate one of God's promises and plead it before Him. We conceive it was thus that David's faith now directed him in the sore strait that he was then in. He knew not how grievously the Lord was provoked against him, nor how things were now likely to go; so he bowed before His throne and left *Him* to determine the case. Many a sorely-stricken soul has obtained relief here when all other spring of comfort have completely failed him, saying with Job "Though He slay me, yet will I trust in Him (13:15).

A sin-entangled soul with guilt burdening his conscience, sees that, in himself, he is unquestionably lost: how the Lord will deal with him he knows not. His signs and tokens are completely eclipsed: he can discern no evidence of God's grace in him, nor of His favour unto him. What is a guilt-bowed soul to do when he is at such a stand? To definitely turn his back upon God would be madness, for "Who hath hardened himself against God and hath prospered?" (Job. 9:4). Nor is there the slightest relief to be obtained for the heart except from and by *Him*, for "who can forgive sins, but God only?" The only recourse, then, is to do as David did: bring our guilty soul into God's presence, wait upon the sovereign pleasure of His grace, and gladly acquiesce in His decision.

"*If* I shall find favour in the eyes of the Lord, He will bring me again, and show me both it and His habitation. But *if* He thus say, I have no delight in thee; behold, here am I, let Him do to me as seemeth good unto Him." Here is an anchor for a storm-tossed soul: though it may not (at once) give rest and peace, yet it secures from the rock of abject despair. To solace the heart with a "who can tell *if* God will turn and repent, and turn away from His fierce anger, that we perish not?" (Jonah 3:9), or a "Who can tell *whether* God will be gracious to me?" (2 Sam. 12:22), is far better than giving way to a spirit of hopelessness. "Who knoweth if He will return and repent, and leave a blessing behind Him"

(Joel 2:14): there the soul must abide until more light from above break forth upon it.

The king also said to Zadok the priest, Are you a seer? Then return to the city in peace, and your two sons with you, Ahimaaz your son, and Jonathan the son of Abiathar. See! I will wait in the plain of the wilderness until word comes from you to tell me. Then Zadok and Abiathar carried the ark of God again to Jerusalem. And they remained there. And David went up by the ascent of Mount Olivet. And he wept as he went up, and had his head covered, and he went barefoot. And of all the people who were with him, each man covered his head. And they went up, weeping as they went. And one told David, saying, Ahithophel is among the conspirators with Absalom. And David said, O LORD, I beseech You, turn the advice of Ahithophel to foolishness. And when David had come to the top, where he worshiped God, behold, Hushai the Archite came to meet him with his coat torn and earth on his head. David said to him, If you pass on with me, then you shall be a burden to me. But if you return to the city and say to Absalom, I will be your servant, O king — I have been your father's servant until now, and now I also will be your servant — then you may defeat the advice of Ahithophel for me. Do you not have there with you Zadok and Abiathar the priests? Then whatever you shall hear out of the king's house, you shall tell it to Zadok and Abiathar the priests. Behold, they have their two sons there with them, Ahimaaz, Zadok's sons, and Jonathan, Abiathar's son. And you shall send to me everything that you hear by them. So David's friend Hushai came to the city. And Absalom came into Jerusalem. — II Samuel 15:27-37.

We resume at the point left off in our last. "The king said also unto Zadok the priest, Art not thou a seer? return into the city in peace, and your two sons with you, Ahimaaz thy son, and Jonathan the son of Abiathar. See, I will tarry in the plain of the wilderness, until there come word from you to certify me" (vv. 27, 28). Though they could not be permitted to minister unto him in holy things, he does not disdain their services; they could further his interests by returning to their post of duty, and from there acquaint him with developments in Jerusalem. What implicit confidence in them was evidenced by this experienced strategist, in revealing to them his immediate plans — the place where he intended to remain for the time being! O that God's servants to-day so conducted themselves that those in trouble would not hesitate to confide in them and seek their counsel. "Zadok therefore and Abiathar carried the ark of God again to Jerusalem: and they tarried there" (v. 29). Blessed obedience: sinking their own wishes, complying with the will of their master.

"And David went up by the ascent of mount Olivet, and wept as he went up, and had his head covered, and he went barefoot" (v. 39). Let not the reader forget what was said in the opening paragraphs of the preceding sections, where we pointed out that the real key to the whole of this passage is to be found in the state of David's heart. Throughout he is to be viewed as *the humble penitent*. God's rebuke was heavy upon him, and therefore did he humble himself beneath His mighty hand. Hence it is that we here see him giving outward expression to his self-abasement and grief for his sins, and for the miseries which he had brought upon himself, his family, and his people. Suitable tokens of his godly sorrow were these, for the covering of his head was a symbol of self-condemnation, while his walking barefooted betokened his mourning: cf. Isa. 20:2, 4; Ezek. 24:17.

"And David went up by the ascent of mount Olivet, and wept as he went up."

How striking is this, coming right after his crossing of the brook Kidron! In the previous article we pointed out five respects in which that foreshadowed our Lord's crossing that same brook on the night of His betrayal. Who can fail to see here another unmistakeable analogy? After His crossing of that doleful brook, our Saviour entered Gethsemane, where His soul was "exceeding sorrowful" and where His supplications were accompanied with "strong crying *and tears*" (Heb. 5:7). Yet while observing the comparison, let us not forget the radical contrast: his own sins were the cause of David's grief, but the sins of His people occasioned Christ's tears.

"And all the people that were with him covered every man his head, and they went up, weeping as they went up" (v. 30). It is our duty to weep with those that weep, and those that were with him were deeply affected by their king's grief. Once again our minds revert to our Saviour's passion, and discover another resemblance between it and David's case here, though it has been strangely overlooked by many. The disciples who accompanied Christ into the Garden failed, it is true, to "watch with Him" for one hour, yet it most certainly was not through indifference, nor because they sought fleshly ease in slumber, for as the Holy Spirit expressly informs us, Christ "found them sleeping *for sorrow*" (Luke 22:45). Thus the weeping people who followed David up Olivet found its counterpart in the sorrowing of those disciples who had accompanied the Saviour unto Gethsemane.

"And one told David, saying, Ahithophel is among the conspirators with Absalom" (v. 31). With the exception of his own son's insurrection, this was the bitterest ingredient in the cup which David was now having to drink. It was no ordinary blow for him to bear, for Ahithophel was no ordinary man. He was one whom the king had taken into his confidence, numbered among his closest friends, and to whom he had shown much kindness. He not only enjoyed the most intimate relations with David concerning the affairs of state, but had close fellowship with him in spiritual things. This is evident from the Psalmist's own statement "We took sweet counsel together, and walked unto the house of God in company" (55:14). Fickle and treacherous is human nature. Our sharpest trials often come from those in whom we have reposed the most trust and to whom we have shown the greatest kindness; yet, on the other hand, the most unlikely friends are sometimes raised up among those from whom we had the least expectations — as the Gittites attached to David: v. 21.

"And one told David, saying, Ahithophel is among the conspirators with Absalom." Troubles rarely come singly: often they crowd one on top of another, as was the case with Job. This sad news was brought to the king just when he was being the most severely tired. Absalom had revolted, and now his 'prime minister' turned traitor at the most crucial moment. It was a vile requital for the king's generosity to him. Here again we may perceive these historical incidents shadowing forth events even more solemn and frightful in connection with our blessed Lord, for Ahithophel is undoubtedly a striking type of Judas, who, after being admitted to the inner circle of Christ's disciples, basely turned against Him and went over to the side of His enemies. Sufficient, then, for the disciple to be as his Master: if *His* charity was rewarded with cruel treachery, let *us* be prepared for similar treatment.

How keenly David felt the perfidy of Ahithophel is evident from several statements in the Psalms which obviously refer to him. In the 41st he mentions one evil after another which afflicted him, and finishes with "Yea, mine own familiar friend, in whom I trusted, which did eat of my bread, hath lifted up his heel against me" (v. 9) — that was the climax: anything worse could scarcely be imagined, as the opening "Yea," suggests. Ahithophel had not only forsaken David in his hour of need, but had gone over to the side of his foe. The "lifted up his heel against me" is the figure of a horse which has just been fed by its master, and then lashing out with his feet, viciously kicks him. More plainly still is his anguish evidenced in "for it was not an enemy that reproached me: then I could have borne it; neither was it he that hated me that did magnify himself against me: then I would have hid myself from him. But it was thou, a man mine equal, my guide, and mine acquaintance" (55:12, 13).

There is still another reference in the Psalms where David laments, "For my love they are my adversaries; but I give myself unto prayer. And they have rewarded me evil for good, and hatred for my love" (109:4, 5). This sad trial of David's was illustrative of what is often the most painful experience of the Church, for her troubles usually begin at home: her open enemies can do her little or no harm until her pretended friends have delivered her into their hands. The statement that David "gave himself to prayer" at once links up with our passage. David's crossing of the Kidron (v. 23), his complete surrender of himself to the will of God (v. 26), his tears (v. 30), and now his *praying*, present one of the most remarkable prefigurations of our Lord's sufferings to be found anywhere in the O.T. In asking the Lord to defeat the counsel of Ahithophel, David recognised and acknowledged that all hearts are in His hands, that He can "make the judges fools" (Job 12:17). There was no suitable opportunity for David to engage in a *lengthy* season of prayer, nor was that necessary, for we are not heard for our much speaking. Apparently, a brief ejaculation was all that now issued from his heart; but it was heard on High!

What a blessed and encouraging example David has here left us! Prayer should ever be the believer's resource, for there is never a time when it is unseasonable. We too may pray for God to bring to nought the crafty counsel of the wicked against His people. We too may come to Him when all appears to be lost, and spread our case before Him. The effectual fervent prayer of a righteous man availeth much, for vain is all worldly wisdom and power against it. So it proved here: though David's petition was a very brief one, yet it met with an unmistakeable answer as 2 Sam. 17:14 shows, where we are told, "And Absalom and all the men of Israel said, The counsel of Hushai the Archite is better than the counsel of Ahithophel; for the Lord had commanded to *defeat* the good counsel of Ahithophel, to the intent that the Lord might bring evil upon Absalom." Let us take encouragement from this incident, then, and *"in everything* by prayer and supplication with thanksgiving, let our requests be made known unto God" (Phil 4:6).

"And it came to pass, that when David was come to the top of the mount, where he worshipped God" (v. 32). This is very blessed and teaches a lovely practical lesson: "weeping must never hinder worshipping" (Matt. Henry). No, why should it; we may worship God in the minor key as truly as in the major. We may adore the Lord as genuinely in the valley of humiliation as from the heights of jubilation. Furthermore, we may worship God as acceptably from the rugged mountain-top as in the most ornate cathedral. This principle was clearly apprehended by the spiritually-minded in O.T. times, as is evident from our passage: though David was away from the tabernacle, he realised that God was still accessible in spirit. Let us, then, grasp this fact, that nothing should prevent us worshipping the Lord, even though we no longer have access to *His public* ordinances. How thankful we should be for such a merciful provision in a day like ours.

"And it came to pass, that when David was come to the top of the mount, there he worshipped God." There are some who believe — we consider with good reason — that David sang the 3rd Psalm as a part of his worship on this occasion, for it bears the title "a Psalm of David when he fled from Absalom his son." It has been well said that "Among all the Psalms of David there is none which more remarkably evidences the triumph of his faith out of the depths of affliction and chastisement than this one" (B.W. Newton). There was no shutting of his eyes to the gravity of his situation, no ignoring the imminency of his danger, for he said, "Lord, how are they increased that trouble me! many are they that rise up against me. Many there be which say of my soul, There is no help for him in God. Selah" (Psa. 3:1, 2).

David described his foes as being numerous, and as boasting there would be no deliverance for him by the Lord. As we have seen (2 Sam. 15:12), the revolt had assumed considerable dimensions, and the conspirators were assured that David's sins had turned away the aid of Heaven from his cause. "But thou, O Lord, *art* a shield for me; my glory, and the lifter up of mine head" (Psa. 3:3): this is most blessed — he opposes their malicious utterances and confident hatred by the conviction that amidst real perils Jehovah was still his defence. With bowed and covered head he had fled from Jerusalem but "Thou art the lifter up of mine head" was his confidence. "Though the dangers were still present, yet in faith he speaks of them as past (Hebrew); the deliverance was yet future, yet he speaks of it as already come" (B.W. Newton).

"I cried unto the Lord with my voice, and He heard me out of His holy hill. Selah (Psa. 3:4). He was an exile from the tabernacle on Zion, and he had sent back the ark to its rest; but though he had to cry to God from the mountain side, He graciously answers from "His holy hill." "He and his men camped amidst dangers, but an unslumbering Helper mounted guard over the undefended slumberers" (A. Maclaren): "I laid me down and slept; I awaked; for the Lord sustained me" (Psa. 3:5). Such was the calm confidence of David, even while multiplied perils were still encircling him. Refreshed by the night's repose, heartened by the Divine protection granted while sheltering in caves or sleeping in the open, the Psalmist breaks forth in triumphant exclamation: "I will not be afraid of ten thousands of people that have set themselves against me round about (Psa. 3:6).

Betaking himself for renewed energy to the weapon of prayer, even before the battle David sees the victory, but ascribed it solely to his God. "Arise, O Lord; save me, O my God: for Thou *hast* smitten all mine enemies upon the cheekbone; Thou *hast* broken the teeth of the ungodly. Salvation belongeth unto the Lord: Thy blessing is upon Thy people. Selah" (Psa. 3:7, 8). "Nor was his confidence in vain. He was restored and allowed again to see Israel in peace — again to prove that God's blessing is upon His people. How precious is the individual use of such a Psalm as this, to every one who, after having backslidden or trespassed, has only turned again to the mercies and faithfulness of God. Even though the tokens of Divine rebuke and chastisement be present on every side, even though every tongue may say 'there is no help for him in God,' such an one may remember David, and again say' 'Thou, O Lord, art a shield for me: my glory, and the lifter up of mine head.' Thus, even the sins and chastisement of God's servants are made blessings in result to His people" (B.W. Newton).

"Behold Hushai the Archite came to meet him with his coat rent, and earth upon his head" (v. 32). From 1 Chron. 27:33 we learn that Hushai was another who had taken a prominent part in the affairs of state, for there it is recorded, "Hushai the Archite was the king's companion." That Hushai was regarded as a man of wisdom is also apparent from the fact that, a little later, Absalom applied to him for advice (2 Sam. 17:5). In the light of what immediately follows, it seems to us that the coming to David of Hushai at this time was *a test*, to manifest whether his confidence lay wholly in the Lord, for it is often His way to so regulate our circumstances as to exhibit the secret workings of our hearts — that we may, subsequently, be humbled thereby, and brought to prize more highly that grace which bears so patiently with us.

"Unto whom David said, If thou passest on with me, then thou shalt be a burden unto me; But if thou return to the city, and say unto Absalom, I will be thy servant, O king; as I have been thy father's servant hitherto, so will I now also be thy servant: then mayest thou for me defeat the counsel of Ahithophel. And hast thou not there with thee Zadok and Abiathar the priests? therefore it shall be, that what thing so ever, thou shalt hear out of the king's house, thou shalt tell it to Zadok and Abiathar the priests. Behold, they have there with them their two sons, Ahimaaz Zadok's son, and Jonathan Abiathar's son; and by them ye shall send unto me every thing that ye can hear. So Hushai David's friend came into the city, and Absalom came into Jerusalem" (vv. 33:37).

"As in water face answereth to face, so the heart of man to man" (Prov. 27:19). Alas, cannot both writer and reader see in the above incident a reflection of his own character? Have there not been times when we confidently committed our cause and case unto the Lord, and then we saw an opportunity where, by fleshly scheming, we thought that we could secure the answer to our prayers? It is far easier to commit our way unto the Lord, than it is to "rest in the Lord and wait patiently for Him" (Psa. 37:5,7). It is *there* that the real test of faith often lies: whether we *leave* things entirely in God's hands, or seek to take matters into our own. Learn, then, that the appearing of a willing Hushai at the critical moment is often permitted to put us to the proof — whether or not our heart be still inclined to lean upon an arm of flesh.

Various attempts have been made seeking to vindicate David for sending Hushai to become a spy for him in Absalom's camp. Strategy may be permissible in warfare, but nothing could justify the king in causing Hushai to act and utter a lie. It is true that God overruled, and through Hushai defeated Ahithophel's counsel, but that no more proves He *approved* of this deception, than did the flowing of water from the smitten rock show God's approbation of Moses' anger. The best that can be said is, "Alas! where shall we find wisdom and simplicity so united in any mere man that we can perceive nothing which admits of censure and needs forgiveness?" (Thos. Scott). There has only been One on this earth in whom there was *no* spot or blemish.

And when David was a little past the top, behold, Ziba the servant of Mephibosheth met him with a couple of asses saddled, and on them two hundred loaves of bread, and a hundred bunches of raisins, and a hundred of summer fruits, and a bottle of wine. And the king said to Ziba, What do you mean by these? And Ziba said, The asses are for the king's household to ride on. And the bread and summer fruits are for the young men to eat. And the wine is so that the ones who are faint in the wilderness may drink. And the king said, And where is your master's son? And Ziba said to the king, Behold, he remains at Jerusalem. For he said, Today the house of Israel shall restore to me the kingdom of my father. Then the king said to Ziba, Behold, All that belonged to Mephibosheth is yours. And Ziba said, I humbly beg you that I may find grace in your sight, my lord, O king. — II Samuel 16:1-4.

"It is human to err." True, yet that does not excuse it, especially where a fellow-mortal is unjustly condemned by us. Appearances are proverbially deceptive: we need to get beneath the surface in order to form a right estimate. Gossip is never to be credited, in fact should not be heeded at all. Only from the mouths of two or more reliable witnesses is an accusation against another to be given a hearing. Even then there must be a fair trial accorded, so that the one accused may know what he is charged with, and have opportunity to defend himself and refute the charge. Only arrant cowards stab in the back or under the cover of darkness. A safe rule to be guided by is never to say anything behind a person's back which you would be afraid to say and are not prepared to substantiate before his face. Alas, how commonly is that rule violated in this evil day! How ready people are to imagine and believe the worst, rather than the best of others — few have escaped this infection.

"Judge not according to the appearance, but judge righteous judgment" (John 7:24). The setting of those words is worthy of note. The Lord Jesus had healed a man on the Sabbath day, and His enemies — ever seeking some pretext to condemn Him — were angry. He had flagrantly disregarded their dicta: He had acted at complete variance with *their* ideas of how the Sabbath should be kept holy. Therefore they at once jumped to the harsh conclusion that the Redeemer had desecrated the Sabbath. Christ pointed out that their verdict was both an arbitrary and superficial one. Circumstances alter cases: as the circumcising of a child on the Sabbath, if that were the eighth day from its birth, (v. 23). It is the motive which largely determines the value of an act, and it is sinful to guess at the motives of others. Moreover, the reign of law must not be suffered to freeze the milk of human kindness in our veins, nor make us impervious to human suffering.

"Judge not according to the appearance, but judge righteous judgment" (John 7:24). Is not this a word which is much needed to-day by both writer and reader. There is a twofold danger to be guarded against. First, to form too favourable a judgment of people, particularly of those who profess to be Christians. Words are cheap, and gushiness is never a mark of reality. That a man calls himself a Christian, and sincerely thinks himself to be so, does not make him one. The fact that he is a great reader of the Bible, a regular attender of religious services, and is sound in his morals, is no proof that he has been born again. "Lay hands suddenly on no man" (1 Tim. 5:22): look for the marks of regeneration and be satisfied you have found them, before you address any one as a Brother or Sister in Christ. It is our own fault if we are imposed upon by

461

wolves in sheep's clothing.

On the other hand, there is just as real a danger of forming too harsh a judgment of people, and imputing to hypocrisy what is genuine. A man is not to be made an offender for a word, nor does he deserve to be snubbed because he fails to fawn upon and flatter you. We must not expect everybody to pronounce *our* shibboleths or see eye to eye with us in everything. A kindly heart often beats beneath a gruff exterior. A babbling brook is very shallow, but still waters run deep. Not all are endowed with five talents. Others may not have had the same opportunities and privileges you have enjoyed. Let not a single action alienate a friend: bear in mind the general tenor of his conduct towards you. Be as ready to forgive as you desire to be forgiven. Remember there is still much in you which grates upon others. When wronged *pray over it* before you pass a verdict. Many a person has afterwards bitterly regretted a hasty decision. Take *all* the circumstances into account and "judge not according to the appearance, but judge righteous judgment."

We have begun this article thus because the passage we are about to consider (2 Sam. 16:1-4) shows us David grievously misjudging one who was affectionately attached to him. David was unwarrantably influenced by "appearances." He gave ear to an unconfirmed slander against an absent one. He at once believed the worst, without affording the accused any opportunity to vindicate himself. It was one to whom David had shown much kindness in the past, and now that a servant brought to him an evil report, the king accepted the same, concluding that the master had turned traitor. It is true that human nature is lamentably fickle, and that kindness is often rewarded with the basest of ingratitude; yet all are not unthankful and treacherous. We must not allow the wickedness of some to prejudice us against all. We should deal impartially and judge righteously of everyone alike: yet only Divine grace — humbly and earnestly sought — will enable us to remain just and merciful after we have been deceived and wronged a few times.

Later, David discovered that he had been deceived (2 Sam. 19:24-30) and was obliged to reverse his harsh verdict; but this did not alter the fact that he had grievously misjudged Mephibosheth and had harboured unjust prejudices against him. And this incident, like many another narrated in Holy Writ, is recorded, my reader, for *our* learning and warning. We are prone to misjudge even our friends, and because of this, are in danger of crediting false reports about them. But there is no reason why we should be deceived, either for or against another: "He that is spiritual discerneth all things" (1 Cor. 2:15 margin). Ah, *there* is the seat of our trouble: it is because we are so unspiritual that we so often judge according to the appearance, and not righteous judgment. A jaundiced eye is incapable of seeing things in their true colours. When the regenerate walk after the flesh, they are just as liable to be imposed upon as are the unregenerate. And this, as we shall see, was the cause of David's sad error.

"And when David was a little past the top of the hill, behold, Ziba the servant of Mephibosheth met him" (2 Sam. 16:1). The topographical reference connects with 15:30 and 32. On leaving Jerusalem David and his little band had crossed the Kidron, and ascended Olivet. They were making for Bahurim (v. 5), which was a low-lying village in the descent from Olivet to the Jordan. Ultimately, they pitched camp at Mahanaim, on the far side of the Jordan (17:24). Thus it will be seen that they were passing through that portion of the land which was allotted to the tribe of Benjamin (see Josh. 18:11-28), which was the territory of *Saul's* tribe, and *that* was surely dangerous ground for him to tread! This is the first point for us to carefully weigh, for it is one of the keys which opens to us the inner significance of our present incident.

There is nothing meaningless in God's Word, even the geographical details often contain deeply important instruction, pointing valuable spiritual lessons, if only we take the trouble to search them out. This is what we have to do here, for the Holy Spirit has given us no direct hint that the direction which David was now taking furnishes a clue to his subsequent conduct. In making for the territory of Saul's tribe, David was (typically) entering upon *the Enemy's ground* — should the reader deem this a rather far-fetched conclusion on our part, we would ask him to note that in the verse which immediately follows our present passage, we are plainly told that there came out 'a man of the family of the house of *Saul.. .and cursed*" David! Surely that was the Devil as a "roaring lion" raging aginst him. Now to come on to the Enemy's ground, my reader, is to give him an "advantage of us" (2 Cor. 2:11), and that is to come under his power; and when under his power our judgment is blinded, and we are quite incapable of judging righteously.

But there is another little detail here, a confirmatory one, which is necessary for us to observe, if we are to view this incident in its true perspective. Our passage opens with the word "And," and common-place and trivial as that may appear, yet it is a vital link in the chain of thought we are now endeavouring to follow out. That "And" tells us we must *connect* what is recorded at the beginning of chapter 16 with that which is narrated at the close of 15. And there, as we saw in the previous article, David was guilty of dishonest subterfuge, counselling the priests to feign themselves the faithful servants of Absalom, when in reality they were David's spies. Therein the king was manifestly acting in the energy of *the flesh*, seeking by his own carnal efforts to "defeat the counsel of Ahithophel" (15:34), instead of leaving it with the Lord to answer his prayer to that end (15:31).

Here, then, is vitally-important practical teaching for you and me, dear reader. If *we* are not to be misguided by superficial appearances and are to judge "righteous judgment," then we must *avoid* these mistakes that David made. The two small details we have dwelt upon above, explain why he so grievously misjudged Mephibosheth. If, then, we are to have clear discernment, which will preserve us from being deceived by glib-tongued imposters and taken in by apparent acts of kindness toward us, we must walk after the Spirit and not after the flesh, and tread the paths of righteousness and not get on to the Enemy's territory. "He that is spiritual discerneth all things" (1 Cor. 2:15): yes, the "spiritual," and not the carnal. As we have said above, it is our *own* fault if we form a wrong judgment of others — due to making the mistakes David did. "If therefore thing eye be single, thy whole body shall be full of light" (Matt. 6:22).

"And when David was a little past the top of the hill, behold, Ziba the servant of Mephibosheth met him, with a couple of asses saddled; and upon them two hundred loaves of bread, and a hundred bunches of raisins, and a hundred of summer fruits, and a bottle of wine" (v. 1). Those who have not followed us throughout this series of sections should turn to 1 Sam. 9, where not a little is recorded of these two men. Mephibosheth was the grandson of Saul, the arch-enemy of David, yet to him David showed great kindness because he was the son of Jonathan (4:4), with whom David had made a covenant that he would not cut off his kindness to his house forever (1 Sam. 20:11-17). In 2 Sam. 9 we read, "The king called to Ziba, Saul's servant, and said unto him, I have given unto thy master's son all that pertained to Saul and to all his house. Thou therefore, and thy sons, and thy servants, shall till the land for him, and thou shalt bring in the fruits, that thy master's son may have food to eat: but

Mephibosheth thy master's son shall eat bread always at my table. Now Ziba had fifteen sons and twenty servants" (vv. 9, 10).

Ziba, then, was a man of some importance, for he had twenty servants, yet both they and his sons were commanded to serve Mephibosheth. This it is which explains his conduct in our present incident: Ziba was not content to be manager of the considerable estate of Mephibosheth, but coveted to be master of it; and covetousness is ever the mother of a brood of other sins. It was so here: so carried away was he by his evil lust, Ziba scorned not to resort to the basest treachery. He concluded that now was a favourable opportunity for furthering his base design. Having laid his plans with serpentine cunning, he put them into execution, and apparently with success. But "The triumphing of the wicked is short, and the joy of the hypocrite but for a moment" (Job 20:5), and so it proved in this case.

Ziba was determined to procure from David a royal grant of his master's estate, and then, whether David or Absalom prevailed in the present conflict, his desire would be secured. To obtain that grant two things were necessary: first, Ziba himself, must obtain favour in the king's eyes; and second, Mephibosheth must be brought into decided disfavour. The opening verse shows the measure Ziba took to accomplish the first. He met the fugitive king and his band with an elaborate present: it was well timed and appropriately selected. Ziba posed as one who was not only loyal to David's cause, but as very solicitous of his welfare and comfort. But as Thos. Scott says, "Selfish men are often very generous in giving away the property of others for their own advantage." Looking at this detail from the Divine side of things, we may see here the mercy of God in providing for His own, as He ever does — even though He employs the *ravens* to feed them!

"And the king said unto Ziba, What meanest thou by these?" (v. 2). David was habitually cautious, and at this critical juncture he had need to be doubly so. His own spoiled son had risen up against him, securing a large following, and when such an one as Ahithophel had gone over to his side, the king knew not whom he could trust. Yet, while this sad situation warranted the utmost caution, it certainly did not justify a readiness to believe the worst of everybody — there is a happy medium between losing all confidence in human nature, and having such a blind trust in men that any charlatan may impose upon us. David did not, then, immediately accept Ziba's present but issued this challenge: was it a subtle trap, or the liberality of a generous man kindly disposed toward him?

"And Ziba said, The asses be for thy king's household to ride on: and the bread and summerfruit for the young men to eat; and the wine, that such as be faint in the wilderness may drink" (v. 2). This was the means used by this wretched Ziba to ingratiate himself with David: "A man's gift maketh room for him, and bringeth him before great men" (Prov. 18:16). Rightly did Matt. Henry ask, "Shall the prospect of advantage in the world, make men generous to be *rich;* and shall not the belief of an abundant recompense in the resurrection of the just, make us charitable to the *poor?*" Surely *that* is the practical lesson for us in this verse: "And I say unto you, Make to yourselves friends of the mammon of unrighteousness; that, when ye fail, they may receive you into everlasting habitations" (Luke 16:9).

"And the king said, And where is thy master's son? And Ziba said unto the king, Behold, he abideth at Jerusalem: for he said, To-day shall the house of Israel restore me the kingdom of my father" (v. 3). Having wormed himself into the king's heart — for being so largely swayed by his emotions, David was peculiarly susceptible to kindness — Ziba now undertook to blacken the character of his master and turn David utterly against him. He represents Mephibosheth as ungrateful, treacherous, and covetous. How often masters and mistresses suffer unjustly from the lies of their servants! "A wicked man taketh a gift out of the bosom to pervert the ways of judgment" (Prov. 17:23). "It is true indeed that David did not *know* that Ziba was wicked. His unexpected kindness came at a time when almost every other hand was either paralysed by terror, or else armed against him in active enmity. No doubt at such a moment, it required great self-possession to pause, and to withhold the tongue from rashly pronouncing judgment. But David was a king, and it behoved him to be wisely cautious" (B.W. Newton).

"Then said the king to Ziba, Behold, thine are all that pertained unto Mephibosheth" (v. 4). David credited the foul calumny and without further inquiry or consideration condemns Mephibosheth, seizes his lands as forfeited, and makes a grant of them to his servant. What a solemn warning is this for us! What pains we should take to confirm what we hear, and thus arrive at the real truth of things. As an old writer quaintly said, "God has given us *two* ears that we may hear *both* sides." But sooner or later the truth *will* come to light, as it did in this case. When at last David returned in triumph to Jerusalem, Mephibosheth met him and had opportunity to vindicate himself. How bitterly must the king have then regretted his hasty verdict and the cruel wrong he had done him by crediting such vile reports against him!

"And Ziba said, I humbly beseech thee that I may find grace in thy sight my lord, O king" (v. 4). Yes, words are cheap, and backbiters are generally flatterers. But note well that Ziba *did not accompany* the fugitive king! No, he thought too much of his own skin for that, and was determined to be on the safe side, no matter what should be the outcome of Absalom's rebellion. "Anxious apparently lest he should suffer if Absalom were to succeed, he seems to have retired to Shimei and the Benjamites, to secure his interests with them; for he was found, when the king returned, in the traim of Shimei — that same Shimei who had cursed David" (B.W. Newton). Thus, when David arrived back again in Jerusalem, Ziba was in the ranks of the king's enemies! — whereas Mephibosheth was among his most loyal subjects.

And when king David came to Bahurim, behold, a man of the house of Saul came out from there, whose name was Shimei, the son of Gera, He came forth and still cursed as he came. And he threw stones at David and at all the servants of king David. And all the people and all the mighty men were on his right hand and on his left. And so said Shimei when he cursed, Come out, come out, you bloody man and man of Belial. The LORD has returned on you all the blood of the house of Saul, in whose place you have reigned. And the LORD has delivered the kingdom into the hand of Absalom your son. And look at you in your mischief, because you are a bloody man! Then Abishai the son of Zeruiah said to the king, Why should this dead dog curse my lord the king? I beg you, let me go over and take off his head. And the king said, What have I to do with you, you sons of Zeruiah? Let him curse, because the LORD has said to him, Curse David. Who then shall say, Why have you done so? And David said to Abishai and to all his servants, Behold, my son, who came forth from my bowels, seeks my life — how much more now should this Benjamite? Let him alone and let him curse, for the LORD has bidden him. It may be that the LORD will look on my affliction, and that the LORD will repay me with good for his cursings this day. —

II Samuel 16:5-12.

In an earlier section we emphasised the fact that in his flight from Jerusalem, David is to be viewed as a contrite penitent. His refusal to stand his ground when Absalom rose up in rebellion against him, is to be attributed not to moral weakness, but to spiritual strength. Apparently this had been preceded by a lengthy and debilitating illness which had hindered him nipping that rebellion while it was in the bud, but the king had recovered by the time the conspiracy had come to a head. No, in his son's rebellion David saw the righteous retribution of God upon his fearful sins against Bathsheba and Uriah, and accordingly he humbled himself beneath His mighty hand. He recognized the ways of God in His moral government, so instead of vainly flinging himself against the bosses of Jehovah's buckler (rebelling and murmuring at His providences), he meekly bowed before His chastening rod. This was "bringing forth fruits meet for repentance" — as lovely, and as acceptable to God, as are "the fruits of righteousness" in their season.

It is, then, in the viewing of David *as an humble penitent* that we obtain the key to most of what is recorded in 2 Sam. 15 and 16. His sin had found him out and brought him to remembrance before the Holy One of Israel, and he bowed his head and meekly accepted His reproofs. It was for this reason that he bade his loyal followers go back, and leave him alone in his trouble. It was in that spirit he had ordered the priests to carry back the ark to Jerusalem — he felt utterly unworthy that *it* should accompany him on his flight. It was in that same spirit, as an humble penitent, he had crossed the Kidron and ascended Olivet barefooted and in tears. It was as *the mourner before God* that David had now turned his face toward the wilderness. All of this has been before us on a previous occasion, but we deemed it necessary to repeat the same, for it explains, as nothing else does, his amazing attitude in the incident we are about to contemplate.

As the fugitive king and his little following began to descend into the valley leading to the Jordan, a man who belonged to the family of the house of Saul came forth, and *cursed* him, charging him with a fearful crime he had never committed. Meeting with no opposition, this wretched creature cast stones at the king and his men. Now David was not the man, naturally speaking, to suffer such indignities to pass unnoticed: why, then, did he now endure them in silence? Abishai, one of the king's followers, asked permission to avenge his master of these insults by slaying the offender; but David restrained him, and suffered Shimei to continue his outrageous conduct. But what seems stranger still, David attributed this humiliating experience unto God Himself, saying *"The Lord* hath said unto him, Curse David" — language which raises a problem of the first magnitude: the relation of God to evil; for David was not guilty of speaking rashly and wickedly, but gave utterance to a most solemn and weighty truth. But to keep to our main thought.

"He saw God in every circumstance, and owned Him with a subdued and reverent spirit. To him it was not Shimei, but the Lord. Abishai saw only the man, and desired to deal with him accordingly. Like Peter afterwards, when he sought to defend his beloved Master from the band of murderers sent to arrest Him. Both Peter and Abishai were living upon the surface, and looking at secondary causes. The Lord Jesus was living in the most profound subjection to the Father: 'the cup which My Father hath given Me, shall I not drink it?' This gave Him power over everything. He looked beyond the instrument to God — beyond the cup to the hand which had filled it. It mattered not whether it were Judas, Herod, Caiaphas, or Pilate; He could say, in all, *'My Father's cup.'* Thus, too, was David, in his measure, lifted above subordinate agents. He looked right up to God, and with unshod feet and covered head, he bowed before Him: 'The Lord hath said unto him, Curse David,' This was enough.

"Now, there are, perhaps, few things in which we so much fail as in apprehending the presence of God, and His dealings with our souls, in every circumstance of daily life. We are constantly ensnared by looking at secondary causes; we do not realise God *in everything*. Hence Satan gets the victory over us. Were we more alive to the fact that there is not an event which happens to us, from morning to night, in which the voice of God may not be heard, the hand of God seen, with what a holy atmosphere would it surround us! Men and things would then be received as so many agents and instruments in our Father's hands; so many ingredients in our Father's cup. Thus would our minds be solemnized, our spirits calmed, our hearts subdued. Then we shall not say with Abishai. 'Why should this dead dog curse my lord the king? let me go over, I pray thee, and take off his head.' Nor shall we, with Peter, draw the sword in natural excitement. How far below their respective masters were both these affectionate though mistaken men! How must the sound of Peter's sword have grated on his Master's ear, and offended His spirit! And how must Abishai's words have wounded the meek and submitting David! Could David defend himself while God was dealing with his soul in a manner so solemn and impressive? Surely not, He dare not take himself out of the hands of the Lord. He was His for life or death — as a king or an exile. Blessed subjection!" (C.H.M.).

"And when the king David came to Bahurim, behold, there came out a man of the family of the house of Saul, whose name was Shimei, the son of Gera, he came forth, and cursed still as he came" (2 Sam. 16:5). What a contrast is this from what was before us in the preceding verse! There we saw the hypocritical Ziba fawning upon David, pretending that he desired to "find grace" in his sight, and addressing him as "my lord, O king." Here we find Shimei "cursing" the king, and denouncing him as "thou man of Belial." Ziba presented David with an elaborate present, whereas Shimei threw stones and cast dust at him. Unto the flatteries of the former David reacted by grievously misjudging Mephibosheth; whereas to the revilings of the latter, he meekly bowed before God — ah, my reader, the Christian has good reason to fear the smiles of the world, far more than he has its frowns.

"And when king David came to Bahurim, behold, there came out a man of the family of the house of Saul, whose name was Shimei, the son of Gera: he came forth, and cursed still as he came." The first book of Samuel furnished the background to this dark scene. Saul had been Israel's king, and upon his death a determined effort had been made to preserve the throne in *his* family: see 2 Sam. 2:8 to 3:2. But the attempt of Abner and the determination of Ishbosheth to reign as king over Israel, was in direct defiance of Jehovah's ordination (1 Sam. 16:1-13; 2 Sam. 2:4). But Shimei disregarded this Divine appointment, and his heart was filled with enmity against David, whom he wrongly regarded as the usurper of the throne. While David was in power, he dared not openly anathematise him — though he hated him just the same; but now he was fleeing from Absalom, Shimei took the opportunity to vent his malice, which shows his utter baseness in taking advantage of David's trouble at this time.

"And he cast stones at David, and at all the servants of king David: and all the people and all the mighty men were on his right hand and on his left" (v. 6). The rank hatred of Shimei's heart now burst forth in full force. With savage vehemence he curses the king, and flings stones and dust in the transports of his

468

fury; stumbling along among the rocks high up in the glen, he keeps pace with the little band in the valley below. But ere passing on, let us not overlook the fact that Bahurim has been mentioned previously in this book: see 2 Sam. 3:16 and context. Did David now recall how the husband from whom he had torn Michal had followed her to this very place, and then turned back weeping to his lonely home? We cannot be sure, but the remembrance of later and more evil deeds now subdued David's spirit, and caused him to meekly submit to these outrageous insults.

"And thus said Shimei when he cursed, Come out, come out, thou bloody man, and thou son of Belial: The Lord hath returned upon thee all the blood of the house of Saul, in whose stead thou hast reigned; and the Lord hath delivered the kingdom into the hand of Absalom thy son: and, behold, thou art taken in thy mischief, because thou art a bloody man" (vv. 7, 8). The different scenes presented in these chapters require to be viewed from various angles, if their manifold signification is to be perceived. This we endeavour to bear in mind as we pass from incident to incident. Shimei is not only to be regarded as the Lord's instrument for chastening David, as a figure of the Devil as "a roaring lion" — raging against David because he had come into the enemy's territory (see preceding section); but also as a type of those who slandered and persecuted Christ Himself. It is this many-sidedness of these historical pictures which gives to them their chief interest for us to-day.

When the parents of the infant Jesus presented Him to God in the temple, old Simeon was moved by the Spirit of prophecy to say, "Behold, this Child is set for the fall and rising again of many in Israel; and for a sign which shall be spoken against. . .that the thoughts of many hearts may be revealed" (Luke 2:34, 35). How truly the terms of this prediction concerning the Antitype were adumbrated in the type. All through his checkered career, but especially that part of it we are now considering, David's various experiences served as occasions that "the thoughts of many hearts might be revealed." Much that was hidden beneath the surface, was forced out into the open. Those who were loyal to him at heart were now unmistakably manifested as his staunch supporters and faithful friends: his "mighty men" continued to cling to him despite the drastic change of his fortunes. It now became clear who really loved him for his own sake. — like Mary and Martha and the apostles in the Gospels. On the other hand, hypocrites were exposed (Ahithophel, the forerunner of Judas), and bitter enemies openly reviled and condemned him — as was the lot of our Lord.

The conduct of Shimei on this occasion was base and vile to the last degree. In the first place, it was in direct defiance of the express commandment of the Lord: "Thou shalt not revile the judges, nor curse the ruler of thy people" (Ex. 22:28); "Curse not the king, no not in thy thought" (Eccl. 10:20). Second, it was despicable beyond words that Shimei should wait to vent his malice upon David till the time when his cup of sorrow was already full, thus adding to his grief: "For they persecute him whom Thou hast smitten; and they talk to the grief of Thy wounded" (Psa. 69:26). Third, the awful charge he now preferred was absolutely false, and against the plainest evidence: so far from David having slain Saul, he had again and again spared his life when he was at his mercy. He was many miles away at the time of Saul's death, and when the tidings of it reached him, he made lamentation for him: (2 Sam. 1:12).

"And thus said Shimei when he cursed, Come out, come out, thou bloody man, and thou man of Belial: the Lord hath returned upon thee all the blood of the house of Saul, in whose stead thou hast reigned; and the Lord hath delivered the kingdom into the hand of Absalom thy son: and, behold, thou art taken in thy to all sins of angels and men, and that not by a bare permission, but such as hath of the holy name of the Lord being found upon the lips of the wicked! — a warning to us that all who make use of the name of Christ do *not* "depart from iniquity" (2 Tim. 2:19). Observe too how Shimei undertook to interpret the Divine dispensations toward David, showing us that wicked men are ever ready to press God's judgments into their service, for they judge right and wrong by selfish interests. May Divine grace preserve both writer and reader from the folly and sin of attempting to philosophise about God's dealings with others.

"Then said Abishai the son of Zeruiah unto the king, Why should this dead dog curse my lord the king? let me go over, I pray thee, and take off his head. And the king said, What have I to do with you, ye sons of Zeruiah? so let him curse, because the Lord hath said unto him, Curse David. Who then shall say, Wherefore hast thou done so?" (vv. 9, 10). Here again the type merges into the antitype, and that in two respects. First, how this well-meant but fleshly suggestion of David's devoted follower reminds us of that request of Christ's disciples concerning those who "did not receive Him," namely, "Lord, wilt Thou that we command fire to come down from Heaven, and consume them, even as Elijah did?" (Luke 9:54). As Christ answered "Ye know not what manner of spirit ye are of," so David restrained Abishai — clear proof he was *not* the "bloody man" Shimei had called him! Second, David refused to return railing for railing, reminding us of "when He (Christ) was reviled, He reviled not again" (1 Pet. 2:23), in this leaving an example for us to follow. But turning from the typical, let *us* consider the practical.

Though the fact itself be not here specificially mentioned, David realized that he *deserved to be* both cursed and stoned, and his consciousness thereof must have taken off the edge from this cutting experience: "Wherefore doth a living man complain, a man for the punishment of his sins?" (Lam 3:39). Though the blood of Saul did not rest upon David, that of Uriah did; this he knew full well, and therefore bowed to God's righteous chastisement, and spared Shimei — both Absalom and Shimei were instruments in the hand of God, justly afflicting him — though the guilt of their conduct belonged to them. A parallel case is found in Aaron: the rememberance of his great wickedness in making the golden calf, composed his mind under the fearful trial of the death of his sons (Lev. 10:1-3) — knowing he deserved yet sorer judgment, he was silent.

"And the king said, What have I to do with you, ye sons of Zeruiah? so let him curse, because the Lord hath said unto him, Curse David" (v. 10). David saw the hand of God in this experience, afflicting him for his sins against Bathsheba and Uriah. Shimei had received a commission from Heaven, to curse David, though that no more excused him or took away his guilt than the crucifiers of Christ were guiltless because they did what God's hand and counsel "determined before to be done" (Acts 2:23; 4:28). God has foreordained *all* that comes to pass in this world, but this does not mean that He regards the wickedness of men with complacency, or that He condones their evil. No indeed. In their zeal to clear God of being the Author of sin, many have denied that He is the Ordainer and Orderer of it. Because the creature cannot comprehend His ways, or perceive how He is the Author of an act without being chargeable with the evil of it, they have rejected the important truth that sin is under the absolute *control* of God, and is as much subject to His moral government, as the winds and waves are directed by Him in the material sphere.

The subject is admittedly a difficult one, and if we are spared, we hope to write more at length upon it in the future. Meanwhile, we content ourself by giving a quotation from the Westminister Confession: "God's providence extendeth itself mischief, because thou art a bloody man" (vv. 7, 8). What a solemn case is this joined with it a most wise and powerful bounding, and other wise *ordering and governing* them, in a manifold disposition unto His own holy ends; yet so as the sinfulness thereof proceedeth only from the creature, and not from God" (chap. 5), The holiness of God is no more sullied by directing the activities of evil men, than the beams of the sun are defiled when they shine upon a filthy swamp. The hatred of his heart belonged to Shimei himself, but it was God's work that that hatred should settle so definitely on David, and show itself in exactly the manner and time it did.

"And David said to Abishai, and to all his servnats, Behold, my son, which came forth of my bowels, seeketh my life: how much more now may this Benjamite do it? let him alone, and let him curse; for the Lord hath bidden him. It may be that the Lord will look on mine affliction, and that the Lord will requite me good for his cursing this day" (vv. 11, 12). Two further considerations are here presented: David calmed himself under the lesser affliction of Shimei's cursing him, by reminding himself of the greater trial of Absalom's rising up against him. And he sought comfort in the possibility that God might yet overrule this trouble for his own ultimate blessing. The *practical* value of this incident is, the valuable teaching it contains on how a saint ought to conduct and console himself under severe trials. Let us summarize. First, David comforted himself with the thought that his sins deserved sorer chastisement than he was receiving. Second, he looked beyond the afflicting instrument, to the righteous hand of God. Third, he considered the minor affliction unworthy of consideration in view of the major. Fourth, he exercised *hope* that God would yet bring "good" out of evil. May grace be granted us to do likewise.

And as David and his men went by the way, Shimei went along on the hillside over across from him, and cursed as he went, and threw stones at him, and threw dust. And the king, and all the people who were with him, arrived weary. And they refreshed themselves there. And Absalom and all the people, the men of Israel, came to Jerusalem. And Ahithophel went with him. And when Hushai the Archite, David's friend, had come to Absalom, Hushai said to Absalom, Let the king live, let the king live! And Absalom said to Hushai, Is this your kindness to your friend? Why did you not go with your friend? And Hushai said to Absalom, No, but whom the LORD and this people, and all the men of Israel choose, his will I be, and I will stay with him. And, again, Whom should I serve? Should I not serve in the presence of his son? As I have served in your father's presence, so I will be in your presence. Then Absalom said to Ahithophel, Give advice among you as to what we shall do. And Ahithophel said to Absalom, Go in to your father's concubines whom he has left to keep the house. And all Israel shall hear that you are abhorred by your father. Then shall the hands of all who are with you be strong. So they spread Absalom a tent on the top of the house, and Absalom went in to his father's concubines in the sight of Israel. And the advice of Ahithophel, which he advised in those days, was as if a man had inquired at the oracle of God. So was all the advice of Ahithophel, both with David and with Absalom. — II Samuel 16:13-23.

Amid much that is saddening in the next two or three chapters there occasionally shine rays of light through the darkness which overshadows them. The record is mainly concerned with the deeds of David's enemies, but here and there we find chronicled some of the kindly actions of his friends. The depravity of fallen human nature is exhibited again and again, and we behold what fearful depths of iniquity men will fall into when not immediately restrained from above. God righteously permits the Devil to work freely in the children of disobedience (Eph. 2:2), for man at the beginning deliberately elected to become subject to Satan's sceptre rather than remain in allegiance to his Maker: preferring death to life, darkness to light, bondage to freedom, he is made to suffer the consequences of the same. Nevertheless, the Almighty is over Satan and makes his ragings to subserve His own purpose: "Surely the wrath of man shall praise Thee: the remainder of wrath shalt Thou restrain" (Psa. 76:10) — strikingly illustrated again and again in the various scenes which are to come before us.

The depravity of fallen human nature is not an attractive subject, yet it is a solemn fact confronting us daily, both within and without. Moreover, it explains to us, as nothing else will, the fearful wickedness which abounds on every hand. A corrupt tree can (of itself) product nought but corrupt fruit. That which should really surprise us is not the bountiful harvest which sin is producing in the human family, but rather that so many of its foul blossoms and buds are nipped before they can develop. Now and again God permits some monster of iniquity to run his race without hindrance, to show us what fearful evil man is capable of, and what would be a common occurrence were He to leave Adam's descendants entirely to themselves. The deeds of Ahithophel and Absalom would be duplicated all around us were it not that God puts bridles into the mouths of those who hate Him, and bounds their enmity as truly as He does those of the winds and waves.

But the restraining of man's wickedness is not the sole operation of the Divine government of the human family: from the uncongenial soil of fallen human nature God is also engaged in producing that which makes this world a fit place for His people to live in, For He is doing *all* things for *their* sakes (Rom. 8:28) — His glory and their good being inseparably bound up together. That the saint meets with *any* mercy, justice, or kindness at the hands of the unregenerate is due alone to the grace and power of the Lord. That the believer is at times befriended by those who have not the love of God in their hearts, is as much the product and marvel of Divine power as His creating an occasional oasis in the desert. There are times when the Lord makes the leopard to "lie down with the kid, and the calf and the young lion and the fatling together" (Isa. 11:6). There are times when He causes the ravens to feed His servants. Yet, whatever be the instruments God is pleased to use, the language of the believer should be *"Thou* preparest a table before me in the presence of mine enemies" (Psa. 23:5).

Thus, amid the hardships and sufferings which his enemies inflicted upon David, we are also to note the reliefs and kindly supplies which God moved others to furnish him and his men. It was so in the experience of his blessed Son: if on the one hand we read that He "had not where to lay His head," on the other we are told "And many others (of the women) which ministered unto Him of their substance" (Luke 8:3). It was so in the history of the apostle Paul: if on the one hand he sometimes experienced "hunger and thirst. . .cold and nakedness" (2 Cor. 11:27), at others it could be recorded "The barbarous people showed us no little kindness: for they kindled a fire, and received us everyone, because of the present rain, and because of the cold. . .who also honoured us with many honours: and when we departed, they laded us with such things as were necessary" (Acts 28:2, 10). And has it not been thus in the lives of both writer and reader? Undoubtedly; sweets and bitters, disappointments and pleasant surprises, have been intermingled: "In the day of prosperity be joyful, but in the day of adversity consider: God also hath *set the one over against the other"* (Eccl. 7:14).

"And the king, and all the people that were with him, came weary, and refreshed themselves there" (16:14): that is, at Bahurim (v. 5). After their long and arduous journey from Jerusalem, David and his band of loyal followers pitched camp and obtained a much-needed rest. At the same time "Absalom, and all the people of the men of Israel, came to Jerusalem and Ahithophel with him" (v. 15) David and his retinue having left the way wide open for Absalom to take possession of the royal city whenever he pleased. There were none to oppose him. Accordingly he came, and no doubt felt much elated by this initial success, promising himself that the whole country would soon be his: "God suffers wicked men to prosper a while in their wicked plots, even beyond their expectation, that their disappointment may be the more grievous and disgraceful" (Matt. Henry).

"And it came to pass, when Hushai the Archite, David's friend, was come unto Absalom, that Hushai said unto Absalom, Let the king live, Let the king live (margin). And Absalom said to Hushai, Is this thy kindness to thy friend? why wentest thou not with thy friend? and Hushai said unto Absalom, Nay; but whom the Lord, and this people, and all the men of Israel, choose, his will I be, and with him will I abide. And again, whom should I serve? should I not serve in the presence of his son? as I have served in thy father's presence, so will I be in thy presence"(vv. 16-19). This is the sequel to what was before us in 15:32-37: Hushai, at some risk to himself, ventured into the lion's den, in order to serve and help David. His conduct on this occasion raises a problem, one which the commentators have differed widely upon. Some have argued that, on the worldly principle of "all is fair in love and war," Hushai was fully justified in his dissimulation: others have condemned him, without qualification, as an unmitigated liar; while a few have been so puzzled they withheld a judgment.

Let it be pointed out, first, that Hushai did *not* say "Let king Absalom live;" and when challenged concerning his infidelity to David, he did not reply "I have done with thy father, and am now devoted solely to *thee* and thy cause:" his language was ambiguous, capable of a double construction. While that somewhat modified his offence it by no means cleared Hushai, for his language was intended to mislead, and therefore was chargeable with duplicity. That his intention was a good one, and that his efforts succeeded, by no means exonerated him. "Results" are not the criterion by which we should determine the rightness or wrongness of anything. Bear in mind it is the *human* side of things we are now considering — from the Divine side, God suffered the pride of Absalom's heart to deceive him: he fondly imagined that David's best friends were so in love with himself that they gladly took the present opportunity to flock to his banner; and therefore he construed Hushai's words in favour of himself.

The above incident is recorded as a warning, and *not* for our imitation. It shows that something more than a good motive is necessary in order for a deed to be right in the sight of God. This is an important principle for us to weigh, for not a few to-day excuse much that is wrong by saying "Well, his intentions were good." While it be true that the motive often determines the value of an act, yet *other* principles and considerations must also regulate us. For instance, in seeking to carry out our good intentions, we must use *the right means*. It is praiseworthy for a parent to seek food for his hungry children, yet he or she must not steal the same. *This* was where Hushai failed: the desire to help David did not warrant his playing the part of a hypocrite. "For our rejoicing is this: the testimony of our conscience, that in *simplicity and godly sincerity*, not with fleshly wisdom, but by the grace of God, we have had our conversation in the world" (2 Cor. 1:12) is the Christian's standard. It is never right to do wrong.

The principal means which the believer should employ in every time of trouble and emergency, is *prayer*: presenting his case in humble and trustful confidence to Him with whom there are no difficulties, leaving Him to undertake for us as seemeth Him best. This is what David had done at first (2 Sam. 15:31); but, later, he spoiled it by resorting to a carnal policy (15:34). Ere passing on let us note how Absalom's challenge to Hushai may be taken to heart by ourselves in a higher sense: "Men who admire themselves will be easily deceived by those who profess an attachment to them; yet they readily discern those faults in others, of which themselves are far more notoriously guilty, and are apt to express astonishment at them. If a zealous disciple of Christ commit evident wickedness, even profligates will exclaim 'Is this thy kindness to thy Friend?' But, alas, how often might the Saviour Himself address each of us in these words, to our shame and confusion! And how often should we thus check ourselves, and remember our ingratitude, to our deep humiliation" (T. Scott). Unfaithfulness to Christ is a species of unkindness to our best Friend! What a theme that is for a practical sermon!

We have, in a former section, already made allusion to the revolting episode recorded in the closing verses of 2 Sam. 16, so few brief remarks on it here will suffice. "Then said Absalom to Ahithophel, Give counsel among you what we shall do" (v. 20). First, we note that Absalom did not seek unto the custodians of the ark (which David had sent back to Jerusalem) for guidance, for he had no concern for the will of Jehovah: throughout the entire piece he acts as an infidel, a blatant rebel. Second, the obvious design of Ahithophel in so evilly advising Absalom — which, as Matt. Henry rightly says was as though he enquired "at the oracle of Satan" rather than "of God" (v. 21) — was to get his new master to so conduct and commit himself that all hope of forgiveness by David would be out of the question. Third, but, behind the scenes, was the overruling hand of God, fulfilling His own word (2 Sam. 12:11) and chastising David for his wickedness — that he had these "concubines" in addition to a plurality of wives, is a sad reflection upon the Psalmist.

"Moreover Ahithophel said unto Absalom, Let me now choose out twelve thousand men, and I will arise and pursue after David this night: And I will come upon him while he is weary and weak handed, and will make him afraid: and all the people that are with him shall flee; and I will smite the king only: and I will bring back all the people unto thee: the man whom thou seekest is as if all returned: so all the people shall be in peace" (17:1-3). It may be thought that this vile suggestion was prompted by the feelings of private animosity, for, as previously pointed out, Bathsheba was the grand-daughter of Ahithophel, and therefore he would desire to personally avenge the wrong done to his family. But whether this be the case or no, as a politic man Ahithophel would be quick to recognize that delay was dangerous, and that if Absalom desired the removal of David from his path, there must be swift action, and a striking while his father and men were tired and low spirited.

Those who surrounded the wicked Absalom at this time, understood clearly that nothing short of the death of David and the seizing of the throne for himself would satisfy his covetousness: the only matter to be determined was the best way in which to accomplish this base design. Consequently, when Ahithophel voiced his evil counsel, there were none that raised hands of holy horror, none who so much as objected to the *gross injustice* of such a course. Not long ago Absalom himself had fled for a crime, and David contented himself by allowing his son to remain in exile, though he deserved death; nay, he craved his return. But so utterly devoid was Absalom of natural affection, so incapable of ingratitude, that he thirsts for David's blood. See, my reader, what human nature is capable of (yours and mine not excepted) when God leaves us entirely to ourselves. How far, far astray are they who deny the solemn truth of the total depravity of fallen man!

The scheme propounded by Ahithophel had much to commend itself to a man of such a designing type as Absalom. It would not serve his purpose for there to be a wholesale massacre of his subjects — the Philistines were too near and numerous to unnecessarily weaken his forces. Let the king himself be smitten, and his followers will readily capitulate. "Smite the shepherd and the sheep will be scattered, and be an easy prey to the wolf" was the principle of Ahithophel's plan. It has been pointed out by others that there was a close resemblance (if not an actual foreshadowment) here to the policy suggested by Caiaphas: "Now consider that it is expedient for us that *one man* should die for the people, and that the whole nation perish not" (John 11:50). So too the language of others of Christ's enemies was "This is the Heir: come, let us kill Him, and the inheritance shall be ours" (Mark 12:7).

"And the saying pleased Absalom well, and all the elders of Israel" (v. 4). The desperate wickedness of the cold-blooded proposal of Ahithophel to "smite" — slay — God's anointed, so far from filling Absalom with horror, met with his hearty approval. If "the path of the just is as the shining light, that shineth more and more unto the perfect day" (Prov. 4:18), it is equally true that evil men and seducers wax worse and worse. The falling stone gathers momentum, and the further it rolls down hill, the greater is its velocity. So it is with one who has thoroughly sold himself to the Devil; he gives his wretched victims no rest, but urges them on from crime to crime, until their cup of iniquity is full. Satan is a merciless taskmaster, who ever demands an increasing tale of bricks from his slaves. How earnestly we should pray to be delivered from the Evil one!

"Then said Absalom, Call now Hushai the Archite also, and let us hear likewise what he saith"(v. 5). This is surely very striking. In the previous instance Absalom had acted promptly on the evil counsel of Ahithophel (16:22), why, then, did he not do so now? The proposal made had "pleased him well," yet he hesitated and consulted with Hushai, the secret friend of David. It was not that Hushai took the initiative and pushed himself forward: it was Absalom himself who *sought* to know his mind. What a proof that "the king's heart is in the hand of the Lord, as the rivers of water: He turneth it whithersoever *He* will" (Prov. 21:1). "The Lord had appointed to defeat the good (politic) counsel of Ahithophel" (v. 14), yet He accomplished this not by physical force, but by the working of natural laws. Absalom appeared to act quite freely in following out the thought that had entered his mind, nevertheless a Divine hand was directing him, unknown to himself. Man is free to act only within the circumference of the Divine decrees.

It was at this critical moment, when the doom of David appeared to be as good as sealed, that his faithful follower was given the opportunity of befriending him. How blessedly God *times* His interventions. He is never too early, and never too late. It is the impatience of unbelief and the fretfulness of self-will which so often makes us th'. he Lord is tardy. Often God "waits that He may be gracious" (Isa. 30:) order to bring us to the end of ourselves, and that the deliverance may mo. vidently appear to be from Himself. At other times, He delays His interposition on behalf of His own for the greater chargrin and dismay of their enemies. Hushai did not fail David at this critical moment, but by clever and plausible arguments caused Absalom to change his mind, and postpone an immediate attack upon the fugitive king. This accomplished his object, for any delay on the part of Absalom afforded David an opportunity to rest his weary men, add to his forces, and station them to best advantages. But more of that in our next.

In working out His own eternal designs, in ministering to the spiritual and temporal needs of His people, and in delivering them from their enemies, God acts as sovereign, employing subordinate agents or dispensing with them as He pleases. That He is *not* restrained by the lack of means is evident from His feeding two million Israelites in the wilderness for the space of forty years, by giving them bread from heaven; and from other signal instances recorded in His Word. Nevertheless, generally, He is pleased to make use of means in the accomplishment of His everlasting decrees. Oftentimes those means are very feeble ones, altogether inadequate in themselves for accomplishing the ends they do — to show us that their sufficiency lies in Him who deigns to make use of them. Where human agents are employed by God, their unmeetness and unworthiness is often very apparent, and this, that we may glory not in them, but in the One who condescends to place His treasure in earthen vessels. Unless this principle be clearly recognised by us, we are very apt to stumble at the manifest faults in the instruments God employs.

God has never had but one perfect Servant on this earth, and His surpassing excellency is made the more conspicuous by the numerous imperfections of all others. Yet we must not take delight in looking for or dwelling upon the blemishes of those God made use of — like unclean birds seeking carrion to feed upon. Who are we, so full of sin ourselves, that we should throw stones at others? On the other hand, the faults recorded in Scripture of those whom God used in various ways, must not be made a shelter behind which we hide, in order to excuse our own sins. It is the bearing in mind of these obvious rules which often occasions a real difficulty to the minister of God, whether his preachings be oral or written. It is his duty to use *as warnings* the faults of Biblical characters; yet, alas, in doing so, he frequently has occasion to *condemn himself*; yet that is beneficial if it truly humbles him before God.

And Ahithophel said to Absalom, Now let me choose out twelve thousand men, and I will arise and pursue after David tonight. And I will come on him while he is weary and weak-handed, and I will make him afraid. And all the people who are with him shall flee. And I will strike the king only. And I will bring back all the people to you. The man whom you seek is as if all returned — so all the people shall be in peace. And the saying pleased Absalom very much, and all the elders of Israel. Then Absalom said, Now call Hushai the Archite also, and let us hear likewise what is in his mouth. And when Hushai had come to Absalom, Absalom spoke to him, saying, Ahithophel has spoken in this way — shall we do his word? If not, you speak. And Hushai said to Absalom, The advice which Ahithophel has given is not good at this time. For, Hushai said, you know your father and his men, that they are mighty men, and they are chafed in their minds, like a bear robbed of her whelps in the field. And your father is a man of war and will not stay the night with the people. Behold, he is hidden now in some pit, or in some place. And when some are overthrown at the first, whoever hears it will say, There is a slaughter among the people who follow Absalom. And also he who is strong, whose heart is like the heart of a lion, shall utterly melt. For all Israel knows that your father is a mighty man, and they who are with him are mighty men. Therefore I advise that all Israel be generally gathered to you, from Dan even to Beer-sheba, like the sand that is by the sea for multitude — and then that you go to battle in your own person. So we shall come on him in some place where he shall be found, and we will light on him like the dew falls on the ground — and of him and of all the men that are with him there shall not be left so much as one. Moreover, if he has gotten into a city, then all Israel shall bring ropes to that city, and we will draw it into the river until there is not one small stone found there. And Absalom and all the men of Israel said, The counsel of Hushai the Archite is better than the counsel of Ahithophel. For the LORD had appointed to defeat the good counsel of Ahithophel, to the intent that the LORD might bring evil on Absalom. — II Samuel 17:1-14.

We are now to consider the means used by God in delivering His servant from the murderous designs of his enemies. If there had been a Jonathan in Saul's palace to plead his cause and give him intelligence of his father's plans, so now God raised up an Hushai at the headquarters of Absalom to render him aid and forward him notice of what was impending. Reliable nessengers to carry these important tidings from him to David were present in the persons of the two priests, whom David had sent back to Jerusalem in order to there serve his interests; though they had been obliged to lodge outside the city at Enrogal, where a servant-girl communicated, in turn, with them. Yet one other link in the chain was required in order for the contact to be established: the two priests were seen as they started out on their mission, and were pursued by Absalom's men; but a protector was raised up for them, and they escaped. Thus, in this one instance God made use of a prominent politician, two priests, a maid-servant, and a farmer and his wife.

"Then said Absalom, call now Hushai the Archite also, and let us hear likewise what he saith. And when Hushai was come to Absalom, Absalom spake unto him, saying, Ahithophel hath spoken after this manner: shall we do after his saying? if not, speak thou" (2 Sam. 17:5, 6). Let it not be forgotten that "the counsel of Ahithophel, which he counselled in those days, was as if a man had enquired at the oracle of God: so was all the counsel of Ahithophel, both with David and with Absalom" (16:23). Is it not, then, truly remarkable that

Absalom did not act promptly on his advise, instead of now conferring with Hushai; the more so as the plan propounded by Ahithophel had "pleased Absalom well, and all the elders of Israel" (v. 4). There is only one satisfactory explanation: God had decreed otherwise! This is far more, my reader, than an incident in ancient history: it furnishes an example *of how* God regulates the affairs of nations to-day. Have we not witnessed individuals as devoid of all natural affections, as godless, as ruthless, as unscrupulous as was Absalom, who have *forced themselves* into the high places of national and international affairs!

Yes, my reader, what the Holy Spirit has recorded here in 2 Sam. 17 is something of much greater importance than an episode which transpired thousands of years ago. The anointed eye may discern in and through it the light of Heaven being shed upon the political affairs of earth. God governs as truly in the houses of legislature and in the secret conferences of rulers and diplomats, as He does the elements and the heavenly bodies: He it is who rules their selfish schemings and over-rules the counter plans of others. It was so here in Jerusalem in the long ago; it is so, just as actually now, at London, Washington, Paris, Moscow, Berlin, and Rome. The very reason why the Spirit has chronicled our incident in the imperishable pages of Holy Writ is that God's people in all succeeding generations might know that "the Most High ruleth in the kingdom of men, and giveth it to whosoever He will" (Dan. 4:17, 25, 32) — alas, that through the ignorance and unfaithfulness of the modern pulpit so many believers are now deprived of that comforting assurance.

God's Word is a *living* Word, and not an obsolete history of things which took place in the far-distant past. It is to our own irreparable loss if we fail to turn its light upon the mysteries of life and the "dark places of the earth." And surely there are no darker places than the conference chambers of politicians and international diplomats: God "setteth up over the kingdom of men, *the basest* of men" (Dan. 4:17), where His claims and the interests of His people are either totally ignored or blatantly defied; yet, even *there* the Most High is supreme, and has *His* way. Only so far are they allowed to go in their evil schemings and greedy plannings. If on the one hand there is a bloodthirsty Ahithophel (a military leader) who urges the modern dictator to the shedding of innocent blood, on the other hand God raises up an Hushai (though his name may not appear in our newspapers), who restrains and checks by advising cautious delay, and *his* counsel is made (by God) to thwart or modify the more extreme measures of the former. In the Day to come we shall find that 2 Sam. 17 has often been duplicated in the politics of this world, particularly in those of Europe.

"And Hushai said unto Absalom, The counsel that Ahithophel hath given is not good at this time" (v. 7). Hushai was put to rather a severe test. In the first place, Absalom had already evidenced some suspicion of his loyalty to himself, when he first appeared on the scene (16:17). In the second place, Ahithophel had just advanced a plan which met with general approval. And in the third place, to criticise the scheme of Ahithophel might well be to increase Absalom's suspicion against himself. But he stood his ground, and at some risk to himself, did what he could to befriend David. He came right out and boldly challenged the counsel of his rival, yet he prudently took the edge off the blow by his modification of "at this time." His language then is skillfully chosen. Thus Absalom discovered that his counsellors did not agree — it is by diversity of views and policies that a balance is preserved in the affairs of human government.

"For, said Hushai, thou knowest thy father and his men, that they be mighty men, and they be chafed in their minds, as a bear robbed of her whelps in the field: and thy father is a man of war, and will not lodge with the people" (v. 8). In these words Hushai artfully suggests that Ahithophel was seriously misjudging the ease of his task. He had lightly and bumptiously declared "I will smite the king only" (v. 2). But *that* was not such a simple task as Ahithophel supposed. David was something more than a pasteboard monarch: he was a man of great courage and much experience in the arts of warfare. Moreover, he was accompanied by valiant warriors, who were in an angry mood over the shameful necessity of their beloved master's flight from Jerusalem, and would not stand idly by while he was slaughtered. Absalom had better pause and face the very real difficulties of the situation, for it is often a fatal mistake to under-estimate the strength of an adversary. To sit down first and count the cost (Luke 14:28), is always a prudent course to follow. Rash and ill-considered measures are likely to meet with failure. But much grace is needed in this feverish age to act thoughtfully and cautiously, and not rush blindly ahead.

"Behold, he is hid now in some pit, or in some other place; and it will come to pass, when some of them be overthrown at the first, that whosoever heareth it will say, There is a slaughter among the people that followeth Absalom" (v. 9). The fugitive king was not the type of man to seek his ease: he "will not lodge with the people," but rather will he, as a seasoned warrior, resort to subtle strategy, and lie in a well-chosen ambush, from which he will unexpectedly spring out, and slay at least the foremost of Ahithophel's men. And *that* would seriously prejudice Absalom's cause, for the news would quickly go forth that David was victor in the field. The practical lesson which this points for us, is, that we must not commit the folly of under-estimating the strength and sublety of our spiritual enemies, and that we must carefully consider what are the best ways and means of overcoming them. Our lusts often secretly hide themselves, and then spring forth when they are least expected. Satan generally attacks us from an unlooked-for quarter. He has had far more experience than we, and we need to tread very cautiously if he is not to gain a serious advantage over us.

"And he also that is valiant, whose heart is as the heart of a lion, shall utterly melt: for all Israel knoweth that thy father is a mighty man, and they which be with him are valiant men" (v. 10). Hushai is here pressing upon Absalom what would inevitably follow if that should eventuate which he had mentioned in the previous verse. In case David succeeded in springing a trap and the advance guard of Ahithophel's proposed expedition were slain, as would most probably happen when pitted against such a wily antagonist as the conqueror of Goliath, only one course would surely follow — the entire force sent against David would be demoralized. The inexperienced men Ahithophel led, though superior in numbers, would now feel they were no match for the braves in the king's forces, and they would be utterly dismayed. That would be fatal to Absalom's cause, as a very little reflection must make apparent. Human nature is very fickle, and men in the mass are even more easily swayed than are individuals: it takes very little to turn the tide of public opinion.

"Therefore I counsel that all Israel be generally gathered unto thee, from Dan even to Beersheba, as the sand that is by the sea for multitude; and that thou go to battle in thine own person" (v. 11). This was the only logical inference to draw from the preceding premises. The "twelve thousand men" Ahithophel asked for (17:1) were altogether inadequate for success against such a general as David and against such renowned men as he commanded. Absalom must mobilize the entire manhood of the nation, and overwhelm his father by sheer force of numbers. Incidentally, observe that "as the sand that is by the sea for multitude" is a *hyperbolical* expression to denote a considerable company, and is *not* to be taken as its face value. This same figure is used again in "I will multiply thy seed as the stars of the heaven, and as the sand which is upon the sea shore" (Gen. 22:17), "And they went out, they and all their hosts with them, much people, even as the sand that is upon the sea shore in multitude" (Josh. 11:4), "And the Midianites and the Amalekites and all the children of the east lay along in the valley like grasshoppers for multitude, and their camels were without number" (Judges 7:12). Therefore, if Scripture is to be interpreted by Scripture the "great multitude which no man could number" of Rev. 7:9 must be taken as a hyperbole and *not* interpreted literally.

In counselling Absalom to undertake a general mobilization, or the gathering together of an overwhelming force, Hushai was obviously "playing for time." The longer he could induce Absalom to delay taking military action against the one he was befriending, the better would his real object be achieved. The slower Absalom was in moving, the more time would David have for putting a greater distance between himself and Jerusalem, to increase his own forces, and to select to best advantage the site for the coming conflict. The entire design of Hushai was to counter Ahithophel's proposed "I will arise and pursue David *this* night" (v. 1). To further strengthen his argument Hushai suggests that Absalom should "go to battle in thine own person" (v. 11) — take the place of honour, and lead your own men. Indirectly, he was intimating that Ahithophel's project had only his *own* ends (private revenge) and personal glory in view: not his "I will arise," "I will come upon him," "I will smite the king" (vv. 1, 2). Hushai knew well the kind of man he was dealing with, and so appealed to the pride of his heart.

As we shall (D.V.) see from the sequel, it was this very detail which issued in Absalom's losing his own life. Had he followed the counsel of Ahithophel he would have remained at Jerusalem, but by accepting the advice of Hushai to go to battle in his own person, he went forth to his death. How true it is that "God taketh the wise in their own craftiness, and the counsel of the froward is carried headlong" (Job 5:13)! No doubt Absalom was priding himself in his prudence by obtaining the advice of both these experienced counsellors, yet that was the very thing that led to his destruction. The suggestion of Hushai appealed to his personal vanity, and by yielding thereto we are shown here that "Pride goeth before destruction." If God has placed you, my reader, in humble circumstances and in a lowly position, envy not those who take the lead, and aspire not to a place of worldly dignity and carnal honours.

"So shall we come upon him in some place where he shall be found, and we will light upon him as the dew falleth on the ground: and of him and of all the men that are with him there shall not be left so much as one" (v. 12). This completes the thoughts begun at the start of the preceding verse: by means of an enormous force we shall be able to fall upon David and his followers and utterly annihilate them: neither strategy nor valour will be of any avail against such overwhelming numbers. Such counsel as this was not only calculated to appeal to Absalom himself, but also to the unthinking masses: there would be little danger to themselves; in fact, such a plan seemed to guarantee success without any risk at all: "There is safety in numbers" would be their comforting slogan. Note Hushai's artful use of the plural number: "So shall *we* come upon him" and "*we* will light upon him" in sharp contrast from the threefold "I" of Ahithophel.

"Moreover, if he be gotten into a city, then shall all Israel bring ropes to that city, and we will draw it into the river, until there be not one small stone found there" (v. 13). Thus Hushai sought to close the door against every possible objection. Should David and his men take refuge in some city, and fortify it, instead of hiding in a pit or wood (v. 9), *that* would prove no obstacle to such a host as we should take against him. We will not endanger our men by seeking to force a way in, but, by main force, drag the city and its people into the river — this, of course, was not to be taken seriously, but was intended to raise a laugh. It was simply designed to signify that by no conceivable means could David either defy or escape them.

"And Absalom and all the men of Israel said, The counsel of Hushai the Archite is better than the counsel of Ahithophel. For the Lord had appointed to defeat the good (politic) counsel of Ahithophel, to the intent that the Lord might bring evil upon Absalom" (v. 14). The second half of this verse explains the first. The prudent advice of Ahithophel was rejected, and the plausible but foolish measures of Hushai were accepted — foolish because they involved so much delay. The same thimg has happened scores of times in the affairs of nations, and for a similar reason. Folly often prevails over wisdom in the counsels of princes and in the houses of legislators. Why? Because *God* has appointed the rejection of sound counsel in order to bring on nations the vengeance which their crimes call down from Heaven. It is *thus* that God rules the world by His providence. See that grave senator, or that sage diplomat: he rises and proposes a course of wisdom; but if God has appointed to punish the nation, some prating fanatic will impose his sophisms on the most sagacious assembly.

Then Hushai said to Zadok and to Abiathar the priests, This and this Ahithophel advised Absalom and the leaders of Israel, and this and this I have advised. Now therefore send quickly and tell David, saying, Do not stay in the plains of the wilderness to night, but speedily pass over, lest the king be swallowed up, and all the people who are with him. Now Jonathan and Ahimaaz stayed by Enrogel, for there they might not be seen to come into the city. And a girl went and told them, and they went and told king David. But a lad saw them and told Absalom. But both of them went away quickly, and came to a man's house in Bahurim, who had a well in his court, into which they went down. And the woman took and spread a covering over the well's mouth, and spread ground grain on it, and the thing was not known. And when Absalom's servants came to the woman of the house, they said, Where are Ahimaaz and Jonathan? And the woman said to them, They have gone over the brook of water. And when they had searched and could not find them they returned to Jerusalem. And after they had departed, they came up out of the well and went and told king David. And they said to David, Arise and pass quickly over the water, for this is what Ahithophel has advised against you. Then David and all the people who were with him arose. And they passed over Jordan. By the morning light there was not one of them that had not gone over Jordan. And when Ahithophel saw that his counsel was not followed, he saddled his ass and arose and went home to his house, to his city, and put his household in order. And he hanged himself and died and was buried in the tomb of his father. Then David came to Mahanaim. And Absalom passed over Jordan, he and all the men of Israel with him. And Absalom made Amasa captain of the army instead of Joab. This Amasa was the son of a man named Ithra, an Israelite, who went in to Abigail the daughter of Nahash, sister to Zeruiah, Joab's mother. So Israel and Absalom pitched in the land of Gilead. And when David had come to Mahanaim, it came to pass that Shobi the son of Nahash of Rabbah, of the children of Ammon, and Machir the son of Ammiel of Lodebar, and Barzillai the Gileadite of Rogelim, brought beds and basins and earthen vessels, and wheat and barley and flour and parched grain, and beans and

lentils and other parched food,and honey and butter and sheep and cheese from
cows, for David and for the people who were with him to eat. For they said. The
people are hungry and weary and thirsty in the wilderness. II Samuel 17:15-29.

We have seen how God made use of Hushai, David's friend, to defeat the
counsel which Ahithophel had proposed to Absalom. This meant a short
breathing space was afforded the fugitive king. Hushai at once took steps to
acquaint his master with his success (17:15, 16). The two priests who served as
messengers were obliged to take refuge in a farmer's house at Bahurim, hiding in
a well, which his wife covered — how many strange and unexpected places have
sheltered the servants of God from their enemies only the Day to come will fully
reveal. Incidentally, let us note how this episode teaches us that so far from
acting rashly and presumptuously, we should always avail ourselves of any lawful
means which a merciful providence supplies for us. True faith never leads to
fanaticism or fatalism, but moves us to act with prudence and with good
judgment.

It was well that the two messengers had taken this precaution, for they were
pursued and tracked to the place where they were hiding, but through the
woman's prevarication their enemies were sent on a false trail. "And it came to
pass, after they (the pursuers) were departed, that they came up out of the well,
and went and told king David, and said unto David, Arise, and pass quickly over
the water; for thus hath Ahithophel counselled against you. Then David arose,
and all the people that were with him, and they passed over Jordan: by the
morning light there lacked not one of them that was not gone over *Jordan"*
(17:21, 22). "This was a remarkable instance of God's providential care over His
servant and his friends, that not one was lost, or had deserted, out of the whole
company; and he was in this a type of Christ, who loses none of His true
followers" (Thos. Scott). For the antitype see John 18:8, 9.

It was at this time, most probably, that David wrote the 42nd and 43rd Psalms.
They were composed at a season when he was deprived of the benefit and
blessing of the public means of grace. This loss he felt keenly (42:4), but hoping
in God and earnestly supplicating Him, he looked forward to the time when he
would be again permitted to enter His holy courts with joy and thanksgiving
(43:3, 4). These Psalms bring before us in a most blessed way the exercises of
soul through which David passed at this season, and the persevering efforts he
made to retain his hold upon God. They show us that though a fugitive, pressed
almost beyond endurance by sore trials, nevertheless he maintained his
intercourse with the Lord. They reveal the grand recourse which the believer has
in every time of trouble — something to which the poor worldling is a complete
stranger — namely, the privilege of unburdening his heart unto One who is of
tender mercy, great compassion, and who has promised to sustain (Psa. 55:22)
when we cast our burden upon Him.

The first two verses of Psa. 42 express the deep longing of a spiritual heart for
communion with God in the house of worship: it is only when deprived of such
privileges that we come to value them as we should — just as a parched throat is
the one which most relishes a glass of water. In v. 3 he tells the Lord how keenly
he had felt the mocking jibes of his blasphemous foes. Then he recalls the vivid
contrast from previous experience, when he, though king, had gone with the
multitude to the tabernacle and joined in celebrating God's praise. Challenging
himself for his despondency, he seeks to raise his spirits. But soon dejection
returns and he cries "O my God, my soul is cast down within me" (v. 6). Then it
was he added "therefore will I *remember Thee* from the land of *Jordan,* and of

the Hermonites, from the little hill" yes, though cut off from the public means of grace, though plagued with sore trials, he will not forget his best Friend.

In the remaining verses we find the Psalmist freely unburdening himself to God. As Spurgeon said, "It is well to tell the Lord how we feel, and the more plain the confession the better: David talks like a sick child to his mother, and we should seek to imitate him." So closely is the 43rd Psalm connected with the one preceding, that in one or two of the older manuscripts they are coupled together as one: that it was written during the same period is evident from vv. 3, 4. In it we find David begging God to undertake for him, to "plead his cause against an ungodly nation," to "deliver him from the deceitful and unjust man" — the reference being to Ahithophel or Absalom, or both. He is distressed at his own despondency and unbelief, prays for a fresh manifestation of the Divine presence and faithfulness (v. 3), asks for such a deliverance as would permit his return to God's house, and closes with an expression of assurance, that, in the end, all would turn out well for him.

"And when Ahithophel saw that his counsel was not followed, he saddled his ass, and arose, and gat him home to his house, to his city, and put his household in order, and hanged himself, and died, and was burried in the sepulchre of his father" (2 Sam. 17:23). Unspeakably solemn is this. What a contrast is here presented: in the preceding verse we see the temporal deliverance of David and all his men; here we behold his chief enemy flinging himself into eternal destruction by his own mad act. Significantly enough "Ahithophel" signifies "the brother of a fool," and none exhibit such awful folly as those who are guilty of self-murder. Ahithophel did not commit this unpardonable crime on the spur of the moment, but with full deliberation, journeying to his own home to accomplish it. Nor was he bereft of his senses, for he first duly settled his affairs and arranged for the future of his family before destroying himself.

But *why* should Ahithophel have proceeded to such desperate measures? Ah, my reader, there is something here which needs to search *our* hearts. That upon which he had *chiefly doted* was now turned to ashes, and therefore he no longer had any further interest in life: his household "gods" were, so to speak, stolen from him, his "good thing" was gone, and therefore his temple lay in ruins. Hitherto his counsel was regarded "as if a man had enquired at the oracle of God" (16:23), but the advice of Hushai was now preferred before his. The high esteem in which he had been held for his political acumen, his wisdom in the affairs of state, was everything to him, and when Absalom passed his advice by (17:14) it was more than the pride of his heart could endure. To be slighted by David's usurper meant that he was now a "back number;" to be thus treated before the people was too humiliating for one who had long been lionized by them.

Do we not behold the same Satanic egotism in Saul. When Samuel announced to him that the Lord had rejected him from being king, what was his response? Why, this: "Then he said, I have sinned: yet *honour me now*, I pray thee, before the leaders of my people, and *before Israel*" (1 Sam. 15:30). Ah, it was the praise of man, and not the approbation of God, which meant everything to him. Thus it was with Ahithophrel: an intolerable slur had been cast upon his sagacity, and his proud heart could not endure the idea of having to play second fiddle to Hushai. What point this gives to that exhortation, "Thus saith the Lord, Let not the wise man glory in his wisdom, neither let the mighty man glory in his might, let not the rich man glory in his riches; but let him that glorieth glory in this, that he understandeth and knoweth Me, that I am the Lord which exercise loving-kindness, judgment, and righteousness, in the earth: for in these things I delight, saith the Lord" (Jer. 9:23, 24). Observe the justice of God in suffering Ahithophel to come to such an end: he plotted the violent death of David, and now was fulfilled that word "his mischief shall return unon his own head, and his violent dealing shall come down upon his own pate" (Psa. 7:16).

O that we may really take this to ourselves, so that we honestly examine our hearts, and ascertain upon what it is, really, chiefly set. What did anything avail Haman, while Mordecai sat at the gate? is another illustration of the same evil principle. What a solemn lesson all of this reads to us! Have we, my reader, some earthly idol — be it riches, honour, fame, or even a loved one — around which the tendrils of the soul are so entwined that if *it* be touched, our very *life* is touched; if *it* be taken away, life is for us no longer worth living.Where is our ruling passion fixed? on what is it centered? Is it some object of time and sense, or One who is eternal and immutable? What "treasure" are we laying up day by day? Is it one that the hand of man or the hand of death may soon take from us, or that which is "eternal in the heavens?" Seek to answer this question in the presence of the Lord Himself.

"Then David came to Mahanaim" (v. 24). This was one of the cities of the Levites in the tribe of Gad (Josh. 13:26). What sacred memories were associated with this place we may discover by a reference to Gen. 32. It was at this very place that Jacob had stopped on his return from sojourning so long with Laban. He was on his way toward the unwelcome meeting with Esau. But it was there that "the angels of God met him!" With faith's discernment, Jacob perceived that this was "a token for good" from the Lord: "and when Jacob saw them, he said, This is God's host, and he called the name of that place Mahanaim" or "two hosts" — if God were for him, who could be against him! It was *this* place, then, that David now made his headquarters, where he increased his forces, and gathered together an army with which to oppose the rebels.

By this time the first force of the disaster had spent itself, and when David had succeeded in getting his forces safely across the Jordan, on the free uplands of Bashan, his spirits rose considerably. The 42nd and 43rd Psalms reflect the struggle which had taken place within him between despair and hope, but as we have seen, the latter eventually triumphed. Now that Mahanaim was reached, he determined to make a definite stand. No doubt the sacred memories associated with this place served to further hearten him, and when the news reached him of Ahithophel's defection from Absalom and his subsequent suicide, he had good ground to conclude that the Lord was not on the side of the enemies. As the time went on, it became increasingly evident that the leaders of the rebellion were lacking in energy, and that every day of respite from actual fighting diminished their chances of success, as the astute Ahithophel had perceived.

"And Absalom passed over Jordan, he and all the men of Israel with him...so Israel and Absalom pitched in the land of Gilead" (vv. 24, 26). At last the perfidious Absalom proceeds to carry out his vile designs. Not content with having hounded his fond parent from Jerusalem, and driven him to the utmost corner of his kingdom, nothing will satisfy him but removing David from the world itself. See to what fearful lengths Satan will lead one who is fully yielded to his sway. He was guilty of high treason. With eager mind and brutal heart he determined to deprive his father of his life. His awful conspiracy had now reached its consummation. He set his army in battle array against David. He was willing to play the part of paracide, to stain his hands with the blood of a loving father who had been too long-suffering with him.

"And Absalom made Amasa captain of the host instead of Joab: which Amasa was a man's son, whose name was Ithra an Israelite, that went in to Abigail the daughter of Nahash, sister to Zeruiah Joab's mother" (v. 25). Joab, the commander-in-chief of Israel's army (1 Chron. 20:1), had remained loyal to his master, so that Absalom had perforce to appoint a new general to take charge of his forces: the wicked are not allowed to have everything their own way —

Divine providence generally puts a cog in their wheel. There is some difficulty in deciphering the details of this verse; as the marginal readings intimate. The one selected by Absalom as captain of his host was, originally, "Jether an *Ishmaelite*," who had seduced the half-sister of David — suitable character for the present position! Later, he was known as "Ithra an Israelite," Matt. Henry suggesting that he had become such by "some act of state — naturalized." Such a selection on the part of Absalom was fully in accord with his own rotten character.

"And it came to pass, when David was come to Mahanaim, that Shobi the son of Nahash of Rabbah of the children of Ammon, and Machir the son of Ammiel of Lodebar, and Barzillai the Gileadite of Rogelim, brought beds, and basons, and earthern vessels, and wheat, and barley, and flour, and parched corn, and beans, and lentils, and parched pulse, and honey, and butter, and sheep, and cheese of kine, for David and for all the people that were with him to eat: for they said, "The people is hungry, and weary, and thirsty, in the wilderness" (vv. 27-29). Here the scene changes again, and from the malice of David's foes our attention is directed to the kindness of his friends. What vivid contrasts these chapters abound in! And is it not thus in all earthly life? How can it be otherwise in a world which is ruled by Satan, but overruled by God.

There is something striking and touching in connection with each of the three men mentioned here, who brought such a lavish present to David. "Shobi was the brother of him, concerning whom David had said, 'I will *show kindness* to Hanun the son of Nahash' " (10:2) so, with the measure he had meted out to this Gentile, it is measured to him again. Ah, has not God promised that he who watereth others, shall himself be watered! "Machir the son of Ammiel of Lodebar" was the man who had given shelter to Mephibosheth (9:5): the king had relieved him of this trust by giving Mephibosheth a place at his own table (9:11), and now Machir shows his gratitude by providing for David's table. Concerning "Barzillai" we read that he was "a very aged man, even four score years old" (19:22), yet he was not too aged to now minister unto David's needs. He will come before us again (D.V.) in the sequel.

Let this pleasing incident be contemplated in the light of David's prayers, recorded in Psalms 42 and 43. This was a most evident answer from God, who did not forget His servant in this hour of his emergency. Once again a kind providence moved different ones to befriend the fugitive king and his forces. Weary from their long march, ill provisioned for what lay before them, bountiful supplies are now freely given to them. As Matt. Henry pointed out, "He did not put them under contribution, did not compel them to supply him, much less plunder them. But, in token of their dutiful affection to him, their firm adherence to his government, and their sincere concern for him in his present straits, of their own good will, they brought in plenty of all that which he had occasion for. Let us learn hence to be generous and open-handed, according as our ability is, to all in distress, especially great men, to whom it is most grievous, and good men, who deserve better treatment."

How often it falls out that God moves strangers to comfort His people when they are denied it from those much nearer to them. There is a law of compensation which is conspicuously exemplified in the Divine government of human affairs. A balance is strikingly preserved between losses and gains, bitter disappointments and pleasant surprises. If an heartless Pharaoh determines to slay the children of the Hebrews, his own daughter is constrained to care for Moses. If Elijah has to flee from Palestine to escape the fury of Ahab and Jezebel, a widow at Zarephath is willing to share her last meal with him. If the parents of Jesus Christ were poverty stricken, wise men from the East come with a gift of "gold," which made possible their flight and sojourn in Egypt. If a man's foes be those of his own household, friends are raised up for him in the most unexpected quarters. Let us not, then, dwell unduly upon the former; and let us not fail to be grateful and return thanks for the latter.

And David numbered the people who were with him, and set captains of thousands and captains of hundreds over them. And David sent forth a third of the people under the hand of Joab, and a third under the hand of Abishai the son of Zeruiah, Joab's brother, and a third under the hand of Ittai the Gittite. And the king said to the people, I will also surely go out with you myself. But the people answered, You shall not go. For if we run away, they will not care for us. Neither if half of us die, will they care for us. But now you are worth ten thousand of us. Therefore now it is better that you remain to help us from the city. And the king said to them, I will do what seems best to you. And the king stood by the side of the gate, and all the people came out by hundreds and by thousands. And the king commanded Joab and Abishai and Ittai, saying, For my sake be gentle with the young man, with Absalom. And all the people heard when the king gave all the captains charge concerning Absalom. So the people went out in the field against Israel. And the battle was in the woods of Ephraim, where the people of Israel were killed before the servants of David. And there was a great slaughter that day of twenty thousand men. For the battle was scattered there over the face of all the country. And the woods devoured more people that day than the sword devoured. And Absalom met the servants of David. And Absalom rode on a mule, and the mule went under the thick boughs of a great oak. And his head caught hold of the oak, and he was taken up between the heaven and the earth. And the mule which was under him went away. But a certain man saw it and told Joab, and said, Behold, I saw Absalom hanged in an oak. And Joab said to the man who told him, And, behold, you saw him, and why did you not strike him there to the ground? And I would have given you ten shekels of silver and a girdle. And the man said to Joab, though I should receive a thousand shekels of silver in my hand, yet I would not put forth my hand against the king's son. For in our hearing the king charged you and Abishai and Ittai, saying, Beware that none touches the young man Absalom. — II Samuel 18:1-12.

"The triumphing of the wicked is short, and the joy of the hypocrite but for a moment" (Job 20:5) — often so even when measured by human and temporal standards: how much more so in the light of Eternity! Alas, that our hearts are so little affected by that unspeakably solemn consideration— *a never-ending future:* enjoyed under the blissful approbation of God, or endured beneath His frightful curse. What are the smiles and honours of men worth, if their sequel be the everlasting frown of the Almighty? The pleasures of sin are but "for a season" (Heb. 11:25), whereas the pleasures which are at God's right hand are "for ever more" (Psa. 16:11). Then what shall it profit a man if he should gain the whole world, and lose his own soul? Yet how many, like Esau of old, place more value upon a mess of pottage than the blessings of Heaven. How many, like Ahab, will set themselves to do evil in order for a brief moment of pleasure of fame.

"The triumphing of the wicked is short." Yes, and so it proved with David's wretched son. Absalom had laid his plans carefully, executed them zealously, and had carried them out without any compunction (2 Sam. 15:1, 2, 5). He had taken a mean advantage of his father's indisposition and had stolen the hearts of many of his subjects from him. He aspired to the kingdom, and now determined to sieze the throne for himself (15:10). He had assembled his forces at Jerusalem, and had the powerful Ahithophel to counsel him. He had ruthlessly determined that his father's life must be sacrificed to his ambition, and had now gone forth at the head of the army to accomplish his death (17:24). His triumph seemed to be assured, but unknown and unsuspected by himself, he was going forth to meet his own tragic but fully merited doom.

"And David numbered the people that were with him, and set captains of thousands and captains of hundreds over them" (2 Sam. 18:1). As Ahithophel had foreseen, the delay of Absalom had afforded David the opportunity to greatly augment his forces. Though considerable numbers had joined the rebel, yet there must have been many scattered throughout Israel who still remained loyal to David, and as the news of the insurrection spread abroad, no doubt hundreds of them took up arms and went forth to assist their fugitive king. That his army had, by this time, been greatly strengthened, is clear from the terms of this verse. David now proceeded to muster and marshal his re-inforcements so that they might be used to the best advantage. He girded on the sword with some of the animation of early days, and the light of trustful valour once more shone in his eyes.

It seems quite clear that, by this time, David had no fear of what the outcome would be of the coming conflict. He had committed his cause to God, and looked forward with confidence to the issue of the impending battle. The striking answer which God had given to his prayer that the counsel of Ahithophel might be turned to foolishness, must have greatly strengthened his faith. His language at the close of both the 42nd and 43rd Psalms (composed at this period) witness to his hope in the living God. Yet let it be duly noted that strong faith did not produce either sloth or carelessness. David acted with diligence and wisdom: marshalling his forces, putting them in good order, dividing them to best advantage, and placing them under the command of his most experienced generals. In order to insure success, our responsibility is to employ all lawful and prudent means. Declining to do so is presumption, and not faith.

"And David sent forth a third part of the people under the hand of Joab, and a third part under the hand of Abishai the son of Zeruiah, Joab's brother, and a third part under the hand of Ittai the Gittite" (v. 2). How true it is that there is nothing new under the sun. Military tactics were conducted along the same lines then as they are now: David disposed his forces into a central army, with right and left protecting flanks. "And the king said unto the people, I will surely go forth with you myself also" (v. 2). David was not lacking in courage, and was ready and willing to share any danger with his men. Yet we believe there was something more than bravery evidenced by these words: was he not anxious to be on the spot when the crisis arrived, so that he could protect his wayward son from the fury of his soldiers! Yes, we see here the father's heart, as well as the king's nobility.

"And the king said unto the people, I will surely go forth with you myself also." His desire was still upon Absalom, judging that his presence might help to shield him, for he was of too soft a heart to disown the feelings of a father, even toward one who had risen up in rebellion against him. Yet it seems to us that there was something of a deeper character which prompted David at this time. He would feign go forth himself because he realized that it was *his sin* which had brought all this trouble upon the land, and he was far too noble minded to let the risks of battle find any in the foreground but himself. Let not the reader forget what we pointed out several times in the preceding sections, namely, that it is *as the humble penitent* David is to be viewed throughout this connection: this it is which supplied the key to various details in these incidents.

"But the people answered, Thou shalt not go forth: for if we flee away, they will not care for us; neither if half of us die, will they care for us: but now *thou* art worth ten thousand of us, therefore now it is better that thou succour us out of the city" (v. 3). This is indeed beautiful. David had shown his affection for his faithful followers, and now they evidence theirs for him. They would not hear of their beloved king adventuring himself into the place of danger. How highly they esteemed him! and justly so: he was not only possessed of qualities which could well command, but of those which held the hearts of those who knew him best. The deep veneration in which he was held comes out again at a later date, when he was hazarding his life in battle with the Philistines: his men sware to him saying, "*Thou* shalt go no more out with us to battle, that thou quench not the light of Israel" (21:17). He was their "light:" thier leader, their inspirer, their joy, the honoured and loved one, in favour with God and man.

"And the king said unto them, What seemeth you best I will do. And the king stood by the gate side, and all the people came out by hundreds and by thousands" (v. 4). "He might be more serviceable to them by tarrying in the city, with a reserve of his forces there, whence he might send them recruits — that may be a position of real service, which yet is not a position of danger. The king acquiesced in their reasons, and changed his purpose. It is no piece of wisdom to be stiff in our resolutions, but to be willing to hear reason, even from our inferiors, and to be overruled by their advice, when it appears to be for our own good. Whether the people's prudence had an eye to it or no, God's providence wisely ordered it, that David should not be in the field of battle; for then his tenderness had certainly interposed to save Absalom's life, whom God had determined to destroy" (M. Henry).

Personally, we regard the king's acquiescence as another indication of his *chastened heart*. There is nothing that more humbles and meekens the soul than a spirit of genuine repentance, as nothing more tends to harden and swell with self-importance than the absence of it. He who is blind to his own faults and failings, is unprepared to listen to the counsels of others: an unbroken will is self-assertive and impervious to either the feelings or wishes of his fellows. But David was sorrowing over his past sins, and that made him tractable and in a condition to yield to the desire of his men. As he stood at the gate, watching his army go forth to the battle of the wood of Ephraim, victory or defeat would be much the same to him. Whatever the outcome, the cause must be traced back to his *own* wrong doing. He must have stood there with a sad remembrance of that other battle, in which a devoted servant had fallen, as one murdered by his own hand (2 Sam. 11:24).

"And the king commanded Joab and Abishai, and Ittai, saying, Deal gently for my sake with the young man, even with Absalom. And all the people heard when the king gave all the captains charge concerning Absalom" (v. 5). So great was David's love for his wayward son that, even now, he sought to deliver him from the stroke of death. He knew that Absalom was an excuseless rebel, who sought his life and throne, who had proven himself to be the very incarnation of iniquitous ingratitude, of unfeeling cruelty, of unadulterated wickedness, of Satanic ambition. He was guilty of treason of the vilest sort, and his life by every law of justice was entirely forfeited; yet in spite of all, the heart of David remained steadfast unto him. There is nothing recorded in Holy Writ which exhibits so vividly the depth and power of human affection, nothing which displays so touchingly *love for the utterly unworthy*. Therefore, is it not designed to turn our thoughts into a higher and purer Love!

Yes, see this aged parent, driven from his home, humiliated before his subjects, stricken "to the very depths of his heart by the murderous hatred of the son whom he had forgiven and honoured, loving this worthless and Devil-driven youth with an unchanged devotion, that sought to save him from his just and impending doom. Yet wonderful as this was, it provides only a faint shadow of the amazing love of Christ, which moved Him to set His heart upon "His own," even while they were totally depraved, utterly corrupt, dead in trespasses and sins. God commended His love toward us by the death of His Son (Rom. 5:8), and it was for the rebellious and the ungodly that He was crucified. Nor can anything ever separate us from that love: no, "Having loved His own which were in the world, He loved them unto the end" (John 13:1). Verily, such love "passeth knowledge."

"So the people went out into the field against Israel: and the battle was in the wood of Ephraim" (v. 6). This statement has presented quite a problem to the commentators, some going so far as to (irreverently) say there was a slip of the historian's pen. As we have seen, both David and Absalom had crossed the Jordan and were now "in the land of Gilead" (17:22, 26), which was on the eastward side of the river; whereas *their* territory lay wholly on the west of it. How, then, ask the sceptics, could this battle be said to have taken place in "the wood of Ephraim?" Did the narrator err in his geography? Certainly not: it is the critics who display their ignorance of sacred history.

We do not have to go outside of the Scriptures in order to discover the solution to this "serious difficulty." If we turn back to Judges 12, we discover that an attack was made by "Ephraimites" upon Jephthah in the land *of Gilead,* under pretense of a wrong being done them when *they* were not invited by the latter to take part in his successful invasion of Ammon. Jephthah sought to soothe his angry assailants, but in vain. A battle was fought near "the passages of the Jordan" (Judges 12:5), and Ephraim met with fearful slaughter: in all forty-two thousand of their men being put to death. Now an event so fearful was not likely to pass away without some memorial, and what more natural than to name their grave, the Aceldama of their tribe, by this name "the wood of Ephraim" in the land of Gilead!

For a short while the battle was furious, but the issue was not long left in doubt: the rebels suffering a heavy defeat: "The people of Israel were slain before the servants of David, and there was there a great slaughter that day of twenty thousand men. For the battle was there scattered over the face of all the country: and the wood devoured more people than the sword devoured" (vv. 7, 8). "Now they smarted justly for their treason against their lawful prince, their uneasiness under so good a government, and their base ingratitude to so good a governor; and found what it was to take up arms for an usurper, who with his kisses and caresses had wheedled them into their own ruin. Now where are the rewards, the preferments, the golden days, they promise themselves from him? Now they see what it is to take counsel against the Lord and His anointed, and to think of breaking His bands asunder" (M. Henry).

Most evident was it on which side the Lord was. All was confusion and destruction in the ranks of the apostate. The anointed eye may discern the hand of God as manifest here as, on a former occasion, it has been at Gibeon: as there the "hailstones," so here the "wood" devoured more than the sword. No details are given, so it is useless to conjecture whether it was pits and bogs or the wild beasts that infested those forests: sufficient that it was God Himself who fought against them — conquering them by a much smaller force than their own, and then, their being pursued by His destructive providences when they sought to escape the sword. Nevertheless, such wholesale slaughter of Israel — in view of their surrounding enemies — was a serious calamity for David's kingdom.

And meanwhile, what of the arch-traitor himself? Ah, he is dealt with separately, and that, in a manner which still more conspicuously displayed God's hand: he was "made a show of openly." "And Absalom rode upon a mule, and the mule went under the thick boughs of a great oak, and his head caught hold of the oak, and he was taken up between the heaven and the earth; and the mule that was under him went away" (v. 9). Those boughs, like the hands of a giant, gripped him, holding him fast either by his neck or by his luxuriant hair (2 Sam. 14:26). His beast continued its progress, leaving him there, as though glad to be rid of such a burden. There he was suspended, between heaven and earth, to intimate he was fit for neither. Behold the striking providence of this: "*Cursed* is every one that hangeth on a tree" (Gal. 3:13)! There he hung as an object of shame, filled with terror, incapable of delivering himself, unable to either fight or flee. He remained in this direful situation for some considerable time, awaiting with horror his merited doom.

Full opportunity was now afforded him to meditate upon his crimes and make his peace with God. But, alas, so far as the sacred record informs us, there was no contrition on his part, nothing to intimate that he now felt unfit to either live or die. As God declared of Jezebel "I gave her space to repent of her fornication, and she repented not" (Rev. 2:21), so the life of Absalom was spared a few more hours, but no hint is given us that he confessed his fearful sins to God before being summoned into His holy presence. No, God had no place in his thoughts; as he had lived, so he died — defiant and impenitent. His father's love, tears, and prayers were wasted on him. Absalom's case presents to us one of the darkest pictures of fallen human nature to be met with in the whole of God's Word.

A more melancholy and tragic spectacle can scarcely be imagined than Absalom dangling from the boughs of that tree. Deserted by his fellows, for they had one and all left him to his fate; abandoned by God, now that the cup of his iniquity was filled; a prey to remorse, for though utterly heartless and consciencless, his thoughts now must have been of the gloomiest nature. Quite unable to free himself, he was compelled to wait, hour after hour, until some one came and put an end to his wretched life. What an unspeakably solemn object lesson is this for the young people of our day! How clearly the fearful end of Absalom demonstrates the Lord's abhorrence of rebellion against parents! God's Word tells us that it is *the fool* who "despiseth his father's instruction" (Prov. 15:5), and that "whoso curseth his father or his mother, his lamp shall be put out in obscure darkness" (Prov. 20:20); and again, "The eye that mocketh at his father, and despiseth to obey his mother, the ravens of the valley shall pick it out, and the young eagles shall eat it" (Prov. 30:17).

The sands of his hour glass had now almost run out. "And a certain man saw it, and told Joab, and said, Behold, I saw Absalom hanged in an oak" (v. 10). This man had beheld Absalom's tragic plight, but had made no effort to extricate him: instead, he went and reported it to the general. "And Joab said unto the man that told him, And behold, thou sawest him, and why didst thou not smite him there to the ground? and I would have given thee ten sheckels of silver and a girdle. And the man said unto Joab, Though I should receive a thousand shekels of silver in mine hand, yet would I not put forth mine hand against the king's son: for in our hearing the king charged thee and Abishai and Ittai, saying, Beware that none touch the young man Absalom" (vv. 11, 12). And here we must stop: amidst so much that is revolting: it is a welcome contrast to behold the obedience of this man to his royal master.

Otherwise I should have dealt falsely with my own life, for there is no matter

hidden from the king, and you yourself would have set yourself against me.
Then Joab said, I cannot stay here with you this way! And he took three darts in
his hand and thrust them through the heart of Absalom while he was still alive in
the middle of the oak. And ten young men who bore Joab's armor surrounded
and struck Absalom, and killed him. And Joab blew the trumpet, and the people
returned from pursuing Israel. For Joab held back the people. And they took
Absalom and threw him into a great pit in the woods. And they laid a very great
heap of stones on him. And all Israel fled, each one to his tent. Now Absalom in
his lifetime had taken and reared up for himself a pillar, which is in the king's
valley — for he said, I have no son to keep my name in remembrance. And he
called the pillar after his own name. And it is called until this day, Absalom's
place. Then Ahimaaz the son of Zadok said, Now let me run and bear the news
to the king, how the LORD has avenged him of his enemies. And Joab said to
him, You shall not bear news today, but you shall bear good news some other
day. But today you shall bear no news, because the king's son is dead. Then Joab
said to Cushi, Go tell the king what you have seen. And Cushi bowed himself to
Joab and ran. Then Ahimaaz the son of Zadok said yet again to Joab, Come
what may, please let me also run after Cushi. And Joab said, Why will you run,
my son, since you have no good news ready? But he said, Come what may, let
me run! And he said to him, Run. Then Ahimaaz ran by the way of the plain
and ran past Cushi. — II Samuel 18:13-23.

In our last we left Absalom caught in an oak, suspended in the air, unable to free himself. His predicament was indeed a desperate one, for all his followers had forsaken him. What was to be the sequel? David had given express instructions to his generals, "Deal gently for my sake with the young man, even with Absalom" (2 Sam. 18:5). In that charge we see expressed the weakness of a doting father, rather than the uncompromising faithfulness of a monarch. It was not for the interests of his kingdom that such an insurrectionist should be spared, for none could tell how soon he would occasion further trouble. Sentiment ought never to override the requirements of righteousness, yet often it is far from easy to perform the latter when they come into conflict with the yearnings of the former. By yielding to his paternal feelings and giving such counsel to his men, David created a difficulty which should never have been raised.

"And a certain man saw it, and told Joab, and said, Behold, I saw Absalom hanged in an oak" (2 Sam. 18:10). The commentators differ considerably in their estimations of what is recorded in this verse and those which immediately follow. Some criticize this man for his timidity in refusing to take matters into his own hands and rid the earth of such a wretch; others go to an opposite extreme and blame him as a sneak for revealing the situation to Joab, knowing that he would have no scruples against killing Absalom. Personally, we consider he did the right thing in taking this middle course. It was not for him, as a private person, to fly in the face of the king's charge, and act as public executioner; nor was it the thing for him to conceal from the general-in-charge the helpless position in which the arch-enemy of David was now placed: all of which illustrates what was said at the close of the preceding paragraph.

"And Joab said unto the man that told him, And, behold, thou sawest him, and why didst thou not smite him there to the ground? and I would have given thee ten shekels of silver, and a girdle" (v. 11). Those words were evidently uttered rashly on the spur of the moment, for when Joab had listened to the man's reply, he did not further upbraid him. Joab failed to realise the quandary in which David's command had placed this man, or perhaps he was constitutionally incapable of appreciating the conscientious scruples which regulated others — which seems the more likely in the light of what follows. What a coarse and mercenary spirit his words betrayed! As though a monetary reward should have been sufficient inducement for any one to have slain Absalom in cold blood. One cannot expect such a gross materialist to value the finer sensibilities of others.

"And the man said unto Joab, Though I should receive a thousand shekels of silver in mine hand, yet would I not put forth mine hand against the king's son: for in our hearing the king charged thee and Abishai and Ittai, saying, Beware that none touch the young man Absalom. Otherwise I should have wrought falsehood against mine own life: for there is no matter hid from the king, and thou thyself wouldest have set thyself against me" (vv. 12, 13). This unnamed man was not to be intimidated by the fierce Joab, but boldly stood his ground and frankly avowed the principles which had regulated his conduct. Though it was not a lawful command which the king had imposed upon his subjects, yet this one respected the authority of his royal master. Moreover, as he shrewdly pointed out, what advantage would he receive from the largest reward if the penalty for his action were the forfeiting of his own life? That was an argument which admitted no answer, acknowledged by Joab's abruptly terminating the conversation under the plea of haste.

"Then said Joab, I may not tarry thus with thee. And he took three darts in his hand, and thrust them through the heart of Absalom, while he was yet alive in the midst of the oak" (v. 14). Joab will come before us again (D.V.) in the chapters that follow, but this seems as good a place as any to offer some remarks upon his character. It has been rightly said that "Among the followers and closest adherents of David, Joab was one. He was early found with David in the cave. Whilst Jonathan tarried in the court of Saul, Joab was sharing the hardships and dangers of David in the wilderness. Throughout all his subsequent dangers, he stood like a lion at his side, and if extent of outward service were regarded, David perhaps had no such servant as he. Yet in order to serve David aright, it was necessary to have respect not to his office merely, but also to appreciate the character of him who bore that office; to love him for *his own* as well as for the office sake, and above all, to remember that no real service could be rendered to David, except God were reverently regarded and reverently obeyed" (B.W.Newton).

It is possible for one to serve, because of the dignity of his office, one whose excellency as an individual we have no regard for. In such an event, our service, no matter however energetic, will probably have its springs in self-interest, and its course will be marked by self-will and pride. Such indeed was the case with Joab: he was zealous in maintaining the support of David's throne, yet he was ever alive to the maintenance of his own personal interests. He deemed it best that the crown should rest on David's brow, because by so doing his own fortunes were furthered. No matter how definitely or plaintively David might express his desires, Joab never hesitated, when the opportunity arose, to outrage the king's feelings or defy his will if he could thereby gain his own ends without at the same time compromising the stability of the throne. In such a course, Joab regarded neither David nor God.

No one can read carefully the sacred narrative without perceiving that in the latter years of his reign David was little more than a *nominal* king. He seems to have come thoroughly under the power of Joab, the captain of his armies: on the one hand he was too suspicious to trust him, and on the other too weak to dismiss him. It is both interesting and instructive to trace out *the occasion and cause* whereby Joab established such a despotic control over his royal master. Nor is this by any means a complicated task: "David wrote a letter *to Joab*, and sent it by the hand of Uriah. And he wrote in the letter, saying, Set ye Uriah in the forefront of the hottest battle, and retire ye from him, that he may be smitten, and die" (2 Sam. 11:14, 15). By making Joab the partner and secret agent of his guilty plot concerning Uriah, David sold himself into his hands: in that fatal letter he forfeited his liberty, surrendering it to this unscrupulous accomplice.

By temperament Joab was a daring and energetic man: a bold fighter in lawless times. The faction of Saul's house was so strong that at the beginning of his reign David could scarcely call the throne his own, or choose his servants according to his own pleasure. Joab was an able warrior, and though he sometimes avenged his own private quarrels at the expense of his sovereign's honour, thereby vexing him at heart, yet he was too strongly entrenched to be displaced. Nevertheless, at that time David was not afraid to open his mouth and rebuke him for his slaying of Abner. Nay, he openly asserted his authority by *compelling* Joab to rend his clothes, put on sackcloth, and mourn before this very Abner (2 Sam. 3:28-31) — a most humiliating experience for one of his proud heart, and which made it unmistakably manifest that David was as yet supreme in his own dominions.

Circumstances might still constrain David to employ this renowned warrior, and he had not — short as had then been his reign — yielded himself up to this imperious subject. On the contrary, as his own cause waxed stronger and stronger, and the remnant of Saul's party dispersed, he became the king of Israel in fact as well as in name, so that his throne was established not only by law, but by public opinion too, for we are told that "whatsoever the king did, pleased all the people" (2 Sam. 3:36). Consequently, he was now in the condition to rule for himself, and this he did, for a little later we find him appointing this officer to be the commander of his army by his *own* decision, and that simply because Joab was the one who won that rank, when it was promised by David as the reward to any individual in his host who should be the first to get up to the gutter and smite the Jebusites at the storming of Zion (2 Sam. 5:8).

We have only to read carefully through the 8th and 10th chapters of 2 Sam., in which are narrated the bold achievements of David at this bright period of his life, his prowess abroad and his strong policy at home, the energy he instilled into the national character, and the respect he commanded for it throughout all the surrounding countries, to perceive that he reigned without restraint and without a rival. But then came his fearful fall, that evil sowing from which he reaped so bitter a harvest. From that point onwards we may discern how Joab usurped by degrees an authority which he had not before. More and more he took matters into his own hands, executing or disregarding David's orders as suited his own designs; until finally, we shall see (D.V.) he dared to conspire against his very throne and the rightful successor of his line.

An incident recorded in 2 Sam. 14 well illustrates what we have pointed out above. There we see the hands of David tied, his efforts to free himself from this oppressor both feeble and ineffectual, and his punishment of Absalom successfully resisted, for it was Joab, through the widow of Tekoah, who clamoured for the recall of Absalom from his banishment. The suspicions of the king were aroused, for he asked "Is not the hand of *Joab* with thee in all this?" (14:19), nevertheless, he yielded to his will. It seems that this move on Joab's part was without any other design than to embarass the king and force him to do that which could only lower him in the estimation of his subjects. Certainly he had no love for Absalom as the sequel clearly shows.

During Absalom's rebellion, Joab, as might have been expected, was loyal to the cause of David, for he had no desire to see *his* government overthrown and one of another order take its place. Joab knew full well what was in the heart of Absalom, and therefore he was prepared to resist him with all his might. He wished to have the present government of Israel continued, and that in David's own person, yet it was out of no love for David that he now fought against Absalom. This is evident from his open defiance of the express charge which the king had given his generals: "Deal gently for my sake with Absalom." But Joab heeded not, for he had lost all respect for David's commands. Nothing could be more deliberate than his infraction of this one — probably the most imperious which had ever been laid upon him. It was not in the fury of the fight that he forgot his commission of mercy, but in cold blood he deliberately went to the place where Absalom was hanging helpless and slew him.

No, if Joab had loved David and regarded him as his friend, he had never recklessly despised the anguish of David's heart and made him cry, "Would God I had died for thee, O Absalom, my son, my son." Whatever may be said about his conferring a public benefit by the removal of this reprobate ringleader, the fact remains that Joab no longer cared anything for a king *whose guilty secret he shared.* He thrust Absalom through the heart with his three darts, and then made his way, with contenance unabashed, into the chamber of his royal master, where David was lamenting the death of his son. As we shall see, the sequel is a piece with what preceded: Joab imperious and heartless; David, once so regnant, abject in spirit and tame to the lash. How had the mighty fallen! Into what public humiliation as well as personal sorrows had his deed of lust and blood now sunk him down!

"And they took Absalom, and cast him into a great pit in the wood, and laid a very great heap of stones upon him: and all Israel fled every one to his tent" (2 Sam. 18:17). What an ending is this! hanged in a tree, abandoned by his followers, dispatched by Joab, and now his body treated with the utmost contempt. Instead of receiving the honourable burial of a king's son, he was ignominiously dealt with as a criminal: the casting of him into a great pit intimated their valuation of his carcass, while their laying upon him a great heap of stones signified that he ought to have been stoned to death as a rebellious son (Deut. 21:18, 21).

"Now Absalom in his lifetime had taken and reared up for himself a pillar, which is in the king's dale: for he said, I have no son to keep my name in remembrance: and he called the pillar after his own name: and it is called unto this day, Absalom's place" (v. 18). What a striking and solemn contrast do these two verses present, and what a forcible illustration do they supply of that principle "whosoever exalteth himself shall be abased" (Luke 14:11): so it was in the history of Haman and of Nebuchadnezzar, and such was the case here. Absalom had three sons (2 Sam. 14:27), but they had predeceased their father, and therefore he sought to perpetuate his memory by setting up this pillar to honour his name, by the side of which he doubtless intended that his body should be interred. Alas, how vain are some men to attract the notice of future generations, who are at no pains to seek the approbation of God. But even in death Absalom was thwarted: "a great heap of stones" as a monument of his villany was all that marked his resting-place.

"Then said Ahimaaz the son of Zadok, Let me now run, and bear the king tidings, how that the Lord hath avenged him of his enemies" (v. 19). Ahimaaz was the son of Zadok the priest (2 Sam. 15:27), who was deeply devoted to

David. He was one of the two men who had endangered their lives in the kings service by bringing him tidings of Absalom's plans (17:17-21). That he was a godly soul is intimated by the language which he used on this occasion, for instead of flattering Joab by congratulating him for his bringing the conflict to a triumphant issue, he ascribes the success to the Lord. How often God is forgotten in the flush of victory, and instead of exclaiming *"His* right hand, and *His* holy arm, hath gotten Him the victory" (Psa. 98:1), proud man attributes the defeating of his enemies to his own strength, vigilance or skill. In such an hour it is for the servant of God to lift up his voice and make known the truth that the glory belongs to God alone.

"And Joab said unto him, Thou shalt not bear tidings this day, but thou shalt bear tidings another day: this day thou shalt bear no tidings because the king's son is dead" (v. 20). In the light of what follows it is not easy to determine what it was that influenced Joab to refuse the request of Ahimaaz, for immediately afterward he bids another man go and tell the king what he had seen, and when Ahimaaz renewed his request, after a slight demur Joab granted it. It is possible that Joab feared for the life of Ahimaaz and considered he was too valuable a man to be thrown away, for the name of the selected messenger ("Cushi") suggested that he was an Ethiopian — probably an African slave. Joab knew that David was an impulsive and quick-tempered man, and remembered the fate which overtook the one who bore to him the tidings of Saul's death (2 Sam. 1:15), and therefore he probably thought that a similar vengeance might be visited upon the one who should inform him of Absalom's death.

"Then said Ahimaaz the son of Zadok yet again to Joab, But howsoever let me, I pray thee, also run after Cushi. And Joab said, "Wherefore wilt thou run, my son, seeing that thou hast no tidings ready?" (v. 22). The marginal renderings of this verse seem to decidedly confirm what we have just said above. The words of Ahimaaaz, "But howsoever" are literally "be what may:" whatever be the risk of incurring the king's fury, I am quite willing to face it. Joab's "Wherefore wilt thou, *my son,*" indicates that he held Ahimaaz in some esteem, and his "thou hast no tidings ready" is really "no tidings *convenient,*" which intimates he sought to discourage him from being the bearer of news which would be so unwelcome to David. And why, it may be asked, was Ahimaaz anxious to serve as messenger on this fateful occasion? We believe it was because he was so devoted to the king that he wished, so far as was possible, to tactfully *lighten the blow*. This he did, for instead of bluntly blurting out that Absalom had been slain he simply said, "Blessed be the Lord thy God, which hath delivered up the men that lifted up their hand against my lord the king" (v. 28).

And David sat between the two gates. And the watchman went up to the roof over the gate to the wall and lifted up his eyes and looked. And, behold, a man ran alone. And the watchman cried and told the king. And the king said, If he is alone, there is news in his mouth. And he came apace and drew near. And the watchman saw another man running. And the watchman called to the porter and said, Behold, another man running alone. And the king said, He also brings news. And the watchman said, I see the running of the first is like the running of Ahimaaz the son of Zadok. And the king said, He is a good man come with good news. And Ahimaaz called and said to the king, Peace be to you! And he fell down on his face before the king and said, Blessed by the LORD your God, who has delivered up the men who lifted up their hand against my lord the king. And the king said, Is the young man Absalom safe? And Ahimaaz answered, When Joab sent the king's servant, and your servant, I saw a great uproar, but I did not know what it was. And the king said, Turn aside, stand here. And he turned aside and stood still. And, behold, Cushi came, And Cushi said, Good news, my lord the king — for the LORD has avenged you this day of all those who rose up against you. And the king said to Cushi, Is the young man Absalom safe? And Cushi answered, May the enemies of my lord the king, and all who rise against you to do you hurt, be as that young man is. And the king was much moved and wept as he went, he said this — O my son Absalom, my son, my son Absalom! O that I had died for you, O Absalom, my son, my son!

Man is a composite creature, possessing a soul as well as a spirit. God has bestowed upon him an emotional nature as well as a rational principle. True, in some persons the passions are much stronger, while in others the intellectual faculty is more prominent; but whichever be the case, we should seek to preserve the balance between their play and interplay. The emotions must not be allowed to run away with us, for if they do we shall be incapacitated for clear thinking and prudent actions. On the other hand, the emotions are not to be utterly crushed, or we shall degenerate into callous cynics and cold intellectual machines. There is a happy medium between epicurianism and stoicism, yet it can only be attained by constant watchfulness and self-discipline. The regular management of our unruly passions is essential if we are to obtain the mastery of them, and not be mastered by them.

Stoicism or the complete suppression of our emotions receives no countenance from the teachings of Holy Writ. How could it, seeing that the Author of Scripture is the One who has endowed us with an emotional nature! God's Word and His works do not contradict each other. Let it be remembered that it is recorded of the Perfect Man that He *wept* by the graveside of Lazarus and made lamentation over the doomed city of Jerusalem. He who created muscles in the face which are only called into action by a hearty laugh and a tear-duct for the eye, meant that each should be used in their season. They who are physically incapable of breaking out into a healthy sweat, suffer far more than those who perspire freely in hot weather; and they who weep not when a great sorrow overtakes them, incur the danger of something snapping in their brains. Laughter and tears are nature's safety valves; they ease nervous tension, much as an electric storm relieves a heavily-charged atmosphere.

Nevertheless, it remains that our emotions are to be disciplined and regulated. "Keep thy heart with all diligence" (Prov. 4:23): an essential part of the task that involves, is the government of our passions and emotions — anger is to be curbed, impatience subdued, covetousness checked, grief and joy tempered. One of the things we are bidden to mortify is "inordinate affection" (Col. 3:5), and that includes not only unholy lustings, but also excessive desires after lawful things. "Set your affection on things above, not on things on the earth" (Col. 3:2): that does not mean it is wrong for us to have any love for earthly objects, but it does mean that such love is to be regulated and subordinated to Divine and spiritual things. Responsibility attaches as much to our inner life as it does to our outward.

Rejoicing and merrymaking are seasonable at a wedding or a birth, while grief and lamentation are natural at the death of a loved one; yet even on such occasions we are required to hold our emotions within due bounds. If on the one hand we are bidden to "rejoice with trembling" (Psa. 2:11), on the other hand we are exhorted to "sorrow not, even as others who have no hope" (1 Thess. 4:13). The subject is admittedly a delicate one, yet is it one of practical importance. Intemperate grief is as unjustifiable as is intemperate joy. The hand of God is to be viewed in that which occasions the one as truly as that which occasions the other: if He is the One who gives, He is equally the One who takes away; and the more the heart recognizes this, the less likely are we to overstep the bounds of propriety by yielding to uncontrolled passion.

That God takes notice of inordinate grief may be seen from the case of Samuel mourning for Saul. Samuel is one of the brightest characters of which we have record in Scripture, yet he failed at this point. The thought of God's having rejected Saul from being king, so moved the bowels of natural affection in the prophet that he sat up all night weeping for him (1 Sam. 15:11), yea, he continued mourning until the reproof of Heaven stopped the torrent of his tears. "And the Lord said unto Samuel, How long wilt thou mourn for Saul, seeing I have rejected him from reigning over Israel?" (1 Sam. 16:1) — had such grief been acceptable to God, He surely had not rebuked him for the same! This incident is recorded for our learning and warning.

The hour of emergency is what usually brings to light that which is to be found within us. It is not the ordinary routine of life, but *the crises* which reveal character: not that the crisis changes or makes the man, but rather that it affords opportunity to display the benefits of previous discipline or the evils of the lack of the same. Therefore it is of little or no use to bid a person control himself or herself when deeply agitated over an unusual experience, for one who has never learned to govern himself day by day, cannot begin doing so under exceptional circumstances. Here, then, is the answer to the question, How am I, especially if of a passionate nature, to *avoid* inordinate joy or sorrow? A person cannot change his disposition, but he can greatly modify it, if he will take pains to that end.

"He that is slow to anger is better than the mighty: and he that *ruleth his spirit* than he that taketh a city" (Prov. 16:32): it is this ruling of our spirits which is the subject we are attempting to develop: the mind perceiving the needs and the will exerting itself to govern our emotions. Inordinate grief is the outcome of inordinate love, and therefore we need to watch closely over our affections and bring reason to bear upon them. We must discipline ourselves daily and control our emotions over little things, if we are to control ourselves in the crises of life. As the twig is bent, so the bough grows. The longer we allow our passions to run riot, the harder will it be to gain control of them. Much can be done by parents in training the child to exercise self-control and be temperate in all things.

Does not the reader now perceive the practical importance of what has been before us? How many there are who go entirely to pieces when some grief or calamity overtakes them. And why is this? Because they have no self-control: they have never learned to govern their emotions. But *can we* rule our spirits? Certainly; yet not in a moment, nor by spasmodic efforts, but only by the practice of daily and *strict self-discipline*. Form the habit, then, of keeping tab on your desires, and check them immediately you find they are going out after forbidden objects. Watch your affections, and bring reason to bear upon them: see that they do not become too deeply attached to anything down here: remember the more highly you prize an object, the more keenly will you feel the loss of it. Seek to cultivate a mild and even disposition, and when provoked, assure yourself such a trifle is unworthy of perturbation. Paul could say, "all things are lawful for me, but I will not be brought under the power of any" (1 Cor. 6:12) — that was *his own* determination.

The pertinency of what has been before us will appear as we resume our consideration of David. The reader will remember that we last viewed him disposing of his forces, and then commanding his generals "Deal gently for my sake with the young man, even with Absalom" (2 Sam. 18:1-5). Two things are to be noted. First, David was under no qualms of the issue of the conflict, no fear that the battle would go against him. As we pointed out in a previous section, the 42nd and 43rd Psalms (composed at this time) show that he had overcome his despondency and doubts, and again had confidence in God. Second, we behold again the doting father: not only in referring to Absalom as "the young man" (he had had at least four children: 14:27), but in laying such an unlawful charge upon his officers he allowed sentiment to override the requirements of righteousness.

"And David sat between the two gates: and the watchman went up to the roof over the gate unto the wall, and lifted up his eyes, and looked, and behold a man running alone" (2 Sam. 18:24). What a pathetic picture is presented here: the aged king and tender parent anxiously waiting for news? He must have known, deep down in his heart, that the providence of God would execute that just punishment which he had been too weak to inflict upon the evil doer; yet, doubtless, he hoped against hope that the guilty one would escape. Moreover, as he sat there with plenty of time for meditation, he must have reflected upon *his own sins*, and how they were responsible for this unhappy conflict, which seriously threatened to permanently split the Nation into two opposing factions. If only we would look ahead more and anticipate the consequences of our actions, how often we should be deterred from entering upon a mad and sinful course.

"And the watchman cried, and told the king. And the king said, If he be alone, there is tidings in his mouth. And he came apace, and drew near. And the watchman saw another man running: and the watchman called unto the porter, and said, Behold another man running alone. And the king said, He also bringeth tidings" (vv. 25, 26). Within a short time at most the king's anxiety was to be relieved, and he would know the best or the worst. When the watchman upon the walls reported that a single runner was approaching, followed by another lone individual, David knew that his forces had not been defeated, for in that case, his men had fled before the enemy in confusion, and had come back in scattered groups. These persons were evidently special messengers, bringing report to the king: God had prohibited the multiplying of horses in Israel, so that these couriers came on foot.

"And the watchman said, Me thinketh the running of the foremost is like the running of Ahimaaz the son of Zadok. And the king said, He is a good man, and cometh with good tidings" (v. 27). It will be remembered that Joab had first dispatched Cushi and then had yielded to the importunity of Ahimaaz to follow him, but the latter taking a short cut and being the swifter of the two, "overran Cushi" (v. 23). Upon hearing that the son of the priest was approaching, David concluded he was the bearer of favourable news. As other writers have pointed out, this illustrates an important principle: those who bear good tidings should themselves be good men. Alas, what incalculable harm has often been wrought and the Gospel brought into contempt by the inconsistent and worldly lives of many who proclaim it. How needful it is that the servants of Christ should practice what they preach, and secure the confidence of those who hear them by a reputation for integrity and righteousness. "In all things showing thyself a pattern of good works" (Titus 2:7).

"And Ahimaaz called, and said unto the king, All is well. And he fell down to the earth upon his face before the king, and said, Blessed be the Lord thy God, which hath delivered up the men that lifted up their hand against my lord the king" (v. 28). Truly this was "a good man" indeed, who both feared God and honoured the king (1 Pet. 2:17). First, his "all is well" was to assure David that his forces had been successful; then he rendered obeisance to his royal master, and honoured God by ascribing the victory to Him. This was both pious and prudent, for his words were calculated to turn David's mind from Absalom unto the Lord, who had so mercifully interposed to defeat his counsels. Herein is a most important lesson to be heeded by those who have to break the news of the death of a loved one: seek to direct the heart of the grief stricken to Him in whose hands alone are "the issues from death" (Psa. 68:20).

"And the king said, Is the young man Absalom safe? And Ahimaaz answered, When Joab sent the king's servant, and me thy servant, I saw a great tumult, but I knew not what it was. And the king said unto him, Turn aside, and stand here. And he turned aside, and stood still" (vv. 29, 30). David's question showed he was more concerned about the welfare of his wicked son than he was over the well-being of his kingdom: that was natural no doubt, nevertheless it was a serious failure — those who serve the public are often called on to set aside their own private feelings and interests. Ahimaaz avoided giving a direct reply to the king: he was deeply attached to him, and no doubt wished to spare his feelings as far as possible; yet that did not excuse him if he resorted to prevarication. We are never justified in telling an untruth: no, not even to relieve the suspense of an anxious soul or to comfort a bereaved one.

"And, behold, Cushi came; and Cushi said, Tidings, my lord the king: for the Lord hath avenged thee this day of all them that rose up against thee. And the king said unto Cushi, Is the young man Absalom safe? And Cushi answered, The enemies of my lord the king, and all that rise against thee to do thee hurt, be as that young man is" (vv. 31, 32). The second courier now arrived and confirmed the word of Ahimaaz that the Lord had graciously undertaken for the king. His language too was pious, though not so fervent as that of the former. It was couched also in general terms, so that David had to repeat the question concerning his son. His query now received a definite reply, though the harrowing details were wisely withheld. Cushi did not mention Joab's having thrust the three darts into Absalom's heart, nor that his body had been contemptuously cast into a pit and covered with a great heap of stones. Instead, he merely intimated that Absalom was now safe in the grave, where he could work no more harm against the kingdom, whither Cushi loyally desired all other traitors might be.

"And the king was much moved, and went up to the chamber over the gate, and wept; and as he went, thus he said, O my son Absalom! my son, my son Absalom! would God I had died for thee, O Absalom, my son, my son!" (v. 33). Gratitude that his kingdom had been delivered was completely submerged by overwhelming grief for his wayward child. Probably this was one of the most pathetic lamentations that ever issued from a stricken heart, yet its extravagance and impiety cannot rightly be extenuated. David's inordinate affection for Absalom now found expression in inordinate grief. His passions carried him completely away, so that he spake unadvisedly, rashly, with his lips. No doubt his sorrow was made more poignant by the realization that Absalom's soul was lost, for there is no hint whatever that he sought to make his peace with God; yet that in nowise warranted such an inconsiderate outburst.

Matt. Henry ably analysed and summarized this sin of David's. "He is to be blamed. 1. For showing so great a fondness for a graceless, however handsome and witty, son, that was justly abandoned both of God and of man. 2. For quarreling, not only with Divine Providence, the disposals of which he ought silently to acquiesce in, but Divine justice, the judgments of which he ought to adore and subscribe to: see how Bildad argues, 'If thy children have sinned against Him, and He hath cast them away in their transgression (thou shouldest submit) for doth God pervert judgment?' (Job 8:3, 4 and compare Lev. 10:3). 3. For opposing the justice of the Nation, which, as king, he was entrusted with the administration of, and which, with other public interests, he ought to prefer before any natural affection.

"4. For despising the mercy of his deliverance, and the deliverance of his family and kingdom, from Absalom's wicked designs, as if this were no mercy, nor worth giving thanks for, because it cost the life of Absalom. 5. For indulging a strong passion, and speaking unadvisedly with his lips. He now forgot his own reasoning upon the death of another child (can I bring him back again?) and his own resolution to keep 'his mouth as with bridle when his heart was hot within him;' as well as his own practice at other times, when he 'quieted himself as a child that was weaned from his mother.' "

The practical warnings from this incident are obvious. David had allowed his inordinate affection for Absalom to hinder the discharge of his public duty. First, in failing to inflict the penalty of the Divine law for Absalom's murder of Ammon. Second, in allowing him to return from banishment. The claims of God must prevail over all natural inclinations: fleshly sentiment, and not a concern for God's glory, moved David to send for his son. As chief magistrate in Israel he condoned his grievous offences. His inordinate love terminated in this inordinate grief. How we need to watch and pray against excessive affection, the indulging of wayward children, and passionate outbursts in times of stress and strain. Doubly we need to keep a strict guard upon ourselves when that is removed from us which is very dear to us: much grace is required to say with Job "Blessed be the name of the Lord.

And Joab was told, Look, the king is weeping and mourning for Absalom. And the victory that day was turned into mourning to all the people. For the people heard it said that day how the king was grieved for his son. And the people went up secretly into the city that day, as people who are ashamed steal away when they flee in battle. But the king covered his face, and the king cried with a loud voice, O my son Absalom, O Absalom, my son, my son! And Joab came into the house to the king and said, You have today shamed the faces of all your servants — for they have saved your life and the lives of your sons and your daughters today, the lives of your wives, and the lives of your concubines — in that you love your enemies and hate your friends! For you have shown today that you neither regard princes or servants. For today I see that if Absalom had lived and all of us had died today, then it would have pleased you very much! Now therefore get up and go forth. Speak comfortably to your servants. For I swear by the LORD if you do not go forth, there will not one stay with you tonight, and that will be worse to you than all the evil which befell you from your youth until now. Then the king arose and sat in the gate. And they told it to the people, saying, Behold, the king sits in the gate! And all the people came before the king. (For Israel had fled, every one to his tent.) And all the people judged themselves throughout all the tribes of Israel, saying, The king saved us out of the hand of our enemies, and he delivered us out of the hand of the Philistines. And now he has fled out of the land from Absalom. And Absalom, whom we anointed over us, is dead in battle. Now therefore why do you not speak a word about bringing the king back? And David the king sent to Zadok and to Abiathar the priests, saying, Speak to the elders of Judah, saying, Why are you the last to bring the king back to his house, since the speech of all Israel has come to the king, to his house. You are my brothers and my flesh. Why then are you the last to bring back the king? And you say to Amasa, Are you not of my bone and of my flesh? May God do so to me, and more also, if you are not captain of the army before me continually instead of Joab. And he bowed the heart of all the men of Judah, even as one man, so that they sent to the king, saying, Return, you and all your servants. So the king returned and came to Jordan. And Judah came to Gilgal to go to meet the king, to conduct the king over Jordan. — II Samuel 19:1-15.

It will be remembered that in our last we were occupied with the effects which the advance messengers of Joab had upon David. Those special couriers informed him of the defeat and death of Absalom (2 Sam. 18), and the king at once broke down and gave way to bitter lamentations. No doubt this was natural, and to be expected, for the insurrectionist was his own son, though an utterly unworthy one; yet while an outburst of sorrow was excusable, inordinate grief was not so. In writing upon this subject care needs to be taken by us, so as to prevent the reader, as far as we can, from drawing wrong conclusions. Inordinate grief is neither the depths to which we may be shaken nor the copiousness of our tears, for that is largely a matter of personal temperament and the state of our health.

Inordinate grief is when we so far lose control of ourselves that we become guilty of hysterical outbursts which ill become a rational creature, and uttering intemperate expressions, which displease the Lord and offend those who have His fear upon them. Especially should the Christian ever seek to set before others an example of sobriety, checking everything which savours of insubordination to God. Again; we are guilty of inordinate grief when we allow a

500

sorrow to so overwhelm us that we are rendered incapable of discharging our duty. Particularly is this the case with those who occupy a public position, upon whom others are dependent or influenced thereby. In David's case he failed at each of these points, being guilty of a violent outburst of his passions, using intemperate language, and taking issue with God's providential will.

In due time Joab and his victorious army arrived at Mahanaim, to receive the congratulations of the king and wait upon him for further instructions. But instead of meeting them with warm gratitude for the signal service they had rendered him and his kingdom, David conducted himself in such a way as to make the army conclude the sovereign was filled with regret at their achievements. Consequently, instead of there being joyous celebrations over the victory, the spirit of the camp was greatly dampened. Instead of being thankful that his kingdom had been mercifully delivered, David was completely overwhelmed with grief over the death of his wayward son, and all were made to suffer in consequence. The deplorable effects this produced will now be considered by us.

"And it was told Joab, Behold the king weepeth and mourneth for Absalom. And the victory that day was turned into mourning unto all the people: for the people heard say that day how the king was grieved for his son. And the people gat them by stealth that day into the city, as people being ashamed steal away when they flee in battle. But the king covered his face, and the king cried with a loud voice, O my son Absalom! O Absalom, my son, my son!" (2 Sam. 19:1-4). "The excessive indulgence of any passion (grief by no means excepted), not only offends God, but betrays men into great imprudences in their temporal concerns. They who have faithfully served us expect that we should appear pleased with them, and thankful for their services; and many will do more for a smile and a kind word from their superiors, than for a more substantial recompense; and be much grieved and disheartened if they think themselves frowned on" (Thos. Scott).

This was no time for David to yield to his private sorrows: public interests urgently required him to bestir himself and grip the helm of state with a firm hand. A most serious and critical situation confronted him, which called for prompt and decisive action. Absalom's rebellion had rent the kingdom asunder, and only a prudent policy, swiftly executed, could hope to restore peace and unity again. There had been a widespread revolt, and David's throne had been shaken to its very foundations. The king himself had been forced to flee from Jerusalem and his subjects had become divided in their interests and loyalty. But God had graciously intervened: the arch-rebel was slain and his forces utterly routed. This was the hour, then, for David to assert his authority, press upon the people the honour of Jehovah's name, take charge of things, and take full advantage of the situation which had swung things so markedly into his favour.

As soon as he had received confirmation that Absalom and his forces had been defeated, David's only wise course was to return immediately to Jerusalem. To set up his court once more in the royal city, while the rebels were in confusion and before they could rally again, was but the part of common prudence — how else could the insurrectionists be cowed and the unity of the nation be restored? But now grief paralyzed him: beclouding his judgment, sapping his energy, causing him to conduct himself most injudiciously. Never was there a time when he more needed to hold the hearts of his soldiers: it was essential to his royal interests that he should secure their respect and affection; but by keeping himself in close mourning, he not only dampened the spirits of his strongest supporters, but acted as though he disapproved of what they had done.

"And it was told Joab, Behold, the king weepeth and mourneth for Absalom. And the victory that day was turned into mourning unto all the people: for the people heard say that day how the king was grieved for his son." "The people will take particular notice of what their princes say and do: the more eyes we have upon us, and the greater our influence is, the more need we have to speak and act wisely, and to govern our passions strictly" (Matt. Henry). David ought to have been ashamed of his sorrowing over such a worthless and wicked son, and done his utmost to subdue and hide it. See how the people reacted: they "gat them by stealth that day into the city, as people being ashamed steal away when they flee in battle." Out of respect for their sovereign they would not rejoice while he continued to mourn, yet they must have felt deeply how little their efforts on his behalf were really appreciated.

"But the king covered his face, and the king cried with a loud voice, O my son Absalom! O Absalom my son, my son!" This was not the initial outburst of David's anguish, but the prolonged hugging to himself of his sorrow after the army had returned. The king was quite overcome, insensible to the pressing requirements of the hour and the needs of his subjects. This is what inordinate grief produces: it makes one so self-centered that the interests of others are ignored. It thoroughly unfits for the discharge of our duties. It so takes the eye off God that we are wholly occupied with distressing circumstances. It is in such an hour that we need to take hold of and act out that oft-repeated injunction "Be strong and of a good courage." Inordinate grief will not restore the dead, but it will seriously injure the living.

David's conduct displeased the Lord, and He used an unwelcome instrument to bestir the king to a renewed sense of his responsibility, for it is from this angle that we must first view Joab's attack upon David. "When a man's ways please the Lord, He maketh even his enemies to be at peace with him" (Prov. 16:7): yes, "maketh," for our enemies are as much under the immediate control of the Most High as are our best friends. True it is that every attack made upon us by our foes is not, necessarily, an indication that we have offended God, yet oftentimes it *is* so, and therefore it is the part of wisdom for us to always regard the attacks of our enemies as being God's rod reproving us, and for us to examine our ways and judge ourselves. Did not God make Abimelech to be at peace with Isaac (Gen. 26:26-30) and Esau with Jacob (Gen. 33), then He could have easily softened the heart of Joab toward David; that He did *not* do so, intimates He was displeased with him for his inordinate grief.

"And Joab came into the house to the king and said, Thou hast shamed this day the faces of all thy servants, which this day have saved thy life, and the lives of thy sons, and of thy daughters, and the lives of thy wives, and the lives of thy concubines; In that thou lovest thine enemies and hatest thy friends. For thou hast declared this day, that thou regardest neither princes nor servants: for this day I perceive that if Absalom had lived, and all we had died this day, then it had pleased thee well" (vv. 5, 6). As we have pointed out in the previous section, Joab, during the later years of his life, was far from being friendly disposed toward David, and though he served at the head of his army, self-interest and not loyalty to the king was what actuated him. He was therefore quick to sieze this opportunity to assert his arrogance, and not sparing David's feelings at all, he strongly berated him for his present selfishness and inertia. True, he was justified in remonstrating with David on the impropriety of his conduct, yet that by no means excused his pride and insolence. Though there was much force in what Joab said, yet he sadly failed to show that respect which was due his master.

"Now therefore arise, go forth, and speak confortably unto thy servants: for I swear by the Lord, if thou go not forth, there will not tarry one with thee this night: and that will be worse unto thee than all the evil that befell thee from thy youth until now" (v. 7). David's duty was here plainly if roughly pointed out to him: he ought to present himself at once before those faithful troops who had endangered *their* lives for the preservation of *his*. Let the king now bestir himself and delay no longer, but go forth and publicly congratulate their success and thank them heartily for their services. The painful alternative must not be ignored: there was grave danger of a further and worse revolt. If the king persisted in selfish ingratitude, he would lose the respect of his staunchest supporters, and then he would be left without any to further his interests. Sometimes God makes use of a rough hand to arouse us from our lethargy, and we should be thankful that He cares sufficiently for us to do so.

Joab had pressed upon David the claims of his people, and the king was duly aroused. So far from being angry at and refusing the counsel which he had received, David acted promptly upon it and took his proper place. "Then the king arose, and sat in the gate, And they told unto all the people, saying, Behold, the king doth sit in the gate. And all the people came before the king: for Israel had fled every man to his tent" (v. 8). A wise man will seek to profit from good advice, no matter who may proffer it or how unkindly it may be given — shall I refuse an important letter because I dislike the appearance or manners of the postman! "When we are convinced of a fault we must amend, though we are told it by our inferiors, and indecently, or in heat and passion" (Matt. Henry). Was David looking back to this incident when he wrote, "Let the righteous smite me; it shall be a kindness; and let him reprove me: it shall be an excellent oil, which shall not break my head" (Psa. 141:5)?

"And all the people were at strife throughout all the tribes of Israel, saying, The king saved us out of the hand of our enemies, and he delivered us out of the hand of the Philistines, and now he is fled out of the land for Absalom. And Absalom, whom we anointed over us is dead in battle. Now therefore why speak ye not a word of bringing the king back?" (vv. 9, 10). These verses show clearly the timeliness of Joab's intervention and the deplorable state the kingdom of Israel was now in. A house divided against itself cannot stand: strong and swift measures were now called for. Many of the people still desired the return of their king, though they were too dilatory to do more than talk, and ask why a message was not sent urging him to come to Jerusalem. It is generally thus: those who are friendly disposed toward us lack the energy to *act* on our behalf.

The tribes of Israel were conscious of their predicament: they were without a competent head. David undoubtedly possessed the best claims: he had proved himself a valiant and successful leader, delivering them from their powerful foes. Yet, when his son turned traitor and many of his subjects had joined forces with him, the king fled. But Absalom was now dead, and his army had been defeated. A "strife" ensued: probably the people blamed their elders for not taking the initiative and communicating with David, to assure him of their repentance and renewed fealty; while the elders threw the blame on the people because of their recent disloyalty. Mutual recriminations got them nowhere; meanwhile no definite steps were taken by them to urge David's return to the capital.

"And king David sent to Zadok and to Abiathar the priests, saying, Speak unto the leaders of Judah, saying, Why are ye the last to bring the king back to his house. Ye are my brethren, ye are my bones and my flesh: wherefore then are ye the last to bring back the king?" (vv. 11,12). When David learned of the favourable sentiment which existed, generally, throughout Israel toward him, he threw the onus on the elders of his own tribe. "We do not always find the most kindness from those whom we have the most reason to expect it" (Matt. Henry). Alas, how true that is. How often we find that those who are bound to us by the closest ties and upon whom we have the greatest claims, are the first to fail and the last to help us. Perhaps one reason why this incident is recorded is that it may warn us not to expect too much even from our spiritual brethren — the less we expect, the less will be our disappointment.

That Judah, his own tribe, was so lacking in affection or enterprise, suggests that they too had been seriously implicated in the recent rebellion; and now they were either too slack to make suitable overtures to their king, or else they feared they had wronged him so grievously by siding with Absalom that there was no hope of regaining his favour. By employing two of the priestly family to negotiate with the elders of Judah, David evidenced both his prudence and piety. As God-fearing men, Zadok and Abiathar were trusted by the king and respected by the best of people, and therefore there would be no suspicion on either side that they were working from self-interests. It is always wise and well for us to enlist the aid of those most looked up to for their uprightness when it becomes necessary for us to use intermediaries.

"And say ye to Amasa, Art thou not of my bones, and of my flesh? God do so to me, and more also, if thou be not captain of the host before me continually in the room of Joab" (v. 13). Though Amasa was the son of David's sister (1 Chron. 2:17). Absalom had set him over the rebel army (2 Sam. 17:25), and therefore he was the leader of an influential party whom David desired to win. Moreover, he was determined to strip the haughty and intolerable Joab of his power, if that were at all possible; yet he was very unwise in making known his purpose, for though Amasa accepted David's offer, yet on the very first military enterprise on which he was dispatched, Joab met and murdered him (2 Sam. 20:10). By singling out Amasa for special notice — owning him as his kinsman and promising to make him general of all his forces if he now stood by the king's cause — David gave clear intimation that he was ready to *pardon* those who had most grievously wronged him.

"And he bowed the heart of all the men of Judah, even as the heart of one man; so that they sent this word unto the king, Return thou and all thy servants" (v. 14). There is some difference of opinion as to whether the "he" refers to David, Amasa, or the Lord Himself. Personally, we believe it signifies the latter. First, because "God" is directly mentioned in v. 13; second, because had the reference been to David it had said "so they sent this word unto *him*" etc; third, because we have no reason to suppose that Amasa was sufficiently prominent or powerful to affect "all the men of Israel." Finally, because it is God's prerogative alone to regulate the heart (Prov. 21:1). No doubt God, instrumentally, made use of the persuasions of the priests and of Amasa to influence them; nevertheless their spontaneity and unanimity must be ascribed unto him who sways all His creatures.

"So the king returned, and came to Jordan" (v. 15). David did not move until he was assured that the people really desired his return: he was unwilling to be king of those who welcomed him not. In this we have typically illustrated an important truth: "Our Lord Jesus will rule in those who invite Him to the throne of their hearts, and not till He *is* invited. He first *bows the heart* and makes it willing in the day of His power, and then *rules* in the midst of His enemies: Psa. 110:2, 3" (Matt. Henry).

And Shimei the son of Gera, a Benjamite, who was of Bahurim, hurried and came down with the men of Judah to meet king David. And there were a thousand men of Benjamin with him, and Ziba the servant of the house of Saul, and his fifteen sons and his twenty servants with him. And they went over Jordan before the king. And a ferryboat went over to carry the king's household over, and to do what he thought good. And Shimei the son of Gera fell down before the king as he had come over Jordan. And he said to the king, Let not my lord charge iniquity to me. Do not remember the perverse way your servant acted in the day that my lord the king went out of Jerusalem, so that the king should take it to his heart. For your servant knows that I have sinned. Therefore, behold, I have come today, the first of all the house of Joseph to go down to meet my lord the king. But Abishai the son of Zeruiah answered and said, Shall not Shimei be put to death for this, because he cursed the LORD's anointed? And David said, What do I have to do with you, you sons of Zeruiah, that you should be my foes today? Shall there be any man put to death today in Israel? For do I not know that I am king over Israel today? Therefore the king said to Shimei, You shall not die, And the king swore to him. — II Samuel 19:16-23.

What a bewildering maze does the path of life present to many a soul: its twistings and turnings, its ups and downs, its advances and retreats are often too puzzling for carnal wisdom to solve. True it is that the lives of some are sheltered ones, with little of adventure and still less of mystery in them; yet it is far otherwise for others, with their journeyings hither and thither. But in the light of Scripture the latter should not be surprised. One has only to read the biographies of the patriarchs to discover how often they were called upon to strike their tents, move from place to place, traverse and then re-traverse the same path. The experiences of David, then, were in this respect, far from being exceptional: nor should any child of God deem it passing strange if he too finds himself retracing his steps and returning to the same place which he left months or years ago.

Amid the strange vicissitudes of life how comforting it is for the saint to be assured that "the steps of a good man are ordered by the Lord" (Psa. 37:23). Ah, it was David himself, who, by the Spirit of inspiration, originally penned those words. He realized that a predestinating God had first decreed and then ordered his entire journey through this world. Happy, thrice happy, the soul who by faith lays hold of this grand truth. To be fully assured that neither fickle fortune nor blind fate, but his all-wise and loving Father has mapped out his course supplies a peace and poise to a believing heart such as nothing else can give. It softens disappointment, affords comfort in sorrow, and quiets the storm within; yet it is only as faith is *in exercise* that those peaceable fruits of righteousness are produced in us. An evil heart of unbelief deprives one of such consolation, placing him on the same level as the poor worldling, who has no light to disperse his gloom.

In previous sections we spent some little time in dwelling upon the various sad incidents which marked David's journey from Jerusalem to the Jordan, and from there to Mahanaim; now we are to contemplate the brighter side of things as the king retraced his steps. The contrasts presented are indeed striking, reminding us of the welcome spring and genial summer after a long and dreary winter. The analogies which exist between the seasons of the year and the different stages and experiences of life have often been dwelt upon, yet not too often, for there are many salutary lessons to be learned therefrom. Some dyspeptic souls seem more in their element when dwelling upon that which is sad and sombre, just as there are those (because they suffer from the heat) who are glad when summer is over. Another class determine to be occupied only with that which is cheerful and gay, refusing (to their own loss) to face that which is serious, sober and solemn — just as some people always grumble when the weather is wet, failing to realize the rain is as needful as the sunshine.

It is much the same with those preachers who attempt to trace out the experiences of a Christian. Some who delineate the inward history of a believer, or what *they* consider it should consist of, disproportionately dwell upon his assurance, peace and joy; while others over-emphasize his painful conflicts and defeats, his doubts and fears. The one is as harmful as the other, for in either case only a caricature of the truth is presented. The one would rapidly skim over the distressing incidents which occasioned David's flight from Jerusalem to the Jordan, and those which attended him on the way to Mahanaim; while the other would expatiate fully thereon, but say little upon his happier lot as he returned from his exile to the capital. Let us diligently seek to avoid such lopsidedness, and preserve the balance in all things, so that as we should be equally thankful for each of the passing seasons of the year, we will endeavour to profit from the every-varying circumstances of life through which we are called upon to pass.

If David had passed through a season of gloom and tragedy, he was now to encounter some pleasant and gratifying experiences. If he had met with the ingratitude and unjust reproaches from some of his subjects, he was now to be the recipient of a hearty welcome and the appreciative homage of others. How the tide of public opinion ebbs and flows: one moment exclaiming "no doubt this man is a murderer," and the next one changing their minds and saying "that he was a god" (Acts 28:4-6). How this should warn us against placing any reliance upon the creature! How thankful we should be when God is pleased to incline any to be favourably disposed towards us. On occasions the crowd changes from friendliness to hostility, at other times the converse is the case. So it was at the stage we have now reached in our hero's history.

"So the king returned and came to Jordan" (2 Sam. 19:15). What a change had been wrought since David had last stood on the banks of this river. Then he was fleeing from Absalom, who had captured the hearts of many in Judah; now the rebel was dead, and God had so reinstated David in the affections of the royal tribe, that all the men of Judah had sent word unto him "Return thou, and all thy servants" (v. 14). Assured that God was with him, and that he could rely upon the loyalty of his people, David left Mahanaim where his temporary camp had been set up, and betook himself as far as this famous stream. He had been slow in acting, partly because he wished to make sure of his ground, by ascertaining whether or not the people still desired him to reign over them. Not by force of arms, but by the wishes of his subjects was he determined to hold his position.

"And Judah came to Gilgal, to go to meet the king, to conduct the king over Jordan," (v. 15). It will be recalled that David had sent Zadok and seems a pity that there had been no joint conference with the heads of the other tribes. "It would have been better if they had conferred with their brethren, and thus acted in concert, as this would have prevented many bad consequences" (Thos. Scott). Even though it had involved further delay, joint action on the part of Israel would have been far more satisfactory. Nothing is gained by partiality: those slighted nurse their grievance, and sooner or later express their dissatisfaction and cause trouble. Thus it proved with the Nation, for less than a century later ten of its tribes separated, and were never again restored.

"And Judah came to Gilgal, to go to meet the king, to conduct the king over Jordan." The place where the men of Judah now met David was associated with memorable events. It was there that Joshua had, by the command of the Lord, circumcised those of Israel who had been born in the wilderness, so that "the reproach of Egypt" was rolled away from them (Josh. 5:2-9); and it was from that incident it derived its name, for Gilgal means "rolling away." How appropriate the chosen venue, for the reproach of Judah's infidelity was rolled away as they now renewed their fealty to David. Again; at a later date we read, "Then said Samuel to the people, Come, and let us go to Gilgal, and *renew the kingdom there*" (1 Sam. 11:14) – thus was history now virtually repeating itself.

"And Shimei the son of Gera, a Benjamite, which was of Bahurim, hasted and came down with the men of Judah to meet king David" (v. 16). What pleasant surprises we sometimes have amid life's disappointments! This is the last man of all who might have been expected to be among those who came to welcome the king, for Shimei was the one who had reviled and cursed him on his outward journey (2 Sam. 16:5, 6). The commentators attribute Shemei's friendly advances on this occasion to nothing more than carnal prudence or an instinct of self-preservation, but this we think is quite a mistake – he seems to have been in no danger of his life, for the next verse informs us there were a thousand men of Benjamin with him. No, in the light of v. 14 we believe this is another instance of God's making his enemies to be at peace with him when a man's ways please the Lord.

"And there were a thousand men of Benjamin with him, and Ziba the servant of the house of Saul, and his fifteen sons and his twenty servants with him; and they went over Jordan before the king" (v. 17). Well did Matt. Henry suggest "Perhaps Jordan was never passed with so much solemnity, nor with so many remarkable occurrences, as it was now, since Israel passed it under Joshua." It was almost as surprising for the lying Ziba to present his obeisance to the king on this occasion, as it was for Shimei, for if the one had reviled him with a foul tongue, the other, by his wicked imposition (2 Sam. 16:1-4) abused him with a fair one. No doubt he was anxious to establish himself more firmly in the king's favour ere Mephibosheth should undeceive him.

"And there went over a ferry-boat to carry over the king's household, and to do what he thought good" (v. 18). "This is the only place in which a *boat* for passing over a river is mentioned. Bridges are not mentioned in Scripture. Rivers were generally *forded* at that time" (Thos. Scott). "And Shimei the son of Gera fell down before the king, as he was come over Jordan" (v. 18). See here a signal demonstration of the power of God: nothing is too hard for Him: He can subdue the most rebellious heart. What wonders are wrought by the Spirit even in the reprobate, for upon them too He puts forth both His restraining and constraining operations: were it not so, the elect could not live in this world at all. Yet how feebly is this realized today, even by the saints. How little is the hand of God beheld by them in the subduing of their enemies' hatred and in making others to be friendly and kind toward them. A spirit of atheism, which would exclude God from all human affairs, is more and more infecting this evil generation.

"And said unto the king, Let not my lord impute iniquity unto me, neither do thou remember that which thy servant did perversely the day that my lord the king went out of Jerusalem, that the king should take it to his heart. For thy servant doth know that I have sinned: therefore, behold, I am come the first this day of all the house of Joseph to go down to meet my lord the king" (vv. 19, 20). Let us see in this incident a typical picture of the penitent sinner casting himself upon the mercy of David's greater Son and Lord. This is exactly what takes place at a genuine conversion: "Let the wicked forsake his way, and the unrighteous man his thoughts; and let him return unto the Lord, and He will have mercy upon him; and to our God, for He will abundantly pardon" (Isa. 55:7). This is the course which Shimei now followed: he ceased his defiant conduct, threw down the weapons of his warfare against David, acknowledged his grievous offences, cast himself at the king's feet, thereby avowing his willingness to be subject to his royal sceptre. Saving mercy is not to be obtained any other way. There must be a complete right-about-face: contrition and confession are as imperative as is faith in Christ.

Have you, my reader, really and truly surrendered yourself to the Lordship of Christ? If you have not, no matter what you believe, or how orthodox the profession you make, you are yet in your sins and on your way to eternal perdition. Make no mistake on this point, we beseech you: as you value your soul, examine thoroughly the foundations of any hope of salvation which you may cherish. If you are living a life of self-pleasing, and are not in subjection to the commandments of Christ, then are you in open revolt against Him. There must be a complete break from the old life of worldliness and carnal gratification, and the entering into a new relationship with God in Christ, namely, a submitting to His holy will and the ordering of all your conduct thereby. You are either living for self, or striving to serve and please God; and in your heart you *know* which course you are following. Being religious on the Sabbath and irreligious the other six days will avail you nothing.

"But Abishai the son of Zeruiah answered and said, Shall not Shimei be put to death for this, because he cursed the Lord's anointed?" (v. 21). Abishai was brother to the arrogant Joab and possessed much of his domineering spirit. He was the one who had offered to slay Shimei at the time he had reviled David (2 Sam. 16:9): mercy was foreign to his nature, and even though Shimei now publicly acknowledged his offence and besought the king's pardon, this son of Zeruiah thirsted for his blood. May we not consider this line in our typical picture as illustrative of the principle (cf. Luke 9:42; 15:2 etc.) that there are some ready to oppose whenever a sinner takes his true place before God. If there are those who complain that the way of salvation is made too easy when the *grace* of God is emphasized, there are others who argue that salvation by works is being inculcated when the *righteousness* of God and the claims of Christ are duly pressed.

"And David said, What have I do to with you, ye sons of Zeruiah, that ye should this day be adversaries unto me? shall there any man be put to death *this* day in Israel? for do not I know that I am this day king over Israel? Therefore the king said unto Shimei, Thou shalt not die. And the king sware unto him" (vv. 22, 23). It is indeed blessed to mark how David's soul loathed the evil suggestion made by Abishai. That son of Zeruiah — whose heart had never been broken before God, and therefore was devoid of His compassions — was far too blind to perceive that this was no time for the enforcing of unmingled justice. But it was far otherwise with David: "Blessed are the merciful, for they shall obtain mercy" (Matt. 5:7): he had received wondrous mercy from the Lord, and now he exercised mercy unto this wretched Shimei, and in return for this he shall obtain further mercy from God. Let us not ignore that searching word, "If ye forgive men their trespasses, your heavenly Father will also forgive you; but if ye forgive not men their trespasses, neither will your Father forgive your trespasses" (Matt. 6:14, 15). God communicates grace to His people in order to make them gracious — reflectors of Himself.

Feign would we dwell for a moment longer on the lovely spirit which now actuated our hero. In previous sections of 1 and 2 Sam. we have beheld the grace of God *towards* David — electing, exalting, pardoning and preserving him; so too have we seen the grace of God working *in* him. It was the general rule of his life, giving character to his dealings with others, as it had thus given character to God's dealings with him. Being called to enter into blessing, he rendered blessing. When he was reviled, he reviled not again (1 Sam. 17:28); when persecuted, he threatened not, but suffered it (1 Sam. 19:31). Never do we read of him seeking his own advancement or honour: when tidings reached him of the death of Saul, he wept instead of rejoicing; in the fall of Abner and Ishbosheth, it is only the sorrow and fasting of David we hear of. So it is, in varying measure, with all Christians: notwithstanding the detestable workings of the flesh, there are also the precious fruits of the Spirit — seen and approved of by God, if not always observable by others or congizable to ourselves.

This was the man after God's own heart, and in every scene in which he was called to take a part — save when he was, for a while, turned aside by Satan — we behold him seeking not his own aggrandizement or even vindication, but serving in grace and kindness. A most blessed example of this was before us when pondering 2 Sam. 9. He would be an emulator or follower of God (Eph. 5:1), as a dear child. So it was when Abishai was for exacting bare righteousness: but mercy had rejoiced over judgment towards himself in the heart of the Lord, and nothing but the same is now beheld in the heart of David. Divine grace had not only pardoned his grievous sins against Uriah, but had now delivered him from the murderous designs of Absalom; how, then, could he consent to the death of even his worst enemy! Ah, my reader, Divine grace not only forgives sins, but it also transforms sinners: taming the lion, making gentle the wolf. Thereby the Divine "workmanship" (Eph. 2:10) is made manifest.

But let us look again beyond David to that blessed One of whom he was so eminent a type. In what has just been before us we are presented with a lovely picture of *the Gospel*. The grand truth of the Gospel is that Christ "receiveth sinners." Yes, He not only spares, but welcomes His worst enemies, and freely pardons them. Nevertheless, they must seek Him, surrender to His Lordship, take their place before Him in the dust as penitents, confessing their sins, and casting themselves on His sovereign mercy. This is what Shimei did. He determined to make his peace with David, came to him, and did obeisance before him; and we read that the king said "Thou shalt not die." And this, dear reader, is what the King of kings will say of you, if you throw down the weapons of your warfare against Him and exercise faith in Him. May the Spirit of God graciously cause some unsaved reader to do so.

And Mephibosheth the son of Saul came down to meet the king. And he had neither dressed his feet, nor trimmed his beard, nor washed his clothes, from the day the king departed until he came in peace. And when he had come to Jerusalem to meet the king, the king said to him, Why did you not go with me, Mephibosheth? And he answered, My lord, O king, my servant deceived me. For your servant said, I will saddle me an ass so that I may ride on it and go to the king — because your servant is lame. And he has been backbiting your servant to my lord the king. But my lord the king is as an angel of God. Therefore do what is good in your eyes. For all of my father's house were but dead men before my lord the king. Yet you set your servant among those who ate at your own table. What right then have I to cry to the king any more? And the king said to him, Why do you speak any more of your matters? I have said, You and Ziba divide the land. And Mephibosheth said to the king, Yes, let him take all, because my lord the king has come in peace to his own house. And Barzillai of Gilead came down from Rogelim and went over Jordan with the king to conduct him over

Jordan. Now Barzillai was a very aged man, eighty years old. And he had provided food for the king while he was lying at Mahanaim — for he was a very great man. And the king said to Barzillai, Come over with me and I will feed you with me in Jerusalem. And Barzillai said to the king, How long do I have to live, that I should go up with the king to Jerusalem? I am eighty years old today, and can I discern between good and evil? Can your servant taste what I eat or what I drink? Can I any more hear the voice of singing men and singing women? Why then should your servant be still a burden to my lord the king? Your servant will go a little way over Jordan with the king. And why should the king repay me for it with such a reward? I beg you, let your servant turn back again so that I may die in my own city and be buried by the grave of my father and of my mother. But behold your servant Chimham, let him go over with my lord the king. And do to him what shall seem good to you. And the king answered, Chimham shall go over with me, and I will do to him that which shall seem good to you. And whatever you shall ask of me, that I will do for you. And all the people went over Jordan. And when the king had come over, the king kissed Barzillai, and blessed him. And he returned to his own place. Then the king went on to Gilgal, and Chimham went with him. And all the people of Judah were bringing the king, and also half the people of Israel. And, behold, all the men of Israel came to the king, and said to the king, Why have our brothers the men of Judah stolen you away, and have brought the king and his household, and all David's men with him, over Jordan? And all the men of Judah answered the men of Israel, Because the king is near of kin to us. Why then are you angry for this matter? Have we eaten at all at the king's cost? Or has he given us any gift? And the men of Israel answered the men of Judah and said, We have ten parts in the king, and we also have more right in David than you. Why then did you despise us, so that our advice should not be sought first in bringing back our king? And the words of the men of Judah were more fierce than the words of the men of Israel. — II Samuel 19:24-43.

We continue to trace out the progress of David on his way back from Mahanaim to Jordan, and thence to Jerusalem. A number of incidents occurred which intimated the change in his fortunes. Many of those who forsook the king in the time of adversity, now flocked around him in the day of his prosperity. Yet these were not all fair-weather friends; some had rendered him real service when the storm burst upon him; others, who had been hindered from so doing, had nevertheless remained loyal to him and now came to welcome him as he returned from exile. Each of these incidents possesses a charm all its own. At the close of our last we viewed the lovely magnanimity of our hero unto Shimei, the man who had cursed him; next we behold his wisdom and fidelity.

"And Mephibosheth the son of Saul came down to meet the king, and had neither dressed his feet, nor trimmed his beard, nor washed his clothes, from the day the king departed until the day he came again in peace" (2 Sam. 19:24). This is very touching. Mephibosheth, it will be remembered, was the grandson of Saul, David's arch-enemy. For his father Jonathan's sake, Mephibosheth had received such kindness at the king's hands that he was accorded a place at his table (2 Sam. 9). Mephibosheth was practically a cripple, being lame on both his feet (2 Sam. 9:3 and cf. 4:4). In the day of David's sore need, Mephibosheth had prepared an elaborate and serviceable present, and had ordered his servant to saddle an ass that he might ride unto the fugitive king. But instead of obeying orders, the servant, Ziba, had himself ridden to the king, offered the present as a gift from himself, and had then grievously slandered and lied about his master (2

Sam. 16:1-4). All through the time of his absence David had laboured under a misapprehension of the loyalty of Mephibosheth; but now the truth was to be revealed.

What is recorded about Mephibosheth here in v. 24 clearly denoted his devotion to David in the hour of his rejection and humiliation. So real and so great had been his grief at the sorry pass to which the king had been reduced, that Mephibosheth had utterly neglected his own person. Instead of seeking to feather his own nest, he had genuinely mourned David's absence. This is very beautiful, and is recorded for our learning, for everything in the O.T. has a lesson for *us*, if only we have eyes to see and a heart to receive. The practical lesson in this incident for the believer to-day is found in those words of Christ's, "The days will come when the Bridegroom shall be taken from them, and then shall they fast" (Matt. 9:15) — it becomes us to *mourn* during the King's absence! Note how the apostle rebukes the Corinthians because they were "full," "rich," and had "reigned as kings" (1 Cor. 4:8).

"The king said unto him, Wherefore wentest thou not with me, Mephibosheth?" (v. 25). First, let it be noted that David did not turn away from him in anger or disgust, refusing him a hearing. Probably the king was surprised to see him at all after the false impression that Ziba had conveyed to him. But the present condition of Mephibosheth must have made quite an impression, so the king gave him opportunity to explain and vindicate himself. An important lesson this for *us* to heed. We must ever seek to be fair and impartial, and ready to hear *both* sides. It is obviously unjust to give credence to a report received behind a person's back, and then refuse to hear his explanation face to face.

Mephibosheth gladly availed himself of the opportunity now given, and proceeded to make an unvarnished statement of the facts (vv. 25, 26). He employed the most respectful and affectionate language — an example we also do well to heed if placed under similar circumstances, for nothing is gained, and our cause is rather weakened than strengthened, if we hotly condemn our questioner or judge for being so ready to believe evil of us. "But my lord the king is as an angel of God: do therefore what is good in thine eyes" (v. 27). Herein Mephibosheth expressed his confidence in David's wisdom and justice. He was satisfied that once his royal master heard both parties and had time to reflect upon the merits of the case, he would not be imposed upon; and therefore he was not afraid to leave himself in David's hands.

Next, Mephibosheth owned the utter unworthiness of himself and family, and acknowledged the signal grace that had been shown him. "For all of my father's house were but dead men before my lord the king, yet didst thou set thy servant among them that did eat at thine own table. What right therefore have I yet to cry any more unto the king?" (v. 28). "This shows that Ziba's suggestion was improbable: for could Mephibosheth be so foolish as to aim higher, when he fared so easily, so happily, as he did?" (Matt. Henry). This was powerful reasoning. By the king's clemency Mephibosheth had already been amply provided for: why, then, should he aspire unto the kingdom? It was not as though he had been slighted and left portionless. Having been adopted into the king's family circle, it had been utter madness to deliberately court the king's displeasure. But he would refrain from any further self-vindication.

"And the king said unto him, Why speakest thou any more of thy matters? I have said, Thou and Ziba *divide* the land" (v. 29). It seems strange that the commentators completely miss the force of this, considering that David was quite unconvinced by Mephibosheth's defence, yea, themselves regarding it as weak and unsatisfactory. We feel, then, we must labour the point a little. First, the words of David on this occasion cannot possibly mean that his previous decision remained unaltered, that the verdict he had given in the past must stand. And for this simple but conclusive reason: David had given no such orders previously! If we turn back to the occasion when the servant had deceived the king, we find that he said, "Behold, thine are *all* that pertained unto Mephibosheth" (16:4).

But now: since David did *not* confirm here the order he had given in 16:4, how are we to understand his words? Was he so puzzled by the conflicting statements of Ziba and Mephibosheth that he knew not which to believe, and so suggested a *division* of the land as a fair compromise? Surely not; for that had been grossly unjust to both of them. What then? This: David said what he did not in any harshness, but in order to *test* Mephiboseth's heart and draw out his affections. Obviously a false and mercenary Mephibosheth would have cried out, Yes, yes, that is a very satisfactory settlement. But not such was the language of the true and devoted Mephibosheth.

Have we not a similar case in the puzzling situation presented to Solomon by the two harlots? Both of those women gave birth to a child: one overlying and smothering her's, and then stealing the remaining one. When the two women appeared before the king, each claimed to be the mother of the surviving child. What did Solomon say? This, *"Divide* the living child in two, and give half to the one, and half to the other" (1 Kings 3:25) — the very proposal David made unto Mephibosheth! And how did the suggestion work out? Why, the imposter was quite willing to the arrangement, but the actual mother of the living child at once cried out, "O my lord, give *her* the living child, and in no wise slay it" (v. 26). And so it was here, as the sequel shows.

"And Mephibosheth said unto the king, Yea, let *him* take *all*, forasmuch as my lord the king is come again in peace unto his own house" (v. 30). How clearly that evidenced the unfeigned and disinterested character of his love! All he wanted was David's own company. Now that the king was restored, nothing else mattered. To be in David's own presence meant far more to Mephibosheth than any houses or lands. A later incident *confirms* the fact that Mephibosheth had *not* been cast out of the king's favour, for when seven of Saul's descendants were slain as a satisfaction for his sin in the slaughter of the Gibeonites, it is expressly recorded that "The king spared Mephibosheth (21:7)! And what of the wicked Ziba? He was allowed to go away unpunished, as Shimei had been, for David marked his appreciation of his restoration by the gracious remission of the injuries done to him.

"And Barzillai the Gileadite came down from Rogelim, and went over Jordan with the king, to conduct him over Jordan. Now Barzillai was a very aged man, even fourscore years old: and he had provided the king of sustenance while he lay at Mahanaim; for he was a very great man" (vv. 31, 32). This befriending of the king in the hour of his need came before us as we pondered the closing verses of chapter 17. There is no doubt that in ministering so freely to David and his men, Barzillai had done so at considerable risk to himself, for had Absalom prevailed there is little doubt that he had been made to suffer severely for his pains. It is touching to see him here, in his feebleness, taking such a journey to conduct his beloved monarch across the Jordan.

"And the king said unto Barzillai, Come thou over with me, and I will feed thee with me in Jerusalem" (v. 33). Deeply did the king appreciate the loyalty, generosity, and welcome of his aged subject, and accordingly desired that he should participate in the feast which was to mark his restoration. But Barzillai had other thoughts. He felt, and rightly so, that one so near to death should be engaged in more serious and solemn exercise than festive jollifications. Not but there is a time to feast as well as a time to fast, yet such was hardly a suitable occupation for a man so close to the brink of eternity. The aged should be done with carnal pleasures, and set their thoughts and affections on something more enduring and satisfying than the best this earth has to offer.

"But behold thy servant Chimham: let him go over with my lord the king, and do to him what shall seem good to thee" (v. 37) — apparently this was one of his sons or grandsons. Barzillai was no austere cynic who cherished a dog-in-the-manger attitude toward the rising generation. "They that are old must not begrudge young people those delights which they themselves are past the enjoyment of, nor oblige them to retire as *they* do" (Matt. Henry). If on the one hand those of experience should do what they can to warn and shield their juniors from carnal follies and the snares of this world, on the other hand they must guard against that extreme which would deprive the young of those lawful pleasures which they themselves once participated in. It is easy for some dispositions to develop selfishness and crabbedness under a supposed concern of protecting those under their charge. Such, we take it, is one of the lessons here inculcated in Barzallai's response to the king's invitation.

"And the king answered, Chimham shall go over with me, and I will do to him that which shall seem good unto thee: and whatsoever thou shalt require of me, that will I do for thee" (v. 38). David at once fell in with Barzillai's suggestion, for he was anxious to repay his kindness. It is our duty to do what we can in assisting the children of those who befriended us, when we were in need. It is beautiful to read how that when the aged David was giving instruction to Solomon, he made special mention of the descendants of Barzillai: "But show kindness unto the sons of Barzillai the Gileadite, and let them be of those that eat at my table: for so they came to me when I fled because of Absalom thy brother" (1 Kings 2:7). Nor was this all that David had done, as the sequel will show.

In his remarkable little work "Scripture Coincidences", J.J. Blunt points out how that Chimham is mentioned by the prophet Jeremiah, and in that incidental manner common to hundreds of similar allusions in the Word which so evidently bear the stamp of truth upon them. This argument for the Divine inspiration of the Scriptures produces a stronger conviction than any external evidence. There is an exact coincidence observable by allusions to particular facts which demonstrates perfect consistency *without* contrivance or collusion. As we have seen, Chimham accompanied David to Jerusalem, but what the king did for him, beyond providing a place for him at his table and recommending him to the care of Solomon, does not appear. Nothing further is said about him in the historical books of the O.T. But in Jer. 41 his name again appears. An account is there given of the murder of Gedaliah, the officer whom Nebuchadnezzar had left in charge of Judea as its governor, when he carried away captive the more wealthy of its inhabitants. The Jews, fearing the consequences of their crime, and apprehending the vengeance of the Chaldeans, prepared for flight: "And they departed, and dwelt in the habitation of *Chimham*, which is by *Bethlehem* to go to enter into Egypt" (Jer. 41:17).

"It is impossible to imagine anything more incidental than the mention of this estate near Bethlehem, which was the habitation of Chimham; yet how well does it tally with the spirit of David's speech to Barzillai some four hundred years before! What can be more probable, than that David, whose birth-place was this very Bethlehem, and whose patrimony in consequence lay there, having undertaken to provide for Chimham, should have bestowed it in whole, or in part, as the most flattering reward he could confer, a personal, as well as a royal, mark of favour, on the son of the man who had saved his life, and the lives of his followers in the hour of their distress; and that, to the very day when Jeremiah wrote, it should have remained in the possession of the family of Chimham and be called after his own name" (J. J. Blunt).

"Then the king went on to Gilgal, and Chimham went on with him: and all the people of Judah conducted the king, and also half the people of Israel. And, behold, all the men of Israel came to the king, and said unto the king, Why have our brethren the men of Judah stolen thee away, and have brought the king, and his household, and all David's men with him, over Jordan?" (vv. 40, 41). By the time that David had crossed the Jordan many of the elders and people of Israel came to bring back the king, only to discover they had been anticipated. The officers of Judah had taken the lead in this, and had failed to notify the Ten Tribes of their intentions. This omission was strongly resented, for those of Israel felt they had been slighted, yea, that a serious reflection was cast upon their loyalty to the king.

"And all the men of Judah answered the men of Israel, Because the king is near of kin to us: wherefore then be ye angry for this matter? have we eaten at all of the king's cost? or hath he given us any gift? And the men of Israel answered the men of Judah, and said, We have ten parts in the king, and we have also more right in David than ye: why then did ye despise us, that our advice should not be first had in bringing back our king? And the words of the men of Judah were fiercer than the words of the men of Israel" (vv. 42, 43). Alas, what is poor human nature. If these Israelites were so desirous that the king should be honoured, why be peeved because others had preceded them? O what mischief issues from pride and jealousy. How quick many are to take umbrage at the least seeming slight. How we need to watch against the workings of our own pride, and endeavour to avoid giving offence to the pride of others. But let us, in closing, contemplate a deeper significance possessed by the incidents which have been before us.

"But here again some glimpses may be discerned of the glorious character and kingdom of David's Son and Lord. Being anointed by the Father to be His King upon His holy hill of Zion, He reigns over a willing people, who deem it their privilege to be His subjects. Once indeed they were rebels (and numbers of their associates perish in rebellion): but when they became sensible of their danger, they were fearful or reluctant to submit unto Him; till His ministers, by representing His tender love, and His promises of pardon and preferment, through the concurring influences of His Spirit, bowed their hearts to an humble willingness that He should reign over them; then He readily pardoned and accepted them, and upon no account will He cast out or cut off the greatest offender who cries for mercy. He will recompense those, who from love to Him, feed His servants; He will assign them a place in His holy city. Alas that it must be added, that while the king himself is so plenteous in mercy, many of His professed subjects are envious and contentious with each other, and quarrel about the most trivial concerns, which prevent much good, and does immense mischief" (T. Scott).

And there happened to be there a man of Belial whose name was Sheba, the son of Bichri, a Benjamite. And he blew a trumpet and said, We have no part in David, neither do we have any inheritance in the son of Jesse. Every man to his tents, O Israel! So every man of Israel went up after David, and followed Sheba the son of Bichri. But the men of Judah clung to their king, from Jordan even to Jerusalem. And David came to his house at Jerusalem. And the king took the ten women, his concubines, whom he had left to keep the house, and put them in ward and fed them but did not go in unto them. So they were shut up till the day of their death, living in widowhood. Then the king said to Amasa, Gather to me the men of Judah within three days, and you be present here. So Amasa went to gather Judah. But he stayed longer than the set time which he had appointed him. And David said to Abishai, Now Sheba the son of Bichri shall do us more harm than Absalom. You take your lord's servants and pursue after him, lest he get himself into fenced cities and escape us. And Joab's men went out after him, and the Cherithites, and the Pelethites, and all the mighty men. And they went out of Jerulem to pursue after Sheba the son of Bichri. When they were at the great stone which is in Gibeon, Amasa came to meet them. And Joab was girded with his war-coat, which he had put on. And on it was a girdle with a sword fastened on his loins, in the sheaf of it. And as he went forth, it fell out.
— II Samuel 20:1-8.

There had been not a little to offset David's grief over the revolt and death of Absalom. As we have seen, his journey back to Jerusalem was marked by several incidents which must have brought satisfaction and joy to the king's heart. The radical change in the attitude of Shimei towards him, the discovery that after all the heart of Mephibosheth beat true to him, the affectionate homage of the aged Barzillai, and the welcome from the elders and men of Judah, were all calculated to cheer and encourage the returning exile. Things seemed to have taken a decided turn for the better, and the sun shone out of a clear sky. Yes, but the clouds have a habit of returning even after a heavy rain. And so it was here. A dark cloud suddenly appeared on David's horizon which must have caused him considerable uneasiness, presaging as it did the gathering of another storm.

The leaders of the Ten Tribes had met David at Gilgal, and a dispute at once ensued between them and the men of Judah. This was the fly in the ointment. A foolish quarrel broke out between the two factions over the matter of bringing back the king. "It was a point of honour which was being disputed between them, which had most interest in David. 'We are more numerous' say the elders of Israel. 'We are nearer akin to him' say the elders of Judah. Now one would think David very safe and happy when his subjects are striving which should love him best, and be most forward to show him respect; yet even that strife proved the occasion for a rebellion" (Matt. Henry). No sooner was one of David's trials over than another arises, as it were, out of the ashes of the former.

Ah, my reader, we must not expect to journey far in this world without encountering trouble in some form or other; no, not even when the providence of God appears to be smiling upon us. It will not be long before we receive some rude reminder that "this is not your rest." It was thus in the present experiences of our hero: in the very midst of his triumphs he was forced to witness a disturbance among his leading subjects, which soon threatened the overthrow of his kingdom. There is nothing stable down here, and we only court certain disappointment if we build our hopes on anything earthly or think to find satisfaction in the creature. Under the sun is but "vanity and vexation of spirit." But how slow we are to really believe that melancholy truth; yet in the end we find it *is* true.

We closed our last section with a quotation which called attention to the typical significance of the incidents recorded in 2 Sam. 19; the opening verses of 20 may be contemplated as bearing out the same line of thought. Christ's visible kingdom on earth is entered by profession, hence there are tares in it as well as wheat, bad fish as well as good, foolish virgins as well as wise (Matt. 13 and 25). This will be made unmistakably manifest in the Day to come, but even in this world God sometimes so orders things that profession is tested and that which is false is exposed. Such is the dispensational significance of the episode we are now to consider. The Israelites had appeared to be very loyal and devoted to David, yea, so much so that they were hurt when the men of Judah had, without consulting them, taken the lead in bringing back the king.

But how quickly the real state of their hearts was made apparent. What a little thing it took to cause their affection for David not only to cool off but to completely evaporate. No sooner did an enemy cry "to your tents, O Israel," than they promptly responded, renouncing their professed allegiance. There was no reality to their protestation of fealty, and when the choice was set before them they preferred a "man of Belial" rather than the man after God's own heart. How solemnly this reminds us of the multitudes of Israel at a later date: first crying out "Hosanna to the Son of David, Blessed is He that cometh in the name of the Lord" (Matt. 21:9) and a short time after, when the issue was drawn, preferring Barabbas to Christ. And how often since then, especially in times of trial and persecution, have thousands of those who made a loud profession of Christianity preferred the world or their own carnal safety.

"And there happened to be there a man of Belial, whose name was Sheba, the son of Bichri, a Benjamite: and he blew a trumpet, and said, We have no part in David, neither have we inheritance in the son of Jesse; every man to his tents, O Israel" (2 Sam. 20:1). Alas! how often it appears that in a happy concourse of those who come together to greet and do homage to David there is "a son of Belial" ready to sound the trumpet of contention. Satan knows full well that few things are better calculated to further his own base designs than by causing divisions among the people of God. Sad it is that we are not more upon our guard, for we are not ignorant of his devices. And to be on our guard means to be constantly mortifying pride and jealousy. *Those* were the evil roots from which this trouble issued, as is clear from the "that *our* advice should not *first* be had in bringing back our king" (19:43).

"And the words of the men of Judah were fiercer than the words of the men of Israel" (19:43). This was only adding fuel to the fire. "A soft answer turneth away wrath, but grievous words stir up anger" (Prov. 15:1). If the spirit of jealousy prevailed among the leaders of Israel, pride was certainly at work in the hearts of the elders of Judah, and when those two evils *clashed*, anger and strife quickly followed. It is solemn to observe that God Himself took notice of and recorded in His Word *the fierceness* of the words of the men of Judah — a plain intimation that He now registers against *us* that language which is not pleasing unto Him. How we need to pray that God would set a watch before our mouths, that the door of our lips may be kept from allowing evil to pass out.

"And there happened to be a man of Belial, whose name was Sheba, the son of Bichri, a Benjamite; and he blew a trumpet, and said, We have no part in David, neither have we inheritance in the son of Jesse." Sheba belonged to the tribe of Saul, which had bitterly begrudged the honour done to Judah, when the son of

Jesse was elected king. The Benjamites never really submitted to the Divine ordination. The deeper significance of this is not hard to perceive: there is a perpetual enmity in the Serpent's seed against the antitypical David. How remarkably was this mysterious yet prominent feature of Christ's kingdom adumbrated in the continued opposition of the house of Saul against David: first in Saul himself, then in Ishbosheth (2 Sam. 2:8, 9; 3:1 etc.), and now Sheba. But just as surely as David prevailed over all his enemies, so shall Christ vanquish all His foes.

"And he blew a trumpet, and said, We have no part in David, neither have we inheritance in the son of Jesse: every man to his tents, O Israel." See how ready is an evil mind to place a false construction upon things, and how easily this can be accomplished when determined so to do. The men of Judah had said "the king is near of kin to us" (19:42), but this son of Belial now perverted their words and made them to signify "We have *no* part in David" whereas they intended no such thing. Then let us not be surprised when those who secretly hate us give an entirely false meaning to what we have said or written. History abounds in incidents where the most innocent statements have been grossly wrested to become the means of strife and bloodshed. It was so with the Lord Jesus Himself: see John 2:19-21 and compare Matt. 27, 26: 61, 62 — sufficient then for the disciple to be as his Master. But let the Christian diligently see to it that he does not let *himself* (or herself) be used as a tool of Satan in this vile work.

"Every man to his tents, O Israel." This call put them to the proof testing their loyalty and love to David. The sequel at once evidenced how fickle and false they were. "So every man of Israel went up from after David, and followed Sheba the son of Bichri" (v. 2). Hardly had they returned to their allegiance, than they forsook it. How utterly unreliable human nature is, and how foolish are they who put their trust in man. What creatures of extremes we be: now welcoming Moses as a deliverer, and next reviling him because the deliverance came not as easily and quickly as was expected; now glad to escape from the drudgery of Egypt, and a little later anxious to return thither. What grace is neeeded to *anchor* such unstable and unreliable creatures.

"So every man of Israel went up from after David, and followed Sheba the son of Bichri" (v. 2). Nothing is told us as to whether or not David himself had taken any part in the debate between the elders of Israel and of Judah, or whether he had made any attempt to pour oil on the troubled waters. If he did, it appears that he quite failed to convince the former, for they now not only refused to attend him any further on his return to Jerusalem, but refused to own him as their king at all. Nay more, they were determined to set up a rival king of their own. Thus the very foundations of his kingdom were again threatened. Scarcely had God delivered David from the revolt of Absalom, than he was now faced with this insurrection from Sheba. And is it not thus in the experience of David's spiritual seed: no sooner do they succeed in subduing one lust or sin, than another raises its ugly head against them.

"But the men of Judah clave unto their king, from Jordan even to Jerusalem" (v. 2). It is blessed to find there were some who remained loyal to David, refusing to forsake him even when the majority of his subjects turned away from him. Thus, though the test exposed the false, it also revealed the true. So it ever is. And *who* were the ones that remained steadfast to the king? Why, the men of his own tribe, those who were related to him by *blood* The typical significance of this is obvious. Though in the day of testing there are multitudes who forsake the royal banner of the antitypical David, there is always a remnant which Satan himself cannot induce to apostatize, namely, those who are Christ's brethren spiritually. How beautifully was that here illustrated.

"And David came to his house at Jersualem; and the king took the ten women his concubines, whom he had left to keep the house, and put them in ward, and fed them, but went not in unto them. So they were shut up unto the day of their death, living in widowhood" (v. 3). Here we see one of *the gains* resulting from the severe chastening that David had undergone. As we have seen in earlier chapters, David had multiplied wives and concubines unto himself contrary to the law of God, and they had proved a grief and a shame to him (15:16; 16:21, 22). God often has to take severe measures with us ere we are willing to forsake our idols. It is good to note that from this point onwards we read nothing more of concubines in connection with David. But how solemn to discover, later, that this evil example which he had set before his family, was followed by his son Solomon — to the drawing away of his heart from the Lord. O that parents gave more heed to the Divine threat that their sins shall surely be visited upon their descendants.

"Then said the king to Amasa, Assemble me the men of Judah within three days, and be thou here present" (v. 4). Though the men of Judah had not followed the evil example of the Ten Tribes in their revolt against the king, yet it appears from this verse that many of them were no longer in attendance upon David, having no doubt returned unto their own homes. Considering the circumstances, it seems that they put their own comfort and safety first, at a time when their master's regime was seriously threatened. "Though forward enough to attend the king's triumphs, they were backward enough to fight his battles. Most love a loyalty, as well as a religion, that is cheap and easy. Many boast of their being akin to Christ that yet are very loath to venture for Him" (Matt. Henry). On the other hand let it not be forgotten that it is not without reason the Lord's people are called "sheep" — one of the most *timid* of all animals.

"Then said the king to Amasa, Assemble me the men of Judah within three days, and be thou here present." This shows the uneasiness of David at Sheba's rebellion and his determination to take strong and prompt measures to quell it. Amasa, it may be pointed out, had been the "captain of the host" for Absalom against David (17:25), yet he was near akin unto the king. He was the one whom David had intended should replace Joab as the commander of his armies (19:13), and the rebellion of Sheba now supplied the opportunity for the carrying out of this purpose. Having received a previous notification of the king's design may have been the main reason why Amasa, though an Israelite, did not join forces with the insurrectionists. He saw an opportunity to better his position and acquire greater military honour. But, as we shall see, in accepting this new commission, he only signed his own death-warrant — so insecure are the honours of this world.

It is very much to be doubted whether David's choice was either a wise or a popular one. Since Amasa had filled a prominent position under Absalom, it could scarcely to expected that the man whom Joab had successfully commanded would now relish being placed in subjection to the man who so recently had been the enemy of their king. It is this which, most probably, accounts for the delay, or rather Amasa's lack of success in carrying out the king's orders, for we are told "So Amasa went to assemble the men of Judah: but he tarried longer than the set time which he had appointed him" (v. 5). As Scott says, "The men of Judah seemed to have been more eager in disputing about their king, than to engage in battle under Amasa." This supplied a solemn warning for Amasa, but in the pride of his heart he heeded it not.

"And David said to Abishai, Now shall Sheba the son of Bichri do us more harm than did Absalom: take thou thy lord's servants, and pursue after him, lest he get him fenced cities, and escape us" (v. 6). It had already been clearly demonstrated that Sheba was a man who possessed considerable influence over the men of Israel, and therefore David had good reason to fear that if he were allowed to mature his plans, the most serious trouble would be sure to follow. His order to Amasa shows that he was determined to frustrate the insurrectionists by nipping their plans while they were still in the bud, by sending a powerful force against them. Chafing at the delay occasioned by Amasa's lack of success in promptly collecting an army, David now gave orders to Abishai to take command of the regular troops, for he was determined to degrade Joab.

"And there went out after him Joab's men, and the Cherithites, and the Pelethites, and all the mighty men: and they went out of Jerusalem to pursue after Sheba the son of Bichri" (v. 7). This, we take it, defines "thy lord's servants" of the previous verse, namely, the seasoned warriors which Joab had formerly commanded. Though he had no intention of employing Joab himself on this occasion. David gladly availed himself of his trained men. Abishai was a proved and powerful officer, being in fact brother to Joab. All seemed to be now set for the carrying out of David's design, but once more it was to be shown that though man proposes it is God who disposes. Even great men, yea, kings themselves, are often thwarted in their plans, and discover they are subordinate to the will of Him who is the King of kings. How thankful we should be that this is so, that the Lord in His infinite wisdom ruleth over all.

"When they were at the great stone which is in Gibeon, Amasa went before them" (v. 8). It seems this was the appointed meeting-place for the concentrated forces of David. Amasa now arrived on the scene at the head of the men which he had mustered, and promptly placed himself in command of the army. But brief indeed was the moment of his military glory, for no sooner did he reach the pinnacle of his ambition than he was brutally dashed therefrom, to lay weltering in his own blood. "Vain are earthly distinctions and preferments, which excite so much envy and enmity, without affording any additional security to man's uncertain life: may we then be ambitious of that honour which cometh from God only" (Thos. Scott).

And Joab said to Amasa, Are you well, my brother? And Joab took Amasa by the beard with the right hand to kiss him. But Amasa took no heed to the sword that was in Joab's hand. So he struck him with it in the fifth rib, and shed out his bowels to the ground. And he did not strike him again. And he died. So Joab and Abishai his brother pursued after Sheba the son of Bichri. And one of Joab's men stood by him and said, He who favors Joab, and he who is for David, go after Joab! And Amasa wallowed in blood in the middle of the highway. And when the man saw that all the people stood still, he moved Amasa out of the highway into the field, and threw a cloth over him — when he saw that everyone who came by him stood still. When he was moved out of the highway, all the people went on after Joab, to pursue after Sheba the son of Bichri. And he went through all the tribes of Israel to Abel, and to Bethmaachah and all the Berites. And they were gathered together, and went after him too. And they came and besieged him in Abel of Bethmaachah. And they threw up a bank against the city. And it stood in the trench. And all the people who were with Joab battered the wall to throw it down. Then a wise woman cried out of the city, Hear, Hear!

I beg you, say to Joab: Come near here so that I may speak with you. And when he had come near her, the woman siad, Are you Joab? And he answered, I am. Then she said to him, Hear the words of your servant. And he answered, I hear. Then she spoke, saying, They plainly spoke in the beginning, saying, Surely they will ask of Abel, and so make an end of the matter. I am peaceable and faithful in Israel. You seek to destroy a city and a mother in Israel. Why will you swallow up the inheritance of the LORD? And Joab answered and said, Far be it, far be it from me, that I should swallow up or destroy. The matter is not so. But a man of Mount Ephraim, Sheba the son of Bichri by name, has lifted up his hand against the king, against David. Only deliver him, and I will depart from the city. And the woman said to Joab, Watch! His head shall be thrown to you over the wall. Then the woman went to all the people in her wisdom. And they cut off the head of Sheba the son of Bichri and threw it out to Joab. And he blew a trumpet, and they scattered from the city, each man to his tent, And Joab returned to Jerusalem to the king. Now Joab was over all the army of Israel. And Benaiah the son of Jehoiada was over the Cherethites and over the Pelethites. And Adoram was over the tribute. And Jehoshaphat the son of Ahilud was recorder. And Sheva was scribe. And Zadok and Abiathar were the priests. And also Ira the Jairite was a chief ruler around David. — II Samuel 20:9-26.

In previous sections it has been pointed out that Joab was a man of a fierce and intractable spirit, and that he was ungodly and unscrupulous in principle. Once David had placed himself in his power (by making him his secret agent in the death of Uriah: 2 Sam. 11:14, 15), he thenceforth took matters more and more into his own hands, executing or disregarding the king's orders as best suited himself. Imperious and ruthless to the last degree, Joab would brook no interference with his own policy. Devoid of natural feeling, fearing neither God nor man, he hesitated not to slay any who stood in his way. Fearfully does his arrogance, treachery, and brutality appear in the incident which is to be before us. Feign would we pass by an episode so revolting, yet it is recorded in Holy Writ, and therefore it must contain some message that is needed by us.

We have also seen how that, at length, David made a determined effort to strip Joab of his power, by removing him from the head of the army. Accordingly Amasa was selected as the one to replace him. But the king's design was thwarted, frustrated by one of the vilest deeds chronicled in the Scriptures. Under pretence of paying obeisance to the new general, Joab thrust him through with the sword. Such an atrocity staggers the thoughtful, making them to wonder why God suffers such outrages to be perpetrated. This is indeed one of the dark mysteries of Divine providence — why the Lord permits such monsters of wickedness to walk the earth. Faith is assured that He must have some sufficient reason. Though often God giveth "no account of His matters" (Job 33:13), yet His Word does indicate, more or less clearly, the general principles which regulate His governmental dealings.

Much help is afforded upon the mystery of Providence when it is perceived that God makes "all things *work together*" (Rom. 8:28). When incidents are contemplated singly they naturally appear distorted, for they are viewed out of their proper perspective; but when we are able to examine them in relation to their antecedents and consequents, usually their significance is much more evident. The detached fragments of life are meaningless, bewildering, staggering; but put them together, and they manifest a design and purpose. Much in the present finds its explanation in that which preceded it in the past, while much in the present will also become intelligible by the sequel in the future — "What I do thou knowest not now; but thou shalt know hereafter" (John 13:7). If these principles were more steadily borne in mind, we should be less non-plussed by startling occurrences.

Our present incident is a case in point. Viewed by itself apart, the brutal murder of Amasa is indeed overwhelming, as to why God should permit him to come to such a fearful end. But viewed in relation to other things, contemplated in connection with that inexorable but righteous principle of sowing and reaping, light is cast on that dark scene. If we take the trouble to go back from effect to cause, we shall find that God had a just reason for employing Joab to thwart David's purpose, and that in meeting with such a death Amasa but received his just deserts. If this can be demonstrated, then we may perceive much more clearly why this revolting incident is recorded in Holy Writ; for since it is evident that God had a sufficient reason for suffering *this* tragedy to occur, we may rest the better assured that He has His own wise ends in things which often appear so puzzling and appalling to us in the world to-day.

There was a reason why God permitted Jacob to be so basely deceived about the fate of his beloved Joseph (Gen. 37:31-35): he was but reaping what he had sown in the deceiving of his father Isaac (Gen. 27). There was a reason why God permitted the Egyptians to treat the Hebrews with such cruelty and severity (Ex. 1 and 5): they were His instruments in punishing them for their idolatry and their refusal to heed the Divine call to cast away the heathen abominations with which they had defiled themselves (Ezek. 20:7, 8). There was a reason why God permitted Doeg to brutally slay no less than eighty-five of the priestly family (1 Sam. 22:18): it was the execution of the solemn judgment which He pronounced upon the house of Eli (1 Sam. 2:31-36; 3:12-16), the sins of the fathers being visited upon the children. There is a reason why God has permitted the Jews to be more hated and persecuted throughout this Christian era than any other people: the guilt of Christ's crucifixion rests on them and their children (Matt. 27:25).

"The curse causeless shall not come" (Prov. 26:2). While God is absolute sovereign and exercises His justice or His mercy as and when He pleases, yet He acts not arbitrarily: He neither punishes the innocent, nor does He pardon the guilty without reparation — i.e. through a Substitute. Hence, we may rest assured that when the Divine curse falls upon a person, there is due cause for the same. But let not the reader misunderstand us: we do not wish to imply that any of *us* are capable of ascertaining the reason or reasons which lie behind any calamity that may overtake either ourselves or any of our fellows. On the contrary, it lies entirely outside of our province to explain the mysteries of Divine Providence, and it would be the height of presumption to say *why* an affliction has been sent upon another — the book of Job warns loudly against such a procedure.

No, what we have been seeking to do is to point out that the most mysterious of Divine Providences, the most appalling events in history — whether involving individuals only or nations — *have* a satisfactory explanation, that God *has* sufficient reason for all that He does or permits. And in His Word He has graciously made this evident, by revealing in instance after instance, the obvious connection between sowing and reaping, True, He has by no means done so in every case, for God has not written His Word either to vindicate His own character and conduct or to satisfy our curiosity. Sufficient is said in His Word to show that God is infinitely worthy of our utmost confidence, so that we should say with him whose faith was tried in a way and to an extent that few ever have been, "Though He slay me, yet will I trust in Him."

We have followed out the present train of thought because some are so overwhelmed by the shocking things which take place in the world from time to time, that their faith is shaken. They know that so far from its affording any solution to the problem, to affirm that *God* has no connection with such things, is a serious error — denying His present government over and control of the wicked. Nay, it is because they recognize that God actually permits these outrages, that they find it so difficult to harmonize this with His revealed character. We have called attention to some outstanding cases because they are to be regarded as *examples* of a general principle. Retributive justice is one of the Divine perfections, and though we are often far too short-sighted to perceive its workings, nevertheless, we may have implicit confidence in its operations, and as it is regulated by Omniscience, we know it makes no mistakes.

Resuming now at the point where we left off in our last: "When they were at the great stone which is in Gibeon, Amasa went before them" (2 Sam. 20:8). It will be remembered that in connection with David's journey back to Jerusalem, upon his crossing of the Jordan, there had occurred a sharp controversy between the elders of Judah and the elders of Israel. The old spirit of rivalry and jealousy was stirred up, and an evil man, by name of Sheba, who belonged to the tribe of Saul, sought to capitalize the situation, and called upon those belonging to Israel to abandon the cause of David. In this he was, for the moment, successful, for we are told, "So every man of Israel went up from after David, and followed Sheba the son of Bichri" (v. 2). This threatened the most serious consequences, and unless Sheba's plans were nipped in the bud, David would be faced with another rebellion.

The king recognized the danger, and at once took measures to meet it. Now was the opportunity, he felt, to put into execution the plan which he had formed for the removing of Joab from the head of the forces. Calling Amasa to him, he said, "Assemble me the men of Judah within three days, and be thou here present." As we saw, there was some delay, so "David said to Abishai, Now shall Sheba the son of Bichri do us more harm than did Absalom: take thou thy lord's servants, and pursue after him, lest he get him fenced cities, and escape us." Then we are told, "And there went out after him Joab's men, and the Cherethites, the Pelethites, and all the mighty men: and they went out of Jerusalem, to pursue after Sheba." They had some distance to go, and apparently the great stone in Gibeon was to be the gathering-point of David's forces, for "when they were at the great stone which is in Gibeon, Amasa went before them." By this we understand that the men whom Amasa, according to David's orders, now took charge of the entire expedition.

"And Joab's garment that he had put on was girded unto him, and upon it a girdle with a sword fastened upon his loins in the sheath thereof; and as he went forth it fell out" (v. 8). It seems from this that Joab had accompanied the soldiers in a private capacity. He pretended to gladly submit to the new arrangement, and to be full of zeal for David's cause, prepared to do his part in preventing another general uprising. But outward appearances are often deceptive. In reality, Joab was determined to avenge the dishonour done to him and assassinate the one who had been appointed to displace him. As he advanced to greet the new commander-in-chief, his sword fell out of its sheath, and to prevent its falling to the ground he caught it in his left hand. It looked as though the sword had become unsheathed by accident, but the sequel shows it was by design, and was but a subtle devise to cloak his vile purpose.

"And Joab said to Amasa, Art thou in health, my brother? And Joab took Amasa by the beard with his right hand to kiss him. But Amasa took no heed to the sword that was in Joab's hand: so he smote him therewith in the fifth rib, and shed out his bowels to the ground, and struck him not again; and he died"

(vv. 9, 10). How the real character of Joab was here displayed! Treacherous, ruthless, blatant, utterly hardened. Amasa was his own cousin, yet ties of blood meant nothing to this callous wretch. Amasa had been definitely appointed by the king to lead his forces, but the royal authority counted for naught to Joab. Moreover, it was in front of all the troops that Joab committed this awful crime, caring not what they thought nor afraid of what they might do. Thoroughly lawless and defiant, he never hesitated to take matters into his own hands and crush whoever stood in his way.

Viewed as an isolated event, here was a most appalling crime. A man in the path of duty brutally murdered without a moment's warning. And yet a holy God permitted it, for most certainly He could have prevented it had He so pleased. Why, then, did He suffer David's purpose to be so rudely thwarted? and why was Joab allowed to slay Amasa? The two questions are quite distinct, and must be considered separately. Unspeakably solemn though the subject be, yet earlier events cast their light on this dark scene. After David's murder of Uriah God had said, "the sword shall never depart from thine house" (2 Sam. 12:10), and Amasa was David's *own nephew*: see 2 Sam. 17:25 and compare 1 Chron. 2:13, 16. "Be sure your sin will find you out" (Num. 32:23). It found David out: in the death of Bathsheba's child, in the raping of Tamar; in the murder of Ammon, in the death of Absalom, and now in the slaying of Amasa.

And what of Amasa himself? Ah, was he one who had served the king with unswerving loyalty? No indeed, far from it. And what of the stock from which he came? Were his parents pious, so that the blessing of the Lord might be expected upon their offspring? And again the answer is no. "And Absalom made Amasa captain of the host instead of Joab" (2 Sam. 17:25). Thus, Amasa had not only failed David at the most critical juncture, but he had taken an active and prominent part against him. And now he was slain, justly slain, by one who had fought *for* the king. 2 Sam. 17:25 also tells us, "Which Amasa was a man's son, whose name was Ithra an Israelite, that went in to Abigail the daughter of Nahash, sister to Zeruiah, Joab's mother" so that here again it was a case of the sins of the parent being visited upon the child. Thus, revolting though this episode be, we may see in it the righteous judgment of God.

"So Joab and Abishai his brother pursued after Sheba the son of Bichri. And one of Joab's men stood by him, and said, He that favoureth Joab and he that is for David, let him go after Joab" (vv. 10, 11). This was playing politics with a vengeance, pretending that fealty to David demanded that the army should follow the leadership of Joab — how often the people are induced to follow a course which is evil under the impression that they are furthering a righteous cause! Why, these soldiers had just seen Joab slay the very man whom the king had called to head his forces: how, then, could they be for David if they followed this murderer? But, few people think for themselves, and fewer still are regulated by moral principle. The great majority are easily imposed upon, accepting what any glib-tongued or forcible leader tells them.

"And Amasa wallowed in blood in the midst of the highway. And when the man saw that all the people stood still, he removed Amasa out of the highway into the field, and cast a cloth upon him, when he saw that every one that came by him stood still. When he was removed out of the highway all the people went on after Joab, to pursue Sheba the son of Bichri" (vv. 12, 13). Though none had raised a hand against the cold-blooded murderer, they had sufficient decency to stand their ground until the body of his victim was removed from the public highway and respectfully covered. This done, they unanimously followed Joab. He might be impetuous and imperious, still he was a valiant warrior, and in the eyes of these soldiers, *that* covered a multitude of sins. Moreover, was he not pursuing Sheba, the enemy of their king; there could not, then, be anything radically wrong with him. Such has often been the superficial logic of the multitude, as the testimony of history abundantly illustrates. Yet faith discerns One behind the scenes working all things after the counsel of His own will.

Sheba had meanwhile taken refuge in the "city," or fortified town of Abel. Thither came Joab and his forces to besiege it, battering upon the outer wall to throw it down. Whereupon a "wise woman" of the city expostulated with Joab, protesting against the needless destruction of the town and the slaying of its inhabitants, reminding him that by so doing he would "swallow up the heritage of the Lord" (v. 19). Joab at once made it known that all he was after was the capture of the arch-rebel against David, assuring the woman that as soon as that son of Belial was delivered up to him, he and his forces would withdraw. Accordingly, Sheba was executed and his head thrown over the wall. Thus perished one more of those who set themselves against the Lord's anointed. "Evil shall hunt the violent man to overthrow him" (Psa. 140:11).

The readiness of Joab to heed the wise counsel of the woman of Abel is not to be taken as a redeeming feature on this occasion, still less as conflicting with what we have said above about his ge. al character. Joab had no personal grievance against the inhabitants of that city: had *that* been the case, it had indeed gone hard with them. Moreover, to have made a wholesale slaughter of those innocent Israelites, would obviously have been against the interests of the kingdom at large, and Joab was too politic to be guilty of so grave a blunder. "And Joab returned unto Jerusalem unto the king" (v. 22). Unabashed at his crime, conscious of the guilty hold which he had over him, Joab feared not to face his royal master. Thus was David's purpose thwarted, and as though to particularly emphasize the fact, the chapter closes by saying, "Now Joab was over all the hosts of Israel" etc. (v. 23).

Then there was a famine in the days of David three years, year after year. And David inquired of the LORD. And the LORD answered, It is for Saul, and for his bloody house, because he killed the Gibeonites. And the king called the Gibeonites and spoke to them. Now the Gibeonites were not of the children of Israel, but of the remnant of the Amorites. And the children of Israel had sworn to them. And Saul sought to kill them in his zeal to the children of Israel and Judah. Therefore David said to the Gibeonites, What shall I do for you? And with what shall I atone for this, so that you may bless the inheritance of the LORD? And the Gibeonites said to him, We will have no silver or gold from Saul, or from his house. Neither shall you kill any man in Israel for us. And he said, What you shall say, that I will do for you. And they answered the king, The man who destroyed us, and who devised against us, that we should be destroyed from remaining in any of the borders of Israel — let seven men of his sons be delivered to us, and we will hang them up to the Lord in Gibeah of Saul, chosen of the LORD. And the king said, I will give them. But the king spared Mephibosheth, the son of Jonathan the son of Saul, because of the LORD's oath that was between them, between David and Jonathan the son of Saul. But the king took the two sons of Rizpah the daughter of Aiah, whom she bore to Saul, Armoni and Mephibosheth — and the five sons of Michal the daugher of Saul, whom she brought up for Adriel the son of Barzillai the Meholathite — and he delivered them into the hands of the Gibeonites. And they hanged them in the hill before the LORD. And they fell, all seven together, and were put to death in the days of harvest, in the first days, in the beginning of barley harvest. And Rizpah the daughter of Aiah took sackcloth and spread it for herself on the rock, from the beginning of harvest until water dropped on them out of heaven. And she did not allow either the birds of the air to rest on them by day, or the beasts of the field by night. And it was told David what Rizpah the daughter of Aiah, the concubine of Saul, had done. And David went and took the bones of Saul and the bones of Jonathan his son from the men of Jabesh-gilead, who had stolen them from the street of Bethshan, where the Philistines had hanged them when the Philistines had slain Saul in Gilboa. And he brought the bones of Saul and the bones of Jonathan his son up from there. And they gathered the bones of those who were hanged. And they buried the bones of Saul and Jonathan his son in the country of Benjamin in Zelah, in the tomb of his father Kish. And they did all that the king commanded. And after that, God heeded prayer for the land. And the Philistines had war still again with Israel. And David went down, and his servants with him, and fought against the Philistines. And David became faint. And Ishbi-benob, who was of the sons of the giant, the weight of whose spear was three hundred shekels of brass in weight, he being girded with a new sword thought to kill David. But Abishai the son of Zeruiah came to his aid and struck the Philistine and killed him. Then the men of David swore to him, saying, You shall not go out to battle with us any more, so that you do not put out the light of Israel. And after this there was again a battle with the Philistines at Gob. Then Sibbechai the Hushathite killed Sippai, who was of the sons of the giant. And there was again a battle with the Philistines in Gob, where Elhanan of Bethlehem, the son of Jaare-oregim, killed the brother of Goliath the Gittite, the staff of whose spear was like a weaver's beam. And there was yet again a battle in Gath, where there was a man of great stature who had six fingers on each hand, and six toes on each foot, twenty-four in number. And he also was born to the giant. And when he defied Israel, Jonathan the son of Shimea, the brother of

David, killed him. These four were born to the giant in Gath, and fell by the hand of David, and by the hand of his servants. — II Samuel 21:1-22.

There does not seem to be much in common between the murder of Amasa and the famine which afflicted the land of Israel, yet that the contents of 2 Sam. 20 and 21 are definitely linked together is clearly intimated by the opening "Then" of the latter. What that connection is, a little reflection should make clear: that which is now to be before us supplies a further illustration of the principal thought developed in our last. It is *the retributive justice* of God which is again seen in exercise. There it had to do with an individual; here it affected a whole nation. Valuable light is here shed upon the subject of the Divine government of this world, for we are not only given to see how that God fully controls even its physical history, but are also shown something of the moral principles which regulate His procedure. So far from that government being a capricious one, it is regulated by definite design and method. It is the noting of this which supplies the key to the philosophy of history.

"Then there was a famine in the days of David three years, year after year" (2 Sam. 21:1). When faced with droughts and famines, the scientists (so called) and other wiseacres prate about planetary disturbances, sun-spots, the recurring of astronomical cycles, etc., but the Christian looks beyond all secondary causes and discerns the Maker of this world directing all its affairs. And thus the simplest believer has light which the most learned of this world's savants possess not. They, and all who follow them, leave God out of their thoughts, and therefore the light which is in them is darkness, and how great is that darkness. It is only the eye of faith which sees the hand of the Lord in everything, and where faith is in exercise there is secured a satisfying restingplace for the heart.

"And David enquired of the Lord" (v. 1). Wise man: he declined to lean unto his own understanding. Nor did he, like the monarchs of Egypt and Babylon before him, send for the astrologers and soothsayers. There was no need to, when he had access to the living God. The pity is that he did not consult Him earlier, instead of waiting till the situation got really desperate. By enquiring of the Lord in the time of trouble, David left us an example which we do well to follow. The Sender of trouble is the only One who can remove it; and if it be not His pleasure to remove it, He is the One who can show us how best to meet it. He did so for David; and He will for us, if we seek Him aright — that is, with an humble, penitent, yet trustful heart.

Troubles do not come by haphazard. The poor worldling may talk of his "bad luck" and "ill fortune," but the believer ought to employ more God-honouring language. He should know that it is his *Father* who orders all his circumstances and regulates every detail of his life. Therefore, when famine comes upon him — be it a spiritual or a financial one — it is both his privilege and his duty to seek unto the Lord and ask, "Show me wherefore Thou contendest with me" (Job 10:2). When the smile of God is withdrawn from us, we should at once suspect that something is wrong. True, His favour is not to be measured by His material benefits; and true also that His withholding of them does not always indicate His displeasure. No, He may be testing faith, developing patience, or preparing us for an enlarged trust. Nevertheless, it is always the part of wisdom to think the worst of ourselves, for the promise is "seek ye first the kingdom of God and His righteousness, and all these (material) things shall be added unto you. (Matt. 6:33).

"And the Lord answered, It is for Saul, and for his bloody house because he slew the Gibeonites" (21:1). The Lord did not turn a deaf ear unto David's enquiry, even though it was such a tardy one. How longsuffering He is with His own! How many of us have been like David in this! samrting under the chastening rod of God, yet allowing a lengthy interval to pass before we definitely enquired of God as to its cause. Rightly did the poet say, "O what peace we often forfeit, O what needless pains we bear, All because we do not carry, everything to God in prayer." Yes, oftentimes they are quite 'needless," for if God shows us what is wrong, and we put matters right, His rod will quickly be removed.

It is solemn to note that the controversy which the Lord had with Israel at this time was not over some recent thing, but one which had been committed years previously; yet was it one that had never been put right. God does not forget, if we do. Many afflictions, both upon individuals and upon nations, are expressly sent by Him for the purpose of "bringing to remembrance" the sins of the past. In the case before us Israel was now suffering because of the transgression of Saul, for it is an unchanging principle in the Divine government that God deals with nations according to the conduct of their rulers or responsible heads. No truth is more clearly revealed in Scripture than this, and the same is plainly exemplified in the history of the world all through this Christian era. Nor need this fact and principle at all surprise us, for in the great majority of instances the rulers follow that policy which will best please their subjects.

The earlier history supplies no record of that which occasioned this calamity upon the nation. We mention this in order to correct the assertion which is often made in some quarters that Scripture always explains Scripture, by which it is meant that every verse or statement in the Word may be understood by some other statement elsewhere. As a general principle this is true, yet it is by no means without exception, and therefore it needs qualifying. The above is an example of what we mean: there is no historical account of Saul's slaying the Gibeonites. Nor is this example by any means an isolated one. Paul said "thrice I suffered shipwreck, a night and a day have I been in the deep" (2 Cor. 11:25), yet we know not when and where this occurred. In connection with the giving of the law at Sinai "Moses said, I exceedingly fear and quake" (Heb. 12:21), but there is no record in the O.T. of this. Heb. 13:23 tells of Timothy being "set at liberty," yet his imprisonment is nowhere recorded in Scripture.

"Now the Gibeonites were not of the children of Israel, but of the remnant of the Amorites; and the children of Israel had sworn unto them" (v. 2). The allusion is to what is found in Josh. 9. It will be remembered that after Joshua had overthrown Jericho and Ai the inhabitants of Gibeon were afraid, and resorted to dishonest strategy. They succeeded in deceiving Joshua. After telling a plausible tale, the Gibeonites offered to become the servants of Israel. And we are told "And Joshua made peace with them, and made a league with them, to let them live: and the princes of the congregation sware unto them" (Josh. 9:15). A little later, Israel learned that they had been deceived, that instead of the Gibeonites being travellers from a far country (as they had affirmed) they were really Canaanites. The sequel is very striking and contains a lesson which governmental leaders would do well to take to heart to-day.

Three days later, as they continued their advance, the Israelites reached the cities of the Gibeonites, and we are told "And the children of Israel smote them not, because the princes of the congregation had sworn unto them by the Lord God of Israel" (v. 18). The heads of the nation respected the solemn treaty into which they had entered with the Gibeonites. Then they were put to a more severe test: "And all the congregation murmured against the princes" (v. 18). The common people urged their leaders to regard that treaty as a scrap of paper

— human nature was just the same then as it is now: unprincipled, blind to its own highest interests, utterly selfish, indifferent to the Divine approval. But in the merciful providence of God, Israel at that time was favoured with conscientious leaders, who refused to yield to the popular clamour and do that which they knew was wrong.

"But all the princes said unto all the congregation, We have sworn unto them by the Lord God of Israel: now therefore we may not touch them. This we will do to them; we will even let them live, lest wrath be upon us, because of the oath which we sware unto them" (vv. 19, 20). What a mercy it is when the responsible heads of the nation are God-fearing men, whose word is their bond, who cannot be induced to forsake the paths of righteousness. And my reader, how we need to *pray* (as we are commanded to do: 1 Tim. 2:1, 2) for all in authority over us, that God will make them honest, just, truthful, and that He will keep them steadfast in the performance of duty. Their position is no easy one: they are in need of Divine grace, and prayer is the appointed channel through which supplies of grace are communicated — to the ministers of state as truly as to the ministers of the Gospel. Then instead of criticizing and condemning them, let us hold up their hands by daily supplication for them.

Joshua confirmed the stand taken by the "princes" — the heads of the tribes. Calling the Gibeonites unto him, he asked why they had beguiled him. Whereupon they confessed it was out of fear for their very lives that they had resorted to the imposture; and then cast themselves upon his mercy and fidelity. "And so did he unto them, and delivered them out of the hand of the children of Israel, that they slew them not. And Joshua made them that day hewers of wood and drawers of water for the congregation, and for the altar of the Lord, even unto this day" (vv. 26, 27). From that time onwards, the Gibeonites remained in Israel's midst, acting as their servants — a peaceful and useful people, as Neh. 3:7 and other passages intimate.

"And Saul sought to slay them in his zeal to the children of Israel and Judah" (2 Sam. 21:2). In utter disregard for the solemn treaty which guaranteed their security, Saul determined to exterminate these Gibeonites; but this was done not out of zeal for the Lord, but "in his zeal to the children of Israel." How perverse human nature is! God had given Saul no commission to slay the Gibeonites, but He *had* commanded him to destroy the Philistines and Amalekites; but this he left undone. Ah, the extirpation of the Philistines was a difficult and dangerous task, for they were a well-armed and powerful people, fully prepared to resist; whereas the Gibeonites were an easy prey. And is there not much fleshly zeal being displayed in corrupt Christendom to-day? — thousands engaged in work to which God has never called them, whilst neglecting the great task He *has* assigned them. What numbers of the rank and file of professing Christians are now busy in seeking to "win souls to Christ," while neglecting the mortifying of their fleshly and worldly lusts — ah, the former is far easier than the latter.

Saul, then, broke public faith with the Gibeonites, for the solemn covenant entered into with them by Joshua assured their preservation. This is clear from v. 5, for while v. 2 says only that he "sought to slay them," here the Gibeonites referred to him as "the man that consumed us, and that devised against us, that we should be destroyed from remaining in any of the coasts of Israel," which is an amplification of the Lord's words, "It is for Saul, and for his bloody house, because he slew the Gibeonites" (v. 1). This brought down heavy guilt upon the nation, which had not been expiated by the punishment of the guilty. The three years' famine which now came upon the land was proof of this. "It pleased God in this manner, and so long after, to proceed against the nation for it: to show

His abhorrence against such crimes; to teach rulers to keep at a distance from similar offences themselves, and to punish them in others; and to intimate that the chief punishment of sin is *after* the death of the offenders" (T. Scott).

The fact that God waited so many years before He publicly evidenced His displeasure against Israel for this heinous transgression, manifested His long sufferance, granting them a lengthy space for repentance. But they repented not, and now He made them to realize that He had neither overlooked nor forgotten their crime. Learn then, my reader, that the passage of time does not remove or lessen the guilt of sin. Let us also learn what a solemn thing it is for a strong nation to go back upon its pledged word when they have promised protection to a weak people. This is something which the present government of Great Britain needs to take to heart, for if they should violate their promises to protect the lives and property of the Jews in Palestine, then we may most certainly expect the righteous judgment of God to fall heavily on our land.

God made known unto David the reason for his present controversy with Israel, that he might take proper measures for expiating the national guilt. As a God-fearing man, David at once recognised the binding obligation of the league Joshua had made with the Gibeonites, and the nations's guilt in violating the same. Accordingly "David said unto the Gibeonites, What shall I do for you? and wherewith shall I make the atonement, that ye may bless the inheritance of the Lord" (v. 3). This was but fair: they were the ones who had been wronged, and therefore it was but just that they should be given the opportunity for deciding what form the reparation should take. Incidentally, let it be carefully noted that this is still another passage which plainly teaches that "atonement" is made for the express purpose of turning away the displeasure of the Lord — there is no thought of at-one-ment or reconciliation here, for the Gibeonites were not alienated from Him!

"And the Gibeonites said unto him, We will have no silver nor gold of Saul, nor of his house; neither for us shalt thou kill any man in Israel" (v. 4). Most generous and noble was their reply. It showed they were neither mercenary nor spiteful: they neither desired to turn this situation to their own material advantage, nor did they harbour a spirit of revenge. For centuries they had acted as servants, and now that Israel had broken the covenant they might well have demanded their freedom. How their unselfishness puts to shame the greedy, grasping spirit of this much-vaunted twentieth century! It is not often that the poor are free from covetousness and avarice — the great majority are not poor from choice, but from necessity of circumstances. No wonder the Lord was ready to plead the cause of so meek and mild a people.

"And he said, What ye shall say, that will I do for you. And they answered the king, The man that consumed us, and that devised against us that we should be destroyed from remaining in any of the coasts of Israel; let seven men of his sons be delivered unto us, and we will hang them up unto the Lord in Gibeah of Saul, whom the Lord did choose" (vv. 5, 6). Here we perceive their spiritual intelligence and piety. Their asking for "seven" of the descendants of Saul showed they understood that number signified completeness. Their suggestion that these seven men should be "hanged," intimated that they knew this form of death betokened accursedness (Deut. 21:23). Their words "hang them up before the Lord in Gibeah" evinced their knowledge that satisfaction must be offered unto God's justice before His wrath could be turned away from Israel. Their declaration "Saul, whom the Lord did choose" was an open acknowledgement of the sovereignty of God. Their offer "*we* will hang them up unto the Lord" was very magnanimous — willing to spare David, and themselves bear any public criticism which was likely to be offered.

But let us now notice the nobility of David's conduct in this connection. First, in his enquiring of the Lord as to the reason why the famine had been sent on his land. Those who have followed us throughout this lengthy series will recall how often this grace was seen in him — signal evidence of his piety. Second, in his readiness to consult with the Gibeonites. How many a man would have considered it beneath his dignity to hold conference with menials! — but humility was another grace which shone brightly in David. Third, in his fairness. An unscrupulous man would have disputed their claim, saying that the league made in the days of Joshua was long since obsolete. Fourth, in his consenting to their proposal. We know from other passages that he was sentimentally attached to the family of Saul, but with him the claims of justice superseded all personal considerations. Finally, his fidelity to the promise he had made to Jonathan: "But the king spared Mephibosheth, the son of Saul, because of the Lord's oath that was between them" (v. 7) and cf. 1 Sam. 15:20, 42.

"Then there was a famine in the days of David three years, year after year: and David inquired of the Lord. And the Lord answered, It is for Saul and for his bloody house, because he slew the Gibeonites" (2 Sam. 21:1). In our last we sought to show that this occurrence supplies a definite illustration or example of God's governmental ways with the nations. On this occasion He was dealing with Israel for a crime which they had committed many years previously. That crime respected their violation of a treaty which had been entered into between themselves and the Gibeonites in the days of Joshua. King Saul had ruthlessly ignored that solemn obligation, and instead of protecting the weak had brutally sought to exterminate them, thus bringing down upon his own house and upon the nation the holy wrath of the Lord.

God does not always manifest His displeasure at once, either against individuals or nations; instead, He usually gives "space for repentance" (Rev. 2:21). But alas, so perverse is fallen human nature that, instead of improving the Divine mercy, it perverts the same: "Let favour be showed to the wicked, yet will he not learn righteousness" (Isa. 26:10). No, instead of "learning righteousness" man only adds iniquity to iniquity: "Because sentence against an evil work *is not executed speedily*, therefore the heart of the sons of men is fully set in them to do evil" (Eccl. 8:11). Men regard God's patience as indifference to their sins, thereby emboldening themselves in their wickedness: "These things hast thou done, and I kept silence: thou thoughtest that I was altogether such an one as thyself; but I will reprove thee, and set them in order before thine eyes" (Psa. 50:21). Yes, sooner or later, God will "reprove" — exhibiting His holiness, exercising His retributive justice. It was so here. Though Saul was now dead, yet his house was made to feel God's avenging hand.

When David inquired the reason why God had sent this protracted famine upon the land of Israel, He made known to him the cause thereof. The king thereupon entered into a conference with those who had been wronged, and invited them to state what reparation should be made for Saul's outrages upon their people. Their response was very striking, illustrating the fact that those from whom it is to be the least expected often evince much more magnanimity than others who have enjoyed far greater privileges. The Gibeonites made it known that they sought no pecuniary gain, being far more concerned that the Divine justice should be compensated: "Let seven men of his sons be delivered unto us, and we will hand them up *unto the Lord* in Gibeah of Saul, whom the Lord did choose" (2 Sam. 21:6).

Let it be duly noted, first, that the Gibeonites had for many years held their peace, neither complaining to David for the unredressed wrong Saul had done them, nor disturbing the kingdom by their protests and demands. It was not until the Lord had interposed on their behalf, and until David himself had inquired what satisfaction should be made for the grievous wrong which had been done them, that they preferred the above request. It was in no blood-thirsty and vindictive spirit they now spoke. Their request was neither unjust nor unreasonable: they asked for no lives but those of Saul's own family: he had done the wrong, and therefore it was but right that *his house* should pay the price. To this day, the heirs may be lawfully sued for their parents' debts. True, in the ordinary course of things, children are not to be slain for the crimes of their father (Deut. 24:16), but the case of the Gibeonites was altogether extraordinary.

Furthermore, it must be borne in mind that the Lord had definitely intervened on behalf of these injured ones, and therefore what is here before us should be considered from the *Divine* viewpoint. However shocking this incident may appear to us, or however contrary to our sense of the fitness of things, let us beware of condemning or even criticising that which the Most High inspired. "God had made Himself an immediate party to the cause, and, no doubt, put it into the hearts of the Gibeonites to make this demand. . .Let parents take heed of sin, especially the sin of cruelty and oppression, for their children's sake, who may be smarting for it by the just hand of God, when they are in their graves. Guilt and a curse are a bad entail on a family" (Matt. Henry). A most solemn warning was furnished for all future generations in this tragic incident.

Finally, let it not be overlooked that God owned what was done on this occasion: "And after that God was entreated for the land" (v. 14). God's judgments are not subject to those rules which human judgments are to be regulated by, nor does He stand in need of any apology from us. Jehovah's actions are not to be measured by our petty tapelines. Where we cannot understand His ways, we must bow silently before Him, assured that He will yet fully vindicate Himself and at the finish close the mouth of every rebel who now quarrels with His providences. However, it should not be overlooked that, in this particular punishment which fell upon Saul's descendants, it was by no means a case of innocent and unoffending members of his house being dealt with, for God Himself speaks of them as a "bloody house" (v. 1) — they were actuated by their father's cruel spirit and walked in his steps.

"Let seven men of his sons be delivered unto us, and we will hang them up unto the Lord in Gibeah of Saul whom the Lord did choose" (v. 6). Notice the "whom *we* will hang up," which showed their consideration for the king: they were quite willing to bear the odium of the execution. As we have already pointed out, this was not for the gratification of personal revenge — "not for us shalt thou kill any man in Israel" (v. 4). "Hang them up *unto the Lord*" — as a sacrifice unto His justice, and also as a warning unto Israel to molest them no more. "In Gibeah of Saul" — as an object lesson to those who had assisted him in his persecution and slaughter of the innocent. "And the king said, I will give them" (v. 6). Obviously David had never consented to their proposal had it been wrong in the sight of God. Inasmuch as the selection of these seven men was left to David, opportunity was afforded him to spare the son of Jonathan (v. 7).

"But the king took the two sons of Rizpah the daughter of Aiah, whom she bare unto Saul, Armoni and Mephibosheth; and the five sons of Michal the daughter of Saul, whom she brought up for Adriel the son of Barziallai the Meholathite" (v. 8). The first two were Saul's own sons, which he had by a concubine. The other five were grandsons which his daughter had borne to

Adriel, but who had been brought up by their aunt. Let it be recalled that the mother of these five men had been promised to David by her father, but he treacherously gave her to Adriel, with the intention of provoking the sweet singer of Israel (1 Sam. 18:19). Herein we may perceive more clearly the workings of Divine justice. Commenting on this particular point Joseph Hall said, "It is a dangerous matter to offer injury to any of God's faithful ones: if their meekness have easily remitted it, God will not pass it over without a severe rebuke, though it may be long afterwards.

"And he delivered them into the hands of the Gibeonites" (v. 9). We are well aware that, in this sentimental age and when capital punishment is being more and more opposed, many will consider David did wrong in carrying out the wishes of the Gibeonites. Some have so perversely wrested this incident that they have not hesitated to charge David with seizing the opportunity to wreak his own spite upon an old enemy. But surely it is evident to all right-minded people that David could do no other: it was not from any private animosity which he bore to the house of Saul, but that obedience to God required his compliance with the request of the Gibeonites, while his having at heart the good of the Nation left him no other alternative. "Those executions must not be complained at as cruel which are become necessary in the public welfare. Better that seven of Saul's bloody house be hanged, than that all Israel should be famished" (Matt. Henry).

"And they hanged them in the hill before the Lord: and they fell all seven together, and were put to death in the days of the harvest" (v. 9). "As these persons were hanged by the express appointment of God for an anathema, an accursed thing, a national atonement to Divine justice, they were left on the tree or gibbet till some tokens of the Lord's reconciliation were afforded by seasonable rains" (T. Scott). Yet here again we may perceive the absolute sovereignty of Jehovah, and His superiority to all restrictions. Though He had expressly forbidden magistrates to slay children in order to avenge the crimes of their parents (Deut. 24:16), nevertheless, God Himself is bound by no such limitations. He had also given command to Israel, "If a man have committed a sin worthy of death, and he be to be put to death, and thou hang him on a tree; his body shall *not remain* all night upon the tree, but thou shalt in any wise bury him that day, for he that is hanged is accursed of God" (Deut. 21:22, 23); yet here we see the Lord moving David to do exactly the contrary! Why? if not to make it plain that He Himself is *above* all Law, free to do just as He pleases.

"And were put to death in the days of harvest, in the first days, in the beginning of barley harvest" (v. 9). Every detail here evidenced the superintending hand of the Lord. First, the *place* appointed for this execution, namely, in Saul's own city, so that the seven victims were, practically speaking, put to death on their own doorstep. Second, the *manner* of their execution, which was by hanging before the Lord, to demonstrate they were accursed in His sight. Third, the *time* of their execution, namely, "in the days of harvest." Those days were selected to make it the more manifest that they were being sacrificed for the specific purpose of appeasing God's wrath, which had for three years withheld from them harvest mercies, and to obtain His favour for the present season. Who, then, can reasonably doubt that every thing was here done according to the Divine ordering.

But is there not also an important practical lesson for *us*? Surely there must be, for the natural ever adumbrates the spiritual. Nor should it be difficult to ascertain what is here figuratively set forth. While those bloody sons of Saul were spared, the mercies of God were withheld; but when they had been hanged,

"God was entreated for the land" (v. 14). And is it not the same with us to-day individually? If we fail to deny self, and on the contrary indulge our corruptions, how can we expect the smile of the Lord to be upon us? "Your iniquities have turned away these things, and your sins have withholden good things from you" (Jer. 5:25). Do we sufficiently realize, dear reader, that the One with whom we have to do is the thrice Holy God? If we play with fire we must expect to get our fingers burned, and if we trifle with sin and trample upon the Divine precepts, we shall suffer severely.

We are well aware that *this* aspect of the Truth is not a very palatable one. Those who lead a life of self-pleasing wish to hear only of the grace of God. But does not the very grace of God teach us *to deny* "ungodliness and worldly lusts" and to "Live soberly, righteously, and godly, in this present world" (Titus 2:12)! Grace is given not to countenance evil doing, but to counteract the workings of an evil nature. Grace is given to enable its recipient to pluck out right eyes and cut off right hands: in other words, it is a supernatural principle which produces supernatural effects. Is it doing so in you and me? or are we after all our profession, strangers to it? Have we diligently sought to use the grace already imparted? If not, can we really expect more grace until we penitently confess our failures and put right with God what we know to be displeasing in His sight.

We are also well aware that this aspect of the Truth is utterly ignored by the great majority of preachers and "Bible teachers" to-day, who instead of pressing the holy claims of God and rebuking self-indulgence, are seeking either to amuse or soothe their hearers in their sins. It is not that we are inculcating a strange doctrine, introducing that which opposes Divine grace. No, those servants of God in the past who most extolled the grace of God, also maintained the requirements of His righteousness. As a sample of what we have in mind take these words of Matt. Henry's on 2 Sam. 21:19, "There is no way of appeasing God's anger but by mortifying and crucifying our lusts and corruptions. In vain do we expect mercy from God, unless we do justice upon our sins." What have we said above which is any stronger than that? If there was no other way of placating God's wrath than the slaying of Saul's sons, so now our sins must be put to death if His approbation is to be enjoyed.

"Then there was a famine in the days of David, three years, year after year." Is that nothing more than an item of ancient history? Has it no voice for us to-day? Does it not accurately describe the actual experience of many a backslidden Christian? Is it not pertinent to the case of some of our readers? Has there not long been a famine *in your soul*, dear friend? Ah, there *is* indeed a most important practical application of the above incident to our low lives. If you are painfully aware that such is the case with you, are you not desirous of that famine being removed? Then take to heart what has been before us above: put matters right with God — banish from your life that which withholds from you His approval. "He that covereth his sins shall not prosper; but whoso confesseth and forsaketh them shall have mercy" (Prov. 28:13).

"And Rizpah the daughter of Aiah took sackcloth, and spread it for her upon the rock, from the beginning of harvest until water dropped upon them out of heaven, and suffered neither the birds of the air to rest on them by day, nor the beasts of the field by night" (v. 10). It is touching to behold this poor mother keeping so lengthy a vigil over the corpses of her two sons. True, she made no attempt to cut down the bodies, thereby evidencing her submission to the righteous judgment of God; yet was she not guilty of inordinate grief? As Matthew Henry says, "She indulged her grief, as mourners are apt to do, to no good purpose. When sorrow, in such cases, is in danger of excess, we should rather study how to divert and pacify it, rather than humour and gratify it. Why should we thus harden ourselves in sorrow?"

"And David went and took the bones of Saul and the bones of Jonathan his son from the men of Jabesh-gilead, which had stolen them from the street of Beth-shan, where the Philistines had hanged them, when the Philistines had slain Saul in Gilboa. And he brought up from thence the bones of Saul and the bones of Jonathan his sons, and they gathered the bones of them that were hanged. And the bones of Saul and Jonathan his son they buried in the country of Benjamin in Zelah, in the sepulchre of Kish his father" (vv. 12-14). This respectful interment of the bones of Saul and his descendants by the king, is clear proof that David had not been actuated by a spirit of spite and revenge when he had delivered them up to the Gibeonites. But what, let us ask, is the spiritual lesson *for us* in this detail? If those sons of Saul may justly be taken as a figure of our sins (that which withholds God's blessings from us), and if the slaying of them adumbrates the believer's mortification of his lusts, then surely it is no far-fetched phantasy to regard the interment of their bones as indicating we are to *bury in oblivion* those disgraceful things of the past: "Never open thy mouth any more because of thy shame, when I am pacified toward thee" (Ezek. 16:63). Instead of holding up to the public view — under the pretence of "giving your testimony" — those things we hope are under the blood, let us draw a veil over them.

The last eight verses of our chapter give a brief summary of the events which occurred during the closing years of David's reign. That which is most prominent in them is, the further battles which took place between Israel and the Philistines, and the slaying of certain antagonistic giants. Here, too, the spiritual application is not difficult to perceive. There is *no furlough* in the fight of faith! The flesh continues to lust against the spirit till the end of our earthly pilgrimage, and therefore the work of mortification is to go on till God calls us to our rest. When the seven sons of Saul have been put to death, other foes (lusts) will seek to prevail against us, and they too must be resisted, and (by grace) be overcome. Let it be duly noted that, though David grew old and feeble, he did not grow indolent (vv. 15, 22)! The mention of the "giants" at *the close* of the chapter, intimates that the most powerful of our enemies are reserved for the last great conflict: yet through our "David" we shall be more than conquerors.

CHAPTER 22.

And David spoke to the LORD the words of this song in the day that the LORD had delivered him out of the hand of all his enemies, and out of the hand of Saul. And he said, The LORD is my Rock, and my Fortress, and my Deliverer. The God who is my Rock, in Him will I trust. He is my Shield, and the Horn of my salvation, my High Tower, and my Refuge, my Saviour. You save me from violence. I will call on the LORD, who is worthy to be praised. So shall I be saved from my enemies. — II Samuel 22:1-4.

2 Samuel 22 opens with the word "And," which at once suggests there is a close connection between its contents and what has immediately preceded. The chapter which is now to be before us records David's grand psalm of thanksgiving, and, as its opening verse intimates, it was sung by him in celebration of the signal deliverances which God had granted him from his many enemies. In the previous chapter we had an account of the execution of the sons of Saul, followed by a summary of Israel's victories over the Philistines and the slaying of a number of their giants. In our last section we sought to point out the spiritual application of these things, as they bear upon the lives of Christians to-day, and the same line of thought is to be followed as we enter the present chapter. It is this looking for the *practical bearing* of the Scriptures upon ourselves which is so sorely needed, and which, alas, is now so much neglected by the present generation; only thus do we make the Bible a *living* Book, suited to our present need.

The spiritual and practical link of connection between 2 Sam. 21 and 22 is not difficult to perceive. As was shown in our last, the execution of the sons of Saul (seven in number, for the work must be done *completely*) is to be regarded as a figure of the believer's mortifying his lusts, and the conflicts which followed between Israel and the Philistines, David and the giants, symbolizes the fact that that warfare with sin which the saint is called upon to wage, continues till the end of his earthly course. Now the work of mortification is indeed a very painful one, nevertheless it issues in a joyful sequel. The plucking out of right eyes and the cutting off of right hands doubtless produces many a groan, yet will they be followed by melodious thanksgiving. Death figures prominently in 2 Sam. 21, but 2 Sam. 22 opens with a "Song!" Here, then, is the obvious connection: when *death* be written upon our lusts, music will fill the heart; when that which is displeasing to God has been put away, the Spirit will tune our souls to sing Jehovah's praise.

It is a most interesting and instructive study to trace out the sacred "Songs" of Scripture, paying particular attention to their *setting*. The first one is recorded in Ex. 15. We read not of the Hebrews celebrating the Lord's praises while they were in Egypt, but only of their sighing and groaning (Ex. 2:23, 24). But when they had been delivered from the house of bondage and their foes had been drowned in the Red Sea, a pean of worship ascended from their heart. Again, we read of Israel singing when the Lord supplied them with water (Num. 21:17). Moses ended his wilderness wanderings with a song (Deut. 31:22). Upon Israel's victory over the Canaanites they sang a song (Judges 5:1). Job speaks of God giving "songs in the night" (35:10) — a real, if a rare, experience, as many saints can testify. The Psalmist said, "Thy statutes have been my songs in the house of my pilgrimage" (119:54).

There is a most marked similarity between the Song of David in 2 Sam. 22 and the 18th Psalm (observe the latter's superscription), indeed so close is the resemblance that almost all of the commentators have regarded them as being one and the same, attempting to account for their verbal variations (which though incidental are by no means few in number) on the supposition that the latter is a revised edition of the former. But such an assumption does not seem at all satisfactory — to us it appears a serious slight upon Divine inspiration: surely the Holy Spirit never needs to make any emendations! We therefore greatly prefer the view of C. H. Spurgeon: "We have another form of this 18th Psalm with slight variations, in 2 Sam. 22, and this suggests the idea that it was sung by him on different occasions when he reviewed his own remarkable history, and observed the gracious hand of God in it all."

This particular Song of David is no exception to a general if not an invariable feature which marked all his inspired minstrelsy, in that we may see in it both a surface and a deeper allusion, both an historical and a prophetic significance. All doubt upon this point is definitely removed by the testimony of the N.T., for there we find two of its verses quoted from as being the very words of Christ Himself, thus making it plain that a greater than David is here. In its deeper meaning it is the utterance of the Spirit of Christ in David, making special reference to His triumph over death by the mighty power of God (Eph. 1:19). David thankfully recounts the glorious actings of God on his behalf, yet in such language as rises above himself, to his Son and Lord, against whom all the powers of darkness were concentrated.

"And David spake unto the Lord the words of this song, in the day that the Lord had delivered him out of the hand of all his enemies, and out of the hand of Saul" (2 Sam. 22:1). One of the outstanding features of the checkered career of David was the large number of his foes, both from the surrounding nations and among his own people, the chief of all being Saul — the most formidable, malicious, and inveterate. Nor should this unduly surprise us, even though, as Matthew Henry tersely expressed it, "David was a man after *God's* heart, but not after *man's* heart: many were those who hated him." Why was this? First, God so ordered it that he might be an eminent type of Christ, who, throughout the ages has been "despised and rejected of men." Second, that thereby God might display the more conspicuously His faithfulness and power in preserving His own. Third, because this is generally the experience of the saints.

"And David spake unto the Lord the words of this song, in the day that the Lord had delivered him out of the hand of all his enemies, and out of the hand of Saul." Therefore was he well qualified experimentally to declare, "Many are the afflictions of the righteous, but the Lord delivereth him out of them all" (Psa. 34:19). The Lord's "deliverance" of David from his many foes assumed a great variety of forms: sometimes in one way, sometimes in another, for the Almighty is not limited to any particular means or method. On occasions He employs human instruments; and again, He wrought without them. Let this encourage the tried and Satan-harassed believer. Though every avenue of escape seem fast shut to your eyes, yet remember that closed doors are no barrier to the Lord (John 20:26). When the long drought completely dried up the water which sustained Elijah at Cherith, God maintained him with oil at Zarephath.

This too is written for our learning and comfort. As we have traced the life of David through the two books of Samuel, we have seen him in some sore straits: again and again it looked as though his foes must surely prevail against him; yea, on one occasion, he himself dolefully declared, "I shall now perish one day by the hand of Saul" (1 Sam. 27:1). Yet he did not! No, One infinitely mightier than Saul was watching over him. And this is equally the case with you and me, dear reader, if we belong to Christ: the combined forces of Hell shall never prevail against us; the united assaults of the flesh, the world, and the Devil cannot destroy us. Why? "Because greater is He that is in you, than he that is in the world" (1 John 4:4). Then why should we be so fearful? let us seek grace to rest on that sure promise, "God is our refuge and strength, a very present help in trouble" (Psa. 46:1).

Observe well David's *response* to these Divine interpositions on his behalf: deliverance calls for thanksgiving. This is the very least we can render unto the Lord in return for all His benefits. Nor should there be any tardiness in discharging this delightful obligation: gratitude must issue promptly in praise. It did so with the sweet singer in Israel, and it should also with us. Then let us take to heart this word, "And David spake unto the Lord the words of this song *in the day* that the Lord had delivered him." We ought to present unto God a sacrifice of praise while His mercies are fresh and the heart is duly affected by them. We are not slow in crying to God when imminent danger threatens us: then let us be just as prompt in acknowledging His goodness when His delivering hand is extended to us.

Many of the commentators are of the opinion that this Sacred Song was composed by David at an *early* date in his life, but personally we fail to see anything in the Scriptures which supports such a view. The very fact that the Holy Spirit has expressly told us it was uttered by David when "The Lord had delivered him out of the hand of *all* his enemies," is surely a plain intimation that it was uttered by him late in life — the added words "and out of the hand of Saul" do not modify this view when the mention of him is regarded as being intended for the purpose of *emphasis*, he being his predominant foe. The main divisions of the Song are fairly clearly defined. First, is the preface, in which David is occupied with extolling Jehovah's perfections: vv. 1-4. Second, he magnifies the Lord for His delivering mercies: vv. 5-20. Third, he expressed the testimony of a clear conscience: vv. 21-28. Fourth, he concludes with a prophetic anticipation of the glorious triumphs of the Messiah: vv. 29-45.

"And he said, The Lord is my rock, and my fortress, and my deliverer" (v. 2). David begins by adoring Jehovah. He does so on the ground of his personal relation to Him, for all the benefits he had received, he bases upon his relation to God. Observe that in vv. 2, 3, he uses the personal pronoun no less than nine times. It is a grand thing when we have the assurance and can feelingly say, "The Lord is *my* Rock." While our enemies are not upon our heels wounding us sorely, threating our very life, we sometimes do not have this blessed assurance; but when God's delivering grace is experienced afresh by us, new hope is kindled in the soul. "The Lord is my Rock and my Fortress." "Dwelling among the crags and mountain fastnesses of Judea, David had escaped the malice of Saul, and here compares his God to such a place of concealment and security. Believers are often hidden in their God from the strife of tongues and the fury of the storm" (C. H. Spurgeon).

"And he said, The Lord is my rock, and my fortress, and my deliverer." Let us not miss *the connection* between this and the preceding verse: they that trust God in the path of duty, will ever find Him a very present help in the greatest of dangers. And David *had* trusted God, with a faith which wrought miracles. Recall, for example, his intrepidity in facing Goliath. All Israel were afraid of the Philistine giant, so that none — not even Saul — dared to accept his haughty challenge. Yet David, though then but a youth, hesitated not to engage him in mortal combat, going forth to meet him without any material armour, and with naught but a sling in his hand. And wherein lay his strength? What was the secret of his courage and of his success? It was at once revealed in the words with which he met the enemy's champion: "thou comest to me with a sword, and with a spear, and with a shield; but I come to thee in the name of the Lord of hosts, the God of the armies of Israel" (1 Sam. 17:45)!

And is *that*, my reader, nothing more than a striking incident of ancient history? Has it no message for our hearts? Is not God the same to-day: ready to respond to a faith that dares! Is it not written "if thou canst believe, all things are possible to him that believeth" (Mark 9:23)? Do we really believe this? If so, are we earnestly begging God to increase our faith? Faith is invincible, because it lays hold of One who is omnipotent. Faith is the hand which grasps the Almighty, and is anything too hard for Him! Is it not also written "according unto your faith be it unto you" (Matt. 9:29). Ah, does not that explain why it is we so often meet with defeat, why it is that our enemies prevail against us? O for faith in the living God, faith in the efficacy of Christ's mediation, to vanquish our lusts.

Yes, most important is it that we should heed the connection between the first two verses of our chapter: the deliverances David had from his enemies, and his implicit confidence in God. Nor was he by any means alone in this experience. It was by the miracle-working power of God that the three Hebrews were delivered from Babylon's fiery furnace. Yes, but that Divine power was put forth in response to their faith: "our God whom we serve is able to deliver us from the burning fiery furnace, and He will deliver us out of thine hand, O king" (Dan. 3:17). So again with Daniel himself, yet how often *this* particular is overlooked. From early childhood most of us have been familiar with that Divine marvel which preserved the prophet from the lions, but how many of us have noticed those words, "So Daniel was taken up out of the den, and no manner of hurt was found upon him, *because he believed in his God*" (6:23).

"And he said, the Lord is my rock, and my fortress, and my deliverer" (v. 2). When almost captured, the Lord's people are rescued from the hand of the mighty by One who is mightier still. God never fails those who really exercise faith in Him: He may indeed severely test, but He will not suffer them to be "utterly cast down." As our "Rock" God is the strength and support of His people, the One on whom they build their hopes, the One who affords shade from the burning heat of the desert. As our "Fortress" God gives His people shelter from their assailants, supplying protection and security — "The name of the Lord is a strong tower: the righteous runneth into it, and is safe" (Prov. 18:10). As our "Deliverer" God saves us from ourselves, redeems us from the damning power of sin, rescues us from the roaring lion, secures us against the second death.

"The God of my rock: in Him will I trust: He is my shield, and the horn of my salvation, my high tower, and my refuge, my saviour; Thou savest me from violence! (v. 3). This piling up of metaphors indicates the strong assurance which David had in the Lord, the realization of His sufficiency to meet his every emergency and supply his every need. He saw in God one who was infinitely worthy of his fullest confidence: no matter how critical his circumstances, how desperate his situation, how numerous or powerful his foes, and how great his own weakness, Jehovah was all-sufficient. Such too ought to be *our* confidence in God. Yea, we have more ground to rest *our* faith upon than ever David had. God is now revealed as the (penitent) sinner's Friend, as He never was then. In Christ He is revealed as the Conqueror of sin, the Vanquisher of death, the Master of Satan. Then have we not cause to exclaim "in Him will I *trust*." O that this may become more and more of an actuality in the lives of both writer and reader.

"The God of my rock: in His will I trust: He is my shield, and the horn of my salvation, my high tower, and my refuge, my saviour; Thou savest me from violence." These energetic figures of speech, which rise above the level of ordinary prose, reveal what God is to His believing people, for only as *faith* is lively and vigorous is He viewed thus. He is "my Shield" with which to ward off every attack: faith interposes Him between our souls and the enemy. He is "the Horn of my salvation," enabling me to push down my foes, and to triumph over them with holy exultation. He is "my high Tower:" a citadel placed upon a high eminence, beyond the reach of all enemies, from which I may look down on them without alarm. He is "my Refuge" in which to shelter from every storm. He is "my Saviour" from every evil to which the believer is exposed. What more do we need! what more can we ask! O for faith's realization of the same in our souls. "Thou savest me from violence:" again we would press the point that this is in response to faith — "He shall deliver them from the wicked, and save them, *because they trust in Him*" (Psa. 37:40).

"I will call on the Lord, who is worthy to be praised: so shall I be saved from mine enemies" (v. 4). As an unknown writer has said, "The armour of a soldier does him no service except he put it on; so, no protection from God is to be expected, unless we apply ourselves to prayer." It is faith which girds on the spiritual armour: it is faith which finds all its resource in the Lord. "I will *call* on the Lord, who is worthy to be praised: *so* shall I be saved from mine enemies:" note carefully the words which we have placed in italics. This affords abundant confirmation of all we have said above: to "call upon the Lord" is to exercise faith in Him, such faith as praises Him *before* the victory — SO shall we be saved from our enemies: by God's mighty power in response to believing prayer and sincere praise.

When the waves of death encircled me, the floods of ungodly men made me afraid. The sorrows of hell hemmed me in. The snares of death went in front of me. In my distress I called on the LORD and cried to my God. And He heard my voice out of His Temple, and my cry entered into His ears. Then the earth shook and trembled. The foundations of heaven moved and shook because He was angry. Smoke went up out of His nostrils, and fire out of His mouth devoured. Coals were kindled by it. And He bowed the heavens and came down. And darkness was under His feet. And He rode upon a cherub and did fly. And he was seen on the wings of the wind. And He made darkness coverings around Him, dark waters, thick clouds of the skies. Through the brightness before Him were coals of fire kindled. The LORD thundered from heaven, and the Most High uttered His voice. And He sent out arrows and scattered them — lightning, and troubled them. And the channels of the sea appeared, the foundations of the world were uncovered, at the rebuking of the LORD, at the blast of the breath of His nostrils. He sent from above, He took me. He drew me out of many waters. He delivered me from my strong enemy, from those who hated me — for they were too strong for me. They went before me in the day of my calamity, but the LORD was my stay. He brought me forth also into a large place. He delivered me because He delighted in me. — II Samuel 22:5-20.

As pointed out in our last, the main divisions of David's sacred song in 2 Sam. 22 are more or less clearly marked. In the first (vv. 1-4) he is occupied with extolling Jehovah's perfections: this section we have already considered. In the second (vv. 5-20), which is now to be before us, he magnifies the Lord for His delivering mercies. This section of the Song is couched in highly figurative and poetic language; which indicates how deeply stirred were the emotions of its inspired composer. Its contents may be regarded in a threefold way. First, as depicting the physical dangers to which David was exposed from his human foes. Second, the deep soul distress which he experienced from his spiritual enemies. Third, the fearful suffering through which Christ passed while acting as the Substitute of His people, and the awe-inspiring deliverance which God wrought for His servant. We will endeavour to consider our passage from each of these viewpoints.

"When the waves (pangs) of death compassed me, the floods of ungodly men made me afraid, the sorrows (cords) of Hell compassed me about; the snares of death prevented (anticipated) me" (2 Sam. 22:5, 6). Thus opens this second division: that which it so vividly portrayed is the large number and ferocity of his enemies, and the desperate danger to which David was exposed by them. First, he employed the figure of an angry sea, whose raging waves menaced him from every side, until his frail craft was in immediate prospect of being swamped by them. Next, he likened his lot to one who was marooned on some piece of low-lying ground, and the floods rapidly rising higher and higher, till his destruction seemed certain. The multitude of the wicked pressed him sorely on every side. Then he resembled his plight to one who had already been taken captive and bound, so that the very cords of death seemed to be upon him. Finally, he pictures his case as a bird that had been caught in the fowler's snare, unable to fly away.

The above references were to the attempts made by Saul, Abner, and Absalom to capture and slay David. So fierce were their attacks, so powerful the forces they employed against him, so determined and relentless were his foes, that David here acknowledged they "made me afraid." "The most sea-worthy bark is sometimes hard put to it when the storm flood is abroad. The most courageous man, who as a rule hopes for the best, may sometimes fear the worst" (C. H. Spurgeon). Strong as his faith generally was, yet on one occasion unbelief prevailed to such an extent that David said, "I shall now perish one day by the hand of Saul" (1 Sam. 27:1). When terrors from without awaken fears within, our case is indeed a miserable one: yet so it was with Moses when he fled from Egypt, with Elijah when he ran away from Jezebel, with Peter when he denied his Lord.

But these lamentations of David are also to be construed *spiritually*: they are to be regarded as those harrowing exercises of soul through which he passed in his later years: Psalms 32 and 51 cast light upon them. "The sorrows (cords) of Hell compassed me about; the snares of death anticipated me:" such was the anguish of his soul under the lashings of a guilty conscience. "The temptations of Satan and the consciousness of his sins filled him with fears of wrath and dreadful apprehensions of future consequences. He felt like a malefactor bound for execution, whose fetters prevent him from attempting an escape, for whose body the grave hath certainly opened her mouth, and who is horribly alarmed lest the pit of hell should swallow up his soul" (Thos. Scott). Fearful beyond words is the suffering through which many a backslider has to pass ere he is restored to fellowship with God — one who has experienced it will not deem the language of these verses any too strong.

But there is something deeper here than the trials David encountered either from without or within: in their ultimate sense these verses articulate the groanings of the Man of sorrows as He took upon Him the obligations and suffered in the stead of His people. As we pointed out in our last, two of the verses of this Song are quoted in the N.T. as being the very words of Christ Himself: "In Him will I trust" (v. 3).) is found in Heb. 2:13, and "I will give thanks unto Thee, O Lord, among the heathen (Gentiles), and I will sing praises unto Thy name" (v. 50) is found in Rom. 15:9, "The Messiah our Saviour is evidently, over and beyond David or any other believer, the main and chief subject of this Song; and while studying it we have grown more and more sure that every line has its deeper and profounder fulfilment in Him" (C. H. Spurgeon). Let this be kept before us as we pass from section to section, and from verse to verse.

"When the waves (pangs) of death compassed Me, the floods of ungodly men made Me afraid; the sorrows (cords) of Hell compassed Me about; the snares of death anticipated Me." Here was the Spirit of Christ speaking prophetically through the Psalmist, expressing the fierce conflict through which the Redeemer passed. Behold Him in Gethsemane, in the judgment-halls of Herod and Pilate, and then behold Him on the cross itself, suffering horrible torments of body and anguish of soul, when He was delivered into the hands of wicked men, encountered the fierce assaults of Satan, and endured the wrath of God against Him for our sins. It was then that He was surrounded by the insulting priests and people. His "My soul is exceeding sorrowful, even unto death" (Matt. 26:38) was but an echo of these words of David's song.

"In my distress I called upon the Lord, and cried to my God: and He did hear my voice out of His temple, and my cry did enter into His ears" (v. 7). Here we behold God's suffering servant making earnest supplication to Heaven. The one so sorely pressed by his enemies, that the eye of sense could perceive not a single avenue of escape, yea, when death itself immediately threatened him, seeks relief from above, and so it should be with us: "Is any among you afflicted? let him pray" (James 5:13). Ah, it is then he is most likely to really *pray*: cold and formal petitions do not suit one who is in deep trouble — alas that so often nothing short of painful trial will force fervent supplications from us. An old writer expressed it, "Prayer is not eloquence, but earnestness; not the definition of earnestness, but the feeling of it; it is the cry of faith in the ear of mercy:" yet either pangs of body or of soul are usually needed before we will cry out in reality.

"In my distress I called upon the Lord, and cried to my God: and He did hear my voice out of His temple, and my cry did enter into His ears" (v. 7). So many neglect prayer when they are quiet and at ease, but as the Lord declares, "In their affliction they *will* seek Me early" (Hos. 5:15). Yet it is well if we *do* seek unto God in our affliction, instead of sulking in rebellion, which is to forsake our own mercy. The Lord is a very present help in trouble, and it is our holy privilege to prove this for ourselves. The Hebrew word for "cried" here is a very expressive one, signifying such a cry as issues from one in a violent tempest of emotion, in the extremity of grief and anxiety: in fact Alex. Maclaren renders it "shriek." David was all but sinking and could only give vent to an agonized call for help.

"Prayer is that postern gate which is left open even when the city is straitly besieged by the enemy: it is that way upward from the pit of despair to which the spiritual miner flies at once, when the floods from beneath break forth upon him. Observe that he 'calls,' and then 'cries;' prayer grows in vehemence as it proceeds. Note also that he first invokes his God under the name of Jehovah, and then advances to a more familiar name, 'my God:' thus faith increases by exercise, and he whom we at first viewed as Lord is soon seen to be our God in covenant. It is never an ill time to pray; no distress should prevent us from using the Divine remedy of supplication" (C. H. Spurgeon).

"In my distress I called upon the Lord, and cried to my God." The fulfilment of these prophetic words in the case of our suffering Redeemer is well known to all who are acquainted with the four Gospels. Blessed indeed is it to behold that One, who was supremely the Man after God's own heart, betaking Himself to prayer while His enemies were thirsting for His blood. The deeper His distress, the more earnestly did He call upon God, both in Gethsemane and at Calvary, and as Heb. 5:7 tells us, "Who in the days of His flesh, when He had offered up prayers and supplications with strong crying and tears unto Him that was able to save Him from death, and was heard in that He feared." Let us not hesitate, then, to follow the example which He has left us, and no matter how hardly we are pressed, how desperate be our situation, nor how acute our grief, let us unburden ourselves to God.

"And He did hear my voice out of His temple, and my cry did enter into His ears." This is in explanation of all that follows: the gracious interpositions of the Lord on David's behalf and the wondrous deliverances He wrought for him, were *in answer to prayer*. God's lending a willing ear to the cry of His distressed child is recorded for our encouragement. It is indeed deplorable that we are often so prayerless until presure of circumstances force supplication out of us, yet it is blessed to be assured that God does not then (as well He might) turn a deaf ear unto our calls; nay, such calls have the greater prevalency, because of their sincerity and because they make a more powerful appeal unto the Divine pity. Let the fearing and despondent believer read through the 107th Psalm and mark how frequently it is recorded that the redeemed "cry unto the Lord in their trouble," and how that in each instance we are told "He delivered them." Then do *you* cry unto Him, and be of good courage.

"Then the earth shook and trembled: the foundations of heaven moved and shook, because He was wroth" (v. 8). David's prayer was answered in a most effectual manner by the providential interpositions which Jehovah made on his behalf. In a most singular and extraordinary way the Lord appeared for his relief, fighting for him against his enemies. Here again David adorned his poem with lively images as he records God's gracious intervention. The mighty power of God was now exercised for him: such language being employed as to intimate that nothing can resist or impede Him where He acts for His own. God was now showing Himself to be strong on behalf of His oppressed but supplicating servant. See here, dear reader, the response of Heaven to the cry of faith. "Then the earth shook and trembled:" Let these words be pondered in the light of "And at midmight Paul and Silas *prayed* . . . and suddenly there was a great earthquake, so that the foundations of the prison were *shaken*, and immediately all the doors were opened and every one's bands were loosed" (Acts 16:25,26)!

Again we would remind the reader that a greater than David is to be kept before us as we pass from verse to verse of this Psalm. "Then the earth shook and trembled: the foundations of heaven moved and shook, because He was wroth:" who can fail to be reminded of the supernatural phenomena which attended the death and resurrection of David's Son and Lord? He too had called upon Jehovah in His deep distress, "And was heard" (Heb. 5:7). Unmistakable was Heaven's response: "from the sixth hour there was darkness over all the land unto the ninth hour. . .Jesus, when He had cried again with a loud voice, yielded up the spirit. And, behold, the veil of the temple was rent in twain from the top to the bottom; and the earth did quake, and the rocks rent; and the graves were opened" (Matt. 27:45, 50-52). Yes, the earth literally "shook and trembled"! As another has rightly said, "Tremendous was the scene! Never before and never since was such a battle fought, or such a victory gained, whether we look at the contending powers or the consequences resulting. Heaven on the one side, and Hell on the other: such were the contending powers. And as to the consequences resulting, who shall recount them?"

"There went up a smoke out of His nostrils, and fire out of His mouth devoured: coals were kindled by it. He bowed the heavens also, and came down, and darkness was under His feet" (vv. 9, 10). These expressions are borrowed from the awe-inspiring phenomena which attended the appearing of Jehovah upon mount Sinai: compare Ex. 19:16-18. It was Jehovah the Avenger appearing to vindicate His servant and vanquish his enemies. David considered that is his case the Lord God manifested the same Divine perfections which He had displayed of old at the giving of the Law. We cannot do better here than quote from Matt. Henry's comments on the spiritual significance of the vivid imagery which was here employed by the Psalmist.

"These lofty metaphors are used. First, to set forth the glory of God, which was manifested in his deliverance: His wisdom and power, His goodness and faithfulness, His justice and holiness, and His sovereign dominion over all the creatures and all the counsels of men, which appeared in favour of David, were as clear and bright a discovery of God's glory to an eye of faith, as those would have been to an eye of sense. Second, to set forth God's displeasure against his enemies: God so espoused his cause, that he showed Himself an Enemy to all his enemies; His anger is set forth by a smoke out of His nostrils, and fire out of His mouth. Who knows the power and terror of His wrath! Third, to set forth the vast confusion which his enemies were put into and the consternation that seized them; as if the earth had trembled and the foundations of the world had been discovered. Who can stand before God, when He is angry? Fourth, to show how ready God was to help him: He 'rode upon a cherub, and did fly' (v. 11). God hastened to his succour, and came in to him with seasonable relief."

' And He rode upon a cherub, and did fly; and He was seen upon the wings of the wind" (v. 11). Though the Lord "wait that He may be gracious" (Isa. 30:18), and some times sorely tries faith and patience, yet when His appointed time comes, He acts swiftly. "And He made darkness pavilions round about Him, dark waters and thick clouds of the skies" (v. 12): just as that pillar of fire which gave light to Israel was "a cloud and darkness" to the Egyptians (Ex. 14:20), so were the providential dealings of the Lord unto the enemies of David. The One who is pleased to reveal Himself unto His own, conceals Himself from the wicked, and hence the fearful portion of those who shall be everlastingly banished from the presence of the Lord is represented as "the blackness of darkness forever."

"Through the brightness before Him were coals of fire kindled. The Lord thundered from Heaven, and the Most High uttered His voice. And He sent out arrows, and scattered them; lightning, and discomfited them. And the channels of the sea appeared, the foundations of the world were discovered, at the rebuking of the Lord, at the blast of the breath of His nostrils" (vv. 13-16). All of this is an amplification of "because He was wroth" (v. 8). Nothing so arouses Jehovah's indignation as injuries done to His people: he who attacks them, touches the apple of His eye. True, God is not subject to those passions which govern His creatures, yet because He hates sin with a perfect hatred and sorely punishes it, He is often represented under such poetic imagery as is suited to human understanding. God is a God to be feared, as those who now trifle with Him shall yet discover. How shall puny men be able to face it out with the Almighty, when the very mountains tremble at His presence! Satan-deluded souls may now defy Him, but their false confidence will not support or shelter them in the dread day of His wrath.

"He sent from above, He took me; He drew me out of many waters; He delivered me from my strong enemy, and from those that hated me: For they were too strong for me" (vv. 17, 18). Here is the happy issue to David's prayer and the Lord's response. Observe, first, that David gives God the glory by unreservedly ascribing his deliverance unto Him. He looked far above his own skill in slinging the stone which downed Goliath and his cleverness in eluding Saul: "*He* sent. . .*He* took me, He drew me. . .*He* delivered me" gives all the honour unto Him to whom it was truly due. Note, second, the particular reason mentioned by David as to why the Lord had intervened on his behalf: "*for* they were too strong for me" — it was his confessed weakness and the strength of his foes that made such a powerful appeal to God's pity: compare the effectual plea of Jehoshaphat: "O our God, wilt Thou not judge them? for we have no might against this great company that cometh against us" (2 Chron. 20:12). Finally, while the "strong enemy" of v. 18 is an allusion to either Goliath or Saul, yet David's deliverance from them but prefigured *Christ's* victory over death and Satan, and here He ascribed that victory unto His God.

The second section of David's song glides so smoothly into the third that there is scarcely a perceptible break between them: in the one he recounts the Lord's gracious deliverances of him from his numerous and relentless enemies; in the other he states the reasons why He had intervened on his behalf. A few more words now on the closing verses of the former: "He sent from above, He took, me; He drew me out of many waters; He delivered me from my strong enemy, and from them that hated me: for they were too strong for me" (2 Sam. 22:17, 18). Here he freely ascribes unto God the glory of his deliverances: extolling His goodness, power, faithfulness, and sufficiency. If God be for us, it matters not who be against us. Torrents of evil shall not drown the one whose God sitteth upon the floods to restrain their fury. He has but to speak and the winds are calmed, the downpour ceases, and the floods subside; true alike physically and morally.

"They prevented me in the day of my calamity: but the Lord was my stay" (v. 19). This is a parenthetical statement between vv. 18 and 20, wherein the writer refers to the determined efforts of his foes to prevent his escape and ensure his destruction. "When David had framed any plan for secreting or securing himself in the day of his calamity, his enemies employed every method of treachery and malice to prevent his success. Thus the men of Keilah were ready to deliver him to Saul (1 Sam. 23:7-12) and the Ziphites repeatedly informed on Him (1 Sam. 26:1, 2): and therefore, notwithstanding his own prudence and activity, he must have been cut off if the Lord Himself had not protected him by His own immediate and extraordinary interpositions" (T. Scott). "But (blessed "but!") The Lord was my stay:" his support, the One on whom he rested — nor was his confidence disappointed. When the Enemy rages most fiercely against us, then is the time to lean most heavily upon the everlasting arms.

"He brought me forth also into a large place: He delivered me, because He delighted in me" (v. 20). It is here that the third division of this inspired song really begins, the main purpose of which is to vindicate David, by showing that he had done nothing to provoke or deserve the fierce attacks which had been made upon him; and to affirm that God had acted in righteousness in favouring him with deliverance. But before taking up this leading thought, let us observe and admire the ways of the Lord. God does not leave His work half done, for after He has defeated the foe, He leads the captive out into liberty. After pining for years in the prison, Joseph was advanced to the palace; from the cave of Adullum, David was elevated to the throne. This illustrates and exemplifies a most important and blessed principle in the dealings of God with His people, and when laid hold of by faith and hope it affords unspeakable comfort to the oppressed and despondent.

The prison ever precedes the palace in true spiritual experience, not only at our first awakening, but repeatedly throughout the Christian life. The soul is shut up in confinement, before it is brought forth "into a large place." The spirit of bondage is experienced before we receive the Spirit of adoption, whereby we cry "Abba, Father" (Rom. 8:15). Our frail craft is made to battle long against the angry waves, before the Lord appears for our relief (Matt. 14:22-23). Bear this steadily in mind, dear reader, while you are passing through the day of calamity: "Being confident of this very thing, that He which hath begun a good work in you, *will complete it*" (Phil. 1:6). Enlargement of spirit will be the more appreciated after a season of sorrowful confinement. Remember, then, that Joseph did not die in prison, nor did David *end* his days in the cave of Adullum: "Weeping may endure for a night, but joy cometh in the morning." Sometimes we are granted a foretaste of that joy even in this vale of tears; but even if we are not, all weeping shall end when the night is over.

Once again we would remind ourselves that the *antitypical David* must be kept before us as we pass from verse to verse of this song, for the experiences of the members is identical with those which were endured by the Head of the mystical Body. Christ too could say, "They prevented Me in the day of My calamity: but the Lord was My stay" (v. 19). Never forget that the Redeemer Himself passed through a day of calamity: why, then, should the redeemed think it a strange thing if they too encounter the same? *He* was beset by merciless foes: His liberty was taken away when they arrested Him: He was buffeted and scourged — sufficient, then, for the disciple to be as his Master. O that we also may be able to say with Him "but the Lord was My stay." Yes, He too could say, "He brought Me forth also into a large place: He delivered Me, because He delighted in Me." Yes, He was delivered from the grave, removed from this earth, and given the position of honour and glory at God's right hand; and this, because God delighted in Him: Isa. 42:1.

The LORD rewarded me according to my righteousness, according to the cleanness of my hands He has rewarded me. For I have kept the ways of the LORD and have not wickedly departed from my God. For all His judgments were before me. And as for His laws, I did not depart from them. I was also upright before Him, and have kept myself from my iniquity. Therefore the LORD has rewarded me according to my righteousness, according to my cleanness in His eyes. With the merciful You will show Yourself merciful; with the upright man You will show Yourself upright. With the pure You will show Yourself pure; and with the perverse You will show Yourself perverse. And You will save the afflicted people, but Your eyes are on the proud so that You may bring them down. — II Samuel 22:21-28.

It is a great mistake to confine our attention, as some have done, to the antitypical David in this passage. For example, in his comments upon this portion of David's song, C.H.M. said, "These verses (21-25) prove that in this entire song, we have a greater than David. David could not say 'The Lord rewarded me according to my righteousness, according to the cleanness of my hands did He recompense me.' How different is this language from that of the 51st Psalm. There it is 'Have mercy upon me according to Thy lovingkindness, according to the multitude of Thy tender mercies.' This was suitable language for a fallen sinner, as David felt himself to be. He dare not speak of his righteousness, which was as filthy rags; and as to him recompense, he felt that the Lake of Fire was all that he could in justice claim upon the ground of what he was. Hence, therefore, the language of our chapter is the language of Christ, who *alone* could use it" (The Life and Times of David, King of Israel).

Such confusion of thought is really inexcusable in one who posed as a teacher of preachers, and who was so fond of criticizing and condemning the expositions of servants of God which issued from pulpits in what he dubbed the "sects" and "systems" of Christendom. One might just as well affirm that "I have fought a good fight, I have finished my course, I have kept the faith" (2 Tim. 4:7) is "the language of Christ, who alone could use it." And then add "how different is the language of Paul in Phil. 3:" "What things were gain to me, those I counted loss for Christ. Yea doubtless, and I count all things but loss for the excellency of the knowledge of Christ Jesus my Lord: for whom I have suffered the loss of all things, and do count them but dung, that I may win Christ; and be found in Him, not having mine own righteousness, which is of the law, but that which is through the faith of Christ" (vv. 7-9). The simple fact is that the apostle was speaking from two radically different viewpoints in those respective passages: in Phil. 3 he defines the ground of his *acceptance* before God, whereas in 2 Tim. 4 he refers to his *ministerial fidelity*. It was thus with David: in Psa. 51 he states the basis on which he sought God's forgiveness; in 2 Sam. 22:21-25 he relates his innocence in connection with his enemies.

We hardly expect one who belonged to the religious school that Mr. Mackintosh did, to be capable of drawing theological distinctions, but we *are* surprised to find such an able exegete as Alex. Maclaren erring on this same point. He too failed to grasp the Psalmist's scope or object in the passage which we are now considering, as is clear from his remarks thereon in his otherwise helpful work on "The life of David as reflected in his Psalms." It was his mistaking of the purport of these verses (20-25 — repeated in substance in Psa. 18:19-24) which caused him to argue that this song (and Psalm) must have been written before his awful sin in connection with Uriah: "The marked assertion of his own purity, as well as the triumphant tone of the whole, neither of which characteristics correspond to the sad and shaded years after his fall, point in the same direction" (p. 154).

"He brought me forth also into a large place: He delivered me, because He delighted in me." The "large place" is in designed contrast from the cramped confinement of the caves in which David had been obliged to dwell when his enemies were so hotly pursuing him: it may also refer to the vast extent of his dominions and the great riches he was blest with. God not only preserved, but prospered him, granting him liberty and enlargement. The Lord not only displayed His power on behalf of His servant, but also manifested His particular favour toward him: this is intimated in "He delivered me, because He delighted in me," which signifies that God acted not from His general providence, but from His covenant love. Should it be asked, How would David know this? The answer is, by the communications of Divine grace and comfort in his soul which accompanied the deliverances, and by the communion he had with God in them.

"The Lord rewarded me according to my righteousness; according to the cleanness of my hands hath He recompensed me" (v. 21). It seems strange that these words have perplexed any one with a spiritual mind, for if they be not strained beyond their original and obvious intention, there is nothing in them to occasion any difficulty. Let them be read in the light of their context, and they are plain and simple. David was alluding to God's delivering of him from Goliath and Saul, and from others of his foes: what had been his conduct toward *them*? Had he committed any serious crimes which warranted their hostility? Had he grievously wronged any of them? Had they justly or unjustly sought his life? His own brother preferred a charge against him (1 Sam. 17:28) just before he engaged Goliath, and from several of the Psalms there seems to be good ground for concluding that Saul accused him of pride, covetousness and treachery. But what real basis was there for such? Read the record of David's life, and where is there a hint that he coveted the throne or hated Saul?

No, the fact of the matter is that David was entirely innocent of any evil designs against any of those who persecuted him. Further proof of this is found in one of his prayers to God: "Let not them that are mine enemies *wrongfully* rejoice over me, neither let them wink with the eye that hate me *without* a cause" (Psa. 35:19). It was because he had neither given his enemies just cause for their persecution, and because so far from retaliating, he had borne them no malice, that he enjoyed the testimony of a good conscience. David's character had been grievously aspersed and many hideous things laid to his charge; but his conduct had been upright and conscientious to an uncommon degree. "In all his persecutions by Saul, he would not injure him or his party; nay, he employed every opportunity to serve the cause of Israel, though rewarded by envy, treachery, and ingratitude" (T. Scott). When maligned and oppressed by men, it is an inestimable consolation to have the assurance of our own hearts of our innocence and integrity, and therefore we should spare no pains in exercising ourselves "to have always a conscience void of offence toward God and men" (Acts 24:14).

In saying "The Lord rewarded me according to my righteousness" David enunciated one of the principles operative in the Divine government of this world. "Albeit that the dispensations of Divine grace are to the fullest degree sovereign and irrespective of human merit, yet in the dealings of Providence there is often discernible a rule of justice by which the injured are at length avenged and the righteous ultimately delivered" (C. H. Spurgeon). That statement manifests an intelligent grasp of the view point from which David was writing, namely, the *governmental ways of* God in time, and not the ground upon which He saves eternally. These declarations of the Psalmist had nothing whatever to do with his justification in the high court of Heaven, but concerned the innocency and integrity of his conduct toward his enemies on earth, because of which God delivered him from them.

"For I have kept the ways of the Lord, and have not wickedly departed from my God" (v. 22). We regard David as continuing to refer unto how he had conducted himself during the time that his life had been in danger. Certainly his language here is not to be taken absolutely, nor even as a relative declaration upon his life as a whole. Notwithstanding the provocations he received from Saul, and later from Absalom, and notwithstanding the efforts which we doubt not Satan made at such seasons to make him question God's goodness and faithfulness, tempting him to cast off allegiance to Him, David persevered in the paths of righteousness and refused to apostatise. The Psalms written by him at these trying periods of his life make it unmistakably clear that David's piety waned not, despite the most aggravating circumstances.

"For all His judgments were before me: and as for His statutes, I did not depart from them" (v. 23). "His conscience witnessed to him that he had ever made the Word of God his rule, and had kept to it. Wherever he was, God's judgments were before him, and his guide; whithersoever he went, he took his religion along with him; and though he was forced to depart from his country, and sent, as it were, to serve other gods, yet, as for God's statutes, he did not depart from them, but kept the way of the Lord and walked in it" (Matt. Henry). This was sure evidence of the genuineness of his piety. It is comparatively easy to discharge the external duties of religion while we are at home, surrounded by those likeminded, but the real test of our sincerity comes when we go abroad and sojourn among a people who make no profession. David not only worshipped God while he abode at Jerusalem, but also while he tarried in the land of the Philistines.

"I was *also* upright before *Him*, and have kept myself from mine iniquity" (v. 24). This declaration manifestly clinches the interpretation we have made of the preceding verses: in them he had referred solely to his conduct unto his *enemies*, which conduct has been strictly regulated by the Divine statutes: particularly had he heeded "thou shalt not kill" when Saul was in *His* sight *too* he had acted blamelessly toward his foes. "Sincerity is here claimed; sincerity, such as would be accounted genuine before the bar of God. Whatever evil men might think of him, David felt that he had the good opinion of God" (C.H. Spurgeon). Various explanations have been given of "mine iniquity:" but in the light of the context, we regard the reference as being to David's refusal to slay Saul when in his power.

"Therefore the Lord hath recompensed me according to my righteousness; according to my cleanness in His eyesight" (v. 25). They greatly err who suppose that David here gave vent to a boastful spirit: he was pleading his innocency before the bar of *human* equity. A man is not guilty of pride in knowing that he *is* truthful, honest, merciful; no, nor when he believes that God rewards him in providence because of these virtues, for such is a most evident matter of fact. Yea, so patent is this, that many of the ungodly recognize that honesty is the best policy for this life. It *would be* self-righteousness to transfer such thoughts from the realm of providential government into the spiritual and everlasting kingdom, for *there* grace reigns not only supreme, but alone, in the distribution of Divine favours. A godly man with a clear conscience, who knows himself to be upright, is not required to deny his consciousness, and hypocritically make himself out to be worse than he is.

Having shown how the above verses may be understood, relatively, of David himself, let us very briefly point out how they applied to Christ without any qualification. "I have kept the ways of the Lord:" when tempted to forsake them, He indignantly cried, "get thee hence Satan." "And have not wickedly departed from My God:" "Which of you convinceth Me of sin?" (John 8:46) was His challenge to His enemies. "For all His judgments were before Me:" "I have given unto them the words which Thou gavest Me" (John 17:8) He affirmed. "I was also upright before Him:" "I do always those things that please Him" (John 8:29) was His declaration. "And have kept Myself from Mine iniquity:" so far from slaying those who came to arrest, He healed one of them (Luke 22:51). "Therefore the Lord hath recompensed Me according to My righteousness:" "Thou lovest righteousness, and hatest wickedness: therefore God, Thy God, hath anointed Thee with the oil of gladness above Thy fellows" (Psa. 45:7) is the Spirit's confirmation.

"With the merciful Thou wilt show Thyself merciful, and with the upright man

Thou wilt show Thyself upright. . . But Thine eyes are upon the haughty, that Thou mayest bring them down" (vv. 26-28). These verses announced a general principle in God's government of this world: we say "general," for God exercises His sovereign discretion in the actual application of it. If on the one hand we are told that some of the O.T. heroes of faith "quenched the violence of fire, escaped the edge of the sword," etc , yet we also read "others had trial of cruel mockings. . .were stoned," etc. (Heb. 11:36-37). The Baptist was beheaded and Stephen stoned, yet Peter and Paul were miraculously delivered from their enemies.

For You are my lamp, O LORD. And the LORD will lighten my darkness. For by You I have run through a troop. By my God I have leaped over a wall. As for God, His way is perfect. The word of the LORD is tried. He is a shield to all those who trust in Him. For who is God, except Jehovah? And who is a rock except our God? God is my strength and power, and He makes my way perfect. He makes my feet like hinds' feet and sets me on high places. He teaches my hands to war, so that a bow of steel is broken by my arms. You have also given me the shield of Your salvation, and Your gentleness has made me great. — II Samuel 22:29-36.

In this Song David is celebrating the wondrous deliverances from his many enemies which he had experienced by the goodness and power of Jehovah. But unless we carefully bear in mind his particular viewpoint therein, we shall utterly fail to contemplate those experiences in their proper perspective. David was not here furnishing an outline of his entire history, but instead, confines himself to one particular phase thereof. Because they lay *outside* his present scope, he says nothing about his own sad failures and falls, rather does he restrict himself to what the Lord had wrought for and by him. There *are* passages, many of them, both in the historical books, and in the Psalms, wherein we hear him confessing his sins and bewailing his transgressions; but in this Song he recounts his victories over and vanquishing of his foes, not by his own prowess, but by Divine enablement.

In what has just been pointed out there is a most important lesson for the believer to take to heart. If there be times (as there certainly are) when the Christian may feelingly appropriate to his own use the mournful language of Psa. 38 and the abasing confessions of Psa. 51, it is equally true that there are times when he should employ the triumphant tones of Psa. 18, which is almost identical with 2 Sam. 22, In other words, if there be occasions when the saint can only sigh and groan, there are also seasons when he should sing and celebrate his triumphs, for David has left us an example of the one as truly as he has of the other. Nor should such singing be limited to the days of our "first love," the joy of our espousal. This Song was composed by David in his declining years: as he reviewed his checkered career, despite his own failings and falls, he perceived how, after all, he was "more than conqueror through Him that loved him" (Rom. 8:37).

If on the one hand there be a large class of Satan-deceived professors who are fond of trumpeting forth their own achievements and of advertising their fancied victories over sin, there is on the other hand a considerable proportion of the Lord's people who are so occupied with their downfalls and defeats, that they are sadly remiss in recounting the Lord's triumphs in them and by them. This ought not to be: it is robbing the Lord of that which is His due; it is a morbidity which causes them to lose all sense of proportion; it conveys to others an erroneous conception of the Christian life. It is a false humility which shuts our eyes to the workings of Divine grace within us. It is the presence and exercise of a true humility that takes notice of our successes and conquests so long as it is careful to lay all the trophies of them at the Lord's feet, and ascribe to Him alone the honour and glory of the same.

Let those who are engaged in fighting the good fight of faith remember that this is not the work of a day, but the task of a lifetime. Now in a protracted war success does not uniformly attend the efforts of that side which is ultimately victorious. Far from it. It usually falls out that many a minor skirmish is lost; yea, and sometimes a major one too, before the issue is finally determined. At times, even the main army may have to fall back before the fierce onslaughts of the enemy. There are severe losses, sad disappointments, heavy sacrifices, the receiving of many wounds, before success is ultimately achieved. Why do we forget these well known facts when it comes to our spiritual warfare? They apply with equal force thereto. Even under the inspired leadership of Joshua, Israel did not conquer and capture Canaan in a day, nor in a year; nor without drinking the bitters of defeat as well as tasting the sweets of victory.

We are well aware that one of the principal hindrances against our rendering to God the praise which is His due, for the victories He has given us over our enemies, is a sense of *present* defeat. But if we are to wait till *that* be removed, we shall have to wait till we reach Heaven before we sing this Song, and obviously that is wrong, for it is recorded for us to use here on earth. Ah, says the desponding reader: others may use it, but it is not suitable to such a sorry failure as I am; it would be a mockery for *me* to praise God for my triumphs over the Enemy. Not so fast, dear friend: ponder these questions. Are you not still out of Hell? — many of your former companions are not! Though perhaps tempted to do so, has Satan succeeded in causing you to totally apostatise from God? — he has many others! Have you been deceived and carried away by fatal errors? — millions have! Then what cause have you to thank God for such deliverances!

As the believer carefully reviews the whole of his career, while on the one hand he finds much to be humbled at in himself, yet on the other hand he discerns not a little to be elated over in the Lord. Thus it was with David. Though there had been tragic failures, there were also blessed successes, and it was these he celebrated in this Song. After affirming that God had acted righteously in favouring him as He had (vv. 20-28), the purely personal tone is again resumed and he bursts forth into joyful strains of praise. The leading difference between the second half of this Song from its first is easily ascertained by attention to its details: in the former David dwells on God's delivering him *from* his enemies (see vv. 3, 17), in the latter half he recounts his victories *over* his enemies: in each the glory is ascribed alone to Jehovah. In the first David was passive — God's arm alone was his deliverance; in the second he is active, the conquering king, whose arm is strengthened for victory by God.

"For Thou art my lamp, O Lord; and the Lord will lighten my darkness" (2 Sam. 22:29). This is the verse which links together the two halves of the Song. At first sight the force of its connection is not very apparent, yet a little reflection will ascertain its general bearing. David's path had been both a difficult and a dangerous one. At times it was so intricate and perplexing, he had been quite unable to see whither it was leading. More than once the shadows had been so dark that he had been quite at a loss to discern what lay ahead. Once and again there had been much which tended to cast a heavy gloom upon David's soul, but the Lord had graciously relieved the tension, supplying cheer in the blackest hour. It is to be remembered that with the Orientals the "lamp" is used for *comfort* as much as for illumination — many of them will stint themselves of food in order to buy oil; which helps us to understand the figure here used.

"For Thou art my lamp, O Lord." This is the grand recourse of the believer in seasons of trial: he can turn unto One to whom the poor worldling is a total stranger; nor will he turn to Him in vain, for God is "a very present help in trouble." It is then that the oppressed and depressed saint proves Him to be "the Father of mercies and the God of all comfort" (2 Cor. 1:3). Though his night be not turned into day, yet the welcome radiance of God's countenance affords such cheer as to sustain the trembling heart in the loneliest and saddest hour. In the cave of Adullam, in the hold of Rephaim, in the fastnesses of Mahamaim, the Lord had been his solace and support; and now that old age drew near, David could bear witness "Thou art my lamp, O Lord." And is not this the testimony of both writer and reader? Have we not abundant cause to witness to the same glorious fact!

"And the Lord *will* lighten my darkness." This was the language of faith and hope: He who had so often done this for David in the past, would not fail him in the future. No matter how dense the gloom would be, there should be a break in the clouds. That which is incomprehensible to the natural man is often made intelligible to the spiritual. That loss of health, financial disaster, or family bereavement: yes, but "the secret of the Lord is with them that fear Him." Divine providence is often a mysterious deep, but God is his own interpreter, and He will make plain what before was obscure. Particularly is this the case with the believer's being plagued so fiercely and so frequently by his enemies. Why should his peace be so rudely disturbed, his hope dampened, his hopes shattered? Why should the conflict so often go against him and humiliating defeat be his portion? Here too we can confidently affirm "the Lord will lighten my darkness:" if not now, in the hereafter.

"For by Thee I have run through a troop: by my God have I leaped over a wall" (v. 30). Occurring as they do in the second half of this Psalm, we do not (as some) regard these words as referring to David's escapes from his enemies, but to his vanquishing of them. It was not that he was almost surrounded by hostile forces and then managed to find a loophole, or that he was driven into some stockade and then climbed over it; rather that he successfully attacked them. Instead of picturing the difficulties from which David extricated himself, we consider this verse portrays his foes as occupying two different positions: in the open field, sheltering behind some battlement; and his prevailing over them in each case. The leading thought seems to be that the Christian warrior must expect to have a taste of *every form* of fighting, for at times he is required to take the offensive, as well as the defensive. A "troop" of difficulties may impede his progress, a "wall" of opposition obstruct his success: by Divine enablement he is to master both.

"As for God, His way is perfect" (v. 31). What a glorious testimony was this from one who had been so severely tried by His adverse providences! Severely as he had been buffeted, rough as was the path he often had to tread, David had not a word of criticism to make against God for the way He had dealt with him; so far from it, he vindicated and magnified Him. What a restingplace it is for the heart to be assured that all the Divine actions are regulated by unerring wisdom and righteousness, infinite goodness and patience, inflexible justice and tender mercy. "The Word of the Lord is tried" like silver refined in the furnace. Tens of thousands of His people have, in all ages and circumstances, tested and proved the sufficiency of God's Word for themselves: they have found its doctrine satisfying to the soul, its precepts to be their best interests to follow, its promises absolutely reliable. "He is a buckler to all them that trust in Him" (v. 31): the covenant-keeping Jehovah is a sure Shield of protection to His warring people.

"For who is God, save the Lord? and who is a rock, save our God?" (v. 32). There is none to be compared with Him, for there is none like unto Him: all others worshipped as deities are but counterfeits and pretenders. "Who is like unto Thee, O Lord, among the gods? who is like Thee, glorious in holiness, fearful in praises, doing wonders?" (Ex. 15:11). Who else save the living and true God creates, sustains, and governs all creatures? He is perfect in every attribute, excellect in every action. The opening "for" may be connected both with v. 30 and v. 31: "by my God have I leaped over a wall," for there is none else enables like Him; "He is a buckler to all that trust in Him," for He, and He alone, is reliable. Where can lasting hopes be fixed? where is real strength to be found? where is refuge to be obtained? In the Rock of Ages, for He is immoveable and immutable, steadfast and strong.

"God is my strength and power; and He maketh my way perfect" (v. 33). By Him David had been energised and enabled, upheld and preserved, both as a pilgrim and as a warrior. How often the Christian soldier has grown weary and faint, when fresh vigour was imparted: "strengthened with might by His Spirit in the inner man." How often the task before us seemed impossible, the difficulties insurmountable, when such might was ours that we mounted up with wings as eagles and ran and were not weary. Nor can we take any credit for this to ourselves: God Himself is our strength and power, both physically and spiritually. "He maketh my way perfect," by which we understand David to mean that his course had been successful. There is a real sense in which each believer may make these words his own: because his steps are ordered by the Lord and because his path shineth more and more unto "the perfect day."

"He maketh my feet like hinds' feet; and setteth me upon my high places" (v. 34). "As hinds climb the craggy rocks and stand firm upon the slippery summit of the precipice, so David had been upheld in the most slippery paths and advanced to his present elevated station by the providence and grace of God" (Thos. Scott). The feet of certain animals are specially designed and adapted by the figure of this verse. First, God fits the believer for the position which He has appointed him to occupy, no matter how honourable and hazardous. Second, God furnished him with alacrity and agility when the King's business requireth haste, for speed as well as sureness of foot characterises the hind. Third, God protects and secures him in the most dangerous places: "He will keep the feet of His saints" (1 Sam. 2:9).

"He teacheth my hands to war, so that a bow of steel is broken by mine arms" (v. 35). Whatever skill he possessed in the use of weapons, David, gratefully ascribed it unto Divine instruction. The general principle here is of wide application: the artizan, the musician, the housewife, should thankfully acknowledge that it is God who has imparted dexterity to his or her fingers. In its higher significance this verse has reference to Divine wisdom being imparted to the Christian warrior in the use of the armour which grace has provided for him. As it is in the natural, so it is in the spiritual: weapons, whether the offensive or defensive ones, are of little avail to us till we know how to employ them to advantage. "Take unto you the whole armour of God, that ye may be able to withstand in the evil day" (Eph. 6:13) not only means appropriate to yourself the panoply which God furnished, but also look to Him for guidance and help in the use of the same. The second half of our verse seems to indicate that David, like Samson, was at times endued with more than ordinary strength.

"Thou hast also given me the shield of Thy salvation" (v. 36). Here we find David looking higher than the material and temporal blessings which God had so freely granted him, to those special favours reserved for His own elect. There are common gifts of Providence bestowed upon the wicked and the righteous alike, but there are riches of grace communicated only to the high favourites of Heaven, that infinitely surpass the former. What are bodily deliverances worth if the soul be left to perish! What does protection from human foes amount to, if the Devil be permitted to bring about our eternal destruction! David was not only granted the former, but the latter also. Here is a plain hint that we should seek after the higher meaning throughout this Song and interpret it spiritually. Let it be noted that this is not the only place in it where God's "salvation" is referred to: see vv. 47, 51.

"And Thy gentleness hath made me great" (v. 36). The Hebrew word which is here rendered "gentleness," is one of considerable latitude and has been variously translated. The Septuagint has "Thy discipline," or Fatherly chastening; another gives "Thy goodness," referring to the benevolence of God's actions; still another, and more literally, "Thy condescension." They all amount to much the same thing. This acknowledgment of David's is very blessed: so far was he from complaining at the Divine providences and charging God with having dealt with him harshly, he extols God's perfections for the pains that had been taken with him. David owns that God had acted toward him like a tender parent, tempering the rod with infinite patience; he affirmed that God had graciously sanctified his afflictions to him. Though he had been raised from the sheepcote to the throne and had become great in prosperity and power, a successful conqueror and ruler, he fails not to give God all the glory for it.

You have enlarged my steps under me, so that my feet did not slip. I have pursued my enemies and destroyed them and turned not again until I had finished them. And I have crushed them and wounded them so that they could not rise. Yea, they have fallen under my feet. For You have girded me with strength to battle. You have subdued under me those who rose up against me. You have also given me the necks of my enemies, so that I might destroy those who hate me. They looked, but there was none to save. They looked to the LORD, but He did not answer them. Then I beat them as small as the dust of the earth, I stamped them like the mire of the street and spread them abroad. You have also delivered me from the strivings of my people, You have kept me the head of the heathen. A people I knew not shall serve me. Strangers shall submit themselves to me. As soon as they hear, they shall obey me. Strangers shall fade away, and they shall be afraid out of their strongholds. The LORD lives! And blessed be my Rock, and exalted be the God, the Rock of my salvation. It is God who avenges me and who brings down the people under me, and who brings me forth from my enemies. You also have lifted me up on high above all those who rose up against me. You have delivered me from the violent man. Therefore I will give thanks to You, O LORD, among the heathen, and I will sing praises to Your name. He is the Tower of salvation for His king, and He shows mercy to His anointed, to David and to his seed, forevermore. — II Samuel 22:37-51.

If we are now to complete our exposition of this Song we must dispense with our usual introductory remarks: we therefore proceed at once to our next verse. "Thou hast enlarged my steps under me, so that my feet did not slip" (2 Sam. 22:37). Here David praises the Lord because He had not only preserved but prospered him too, blessing him with liberty and expansion — compare v. 20. From the narrow mountain pass and the confinement of caves, he had been brought to the spacious plains, and there too he had been sustained, for the latter has its dangers as well as the former: "It is no small mercy to be brought into full Christian liberty and enlargement, but it is a greater favour still to be enabled to walk worthily in such liberty, not being permitted to slide with our feet" (C.H. Spurgeon). To stand firm in the day of adversity is the result of grace upholding, and that aid is no less needed by us in seasons of prosperity.

"I have pursued mine enemies, and destroyed them: and turned not again until I had consumed them" (v. 38). David was here alluding to occasions like that recorded in 1 Sam. 30: the Amalekites thought themselves clear away with their booty (v. 2), but when David's God guided him in pursuit, they were soon overtaken and cut in pieces (vv. 16-18). It is not sufficient that the believer stand his ground and resist the onslaught of his foes. There are times when he must assume the offensive and "pursue" his enemies: yea, as a general principle it holds good that attack is the best means of defense. Lusts are not only to be starved, by making no provision for them, they are to be "mortified" or put to death. God has provided the Christian warrior with a sword as well as with a shield, and each is to be used in its season. Observe that v. 38 follows v. 37: there must be an enlargement and revival before we can be the aggressors and victors.

"And I have consumed them, and wounded them, that they could not arise: yea, they are fallen under my feet" (v. 39). This calls attention to the *completeness* of the victories which the Lord enabled David to achieve. But does not this present a serious difficulty to the exercised saint? How far, far short does *his* actual experience come to this! So far from his enemies being consumed and under his feet, he daily finds them gaining the ascendency over him. True; nevertheless, there *is* a real sense in which it is his holy privilege to make these words his own: they are the language of *faith*, and not of sense. The terms of this verse may be legitimately applied to the judicial slaughter of our foes: we may exult over sin, death, and hell having been destroyed by our conquering Lord! Forget not His precious promise "because I live, ye shall live also" (John 14:19): His victory in the past, is the sure guarantee of our complete victory in the future.

"For Thou hast girded me with strength to battle: them that rose up against me hast Thou subdued under me" (v. 40). David had been both vigorous and valiant, yet he takes no credit to himself for the same. He freely acknowledges that it was God who had qualified him for his warfare, who had given him ability therein, and who had crowned his efforts with such success. Any measure of liberty from sin and Satan which we enjoy, any enlargement of heart in God's service, our preservation in the slippery paths of this enticing world, are cause for thankfulness, and not ground for glorying in self. It is true that *we* have to wrestle with our spiritual antagonists, but the truth is that the victory is far more the Lord's than ours. It has long been the conviction of this writer, both from his own experience and the close observation of many others, that the principal reason why the Lord does not grant us a much larger measure of present triumph over our spiritual foes, is because we are so prone to be self-righteous over the same. Alas how deceitful and wicked are our hearts.

"Thou hast also given me the necks of mine enemies, that I might destroy them that hate me" (v. 41). There is no doubt that such will be our pean of praise in Heaven in a far fuller sense that ever it is in this world. Do we not get more than a hint of this in Rev. 15:1-3, where we are told that "those that had gotten the victory over the Beast," etc, sing "the song of Moses, the servant of God (see Ex. 15) and the song of the Lamb." Meanwhile, it is our blessed privilege to rest upon the Divine promise: "The God of peace shall bruise Satan under your feet shortly" (Rom. 16:20). Rightly did Adams the Puritan when commenting on this verse in our Song, exhort his hearers "Though passion possess our bodies, let patience possess our souls." In a protracted warfare *patience* is just as essential as is valour or skill to use our weapons. The promise of ultimate salvation is made only unto those who "endure to the end." In due season we shall reap if we faint not. The fight may be a long and arduous one, but the victor's crown will be a grand recompense. Then look above the smoke and din of battle to the Prince of Peace who waits to welcome thee on High.

"They looked, but there was none to save; even unto the Lord, but He answered them not" (v. 42). The Companion Bible has pointed out that there is here a play on words in the Hebrew, which may be rendered thus in English: They cried with fear, but none gave ear. They called both to earth and heaven for help, but in vain. God heeded them not for they were His enemies, and sought Him not through the Mediator; being given up by Him, they fell an easy prey to David's righteous sword. "Prayer is so notable a weapon that even the wicked will take to it in their fits of despair. But men have appealed to God against His own servants, but all in vain: the kingdom of heaven is not divided, and God never succours His foes at the expense of His friends. There are prayers to God which are no better than blasphemy, which bring no comforting reply, but rather provoke the Lord unto greater wrath" (C. H. Spurgeon).

"Then did I beat them as small as the dust of the earth: I did stamp them as the mire of the street, and did spread them abroad" (v. 43). Let not the *connection* between this and the preceding verse be missed — emphasised by its opening "Then." It shows us how utterly helpless are those who are abandoned by God, and how fearful is their fate — compare the case of King Saul: 1 Sam. 28:6 and 30:3, 4! The defeat of those nations which fought against David was so entire that they were like powders pounded in the mortar. Thos. Scott saw in this verse, and we think rightly so, a reference to "the inevitable destruction which came upon the Jews for crucifying the Lord of glory and rejecting the Gospel. They cried, and they still cry, to the Lord to save them, but refusing to obey His beloved Son, He vouchsafes them no answer." How accurately did the figures of this verse depict the tragic history of *the Jews*: "dust" which is scattered by the wind to all parts of the earth; "mire" that is contemptuously trampled underfoot!

"Thou also hast delivered me from the strivings of my people, Thou hast kept me to be head of the heathen: a people which I knew not shall serve me" (v. 44). In the first clause David refers to the intense strife which had so gravely threatened and menaced his kingdom. There had been times when internal dissensions had been far more serious and dangerous than anything which the surrounding nations threatened; nevertheless God had graciously preserved His servant from their malice and opposition. Thus it is with a Christian warrior: though he be opposed from without by both the world and the Devil, yet his greatest danger comes from *within* — his own corruptions and lusts are continually seeking his overthrow. None but God can grant him deliverance from his inward foes, but the sure promise is "He which hath begun a good work in you will finish it" (Phil. 1:6). The same principle holds true of *the minister*: his acutest problems and trials issue not from without the pale of his church, but from its own members and adherents; and it is a great mercy when God gives peace within.

"Thou hast kept me to be head of the heathen: a people which I knew not shall serve me." God's signal preservation of David intimated that he was designed and reserved for an important and imposing position: to rule over the twelve tribes of Israel, notwithstanding all the opposition the Benjamites had made against him, and to be exalted over heathen nations also: the decisive defeats of the Amalekites and Philistines were regarded as the pledge of still more notorious triumphs. The practical lesson inculcated therein is one of great importance: hereby we are taught that the unchanging faithfulness of God should encourage us to view all the blessings which we have received at His hands in the past as the earnest of yet greater favours in the future. God hath not preserved thee thus far, my faint-hearted brother, to let thee founder at the end. He who did sustain thee through six trials declares "in seven there shall no evil touch thee" (Job 5:19). Say, then, with the apostle, "Who hath delivered us from so great a death, and doth deliver; in whom we trust that He will *yet deliver us*" (II Cor. 1:10).

"Strangers shall submit themselves unto me: as soon as they hear, they shall be obedient unto me" (v. 45). It will be observed that in this verse, as well as in the second half of the preceding one, that our translators have made a change of tense from the present to the future. Opinions vary considerably as to where the last section of the Song really commences, in which memory passes into hope, in which the successes of the past are regarded as the guarantee of still greater triumphs in the future. God had been David's "buckler" (v. 31), his "strength and power" (v. 33), His condescension had made him great (v. 36), He had given him the necks of his enemies (v. 41): from all of which he draws the conclusion that God had still grander blessings in store for him. There can be little room for doubt that in the verses we are now pondering David was carried forward by the Spirit of prophecy unto this N.T. era, his own kingdom being the symbol and portent of the spiritual reign of his Son and Lord.

The only matter on which there is any uncertainty is the precise point in this Song where the historical merges into the prophetical, for the Hebrew verb does not, as in English, afford us any help here. As we have seen, Thos. Scott considers that v. 43, at least, should be included in this category. Alex. Maclaren suggested, "It is perhaps best to follow many of the older versions, and the valuable exposition of Hupfield, in regarding the whole section from v. 38 of our translation as the expression of the trust which past experience had wrought." Personally, we consider that too radical: we are on much safer ground if we take the course followed by the A.V. and regard v. 44 as the turning point, where it is evident David was conscious that his kingdom was destined to be extended further than the confines of Palestine: strange tribes were to submit unto him and crouch before him in subjection.

Not only were the severe conflicts through which David passed and the remarkable victories granted to him prefigurations of the experiences of Christ, both in His sufferings and triumphs, but the further enlargements which David expected and his being made head over the heathen, foreshadowed the Redeemer's exaltation and the expansion of His kingdom far beyond the bounds of Judaism. First, the antitypical David had been delivered from the strivings of his Jewish people (v. 44), not by being preserved from death, but by being brought triumphantly through it, for in all things He must have the pre-eminence. Second, He had been made Head of the Church, which comprised Gentiles as well as Jews. Third, those who had been "strangers" (v. 45) to the commonwealth of Israel, submitted to the sound of His voice through the Gospel and rendered to Him the obedience of faith. Fourth, Paganism received its death-wound under the labours of Paul, its pride being humbled into the dust: such we take it is the prophetic allusion in v. 46.

"As soon as they hear, they shall be obedient unto Me" (v. 45). "In many cases the Gospel is speedily received by hearts apparently unprepared for it. Those who have never heard the Gospel before, have been charmed by its first message, and yielded obedience to it; while others, alas! who are accustomed to its joyful sound, are rather hardened than softened by its teachings. The grace of God sometimes runs like fire among the stubble, and a nation is born in a day. 'Love at first sight' is no uncommon thing when Jesus is the wooer. He can write Caesar's message without boasting, 'Veni, vidi, vici'; His Gospel is in some cases no sooner heard than believed. What inducements to spread abroad the doctrine of the cross" (C. H. Spurgeon).

"Strangers shall fade away, and they shall be afraid out of their close places" (v. 46). "Out of their mountain fastnesses the heathen crept in fear to our allegiance to Israel's king; and even so, from the castles of self-confidence and the dens of carnal security, poor sinners come bending before the Saviour, Christ the Lord. Our sins which have entrenched themselves in our flesh and blood as in impregnable forts, shall yet be driven forth by the sanctifying energy of the Holy Spirit, and we shall serve the Lord in singleness of heart" (C.H. Spurgeon).

"The Lord liveth: and blessed be my Rock; and exalted be the God of the rock of my salvation" (v. 47). After offering praise for past conquests and expressing his confidence in future victories, David returned to the more direct adoration of God Himself. Some of the glorious names of Deity which he had heaped together at the beginning of his Song, are now echoed at its close. The varied experiences through which he had passed had brought to the Psalmist a deeper knowledge of his living Lord: the One who had preserved Noah and ministered to Abraham long before, was his God too: swift to hear, active to help. One of the lesser known Puritans commented thus on this verse: "Honours die, pleasures die, the world dies; but the Lord *liveth*. My flesh is as sand, my fleshly life, strength, and glory is as a word written on sand; but blessed be my *Rock*. Those are but for a moment; this stands for ever; the curse shall devour those, everlasting blessings on the head of these." (P. Sterry).

"It is God that avengeth me, and that bringeth down the people under me; and that bringeth me forth from mine enemies. Thou also hast lifted me up on high above them that rose up against me; Thou hast delivered me from the violent man" (vv. 48, 49). Here David recurs to the dominant sentiment running through this Song: all his help was in God and from God. To take matters into our own hands and seek personal revenge, is not only utterly unbecoming in one who has received mercy from the Lord, but it is grossly wicked, for it encroaches upon a prerogative which belongs alone to Him. Moreover, it is quite unnecessary, for in due time the Lord will avenge His wronged people. Though we may join with Stephen in praying "Lord, lay not this sin to their charge," yet when Divine justice takes satisfaction upon those who have flouted His law, the devout heart will return thanks. After the battle at Naseby, in a letter to the Speaker of the House of Commons, Oliver Cromwell wrote, "Sir, this is none other than the hand of God, and to Him alone belongs the glory, wherein none are to share with Him."

'Therefore I will give thanks unto Thee, O Lord, among the heathen and I will sing praises unto Thy name" (v. 50). What an example does David here set us of a holy soul making its boast in God in the presence of ungodly men. There is a happy medium between an unseemly parading of our piety before unbelievers and a cowardly silence in their presence. We must not suffer the despisers of God to shut our mouths and stifle our praises; especially is it our bounden duty to bow our heads and "give thanks unto the Lord" before partaking of a meal, even though we are "among the heathen." Be not ashamed to acknowledge thy God in the presence of His enemies. This verse is quoted by the apostle and applied to Christ in Rom. 15:9, which affords clear proof that David had his Antitype before him in the second half of this Song.

"He is the tower of salvation for His king; and showeth mercy to His anointed, unto David, and to his seed for evermore" (v. 51). David contemplated God not only as "the rock of his salvation" — the One who under-girded him, the One on whom all his hopes rested — but also as "the tower of salvation" — the One in whom he found security, the One who was infinitely elevated above him. Though saved, he yet had need of being shown "mercy"! The last clause indicates that he was resting on the Divine promise of II Sam. 7:15, 16, and supplies additional evidence that he had here an eye to Christ, for He alone is his "Seed for evermore."

Now these are the last words of David. David the son of Jesse said (and the man who was raised up on high, the anointed of the God of Jacob, and the sweet psalmist of Israel, said), The Spirit of the LORD spoke by me, and His word was in my tongue. The God of Israel said, The Rock of Israel spoke to me — he who rules over men must be just, ruling in the fear of God. And he shall be like the light of the morning, when the sun rises, even a morning without clouds — like the tender grass springing out of the earth by clear shining after rain. Although my house is not so with God, yet He has made with me an everlasting covenant, ordered in all things, and sure. For this is all my salvation, and all my desire, although He does not make it grow. But the sons of Belial shall all of them be like thorns thrust away, because they cannot be taken with hands. But the man who shall touch them must be fenced with iron and the staff of a spear. And they shall be utterly burned with fire in the same place. — II Samuel 23:1-7.

The passage for our present consideration (2 Sam. 23:1-7) presents somewhat of a difficulty, especially to those who are not accustomed to the drawing of distinctions and the taking of words relatively as well as absolutely. It opens by telling us "These be the last words of David," when in fact the close of the patriarch's life was not yet reached. It seems strange that we should read of this here, when so much else is recorded in the chapters which follow, for we naturally associate the "last words" of a person with his closing utterances as life is expiring. Nor is the difficulty decreased when we note what vastly different language is upon his lips in 1 Kings 2:9. Thos. Scott suggested that "perhaps he repeated them in his dying moments as the expression of his faith and hope and the source of his consolation." This may be the case, for very likely such sentiments were in his heart and mouth again and again during his declining days.

However, it seems to us that 2 Sam. 23 refers to "the last words of David" not so much as those merely of *a man*, but rather as being a *mouthpiece* of God, thus forming a brief appendix to his Psalms. That our passage concerns the final inspired utterance of David appears to be quite plain from the specific terms used in it. First, he makes definite mention of himself as "the sweet Psalmist of Israel" (v. 1), which obviously refers to his official character as the Lord's servant and seer. Second, he states "the Spirit of the Lord spake by me, and His Word was in my tongue" (v. 2), which language could only be used of one appointed to formally deliver the oracles of God, of one so completely controlled by the Holy Spirit that his utterance was a Divine revelation. Third, what he said in vv. 3, 4 looked beyond himself, being a prophetic announcement concerning the antitypical "Ruler" — proof that he was "moved by the Holy Spirit." Further, there is nothing in the chapters following which indicate David was giving forth a formal utterance by Divine revelation.

There is still another distinction which may be drawn, that clears away any remaining difficulty from our passage. Not only are we to distinguish between David's utterances as a man and as the mouthpiece of Jehovah, but also between his acts and words looked at *historically* and considered *typically*. In the course of this lengthy series of chapters we have pointed out again and again that in many (though by no means in all) of his experiences David is to be viewed *representatively*, as treading the same path and encountering the temptations and trials common to all the saints as they pass through this wilderness of sin. 1 Kings 1 gives us the historical close of the patriarch's life, the last utterance of the aged king being "but his hoar head bring thou down to the grave *with blood.*" "Blood" is the final word on the lips of the dying warrior, a "man of war" from his youth, as Philistine enemies and Amalekite foes could testify.

But in 2 Sam. 23 we are permitted to gaze upon the other side of the picture, a most blessèd and refreshing one. Here, the Spirit of God brings before us not "the man of war" (1 Sam. 16:18), but "the man after God's own heart," the one who had found favour in His eyes and had been loved with an everlasting love, and thus the representative of His chosen people. Here we listen to the holy breathings of the saint, and the scene becomes to us a "gate of heaven." As the believer draws near the end of his wilderness journey, like David, he reviews the Lord's goodness, dwells upon the amazing grace which lifted him from the dunghill and made him to sit in the heavenlies in Christ (v. 1), and while he laments the spiritual condition of some near and dear to him and his own failure to grow in grace as he ought, yet he found unspeakable comfort in the fact that God had made with him an everlasting covenant.

"Now these be the last words of David" (2 Sam. 23:1). Rightly did Matt. Henry point out that "When we find death approaching, we should endeavour both to honour God and to edify those about us with our last words. Let those who have had long experience of God's goodness and the peacefulness of wisdom's ways, when they come to finish their course, leave a record of that experience and bear their testimony to the truth of the promise." It is not all who are granted a clear token of their approaching dissolution or given a season of consciousness, so that they may clearly avow their faith and hope; but when such *is* afforded, their duty and privilege is plain. David thus acquitted himself to the glory of God and the comfort of His people, and everything else being equal, so should we.

"David the son of Jesse said, and the man who was raised up on high, the anointed of the God of Jacob, and the sweet psalmist of Israel, said" (v. 1). The Hebrew word for "said" (twice used in this verse) signifies to speak with assurance and authority, thus confirming what we have pointed out above concerning the Divine character of this utterance. David described himself, first, by the lowliness of his origin — "the son of Jesse," unknown amongst those arrayed in purple and fine linen. The stock from which he came was indeed an humble one, for when it was asked in Saul's court "whose son is he?" the answer was returned "O king, I cannot tell" (1 Sam. 17:55); and so David had to answer for himself, "I am the son of thy servant Jesse, the Bethlehemite" — a small and despised house, and he the least in that house. Typically speaking, this is the believer owning his humble origin, looking back to the hole of the pit from which he was digged.

"And the man that was raised up on high:" here he makes mention, secondly, of the dignity of his elevation. Though of such mean parentage, from one of the humblest of Saul's subjects, yet he found favour in the sight of the Lord, being exalted to the throne and made ruler over all Israel. The nearer the believer approaches the close of his life, the more is his heart made to wonder at the sovereign grace of God for laying hold of one so utterly unworthy and raising him to a position of dignity and honour above that occupied by the holy angels. Third, David described himself as "the anointed of God:" as such he was again the typical believer, for of Christians it is written, "Now He which stablisheth us with you in Christ, and hath *anointed* us, is God" (2 Cor. 1:21). Finally, "and the sweet psalmist of Israel:" that of course refers to his official character, and yet this too is representative: though he composed the Psalms, they are for our use (James 5:13).

"The Spirit of the Lord spake by me, and His word was in my tongue" (v. 2). Though it be useless for us to attempt any explanation of the rationale of Divine inspiration, yet this is one of many statements found in Holy Writ which serves to define its nature and extent. When we come face to face with the conjunction of the Divine and the human, we confront that which transcends the grasp of the finite mind; nevertheless by the aid of what is revealed we may make certain postulates, so as to guard against error at either extreme. The Scriptures are indeed the very Word of God, inerrant and imperishable, yet the instrumentality of the creature was employed in the communication and compilation of them. The mouth uttering it was human, but the message was Divine; the voice was that of man, but the actual words those of God Himself.

"Holy men of God spake as they were moved by the Holy Spirit" (2 Pet. 1:21). Those holy men were the actual mouthpieces of the Almighty: their utterances were so absolutely controlled by Him that what they said and wrote was a perfect expression of His mind and will. It is not simply that their minds were elevated or their spirits sublimated, but that their very tongues were regulated. It was not merely that their wills received a supernatural impulse or that their minds were Divinely illuminated, but the very words of their message was conveyed to them. Nothing less than this can be gathered from the verse before us: when David affirmed God's Word was "in his tongue," far more is denoted than that a concept was conveyed to his mind and he left free to express it in his own language. Nothing less than their *verbal inspiration* is predicated of the Scripture themselves — compare 1 Cor. 2:13.

"The God of Israel said, the Rock of Israel spake to me, He that ruleth over men must be just, ruling in the fear of God" (v. 3). The older writers saw in these verses, and we believe rightly so, a reference to the blessed Trinity. First, in v. 2 David affirmed "the Spirit of the Lord spake by me," and that a Divine person rather than a spiritual inflation was denoted is plain from "and *His* word was in my tongue." Second, "the God of Israel said:" that is, God the Father spake, as a reference to Heb. 1:1, 2 makes clear. Third, "the Rock of Israel spake to David" alludes to the Son, in His mediatorial capacity, of whom it was predicted, "And a Man shall be as a hiding place from the wind, and a covert from the tempest as rivers of water in a dry place, as the shadow of a great rock in a weary land" (Isa. 32:2). Though a fuller and brighter manifestation of the Godhead has been made under Christianity, nevertheless the Tri-unity of God was definitely revealed in the O.T. Scriptures.

There is a distinction to be drawn between what is recorded in the verse preceding and in v. 3: there it was "the Spirit of the Lord spake *by* me," here "spake *to* me" — that relates to what he was moved to record by Divine inspiration (principally in the Psalms), this a more personal message for himself and family. "Let ministers observe that those by whom God speaks to others are concerned to hear and heed what the Spirit speaks to themselves. They whose office it is to teach others their duty, must be sure to learn and do their own" (Matt. Henry). Particularly must due attention be paid unto these two things: "He that ruleth over men must be just, ruling in the fear of God." The immediate reference is to civic leaders, but the principle applies strictly to ecclesiastical ones too: impartiality and righteousness ought ever to characterise both magistrate and minister alike, while the office of each is to be discharged in the awe of Him to whom an account will yet have to be rendered.

"And he shall be as the light of the morning, when the sun riseth, even a morning without clouds; as the tender grass springing out of the earth by clear shining after rain" (v. 4). Here is the blessing and prosperity assured to those who faithfully discharge their obligations, keeping both tables of the Law. "Light is sweet and pleasant, and he that does his duty shall have the comfort of it; his rejoicing will be the testimony of his conscience. Light is bright, and a good prince (or minister) is illustrious; his justice and piety will be his honour. Light is a blessing, nor are there greater and more extensive blessings to the public than princes that rule in the fear of God. It is like 'the light of the morning,' which is most welcome after the darkness of the night; so was David's government after Saul's. It is likewise compared to the tender grass, which the earth produces for the service of men; it brings with it a harvest of blessings" (Matt. Henry).

Verses 3 and 4 can also be rightly regarded as a Messianic prophecy, for the Hebrew may be rendered "There shall be a Ruler over men which is just, ruling the fear of God." The qualities essential in the one who is to rule for God's glory and His people's good, are righteousness and dependence — found alone in their perfection in that blessed One who came not to do His own will, but the will of Him who sent Him. Saul wielded the power for himself; David had to hang his head and own "my house be not so with God" (v. 5); which requires us to turn to Christ. He orders the affairs of the Father's kingdom according to the Divine will. He is "as the light of morning" because "the Light of the world," and "as the tender grass" because He is "the Branch of the Lord" and the Fruit of the earth (Isa. 4:2).

"Although my house be not so with God" (v. 5). Here again the historical merges into the typical. After the prophetic foreview just granted him, David turned his reflections upon himself and his own house, and sorrowed over the state of the same. "By his own misconduct, his family was much less religious and prosperous than it might have been expected, and both he and Israel had suffered many things in consequence. Several grievous and scandalous events had occurred: matters were not yet as he could wish, and he seems to have had his fears concerning his descendants, who should succeed him in the kingdom" (T. Scott). Grief, then, was mingled with His joy, and dismal forebodings cast a dark shadow over his lot.

As the believer nears the end of his course, he not only meditates upon the lowliness of his original estate and then the elevated position to which sovereign grace has lifted him, but he also reviews his follies, bemoans his failures, and sorrows over the wretched returns he has made unto God's goodness. This is the common experience of the pious: as they journey through this wilderness they are sorely tried and exercised, pass through deep waters, experience many sharp conflicts, and are often at a loss to maintain their faith.

> "Favour'd saints of God,
> His messengers and seers,
> The narrow path have trod,
> 'Mid sins, and doubts, and fears."

And at the end they generally have to mourn over the graceless condition of some that are nearest and dearest to them, and exclaim "Although my house be not so with God."

"Yet He hath made with me an everlasting covenant, ordered in all things, and sure" (v. 5). Blessed antithesis. The opening "yet" is placed over against the "although" at the beginning of the previous clause: it is the faithfulness of God set in delightful contrast from David's failures. It illustrates most solemnly the awe-inspiring sovereignty of God: Divine justice had been meted out to his foes,

Divine grace had dealt with himself. At least one of his children had evidenced himself to be among the reprobate, but God had entered into an eternal compact of peace with the father. Here was indeed sweet consolation for his poor heart. The allusion is to that covenant of grace which God made with all His people in Christ before the foundation of the world. That covenant is from everlasting in its contrivance, and to everlasting in its consequences.

That everlasting covenant is so "ordered" as to promote the glory of God, the honour of the Mediator, and the holiness and blessing of His people. It is "sure" because its promises are those of Him who cannot lie, because full provision is made in it for all the failures of believers, and because its administration is in the hands of Christ. "For this is all my salvation." David rightly traced his salvation back to "the everlasting covenant:" alas that so many to-day are ignorant of this inexhaustible well of comfort. It is not enough that we go back to the hour when we first believed, nor even to the cross where the Saviour paid the price of our redemption; to the everlasting covenant we must look, and see there God graciously planning to give Christ to die for His people and impart the Spirit to them for quickening and the communicating of faith. This is "all our salvation" for it entirely suffices, containing as it does a draft of all the salvation-acts of Father, Son, and Holy Spirit.

In consequence of the nature, fulness, and sufficiency of the everlasting covenant, it must be "all my desire:" that is, obtaining by the Spirit's help an assurance of my personal interest in its grand promises. "Although He make it not to grow." First, with reference to his house: "in number, in power; it is God that makes families to grow, or not to grow (Psa. 107:41). Good men have often the melancholy prospect of a declining family, David's house was typical of the Church of Christ. "Suppose this be not so with God as we could wish: suppose it be diminished, distressed, disgraced, and weakened by errors and corruptions, yea, almost extinct, yet God has made a covenant with the church's Head, that He will preserve to Him a seed: this our Saviour comforted Himself with in His sufferings: Isa. 53:10, 12" (Matt. Henry). Second, with reference to himself: he had received the grace of the covenant, but it had not flourished in him as could be desired — his own neglect being the criminal cause.

David concluded (vv. 6, 7) with a most solemn reference to the awful fate awaiting the reprobate. Destitute of faith, self-willed, unconcerned about God's glory, despising and ill-treating His servants, righteous retribution shall surely fall upon them. "As thorns thrust away" is a figure of their rejection by God; ultimately they shall be "utterly burnt with fire." It was a prediction of the eternal undoing of all the implacable enemies of Christ's kingdom.

These are the names of the mighty men whom David had: The Tachmonites who sat in the seat, chief among the captains — the same was Adino the Eznite. He lifted up his spear against eight hundred, whom he killed at one time. And after him was Eleazar the son of Dodo the Ahohite, one of the three mighty men with David. When they defied the Philistines who were gathered together there to battle, and the men of Israel had gone away, he arose and struck the Philistines until his hand was weary, and until his hand clung to the sword. And the LORD wrought a great victory that day. And the people returned after him only to spoil. And next was Shammah the son of Agee the Hararite. And the Philistines were gathered together into a troop, where there was a piece of ground full of lentils. And the people fled from the Philistines. But he stood in the middle of the ground, and defended it, and killed the Philistines. And the LORD wrought a great victory. — II Samuel 23:8-12.

The last thirty-two verses of 2 Sam. 23 have received comparatively scant attention from those who are accustomed to read the Scriptures, and even most of the commentators are nearly silent upon them. Probably the average Christian finds it somewhat difficult to glean much from them which he feels is really profitable to his soul. A number of men are enumerated — some of them mentioned in earlier chapters, but the great majority otherwise quite unknown to us — and one or two of their deeds are described; and then the second half of our chapter is taken up with a long list of names, which most people are inclined to skip. Nevertheless, these very verses are included in that Divine declaration "Whatsoever things were written *afore time* were written for *our learning*" (Rom. 15:4); and it is therefore to the dishonour of God and to our own real loss if we ignore this passage.

There is nothing meaningless in any section of Holy Writ: every part thereof is "profitable" for us (2 Tim. 3:16, 17). Let us therefore settle it at the outset that this passage contains valuable instruction for us to-day, important lessons which we do well to take to heart. Let us, then, humbly bow before God and beg Him to open our eyes, that we may behold "wondrous things" in this part of His Law. Let us gird up the loins of our minds, and seek to reverently ponder and spiritually meditate upon its contents. Let us bear in mind the law of the context, and endeavour to ascertain the relation of this passage to the verses immediately preceding. Let us duly take note of how these "mighty men of David" are classified, and try to discover what is suggested thereby. Let us look beyond the historical and trace out what is *typical*, at the same time setting bounds to our imagination and being regulated by the Analogy of Faith.

Before entering into detail, let us point out some of the general lessons inculcated — suggested, in part, by the brief notes of Matt. Henry. First, the catalogue which is here given us of the names, devotion and valour of the king's soldiers is recorded for the honour of David himself, who trained them in their military arts and exercises, and who set before them an example of piety and courage. It enhances the reputation of, as well as being an advantage, when a prince is attended and served by such men as are here described. So it will be in the Day to come. When the books are opened before an assembled universe and the fidelity and courage of God's ministers is proclaimed, it will be principally for the glory of their Captain, whom they served and whose fame they sought to spread, and by whose Spirit they were energized and enabled. Whatever crowns His servants and saints receive from God, they will be laid at the feet of the Lamb, who alone is worthy.

Second, this inspired record is made for the honour of those worthies themselves. They were instrumental in bringing David to the crown, of settling and protecting him in the throne, and of enlarging his conquests; and therefore the Spirit has not overlooked them. In like manner, the faithful ministers of God are instrumental in the establishing, safe-guarding, and extending the kingdom of Christ in the world, and therefore are they to be esteemed highly for their works' sake, as the Word of God expressly enjoins. Not that they desire the praise of men, but "honour to whom honour is due" is a precept which God requires His people to ever observe. Not only are the valorous soldiers of Christ to be venerated by those of their own day and generation, but posterity is to hold them in high regard: "The memory of the just is blessed." In the Day to come each of them shall "have praise of God" (1 Cor. 4:5).

Third, to excite those who come after them to a generous emulation. That which was praiseworthy in the sires should be practised by their children. If God is pleased to hereby express His approbation of the loyalty and love shown unto David by his officers, we may be sure that He is pleased now with those who strengthen the hands of His ministers, be they in the civil or the ecclesiastical realm. Those alive to-day should be inspired and encouraged by the noble deeds of heroes of the past. But to raise the thought to a higher level: if those men held David in such great esteem that they hesitated not to hazard their lives for his sake, how infinitely more worthy is the antitypical David of the most self-denying sacrifices and devotion from His servants and followers. Alas, how sadly they put most of us to shame.

Fourth, to show how much genuine religion contributes to the inspiring men with true courage. David, both by his Psalms, and by his offerings for the service of the temple, greatly promoted piety among the grandees of the Kingdom (see 1 Chron. 29:6), and when they became famous for piety, they became famous for bravery. Yes, there is an inseparable connection between the two things, as Acts 4:13 so strikingly exemplifies: even the enemies of the apostles "took knowledge of them that they had been with Jesus" when they "saw their *boldness.*" He who truly fears God, fears not man, It is written. "The wicked flee when no man pursueth: but the righteous are bold as a lion" (Prov. 28:1). History, both sacred and secular, abounds in examples of how pious leaders imbued their men with courage: Abraham, Joshua, Cromwell, being cases in point. From the record of their exploits courage should be inspired *in us.*

Let us now inquire, What is the connection between our present portion and the one preceding it? This is a principle which should never be neglected, for the ascertaining of the relation of one passage to another often throws light upon its typical scope, as well as supplies a valuable key to its interpretation. Such is the case here. The first seven verses of 2 Sam. 23 are concerned with "the last words of David," and what follows is virtually an honour role of those who achieved fame in his service. What a blessed foreshadowment of that which will occur when the earthly kingdom of the antitypical David comes to an end. Then shall His servants receive their rewards, for the righteous Judge will then distribute the crowns of life" (Rev. 2:10), cf "righteousness" (2 Tim. 4:8), and of "glory" (1 Pet. 5:4). Then shall He pronounce His "well done thou good and faithful servant, enter thou into the joy of thy Lord." Let therefore those now engaged in fighting the Lord's battles be faithful, diligent, and valorous, assured that in due course they will be richly compensated.

"These be the names of the mighty men whom David had: The Tachmonite that sat in the seat, chief among the captains; the same was Adino the Eznite: he lifted up his spear against eight hundred, whom he slew at one time." (2 Sam. 23:8). When God calls a man to perform some special service in the interests of His kingdom and people, He also graciously raises up for him those who support his cause and strengthen his hands by using their influence on his behalf. Some of those helpers obtain the eye of the public, while others of them are far more in the background; but at the end each shall receive due recognition and proportionate honour. It was so here. David could never have won the victories he did, unless a kind Providence had supplied him with loyal and courageous officers. Nor had men like Luther and Cromwell performed such exploits unless supported by less conspicuous souls. Thus it has ever been, and still is. Even such a trivial work as the ministry of this book is only made possible by the co-operation of its readers.

The first one mentioned of David's mighty men is Adino the Eznite. He is described as "The Tachmonite that sat in the seat, chief among the captains," by which we understand that he presided over the counsels of war, being the king's chief military adviser. In addition to his wisdom, he was also endowed with extraordinary strength and valour, for it is here stated that he "lifted up his spear against eight hundred, whom he slew at one time." His case seems to have been one similar to that of Samson's — a man endued with supernatural strength. Typically, he reminds us of Paul, *the chief* of the apostles, who was not only enriched with unusual spiritual wisdom, but was mightier than any other in the pulling down of the strongholds of Satan; but whereas the one was famous for the taking of life, the other was instrumental in the communicating of life.

"And after him was Eleazar the son of Dodo the Ahohite, one of the mighty men with David, when they defied the Philistines that were there gathered together to battle, and the men of Israel were gonè away" (v. 9). Here is the second of David's worthies, one who acquitted himself courageously in an hour of urgent need. Nothing is said of him elsewhere, save in what some term "the parallel passage" of 1 Chron. 11. This son of Dodo was one of the heroic triumvirate that enabled their royal master to successfully defy the assembled Philistines, and that at a time when, for some reason or other, the king's army was "gone away." Eleazar refused to flee before the massed forces of the enemy, and he not only nobly stood his ground, but took the offensive, and with his confidence in the living God fell upon and slew hundreds of them.

The Spirit has placed special emphasis upon the noteworthiness of Eleazar's prowess by informing us it was exercised on an occasion when "the men of Israel had gone back." *That* is the time for true courage to be manifested. When through unbelief, lack of zeal, or the fear of man, the rank and file of professing Christians are giving way before the forces of evil, then is the opportunity for those who know and trust the Lord to be strong and do exploits. It does not require so much courage to engage the enemy when all our fellow-soldiers are enthusiastically advancing against them, but it takes considerable grit and boldness to attack an organized and powerful foe when almost all of our companions have lost heart and turned tail.

God esteems fidelity and holy zeal far more highly in a season of declension and apostasy than He does in a time of revival. A crisis not only tests, but reveals a man, as a heavy storm will make evident the trustworthiness or otherwise of a ship. What is here recorded to the lasting honour of Eleazar makes us think of the beloved Paul. Again and again he stood almost alone, yet he never made the defection of others an excuse for the abating of his own efforts. On one occasion he had to lament, "This thou knowest, that all they which are in Asia be turned away from me" (2 Tim. 1:15). Later, in the same epistle he wrote "At my first answer my man stood with me, but all men forsook me: I pray God that it may not be laid to their charge. Notwithstanding *the Lord* stood with me, and strengthened me" (4:16, 17). Let the servants of God to-day take heart from these blessed examples.

"He arose, and smote the Philistines until his hand was weary, and his hand clave unto the sword" (v. 10). Let it be duly noted that Eleazar did not stop when his work was half done, but went on prosecuting the same as long as he had any strength remaining. "Thus, in the service of God, we should keep us the willingness and resolution of the spirit, notwithstanding the weakness and weariness of the flesh; faint, yet pursuing (Judges 8:4); the hand weary, yet not quitting the sword" (M. Henry). Alas, in this age of ease and flabbiness, how readily we become discouraged and how quickly we give in to difficulties. O to heed that emphatic call "Be not weary in well doing: for in due season we shall reap, if we faint not" (Gal. 6:9). Such incidents as these are recorded not only for our information but also for our inspiration, that we should emulate their noble examples; otherwise they will put us to shame in the Day to come.

"And the Lord wrought a great victory that day." It is the *daring* of faith which He ever delights to honour, as He had so signally evidenced a few years previously, when David as a stripling had challenged and overcome the mighty Goliath. It is the *perseverance* of faith which the Lord always rewards, as was strikingly demonstrated after Israel had marched around the walls of Jericho thirteen times. No doubt God struck this army of the Philistines with a terror as great as the courage with which He had endowed this hero. It is ever God's way to work at both ends of the line: if He raises up a sower He also prepares the soil; if He inspires a servant with courage He puts fear into the hearts of those who oppose him. Observe how the glory of the victory is again ascribed to the Lord, and carefully compare Acts 14:27 and 21:19. "And the people returned after him only to spoil" (v. 10). How like human nature was this: they *returned* when there was "spoil" to be had!

"And after him was Shammah the son of Agee the Hararite. And the Philistines were gathered together into a troop, where was a piece of ground full of lentiles: and the people fled from the Philistines" (v. 11). This incident concerned an armed force of Israel's enemies who were out foraging, and who struck such terror into the hearts of the country side that the peaceful locals fled. But there was one who refused to yield unto the marauders, determined to defend the food supply of his people, and under God, he completely routed them. Here is another courageous man of whom we know nothing save for this brief reference: what a hint it furnishes that in the Day to come many a one will then have honour from God who received scant notice among his fellows. No matter how obscure the individual, or how inconspicuous his sphere of labour, nothing that is done in faith, no service performed for the good of His people, is forgotten by God. Surely this is one of the lessons written plain across this simple but striking narrative.

"But he stood in the midst of the ground, and defended it, and slew the Philistines: and the Lord wrought a great victory" (v. 12). How this reminds us of what is recorded in Acts 14:3: "Long time therefore abode they speaking *boldly* in the Lord, which gave testimony unto the Word of His grace, and granted signs and *wonders* to be done by their hands." Then let us heed that Divine injunction, "Be strong in the Lord, and in the power of His might. Put on the whole armour of God, that *ye* may be able to stand against the wiles of the devil" (Eph. 6:10, 11). Let us duly observe how, once more, the victory is ascribed to the Lord. No matter how great the ability and courage of the instruments, all praise for the achievement must be rendered alone unto God. "Let not the wise man glory in his wisdom, neither let the mighty man glory in his might, let not the rich man glory in his riches" (Jer. 9:23), for what has he that he did not first receive from above! How needful is this exhortation in such a day as ours, when pride is so much in the saddle and men's persons are "had in admiration." God is jealous of His glory and will not share it with the creature, and His Spirit is quenched if we do so.

And three of the thirty chief men went down and came to David in the harvest time into the cave of Adullam. And the troop of the Philistines pitched in the valley of Rephaim. And David was then in a stronghold, and the fort of the Philistines was then in Bethlehem. And David longed and said, Oh that someone would give me a drink from the water of the well of Bethlehem which is by the gate! And the three mighty men broke through the army of the Philistines, and drew water out of the well of Bethlehem, which was by the gate, and took it and brought it to David. Nevertheless he would not drink of it, but poured it out to the LORD. And he said, Be it far from me, O LORD, that I should do this — is this not the blood of the men who went in danger of their lives? Therefore he would not drink it. These three mighty men did these things. And Abishai the brother of Joab, the son of Zeruiah, was chief among three. And he lifted up his spear against three hundred and killed them, and had the name among three. Was he not most honouable of three? Therefore he was their captain. However he did not attain to the first three. And also Benaiah the son of Jehoiada, the son of a mighty man, of Kabzeel, who had done many acts — he killed two lion-like men of Moab. He also went down and killed a lion in the middle of a pit in time of snow. And he killed an Egyptian, a goodly man. And the Egyptian had a spear in his hand, but he went down to him with a staff and plucked the spear out of the Egyptian's hand. And he killed him with his own spear. These Benaiah the son of Jehoiada did, and had the name among three mighty men. He was more honorable than the thirty, but he did not attain to the first three. And David set him over his guard. Asahel the brother of Joab was one of the thirty. So were Elhanan the son of Dodo of Bethlehem — Shammah the Harodite — Elika the Harodite — Helez the Paltite — Ira the son of Ikkesh the Tekoite — Abiezer the Anethothite — Mebunnai the Hushathite — Zalmon the Ahohite — Maharai the Netophathite — Heleb the son of Baanah, a Netophathite — Ittai the son of Ribai out of Gibeah of the children of Benjamin — Benaiah the Pirathonite — Hiddai of the brooks of Gaash — Abialbon the Arbathite, Azmaveth the Barhumite — Eliahba the Shaalbonite, of the sons of Jashen-Jonathan — Shammah the Hararite — Ahiam the son of Sharar the Hararite — Eliphelet the son of Ahasbai, the son of Maachathite — Eliam the son of Ahithophel the Gilonite — Hezrai the Carmelite — Paarai the Arbite — Igal the son of Nathan of Zabah — Bani the Gadite — Zelek the Ammonite — Naharai the Beerothite, armor-bearer to Joab the son of Zeruiah — Ira an Ithrite — Gareb an Ithrite — Uriah the Hittite — thirty- seven in all. — II Samuel 23:13-39.

2 Sam. 23 supplies a vivid illustration of the great variety of spiritual gifts and graces which God bestows upon His people in general and on His ministers in particular. All are not called to engage in the same specific form of service, and therefore all are not alike qualified. We see this principle exemplified in the natural sphere. Some have a special aptitude for certain avocations, while others are fitted for entirely different ones: those who find it easy to work a typewriter or keep books, would be quite out of their element if they attempted to do the work of a farmer or carpenter. So it is in the spiritual realm: one is called to some particular sphere and is endowed accordingly, while another is appointed to a different function and is suitably equipped for it; and naught but confusion would follow if the latter attempted to discharge the duties of the former.

"Every man hath his proper gift of God: one after this manner, and another after that" (1 Cor. 7:7), but whether our talents be more or fewer it is our duty to use and improve the same for the good of our generation. "But all these worketh that one and the selfsame Spirit, dividing to every man severally as He will" (1 Cor. 12:11), and therefore we must be content with the gifts and position which God has allotted us, neither despising those below nor envying those above us. There are various degrees of usefulness and eminence among Christians, just as there were different grades of honour among those worthies of David. Of one of them we read, "Therefore he was their captain, howbeit he attained not unto the first three" (v. 19), and later in the chapter we are given a list of another thirty who occupied a yet lower rank. First in eminence were the apostles; next to them were the Reformers; and below them are those who have followed during the last four centuries.

Throughout the long and checkered career of David there were two things to cheer and comfort him: the unchanging faithfulness of God and the loving devotedness of his servants. Another has pointed out that at the close of Paul's career he had the same spring of solace to draw from. "In his second epistle to Timothy he glances at the condition of things around him: he sees the 'great house', which assuredly was not so with God as He required it; he sees all that were in Asia turned away from him; he sees Hymeneus and Philetus teaching false doctrine, and overthrowing the faith of some; he sees Alexander the coppersmith doing much mischief; he sees many with itching ears, heaping to themselves teachers, and turning away from the truth to fables; he sees the perilous times setting in with fearful rapidity; in a word, he sees the whole fabric, humanly speaking, going to pieces; but he, like David, resting in the assurance that 'the foundation of God standeth sure', and he was also cheered by the individual devotedness of some mighty man or other, who, by the grace of God, was standing faithful amid the wreck. He remembered the faith of a Timothy, the love of an Onesiphorus; and moreover, he was cheered by the fact there would be a company of faithful men in the darkest times who would call on the Lord out of a pure heart."

In the preceding section we called attention to the logical connection of 2 Sam. 23 with the previous chapter, where "the last words of David" (his final inspired and official message) are recorded. We may also notice that our present passage comes immediately after David's reference to the "Everlasting Covenant" which Jehovah had made with him (v. 5). How significant is this, and what blessed instruction it conveys to us. The two things are intimately, yea inseparably connected: the eternal counsels of God's grace and His providing us with all needed assistance while we are in a time state. In other words, that "Everlasting Covenant" which God made with His elect in the person of their Head guarantees the supply of their every need in this world, the interposition of the Lord on their behalf wherever required, and the raising up of faithful friends to help in each hour of emergency. Thus David found it, as the verses before us amply demonstrate.

If the Spirit of God has been pleased to chronicle some of the bravest exploits of David himself, He has not been altogether silent upon the heroic achievements of those who stood loyally by him when he was menaced by his numerous foes. This too adumbrated something yet more blessed in connection with the antitypical David and His officers. Some of their deeds of devotion may not be known among men, or at most little valued by them, but they are recognised and recorded by *God*, and will yet be publicly proclaimed from His throne. We should have known nothing of these deeds of David's worthies had not the Spirit here described them. So, many a heart which now throbs with affection for Christ of which the world is not cognizant, and many a hand which is stretched forth in service to Him which is unnoticed by the churches, will not pass unheeded in the Day to come.

In our last section we dwelt upon the exploits of the first triumvirate of David's mighty men — Adino, Eleazar and Shammah (vv. 8-12): our present passage opens with a most touching incident which records (we believe) another heroic enterprise in which the same three men acted together. We are told "And three of the thirty chiefs went down and came to David in the harvest time into the cave of Adullam: and the troop of the Philistines pitched in the valley of Rephaim" (v. 13). This most probably takes us back to what is narrated in 1

Sam. 22, when the uncrowned son of Jesse was a fugitive from the murderous designs of King Saul. It was not, then, in the hour of his popularity and power that these three officers betook themselves unto David, but in the time of his humiliation and weakness, while taking refuge in a cave, that they espoused his cause. No fair weather friends were these, but disinterested and unselfish supporters.

"And David was then in a hold, and the garrison of the Philistines was then in Bethlehem" (v. 14). How strangely varied is the lot of those who are beloved of God! what ups and downs in their experience and circumstances! Bethlehem was the place where David was born — presaging the incarnation of his Son the Lord; but now it was occupied by the enemies of God and His people: how many a dwellingplace which once gave shelter to an eminent servant of God is now the abode of worldlings. From the fertility and peacefulness of Bethlehem David was forced to flee and seek refuge in a cave: then let us not be cast down if a lowly and uncongenial habitation be our portion. But David was not forgotten by the Lord, and He graciously moved the hearts of others to seek him out and proffer their loving service. Take heart, then, lonesome believer: if God does not raise up earthly friends for thee, He will doubly endear Himself to thine heart.

"And David longed, and said, Oh that one would give me drink of the water of the well of Bethlehem, which is by the gate!" (v. 15). Some of the Puritans believed that David was not here expressing his desire for literal water, but rather for the Messiah Himself, who was to be born at Bethlehem. Though this does not appear to be borne out by what follows, yet it is surely significant that such excellent and desirable water was to be found there. Bethlehem means "the house of bread," and as the Lord Jesus declared, He is in His own blessed person both the Bread of Life and the Water of Life — the sustainer and refresher of the new man. Personally, we agree with Matthew Henry that what is recorded in this verse "seems to have been an instance of his weakness," when he was dissatisfied with what Divine providence had supplied, giving way to inordinate affection and yielding to the desires of mere nature.

It was summer time, when the weather was hot and trying, and David was thirsty. Perhaps good water was scarce at Adullam, and therefore David earnestly cried "Oh that one would give me drink of the water of the well of Bethlehem." Ture, it is natural to hanker after those things which Providence withholds, and such hankering is often yielded to even by godly men in an unguarded hour, which leads to various snares and evils. "David strangely indulged a humour which he could give no reason for. It is folly to entertain such fancies, and greater folly to insist upon the gratification of them. We ought to check our affections when they go out inordinately toward those things which are more pleasant and grateful than others" (Matt. Henry). The best way, and perhaps the only one, of doing this is by heeding that injunction "giving thanks always for all things unto God" (Eph. 5:20), thereby evidencing we are content with such things as we have — instead of lusting after those we have not.

"And the three mighty men brake through the host of the Philistines, and drew water out of the well of Bethlehem, that was by the gate, and took it, and brought it to David" (v. 16). What proof this gave of how highly these brave men valued their leader, and how ready they were to face the greatest of dangers in his service. It must be remembered that at this time David was uncrowned, a fugitive from Saul, and in no position to reward their valorous efforts on his behalf. Moreover, no command had been issued, no one in particular was commissioned to obtain the water from Bethlehem: it was enough for them that their beloved master desired it. How little they feared the Philistines: so absorbed were they in seeking to please David, that terror of the enemy had no, place in their hearts! Do they not put all of us to shame? How feeble in comparison is our devotedness to the antitypical David! How trifling the obstacles which confront us from the peril which menaced them.

"Nevertheless he would not drink thereof, but poured it out unto the Lord" (v. 16). Very blessed is this, and a lovely sequel to what has just been before us. Those three men had spontaneously responded to the known wish of their leader, and, not counting their lives dear unto themselves, they had — whether by use of the sword or by strategy we are not told, but most likely the former — obtained and brought back to David the longed-for refreshment. Such devotion to his person and such daring on their part was not lost upon David, and being recovered from his carnal lapse and seeing things now with a spiritual discernment, he deemed that water a sacrifice too costly for any but Jehovah Himself, and hence he would not suffer the sweet odour of it to be intercepted in its ascent to the throne of God.

"And he said, Be it far from me, O Lord, that I should do this: is not this the blood of the men that went in jeopardy of their lives? therefore he would not drink it. These things did these three mighty men" (v. 17). This is ever one of the marks of a gracious man. When he is conscious of making a mistake or committing folly, he does not feign ignorance or innocence, but acknowledges and seeks to correct the same. The outstanding characteristic of regeneration is that where this miracle of grace is wrought an *honest heart* is ever the evidence of the same. It is those who are under the full sway of Satan who are crafty, deceitful, and serpentine in their ways. Those whom Christ saves He conforms unto His image, and *He* was without guile. David was now ashamed of his inordinate desire and rash wish, and regretted exposing his brave officers to such peril on his behalf. This is another mark of the genuine child of God: he is not wholly wrapped up in himself.

Sin and self are synonymous terms for as someone has quaintly pointed out the centre of SIN is "I," that is why when the Church confesses "all we like sheep have gone astray," she defines it by saying "we have turned every one to *his own* way." If sin and selfishness are synonymous, grace and unselfishness are inseparable, for when the love of God is shed abroad in the heart there is awakened a genuine concern for the good of our fellows, and therefore will the Christian seek to refrain from what would injure them. "Upon reflection and experience, a wise man will be ashamed of his folly, and will abstain not only from unlawful indulgences, but from those also which are inexpedient and might expose his brethren to temptation and danger." (Thos. Scott).

"And Abishai, the brother of Joab, the son of Zeruiah was chief among three. And he lifted up his spear against three hundred, and slew them, and had the name among three" (v. 18). We are not here informed when or where this extraordinary feat was accomplished, but from the analogy supplied by the other examples in this chapter, we know it was performed by Divine enablement, for the public good, and in the service of David. It is solemn to note that Abishai's more famous, and yet infamous, brother, has no place in this role of honour, illustrating the solemn truth that if "the memory of the just is blessed" yet "the name of the wicked shall rot." "Was he not most honourable of the three? therefore he was their captain: howbeit he attained not unto the first three" (v. 19). These degrees of eminence and esteem exemplify the fact that men are not designed to all occupy a common level: the theory of "socialism" receives no countenance from Scripture.

"And Benaiah the son of Jehoiada, the son of a valiant man, of Kabzeel, who had done many acts, he slew two lionlike men of Moab" (v. 20). It is good to see the sons walking in the steps of their sires when a noble example has been set before them: God takes notice of the one as much as the other. Those men of Moab might be fierce and powerful, but nothing daunted, Benaiah went forth and slew them. This too is recorded for our encouragement: no matter how strong and furious be our lusts, in the strength of the Lord we must attack and mortify them. "He went down also and slew a lion in the midst of a pit in time of snow" (v. 20). Amid the frosts of winter our zeal is not to be relaxed. Nor must the soldiers of Christ expect to always have plain sailing: even when engaged in the best cause of all, formidable obstacles will be encountered, and the soldiers of Christ must learn to endure hardness and aquit themselves like men.

"And he slew an Egyptian, a goodly man: and the Egyptian had a spear in his hand; but he went down to him with a staff, and plucked the spear out of the Egyptian's hand and slew him with his own spear" (v. 21). If his slaying of the lion is a figure of the servant of Christ successfully resisting the Devil (1 Pet. 5:8), his vanquishing of this Egyptian (spoken of in 1 Chron. 11:23 as a "man of great stature") may well be regarded as a type of the minister of God overcoming the world, for in Scripture "Egypt" is ever a symbol of that system which is hostile to God and His people. And how is victory over the world obtained? We need go no farther than this verse to learn the secret: by maintaining *our pilgrim character*, for the "staff" is the emblem of the pilgrim. If the heart be fixed upon that fair Land to which we are journeying, then the shows of this "vanity fair" will possess no attraction for it. The world is overcome by "faith" (1 John 5:4): a faith which grasps the good of God's promises enables us to reject the evils of this world.

"These things did Benaiah the son of Jehoiada, and had the name among three mighty men. He was more honourable than the thirty, but he attained not to the first three. And David set him over his guard" (vv. 22, 23). Once again we are reminded that there is a gradation among the creatures and servants of God: there is no such thing as equality even among the angels. How wrong it is, then, for any of us to be dissatisfied with the status and position which the sovereign will of God has assigned to us: let us rather seek grace from Him to faithfully discharge our duties, however exalted or lowly be our station in life. Our chapter ends with a list of thirty men who were in the third grade: the first being Asahel (v. 24) and the last Uriah (v. 30), the former being murdered by Joab and the latter being sent to his death by David — deliverance from one danger is no guarantee that we shall escape from another.

CHAPTER 24.

And again the anger of the LORD was kindled against Israel, and He moved David against them to say, Go count Israel and Judah. For the king said to Joab the captain of the army, who was with him, Go around through all the tribes of Israel, from Dan to Beer-sheba, and count the people so that I may know the number of the people. And Joab said to the king, Now may the LORD your God add to the people however many they be, a hundred times as many, and may it be that the eyes of my lord the king may see. But why does my lord the king delight in this thing? But the king's word prevailed against Joab, and against the captains of the army. And Joab and the captains of the army went out from the presence of the king to number the people of Israel. And they passed over Jordan and pitched in Aroer, on the right side of the city that lies in the middle of the river of Gad, and toward Jazer. Then they came to Gilead, and to the land of Tahtim-hodshi. And they came to Dan-jaan, and around to Sidon. And they came to the stronghold of Tyre and to all the cities of the Hivites and of the Canaanites. And they went out to the south of Judah, to Beer-sheba. So when they had gone through all the land, they came to Jerusalem at the end of nine months and twenty days. And Joab gave up the sum of the number of the people to the king. And there were in Israel eight hundred thousand strong men who drew the sword. And the men of Judah were five hundred thousand men. — II Samuel 24:1-9.

We are about to look at one more of the dark chapters in David's life, though it has a much brighter ending than had some of the others. It concerns an episode which though simple and plain in some of its features, is in other respects shrouded in deep mystery; nor do we profess to be able to fully solve it. The incident which is narrated in 2 Sam. 24 concerns the purpose which David formed for numbering Israel and Judah, in order that he might know the exact fighting strength of his people. Apparently this was quite an innocent undertaking, yet it promply met with disfavour and opposition from the commander and officers of his army. A little later David himself acknowledged that therein he had "sinned greatly," and the Lord Himself manifested His sore displeasure by slaying no less than seventy thousand of his men by a pestilence.

On two occasions the Lord Himself had directed Moses to number the people. First in connection with their encampment in the Wilderness (Num. 1), and later it was enjoined with special reference to the allotments which the different tribes were to receive in Canaan (Num. 26:2). On each occasion Moses numbered the male Israelites from twenty years old and upwards, "all that were able to go forth to war" — the fighting strength of the Congregation being thereby ascertained. We mention this because it would thus appear that David had clear precedent to warrant his procedure. It is true that after Israel settled in Canaan God never again issued a command for His people to be numbered, and while we are not informed that He gave any such order to our hero at this time, yet we *are* told that the Lord "moved David against them to say, Go, number Israel and Judah" (v. 1).

We are not left in any doubt that on this occasion David committed a grave fault, yet wherein lay the *evil* of it is not so certain. Varied indeed have been the conjectures formed and the explanations advanced by different writers thereon. Some have drawn the inference from 1 Chron. 27:23, 24 that David's sin lay in numbering those who were *under* twenty years old (yet sufficiently developed as to be able to bear arms), and that because his act was thus illegal it was not

573

formally entered in the state records. Others conclude from the same passage that he erred in numbering the people at all, that his act sprang from *unbelief* in the promises of God to the patriarchs that their seed should be as innumerable as the sand of the seashore. Others think that he was guilty of *presumption*, acting without any instruction from God. Others think that the fault lay in his failure to require the half shekel, which was to be paid for the service of the sanctuary when the people were numbered, as "a ransom for their souls" (Ex. 30:12).

Now we are not one of those who take pleasure in pitting the interpretations of one expositor against another, rather do we prefer to combine them when this seems permissible and helpful. In the absence of any authoritative word from God as to the precise nature of David's sin in the case before us, we shall, as we proceed to comment upon it, bear in mind these several views, which may well supplement each other. One other explanation has been advanced, which impresses us personally most strongly of all, namely, that it was *pride of heart* which moved Israel's king to here commit such folly. If he was intoxicated with the successes which Heaven had granted to his arms, and was more occupied with them than their Giver, then that would readily account for this disastrous lapse, for "pride goeth before destruction, and a haughty spirit before a fall."

Some light may be cast on this mysterious episode by taking into account the relative period in David's history at which it occurred. As the previous chapters have informed us, the sword of David and of Israel had been successful over all their enemies. The Philistines had been subdued, Moab had brought gifts, garrisons had been stationed in Damascus, and the Syrians as well as the Edomites had become their servants. To such a remarkable extent had his arms been permitted to triumph, that we are told, "And the fame of David went out into all lands; and the Lord brought the fear of him upon all nations" (1 Chron. 14:17). Naught of the good of which Jehovah had spoken to him had failed. But David was human, a man of like passions with us. Man — no matter who he be — if left to himself is quite incapable of holding a blessing, as was clearly demonstrated in Eden at the beginning. The fuller be our cup of joy, the steadier the hand required to hold it.

The history of David's sin is stated thus, "And again the anger of the Lord was kindled against Israel, and He moved David against them to say, Go, number Israel and Judah" (2 Sam. 24:1), or as 1 Chron. 21:1 gives it, "And Satan stood up against Israel, and provoked David to number Israel." Those two statements are not, as some have foolishly supposed, contradictory, but are complementary. Though God is not the Author of sin, and can never be charged with evil, yet as the Governor of the universe He is the Controller and Director of it, so that when it serves His righteous purpose even Satan and his hosts are requisitioned by Him: 1 Kings 22:20-22; Ezek. 14:9, etc. In this instance it is clear at least that God permitted Satan to tempt David, and David being left to himself yielded to the temptation and sinned. Moreover, the fact that David yielded so readily, and so obstinately rejected the counsel of his servants, seems to indicate that he had not been walking with holy watchfulness before God.

It was a remarkable juncture in the history of David. The ancient foes of Israel, after centuries of conflict, had at last succumbed. Even the powerful sons of Goliath had been so crushed by his vanquisher that they no longer made any effort to antagonize. But not only had the surrounding nations been subdued, they were despoiled, and the huge quantities of gold which had been taken from them was dedicated unto the Lord (see 1 Chron. 18:11; 20:4). "Triumphs had been gained and a rest attained such as Israel had never known before. The sword was about to be sheathed and the reign of Solomon (the typical Prince of

Peace) was at hand. The Ark of God, ceasing from its lengthy wanderings, was no longer to dwell in curtains. The Temple was about to be built. Israel was to be gathered there in solemn and associated worship, and God's house was to be filled with His glory. It was a bright and blessed era, but it was only a typical and shadowy one" (B. W. Newton).

Ah, that was the very point: this wonderful juncture in Israel's history was but "a typical and a shadowy" one, and therefore it made all the difference whether it were viewed by the eye of faith or with the eye of sense. To those who contemplated it with the eye of faith, and saw therein a blessed foreshadowment of a yet distant future, it afforded holy encouragement, strengthening them in patient endurance and hope. But to those who looked upon this successful period with the eye of sense, it could prove only a snare. As another has pointed out, "When the feelings of nature predominate (and they always do predominate when faith is not in vigorous exercise), triumph or success even when recognised as a gift of God's undeserved mercy, will, nevertheless, be so used as to exalt ourselves. As weeds flourish under sunshine and showers, so when there is not watchfulness, the tendencies of our nature germinate under mercies."

This, it seems to us, is the chief practical lesson inculcated by our present passage. It points a most solemn warning against *the dangers of success*. If adversity carries with it a measure of menace to the spiritual life, the perils of prosperity are far greater. If through our unwatchfulness the former leads to discontent and murmuring, the latter will, unless we be doubly on our guard, issue in self-complacency and self-sufficiency. It is when we are brought low, by losses and trials, that we are the most cast upon God; as it is when success crowns our efforts and our barns are well filled, that we are most apt to walk independently of Him. Little wonder, then, that the Lord intrusts few of His people with much of this world's goods. The same applies to spiritual blessings: if earnests of a coming rest are granted, they will be regarded as realities instead of foreshadowings, and then we shall rest before our time to rest be come — instead of continuing to press forward.

It seems likely that David had fallen into this snare, encouraging imaginations which were completely at variance with the actual facts of both his own and Israel's actual condition: that is, utterly inconsistent with the truth that their national prosperity was but typical and transitory. In the first place, to number the people was but the natural act of one who had persuaded himself that Israel had entered upon a period of stable and permanent rest. In the second place, to number the people was an act indicative of ownership, and it was obviously wrong for David to regard Israel as though they were *his* people, whom it was legitimate to number as *his* inheritance and strength. Instead, he should have viewed them as the congregation and inheritance of Jehovah, to be numbered only when He gave the command. Finally, he ought to have looked upon them as Jehovah's *redeemed* inheritance, and therefore never to be numbered without a typical ransom for the soul of each being rendered to God.

The Divine statute was very definite on this point: "When thou takest the sum of the children of Israel after their number, then shall they give every man *a ransom for his soul* unto the Lord, when thou numberest them; that there be no plague among them, when thou numberest them. . .And thou shalt take the atonement money of the children of Israel and shalt appoint it for the service of the tabernacle of the congregation, that it may be a memorial unto the children of Israel before the Lord to make an atonement for your souls" (Ex. 30:12, 16). "The very mention of the 'atonement money' was sufficient to banish every feeling of pride or independency both from him who numbered and from those who were numbered amongst the congregation of Jehovah: for 'according to Jehovah's fear so is His wrath': that is, the nearer we draw to Jehovah to fear and to serve Him, the more do we supply occasions for His displeasure and wrath, for the higher and holier the service, the more does our natural sinful incompetency appear.

"The very fact of being His congregation, appointed to draw nigh to Him and serve Him in His holiness, must entail chastisement and plague on all numbered as His people, unless atonement interposed and provided a ransom for the soul. If David unbidden, and in unholy elation of heart presumed to number Israel as if there had been in them a strength that needed not to fear any chastisement, or dread any abasement, it is no wonder that the atonement money would have been withheld. It seems to have been utterly forgotten. No mention is made thereof. He seems not to have recollected the words 'that there be no *plague* among them when thou numberest them.' Israel was numbered as if they could forego that protection of grace which the atonement money signified, and stand firm on the basis of that strength which in their recent triumphs had been so marvellously exhibited" (B.W. Newton).

But we must now look at this strange and solemn incident from another angle, from the side presented to us in 1 Chron. 21:1, where we are permitted a glimpse behind the veil: "And Satan stood up against Israel, and provoked David to number Israel." Expositors have pointed out that these words "stood up" (carefully compare Zech. 3:1) have a forensic force, being an expression which alludes to the posture of those who accuse or charge another person with a crime in a court of law. In Rev. 12:10 Satan is expressly designated "the accuser of our brethren," which office we behold him discharging in Job. 1:9-12. All these passages are admittedly deeply mysterious, yet in the light of them it appears that the spiritual condition of Israel at this time gave the Adversary an advantage, and that he promptly used the same by representing their condition to the Lord as a reason why they should be *punished.*This seems to be clearly borne out by the terms of 2 Sam. 24:1.

"And again the anger of the Lord was kindled against Israel, and He moved David *against them* to say, Go, number Israel and Judah." "The Israelites had offended God by their ungrateful and repeated rebellions against David, by not duly profiting under the means employed for the revival of religion; and probably by that pride, luxury, and ungodliness, which generally springs from great prosperity. They had before, in a famine which lasted three years, experienced the effects of the Divine displeasure, and it is likely they had not been amended by the correction: but some think that the sin immediately intended was the setting up of Absalom for king, and rebelling against David. This, David had cordially forgiven; but it was a national defection from God, which He did not judge it proper to leave unpunished. So that 'again the anger of the Lord was kindled against Israel', and He permitted Satan to tempt and prevail against David, that in *chastising* him, He might *punish* them" (Thos. Scott).

The Nation at large was not made up of those who walked by faith and trode the path of the Divine statutes. Very far from it, as is clearly intimated by David's prayer, "Help Lord, for the godly man ceaseth; for the faithful fail from among the children of men" (Psa. 12:1). From 2 Sam. 23:6 it is also plain that the "sons of Belial" were strong and numerous in the midst of Israel, so that we need not be surprised that the signal triumphs which had been vouchsafed them should have awakened in the hearts of the majority a proud and self-sufficient arrogance, which was bound to affect their fellows, and which thus called forth the sore displeasure of God. Nothing gives Satan so easy an approach to and such an advantage over us as when we are swelled by a sense of our self-importance. Few things are more detestable unto God than a heart that is inflated by egotism: note how the seven things which He hates is headed by "A proud look" (Prov. 6:16-19). How urgently we need to heed the exhortation of Christ and take His yoke upon us and learn of Him who is "meek and lowly in heart."

It is indeed solemn to see one so near the end of his earthly pilgrimage, one who had (in the main) for so many years walked so closely with God, now giving place to the Devil and being overcome by him. What proof is this that neither age nor experience is (in itself) any safeguard against his attacks. As long as the believer is in this world the great Enemy of our Souls has access to us, is often permitted to work upon our corruptions, and under certain restrictions to tempt us. And therefore it is we are called upon to "Humble yourselves therefore under the mighty hand of God, that He may exalt you in due time: casting all your care upon Him, for He careth for you, Be sober, be vigilant; because your adversary the Devil, as a roaring lion, walketh about, seeking whom he may devour: whom resist steadfast in the faith" (1 Pet. 5: 6-8). We have purposely quoted the whole of that passage because it is imperative that we heed the order of its several precepts: we cannot obey those in v. 8 unless and until we respond to those in vv. 6, 7.

There never comes a time, then, when the saint on earth can dispense with any part of the armour which God has provided, nor when he may relax his vigilance against his untiring and remorseless Adversary. If the time of youth be dangerous because of hot passions, the season of old age is imperilled by the surgings of pride: therefore must we watch and pray always lest we enter into temptation. And, the higher be the rank of the saint, the more important and influential be the office he holds, then the greater is his need to be doubly on his guard. It has ever been Satan's way to level his principal attacks against those who are eminent for usefulness, knowing full well that if he can encompass *their* downfall, many others will be involved either in his sin or in his sufferings.

The Word of God supplies us with two separate accounts of David's sin in numbering the people: one in 2 Sam. 24 and the other in 1 Chron. 21, and both of them need to be carefully pondered by us if we are to have the advantage of all the light the Lord has vouchsafed us on this mysterious incident. Infidels have appealed to these two chapters in an endeavour to show that the Scriptures are unreliable, but their efforts to do so are utterly vain: what they, in their blindness, suppose to be discrepancies are in reality supplementary details, which enable us to obtain a more comprehensive view of the various factors entering into this incident. Thus once more God taketh the wise in their own craftiness and makes the wrath of man to praise Him, for the attempt of His enemies to pit 1 Chron. against 2 Sam. 24 has served to call the attention of many of His people to a companion passage which otherwise they had probably overlooked.

The first help which 1 Chron. 21 affords us is to indicate the moral connection between David's folly and that which *preceded* it. 1 Chron. 21 opens with the word "And," which bids us look at the immediate context — one which is quite different from that of 2 Sam. 24. 1 Chron. 20 closes with "These were born unto the giant in Gath; and they fell by the hand of David, and by the hand of his servants" (v. 8). That closes a record of notable exploits and victories which David and his mighty men had obtained over their foes. And then we read, "And Satan stood up against Israel, and provoked David to number Israel" (1 Chron.

21:1). Is not the connection obvious; flushed with his successes the heart of David was lifted up, and thus the door was opened for Satan to successfully tempt him. Let us seek to constantly bear in mind that, the only place where we are safe from a fall is to lie in the dust before God.

Some have wondered wherein lay David's sin in taking this military census. But is it not plain that, as king over all Israel and victorious over all his enemies, he wished to know the full numerical strength of the Nation? — losing sight of the fact that his strength lay wholly in that One who had multiplied his power and given him such success. Would it not also serve to strike terror into the hearts of the surrounding nations for there to be publicly proclaimed the vast number of men capable of taking up arms that David had under him? But if this was one of the motives which actuated the king, it was equally unnecessary and unworthy of him, for God is well able to cause His fear to fall upon those who oppose us without any fleshly efforts of ours to that end — efforts which would deprive Him of the glory were He to grant them success. What honour does *the Lord* get as the Protector of any nation while they boast of and rely on the vastness of their armaments?

But David was far from being alone in this folly, for as 2 Sam. 24:1 tells us, "And again the anger of the Lord was kindled *against Israel*, and He moved David against them." The Lord had a controversy with the Nation. He had dealt governmentally with David and his house (chaps. 12-21), as He had likewise with Saul and his house (21), and now His grievance is more immediately with Israel, whom He chastised through the act of their king — the "again" looks back to 1 Chron. 21:1. No one particular sin of Israel's is mentioned, but from David's Psalms we have little difficulty in ascertaining the general state of his subjects. Ever prone to remove their eyes from Jehovah, there is little room for doubt that the temporal successes which God had granted them became an occasion to them of self-congratulation, and like the children of this world, in the unbelief of self-confidence, they were occupied with their own resources.

The second help which 1 Chron. 21 affords us is the information which it supplies that *Satan* was instrumental in moving David to commit this great folly. Not that this in any wise excused David or modified his guilt, but because it casts light on the governmental ways of God. "In the righteous government of God rulers and their subjects have a reciprocal influence on one another. Like the members in the human body, they are interested in each other's conduct and welfare; and cannot sin or suffer without mutually affecting each other. When the wickedness of nations provokes God, He leaves princes to adopt pernicious measures, or to commit atrocious crimes, which bring calamities on the people: and when the ruler commits iniquity, he is punished by the diminuation of his power, and by witnessing the distresses of his subjects. Instead therefore of mutual recriminations under public calamities, however occasioned, all parties should be reminded to repent of their own sins, and to practise their own duties. Princes should hence be instructed, even for their own sakes, to repress wickedness and to promote righteousness in their dominions, as well as to set a good example: and the people, for the public benefit, should concur in salutary measures, and pray continually for their rulers." (T. Scott).

The solemn principles which are illustrated in the above quotation are of wide ramification and go far to explain many a painful incident which often surely puzzles the righteous. For example, only the Day to come will reveal how many ministers were permitted by God to fall into public disgrace because He had a controversy with *the churches* over which they were set as pastors. God left David to himself to be tempted by Satan because He was displeased with his subjects and determined to chastise them. In like manner, He has left more than one minister of the Gospel to himself, to be tried and tripped up by the Devil, because He had a grievance against the people he served, so that in the fall of their leader the pride of the people was humiliated. Yet, be it said emphatically, this is in nowise a case of making the *innocent* suffer because of the guilty: the pride of David's own heart left him an easy prey to the Enemy.

"For the king said to Joab the captain of the host, which was with him, Go now through all the tribes of Israel, from Dan even to Beersheba, and number ye the people, that I may know the number of people. And Joab said unto the king, Now the Lord thy God add unto the people, how many so ever they be, a hundredfold, and that the eyes of my lord the king may see it: but why doth my lord the king delight in this thing?" (2 Sam. 24:2, 3). From the human side of things, it seems strange that Joab should have been the one to demur against David's act of vain glory. As we have seen in earlier chapters, Joab was a man of blood and eminently one of the children of this world, as the whole of his career makes plain; yet was he quick to see, on this occasion, that the step David proposed to take was one fraught with grave danger, and therefore did he earnestly remonstrate with the king.

It is indeed striking to find that this infatuation of David was met by an objection from the commander of his army. Not that it was the ungodliness of David's project which filled Joab with horror: rather that he realised the impolity of it. As we pointed out in the preceding section, after Israel entered into Canaan God never gave a command for the numbering of His people, and there was no occasion now for a military census to be taken. Joab was conscious of that and expostulated with his master, being wiser in his generation. This serves to illustrate a solemn principle: many a man of the world exercises more common sense than does a saint who is out of communion with God and under the power of Satan. This fact is written large across the pages of Holy Writ and a number of examples will no doubt come to mind if the reader meditates thereon.

The force of Joab's objection to David's plan was, why take delight in such a thing as ascertaining the precise numerical strength of your army, and thereby run the danger of bringing down Divine judgment upon us? Thus this child of the world perceived what David did not. Most solemn is the lesson which is here pointed for the Christian. It is in *God's light* that we "see light" (Psa. 36:9), and when we turn away from Him we are left in spiritual darkness. And as the Lord Jesus exclaimed, "If therefore the light that is in thee be darkness, how great is that darkness!" (Matt. 6:23). A believer who is out of fellowship with the Lord will make the most stupid blunders and engage in crass folly such as a shrewd unbeliever would disdain. This is part of the price which he has to pay for wandering from the narrow path.

But we must now look at Joab's opposition of David's plan from the *Divine* side. Had David been walking with holy watchfulness before the Lord he had not yielded so readily to Satan's temptation, still less had he been prepared to act contrary to the express requirements of Ex. 30:12-16. Nevertheless, God did not now utterly forsake David and give him up fully to his heart's lusts. Instead, He placed an obstacle in his path, in the form of Joab's (probably, most unexpected) opposition, which rebuked his folly, and rendered his sin still more excuseless. Behold here, then, the wondrous mingling of the workings of Divine sovereignty and the enforcing of human responsibility. God decreed that Pilate should pass the death-sentence upon Christ, yet He gave him a most emphatic deterrent through his wife (Matt. 27:19). In like manner, it was God's purpose to chastise Israel through the folly of their king, yet so far from approving of

David's act He rebuked him through Joab.

Yes, remarkable indeed are the varied factors entering into this equation, the different actors in this strange drama. If on the one hand the Lord suffered Satan to tempt His servant, on the other hand He caused Joab to deter him. It was David's refusal to listen to Joab — backed up by his officers (v. 4) — which rendered his sin the greater. And is not the practical lesson plain for us! When we are meditating folly and a man of the world counsels us against it, it is high time for us to "consider our ways." When the merciful providence of God places a hindrance in our path, even though it be in the form of a rebuke from an unbeliever, we should pause in our madness, for we are in imminent danger to ourselves and probably to others as well.

"Notwithstanding the king's word prevailed against Joab, and against the captains of the host" (v. 4). Joab perceived that David's purpose sprang from carnal ambition and that it was against the public interest, and accordingly he remonstrated with him. When that failed he summoned to his aid the additional pleas of the captains of the army. But all in vain. David's mind was fully made up, and in self-will he committed this grievous sin. "When the mind, instead of taking a comprehensive view of all the circumstances before it, persists in viewing them partially in some favourite aspect, it is astonishing how blind it may become to things obvious as the day to every one who has no such bias to warp his judgment. David's soul, whilst absorbed in contemplating the might and triumphs of Israel, had no desire to consider other circumstances, the consideration of which would leave on the heart a sense of weakness — not of strength" (B.W. Newton).

How merciful is God to raise up those who oppose us when we anticipate doing that which is displeasing to Him! Yet how often, in the pride of our hearts and the stubbornness of our wills do we resent such opposition. Everything that enters our lives contains a message from God if only we will pause and listen to it, and many a thorny path should we have escaped if only we had heeded that hedge which Divine providence placed in our way. That hedge may take the form of a friendly word of advice from those around us, and though we are far from suggesting that we should always follow out the same, yet it is for our good that we prayerfully weigh it before God. If we do not, and in our self-will force our way through that hedge, then we must not be surprised if we get badly torn in the process. How much better had it been both for David and his subjects to have responded to the council of Joab and his officers.

"And Joab and the captain of the host went out from the presence of the king. to number the people of Israel" (v. 4). On other occasions Joab had lent himself readily to the furthering of the king's evil designs (2 Sam. 11:16; 14:1, 2), but at this time he carried out his orders with great reluctance. How strongly he was opposed to David's policy appears from "the king's word was abominable to Joab" (1 Chron. 21:6). The service on which Joab now embarked was most distasteful to him, nevertheless he carried it out, for it was "of the Lord" (as v. 1 shows) that he should do so. Yet that did not excuse him; the less so when he clearly perceived the wrongfulness of it. What God has decreed must come to pass, nevertheless the entire guilt of every wicked deed rests upon him who performs it. It is never right to do wrong, and Joab certainly ought to have declined having any part in such an evil course.

Joab commenced his distasteful task in the remotest sections of Palestine, and took his time about it, perhaps hoping that long ere it was completed the king would repent him of his folly. The compilers of the census first numbered the inhabitants of the country to the east of Jordan, from thence proceeding to the northern part of Canaan, and finishing up in the region to the west of Jordan (vv. 5-7). They compiled a complete register of all the men capable of taking up arms, excepting only the Levites and the Benjamites: the former because their sacred vocation exempted them from military service; the latter, probably because they could not yet be relied upon to render whole-hearted devotion to David (compare 2:28; 3:1, etc). Nearly ten months were spent on this task: how patient the Lord is and how great His mercy in giving us "space for repentance" — alas, how great is our madness and sin in refusing to repent.

"So when they had gone through all the land, they came to Jerusalem at the end of nine months and twenty days. And Joab gave up the sum of the number of the people unto the king: and there were in Israel eight hundred thousand valiant men that drew the sword; and the men of Judah were five hundred thousand men" (2 Sam. 24:8, 9). The careful student will note that the figures given here are different from those found in 1 Chron. 21:5 — a variation which sceptics are quick to seize upon as one of the "errors the Bible is full of;" but most deplorable is it to find that some of the orthodox commentators solve "the difficulty" by suggesting that the records were "inaccurate." The fact is that the two classifications are quite different, the one supplementing the other. It is to be carefully observed that 2 Sam. 24 qualifies the first total by "there were in Israel 800,000 *valiant* men," whereas 1 Chron. 21:5 only says 1,100,000 "men that drew the sword" in Israel, so that an additional number to the "valiant men" was there included! Again; in Chron. the men of Judah "were 470,000 that drew sword," whereas in 2 Sam. 24 the "men of Judah were 500,000 — evidently 30,000 drew not the sword.

It is striking to note that the Hebrews had not multiplied nearly so much during their five hundred years' residence in Canaan as they did in their briefer sojourn in Egypt; nevertheless, that such a vast multitude were sustained in such a narrow territory is clear evidence of the remarkable fertility of the Country — a land flowing with milk and honey. Whether the total figures which Joab presented to his royal master reached his expectations, or whether they mortified his pride, we are not told; but probably his subjects were not so numerous as he had expected. It usually follows that when we set our hearts upon the attaining of some earthly object, the actual realisation of our quest proves to be but a chimera. But such disappointments ought only to serve in weaning our affections from things below, to fix them on things above which alone can satisfy the soul. Alas, how slow we are to learn the lesson.

And David's heart struck him after he had numbered the people. And David said to the LORD, I have sinned greatly in what I have done. And now, I beseech You, O LORD, take away the iniquity of Your servant, for I have done very foolishly. For when David was up in the morning, the word of the LORD came to the prophet Gad, David's seer, saying, Go and say to David, Thus says the LORD, I offer you three things. Choose one of them, so that I may do it to you. So Gad came to David and told him. And he said to him, Shall seven years of famine come on you and on your land? Or will you flee three months before your enemies while they pursue you? Or shall there be three days' plague in your land? Now advise, and see what answer I shall return to Him who sent me. And David said to Gad, I am in much distress. Let us fall now into the hand of the LORD, for His mercies are great. And do not let me fall into the hand of man. — II Samuel 24:10-14.

"When thou takest the sum of the children of Israel after their number, then shall they give every man a ransom for his soul unto the Lord, when thou numberest them; that there be no *plague* among them, when thou numberest them" (Ex. 30:12). In the absence of any commission from God to do so, David not only did wrong in yielding to the pride of his heart by insisting that a military census should be taken of Israel, but he also erred grievously in the way it was carried out. This it is which explains to us why Divine judgment followed upon his being so remiss, and why that plague fell on all the Nation, for the Law laid the responsibility on every individual alike. The amount of the required "ransom" was so small (a shilling — a quarter) that it lay within the capacity of the poorest. "The rich were not allowed to give more, thus teaching us that all mankind are, in this matter, equal. All had sinned and come short of the glory of God: therefore all needed, equally needed, a ransom.

"This numbering was a solemn ceremonial that could not be done quickly, as we see by the first chapter in the book called Numbers. Therefore there was time for the officers to have looked up in the Law what was required of them. For a man to present himself to God without a ransom was a solemn and dangerous thing to do. The fact that the result, which they were warned by this law to avoid, came upon them, shows us that we are expected to read the Word, and that God will not contradict His own Word. As Paul warns us, 'If we believe not, yet He abideth faithful; He cannot deny Himself': 2 Tim. 2:13" (C. H. Bright). How loudly ought this incident to speak unto us in this flesh-pleasing and God-defying age: to ignore the requirements of the Divine Law is to court certain disaster — true alike for the individual and for the nation.

"So when they had gone through all the land, they came to Jerusalem at the end of nine months and twenty days. And Joab gave up the sum of the number of the people unto the king" (2 Sam. 24:8, 9). For nine long months the pride of David's heart deceived him, as alas, lust had before dimmed his eyes the same length of time (2 Sam. 11, 12). During this season his conscience slumbered, and there was no exercise of it before God over his action — such is ever the case when we are caught in the toils of Satan. Does it strike us as well nigh incredible that one so favoured of God and one who had so signally honoured Him in the general course of his life, should now have such a deplorable and protracted lapse? Let each of us answer the question out of his checkered experience. We doubt not that the majority of our Christian readers will hang their heads with shame, as they are conscious of similar backslidings in their own history; and if perchance a minority have been preserved from such falls, well may they marvel at the distinguishing Mercy which has been vouchsafed them.

"And David's heart smote him after that he had numbered the people" (v. 10). This indicated that he was a regenerate soul, for it is ever one of the marks of a true believer to repent of his misdeeds, for though on the one hand the flesh lusteth against the spirit, on the other spirit (the nature received at the new birth) is contrary to the flesh, and delights not in its works. For almost a year David appears to have been indifferent to his sin, but now he is conscious of his wickedness, without, so far as we are informed, any human instrument convicting him of the evil which he had done. It is good to see that though he had remained so long in the path of self-will, yet his heart was not obdurate: though his conscience had indeed slumbered, yet it was not dead. It is cause for real thanksgiving when we find that we have hearts which smite us for wrong doing.

We are not here told what it was that aroused David from his spiritual stupor and caused his heart to smite him: simply the bare fact is stated. Here again is where we receive help by comparing the supplementary account furnished by 1

Chron. 21, for there we are told "And God was displeased with this thing; therefore He smote Israel. And David said unto God, I have sinned greatly" (vv. 7, 8). In 2 Sam. 24 David's confession of his sin (v. 10) *followed* his contrition, so that a careful comparison of the two passages enables us to ascertain that the chiding from his heart was the effect of the Lord's being displeased at what he had done. This is one of many illustrations which serves to bring out the characteristic differences of the two books: the one is mainly exoteric, the other largely esoteric: that is to say, 1 and 2 Sam. narrates the historical facts, whereas 1 and 2 Chron. generally reveals the hidden springs from which the actions proceed.

"And God was displeased with this thing; therefore He smote Israel" (1 Chron. 21:7). Here we learn how *God* regarded the policy David had pursued: He was offended, for His Law had been completely disregarded. "And He smote Israel:" observe particularly that this comes *before* David's confession of his sin (v. 8), and before God "sent pestilence upon Israel" (v. 14). Ere God caused the plague to fall upon the Nation, He first smote David's heart! He did not turn His back upon David! As another has pointed out "The whole system of Israel, by this national transgression, was now defiled and tainted, and ripe for severity or judgment: this pride was the giving up of God, and God would have been dealing righteously had He at once laid Israel aside, as He did Adam, in such a case." Instead, He acted here in sovereign grace.

No, the Lord was far from utterly forsaking David. Put together the two statements, and in this order, "And God was displeased with this thing; therefore He smote Israel" (1 Chron. 21:7), "And David's heart smote him after he had numbered the people" (2 Sam. 24:10). Do not these two statements stand related as cause to effect? the one revealing the Lord's working, the other showing the result produced in his servant. God now smote David's heart, making him to feel His sore displeasure. David, as a child of God, might be tempted, overtaken in a fault, and thus brought to shame and grief; but could he be left impenitent? No; no more than Peter was (Luke 22:32). The reprobate are given up to hardness of heart; but not so the righteous; the Lord would not suffer David to remain indifferent to his sin, but graciously wrought conviction and contrition within him. And so far from David's conscience being as one which had been "seared with a hot iron" (1 Tim. 4:2), it was sensitive and quick to respond to the influences of God's Spirit.

"And David's heart smote him after that he had numbered the people. What a warning is this for us. How it should speak to *our* hearts! What a solemn and salutary lesson does it point: the very thing which David imagined would bring him pleasure, caused him pain! This is ever the case: to listen unto Satan's temptations is to court certain trouble, to be attracted by the gilt on the bait he dangles before us, will be our inevitable undoing. It was so with Eve, with Dinah (Gen. 34:1, 2), with Achan. Indulging the pride of his heart, David fondly supposed that to secure an accurate knowledge of the full military strength of his kingdom would prove gratifying; instead, he now grieves over his folly. What insanity it is for us to invest folly with the garb of satisfaction: not only will a sense of sin dampen the Christian's carnal joy, but "at the last it biteth like a serpent, and stingeth like an adder" (Prov. 23:32.)

"And David's heart smote him after that he had numbered the people." What a now, I beseech Thee, O Lord, take away the iniquity of Thy servant, for I have done very foolishly" (v. 10). David had been convicted by the Spirit, and as heavy sense of guilt oppressed him — ever an intolerable burden to a renewed soul. Sensible of his wrongdoing, he earnestly sought forgiveness of the Lord.

Where Divine grace possesses the heart, the conscience of a saint, upon reflection, will reprove him for his transgressions. It is at this point there appears the great difference between the regenerate and the empty professor or religious hypocrite. The latter may afterwards have a realisation of his madness and suffer keen remorse therefrom, but he will not get down in the dust before God and unsparingly condemn himself; instead, he invariably excuses himself by blaming his circumstances, his associates, or those lusts which are now his master. This is one of the outstanding characteristics of depraved human nature: Adam took not upon himself the blame for his fall, but sought to throw the onus of it upon his wife, and she upon the Serpent.

But it is far otherwise with those who have been made the subjects of a miracle of grace. One who is born again has been given an honest heart, and one of the plainest evidences of this is that its possessor is honest with himself, and with his fellows, and above all, with God. An honest soul is sincere, open, candid, abhorring deception and lies. Therefore in unmistakable contrast from the hypocrite the genuine believer will, upon realising his transgressions, humble himself before the Lord, and with unfeigned contrition and fervent prayers seek His forgiveness, sincerely purposing by His grace to return no more to his folly. Wondrous indeed is the ministry which grace performs, making our very pride to be an occasion of increasing our humility! Thus it was with David. The same appears again in the case of Hezekiah: "Hezekiah rendered not again according to the benefit done unto him: for his heart was lifted up: therefore was wrath upon him, and upon Judah and Jerusalem. Notwithstanding, Hezekiah *humbled* himself for the *pride* of his heart" (2 Chron. 32:25, 26).

"And David said unto the Lord, I have sinned greatly in that I have done: and now, I beseech Thee, O Lord, take away the iniquity of Thy servant, for I have done very foolishly." It is by the depth of his conviction, the sincerity of his repentance, and the heartiness of his confession, that the child of God is identified. So far from making any attempt to extenuate himself, so far from throwing the blame upon Satan (who had tempted him), David unsparingly condemned *himself.* To others it might seem a small thing that he had done. But David felt he had "sinned greatly." Ah, he now saw his deed in the light of God's holiness. In true confession of sin we do not spare ourselves or minimize our misdemeanors, but frankly and feelingly acknowledge the enormity of them. "I have done very foolishly" David owned, for what he had done was in the pride of his heart, and it was veritable madness for him to be vain of his subjects when they were *God's* people, as it is insane for the Christian to be proud of the gifts and graces which the Spirit has bestowed upon him.

"For (Heb. "And") when David was up in the morning, the word of the Lord came unto the prophet Gad, David's seer" (v. 11). This seems to indicate that David's confession had been made during the hours of darkness. God "giveth His beloved sleep" (Psa. 127:2), and likewise He withholds it when it serves His purpose. And it is always for our *good* (Rom. 8:28) that He does so, whether we perceive it or no. Sometimes He "giveth songs in the night" (Job 35:10); we read too of "visions of the night" (Job 4:2, 13); but at other times God removes sleep from our eyes and speaks to us about our sins. Then it is we can say with Asaph, "My sore ran in the night, and ceased not: my soul refused to be comforted" (Psa. 77:2), and then it is that we have a taste of David's experience: "I am weary with my groaning; all the night make I my bed to swim; I water my couch with my tears" (Psa. 6:6). But whatever be God's object in withholding sleep, it is blessed when we can say, "By night on my bed *I sought Him* whom my soul loveth" (Song of Sol. 3:1).

"And when David was up in ·the morning, the word of the Lord came unto the prophet Gad, David's seer, saying, Go and say unto David, Thus saith the Lord, I offer thee three things: choose thee one of them, that I may do it unto thee" (vv. 11, 12). The solemn exercises of David's heart during the night season were to prepare him for God's message of judgment. He had been made to taste something of the bitterness of his folly while others were slumbering, but now he is to know more definitely how sorely displeased God was. When the Lord is about to send us a special message, be it one of cheer or of reproof, He first fits the heart to receive it. When the morning broke, the Lord commissioned Gad to deliver His ultimatum to the king. Gad was a prophet, and he is here designated "David's seer" because he was one who, on certain occasions, was wont to counsel him in the things of God — cf. 1 Sam. 23:5. At this time he had to deliver a far-from-pleasant message — such often falls to the lot of God's servants.

His heavenly Father must correct David, yet He graciously gave him leave to make choice whether it should be by famine, war, or pestilence; whether it should be a long-protracted judgment or a very brief yet terribly severe one. Matt. Henry suggested that the Lord had a fourfold design in this. First, to humble David the more for his sin, which he would see to be exceeding sinful, when he came to consider that each of the judgments were exceeding dreadful. Second, to upbraid him for the proud conceit he had entertained of his own sovereignty over Israel: he had become so great a monarch that he might now do whatever he would: very well, says God, choose which of these three things you prefer. Third, to grant him some encouragement under the chastisement: so far from the Lord having utterly disfellowshipped him, He let him decide what He should do. Fourth, that he might more patiently endure the rod seeing it was one of his own selection.

"So Gad came to David, and told him, and said to him, Shall seven years of famine come unto thee in thy land? or wilt thou flee three months before thine enemies, while they pursue thee? or that there be three days' pestilence in thy land? now advise, and see what answer I shall return to Him that sent me" (v. 13). Here is the third thing connected with this incident which is apt to greatly puzzle the casual reader. First, that such an apparently trifling act on David's part should have so sorely displeased the Lord. Second, that He suffered Satan to tempt David, and then was angry with him for doing as the Tempter suggested. These we have already considered. And now, after David had been convicted of his sin, sincerely repented of the same, had confessed it, and sought the Lord's forgiveness, that judgment should fall so heavily upon him. It is really surprising that so many of the commentators when dealing with this "difficulty" fail to bear in mind the opening sentence of the chapter — the key to all that follows: "And again the anger of the Lord was kindled against *Israel.*"

God had a controversy with the Nation, and this it is which accounts for the character of His governmental dealings with them. His judgment could not be averted, and therefore He punished their pride and rebellion by leaving them to suffer the consequences of their king's following out the natural impulse of his heart. But there are several other aspects of the case which must be borne in mind. David's sin had not been a private but a *public* one, and though God forgave him as to his personal concern, yet he had to be publicly humiliated. Again, while God remits the penal and eternal consequences of sin unto a contrite saint, yet even penitents are chastised and often made to smart severely in this world for their folly. Though God be longsuffering, He will by no means clear the guilty. True, His gifts and calling are without repentance (Rom. 11:29), and unto His own His compassions fail not (Lam. 3:22); yet, the righteousness of His government must be vindicated.

What has last been pointed out holds good in all dispensations, for God's "ways" change not. Correction is ever a characteristic of the Covenant, for whom the Lord loveth He chasteneth" (Heb. 12:6). Had David walked in his integrity and in humility before God, he would have been spared severe discipline, but now he must bear the rod. "Then will I visit their transgression with the rod, and their iniquity with stripes; nevertheless My loving kindness will I not utterly take from him, nor suffer My faithfulness to fail" (Psa. 89:32, 33): that clearly states the principle. "And David said unto Gad, I am in a great strait: let us fall now into the hand of the Lord; for His mercies are great; and let me not fall into the hands of man" (v. 14). Here was his wise decision.

It will be remembered that in the last two sections upon the life of David we chose for their title "His Final Folly," but here we are to be occupied with his wise decision. What a strange mingling there is in the life of the believer of these two things — clearly exemplified in the recorded history of both Old and N.T. saints. This it is which often makes the experiences of a Christian to be so perplexing to him; yet the explanation thereof is not difficult to determine. There are two opposing principles operating within him; the "flesh" and the "spirit," and if one be essentially evil, it is also the cause of all his folly; while if the other be intrinsically holy, it is the spring of all true wisdom. Hence it is that in the Scriptures (outstandingly so throughout the book of Proverbs) sin and folly are synonymous terms, while holiness and wisdom are used interchangeably.

It is only by an unsparing and ceaseless judging of ourselves and by the maintenance of close and constant fellowship with God, that indwelling sin can be suppressed and ourselves preserved from deeds of madness. When communion with the Holy One is broken, we have forsaken the Fountain of wisdom, and then we are left to follow a course from which even the "common sense" of the worldling frequently deters him. We have seen this most solemnly illustrated in the case of David. First, he had allowed his heart to be lifted up over the strengthening and extension of his kingdom and by the great successes which had attended his arms. This led to the folly of his causing a needless military census to be taken of his subjects, without any Divine authorization. Worse still, he persisted in this mad course against the express remonstrance of his officers. And worst of all, he failed to meet the requirements of Ex. 30:12 and provide the necessary ransom.

Painful as it is to dwell upon the failures of so eminent a servant of God, yet the same will prove beneficial to us if we duly take to heart such a solemn warning, and learn therefrom to walk more softly before God. The same evil tendencies lie within both the writer and reader, and it is only as we are truly humbled by such a realisation and are moved to deeper self-distrust and self-loathing, and only as we are led to more earnestly and definitely seek God's subduing and preserving grace, that we shall ourselves be kept from falling into similar evils. These O.T. histories are not merely given for information, but for our edification, and growth is possible only by feeding on God's Word. Feeding on the Word means that we appropriate and masticate it; taking it unto ourselves and assimilating the same.

But alas, David fell; and so have we. Who amongst us dares to say that he has never followed a course of folly since he became a Christian? that he has never been guilty of God-dishonouring acts of madness? But as we are now to see, David recovered his sanity, and once more again acted wisely. It was what lay *between* these two things which we would again call attention to, for it is at this very point that most important and precious practical instruction is furnished us. Surely those Christians who have entered the paths of folly desire to tread once more the ways of wisdom. Does it not behove us, then, to attend closely unto our present narrative and observe the several steps by which the one path is left and the other path returned unto? How gracious of the Holy Spirit in here revealing to us the way of recovery and the means of restoration.

And what, my reader, do you suppose is the first step which leads us back into communion with God? what the particular exercise which recovers us from the disease of folly? If you have any acquaintance with Divine things the answer will promptly be forthcoming, for the history of your own experience will prompt it. "And David's heart smote him after that he had numbered the people" (2 Sam. 24:10). We have previously commented upon this verse, so our remarks thereon must be brief. Yet once more we would point out what a mercy it is when an erring saint finds his heart reproving him for his madness and weighed down with a sense of guilt, for this is both a mark of regeneration and a sign that the Lord has not abandoned him — given him up to total hardness and blindness. But it is as intimating the first step in David's recovery that we would now particularly consider the verse.

"And David's heart smote him." This is basic and indispensable. There can be no real restoration to communion with a holy God until we unsparingly condemn ourselves for the lapse; that thing which broke the communion must be judged by us. God never forgives, either sinner or saint, where there is no repentance; and one essential ingredient in repentance is *self-judgment*. "If My people which are called by My name shall humble themselves, and pray, and seek My face, and turn from their wicked ways; then will I hear from heaven, and will forgive their sin, and will heal their land" (2 Chron 7:14). The first thing, then, is the humbling of ourselves, and that is what repentance is; it is the taking of sides with God against ourselves and sorrowing over our wickedness. Thus it is the tears of contrition which cleanse the eyes of our heart from the grit of folly, and enable them once more to look on things with the vision of prudence.

And what, dear reader, do you suppose is the next step in the return to the ways of wisdom? And again the answer is very simple; where there is a true and honest judging of self, there will also be an humble and contrite owning of the fault to God. Consequently we find in the passage quoted above (2 Chron. 7:14) that immediately after, If My people "shall humble themselves" is, "and pray and seek My face." This is exactly what we find poor David did; "And David said unto the Lord, I have sinned greatly in that I have done; and now, I beseech Thee, O Lord, take away the iniquity of Thy servant; for I have done very foolishly" (v. 10). He made honest confession of his transgression, emphasising the greatness of his folly. And this is what every backslider must do before he can be recovered from his madness and restored to fellowship with the Lord.

It is to be observed that coupled with David's confession of sin to the Lord was his request "take away the iniquity of Thy servant." By that petition at least three things were denoted. First, remit the guilt of the same, both from before Thine accusing Law and the weight of the same upon my conscience. Second, cleanse the defilement thereof, both from before Thy holy sight and in my polluted soul. Third, cancel or annul the governmental consequences of my crime, so that I may not be punished for it. We need to be clear upon these distinctions, for they are something more than mere technicalities. Now where the holy requirements of God have been duly met and He is pleased to bestow a pardon, the first two of these elements are always included; guilt is blotted out and defilement is cleansed. But the third by no means always obtains.

God ever reserves to Himself the sovereign right to mete out the governmental consequences of our sins as best subserves His glory and the accomplishment of His eternal purpose. So far as the believer himself is concerned, those consequences are not penal but disciplinary, visited upon him not in wrath but in love. Yet it must not be forgotten that wider interests are involved than our own personal ones. Were God to remit all the consequences of sin every time a believer committed a flagrant offence and then sincerely repented of and confessed the same, what impression would be received by men in general! Would not the ungodly draw the conclusion that the Lord regarded transgressions as trifles and was indifferent to our conduct? Thus it is that, as the moral Ruler of this world, God often gives solemn tokens of His disapproval of our sins by making us suffer some very painful effects of them in this life.

Yet it would be a great mistake for an afflicted saint to draw the inference from what has just been said, that such tokens in his present life of God's displeasure are so many evidences that the sins he has penitently confessed are still unpardoned. A striking case in point occurs in the earlier life of David himself. After he had transgressed so grievously in the matter of Uriah's wife, the prophet was sent to charge him with his crime. Whereupon David acknowledged "I have sinned against the Lord," and none who have read seriously the 51st Psalm can doubt either the sincerity or the depth of his repentance. Accordingly Nathan told him "the Lord also hath put away thy sin, thou shalt not die." Yet he at once added, "Howbeit, because by this deed thou hast given great occasion to the enemies of the Lord to blaspheme, the child also that is born unto thee shall surely die" (2 Sam. 12:14).

A much commoner example is met with in the case of those who in their unregenerate days lived reckless and profligate lives. Upon their conversion God graciously remits the guilt of their sins, cancelling the penal consequences of the same so far as eternity is concerned, as He also cleanses them from all the defilements thereof. But it is rare indeed that a debauchee is given back again the health and strength which he had squandered in riotous living; rather is he (in the vast majority of cases, at least) left to now reap in his body the wild oats sown in his mad youth. So it was with David in the matter of his awful crime against Uriah; the "sword" of God's displeasure was not sheathed, but was used against him and his household during the remainder of his earthly pilgrimage.

In the instance now before us, the prophet Gad was sent unto David to say unto him, "Thus saith the Lord, I offer thee three things: choose thee one of them, that I may do it unto thee. So Gad came to David and told him, and said unto him, Shall seven years of famine come unto thee in thy land? or wilt thou flee three months before thine enemies, while they pursue thee? or that there be three days' pestilence in thy land? now advise, and see what answer I shall return to Him that sent me" (2 Sam. 24:12, 13). It must be borne in mind (as we pointed out more than once in our sections on the earlier verses of this chapter) that the Lord had a grievance against Israel, and therefore His governmental displeasure could not be averted by David's prayer. Divine judgment must fall upon the Nation which had so grievously provoked the Lord, but the form in which it was to come lay with David to choose, though within the prescribed limits.

"And David said unto Gad, I am in a great strait; let us now fall into the hand of the Lord" (v. 14). David was now made to taste the bitterness of his sin, yet it is most blessed to see that he neither hardened his heart nor murmured against God when he heard the terrifying message of the Prophet. His beautiful response thereto clearly evidenced the genuineness of his repentance and the sincerity of his confession. This is another point in our narrative which we do well to heed, for alas our hearts frequently deceive us therein. How often have we mourned over our iniquities and acknowledged them unto the Lord, and then have fretted and fumed when made to feel the governmental consequences of the same — thereby manifesting the superficiality of our repentance and the dishonesty of our confession.

As we have said in a previous paragraph, genuine repentance is a taking sides with God against ourselves. It is not only the unsparing condemnation of ourselves and a sorrowing for having displeased the Lord, but it is also a heart-felt acknowledgment that we richly deserve to receive the due reward of our iniquities. It is the recognition and acknowledgment that God will be righteous in making us smart severely under His chastening hand. But it is the sequel which will show how genuine or else how disingenuous is our confession; it is how we carry ourselves under the rod itself; whether meekly or rebelliously — that evidences the reality and depth of our self-judgment. Let us not forget that Pharaoh, king of Egypt, owned "I have sinned against the Lord your God" (Ex. 10:16), yet as soon as the plagues of Jehovah returned to his land, he again hardened his heart.

His heavenly Father must correct David himself, yet He graciously permitted him to determine whether it should be a long protracted or a very brief yet terribly severe one. "Years of famine he and Israel had recently experienced. For three years had that scourge prevailed. What misery would seven years of it inflict on them all. During this period a Sabbatical year would fall, throughout which the land must rest, and the Nation would have to pass through it without the gracious provision of the sixth's years prolific crop. Seven years' famine would have been a heavy infliction indeed, as the history of such a scourge in the days of Joseph had made plain. Flight before his enemies was not an unknown trial to David. Years of harassment at the hands of Saul he had experienced, and flight before Absalom he had known. Those trials, we may be sure, were not forgotten, though they were ended; and they must have taught him of what men were capable, if allowed by God to pursue him" (C. E. Stuart.)

In the previous section we quoted from Matt. Henry, who pointed out that the Lord had a fourfold design in presenting unto David the choice of what particular form His judgment should take, namely; — First, to humble David for his sin, which he would see to be exceedingly sinful, when he discovered what dreadful judgment it entailed. Second, to upbraid him for his pride; he had acted in self-will, deeming himself so great a monarch that he could do as he pleased; now he is bidden to exercise his choice in selecting from these dread alternatives. Third, to grant him some encouragement under the chastisement; as far from the Lord having totally deserted his servant, he is granted the power to decide what He should do. Fourth, that he might more patiently endure the rod, seeing it was one of his own choosing. To these we would add, fifth, to try out his heart and give opportunity for the exercise and exhibition of his *faith*.

"Let us now fall into the hand of the Lord; for His mercies are great; and let me not fall into the hand of man" (v. 14). What proof was this that David had recovered his sanity. The wise decision which he now made clearly demonstrated his recovery from the paths of folly and his return to the ways of prudence. And how this illustrates once more the blessed fact that God ever honours those who honour Him. And let it be clearly grasped by us all, that we *do* honour God when we humble ourselves before Him and penitently confess our sins. And one of the ways in which He honours us in return is to grant us a renewed power of spiritual discernment, by which our hearts are drawn out to Him in warmer love and assurance, and by which we obtain a fuller realisation of the greatness of His mercies. How much we miss, dear reader, by refusing to judge ourselves and take our place in the dust before the Throne of Grace! How wondrous are the ways of Jehovah. He had not only dealt with David's conscience, but He now drew out unto Himself the affections of his heart! He not only brought him to repentance, but He called forth the faith of His beloved servant — the order of which is ever the same. There must be repentance before there can be faith (Mark 1:15, Matt. 21:32)! for it is impossible for an hard and impenitent heart to truly trust in the Lord. Thus we may learn that it is impenitency for our sins which lies at the root of our wicked unbelief. But after David *had* repented, the Lord (as we have said above) granted him the opportunity to display his faith. And what a grand exhibition of it he now gave. What acquaintance with the confidence in the Divine character do these words breathe, "Let us fall now into the hand of the Lord"!

Ah, my reader, even when the Lord is sorely chastening us for our faults, He is infinitely more gracious, more faithful, more deserving of our trust than is any creature. "And let me not fall into the hand of man." Poor David had had abundant experience of what man was capable of. His own brethren had been jealous of and had cruelly slandered him (1 Sam. 17:28). Saul had evilly requited him for his kindness. Ahitophel had basely deceived him and betrayed his trust. His beloved son had risen up in rebellion against him and almost succeeded in dethroning him. Good reason, then, had he to say "Let me not fall into the hand of man": unstable, treacherous, cruel man. And so says the writer after thirty years of Christian experience: "Let me not fall into the hand of man" — least of all religious man. No, let us rather "fall into the hand of the Lord, for HIS mercies *are* great."

So the LORD sent a plague on Israel from the morning even till the time appointed. And there died from the people, from Dan to Beer-sheba, seventy thousand men. And when the angel stretched out his hand on Jerusalem to destroy it, the LORD turned from the evil, and said to the angel who destroyed the people, It is enough. Now stay your hand. And the angel of the LORD was by the threshing-place of Araunah the Jebusite. And David spoke to the LORD when he saw the angel who struck the people, and said, Lo, I have sinned, and I have done wickedly. But these sheep, what have they done? I beg You, let Your hand be against me and against my father's house. And Gad came that day to David and said to him, Go up! Rear an altar to the LORD in the threshing-floor of Araunah the Jebusite. And David went up, according to the saying of Gad, as the LORD commanded. And Araunah looked and saw the king and his servants coming on toward him. And Araunah went out and bowed himself before the king, with his face on the ground. — II Samuel 24:15-20.

It is both interesting and instructive to note in how many different characters David is brought before us in 2 Sam. 24. First, as the proud and haughty one: which may be inferred from the opening "And" of the chapter (following upon his remarkable victories, and the extension of his kingdom), and confirmed in Psa. 30:6, which refers to this very time, and will (D.V.) be considered by us in a later section. Second, the tempted one, as 1 Chron. 21:1 more definitely shows. Third, as the foolish one, deciding upon a military census when there was no need or Divine commission for it. Fourth, the intractable one, when he stubbornly refused to yield unto the counsel of his officers or listen to their remonstrance (vv. 3, 4), determining to have his own way. The logical order in these downward steps is apparent on the surface.

Now on the other side, we behold him, fifth, as the penitent one, mourning over his sins and confessing the same to God (v. 10). Sixth, as the submissive one; not murmuring against the severity of God as he heard the terrible pronouncement of the prophet, but meekly bowing to the Divine verdict. Seventh, the prudent one: preferring to fall into the hand of the Lord rather than into the hand of man. Eighth, as the believing and confident one: recognising and owning the greatness of the Divine mercies (v. 14). Ninth, as the chastened one: the judgment of God falling upon his beloved subjects (v. 15), which he felt more keenly than had the rod descended upon himself and his own house. Tenth, as the intercessor before God; stepping into the breach and making supplication for his afflicted kingdom. Here, too, we may perceive clearly the logical sequence of these things.

It is, however, in this last character, as *the intercessor* before God, that we are now to specially consider David. But we shall miss one of the most striking points in connection therewith, and one of the most instructive and valuable lessons for our own hearts therein, if we fail to observe very particularly the order before us. It is not every believer who has power with God in prayer. Far from it; rather are there, alas, very few who can prevail with the Lord in their supplications on the behalf of others. Nor is the reason for this far to seek: they possess not the requisite qualifications. They do not have those marks which fitted David on this occasion. If we are walking contrary to the Divine commandments (1 John 3:22), or there be unmourned and unconfessed sin in our lives, then the Lord will not hear us (Psa. 66:18).

We sincerely trust the reader does not weary of our so often calling attention to the order of events in a narrative, for very often lessons of fundamental importance are thereby inculcated. It is so in the case before us. It is by duly noting *what preceded* David's prevailing intercession, that we learn how we may become successful supplicants on behalf of others. First, there must be a putting right of what in our own lives is displeasing to a holy God: by a genuine contrition for and humble acknowledgement to Him of our offences. Second, there must be entire submission beneath His chastening hand, meekly bowing to His righteous rod. Third, an implicit confidence in His wisdom, faithfulness, and goodness, so that we freely yield ourselves into His hands. Fourth, a real persuasion of the greatness of His mercies, laying hold thereof by faith and pleading the same before Him.

"So the Lord sent a pestilence upon Israel from the morning even to the time appointed: and there died of the people from Dan even to Beer-sheba seventy thousand men" (2 Sam. 24:16). First of all, let us note how exactly the punishment answered to the crime! Penitent though he was, yet David must be corrected; and as his offence had been a public one, so is the retribution. But it is indeed striking to see that the rod of God fell in the very place of His servant's transgression. David had doted upon his thousands, and his thousands must be drastically reduced! God now numbered to the sword, those whom David had numbered to his self-complacency — one twentieth (cf. v. 9) being slain. Clearly, then, it was *the pride* of David against which this Divine judgment was directed. "Whatever we idolize or grow proud of, God will generally take from us, or else convert it into a cross" (T. Scott).

Yet it is also to be noted that God's scourge fell immediately upon the people themselves, for it was against *them* Jehovah had a controversy (v. 1). "A solemn time it must have been. Pestilence was walking in darkness, and destruction was wasting at noonday. The destroying angel was actively at work, and no man was able to withstand him. Throughout the length and breadth of the land death was claiming its victims. Who would next be struck no one could tell. No remedy availed to cure the sick. No intercession, however urgent, succeeded in preserving the life of a beloved one. All joy must have fled: all energy for ordinary pursuits must have been paralysed. God was working, and in power. Of old He had laid bare His arm, and worked in power on behalf of Israel; now His hand was outstretched, but in this deadly way *against* them. Could any charge Him with injustice? No, They deserved the chastisement, though David's act in numbering them was the proximate cause for this visitation. Helpless, how helpless were they all. Their only hope was in the mercy of God" (C. E. Stuart).

Let us see in this solemn incident a demonstration of how easily God can reduce the haughtiest of sinners: the "day of the Lord" (His acting in judgment) is ever upon those who are proud and lifted up: (Isa. 2:12). Then how greatly are we indebted daily to His longsufferance! Stout-hearted rebels, who carry themselves with such effrontery against the Most High, little realize how much they owe to His wondrous patience; but they shall yet discover there are limits even to that. Some one had pertinently pointed out that, "If the power of angels be so terrible — a single one smiting with death seventy thousand Israelites in a single day — what is that of the all-mighty Creator!" Rightly then does He ask "Can thine heart endure, or can thine hands be strong, in the day that I shall deal with thee?" (Ezek. 22:14).

"So the Lord sent a pestilence upon Israel from the morning even to the time appointed." This expression "the time appointed" can mean either the close of the third day or, as many think, the season of the evening sacrifice of the first day. The Heb. may be literally rendered "till the time of appointed assembly," that is, the hour set apart for the meeting together of Israel for the evening worship. The renowned scholar Hengstenberg remarks as follows: "The calamity according to 2 Sam. 24:16 lasted from morning till the time of meeting, by which we are to understand 'the evening religious assembly' — compare 1 Kings 18:29, 36; 2 Kings 16:15." But altogether apart from the meaning of the Hebrew, there are two considerations which seem to require this rendering. First, because the phrase "till the time appointed" stands in opposition to "from the *morning.*" Second, from the statement in the next verse, "The Lord repented Him of the evil."

The last-quoted clause appears to us to plainly denote that He did not go to the full length of the judgment announced. Yet even in that brief period there fell of Israel seventy thousand, in as many hours as Joab had taken months in numbering the people. But by the mercy of God the duration of the awful pestilence was contracted. Judgment is God's "strange work," for He delighteth in mercy, yet His mercy never ignores the requirements of His holiness nor sets aside the demands of His justice. And most blessedly may we perceive here the meeting-place of these two grand sides of the Divine character. It was the sweet savour of the evening sacrifice which stayed the desolating plague! What a wondrous foreshadowing was this — brought out still more plainly in what follows — of that which is set forth without veil or symbol in the N.T. The Cross of Christ is where the varied attributes of God all shine forth in blended harmony.

"And when the angel stretched out his hand upon Jerusalem to destroy it, the Lord repented Him of the evil" (v. 16). Let us first remove a misapprehension at this point. Enemies of the Truth have not been slow to seize upon this reference to the Lord's repenting (and similar passages, such as Gen. 6:6; 1 Sam. 15:11, etc.), and have drawn the wicked inference that God is fickle, subject to changes of mind like the creature is. Arminians misuse such verses in their vain efforts to overthrow the doctrine of foreordination. But nothing is more clearly revealed in Holy Writ than the *immutability* of God. "God is not a man, that He should lie; neither the son of man, that He should repent: hath He said, and shall He not do it?" (Num. 23:19); "But He is in one mind, and who can turn Him? and what His soul desireth, even that He doeth" (Job 23:13); "For I am the Lord: I change not" (Mal. 3:6); "Every good gift and every perfect gift is from above, and cometh down from the Father of lights, with whom is no variableness, neither shadow of turning" (James 1:17). It is impossible for language to be more explicit, emphatic, and unequivocal. If such definite declarations do not mean what they say and are not to be understood at their face value, then it is a waste of time to read the Bible.

Now it is quite obvious to any spiritual mind that the Scriptures cannot contradict themselves, and that there is perfect harmony (whether we can perceive it or no) between those verses which appear to conflict with each other. When we are unable to discern their complete accord, then it is the part of wisdom to acknowledge our ignorance and wait upon God for fuller light. And while so doing, those passages which perplex us must be subordinated to others which are plain to us. Thus we may rest assured that those declarations which so positively affirm God's immutability or unchangeableness are to be regarded absolutely without any qualification, whereas those which seem to speak of His changing His mind are to be taken relatively and figuratively. If Arminians deem this a begging of the question, then we ask them, Does not the express declaration of 1 Sam. 15:29 *oblige us* to interpret 1 Sam. 15:11 in a non-natural sense? Certainly the Holy Spirit would not contradict Himself within the scope of two verses of the same chapter!

The fact of the matter is that God often condescends to employ anthropomorphisms in His Word, that is, He graciously accommodates Himself to our limited capacities and *speaks after the manner of men.* Thus we read of Him being "wearied" (Isa. 42:24, Mal. 2:17), yet in another place we are told "the Creator fainteth not, neither is weary" (Isa. 40:28). In Deut. 32:27 Jehovah speaks as "fearing the wrath of the enemy," which is manifestly a figure of speech. Again, in Psa. 78:65 we read, "The Lord awaked as one out of sleep," yet we know full well that He never slumbers. In Isa. 59:16 it is said that He "wondered," yet nothing can take Him by surprise. Jeremiah 7:13 pictures Him as "rising early," to denote His earnestness. And so we might go on. The "repenting" of the Lord in 2 Sam. 24:16 signifies no change of mind, but intimates an alteration in His *outward* course — the cessation of His judgment.

"And when the angel stretched out His hand upon Jerusalem to destroy it, the Lord repented Him of the evil." Scripture is many-sided and it is only by carefully comparing one passage with another that we are enabled to obtain the full light upon any given incident. Such is the case before us here. Above, we have called attention to the significant and blessed fact that the destructive plague upon Israel was stayed at the hour of the evening sacrifice. Now we would point out another and supplementary angle. Of old the Lord had declared concerning Israel, "If they shall confess their iniquity, and the iniquity of their fathers, with their trespass which they have trespassed against Me, and that also they have walked contrary unto Me; and that I also have walked contrary unto them. . .If then their uncircumcised hearts be humbled, and they then *accept of the punishment* of their iniquity: then will I remember My covenant with Jacob, Isaac and Abraham" (Lev. 26:40-42). This was exactly what David had, in principle, done. He not only confessed his iniquity and humbled his heart (v. 10), but also bowed to God's rod "accepting the punishment" (v. 14). So that it was now in *covenant faithfulness* Jehovah acted in causing the plague to cease!

"And when the angel stretched out his hand upon Jerusalem to destroy it, the Lord repented Him of the evil." In the supplementary account supplied us in 1 Chron. 21 we are told, "And David lifted up his eyes, and saw the angel of the Lord stand between the earth and the heaven, having a drawn sword in his hand stretched out over Jerusalem" (v. 16). That "drawn sword" was the emblem of Divine justice. How it reminds us of those solemn words of Jehovah, "Awake O Sword, against My Shepherd, and against the Man that is My Fellow, saith the Lord of hosts: smite the Shepherd" (Zech. 13:7). And how striking the contrast between the two passages. There in Zech., the sword was, as it were, slumbering, and was called to "Awake." Why? because it was against the Holy One: there was nothing in Him personally the "sword" could find fault with! But different far was it here with guilty Israel: the sword needed no awaking, but was drawn in the angel's hand.

"And when the angel stretched out his hand upon Jerusalem to destroy it, the Lord repented Him of the evil, and said to the angel that destroyed the people, It is enough: stay now thine hand" (v. 16). How blessedly this presents to us once more the precious truth, which is the sure ground of all our hopes, that with our God "mercy rejoiceth against judgment" (James 2:13). The whole system of Israel had exposed itself to the wrath of the Lord. He might have broken it at once as a vessel wherein was no pleasure. He might have taken away His vineyard from His unthankful and wicked husbandmen: but "mercy rejoiceth against judgment" in the heart of their God, and therefore He commanded the destroying angel to stay his hand. And why? God's holiness had been satisfied, His justice had been appeased. "It is enough:" stay now thine hand:" how these words remind us of that blessed utterance of our Saviour's "It is finished" — proclaiming the glorious truth that all the claims of God are now fully met.

"And David spake unto the Lord when he saw the angel that smote the people, and said, Lo, I have sinned, and I have done wickedly: but these sheep, what have they done? let Thine hand, I pray Thee, be against me, and against my father's house" (v. 17). The exact point at which this intercession occurred is made much plainer in 1 Chron. 21. There we learn there were two distinct parts or stages to the Divine judgment. First, we are told "So the Lord sent pestilence upon Israel: and there fell of Israel seventy thousand men" (v. 14): this was accomplished by angelic agency as is clear from 2 Sam. 24, and it was terminated at the time of the evening sacrifice, and that, by the Covenant faithfulness of Jehovah. Second, "And God sent an angel unto Jerusalem to destroy it" (v. 15) — a separate thing from the preceding. "And David lifted up his eyes and saw the angel of the Lord. . .then David and the elders of Israel, who were clothed in sackcloth, fell upon their faces. And David said unto the Lord "Is it not I that commanded the people to be numbered? even I it is that have sinned and done evil indeed" (vv. 16, 17). It was at that critical moment he stepped into the breach and made successful intercession.

First, let us notice that David did not here make the fatal mistake of supplicating the *angel:* no, he was better instructed than are the poor deluded Papists of our day. Second, observe that David did not throw the blame upon the Nation, but criminated himself. "Most people, when God's judgments are abroad, charge others with being the cause of them, and care not who falls by them, so *they* can escape; but David's penitent and public spirit was otherwise affected" (Matt. Henry). This is most beautiful and striking. David took the blame entirely upon himself: "Is it not I that commanded the people to be numbered? even I it is that have sinned and done evil indeed" — it was as though he could not paint his own faults in sufficiently dark colours. "As for these sheep, what have they done?" How dear were they to his heart! No charge would he prefer against them. "Let Thine hand, I pray Thee, O Lord, be on me and on my father's house; but not on Thy people, that they should be plagued" (v. 17): smite their shepherd, but spare the flock, O Lord.

We were obliged to omit several points of importance at the close of our last section, so we will commence here at the stage where we then left off. There we called attention to an essential detail — one which, so far as we can discover, has escaped the notice of all the commentators — namely, that God's judgment upon Israel was twofold, or in two distinct stages; and we would also observe that this corresponded exactly with David's sin. First we are told "The Lord sent pestilence upon Israel: and there fell of Israel seventy thousand men" (1 Chron. 21:14). In Samuel's account it reads "there died of the plague from Dan *even to Beer-sheba* seventy thousand men." How remarkably did the punishment fit the crime, for David had commanded Joab "Go now through all the tribes of Israel, from Dan *even to Beer-sheba,* and number ye the people" (v. 2). It will be remembered that the account of the census-taking closed by saying, "So when they had gone through all the land, they came to *Jerusalem* at the end of nine months and twenty days."

Second, "And God sent an angel unto *Jerusalem* to destroy it" (1 Chron. 21:15). Samuel tells us, "and when the angel stretched out his hand upon Jerusalem to destroy it, the Lord repented Him of the evil" (v. 16), and follows with David's prayer. But the account in Chronicles evidently observes a closer chronological order, for there we read, "And David lifted up his eyes, and saw the angel of the Lord stand between the earth and the heaven, having a drawn sword in his hand stretched out over Jerusalem. Then David and the elders of Israel, who were clothed with sackcloth, fell upon their faces. And David said unto God, "Is it not I that commanded the people to be numbered?" (vv. 16, 17). The dreadful spectacle of the avenging angel, about to fall upon the holy city, deeply affected David. He had previously repented of and confessed his sin, but the calamity which now threatened the capital itself, caused him to pour out his heart afresh unto the Lord, both in humble contrition and earnest supplication.

"And David said unto God, Is it not I that commanded the people to be numbered? even I it is that have sinned and done evil indeed." What blessed self-abnegation was this. David takes the entire blame unto himself, adding "but as for these sheep, what have they done?" Rightly did Matt. Henry answer the question by saying, "Why, they had done much amiss: it was *their* sin which had provoked Jehovah to leave David to himself, as He did." ' Let Thine hand, I pray Thee, O Lord my God, be on me, and on my father's house" (v. 17). How nobly did David here stand in the breach, and that, at his own cost. He not only shouldered the guilt, but was willing to bear the retribution.

As we pointed out in our last section, it was as though David said, Smite me, the shepherd, but let the flock be spared. Ah, but *that* could not be: God would not allow David to suffer in the stead of all Israel. No, none could fill that awful and honourable place of substitution but David's Son and Lord. Nevertheless, we see how grandly he, in spirit, foreshadowed the good Shepherd, who, that they might be rich, Himself became poor, and actually took upon Himself the sins of His sheep and died in their room. "But not on Thy people, that they should be plagued" (v. 17). Is it not lovely to behold David here referring to Israel not as "the people," but as "Thy people." In his folly he had regarded them as *his* people, but in his wisdom he now saw them as the *Lord's*.

Let us point out just here that the confession and prayer of David on this occasion should be taken to heart by every minister of the Gospel. In his comments, T. Scott applied the principle of David's heart-exercises to preachers thus, "While ministers mourn over the state of their congregations, they may sometimes profitably enquire whether their own supineness, pride, want of zeal and simplicity, their self-indulgence or conformity to the world, do not bring a secret blight upon their labours, although more open evils do not bring a blot upon their profession? and whether the people's souls are not suffering for their correction, and bring them to deeper humiliation, greater fervency in prayer, and a more spiritual frame of mind and devotedness to God. And surely we should choose to be chastened in our own persons, rather than that the blessing should be withheld from our congregations: for though the Lord is righteous in these dispensations, yet the people have not deserved *at our hands*, that we should occasion this evil to them. Grace teaches men to condemn themselves rather than others, and to seek the interests of their fellows in many respects before their own: and earnest prayers offered in this temper of mind, by those who unreservedly cast themselves on the mercies of the Lord are very prevalent."

Returning now to the case of David, we may observe that his supplication prevailed with God. Such deep humiliation, such unsparing acknowledgement of his faults, such utter self-abnegation and such tender pleading for the people, touched the heart of Him who is filled with compassion. If the unselfishness of Moses prevailed at another grave crisis in their history, when he asked God to blot him out of His book (Ex. 32:32) rather than that the nation should be destroyed; equally so did the readiness of David for God's judgment to fall upon himself and his house instead of his subjects, turn the tide; for it was in direct answer to his pleading that God said to the angel "stay now thine hand." This gives beautiful completeness to our type, portraying as it does the efficacy of our great High Priest's intercession on behalf of His people.

There is one other point of deep practical importance to be noted here. "God sent an angel unto Jerusalem to destroy it, and as he was destroying (or as 2 Sam. 24:16 puts it "when the angel stretched out his hand upon Jerusalem *to* destroy it"), the Lord beheld, and He repented Him of the evil" (1 Chron. 21:15). And *what was it* that He now "beheld"? Why, David and his servants, "clothed in sackcloth," fallen "upon their faces" (v. 16)! It was not simply that He "saw," but *"beheld"* — with concentrated attention. And then follows immediately David's supplication. Here, then, is the final lesson: it is the one clothed with sackcloth, on his face in the dust, whose intercession prevails with God! In other words, it is the one who is thoroughly humbled, who is brought to the place of self-loathing, and who takes upon his own spirit the afflictions of others, who alone is qualified to plead on their behalf.

Were we asked whose prayers we would rather have on our behalf, we should unhesitatingly reply, Not those who are in raptures on the mountain top, but those who are mourning before God over their own sins and the sufferings of others. Personally, we appreciate far more highly the supplications of those who are (spiritually speaking) clothed in sackcloth, than those arrayed in their wedding garments. It is the absence of the "sackcloth" which renders ineffectual the prayers of so many to-day. Here, then, is holy encouragement for those of God's people who are bowed in the dust before Him: if we have repented of and confessed our sins, and are truly humbled before Him, then is the very time to intercede for other tried souls. Finally, observe the prompt compliance of the angel to the Lord's order "stay thine hand:" if celestial creatures are so obedient to their Maker's word, how promptly should *we* respond to His revealed will.

"And Gad came that day to David, and said unto him, Go up, rear an altar unto the Lord in the threshing floor of Araunah the Jebusite (2 Sam. 24:18). If we compare at this point the supplementary account we learn that, "Then the angel of the Lord commanded Gad to say to David, that David should go up, and set up an altar unto the Lord" (1 Chron. 21:18). The relief, then, for David in this dark hour was announced (through Gad) by the avenging angel, and thus we may say once more that the eater himself yielded meat, the strong one sweetness (Judges 14:14). Most blessed indeed was this, for an "altar" calls for an accepted worshipper, and the Lord would not have given directions for the one, if He had not provided the other. Thus it was with the very first worshipper: "And the Lord had respect unto Abel and to his offering" (Gen. 4:4) – his person was first accepted and then his sacrifice; and here the Lord's readiness to accept an offering at the hands of David was proof that David himself had been received.

This Divine direction for David to now erect an altar, denoted, first, that God was thoroughly reconciled to him, and therefore might he infer with Manoah's wife "If the Lord were pleased to kill us, He would not have received a burnt offering and a meal offering at our hands" (Judges 13:23). Second, that peace between God and guilty sinners is effected by sacrifice, and not otherwise than by Christ, the great Propitiation. Thus, while God's mercy rejoiced against judgment on this solemn occasion, yet He made it abundantly clear that His grace reigns through righteousness (Rom. 5:21) and not at the expense of it. It is the blood which maketh an atonement for the soul (Lev. 17:11), because it is the blood which placates the retributive justice of God. Third, that when God's judgments are graciously stayed, we ought to acknowledge it with thankfulness to His praise: "I will praise Thee: though Thou wast angry with me" (Isa. 12:1).

It will be remembered 2 Sam. 24:16 informed us that when the angel of the Lord stretched out his hand upon Jerusalem to destroy it, he was "by the threshingfloor of Araunah." The peaceful occupation of this Gentile (for he was a Jebusite), quietly continuing to thresh his wheat on the floor of his own isolated garner (1 Chron. 21:20) *without* the walls of Jerusalem, stands out in marked contrast from the troubled scene *within* the city, where David and the elders of Israel clothed in sackcloth, fell on their faces. Nevertheless, Araunah too was threatened, for the avenging angel drew nigh to and stood over the peaceful threshingfloor itself, and as 1 Chron. 21 tells us "Ornan (Araunah) turned back, and saw the angel; and his four sons with him hid themselves" (v. 20). But the angel smote them not: telling us most blessedly, in figure, that Gentiles as well as Jews are delivered from judgment on the ground of the Antitypical Sacrifice.

The tranquil plot of ground of Araunah was not to be the scene of judgment, but was ordained to be the place of grace, forgiveness, and peace. And *where* was that threshingfloor situated? Most significantly, on Mount Moriah. We are not left in any doubt upon this point, though the information is supplied neither in 2 Sam. 24 nor 1 Chron. 21 – not for lazy people is the Bible written! "Then Solomon began to build the house of the Lord at Jerusalem in mount Moriah, where the Lord appeared unto David his father, in the place that David had prepared in the place of Araunah the Jebusite" (2 Chron. 3:1). And Moriah, as its name intimates, was the very place where Jehovah appeared as "Jehovah-jireh" to Abraham, and where – true to His covenant name – He appeared to meet and provide for the need of David. How very remarkable and inexpressibly blessed: Moriah was and continued to be the place of sovereign *grace!*

Moriah was the mount to which Abraham went when commanded to offer up Isaac. In Gen. 22:14 we read, "And Abraham called the name of that place Jehovah-jireh: as it is said to this day, in the mount of the Lord it shall be seen." i.e. seen as the Provider, or as Gesenius, the celebrated Hebraist, renders it "in the mount of Jehovah it shall be provided." B.W. Newton tells us that Moriah is "a name derived from the same root, and signifies the place of appearing, i.e. of the appearance of Jehovah as the Provider. It should be observed that all the thoughts connected with Moriah and the provision there made, are to be traced back to the words of Abraham, "my son, God will provide (Heb. "for" Himself a lamb for a burnt offering — Gen. 22:8)."

But now observe the contrast. Confiding implicitly in God, even when he understood not the reason of His commands, Abraham went to Moriah to give full proof of his faith and obedience. Far otherwise was it with poor David. He went there as one whose disobedience had encompassed him with sorrow, judgment and death. He came clothed with sackcloth, bowed down by anguish. He came because he saw the sword of the avenging angel drawn against him and his people. He came as the "troubled one," as one who needed to be delivered from "going down to the Pit" (Psa. 30:3). True, Abraham was afflicted, yet how different was the sorrow of the consciously-obedient Abraham from the consciously-disobedient David! Nevertheless, David found on Moriah the same God that there met Abraham. In the very place where Abraham by a countermand from Heaven was stayed from slaying his son, the angel by a like countermand was stayed from destroying Jerusalem!

"And Gad came that day to David, and said unto him, Go up, rear an altar unto the Lord in the threshingfloor of Araunah the Jebusite" (v. 18). It is to be duly noted that the "altar" was *God's* thought and not David's. This is very blessed, telling us that the initiative is ever with God in all salvation matters. God is the great Provider: our privilege is to accept His gracious provision. Christ — to whom the altar pointed — was the gift of God and not the product of man. We love Him because He first loved us. And how gracious He was not to keep David in suspense a whole day, nor even hour. No sooner had he sought unto God, and He immediately responded. The ark was then at mount Zion and the tabernacle at Gibeon (2 Chron. 1), but David was bidden to go neither to the one nor the other.

"And David, according to the saying of Gad, went up as the Lord commanded" (v. 19). What beautiful completeness this gives to all that has been before us. The penitent, prudent, submissive, and supplicating one, is now seen as the *obedient* one. How could it be otherwise? He who is, spiritually speaking, clothed with sackcloth, does not follow a course of self-will and self-pleasing. David made no demur against being told to seek unto this Gentile and ask a favour at *his* hands. A truly meek heart neither reasons about nor objects to the Divine demands, but complies promptly. Here, then, is the final mark of the prevailing intercessor: he who has power with God in prayer (after his recovery from folly,) is one that now treads the path of obedience. If God is to respond to our petitions, we must respond to His precepts.

In closing, let us call attention to one other point of analogy between the experiences of Abraham and David on this memorable mount, the one which is most pertinent of all to our present subject — David's grand reward. God called the patriarch to Moriah not only that he might there give proof of his faith and obedience, but more especially that this trial of Abraham might be the occasion of unfolding to him (and through him, to us) a fuller revelation of His own ways *in grace:* for as we now know, the touching drama there enacted provided a striking adumbration of the Father Himself not sparing His own beloved Son, but freely delivering Him up for all His people. In like manner, God not only provided a substitute for David on Moriah, but He there vouchsafed him a revelation of the counsels of His grace. Moriah was not only the place where David obtained forgiveness for his sins, but it was also made to him the place of *honour and blessing.*

Upon the altar he there erected, David "offered burnt offerings and peace offerings" (1 Chron. 21:26). Nor did he do so in vain: the Lord "answered him from heaven by fire" — in token of His approval and acceptance. But more: this was the time when and the place where he received commission to prepare for the building of God's House. "Then David said, This is the house of the Lord God, and this is the altar of the burnt offering for Israel" (1 Chron. 22:1)

Now it was that David learned where was the sacred spot which Jehovah had chosen for the site of *the Temple.* This, then, was David's grand reward: unto *him* and not to any of the prophets, nor even to the high priest, was given the holy privilege of entering into God's mind concerning His House and to make provision for the same! How true it is, dear reader, that God ever honours those that honour Him — even though it be by appearing before Him in sackcloth: though He does not always make His approbation so evident to our senses as He did here to David's

And Araunah said, Why has my lord the king come to his servant? And David said, To buy the threshing-floor from you, to build an altar to the Lord, so that the plague may be stayed from the people. And Araunah said to David, Let my lord the king take and offer up what seems good to him. Behold, here are oxen for burnt sacrifice and threshing instruments and other instruments of the oxen for wood. All these things did Araunah, like a king, give to the king. And Araunah said to the king, May the Lord your God accept you. And the king said to Araunha, No, but I will surely buy it from you at a price. Neither will I offer burnt offerings to the Lord my God of that which does not cost me anything. So David bought the threshing-floor and the oxen for fifty shekels of silver. And David built there an altar to the Lord and offered burnt offerings and peace offerings. So the Lord was entreated for the land, and the plague was stayed from Israel. — I Samuel 24:21-25.

"And Gad came that day to David and said unto him, Go up, rear an altar unto the Lord in the threshingfloor of Araunah the Jebusite. And David, according to the saying of Gad, went up as the Lord commanded" (2 Sam. 24:18, 19). Here we behold David's trustful and thankful acceptance of the mercy vouchsafed him. He received not the grace of God in vain, but complied promptly with His revealed will. To unbelief it would seem too good to be true that God's displeasure was now appeased; but faith laid hold of the prophet's word, knowing that an "altar" spoke of propitiation and acceptance. And this is ever the way with those who have truly repented of their sins and humbled themselves before the Lord. Satan may seek to persuade them that they have transgressed beyond the hope of forgiveness, but sooner or later the heart of the Christian will turn again to the Antitypical Altar, and overcome the Adversary with the blood of the Lamb (Rev. 12:11).

How different, for the moment, was the attitude of Araunah: "And Araunah turned back, and saw the angel; and his four sons with him *hid* themselves" (1 Chron. 21:20). This is in direct contrast, and presents to us a most important truth. On the one hand, the case of Araunah terror- stricken with the sight of the destroying angel, tells us that no flesh can stand naked, as in its own resources, before the Lord. On the other hand, David here exemplified the fact that penitent sinners may confidently draw nigh to Him in the power of simply believing in His wondrous grace. At this time the greatness of God's mercy had not been revealed to Araunah : he knew nothing of the "altar" that was to be set up in his threshingfloor, and therefore, as nakedly a creature in the sight of God — like Adam before Him in such a case — he hid himself.

But David *had* revealed to him the remedy, which mercy rejoicing against judgment had provided, and therefore he hesitated not. Though shamed and humbled, he immediately responded to Gad's message, and "went *up*" — significant word (cf. Gen 13:1-3, etc.) — delivered from the mire into which he had fallen. The angel's "sword," *still unsheathed,* had no alarms for him now, for he goes to the very place where he stood (1 Chron. 21:16)! Is not this remarkable? the very spectacle which filled Araunah with fear, had no terror for David. Believing, he was neither ashamed nor confounded. Consequently we see in his action here no disturbance of the flesh, but all is quietness and assurance as he rested on the Word of God. What a lesson is there here for our needy hearts. Alas, what cowards we are! What trifles we allow to affright us. O for more confidence in the living God, more reliance upon His promises; less occupation with what intimidates the flesh.

"And as David came to Araunah, Araunah looked and saw David, and went out of the threshingfloor and bowed himself to David with his face to the ground" (1 Chron. 21:21). Let us not lose sight of the blessed *humility* of David here — ever a prominent spiritual grace in his character and conduct. Does the reader perceive to what we now call attention? It is this: David did not treat with Araunah mediately, through one of his underlings, but *directly*. Was not this in perfect keeping with the "sackcloth?" He still took the place of self-abnegation. Ah, dear friends, it is the emptied vessel which God fills. Rightly did Matt. Henry declare, "Great men will never be less respected for their humility, but the more." Those who are self-important and pompous only display their littleness and meanness.

"And Araunah said, wherefore is my lord the king come to his servant? And David said, To *buy* the threshingfloor of thee, to build an altar unto the Lord, that the plague may be stayed from the people" (2 Sam. 24:21). Here we behold David as the *righteous* one. Though he was a king, and though he had received commandement from the Lord to build an altar at this particular place, nevertheless he insisted upon making fair payment to this man, even though a Gentile. This is ever a mark of true spirituality: those who walk with God, are honourable in dealing with their fellowmen. "Owe no man anything (Rom. 12:8) is a necessary application of "thou shalt love thy neighbour as thyself." Neither high office nor pressure of circumstances can justify one in taking an unfair advantage of another. Nothing lower than "in all things willing to *live honestly*" (Heb. 13:18) must be the Christian's standard. Those who attended Christ most closely during the days of His public ministry, neither imposed upon the kindness of others nor begged favours, but *bought* their food (John 4:8).

"And Araunah said unto David, let my lord the king take and offer up what seemeth good unto him: behold, here be oxen for burnt sacrifice, and threshing instruments and other instruments of the oxen for wood" (v. 22). The language of 1 Chron. 21:23 is yet more definite: "Take it to thee, and let my lord the king do that which is good in his eyes: lo, I *give* thee the oxen also for burnt offerings, and the threshing instruments for wood, and the wheat for the meat offering; I give it *all.*" What noble generosity was this! But we prefer to look at Araunah's liberality from the Divine side — when any one befriends us, we should ever discern *the Lord's* prompting such kindness. But what we would particularly emphasize now is, that here we have another illustration of the principle that when God works, he always works at *both ends* of the line. He who wrought in David a readiness to comply with His request, was the Same as now moved Araunah to meet him more than half way. If He sends Elijah to Zarephath, He makes a widow willing to share her portion with him. There is great encouragement in this if faith lays hold of the same. If God continues to grant us messages, He will continue to prepare hearts to receive them.

"All these things did Araunah, as a king, give unto the king. And Araunah said unto the king, The Lord thy God accept thee (v. 23). Some have drawn the conclusion from these words that Araunah himself was of royal stock, for the Jebusites were the original owners of Zion (2 Sam. 5:6-9), but there is nothing else in Scripture to support this view. Rather do we understand our verse to signify that Araunah acted with royal munificence. A most laudable contention it was between a good king and a good subject. Since it was to David, and since it was for the Lord, Araunah would not sell, but give. On the other side, David, since it was for the Lord, would not take, but pay. So far from his words "The Lord thy God accept thee" denoting that he was not himself a believer in and worshipper of Jehovah (as if an idolator had been permitted to dwell on mount Zion!) they evidence that Araunah was possessed of faith and spiritual intelligence.

"And the king said unto Araunah, Nay; but I will surely buy it of thee at a price: neither will I offer burnt offerings unto the Lord my God of that which doth cost me nothing" (v. 24). Here again we should view things from the standpoint of the Divine workings. God's moving Araunah to act so magnanimously afforded David an opportunity to display his devotedness to the Lord. A gracious heart will not serve God with that which costs him nothing, nor will he deem that true piety which involves no sacrifice. This is the fruit of *faith.* Carnal nature begrudges everything, and says with Judas "To what purpose is this waste?" but faith will not withhold from God its Isaac (Heb. 11:17). It is also the fruit of *love,* which deemeth nothing too good for the Lord — witness the woman with her precious spikenard. The denial of self and the mortification of his lusts are the unfailing marks of a genuine saint. How these words of David need to be laid to heart in this flesh-pleasing age!

"So David bought the threshingfloor and the oxen, for fifty shekels of silver" (v. 24). As usual, infidels have called attention to the "discrepancy" in 1 Chron. 21, where we are told "So David gave to Araunah for the place six hundred shekels of gold by weight" (v. 25). But two different things are in view. Samuel mentions David buying the threshingfloor and the oxen, whereas Chronicles refers to his purchase of "the place," which probably signifies the whole of his land — which afterwards becomes the extensive site for the temple. It is to be noticed that for the former David paid in "silver," which speaks of *redemption;* whereas for the latter he gave "gold," the emblem of *Divine glory.* Spiritually speaking we do not learn the value of the "gold," until we are experimentally acquainted with the "silver." The amount of the gold was twelve times as great as that of the silver, showing this was for the complete number of Israel's tribes, and typifying the entire Body of Christ.

"And David built there an altar unto the Lord, and offered burnt offerings and peace offerings" (v. 25). This supplies the final line to our typical picture, for here we behold David as the accepted worshipper. "Accepted" we say, for 1 Chron. 21 tells us that the Lord, "answered him from heaven by fire upon the altar of burnt offering" (v. 26), which announced that his sacrifice had been received on High (cf. Lev. 9:24; 1 Kings 18:28,29; 2 Chron. 7:1-3). Thus does the God of all grace delight to honour those who confide in Him, by granting tokens of His approbation. But note well the *strength* of David's faith and the heartiness of his thanksgiving: he offered on that altar not only burnt offerings, but peace offerings as well. Now the "peace offering" spoke of *communion*, for (while the burnt offering was wholly consumed upon the altar) *this* was shared in by God, all the males of the priesthood, and that of the offerer himself (Lev. 7:6, 15) — each had their portion.

"And the Lord commanded the angel; and he put up his sword again into the sheath thereof" (1 Chron. 21:27). So the Lord was intreated for the land, and the plague was stayed from Israel" (2 Sam. 24:25). What a remarkable *ending* is this to the second book of Samuel! The atoning sacrifice appeasing the just displeasure of God, the erring one restored to full communion with Him, and the discovery made to David of the place where the temple was to be built and the worship of Israel subsequently to be carried on. Sorrow was turned into joy for all who had their portion of the peace offerings that day. What thoughts must then have occupied their hearts as they partook of that sacrifice according to Divine appointment: they feasted on the very offering which God had accepted. 2nd. Sam., then, closes by showing us David *in full fellowship with the Lord.* What a blessed foreshadowment of Eternity! How it reminds us to the closing words of the parable of the Prodigal Son: "Bring hither the fatted calf, and kill it; and let *us* eat, and be merry" (Luke 15:23)!

In addition to the two historical accounts furnished us by 2 Sam. 24 and 1 Chron. 21, Psa. 30 (composed very shortly afterwards) throws further light on the exercises of David's heart at that time. As C.H. Spurgeon pointed out in his introductory remarks upon Psa. 30, "A Psalm and Song at the Dedication of the House of David; or rather, A Psalm : a Song of Dedication for the House. By David." It is "A Song of *faith* since the house of Jehovah, here intended, David never lived to see. A Psalm of *praise,* since a sore judgment had been stayed and a great sin forgiven." The translation and punctuation of the title to this 30th Psa. is definitely settled for us by David's own words in 1 Chron. 22: "Then David said, This is the house of the Lord God (referring to Araunah's threshingfloor) and this the altar of the burnt offering for Israel" (v. 1).

"I will extol Thee, O Lord; for Thou hast lifted me up, and hast not made my foes to rejoice over me" (Psa. 30:1). This Psalm is a "song" and not a complaint. An experimental realization of the joy of deliverance contrasted from previous anguish, is its characteristic note. The "foes" to which David refers are to be understood of evil spirits as well as Satan's serfs among men: they are ever ready to rejoice at the falls, griefs, and chastisements of those who fear God. For having recovered him from his fall and thus saving him from utter discomfiture before his enemies, David praised God.

"O Lord my God, I cried unto Thee, and Thou hast healed me. O Lord, Thou hast brought up my soul from the grave: Thou hast kept me alive, that I should not go down to the pit" (vv. 2, 3). It is beautiful to see how David had owned Him according to His covenant title, for as we pointed out in our last, it was in His covenant faithfulness that Jehovah had acted when He caused the desolating pestilence to cease. His "I cried unto Thee" tells of the acuteness of his distress: he was too agitated to *pray,* yet he poured out his soul unto Him who understands the language of inarticulate groans. So desperate had been his plight, and so signal the Lord's intervention in mercy, David felt as one who had been recovered from the dead.

"Sing unto the Lord, O ye saints of His, and give thanks at the remembrance of His holiness. For His anger endureth but a moment; in His favour is life: weeping may endure for a night, but joy cometh in the morning" (vv. 4, 5). It was not only in mercy but in holiness God had acted, as His bidding David to erect an altar clearly evidenced. Does not the Psalmist teach us here a much-needed lesson? How often we praise the Lord for His goodness, His longsufferance, His restoring grace; but how rarely we bless Him for His *holiness*, which is chief among His perfections! David found cause for rejoicing in the brevity of the Divine judgment: the plague had lasted but a few hours, but His favour is life everlasting. What a mercy it is that His chastisements (even if continued to the end of our earthly course) are but "for a moment" (2 Cor. 4:17), in contrast from the eternity of bliss which awaits His beloved.

"And in my prosperity I said, I shall never be moved. Lord, by Thy favour Thou hast made my mountain to stand: Thou didst hide Thy face, and I was troubled" (vv. 6, 7). How clearly this confirms the exposition we gave, tracing back David's folly in numbering the people to the *pride* of his heart. Here is plainly revealed to us the secret of his sad fall. It is true that he had not attributed the success of his arms to anything in himself, or his men, but rather had freely ascribed the victories to the Lord's favour (2 Sam. 22:1, 48-50), yet he fondly imagined that God had made his kingdom invincible, one that would never be overthrown. And the Lord had hidden His face, as He always does when we forsake the place of conscious weakness and dependency upon Him. And poor David was "troubled" — brought to confusion and dismay, for no "mountain," however firm, can yield a saint satisfaction when the smile of Jehovah's countenance is concealed from him. What a warning is there here for us against cherishing a sense of carnal security.

"I cried to Thee, O Lord: and unto the Lord I made supplication" (v. 8). "Prayer is the unfailing resource of God's people. If they are driven to their wits' end, they may still go to the mercy-seat. When an earthquake makes our mountain tremble, the throne of grace still stands firm, and we may come to it" (C.H. Spurgeon). On a former occasion at Ziklag, when David was deeply distressed, for the people had spoken of stoning him, he had "encouraged himself in the Lord" (1 Sam. 30:6); so now he sought for refuge in God, and the Divine faithfulness failed him not. Not in vain do believers commit themselves into the hands of the Lord.

"What profit is there in my blood, when I go down to the pit? Shall the dust praise Thee? shall it declare Thy truth? Hear, O Lord, and have mercy upon me: Lord, be Thou my Helper" (vv. 9, 10). The intensity of David's sufferings are plainly discovered to us here. Outwardly he was clothed in sackcloth, but that was a feeble expression of his inward anguish. As the king of Israel, it had specially devolved upon him to honor the Divine statutes, but he had broken them, and caused his subjects to do so too. Just retribution had fallen upon his kingdom. Plaintively does he plead with Jehovah: would his death promote God's cause on earth? would it issue in Divine adoration? Let then mercy rejoice against judgment.

"Thou hast turned for me my mourning into dancing: Thou hast put off my sackcloth, and girded me with gladness; to the end that my glory may sing praise to Thee, and not be silent. O Lord my God, I will give thanks unto Thee forever" (vv. 11,12). Here is further proof (if any be needed) that this 30th

Psalm treats of the same period of David's life as is before us 2 Sam. 24. And a grand finale do its closing verses supply. David had begged God to be gracious unto him, and He was gracious. Such wondrous mercy made "glory" vocal with the voice of ceaseless thanksgiving, for GLORY is to be the dwellingplace of redeemed and rescued sinners — those who have, like David, proved for themselves the greatness and sufficiency of the Lord's mercies. "I will give thanks unto Thee forever": such will be our employ in Glory, and all because of *Sacrifice*. Verses 11, 12 are true of Christ Himself, and therefore of the members of His Body also.

CONCLUSION TO THE LIFE OF DAVID.

1 Kings

The public life of David had been a stormy one throughout, nor was he permitted to end his career in tranquility — such is generally the lot of those in high station, who are ignorantly envied by so many. Even in his declining days, when the infirmities of old age were upon David, serious trouble broke out in his kingdom, so that both the public peace was jeopardized and his own family circle again threatened by the assassin. Another of his own sons now set himself not only against the will of his father, but also against the declared purpose of God; in which he was abetted by those who had long held positions of honour under the king. No doubt we should look deeper and see here a setting forth of the conflict which obtains in a higher realm: the enmity of the Serpent against the woman's Seed and his opposition to the will of God concerning His kingdom. But it is with that which refers more immediately to David we shall concern ourselves.

The record of what we have referred to above is found in 1 Kings 1. That chapter opens by presenting to us the once virile and active king now going the way of all the earth: his natural spirits dried up, no longer able to attend to public affairs. The events chronicled therein occurred very near the close of David's eventful career. Though not yet quite seventy he is described as "old and well stricken in years." Though blest with a vigorous constitution, the king was thoroughly worn out: among the contributing causes, we may mention the strenuous life he had lived and the heavy domestic griefs which had fallen upon him. That he was still dearly beloved by his followers is evident from their kindly if ill-advised efforts for his comfort (vv. 1-3). David's falling in with their plan, shows him taking the line of least resistance, apparently out of deference to the wishes of his attendants. It was a device which has been resorted to in various climes and ages, yet surely it was one which did not become a child of God.

Old age as well as youth has its own particular snares, for if the danger of the latter is to disdain the advice of seniors and be too self-willed, the infirmities of the former place them more in the power of their juniors and they are apt to yield to arrangements which their consciences condemn. It is not easy to deny the wishes of those who are tending us, and it seems ungrateful to refuse well-meant efforts to make our closing days more comfortable. But while on the one hand the aged need to guard against irritability and a domineering spirit, yet on the other they must not be a willing party to that which they know is wrong. Legitimate means of restoring health and for prolonging our days should be employed, but unlawful measures and anything having the appearance of evil or which may become an occasion of temptation to us, should be steadfastly refused, no matter by whom it is proposed.

The Lord's *displeasure* against David's weakness in consenting to the carnal counsel of his friends, is plainly marked in the immediate sequel, Serious trouble now arose from yet another of his sons. It is true that this was the fruit of his earlier laxity in ruling his children, for he was much too easy-going with them: yet *the time* when this impious insubordination occurred leaves us in no doubt that it is to be regarded as a Divine chastening of David for being a party to such a questionable procedure as that to which we have briefly alluded above. *"Then Adonijah the son of Haggith exalted himself, saying, I will be king: and he prepared him chariots and horsemen, and fifty men to run before him"* (1 Kings 1:5). Nothing is more conspicuous throughout the whole history of David than that, whenever a believer sows to the flesh, he will most certainly of the flesh reap corruption; and another solemn example of this is here before us.

David was now stricken in years, and the time for one to succeed him to the throne has well-nigh arrived. Yet is was for Jehovah alone to say who that one should be. But Adonijah, the oldest living son, determined to be that successor. Nor is this to be wondered at, for "His father had not displeased him at any time in saying, Why hast thou done so?" (v. 6). David had permitted him to have his own way. He never crossed his will, never inquired the motive of his actions, nor at any time rebuked him for his folly. In allowing his son to be guided by his own unbridled will, David sadly failed to exercise his parental authority and to fulfil his parental responsibility; and bitterly did he now pay for his folly, as many since have also been made to do.

That which immediately follows v. 6 is recorded for our learning, and a most solemn warning does it point for our own day, when so many fond parents are allowing their children to grow up with little or no restraint placed upon them. They are only preparing a rod for their own backs. God Himself has forbidden parents to refrain from chastening their children when they need it: "Withhold not correction from the child: for if thou beatest him with the rod, he shall not die" (Prov. 23:13). And again, "He that spareth his rod hateth his son: but he that loveth him chasteneth him betimes" (Prov. 13:24). And yet again, "Chasten thy son while there is hope, and let not thy soul spare him, for his crying" (Prov. 19:18). Because of his parental neglect David himself was in large measure responsible for the lawlessness of his son. Lax and indulgent parents must expect willful and wayward children, and if they despise the infirmities of their sires and are impatient to get possession of their estates, that will be all which they deserve at their hands.

David's unruly son now determined to exalt himself, even though he certainly knew that Solomon had been appointed by God to succeed David in the kingdom (2 Sam. 7:12-16; 1 King 2:15-18). "Then Adonijah the son of Haggith exalted himself, saying, I will be king: and he prepared nim chariots and horsemen, and fifty men to run before him" (v. 5). In this magnifying of his state, he followed the evil example of his rebellious brother Absalom (2 Sam. 15:1) — a solemn warning this for older brothers to set their younger ones a good example. Adonijah dared to usurp the throne of Israel: he made a feast, gathered the people about him, and incited them to proclaim him as king (vv. 7-9, 25). In this too he was again following the example of Absalom (2 Sam. 15:10), confident that where his brother had failed, he would now succeed. But like Absalom before him, Adonijah reckoned without God: "The Lord bringeth the counsel of the heathen to naught: He maketh the devices of the people of none effect. The counsel of the Lord standeth forever" (Psa. 33:10,11).

Nevertheless, for a time it looked very much as though the daring revolt of Adonijah would be successful, for both Joab the commander of the army and Abiathar the priest, threw in their lot with him (v. 7). Thus does God often allow the wicked to prosper for awhile, yet their triumphing is but short. Joab, as we have seen in other connections, was a thoroughly unprincipled and ungodly man, and no doubt the impious Adonijah was more congenial to his disposition than Solomon would be. Moreover if this son of Haggith obtained the kingdom, then his own position would be secure, and he would not be displaced by a successor to Amasa (2 Sam. 19:13). So too Abiathar the high priest seems to have been less regarded by David than Zadok was (2 Sam. 24:25), and probably he feared that Solomon would set his family aside for the line of Eliazar to which Zakok belonged.

Characters like Joab and Abiathar are ever actuated by selfish motives, though individuals like Adonijah often flatter themselves that the service of such is rendered out of love or esteem for their persons, when in reality very different considerations moves them. Disinterested loyalty is a very rare thing, and where found it cannot be valued too highly. Those in eminent positions, whether in church or state, are surrounded by mercenary sychophants, who are ever eager to turn to their own advantage every thing which transpires. It matters nothing to Joab and Abiathar that their royal master was a pious and faithful one, who had steadily sought the good of the kingdom, or that Adonijah was a grasping and lawless semi-heathen; they were ready to forsake the one and espouse the other. So it is still: that is why those in high places are afraid to trust the ones nearest to them in office.

"There are many devices in a man's heart: nevertheless the counsel of the Lord, that shall stand" (Prov. 19:21). No planning on man's part can thwart the purpose of the Most High. Saul had proved that; so too had Absalom; so now shall Adonijah. Yet the Lord is pleased to use human instruments in bringing His counsel to pass. He always has His man ready to intervene at the critical moment. In this instance it was Nathan the prophet: "Wherefore Nathan spake unto Bathsheba the mother of Solomon, saying, Hast thou not heard that Adonijah the son of Haggith doth reign, and David our lord knoweth it not?" (v. 11). Nathan had been faithful in rebuking David for his sin in former days (2 Sam. 11:7-12), he was faithful now in recalling to him the promise he had made concerning Solomon. He interviewed Bathsheba and persuaded her to go unto David and remind him of his oath (vv. 11-13), and arranged that while she was speaking to the king, he also would come into his presence and confirm her testimony (v. 14).

It is blessed, both from the Divine and human side, to see how readily and how graciously Bathsheba responded to Nathan's suggestion. From the Divine side, we may behold how that when God works He works at both ends of the line: if the prophet gave counsel under Divine prompting, the queen was willing in the day of God's power, as David also yielded thereto — each acted under Divine impulse, yet each acted quite freely. From the human side, we may note that Bathsheba made no demur to Nathan's counsel but readily acquiesced. Though David was her husband she "bowed and did obeisance to the king" and addressed him as "my lord" (vv. 16, 17), thereby evidencing that she was a true daughter of Abraham. First she reminded him of his solemn oath that Solomon should reign after him (v. 17). Then she acquainted him with the revolt of Adonijah (v. 18). Next she assured the king that Nation awaited an authoritative word from him about the accession; and ended by warning him that if he failed in his duty she and Solomon would be in grave danger of their lives.

"And, lo, while she yet talked with the king, Nathan the prophet came in" (v. 22). It was something more than a politic move on Nathan's part to appear before the king at the psychological moment and second what Bathsheba had just said. It was an act of obedience to the Word of God, for the Divine Law required that matters of solemn moment must be confirmed by one or more witnesses. "One witness shall not rise up against a man for any iniquity, or for any sin, in any sin that he sinneth: at the mouth of two witnesses, or at the mouth of three witnesses, shall the matter be established" (Deut. 19:15). The same principle was insisted upon by Christ on more than one occasion, and therefore it is binding on us to-day. Much needless trouble had been avoided in the church (Matt. 18:16), many a false accusation had been exposed (John 8:13, 17), many a breach had been healed (2 Cor. 13:1), and many an innocent servant of God had been cleared (1 Tim. 5:19), if only this principle had been duly heeded.

According to his promise to Bathsheba Nathan entered the king's presence and bore out what she had just told him. The prophet showed how urgent the situation was. First, he declared that the supporters of the revolter were so confident of success that they were even now saying "God save king Adonijah" (v. 25). Second, he pointed out the ominous fact that neither himself nor Zadok the priest, Benaiah or Solomon had been invited to the feast (v. 26), which made evident his lawless designs: neither the will of God nor the desire of his father were going to be consulted. Third, he endeavoured to get the aged David to take definite action before it was too late. He asks the king point blank if this thing was being done with his approval (v. 27), to make him realise the better what blatant insolence Adonijah and his party were guilty of in thus acting without authority from the crown. Thus did he make clear to David his public duty.

It was now that the real character of David asserted itself. Weak he was in the ruling of his own household, but ever firm and fearless where the interests to God's kingdom were concerned. Nothing could induce him to resist the revealed will of the Lord for Israel. First, he now acknowledged again the faithfulness of God unto himself: "And the king sware, and said, As the Lord liveth, that hath redeemed my soul out of all distress" (v. 29). The Lord is the Deliverer of all who put their trust in Him, and repeatedly had He delivered David out of the hands of his enemies. Second, God's faithfulness to David now inspired him to be faithful to his covenant promise concerning Solomon: "Even as I sware unto thee by the Lord God of Israel, saying, Assuredly Solomon thy son shall reign after me, and he shall sit upon my throne in my stead; even so will I certainly do this day" (v. 30). Most blessed is this: whatever danger his own person might be threatened with, he hesitated not.

In what immediately follows we are informed of the decisive measures taken by David to overthrow the plot of Adonijah. "Call me Zadok the priest, and Nathan the prophet, and Benaiah the son of Jehoiada. And they came before the king. The king also said unto them, Take with you the servants of your lord, and cause Solomon my son to ride upon mine own mule, and bring him down to Gihon: and let Zadok the priest and Nathan the prophet anoint him there king over Israel: and blow ye with the trumpet and say, God save king Solomon. Then ye shall come up after him, that he may come and sit upon my throne: for he shall be king in my stead: and I have appointed him to be ruler over Israel and over Judah" (vv. 32-35). Orders were given for the proclaiming of Solomon: he was to be set upon the royal mule, formally anointed, and duly proclaimed king. This important transaction was entrusted to men of God who had proved themselves in His service. Solomon would thus have the necessary authority for conducting state affairs until David's decease, after which there would be no uncertainty in the public mind as to his rightful successor.

"And Benaiah the son of Jehoaida answered the king, and said, Amen: the Lord God of my lord the king say so too. As the Lord hath been with my lord the king, even so be He with Solomon, and make his throne greater than the throne of my lord king David" (vv. 36, 37). The measures proposed by the king met with the hearty approval of his advisers. Speaking in the name of the others, Benaiah expressed their complete satisfaction in the royal nomination: his "Amen" shows the original meaning and emphasis of this term — it was faith's affirmation, assured that God would make good His promise. Benaiah's language was that of fervent piety, for he realised that the plans of his master, no matter how wise and good, could not be carried to a successful conclusion without the blessing of Divine providence — alas that this is so largely lost sight of to-day. He added the earnest prayer that God would bless Solomon's reign even more than He had his father's.

The orders which David had given were promptly executed. Solomon was brought in state to the place appointed and was duly anointed. This gave great joy and satisfaction to the people. "And all the people came up after him, and the people piped with pipes and rejoiced with great joy, so the earth rent with the sound of them" (v. 40): thereby they evidenced their cheerful acceptance of him as David's successor. In like manner, all who belong to the true Israel of God gladly own the Lordship of His Son. The sequel was indeed striking. No sooner was Solomon acclaimed by the loyal subjects of David, than news thereof was borne to Adonijah and his fellow-conspirators (vv. 41, 42). Instead of ending in joy, the feast of the rebel terminated in consternation: "And all the guests that were with Adonijah were afraid, and rose up, and went every man his way. And Adonijah feared because of Solomon, and arose, and went, and caught hold on the horns of the altar" (vv. 49, 50). Thus did the Lord graciously show Himself strong on David's behalf to the end of his course.

In closing we would call attention to a most blessed typical picture, in which both David and Solomon are needed to give it completeness — compare the joint-types supplied by Joseph and Benjamin, Moses and Aaron, Elijah and Elisha. First, David had been successful as "a man of war" (1 Chron. 28:3), for by him the Lord so overcame the enemies of Israel as to "put them under the sole of his feet" (1 Kings 5:3): in like manner the Lord Jesus by His death and resurrection was victorious over all His foes (Col. 2:14, 15). Second, Solomon had been chosen and ordained to the throne before he was born (1 Chron. 22:9): so too Christ was the Elect of God from all eternity" (Isa. 42:1). Third, Solomon rode on a mule, not as a warrior, but in lowly guise: so did Christ (Matt. 21:1-9). Fourth, he was anointed with the sacred oil — type of the Spirit: so Christ received the Spirit in His fulness at His ascension (Acts 2:33; Rev. 3:1). Finally, rest and quietness was granted unto Israel throughout Solomon's reign (1 Chron. 22:19): so Christ is now reigning as "the Prince of peace" over His people.

The sand in David's hour-glass was running very low; the time appointed for his departure from this world had almost arrived; yet it is beautiful to behold him using his remaining strength in the service of God, rather than rusting out amid the shadows. The sun of his life had often been temporarily overcast, but it set in golden splendour, illustrating that word, "Better is the end of a thing than the beginning thereof" (Eccl. 7:8). The revolt of Adonijah was the last dark cloud to pass across his horizon, and it was quickly dissolved, to give place to blue skies of peace and joy. The final scenes are painted in roseate colours and the exit of our patriarch from this world was one which well fitted the man after God's own heart, Blessed is it to see him using his fast-failing energies in setting in order the affairs of the kingdom and to mark how the glory of the Lord and the good of his people was that which now wholly absorbed him.

The Holy Spirit has dwelt at quite some length upon the closing acts of David's reign, supplementing the briefer account given in 1 Kings by furnishing much fuller details in 1 Chron. It is to these supplementary accounts we now turn. In them we, first, behold him completing the extensive preparations he had made for the building of the temple. Second, his giving solemn charge unto Solomon concerning the erection of the Lord's house, concerning his own personal conduct, and concerning the removal of his enemies. Third, his charge to the princes to stand by and assist his son. Fourth, his ordering of the priesthood in their courses. Fifth, his charge to the officers of the Nation. Sixth, his entrusting to Solomon the pattern or plan of the temple which he had received from God. Seventh, his final charge to the whole congregation. Most carefully did David prepare for the end of his reign and for the welfare of his successor.

"And David said, Solomon my son is young and tender, and the house that is to be builded for the Lord must be exceeding magnifical of fame and glory, throughout all countries: I will therefore now make preparation for it. So David prepared abundantly before his death" (1 Chron. 22:5). The dearest desire of his heart had been to erect a permanent house for the worship of God, and a tremendous amount of materials had he already acquired and consecrated to that end. But his wish was not granted: another was to have that peculiar honour; yet he did not, like so many peevish persons when their wills are crossed, mope and fret, and then lose all interest in the Lord's service; but readily acquiesced in God's will and continued his preparation. Yea, so far from advancing age and increasing infirmities deterring him, they quickened him to increase a diligence and effort.

The extent and value of the materials which David had gathered for the temple may be seen by "Now, behold, in my trouble I have prepared for the house of the Lord a hundred thousand talents of gold, and a thousand thousand talents of silver; and of brass and iron without weight; for it is in abundance; timber also and stone have I prepared" (1 Chron. 22:14). These were all ready to hand for his successor, who made good use of the same. What encouragement is there here for us: much good may appear after our death, which we were not permitted to witness during our life. Often we grieve because we see so little fruit for our labour, yet if we are diligent in preparing materials, others after us may build therewith. Then let us sow beside all waters, and confidently leave the outcome with God. Those who are mature and experienced should consider the younger ones who are to follow, and furnish all the help they can to make the work of God as easy as possible for them.

We turn next to the charges which David gave to his son. The first concerned his building of the temple, for this lay most of all upon his heart. "Then he called for Solomon his son, and charged him to build a house for the Lord God of Israel. And David said to Solomon, My son, as for me, it was in my mind to build a house unto the name of the Lord my God. But the word of the Lord came to me, saying, Thou hast shed blood abundantly, and hast made great wars: thou shalt not build a house unto My name because thou hast shed much blood upon the earth in My sight" (1 Chron. 22:6-8). Here we see how jealous God was of His types — as was also evidenced by His displeasure against Moses for striking the rock (on the second occasion) instead of speaking to it; and by His smiting Gehazi with leprosy for seeking a reward from the healed Naaman. The erection of the temple was a figure of Christ building His Church, and this

He does not by destroying men's lives, but by saving them.

Continuing the "word" which David had received from the Lord, he adds, "Behold, a son shall be born to thee, who shall be a man of rest; and I will give him rest from all his enemies round about: for his name shall be Solomon (Peaceable), and I will give peace and quietness unto Israel in his days. He shall build a house for My name; and he shall be My son, and I will be his Father; and I will establish the throne of his kingdom over Israel forever. Now, my son, the Lord be with thee, and prosper thou and build the house of the Lord thy God, as He hath said of thee" (vv. 9-11). In what follows David enjoined his son (v. 13) to keep God's commands and to take heed to his duty in everything. He must not think that by building the temple he would secure a dispensation to indulge the lusts of the flesh. Nay, let him know that though king of Israel, he was himself a subject of the God of Israel, and would be prospered by Him in proportion as he made the Divine Law his rule (cf. Josh. 1:8).

A little later he addressed him thus: "And thou, Solomon my son, know thou the God of thy father, and serve Him with a perfect heart and with a willing mind: for the Lord searcheth all hearts and understandeth all the imaginations of the thoughts: if thou seek Him He will be found of thee but if thou forsake Him He will cast thee off forever. Take heed now; for the Lord hath chosen thee to build a house for the sanctuary: be strong and do it" (1 Chron. 28:9, 10). How concerned David was that his son should be pious. Faithfully did he set before him the inevitable alternative: blessing if he served the Lord, woe if he turned away from Him. Here was a case where Divine foreordination had made irrevocably certain the end, and yet where human responsibility was insisted upon. The perpetuity of God's kingdom to David's posterity was absolutely assured in Christ, yet the entail of the temporal kingdom was made contingent on the conduct of David's descendents: if they were self-willed and remained disobedient, the entail would be cut off.

The same note of contingency is struck again unmistakably in "*If* thy children take heed to their way, to walk before Me in truth with all their heart and with all their soul, there shall not fail thee (said He) a man on the throne of Israel" (1 Kings 2:4). Alas, we know from the sequel what happened: God punished the idolatry of Solomon by the defection of the ten tribes from his son, till ultimately the family of David was deprived of all royal authority. It has been thus all through the piece: man has utterly failed in whatever trust God has committed to him: sentence of death was written upon the prophetic, the priestly, and the kingly office in Israel. Was then the Divine purpose thwarted? No indeed; that could not be; the counsels of God are made good in the Second Man and not in the first. It is in and by and through *Christ* the Divine decrees are secured. And as it is in the Second Man and not in the first, so it is in a *heavenly* realm and not in the earthly that the O.T. promises find their fulfillment. Christ, according to the flesh, was made to the seed of David, and in Him the kingdom of God is *spiritually* realized.

"And David said to Solomon his son, Be strong and of good courage, and do it: fear not nor be dismayed, for the Lord God, even my God, He will not fail thee nor forsake thee until thou hast finished all the work for the service of the house of the Lord" (1 Chron 28:20). It is noteworthy that that to which David principally exhorted his son was firmness and boldness. *Courage* is one of the graces most needed by the servants of God, for the Devil as a roaring lion will ever seek to strike terror into their hearts. This was the charge given to Joshua when called to succeed Moses: "Only be thou strong and very courageous, that thou mayest observe to do according to the Law" (Josh. 1:7). To His servant the prophet the Lord said, "Fear them not, neither be dismayed at their looks, though they be a rebellious house" (Ezek. 3:9): the frowns of those who hate the Truth are no more to be regarded than the flattery of those who would quench the Spirit by puffing us up with a sense of our own importance. "Fear not them that kill the body, but are not able to kill the soul: but rather fear Him which is able to destroy both soul and body in Hell" (Matt. 10:28) said Christ to his apostles — gifts are of no avail if we lack courage to use them.

The charge which David gave to Solomon concerning his old enemies is recorded in 1 Kings 2. "Moreover thou knowest also what Joab the son of Zeruiah did to me, and what he did to the two captains of the hosts of Israel, unto Abner the son of Ner, and unto Amasa the son of Jether, whom he slew and shed the blood of war in peace, and put the blood of war upon his girdle that was about his loins and in his shoes that were on his feet. Do therefore according to thy wisdom, and let not his hoar head go down to the grave in peace. . .and behold thou hast with thee Shimei. . .which cursed me with a grievous curse. . .now therefore hold him not guiltless" etc. (vv. 5-9). These orders are not to be regarded as issuing from a spirit of private revenge, but rather with a regard for the glory of God and the good of Israel. Joab had long deserved to die for his cold-blooded murders, and the part he had recently played in aiding the revolt of Adonijah. While such men as he and Shimei lived they would be a continual *menace* to Solomon and the peacefulness of his reign.

The charge David made to the princes is found in 1 Chron. 22: "David also commanded all the princes of Israel to help Solomon his son, saying, Is not the Lord your God with you? and hath He not given you rest on every side? for He hath given the inhabitants of the land into mine hand; and the land is subdued before the Lord and before His people. Now set your heart and your soul to seek the Lord your God; arise therefore and build ye the sanctuary" (vv. 17-19). Once more we see how deeply concerned David was that the honour of Jehovah should be promoted by the erection of a suitable dwelling-place for His holy ark, and therefore did he command the princes to give whatever aid they could to his son in this undertaking. Monarchs can only forward the work of God in their dominions as they are supported by those nearest to them in high office. David urged upon them their obligations by insisting that gratitude to God for His abundant mercies called for generosity and effort on their part. He bids them be zealous by fixing their eyes of God's glory and making His favour their happiness. When the Lord truly possesses the heart neither sacrifice nor service will be begrudged.

From 1 Chron. 23 and the chapters which follow we learn of the considerable trouble David went to in fixing the arrangements for the temple services and putting in order the offices of it, in which he prepared for the house of God as truly when he laid up silver and gold for it. It is noticeable that the tribe of Levi had multiplied almost fourfold (23:3; and cf. Num 4:46-48), which was a much greater increase than in any other tribe. It was for the honour of Jehovah that so great a number of servants should attend His house — an adumbration of the countless millions of angels which wait upon the Heavenly Throne. A detailed account is supplied of the distribution of the priests and Levites into their respective classes and of their duties, such particularization showing us that God is a God of order, especially in matters pertaining to His worship. The distribution of the officers was made by lot (24:5, etc) to show that all was governed by the Divine will (Prov. 16:33). The priesthood was divided into twenty-four courses (24:18), a figure perhaps of the "twenty-four elders" of

Rev. 4:4.

"Then David gave to Solomon his son the pattern of the porch and of the house thereof. . .And the pattern of all that he had by the Spirit of the courts of the house of the Lord. . .All this, said David, the Lord made me understand in writing by His hand upon me, even all the works of this pattern" (1 Chron. 28:11, 12, 19). David had received full instructions from God concerning the design of the temple and how everything was to be ordered in it: nothing was left to chance or the caprice of man, nor even to the wisdom of Solomon; all was Divinely prescribed. Moses had received a similar pattern for the building of the tabernacle (Ex. 25:9) both of them being a figure of Christ and heavenly things. But the worship of God in this Christian era is in marked contrast from that which obtained under the Mosaic economy: in keeping with the much greater liberty which obtains under the New Covenant, precise rules and detailed regulations for the external worship of God in every circumstance are nowhere to be found in either the Acts or the Epistles.

The charge which David gave to the Congregation was the longest of any. First, he warned them that Solomon was of tender years — less than twenty — and therefore very young to assume such heavy responsibilities (1 Chron. 29:1). Second, he reminded them how he had himself "prepared with all his might for the house of his God" (v. 2), having "set his affection" thereon, and urged his hearers to emulate his example by giving of their substance unto the Lord (v. 5). Both the leaders (vv. 5-8) and the people (v. 9) responded "willingly" and liberally, so that David "rejoiced with great joy." Then he magnified the Lord in these notable terms, "Thine, O Lord, is the greatness, and the power, and the glory, and the victory, and the majesty: for all that is in the heaven and in the earth is Thine; *Thine* is the kingdom, O Lord, and Thou art exalted as Head above all. Both riches and honour come of Thee, and Thou reignest over all; and in Thine hand is power and might" (vv. 11, 12).

The *deep humility* of the man was again evidenced when David added, "But who am I, and what is my people, that *we* should be able to offer so willingly after this sort? for all things come of Thee, and of Thine own have we given Thee. For we were strangers before Thee, and sojourners as were all our fathers: our days on the earth are as a shadow, and there is none abiding. O Lord our God, all this store that we have prepared to build Thee a house for Thine holy name cometh of *Thine hand*, and is all Thine own " (vv. 14-16). Beautiful is it to hear the king in his last words giving honour to whom honour is due. "And David said to all the congregation, Now bless the Lord your God. And all the congregation blessed the Lord God of their fathers, and bowed down their heads, and worshipped the Lord, and the king. And they sacrificed sacrifices unto the Lord. . .And they did eat and drink before the Lord on that day with great gladness" (vv. 20-22). What a grand finale was this to the reign of David: the king surrounded by his subjects engaged in joyfully worshipping the King of kings!

"Now the days of David drew nigh that he should die" (1 Kings 2:1): not that extreme old age necessitated his demise, but because his appointed time had arrived. The length of our sojourn on this earth is not determined by the care we take of our health (though human responsibility requires that we abstain from all intemperance and recklessness), nor upon the skill of our physicians (though all lawful means should be employed), but upon the sovereign decree of God. "Man that is born of a woman is of few days. . .His days are *determined*, the number of his months are with Thee, Thou hast appointed his bounds that he cannot pass" (Job. 14:1, 5). No, when the Divinely-ordained limit is reached, all the doctors in the world cannot prolong our life a single moment. Thus we are told of Jacob, "The time drew nigh that Israel *must* die" (Gen. 47:29) — "must" because God had decreed it. So it was with David: he had fulfilled God's purpose concerning him, his course was finished, and he could now enter into his eternal rest.

"And he charged Solomon his son, saying, I go the way of all the earth" (1 Kings 2:1). He realised that his end was very near, yet he was not diffident to own it nor afraid to speak of dying. He calmly referred to his decease as a "way": it was not only an exit from this world, but an entrance into another and better one. He speaks of his death as "the way of all the earth:" from the earth its dwellers are taken, and to it they return (Gen. 3:19). Even the heirs of Heaven (except those alive at Christ's return: 1 Cor. 15:51) must pass through the valley of the shadow of death, yet they need fear no evil. In like manner Paul spoke of his "departure" (2 Tim. 4:6), using a nautical term which refers to a ship being loosed from its moorings: so at death the soul is released from the cables which bound it to the shores of time, and it glides forth into eternity.

David made all the preparations for his departure with unruffled composure because he knew that death did not end all. He knew that as soon as he drew his last breath, the angels of God (Luke 16:22) would convey him into the abode of the redeemed. He knew that the moment his soul was absent from the body, he would be present with the Lord (2 Cor. 5:19). He knew that in the grave his flesh should rest "in hope" (Psa. 16:9), and that in the morning of the resurrection he should come forth fully conformed to the image of his Saviour (Psa. 17:15). "And he died in a good old age, full of days, riches, and honour: and Solomon his son reigned in his stead" (1 Chron. 29:28). His epitaph was inscribed by the Holy Spirit: "For David, after he had served his own generation by the will of God, fell on sleep" (Acts. 13:36). May we too be enabled to serve our generation as faithfully as David did his.

www.ingramcontent.com/pod-product-compliance
Lightning Source LLC
Chambersburg PA
CBHW070942150426
42812CB00063B/2723